SECOND
EDITION

Introduction to Hospitality

John R. Walker, D.B.A., FMP.

Marshall Professor and Director
Hotel, Restaurant, and Tourism Management
United States International University
San Diego, California

Prentice Hall
Upper Saddle River, New Jersey 07458

Library of Congress Cataloging-in-Publication Data
Walker, John R.
    Introduction to hospitality / John R. Walker. — 2nd ed.
        p.   cm.
    Includes index
    ISBN 0-13-917881-3
    1. Hospitality industry—Management.   I. Title
TX911.3.M27W35   1999
647.94'068—dc21
                                                        99-23053
                                                        CIP

Production Editor: Michael Jennings/Carlisle Publishers Services
Production Liaison: Eileen M. O'Sullivan
Acquisitions Editor: Neil Marquardt
Editorial Assistant: Jean Auman
Director of Manufacturing & Production: Bruce Johnson
Managing Editor: Mary Carnis
Designer: Laura Ierardi
Marketing Manager: Frank Mortimer, Jr.
Cover Design: Bruce Kenselaar
Cover Illustration: B. J. Faulkner
Interior Design: Kevin Kall
Art Director: Marianne Frasco
Manufacturing Manager: Ed O'Dougherty
Formatting/Page make-up: Carlisle Communications, Ltd.
Printer/Binder: R.R. Donnelley-Willard

© 1999, 1996 by Prentice-Hall, Inc.
Simon & Schuster/A Viacom Company
Upper Saddle River, New Jersey 07458

Printed in the United States of America

10 9 8 7 6 5 4 3 2 1

ISBN 0-13-917881-3

Prentice-Hall International (UK) Limited, *London*
Prentice-Hall of Australia Pty. Limited, *Sydney*
Prentice-Hall Canada Inc., *Toronto*
Prentice-Hall Hispanoamericana, S.A., *Mexico*
Prentice-Hall of India Private Limited, *New Delhi*
Prentice-Hall of Japan, Inc., *Tokyo*
Simon & Schuster Asia Pte. Ltd., *Singapore*
Editoria Prentice-Hall do Brasil, Ltda., *Rio de Janeiro*

Contents

CHAPTER 1

Hospitality: A Historical Perspective 2-3

CHAPTER 2

Tourism 30–31

CHAPTER 3

The Hotel Business: Development and Classification 76–77

CHAPTER 4

Hotel and Rooms Division Operation 118–119

CHAPTER 5

Hotel Operations: Food and Beverage Division 162–163

CHAPTER 6

The Restaurant Business: Development and Classification 194–195

CHAPTER 7

Restaurant Operations 232–233

CHAPTER 8

Managed Services 266–267

CHAPTER 9

Beverages 292-293

CHAPTER 10

Recreation and Leisure 326-327

CHAPTER 11

The Gaming Entertainment Industry 350-351

CHAPTER 12

Meetings, Conventions, and Expositions 378–379

CHAPTER 13

Marketing, Human Resources, and Culture 404–405

CHAPTER 14

Leadership and Management 436–437

Preface

Hospitality management is an exciting professional discipline. *Introduction to Hospitality* is a comprehensive tour through the fascinating and challenging related fields in the hospitality industry: travel and tourism, lodging, food service, meetings, conventions and expositions, leisure and recreation. The book also discusses marketing, human resources, leadership, and management and how they apply to hospitality management.

This text is designed for hospitality management professionals of tomorrow. By dynamically involving the readers in each step of this exciting journey, *Introduction to Hospitality* invites students to share the unique enthusiasm surrounding the field of hospitality.

The increase in globalization is reflected in the hospitality industry. Through the stories and examples presented in the text, readers are encouraged to share the deep appreciation for, and gain exposure to, the diversity of existing traditions and cultures.

Other features unique to this book include the following:

- ✔ The thorough identification and analysis of trends, issues, and challenges that will have a significant impact on hospitality into the twenty-first century
- ✔ The scope of coverage and the international perspective on present and future industry issues
- ✔ The presentation and description of numerous career opportunities in hospitality
- ✔ Numerous suggestions for educational and professional development

This wide variety of learning tools provides a fundamental aid to students and encourages their active participation in the course.

Features of the Chapters

Chapter 1

"Hospitality: A Historical Perspective" introduces and presents a brief historical overview of the hospitality industry, describing the evolution of hospitality from Greek and Roman times to the present day.

Chapter 2

"Tourism" outlines the scope of tourism and identifies the major influences on the increase of tourism, the various travel modes, and the key organizations and the role they play from a global to a local perspective.

Chapter 3

"The Hotel Business: Development and Classification" illustrates the various forms of hotel development, the different types of hotels, their classification, and ways hotels cater to the business and leisure travel markets.

Chapter 4

"Hotel and Rooms Division Operation" provides a hands-on perspective that details the rooms division department functions and activities. A complete overview of the guest cycle from reservations to checkout is included. The chapter also outlines the duties and responsibilities of key executives and department heads.

Chapter 5

"Hotel Operations: Food and Beverage Division" details the food and beverage departments and illustrates the duties and responsibilities of the key food and beverage executives.

Chapter 6

"The Restaurant Business: Development and Classification" traces the history and development of the restaurant business. Restaurant development from operating philosophy and mission statements to market, concepts, location, ambiance, menu planning, and classification of restaurants is discussed.

Chapter 7

"Restaurant Operations" focuses on the operations of a restaurant. The chapter discusses forecasting, purchasing, receiving, storage/issuing, food production, and service. Budgeting, controllable expenses, restaurant accounting, operating ratios, and controls are also discussed.

Chapter 8

"Beverages" presents the various types of wines and wine making, beer and the brewing process, spirits, nonalcoholic beverages, bars, beverage management, and liquor liability and the law.

Chapter 9

"Managed Services" outlines the different noncommercial food service segments and describes the factors that distinguish noncommercial food service operations from commercial ones. Characteristics and trends in airline, military, elementary and secondary schools, colleges and universities, healthcare, business, and industry food service are illustrated.

Chapter 10

"Recreation and Leisure" introduces recreation, leisure, and wellness as essential to our cultural, moral, and spiritual well-being. Government-sponsored recreation, national parks, and public recreation agencies are illustrated together with commercial recreation/theme parks and clubs. Noncommercial recreation in the form of voluntary organizations, campus, armed forces, employee recreation, and recreation for special populations are discussed.

Chapter 11

The Gaming Entertainment Industry reviews the history of gaming entertainment and examines the size and scope of the industry. The key players are identified and exciting entertainment projects are discussed together with careers and the relationship of the gaming industry to hotels, food and beverage, casino, and retail operations.

Chapter 12

"Meetings, Conventions, and Expositions" introduces readers to the different types of meetings, conventions, and expositions. Meeting planners, convention and visitors bureaus, event management, and specialized services are also covered in detail.

Chapter 13

"Marketing, Human Resources, and Culture" presents the elements of marketing, sales, human resources, and culture that are common to all segments of the hospitality industry.

Chapter 14

"Leadership" provides the reader with an overview of the characteristics and attributes of leaders, and offers a comparison of the different styles of leadership. Hospitality leaders such as Wayne Calloway, CEO of PepsiCo.; Herb Kelleher, president and CEO of Southwest Airlines; Ray Kroc, founder of McDonald's; Bill Fisher, executive director, National Restaurant Association; Isadore Sharp, president and CEO of Four Seasons Hotels and Resorts; John Martin, president and CEO of Taco Bell Corporations; and Van E. Eure, president of The Angus Barn Restaurant, offer their insights into successful leadership. Ethical, moral, and social responsibilities in business are also discussed. "Management Service and Professionalism" focuses on corporate philosophy, culture, mission, goals, and objectives. Emphasis is placed on key management functions, service, total quality management, and professionalism.

Learning Tools

Each chapter contains a number of tools designed to assist in the learning process.

- ✔ *Learning objectives* that help the reader focus on the main points discussed in the chapter
- ✔ *Benchmarking,* with individuals and corporate examples of excellence
- ✔ *Personal profiles,* focusing on the achievements and contributions to the industry by individuals who represent success models, such as Auguste Escoffier, Patti Roscoe, Steve Wynn, Jim Gemignani, Herman Cain, Richard Melman, Robert Mondavi, Walt Disney, Carol Wallace, Carroll Armstrong, and Herb Kelleher
- ✔ *Industry profiles* that provide extensive input from industry professionals, such as the Hospice de Beaune, Club Med, Carlson Companies, Hyatt Hotels, Sheraton Hotels, TGI Friday's, Joseph E. Seagram and Sons, The Disney Corporation, Las Vegas Convention and Visitor Authority, Marriott Corporation, and The Ritz-Carlton Hotel Corporation
- ✔ *A day in the life,* which selects key hospitality individuals and real-life accounts that provide exposure to the issues and challenges one might have on the job
- ✔ *Summaries* that correspond to the chapter learning objectives
- ✔ *Key words and concepts,* provided to help the reader internalize the various topics presented in the chapter
- ✔ SCANS (Secretary's Commission on Achieving Necessary Skills)–related critical thinking *Exercises* that help readers master the material presented and apply what they have learned
- ✔ A Glossary that explains the meaning of special words used throughout the text
- ✔ Case studies allow students to use their critical thinking and analysis skills in handling realistic industry situations

The extensive supplement package includes the following:

✔ *An instructor's manual* that contains teaching notes and interactive class exercises

✔ *A free powerpoint software presentation package*

✔ *Color overheads* of selected charts and graphs from the text are also available on the powerpoint software presentation package.

✔ *A computerized test bank* that consists of multiple choice, matching, and fill-in-the-blank questions

✔ *A video* highlighting hospitality organizations that is keyed specifically to the text. The video provides insight into the hospitality industry and offers students a glimpse of the opportunities, issues, and challenges that lie ahead.

Special thanks to the many colleagues and students who offered suggestions for the improvement of this text.

All of these features were designed to stimulate and promote student involvement, participation, and interaction with the course. I hope you will derive as much pleasure from reading the text as I did from writing it.

John R. Walker
San Diego, California
November 1997

Chapter opening Photo Credits

1. Hospice de Beaune, French Tourist Office; 2. A Cote d'Azure beach, French Tourist Office; 3. Hotel del Coronado, Hotel del Coronado, San Diego, CA.; 4. Banff Springs Hotel, Banff Springs Hotel, Alberta, Canada; 5. A Marriott Hotel dinner table setting, Marriott Hotels; 6. Remi Restaurant, New York, Adam D. Tihany. Photo credit, Peter Paige; 7. A TGI Friday's Restaurant, TGI Friday's; 8. A non-commercial foodservice operation, ARAMARK; 9. A Napa Valley winery, Robert Mondavi; 10. Yellowstone National Park, Yellowstone National Park; 11. San Diego Convention Center, San Diego Convention Center; 11. New York, New York Hotel; 13. A Human Resources Director, Sheraton Grande Torrey Pines; 14. Herman Cain, Chairman of the Board, Godfather's Pizza, and President and CEO, The National Restaurant Association.

Additional Photo Credits

Chapter 1 Escoffier (Courtesy of UPI/The Bettmann Archive)

Chapter 2 Model T-Ford (Courtesy of The Bettmann Archive)

Chapter 3 Conrad Hilton (Courtesy of Hilton Hotels Corporation)
U.S. Grant Hotel, San Diego, CA (Courtesy of U.S. Grant Hotel, San Diego, CA)

Banff Springs Hotel (Courtesy of Banff Springs Hotel)

Morena Valley Travelodge (Courtesy of Forte Hotels)

The Mirage Hotel and Casino (Courtesy of Mirage Resorts Incorporated)

MGM (Courtesy of MGM Grand Casino and Theme Park)

Fairfield Inn and Residence Inn (Courtesy of Marriott)

Cesar Ritz (Courtesy of The Bettmann Archive)

Chapter 4 Ritz-Carlton Interior (Courtesy of Ritz-Carlton Hotel Company)

Hyatt Hotels (Courtesy of Hyatt Hotels and Resorts)

Clarion Hotel Bayview (Courtesy of Clarion Hotel Bayview)

Chapter 5 Old King Cole Bar (Courtesy of St. Regis Hotel)

Chapter 6 The Eccentric and Papagus (Courtesy of Steinkamp/Ballogg, Chicago)

Tavern on The Green (Photo Credit: © Gayle Gleason, 1990. Courtesy of Tavern on the Green)

Chapter 7 T.G.I. Friday's (Courtesy of T.G.I. Friday's)

Chapter 9 Napa Valley (Courtesy of The Napa Valley Wineries Association)

Robert Mondavi (Courtesy of Robert Mondavi Winery)

Bernini's (Courtesy of Bernini's)

Chapter 10 New York Marathon (Courtesy of Reuters/Bettmann)

Banff Springs Hotel and Park (Courtesy of Banff Springs Hotel)

Chapter 12 Jacob K. Javits Convention Center (Courtesy of Jacob K. Javits Convention Center)

Chapter 13 Marriott International, Inc. (Courtesy of Marriott International)

Chapter 14 Martin Luther King, Jr. (Courtesy of UPI/Bettmann)

Acknowledgments

This book is dedicated to you—the students, instructors, and professors—and to the industry professionals, many of whom contributed to this text.

To your success.

For the second edition, the text has been completely updated to incorporate the many changes that have taken place over the past few years in the hospitality industry. A section on trends and mini case studies have been added to chapters two to fourteen. In addition, several more profiles have been added to each chapter. A new chapter on Gaming Entertainment has enhanced the text, in response to several requests. The instructor's manual has also been revised and has additional critical thinking exercises for classroom use.

Thanks also goes to all my CHRIE colleagues, many of whom encouraged me to undertake this project and made valuable suggestions. In particular, I would like to thank Professor Jennifer Aldrich of Johnson & Wales University who has done a great job on the instructor's manual. She has created an invaluable guide for instructors teaching this course.

This book would not have been possible without the extraordinary help of Michael Thorpe, Elena Cormio, Tania Saenz, Nicole Daane, Jennifer Mariscal, Melanie Mariscal, Rachel Martin, Dr. Jon Kingsbury, James Lorenz, Dr. Jay Schrock for his work on Chapter 4, Dr. Ken Crocker, Patti Cocoren, Dan Piotrowski, Kathleen Doeller, Edward Inskeep, Dr. Ellis Norman, Chuck Hamburg, Sheri Henderson, Steve Cenicola and Professor Peter Zuccilli, who worked so diligently on numerous key aspects of this project. I am very grateful to the following reviewers, whose comments and suggestions considerably improved the text:

Jennifer Aldrich
Johnson & Wales University
Providence, Rhode Island
Maureen Blesson
Morris County Community College
Randolph, New Jersey
Carl Boger
Kansas State University

Carl Braunlich
  Purdue University
  West Lafayette, Indiana
Melissa Dallas
  Seattle Central Community College
Evan Enowitz
  Grossmont College
  San Diego, California
Tom Jones
  University of Nevada–Las Vegas
Carol Kizer
  Columbus State Community College
  Columbus, Ohio
Daniel J. Mount
  Pennsylvania State University
  University Park, Pennsylvania
Jay Schrock
  San Francisco State University
Andrew Schwarz
  Sullivan County Community College
  Loch Sheldrake, New York
Robert C. Bennett
  Delaware County Community College
Jon Fields
  South Dakota State University
Nels Oman
  Jackson Community College
Richard M. Lagiewski
  SUNY-Plattsburgh
Kathleen A. Doeller
Andrew Hale Feinstein
  Pennsylvania State University
Charles Latour
  Northern Virginia Community College

A special thank you goes to Dr. Carl Braunlich, of Purdue University, for the excellent chapter on Gaming Entertainment.

Finally, special thanks to Robin Baliszewski and Neil Marquardt, whose vision and encouragement were an inspiration, to Eileen O'Sullivan, production liaison, whose attention to detail and expertise added much to this project, and to the rest of the Prentice Hall staff, who were a pleasure to work with. In addition, I would like to thank Michael Jennings of Carlisle Publishers Services for outstanding editorial services as project editor.

About the Author

Dr. John R. Walker is professor and director of the Hotel, Restaurant and Tourism Management Program at the United States International University in San Diego, California. John's fifteen-years industry experience includes management training at the Savoy Hotel London. This was followed by terms as food and beverage manager, assistant rooms division manager, catering manager, and general manager with Grand Metropolitan Hotels, Selsdon Park Hotel, Rank Hotels, Inter-Continental Hotels, and the Coral Reef Resort Barbados, West Indies.

For the past seventeen years he has taught at two- and four-year schools in Canada and the United States. In addition to being a hospitality management consultant, he has been published in *The Cornell Hotel Restaurant Administration Quarterly* and *The Hospitality Educators Journal*. He is co-author of *The Restaurant: from Concept to Operation*, with Dr. Donald Lundberg, published by John Wiley & Sons in 1993. Dr. Walker is an editorial advisory board member for Progress in Tourism and Hospitality Research, published by John Wiley & Sons. John is a past president of the Pacific chapter of the Council on Hotel, Restaurant, and Institutional Education (CHRIE). He is a certified hotel administrator and a certified food service management professional.

Introduction to Hospitality

Hospitality: An Historical Perspective

1

After reading and studying this chapter you should be able to do the following:

- ✔ Describe the evolution of the hospitality industry
- ✔ Relate the evolution of the lodging and foodservice industry to world events
- ✔ Describe the history of restaurants

The concept of hospitality is as old as civilization itself. Its development from the ancient custom of breaking bread with a passing stranger to the operations of today's multifaceted hospitality conglomerates makes fascinating reading.

The word *hospitality* comes from *hospice,* an old French word meaning "to provide care/shelter for travelers." The most famous hospice is the Hospice de Beaune in the Burgundy region of France, also called the Hotel Dieu or the House of God. It was founded as a charity hospital in 1443 by Nicolas Rolin, the chancellor of Burgundy, as a refuge for the poor. During the time of his power, he was regarded as an extremely efficient tax collector, one of the most assiduous Burgundy had ever had. King Louis XI sarcastically remarked that it was very right that Rolin was the one to have constructed a house for the poor, since he had made so many of them!

The Hospice de Beaune is located in one of the most beautiful regions in France, the Côte de Beaune, located in northeastern France near Dijon. The Côte de Beaune owes its name to the town it embraces, Beaune, a center of about sixteen thousand people. A thriving community during the Roman ages, Beaune became an important city in Burgundy during the Middle Ages. Today Beaune is rightly considered the capital of the Burgundian wineland. The wines of the Côte de Beaune are among the finest of their type. The delicacy of the reds compensates for the slight lack of fullness, thus making them particularly appropriate to accompany dishes of subtle flavor. The whites are commonly regarded as the finest in the world.

Something about the fine wines also appears to inspire the muses: Where good wines are made, literature, music, poetry, cuisine, and architecture flourish. The extravagance of the architecture of the Hospice de Beaune is staggering, with ornate fretwork, gabled courtyards, and a dazzling polychrome tile roof. The medieval structure of the outside is mirrored in the inside; however, the building hides modern, twentieth-century medical devices, such as X-ray machines and operating rooms. The Hospice is enriched by a remarkable art collection, which displays distinguished pieces such as Roier van der Weyden's "Last Judgment."

The hospital is still functioning, partly because of its role in the wine world. Throughout the centuries, several Burgundian landowners have donated vineyards to the Hospice to help pay for maintaining its costs. Every autumn the wines from these vineyards—about a hundred acres of vines—are sold at a characteristic and colorful wine auction on the third Thursday in November, which determines the prices for the next year's Burgundy wines.

Ancient Times

Greece and Rome

Mention of hospitality—in the form of taverns—is found in writings dating back to ancient Greece and Rome, beginning with the Code of Hammurabi (circa 1700 B.C.). It is evident from these references that these taverns were also houses of pleasure. The reputation of these establishments was far from savory. The Code required owners to report any customers who planned crimes in their taverns. The penalty for not doing so was death, making tavern-keeping in those times a hazardous occupation. The death penalty could be imposed merely for watering the beer!

Increased travel and trade made some form of overnight accommodations an absolute necessity. Because travel was slow and journeys long and arduous, many travelers depended solely on the hospitality of private citizens.[1]

In the Greek and Roman empires, inns and taverns sprang up everywhere. The Romans constructed elaborate and well-appointed inns on all the main roads. Marco Polo later proclaimed these inns as "fit for a king." They were located about twenty-five miles apart to provide fresh houses for officials and couriers of the Roman government and could only be used with special government documents granting permission. These documents became revered status symbols and were subject to numerous thefts and forgeries. By the time Marco Polo traveled to the Far East, there were 10,000 inns.

Some wealthy landowners built their own inns on the edges of their estates. These inns were often run by household slaves. Nearer the cities, inns and taverns frequented by less affluent citizens were run by freemen or by retired gladiators who would invest their savings in the "restaurant business" in the same way that so many of today's retired athletes open restaurants.

The first "businessman's lunch" is reputed to have been the idea of Seqius Locates, a Roman innkeeper, in 40 B.C. Locates devised this idea for ships' brokers who often were too busy to go home for their midday meals.

Innkeepers, as a whole, were hardly the Conrad Hiltons of their day. They were not admitted to military service, could not usually bring a legal action in court, could not take an oath, nor could they act as guardians for children. The morals of anyone who worked at an inn were automatically suspect.

However, Roman cooks considered themselves superior beings and gave themselves splendid titles. During the reign of Hadrian (A.D. 117–138), cooks and chefs even established their own elite academy on the Palatine Hill in Rome.

Inns for the common folk were regarded as dens of vice, where degenerate aristocrats might go slumming. Generally, the upper classes sought their thrills in the public baths. By the time Caligula came to power in A.D. 37, these baths were open around the clock, mixed bathing was common, and wine flowed freely. Attached to the baths were sumptuous dining rooms available for parties. Banquets, both public and private, eventually became so elaborate and wasteful that Sumptuary Laws were passed to restrict the amounts Romans spent on food and drink.

In ancient Persia, traveling was done in large caravans, which carried elaborate tents for use along the caravan routes. Occasionally, these caravans stopped at *Khans*—combinations of stables, sleeping accommodations, and fortresses—which provided shelter from the elements—such as sandstorms—and also against enemies who found it easy to attack caravans. During this period, accommodations in Asia far surpassed those of the Western World. Trade was brisk, and so was travel. The Chinese posting system was superior to that of the Romans, although mainly confined to those travelers of means.

As the Roman Empire flourished, travelers included merchants, scholars, and actors who stayed at inns and taverns. Often people slept on straw with the animals to keep warm.

After the fall of the Roman Empire, public hospitality for the ordinary traveler became the province of religious orders. In Britain, for instance, inns catered more to the drinker than to the traveler, and traveling was discouraged. Those who did travel were mainly connected with the Royal Court or the Church and were hardly interested in the primitive accommodations provided by wayside inns. In these times, many travelers were missionaries, priests, and pilgrims, traveling to holy places such as temples. Consequently, inns were located close to these religious sites. The accommodations were very basic and were operated by slaves of the priests and holy men of the temples.

Medieval Times

On the European Continent, Charlemagne established rest houses for pilgrims in the eighth century; the sole purpose of several orders of knighthood was to protect pilgrims and provide hospitality on their routes. One such rest house, an abbey at Roncesvalles, advertised services such as a warm welcome at the door, free bread, a barber and cobbler, cellars full of fruit and almonds, two hospices with beds for the sick, and even a consecrated burial ground.

Monasteries were plain but often of a quality superior to that found elsewhere along the road. Monks usually raised their own provisions on the monastery grounds; kitchens were cleaner, better organized, and less chaotic than those in private households; and the brothers even devised a crude system of accounting to determine feeding costs. As a result, pilgrims and vagrants often fared better than the nobility.

Medieval guilds also held open houses to receive pilgrims. Accommodations in medieval guilds were much like those of the monasteries. In fact, the famous Hanseatic League operated a residence in London called *The Steelyard;* the rules for league members were as strict as those for any monk—except that these highly ambitious merchants were not required to take a vow of poverty.

In 1282, the innkeepers of Florence, Italy, incorporated a guild or association for the purpose of business. The inns belonged to the city, which sold three-year leases at auction. They must have been profitable, because by 1290, there were eighty-six innkeepers as members of the guild.

In England, the stagecoach became the favored method of transportation. A journey from London to a city like Bath took three days, with several stopovers at inns or taverns that were also called *post houses.* Today, the journey from London to Bath takes two and one-half hours by car.

As travel and travelers increased during the Middle Ages, so did the number of wayside inns in Europe; yet, they were primitive affairs by today's standards. Guests often slept on mattresses strewn in what today would be the lobby. Each person either ate what they had brought with them or what they could purchase from the house. The fare was usually bread, meat, and beer, but it varied occasionally with fish or capon.

As the quality of the inns improved, more people began to travel. Many of the travelers were wealthy people, accustomed to the good life; their expectations demanded that inns be upgraded. Some of these inns, however, were inclined to be rowdy, and patrons frequenting taverns in a port area were likely to wake up at sea—"shanghaied" (a practice of forcibly obtaining a crew for ships headed toward Asia).

Chaucer's fourteenth-century Canterbury pilgrims gathered in the famed Tabard Inn in London to dine and revel before and after visiting the shrine of St. Thomas à Becket. The best teller of tales during the pilgrimage was rewarded with a free meal and feted by the host, Harry Bailey. He went along on the pilgrimage to judge the best raconteur himself.

One of the first European hotels, the Hotel de Henry IV, was built in Nantes in 1788, at a cost of $17,500. At that time, this was considered a vast sum of money for the sixty beds, considered the finest in Europe.

No discussion of medieval hospitality would be complete, however, without mention of the royal and noble households themselves, which often served hundreds of guests at each meal. Although à la carte dining was practically unknown until the nineteenth century, these households practiced what might be called discriminatory feeding, where different meals were served to persons of different rank. Nobles got the best, of course; an early household book records no less than ten grades of breakfast being served at a single morning meal.

Sanitary standards in these kitchens were appalling, with food supplies poorly stored and overflowing onto the floor, refrigeration unheard of, dogs and children playing freely among the provisions, and dozens of kitchen helpers milling about. To add to the confusion, the food handlers themselves frequently had questionable sanitary habits, so communicable diseases spread freely, to rich and poor alike.

Often, dozens of dishes were prepared for a single meal, elaborately served, but eaten with less than proper ceremony. Forks were unknown. Catherine de Medici allegedly introduced forks to the French court in the sixteenth century, but their use did not become commonplace for another 200 years. Fingers dipped and slipped and splashed in sauces and among tidbits. Knives doubled as both cutting and feeding utensils. Food was eaten from trenchers, which could be made either of wood or pieces of four-day-old bread pared smooth and cut into thick squares.

Despite this, medieval hosts, who naturally knew nothing of germs and sanitation, forks or fingerbowls, set forth their own rules for public suppers, few of which would seem out of place today.

1. Meals should be served in due time: not too early, not too late.
2. Meals should be served in a conveyable place: large, pleasant, and secure.
3. He who maketh the feast should be of the heart and glad cheer.
4. Meals should consist of many diverse messes so that who like not of one may taste another.
5. There should be diverse wines and drinks.

6. Servants should be courteous and honest.
7. There should be natural friendship and company among the diners.
8. There should be mirth of song and instruments of music.
9. There should be plenty of light.
10. The deliciousness of all that is set on the board should be guaranteed.
11. Men should eat by leisure and not too hastily.
12. Without harm and damage every man should be prayed to the dinner.
13. Each diner should rest after supper.[2]

Who could argue with rules such as these?

In the late sixteenth century, a type of eating place for commoners called an *ordinary* began to appear in England. These places were taverns serving a fixed-price, fixed-menu meal at a long common table. Ordinary diners could not be choosy, nor did they often question what they were eating. Frequently, the main dish served was a long-cooked, highly seasoned meat-and-vegetable stew. Culinary expertise was limited by the availability and cost of certain ingredients. Few diners had sound teeth, and many had no teeth at all, so the meal had to be gummable as well as edible. Fresh meat was not always available; spoiled meat was often the rule rather than the exception. Spices helped not only to preserve meat but to disguise the flavor of gamey or "high" meat.

Coffee Houses

During the sixteenth century, two "exotic" imports began to influence the culinary habits of Western Europe: coffee and tea. These beverages, so integrated into the twentieth-century way of life, were once mere taste curiosities. Tea developed much more slowly than coffee as a common beverage and attained widespread use most notably in England—and there not even until the mid-nineteenth century.

Travelers to Constantinople (now known as Istanbul, Turkey) enjoyed coffee there and brought it back to Europe. By the end of the sixteenth century, coffee had become noticed enough to bring about the censure of the Roman Catholic Church, which called it the wine of Islam, an infidel drink. When Pope Clement VIII tasted the drink, he is reputed to have remarked that the Satan's drink was too delicious to leave to the heathens so he made a Christian beverage of it.

During the next century, coffee houses sprang up all over Europe. By 1675, Venice had dozens of coffee houses, including the famous Café Florian on the piazza San Marco, still filled to capacity today. The first English coffee house was opened by an Armenian refugee in St. Michael's Alley, London, in 1652.

When the siege of Vienna by the Turks was lifted in 1683, a gentleman (named Kolschitski, by some accounts) who was credited with saving the city from destruction received permission to open Central Europe's first coffee house. It was here that the first cup of coffee sweetened with honey and lightened with milk was served.

Coffee houses, the social and literary centers of their day and the forerunners of today's cafes and coffee shops, served another even more useful (though less obvious) purpose: They helped to sober up an entire continent.

Café Florian (Courtesy Café Florian.)

In a day when water was vile, milk dangerous, and carbonated beverages centuries in the future, alcoholic drinks were the rule rather than the exception. Children were weaned on small amounts of beer and wine mixed with water (a custom occasionally observed in France). Adults drank amounts measured in gallons. Queen Elizabeth I's ladies-in-waiting, for instance, were allowed a breakfast ration of two gallons of ale. Drunkenness was rampant.

As sobering as coffee houses were, they nevertheless had their detractors. Women abhorred them because, like most public ventures, they were strictly male affairs. Women circulated petitions, to no avail, attacking coffee as a cause of illness, even death; yet coffee houses flourished.

Coffee was generally served in a dish or small bowl, a little larger than to-day's coffee cup, without a handle. Coffee houses were famous for their con-vivial atmosphere; one could sit at a table near a warm fire, meet friends, have a hot, aromatic drink, and discuss the affairs of the day, a tradition that has not changed much through the years.

Hospitality on the Road

At about the time coffee houses began blossoming in cities and towns all over Europe, the advent of stagecoach travel was revolutionizing hospitality on the road. The longer and colder the trip, the greater the bouncing and jouncing, the more welcoming the passengers found the wayside inn, and the great tradition of the British stagecoach inn was born. In the cities, the more well-to-do traveler, who went on horseback or in his or her own carriage, did not stay in the same inns frequented by the coaches and their passengers. Poorer travelers who journeyed on foot had difficulty finding any kind of accommodations at all.

In rural sections, one inn served all travelers, although sharp distinctions were apparent in the treatments meted out. Travelers of means were served in the dining room or in their chambers. Poorer travelers invariably had to eat with the landlord and his family in the kitchen, and they were served the ordinary fare (what the French call *table d'hote* or *table of the host*) at a nominal cost. Wealthier guests could order special dishes à la carte and visit the kitchen to see that they were properly prepared. The fare varied with the region, each having its own specialties to tempt visitors' palates.

Inns on the European continent in no way approached the supremacy of the British variety. Even in an age where travelers got little in the way of comfort, most continental travelers were appalled at what they found, especially compared with British accommodations. Even in France, a country with high culinary standards even then, *les auberges du pays* were known for the poor quality of their food and the high quantity of their vermin.

Eighteenth Century

The New World

Colonial inns and taverns were based on the British type, and the British at this time maintained the highest standards of public accommodations in the western world. Although there is some evidence that a tavern was built in Jamestown, Virginia, during the early days of the settlement, it was the Dutch who built the first known tavern—the Stadt Huys—in Nieuw Amsterdam (New York) in 1642.

Early colonial inns and taverns in America are steeped as much in history as they are in hospitality. The year after the Dutch East India Company opened the Stadt Huys, Kreiger's Tavern opened on Bowling Green. During the American Revolution, this tavern, then called the King's Arms, became the headquarters of British General Gage.

The even more famous Fraunces Tavern was the Revolutionary headquarters of General George Washington, and was the place in which he made his famous Farewell Address. It is still operating.

As the colonies grew from scattered settlements to towns and cities, more and more travelers appeared, along with more accommodations to serve them. In New York and New England, these accommodations were also usually called *taverns*. In Pennsylvania, they were called *inns* and, in the South, *ordinaries*. There were regional differences among these accommodations as well.

The local inn/tavern/ordinary in the Colonies soon became a gathering place for residents, a place where they could catch up on the latest gossip, keep up

Fraunces Tavern (Courtesy Fraunces Tavern.)

with current events, hold meetings, and conduct business. The innkeeper, unlike the landlord of Roman times, was often the most respected member of the community and was always one of its more substantial citizens. The innkeeper usually held some local elected office and sometimes rose much higher than that. John Adams, the second president of the United States, owned and managed his own tavern between 1783 and 1789.

Little wonder that colonial inns and taverns, in addition to their social functions, became ammunition storage depots, meeting places for the Revolutionary underground, and occasionally recruiting offices for pirates, who especially liked to frequent ordinaries along the Southeastern coastline. Many a cutthroat began his career in a public house in Charleston or Savannah.

The Revolutionary War did little to change the character of these public places. They maintained their position as social centers, political gathering places, newsrooms, watering holes, and travelers' rests; now, however, these same places were going by different names—hotels—that reflected a growing French influence in the new nation.

The French Revolution

The French Revolution took place at approximately the same time the American colonies were fighting for independence. Among many other effects, the French Revolution helped to change the course of culinary history.

France is now a nation that awaits with bated breath the Michelin's annual selection of three-star restaurants. Thus, it is hard to believe that only slightly more than 200 years ago, only one restaurant worthy of that rating existed in all of Paris—indeed, in all of France. The Tour d'Argent opened in 1533, and for more than two centuries it was unique. Inns served meals, of course, but they were not primarily eating places, as was the Tour d'Argent. Only the *traiteurs,* or caterers, were allowed by law to sell cooked meat to the public, and they were limited to cooking for banquets.[3]

M. Boulanger, "the father of the modern restaurant," sold soups at his all-night tavern on the Rue Bailleul. He called these soups *restorantes* (*restoratives*), which is the origin of the word *restaurant.* However, Boulanger was hardly content to let his culinary repertoire rest there. In 1767, he challenged the *traiteurs'* monopoly by creating a "soup" of sheep's feet in a white sauce. The *traiteurs* guild sued, and the case went to the French Parliament. Boulanger won, and soon his restaurant, Le Champ d'Oiseau, was restoring hundreds of patrons from the ravages of hunger with its succulent, well-prepared dishes.[4]

One of these dishes, boulangere potatoes, was a dish of sliced potatoes in stock that was baked in the bread bakers' oven. Boulanger allowed people from the neighborhood to use the heat of his oven to cook their potatoes after the bread was done.

In 1782 the Grande Taverne de Londres, a true restaurant, opened on the Rue de Richilieu; three years later, Aux Trois Freres Provencaux opened near the Palais-Royal. By 1794, when heads were literally rolling in Paris, there were 500 restaurants. Although it really cannot be said the French Revolution was responsible for the invention of the restaurant, it was responsible for the propagation of the concept. Except for a few faithful retainers, the chefs of the noble houses of France were scattered by the Revolution. Some stayed in France; some went to other parts of Europe; many crossed the Atlantic to America, especially to New Orleans, the one truly French corner of the New World. They almost all went into the restaurant business.

The chefs brought their culinary traditions with them. Soon the plain, hearty fare of the British and the primitive cooking of the Americans were laced with sauces piquantes and *pots au feu.* Other countries, too, felt the effects of French culinary artistry, and most absorbed some of the principles of French cooking into their own. Exceptions were the Italians, who had developed their own very strong culinary traditions and felt, with a great deal of justification, that French cooking was itself derived from the Italian.

French cuisine was not immediately embraced even by the two nations who stood to benefit most by it—Great Britain and the United States. French cooking was point-blank better than the British, and British cooks felt naturally threatened and became extremely chauvinistic and protective toward their culinary traditions. The United States, however, had no such traditions to uphold; the Puritans simply considered French cooking sinful. The plain cooking heritage had stuck, and travelers from abroad felt that Americans did not treat their abundant raw materials properly when they prepared them.

In 1784, during a five-year period as an envoy to France, Thomas Jefferson acquired a taste for French cuisine. He later enticed a French chef to the

Court of the Two Sisters (Courtesy Court of the Two Sisters.)

White House and paid handsomely for his expertise. This act stimulated interest in French cuisine and enticed U.S. tavern owners to offer better quality and more interesting food.

During this time, several French chefs emigrated to the United States. Many found their way to New Orleans, which was a French enclave. In fact, New Orleans is named after a French city and, over the years, was occupied by Britain, Spain, France, and America. One famous restaurant in New Orleans is the Court of the Two Sisters. It has the names of prisoners from the various wars inscribed on the walls of the entrance way.

Nineteenth Century

By the early 1800s, the English had begun to borrow the concept of the restaurant from their French neighbors. The English restaurant was a lofty place, brimming with haute cuisine, haute decor, and haughty service, and affordable by only a few.

Restaurants in Europe continued to flourish. In 1856, Antonin Careme published *La Cuisine Classique* and other volumes detailing numerous dishes and their sauces. The grande cuisine offered a carte (or list) of suggestions available from the kitchen. This was the beginning of the à la carte menu.

In 1898 the Savoy Hotel opened in London. The general manager was the renowned Cesar Ritz (today, the Ritz-Carlton hotels bear his name) and the Chef des Cuisines was Auguste Escoffier. Between them they revolutionized hotel restaurants. Escoffier was one of the greatest chefs of all time. He is best known for his classic book *Le Guide Culinaire,* which simplified the extraordinary works of Careme. He also installed the kitchen Brigade System.

The Americans used their special brand of ingenuity to create something for everyone. By 1848, a hierarchy of eating places existed in New York City. At the bottom was Sweeney's "sixpenny eating house" on Ann Street, whose proprietor, Daniel Sweeney, achieved questionable fame as the father of the greasy spoon. Sweeney's less-than-appetizing fare ("small plate sixpence, large plate shilling") was literally thrown or slid down a well-greased path to his hungry customers, who cared little for the social amenities of dining.

The next step up was Brown's, an establishment of little more gentility than Sweeney's, but boasting a bill of fare, with all the extras honestly marked off and priced in the margin, and waiters who would occasionally pass within hearing range to attend a customer's wants.

The famous Delmonico's was at the top of the list of American restaurants for a long time. Delmonico's was known as the only expensive and aristocratic restaurant in the United States. From the day the Delmonico family opened its first coffee and pastry shop at 23 William Street in 1827 until the farewell meal was served in Delmonico's Restaurant at 5th Avenue and 44th Street in 1923 (due to Prohibition), the name was synonymous with fine food, exquisitely prepared and impeccably served—the criteria by which all like establishments were judged.

Personal Profile: Auguste Escoffier (1846–1935)

Auguste Escoffier is considered the patron saint of the professional cook. Called the "emperor of the world's kitchens," he is considered as a reference point and a role model for all chefs. His exceptional culinary career began at the age of thirteen, when he apprenticed in his uncle's restaurant. He worked until 1920, and retired to die quietly at home in Monaco in 1935. Uneducated, but a patient educator and diligent writer, he was an innovator who remained deeply loyal to the regional and bourgeois roots of French cookery. He exhibited his culinary skills in the dining rooms of the finest hotels in Europe, including the Place Vendome in Paris and the Savoy and Carlton hotels in London.

Escoffier

When the Prince of Wales requested something light but delicious as late dinner after a night in the Casino in Monte Carlo, Auguste Escoffier responded with *poularde Derby*, a stuffed chicken served with truffles cooked in champagne, alternating with slices of butter-fried *foie gras*, its sauce basted with the juices from the chicken and truffles. Another interesting anecdote regarding the chef's originality in making sauces tells of a special dinner for the Prince of Wales and Kaiser Wilhelm. Escoffier was asked to create a special dish to honor such an occasion. Struggling with an apparent loss of creativity until the night before the event, the chef finally noticed a sack of overripe mangos, from which he created a sauce that he personally came out from the kitchen to serve. As he placed the plate on the table, he looked at the Kaiser and with a wicked smile said, "*zum Teufel*"—to the devil. Then was born sauce diabla, today a favorite classic sauce. Escoffier's insistence on sauces derived from the cooking of main ingredients was revolutionary at the time and in keeping with his famous instruction: *faites simple*—keep it simple.

In fact, in his search for simplicity, Escoffier reduced the complexity of the work of Careme, the "cook of kings and king of cooks," and aimed at the perfect balance of a few superb ingredients. In *Le Livre des Menus* (1912), Escoffier makes the analogy of a great dinner as a symphony with contrasting movements that should be appropriate to the occasion, the guests, and the season. He was meticulous in his kitchen, yet wildly imaginative in the creation of exquisite dishes. In 1903, Escoffier published *Le Guide Culinaire,* an astounding collection of more than 5,000 classic cuisine recipes and garnishes. Throughout the book, Escoffier emphasizes technique, the importance of a complete understanding of basic cookery principles, and ingredients he considers to be essential to the creation of great dishes.

Escoffier's refinement of Careme's *grand cuisine* has been so radical as to credit him with the development of a new cuisine referred to as *cuisine classique.* His principles have been reinstated by successive generations, most emphatically by the *novelle cuisine* brigade. Francois Fusero, *chef de cuisine* at the Hotel Hermitage, Monte Carlo, regards Escoffier as his role model, and he schools his chefs in Escoffier's style: No detail is left to chance.

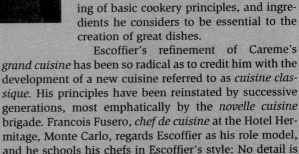

Delmonico's served Swiss-French cuisine and became the focus of American gastronomy (the art of good eating). Delmonico's is also credited with the innovation of the bilingual menu, Baked Alaska, Chicken à la King, and Lobster Newberg. The Delmonico steak is named after the restaurant. Realizing that his customers would have difficulty ordering from a menu printed entirely in French, John Delmonico paid a linguist, Robert Greenhow, $100 to translate the French menu into an English bill-of-fare, with the menu and its translation printed side by side. This custom has survived and even expanded with the years. Delmonico's changed the way Americans ate.

More and more, eating places in the United States and abroad catered to residents of a town or city and less to travelers forced to make do with wayside fare. The custom of eating out for its own sake had arrived.

Hotel del Coronado (Courtesy Hotel del Coronado, San Diego, California.)

Other American cities had their own hotel-palaces: Chicago had the Palmer House; New Orleans had the St. Charles and St. Louis hotels; St. Louis had the Planter's Hotel. The Hotel del Coronado in San Diego is a historic landmark. The "Hotel del's" unique architectural style has contributed to its worldwide fame. Philadelphia, Baltimore, Washington, D.C., and Buffalo all had their fashionable hostelries, each one the last word in gilt-edge opulence. Sometimes they were filled with "antiques" of questionable origin and decorations of questionable taste. The one thing that could not be called questionable was the food. By 1852, any first-class hotel worth its guest register had a French chef. Americans were reputed not to be too fond of "fussy" French meals, with their souffles and sauces, but those who frequented these hotels would have been loathe to admit it. Although the modern hotel was admittedly an American invention, the Europeans had made some contributions of their own. For instance, there was the European plan, which meant a guest need not pay for both room and meals in one lump sum, but could pay for only the room and order the meals separately from an à la carte menu, or eat elsewhere, if preferred.

Although big cities of the nineteenth century had their marble palaces, small towns had their serviceable imitations. Resort areas like Saratoga Springs, New York, and White Sulphur Springs, West Virginia, offered a whole new world of social and sensual pleasures. Yet, west of St. Louis, there was still no such thing as a decent night's lodging or a square meal. It's said, however, that the cafeteria concept originated in the California Gold Rush, when prospectors, eager to return to their claims, stood in line to be served from big communal bowls and pots rather than wait their turn at table.

By the 1870s, general conditions in the West had begun to civilize; unfortunately, the quality of the hospitality had not improved correspondingly. Rail travelers were warned to bring along nonperishable viands (foods) that could last several days. There were no dining cars or vendors. Meals were served in grimy lunchrooms, whose greedy proprietors often split their profits with train workers to ensure that the "all aboard" would sound before passengers had a chance to eat. The exact same reheated food was often served to three or four trainloads.

In 1876, Fred Harvey opened a small railway restaurant on the second floor of the Santa Fe railway depot in Topeka, Kansas. The restaurant was different from others of its kind in that it featured good, well-cooked food, spotless facilities, and courteous service. Business boomed.

Later that same year, Harvey opened his first hotel in Florence, Kansas, on the Santa Fe railway. During the 1880s and 1890s, Harvey Houses opened every 100 miles along the Santa Fe. They were renowned not only for genteel accommodations, incomparable seven-entree meals, and superb service, but also for their famous "Harvey Girls." These attractive, well-trained servers were recruited from good homes in the East, and eventually contributed more than their share to taming the untamed West. Thousands found husbands and settled from Kansas to California. "Grandma was a Harvey Girl" is today proclaimed proudly by many of the West's first families.

One could say that the nineteenth century saw more innovations in hospitality than in all previous recorded history. Women began to dine out in most of the Western world's distinguished restaurants. The famed Cesar Ritz, whose last name has entered the vocabulary as a synonym for the ultimate in luxury, made restaurant dining at London's Savoy almost a must for the fashionable aristocracy of both sexes. For those not so formally disposed, the "grill room," another English concept, made informal dining possible in a congenial, well-appointed atmosphere.

In the nineteenth century, better methods of preserving food through canning and vacuum packing made out-of-season culinary delights commonplace on tables everywhere. Many contributed to this development, primarily Napoleon I, who in 1809 awarded a prize of 12,000 francs (nearly a quarter of a million dollars in modern currency) to a man named Nicholas Appert for inventing a process to keep foodstuffs edible when preserved in glass jars. Napoleon's motivations were military rather than altruistic, as his armies were depleted as much by deficiency diseases and starvation as from wounds.

There was also an enormous growth in mass feeding. In schools, until the nineteenth century, no one had ever considered lunches for schoolchildren, because there were so few children who went to school. For those few who were fortunate enough to attend college, there had been a tradition of student hostels both in England and on the European Continent since sometime in the twelfth century. Through the centuries these hostels—sometimes run by the students themselves, sometimes through endowments, sometimes by the school—had provided some sort of living quarters and sustenance for the student population. Eventually, many of them evolved into the houses, clubs, fraternities, and sororities of today.

It was not until the Industrial Revolution freed great numbers of children from child labor that the school-age population increased to where feeding children of an elementary school age became a problem. Canteens for schoolchildren started in France in 1849. In 1865, Victor Hugo, the famous French author, started school feeding in England by providing hot lunches at his home in Guernsey for the children of a nearby school. In 1853, the Children's Aid Soci-

ety in New York opened an industrial school and offered food to all consumers. Some decades later,
men and women concerned with nutrition for children sponsored the development of school lunch-
room programs in several urban centers; state extension services, PTAs, and other organizations saw
to it that these services were available in rural
schools as well.

P.J. Clarke's (Courtesy P.J. Clarke's.)

The nineteenth century also saw the development of hospital feeding that did not kill as many
patients as it helped cure. For this the world owes
another great debt of gratitude to Florence Nightin-
gale, who was the founder of dietetics as well as
modern nursing. In the diet kitchen she set up at the
hospital at Scutari (now part of Istanbul) during the
Crimean War, she replaced the ill-cooked, ill-served fare with punctual and
more appetizing meals.

The nineteenth century also saw the birth of the ice cream soda, and marble-
topped soda fountains began to make their appearances in so-called ice cream
parlors.

This century brought about enormous changes in our traveling and eating
habits. Tastes have been refined and expanded in the twentieth century, but it
is interesting to note how many restaurants have stood the test of time.

Thirty-five restaurants in New York City have celebrated their one-hundredth
birthdays. One of them, P.J. Clarke's, established in 1890, is a "real" restaurant-
bar that has changed little in its hundred years of operation. On entering, one
sees a large mahogany bar, its mirror tarnished by time, the original tin ceiling,
and the tile mosaic floor. Memorabilia ranges from celebrity pictures to Jessie,
the house fox terrier that customers had stuffed when she died and who now
stands guard over the ladies' room door. Guests still write their own checks at
lunch time, on pads with their table numbers on them (this goes back to the
days when one of the servers could not read or write and was struggling to memorize orders).[5]

Twentieth Century

In 1921, Walter Anderson and Billy Ingraham began the White Castle hamburger chains. The name White Castle was selected because white stood for purity and castle for strength. The eye-catching restaurants were nothing more
than stucco building shells, a griddle, and a few chairs. People came in droves,
and within ten years White Castle had expanded to 115 units.[6]

Marriott's Hot Shoppe and root beer stands opened in 1927. About this time,
the drive-in roadside and fast food restaurants also began springing up across
America. The expression *car hop* was coined because as an order taker approached

an automobile, he or she would hop onto the auto's running board. The drive-in became an established part of Americana and a gathering place of the times.

In 1925, another symbol of American eateries, Howard Johnson's original restaurant, opened in Wollaston, Massachusetts.

After the stock market crash of 1929 and the Depression, America rebounded with the elegance and deluxe dining of the 1930s à la Fred Astaire. The Rainbow Room opened in 1934. This art deco restaurant championed the reemergence of New York as a center of power and glamour.

Trader Vic's opened in 1937. Although the idea was borrowed from another restaurant known as the Beachcomber, Trader Vic's became successful by drawing the social elite to the Polynesian theme restaurant where Vic concocted exotic cocktails including the Mai-tai, which he invented.[7]

At the World's Fair in 1939, a restaurant called Le Pavillion de France was so successful that it later opened in New York. By the end of the 1930s, every city had a deluxe supper club or night club.

The Four Seasons opened in 1959. The Four Seasons was the first elegant American restaurant that was not French in style. It expressed the total experience of dining, and everything from the scale of the space to the tabletop accessories was in harmony.[8]

The Four Seasons was the first restaurant to offer seasonal menus (summer, fall, winter, spring) (see Figure 1–1), with its modern architecture and art as a theme. Joe Baum, the developer of this restaurant, understood why people go to restaurants—to be together and to connect with one another. It is very important that the restaurant reinforce why customers chose it in the first place. Restaurants exist to create pleasure, and how well a restaurant meets this expectation of pleasure is a measure of its success.[9]

The savvy restauranteur is adaptable. Being quick to respond to changing market conditions has always been the key to success in the restaurant business. An interesting example of this was demonstrated in the early 1900s by the operator of Delmonico's. As business declined during a recession in the 1930s, Delmonico's opened for breakfast, then began delivering breakfast, lunch, dinner, and other fare to Wall Street firms for late-evening meetings. Next, he turned his attention to the weekends when Wall Street was quiet. He built up a weekend catering business and developed a specialty of weddings. Later, he connected with tour groups going to Ellis Island and encouraged them to stop off for meals.[10]

Following World War II, North America took to the road. There was a rapid development of hotels and coffee shops. They sprang up at almost every highway intersection.

The 1950s witnessed incredible growth in both air and road transportation. Cross-continental flights were not only more frequent, but took much less time. In 1958, the Boeing 707 enabled faster trans-Atlantic flights. Pan-Am began offering daily eight-hour flights from New York to Paris. The 1950s also saw the emergence of a new phenomenon—"fast food."[11]

In the 1960s, as a result of a booming economy, business and leisure travel grew. The Boeing 727 could carry 125 passengers at up to 600 mph. Fine dining became more popular—business people liked to eat well. Mass tourism

DINNER

We Suggest That You Order The Dessert Soufflé
At The Beginning Of The Meal

COLD APPETIZERS

Parma PROSCIUTTO with Poached Pears	17.00	A Service of SHRIMP	19.00
Breast of QUAIL Salad with Chestnuts	15.50	LITTLENECKS, A Platter	13.00
Smoked Scottish SALMON Roulade with Caviar	25.00	Cherrystone CLAMS	13.00
Roasted PEPPERS, Mozzarella and Basil	15.00	CRAB Lump Cocktail	19.00
TUNA Carpaccio with Ginger and Coriander	17.00	A Selection of OYSTERS	15.00
		Smoked Scottish SALMON	25.00
		Beluga CAVIAR	90.00

HOT APPETIZERS

LOBSTER Ravioli	20.00
RISOTTO Cake with Wild Mushrooms	15.00
Sautéed Fresh FOIE GRAS	25.00
Crisp SHRIMP with Mustard Fruits	19.50

SOUPS

SEAFOOD Gumbo with Okra	10.50
PHEASANT Consommé	9.50
Pumpkin BISQUE with Pepitas	9.50

THIS EVENING'S ENTREES

Grilled Curried SWORDFISH with Pickled Vegetables 37.50
Seared SALMON with Braised Belgium Endive, Saffron Vinaigrette 38.50
CRABMEAT Cakes with Mustard Sauce 37.50
Maine LOBSTER: Broiled, Poached or Steamed 42.00
DOVER SOLE Meunière or Broiled 45.00
Breast of PHEASANT Braised in Port with Mashed Potatoes 35.00
Médallion of VENISON with Stuffed Savoy Cabbage and Cranberries 40.00
Grilled LAMB CHOPS with String Beans 37.00
Sautéed CALF'S LIVER with Olives and Avocado 34.00
VEAL Four Seasons with Crabmeat and Artichokes 42.00
Black Angus Skillet STEAK with Smothered Onions 40.00
Grilled FILET MIGNON, Béarnaise and Snow Peas 40.00
A Skewer of Grilled VEGETABLES and WILD MUSHROOMS, Bulgur and Avocado 30.00

FOR TWO (PER PERSON)

Roast Darn of SALMON with Herb Sauce 39.50
Crisp Farmhouse DUCK: au Poivre or with Apple and Cinnamon Compote 39.50
Roast Rack of LAMB with Zucchini and Pepper Timbale 42.00
CHATEAUBRIAND with Béarnaise, Snow Peas and Wild Mushrooms 45.00

SPA CUISINE ®

APPETIZERS:	BAY SCALLOPS Seviche 14.00
MAIN COURSES:	Grilled Filet of LAMB with Corona Beans and Broccoli 33.00
DESSERT:	APRICOT Semifreddo 8.50

SALADS, VEGETABLES AND POTATOES

Caesar SALAD	11.50	WILD RICE with Pine Nuts	9.00
Wilted SPINACH and Bacon	9.50	SNOW PEA Pods with Shoyu	8.00
Winter GREENS	9.00	Creamed SPINACH	7.00
Stuffed Savoy CABBAGE	9.00	Mashed POTATOES	6.50
Sautéed WILD MUSHROOMS	9.50	Baked POTATO	6.00
		ROESTI	6.50

DESSERTS

A Selection from the DESSERT WAGON	8.50
SHERBETS and ICE CREAMS	6.50
Choice of APPLE CINNAMON, CRANBERRY	
ORANGE or CHOCOLATE and KAHLUA Soufflé	8.50

BEVERAGES

A Variety of TEAS	3.50
COLOMBIAN COFFEE	3.50
CAFE Cognac Chantilly	8.50
IRISH COFFEE	8.50
ESPRESSO	3.50

THE FOUR SEASONS

Figure 1–1 *Four Seasons Menu*

The Four Seasons Restaurant (Courtesy Four Seasons Restaurant.)

began as millions could afford vacations and had the urge to travel. TWA purchased Hilton International and began offering package tours.[12]

The 1970s saw the introduction of new establishments like Taco Bell, TGI Fridays, Houston's, and Red Lobster in the restaurant industry and Days Inn, Super 8 Motels, and Comfort Inns in the lodging industry. Corporations like Four Seasons, Canadian Pacific, Marriott, Hyatt, Sheraton, Hilton, Radisson, Ramada, and other high-end chains expanded in North America and, in some cases, overseas.

In the 1980s, tourism and travel continued to increase dramatically. The Baby Boomers began to exert influence through their buying power. Distant exotic destinations and resorts became even more accessible and more popular.

The 1990s began with the recession that had started in 1989. The Gulf War contributed to the downturn that the industry experienced. As organizations strived for profitability, they downsized and consolidated.

Since 1993, the economic recovery has proved very strong, and, with the maturing of the industry, a number of mergers and acquisitions have taken place. Many corporations experiencing near saturation in North America have expanded overseas. Eastern Europe and China have opened up. These and other trends are discussed in more detail in following chapters.

Hospitality and Tourism Pioneers

The hotel industry has a number of outstanding individuals who have made a significant contribution to the growth and development of the profession. Among the better-known hotel pioneers of the late-nineteenth and early-twentieth century are Ellsworth Statler, Conrad Hilton, Ernest Henderson, Howard

Johnson, and J. Willard (Bill) Marriott. Cesar Ritz's story is a good example of an industry pioneer.

Cesar Ritz

Cesar Ritz

Cesar Ritz was a legend in his own time; yet, like so many of the early industry leaders, he began at the bottom and worked his way up through the ranks. In his case it did not take long to reach the top because he quickly learned the secrets of success in the hotel business. His career began as an apprenticed hotel keeper at the age of fifteen. At nineteen he was managing a Parisian restaurant. Suddenly, he quit that position to become an assistant waiter at the famous Voisin restaurant. There he learned how to pander to the rich and famous. In fact, he became so adept at taking care of the guests—remembering their likes and dislikes, even their idiosyncrasies—that a guest would ask for him and want to only be served by him.

At twenty-two, he became manager of the Grand National Hotel in Lucerne, Switzerland, one of the most luxurious hotels in the world. It was not very successful at the time Ritz became manager, but with his ingenuity and panache he was able to attract the "in" crowd to complete a turnaround. After eleven seasons, he accepted a bigger challenge: the Savoy Hotel in London, which had only been open a few months and was not doing well. Cesar Ritz became manager of one of the most famous and luxurious hotels in the world at the age of thirty-eight.

Once again, his flair and ability to influence society quickly made a positive impression on the hotel. To begin with, he made the hotel a cultural center for the high society. Together with Escoffier as executive chef, he created a team that produced the finest cuisine in Europe in the most elegant of surroundings. He made evening dress compulsory and introduced orchestras to the restaurants. Cesar Ritz would spare no expense in order to create the lavish effect he sought. On one occasion he converted a riverside restaurant into a Venetian waterway, complete with small gondolas and gondoliers singing Italian love songs.[13]

Ritz considered the handling of people as the most important of all qualities for a hotelier. His imagination and sensitivity to people and their wants contributed to a new standard of hotel keeping. The Ritz name remains synonymous with refined, elegant hotels and service.[16] However, Ritz drove himself to the point of exhaustion, and at age fifty-two, he suffered a nervous breakdown.

Grenelle Foster

Foster

"Ask Mr. Foster," the oldest U.S. travel agency, began in 1888 when Ward Grenelle Foster opened a "travel information office" in St. Augustine, Florida. When the town's residents or travelers had queries concerning directions or visitors' information, they were directed not to the local Seven Eleven, but instead to W. G. Foster's gift shop, where they could "ask Mr. Foster." Foster later adopted this phrase as the name for his small business.

In the 1890s, "Ask Mr. Foster" expanded to all three coasts of the Sunshine State and later to New York and other metropolitan centers. The offices were usually conspicuously located in large buildings, such as hotels and department stores, with heavy foot traffic. The company provided free information and reservations. Their brochure promised to "plan your trip, secure your ticket, make your reservations for hotels, steamers, autos, schools, and railroads—anywhere in the world."

Despite its immense success, Foster decided to sell the business in 1928. It then changed hands several times before it was bought in 1979 by the Carlson Companies, the hospitality conglomerate based in Minneapolis, Minnesota. In 1988, the company had more than 750 offices in forty-six states, and its total sales exceeded that of American Express travel agency sales.[14]

Ellsworth Milton Statler (1863–1928)

Ellsworth Milton Statler is considered by many to be the premier hotelman of all time. He brought a high standard of comfort and convenience to the middle-class traveler at an affordable price. His life story is that of a man overcoming adversity. At age fifteen, with only two years of experience as a bellboy at a leading hotel in Wheeling, West Virginia, Statler became head bellman. Noting the oversized profits gained from the hotel's billiard room and railroad ticket concession, he persuaded the owner to lease him the concessions. A studious promoter, he billed special billiard exhibition games and brought in crowds. Soon he had launched a bowling alley, then a restaurant—*The Pie House*—which was the best in town. By 1894, at the age of thirty-one, Statler was making $10,000 a year and was ready for new fields to conquer.

Buffalo, New York, was the setting for his next venture, one that almost proved to be his undoing. Statler opened a restaurant in the basement of the Ellicott Square Building—a new office building promoted as the "largest in the world." Statler found, however, that Buffalo was an eat-at-home town, and despite an efficient operation, his creditors closed in. With incredible imagination and energy, Statler changed the eating habits of Buffalo's downtown business people. He advertised "All you can eat for twenty-five cents," and in three short years the tide had turned. Statler was in the black and ready for bigger and better things.

He opened a 2,257-room hotel, the Inside-Inn, which was described as the biggest exhibit at the World's Fair in St. Louis. In 1908, Statler opened a 300-room, 300-bathroom hotel in Buffalo, where his genius was seen in many details. Back-to-back rooms used common shafts for plumbing. Every guest room had ice water on tap, a towel hook beside each bathroom, a telephone, and a full-sized closet with its own light. From then on, the Statler story was one of incredible success.

In 1912, Statler built the Cleveland Statler, a property that could handle large business groups, and instituted the policy of "a free newspaper every morning." The kitchens were designed to provide an unhindered traffic flow of food and personnel. The dining rooms were located in close proximity to the kitchen instead of on a lower floor, and guest rooms were decorated with variety but always with related colors. Other Statler innovations included posted room rates, attached bed-headboard reading lamps, radios at no extra charge, and a liberal quantity of towels and writing supplies in all rooms.

"EM," as Statler signed himself, was a dynamo of energy, and no detail of construction or operation was too small for his attention. The Statler Foundation today has assets of many millions.

Thomas Cook and Son

People with knowledge about travel have been arranging trips for others for centuries, but Thomas Cook is credited with being the first professional travel agent.

A wood-turner by trade, Cook was a deeply religious person and a temperance enthusiast. In 1841, he chartered a train to carry 540 people to a temperance convention. Cook arranged the round trip from Leicester to Loughborough, a distance of twenty-two miles, at a shilling per person. Although Cook made no profit for himself, he did realize the potential in arranging travel for other people. From the outset, he saw that the travel business was more than a business—it was an opportunity for education and enlightenment.

In 1845, Cook became a full-time excursion organizer. Reasoning that the five percent commission he received from Midland Countries Railroad was not enough to maintain a solvent business, he became a tour operator and, later, a retailer of tours as well. Dedicated to making tours as convenient and interesting as possible, Cook printed a "handbook of the trip" for an 1845 tour from Leicester to Liverpool. Soon after, he produced coupons that could be used to cover hotel expenses. In 1846, Cook took 350 people by steamer and train on a tour of Scotland, using a touring guide, the first of its kind, prepared especially for the trip. By 1851, Cook's clientele had grown to over 165,000 people. It was that year that Cook made plans to visit London for the first World Exhibition at the Crystal Palace.

After Cook moved his offices to London, he began conjuring up all sorts of imaginative trips. Soon he was arranging "grand circular tours of Europe" with itineraries that included four different countries. He helped popularize Switzerland as a touring center by taking a group through the country in 1863. Soon after the American Civil War, Cook's son, John M. Cook Jr., traveled with a group to the United States and visited New York, Washington D.C., and a handful of Civil War battlefields.

In 1872, Cook achieved another first—an around-the-world trip that took the ten-member group 222 days to complete. Today, the same trip could be taken over a weekend.

Throughout the latter half of the nineteenth century, "The Cook's Tour" included an escorted group expedition, most often conducted by Thomas or one of his sons. After Cook became blind, members of his family took over the business, however, Cook stayed on as manager of the firm. He arranged a trip into Yellowstone Park soon after it opened. In 1875, preparations were finalized for Cook tours to visit Norway, and, then, in collaboration with the P and O Steamship Line, they traveled to India. In the 1890s, the Cooks ran pioneering trips across Europe to Asia via the Trans-Siberian Railroad.

Cook's company was successful partly because he made travel convenient and relatively simple. Another reason was Thomas Cook's enthusiasm for travel as an enlightening venture, not just for the upper class, but for anyone who could afford his much lower prices. In essence, Cook can be credited with making world travel possible for the middle class.

The Cook family was well aware of the elasticity of demand for travel. If the cost was reduced, more people would travel. The more people traveled by a particular mode of transportation, the more likely it was that the cost of transportation could be reduced. For example, by chartering whole trains and steamers and by booking large blocks of rooms, Cook was able to reduce travel expenses considerably. The cost of operating a train, steamship, or airplane that is 100 percent full is only a little more than that of operating one that is 25 percent full, and the cost per seat at 100 percent capacity is substantially less.

The Cooks also pioneered the travel conglomerate (one company engaging in a number of enterprises) long before the term was ever used. Before 1875, the firm had acquired the exclusive right to carry the mail, as well as special travelers and government officials, between the cities of Assiont and Assonan on the Nile.

Upon Thomas Cook's death in 1893, ownership and management of the firm passed to his three sons. The business, by that time, had grown to include three divisions: tourists, banking, and shipping. Later, in 1931, Thomas Cook and Son merged with the Wagon Lit Company, operators of the sleeping car and express trains in Europe. Still, the Cooks continued to do everything possible to make the trip easy for the traveler. Cook's agents often met planes with a car, waiting at the entrance to customs to whisk travelers directly to a reception or anywhere else they wanted to go. The all-inclusive price for a tour made it easier for people to plan vacations and to budget their time and money.

Following World War II, the British government acquired the principle interest in the Thomas Cook and Son Company but later sold it in 1972 for $858.5 million. Today, the Trust Houses Forte, the largest hospitality company in Britain, and the Automobile Association of Britain are part of the owning consortium. The company now has more than 625 offices and 10,000 employees around the world and is composed of five relatively independent divisions. Considered to be the largest of its kind, the company today has manifold interests other than the sale of travel.

We have seen that until the nineteenth century, discretionary travel was limited to a very small percentage of people. This changed dramatically as the Industrial Revolution gave millions of people in North America and Europe some discretionary income. More important, trains and airlines made travel comparatively cheap and convenient. In response to travel demand, entrepreneurs such as Thomas Cook, and later, travel expediters, helped promote and make travel arrangements easier.

Howard Dearing Johnson

Today, Howard Johnson is one of the best-known names in the restaurant and hotel business. The name reflects driving ambition, a desire for excellence, and a prescient perception of the American public. Originally, Johnson worked as a tobacco salesman for his father's company, but when his father passed away in 1925, Johnson was forced to quit school and find a different line of employment. In order to maintain a secure income, he borrowed $500 and took over a drugstore with a small newspaper distributorship in Wallaston, Massachusetts. Although it was highly profitable, Johnson feared that he might lose the newspaper franchise and decided to sell ice cream as well. Business boomed. In the summer, he built little shacks along the Massachusetts beaches and hired boys to sell big ice cream cones and frankfurters for a dime.

Johnson was also one of the first to pioneer franchising in the 1930s. Thanks to his efforts, there were twenty-five Howard Johnson restaurants in 1935 and in 1940, there were 100. In spite of World War II, Johnson's profits continued to soar but not in the highway restaurant business. Johnson instead turned to colleges, and shipping and military units to serve his food. After V-J Day (Victory over Japan) and the signing of the peace treaty that ended the war with Japan in 1947, Johnson reverted back to the highway restaurant business. In fact, it is a tribute to Johnson's drive and ingenuity that at the end of the war he was in better financial condition than he was at the beginning. This success was due in part to his prewar production of ice cream. However, large factors included highway location and cleanliness, and high-quality ice cream and sandwiches served in clean, attractive, and easily identifiable buildings.

In the 1950s, Johnson set a precedent by marketing frozen foods. He built product-specific companies in Boston and Miami where many of the Howard Johnson menu items were created on a production-line basis.

The company entered the lodging industry in 1954 with the franchising of its first motor lodge in Savannah, Georgia. This new venture was a natural offshoot for the restaurant chain, which for nearly thirty years had been highway and family-oriented. As the commercial traveler became a more important segment, recreational facilities, meeting rooms, and banquet rooms were introduced.

In 1959, Howard Sr. abdicated his position as president in favor of his son, telling him to "make it grow." In the years that followed, Johnson's staff grew dramatically in numbers, but despite his renewed efforts, the company failed to attract a fresh constituency. This dilemma found its roots in faulty managerial planning. The company neglected to conduct full-fledged market analyses, relying instead on comment cards.

In 1996, under the new leadership of Howard Johnson President and CEO Stephen H. Phillips, Hospitality Franchise Systems (HFS) launched a plan called "The Future Is Now" to revitalize the brand for the next century. It will allow Howard Johnson properties to capitalize on the improvements in quality, service, and curb appeal that have been achieved during the last few years. A key part of the revitalization is bold, contemporary marketing. While preserving the chain's traditional orange and teal, the new look is set on a bright blue background. Franchisees are also being encouraged to update their building exteriors.

The energetic Phillips, an industry veteran and long-term Howard Johnson franchisee himself, is a strong believer in the strength of the brand. Because of him, they have the longest history in the midmarket segment.[15]

J. Willard Marriott

John Willard Marriott, the second of eight children, was born and raised in Utah. As one may expect in a large family, he took on responsibility at a rather young age, doing odd jobs to earn money and serving two years as a Mormon Missionary by age eighteen. After completing his mission, he enrolled in Weber Junior College and, later, the University of Utah. In order to pay for his education and to help his family financially, he worked at various jobs, such as selling woolen underwear to lumberjacks, managing a bookstore, and teaching high school English.

In 1927, with his wife Alice, Marriott began to sell A&W Root Beer in a stand he personally built in Washington, D.C. Business was slow, particularly when cold weather arrived, so Marriott added hot food to the menu and renamed the stand Hot Shoppe. The concept caught on, making Marriott a millionaire by the age of thirty.

Despite battles with health problems, Marriott remained mentally strong, expanding his business by pioneering in-flight catering at Washington's old Hoover Airfield in 1937. Just two years later, he entered the foodservice management market, providing service to government offices, school cafeterias, and hospitals, and in 1957, Marriott opened the first of many Marriott lodgings. Because of the growing success and the changing image of his company, Marriott renamed his company Marriott Corporation in 1967.

Marriott's son, Bill Jr., officially took over as chief executive officer (CEO) of the Marriott Corporation in 1972. Under the new leadership, the corporation boasted sales in excess of $3 billion by the mid-1980s and had expanded to include resorts, cruise ships, fast food, and senior living communities.

Although Willard Marriott passed away in 1985, Bill Jr. and the Marriott Corporation have continued to be a key asset to the hospitality industry. Through his faith, determination, and family guidance, Willard Marriott began with a root beer stand, founded by necessity, and built it into a multibillion dollar industry.

Ray Kroc

Of all hospitality entrepreneurs, Ray Kroc has been most financially successful. In 1982, he was senior chairman of the board of McDonald's, an organization intent on covering the earth with hamburgers. Among the remarkable things about Kroc is that it was not until age fifty-two that he even embarked on the royal road to fame and fortune.

The original McDonald's concept was created by two brothers, Richard and Maurice, who had no interest in expanding. The McDonald brothers were content with their profitable, yet singular restaurant in San Bernardino, California. However, the golden arches impressed Kroc, as did the cleanliness and simplicity of the operation.

Kroc's organizational skills, perseverance, and incredible aptitude for marketing were his genius. His talent also extended to selecting close associates who were equally dedicated and who added financial, analytical, and managerial skills to the enterprise. Kroc remained the spark plug and master merchandiser until he died in 1984, leaving a multimillion dollar legacy.

Much of Kroc's $400 million has gone to employees, hospitals, and the Marshall Field Museum. It is distributed through Kroc's own foundation. Most importantly, Kroc developed several operational guidelines, including the concepts of "KISS"—Keeping It Simple Stupid—and QSC&V—Quality, Service, Cleanliness, and Value. Kroc's "Never Be Idle a Moment" motto was also incorporated into the business.

Enterprises like McDonald's are not built without ample dedication and Ray Kroc certainly had a wealth of dedication. Today, an average McDonald's franchise can net more than $1 million annually thanks to Kroc's ingenious marketing strategies. In fact, McDonald's Corporation has become so affluent that it was named *Entrepreneur* magazine's number one franchise in 1997.

Isadore Sharp

Isadore Sharp, a first-generation Canadian, is the chairman, president, and founder of Four Seasons Regent Hotels. From one motel on Toronto's Jarvis Street in the early 1960s has grown the world's largest luxury hotel chain—a multi-million-dollar global hotel empire. Four Seasons Regent's success is largely a reflection of the drive, determination, and personal taste and style of Isadore Sharp.

Four Seasons was built slowly, deal by deal. From the first little motel that Sharp literally helped construct, to the complex Asian agreement in which Four Seasons acquired Regent Hotels International Inc., the growth of this company is largely the result of one man's vision. Isadore Sharp (called Issy by friends and family) has created a company that friends and foes alike agree is a model for how Canadian companies can compete globally in an increasingly interconnected world economy.

Isadore Sharp, Chairman of the Board, Four Seasons-Regent Hotels and Resorts

Currently, the Four Seasons manages and owns forty-one hotels around the world and continues to move ahead with more hotel plans in different countries. Isadore Sharp's success is all the more remarkable because he did not inherit vast wealth, and did not rise through the ranks of a major corporation with ready access to international money markets. He is a self-made man, consistent, who has control of his spirit. He believes in excellent quality for both his hotels and his company. Sharp clearly loves his business and credits the Four Seasons Regent team with the successes of the company.

Ruth Fertel

There is no accolade or award for "the first lady of American restaurants," but if there were, Ruth Fertel, founder of Ruth's Chris Steak House, would surely qualify for it.

Ruth's Chris Steak House is the nation's largest upscale restaurant chain with fifty-nine operations—fifty-four in the United States and Puerto Rico, and five internationally—selling more than 11,000 steaks daily and grossing more than $200 million annually. By virtue of this volume, Ruth Fertel is the country's most successful woman restauranteur today.

The Ruth's Chris's success story began on a hunch and a gamble. Born in New Orleans in 1927, Fertel earned a degree in chemistry with a minor in physics at Louisiana State University at the age of nineteen. She taught briefly at McNeese Junior College in Lake Charles, Louisiana, but left to marry and raise a family. Fourteen years later, and by then divorced, she reentered the work force as a lab technician at Tulane Medical School. After four years, she was convinced that she could not earn enough to send her two sons to college and so, in 1965, she decided to go into business for herself. While scanning the classified section of the local newspaper, Fertel found an ad for a steak house that was for sale. Although she had no prior experience and limited funds, she decided to try it despite the advice of her lawyer, her banker, and her best friend to the contrary. She mortgaged her home to buy the small restaurant, which was then called Chris Steak House.

Fertel

Fertel compensated for her lack of experience with plain hard work. In the first six months, she more than doubled her previous annual salary. Her restaurant soon became popular with the city's media personalities, political leaders, sports figures, and business people. The name "Ruth's Chris" became synonymous with fine, quality steaks.

In 1977, at the urging of a loyal customer, Fertel granted her first franchise for a locally owned Ruth's Chris Steak House. Today, twenty-four restaurants are company owned and thirty-five are franchised.

Fertel attributes her success to the way she treats her customers and associates—as she would want to be treated—and to her basic "gut feeling" that has been responsible for successful decisions throughout the years.

The consistent quality of the meat she serves has also contributed to her success. Through the years, she has stuck with the same suppliers and served nothing but the finest foods on the market.

Conclusion

The exclusive restaurant of yesterday may still be the exclusive restaurant of today, but the less affluent citizen can choose from a staggering array of eating places ranging from the almost-exclusive to the almost-greasy spoon.

What people have today is choice; it is truly a world in which the automobile and airplane have made almost any place in the world accessible to the average citizen. It is a world with more people who expect to have better accommodations, food, entertainment, recreation, and leisure.

Summary

1. The first references to hospitality can be traced back to ancient Greece and Rome, when increased travel and trade made some form of overnight accommodation a necessity.

2. The Romans developed a well-appointed postal system. The ancient Persians created a combination of stables and sleeping accommodations called Khans, which served traveling caravans.

3. During the Middle Ages, hospitality started to become more organized with the creation of a restaurant guild. In England, the stagecoach became the favorite method of transportation.

4. Many values established for hospitality during medieval times can still be applied today, such as friendly service, nice atmosphere, and plenty of food. Compared with today, sanitary standards were rather poor and accommodations primitive.

5. The sixteenth century introduced two exotic imports, coffee and tea, to Europe. Coffee houses not only became social gathering places but also helped to sober up an entire continent.

6. During the Middle Ages, most inns distinguished themselves in their treatment of common and noble travelers. This led to the creation of the ordinary, a tavern that served a fixed menu at a fixed price to the common folk.

7. As colonies developed into towns, traveling increased. Taverns became a social and political gathering place reflecting a growing French influence.

8. The French Revolution influenced the culinary development by establishing the first restaurant in the New World and bringing French cuisine to America.

9. The nineteenth century created concepts such as à la carte dining, mass feeding, better preservation, and ice

cream parlors, and established the custom of eating out.

10. Advanced technology and transportation in the twentieth century has opened up the world to almost every-one. People expect a wide range of dining choices, including excellent service, food, accommodations, and entertainment. This fast-paced century also created the fast-food industry.

Review Exercises

1. Explain the origin of the term *hospitality*.
2. Give a brief overview of the development of hospitality from ancient Rome to the New World.
3. What values of hospitality that existed during the Middle Ages are still valued today? Name one concept that originated during that time and still exists today.
4. Explain how the respectability of innkeepers changed from ancient Rome until modern times and how this related to the evolution of the lodging industry.
5. Explain the importance of the French Revolution in the history of restaurants.
6. What is the concept of modern hospitality?

Key Words and Concepts

À la carte	French Revolution	Khans	Rest houses
Boulanger	Guild	Marco Polo	Cesar Ritz
Coffee houses	Hospice	Monasteries	Table d'hote
Delmonico's	Hospitality	Ordinary	Taverns
European plan			

Notes

[1] This section draws on William S. Gray and Salvatore C. Liquori, *Hotel and Motel Management and Operations*. Englewood Cliffs, N.J.: Prentice Hall, 1980, pp. 4–5.

[2] *Hospitality Through the Ages*. Corning Glass Works Foodservice Products, Corning, N.Y. 14830.

[3] In those days a number of guilds existed as societies of merchants or tradespeople whose purpose was to promote and protect their common interests.

[4] Linda Glick Conway (ed.), *The Professional Chef*, 5th ed. Hyde Park, N.Y.: The Culinary Institute of America, 1991, p. 5.

[5] Ibid.

[6] John Mariani, *America Eats Out*. New York: William Morrow, 1991, pp. 122–124.

[7] Ibid.

[8] Martin E. Dorf, *Restaurants That Work*. New York: Whitney Library of Design, 1992, p. 9.

[9] Ibid.

[10] Ibid.

[11] Richard A. Wentzel, "Leaders of the Hospitality Industry or Hospitality Management," *An Introduction to the Industry*, 6th ed. Dubuque, Iowa: Kendall/Hunt, 1991, p. 29.

[12] This section draws on Lundberg, op. cit., pp. 33–34.

[13] Richard A. Wentzel, "Leaders of the Hospitality Industry or Hospitality Management," *An Introduction to the Industry*, 6th ed. Dubuque, Iowa: Kendall/Hunt, 1991, p. 29.

[14] Donald E. Lundberg, *Tourist Business*, New York: Van Nostrand Reinhold, 1990.

[15] This section draws from Donald E. Lundberg, *The Hotel and Restaurant Business*, 6th ed. New York: Van Nostrand Reinhold, pp. 268–270.

[16] This section draws on Lundberg, op. cit., pp. 33–34.

Tourism

2

After reading and studying this chapter you should be able to do the following:

✔ Define tourism
✔ Trace the five epochs (or periods) of tourism
✔ Describe the evolution of the major travel modes
✔ Outline the important international and domestic tourism organizations
✔ Describe the economic impact of tourism
✔ Identify promoters of tourism
✔ List reasons why people travel
✔ Describe the sociocultural impact of tourism
✔ Describe ecotourism

What Is Tourism?

Tourism is a dynamic, evolving, consumer-driven force. Tourism is the world's largest industry. This viewpoint may be correct if all the interrelated components are placed under one umbrella, as shown in Figure 2–1.

The World Travel and Tourism Council declares the travel and tourism industry to have the following characteristics:

- ✔ The world's largest industry, with approximately $3.8 trillion in gross output in 1997 and an expected $7.1 trillion by the year 2007
- ✔ The world's leading industrial contribution, producing more than ten percent of the world's Gross National Product (GNP)
- ✔ A leading producer of tax revenues
- ✔ Employer of 262 million people, or ten percent of the global workforce[1]
- ✔ Expected to grow faster than any other sector of world employment[2]

Given the declining manufacturing and agricultural industries, and in many countries the consequent rise in unemployment, it is to the service industries that world leaders should turn for real strategic employment gains.

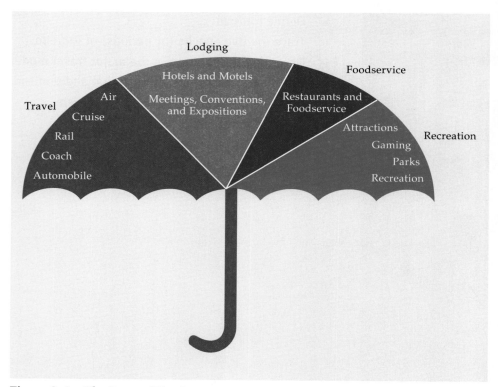

Figure 2–1   *The Scope of Tourism*

Tourism, already the world's largest industry, offers the greatest global employment prospects. This trend is caused by the following factors:

1. The opening of borders
2. An increase in disposable income and vacations
3. Cheaper and more exclusive flights
4. An increase in the number of people with more time and money
5. More people with the urge to travel

According to the World Travel and Tourism Council—the industry's Business Leaders' forum—tourism and travel generates, directly and indirectly, more than ten percent of global gross domestic product (GDP), investment, and employment. It is forecast to grow strongly at 40 to 50 percent in real terms during the next ten years. This means a growth of nearly 2 million jobs in the United States by 2007. Globally, projections are for 700 million visitor arrivals by 2000 and 1 billion by 2010.[3]

The futurist, John Naisbit, says that the global economy of the twenty-first century will be driven by three superservice industries: telecommunications, information technology, and travel and tourism.[4]

The fact that tourism is expected to grow so rapidly presents both tremendous opportunities and challenges. The good news is the variety of exciting career prospects for today's hospitality and tourism graduates. Tourism, although a mature industry, is a young profession. Careful management of tourism and travel will be necessary to avoid repercussions and negativism toward the "pesky" tourist—which is already happening to some extent in Europe, where the sheer number of tourists overwhelms attractions and facilities.

There is an interdependency between the various segments of tourism, travel, lodging, foodservice, and recreation. Hotel guests need to travel in order to reach the hotel. They eat in nearby restaurants and visit attractions. Each segment is, to an extent, dependent upon another for business.

Definition of Tourism

The word *tourism* did not appear in the English language until the early nineteenth century. The word *tour* was more closely associated with the idea of a voyage or perhaps a theatrical tour than with the idea of an individual "traveling for pleasure purposes, which is the accepted use of the word today."[5] *Webster's Tenth Collegiate Dictionary* defines a tourist as "one that makes a tour for pleasure or culture."

Tourism can be defined as the science, art, and business of attracting and transporting visitors, accommodating them, and graciously catering to their needs and wants.[6]

A tourist, by United Nations (U.N.) definition, is a person who stays for more than one night and less than a year. Business and convention travel is included in this definition.

For many developing nations, tourism represents a relatively high percentage of gross national product and an easy way of gaining a balance of trade with other nations.

Tourism means different things to different people. For example, a hotelier might say that tourism is wonderful because it brings guests who fill rooms and restaurants. However, a government official might define it as the economic benefit of more money coming into the country, state, or city. In order to simplify tourism, it is sometimes categorized in terms of the following factors:

Geography: International, regional, national, state, provincial, country, city
Ownership: Government, quasi-government, private
Function: Regulators, suppliers, marketers, developers, consultants, researchers, educators, publishers, professional associations, trade organizations, consumer organizations
Industry: Transportation (air, bus, rail, auto, cruise), travel agents, tour wholesalers, lodging, attractions, recreation
Motive: Profit or nonprofit[7]

Industry practitioners use these categories to identify and interact with the various industry sectors and organizations involved with tourism.

The Five Epochs of Tourism

The historical development of tourism has been divided up into five distinct epochs (or periods),[8] four of which parallel the advent of new means of transportation.

Pre–Industrial Revolution (prior to 1840)
The railway age
The automobile age
The jet aircraft age
The cruise ship age

Pre–Industrial Revolution

As early as 300 B.C., ancient Egyptians sailed up and down the river Nile, carrying huge rocks with which to build pyramids as tombs for their leaders.[9] The Phoenicians were among the first real travelers in any modern sense. In both the Mediterranean basin and the Orient, travel was motivated by trade. However, trade was not the only motivation for travel in these times; commerce and the search for more plentiful food supplies also stimulated travel.[10]

The Roman Empire provided safe passage for travelers via a vast road system that stretched from Egypt to Britain. Wealthy Romans traveled to Egypt and Greece, to baths, shrines, and seaside resorts.[11] The Romans were as curious as modern-day tourists. They visited the attractions of their time, trekking to Greek temples and to places where Alexander the Great slept, Socrates lived, Ajax committed suicide, and Achilles was buried. The Romans also traveled to Egypt to visit the Pyramids, the Sphinx, and the Valley of the Kings—just as today's tourists do.[12] The excavated ruins of the Roman town Pompeii, which was buried by an eruption of Mt. Vesuvius, yielded several restaurants, taverns, and inns that tourists visit even today.

Medieval travel was mostly confined to religious travel, particularly pilgrimages to various shrines: Moslems to Mecca and Christians to Jerusalem and Rome. The Crusades began in 1095 and lasted for the next 200 years, stimulating a cultural exchange that was, in part, responsible for the Renaissance.

Across Europe, travel and trade flourished. With the increase in living standards came a heightened awareness of cultural pursuits. Later, aristocrats undertook Grand Tours of Europe, stopping at major cities for weeks or months at a time. It was considered a necessary part of "rounding out" a young lady's or gentleman's education. Fortunately, travel now has become possible for almost everyone.

The Railway Age

Railroads played a major role in the development of the United States, Canada, and several other countries. The pioneering spirit carried by the railroads opened up the great American West. Prior to the advent of rail travel, tourists had to journey by horse and carriage. By comparison, the railway was more efficient, less costly, and more comfortable. Resort communities came within the reach of a larger segment of the population in North America and Europe. The railroads brought changes in the lodging industry, as taverns along the turnpikes gave way to hotels near the railway stations.

The first railroad was built in the United States in 1830, but only twenty-three miles of rail were laid by the end of that year. In contrast, by 1860, there were 30,626 miles of track. In 1869, rail journey across America was made possible by the transcontinental connection, which enabled the journey to be completed in six days.[13] Before that, such a journey took several months by wagon or several weeks by clipper ships rounding Cape Horn, South America.

To ensure passenger comfort, railroads had excellent dining cars and sleeping berths. Railroads continued to extend their lines into the twentieth century until the Great Depression of the 1930s and World War II. These events began a decline in railroad usage that was accelerated by the invention of the automobile. The freedom of the open road gave automobile travel a competitive advantage over train travel.

In order to prevent a complete collapse of the passenger rail system, the U.S. government created AMTRAK in 1971. AMTRAK is a semipublic organization;

AMTRAK Train (Courtesy AMTRAK.)

Bullet Train (Courtesy Japan Tourist Bureau.)

eight of the fifteen members of its board are selected by the President of the United States, three by the railroads, and four by preferred private stockholders.[14] AMTRAK is subsidized by the U.S. Congress, in amounts ranging from $500 million to $800 million per year; this subsidy represents between 35 and 50 percent of its total revenue.[15] AMTRAK has eliminated many unprofitable lines and improved overall efficiency and service quality. About half of AMTRAK's trains and passengers are in the heavily populated northeastern United States.

Despite these efforts, many passengers opt for the speed and sometimes price advantages of the airlines. To counter this, AMTRAK offers special prices on regional or transcontinental travel. Tour packages are also popular, particularly with retired people who prefer relaxing and watching the ever-changing scenery to driving.

Although rail travel has declined in the United States, railroads in Europe and Asia play far more important roles in passenger and freight transportation. Railroads are more cost-effective and a more efficient means of transportation in densely populated areas. Europeans have developed trains that can travel up to 250 miles per hour. The French Trés Grande Vitesse (TGV, very high speed) runs between Paris and Marseilles in three hours. The channel tunnel (Chunnel) links England with France and enables both trains and automobiles to travel the twenty-three miles of the English Channel.

In Japan, the bullet train can go up to 250 miles per hour. Not all trains go quite that fast, but the ride is remarkably smooth—a beverage glass can rest on a table and not spill. As with the United States, the Japanese and European rail systems are heavily subsidized by their respective governments. However, without such subsidies, the roads and the air would be more congested.

Many Americans visiting Europe take advantage of the Eurailpass. The Eurailpass, which must be purchased from travel agents outside of Europe, allows visitors to travel throughout Europe, with the exception of the United Kingdom. Visitors can get on and off the train at hundreds of cities and enjoy the local attractions.

Automobile Travel

Automobiles evolved from steam engines in the late 1800s, when Karl Benz and Gottlieb Daimler built a factory for internal combustion engines, which is now Mercedes Benz.[16]

In 1891, the production of automobiles began in large numbers. Before long, Henry Ford produced his first vehicle and invented the techniques for making

Model-T Ford

automobiles on an assembly line. By 1914, Henry Ford was producing one Model T Ford every twenty-four seconds.[17] The assembly-line production continues today with the additional help of robots.

The United States has about 150 million autos registered. The country with the next largest amount is Japan, which has about 33 million registered. Figure 2–2 shows the number of motor vehicles registered in various countries.

The call of the great open road and the increased financial ability of more families to purchase automobiles led to a tremendous growth in travel and

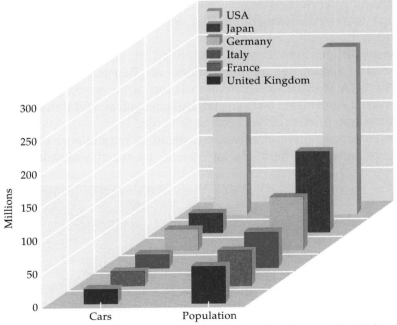

Figure 2–2 *Registered Cars and Population by Country* (R. Walters Somerset, *Travel Industry World Yearbook. The Big Picture—1993*. New York: Child and Waters, 1993.)

tourism. Motels and restaurants sprang up along the highways. The automobile made more places accessible to more people.

Air Travel

The Wright brothers, who enjoyed the hobby of gliding, decided to fit an engine to one of their gliders with movable fins and wingtip controls. To find an engine light enough, they had to build their own. In 1903, they tested their thirteen-horsepower engine. On the first run it lifted the craft in the air for twelve seconds and covered a distance of 120 feet.[18]

In 1909 an airplane crossed the English Channel, and by 1919 a scheduled passenger service began between London and Paris. Realizing that others were about to attempt to cross the Atlantic, Charles Lindbergh persuaded a group of investors in St. Louis to fund construction of a new airplane in San Diego. The "Spirit of St. Louis" was built in sixty days. With 450 gallons of gasoline on board (the tanks even blocked forward visibility), Lindbergh made the first solo crossing of the Atlantic Ocean in 1927. This history-making twenty-eight-hour flight was a major turning point in aviation history. This monumental achievement was a catalyst for massive investment in the airline industry.

The first scheduled air service in the United States began in 1915 between San Diego and Los Angeles. Later, in 1930, the Douglas Company in California introduced the DC-2, which could carry fourteen passengers and fly at a speed of 213 miles per hour. The most renowned airplane, the DC-3, came into service in 1936. To this day, well over 2,000 of them are still flying.[19]

In 1944, an international conference was held in Chicago to establish international air routes and services. American and European delegates disagreed about how much to restrict competition—the Americans pushed for unrestricted competition.

However, seventy airlines from forty nations ratified an important agreement of transportation rates and created the International Air Transportation Association (IATA). The IATA is the major trade association of the world's airlines. Through international agreements on financial, legal, technical, and traffic matters, the worldwide system of air travel became possible.[20]

American and European representatives met again in Bermuda in 1946 to work out a compromise. The Bermuda agreement, by which countries ex-

Spirit of St. Louis

changed benefits, was to later become a model for bilateral negotiations. The "six freedoms of the air" agreed upon in Bermuda were as follows:

- ✔ The right to fly across another nation's territory
- ✔ The right to land in another country for noncommercial purposes
- ✔ The right to disembark passengers and cargo from the carrier's home country in a foreign country
- ✔ The right to pick up passengers and cargo destined for the carrier's home country from a foreign country
- ✔ The right to transport passengers and cargo from one foreign country to another foreign country
- ✔ The right of an airplane to carry traffic from a foreign country to the home nation of that airline and beyond to another foreign country

In 1954, the first Boeing 707 came into service. By 1958, Pan American Airways inaugurated transatlantic flights from New York to Paris. A Boeing 707 could carry 111 passengers over a range of about 6,000 miles at a cruising speed of 600 miles per hour. Also in 1958, McDonnell-Douglas introduced the DC-8, which boasted a similarly impressive performance.

Other aircraft were introduced to handle the medium- and short-range routes. The Boeing 727 was introduced in 1964. It became the workhorse of the U.S. domestic market, carrying 145 passengers at a cruising speed of 600 miles per hour. In 1968, the Boeing 737 established itself as the short-range challenger to the McDonnell-Douglas DC-9. The Boeing 747, introduced in 1970, was the first of the wide-body aircraft. It could transport 400 to 500 passengers at a cruising speed of 600 miles per hour over distances of about 7,000 miles.

A consortium of European countries developed the Airbus. The Airbus A 340 is designed for the long-distance market, and the Airbus A 320 is for the short-distance market.

The Concorde was the first supersonic aircraft, developed at a cost of $3 billion by the British and French governments. However, it has been a financial disaster. The Concorde has a cruising speed of 1,450 miles per hour, vastly reducing time needed to fly from London to New York. A 747 flight leaving at 11 A.M. London time will land at 1:40 P.M. New York time. On a Concorde, a flight leaving at 11:00 A.M. London time will land at 9:50 A.M., New York time. Air France operates the Concorde from Paris, Dakar, and Rio de Janeiro. British Airways (BA) operates Concordes between London and Bahrain and from London to Washington, D.C., or New York.

Boeing 707, 727, 737 (Courtesy Boeing Corporation.)

Boeing 747 (Courtesy Boeing Corporation.)   *Concorde* (Courtesy British Airways.)

Air transportation has further reduced the cost per mile of travel, enabling millions of people to become tourists. As a result, hotels, restaurants, and attractions have grown to keep pace with demand. The speed of air transportation enables vacationers to take intercontinental trips. Europe and Asia are only hours away as are all the cities of North and Latin America.

The Airline Deregulation Act of 1978

Air transportation changed dramatically in 1978. Deregulation transferred the responsibility for airline activity to the Federal Aviation Administration (FAA) and the Department of Transportation (DOT). The purpose of the Deregulation Act was to allow a free market of competition whereby airlines could decide their own fare structures and rates. Deregulation resulted in retrenchment of major air carriers, new airlines, lower airfares, and "megacarriers."[21]

The effects of deregulation were to force several noncompetitive airlines out of business. Pan Am, once the flag bearer of international aviation, lost money and went out of business because it became bloated with too many layers of bureaucracy and too large a payroll. Simply because they had been in business longer, many of the pilots and cabin crew at Pan Am were more highly paid than their competitors. Over the years, costs such as fuel also escalated.

Not only did airlines go out of business, but some were also absorbed by other airlines. For example, Texas Air bought Eastern Airlines, Continental, People's Express, Frontier, and New York Air. They are operated under Continental Airlines.

In the late 1980s, most of the major airlines were in an expansion mode. They incurred heavy debt, spending money on new planes and terminals. This debt service made major airlines vulnerable to price wars, with resultant operational losses.

Over the past few years, major U.S. airlines have lost billions of dollars. One reason is competition from international airlines, several of which are subsidized by their national governments. Although British Airways is the world's largest airline, Air France is central Europe's largest and arguably its steadiest airline. However, Air France lags behind rivals in key areas: controlling costs, starting a frequent-flier plan, and forging meaningful alliances with foreign carriers.[22]

Competition for market share within and to Europe from the United States has intensified. Since 1985, the number of U.S. carriers flying to France has increased from two to eight. This competition has cut Air France's transatlantic market share from 50 percent to 35 percent.[23]

USAir's strategic partnership with British Airways is an example of internationalism that benefits airlines that must compete in a global marketplace. For an airline like USAir to expand into the global market, such a strategic alliance makes sense. Thomas Lagow, USAir's executive vice president of marketing, says that the issue is simple: USAir answers to shareholders, employees, and passengers—if they're happy, that's all that matters.[24]

Alliances of this nature will allow airlines access to each other's feeder markets and to resources that will enable them to flourish in what will ultimately be a worldwide deregulation. A feeder market is a market that provides the source—in this case, passengers for the particular destination.

The complexities of the international business community are illustrated by the fact that Air Canada now owns 28 percent of Continental Airlines. It is possible that these airlines will cooperate if the proposed open skies accord between Canada and the United States takes place.

Ultimately, any major European airline without a strategic alliance in the United States will only limit its own horizons and lose market share.

Major U.S. carriers like TWA and Northwest have been close to bankruptcy for some time. However, they have negotiated salary cuts of up to 15 percent in return for employee representation on the board and 3.5 percent of the company's stock. American Airlines has also worked out a similar cost-reduction package with its employees.[25] At United Airlines, labor proposes to give $3.4 billion in concessions over five years for up to 60 percent of the company's stock, plus significant control over major decisions.[26]

Southwest, a regional carrier, operates more efficiently than the competition despite the fact that its workforce is unionized. Southwest gets more flight time from its pilots than American—672 hours a year versus 371, and racks up 60 percent more passenger miles per flight attendant. These efficiencies have helped Southwest to turn a profit in 1993, while the rest of the industry lost $4 billion.[27]

Regional carriers, such as Southwest, with lower operating costs and consequently lower fares, have forced larger companies to retreat. This has a growing impact on the airline industry.

In order to reduce losses brought about by deregulation, major carriers eliminated unprofitable routes, often those serving smaller cities. New airlines began operating shuttle services between the smaller cities and nearest larger or hub city. This created the hub-and-spoke system (see Figure 2–3).

The Hub-and-Spoke System

In order to remain efficient and cost effective, major U.S. airlines have adopted a hub-and-spoke system. The hub-and-spoke system enables passengers to travel from one smaller city to another smaller city via a hub or even two hubs.

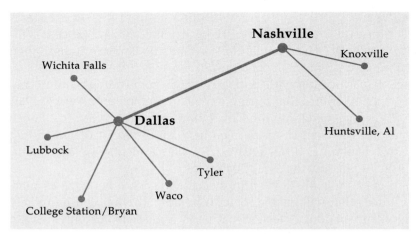

Figure 2–3   *The Hub-and-Spoke System*

Similarly, passengers may originate their travel from a small city and use the hub to reach connecting flights to destinations throughout the world.

The hub-and-spoke system has two main benefits: (1) airlines can service more cities at a lower cost, and (2) airlines can maximize passenger loads from small cities, thereby saving fuel.

Cruise Ships

More than 200 cruise lines offer a variety of wonderful vacations, from the "Love Boat" to freighters that carry only a few passengers. Travelers associate a certain romance with cruising to exotic locations and being pampered all day.

Being on a cruise ship is like being on a floating resort. Accommodations range from luxurious suites to cabins that are even smaller than most hotel rooms. Attractions and distractions range from early morning work-outs to fabulous meals, with nightlife consisting of dancing, cabarets, and possibly gambling. Day life might involve relaxation, visits to the beauty parlor, organized games, or simply reclining in a deck chair by the pool reading a novel. Nonstop entertainment includes language lessons, charm classes, port-of-call briefings, cooking, dances, bridge, table tennis, shuffleboard, and more.

For example, the new Crown Princess is a "super Love Boat" weighing in at 70,000 tons and costing $200 million. This ship is longer than two football fields and capable of carrying up to 1,596 passengers. The Crown Princess was designed by Italian architect Reizo Piano. Its exterior resembles a head of a dolphin, and it features the "Dome," a 13,000-square-foot entertainment complex forward on the top deck. The Dome boasts a casino with blackjack, craps, roulette tables, and masses of slot machines as well as a dance floor, bar, and lounge with wrap-around windows.

Radisson Hotels International has entered the $4.6 billion cruise business with a dramatic catamaran—a twin-hulled ship designed to prevent most of the pitching and rolling that causes seasickness. The new ship, the Radisson Diamond, can carry up to 354 passengers. Completed in 1992 for about $125 mil-

Love Boat (Courtesy Princess Cruise Lines.)

lion, its cost was about 10 to 15 percent higher than a comparable single-hull ship. With rates at about $600 per day, this ship has joined the top end of the cruise market.

The cruise market increased more than 500 percent between 1970 and 1990. However, only about six percent of Americans have been on a cruise. Rates vary from a starting point of $195 per person per day on Carnival Cruise Lines to $600 on the Radisson Diamond. Rates typically are quoted per diem (per day) and are cruise-only figures, based on double occupancy.

There are some 215 ships providing lake, river, but mostly ocean-going cruises. The spectacular new ships with the multideck atriums and razzle-dazzle entertainment cater to the market with incomes of approximately $30,000 and up.

Carnival Cruise Lines is the most successful, financially—netting about 20 percent of sales. It targets adults between the ages of twenty-five and fifty-four, and expects to attract close to 2 million passengers with its spectacular atriums, and round-the-clock activities. Its largest income, other than the fare itself, is from beverage service. Casino income is also high and its casinos are the largest afloat. Carnival hopes that passengers will enjoy buying drinks and putting quarters, or preferably dollars, into the shipboard slot machines. They also hope

Radisson Diamond (Courtesy Carlson Corporation.)

Aft:	Toward the rear or stern of the ship
Beam:	Ship's width at the widest point
Bridge:	Part of the ship where the navigation is done
Bulkhead:	Shipboard name for wall or partition
Cabin:	Name given to a passenger's room
Captain:	Master of the ship; the captain is the final authority and has total responsibility for every aspect of the ship's safety and operations
Companion way:	Flight of stairs
Cruise director:	Individual who plans and directs all shipboard entertainment, including passenger activities, shows, shore excursions
Forward:	Toward the bow or front of ship
Galley:	Seagoing word for kitchen
Gangway:	Ship's boarding ramp
Knot:	Nautical speed (about 1-1/16 of a land mile per hour)
Port side:	Left-hand side of the ship as you face forward
Starboard side:	Right-hand side of the ship as you face forward
Stern:	Aft or rear of the ship
Tonnage:	A customary measure of a ship's size
Wake:	Waves behind a ship

Figure 2–4   *Cruise Lingo*

their passengers will not mind a crowded cabin, since the activities on the ship occupy all of their waking hours and much of the night.

No two ships are alike. Each has its own personality and character. The nationality of the ship's officers and staff contributes greatly to the ship's ambiance. For example, the ships under the Holland America flag have Dutch officers and Indonesian/Filipino crew, and those belonging to the Epirotiki flag have Greek officers and crew.

Casual ships cater to young couples, singles, and families with children. At the other end of the spectrum, ships that appeal to the upscale crowd draw a mature clientele that prefers a more sedate atmosphere, low-key entertainment, and dressing for dinner.

About 4.7 million people took cruises in 1996. Many passengers are remarkably loyal to their particular vessel; as many as half of the passengers on a cruise may be repeat guests.

See Figure 2–4 for examples of cruise lingo.

Most cruise ships sail under foreign flags because they were built abroad for the following reasons:[28]

1. U.S. labor costs for ships, officers, and crew, in addition to maritime unions, are too high to compete in the world market.
2. U.S. ships are not permitted to operate casino-type gambling.
3. Many foreign shipyards are government subsidized to keep workers employed, thereby lowering construction costs.

In addition, cruise ships sail under foreign flags (called "flags of convenience") because registering these ships in countries such as Panama, the Bahamas, and Liberia means fewer and more lax regulations and little or no taxation.

Table 2–1 Passengers Taking a Cruise Longer Than Two Days	
Year	Passengers
1970	500,000
1980	1.4 million
1990	3.6 million
1992	4.4 million (est.)

Perry Hobson, "Analysis of the U.S. Cruise Line Industry," *Tourism Management*, December 1993, p. 454.

Employment opportunities for Americans are mainly confined to sales, marketing, and other U.S. shore-based activities, such as reservations and supplies. On board, certain positions such as cruise director and purser, are sometimes occupied by Americans.

Anecdote

The maître d' on the Love Boat was explaining the dining room staff's duties beginning with breakfast at 6 A.M., followed by lunch and dinner. A student asked, "When does the second shift come on?" The maître d' laughed and said, "There is no second shift." Needless to say, that student's interest declined, especially when he realized the crew would be at sea for months at a time.

Table 2–1 shows the number of passengers taking a cruise lasting more than two days according to the Cruise Lines Association (CLA).

Segmenting the Cruise Market

There are marked differences between the segments of the cruise industry.

Mass Market: Generally people with incomes in the $20,000 to $39,000 range, interested in an average cost per person of between $125 and $200 per day, depending on the location and size of the cabin.

Middle Market: Generally people with incomes in the $40,000 to $59,000 range, interested in an average cost per person of $200 to $350 per day. This is the largest part of the market. These ships are capable of accommodating 750 to 1,000 passengers. The middle market ships are stylish and comfortable with each vessel having its own personality that caters to a variety of different guests. Among the cruise lines in the middle market are Princess Cruises, Norwegian Cruise Lines, Royal Caribbean, Holland America Lines, Windstar Cruises, Cunard Lines, and Celebrity Cruises.

Luxury Market: Generally people with incomes higher than $60,000, interested in an average cost per person of more than $350 per day. In this market, the ships tend to be smaller, averaging about 700 passengers, with superior appointments and service. What constitutes a luxury cruise is partly a matter of individual judgment, partly a matter of advertising and public relations. The ships that received the top accolades from travel industry writers and others who assign such ranks, cater only to the top two percent of North American income groups. Currently, the ships considered to be in the very top category are The Sea Goddess I, the Sea Goddess II, Seabourn Spirit, Seabourn Legend, Seabourn Pride, Crystal Harmony, Crystal Hanseatic, Radisson Diamond, Silver Wind, and Song of Flower. These six-star vessels have sophisticated cuisine, excellent service, far-reaching and imaginative itineraries, and highly satisfying overall cruise experiences.

A current trend in the cruise industry is toward merging, or consolidation, of cruise lines. As any market matures, there is a tendency towards consolidation, which allows for greater economy of scale. This, in turn, leads to more efficient marketing and cost savings, by virtue of the size of the organization. For example, increased purchasing power could result in substantial savings.

Tourism Organizations

Governments are involved in tourism decisions because tourism involves travel across international boundaries. Governments regulate the entrance and exit of foreign nationals. They become involved in the decisions surrounding national parks, heritage, preservation, and environmental protection, as well as cultural and social aspects of tourism. Tourism is to some extent an international ambassador, fostering goodwill and closer intercultural understanding among the peoples of the world.

International Organizations

Looking first at the macro picture, the World Tourism Organization (WTO) is the most widely recognized organization in tourism today.[29] The WTO is the only organization that represents all national and official tourism interests among its allied members.

The International Air Transportation Association (IATA) is the global organization that regulates almost all international airlines. The purpose of IATA is to facilitate the movement of people and goods via a network of routes. In addition to tickets, IATA regulations standardize waybills and baggage checks and coordinate and unify handling and accounting procedures to permit rapid interline bookings and connections. The IATA also maintains stability of fares and rates.

International Civil Aviation Organization (ICAO) is comprised of more than eighty governments. ICAO coordinates the development of all aspects of civil aviation, specifically with regard to the formulation of international standards and practices.

Each of several international development organizations shares a common purpose that includes tourism development. The better known organizations include the following:

The World Bank (WB), which lends substantial sums of money for tourism development. Most of this money is awarded in the form of low-interest loans to developing countries.

The International Bank for Reconstruction and Development, which is similar to the World Bank.

United Nations Development Program (UNDP), which assists countries with a variety of development projects, including tourism

Organization for Economic Cooperation and Development (OECD), which was established by an international convention signed in Paris in 1960. The purpose of the OECD is to do the following:

1. Achieve the highest sustainable economic growth and employment, and a rising standard of living in member countries while maintaining financial stability—thus contributing to the development of the world economy
2. Contribute to sound economic expansion in member as well as non-member countries through economic development
3. Contribute to the expansion of world trade on a multilateral, nondiscriminating basis, in accordance with international obligations

The OCED's tourism committee studies various aspects of tourism, including tourism problems, and makes recommendations to governments. The committee also works on standard definitions and methods of data collection, which are published in an annual report entitled "Tourism Policy and International Tourism in OECD Member Countries."

Other banks and organizations with similar interests include the Asian Development Bank, Overseas Private Investment Corporation, Inter-American Development Bank, and Agency for International Development.

The Pacific Area Travel Association (PATA) represents thirty-four countries in the Pacific and Asia that have united behind a common goal: excellence in travel and tourism growth. PATA's accomplishments include shaping the future of travel in the Asia/Pacific region; it has had a remarkable record of success with research, development, education, and marketing.

Domestic Organizations

The United States Travel and Tourism Administration (USTTA) is the main government agency in the United States responsible for the promotion of tourism. USTTA was established in 1981 by the National Tourism Policy Act. The mission of USTTA is to develop travel to the United States from other countries, expand growth of the U.S. travel industry, and encourage foreign exchange earnings. USTTA is responsible to the Secretary of Commerce, whose job it is to coordinate the various governmental policies, issues, and programs that affect tourism development.

The Travel Industry of America (TIA) is the national association that speaks for the common interests and concerns of all components of the U.S. travel industry. Its mission is to benefit the whole U.S. travel industry by unifying its goals, coordinating private sector efforts to encourage and promote travel to and within the United States, monitoring government policies that affect travel and tourism, and supporting research and analysis in areas vital to the industry. Established in 1941, TIA's membership represents more than 2,000 travel-related businesses, associations, and local, regional, and state travel promotion agencies of the nation's 6.02-million-employee travel industry.

State Offices of Tourism

The next level of organizations concerned with tourism is the state office of tourism. State offices of tourism are charged by their legislative bodies with the orderly growth and development of tourism within the state. They promote information programs, advertising, publicity, and research in terms of their relationship to the recreation and tourism attractions in the state.

City-Level Offices of Tourism

Cities have also realized the importance of the "new money" that tourism brings. Many cities have established convention and visitors bureaus (CVBs) whose main function is to attract and retain visitors to the city. The convention and visitors bureaus comprise representatives of the city's attractions, restaurants, hotels and motels, and transportation. These bureaus are largely funded by the transient occupancy tax (TOT) that is charged to hotel guests. In most cities, the TOT ranges from 8 percent to 18 percent. The balance of funding comes from membership dues and promotional activities.

The Economic Impact of Tourism

The World Travel and Tourism Council, a Brussels-based organization, commissioned a study from the Wharton Economic Forecasting Association. Their report put the total gross output for travel and tourism at $3.8 trillion in 1997 and estimated that it will be $7.1 trillion in 2007, or more than ten percent of the World's gross national product (GNP). Tourism, says the study, grows about twice as fast as world GNP. Of the industry's total world spending, about 31 percent takes place in the European Community and 30 percent on the North American continent.

International arrivals, according to the WTO, were 592 million in 1996. It is estimated that they will reach 702 million in 2000, 1 billion in 2010, and 1.6 billion by 2020—more than triple the 475 million people who traveled abroad in 1992.

In 1994, an estimated 46 million overseas residents visited the United States. Nearly every state publishes its own tourism economic impact study. New York, for example, estimates its tourism revenue to be $36.7 billion; Florida, about $49.3 billion; Texas, $31 billion; and California, just over $50 billion. Tourism is Hawaii's biggest industry with revenues of $21.9 billion.

The National Travel and Tourism Awareness Council's annual "The Tourism Work for America Report" indicates that travel and tourism is one of the nation's leading sectors. Statistics include the following:

✔ Domestic and international travelers spend about $500 billion on travel-related expenses (e.g., lodging, food, and entertainment) in the United States annually.

✔ Seven million people are directly employed in the industry, making travel and tourism the nation's second largest employer, after health services.

✔ Travel generates about $60 billion in tax receipts.

✔ Spending by international visitors within the United States is about $21 billion more than is travel-related spending by Americans outside the United States.

✔ Nearly 45 million international travelers visit the United States each year.

Travel and tourism supports more than 200 million jobs worldwide. This represents about 12 percent of the global workforce, according to the World Travel and Tourism Council (WTTC). By employing approximately one out of every ten workers, travel and tourism is the world's largest employer and is the largest industry. The estimates are that by the year 2000, these jobs will account for $2 trillion, or 11 percent, of all employee wages and sales worldwide.

The Multiplier Effect

Tourists produce secondary impacts beyond their original expenditures. When a tourist spends money to travel, to stay in a hotel, or to eat in a restaurant, that money is recycled by those businesses to purchase more goods, thereby generating further use of the money. In addition, employees of businesses who serve tourists spend a higher proportion of their money locally on various goods and services. This chain reaction continues until there is a *leakage,* meaning that money is used to purchase something from outside the area. Figure 2–5 (next page) illustrates the multiplier effect.

"Most developed economies have a multiplier effect between 1.7 and 2.0."[30] This means that the original money spent is used again in the community between 1.7 and 2.0 times.

Tour Operators

The National Tour Association estimates that nearly 500,000 tours were conducted by 1,636 U.S. tour operators during 1992. These tours carried 16.5 million passengers, who spent an average of $118.38 per passenger per day on both one-day and multiday tours.

Promoters of Tourism

Travel Agencies

A travel agent is a middle-person who acts as a travel counselor and sells on behalf of airlines, cruise lines, rail and bus transportation, hotels, and auto rental companies. Agents may sell individual parts of the overall system or several

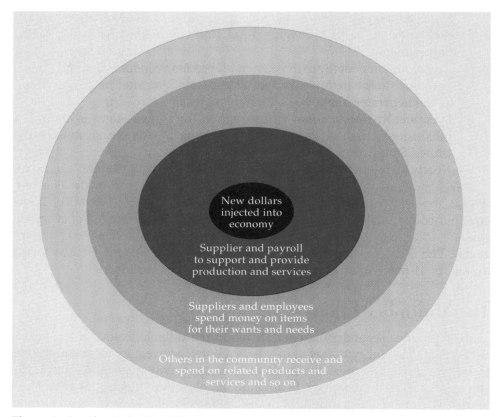

Figure 2–5   *The Multiplier Effect*

elements, such as air and cruise tickets. The agent acts as a broker, bringing together the client (buyer) and the supplier (seller). An agent has quick access to schedules, fares, and advice for clients about various destinations.

The first U.S. travel agents emerged in the 1880s, selling steamship and rail tickets and some arranged tours. "Ask Mr. Foster," the oldest U.S. travel agency got its name because a Mr. Foster opened a travel information office in St. Augustine, Florida. Anyone in the area who had any travel questions was told to "Ask Mr. Foster." As business grew, more offices opened and Mr. Foster decided to adopt the phrase as a business slogan. Eventually, offices opened in various parts of Florida and spread to New York and other major U.S. cities.

The American Society of Travel Agents (ASTA) has 28,000 members in 168 countries that include both travel agencies and travel suppliers. Total airline sales processed by travel agencies reached $51 billion in 1992. The Airlines Reporting Corporation (ARC) reports that travel agencies had 32,147 retail locations in 1992. The average travel agency's yearly sales are about $3 million. According to *Travel Weekly Magazine,* the top fifty travel agencies in terms of sales generated (approximately $25 billion in revenue) represent 30 percent of total agency sales.

Agents use computer reservation systems (CRS) to access availability and make bookings. In the United States, the main vendors are as follows:

1. Sabre, which is owned by American Airlines and has more than 100,000 terminals and a 37.4 percent market share
2. Apollo, which is owned primarily by United Airlines and has a similar market share by location but fewer terminals
3. Worldspan, which is shared by four companies (Delta, Northwest, TWA, and Abacus) and has a 19.3 percent market share with 8,500 sites in the United States
4. System One, which is owned by Continental Airlines and has a 14.9 percent marketshare and 6,800 locations.[31]

According to the American Society of Travel Agents (ASTA), a travel agent is more than a ticket seller. Agents serve their clients in the following ways:
- ✔ Arranging transportation by air, sea, rail, bus, car rental, etc.
- ✔ Preparing individual itineraries, personally escorted tours, group tours, and prepared package tours
- ✔ Arranging for hotel, motel, and resort accommodations; meals; sightseeing tours; transfers of passengers and luggage between terminals and hotels; and special features such as tickets for music festivals, the theater, etc.
- ✔ Handling and advising on many details involved with travel, such as insurance, travelers checks, foreign currency exchange, documentary requirements, and immunizations and other inoculations
- ✔ Using professional know-how and experience (e.g., schedules of air, train, and bus connections, rates of hotels, quality of accommodations, etc.)
- ✔ Arranging reservations for special-interest activities, such as group tours, conventions, business travel, gourmet tours, sporting trips, etc.[32]

Approximately 43,000 travel agencies are currently operating in the United States, up from 29,548 in 1987. The average agency has between four and seven full-time employees. The average starting salaries are $12,000. The average salary for an agent with three to five years service is $18,000. Agents with ten plus years average $25,007. Managers make an average of $23,000. Twenty-one percent of agents receive commissions ranging between 6 and 11 percent of their sales. The average sales volume per agency is as follows:[33]
- ✔ 33 percent of agencies have sales of less than $1 million
- ✔ 26 percent of agencies have sales between $1 and $3 million
- ✔ 27 percent of agencies have sales between $2 and $5 million
- ✔ 14 percent of agencies have sales of more than $5 million

Agencies make their money on commissions. They usually make 10 percent on air travel within the United States and about 11 percent on international travel. Commission on hotel accommodations ranges from 10 to 15 percent and commission on cruise packages ranges from 11 to 14 percent.

Commission Caps

In 1995, the airlines imposed a commission cap of $50 for a domestic flight and 8 percent for an international booking. This restriction forced several agencies to close. During the first quarter of 1996, 505 full-service agency locations shut down—a 59 percent jump from the previous year.[34] Other agencies were forced to increase the scope of services offered. Now, cruise line officials are also look-ing at travel agent commission rates, which they feel are too high. Rick Sasso, Celebrity's president, observes that if bookings start to become a normal prac-tice on the Internet, a client might still pick up the booking at a travel agency. Cruise lines could tell an Internet broker that they have booked and that they may go to any travel agent to pick up the document. In that case, the level of commission would probably be about five percent, approximately half the nor-mal commission.

Travel Corporations

There are a number of large and successful travel corporations—the largest be-ing American Express Travel Services. American Express (AMEX) is a corpora-tion that has a travel services division with locations worldwide. Each location is licensed and bonded with the International Air Transportation Association (IATA), which provides travel services and tickets through the corporation. The travel services division provides other services including foreign currencies, AMEX traveler's checks in different currencies, and gift checks. Currently, the travel ser-vices division is trying to promote foreign currencies to increase revenues.

The majority of American Express Travel Services' revenues is generated in business travel through corporate accounts. The airlines give the travel agency an override to portion with the corporate client. The business contract is indi-vidually set up, based on annual travel expenses. For example, if IBM's annual travel expenses are $1 million, the airline will give AMEX a 1.4 percent override commission to split with IBM. AMEX chooses their airline vendors according to who gives the largest override percentage and whose negotiated rates are most appealing. The same policy applies to other vendors in the industry, such as cruise lines. Every travel agent, whether in-house or off-premise, receives a commission from a vendor, based on their annual sales volume. Usually this commission varies, but the standard is ten percent of the sale.

Travel managers for AMEX function as national account managers. Their pay is based on their grade level, region, and market. Their salary also depends on who they service. A small, local clientele generates a lower salary and a broader service center provides a higher salary. Depending on whether they are on- or off-site, a travel manager's salary for AMEX is between $28,000 and $60,000 for corporate clients. The salary range for general public leisure travel is between $28,000 and $48,000. Each travel manager is hired internally and their pay is based mostly on seniority.[35]

American Express Travel on the Internet searches for the best ticket price, or the most convenient flights in the same reservations systems used by thousands of travel agents. In a snap, users can check out the price or search for other op-tions, then book their own reservations on-line. Users can view descriptions of packages to sunny, snow-filled, cultural, or just plain fun destinations, along with full-color photos and a list of amenities. These packages may not be booked on-line. A toll-free number is listed at the site, or consumers may visit an American Express Travel office. Visitors to the site currently have three op-tions: they can book airline tickets, they can view vacation offers, and they can look up the most convenient American Express Travel office. In addition, card members may take advantage of special travel, retail, restaurant, and entertainment offers and shop for a variety of merchandise on another Internet site called ExpressNet.

Corporate Travel Manager

A corporate travel manager is a type of entrepreneur working within the framework of a large corporation. For example, Mitsubishi Electronics, in Cypress, California, was spending about $4 million for travel and entertainment. In addition, twenty-nine field offices operated independently across the United States, Canada, and Mexico. The total expenditure for travel and entertainment was $11 million. Enter John Fazio, recruited by Mitsubishi to improve efficiency and reduce costs. Fazio invited interested agencies to submit proposals based on Mitsubishi's travel needs. The fifteen initial proposals were narrowed to eight; finally two were asked to submit their best and last offers. These offers were evaluated based on Mitsubishi's criteria: technological capabilities, locations, and ability to give personal service.[36]

An interesting trend in corporate travel is agentless booking via electronic mail (E-mail). Travel is initiated at the keyboard, not at the switchboard. Increasingly, technologically savvy corporations are making travel bookings via E-mail. A forerunner in this process is Wal-Mart Stores. Seeking to increase booking efficiency and trim costs, Wal-Mart requested that World Wide develop a system, now known as Quality Agent, to meet their goals. Quality Agent is a Windows-based front end to the reservation system that processes reservations without human intervention. Currently, larger travel agencies are developing similar E-mail programs for their clients.[37]

Travel and Tour Wholesalers

Tour wholesalers consolidate the services of airline and other transportation carriers and ground service suppliers into a tour that is sold through a sales channel to the public.[38] Tour wholesaling came into prominence in the 1960s because airlines had vacant seats—which, like hotel rooms, are perishable. Airlines naturally wanted to sell as many seats as possible and found that they could sell blocks of seats to wholesalers close to departure dates. These tickets were for specific destinations around which tour wholesalers built a tour. Wholesalers then sold their tours directly through retail agents.

The tour wholesale business is concentrated with about one hundred independent tour wholesalers; however, ten major companies account for about 30 percent of the industry's business. Tour wholesalers offer a wide range of tours at various prices to many destinations. This segment of the industry is characterized by three key types of wholesalers:

1. An independent tour wholesaler
2. An airline working in close cooperation with a tour wholesaler
3. A retail travel agent who packages tours for his or her clients

In addition, incentive travel houses and various travel clubs round out the tour wholesale business.[39]

Certified Travel Counselor (CTC)

Leading experts in the travel industry worked together to form an Institute of Certified Travel Agents (ICTA). The ICTA offers specialized professional studies for those seeking higher proficiency in the travel industry. The professional designation of CTC is awarded to individuals who have successfully passed examinations and who have five years full-time experience in a travel agency or in the marketing and promotion of travel.[40]

National Offices of Tourism (NOT)

National offices of tourism seek to improve the economy of the country they represent by increasing the number of visitors and consequently their spending in the country. Connected to this function is the responsibility to oversee and ensure that hotels, transport systems, tour operators, and tour guides maintain high standards in the care and consideration of the tourist.[41] The main activities of NOTs are as follows:

- ✔ Publicizing the country
- ✔ Assisting and advising certain types of travelers
- ✔ Creating demand for certain destinations
- ✔ Supplying information
- ✔ Ensuring that the destination is up to expectations
- ✔ Advertising[42]

Destination Management Companies (DMCs)

A destination management company is a service organization within the visitor industry that offers a host of programs and services to meet clients' needs. Initially, a destination management sales manager concentrates on selling the destination to meeting planners and performance improvement companies (incentive houses).

The needs of such groups may be as simple as an airport pick-up or as involved as an international sales convention with theme parties. DMCs work closely with hotels; sometimes DMCs book rooms, and other times hotels request the DMC's know-how on organizing theme parties.

Patricia Roscoe, Chairperson of Patti Roscoe and Associates (PRA), says that meeting planners often have a choice of several destinations and might ask, "Why should I pick your destination?" The answer is that a DMC does everything, including airport greetings, transportation to the hotel, VIP check-in, theme parties, sponsoring programs, organizing competitive sports events, and so on, depending on budget.

Personal Profile: Patti Roscoe

Patricia L. Roscoe, Chairperson of Patti Roscoe and Associates (PRA) and Roscoe/Coltrell Inc. (RCI), landed in California in 1966, charmed by the beautiful San Diego sun compared to the cold winters in Buffalo, New York, her hometown. She was a young, brilliant middle manager who was to face the challenges of a time period when women were expected to become either nurses or teachers. She became involved with the hotel industry, working for a large private resort hotel, the Vacation Village. Those were the years to be remembered. She gained a very thorough knowledge of Southern California tourism, as well as of the inherent mechanisms of the industry. With the unforgettable help and guidance of her manager, she began to lay the foundations of her future career as a very successful leader in the field. The outstanding skills that she learned are, in fact, the very basis of her many accomplishments.

The list of her awards and honors is astounding: She earned the prestigious CITE distinction (Certified Incentive Travel Executive), she was named San Diego Woman of Accomplishment in 1983, and in February, 1990, Ms. Roscoe was honored as San Diego's 1989 Allied Member of the Year during the tourism industry Gold Key Awards. In 1990, she was given the Wonder Woman Award by the U.S. Small Business Administration for her outstanding achievements in the field. In 1993, the San Diego Convention and Visitors Bureau conferred on her the prestigious RCA Lubach Award for her contributions to the industry.

She is also extremely involved in civic and tourism organizations, including the Rotary Club, the American Lung Association of San Diego and Imperial Counties, and the San Diego Convention and Visitors Bureau.

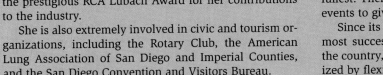

Patti Roscoe

The key to her success perhaps lies in her remarkable skills of interacting with people. It is the human resources, in fact, that represent the major strength of PRA. Its employees are experienced, dedicated, and service oriented. But what makes them so efficient is their dedication to working together as a team. Patti Roscoe guides, inspires, and motivates these teams. She is a self-admitted "softy," a creative and emotional leader who enjoys training her employees and following their growth step by step, to eventually give them the power of initiative they deserve, as a tool to encourage their creativity and originality. She constantly seeks to balance the concept of teamwork with the individual goals and private lives of her employees. It is through the achievement of such a balance that a profitable, healthy community is preserved. PRA is a bit more than a community, however: It is a family, and just like a mother, Patti's formula is discipline and love. At the same time, Patti's leading efforts are aimed at training her employees to "think outside of the box," and "keep one's view as broad as possible," which is the only way to rise above the commonplace, the rhetorical, and the trivial, to escape provincialism, and thus become unique individuals.

That's how the magic is done. PRA excels in creating "something that becomes exclusively yours—that has never been done before." PRA is decentralized into service teams to foster an entrepreneurial environment in which initiative and creativity can be boosted to the fullest. Therefore, PRA staff design personalized, unique events to give their customers an unforgettable time.

Since its opening in 1981, PRA has become one of the most successful destination management companies in the country, providing personal, caring service characterized by flexibility and creativity.

Sales managers associated with DMCs obtain leads, which are potential clients, from the following sources:

- ✔ Hotels
- ✔ Trade shows
- ✔ Convention and visitors bureaus
- ✔ Cold calls
- ✔ Incentive houses
- ✔ Meeting planners

Each sales manager has a staff or team that would include the following:

Special events manager, who will have expertise in sound, lighting, staging, and so on

Accounts manager, who is an assistant to the sales manager

Operations manager, who coordinates everything, especially on-site arrangements, to ensure that what is sold actually happens.

For example, Patti Roscoe's destination management company recently organized meetings, accommodations, meals, beverages, and theme parties for 2,000 Ford Motor Company dealers in nine groups over three days.

Roscoe also works closely with incentive houses, such as Carlson Marketing or Meritz Travel. These incentive houses approach a company and offer to evaluate and set up incentive plans for the sales team, including whatever it takes to motivate them. Once approved, Carlson contacts a destination management company and asks for a program.

In conclusion, thousands of companies and associations hold meetings and conventions all over the country. Many of these organizations use the services of professional meeting planners, who in turn seek out suitable destinations for the meetings and conventions.

Why People Travel

There are many reasons why people travel, however they fall under two main headings: travel for pleasure and travel for business. Research indicates that when consumers are asked what they associate most with success and accomplishment, the number one response is travel for pleasure.

Among the reasons people travel for pleasure are the following:

- Visiting friends and relatives
- Health
- Enlightenment, education
- Beauty, nature, and national parks
- Religion
- Indulgence
- Sports
- Festivals
- Shopping
- Fun of the trip
- Gaming
- Adventure
- Heritage
- Ecotourism
- Attractions

Pleasure Travel

Sixty-nine percent of domestic travel is for pleasure purposes. Approximately 636.4 million person-trips were taken for pleasure during 1992, according to the United States Travel Data Center's (USTDC) national travel survey. Nearly half of all the pleasure travelers visited friends and relatives.

The motivation for pleasure travel can be compared to Maslow's hierarchy of human needs. Maslow suggests that people have five sets of basic needs:

1. *Physiological needs:* food, water, oxygen, sex, etc.
2. *Safety needs:* security, stability, order, protection
3. *Love needs:* affection, identification, belonging (family and friends)
4. *Esteem needs:* self-respect, prestige, success, achievement
5. *Self-actualization needs:* self-fulfillment[43]

Some people in their late teens and early twenties may be sun, sand, and sea travelers—the spring break variety. Others may be more interested in the cultural and sporting activities associated with travel—or even the educational aspects.

McIntosh and Charles R. Goeldner suggest that basic travel motivations can be divided into four categories:

1. *Physical motivator:* physical rest, sporting, and beach activities; healthful and relaxing entertainment
2. *Cultural motivator:* the desire for knowledge of other countries—music, art, folklore, dances, paintings, and religion
3. *Interpersonal motivator:* the desire to meet new people; to visit friends or relatives; to escape from the routine, the family, or the neighbor; or to make new friends
4. *Status and prestige motivator:* the desire for recognition, attention, appreciation, and a good reputation[44]

When surveyed, people tend to list the following reasons for travel:
- To experience new and different surroundings
- To experience other cultures
- To rest and relax
- To visit friends and family
- To view, or participate, in sporting/recreational activities

Travel is likely to increase in the coming years, which will have a significant impact on tourism. Some of the reasons for the anticipated increases are as follows:

- *Longer Life Span.* The average person in the United States now has a life expectancy of about seventy-five years. In fact, in just a few years, some baby boomers will be taking early retirement.
- *Flexible Working Hours.* Today, many people work four, ten-hour days and have longer weekends. Of course, many others—especially in the hospitality and tourism industries—work on weekends and have leisure time during the week.

✔ *Early Retirement.* Increasingly, people are being given the opportunity to retire at age fifty-five. This early retirement is generally granted to employees with thirty years of service to their company or government agency.

✔ *Greater Ease of Travel.* Today, it is easier to travel on holidays and weekends, for both business and leisure purposes. Each mode of travel affords increasing opportunities to take advantage of the additional leisure time.

✔ *Tendency to Take Shorter, More Frequent Trips.* People now tend to take shorter, but more frequent, minivacations rather than taking all of their vacation time at once. Europeans generally take much longer vacations than North Americans. For them, four weeks is the normal vacation benefit of new employees, and six weeks is typical after a few years.

✔ *Increase in the Standard of Living.* More people in many developing countries have increased their income and wish to travel. China, with its newfound enterprise zones is producing hundreds of thousands of entrepreneurs who will soon be traveling to foreign countries. Millions of East European residents of the former Soviet Block countries now have the capability and the right to travel. And finally, an additional 300 million people will soon have passports.

Stanley Plog, a respected social scientist, has suggested that travelers can be separated into two extremes: (1) psychocentrics, who prefer familiar travel destinations, and (2) allocentrics, who prefer new and different destinations.

Most travelers fall into a large bell-shaped curve between these two extremes. Figure 2–6 illustrates the types of destinations that psychocentrics and allocentrics are likely to visit. Psychocentrics, as the figure illustrates, prefer to

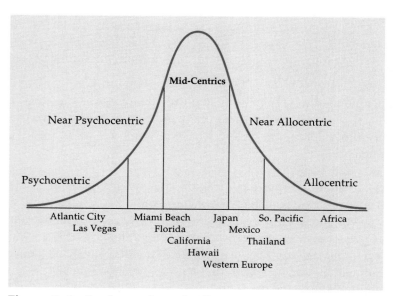

Figure 2–6 *Psychocentric and Allocentric Types of Destinations* (Adapted from Stanley Plog, "Why Destination Areas Rise and Fall in Popularity," a paper presented to the Southern California Chapter of the Travel Research Association, October 10, 1972, as cited in Edward Mayo and Lance Jarvis, The Psychology of Leisure Travel, Boston: CBI Publishing Company, 1981, p. 118.)

travel to well-known destinations that have been visited by millions before. These destinations tend to be constant and predictable. Allocentric personalities tend to be more adventurous, curious, energetic, and outgoing; they will usually be attracted to novel destinations like the South Pacific, Asia, and Africa. Generally, twice as many people are inclined to be allocentric. This has an effect on small-scale tourist areas. First visited by allocentrics, the area (be it a village, town, or resort) then becomes more popular and is forced into becoming more commercialized. Waikiki Beach on Oahu is an example of this—as few as thirty years ago, there were no high-rise hotels there.

Motivations for Travel

Over the course of history, the motivations for most travel have been fairly obvious: religion, conventions, economic gain, war, escape, migration. It would seem that motives for what is left—travel for pleasure—would be straightforward and plainly understandable. This, however, is not the case. Unfortunately, little research has been undertaken to reveal the reasons why people travel and vacation. Because research and an established motivation theory are lacking, the comments included here are necessarily impressionistic and are made principally to stimulate investigation.

Some surprising findings show up in consumer research. A study asked consumers which of twenty-two items they associated with success and accomplishment. The leading choice was "travel for pleasure." As psychologist Abraham Maslow theorized, at the very top of the hierarchy of human needs seem to be those for self-actualization. This desire reflects the fundamental need to develop one's own potential, to gain esthetic stimulation, to create or build one's own personality and character. Certainly there are tremendous variations in what individuals need at the self-actualization level. Millions of people prefer not to travel or vacation because they are more comfortable in their present circumstances. They may be afraid to leave those circumstances, or to take the chance of being injured or victimized while traveling or visiting a strange destination. Other people seem to thrive on the change brought about by travel. Some need the letdown of a quiet vacation; others seek the same pitch of excitement that exists in their workday world. If we hypothesize the need for change, for diversion, for new scenery, for new experiences, then travel and vacationing take their place somewhere near the top of the list of means for meeting these needs. In fact, some psychotherapists posit a basic need for fun and freedom. Pleasure travel is certainly a rich source for fulfilling this need.

Different Places for Different People

Obviously, travelers select destinations for different reasons—climate, history or culture, sports, entertainment, shopping facilities, and so forth. The major appeal of England for Americans seems to be history and culture. American

Express surveyed people going to several destinations—Florida, California, Mexico, Hawaii, the Bahamas, Jamaica, Puerto Rico, the Virgin Islands, and Barbados. Almost half of the respondents were professionals, generally middle-aged, and well educated. Many of them were wealthy travelers who took frequent vacations outside the United States. These respondents ranked the appeals of travel in descending order of importance:

- ✔ Scenic beauty
- ✔ Pleasant attitudes of local people
- ✔ Suitable accommodations
- ✔ Rest and relaxation
- ✔ Air fare cost
- ✔ Historical and cultural interests
- ✔ Cuisine
- ✔ Water sports
- ✔ Entertainment (e.g., nightlife)
- ✔ Shopping facilities
- ✔ Sports (golfing and tennis)

Four basic considerations emerged as factors influencing travel: entertainment, purchase opportunities, climate for comfort, and cost. Even within a group, of course, different factors apply. One individual may select a destination primarily because of opportunities for challenging golf and tennis, another because of the friendly local people, and another because the place offers rest and relaxation. Most of the group would, however, be influenced by air fare costs.

Expectation and Reality

Satisfaction, or dissatisfaction, with the travel experience, of course, depends on how it is viewed by the traveler. A glorious sunset and majestic mountain may be seen as a great bore if an individual is highly gregarious and alone on the trip. The best service in a restaurant with the finest food and decor is meaningless if the person is dyspeptic at the moment. One traveler loves the rain, another despises it. Mountains are one person's delight, heights make another person dizzy. The anthropologist revels in the remote village, the city dweller finds the same place dull. So much depends upon what the person expects of the experience and how he or she actually experiences it.

Travel is an experience, not a tangible object. It results in psychic reward or punishment. It creates pleasant anticipation or aversion, excitement and challenge, or fatigue and disappointment. The anticipation, the experience, and the memory occur in the mind, leaving no tangible evidence as to why travel was undertaken and why the same trip is experienced in so many different ways by different people. Travel literature and films often falsify reality or are shot so selectively that the actual environment is not recognizable by the visitor. The phony shot that makes the pool look longer than it is, the colors that never exist in nature, the lavish buffet that was rigged especially for the photograph, the glorious sunset that occurs once a year—all of this creates expectations that cannot be realized, and leads to disappointment.

Push/Pull Model

An interesting way of modeling travel motivations is to divide them into factors that pull, that is, attractions, and those that push, that is, personal needs. Arlin Epperson, a travel consultant, proposes the push/pull model.

He lists push factors as the intangible desires that are generated from within the person. Examples include those shown in Figure 2–6.

Disney World attracts those motivated by a pull factor. A relaxing week on a Caribbean beach is probably inspired by a push factor. Much travel is likely motivated to some degree by both push and pull factors. For example, a vacation in an isolated mountain cabin would allow for escape, self-discovery, and rest, while at the same time providing scenic beauty.

Business Travel

Half, or more, of all airline travel is undertaken by business travelers. An airline study shows that the business-leisure mix varies widely according to destination area. More than 90 percent of the travel between the United States and the Caribbean is for pleasure. The figure for U.S. mainland to Hawaii pleasure travel is more than 80 percent; for United States–trans-Atlantic flights, about 70 percent; and for United States to Latin America flights, also 70 percent. Pleasure is the predominant reason for slightly more than 60 percent of passengers' flying between the United States and the Asia-Pacific area.

About 60 to 70 percent of the guests who check into Sheraton Hotels around the world are traveling for business reasons. Much business travel is hard work, whether it is travel in one's own automobile, or in the luxury of a first-class seat aboard an airline. A good portion of business travel is, however, mixed with pleasure.

It is difficult to say whether as much as half of his or her time may be spent gambling or gamboling. The trip to Europe may involve contacting potential customers, but it also may allow for sight-seeing or for an evening at the Folies Bergere.

Business travel accounts for approximately half of all travel in the U.S. and is a $156 billion industry. Counted as business travelers are those who travel for business purposes such as meetings; all kinds of sales, including corporate, regional, product, etc.; conventions; trade shows and expositions; and combinations of more than one. In the United States, meetings and conventions alone attract millions of people annually. Sometimes the distinction between business and leisure travel becomes blurred. If a convention attendee in Atlanta decides to stay on for a few days after the conference, are they to be considered a "business" or "leisure" traveler? Business travelers, when compared to leisure travelers, tend to be younger, spend more money, travel further, and travel in smaller groups, but they do not stay as long.

Business travel has increased in recent years due to the growth of convention centers in a number of cities. Similarly, business travelers have given a boost to hotels, restaurants, and auto rental companies. A hotel located near a major convention center often runs a higher occupancy and average daily rate (ADR) than other types of hotels. Business trips to meetings generally last from one to three days. Business travel to attend conventions and trade shows ranges from about five to eight days. For most companies, the third largest controllable expense is business travel and entertainment.

The typical business traveler still resembles the traveling salesperson of old. He or she is 39 years old, married, has a median household income of $40,000 to $50,000, and holds a professional or management job. One in five employed Americans takes at least one overnight business trip each year. Female business travelers, of which there are approximately 15 million, comprise about 27 percent of all U.S. business travelers, and are on the increase. This has prompted hotel operators to take note of the needs and concerns of women business travelers.

Business travel, long the mainstay of airlines and hotels, will likely gradually decline as a percentage of all travel, which includes leisure travel. Leisure travel is forecast to increase due to a favorable economic climate, which in turn produces increased discretionary income. Many people now have more leisure time and higher levels of education, and the cost of travel has remained constant, or dropped, compared to inflation and other costs combined. These factors indicate a bright future for the travel industry.

An analysis of business travel costs by the *Wall Street Journal* tracks travel prices with the weekly Dow Jones Travel Index, which looks at average business and leisure fares on twenty major routes, as well as the cost of hotel rooms and car rentals. An annual increase in travel costs of four percent is significant for a group who spends upwards of $130 billion a year in travel. Bob Litchman, head of corporate travel at Bay Networks in Santa Clara, California, says a four percent increase would add $600,000 to his domestic travel budget. Business travelers pay most of the increases, economists say, because they are the passengers who really contribute to an airline's earnings. The major domestic airlines receive thirty-three cents per passenger per mile for full-fare tickets—more than twice what they get for discounted tickets. In other words, airlines sometimes lose money on their leisure travelers and make money with their business travelers.

An increasing number of business travelers are able to make their own travel arrangements on-line. For example, in the middle of a client meeting Suzie Aust, a meeting consultant, realizes that she has forgotten to book the next day's flight. She pulls out her laptop, gets on-line, and books the flight. Corporate America is worried about travelers like Suzie because they are often able to skirt corporate policies when making their own reservations. Some companies use a product from Microsoft and American Express. Code-named Rome, the product will allow companies to control their own travelers by insisting that employees buy their own tickets through American Express. Needless to say, American and United Airlines are each rolling out similar products. Ed Gilligan, president of corporate services for American Express, estimates that American companies lose $15 billion a year due to deviations from corporate policy. And the portion of that sum lost to on-line reservation systems is "ramping up quickly," he says. Between 786,000 and 1.8 million business travelers are wired, according to Addison Schonland, director of aviation, travel, and marketing for CIC Research, in San Diego. The Eastman Group, a Newport Beach, California, management consulting and travel software group, predicts that by 2001, approximately 65 percent of travel will be ticketless and by 2006, 99 percent of all airline travel will be ticketless.

Hotels are, for many business travelers, supposed to be a home away from home. However, in some cases, they are more like the office away from the office. For hotels that are aiming to please their business travelers, they must not overlook the homier touches such as feather pillows and old-fashioned innkeeping virtues: cleanliness, comfort, safety, attentive service, and peace and quiet.

Trends in Business Travel

Businesses are trimming perks for their employees, and more business travelers are spending weekends on the road and more nights in economy hotels, according to an American Express survey. The survey indicates the following:

- ✔ Seventy-eight percent of companies require employees to take the lowest reasonable airfare available, up from 69 percent when the survey was last done in 1994. That means more employees are flying in and out of less-convenient airports, and they are taking connecting, instead of nonstop, flights.
- ✔ Thirty-seven percent make employees stay over a Saturday night when it will reduce the airfare.
- ✔ Seventy-seven percent impose a size limit on rental cars, up from 70 percent.
- ✔ Fourteen percent regularly make employees stay in economy hotels such as Hampton Inn or Courtyard by Marriott.

There will be an increase in ticketless travel and rental car navigation systems, and Boeing will launch the 777, its first new jet in more than a decade.

For frequent flyers, American Airlines has introduced frequent-flyer mileage for home mortgages—a mile is earned for every dollar of interest paid. This is in addition to one mile for every dollar spent on long distance calls placed with MCI and one mile for every dollar charged on the Citibank Visa Card. Experts agree that almost all of the new mileage promotions will come from nonflying activities.

The number of female business travelers will increase, and airlines, hotels, restaurants, car rental agencies, and associated businesses will need to pay increasing attention in order to exceed their expectations.

Social and Cultural Impact of Tourism

From a social and cultural perspective, tourism can leave both positive and negative impacts on communities. Undoubtedly, tourism has made significant contributions to international understanding. World tourism organizations recognize that tourism is a means of enhancing international understanding, peace, prosperity, and universal respect for, and observance of, human rights and fundamental freedom for all without distinction as to race, sex, language, or religion. Tourism can be a very interesting sociocultural phenomenon. Seeing how others live is an interest of many tourists, and the exchange of sociocultural values and activities is rewarding.

Providing that the number of tourists is manageable and that they respect the host community's sociocultural norms and values, tourism provides an opportunity for a number of social interactions. A London pub or a New York café are examples of good places for social interaction. Similarly, depending on the reason for the tourist visit, myriad opportunities are available to interact both socially and culturally. Even a visit to another part of the United States would be both socially and culturally stimulating. For example, New Orleans has a very diverse social and cultural heritage. Over the years, the city has been occupied by Spanish, French, British, and Americans. The food, music, dance, and social norms are unique to the area.

However, sociocultural problems can also result from tourism. Imagine the feelings of an employee in a developing country who earns perhaps $5 per day when he or she sees wealthy tourists flaunting money, jewelry, and a lifestyle not obtainable. Another example might be nude or scantily clad female tourists sunbathing in a Moslem country. Critics argue that, at best, tourism dilutes the culture of a country by imposing the culture of the mass tourism market. Most of the food prepared in the Western-style hotels is American or European, with perhaps the addition of an Americanized local dish.

Most resorts offer little opportunity for meaningful social interaction between the tourist and the host community. Developers build the hotel (which can cause disruptions as well as create opportunities); likely as not, an international hotel company will manage the hotel, which may mean that the top positions are filled by non-natives, leaving only the lower positions to the locals.

Proponents of the sociocultural benefits of tourism are able to point out that tourism is a clean and green industry, that some hotels are built with great concern for the environment and use local craftspeople, designers, and materials in order to harmonize with the locals. Tourism brings new revenue to the area; it also creates and maintains higher levels of employment than if there were no tourism. In some countries, a hotel may be restricted as to the number of foreigners it employs and the length of their contracts. This allows for the promotion of the local employees to higher positions. Tourism may act as a catalyst for the development of the community because taxes help the government provide other services such as schools, hospitals, and so on. In addition, tourists often enjoy the cultural exchanges they have at all levels in the community. The excursions, shopping, dancing, and so on serve to embellish the tourists' experiences.

Tourism is not likely to have a significant sociocultural impact in developed countries, where the economy is active and well-diversified.[45] The most noticeable change in established value patterns and behavior occurs when tourism is a major contributor to the gross national product.

In some developing countries tourism is a major contributor to the GNP. However, tourism may contribute to the generation gap between the young, who are quick to adapt to the ways of the tourists, and the older people, who hold more traditional values.

Efforts to preserve the cultural heritage of a community may be further eroded when tourist "junk" is imported and offered for sale to tourists. In every society, people have opposing points of view about tourism development and cultural heritage preservation. The important thing to remember is to strike a balance between what is appropriate for a destination in terms of the number of tourists and the type of tourists that the community is capable of sustaining.

An example of how tourism can have a negative impact is shown in the center of Paris, in the once-beautiful park known as the Bois de Bologna, which now looks more like a refugee camp. Tourists have been allowed to take over with a massive campsite that includes dilapidated trailers, laundry hanging on makeshift clotheslines, and pets along for the vacation. This is a real shanty town in the heart of one of the world's most beautiful cities.

Further examples of tourism pollution include the famous beaches in the south of France. The Cote d'Azure for years has been a popular haunt of the rich and famous. Cities like Nice, St. Tropez, and Juez le Pain became celebrity hangouts once they were discovered in the 1950s and 1960s. Now at the height of the season, public beaches are wall-to-wall people. Private beaches will rent a parasol and a $6' \times 4'$ plot for the day for approximately $40.

The effects of too many tourists have necessitated that the famous Cathedral of Notre Dame restrict the number of visitors to 400 per day, down from several thousand. The sheer number of visitors was causing serious problems for the building.

Similarly, the prehistoric cave paintings at Lascoux in southwest France were closed in 1964 to prevent further deterioration of the paintings. Human breath, which gives off CO_2, is harmful to paint. Now, its replica, Lascoux II, which was built to allow visitors a chance to experience the caves, is in trouble for the same reason.

Just imagine what will happen when another 300 million people become tourists by virtue of increasing standards of living and more people obtaining passports. Currently only 10 percent of the U.S. population has passports. The

Beach Scenes Cote d'Azure (Used with permission of the French Government Tourist Office).

Corporate Profile: Club Med

In 1950, a Belgian diamond cutter and water polo champion conceived the first Club Med village, funded with army surplus tax money, on the little Spanish island of Majorca. The goal of that first resort was to unite people from diverse backgrounds, encourage them to share a good time, and offer them a unique escape from the stress and the tension of the everyday events of post-World War II Europe. The first adventurous vacationers to experience that new environment were mostly young couples or singles, living together in a beautiful natural setting, enjoying the atmosphere of camaraderie and no worries, playing sports, or just simply relaxing on a warm soft beach.

The following decade was a particularly profitable one, because of the overall social climate that characterized the 1960s. The young generation, generally speaking, was wrapped up in a whirl of ideals, such as peace, communion, and the sharing of feelings and experiences, all in the framework of a return to nature. The so-called flowerchild phenomenon saw the young long for a return to primitive purity, innocence, and freedom of expression. It is not surprising, then, that Club Med's clientele rose by 500 percent in that decade. In fact, the features that characterized the resorts made them just the right environment to meet the needs of this target market. Club Med began its expansion throughout the Mediterranean coastlines and islands, including Greece and Italy. Centers began to spring up on the coasts of Africa and the Middle East. Today Club Med—short for Mediterranean—has more than one hundred resorts and vacation villages around the world, hosted by twenty-eight countries in the Mediterranean as well as in the Caribbean, Africa, Mexico, the Bahamas, South Pacific, South America, Asia, and the United States. The little village in Majorca blossomed into a colorful, joyful, sunny, colossal empire: Club Med is the world's largest vacation village organization and the ninth largest hotel chain, with 93,000 beds and 20,000 employees. More than 9 million guests have come to the villages since 1950.

Today's philosophy doesn't differ much from the original one. Club Med intends to provide a spectacular natural setting in which its guests can enjoy life and its amenities, away from the troubles and the worries of the everyday frantic rat race. The theme on the printed advertisements points straight to this: "Club Med: Life as it should be." Sports, various entertaining activities, good food, real concern for guests' needs, and a carefree lifestyle worked wonders. Imagine all of these amenities in the context of white sand beaches and a clear blue sea that seems to stretch out indefinitely to meet a virtually cloudless sky at the horizon.

Club Med's original formula was copied by several other organizations in the travel and tourism industry. The increased competition caused Club Med to revise its management strategies and develop a different product in order to gain and hold market share. Changes in the industry were accompanied by social changes. As the years went by, the baby boomers of the 1960s and 1970s grew up, got married, and began to travel with their families. The target market thus changed again, and the necessity to change along with the market was promptly acknowledged.

The policy Club Med's managers embraced was one of differentiation and flexibility. Through assiduous market research, studies, and surveys, Club Med identified the continuously changing needs and characteristics of both the market and the clientele. On the basis of their results, they were able to take effective action to keep up with such evolution. Marketing strategies therefore were re-elaborated, and the product Club Med offers was repackaged according to the demands of the industry, while still remaining faithful to the original philosophy. The image of Club Med was also reconsidered in order to determine the most appropriate one at all times.

Other significant changes included an entrance into the cruise business—Club Med I is a luxurious cruise ship that offers the excitement of yachting (thanks to a retractable platform that allows activities such as waterskiing, diving, etc.) together with the comforts of the cruise. Activities within the village were also improved and upgraded, following the guests' requests for more in-depth sports teaching, more amenities in the rooms, specialized restaurants, more security, and communication tools.

The clientele target was also widened: Club Med now attempts to attract customers other than the original youth/couples. As a consequence, the individual villages were updated by specializing in a particular area. Although all clubs offer the same basic services, some focus mainly on sports, some on tours and excursions, some on convention and meeting facilities, some on entertainment, and so on. Customers now range from sports enthusiasts to families (mini-clubs and baby-clubs were recently established), honeymooners, and corporate clients. The new trend at the moment is that of finding ways to attract the older clientele.

Club Med also has had another innovative idea: Wild Card, which offers a bargain rate to vacationers who don't mind gambling on which village they visit. Wild Card confirms participants on a one-week vacation at one of Club Med's Villages in the Bahamas, Caribbean, or Mexico for $999 per person, double occupancy; this is a savings of up to $500 over the weekly standard rate. Included is the price of the airfare from specified gateway cities.

Wild Card presents a win-win situation. Club Med wins because it can utilize vacant space on air charters and accommodations; guests win because they get a great vacation at a bargain price. As a result, about 75 percent of Wild Card bookings are from first-time guests. This means a great deal of new business is being generated in addition to Club Med's 50 percent repeat business rates—one of the highest in the resort industry.[1]

To cope with the changes and implementations in the global structure of the villages, human resources staff (GOs—gentle organizers, etc.) also have been selected and trained more thoroughly. GOs come from all over the world; they must have some foreign language proficiency (to keep up with an extremely cosmopolitan clientele), skills in sports or entertainment, and, most of all, be extremely enthusiastic and very people oriented. In fact, the spirit of the village depends almost entirely on the creative ideas and contact generated by the staff.

Overall, Club Med has shown a very remarkable ability to reinvent itself according to the continuous evolution of the market and society. The genuine commitment to excellence that has been demonstrated should help Club Med retain its status as the ultimate destination resort organization.

[1]Joel Sleed, "Club Med Tells Its Customers Where to Go," *San Diego Union-Tribune*, February 4, 1993, p. D4.

The Prehistoric Cave Paintings at Lascoux (Used with permission of the French Government Tourist Office.)

population of Eastern Europe and the nouveau riche of the Pacific Rim countries will substantially add to the potential number of tourists.

Ecotourism

Within the past few years, the tourism industry has witnessed a phenomenon that continues to take tourists and industry leaders alike by storm. *Ecotourism,* often dubbed "adventure tourism," "responsible tourism," or "sustainable tourism," has become the fastest growing segment within the world's largest industry. For

Giraffes and other wildlife in Africa—one example of Ecotourism

tourists, it is the latest trend. For ecologists, scientists, and students, it is a life-long dream. And for the tourism industry leaders, it is a potentially prosperous business. But amidst the awe of what ecotourism can provide, there has been much confusion and controversy as to what ecotourism actually is and whether it actually works.

Although the term may be new—it has only been in existence for about a decade—the concept has been alive for much longer. There is no true definition of what ecotourism really is, perhaps because it is difficult to describe and because there have been many distinct interpretations of the concept. Whether it is called ecotourism, adventure tourism, or nature travel, the definitions contain elements and concepts that are associated with what is known as sustainable development.[46] It is believed that tourism—ecotourism in particular—is a key tool in achieving sustainable development, which is "to meet the needs of the present without compromising the ability of the future generations to meet their own needs."[47] One of the most widely accepted descriptions is that of The Ecotourism Society, an organization based in the United States, in which ecotourism is described as "responsible travel to natural areas that conserves the environment and sustains the well-being of the local people."[48]

In the early 1970s, people in several remote areas of the world saw that tourism could be important, however they did not want to destroy the exotic environment that surrounded them. One such place was Cancun, Mexico. At the time, Cancun was a prime beach location, but the number of tourists was not very high. Unlike today, there were more natives than visitors. Developers recognized the potential Cancun had and "drew up a master plan that placed priority on environmental protection."[49] Unfortunately, Mexico began to experience political and economic instability. The recession caused the government and business leaders to scramble to find a way to bring money into the economy—specifically, U.S. dollars. Tourism in Mexico was, then, one of the few industries in the country that showed signs of growth. Instead of having environmentally friendly attractions, however, as Cancun was meant to have, it was sacrificed in order to make room for large-scale development.[50]

As a result, the natives were moved off their homeland and pushed onto the side of a mountain. They live in what looks like cardboard shacks and do not have running water or a sewage system. The area beaches are becoming cluttered with travelers and garbage and the reef that is found off of the coastline has been damaged by ships coming into the wharf. Water treatment is insufficient and it is practically impossible to meet the growing capacity requirements.[51] Mass tourism has proven to be destructive.

As similar stories become known to the world, ecologists, together with tourism leaders, realize how important it is to preserve the environment so that generations to come can continue to enjoy earth's natural beauty. Because of this, most ecotourism destinations can be found in areas with vast natural surroundings and plentiful flora and fauna. Places like deserts, tropical rainforests, coral reefs, and ice glaciers are prime locations. Also important in ecotourism is the presence of a culture that is unique to the visitor. The focus of ecotourism is to provide tourists with new knowledge about a certain natural area and the culture that is found within, along with a little bit of adventure. As for the natives, ecotourism is to help improve the local economy and conservation efforts. All parties are to gain a new appreciation for nature and people.

Thus far, ecotourism projects tend to be developed on a small scale. It is much easier to control such sites, particularly because of limits that are normally set upon the community, the local tourism business, and the tourists. Limitations may include strict control of the amount of water and electricity being used, tougher recycling measures, regulating park and market hours, and more importantly, limiting the number of visitors to a certain location at one time, and limiting the size of the business. Another reason ecotourism projects are kept small is to allow more "in depth" tours and educational opportunities.

Generally speaking, most of the more popular ecotourism destinations are located in underdeveloped and developing countries. As vacationers are becoming more adventurous and are visiting remote, exotic places, inclusively, they are participating in activities that, hopefully, impact nature, host communities, and themselves, in a positive manner. However, because of the growing interests of travelers, many developed countries are following the trend. It is apparent from Yellowstone National Park in the United States to the Mayan Ruins of Tikal in Guatemala; from the Amazon River in Brazil to the vast Safari lands of Kenya; from the snow-capped Himalayas in Nepal to the sultry jungles of Thailand; and from the Great Barrier Reef in Australia to the massive ice glaciers in Antarctica. There is no doubt that this is an attractive trend in many parts of the world.

Some of the more successful examples of ecotourism can be found in Central America, the Caribbean, Africa (particularly in Kenya), and Nepal. For instance, "Mundo Maya" is a unique project in that it is a joint endeavor comprising of the countries in which the Maya civilization was, and still is, found. These countries include Belize, El Salvador, Guatemala, Honduras, and the five Mexican states of Quintana Roo, Yucatán, Campeche, Tabasco, and Chiapas. "The area's countless tourist attractions reflect the geographical diversity of the Maya World and its rich, cultural heritage, both ancient and modern. . . ."[52] Tourists can climb the massive, stone pyramids; sit in one of the housing rooms; hike through the jungles; watch for exotic birds, howling monkeys, and other animals; and, in some places, see the coral reefs in the Caribbean coastline. What is especially appealing about Mundo Maya is that the traveler can visit one area or country at a time or take a package that includes every country and major attraction.[53]

Another prosperous site is the U.S. Virgin Islands. Here, developer Stanley Selengut designed an "ecoresort" with the idea that ecotourism does not have to be as big as traditional tourism. Specifically, ecotourism should be more conscious of the damage it causes, or may cause, in an area that is virtually virgin and very fragile. Maho Bay Camps is a series of "luxury" tent/cottages scattered strategically about the island. The camps are not luxurious, but they are sufficiently equipped to accommodate guests, and include communal bathrooms. For the more upscale-minded, Selengut opened a second resort, with private bathrooms, called Harmony, which is made almost entirely from recycled products.

Africa's tourism industry, especially ecotourism, is growing tremendously. The most popular activity is a Safari tour, in which visitors can see, up close, wildlife like elephants, gazelles, lions, tigers, buffaloes, cheetahs, and many others. Kenya is an important destination for safaris. Also popular in Africa are the rich rain forests of Rwanda and Zaire, home to several endangered primates, like the mountain gorillas. These animals, and the area, gained much recognition when Dian Fossey lived in the jungles to study the gorillas.[54]

Thousands of miles away, ecotourism is becoming popular in Southeast Asia, where places like Malaysia, Thailand, and the Philippines are developing tourism programs based on environmental conservation and protection. As with other regions of the world that are covered by dense rain forests, Southeast Asia is home to a vast variety of wild flora and fauna. River boat rides and visiting small villages that dot the islands are also quite popular.

As a result of the concerns about and interests in ecotourism, many conferences have been held to inform the general population and, particularly, the tourism professionals and ecologists about the advantages and disadvantages of ecotourism. Conferences also provide advice and suggestions for running a successful ecotourism attraction. The 1992 Earth Summit, presented by the United Nations in Rio de Janeiro, Brazil, focused on the environment and development in general with tourism being the key to accomplishing sustainable development throughout the world. The Earth Summit also produced Agenda 21, which addresses issues pertaining to the environment and sustainable development and is intended to prepare the world to successfully meet the challenges in the coming century.

The World Conference on Sustainable Tourism, held in Spain in 1995, dealt specifically with tourism and resulted in the Charter of Sustainable Tourism. It recognized "the objective of developing a tourism [industry] that meets economic expectations and environmental requirements, and respects not only the social and physical structure of the location, but also the local population".[55] It also emphasizes that "environmentally and culturally vulnerable spaces, both now and in the future, should be given special priority . . . for sustainable tourism development".[56] Sustainable tourism, especially ecotourism, can be a main source of worldwide promotion of sustainable development geared toward tourists and communities in all countries.

Trends in Tourism and Travel

- ✔ Ecotourism, sustainable tourism, and heritage tourism will continue to grow in importance.
- ✔ Globally, the number of tourist arrivals will continue to increase by about eight percent per year, topping 1 billion by 2010.

✔ Governments will increasingly recognize the importance of tourism not only as an economic force, but also as a social-cultural force of increasing significance.

✔ More bilateral treaties are being signed, which will make it easier for tourists to obtain visas to visit other countries.

✔ The promotion and development of tourism is moving from the public sector (government) to the private sector (involved industry segments).

✔ Internet bookings will increase.

✔ Franchising of travel agencies and home-based travel agents will increase.

✔ Technology will continue to advance allowing even more information to be available more quickly to more places around the world.

✔ Marketing partnerships and corporate alliances will continue to increase.

✔ Employment prospects will continue to improve.

✔ Ticketless air travel will become commonplace.

Airline Commission Caps

Travel agents have begun legal action and public campaigns to combat United Airlines' decision to lower commissions for writing tickets, and have warned of higher ticket costs if other airlines followed United's example. United recently lowered the commission rate on tickets for domestic flights from ten percent to eight percent, retaining a $50 cap for a roundtrip fare. International commissions also fell to eight percent from ten percent, with no cap on payments.

Southwest Airlines announced it will not follow United's decision; TWA has, as yet, made no decision; and other major airlines have declined to comment. Airlines analysts predict that most will follow United. The other airlines appear to be temporarily letting United take the heat.

As consumers begin to balk at rising ticket prices and Wall Street presses for continued earnings growth, airlines must cut costs by turning to their second largest expense, the $12 billion spent annually for costs such as travel agent commissions. It has become clear that airlines can do nothing about fuel prices and can do very little, if anything, about labor costs. The only area that airline management has any power over is the area of distinction expenses.

American Express Corporate Services Agencies, which books mostly business travelers, warned that if other airlines follow suit, some travel agencies will go out of business. That would send more businesses to airlines' reservation agents, who do not offer the lowest available fares from all carriers, or could result in travel agents passing costs along to consumers.

The American Society of Travel Agents, which represent 27,000 agents, and The Association of Retail Travel Agents, a trade group that represents 4,000 travel agents, have announced they will seek U.S. congressional approval to allow small, "business-sized" travel agents to bargain collectively with the major airlines and to steer customers to "friendly" airlines when negotiating fails. The associations believe that the cut in commissions in less than three years is a slap in the face, since airlines are earning record profits.

After the introduction of the initial cap of $25 for one-way domestic tickets and $50 for round-trip tickets, many agents complained caps would eliminate jobs and reduce earnings. A class action lawsuit followed on behalf of 33,000 travel agents, alleging price fixing. Some travel agents also steered customers away from other airlines such as Delta in retaliation.

In September 1996, American, Delta, Northwest, and United agreed to pay $72 million in cash to settle the lawsuit.[57]

Discussion Questions

1. If you owned a travel agency, what would your reaction to the reduced commission cap be?
2. What options would you consider?

Developing the San Diego Waterfront

Description of the Existing Situation and Issues

San Diego, California has a diversified economic base with tourism as an important component of the economy. In 1996, the city hosted about 14 million tourists who spent some $4 billion, and tourism is steadily expanding each year. Most tourists are domestic, although a fair number of foreigners also visit the city. The attractions for tourists in San Diego are the mild Mediterranean-type climate; attractive natural setting; beaches developed with resort and park facilities; and major attractions including Sea World, the world-famous San Diego Zoo and Wild Animal Park, interesting and well-preserved historic areas, and picturesque shopping districts. A variety of resort and urban hotels have been developed, the most notable being the historic Hotel del Coronado. The policy of government, which is supported by most residents, is for the continued but controlled development of tourism as a major source of income and employment.

A major focal point for tourism development is the downtown area located next to the waterfront of San Diego Bay. As a result of concerted planning efforts and substantial investment during the past several years, the San Diego downtown is undergoing new development and redevelopment. Changes include a recently completed convention center; the preservation and renovation of numerous shops and restaurants in the historical Gaslamp Quarter; the development of a maritime museum on the waterfront of historic ships; the Seaport Village shopping and restaurant complex and related park, also located on the waterfront; and others. New urban residential complexes are also developing. In response to the revitalization of downtown, several new high-rise hotels have been developed and some historic hotels have been renovated to provide good quality tourist facilities. Many conferences and conventions are now being attracted to the downtown and this area, with its interesting features, has become an important center for tourism for both business conferences and holiday tourists.

San Diego recognizes the importance of its waterfront and the views it affords as a major attraction for both residents and tourists. If properly conserved and carefully developed, waterfronts give an urban area a unique character. However, in the case of San Diego, and some other cities, the economic pressure to develop prime waterfront sites can lead to cutting off public access to the waterfront, thereby preempting waterfront areas from public use and blocking views of the water from inland downtown buildings. In San Diego, the new convention center already stretches along a considerable length of the waterfront and plans are to expand it further along this area. New high-rise hotels near the convention center are blocking waterfront access and views of the bay, and more hotels have been proposed for this area. Expansion is planned for the popular Seaport Village, however this complex is low-rise and does not greatly impinge on views. It is designed to provide pedestrian access along the waterfront. Other projects are being considered for development on the waterfront. Thus, there is the dilemma of the waterfront area, the most significant natural feature of the downtown environment, not being effectively integrated into development patterns because of economic development pressures. At the same time, many persons recognize the need to preserve public access, use of the waterfront, and views of the bay. The problem relates particularly to the need for careful land-use planning with utmost consideration given to social and economic implications.[58]

Discussion Questions

1. Why is it considered so desirable to develop public and private amenity features on the waterfront and preserve public access to the waterfront and water views in urban areas? From the residents' standpoint? From the standpoint of developing successful tourism?
2. What approach can San Diego take in properly developing its downtown waterfront area both to achieve economic development objectives and to preserve access to and along the waterfront and views of the adjacent bay?
3. If the choice of development of a particular waterfront site lies between developing the site for a high-rise hotel, for which there is proven market demand, or a waterfront public park for use by both residents and tourists, which do you think is the best use of the site? What approaches could be applied to achieve both objectives?

Summary

1. Tourism can be defined as the idea of attracting, accommodating, and pleasing groups or individuals traveling for pleasure or business. It is categorized by geography, ownership, function, industry, and travel motive.

2. The development of tourism started before the Industrial Revolution and continued parallel with the improvement of means of transportation: railway, automobile, aircraft, and cruise ships.

3. Tourism involves international interaction and, therefore, government regulation. Several organizations, such as the World Tourism Organization, are responsible for environmental protection, tourism development, immigration, and cultural and social aspects of tourism.

4. Tourism is the world's largest industry and employer. It affects other industry sectors, such as public transportation, foodservice, lodging, entertainment, and recreation. In addition, tourism produces secondary impacts on businesses that are affected indirectly, which is known as the multiplier effect.

5. Travel agencies, tour operators, travel managers, wholesalers, national offices of tourism, and destination management companies serve as middle persons between a country and its visitors.

6. Physical needs, the desire to experience other cultures, and an interest in meeting new people are some of the motives people have when they travel. Because of flexible work hours, early retirement, and the easy accessibility of traveling, tourism is constantly growing.

7. From a social and cultural perspective, tourism can further international understanding and economically improve a poor country. However, it can also disturb a culture by confronting it with mass tourism, causing the destruction of natural sites. A trend in avoiding tourism pollution is ecotourism.

8. Business travel has increased in recent years due to the growth of convention centers in several cities. As a result, business travelers have given a boost to hotels, restaurants, and auto rental companies. The number of female business travelers is rising as well.

Review Exercises

1. Give a broad definition of tourism and explain why people are motivated to travel.
2. Describe the importance of Benz, Ford, and Lindbergh in the development of tourism.
3. Explain the differences in the development of the European and U.S. railway systems.
4. What is the significance of the Airline Deregulation Act of 1978?
5. Give a brief explanation of the economic impact of tourism. Name two organizations that control or further the economic impact of tourism.
6. Choose a career in the tourism business and give a brief overview of what your responsibilities would be.
7. Discuss the positive and negative impacts that tourism can have on a country in consideration of tourism pollution and ecotourism.
8. What are some of the services offered by travel corporations, such as American Express Travel Services? How does AMEX handle corporate accounts?

Key Words and Concepts

Agenda 21
Airline Deregulation Act of 1978
The Bermuda agreement
Business travel
Commission Caps
Concorde
Conventions and visitors bureaus
Corporate travel manager
Destination management companies
Economic impact of tourism
Ecotourism
Hub-and-spoke system
International Air Transportation Association
International Development Organization
Multiplier effect
National tourism organizations
Pacific Area Travel Association
Pleasure travel
Segmenting the cruise market
Strategic alliance
Sustainable Tourism
Ticketless Travel
Tour operators
Tourism
Tourism promotion organizations
Travel agents
Travel and tours wholesalers
World Tourism Organization

Notes

[1]"Economic Research Highlights from WTTC," World Travel and Tourism Council. http://www.wttc.org.

[2]*American Hotel and Motel Report, 1, 7,* July/August, 1993.

[3]Francisco Fragialli, Secretary General for the World Tourism Organization (WTO), as cited in *Hotel and Motel Management,* vol. 212, no. 13, July 21, 1997.

[4]Richard Kelley, "To Create Jobs, Sumitears Should Take a Breath of Rocky Mountain Air and Promote Tourism." http://www.wttc.org. July 20, 1997.

[5]A. J. Butkarat and S. Meddlik, *Tourism: Past, Present and Future.* London: Heinemann, 1974, p. 3.

[6]Ibid., p. vii.

[7]Robert McIntosh and Charles R. Goeldner, *Tourism Principles, Practices, Philosophies,* 6th ed. New York: John Wiley and Sons, 1990, pp. 11–13.

[8]Ibid.

[9]Edward J. Mayo and Lance P. Jarvis, *The Psychology of Leisure Travel: Effective Marketing and Selling of Travel Services.* Boston: CBI Publishing Company, 1981, p. 5.

[10]Donald E. Lundberg, *The Tourist Business,* 6th ed. New York: Van Nostrand Reinhold, 1990, p. 16.

[11]Ibid.

[12]Lundberg, op. cit., p. 16.

[13]Jan Van Harssel, *Tourism: An Exploration,* 3d ed. Englewood Cliffs, N.J.: Prentice Hall, 1994.

[14]Paul R. Dittmer and Gerald G. Griffen, *The Dimensions of the Hospitality Industry: An Introduction.* New York: Van Nostrand Reinhold, 1993, p. 359.

[15]Lundberg, op. cit., p. 93.

[16]Dittmer and Griffen, op. cit., p. 352.

[17]Ibid.

[18]Van Harssel, op. cit., p. 27.

[19]Ibid.

[20]Ibid.

[21]Dittmer and Griffen, op. cit., p. 365.

[22]Stewart Toy and Andrea Rothman, "Air France: Is This the Right Flight Plan?" *Business Week,* August 2, 1993, p. 48.

[23]Ibid.

[24]Michele McDonald, "USAir's Lagow: BA Link's Strategic Partnership," *Travel Weekly,* August 30, 1993, p. 10.

[25]Kevin Kelly and Aaron Bernstein, "Labor Deals That Offer a Break from Us vs. Them," *Business Week,* August 2, 1993, p. 30.

[26]Ibid.

[27]Marc Levinson, "Something Novel in the Air," *Newsweek,* August 2, 1993, p. 34.

[28]Lundberg, op. cit., p. 102.

[29]McIntosh and Goeldner, op. cit., p. 43.

[30]Robert Christie Mill and Alastair M. Morrison, *The Tourism System: An Introductory Text.* Englewood Cliffs, N.J.: Prentice Hall, 1985, p. 228.

[31]Rick Fairlie, "Dividing the Pies," *Travel Weekly,* November 8, 1993, p. 1.

[32]Courtesy of the American Society of Travel Agents.

[33]Rick Fairlie, "It's in the Mail," *Travel Weekly,* May 31, 1993, p. 32.

[34]ARTA Home Page, April 26, 1996.

[35]Phone interview with an employee of Harvey Golub, President, American Express Travel Services, November 6, 1996.

[36]Based on Stephen Arrendell, "Getting It Together," *Travel Weekly,* May 31, 1993.

[37]Rick Fairlie, "It's in the Mail," op. cit.

[38]Tour Wholesaler Industry Study, Touche Ross & Co., 1976, p. 68, as cited in Mill and Morrison, op. cit., p. 400.

[39]This section draws on McIntosh and Goeldner, op cit., pp. 100–103.

[40]This section draws on Gregory Aryear, *The Travel Agent: Dealer in Dreams,* 3d ed. Englewood Cliffs, N.J.: Prentice Hall, 1989, p. 21.

[41]Ibid., p. 276.

[42]Ibid.

[43]Abraham Maslow, "A Theory of Human Motivations," *Psychological Review,* 50, 1943, pp. 370–396.

[44]McIntosh and Goeldner, op. cit., p. 131.

[45]Van Harssel, op. cit., p. 190.

[46]Internet: "Indigenous Ecotourism and Sustainable Development: The Case Study of Rio Blanco, Ecuador," David T. Schaller. http://www.geog.umn.edu/~shaller/Section2Rio Blanco.html.

[47]Internet: "The Concept of Sustainable Development," Paul Samson, Green Cross International, July 1995. http://greencross. unige.ch/greencross/digiforum/concept.html.

[48]"Tourism's Green Machine," Glenn Hasek. *Hotel and Motel Management,* October 3, 1994, vol. 209, no. 17, pp. 25–26.

[49]"Ecotourism: A Dream Diluted," Mary Farquharson. *Business Mexico,* June 1992, vol. 2, no. 6, pp. 8–11.

[50]Ibid.

[51]Ibid.

[52]Internet: "The Mundo Maya Project," http://www.yucatan. com.mx/mayas/ingles/fsl5.html.

[53]Ibid.

[54]Internet: "Ecotourism: Paradise Gained, or Paradise Lost?" Panos, 1995, Panos. http://www.oneworld.org/panos/panos_ eco2.html.

[55]Ibid.

[56]Ibid.

[57]This case is based on Cliff Edwards, "Travel Agents Assail Commission Cuts." Associated Press, *San Diego Union Tribune,* September 23, 1997, p. 2.

[58]This case is courtesy of Edward Inskeep, a tourism consultant and author with the WTO.

The Hotel Business: Development and Classification

3

After reading and studying this chapter you should be able to do the following:

✔ Describe briefly the development of the U.S. lodging industry
✔ Define the following terms: *hotel franchising, partnerships, leasing, syndicates,* and *management contracts*
✔ Discuss financial aspects of hotel development
✔ Classify hotels by type, location, and price
✔ Explain vertical and horizontal integration
✔ List ways hotels cater to the business and leisure travel markets
✔ Describe the effects of a global economy on the hotel industry

Hotel Development in the United States

Hotels in North America began as inns or taverns, which were vastly different from today's full-service hotels. It is interesting to trace this development over the years, especially from a financial viewpoint.

The industry, as we know it today with a number of high-profile companies, is vastly different from even a generation ago. The taverns in Boston were called "the candles of liberty" by Patrick Henry. In fact, the Green Dragon and the Bunch of Grapes were meeting places for the Sons of Liberty during the American Revolution. The Boston Tea Party was planned in the Green Dragon.[1]

Taverns soon sprang up in all the colonies and became a focal point of the community. They flourished, not only in the major cities, but also along the communication routes known as turnpikes. Later, canals also became a part of the growing transportation system. Naturally, then as now, people on the move required food, beverages, and accommodations.

The first hotel to open in the United States was the seventy-room City Hotel on Broadway, New York City, in 1794. This was followed by others, notably the 170-room Tremont House, which opened in Boston in 1829. The Tremont was the first hotel to have bellpersons, front desk employees, locks on guest-room doors, and free soap for guests.

Perhaps because there was no royalty in the New World, hotels emerged as people palaces. Each new hotel featured a new architectural design, and displayed grand lobbies, ballrooms, superior plumbing, or some other guest convenience—such as elevators, which were first installed in New York's Fifth Avenue Hotel in 1859. Electricity was first used by the Hotel Everett on Park Row in New York.[2]

Transportation changed the nature of the hotel industry. First it was rail travel that prompted hotels to develop as the popular resorts and frontiers opened. From the Hotel del Coronado, near San Diego, California, to the five-star Breakers Resort in Palm Beach, Florida, and the famous Greenbriar Resort in West Virginia, railroads and hotels complemented one another in providing the traveling public with remarkable experiences. In Canada, the Canadian Pacific (CP) railroad enabled passengers to view the spectacular Rocky Mountains. To this day, CP operates the largest chain of Canadian hotels.

The first motel was opened by California architect Arthur Hineman in 1925, in San Luis Obispo, California. This location is about 200 miles north of Los Angeles—a long day's drive in those days. Hineman designed the motel so guests could drive right up to the doors of their rooms or to an adjacent garage. The forty one-story bungalows were grouped around a courtyard. It cost $80,000 to build in its ornate Spanish-mission style, with a three-tiered tower, white pillars, and tree-fringed courtyard—unusually luxurious for the 1920s.

During the Depression of the 1930s, many hotel owners defaulted on their mortgages. As a result, banks and institutions soured on the idea of mortgage loans for hotels. For this reason, few downtown hotels were built after World

The Motel Inn, San Luis Obispo, California

War II, even in the 1950s and early 1960s. Hilton, the preeminent emerging chain at the time, acquired and rebuilt older hotels, like the Stevens in Chicago (now the Chicago Hilton and Towers) and the Plaza in New York City.[3]

The automobile created a wave of hotel and motel construction in the 1940s, 1950s, and 1960s. As Americans began to explore the open road, hotels and motels developed to cater to their accommodation needs. Likewise, air transportation was a catalyst for the development and redevelopment of city hotels and destination resorts. In 1958, the Boeing 707 enabled faster transcontinental and trans-Atlantic flights. Business and leisure travel took off in what was to become the largest worldwide industry.

The vibrant economy of the 1950s meant that there was more disposable income for travel and tourism. With the advent of rail, automobile (car and bus), and air transportation, society became more mobile. This mobility began to transform the industry from small, wholly owned, and independently operated properties to the concepts of development by franchising, partnership, leasing, and management contracts.

Hotel development is linked to the broader economy and the real estate maxim of "Highest and Best Use," that is, which investment will yield the greatest return? If a person or corporation has money to invest, where would it yield the best return? Some could be put in the stock or bond market and some in the property market, but is it best to invest in office buildings, shopping malls, or hotels? Obviously, there are many aspects to consider.

Recently, Arthur Anderson updated its investor study.[4] Many of the organizations said that they were continuing to invest in hotels over other forms of real estate, because hotels are still available for less than replacement costs.

Franchising

Franchising in the hospitality industry is a concept that allows a company to expand more rapidly by using other people's money than if it had to acquire its own financing. The company or franchisor grants certain rights, for example, to use its trademark, signs, proven operating systems, operating procedures and possibly reservations system, marketing know-how, purchasing discounts, and so on for a fee. In return, the franchisee agrees by signing the franchise contract to operate the restaurant, hotel, and so on in accordance with the guidelines set by the franchisor. Franchising is a way of doing business that benefits both the franchisor—who wants to expand the business rapidly—and the franchisee—who has financial backing but lacks specific expertise and recognition. Some corporations franchise by individual outlets and others franchise by territory.

Franchising began in the hotel industry in 1907, when the Ritz Development Company franchised the Ritz-Carlton name in New York City.[5]

Howard Johnson began franchising his hotels in 1927. This allowed for a rapid expansion, at first on the East Coast and later in the Midwest and finally in the mid-1960s into California. Today, there are more than 900 restaurants in the chain.

Holiday Inns (now Holiday Corporation, the largest lodging enterprise in the world) also grew by the strategy of franchising. In 1952, Kemons Wilson, a developer, had a disappointing experience while on a family vacation when he had to pay for an extra room for his children. Therefore, Wilson decided to build a moderately priced family-style hotel. Each room was comfortably sized and had two double beds; this enabled children to stay for free in their parents' rooms. In the 1950s and early 1960s, as the economy grew, Holiday Inns grew in size and popularity. Holiday Inns added restaurants, meeting rooms, and recreational facilities. They upgraded the furnishings and fixtures in the bedrooms and almost completely abandoned the original concept of being a moderately priced lodging operation.

One of the key factors in the successful development of Holiday Corporation was that they were the first company to enter the midprice range of the market. These inns or motor hotels were often located away from the expensive downtown sites, near important freeway intersections and the more reasonably priced suburbs. Another reason for their success was the value they offered: comfort at a reasonable price, avoiding the expensive trimmings of luxury hotels.

About this time, a new group of budget motels emerged. Motel 6 (so named because the original cost of a room was $6 a night) in California slowly spread across the country, as did Days Inn and others. Cecil B. Day was in the construction business and found Holiday Inns too expensive when traveling on vacation with his family. He bought cheap land and constructed buildings of no more than two stories to keep the costs down. These hotels and motels were primarily for the commercial travelers and vacationing families, were located close to major highways, and were built to provide low-cost lodging without frills. Some of these buildings were of a modular construction. Entire rooms were built elsewhere, transported to the site, and placed side-by-side.

It was not until the 1960s that Hilton and Sheraton began to franchise their names. Franchising was the primary growth and development strategy of hotels and motels during the 1960s, 1970s, and 1980s. However, franchising presents two major challenges for the franchisor: maintenance of quality standards and avoidance of financial failure on the part of the franchisee.

It is difficult for the franchise company to state in writing all of the contingencies that will ensure that quality standards are met. Recent franchise agreements are more specific in terms of the exterior maintenance and guest service levels. Franchise fees vary according to the agreements worked out between the franchisor and the franchisee; however, an average agreement is based on 3 or 4 percent of room revenue.

The world's largest franchisor of hotels, with 5,300 hotels, is Hospitality Franchise System (HFS) of Parsippany, New Jersey. Choice Hotels International, ranked second with 3,130 franchised hotels, is a subsidiary of the Blackstone Group, New York. Holiday Inn Worldwide is now the third largest franchisor with 2,082 hotels. Table 3–1 shows franchise hotels among the top ten corporate chains.

Franchising provides both benefits and drawbacks to the franchisee and franchisor. The benefits to the franchisee are as follows:

✔ A set of plans and specifications from which to build
✔ National advertising
✔ Centralized reservation system
✔ Participation in volume discounts for purchasing furnishings, fixtures, and equipment
✔ Listing in the franchisor's directory
✔ Low fee percentage charged by credit card companies

The drawbacks to the franchisee are as follows:

✔ High fees—both to join and ongoing
✔ Central reservations generally producing between 17 and 26 percent of reservations

Table 3–1 Franchised Hotels Among the Top 10 Corporate Chains[1]

Company	Hotels Franchised	Total Hotels
HFS Inc.	5,300	5,300
Choice Hotels International	3,130	3,197
Holiday Inn International	2,082	2,260
Promus Cos.	683	809
Marriott International	604	1,268
Carlson Hospitality Worldwide	416	437
Accor	343	2,465
ITT Sheraton Corp.	204	413
Hilton Hotels Corp.	173	245
Best Western International	N/A	3,654

Source: HOTELS Giants Survey 1997
[1]"Hotels' 325: Corporate 200," *Hotels*, July 1997, p. 46.

Corporate Profiles: HFS Incorporated

In its first year, 1990, Hospitality Franchise Systems Inc. was a company consisting of middle-of-the-market hotel chains Ramada and Howard Johnson. Now HFS Inc. is an empire consisting of a loose confederation of businesses and brands in related services, including hotels, rental cars, real estate, mortgages, and vacation ownership/time-shares. HFS Inc. is a global provider of real estate and travel services, the world's largest franchiser of residential real estate brokerage offices, and the global leader in corporate employee relocation. HFS is also the largest franchiser of hotels and rental cars, the leading provider of vacation time-share exchanges, and the second largest vehicle management company worldwide.

Included under HFS's management are Days Inn, Howard Johnson, Ramada, Knights Inn, Super 8, Travelodge, Villager Lodge, Wingate Inn, Century 21, ERA (Electronic Realty Associates), Coldwell Banker, Avis Rent-a-Car, and PHH Corp. Combined, these businesses account for approximately half a million hotel rooms in the United States, Canada, Latin America, and Europe, and more than 11,500 franchised real estate offices with more than 190,000 brokers in the United States, Mexico, Canada, Puerto Rico, Europe, Africa, and the Asia-Pacific region. Under the leadership of Henry R. Silverman, founder, chairman, and chief executive officer of HFS Inc., company stock has increased nearly 1,400% since its initial offering.

HFS's acquisition policies have been extremely successful, largely because of Silverman's talent and intuition in locating companies "that are either being poorly managed or overstaffed, and then upgrading the management and closing divisions and laying off employees."[1] As a result of the uninterrupted acquisitions, the company's revenue, net income, and profitability have steadily increased for eighteen consecutive quarters. Revenue in the first quarter of 1997 increased 88% to $527 million from $280 million for the first quarter of 1996. Net income increased 111% to $91 million from $43 million in the same quarter.[2]

Although clearly in the consumer services industry, its clients include other businesses and corporations—not individual consumers. As a franchiser, the company licenses the owners and operators of independent businesses to use HFS's brand names, without taking on big business risks and expenses. HFS does not operate hotels or real estate brokerage offices, but instead, provides coordination and services that allow franchisees to retain local control of their activities. At the same time, they benefit from the economies of scale of widely promoted brand names and well established standards of service, national and regional direct marketing, co-marketing programs, and volume purchasing discounts. All HFS brands share "extensive market research, use well-developed technology, such as proprietary reservation systems and, in the case of lodging, a room inventory tracking system, which is extremely technology intensive and eliminates waste."[3] By monitoring quality control and extensively promoting the brand names, HFS offers its independent franchise owners franchise fees that are relatively low compared to the increased profitability they gain.

Through franchising, HFS limits its own risks and is able to keep overhead costs low. Chief Financial Officer Michael P. Monaco says HFS "limits the volatility in the business as best as we can because fees come from revenue, not the franchisee's profitability.[4] CEO Henry Silverman concurs: "Increases or decreases in rate of occupancy have very little impact on us. Our biggest outcome driver is more units—unit growth."[5] A further advantage of being a franchiser of such dimension is that the company is even more protected from the cyclical nature of the economy than are other franchise ventures. In times of prosperity, independent owners are favored, however, that is not the case during a recession. Silverman adds that "cash flow of [owners-operators] will be more volatile than ours. The franchiser's cash flow is relatively more stable and will go up slightly each year with inflation, slightly each year with occupancy and/or royalties, and significantly if you continue growing units."[6]

The critical mass created by all the businesses working together makes HFS more valuable as a whole than as the sum of its parts, gives it outstanding purchasing power and market control, and makes it extremely effective in selling to a wide audience. Although the individual businesses may, at first glance, seem desperate, all the various acquisitions undergone by the company are part of a carefully designed strategy. "What we try to do," CEO Silverman says, "is assemble different brands that have huge internal synergy."[7] "Synergy" is a key word for HFS Inc. It is the magic formula that creates mutual benefits within companies in an industry segment and cross-fertilizes businesses across industries.

Diversification is a common practice in the hotel industry. Marriott, for example, combines hotel properties, foodservices, time-share, and senior living products. However, no other hotel company has had such rapid growth and expansion. But diversification was a necessity as well as a strategic choice. It was precisely HFS's quick expansion as a hotel franchise company that created the need to diversify in order to sustain that growth rate. The businesses the company decided to acquire were carefully selected according to Silverman's view of the peculiar demographics of the North American market. The wave of baby boomers consists of 76 million people who are approaching fifty years of age, and this trend will continue for about ten to twelve more years. In Silverman's view, this clientele consumes primarily two things: travel and residential real estate. In light of this trend, HFS's diversification from the hotel market turned to real estate, mortgage companies, and time-sharing operators.

HFS's future leaves skeptics in doubt. Will HFS be able to sustain and continue this enormous growth? All signs are in favor of it. Again looking at demographics, Silverman anticipates that a possibility for the future may be entering the assisted-living business (a combination of a hotel and a nursing home), which does not have, at this point, enough critical mass to invest in. But, as Silverman stated, "It probably will require some national marketing at some point."[8]

[1]Toni Giovanetti, "HFS, Once Confined to Hotels, Now Encompasses a Global Business Matrix," *Hotel Business*, vol. 6, no. 9, May 7–20, 1997, p. 26.
[2]HFS Incorporated. News Release, May 1, 1997.
[3]Todd Pitock, "The Artful Acquirer," *Journal of Business Strategy*, vol. 18, no. 2, March/April 1997, p. 19.
[4]Ibid.
[5]Philip Hayward, "Silverman on Silverman," *Lodging*, May 1997, p. 49.
[6]Ibid.
[7]John Greenwald, "HFS Stands for Growth," *Time*, March 17, 1997, p. 41.
[8]Hayward, op. cit., p. 50.

✔ Franchisees must conform to the franchisor's agreement
✔ Franchisees must maintain all standards set by the franchisor

The benefits to the franchise company are as follows:

✔ Increased market share/recognition
✔ Up-front fees

The drawbacks to the franchise company are as follows:

✔ The need to be very careful in the selection of franchisees
✔ Difficulty in maintaining control of standards

Franchising continues to be a popular form of expansion both in North America and the rest of the world.

Partnership

Another interesting mode of developmental financing was used by Travelodge: a partnership. Under this plan, a husband and wife who wanted to enter the motel business invested one-half the cost of the motel. The couple received a salary for managing the property, and profits from the operations were divided 50-50 between the company and the couple.[6] Travelodge, now a part of HFS, began and expanded utilizing the partnership arrangement.

Leasing

Leasing became popular in the 1950s and 1960s; it still exists, but to a lesser extent. The leasing arrangement allows both the individual and the chain to enter the market or expand within it. A hotel is leased for a percentage of gross sales, generally 20 to 50 percent.[7] For example, U.S. international hotel expansion began with the lease of the Hotel Caribe Hilton in San Juan, Puerto Rico. The government of Puerto Rico wanted to encourage tourism by having a brand name hotel with management expertise. The government leased the hotel to Hilton in return for two-thirds of the gross operating profit plus marketing expenses.[8]

Several developing countries have adopted the lease concept. In Cuba, all went well until Castro took over after the Cuban Revolution. The Havana Hilton's occupancy dropped to 14 percent, which resulted in a loss. The lessons learned from this led to the management contract, which involved less risk for hotel corporations. Profit-sharing lease agreements became management contracts. A base fee of five percent of gross revenues was introduced, plus an incentive fee of ten percent of the gross operating profit.

In some locations, like Western Europe, the lease was to the hotel corporation's advantage. In London, the Hilton had a twenty-five-year lease, and rent was fixed at eight percent of the original cost with little provision for increase. As a result, Hilton took out almost 75 percent of the gross operating cost.[9]

Leasing may make a comeback with the lack of capital in the current marketplace. Hotel brokers have been looking for new ways to deal with underfinanced properties. Krieger and Snyder of Scottsdale, Arizona, have developed a new type of leasing. Leasing gives the benefits of ownership without the initial capital outlay. The hotel operator or lessee manages the hotel with a lease based on gross guest room revenues. The operator is responsible for insurance, hiring and firing, food and beverage, and the marketing of the hotel. In return, the operator gets a major part of every dollar of room revenue that comes into the hotel and the major part of every increase in revenue.[10]

Syndicates

Syndicates were and still are a popular form of hotel financing. A syndicate involves a group of investors who may (or may not) be friends or acquaintances of the eventual hotel operator. The group arrangement usually allows for a larger investment and a larger property, and naturally allows for the risk to be spread among the syndicate members.

Management Contracts

Management contracts have been responsible for the hotel industry's rapid boom since the 1970s. They became popular among hotel corporations because little or no up-front financing or equity was involved. Even if the hotel corporation was involved in the construction of the hotel, ownership generally reverted to a large insurance company. This was the case with the La Jolla, California, Marriott Hotel. Marriott Corporation built the hotel for about $34 million, then sold it to Paine Webber, a major investment banking firm, for about $52 million on completion. Not a bad return on investment!

The management contract usually allows for the hotel company to manage the property for a period of five, ten, or twenty years. For this, the company receives as a management fee, often a percentage of gross and/or net operating profit, usually about 2 to 4.5 percent of gross revenues. Lower fees in the two percent range are more prevalent today, with an increase in the incentive fee based on profitability. Some contracts begin at 2 percent for the first year, 2.5 the second, and 3.5 the third and for the remainder of the contract.[11] Increased competition among management companies has decreased the management contract fees in the past few years. In recent years, hotel companies increasingly have opted for management contracts because considerably less capital is tied up in managing as compared with owning properties. This has allowed for a more rapid expansion of both the U.S. and international markets.

Hotel management companies often form a partnership of convenience with developers and owners who generally do not have the desire or ability to operate the hotel. The management company provides operational expertise, marketing, and sales clout, often in the form of a centralized reservation system (CRS).

Some companies manage a portfolio of properties on a cluster, regional, or national basis. The largest twenty-five management companies are listed in Table 3–2. Most of these companies manage hotels in the same classifications. This enables them to focus their efforts on managing properties of a similar nature rather than properties in different classifications.

In the early 1990s, because of plummeting real estate values, the high cost of debt service (mortgage payments) and the economic downturn, hotel-operating results and cash flows fell drastically. Recent contracts have called for an increase in the equity commitment on the part of the management company. Between 1988 and 1992, there was an increase from about 25 percent to about 42 percent in chain operators' equity contributions.[12] In addition,

Table 3–2 Top Twenty-five Management Companies

Hotel	Total Properties (1996)
1) Doubletree Hotels Corp.	242
2) Interstate Hotels Corp.	212
3) Richfield Hospitality Services	132
4) Starwood Lodging	75
5) Barrington Hotels and Resorts International	48
6) Carnival Hotels and Resorts	78
7) Queens Moat Houses Plc.	127
8) CDL Hotels	61
9) UniHost Corp.	136
10) Prime Hospitality Corp.	103
11) Tharaldson Enterprises	224
12) Westmont Hospitality Group Inc.	63
13) Servico Inc.	60
14) Southern Sun Hotels	63
15) Remington Hotel Corp.	70
16) Ocean Hospitalities Inc.	65
17) American General Hospitality	64
18) Motels of America Inc.	135
19) Columbia Sussex Corporation	46
20) Winegardner and Hammons Inc.	51
21) John Q. Hammons Hotels	43
22) Grupo Posadas Management	45
23) Gencom American Hospitality	39
24) CapStar Hotels	47
25) Bristol Hotel Management Co.	38

owners increased their operational decision-making options—something seldom done previously.

The strongest trend in contract negotiations is the expansion of the variety of contract provisions. For example, some owners may need or want equity participation. However, they may be unwilling to share control with an equity partner.[13] Generally, a compromise is worked out. Hotel owners focus on management companies with the following characteristics:[14]

- ✔ Experience and reliability
- ✔ Excellence in reporting
- ✔ Communication and human resources
- ✔ Successful strategies for improved profitability
- ✔ Proven ability to meet rigorous operator performance standards

With international expansion, a hotel company entering the market might actively seek a local partner or owner to work within a form of joint venture.

Today, hotel management companies exist in an extremely competitive environment. They have discovered that the hotel business, like most others, has changed and they are adapting accordingly. Today's hotel managers are demanding better bottom-line results and reduced fees. Management companies are seeking sustainability and a bigger share of the business.

The management industry itself is consolidating and institutional owners know they can require management companies, particularly the bigger, more capitalized ones, to actually make contributions to the property—up to ten or twenty percent investments.[15]

Financial Management and Profits

The hotel industry is characterized by a high degree of risk, which primarily is the result of two factors: the cyclical nature of demand and the high degree of capital investment.[16] A greater proportion of profit from hotels comes from the manipulation of real estate rather than from the sale of lodging, food, and beverages.

People construct hotels for a variety of reasons: pride of ownership or ego, profit from building, profit from promoting and financing, or profit from appreciation in value of the property. The great increase in value of the Hilton and Sheraton companies has not come from operating profits but from buying, selling, and tax advantage, and in appreciation of value of the hotels with time. Financial management is the name of the game, and the game is complex.

Perhaps the most amazing corporate development was that accomplished in just twenty-six years by Ernest Henderson. His financial skill, keen analysis, and shrewdness, combined with energy and hard work, catapulted the Sheraton Corporation from very modest beginnings to 154 hotels at his death in 1967. How was this financial success achieved? It was not with Disney's magic wand! Henderson was a capitalist and an opportunist. He bought and sold hotels whenever and wherever a deal could be worked out. The incentives and depreciation won out over ego and sentiment.

Leveraged money was used whenever possible. For example, if the Sheraton Corporation was interested in buying a hotel that had a $100,000 income each year, the corporation might be willing to buy at eight times the income ($800,000). Henderson would borrow half of the $800,000 from a bank or insurance company at 6 percent interest. If the owner would agree to take a second mortgage of $500,000, Sheraton could take over the property for a cash outlay of only $100,000, or a down payment of 12.5 percent.[17]

Creative Financing

The 1970s and 1980s were a difficult time for hotel expansion. Some hotels were planned for questionable markets as companies tried to stretch their abilities to manage fast growth. This situation was brought about by several factors:[18]

- ✓ A period of inflation-fueled expansion from 1976 to 1978, following on the heels of the recession and real estate bust of the mid-1970s
- ✓ A transitional period of stagnation from 1979 to mid-1981, characterized by economic stagflation and rapidly increasing inflation
- ✓ The recession of 1989 to 1993 was characterized by further decreases in productivity, a decreasing rate of inflation, and above-average interest rates

These factors forced lenders to be more active in the financial decision-making process regarding hotel development. Cash-flow decisions became more important, and lenders kept a watchful eye on developers who, until the early 1980s, were generally left to provide an "adequate," unaided return.

The early 1980s were years of extremely high interest rates. It was this critical factor that caused alarm bells to ring because projects were unable to meet the internal rate-of-return standards demanded by the lender as a condition of credit. Consequently, many projects were suspended; others were financed with short-term floating-rate loans.

Another result of the downturn in the economy and overbuilding of first-class properties in most United States cities was a softening of the real estate market. These factors led to what has now become known as *creative* or *portfolio* financing.

Portfolio financing occurs when a number of properties are cross-collateralized and cross-defaulted in a securitized format. This offers both investors and lenders a win-win situation, with greater overall protection against risk than would otherwise be possible with a single property.

By spreading the portfolio pool among more than one location or market (e.g., resort, city center, convention, or resort properties in a variety of locations), the effect of an economic downturn on a particular property will be buffered by other properties. However, care must be exercised when setting up such an arrangement to ensure that if one property were in default of a loan payment, the lender could not automatically foreclose on all the other properties. This creative form of financing will often be able to access funds at a lower rate of interest, one of the critical factors in the success of a hotel venture.

However, in a publicly traded corporation, the chief executive officer's (CEO's) and chief financial officer's (CFO's) primary mission is to maximize the

Personal Profile: Conrad Hilton and Hilton Hotels Corporation

Conrad Hilton "King of Innkeepers" and Master of Hotel Finance

Hilton's success was attributed to two main strategies: (1) hiring the best managers and letting them have total autonomy, and (2) being a cautious bargainer who, in later years, was careful not to overfinance. Conrad Hilton had begun a successful career in the banking business before he embarked on what was to become one of the most successful hotel careers ever.

In 1919, while on bank business in Cisco, Texas, he bought the Mobley Hotel with an investment of $5,000. Hilton rented rooms to oil industry prospectors and construction workers. Because of high demand for accommodations and very little supply, Hilton often rented a room to three or four strangers. On some occasions, he even rented out his own room and slept in a lobby chair.

Because Hilton knew the banking business well and had maintained contacts who would lend him money for down payments on properties, he quickly expanded to seven area hotels. Hilton's strategy was to borrow as much money as possible in order to expand as rapidly as possible. This worked well until the Great Depression of the early 1930s. Hilton was unable to meet the payments on his properties and lost several in bankruptcy proceedings.[1]

Hilton, like many great leaders, had the determination to bounce back. In order to reduce costs, he borrowed money against his life insurance and even worked on the side for another hotel company.

Hilton's business and financial acumen is legendary. *The New York Times* described Conrad Hilton as "a master of finance and a cautious bargainer who was careful not to overfinance" and had "a flawless sense of timing."[2]

Hilton was the first person to notice vast lobbies with people sitting in comfortable chairs not spending any money. So he added the lobby bar as a convenient meeting place and leased out space for gift shops and newsstands. Most of the additional revenue from these operations went directly to the bottom line. The following shows a chronology of Conrad Hilton's and Hilton Corporation's highlights:

1919—Hilton bought the Mobley Hotel.
1925—The first Hilton hotel was built in Dallas, Texas.
1938—Hilton purchased the lease on the Sir Francis Drake Hotel in San Francisco, California. This was the first Hilton outside Texas.

Conrad Hilton

1942—The Town House in Los Angeles became Hilton's headquarters. The Roosevelt and the Plaza in New York became Hilton's first East Coast ventures.
1949—Conrad Hilton bought the lease of Waldorf Astoria in New York and made it successful because he and his organization knew how to run it. Hilton opened the first Hilton International in San Juan, Puerto Rico.
1954—The Statler Hotel Company was bought for $111 million. At this time, this was the largest transaction in the history of the hotel industry.
1960—Conrad Hilton was made chairman of the board of Hilton Hotels Corporation.
1967—Hilton International was acquired by Trans World Airlines.
1971—The Las Vegas Hilton and the Flamingo Hilton marked Hilton's entry into the gaming market.
1977—Ownership of the building and land for the Waldorf Astoria in New York was purchased for a mere $35 million.
1979—Conrad Hilton died at the age of 92. Baron Hilton, Conrad's son, became chairman of the board of directors.
1982—With the addition of 391 rooms, the Las Vegas Hilton became the largest hotel in the world, with 3,174 guest rooms and an extensive gaming area.
1983—Construction began on the Conrad International Hotel and Jupiters Casino on the Gold Coast of Queensland, Australia, the company's first property under Conrad International.
1984—The 1,600-room Anaheim Hilton and Towers opened adjacent to the Anaheim Convention Center in California.
1988—Completion of the renovations at the Hilton Hawaiian Village and the San Francisco Hilton and Towers marked the culmination of Hilton's $1.2 billion restoration and expansion program of its American hotels from coast to coast.
1989—The first Hilton suites property opened in Anaheim, California. The first Crest Hill by Hilton opened in Illinois.
1991—Hilton purchased and announced a massive nine-month renovation of the O'Hare Hilton in Chicago. Hilton established Hilton Grand Vacation Company, a nationwide system of vacation ownership resorts.
1992—Hilton assumed management of the Pointe Resorts in Phoenix, Arizona. Hilton acquired the 2,000-room Bally's Casino Resort in Reno, Nevada.

1993—Hilton Hotels and Hilton Grand Vacations Company commit millions to develop a new generation of "Vacation Ownership" resorts. The first will adjoin the Flamingo Hilton in Las Vegas.

Hilton and its partners, Caesars World, Inc. and Circus Circus Enterprises, Inc., are selected to develop and manage the Casino Windsor in Canada. The alliance marks the first time three world-class gaming companies joined together to offer casino gaming in a major jurisdiction.

1994—Hilton celebrates seventy-five years of innovation, marking the diamond anniversary of company founder Conrad N. Hilton's first hotel purchase, The Mobley.

The Queen of New Orleans riverboat casino, now the Flamingo Casino New Orleans, opened to the public, becoming the first such facility to begin operations on the Mississippi River in New Orleans.

1995—Zip-In Check-In® registration program is launched at more than 220 U.S. Hilton Hotels. Hilton Honors members with guaranteed reservations can now check into a Hilton hotel in thirty seconds or less.

Hilton Hotels' Internet Travel Center opens its site on the World Wide Web. Computer users throughout the world can now make direct reservations and find out about the company programs, special offers, and other information for more than 240 U.S. Hilton and Conrad International hotels worldwide.

Hilton Inns captures fourth consecutive first place ranking as the top midpriced hotel company in the annual *Business Travel News* survey.

1996—Stephen F. Bollenbach is named president and chief executive officer of Hilton Hotels Corporation. Formerly of the Walt Disney Company, this represents the first time in Hilton's history that the CEO position is held by someone whose last name is not Hilton.

Hilton Hotels Corporation becomes the world's largest casino gaming company after the signing of a merger agreement with Bally Entertainment Corporation. The final transaction was approved by both companies' boards of directors, the companies' shareholders, and gaming regulators of several states.

Hilton Hotels Corporation and British company Ladbroke Group PLC (current owners of the Hilton name outside the United States) form a strategic alliance that reunites the famous Hilton brand worldwide for the first time in thirty-two years.

1997—Hilton Hotels Corporation bids for ITT Sheraton.[3]

[1]Paul R. Dittmer and Gerald G. Griffen, *The Dimensions of the Hospitality Industry: An Introduction.* New York: Van Nostrand Reinhold, 1993, pp. 91–92.

[2]Joan Cook, "Conrad Hilton, Founder of Hotel Chain, Dies at 92," *The New York Times*, January 5, 1979, sec. 11, p. 5.

[3]Hilton Hotels' Internet Travel Center, Hilton Press Releases, http://www.hilton.com.

price of the organization's common stock. To do this, the CEO must constantly assess the two key determinants of share price: risk and return. All major hotel financial decisions must be viewed in terms of expected risk, expected return, and their combined impact on share price. These expected values are often difficult to measure; the process requires considerable judgment as well as factual knowledge. In some states, public funds have been used to finance hotel developments. The Westin Hotel in Providence, Rhode Island is a good example. It was built with state funds as part of the convention center project.

Real Estate Investment Trust (REIT)

Real Estate Investment Trusts (REIT) have existed since the 1960s. In those early days, they were mostly mortgage holders. But in the 1980s, they began to own property outright, often focusing on specific sectors like hotels, office buildings, apartments, malls, and nursing homes. Today, about 300 REITs, with a combined market value of $70 billion, are publicly traded. Investors like them because they do not pay corporate income tax and instead are required to distribute at least 95 percent of net income to shareholders. In addition, because they trade as stocks, they are much easier to get into or out of than limited partnerships or the direct ownership of properties. In the hotel industry, REITs are clearly where the action is. In the first six months of 1997, hotel REITs raised about $1 billion in public stock offerings.

The two leading REIT corporations are Patriot American Hospitality and Starwood Lodging Trust. Patriot American Hospitality has acquired Wyndham Hotels, which has become its operating company and given it a well-regarded brand name. Starwood Lodging Trust acquired Westin Hotels and Resorts for $1.4 billion, and outbid Hilton for ITT Sheraton. Patriot and Starwood are the only REITs allowed to both manage and own properties.

Financing Package

The process of determining the required return involves the calculation of the appropriate level of return to compensate the firm for the risk undertaken. Financing for a hotel that is conducive to success requires that the needs and objectives of the developer, operator, and lender or investor be understood and dealt with realistically. The arrangements made depend on the state of the money market; the results of feasibility and market studies; and the strength, credit rating, and reputation of the corporations involved. Generally speaking, about 60 to 80 percent of the total budget required to bring a hotel into being can be raised by debt financing.

It must be recognized that the financing of a hotel is only a part of the total package, albeit an important part. The extent to which the property will be successful will be dependent on the quality of management. The following points may help lay the groundwork for favorable financing:

- Affiliation with a quality franchisor or referral group
- Identification with a national chain through a management contract
- A lease arrangement with a strong, well-recognized hotel operator
- Identification with a national chain by way of a joint-venture agreement
- Conventional first mortgage loans—the most common real estate financing, even for hotels
- Lenders, including insurance companies, commercial banks, investment banks, savings banks, institutional investors, pension funds, syndicates, partnerships, and families

In recent years, hotel financing in North America has experienced an influx of overseas capital; that has been both a blessing and a blight—depending on which type of financial package is agreed to.

One of the dangers of a foreign currency loan is that currency fluctuations may cause an increase or decrease in the amount of the loan repayment. Fortunately, there are safeguards, including having the loan negotiated in U.S. dollars and repaid in U.S. dollars, thereby avoiding any currency fluctuations on the part of the borrower.

Current financing conditions are the most difficult in the industry's history. Viable hotel development opportunities do exist, but developers and franchisors must be creative in locating funding. Having been caught short in the 1980s, lenders are now basing loans on more conservative occupancy and rate projections.[19]

How Some Hotels Become Overvalued

In the mid-1970s, the United States experienced 12 percent inflation and a shortage of good hotel room inventory. Approximately 20,000 new rooms a year were constructed. This meant that there was too much money (demand) chasing too few rooms (supply). Then inflation crept up to 12 percent, with money market accounts yielding 8 to 9 percent. This meant that savings and loan institutions began to become involved in lending for domestic and commercial mortgages. They could lend at 12 to 14 percent while their clients would receive 8 to 9 percent interest on their deposits.

The insurance and pension funds industry, which at the time was cash rich, began to invest heavily in new hotels. Many of these were massive, mixed-use commercial projects consisting of hotels, office blocks, and shopping malls. In some cities, these complexes were not built for the right reasons. America's inner cities had declined in the 1960s and 1970s. However, because hotels are a catalyst for other businesses, every city mayor offered significant benefits to major hotel investments. These benefits included being given land, superstructure, construction, and tax breaks.

The hotel industry is not known as a leading industry; rather, it generally reacts to circumstances. Frequently, the hotel industry is caught by outside forces and swept along. An example of this is the fact that hotels in the 1970s and 1980s were assets managed. This was because the value of the assets—the hotel—increased in value.

In 1981, President Ronald Reagan initiated the Income Recovery Act, which was intended to rebuild America's capital structure. The depreciation period of hotels went from forty to nineteen years, and there was a ten percent tax credit for capital improvement. Thus, as other tax loopholes closed, hotels became a hot investment item. Brokers began syndicating hotels to doctors, lawyers, and other professionals.

The so-called tax laws of 1986 significantly reduced the amount of tax deductions corporations could take on depreciation of property. The Accelerated Cost Recovery System was modified causing the term of depreciation to go from nineteen to thirty-one and one-half years. This legislation had an immediate impact on the bottom lines of hotel corporations. This is still being felt today in the form of increased taxation (or more accurately a decrease in deductions). The recession that began in 1990 indicated that many hotel properties were overvalued. However, the bankers who had lent money did not want to admit that they had overvalued assets; therefore, they denied any problems. Hotel properties became highly leveraged. In fact, many could not service their debt (pay their mortgages). So the savings and loan industry and banks began to experience serious problems as federal regulators became more aware of the situation.

Another interesting example of how a hotel's fortunes go up and down is the U.S. Grant Hotel in San Diego, named after the renowned Civil War general who later became a U.S. president. The hotel opened about a hundred years ago and was successful for a number of years but eventually required an $80 million renovation program in 1986. The hotel then had a succession of owners and management companies—none of whom could pay the debt service. Ultimately, in

U.S. Grant Hotel, San Diego, California.

1994 the owners declared bankruptcy and the hotel was sold at auction for approximately $10 million. This price was considered a bargain for a 285-room property in a prime downtown location. The hotel is now being successfully managed by Joe Dunclafe and Grand Heritage Hotels.

Changes in ownership and management are not uncommon in the hotel business. In light of this, hotel operators, no matter how talented they are, must be cognizant of external factors, such as property values, interest rates, and debt service, that impact the property's operation and profitability.

Other factors fall within the domain of hotel developer; these activities include the overly creative financing that burdened many hotels with unrealistic levels of debt service. Owners, developers, operators, and lenders have each made their own peculiar contribution to today's hospitality industry problems. Some predictions for the lodging industry include a return to basics, global hospitality involvement, and equity/debt restructuring.[20]

In 1991, the industry experienced one of its worst financial operating periods in history. Overall, occupancy was at 60.9 percent and profits were at a record low of $2.8 billion. Since 1992, the hotel business, along with many others, has made a remarkable turnaround from the problems experienced. Due to a robust economy and increased operating efficiencies, hotels are now more profitable than ever before. In 1996, hotels made more profit than in the seven previous years combined.

In the past couple of years, the hotel industry has undergone massive ownership changes—mostly consolidations. The reason for this consolidation, as Bill Marriott, chairman of Marriott International, explains, is globalization. He reasons that medium-sized hotel companies, lacking the critical mass and technological platform needed for worldwide marketing, will seek alliances with larger players who have it.[21]

For instance, Marriott, having acquired Ritz-Carlton and Renaissance Hotels Groups, has entered China and three dozen markets armed with ten hotel brands. Wyndham Hotels have merged with Patriot American Hospitality. Hilton paid $1 billion for Bally but lost out on its bid for ITT Corporation and its Sheraton and Caesars Palace brands to Starwood Lodging Trust. Doubletree became a national chain by merging with Guest Quarters and Red Lion Hotels, but it missed upgrading to being a global player when Marriott trumped its bid for Renaissance Hotels Group.[22] Prince Al-Waleed Bin Talal Bin Abdulaziz Al Saud acquired an interest in Four Seasons Hotels, then bought a controlling interest in Fairmont Hotels, and more recently announced plans to buy Princess Hotels and Resorts.

Available capital has been the driving force of these purchases. From 1991 to 1996, Wall Street raised $16.1 billion in public funds. Private funds are reckoned to be two or three times that amount. In the same period, there were 42 significant mergers and acquisitions; 13 hotel companies that went public; 12 REITs that formed together and purchased more than 350 hotels; and 3,250 individual hotels sold with a value of $23 billion.

Classification of Hotels

According to the American Hotel and Motel Association, the United States lodging industry consists of 46,000 hotels and motels, with a total of 3.3 million rooms. The gross volume of business generated from these rooms is $65 billion.

Unlike many other countries, the United States has no formal government classification of hotels. However, the American Automobile Association (AAA) classifies hotels by diamond award, and the Mobile Travel Guide offers a five-star award. Of the more than 21,000 star-rated establishments, fewer than two percent have been awarded five-star status. The guide currently bestows the five-star award to thirty-five lodging properties.

The AAA has been inspecting and rating the nation's hotels since 1977. Less than two percent of the 19,500 properties inspected annually throughout the United States, Canada, and Mexico earned the five-diamond award, which is the association's highest award for excellence. In 1996, the five-diamond award was bestowed on fifty-two hotels and resorts in twenty states. Twelve of the properties received both the five-diamond and the five-star awards.

AAA uses descriptive criteria to evaluate the more than 24,000 hotels that they rate annually in the United States, Canada, Mexico, and the Caribbean (see Figure 3-1).

- ✓ One-diamond properties have simple roadside appeal and the basic lodging needs.
- ✓ Two-diamond properties have average roadside appeal, with some landscaping and a noticeable enhancement in interior decor.

	◇	◇◇	◇◇◇	◇◇◇◇	◇◇◇◇◇
General	Simple roadside appeal Limited landscaping	Average roadside appeal Some landscaping	Very good roadside appeal Attractive landscaping	Excellent roadside appeal Professionally planned landscaping	Outstanding roadside appeal Professional landscaping with a variety of foliage and stunning architecture
Lobby	Adequate size with registration, front desk, limited seating and budget art, if any	Medium size with registration, front desk, limited seating, carpeted floors, budget art and some plants	Spacious with front desk, carpeted seating area arranged in conversation groupings, good-quality framed art, live plants, luggage carts and bellstation	Spacious or consistent with historical attributes; registration and front desk above average with solid wood or marble; ample seating area with conversation groupings and upscale appointments including tile, carpet or wood floors; impressive lighting fixtures; upscale framed art and art objects; abundant live plants; background music; separate check-in/-out; bellstation	Comfortably spacious or consistent with historical attributes; registration and front desk above average; ample seating with conversation groupings and upscale appointments; impressive lighting fixtures; variety of fine art; abundant plants and fresh floral arrangements; background music; separate check-in/-out; bellstation that may be part of concierge area; concierge desk
Guestrooms	May not reflect current industry standards	Generally reflect current industry standards	Reflect current industry standards	Reflect current industry standards and provide upscale appearance	Reflect current standards and provide luxury appearance
Service	Basic attentive service	More attentive service	Upgraded service levels	High service levels and hospitality	Guests are pampered by flawless service executed by professional staff

Figure 3-1 *Summary of AAA diamond-rating guidelines.* Courtesy of Hotel and Motel Managment.

✔ Three diamonds carry a degree of sophistication through higher service and comfort.
✔ Four diamonds have excellent roadside appeal and service levels that give guests what they need before they even ask for it.
✔ Five-diamond properties have the highest service levels, sophistication, and offerings.

Josette Constantine, manager of AAA inspections, said one word to describe the five-diamond properties is "Wow!"

Even the one-diamond properties provide a valuable listing, Constantine said. One diamond doesn't represent low quality by any means. Almost 40 percent of lodging facilities are not approved for inspection at all because they don't meet the minimum standards of cleanliness, comfort, safety, and maintenance.[23]

Hotels may be classified according to location, price, and type of services offered. This allows guests to make a selection on these as well as personal criteria. A list of hotel classifications follows:

City Center—luxury, first-class, midscale, economy, suites
Resort—luxury, midscale, economy suites, condominium, time-share, convention
Airport—luxury, midscale, economy, suites
Freeway—midscale, economy suites
Casino—luxury, midscale, economy

Alternatively, the hotel industry may be segmented according to price. Figure 3–2 gives an example of a national or major regional brand-name hotel chain in each segment.

City Center Hotels

City center hotels, by virtue of their location, meet the needs of the traveling public for business or leisure reasons. These hotels could be luxury, midscale, business, suites, economy, or residential. They offer a range of accommodations and services. Luxury hotels might offer the ultimate in decor, butler service, concierge and special concierge floors, secretarial services, computers, fax machines, beauty salons, health spas, twenty-four-hour room service, swimming pools, tennis courts, valet service, ticket office, airline office, car rental, and doctor/nurse on duty or on call. Generally, they offer a signature restaurant, coffee shop, or an equivalent name restaurant; a lounge; a name bar; meeting and convention rooms; a ballroom; and possibly a fancy night spot.

City center hotels were constructed in waves; stimulated by government regulations, investors developed hotels when the climate was right. For example, tax incentives for urban renewal projects created favorable economic conditions in the 1960s. This led to the construction of new downtown hotels in many cities. Another boom time for hotel development was the 1980s. Together with convention centers and office buildings, hotels have been one of the catalysts in inner-city revitalization. The Copley Center in Boston and the Peachtree Plaza in Atlanta are examples of this.

Budget $25–$35	Economy $35–$55	Midprice $55–$95	Up Scale $95–195	Luxury $125–$425	All-Suites $65–$125
	Holiday Inn Express	Holiday Inn	Holiday Inn	Crown Plaza	
	Fairfield Inn	Courtyard Inn Residence Inn	Marriott	Marriott Marquis Ritz-Carlton	Marriott Suites
		Days Inn	Omni	Renaissance	
		Radisson Inn	Radisson		Radisson Suites
	Ramada Limited	Ramada Inn	Ramada	Ramada	Ramada Suites
	Sheraton Inn	Sheraton Inn Four Points	Sheraton	Sheraton Grande	Sheraton Suites
			Hyatt	Hyatt Regency Hyatt Park	Hyatt Suites
Sleep Inns	Comfort Inn	Quality Inn	Clarion Hotels		Quality Suites Comfort Suites
		Hilton Inn	Hilton	Hilton Towers	Hilton Suites
		Doubletree Club	Doubletree		Doubletree Suites
Thrift Lodge	Travelodge Hotels	Travelodge Hotels	Forte Hotels	Forte Hotels	
			Westin	Westin	
Sixpence Inn	La Quinta				
E-Z-8	Red Roof Inn				
	Best Western				
	Hampton Inn				Embassy Suites

Figure 3–2 *Hotels by Price Segment*

The St. Regis Hotel in New York is another good example of a city center luxury hotel. An example of a midscale hotel in New York is the Ramada Hotel; an economy hotel is the Days Inn; and a suites property is the Embassy Suites.

Resort Hotels

Resort hotels came of age with the advent of rail travel. Increasingly, city dwellers and others had the urge to vacation in locations they found appealing. Traveling to these often more-exotic locations became a part of the pleasure experience. In the late 1800s, luxury resort hotels were developed to accommodate the clientele that the railways brought.

Such hotels include the famous Greenbrier at White Sulphur Springs, West Virginia, The Hotel del Coronado in Coronado (near San Diego), California, and the Homestead at Hot Springs, Virginia. In Canada, the Banff Springs Hotel and Chateau Lake Louise drew the rich and famous of the day to their picturesque locations in the Canadian Rocky Mountains.

Banff Springs Hotel

The leisure and pleasure travelers of those days were drawn by resorts, beaches, or spectacular mountain scenery. At first, many of these grand resorts were seasonal. However, as automobile and air travel made even the remote resorts more accessible and an increasing number of people could afford to visit, many resorts became year-round properties.

Resort communities sprang up in the sunshine belt from Palm Springs to Palm Beach. Some resorts focused on major sporting activities such as skiing, golf, or fishing; others offered family vacations. Further improvements in both air and automobile travel brought exotic locations within the reach of the population. Europe, the Caribbean, and Mexico became more accessible. As the years passed, some of the resorts suffered because the public's vacation plans changed.

The traditional family month-long resort vacation gave way to shorter, more frequent get-aways of four to seven days. The regular resort visitors became older; in general, the younger guests preferred the mobility of the automobile and the more informal atmosphere provided by the newer and more informal resorts.

In order to survive, the resort hotels became more astute in marketing to different types of guests. For example, some resorts allow no children in the high season because they would interfere with the quiet ambiance for guests who do not want the noise of children. Other resort hotels go out of their way to encourage families; Camp Hyatt is a prominent example. Hyatt hotels have organized a program consisting of a variety of activities for children, thereby giving the parents an opportunity to either enjoy some free time on their own or join their children in some fun activities. Many resort hotels began to attract conventions, conferences, and meetings. This enabled them to maintain or increase occupancy, particularly during the low and shoulder seasons.

Guests go to resorts for leisure and recreation. They want a good climate—summer or winter—in which they can relax or engage in recreational activities. Due to the remoteness of many resorts, guests are a kind of "captured clientele," who may be on the property for days at a time. This presents resort managers with some unique operating challenges. Another operating challenge concerns seasonality—some resorts either do not operate year-round or have periods of very low occupancy. Both present challenges in attracting, training, and retaining competent staff.

Many guests travel considerable distances to resorts. Consequently, they tend to stay longer than at transient hotels. This presents a challenge to the food and beverage manager to provide quality menus that are varied and are presented and served in an attractive, attentive manner. To achieve this, resorts often use a cyclical menu that repeats itself every fourteen to twenty-one days. Also, they provide a wide variety and number of dishes to stimulate interest. Menus are now more health conscious—lighter and low in saturated fats, cholesterol, salt, and calories.

The food needs to be presented in a variety of different ways. Buffets are popular because they give guests the opportunity to make choices from a display of foods. Barbecues, display cooking, poolside, specialty restaurants, and reciprocal dining arrangements with near-by hotels give guests more options.

With increased global competition, not only from other resorts but also from cruise lines, resort managers are challenged to both attract guests and to turn those guests into repeat business, which traditionally has been the foundation of the resorts viability.

In order to increase occupancies, resorts have diversified their marketing mix to include conventions, business meetings, sales meetings, incentive groups, sporting events, additional sporting and recreational facilities, spas, adventure tourism, ecotourism, etc.

Because guests are cocooned in the resort—they expect to be pampered. This requires an attentive, well-trained staff and that is a challenge in some remote areas and in developing countries.

There are a number of benefits in operating resorts. The guests are much more relaxed in comparison to those at transient hotels, and the resorts are located in scenically beautiful areas. This frequently enables staff to enjoy a better quality of life than do their transient hotel counterparts. Returning guests tend to treat associates like friends. This adds to the overall party-like atmosphere, which is prevalent at many of the established resorts.

Vacation Ownership

The Growth of an Industry

From its beginnings in the French Alps in the late 1960s, vacation ownership has become the fastest-growing segment of the U.S. travel and tourism industry, increasing in popularity at the rate of nearly 16 percent each year since 1993.

Vacation ownership is the politically correct way of saying time-share. Essentially, vacation ownership means a person purchases the use of a unit similar to a condominium for blocks of times, usually in weeks. Henry Silverman of HFS, which owns the Indianapolis, Indiana-based Resort Condominiums International (RCI) says that time-share is really a two-bedroom suite that is owned, rather than a hotel room that is rented for a transient night. A vacation club, on the other hand, is a "travel-and-use" product. Consumers do not buy a fixed-week, unit-size, season, resort, or number of days to vacation each year. Instead, they purchase points that represent currency, which is used to access the club's vacation benefits. An important advantage to this is the product's flexibility, especially when tied to a point system. A vacation club is not involved with real-estate ownership in any way, so the point system ties in well with the hotel marketing programs, such as those that reward frequent flyers.[24]

The World Tourism Organization has called time-shares one of the fastest-growing sectors of the travel and tourism industry. Hospitality companies are adding brand power to the concept with corporations like Marriott Vacation Club International, the Walt Disney Company, Hilton Hotels, Hyatt Hotels, Promus' Embassy Suites, Inter-Continental and even Four Seasons participating in an industry that has grown nearly 900 percent since 1980. Still, only about 1.72 percent of all U.S. households own vacation ownership. RCI estimates that the figure could rise to 10 percent within the next decade for households with incomes of more than $50,000. No wonder hotel companies have found this to be a lucrative business.

RCI, the largest vacation ownership exchange (that allows members to exchange vacations with other locations), has more than 2 million member families. Three thousand participating resorts and members can exchange vacation intervals for vacations at any participating resort.[25] Vacation ownership is popular at U.S. resorts from Key West in Florida to Kona in Hawaii and from New York City and Las Vegas to Colorado ski resorts.

Today, more than 3 million households own vacation intervals at nearly 4,500 resorts located in eighty-one countries. Vacationers around the world are turning to vacation ownership resorts as their preferred travel destination, with time-share owners hailing from 174 countries. North America remains the global leader with nearly half of all the participating resorts and approximately 2 million owners. Europe is second with approximately twenty-two percent of owners worldwide and more than 1,000 resorts. Time-share resorts are found around the globe in popular vacation areas near beaches, rivers, lakes, and mountains, and even in major cities.

By locking in the purchase price of accommodations, vacation ownership helps ensure future vacations at today's prices at luxurious resorts with amenities, service, and ambiance that rival any of the world's top-rated vacation destinations. Through vacation exchange programs, time-share owners can travel to other popular destinations around the world. With unparalleled flexibility and fully equipped condominiums that offer the best in holiday luxury, vacation ownership puts consumers in the driver's seat, allowing them to plan and enjoy vacations that suit their lifestyle.

Time-share resort developers today include many of the world's leading hoteliers, publicly held corporations, and independent companies. Properties that combine vacation ownership resorts with hotels, adventure resorts, and gaming resorts, are among the emerging time-share trends. The reasons for purchasing most frequently cited by current time-share owners are the high standards of quality accommodations and service at the resorts where they own and exchange, the flexibility offered through the vacation exchange opportunities, and the cost effectiveness of vacation ownership. Nearly one-third of vacation owners purchase additional intervals after experiencing ownership. This trend is even stronger among long-time owners; 41.2 percent of those who have owned for eight years or longer have purchased additional intervals within the time-share.

What Is Vacation Ownership?

Vacation ownership offers consumers the opportunity to purchase fully furnished vacation accommodations in a variety of forms, such as weekly intervals or points in points-based systems, for a percentage of the cost of full ownership. For a one-time purchase price and payment of a yearly maintenance fee, purchasers own their vacation either in perpetuity or for a predetermined number of years. Owners share both the use and the costs of upkeep of their unit and the common grounds of the resort property. Vacation ownership purchases are typically financed through consumer loans of five to ten years duration, with terms dependent upon the purchase price and the amount of the buyer's down payment. The average cost of a vacation ownership is about $10,500.

Each condominium, or unit, of a vacation ownership resort is divided into intervals, either by the week or by points equivalent, which are sold separately. The condominiums are priced according to a variety of factors, including size of the unit, resort amenities, location, and season. With time-share, owning your vacation is considered a major benefit. Once a majority or other preset percentage is sold to vacation owners, the management of the resort is usually turned over to a Resort Property Owners Association (POA), or Homeowners Association (HOA). The vacation owners then elect officers and take control of expenses, upkeep, and the future of their resort property, including the selection of a management company.

What Are Yearly Maintenance Fees?

Yearly maintenance fees are paid each year to a HOA for the maintenance of the resort. Just like taking care of a home, resort maintenance fees help maintain the quality and future value of the resort property. In a vacation ownership resort, maintenance costs are shared by all owners. They pay for on-site management, unit upkeep and refurbishing, utilities, and maintenance of the resort's common areas and amenities, such as pools, tennis courts, and golf courses. Just like residential condominium owners, they determine the fees through their HOA board of directors. The amount of the yearly maintenance fee typically depends on the size, location, and amenities of the resort. Maintenance fees are assessed and paid annually by each vacation owner.

Today, there are several types of time-share programs from which to choose, enabling consumers to purchase the type of vacation ownership that best matches their lifestyle. Time-sharing, or vacation ownership, describes a method of use and ownership. It denotes exclusive use of accommodations for a particular number of days each year. Usually sold by the week, it is also called interval or vacation interval. The purchase of a time-share interval can take various legal forms. Under a fixed-unit, fixed-week deeded agreement, the purchaser receives a deed allowing the use of a specific condominium at a particular time every year forever, just like buying a house. Benefits may include the tax advantages of ownership, plus a voice in the management of the resort. Under this agreement, the owner may rent, sell, exchange, or bequeath the vacation interval.

Under a right-to-use plan, ownership of the resort remains with the developer. The purchaser reserves the right to use one or more resort accommodations for a specified number of years, ranging generally from 10 to 50 years, after which all use rights return to the developer. These plans come in a variety of forms, most commonly as club membership. Vacation intervals are sold as either fixed or floating time. With fixed time, the unit, or unit type, is purchased for a specific week during the year. That week is reserved for the owner every year, subject to cancellation if the vacation owner does not plan to use it in the given year. Floating time refers to the use of vacation accommodations usually within a certain season of the year, often within a three to four month period, such as spring or summer. The owner must reserve his or her desired vacation time in advance, with reservation confirmation typically provided on a first-come, first-served basis. The purchaser may also receive a deed under a floating-time arrangement. According to a recent national study, approximately 70 percent of time-share condominiums in the United States are sold as floating time. Some price differences are based on demand within each season.

Vacation clubs, or point-based programs, provide the flexible use of accommodations in multiple resort locations. With these products, club members purchase points that represent either a travel and use membership or a deeded real estate product. These points are then used like currency to purchase the various size accommodations, during a certain season, for a set number of days at a participating resort. The number of points needed to access the resort accommodations will vary by the members' demand for unit size, season, resort location, and amenities. A vacation club may have a specific term of ownership or be deeded in perpetuity.

Fractional ownership enables consumers to purchase a larger share of a vacation ownership unit, usually from five to twenty-six weeks. This type of ownership is popular in ski, beach, and island resort areas.

"Lockoff" or "lockout" units allow vacation owners to occupy a portion of the unit and offer the remaining space for rental or exchange. These units typically consist of two bedrooms and two baths, or three bedrooms and three baths.

Split weeks are popular with consumers who prefer shorter vacations. The owner may split use of the interval into two separate visits to the resort, such as one three-night and one four-night stay at two different times of the year. Reservations are usually granted on a first-come, first-served basis and are based on availability.

Biennial ownership, or alternate-year ownership, allows for resort property ownership every other year and costs less than annual ownership at comparable resorts.

The Advantages of Vacation Ownership

Unlike a hotel room or rental cottage that requires payment for each use of rates that usually increase each year, ownership at a time-share property enables vacationers to enjoy a resort, year after year, for the duration of their ownership for only a one-time purchase price and the payment of yearly maintenance fees. Time-share ownership offers vacationers an opportunity to save on the escalating costs of vacation accommodations over the long term, while enjoying all the comforts of home in a resort setting.

Truly a home away from home, vacation ownership provides the space and flexibility to meet the needs of any size family or group. While most vacation ownership condominiums have two bedrooms and two baths, unit sizes range from studios to three, or more, bedrooms. Unlike hotel rooms, there are no charges for additional guests. Also unlike hotels, most units include a fully equipped kitchen with dining area, washer and dryer, stereo, VCRs, and more.

Time-share resort amenities rival those of other top-rated resort properties and may include swimming pools, tennis, Jacuzzi, golf, bicycles, and exercise facilities. Others feature boating, ski lifts, restaurants, and equestrian facilities. Most time-share resorts offer a full schedule of on-site or nearby sporting, recreational, and social activities for adults and children. The resorts are staffed with well-trained hospitality professionals, with many resorts offering concierge services for assistance in visiting area attractions.

Travel the World Through Exchange Vacations

Vacation ownership offers unparalleled flexibility and the opportunity for affordable worldwide travel through vacation ownership exchange. Through the international vacation exchange networks, owners can trade their time-share intervals for vacation time at comparable resorts around the world. Most resorts are affiliated with an exchange company that administers the exchange service for its members. Typically, the exchange company will directly solicit annual membership. Owners individually elect to become members of the affiliated exchange company. To exchange, the owner places his or her interval into the exchange company's pool of resorts and weeks available for exchange and, in turn, chooses an available resort and week from that pool. The exchange companies charge an exchange fee, in addition to an annual membership fee, to complete an exchange. Exchange companies and resorts frequently offer their members the additional benefit of saving or banking vacation time in a reserve program for use in a different year.

One of the largest providers of vacation ownership exchange services, Interval International, has become even larger. Four Seasons Hotels and Resorts has selected the Miami-based company as its vacation exchange partner. Interval, which began more than twenty years ago, has become accustomed to representing premier, independent, and branded vacation resorts worldwide, with affiliations such as Disney Vacation Resorts, Hyatt Vacation Club, and Marriott Vacations Club International.

Airport Hotels

Many airport hotels enjoy a high occupancy because of the large number of travelers arriving and departing from major airports. The guest mix in airport hotels consists of business, group, and leisure travelers. Passengers with early or late flights may stay over at the airport hotel, while others rest while waiting for connecting flights.

Airport hotels are generally in the 200- to 600-room size and are full service. In order to care for the needs of guests who may still feel as if they are in different time zones, room service and restaurant hours may be extended, even offered twenty-four hours. More moderately priced hotels have vending machines.

As competition at airport hotels intensified, some added meeting space to cater to business people who want to fly in, meet, and fly out. Here, the airport hotel has the advantage of saving the guests from having to go downtown.

Freeway Hotels and Motels

Freeway hotels and motels came into prominence in the 1950s and 1960s. As Americans took to the open road, they needed a convenient place to stay that was reasonably priced with few frills. Guests could simply drive up, park outside the office, register, rent a room, and park outside of the room. Over the years, more facilities were added: lounges, restaurants, pools, soft drink machines, game rooms, and satellite TV.

Motels are often clustered near freeway off-ramps on the outskirts of towns and cities. Today, some are made of modular construction and have as few as eleven employees per hundred rooms. These savings in land, construction, and operating costs are passed on to the guest in the form of lower rates.

Casino Hotels

The casino industry is now coming into the financial mainstream, to the point that, as a significant segment of the entertainment industry, it is reshaping the U.S. economy. The entertainment sector has become a very important engine for U.S. economic growth. As a matter of fact, since the recovery of the economy in 1991, entertainment and recreation have provided the biggest boost to consumer spending, thus creating tremendous prosperity in the industry. The fastest-growing sector of the entertainment field is gaming: Chapter 11 discusses gaming in detail.

Full-Service Hotels

Another way to classify hotels is by the degree of service offered: full-service, economy, extended-stay, and all-suite hotels. Full-service hotels offer a wide range of facilities, services, and amenities, including many that were mentioned under the luxury hotel category: multiple food and beverage outlets including bars, lounges, and restaurants; both formal and casual dining; and meeting, convention, and catering services. Business features might include a business center, secretarial services, fax, in-room computer hook ups, and so on.

Most of the major North American cities have hotel chain representation such as Doubletree, Four Seasons, Hilton, Holiday Inn, Hyatt, Marriott, Omni, Ramada, Radisson, Ritz-Carlton, Loew's, Le Meridian, Sheraton, and Westin. Some of these chains are positioning themselves as basic full-service properties. An example of this strategy is Marriott's Courtyard hotels, which have small lobbies and very limited food and beverage offerings. The resulting savings are passed on to the guests in the form of more competitive rates. Thus, the full-service market may also be subdivided into upscale and midpriced hotels.

Economy/Budget Hotels

An economy or budget hotel offers clean, reasonably sized and furnished rooms without the frills of full-service hotels. Chains like Travelodge, Motel 6, Days Inn, and La Quinta became popular by focusing on selling beds, but not meals or meetings. This enabled them to offer rates at about 30 percent lower than the midpriced hotels. The average rate for an economy hotel is about $30 to $50 per night.

Morena Valley Travelodge #982

More recent entrants to this market sector are Promus' Hampton Inns, Marriott's Fairfield, and Choice's Comfort Inns. These properties do not have restaurants or offer substantial food and beverages, but they do offer guests a continental breakfast in the lobby.

Another example of a relatively new budget concept is Microtel. In 1989, despite a credit crunch and a weak economy, a group of entrepreneurs developed a new budget concept called Microtel. Success criteria were developed: The group wanted an economy hotel product, the downside risk had to be limited, and the product would have to demonstrate a competitive advantage over other national budget chains. The result of several months of careful planning and construction was the ninety-nine-room Microtel in Rochester, New York, at a total cost of $2,798,000 or $28,263 per room. The land cost $266,000; construction, interest, taxes, furniture, and equipment cost $2,164,000. The room rates began at $29, and the occupancy was 89.4 percent in the first year. The franchise was sold a year later for a 117 percent return on investment (ROI).[27] This is a remarkable success story that illustrates that entrepreneurs can thrive even in a weak economy.

Fairfield Inn

After enjoying a wave of growth for most of the 1990s, the economy hotel segment may be close to the saturation point. There are about 20,000 properties in this segment with many markets. The economic law of supply and demand rules; if an area has too many similar properties, then price wars usually break out as they try to attract guests. Some will attempt to differentiate themselves and stress value rather than discounting. This adds to the fascination of the business.

Extended-Stay Hotels

Other hotels cater to guests who stay for an extended period. They will, of course, take guests for a shorter time when space is available. However, the majority of guests are long term. Guests take advantage of a reduction in the rates based on the length of their stay. The mix of guests is mainly business and professional/technical, or relocating families.

Residence Inns and Homewood Suites are market leaders in this segment of the lodging industry. These properties offer full kitchen facilities and shopping services or a convenience store on the premises. Complimentary continental breakfast and evening cocktails are served in the lobby. Some properties offer a business center and recreational facilities.

Residence Inn

All-Suite, Extended-Stay Hotels

All-suite hotels typically offer approximately 25 percent more space for the same amount of money as the regular hotel in the same price range. The additional space is usually in the form of a lounge and possibly a kitchenette area.

Embassy Suites, owned and operated by the Promus Corporation; Residence Inns, Fairfield Suites, and Town-Place Suites, all by Marriott; Extended Stay America; Homewood Suites; and Guest Quarters are the market leaders in the all-suites, extended-stay segment of the lodging industry. Several of the major hotel chains have all-suite, extended-stay subsidiaries, including Radisson, Choice Hotels (that dominate the economy all-suite segment with Comfort and Quality Suites), ITT Sheraton Suites, Hilton Suites, Homegate Studios, and Suites by Wyndham Hotels. These properties provide a closer-to-home feeling for guests who may be relocating or attending seminars, or are on work-related projects that necessitate a stay of greater than about five days.

There are now almost 1,000 extended-stay properties. Many of these properties have business centers and offer services like grocery shopping and laundry/dry cleaning. The designers of extended-stay properties realize that guests prefer a home-like atmosphere. Accordingly, many properties are built to encourage a community feeling, which allows guests to informally interact.

Bed and Breakfast Inns

B and Bs, as they are familiarly known, offer an alternative lodging experience to the normal hotel or motel. According to *Travel Assist Magazine,* B and B is a concept that began in Europe and started as overnight lodging in a private home. A true B and B is an accommodation with the owner, who lives on the premises or nearby, providing a clean, attractive accommodation and breakfast, usually a memorable one. The host also offers to help the guest with directions, restaurants, and suggestions for local entertainment or sightseeing.

There are many different styles of B and Bs with prices ranging from about $30 to $300 or more. B and Bs may be as quaint as cottages with white picket fences leading to gingerbread houses, tiny and homey, with two or three rooms available. On the other hand, there are sprawling, ranch-style homes in the Rockies; multistoried town homes in large cities; farms; adobe villas; log cabins;

Luxury—Clarion
Midscale—Quality Inn, Quality Suites
Budget—Comfort Inn, Friendship Inns, Rodeway Inn
Economy—Sleep Inn

Figure 3–3   *Vertical Integration of Choice Hotels*

lighthouses; and many stately mansions. The variety is part of the thrill, romance, and charm of the B and B experience.[26]

Hotel Integration

Vertical Integration

Vertical integration is a trend that began a few years ago. Lodging companies realized that guests' accommodation needs were not just at one level; rather, they seemed to vary by price and facilities/amenities. Almost all major lodging companies now have properties in each segment of the market. An example to illustrate this point is given in Figure 3–3.

Horizontal Integration

Since Pan American opened the first of its Inter-Continental hotels back in the late 1940s, several airlines have opened or managed hotels as a form of horizontal integration. It is a natural progression for an airline, which is transporting passengers, often over great distances, to own and operate hotels for its passengers to stay in. Airlines differ in their strategies toward hotel ownership. For example, Nikko hotels are owned by Japan Airlines. However, American and United Airlines have sold their hotel interests, most likely as a result of financial difficulties they have experienced in recent years.

Marketing Consortium (Referral Organizations)

Marketing consortiums, or referral organizations, are made up of independent hotels who refer guests to each of the other members' hotels. Preferred Hotels Association, also known as Preferred Hotels and Resorts Worldwide, is a consortium of 105 independent, luxury hotels and resorts united to compete with the marketing power of chain operations. It promotes the individuality, high standards, hospitality, and luxury of member hotels. It also provides marketing support services and a reservation center.

Preferred Hotels Association has begun preparing for future trends in the industry. The consortium expects to increase its membership with the reemergence of independent hotels resulting from the advent of affordable technologies. A new, quality-driven advertising campaign is being developed while the group becomes the first to establish an Internet site. The association is using Guest Information Network's Net Software to develop a client database. The database is intended to help the association develop custom-tailored service packages by recording information about clients' preferences and purchasing patterns.

With the decrease in airline commissions, referral organizations, especially those at the luxury end of the market, are well placed to offer incentives to agents to book their clients with the referral group's hotels. An example would be awarding trips to the property for every ten rooms booked. Another would be for the referral hotels to offer, for instance, a 20 percent commission during slow periods. Three luxury Boston-area preferred properties—the Boston Harbor Hotel, the Bostonian Hotel, and the Charles Hotel in Cambridge, Massachusetts—joined recently in promoting a St. Patrick's Day weekend package. Preferred Hotels in Texas—the Mansion on Turtle Creek and Hotel Crescent Court in Dallas, La Mansion Del Rio South in San Antonio, and the Washington Hotel in Fort Worth—have launched a major, year-long promotion, which includes a tie-in with major retail, credit card, and airline partners.

In addition to regional marketing programs, the referral associations that handle reservations for members have joined Galileo International's Inside Availability Service. This gives agents access to actual rates and room availability that is not always available on the standard CRS databases.

Leading Hotels of the World (LHW) was set up in 1928 as Luxury Hotels of Europe and Egypt by thirty-eight hotels, including the London Savoy; the Hotel Royal in Evian, France; and the Hotel Negresco in Nice, France, who were interested in improving their marketing. The organization worked by having hotels advise their guests to use the establishments of fellow members. It then opened a New York office to make direct contact with wealthy American and Canadian travelers wishing to visit Europe or Egypt.

LHW, which is controlled by its European members and always reinvests any profits, acts as an important marketing machine for its members, especially now, with offices around the world providing reservations, sales, and promotional services. All the hotels and offices are connected by a central computer reservation system called ResStar. The number of reservations members receive from Leading Hotel members varies from place to place, but with more than one-hundred hotels waiting to join, it must be beneficial.

Like LHW, Small Luxury Hotels of the World (SLH) is another marketing consortium in which seventy-nine independently owned and managed hotels and resorts are members. For more than thirty years, it has sought to market and sell its membership to the travel industry and to provide an interhotel networking system for all members. Each hotel is assessed and regularly checked to ensure that it maintains the very highest standards.

Best, Biggest, and Most Unusual Hotels and Chains

So which is the best hotel in the world? The answer may depend on whether you watch the "Lifestyles of the Rich and Famous" or read polls taken by a business investment or travel magazine. According to the article "The World's Best Hotels," written for the *Institutional Investor,* the Oriental Hotel in Bangkok, Thailand, was for several years rated number one in the world by a poll of one hundred bankers from around the world. The Oriental was followed by the Regent of Hong Kong, Vier Jahrenzeiten of Hamburg, The Mandarin Oriental of Hong Kong, and the Connaught of London. By 1992, that list had changed, with the Regent Hong Kong and the Bel-Air of Los Angeles being number one and two respectively. Singapore's Shangri-La was third, bringing the total of Asian hotels in the top ten to six.[28] The largest hotel in the world is the 5,505-room MGM Grand in Las Vegas. This, however, will be surpassed by the new Sands Hotel under construction in Las Vegas with an approximate 6,000 rooms, expected to open in 1999. Table 3–3 shows the twenty-five largest hotel chains in the world.[29]

The Best Hotel Chains

The Ritz-Carlton and the Canadian-owned and -operated Four Seasons are generally rated the highest quality chain hotels. In 1993, Ritz-Carlton hotels were awarded the Malcolm Baldrige National Quality Award. Congress created this award in 1987 to promote and recognize quality achievements in U.S. businesses. Named after the late secretary of commerce Malcolm Baldrige, an early proponent of total quality management (TQM), the award is regarded as the ultimate prize among those U.S. companies that pride themselves on the quality of their products and services.[30] Ritz-Carlton has long been recognized as one of the best luxury hotel chains in the industry, however, President and Chief Operating Officer (COO) Horst Schulze wanted more. "We asked ourselves how we could become even better than we were," says Schulze. "The hardest thing for me to do was overcome my ego and admit that I really didn't know how to take the company beyond where it was. Once we did that, the job became easier."

The Ritz-Carlton approach to quality centers on a number of basic but complex principles, many drawn from traditional TQM theory. It is discussed in Chapter 14.

The Most Unusual Hotels

Among the world's most unusual hotels are ones like The Treetops Hotel in one of Kenya's wild animal parks—literally in the treetops. It was at this hotel in 1952 that Queen Elizabeth II learned that she had become queen of England. The uniqueness of the hotel is that it is built on the tops of trees overlooking a wild animal watering hole in the park.

Table 3–3 The Top Twenty-five Corporate Chains as of December 31, 1996

Rank 1996	1995	Corporate Chain Headquarters	Rooms 1996	1995	Hotels 1996	1995
1	1	**HFS Inc.**—Parsippany, NJ USA	**490,000**	509,500	**5,300**	5,430
2	2	**Holiday Inn Worldwide**—Atlanta, GA USA	**386,323**	369,738	**2,260**	2,096
3	3	**Best Western International**—Phoenix, AZ USA	**295,305**	282,062	**3,654**	3,462
4	4	**Accor**—Evry, France	**279,145**	268,256	**2,465**	2,378
5	5	**Choice Hotels International**—Silver Springs, MD USA	**271,812**	249,926	**3,197**	2,902
6	6	**Marriott International**—Washington, DC USA	**251,425**	198,000	**1,268**	976
7	7	**ITT Sheraton Corp.**—Boston, MA USA	**130,528**	129,201	**413**	414
8	9	**Promus Cos.**—Memphis, TN USA	**105,930**	88,117	**809**	669
9	8	**Hilton Hotels Corp.**—Beverly Hills, CA USA	**101,000**	90,879	**245**	219
10	10	**Carlson Hospitality Worlwide**—Minneapolis, MN USA	**91,777**	84,607	**437**	383
11	11	**Hyatt Hotels/Hyatt International**—Chicago, IL USA	**80,598**	79,483	**176**	172
12	12	**Inter-Continental Hotels**—London, England	**69,632**	61,610	**193**	179
13	13	**Hilton International**—Watford, England	**51,305**	52,063	**160**	161
14	15	**Grupo Sol Meliá**—Palma de Mallorca, Spain	**47,371**	46,825	**203**	185
15	14	**Forté Hotels**—London, England	**46,847**	49,183	**259**	270
16	21	**Doubletree Hotels**—Phoenix, AZ USA	**43,555**	28,501	**166**	105
17	18	**Westin Hotels & Resorts**—Seattle, WA USA	**42,897**	40,074	**97**	82
18	16	**Club Méditerranée SA**—Paris, France	**37,906**	45,104	**133**	147
19	19	**Société du Louvre**—Paris, France	**36,059**	32,926	**567**	511
20	20	**La Quinta Inns**—San Antonio, TX USA	**32,096**	30,000	**249**	240
21	23	**Red Roof Inns**—Hilliard, OH USA	**28,000**	26,135	**248**	231
22	22	**Prince Hotels Inc.**—Tokyo, Japan	**26,643**	26,235	**86**	85
23	24	**Tokyu Hotel Group**—Tokyo, Japan	**23,130**	21,870	**109**	84
24	25	**Circus Circus**—Las Vegas, NV USA	**19,585**	20,754	**16**	17
25	30	**Walt Disney Co.**—Burbank, CA USA	**19,415**	16,163	**18**	13

Reprinted with permission from *Hotels*, July 1997

Capsule Hotel

Australia boasts an underwater hotel at the Great Barrier Reef, where guests have wonderful subterranean views from their rooms.

Japan has several unusual hotels. One is a cocoonlike hotel, called Capsule Hotel, in which guests do not have a room as such. Instead, they have a space of about 7 feet by 4 feet. In this space is a bed and a television—which you almost have to operate with your toes! Such hotels are popular with people who get caught up in the obligatory late night drinking with the boss and with visiting professors who find them the only affordable place to stay in expensive Tokyo.

Japan also has love hotels, which are hotels used by couples for a few hours because they have insufficient privacy at home.

The highest hotel in the world, in terms of altitude, is nestled in the Himalayan mountain range at an altitude of 13,000 feet. Weather permitting, there is a marvelous view of Mount Everest. As many as 80 percent of the guests suffer from nausea, headaches, or sleeplessness caused by the altitude. No wonder the hottest-selling item on the room-service menu is oxygen—at $1 a minute.[31]

International Perspective

We are all part of a huge global economy that is splintered into massive trading blocks, such as the European Economic Community (EEC) and the recently formed North American Free Trade Agreement (NAFTA) among Canada, the United States, and Mexico, and comprising a total population of 350 million consumers.

The EEC, with a population of 320 million people in twelve nations, is an economic union that has removed national restrictions not only on trade but also on the movement of capital and labor. The synergy developed between these fifteen member nations is beneficial to all and is a form of self-perpetuating development.[32] As travel, tourism, commerce, and industry have increased within the EEC and beyond, so has the need for hotel accommodations.

NAFTA will likely be a similar catalyst for hotel development in response to increased trade and tourism among the three countries involved. But Argentina, Brazil, Chile, and Venezuela may also join an expanded NAFTA, which would become known as the Americas Trading Block.

It is easy to understand the international development of hotels given the increase in international tourism trade and commerce. The growth in tourism in Pacific Rim countries is expected to continue at the same rate as in recent years. Several resorts are planned in Indonesia, Malaysia, Thailand, Mexico, and Vietnam. Further international hotel development opportunities exist in Eastern Europe, Russia, and the other republics of the former Soviet Union, where some companies have changed their growth strategy from building new hotels to acquiring existing properties.

In Asia, Hong Kong's growth has been encouraged by booming economies throughout Asia and the kind of tax system for which supply-siders hunger. Before sovereignty over Hong Kong reverted back to China, the Hong Kong government levies a flat 16.5 percent corporate tax, a 15 percent individual income tax, and no tax on capital gains or dividends. Several hotel corporations have their headquarters in Hong Kong. Among them are Mandarin Oriental, Peninsula, and Shangri-La, all world-renowned for their five-star status. They are based in Hong Kong because of low corporate taxation and the ability to bring in senior expatriate executives with minimum bureaucratic difficulty.[33]

Seeking to diversify its hotel portfolio globally, New World Hotel (Holdings) Ltd. of Hong Kong bought Ramada, Inc., in 1989. Quickly it sold all but 108 Ramada International properties and fourteen Renaissance hotels in the United States. Ramada International is now expanding primarily in Europe, Asia, and North America. The European market is considered to be the one with the greatest potential because of the common market linkage to other European countries.[34]

In developing countries, once political stability has been sustained, hotel development quickly follows as part of an overall economic and social progression. An example of this would be the former Eastern European countries and former Soviet republics, who for the past few years have offered development opportunities for hotel corporations.

U.S.–International Hotel Development

The future of the lodging industry involves globalization. Companies cannot grow unless they venture beyond the United States. International hotel development took off with the advent of the Boeing 707 in the late 1950s and the 747 in the early 1970s. With the boom in international business and tourism came the need for larger international hotel chains. American hotel chains and their management techniques were in demand by many developing countries who wanted premium-name hotels. Several hotel chains were owned by or in partnership with airlines; some still are. In 1948, the U.S. government, casting about for ways of improving the economy of Latin American countries, asked several hotel companies if they would be willing to build properties in these countries. By the late 1950s, only Pan American Airways had agreed to do so.[35] As a Pan Am subsidiary, Inter-Continental had properties in Venezuela, Brazil, Uruguay, Chile, Colombia, Mexico, Curacao, Cuba, and the Dominican Republic. By 1981, Inter-Continental had eighty-one hotels in about fifty countries. Subsequently, Pan Am sold the Inter-Continental hotel chain to the Saison Japanese Corporation, who later sold it to Grand Metropolitan. Pan Am, after a long decline from its peak, declared bankruptcy and ceased operations in 1992.

Conrad Hilton was another pioneer in U.S. international hotel development. In 1948, he secured the contract to operate the Caribe Hilton in San Juan, Puerto Rico. Hilton won this contract over other U.S. hotel chains primarily because he was the only one to respond with a letter written in Spanish. By 1974, Hilton

International was operating sixty-one hotels (23,263 rooms) in thirty-nine countries outside the continental United States.[36] In 1964, Hilton International Company became a separate company from Hilton U.S.; in 1967, it was bought by TWA. Hilton International is now owned by Britain's Ladbroke Group Plc.

Sheraton Hotel Corporation, a subsidiary of ITT, now has 130,528 rooms and 413 hotels in sixty-two countries. It is second only to Group Accor of France, which operates 279,145 rooms and 2,465 hotels in sixty-six countries under its brands of Novotel, Sofitel, Pullman, Motel 6, and Formule 1.

International Investment in U.S. Hotels

Foreign investors have bought and sold not just individual U.S. hotels but also hotel chains. Bass Plc. (UK) bought Holiday Corporation; Grand Metropolitan (UK) bought Inter-Continental Hotels; Group Accor (France) bought Motel 6.

During the late 1980s and very early 1990s, Japanese investors bought several U.S. hotels. According to Christopher Mead, principal of Mead Ventures, as of 1991, Japanese interests owned all or part of 296 U.S. hotel properties. Mead predicts that the Japanese will continue to invest; the number of U.S. properties in which they have an investment may surpass 400 by the end of the decade.[37]

One interesting statistic to note is the price paid per room. Every $1,000 paid for the purchase or construction of a room equates to $1 in room rate that must be charged to make a reasonable return on investment. By these calculations, the room rate at the hotel Bel Air should be about $1,200 per night. Clearly, the hotel was overvalued and was not purchased to make a profit; more likely prestige and ego were the motivating factors in the purchase decision.

During the second half of the 1980s, Japanese investors were cash rich and in a position to purchase U.S. real estate. This situation was aided by a sharp rise in the value of the yen against the dollar. U.S. land and property was valued far below what it would have been valued in Japan and was perceived to be offered at discount prices. Eventually, however, property, including hotels, became overpriced. An example of this is the La Costa Resort and Spa in La Costa, California. This 470-room property with a golf course was purchased by Sports Shinko in 1986 for $250 million—$531,914 per room. Two interesting things happened with regard to the purchase of this hotel. First, during the few months that elapsed between the signing of the sale documents and the time when the amount was to be paid (the escrow period), the purchaser saved $43 million because of the increase in the value of the Japanese yen compared to the dollar. The second was that the hotel lost $26 million in the first year of operation under the new owner. This was partly because of a lack of "due diligence." An extensive survey of the condition of the hotel would have shown that substantial amounts of money would be necessary to maintain the hotel's condition. The investors were obviously thinking long-term by anticipating that the value of land in southern California would undoubtedly increase in the next few years. Meanwhile, they built and sold a number of high priced condos along the edge of the golf course.

About 1990, Japanese investment in U.S. hotels peaked; others, notably Hong Kong, Taiwan, and Korea, took their place. The Cheng family of Hong Kong recently purchased the forty-property Stouffer hotel chain from Nestle S.A. based

Corporate Profile: Choice Hotels International[1]

This awesome story began in 1968 when Gerald Petitt, a Dartmouth engineering and business student, was seeking summer employment with IBM. He blew the roof off the company's preemployment test scores. The test scores were brought to the attention of Robert C. Hazard, Jr., who at that time was in charge of the Coors Brewery account. This had an appeal for the ski-bum in Petitt, who was originally from Denver. Robert Hazard says that Jerry Petitt did more in one summer for IBM's efforts to design a production system for the brewery than a team of five engineers did in two years.

Robert Hazard decided then, more than twenty-five years ago, to keep this talented person. They progressed in their careers with spells at American Express, Best Western, and eventually went on to Silver Spring, Maryland, where they would take a sleepy, stagnating lodging company called Quality Inns from 300 properties to the 4,000-property Choice brand. Because they had been so successful at Best Western, they were enticed to join Quality in 1980 for equity plus half-million dollar salaries.

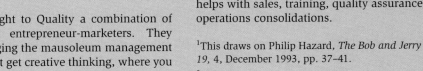

Bob and Jerry brought to Quality a combination of engineer-builders and entrepreneur-marketers. They quickly set about changing the mausoleum management style—"where you don't get creative thinking, where you try to pit good minds against each other." Instead, you get, "What will the chairman think?" and "We can all go along with it—or look for another job."[2]

To illustrate the change of management style, Bob Hazard draws the upside-down management organization, where the bosses are the 92 million guests, 3,000 franchisees, and 37,000 prospective franchises. He and Jerry Petitt, of course, were on the bottom.

The strategy of changing the corporate culture, of taking advantage of emerging technological and management trends with emphasis on marketing-driven management over operations has worked for Choice hotels. The development of brand segmentation was perhaps their best move. Choice Hotels International is now an international hotel franchisor comprising eight brands: Sleep, Comfort, Quality, Clarion, Friendship, Econo Lodge, Mainstay, and Rodeway.

More recently, under President William Floyd, Choice has reorganized, creating Market Area Management teams strategically placed so that licensees can be closer to support staff. Each field staff manager has forty-five properties and helps with sales, training, quality assurance reviews, and operations consolidations.

[1]This draws on Philip Hazard, *The Bob and Jerry Show Lodging*, *19*, 4, December 1993, pp. 37–41.

[2]Ibid, p. 58.

in Switzerland. Cheng Yu-Tung also owns controlling interest in New World Development Co. Ltd. New World is the parent company of the 124-unit Ramada International chain and of New World Hotels, which has eleven properties in Asia. The Chengs also own the Regent and Grand Hyatt hotels in Hong Kong.[38] Needless to say Mr. Cheng is a billionaire.

Trends in Hotel Development

✔ *Capacity control:* Refers to who will control the sale of inventories of hotel rooms, airline seats, auto rentals, and tickets to attractions. Presently, owners of these assets are in control of their sale and distribution, but increasingly control is falling into the hands of those who own and manage global reservation systems and/or negotiate for large buying groups.

Factors involved in the outcome will be telecommunications, software, available satellite capacity, governmental regulations, limited capital, and the travel distribution network.

✔ *Safety and security:* Important aspects of safety and security are terrorism, the growing disparity between the "haves" and "have nots" in the world, diminishing financial resources, infrastructure problems, health issues, the stability of governments, and personal security.

✔ *Assets and capital:* The issues concerning assets and capital are rationing of private capital and rationing of funds deployed by governments.

✔ *Technology:* An example of the growing use of "expert systems" (a basic form of artificial intelligence), would be making standard operating procedures available on-line, twenty-four hours a day, and establishing yield management systems designed to make pricing decisions. Other examples include the smart hotel room and communications ports to make virtual office environments for business travelers; and the impact of technology on the structure of corporate offices and individual hotels.

✔ *New management:* The complex forces of capacity control, safety and security, capital movement, and technology issues will require a future management cadre that is able to adapt to rapid-paced change across all the traditional functions of management.[39]

✔ *Globalization:* A number of U.S. and Canadian chains have developed and are continuing to develop hotels around the world. International companies are also investing in the North American hotel industry.

✔ *Consolidation:* As the industry matures, corporations are either acquiring or merging with each other.

✔ *Diversification within segments of the lodging industry:* The economy segment now has low-, medium-, and high-end properties. The extended-stay market has a similar spread of properties as do all the other hotel classifications.

✔ *Rapid growth in vacation ownership:* Vacation ownership is the fastest growing segment of the lodging industry and is likely to continue growing as the baby boomers enter their fifties and sixties.

✔ *An increase in the number of spas and the treatments offered:* Wellness and the road to nirvana is in increasing demand as guests seek release from the stresses of a fast-paced lifestyle.

✔ *Gaming:* There is an increasing number of hotels coming on-line that are related to the gaming industry.

To Flag or Not to Flag—and If So, Which Flag?

Joy and Bob Brown retired from the military in 1995. They bought a motel near a picturesque New England town. The Cozy Motel is clearly visible and easily accessible from the turnpike. It has 75 rooms that are in good shape, having just been refurbished, and the curbside appeal of fresh paint and attractive landscaping adds to the motel's presentation.

The motel's year-round occupancy is 58 percent, which is about 10 percentage points below the national average. The average daily rate is $38. The Cozy Motel's guests are a mix of business travelers, who are mostly from companies at the nearby business park; a few retirees traveling for pleasure; an occasional bus tour; and some sports teams.

The Browns have asked several major franchise corporations to submit their best offers. The best one indicates that the cost of a franchise application fee is $20,000, and that there is a two percent revenue marketing fee and a reservation fee of $4 per room booked by the Central Reservation System (CRS).

Discussion Questions

1. What would you do in the Brown's situation? Should they sign a franchise agreement or not? Make assumptions, if needed.
2. What terms and conditions of a franchise agreement would be acceptable to you, or to the Browns?
3. What additional information would you, or the Browns, need to know?

Hotel Development

If you were working in the development office of a major hotel corporation, what information would you need to obtain to consider the development of a AAA three-diamond property in a town near you?

Summary

1. Improved transportation has changed the nature of the hotel industry from small, independently owned inns to big hotel and motel chains, operated by using concepts such as franchising, partnership, leasing, and management contracts.
2. The cyclical nature of demand, periods of inflation and recession, and the high degree of capital investment put hotel industries at high risks and call for smart financial management.
3. The financial decisions of a hotel must be based on expected risk, expected return, and their combined impact on common stock. The success of a hotel depends on creative financing combined with quality management.
4. Drastic changes in tax laws, deregulation of the thrift industry, and a softening of regional economics are reasons for the overvaluation of hotels.
5. The future of tourism involves international expansion and foreign investment, often in combination with airlines and with the goal of improving economic conditions in developing countries. It is further influenced by increased globalization, as evidenced by such agreements as NAFTA.
6. Hotels can be classified according to location (city center, resort, airport, freeway, casino), according to the types of services offered, and according to price (luxury, midscale, budget, and economy). Hotels are rated by

Mobil and AAA Awards (five-star or the five-diamond rankings).

7. Every part of the world offers leisure and business travelers a choice of unusual or conservative accommodations that cater to the personal ideas of vacation or business trips.

8. Vacation ownership offers consumers the opportunity to purchase fully-furnished vacation accomodations, similar to condominiums, sold in a variety of forms, such as weekly intervals or point-based systems, for only a percentage of the cost of full ownership. According to the WTO, "timeshares" is one of the fastest growing sectors of the travel and tourism industry.

Review Exercises

1. Describe the development of the motel. What impact did the Great Depression of the 1930s have on the development of the hotel industry?
2. What are the advantages of (a) management contracts and (b) franchising? Discuss their impacts on the development of the hotel industry.
3. Explain the concept of creative financing. What led to the overevaluation of many hotel businesses?
4. In what ways has the trend in globalization affected the hotel industry?
5. Explain how hotels cater to the needs of business and leisure travelers in reference to the following concepts: (a) resorts, (b) airport hotels, and (c) vertical integration.
6. Explain what vacation ownership is. What are the different types of timeshare programs available for purchase?

Key Words and Concepts

All-Suite Extended Stay Hotels	Financing	Leveraged money	Portfolio financing
Bed and Breakfast Inn	First mortgage loans	Marketing Consortiums (referral organizations)	Real Estate Investment Trust (REIT)
Creative financing	Franchise	Management contracts	Recession
Currency fluctuations	Globalization	Money market	Superstructure
Debt service	Inflation	Overvalued	Syndicates
Economic downturn	Interest rates	Partnership	Vacation ownership
	Leasing		

Notes

[1] This section draws from Donald E. Lundberg, *The Hotel and Restaurant Business,* 4th ed. New York: Van Nostrand Reinhold, 1984, p. 24.

[2] Daniel J. Boorstin, *The Americans: The National Experience.* New York: Vintage Books, 1965, p. 139.

[3] Charles A. Bell, "Agreements with Chains-Hotels Companies," *The Cornell Hotel and Restaurant Administration Quarterly, 34,* 1, February 1993, pp. 27–33.

[4] Jeffrey C. Summers, "Available Capital and Strong Industry Economics Fuel Vibrant Market for US Hotel Investors' Acquisitions," *Real Estate Finance Journal.* vol. 12, no. 3, Winter 1997, pp. 91–95.

[5] Lundberg, op. cit., p. 121.

[6] Lundberg, op. cit., p. 48.

[7] Ibid., p. 83.

[8] Ibid., p. 44.

[9] This section draws on Bell, op. cit., pp. 27–33.

[10] Steve Bergsman, "Arizona Company Applies Leasing to Lodging Deals," *Hotel and Motel Management, 206,* 16, September 23, 1991, pp. 2, 29.

[11]James Eyster, "The Revolution in Domestic Hotel Management Contracts," *The Cornell Hotel and Restaurant Administration Quarterly, 34,* 1, February 1993, p. 19.

[12]Ibid.

[13]The International Hotel Association, Paris, "The Management Game: How to Keep One Step Ahead," *Hotels, 27,* 6, May 1993, p. 65.

[14]Heather A. Sanders and Leo M. Renaghan, "Southeast Asia: A New Model for Hotel Development," *The Cornell Hotel and Restaurant Administration Quarterly, 33,* 5, October 1992, pp. 16–23.

[15]Mike Sheridan, "The Rules Have Changed and It's a Whole New Ball Game," *Hotel Management,* vol. 38, no. 7, July 1996, pp. 52–58.

[16]Arbel Avner and Paul Grier, "The Risk Structure of the Hotel Industry," *The Cornell Hotel and Restaurant Administration Quarterly, 28,* 3, November 1987, p. 26.

[17]This section draws on Lundberg, op. cit., p. 76.

[18]James J. Eyster, "Creative Financing in the Lodging Industry, Cornell University," *The Hotel and Restaurant Administration Quarterly, 23,* 4, February 1983, pp. 29–37.

[19]Donald H. Dempsey, "Financing Trends in the Hotel Industry," *Real Estate Finance, 7,* 4, Winter 1991, pp. 74–76.

[20]Michael J. Flannery and Joseph J. Flannery, "Causes of Hotel Industry Distress," *Real Estate Review, 19,* 3, Fall 1990, pp. 35–39.

[21]Tony Dela Cruz, "Globalization, Hot Equity Markets Seen Driving Hotel Consolidation," *Hotel Business,* vol. 6, no. 7, April 7–20, 1997, p. 30.

[22]Ibid.

[23]Julie Miller, "AH&MA Initiates Formal Alliance with AAA," *Hotel and Motel Management,* vol. 212, no. 11, June 16, 1997, p. 15.

[24]Mike Malley, "Timeshare Synergies," *Hotel and Motel Management,* vol. 212, no. 5, March 17, 1997, p. 18.

[25]Robin Taylor Parets, "Getting Their Share," *Lodging,* vol. 22, no. 6, February 1997, pp. 42–45.

[26]This section draws on *Travel Assist Magazine,* "What Is a Bed and Breakfast Inn?"

[27]This section draws on George R. Justus, "Microtel: How 'Simple' Translates into Success," *The Cornell Hotel and Restaurant Administration Quarterly, 32,* 4, December 1991, pp. 50–54.

[28]Lois Madison Reamy, *Institutional Investor, 26,* 10, September 1992, pp. 106–112.

[29]Sally Wolchuk, "World's Largest Hotels," *Hotels,* August 1991.

[30]This section draws on Edward Watkins, "How Ritz-Carlton Won the Baldrige Award," *Lodging Hospitality, 48,* 11, November 1992, p. 22.

[31]Jeannie Realston, "Inn of Thin Air," *American Way,* October 15, 1992.

[32]Belgium, Denmark, France, Germany, Great Britain, Greece, Ireland, Italy, Luxembourg, Portugal, Spain, the Netherlands.

[33]Murray Baily, "Travel Business: Rooms at the Top," *Asian Business, 27,* 9, September 1991, pp. 60–62.

[34]Steve Bergsman, "Ramada International Flourishes Globally," *National Real Estate Investor, 35,* 5, May 1991, pp. 73–75.

[35]Lundberg, op. cit., p. 44.

[36]Ibid.

[37]M. Chase Burritt, "Japanese Investment in U.S. Hotels and Resorts," *The Cornell Hotel and Restaurant Administration Quarterly, 32,* 3, October 1991, p. 64.

[38]Bill Eillette, "Cheng Family Acquires Stouffer," *Hotel and Motel Management, 208,* 7, April 26, 1993, p. 1.

Hotel and Rooms Division Operation

4

After reading and studying this chapter you should be able to do the following:

✔ Describe the functions and departments of a hotel

✔ Trace the guest cycle from reservations to check out

✔ Outline the duties and responsibilities of key executives and department heads

✔ Draw an organizational chart of a hotel and identify the executive committee members

✔ Describe the main functions of the front desk

✔ Describe property management systems and discuss yield management

✔ Calculate occupancy percentages, average daily rates, and actual percentage of potential rooms revenue

✔ Outline the importance of the reservations and guest services function

✔ List the complexities and challenges of the housekeeping and security/loss prevention departments

This chapter describes the function of a hotel and the many departments that constitute a hotel. It also helps to explain why and how the departments are interdependent in successfully running a hotel.

The Functions and Departments of a Hotel

The primary function of a hotel is to provide lodging accommodation. A large hotel is run by a general manager and an executive committee comprised of the key executives who head major departments: rooms division director, food and beverage director, marketing and sales director, human resources director, chief accountant or controller, and chief engineer or facility manager. These executives generally have a regional or corporate counterpart with whom they have a reporting relationship, although the general manager is their immediate superior.

A hotel is made up of several businesses or revenue centers and cost centers. A few thousand products and services are sold every day. Each area of specialty requires dedication and a quality commitment for each department to get little things right all the time. Furthermore, hotels need the cooperation of a large and diverse group of people to do it. Godfrey Bler, the general manager (GM) of the elegant 800-room General Eisenhower Hotel calls it a business of details. Another wise comment comes from Matthew Fox: "If you ignore the little stuff, it will become big stuff."[1]

Hotels are places of glamour that may be awe inspiring. Even the experienced hotel person is impressed by the refined dignity of a beautiful hotel like a Ritz-Carlton or the artistic splendor of a Hyatt. The atmosphere of a hotel is stimulating to a hospitality student. Let us step into an imaginary hotel to feel the excitement and become a part of the rush that is similar to show business, for a hotel is live theater and the GM is the director of the cast of players.

Ritz-Carlton Interior

Hotels, whether they are chain affiliated or independent properties, all exist to serve and enrich society, and at the same time make a profit for the owners. Frequently, hotels are just like pieces of property on a Monopoly board. They often make or lose more money with equity appreciation or depreciation than via operations.

Hotels have been described as people palaces. Some are certainly palatial, and others are more functional. Hotels are meant to provide all the comforts of home to those away from home. A gracious feeling of warmth and welcome is a hotel's most valuable asset. Hotels have personalities that are created by the combined chorus of effort, interest, and sincerity on the part of every member of the staff.[2]

Role of the Hotel General Manager

Hotel general managers have a lot of responsibilities. They must provide owners with a reasonable return on investment, keep guests satisfied and returning, and keep employees happy. This may seem easy, but because there are so many interpersonal transactions and because hotels are open every day, all day, the complexities of operating become challenges that the general manager must face and overcome.

Larger hotels can be more impersonal. Here, the general manager may only meet and greet a few VIPs. In the smaller property, it is easier—though no less important—for the GM to become acquainted with guests, to ensure their stay is memorable, and to secure their return. One way that experienced GMs can meet guests, even in large hotels, is to be visible in the lobby and F&B (food and beverage) outlets at peak times (check-out, lunch, check-in, and dinner time). Guests like to feel that the GM takes a personal interest in their well-being. Max Blouet, who was general manager of the famous George V Hotel in Paris for more than thirty years, was a master of this art. He was always present at the right moment to meet and greet guests. In fact, he often made such a spectacle that other guests would inquire who he was and then would want to meet him. Hoteliers always remember they are hosts.

Rick Segal, vice president of Sheraton's luxury hotel division, credits his success to several things, but the quality he mentions first is paying attention to detail. As general manager of the famous St. Regis Hotel in New York City, he has plenty of opportunities to do just that.

The GM is ultimately responsible for the performance of the hotel and the employees. The GM is the leader of the hotel. As such, she or he is held accountable for the hotel's level of profitability by the corporation or owners.

General managers with a democratic, situational, and participating leadership style are more likely to be successful. There are, however, times when it is necessary to be somewhat autocratic—when crisis situations arise.

To be successful, GMs need to have a broad range of personal qualities. Among those most often quoted by GMs are the following:[3]

Rick Segal, Vice President of ITT Sheraton's Luxury Hotels

- ✔ Leadership
- ✔ Attention to detail
- ✔ Follow-through—getting the job done
- ✔ People skills
- ✔ Patience
- ✔ Ability to delegate effectively

Not surprisingly, a survey of general managers revealed that GMs were hard-working and responsible. Each had overcome difficulties and challenges and each had made sacrifices to become successful. But each was also extremely satisfied doing what he or she was doing.[4]

A successful GM hires the best people. The GM of Chicago's Four Seasons Hotel, Hans Willimann, deliberately hired division heads who knew more about what they were hired for than he did. Willimann says he sets the tone—a structure of excellence—and others try to match it. Once the structure is in place, each employee works to define the hotel commitment to excellence. People who are hired need to be accomplished at what they do, and then they have to fit into the framework of the structure and be compatible with the rest of the group.[5]

As general manager of the Stouffer Wailea Beach Resort, Maui, Hawaii, Donn Takahashi's management philosophy is that to achieve a first-class facility, workers must be viewed as being vital to the operation. He instituted programs designed to cut turnover, engender loyalty, and stave off competition for workers from competing hotels. He says a key to keeping employees happy is making sure there is mutual respect among all levels of workers.[6]

Management functions are generally classified into forecasting, planning, organizing, communicating, and evaluating. Centralized companies such as Marriott give detailed general manager profiles, whereas Hyatt, a decentralized company, does not. Given that the primary purpose of the hotel is to sell rooms and ensure that guests have a wonderful stay, it has been suggested that GMs assume the director-of-sales position and spend up to 75 percent of their time directly involved with sales.[7]

General managers need to understand, empathize, and allow for the cultures of both guests and employees. For example, in the Pacific Rim, spiritual dictates are frequently believed to directly affect hoteliers' profits. At the Westin Kyoto Takaragaike Prince, hotels with floors numbered four or nine are not likely to be very popular. The pronunciation of the number four and the Japanese word for *death* sound the same, and the number nine sounds very similar to *pain* in Japanese.[8]

Often, success can be heavily influenced by the country's culture. For instance, in Southeast Asia, many hoteliers employ Fung Shui experts. Fung Shui is a centuries-old tradition that maintains that placing architectural elements in correct configurations or holding events at correct times pleases spirits. For instance, at the Hyatt Regency Singapore, doors were originally positioned at right angles to the street. A Fung Shui master recognized and told the general manager that the hotel, which was then having problems, would never be successful until the angle was changed. After the doors were repositioned, occupancies began to rise.[9]

About a year after the 850-room megaresort Westin Kauai opened, it became apparent that the "Share the Fantasy" à la Disney theme chosen by management did not fit. After careful consideration, a management-by-values system was introduced. Operating synergistically with the more traditional management by objectives, management by values extracts the moral essences of the local culture and makes them goals of the hotel. Responses from a survey that asked employees to share their values were used to help create a mission statement for the hotel. Management discontinued the Disney model and its vocabulary. Employee uniforms changed from stiff corporate style to flowing Hawaiian clothes.[10]

Management Structure

Management structure differs among larger, midscale, and smaller properties. The midscale and smaller properties will be less complex in their management structures than the larger ones. However, someone must be responsible for each of the key result areas that make the operation successful. For example, a small property may not have a director of human resources, but each department head will have general day-to-day operating responsibilities for the human resources function. The manager will have the ultimate responsibility for all human resources decisions. The same scenario is possible with each of the following areas: engineering and maintenance, accounting and finance, marketing and sales, food and beverage management, and so on.

The Executive Committee

The general manager, using input from the executive committee (Figure 4–1), makes all the major decisions affecting the hotel. These executives, who include the directors of human resources, food and beverage, rooms division, marketing and sales, engineering, and accounting, compile the hotel's occupancy forecast together with all revenues and expenses to make up the budget.

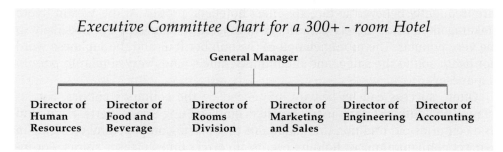

Figure 4–1   *Executive Committee Chart*

They generally meet once a week for one or two hours and might typically cover some of the following topics:

Guest satisfaction
Employee satisfaction
Total quality management
Occupancy forecasts
Sales and marketing plans
Training
Major items of expenditure
Renovations
Ownership relations
Energy conservation
Recycling
New legislation
Profitability

Some GMs rely on input from the executive committee more than others, depending on their leadership and management style. These senior executives determine the character of the property and decide on the missions, goals, and objectives of the hotel. For a chain hotel, this will be in harmony with the corporate mission.

In most hotels, the executive committee is involved with the decisions but the ultimate responsibility and authority rests with the GM. One of the major roles of the committee is communicator, both up and down the line of authority. This helps build interdepartmental cooperation.

The Departments

Rooms Division

The rooms division director is responsible to the GM for the efficient and effective leadership and operation of all the rooms division departments. They include concerns such as the following:

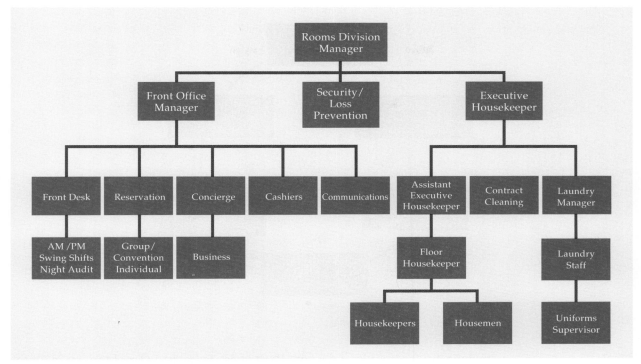

Figure 4–2 *Rooms Division Organizational Chart*

Financial responsibility for rooms division
Employee satisfaction goals
Guest satisfaction goals
Guest relations
Security
Gift shop

The rooms division consists of the following departments: front office, reservations, housekeeping, concierge, guest services, security, and communications. Figure 4–2 shows the organizational chart for a 300-plus-room hotel rooms division.

The guest cycle in Figure 4–3 shows a simplified sequence of events that takes place from the moment a guest calls to make a reservation until he or she checks out.

Front Office

The front office manager's (FOM) main duty is to enhance guest services by constantly developing services to meet guest needs. An example of how some FOMs practice enhancing guest services is to have a guest service associate (GSA) greet guests as they arrive at the hotel, escort them to the front desk, and then personally allocate the room and take the guest and luggage to the room. This innovative way of developing guest services looks at the operation from the guest's perspective. There is no need to have separate departments for doorperson,

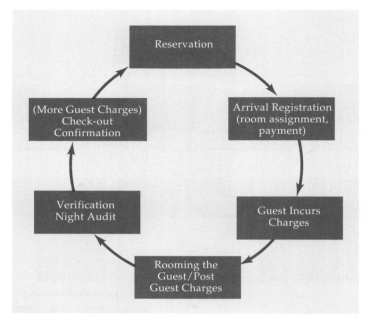

Figure 4–3 *The Guest Cycle*

bellperson, front desk, and so on. Each guest associate is cross-trained in all aspects of greeting and rooming the guest. This is now being done in smaller and midsized properties as well as specialty and deluxe properties. Guest service associates are responsible for the front desk, concierge, PBX, bellpersons, valet, and reservations.

During an average day in a hotel—if there is such a thing—the front office manager performs the following duties:

- ✔ Check night clerk report
- ✔ Review previous night's occupancy
- ✔ Review previous night's average rate

Front Office Manager Reviewing the Arrivals and Departures List

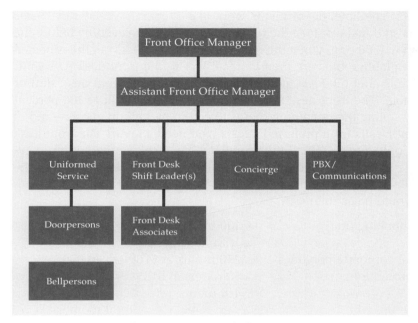

Figure 4–4 *Front Office Organizational Chart*

- ✔ Look over market mix
- ✔ Check complimentary rooms
- ✔ Verify group rooms to be picked up for next thirty days
- ✔ Review arrivals and departures for the day
- ✔ Review the VIP list and prepare preregistration
- ✔ Arrange preregistrations for all arrivals
- ✔ Attend rooms divisions and operations meeting
- ✔ Review arrivals and departures for next day
- ✔ Make staffing adjustments needed for arrivals and departures
- ✔ Review scheduling (done weekly)
- ✔ Meet with lead GSAs (done daily)

In some hotels, the reservations manager and associates report to the director of sales. These positions report to the chief accountant: night auditor, night audit associates, and cashiers.

Figure 4–4 shows an organizational chart for a front office. The front office has been described as the hub or nerve center of the hotel. It is the department that makes a first impression on the guest and one that the guest relies on throughout his or her stay for information and service. Positive first impressions are critical to the successful guest experience. Many guests arrive at the hotel after long, tiring trips. They want to be met by someone with a warm smile and a genuine greeting. If a guest should have a negative experience in checking into a hotel, he or she will be on guard in encounters with each of the other departments. The position's description for a guest service agent details the work performed. Position descriptions for the three main functions of the front office are as follows:

1. To sell rooms. The hotel departments work like a team in a relay race. Sales or reservations staff make or take the room sales up until the evening before the guest's arrival. At 6:00 P.M., when the reservations office closes, all the expected arrivals and available rooms are then handed over to the front desk P.M. shift. Reservations calls after 6:00 P.M. may either be taken by the front desk staff or the 1-800 number. The front desk team will try to sell out (achieve 100 percent occupancy) by selling the remaining rooms to call-in or walk-in guests—and of course the frantic calls from preferred guests who need a favor! The front desk staff must not only aim to sell all the rooms but also achieve the optimum average daily rate (ADR) for the rooms. The ADR is calculated by adding up the rate charged for each room and then dividing by the number of rooms. A simple example would be as follows:

A group booking of	100 rooms at $140 =	$14,000
	10 suites at $250 =	2,500
Individual corporate bookings	250 rooms at $160 =	40,000
Special promotions	50 rooms at $125 =	6,250
Total	410 rooms	$62,750
		Total room sales

$$\$62{,}750 \,/\, 410 = \$153 \text{ Average daily rate}$$

Optimizing the ADR is achieved by "up-selling" and yield management. Up-selling is when the guest service agent/front desk clerk suggestively sells the features of a larger room, a higher floor, or perhaps a better view. Yield management originated in the airline industry where demand also fluctuates. Basically, a percentage of guests who book and send in a deposit in advance will be able to secure a room at a more reasonable price than someone booking a room with just three-days' notice. The price will be even higher for the booking at three-days' notice if demand is good.

Many other factors influence the hotels ability to sell out. Chief among these are *demand,* the number of people needing rooms, and *supply,* the number of available rooms. A good example is the New York Hotel Convention and Trade Show. This event takes place in a city that has a high demand for hotel rooms in proportion to its inventory (number of available rooms). Because there is a fairly constant demand for rooms in New York, special events tend to increase demand to a point that forces up room rates. Another example comes from the airline industry, which always seems to raise prices at the peak travel times (Thanksgiving, Christmas, Easter, and the summer vacation times). They only give special fares when school is in session. Yield management is explained in more detail later in this chapter.

2. To maintain balanced guest accounts. This begins with advance deposits, opening the guest folio (account), and posting all charges from the various departments. Many hotels now have property management systems (PMS)[11] (property management systems are explained in more detail later in this chapter) and point of sale terminals (POS), which are on-line to the front office. This means that guest charges from the various outlets are directly debited to the guest's folio. Payment is either received on guest check-out, or transferred to the "city ledger" (a special account for a company that has established credit with the hotel). This means that the account will be sent and paid within a specified time period. Formerly, the allotted time was at the end of the month, followed by a thirty- or sixty-day grace period for payment to be made. However, most companies now have a goal to keep accounts receivable to a maximum of fifteen to twenty days. This helps the hotel maintain sufficient cash flow to meet its obligations to lenders for mortgage payments and employees' salaries.

A recent innovation to the PMS is in-room check-out. The system allows a guest to check his or her account via the television screen in the room. The guest operates the system via the remote control, verifying all charges and authorizing payment. The total may then be charged to a credit card with a copy sent to the guest, or (for company accounts) to his or her company. Hotels that do not have this feature as part of their PMS sometimes leave a copy of the guest's folio under the door on the last evening. This also allows the guest to check all charges before departure. The guest has the option of calling the desk to inform the cashier that the bill may be sent. Nowadays, because cash flow is so important, payment may be required on receipt of the invoice or a few days later. Credit cards have helped this process by speeding up payment to hotels.

3. To offer services such as handling mail, faxes, messages, and local and hotel information. A constant flow of people approach the front desk with questions. Front desk employees need to be knowledgeable about the various activities in the hotel. The size, layout, and staffing of the front desk will vary with the size of the hotel. A busy 800-room city center property will naturally differ from a country inn. The front desk is staffed throughout the twenty-four hours by three shifts. The hours worked by front desk employees may vary. However, generally the day shift works from 7:00 A.M. until 3:00 P.M., the swing shift runs from 3:00 P.M. until 11:30 P.M., and the graveyard shift/night auditor works from 11:00 P.M. until 7:00 A.M. On a staggered schedule, one person starts at 7:00 A.M. and ends at 3:30 P.M., and another one starts at 2:30 P.M. and goes to 11:00 P.M. This schedule provides time for a smooth handover between the shifts. These few minutes are vital because the shift leaders must exchange essential information such as how the house count is going (how many rooms left to sell), which room changes have been requested but have not been completed, which VIPs are still to arrive and any special arrangements that need to be taken care of (e.g., calling the

Front Desk Associate

manager on duty to escort the guests to their rooms/suites, knowing which guests have serious complaints and therefore need special attention, etc.).

The main duties of the early shift are the following:

1. Check the log book and the previous night's occupancy for no-shows and send information to the accounting office for billing.
2. Conduct a house count and update the forecast (in some hotels this is done by reservations).
3. Decide on the number and mix of rooms to sell (in some hotels this is also done by reservations).
4. Preallocate VIP suites and rooms and block off group or convention rooms.
5. Handle guest check-outs including the following:
    a. Ensure all charges are on guest's folio, especially any last-minute telephone calls and breakfast. (Most medium and large hotels now have a PMS so that the moment a guest incurs charges in the restaurant, the charge will automatically be included on the guest folio. In the old days, some guests would skip off without paying for some charges incurred before check-out.)
    b. Verify the accuracy of the account by going through the various charges with the guest.
    c. Accept the cash or credit as payment.
    d. Tactfully handle any unexpected situation (for example, when the guest says the company is paying for his or her stay and the front desk has received no instructions to that effect).
    e. Send any city ledger accounts to the accounting office—generally this is done when the guest has signed the folio to approve all charges.
6. Politely and efficiently attend to guest inquiries.
7. Note important occurrences in the front office log.
8. Organize any room changes guests may request and follow up.
9. Advise housekeeping and room service of flowers/fruit for VIPs and any other amenities ordered.
10. Check issuing and control of keys.

The desk clerk must be able to work under pressure. Constant interruptions to the actual work of the front desk occur and employees are always on stage; therefore, it is necessary to maintain composure even during moments of apparent panic.

The evening shift duties are the following:

1. Check the log book for special items. (The log book is kept by guest contact; associates at the front office note specific and important guest requests and occurrences such as requests for room switches or baby cribs.)
2. Check on the room status, number of expected check-outs still to leave, and arrivals by double-checking registration cards and the computer in order to update the forecast of the night's occupancy. This will determine the number of rooms left to sell. Nowadays, this is all part of the capability of the PMS.

Major hotel chains offer a number of different room rates, including the following:

rack rate
corporate
association rate
government
encore
cititravel
entertainment cards
AAA
AARP (American Association of Retired Persons)
wholesale
group rates
promotional special

The rack rate is the rate that is used as a benchmark quotation of a hotel's room rate. Let us assume that the Hotel California had a rack rate of $135. Any discounted rate may be offered at a percentage deduction from the rack rate. An example would be a corporate rate of $110, an association rate of $105, and AARP rate of $95—certain restrictions may apply. Group rates may range from $95 to $125 according to how much the hotel needs the business.

Throughout the world there are three main plans on which room rates are based:

AP/American Plan—room and three meals a day
MAP/Modified American Plan—room plus two meals
EP/European Plan—room only, meals extra

Figure 4–5   *Types of Rates*

3. Handle guest check-ins. This means notifying the appropriate staff of any special requests guests may have made (e.g., nonsmoking room or a long bed for an extra tall guest).
4. Take reservations for that evening and future reservations after the reservations staff have left for the day.

Figure 4–5 shows the types of rates offered by hotels.

Night Auditor

A hotel is one of the few businesses that balances its accounts at the end of each business day. Because a hotel is open twenty-four hours every day, it is difficult to stop transactions at any given moment. The night auditor waits until the hotel quiets down at about 1:00 A.M. and then begins the task of balancing the guests' accounts receivable. The other duties include the following:

1. Post any charges that the evening shift was not able to post.
2. Pass discrepancies to shift managers in the morning. The room and tax charges are then posted to each folio and a new balance shown.
3. Run backup reports so if the computer system fails the hotel will have up-to-date information to operate a manual system.
4. Reconcile point-of-sale and PMS to guest accounts. If this does not balance, then the auditor must do so by investigating errors or omissions.

Night Auditor Verifying and Balancing Guest Accounts

Corporate Profile: Hyatt Hotels

When Nicholas Pritzker emigrated with his family from the Ukraine to the United States, he began his career by opening a small law firm. His outstanding management skills led to the expansion of the law firm, turning it into a management company. The Pritzkers gained considerable financial support, which allowed them to pursue their goals of expansion and development. These dreams came into reality with the opening of the first Hyatt Hotel, inaugurated on September 27, 1957.

Today, Hyatt Hotel Corporation is a $2.5 billion hotel management and development company; together with Hyatt International, they are among the leading chains in the hotel industry, with 7.33 percent of the market share.[1] Hyatt has earned worldwide fame as the leader in providing luxury accommodations and high-quality service, targeting especially the business traveler, but strategically differentiating its properties and services to identify and market to a very diverse clientele. This differentiation has resulted in the establishment of four basic types of hotels:

1. *The Hyatt Regency Hotels* represent the company's core product. They are usually located in business city centers and regarded as five-star hotels.
2. *Hyatt Resorts* are vacation retreats. They are located in the world's most desirable leisure destinations, offering the "ultimate escape from everyday stresses."
3. *The Park Hyatt Hotels* are smaller, European-style, luxury hotels. They target the individual traveler who prefers the privacy, personalized service, and discreet elegance of a small European hotel.
4. *The Grand Hyatt Hotels* serve culturally rich destinations that attract leisure business as well as large-

scale meetings and conventions. They reflect refinement and grandeur, and they feature state-of-the-art technology and banquet and conference facilities of world-class standard.

Hyatt Hotels Corporation has been recognized by the *Wall Street Journal* as one of the sixty-six firms around the world poised to make a difference in the industries and markets of the 1990s and beyond. As a matter of fact, the effective management that characterized the company in its early years with the Pritzker family has continued through time. Hyatt Hotels Corporation is characterized by a decentralized management approach, which gives the individual general manager a great deal of decision-making power, as well as the opportunity to stimulate personal creativity and, therefore, differentiation and innovation. The development of novel concepts and products is perhaps the key to Hyatt's outstanding success. For example, the 1967 opening of the Hyatt Regency Atlanta, Georgia, gave the company instant recognition throughout the world. Customers were likely to stare in awe at the twenty-one-story atrium lobby, the glass elevators, and the revolving roof-top restaurant. The property's innovative architecture, designed by John Portman, revolutionized the common standards of design and spacing, thus changing the course of the lodging industry. The atrium concept introduced there represented a universal challenge to hotel architects to face the new trend of grand, wide-open public spaces.

A further positive aspect of the decentralized management structure is the fact that the individual manager is able to be extremely customer-responsive by developing a

This is done by checking that every departmental charge shows up on guest folios.

5. Complete and distribute the daily report. This report details the previous day's activities and includes vital information about the performance of the hotel.
6. Find areas of the hotel where there may be theft or potential theft.

The daily report contains some key operating ratios such as room occupancy percentage (ROP), which is rooms occupied divided by rooms available. Thus, if a hotel has 850 rooms and 622 are occupied, the occupancy percentage is $622 \div 850 = 73.17$ percent. If 375 of the 622 occupied rooms are occupied by two or more persons, then the double or multiple occupancy percentage is

---

thorough knowledge of the guests' needs and thereby providing personalized service—fundamental to achieving customer satisfaction. This is, in fact, the ultimate innkeeping purpose, which Hyatt attains at high levels. Perhaps the most striking result of this forecasting is, again, the introduction of innovative and diversified products and services. For business travelers, for example, Hyatt recently introduced the Hyatt Business Plan, which includes fax machines in every room, twenty-four-hour access to copiers and printers, and other features designed to address the needs of the targeted clientele. Hyatt has also been on the forefront in developing faster, more efficient check-in options, including a phone number, 1-800-CHECK-IN, that allows guests to check in to their hotel rooms by telephone. In addition, the needs of families have been considered as well. The company offers Camp Hyatt, the hotel industry's most extensive children's program.

The other side of Hyatt's success is the emphasis on human resources management. Employee satisfaction, in fact, is considered to be a prerequisite to external satisfaction. Hyatt devotes enormous attention to employee training and selection. What is most significant, however, is the interaction among top managers and operating employees.

Darryl Hartley-Leonard was the company's president in 1989 when he came up with the idea of "In-touch day." On this day, once a year, the company closes its headquarters' office and the senior management spreads out to a hundred Hyatt Hotels in the United States and Canada, "spending time in the trenches"—doing the daily activities of operating employees, taking their front-line positions. Such a strategy is extremely effective: Actually performing the job enables the top executives to learn, first-hand, the challenges and problems of their employees, thus understanding their daily routine and problems. The In-touch day concept provides tangible evidence to employees that the management is not locked into an ivory tower, but is concerned with the improvement of their jobs.

Darryl Hartley-Leonard's leadership was successful. He joined Hyatt in 1964 as a front desk clerk at a Los Angeles Hyatt hotel. After serving in a variety of management positions, he worked his way up to general manager of Hyatt Regency Atlanta (1974); two years later he became a regional vice president. But that was not it. His extraordinary abilities were further recognized and rewarded: Hartley-Leonard was named executive vice president for the corporation in 1978, president in 1986, and chairman in 1994. Currently, Jay Pritzker is the chairman of the Hyatt Hotels Corporation.

[1]The company owns 173 hotels and resorts worldwide: 107 in North America, Canada, and the Caribbeans, and 66 in international locations.

calculated by taking the number of guests minus the number of rooms occupied: $750 - 622 = 128 \div 375 = 34.13$. The ADR is, together with the occupancy percentage, one of the key operating ratios that indicates the hotel's performance. The average daily rate is calculated by dividing the rooms revenue by the number of rooms sold. If the rooms revenue was $75,884 and the number of rooms sold was 662 then the ADR would be $122. See Figure 4-6 for an example of a daily report.

A more recent ratio to gauge a hotel rooms division's performance is the percentage of potential rooms revenue, which is calculated by determining potential rooms revenue and dividing the actual revenue by the potential revenue.

Larger hotels may have more than one night auditor, but in smaller properties these duties may be combined with night manager, desk, or night watchperson duties.

Property Management Systems

Property management systems have greatly enhanced a hotel's ability to accept, store, and retrieve guest reservations, guest history, requests, and billing arrangements. The reservations part of the property management system also provides the reservations associates with information on types of rooms available, features, views, and room rates. A list of expected arrivals can be easily generated. Before the advent of PMSs, it took reservation associates much longer to learn the features of each room and the various room rates, and to make up the arrivals list.

A property management system contains a set of computer software packages capable of supporting a variety of activities in front and back office areas. The four most common front office software packages are designed to assist front office employees in performing functions related to the following tasks:

✔ Reservations management
✔ Rooms management
✔ Guest account management
✔ General management[12]

The reservations management component allows the reservations department to quickly accept reservations and generate confirmations and occupancy forecasts for reservations taken by the hotel directly and by the CRS. Most chain operated or affiliated hotels have a 1-800 number to allow guests to call, without charge, to make reservations anywhere in the United States and, in some cases, overseas. Travel agents also have direct computer access to the central reservations numbers. More than one hundred PMS vendors offer various features, hardware platforms, and operating systems. The various software packages handle some or all of the following:

✔ Reservations
✔ Front desk
✔ Group billing

Clarion Hotel Bayview

Daily Management Report Supplement
January 18, 1995

Daily Report
January 18, 1995

Occupancy%	Today	Avg or %	M–T–D Avg or %		Y–T–D Avg or %	
Rack Rooms	9	2.9%	189	3.37	189	3.37
Corporate Rooms	0	0.0%	103	1.83	103	1.83
Group Rooms	274	87.8%	2,379	42.36	2,379	42.36
Leisure Rooms	3	1.0%	395	7.03	395	7.03
Base Rooms	23	7.4%	348	6.14	345	6.14
Government Rooms	2	0.6%	32	.57	32	.57
Wholesale Rooms	1	0.3%	121	2.15	121	2.15
No-Show Rooms		0.0%	0	.00	0	.00
Comp Rooms	0	0.0%	37	.66	37	.66
Total Occ Rooms & Occ %	312	100%	3,601	64.12	3,601	64.12
Rack	$1,011	$112.33	17,207	91.04	17,207	91.04
Corporate	$0	ERR	8,478	82.31	8,478	82.31
Group	$22,510	$82.15	178,066	74.85	178,066	74.85
Leisure	$207	$69.00	24,985	63.25	24,985	63.25
Base	$805	$35.00	12,063	34.97	12,063	34.97
Govt	$141	$70.59	2,379	74.34	2,379	74.34
Wholesale	$43	$43.00	5,201	42.98	5,201	42.98
No-Show/Comp/Allowance	$0		−914	−24.69	−914	−24.69
Total Rev & Avg Rate	$24,717	$79.22	247,466	68.72	247,466	68.72

Hotel Revenue

Rooms	$24,717		247,466	77.46	247,466	77.46
Food	$1,400		37,983	11.89	37,983	11.89
Beverage	$539		9,679	3.03	9,679	3.03
Telephone	$547		5,849	1.83	5,849	1.83
Parking	$854		11,103	3.48	11,103	3.48
Room Svc II	$70		1,441	.45	1,441	.45
Other Revenue	$1,437		963	1.87	963	1.87
Total Revenue	$29,563		319,484	100.00	319,484	100.00

Figure 4–6 *Daily Report*

Clarion Hotel Bayview

Daily Management Report Supplement
January 18, 1995

Daily Report
January 18, 1995

Cafe 6th & K	Today	Avg or %	M–T–D Avg or %		Y–T–D Avg or %	
Cafe Breakfast Covers	88	57.1%	1,180	47.12	1,180	47.12
Cafe Lunch Covers	43	27.9%	674	26.92	674	26.92
Cafe Dinner Covers	23	14.9%	650	25.96	650	25.96
Total Cafe Covers	154	100.0%	2,504	100.00	2,504	100.00
Cafe Breakfast	$608	$6.91	7,854	6.66	7,854	6.66
Cafe Lunch	$246	$5.72	5,847	8.67	5,847	8.67
Cafe Dinner	$227	$9.86	4,309	6.63	4,309	6.63
Gaslamp Lounge Food			2,431	3.74	2,431	3.74
Total Rev/Avg Check	$1,081	$7.02	20,440	8.16	20,440	8.16
Banquets						
Banquet Breakfast Covers	0	ERR	154	13.24	154	13.24
Banquet Lunch Covers	0	ERR	134	11.52	134	11.52
Banquet Dinner Covers	0	ERR	254	21.84	254	21.84
Banquet Coffeebreak Covers	0	ERR	621	53.40	621	53.40
Total Banquet Covers	0	ERR	1,163	100.00	1,163	100.00
Banquet Breakfast	$0	ERR	980	6.36	980	6.36
Banquet Lunch	$0	ERR	2,997	22.36	2,997	22.36
Banquet Dinner	$0	ERR	4,530	17.84	4,530	17.84
Banquet Coffeebreak	$0	ERR	1,093	1.76	1,093	1.76
Total Rev/Avg Check	$0	ERR	9,600	8.25	9,600	8.25
Room Service						
Room Service Breakfast Covers	13	40.6%	324	48.00	324	48.00
Room Service Lunch Covers	3	9.4%	53	7.85	53	7.85
Room Service Dinner Covers	16	50.0%	298	44.15	298	44.15
Total Covers	32	100.0%	675	100.00	675	100.00
Room Service Breakfast	$119	$9.13	2,665	8.22	2,665	8.22
Room Service Lunch	$29	$9.77	418	7.89	418	7.89
Room Service Dinner	$171	$10.67	2,907	9.75	2,907	9.75
Total Rev/Avg Check	$319	$9.96	5,990	8.87	5,990	8.87

Figure 4–6 *(continued)*

- ✔ Guest history
- ✔ Report writer
- ✔ Travel agent billing
- ✔ Tour operations
- ✔ Housekeeping
- ✔ Yield management
- ✔ Package plans
- ✔ Wholesaler blocks
- ✔ Call accounting interface
- ✔ In-room movie interface
- ✔ Point-of-sale interface
- ✔ Environmental control
- ✔ Central reservations
- ✔ General ledger
- ✔ Accounts payable
- ✔ Condo owner accounting
- ✔ Association management
- ✔ Long-term rentals
- ✔ Timeshare rentals[13]

Medium- to large-sized hotels typically have a minicomputer with front and back office (accounting, control, purchasing) applications. In addition, other hardware platforms may exist within the property, and applications may include back office, point-of-sale, and conference or catering scheduling.[14]

Smaller hotels may use a microcomputer either as a stand-alone system or with a local area network to support the applications.[15]

Marriott hotels have based their property management system on the IBM 173 RISC system/6000. The worldwide installation includes 250 hotels. The goal was to set up a single architecture with one integrated database for sales, catering, human resources, back office, accounting, and front office operations.[16]

Holiday Inn Worldwide (1,600 hotels) has invested more than $60 million installing PMSs in all of its properties. The $60 million covers leasing the Encore PMS for use in all its properties, development of the Holiday Inn Reservation Optimization system, free use of hardware and software for all hotels, and training for employees. The system integrates revenue optimization and customer tracking software to maximize income for the properties and options for the guests.[17]

The advantages of the Holiday Inn Reservation Optimization (HIRO) and EN-CORE are that they include a two-way interface with Holidex (the Holiday Corporation's reservation system) and will automate and simplify front desk procedures. The HIRO system, according to Holiday officials, is the first automated length-of-stay optimization system to be integrated with a central reservation system. This ability to manage length of stay and room type works like this: For example, in August 1991, some 81 percent of the multiple-night requests to Holidex were turned down due to no availability. With HIRO those denials will be turned into room nights and should recover at least $100 million for Holiday Inn.[18]

Until 1993, there were problems with both central reservation systems and property management systems. For example, the most important information about any given property has not been readily available to those in the best position to sell it. Too often, travel agents have been unable to tell if rooms are available and at what price just by looking at the data on the terminal at their desks.[19]

The Hotel Industry Switch Company (THISCO) has created a pathway between the lodging industry's central reservation systems and those of the airlines. THISCO allows the travel agents to look into the hotel database.[20] This system, together with a software package from Anasail, has been installed in Hospitality Franchise Systems, which franchise Days Inn, Ramada, and Howard Johnson brands. Travelodge, Promus, and Choice Hotels have all customized the software for their own uses.

The ultimate goal is for hotels to have access to a global reservations network. Larry Chervenak, a well-known authority on hospitality technology, estimates that more than $3 billion has been invested by various players in the global competition to create reservation systems that will feed more business into hotels.[21]

Hotel systems generally piggyback on the airline systems. The two main airline computer systems, Sabre (American Airlines) and Apollo (jointly owned by United, USAir, Air Canada, and several European airlines), both have developed sophisticated global reservation systems designed to make it easy for the travel agent to make international hotel reservations.

Covla is an example of an international CRS system. It is a subsidiary of the Covla airline system known to U.S. travel agents as Apollo. It enables agents to book hotel reservations around the world. Companies like Ritz-Carlton, Swissotel, and Pan Pacific utilize this system. American Airlines has adopted Qik-Res, a software system developed by Qantas that runs on personal computers (PCs). These user-friendly software systems make it easier for travel agents to make hotel reservations in four easy steps: shop, look, check, and book. Curiously, a recent study suggests that business travelers, who account for almost half of current occupancy levels, are reached directly, with travel agents playing little or no role in formulating property selection.

Another survey, conducted by *Hotel and Motel Management,* shows that business travelers generally make their own hotel reservations 65.2 percent of the time. When it came to choosing a hotel, basic criteria seemed to be important. Although location and price may be the top considerations, cleanliness was rated highest by 91.1 percent of the sample. Comfortable mattresses and pillows were second, with 89.1 percent rating these as important or very important. In terms of brand loyalty, frequent travelers were more likely to specify a particular chain than nonfrequent travelers.[22] It is important to note that business travelers make their own hotel reservations; consequently, the criteria for hotel selection is also important to hotel executives.

The oversupply of rooms has encouraged operators to use information technology to reduce costs and provide better service. The computerized hotel reservation system enables hotels to fill more efficiently the maximum number of rooms on any given day. Reservation programs enable the reservation clerk to provide a high level of personalized service for repeat visitors. Hotels can use yield management systems to maximize revenues by basing the selling price of a room on the expected demand for rooms on a given night.[23]

Yield Management

Yield management is a demand-forecasting technique used to maximize room revenue that the hotel industry borrowed from the airlines. It is based on the economics of supply and demand, which means that prices rise when demand is strong and drop when demand is weak. Thus, the purpose of yield management is to increase profitability. Naturally, management would like to sell every room at the highest rack rate. However, this is not reality, and rooms are sold at discounts on the rack rate. An example would be the corporate or group rate. In most hotels, only a small percentage of rooms are sold at rack rate. This is because of conventions and group rates and other promotional discounts that are necessary to stimulate demand. What yield management does is to allocate the right type of capacity to the right customer at the right price so as to maximize revenue or yield per available room.[24]

Generally the demand for room reservations follows the pattern of group bookings being made months or even years in advance of arrival and individual bookings, which mostly are made a few days before arrival. Figures 4–7 and 4–8 show the pattern of group and individual room reservations.

Group reservations are booked months, even years, in advance. Yield management will monitor reservations and, based on previous trends and current demand, determine the number and type of rooms to sell at what price to obtain the maximum revenue.

The curve in Figure 4–7 indicates the pattern of few reservations being made 120 days prior to arrival. Most of the individual room bookings are made in the last few days before arrival at the hotel. The yield management program will

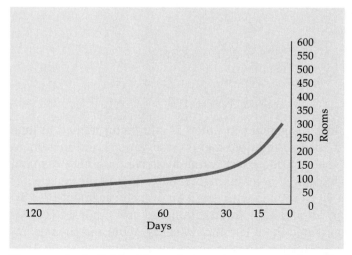

Figure 4–7 *Individual Room Reservations Curve* (Adapted from Sheryl E. Kimes, "The Basics of Yield Management," *The Cornell Hotel Restaurant Administration Quarterly*, November 1989.)

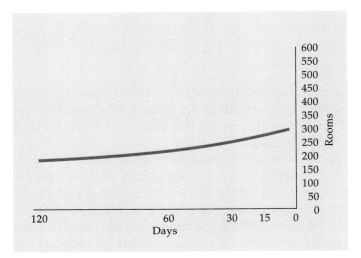

Figure 4–8   *Group Booking Curve*

monitor the demand and supply and recommend the number and type of rooms to sell for any given day, and the price for which to sell each room.

With yield management, not only will the time before arrival be an important consideration in the pricing of guest rooms, but also the type of room to be occupied. For example, there could be a different price for a double, queen, or king room when used for single occupancy. This rate could be above the single rack rate. Similarly, double and multiple room occupancy would yield higher room rates. It works as follows:[25]

Suppose a hotel has 300 rooms and a rack rate of $150. The average number of rooms sold is 200 per night at an average rate of $125. The yield for this property would be

$$\text{Occupancy percentage} = 200 \div 300 = 66.6\%$$

The rate achievement factor is

$$\$125 \div 200 = 62.5\%$$

and the yield would be

$$.666 \times .625 = 41\%$$

The application of yield management in hotels is still being refined to take into consideration factors such as multiple nights' reservations and incremental food and beverage revenue. If the guest wants to arrive on a high demand night and stay through several low demand nights, what should the charge be?

Yield management has been refined with profit analysis by segment (PABS), which uses a combination of marketing information and cost analysis. It identifies average revenues generated by different market segments and then examines the contribution margin for each of the segments considering the cost of making those sales.[26]

There are some disadvantages to yield management. For instance, if a business person attempts to make a reservation at a hotel three days before arrival and the rate quoted in order to maximize revenue is considered too high, this person may decide to select another hotel and not even consider the first hotel when making future reservations.

Revenue per available room, or Rev Par, was developed by Smith Travel Research. It is calculated by dividing room revenue by the number of rooms available. For example, if room sales are $50,000 in one day for a hotel with 400 available rooms, then the formula would be $50,000 divided by 400, or $125. Hotels use Rev Par to see how they are doing compared to their competitive set of hotels. Owners use Rev Par to gauge who they want to run their hotels.

Reservations

The reservations department is headed by the reservations manager who, in many hotels today, is on the same level as the front office manager and reports directly to the director of rooms division or the director of sales. This emphasizes the importance of the sales aspects of reservations and encompasses yield management. Reservations is the first contact for the guest or person making the reservation for the guest. Although the contact may be by telephone, a distinct impression of the hotel is registered with the guest. This calls for exceptional telephone manners and telemarketing skills. Because some guests may be shopping for the best value, it is essential to sell the hotel by emphasizing its advantages over the competition.

The reservation department generally works from 8:00 A.M. to 6:00 P.M. Depending on the size of the hotel, several people may be employed in this important department. The desired outcome of the reservations department is to exceed guest expectations when they make reservations. This is achieved by selling all of the hotel rooms for the maximum possible dollars and avoiding possible guest resentment of being overcharged. Reservations originate from a variety of sources (in rank order with 1 being the highest source of reservations):

1. Telephone to the same property
   a. Fax
   b. Telex
   c. Letter
   d. Cable
2. Corporate/1-800 numbers
3. Travel agents
4. Hotel reservations
5. Meeting planners (may be number one in a convention hotel)
6. Tour operators (may be number one in resort areas)
7. Referral from another company property
8. Airport telephone
9. Walk in

Clearly, reservations are of tremendous importance to the hotel because of the potential and actual revenue realized. Many hotel chains have a 1-800 number that a prospective guest may call without charge to make a reservation at

Central Reservations Office

Hotel Reservations Agent

any of the company properties in the United States and internationally. The corporate central reservations system allows operators to access the inventory of room availability of each hotel in the chain. Once a reservation has been made, it is immediately deducted from the inventory of rooms for the duration of the guest stay. The central reservations system interfaces with the hotel's inventory and simultaneously allows reservations to be made by the individual hotel reservations personnel. A number of important details need to be recorded when taking reservations.

Confirmed reservations are reservations made with sufficient time for a confirmation slip to be returned to the client by mail or fax. Confirmation is generated by the computer printer and indicates confirmation number, dates of arrival and departure, type of room booked, number of guests, number of beds, type of bed, and any special requests. The guest may bring the confirmation slip to the hotel to verify the booking.

Guaranteed reservations are when the person making the reservation wishes to ensure that the reservation will be held. This is arranged at the time the reservation is made and generally applies in situations when the guest is expected to arrive late. The hotel takes the credit card number, which guarantees the payment of the room, of the person being billed. The hotel agrees to hold the room for late arrival. The importance of guaranteed reservations is that the guest will more likely cancel beforehand if unable to show up, which gives more accurate inventory room count and minimizes no-shows.

Another form of guaranteed reservations is advance deposit/advance payment. In certain situations—for example during a holiday—in order to protect itself against having empty rooms (no-shows), the hotel requires that a deposit of either one night or the whole stay be paid in advance of the guest's arrival. This is done by obtaining the guest's credit card number, which may be charged automatically for the first night's accommodation. This discourages no-shows. Corporations that use the hotel frequently may guarantee all of their bookings so as to avoid any problems in the event a guest arrives late, remembering that in cities where the demand is heavy, hotels release any nonguaranteed or nonpaid reservations at 4:00 P.M. or 6:00 P.M. on the evening of the guest's expected arrival.

Communications

Communications CBX or PBX

The communications CBX or PBX includes in-house communications; guest communications, such as pagers and radios; voice mail; faxes; messages; and emergency center. Guests often have their first contact with the hotel by telephone. This underlines the importance of prompt and courteous attention to all calls, because first impressions last.

The communications department is a vital part of the smooth running of the hotel. It is also a profit center because hotels generally add a 50 percent charge to all long distance calls placed from guest rooms. Local calls cost about $0.75 to $1.25, plus tax.

Communications operates twenty-four hours a day, in much the same way as the front office does, having three shifts. It is essential that this department be staffed with people who are trained to be calm under pressure and who follow emergency procedures.

Guest/Uniformed Service

Because first impressions are very important to the guest, the guest service or uniformed staff has a special responsibility. The guest service department or uniformed staff is headed by a guest services manager who may also happen to be the bell captain. The staff consists of door attendants and bellpersons and the concierge—although in some hotels the concierge reports directly to the front office manager.

Door attendants are the hotel's unofficial greeters. Dressed in impressive uniforms, they greet guests at the hotel front door, assist in opening/closing automobile doors, removing luggage from the trunk, hailing taxis, keeping the hotel entrance clear of vehicles, and giving guests information about the hotel and the local area in a courteous and friendly way. People in this position generally receive many gratuities (tips); in fact, years ago, the position was handed down from father to son or sold for several thousand dollars. Rumor has it that this is one of the most lucrative positions in the hotel, even more than the general manager's.

The bellperson's main function is to escort guests and transport luggage to their rooms. Bellpersons also need to be knowledgeable about the local area and all facets of the hotel and its services. Because they have so much guest contact, they need a pleasant, outgoing personality. The bellperson explains the services of the hotel and points out the features of the room (lighting, TV, air conditioning, telephone, wake-up calls, laundry and valet service, room service and restaurants, and the pool and health spa).

Concierge

The concierge is a uniformed employee of the hotel who has her or his own separate desk in the lobby or on special concierge floors. The concierge is a separate department from the front office room clerks and cashiers.

Until 1936, a concierge was not an employee of the hotel but an independent entrepreneur who purchased a position from the hotel and paid the salaries, if any, of his or her uniformed subordinates.[27]

Today's concierge, as one historically minded concierge put it, has come to embody the core of a hotel's efforts to serve guests in a day when the inn is so large that the innkeeper can no longer personally attend to each guest.[28] Luxury hotels in most cities have concierges. New York's Plaza Hotel has 800 rooms and a battery of ten concierges who serve under the direction of Thomas P. Wolfe. The concierge assists guests with a broad range of services such as the following:

- ✔ Tickets to the hottest shows in town, even for the very evening on the day they are requested. Naturally, the guest pays up to about $150 per ticket.
- ✔ A table at a restaurant that has no reservations available.
- ✔ Advice on local restaurants, activities, attractions, amenities, and facilities

Concierge

✔ Airline tickets and reconfirmation of flights
✔ VIP's messages and special requests, such as shopping
Less Frequent Requests:
✔ Organize a wedding on two days' notice
✔ Arrange for a member of the concierge department to go to a consulate or embassy for visas to be stamped in guests' passports
✔ Handle business affairs

What will a concierge do for a guest? Almost anything, *Conde' Nast Traveler* learned from concierges at hotels around the world. Among the more unusual requests were the following:

1. Some Japanese tourists staying at the Palace Hotel in Madrid decided to bring bullfighting home. Their concierge found bulls for sale, negotiated the bulls' purchase, and had them shipped to Tokyo.
2. After watching a guest pace the lobby, the concierge of a London hotel, now operating the desk at the Dorchester, asked the pacer if he could help. The guest was to be married within the hour, but his best man had been detained. Because he was dressed up anyway, the concierge volunteered to substitute.
3. A guest at the Hotel Plaza Athenee in Paris wanted to prevent her pet from mingling with dogs from the wrong side of the boulevard while walking. Madame requested that the concierge buy a house in a decent neighborhood so that her pampered pooch might stroll in its garden unsullied. Although the dog continued to reside at the hotel, Madame's chauffeur shuttled him to the empty house for his daily constitutional.
4. A guest at London's Sheraton Park Tower needed parts for his yacht's Volvo engine for the next morning's sail. Unable to find them in England, the concierge rang the Volvo factory in Sweden and arranged for a messenger from the hotel to fly to Sweden, retrieve the parts, and deliver them late that evening.
5. Dressing for dinner, a guest at the Phoenician in Scottsdale, Arizona, suddenly realized that he had forgotten his shoes. The concierge happened to wear the same size shoe and lent the man his loafers.[29]

The work of the concierge may seem glamorous, especially when seeing Michael J. Fox play a concierge in the movie *For Love or Money*. However, not all hotel concierges earn high salaries, and it does take a few years to learn the ropes. It also takes time to learn who the big spenders are and to build up a clientele who will place their confidence in a particular concierge.

The concierge needs not only a detailed knowledge of the hotel and its services, but also of the city and even international details. Many concierges speak several languages; most important of all, they must want to help people and have a pleasant, outgoing personality. At the Westin St. Francis in San Francisco, a special three-employee department has been created to refine Japanese amenities. This Japanese guest service combines the functions of concierge, front desk, and tour-briefing. Given that one-third of all visitors to San Francisco are international travelers and that most Japanese visitors do not speak English, this progressive approach to guest satisfaction is receiving positive feedback.[30]

Canadian Pacific Hotels

The Canadian Pacific Hotel company started in 1886 with the completion of the Mount Stephen House in Kicking Horse Valley, Canada. William Cornelius Van Horne decided to build a series of "dining stations" along the first Canadian transcontinental railroad to accommodate travelers. During the next year, two more stations were built—Glacier House and Fraser Canyon House—and by 1908, Van Horne had built four more stations.

The look of Van Horne's hotels was remarkable, and travelers enjoyed seeing them. He designed hotels to look like European castles and Canadian author R.G. MacBeth called the hotels "palatial and romantic."

Expansion of Canadian Pacific Hotels continued through the twentieth century, with hotels located in British Columbia, the Rocky Mountains, Urban Alberta, Ontario, Quebec, and Atlantic Canada. Canadian Pacific Hotels currently has a total of twenty-six hotels, with 11,116 rooms and 10,000 employees throughout Canada.

In 1987, Canadian Pacific began to restore all of the hotels to their original grandeur. Each hotel was renovated and refurbished, and rooms, restaurants, and health clubs were added to many of the hotels.

City-Centre hotels are now equipped with modernized business amenities to meet a business traveler's needs. The rooms feature a desk, two phones, a desk drawer organizer with supplies, a fax service, and other services including express check-out. Many hotels contain work centers for business travelers who prefer a place to work other than their room.

Canadian Pacific Hotels are involved in many programs to benefit the residents of Canada. An environmental program that started in 1990, which all hotels in the chain are involved in, is doing great. Canadian Pacific Hotels have set goals for themselves, such as reducing waste and collecting recyclables from the guest rooms. The hotels have reached their goal of being nature-friendly with the help of an environmental consultant. The corporation received the Green Hotelier of the Year award in 1996 for outstanding efforts to improve environmental performance.

Another program that Canadian Pacific is currently involved in is the Adopt-A-Shelter program. Each hotel in

the chain adopts a local women's shelter and donates goods, services, and financial support, mainly used furniture and household items. The relationship between the hotel and the shelter is a continuing one.

The Canadian Pacific Charitable Foundation will also donate $150,000 to the Canadian Women's Foundation during the next three years. This money will help the Women's Foundation set up "Canadian Pacific Violence Prevention Fund," which will help support many violence prevention programs across Canada.

Canadian Pacific Hotels' program to benefit their own workers, Service Plus 2000, is a program designed to redefine their definition of service. Through this program, employees interact with people from different departments to learn about each others' daily activities. General managers also can interact with their employees, who think this is a very positive aspect of the program.

The corporate office of Canadian Pacific Hotels, as well as the individual hotels, have received many awards. They have been recognized for many things, from having outstanding training programs to contributing to the development of the travel and tourism industry. Canadian Pacific Hotels cater to all kinds of travelers from business travelers to vacationers. Personal service and warm hospitality make Canadian Pacific Hotels a leading company in guest satisfaction.

The concierges' organization, which promotes high professional and ethical standards, is the U.P.P.G.H. (Union Professionelle des Portiers des Grand Hotels), more commonly called the *Clefs d'Or* because of the crossed goldkey insignia concierges usually wear on the lapels of their uniforms. The Clefs d'Or has about 4,000 members in twenty-four countries, with approximately 150 U.S. members.[31]

Housekeeping

The largest department in terms of the number of people employed is house-keeping. Up to 50 percent of the hotel employees may work in this department. The person in charge is the executive housekeeper or director of services. Her or his duties and responsibilities call for exceptional leadership, organization, motivation, and commitment to maintaining high standards. The logistics of servicing large numbers of rooms on a daily basis can be challenging.

The importance of the housekeeping department is underlined by guest surveys that consistently rank cleanliness of rooms number one.

The following show the ten rules for effective housekeeping leadership:

1. Utilize people power effectively. Spread responsibilities and tasks to get work done properly and on time.
2. Devise easy methods of reporting work that has to be done. Encourage feedback from all associates and continuous communication with the associates.
3. Develop standard procedures for routine activities. Help associates to develop consistent work habits.
4. Install inventory controls. Control costs for supplies and equipment.
5. Motivate housekeeping associates. Keep high morale, motivation, and understanding.
6. Accept challenges presented by guests and management. Remain unflappable in the face of any request.
7. Involve associates in planning. Encourage associates to use imagination to make the job easier and quicker without changing standards.
8. Increase educational level of staff. Support training, encouragement, and educational classes.
9. Set recruitment programs to develop management trainees. Give trainees opportunities to advance.
10. Cooperate and coordinate with other departments, such as front office, engineering and maintenance, and laundry.

The four major areas of responsibilities for the executive housekeeper are as follows:

1. Leadership of people, equipment, and supplies
2. Cleanliness and servicing the guest rooms and public areas
3. Operating the department according to financial guidelines prescribed by the general manager
4. Keeping records

Executive Housekeeper

An example of an executive housekeeper's day might be as follows:

7:45 A.M. Walk the lobby and property with the night cleaners and supervisors
Check the housekeeping log book
Check the forecast house count for number of check-outs
Check daily activity reports, stayovers, check-ins, and VIPs to ensure appropriate standards
Attend housekeepers' meeting
Meet challenges
Train new employees in the procedures
Meet with senior housekeepers/department managers
Give productivity checks
Check budget
Approve purchase orders
Check inventories
Give room inspections
Review maintenance checks
Interview potential employees
6:00 P.M. Attend to human resource activities, counseling, and employee development

Perhaps the biggest challenge of an executive housekeeper is the leadership of all the employees in the department. Further, these employees are often of different nationalities. Depending on the size of the hotel, the executive housekeeper is assisted by an assistant executive housekeeper and one or more housekeeping supervisors, who in turn supervise a number of room attendants or housekeeping associates (see Figure 4–9). The assistant executive housekeeper manages the housekeeping office. The first important daily task of this position is to break out the hotel into sections for allocation to the room attendants' schedules.

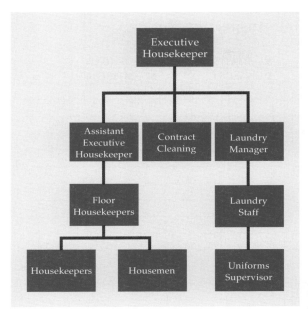

Figure 4–9 *Executive Housekeeping Personnel*

The rooms of the hotel are listed on the floor master. If the room is vacant, nothing is written next to the room number. If the guest is expected to check out, then SC will be written next to the room number. A stayover will have SS, on hold is AH, out of order is XX, and VIPs are highlighted in colors according to the amenities required.

If 258 rooms are occupied and 10 of these are suites (which count as two rooms), then the total number of rooms to be allocated to room attendants is 268 (minus any no-shows). The remaining total is then divided by 17, the number of rooms that each attendant is expected to make up.

Total number of rooms occupied	258
Add 10 for the suites	10
Total number of rooms and suites occupied	268
Less any no-shows	3
	265

Divide 265 by 17 (the number of rooms each attendant services) =
16 (the number of attendants required for that day)

Figure 4–10 shows a daily attendant's schedule.

In order to reduce payroll costs and encourage room attendants to become "stars," a number of hotel corporations have empowered the best attendants to check their own rooms. This has reduced the need for supervisors. Notice how the points are weighted for various items. This is the result of focus groups of hotel guests who explained the important things to them about a room. The items with the highest points were the ones that most concerned the guests.

The assistant executive housekeeper or administrative assistant will assist the executive housekeeper with a number of the duties and will be the anchor-person in the housekeeping office. This is the central headquarters for all

Housekeepers Guest Room Self–Inspection Rating
Inspection Codes:

P – POLISH	R – REPLACE	E – WORK ORDER	S – SOAP SCUM	SM – SMEAR
SA – STAIN	H – HAIR	D – DIRT	DU – DUST	M – MISSING

PART I – GUEST ROOM		S			U	COMMENTS
Entry, door, frame, threshold, latch			1			
Unusual odor OR smoke smell			3			
CLOSET, doors, louvers–containing			1			
Hangers, 8 suits, 4 skirts, 2 bags w/ invoices			2			
Two (2) robes, with info card			2			
Extra TP & FACIAL			1			
One (1) luggage rack			1			
Current rate card			1			
VALET	Shoe Horn & Mitt		2			
DRESSER	LAMP/ SHADE/ BULB		2			
	ICE BUCKET, LID, TRAY		2			
	TWO(2) WINE GLASSES		2			
	Room Service MENU		2			
MINIBAR	TOP, FRONT, 2 Wine glasses/ price list		1			
SAFE	KEY IN SAFE, SIGN		5			
CHECK BEHIND DRESSER			2			
DRAWERS	BIBLE AND BUDDHIST BOOK		1			
	PHONE BOOKS, ATT DIRECTORY		1			
TELEVISION	ON & OFF, CH 19 BEHIND		1			
COFFEE TABLE	REMOTE CONTROL/TEST 1		2			
	T.V. LISTINGS/BOOK MARK		1			
	GLASS TOP/LA JOLLA BOOK		1			
CARPET	VACUUM, SPOTS?		2			
SOFA	UNDER CUSHION/ BEHIND		2			
3 W LAMP	BULB, SHADE & CORD		1			
WINDOWS	GLASS, DOOR, LATCH – C BAR?		2			
CURTAINS	Pull – check seams		1			
PATIO	2 CHAIRS, TABLE & DECK		3			
DESK	2 CHAIRS, TOP, BASE & LAMP/SHADE		5			
	GREEN COMPENDIUM		3			
	Waste paper can		1			
BED	Tight, Pillows, bedspread		5			
	Check Under/SHEETS, PILLOWS		3			
HVAC	Control, setting, vent		1			
SIDE TABLES	Lamps & shade		2			
	Telephone, MESSAGE LIGHT		1			
	Clock Radio CORRECT TIME?		1			
MIRRORS	LARGE MIRROR OVER DRESSER		1			
PICTURES	ROOM ART WORK		1			
WALLS	Marks, stains, etc.		3			

Figure 4–10   *Daily Attendant's Schedule*

Housekeepers Guest Room Self–Inspection Rating

Inspection Codes:

P – POLISH	R – REPLACE	E – WORK ORDER	S – SOAP SCUM	SM – SMEAR
SA – STAIN	H – HAIR	D – DIRT	DU – DUST	M – MISSING

PART II – BATHROOM		S			U		COMMENTS
BATH TUBE/SHOWER							
	GROUT/TILE & EDGE			2			
	ANTISLIP GRIDS			2			
	SIDE WALLS			1			
	SHOWER HEAD			1			
	WALL SOAP DISH			1			
	CONTROL LEVER			1			
	FAUCET			1			
	CLOTHESLINE			1			
	SHOWER ROD, HOOKS			1			
	SHOWER CURTAIN/ LINER			2			
VANITY	TOP, SIDE & EDGE			1			
	SINK, TWO FAUCETS			3			
	3 GLASSES, COASTERS			2			
	WHITE SOAP DISH			1			
	FACIAL TISSUE & BOX			1			
AMENITY BASKET							
	1 SHAMPOO			1			
	1 CONDITIONER			1			
	1 MOISTURIZER			1			
	2 BOXED SOAP			1			
	1 SHOWER CAP			1			
MIRROR	LARGE & COSMETIC			2			
WALLS, CEILING, & VENT				2			
TOILET	TOP, SEAT, BASE & LIP			2			
OTHER	TOILET PAPER, fold			1			
	SCALE AND TRASH CAN			2			
	FLOOR, SWEPT AND MOPPED			3			
	TELEPHONE			1			
BATH LINENS, racks							
	THREE (3) WASH CLOTHS			1			
	THREE (3) HAND TOWELS			1			
	THREE(3) BATH TOWELS			1			
	ONE (1) BATH MAT			1			
	ONE (1) BATH RUG			1			
LIGHT SWITCH				1			
DOOR	FULL LENGTH MIRROR			1			
	HANDLE/LOCK			1			
	THRESHOLD			1			
	PAINTED SURFACE			1			

Figure 4–10 *(continued)*

Housekeeping Associate Making Up a Room

housekeeping operations. The following are some examples from the Sheraton Grande, Torrey Pines, California:

1. All housekeeping associates report here.
2. Section assignments are given.
3. All housekeeping telephone calls are received here.
4. All check-out and in-order rooms are processed here.
5. All guest rooms that are not cleaned by a specified time are reported.
6. All household supplies are issued.
7. Commercial laundry, counting linen, and checking linen may be handled here.
8. Table linen may be issued here.
9. All uniforms and costumes may be issued here.
10. Working records are kept.
11. All housekeeping pass keys are kept and controlled.

Guest room supplies on housekeeping associates' carts are replaced during the night shift. It is suggested that the items given away to the customer are placed on the lower shelf of the cart to discourage guests from collecting souvenirs. Taking calls and relaying information about the rooms is a vital part of the communications necessary for the smooth operation of this busy department.

The evening assistant housekeeper or housekeeper supervisor will take over the office and allocate the turndown sections to the evening. Each attendant has an allocation of sixty-three rooms to turndown and a turndown summary report to complete. The attendants also report back to the housekeeping office any discrepancies, which are in turn forwarded and communicated to the front office. The housekeeping associates clean and service between fifteen and twenty rooms per day depending on the individual hotel characteristics. Servicing a room takes longer in some older hotels than it does in some of the newer properties. Also, service time depends on the number of check-out rooms versus stayovers because servicing check-outs takes longer. Housekeeping associates begin their day at 8:00 A.M., reporting to the executive or assistant executive housekeeper. They are assigned a block of rooms and given room keys, for which they must sign and then return before going off duty.

The role of the executive housekeeper may vary slightly between the corporate chain and the independent hotel. An example is the purchasing of furnishings and equipment. A large independent hotel relies on the knowledge and experience of the executive housekeeper to make appropriate selections, whereas the chain hotel company has a corporate purchase agent (assisted by a designer) to make many of these decisions.

The executive housekeeper is responsible for a substantial amount of record keeping. In addition to the scheduling and evaluation of employees, an inventory of all guest rooms and public area furnishings must be accurately maintained with the record of refurbishment. Most of the hotel's maintenance work orders are initiated by the housekeepers who report the maintenance work order. Many hotels now have a computer link-up between housekeeping and engineering and maintenance to speed the process. Guests expect their rooms to be fully functional, especially at today's prices. Housekeeping maintains a perpetual inventory of guest room amenities, cleaning supplies, and linens.

Productivity in the housekeeping department is measured by the person hours per occupied room. The labor costs per person hour for a full service hotel is $2.00, or twenty minutes of labor for every occupied room in the hotel. Another key ratio is the labor cost, which is expected to be 5.1 percent of room sales. Controllable expenses are measured per occupied rooms. These expenses include guest supplies like soap, shampoo, hand and body lotion, sewing kits, and stationery. Although this will vary according to the type of hotel, the cost should be about $1.75 per room. Cleaning supplies should be approximately $.30 and linen costs $.75, including the purchase and laundering of all linen. These budgeted costs are sometimes hard to achieve. The executive housekeeper may be doing a great job controlling costs, but if the sales department discounts rooms, the room sales figures may come in below budget. This would have the effect of increasing the costs per occupied room.

Another concern for the executive housekeeper is accident prevention. Insurance costs have skyrocketed in recent years, and employers are struggling to increase both employee and guest safety. It is necessary for accidents to be carefully investigated. Some employees have been known to have an accident at home but go to work and report it as a work-related injury in order to be covered by workers' compensation. In order to safeguard themselves to some extent, hotels keep sweep logs of the public areas; in the event that a guest slips and falls, the hotel can show that it does genuinely take preventative measures to protect its guests.

The U.S. Senate Bill 198, known as the Employee Right to Know, has heightened awareness of the storage, handling, and use of dangerous chemicals. Information about the chemicals must be made available to all employees. Great care and extensive training is required to avoid dangerous accidents.

The executive housekeeper must also maximize loss prevention. Strict policies and procedures are necessary to prevent losses from guest rooms. Some hotels require housekeeping associates to sign a form stating that they understand they may not let any guest into any room. Such action would result in immediate termination of employment. Although this may seem drastic, it is the only way to avoid some hotel thefts.

Laundry

Increasingly, hotels are operating their own laundries. This subdepartment generally reports to the executive housekeeper. The modern laundry operates computerized washing/drying machines and large presses. Dry cleaning for both guests and employees is a service that may also come under the laundry department.

Some hotels, especially the smaller and older ones, contract out the laundry service. This is because it is costly to alter an existing hotel to provide space for laundry. Even space itself costs money because the space might be otherwise used for revenue-producing purposes, such as meetings, functions, and so on. In addition, by contracting out, the hotel does not have to own its own linen. It may rent linen and be charged for each piece used. However, operators frequently complain that they receive inferior linen and inconsistent service. Another alternative is for the hotel to purchase its own linen and have it laundered by contract. In either case, the executive housekeeper must ensure that strict control is maintained over linen.

The Chicago Hilton and Towers has installed a semicustomized linen-management and inventory-control system that is expected to save the 1,620-room property between $70,000 and $100,000 annually. The system reduces labor costs by eliminating the need to manually sort linen from the different properties that are served. In addition, because the system provides a perpetual inventory, needs can be anticipated better and overtime costs by housekeeping staff can be minimized.[32]

Much of the heavy work in the housekeeping department is conducted by housepersons. They clean public areas using heavy floor polishers for marble or tile floors, vacuum the corridors on the guest room floors, do carpet shampooing and moving of furniture, and, on occasion, take the linen from the linen room to the floors. The houseperson may also assist the housekeepers with spring cleaning and the turning of mattresses.

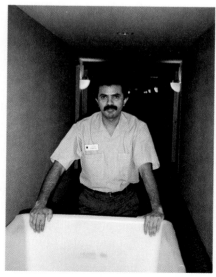

Houseperson

Security/Loss Prevention

The protection of guests and their property is a crucial part of hotel operations. Owner and operators are charged under law to take all reasonable precautions to protect guests from robbery, arson, rape, and other kinds of assault. In addition, innkeepers may be held responsible for injuries to guests during the course of their stay. The courts have awarded huge sums of money to guests that hotels have failed to protect. When a serious incident occurs, it may cost the hotel not only dollars but also its reputation.

Hotel security has to deal with the following responsibilities:

- Emergency procedures
- Guest room security
- Key control
- Loss prevention/locks
- Access
- Alarm systems
- Perimeter control
- Lighting
- Closed circuit
- Safe deposit boxes
- Record keeping

Naturally, prevention is better than cure; thus, the essence of any security program should focus on preventing theft or damage to persons and property.

The security department is largely responsible for reacting to emergency situations. This is an awesome responsibility in today's crime-prevalent society. Most crimes occur between 6:00 P.M. and 3:00 A.M. During this time span, fewer hotel employees are on duty, especially on the guest room floors. Therefore, it is essential for hotels to have established procedures for each kind of emergency.

Guest room security has been upgraded in recent years by the introduction of the electronic room key. This plastic key is encoded at the front desk as the guests check in. These keys are only valid for the duration of the guests' stay and will not open the door after the guests check out. These keys are a definite improvement over a metal key that could easily fall into the wrong hands and allow a thief to gain access to the room at a later date.

Closed circuit television cameras have also helped reduce the number of thefts and assault cases in hotels. Strategically placed cameras will record movements in hotel lobbies, at the cashier's desk, and on the guest room floors. Hidden surveillance cameras are a valuable addition to the security defense. These cameras will also record people's movements without their realizing that they are being observed. These movements are displayed on monitor screens in the security office.

At the Mirage resort hotel in Las Vegas, security concerns are heightened by the cash-intensive casino operation. The Polaroid ID-2000 Plus computer-based electronic security management system plays a central role in supporting the

Mirage's integrated security environment. The system combines advanced database computers and electronic-imaging technologies. This improves efficiency and helps minimize transaction discrepancies.[33]

Lack of security concerning guest room keys is the most serious problem faced by security professionals. In order to prevent problems, the front desk must take inventory of guest room keys whenever guests check out of the hotel. In addition, the front desk staff must verify identity before providing a new key. The most effective way to ensure the security of master keys is to conduct random key checks. Key logs with employees signing keys in and out should be maintained. Some hotels use a card exchange method, whereby employees who require keys are given laminated photo ID cards indicating which keys he or she is permitted to sign out.[34]

In order to reduce robberies, many hotels have installed a personal safe in every guest room in addition to centrally located safe deposit boxes. There are different types of locking devices available: plastic card locks with the combination encoded on them, digital locks with standard numerical keypads on the doors of the safes, or standard key locks equipped with biaxial key locks that can easily be replaced by hotel security.[35]

Trends in Hotel and Rooms Division Operations

- ✔ *Diversity of workforce:* All the pundits are projecting a substantial increase in the number of women and minorities who will not only be taking hourly paid positions, but also supervising and management positions as well.
- ✔ *Increase in use of technology:* Reservations are being made by individuals via the Internet. Travel agents are able to make reservations at more properties. There is increasing simplification of the various property management systems and their interface with POS systems.
- ✔ *Continued quest for increases in productivity:* As pressure mounts from owners and management companies, hotel managers are looking for innovative ways to increase productivity and to measure productivity by sales per employee.
- ✔ *Increasing use of yield management to increase profit by effective pricing of room inventory.*
- ✔ *Greening of hotels and guest rooms:* This includes an increase in recycling and the use of environmentally friendly products, amenities, and biodegradable detergents.
- ✔ *Security:* The survey by the International Hotel Association indicated that guests continue to be concerned about personal security. Hotels are constantly working to improve guest security. For example, one hotel has instituted a womens only floor with concierge and security.

Checking Out a Guest

A guest walked up to the front desk agent in an upscale hotel, ready to check out. As she would normally do when checking out a guest, the agent asked the guest what his room number was. The guest was in a hurry and showed his anxiety by responding, "I stay in a hundred hotel rooms and you expect me to remember my room number?"

The agent then asked for the guest's name, to which he responded, "My name is Mr. Johnstein." After thanking him, the agent began to look for the guest's last name, but the name was not listed in the computer. Because the man had a heavy accent and the agent assumed that she had misunderstood him, she politely asked the guest to spell his last name. He answered, "What? Are you an idiot? The person who checked me in last night had no problem checking me in." Again, the agent looked on the computer to find the guest.

The guest, becoming even more frustrated, said, "I have a plane to catch and it is ridiculous that it has to take this long to check me out. I also need to fax these papers off, but I need to have them photocopied first." The agent responded, "There is a business center at the end of the counter that will fax and photocopy what you need." The guest replied, "If I wanted your opinion, I would have asked you for it. Haven't you ever heard of customer service? Isn't this a five-star hotel? With your bad attitude, you should be working in a three-star hotel. I can't believe they let you work here at the front desk. Haven't you found my name yet?"

The agent, who was beginning to get upset, asked the guest again to spell out his full name. The guest only replied, "Here are my papers I want faxed if you are capable of faxing them." The agent reached to take the papers and the guest shouted, "Don't grab them from my hand! You have a bad attitude, and if I had more time, I would talk to someone about getting you removed from your position to a hotel where they don't require such a level of customer service." The agent was very upset, but kept herself calm in order to prevent the guest from getting angrier.

The agent continued to provide service to the guest, sending the faxes and making the photocopies he had requested. Upon her return, the agent again asked the guest to repeat his last name, since he had failed to spell it out. The guest replied by spelling out his name, "J-o-h-n-s-t-o-n-e." The agent was finally able to find his name on the computer and checked him out, while he continued to verbally attack her. The agent finished by telling the guest to have a nice flight.

Discussion Questions

1. Is it appropriate to have the manager finish the check-out? Or, should the front desk agent just take the heat?
2. Would you have handled the situation in the same manner?
3. What would you have done differently?

Overbooked: The Housekeeping Perspective

It is no secret that in all hotels, the director of housekeeping must be able to react quickly and efficiently to any unexpected circumstances that arise. Stephen Rodondi, executive house-keeper at the Regency in La Jolla, California, usually starts his workday at 8:00 A.M. with a department meeting. These morning meetings help him, and the employees, to visualize their goals for the day. On this particularly busy day, Rodondi arrives at work and is told that three housekeepers have called in sick. This is a serious challenge for the hotel because it is overbooked and has all of its 400 rooms to service.

Discussion Question

1. What should Stephen do to maintain standards and ensure that all the guest rooms are serviced?

Overbooked: The Front Office Perspective

Overbooking is an accepted hotel and airline practice. Many question the practice from various standpoints including ethical and moral. Industry executives argue that there is nothing more perishable than a vacant room. If it is not used, there is no chance to regain lost revenue. Hotels need to protect themselves because potential guests frequently make reservations at more than one hotel or are delayed and, therefore, do not show up.

The percentage of "no-shows" varies by hotel and location, but is often around five percent. In a 400-room hotel, that is twenty rooms, or an average loss of approximately $2,600 per night. Considering these figures, it is not surprising that hotels try to protect themselves by overbooking.

Hotels look carefully at bookings: Who they are for, what rates they are paying, when they were made, whether they are for regular guests or from a major account (a corporation who uses the hotel frequently), etc.

Jill Reynolds, the front office manager at the Regency La Jolla, had known for some time that the 400-room hotel would be overbooked for this one night in October. She prepared to talk with the front desk associates as they came on duty at 7:30 in the morning, knowing it would be a challenge to sell out without "walking" guests. Seldom does a hotel sell out before having to walk a few guests.

The hotel's policy and procedure on walking guests enables the front desk associates to call nearby hotels of a similar category to find out if they have rooms available to sell. If it is necessary to walk a guest, the associate explains to the guest that, regrettably, no rooms are available due to fewer departures than expected. The associate must explain that suitable accommodations have been reserved at a nearby hotel and that the hotel will pay for the room and transportation to and from the hotel. Normally guests are understanding, especially when they realize that they are receiving a free room and free transportation.

On this particular day, the house count indicated that the hotel was overbooked by thirty rooms. Three or four nearby, comparable hotels had rooms available to sell in the morning. Besides walking guests, Jill considered other options, in particular "splitting" the fifteen suites with connecting parlors. If the guests in the suites do not need the parlor, it is then possible to gain a few more "rooms" to sell separately, however roll-away beds must be placed in the rooms. Fortunately, eight parlors were available to sell.

Discussion Question

1. If you were in the same situation, what would you do?

Summary

1. A big hotel is run by a general manager and an executive committee, which is represented by the key executives of all the major departments, such as rooms division, food and beverage, marketing, sales, and human resources.
2. The general manager represents the hotel and is responsible for its profitability and performance. Because of increased job consolidation, he or she also is expected to attract business and to empathize with the cultures of both guests and employees.
3. The rooms division department consists of front office, reservations, housekeeping, concierge, guest services, and communications.
4. The front desk, as the center of the hotel, sells rooms and maintains balanced guest accounts, which are completed daily by the night auditor. The front desk constantly must meet guests' needs by offering services such as mailing, faxing, and messages.
5. The property management system, centralized reservations, and yield management have enabled a hotel to work more efficiently and to increase profitability and guest satisfaction.
6. The communications department, room service, and guest services (such as door attendants, bellpersons, and the concierge) are vital parts of the personality of a hotel.
7. Housekeeping is the largest department of the hotel. The executive housekeeper is in charge of inventory, cleaning, employees, and accident and loss prevention. The laundry may be cleaned directly in the hotel or by a hired laundry service.
8. The electric room key, closed-circuit television cameras, and personal room safes are basic measures to protect the guests and their property.

Review Exercises

1. Briefly define the purpose of a hotel. Why is it important to empathize with the culture of guests?
2. List the main responsibilities of the front office manager.
3. Explain the terms *sell out, American plan,* and *rack rate.*
4. What are the advantages and disadvantages of yield management?
5. Why is the concierge an essential part of the personality of a hotel?
6. Explain the importance of accident and loss prevention. What security measures are taken in order to protect guests and their property?

Key Words and Concepts

Amenities
Average daily rate (ADR)
Central reservations system
Chief accountant/controller
City ledger
Concierge
Confirmed and guaranteed reservations
Daily report
Executive committee
Food and beverage director
General manager
Housekeeping
Human resources director
Inventory control
Marketing and sales director
Property management systems
Reservations
Rev par
Room occupancy percentage
Room rates
Rooms division manager
Security/loss prevention
Yield management

Notes

[1]C. Nebel Eddystone III, *Managing Hotels Effectively: Lessons from Outstanding General Managers.* New York: Van Nostrand Reinhold, 1991, p. 13.

[2]Theodore R. Nathan, *Hotelmanship: A Guide to Hospitality Industry Marketing and Management.* Englewood Cliffs, N.J.: Institute for Business Planning, 1982, p. 16.

[3]Personal conversation with Steve Pelger, General Manager, Hyatt Regency, La Jolla, Calif., November 1994.

[4]Eddystone, op. cit., p. xviii.

[5]Stephen Michaelides, "Narrowing the Margins of Consistency," *Restaurant Hospitality, 76,* 10, October 1992, p. 26.

[6]Stephen G. Michaelides, "The First Resort," *Restaurant Hospitality, 74,* 8, August 8, 1990, pp. 162–166.

[7]Howard Feiertag, "GMs Should Assume Director-of-Sales Duties," *Hotel and Motel Management, 208,* 2, February 1, 1993, p. 14.

[8]Robert Selwitz, "Hoteliers Put Forth Spirited Efforts to Boost Profits," *Hotel and Motel Management, 206,* 15, September 9, 1991, pp. 2, 76.

[9]Ibid.

[10]Kathy Seal, "Westin Kauai Values Values," *Hotel and Motel Management, 206,* 6, April 8, 1991, pp. 2, 68, 82.

[11]PMS is a system of storing and retrieving information on reservations, room availability, room rates. The system may also interface with outlets (restaurants, bars, etc.) for recording guest charges. The accounting functions may also be integrated with a main system. Some hotels may have several systems that interface with one another.

[12]Michael L. Kasavana and Richard M. Brooks, *Managing Front Office Operations.* East Lansing, Mich.: The Educational Institute of the American Hotel and Motel Institute, 1991, p. 112.

[13]Resort Data Processing, Inc., Vail, Colorado 81657.

[14]Brian Katison, "The Politics of PMS," *Hotel and Motel Management, 207,* 11, June 22, 1992, pp. 33–35.

[15]Ibid.

[16]Maryfran Johnson, *ComputerWorld, 26,* 40, October 5, 1992, p. 6.

[17]Megan Row, "The PMS Wars: Holiday and Promos Are Chasing Each Other," *Lodging Hospitality, 48,* 6, June, 1992, p. 32.

[18]Alan Salomon, "Holiday Abuzz with HIRO/ENCORE," *Hotel and Motel Management, 207,* 7, April 27, 1992, pp. 33–34, 60.

[19]Richard Burns, "Lodging," *The American Hotel and Motel Association,* March 1993, p. 19.

[20]Ibid.

21Ibid.

22Pamela A. Weaver and Ken W. McCleary, "Basics Bring 'em Back: Extras Are Appreciated, but Business Travelers Still Value Good Service and Good Management," *Hotel and Motel Management, 206,* 11, June 24, 1991, pp. 29–32, 38.

23Joseph F. Durocher and Neil B. Niman, "Automated Guest Relations That Generate Hotel Reservations," *Information Strategy: The Executives Journal, 7,* 3, Spring 1991, pp. 27–30.

24Shirley Kimes, "The Basics of Yield Management," *The Cornell Hotel Restaurant Administration Quarterly, 30,* 3, November 1989, p. 14.

25Adapted from Michael L. Kasavana and Richard M. Brooks, *Managing Front Office Operations,* 3d ed. East Lansing, Mich.: The Educational Institute of the American Hotel and Motel Association, 1990, p. 390.

26William J. Quain, "Analyzing Sales-Mix Profitability," *The Cornell Hotel and Restaurant Administration Quarterly, 33,* 2, April 1992, pp. 56–62.

27McDowell Bryson and Adele Ziminski, *The Concierge: Key to Hospitality.* New York: John Wiley and Sons, 1992, p. 3.

28Betsy Wade, *The New York Times,* February 21, 1993.

29Nixon O. Jaso, "Your Secrets Are Safe with Me," *Conde' Nast Traveler, 5,* May 1993, p. 26.

30Leslee Jaquette, "St. Francis Caters to Japanese with Guest-Services Program," *Hotel and Motel Management, 207,* 13, July 27, 1992, pp. 6, 29.

31Bryson and Ziminski, op. cit., p. 194.

32Susan M. Bard, "Linen-Management System May Save a Bundle," *Hotel and Motel Management, 206,* 11, June 24, 1991, pp. 27–28.

33Juli Koentopp, "The Mirage Concerning Hotel Security," *Security Management, 36,* 12, December 1992, pp. 54–60.

34Phil Sunstrom, "Unlock the Secret to Key Control," *Security Management, 36,* 11, November 1992, pp. 59–61.

35Joanne A. Straub, "Safe Solution for Hotel Rooms," *Security Management, 36,* 12, December 1992, pp. 51–52.

36Courtesy of Stephen Rodondi, Executive Housekeeper, Hyatt Regency, La Jolla, Calif.

Hotel Operations: Food and Beverage Division

5

After reading and studying this chapter you should be able to do the following:

✔ Describe the duties and responsibilities of a food and beverage director and other key department heads

✔ Describe a typical food and beverage director's day

✔ State the functions and responsibilities of the food and beverage departments

✔ Perform computations using key food and beverage operating ratios

Food and Beverage Management

In the hospitality industry, the food and beverage division is led by the director of food and beverage. She or he reports to the general manager and is responsible for the efficient and effective operation of the following departments:

- ✔ Kitchen/Catering/Banquet
- ✔ Restaurants/Room Service/Minibars
- ✔ Lounges/Bars/Stewarding

The position description for a director of food and beverage is both a job description and a specification of the requirements an individual needs to do the job. Figure 5–1 shows the duties and the average amount of time spent on each one.

In recent years, the skills needed by a food and beverage director have grown enormously, as shown by the following list of responsibilities:

- ✔ Exceeding guests' expectations in food and beverage offerings and service
- ✔ Leadership
- ✔ Identifying trends
- ✔ Finding and keeping outstanding employees
- ✔ Training
- ✔ Motivation
- ✔ Budgeting
- ✔ Cost control
- ✔ Finding profit from all outlets
- ✔ Having a detailed working knowledge of the front of the home operations

These challenges are set against a background of stagnant or declining occupancies and the consequent drop in room sales. Therefore, greater emphasis has been placed on making food and beverage sales profitable. Traditionally, only about 20 percent of the hotel's operating profit comes from the food and beverage divisions. In contrast, an acceptable profit margin from a hotel's food and beverage division is generally considered to be 25 to 30 percent. This figure can vary according to the type of hotel. For example, according to Pannell Kerr Forster, an industry consulting firm, all-suite properties achieve a 7 percent food and beverage profit (probably because of the complimentary meals and drinks being offered to guests).

A typical food and beverage director's day might include the following:

8:30 A.M. Check messages and read logs from outlets and security. Tour outlets, especially the family restaurant (a quick inspection).
Check breakfast buffet, reservations, and shift manager.
Check daily specials.
Check room service.
Check breakfast service and staffing.
Visit executive chef and purchasing director.
Visit executive steward's office to ensure that all the equipment is ready.

POSITION TITLE: *Director of Food and Beverage:*
Food and Beverage
REPORTS TO: *General Manager*

PURPOSE
Directs and organizes the activities of the food and beverage department to maintain high standards of food and beverage quality, service, and merchandising to maximize profits

EXAMPLES OF DUTIES
Average %
of time

10% Plan and direct planning and administration of the food and beverage department to meet the daily needs of the operation

10% Clearly describe, assign, and delegate responsibility and authority for the operation of the various food and beverage subdepartments, for example, room service, restaurants, banquets, kitchens, steward, and so on

10% Develop, implement, and monitor schedules for the operation of all restaurants and bars to achieve a profitable result

10% Participate with the chef and restaurant managers in the creation of attractive menus designed to attract a predetermined customer market

10% Implement effective control of food, beverage, and labor costs among all subdepartments

10% Assist area managers in establishing and achieving predetermined profit objectives and desired standards of quality for food, service, cleanliness, merchandising, and promotion

10% Regularly review and evaluate the degree of customer acceptance of the restaurant and banquet service to recommend to management new operating and marketing policies whenever declining or constant sales imply (1) dissatisfaction by the customers, (2) material change in the make-up of the customer market, or (3) change in the competitive environment

10% Develop (with the aid of subdepartment heads) the operating tools necessary and incidental to modern management principles, for example, budgeting, forecasting, purchase specifications, recipes, portion specifications, menu abstracts, food production control, job descriptions, and so on

10% Continually evaluate the performance and encourage improvement of personnel in the food and beverage department. Planning and administering a training and development program within the department will provide well-trained employees at all levels and permit advancement for those persons qualified and interested in that career development.

Other
Regular attendance in conformance with standards established by management. Employees with irregular attendance will be subject to disciplinary action, up to and including termination of employment.

Due to the cyclical nature of the hospitality industry, employees may be required to work varying schedules to accommodate business needs.

On employment, all employees are required to fully comply with rules and regulations for the safe and efficient operation of facilities. Employees who violate rules and regulations will be subject to disciplinary action, up to and including termination of employment.

Supportive Functions
In addition to performance of the essential functions, employee may be required to perform a combination of the following supportive functions, with the percentage of time performance of each function to be determined solely by the supervisor:

Participate in manager-on-duty coverage program, requiring weekend stayover, constant monitoring, and trouble-shooting problems

Operate word processing program in computer

Perform any general cleaning tasks using standard cleaning products to adhere to health standards

SPECIFIC JOB KNOWLEDGE, SKILLS, AND ABILITIES
The employee must possess the following knowledge, skills, and abilities and be able to explain and demonstrate that he or she can perform the essential functions of the job, with or without reasonable accommodation, using some other combination of skills and abilities:

Considerable skill in complex mathematical calculations without error

Ability to effectively deal with internal and external customers, some of whom will require high levels of patience, information, and the ability to resolve conflicts

Ability to move throughout all food and beverage areas and hospitality suites and continually perform essential job functions

Ability to read, listen, and communicate effectively in English, both verbally and in writing

Ability to access and accurately input information using a moderately complex computer system

Hearing, smelling, tasting, and visual ability to observe and distinguish product quality and detect signs of emergency situations

QUALIFICATION STANDARDS
Education: College degree in related field required. Culinary skills and service background required

Experience: Extensive experience in restaurant, bar, banquet, stewarding, kitchen, sales, catering, and management required

License or certification: No special licenses required

Grooming: All employees must maintain a neat, clean, and well-groomed appearance (specific standards available)

Other: Additional language ability preferred

Courtesy Hilton Hotels.

Figure 5–1 *Job Description of Food and Beverage Director*

	Visit banquet service office to check on daily events and coffee break sequence.
10:00 A.M.	Work on current projects: new summer menu, pool outlet opening, conversion of a current restaurant with a new concept, remodeling of ballroom foyer, installation of new walk-in freezer, analysis of current profit-and-loss (P&L) statements. Plan weekly food and beverage department meetings.
11:45 A.M.	Visit kitchen to observe lunch service and check the "12:00 line," including banquets.
	Confer with executive chef.
	Check restaurants and banquet luncheon service.
	Have working lunch in employee cafeteria with executive chef, director of purchasing, or director of catering.
1:30 P.M.	Visit human resources to discuss current incidents.
2:30 P.M.	Check messages and return calls. Telemarket to attract catering and convention business.
	Conduct hotel daily menu meeting.
3:00 P.M.	Go to special projects/meetings.
	Tour cocktail lounges.
	Check for staffing.
	Review any current promotions.
	Check entertainment lineup.
6:00 P.M.	Check special food and beverage requests/requirements of any VIPs staying at the hotel.
	Tour kitchen.
	Review and taste.
8:00 P.M.	Review dinner specials.
	Check the restaurant and lounges.

A food and beverage director's typical day starts at 8:00 A.M. and ends at 8:00 P.M., unless early or very late events are scheduled, in which case the working day is even longer. Usually, the food and beverage director works Monday through Saturday. If there are special events on Sunday, then she or he works on Sunday and takes Monday off. In a typical week, Saturdays are used to catch up on reading or specific projects.

Food and Beverage Director and Executive Chef Discuss Opeartions

The director of food and beverage eats in his or her restaurants at least twice a week for dinner and at least once a week for breakfast and lunch. Bars are generally visited with clients, at least twice per week. The director sees salespersons regularly, because they are good sources of information about what is going on in the industry and they can introduce leads for business. The director attends staff meetings, food and beverage meetings, executive committee meetings, interdepartmental meetings, credit meetings, and P&L statement meetings.

Food and Beverage Planning

Typically, the monthly forecast for a food and beverage department is prepared between the twelfth and the fifteenth of every month; a budget and forecast for the upcoming years is prepared between July and September. Every January, a planning meeting takes place with all the food and beverage department heads, and the year's special events are planned. These events include Easter, Mother's Day, St. Valentine's Day, St. Patrick's Day, the summer program, Halloween, Thanksgiving, Christmas, New Year's Eve, New Year's Day, and so on.[1]

To become a food and beverage director takes several years of experience and dedication. One of the best routes is to gain work experience or participate in an internship in several food and beverage departments while attending college. This experience should include full-time, practical kitchen work for at least one to two years followed by varying periods of a few months in purchasing, stores, cost control, stewarding,[2] and room service. Additionally, a year spent in each of the following work situations is helpful: restaurants, catering, and bars. After these departmental experiences, a person would likely serve as a department manager, preferably in a different hotel from the one in which the departmental experience was gained. This prevents the awkwardness of being manager of a department in which the person was once an employee and also offers the employee the opportunity to learn different things at different properties. Figure 5–2 shows a career ladder for a food and beverage director.

Kitchen

A hotel kitchen is under the charge of the executive chef; this person, in turn, is responsible to the director of food and beverage for the efficient and effective operation of kitchen food production. The desired outcome is to exceed guests' expectations in the quality and quantity of food, its presentation, taste, and portion size, and to ensure that hot food is served hot and cold food is served cold. The executive chef operates the kitchen in accordance with company policy and strives to achieve desired financial results.

Director of Food and Beverage Go-getters may rise to this position more quickly. It depends on the individual's capability, industry expansion, opportunities, and the labor market.	9 to 15 years
Assistant Food and Beverage Manager	3 to 5 years
Department Manager Kitchen restaurant, room service, stewarding, or cost control	3 to 5 years
Department Experience kitchens, restaurants, lounges, purchasing, cost control, stewarding, room service, and catering	3 to 5 years

Figure 5–2 *Career Ladder to Director of Food and Beverage*

Some executive chefs are becoming kitchen managers; they even serve as food and beverage directors in midsized and smaller hotels. This trend of "right sizing," observed in other industries, euphemistically refers to restructuring organizations to retain the most essential employees. Usually, this means cutting labor costs by consolidating job functions. For example, Michael Hammer is executive chef and food and beverage director at the 440-room Sheraton Grande Torrey Pines Hotel in La Jolla, California. Mike is typical of the new breed of executive chefs: His philosophy is to train his sous chefs—sous being a French word meaning under—to make many of the operating decisions. Mike delegates ordering and hiring and firing decisions; sous chefs are the ones most in control of the group's production and the people who work on their teams. By delegating more of the operating decisions, Mike is developing the chefs de partie (or station chefs) and empowering them to make their own decisions. Mike says, "No decision is wrong—but in case it is unwise, we may talk about it later."

Mike spends time maintaining morale, a vital part of the manager's job. The kitchen staff is under a great deal of pressure and frequently works against the clock. Careful cooperation is the key to success. Mike explains that he does not want his associates to "play the tuba"—he wants them to conduct the orchestra. He does not hold food and beverage department meetings; instead, he meets with groups of employees frequently and problems are handled as they occur. Controls are maintained with the help of software that costs out standard recipes, establishes perpetual inventories,[3] and calculates potential food cost per outlet. Today, executive chefs and food and beverage directors look past food cost to the actual profit contribution of an item. Contribution margin is the dollar differential between the cost and the sales price of a menu item. For example, if a pasta dish costs $2.75 and sells for $8.75, the contribution is $6.00. If a chicken dish costs $3.25 and sells for $12.95 the contribution is $9.70, or $3.70 more. Labor cost benchmarks are measured by covers-per-person-hour. For example, in stewarding, it should take no more than one person hour to clean 37.1 covers.

Executive Chef

Mike and his team of outlet managers have interesting challenges, such as staffing for the peaks and valleys of guests' needs at breakfast. Most guests want breakfast between 7:00 and 8:30 A.M., requiring organization to get the right people in the right place at the right time to ensure that meals are prepared properly and served in a timely manner.

At the Sheraton Grande Torrey Pines, executive chef Mike Hammer's day goes something like the following:

1. Arrive at 6:00 to 7:00 A.M. and walk through the food and beverage department with the night cleaners.
2. Check to make sure the compactor is working and the area is clean.
3. Check that all employees are on duty.
4. Ask people what kind of challenges they will face today.
5. Sample as many dishes as possible, checking for taste, consistency, feel, smell, and overall quality.

Breakfast Service

6. Check walk-ins.
7. Recheck once or twice a day to see where department stands production-wise—this eliminates overtime.
8. Approve schedules for food and beverage outlet.
9. Keep a daily update of food and beverage revenues and costs.
10. Forecast the next day's, week's, and month's business based on updated information.
11. Check on final numbers for catering functions.

Corporate Profile: Four Seasons Regent Hotels

In 1960, Isadore Sharp opened the first Four Seasons Hotel on Jarvis Street in downtown Toronto, Canada. Today, Four Seasons Hotels and Resorts is currently the world's largest operator of medium-sized, luxury hotels, managing thirty-nine hotels in sixteen countries, under the brand names Four Seasons and Regent. Some properties, however, do not carry the brand names, such as the Ritz-Carlton in Chicago and the Pierre in New York.

By retaining absolute control of the company throughout its history, Isadore Sharp has been able to create and maintain a well-defined culture of consistently providing quality and refinement. "Sharp is a perfectionist, and the reputation of the company has grown out of his personality."[1] Sharp has established a "zero defects" culture, in which class is obtained with simplicity, and excellence is clearly distinguished from extravagance. Taste, elegance, and style are defining features of all Four Seasons properties. Their standards of impeccable service are deeply rooted and upheld by all employees and are tailored to appeal to the luxury segment of the business and leisure travel markets.

Isadore Sharp's understanding of what modern travelers want from a hotel has positioned Four Seasons as the first choice of many business travelers. They can expect their check-in to be fast and efficient, the rooms to be luxurious, the laundry to be back on time, and the food to be very good. Genuinely caring about the needs of the guests has led to

the introduction of many innovative services that have made Four Seasons a benchmark for quality and service. For example, the company was the first to introduce in-room amenities and company-wide concierge services.

Quality in every aspect of the business translates into excellent food and beverage. Each of the restaurants in all of the Four Seasons properties were designed to lead the local fine-dining market and to demolish the stereotype of the mediocre, overpriced hotel restaurant.[2] Sharp recalls that when his first hotels were opened, the industry generally considered hotel restaurants a guaranteed loss, thus, the idea was to offer the bare minimum. However, Sharp was a novice in the hotel industry. "We didn't know the rules. Nobody told us that you couldn't make money in a hotel restaurant, so we went out and did it."[3] Four Seasons successfully challenged the hotel food stigma. Its restaurants serve imaginative and attractive dishes that suit the tastes of both the local guests and the international clientele.

Once again, meeting the guests' needs was accomplished in 1984 with the introduction of alternative cuisine—stylish and flavorful items prepared with an eye on proper nutrition—designed for the frequent business traveler who spends many nights in hotel rooms and would appreciate lighter menu options.

Alternative cuisine was conceived by diet and nutrition expert Jeanne Jones, one of the country's leading authors and consultants on the gourmet approach to good

Financial results are generally expressed in ratios, such as food cost percentage—the cost of food divided by the amount of food sales. In its simplest form, an example would be the sale of a hamburger for $1.00. If the cost of the food was $.30 then the food cost percentage would be 30 percent, which is about average for many hotels. The average might be reduced to 27 percent in hotels that do a lot of catering. As discussed later in this section, in determining the food and beverage department's profit and loss, executive chefs and food and beverage directors must consider not only the food cost percentage but also the

---

nutrition, who then passed the concept on to Four Seasons chefs. Alternative cuisine is a method of preparation that creates nutritionally balanced dishes with reduced levels of cholesterol and sodium, without sacrificing quality, originality, taste, or presentation. The principles of alternative cuisine are achieved by:

- ✔ *reducing fats,* using low-fat content ingredients and avoiding high-fat dairy products, oils, mayonnaise, etc.
- ✔ *reducing sodium* by reducing salt, high-sodium foods such as olives, pickles, and Parma ham, and by avoiding any unnatural flavoring
- ✔ *reducing cholesterol* by carefully limiting animal meats, avoiding organ meats, skin of poultry, egg yolks, etc.

Instead, Four Seasons chefs emphasize the use of foods containing animal protein (fish, poultry, and selected meats such as veal, flank steaks, game), complex carbohydrates (vegetables, salads, starch), simple carbohydrates (fruits), and fiber (whole grain breads, rice, pasta, cereal). The lower levels of salt used in alternative cuisine are compensated for by using herbs and reduction to give dishes full aroma and taste. The protein-rich items (meats, fish) are often in smaller quantities to reduce the calorie count and are offered with plenty of vegetables.[4] The results are pleasing to the health-conscious traveler. A typical two-course alternative cuisine lunch can have as few as 500 calories. A three-course dinner can count as little as 650.

Another culinary innovation at Four Seasons-Regent properties is the Home Cooking Program introduced in 1996. The company's chefs recognized that business travelers who are often forced to eat in restaurants while on the road, are almost exclusively exposed to gourmet menu items and would appreciate the chance to choose simpler, "home cooking" dishes. Some of the menu of-

ferings introduced include chicken noodle soup, chicken pot pie, bread pudding, meatloaf and mashed potatoes, and deep-dish apple pie. The program has been very successful so far. At the Four Seasons Hotel Toronto, for example, 60 percent of all room service orders include selections from their "Home Style Classics" menu. The recipes are very often the chefs' own—passed down to them by their grandmothers. At the Four Seasons Hotel Seattle, Executive Chef Sear has introduced recipes that were taught to him by his 101-year-old grandmother, including herb potatoes, pot roast, and steamed batter puddings. Some of Grandmother Sear's recipes date back to World War II, and her cookbook is one of Chef Sear's most prized possessions, to which he often refers.

Tony Ruppe, executive chef at the Four Seasons Hotel Houston, talks about the fundamentals of cooking as he learned them in his grandparents' kitchen in Oklahoma, recalling "the flavor of things, the freshness of vegetables and fruits. Real simple cooking with lots of tender loving care."[5]

These food and beverage innovations have contributed to Four Seasons-Regent Hotel restaurants ranking among the top restaurants in their respective cities. They reflect the company's single-minded commitment to quality and guest satisfaction in all aspects of the hotel experience.

[1]Corby Kummer, "A Man for Four Seasons." *Connoisseur,* February 1990.
[2]James Scarpa, "Rich Harvest." *Restaurant Business,* September 1, 1989.
[3]Ibid.
[4]This section adapted from Four Seasons-Regent Hotels and Resorts News, "Alternative Cuisine."
[5]This section adapted from Four Seasons-Regent Hotel and Resorts News, "Four Seasons Regent Offers Guests a Taste of Home with Its New Home Cooking Program," December 1996.

Personal Profile: Jim Gemignani, Executive Chef

Jim Gemignani is executive chef at the 1,500-room Marriott Hotel in San Francisco. Chef Jim, as his associates call him, is responsible for the quality of food, guest, and associate satisfaction and for financial satisfaction in terms of results. With more than 200 associates in eight departments, Chef Jim has an interesting challenge. He makes time to be innovative by researching food trends and comparative shopping. Currently, American cuisine is in, as are free-standing restaurants in hotels. An ongoing part of American cuisine is the healthy food that Chef Jim says has not yet found a niche.

Hotels are building identity into their restaurants by branding or creating their own brand name. Marriott, for example, has Pizza Hut pizzas on the room service menu. Marriott hotels have created their own tiers of restaurants. JW's is the formal restaurant, Tuscany's is a Northern Italian-themed restaurant, The American Grill has replaced the old coffee shop, and Kimoko is a Japanese restaurant. As a company, Marriott decided to go nationwide with the first three of these concepts.

Jim Gemignani

This has simplified menus and improved food quality and presentation, and yet regional specials allow for individual creativity on the part of the chef.

When asked about his personal philosophy, Chef Jim says that in this day and age, one needs to embrace change and build teams; the guest is an important part of the team. Chef Jim's biggest challenge is keeping guests and associates happy. He is also director of food service outlets, which now gives him a front-of-the-house perspective. Among his greatest accomplishments are seeing his associates develop—twenty are now executive chefs—retaining 96 percent of his opening team, and being voted Chef of the Year by the San Francisco Chef's Association.

Chef Jim's advice: "It's tough not to have a formal education, but remember that you need a combination of 'hands on' and formal training. If you're going to be a leader, you must start at the bottom and work your way up; otherwise, you will become a superior and not know how to relate to your associates."

contribution margin of menu items. Another important cost ratio for the kitchen is labor cost. The labor cost percentage may vary depending on the amount of convenience foods purchased versus those made from scratch (raw ingredients). In a kitchen, this may be expressed as a percentage of food sales. For example:

Food Sales $1,000
Labor Costs $250
The formula is cost/sales × 100 or 250/1,000 = 25 percent labor cost

An executive chef has one or more sous chefs. Because so much of the executive chef's time is spent on administration, sous chefs are often responsible for the day-to-day running of each shift. Depending on size, a kitchen may have several sous chefs: one or more for days, one for evenings, and another for banquets.

Under the sous chefs is the chef tournant. This person rotates through the various stations to relieve the station chef heads, also known as chefs de partie (see Figure 5–3). These stations are organized according to production tasks, based on the classic "brigade" introduced by Escoffier. The brigade includes the following:

English	French	Pronunciation
Sauce chef	Saucier	sau*see*ay
Fish chef	Poissonier	pwa*so*ay
Roast chef	Rotisseur	ro*tee*sur
Relief chef	Tournant	tour*nant
Vegetable chef	Entremetier	aun*tre*me*tee*ay
Pastry chef	Patissier	pa*tis*see*ay
Pantry chef	Garde manger	gard*mon*zhay

Figure 5–3   *Chefs de Partie*

Sauce chef, who prepares sauces, stews, sautes, hot hors d'oeuvres

Roast chef, who roasts, broils, grills, and braises meats

Fish chef, who cooks fish dishes

Soup chef, who prepares all soups

Cold larder/pantry chef, who prepares all cold foods: salads, cold hors d'oeuvres, buffet food, and dressings

Banquets chef, who is responsible for all banquet food

Pastry chef, who prepares all hot and cold dessert items

Vegetable chef, who prepares vegetables (this person may be the fry cook and soup cook in some smaller kitchens)

(Soup, cold larder, banquets, pastry, and vegetable chefs' positions may be combined in smaller kitchens.)

Hotel Restaurants

A hotel may have several restaurants or no restaurant at all; the number and type of restaurants varies as well. A major chain hotel generally has two restaurants: a signature or upscale formal restaurant and a casual coffee-shop type of restaurant. These restaurants cater to both hotel guests and to the general public. In recent years, because of increased guest expectations, hotels have placed greater emphasis on food and beverage preparation and service. As a result, there is an increasing need for professionalism on the part of the hotels' personnel.

Hotel restaurants are run by restaurant managers in much the same way as other restaurants. Restaurant managers are generally responsible for the following:

- ✔ Exceeding guest service expectations
- ✔ Hiring, training, and developing employees
- ✔ Setting and maintaining quality standards
- ✔ Marketing
- ✔ Room service, minibars, or the cocktail lounge
- ✔ Presenting annual, monthly, and weekly forecasts and budgets to the food and beverage director

Hotel Restaurant Lunch Restaurant Veranda, Four Seasons, Milano

Hotel Restaurant Dinner Gardens Restaurant, Four Seasons Los Angeles at Beverly Hills

Some restaurant managers work on an incentive plan with quarterly performance bonuses. Hotel restaurants present the manager with some interesting challenges because hotel guests are not always predictable. Sometimes they will use the hotel restaurants, and other times they will dine out. If they dine in or out to an extent beyond the forecasted number of guests, problems can arise. Too many guests for the restaurants results in delays and poor service. Too few guests means that employees are underutilized, which can increase labor costs unless employees are sent home early. Fortunately, over time, a restaurant manager keeps a diary of the number of guests served by the restaurant on the same night the previous week, month, and year. The number (house count) and type of hotel guest (e.g., the number of conference attendees who may have separate dining arrangements) should also be considered in estimating the number of expected restaurant guests for any meal. This figure is known as the *capture rate,* which when coupled with historic and banquet activity and hotel occupancy, will be the restaurant's basis for forecasting the number of expected guests.

Most hotels find it difficult to coax hotel guests into the restaurants. However, many continuously try to convert food service from a necessary amenity to a profit center. The Royal Sonesta in New Orleans offers restaurant coupons worth $5 to its guests and guests of nearby hotels. Another successful strategy, adopted by the Plaza Athenee in New York, is to show guests the restaurants and explain the cuisine before they go to their rooms. This has prompted most guests to dine in the restaurant during their stay. At the Sheraton Boston Hotel and Towers, the restaurants self-promote by having cooking demonstrations in the lobby: The "onsite" chefs offer free samples to hotel guests.[4]

Progressive hotels, such as the Kimco Hotel, in San Francisco, ensure that the hotel restaurants look like free-standing restaurants with separate entrances. They also charge the restaurants rent and make them responsible for their own profit and loss statements.[5]

Compared with other restaurants, some hotel restaurants offer greater degrees of service sophistication. This necessitates additional food preparation and service skills and training. Compared to free-standing/independent restaurants, it is more difficult for hotel restaurants to operate at a profit. They usually are open from early morning until late at night and are frequently underpatronized by hotel guests who tend to prefer to eat outside of the hotel at independent restaurants.

Bars

Hotel bars allow guests to relax while sipping on a cocktail after a hectic day. This opportunity to socialize for business or pleasure is advantageous for both guests and the hotel. Because the profit percentage on all beverages is higher than on food items, bars are an important revenue source for the food and beverage departments. The cycle of beverages from ordering, receiving, storing, issuing, bar stocking, serving, and guest billing is complex, but, unlike restaurant meals, a beverage can be held over if not sold. An example of a world-famous hotel bar is The King Cole Bar in the St. Regis Hotel in New York City. This bar has been a favored New York "watering hole" of the rich and famous for many years. The talking point of the bar is a painted mural of Old King Cole, the nursery rhyme character.

Bar efficiency is measured by the pour/cost percentage. Pour cost is obtained by dividing the cost of depleted inventory by sales over a period of time. The more frequently the pour cost is calculated, the greater the control over the bar.[6]

Food and beverage directors expect a pour cost of between 16 and 24 percent. Generally, operations with lower pour costs have more sophisticated control systems and a higher-volume catering operation. An example of this would be an automatic system that dispenses the exact amount of beverage requested via a pouring gun, which is fed by a tube from a beverage store. These systems are expensive, but they save money for volume operations by being less prone to pilferage, overpouring, or other tricks of the trade. Their greatest savings comes in the form of reduced labor costs; fewer bartenders are needed to make the same amount of drinks. However, the barperson may still hand pour premium brands for show.

Hotel bars are susceptible to the same problems as other bars. The director of food and beverage must set strict policy and procedure guidelines and see to it that they are followed. In today's litigious society, the onus is on the operator to install and ensure responsible alcohol service. If a guest becomes intoxicated and is involved in an accident, the server of the beverage, the barperson, and the manager may all be liable.

Another risk bars encounter is pilferage. Employees have been known to steal or tamper with liquor; they could, for example, dilute it with water or colored liquids, sell the additional liquor, and pocket the money. There are several other ways to defraud a bar. One of the better-known ways is to overcharge guests for beverages. Another is to underpour, which gives guests less for their money. Some bartenders overpour measures in order to receive larger tips. The best way

Old King Cole Bar, The St. Regis Hotel

to prevent these occurrences is to have a good control system, which should include shoppers—people who are paid to use the bar like regular guests, except they are closely watching the operation.

In a large hotel there are several kinds of bars:

The lobby bar: This convenient meeting place was popularized when Conrad Hilton wanted to generate revenue out of his vast hotel lobby. Lobby bars, when well managed, are a good source of income.

The restaurant bar: Traditionally, this bar is away from the hubbub of the lobby and offers a holding area for the hotel's signature restaurant.

The service bar: In some of the very large hotels, restaurants and room service have a separate backstage bar. Otherwise, both the restaurant and room service are serviced by one of the regular beverage outlets, such as the restaurant bar.

The catering and banquet bar: This bar is used specifically to service all the catering and banquet needs of the hotel. These bars can stretch any operator to the limit. Frequently, several cash bars must be set up at a variety of locations; if cash wines are involved with dinner, it becomes a race to get the wine to the guest before the meal, preferably before the appetizer. Because of the difficulties involved in servicing a large number of guests, most hotels encourage inclusive wine and beverage functions in which the guests pay a little more for tickets that include a predetermined amount of beverage service. Banquet bars require careful inventory control. The bottles should be checked immediately after the function, and, if the bar is very busy, the bar manager should pull the money just before the bar closes. The breakdown of function bars should be done on the spot if possible to help prevent pilferage.

The banquet bar needs to stock not only large quantities of the popular wines, spirits, and beers but also a selection of premium spirits and after-dinner liqueurs. These are used in the ballroom and private dining rooms in particular.

The pool bars: Pool bars are popular at resort hotels where guests can enjoy a variety of exotic cocktails poolside. Resort hotels that cater to conventions often put on theme parties one night of the convention to allow delegates to kick back. Popular themes that are catered around the pool might be a Hawaiian luau, a Caribbean reggae night, Mexican fiesta, or country and western events. Left to the imagination, one could conceive of a number of theme events.

Minibars: Minibars are small, refrigerated bars in guest rooms. They offer the convenience of having beverages available at all times. For security, they have a separate key, which may be either included in the room key envelope at check-in or withheld according to the guest's preference. Minibars are typically checked and replenished on a daily basis. Charges for items used are automatically added to the guest folio.

Night clubs: Some hotels offer guests evening entertainment and dancing. Whether formal or informal, these food and beverage outlets offer a full beverage service. Live entertainment is very expensive. Many hotels are switching to operations with a DJ or where the bar itself is the entertainment (e.g., sports bar). Directors of food and beverage are now negotiating more with live bands, offering them a base pay (below union scale) and a percentage of a cover charge.

Sports bars: Sports bars have become popular in hotels. Almost everyone identifies with a sporting theme, which makes for a relaxed atmosphere that complements contemporary lifestyles. Many sports bars have a variety of games such as pool, football, bar basketball, and so on, which, together with satellite-televised sporting events, contribute to the atmosphere.

Stewarding Department

The chief steward is responsible to the director of food and beverage for the following functions:

✔ Cleanliness of the back of the house (all the areas of the back stage that hotel guests do not see)
✔ Maintaining clean glassware, china, and cutlery for the food and beverage outlets
✔ Maintaining strict inventory control and monthly stock check
✔ Maintenance of dishwashing machines
✔ Inventory of chemical stock
✔ Sanitation of kitchen, banquet isles, storerooms, walk-ins/freezers, and all equipment
✔ Pest control and coordination with exterminating company
✔ Forecasting labor and cleaning supplies

A Chief Steward Checking the Silver Inventory

In some hotels the steward's department is responsible for keeping the kitchen(s) clean. This is generally done at night to prevent disruption of the food production operation. A more limited cleaning is done in the afternoon between the lunch and dinner services. The chief steward's job can be an enormous and thankless task. In hotels this involves cleaning up for several hundred people three times a day. Just trying to keep track of everything can be a headache. Some hotels have different patterns of glasses, china, and cutlery for each outlet. The casual dining room frequently has an informal theme, catering and banqueting a more formal one, and the signature restaurant, very formal place settings. It is difficult to ensure all of the pieces are returned to the correct places. It is also difficult to prevent both guests and employees from taking souvenirs. Strict inventory control and constant vigilance helps keep pilferage to a minimum.

Catering Department

Throughout the world's cultural and social evolution, numerous references have been made to the breaking of bread together. Feasts or banquets are one way to show one's hospitality. Frequently, hosts attempted to outdo one another with the extravagance of their feasts. Today, occasions for celebrations, banquets, and catering include the following:

- State banquets, when countries' leaders honor visiting royalty and heads of state
- National days
- Embassy receptions and banquets
- Business and association conventions and banquets
- Gala charity balls
- Company dinner dances
- Weddings

Catering has a broader scope than banquets. *Banquets* refers to groups of people who eat together at one time and in one place. *Catering* includes a vari-

Catering Office and Director

ety of occasions when people may eat at varying times. However, the terms are often used interchangeably.

For example, catering departments in large, city-center hotels may service the following events in just one day:

✔ A Fortune 500 company's annual shareholders meeting
✔ An international loan-signing ceremony
✔ A fashion show
✔ A convention
✔ Several sales and board meetings
✔ Private luncheons and dinner parties
✔ A wedding or two

Naturally each of these requires different and special treatment. Hotels in smaller cities may cater the local chamber of commerce meeting, a high school prom, a local company party, a regional sales meeting, a professional workshop, and a small exhibition.

Catering may be subdivided into on-premise and off-premise. In off-premise catering, the event is catered away from the hotel. The food may be prepared either in the hotel or at the event. The organization chart in Figure 5–4 shows how the catering department is organized.

The dotted lines show cooperative reporting relationships and continuous lines show a direct reporting relationship. For example, the banquet chef reports directly to the executive chef but must cooperate with the director of catering and the catering service manager.

The director of catering is responsible to the food and beverage director for selling and servicing, catering, banquets, meetings, and exhibitions in a way that exceeds guests' expectations and produces reasonable profit. The director of catering has a close working relationship with the rooms division manager because the catering department often brings conventions, which require rooms, to the hotel. There is also a close working relationship with the executive chef. The chef plans the banqueting menus but the catering manager must ensure that they are suitable for the clientele and practical from a service point of view. Sometimes they work together in developing a selection of menus that will meet all the requirements, including cost and price.

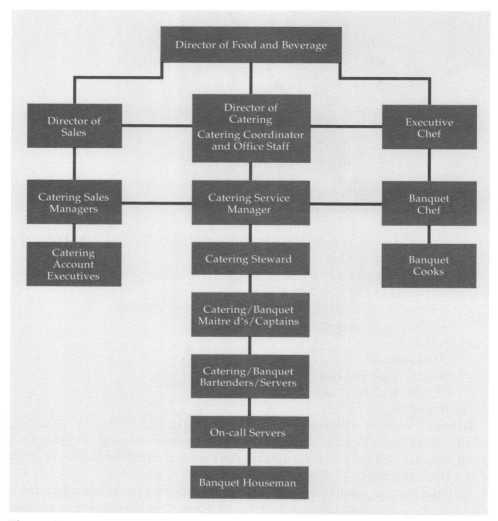

Figure 5–4   *Organization of the Catering Department*

The director of catering must be able to do the following:

1. Sell conventions, banquets, and functions
2. Lead a team of employees
3. Together with input from team members, make up departmental goals and objectives
4. Set individual and department sales and cost budgets
5. Set service standards
6. Ensure that the catering department is properly maintained
7. Be extremely creative and knowledgeable about food, wine, and service
8. Be very well versed in the likes and dislikes of various ethnic groups, especially Jewish, Middle Eastern, and European

Position Profile

The director of catering is required to have a variety of skills and abilities as shown in the following:

Technical
- ✔ A thorough knowledge of food and beverage management including food preparation and service
- ✔ Selling conventions, functions, and banquets
- ✔ The ability to produce profit
- ✔ Setting individual and department sales and cost budgets

Leadership
- ✔ Leading a team of employees
- ✔ Setting departmental mission, goals, and objectives
- ✔ Training the department members in all facets of operations
- ✔ Setting service standards
- ✔ Ensuring that the catering department is properly maintained

The catering department is extremely complex and demanding; the tempo is fast and the challenge to be innovative is always present. The director of catering in a large city hotel should, over the years, build up a client list and an intimate knowledge of the trade shows, exhibitions, various companies, groups, associations, and SMERF organizations (social, military, education, religious, and fraternal market). This knowledge and these contacts are essential to the director of catering's success, as is the selection of the team members.

The main sales function of the department is conducted by the director of catering (DOC) and catering sales managers (CSMs). Their jobs are to optimize guest satisfaction and revenue by selling the most lucrative functions and exceeding guests' food and beverage and service expectations.

The DOC and catering sales managers obtain business leads from a variety of sources, including the following:

The hotel's director of sales: She or he is a good source of event bookings because she or he is selling rooms, and catering is often required by meetings and conventions.

GMs: These are good sources of leads as they are very involved in the community.

The corporate office sales department: If, for example, a convention were held on the East Coast one year at a Marriott hotel and by tradition the association goes to the West Coast the following year, the Marriott hotel in the chosen city will contact the client or meeting planner. Some organizations have a selection of cities and hotels bid for major conventions. This ensures a competitive rate quote for accommodations and services.

The convention and visitors bureau: Here is another good source of leads because its main purpose is to seek out potential groups and organizations to visit that city. In order to be fair to all the hotels, they publish a list of clients and brief details of their requirements, which the hotel catering sales department may follow up on.

Enquiry: Incoming calls
   From prospective clients
   Director of marketing and sales
   Corporate sales office
   Cold calls by catering sales manager to seek prospective clients
Check for space available in the "bible"* or the computer program
Confirm availability and suggest menus and beverages. Invite clients to view hotel when it
   is set up for a similar function
Catering prepares a contract and creates a proposal and a pro-forma invoice for client.
   This enables client to budget for all costs with no surprise.
Catering manager makes any modifications and sends client a contract detailing events,
   menus, beverages, and costs.
Client confirms room booking, menus, and beverages by returning the signed contract.

*The bible is the function book in which a permanent record is maintained of each
function room's availability, tentative booking, or guaranteed booking.

Figure 5–5   *Booking a Function*

Reading the event board of competitive hotels: The event board is generally
   located in the lobby of the hotel and is frequently read by the competition. The CSM then calls the organizer of the event to solicit the business
   the next time.

Rollovers: Some organizations, especially local ones, prefer to stay in the
   same location. If this represents good business for the hotel, then the
   DOC and GM try to persuade the decision makers to use the same hotel
   again.

Cold calls: During periods of relative quiet, CSMs call potential clients to inquire if they are planning any events in the next few months. The point
   is to entice the client to view the hotel and the catering facilities. It is
   amazing how much information is freely given over the telephone.

Figure 5–5 shows the steps involved in booking a function.

The most frequent catering events in hotels are the following:
✔ Meetings
✔ Conventions
✔ Dinners
✔ Luncheons
✔ Weddings

For meetings, a variety of room set-ups are available, depending on a client's
needs. The most frequently selected meeting room set-ups are as follows:

Theater style: Rows of chairs are placed with a center group of chairs and
   two aisles. Figure 5–6 shows a theater-style set-up with equipment centered on an audiovisual platform. Sometimes multimedia presentations,
   requiring more space for reverse image projections, reduce the room's
   seating capacity.

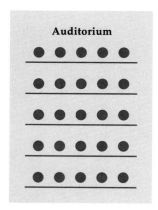

Figure 5–6   *Theater-Style Seating*

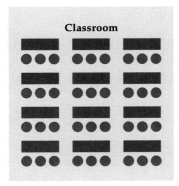

Figure 5–7 *Classroom-Style Seating*

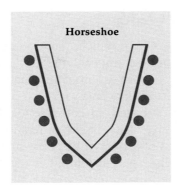

Figure 5–8 *Horseshoe-Style Seating*

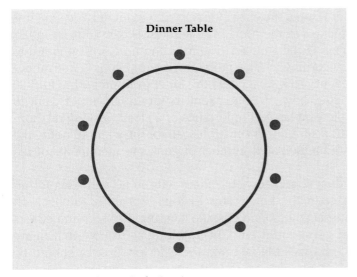

Figure 5–9 *Dinner-Style Seating*

Classroom style: As the name suggests, tables, usually slim 18″ ones, are used because meeting participants need space to take notes. Classroom-style set-up usually takes about three times as much space as theater style, and takes more time and labor to set up and break down. Figure 5–7 shows a classroom-style set-up.

Horseshoe style: This type of meeting set-up (Figure 5–8) is frequently used when interaction is sought among the delegates, such as training sessions and workshops. The presenter or trainer stands at the open end of the horseshoe with a black or white board, flip chart, overhead projector, and video monitor and projector.

Dinner style: Dinners are generally catered at round tables of eight or ten persons for large parties and on boardroom-style tables for smaller numbers. Of course, there are variations of this set-up (see Figure 5–9).

Catering Event Order

A catering event order (CEO), which may also be called a banquet event order (BEO), is prepared/completed for each function to inform not only the client but also the hotel personnel about essential information (what needs to happen and when) to ensure a successful event.

The CEO is prepared based on correspondence with the client and notes taken during the property visits. Figure 5–10 shows a CEO and lists the room's layout and decor, times of arrival, if there are any VIPs and what special attention is required for them, i.e., reception, bar times, types of beverages and service, cash or credit bar, time of meal service, the menu, wines, and service details. The catering manager or director confirms the details with the client. Usually, two copies are sent, one for the client to sign and return and one for the client to keep.

An accompanying letter thanks the client for selecting the hotel and explains the importance of the function to the hotel. The letter also mentions the guaranteed-number policy. This is the number of guests the hotel will prepare to serve, and will charge accordingly. The guaranteed number is given about seven days prior to the event. This safeguards the hotel from preparing for 350 people and having only 200 show up. The client, naturally, does not want to pay for an extra 150 people—hence the importance of a close working relationship with the client. Contracts for larger functions call for the client to notify the hotel of any changes to the anticipated number of guests in increments of ten or twenty.

Experienced catering directors ensure that there will be no surprises for either the function organizer or the hotel. This is done by calling to check on how the function planning is going. One mistake catering directors sometimes make is accepting a final guest count without inquiring as to how that figure was determined. This emphasizes the fact that the catering director should be a consultant to the client. Depending on the function, the conversion from invitations to guests is about 50 percent. Some hotels have a policy of preparing for about three to five percent more than the anticipated or guaranteed number. Fortunately, most events have a prior history. The organization may have been at a similar hotel in the same city or across the country. In either case, the catering director or manager will be able to receive helpful information from the catering director of the hotel where the organization's function was held previously.

The director of catering holds a daily or weekly meeting with key individuals who will be responsible for upcoming events. Those in attendance should be the following:

Director of catering
Executive chef and/or banquet chef
Beverage manager or catering bar manager
Catering managers
Catering coordinator
Director of purchasing

SHERATON GRANDE TORREY PINES
BANQUET EVENT ORDER

POST AS:	U.S.I.U. WELCOME BREAKFAST	CHERI WALTER
EVENT NAME:	MEETING	
GROUP:	UNITED STATES INTERNATIONAL UNIVERSITY	
ADDRESS:	10455 POMERADO ROAD	BILLING:
	SAN DIEGO, CA 92131	
PHONE:	(619) 635-4627	DIRECT BILL
FAX:	(619) 635-4528	
GROUP CONTACT:	Dr. John Walker	**Amount Received:**
ON-SITE-CONTACT:	same	

DAY	DATE	TIME	FUNCTION	ROOM	EXP	GTE	SET	RENT
Wed	January 25, 1995	7:30 AM – 12:00 PM	Meeting	Palm Garden	50			250.00

BAR SET UP:

N/A

WINE:

FLORAL:

MENU:

MUSIC:

7:30 AM CONTINENTAL BREAKFAST

Freshly Squeezed Orange Juice, Grapefruit Juice and
   Tomato Juice
Assortment of Bagels, Muffins, and Mini Brioche
Cream Cheese, Butter, and Preserves
Display of Sliced Seasonal Fruits
Individual Fruit Yogurt
Coffee, Tea, and Decaffeinated Coffee

PRICE:_____

AUDIO VISUAL:
–OVERHEAD PROJECTOR/SCREEN
–FLIPCHART/MARKERS
–VCR/MONITORS

PARKING:

HOSTING PARKING, PLEASE PROVIDE VOUCHERS

11:00 AM BREAK

Refresh Beverages as needed

LINEN:
HOUSE

SETUP:
–CLASSROOM-STYLE SEATING
–HEAD TABLE FOR 2 PEOPLE
–APPROPRIATE COFFEE BREAK SETUP
–(1) 6' TABLE FOR REGISTRATION AT ENTRANCE
   WITH 2 CHAIRS, 1 WASTEBASKET

All food and beverage prices are subject to an 18% service charge and 7% state tax. Guarantee figures, cancellations, changes must be given 72 hours prior or the number of guests expected will be considered the guarantee. To confirm the above arrangements, this contract must be signed and returned.

ENGAGOR SIGNATURE _____ DATE _____

BEO # 003069

Figure 5–10 *Catering Event Order* (Courtesy of Sheraton Grande Torrey Pines.)

Chief steward
Audiovisual representative

The purpose of this meeting is to avoid any problems and to be sure that all the key staff know and understand the details of the event and any special needs of the client.

Catering Coordinator

The catering coordinator has an exacting job in managing the office and controlling the "bible" or function diary. She or he must see that the contracts are correctly prepared and check on numerous last-minute details, such as whether or not flowers and menu cards arrive.

Catering Services Manager

The catering services manager (CSM) has the enormous responsibility of delivering higher-than-expected service levels to guests. The CSM is in charge of the function from the time the client is introduced to the CSM by the director of catering or catering manager. This job is very demanding because several functions always occur simultaneously. Timing and logistics are crucial to the success of the operation. Frequently, there are only a few minutes between the end of a day meeting and the beginning of the reception for a dinner dance.

The CSM must be liked and respected by guests and at the same time be a superb organizer and supervisor. This calls for a person of outstanding character and leadership—management skills that are essential for success. The CSM has several important duties and responsibilities including the following:
- Directing the service of all functions
- Supervising the catering housepersons in setting up the room
- Scheduling the banquet captains and approving the staffing levels for all events
- Cooperating with the banquet chef to check menus and service arrangements
- Checking that the client is satisfied with the room set-up, food, beverages, and service
- Checking last-minute details
- Making out client bills immediately after the function. Adhering to all hotel policies and procedures that pertain to the catering department. This includes responsible alcoholic beverage service and adherence to fire code regulations.
- Calculating and distributing the gratuity and service charges for the service personnel
- Coordinating the special requirements with the DOC catering manager and catering coordinator

Room Service/In-Room Dining

The term *room service* has for some time referred to all service to hotel guest rooms. Recently, some hotels have changed the name of room service to *in-room dining* to present the service as more upscale. The intention is to bring the dining experience to the room with quality food and beverage service.

A survey of members of the American Hotel and Motel Association showed that 56 percent of all properties offer room service and that 75 percent of airport properties provide room service. Generally, the larger the hotel and the higher the room rate, the more likely it is that a hotel will offer room service.

Economy and several midpriced hotels avoid the costs of operating room service by having vending machines on each floor and food items like pizza or Chinese food delivered by local restaurants. Conversely, some hotels prepare menus and lower price structures that do not identify the hotel as the provider of the food. As a result, the guests may have the impression that they are ordering from an "outside" operation when they are in fact ordering from room service.

The level of service and menu prices will vary from hotel to hotel. The Sheraton Grande at Torrey Pines, California, has butler service for all guest rooms without additional charge. This has become the trademark of the hotel.[7]

A few years ago, room service was thought of as a necessary evil, something that guests expected, but which did not produce profit for the hotel. Financial pressures have forced food and beverage directors to have this department also contribute to the bottom line. The room service manager has a difficult challenge running this department, which is generally in operation between sixteen and twenty-four hours a day. Tremendous effectiveness is required to make this department profitable. Nevertheless, it can be done. Some of the challenges in operating room service are as follows:

Delivery of orders on time—this is especially important for breakfast, which
  is by far the most popular room service meal
Making room service a profitable food and beverage department
Avoiding complaints of excessive charges for room service orders

Butler Service

There are many other challenges in room service operation. One is forecasting demand. Room service managers analyze the front desk forecast, which gives details of the house count and guest mix—convention, group, and others for the next two weeks. The food and beverage forecast will indicate the number of covers expected for breakfast, lunch, and dinner. The convention resumés will show where the convention delegates are having their various meals. For example, the number of in-house delegates attending a convention breakfast can substantially reduce the number of room service breakfast orders. Experience enables the manager to check if a large number of guests are from different time zones, such as the West or East coasts or overseas. These guests have a tendency to either get up much earlier or much later. This could throw room service demands off balance. Demand also fluctuates between weekdays and weekends; for example, city hotels may cater to business travelers, who tend to require service at about the same time. However, on weekends, city hotels may attract families, who will order room service at various times. Resort guests, usually couples and families, are more relaxed and less likely to require twenty-four-hour room service. At airport hotels, however, people come and go and want to eat at all times.[8]

Once the forecast has been determined, the manager can begin to plan to meet the expected demand. The challenge of planning for the room service operation includes the following:

Planning the amount of equipment that will be required. Items like room service carts, trays, and cutlery need to be considered.

Staffing schedules need to be carefully planned so as to ensure maximum efficiency. A balance needs to be struck between having people standing around and being rushed off their feet. When planning the schedule, managers check the work load on the forecasts to determine how many different types of set-ups will be required (e.g., how many executive bars will have to be set up and replenished with fresh garnishes and ice, how many in-room dinners are expected, and how many amenities will need to be made up and placed in guest rooms).

The room service menu requires careful planning. The challenge here is that the food must not only keep its presentation, but it must also have longevity. Room service menus are generally quite mainstream because of the wide variety of guests. Even in a five-star hotel, it is virtually impossible to take hamburgers off the menu because hamburgers are a favorite food item for children. Most dishes that room service offers are items selected from the restaurant menu, thereby avoiding too much additional preparation.

Pricing the menu calls for judgment and a balancing act between charging a realistic amount and having prices appear too high, which might discourage guests from ordering.

In a structured environment, the organizational challenge of room service management consists of mise en place, arranging everything in the correct place and ready for action. The system for guests' ordering is organized in two main ways: by telephone and by doorknob hangers for breakfast orders. The room service order taker takes the order and makes out a bill, giving one copy to the kitchen and one to the servers. During quieter periods, the room service order taker helps with setting up the trays and carts. Running an operation in which each person has set duties contributes to the efficient running of the department.

To avoid problems with late delivery of orders, a growing number of hotels have dedicated elevators to be used only by room service during peak periods. At the 550-room Intercontinental Hotel in London, up to 350 room service breakfasts are served per day; there the elevator is a mobile continental breakfast service kitchen. At the 565-room Stouffer Riviera Chicago, director of food and beverage Bill Webb has a solution: Rapid action teams (RAT) are designated food and beverage managers and assistants who can be called on when room service orders are heavy.

Westin Hotels recently introduced Service Express, an innovation that allows a customer to address all needs (room service, housekeeping, laundry, and other services) with a single call. In addition, new properties are designed with the room service kitchen adjacent to the main kitchen so that a greater variety of items can be offered.

Hotels are also looking at sous-vide (airtight pouches of prepared food that can be quickly reheated). The food quality is good and the food can be prepared in advance during quiet times. Sous-vide works well for fish and almost anything except grilled dishes; it could streamline late-night service, especially at airport hotels, where a layover can mean one hundred people clamoring for dinner at midnight.

Some properties, in an effort to make room service more cost effective, have introduced more vending machines on guest floors. This gives guests a wider selection of food and beverage items at a lower cost without waiting.[9]

The challenge of speedy and accurate communication is imperative to a successful room service operation. This begins with timely scheduling and ends with happy guests. In between is a constant flow of information that is communicated by the guest, the order taker, the cook, and the server.

Another challenge is to have well-trained and competent employees in the room service department. From the tone of voice of the order taker and the courteous manner with which the order is taken to the panache of the server for the VIP dinners, training makes the difference between ordinary service and outstanding service. With training, which includes menu tasting with wine and suggestive selling, an order taker becomes a room service salesperson. This person is now able to suggest cocktails or wine to complement the entree, and can entice the guest with tempting desserts. The outcome of this is to increase the average guest check. Training also helps the set-up and service personnel hone

1. Make sure the table is properly set, and the order is correct before knocking on the door.

2. Knock on the door three times and immediately say "Good evening. This is room service."

3. As the guest opens the door, greet the guest appropriately. Always ask if you may enter.

4. On entering the room, ask the guest where she or he would like to dine this evening.

5. Present the order, and recommend other menu items.

6. Ask whether the guest would prefer the entrees to remain in the hot box if the order has salads or appetizers. If so, extinguish the sterno in the hot box and explain its use. If the guest would like you to take out the hot box, do so, but in a conservative manner. Never lift the hot box over the table and/or guest. Leave a service towel for the guest.

7. During this entire time it is important to mention that the room service server should be reading the customer they are servicing. Always remain courteous and friendly.

8. Ask the guest if he or she would like the wine opened and poured. Ask the same for beer, coffee/tea, soda, and so on.

9. On exiting, ask the guest to call room service for removal of tray/table, or if any further assistance is needed. Thank them for using room service.

Figure 5–11   *Evening Room Service*

their skills to enable them to become productive employees who are proud of their work.

An example of the steps of service for an evening room service associate is given in Figure 5–11.

Trends in Food and Beverage Operations

- ✔ The use of branded restaurants instead of hotels operating their own restaurants.
- ✔ Hotels opting not to offer food and beverage outlets. These are usually smaller to midsized properties that may have restaurants on the same lot nearby.
- ✔ Making restaurants and beverage outlets more casual.
- ✔ Using themes for a restaurant. For example, one major hotel chain has adopted a northern Italian theme in all of its restaurants.
- ✔ Standardized menus for all hotel restaurants in a chain.
- ✔ Many hotels are converting one of the beverage outlets into a sports-themed bar.

Ensuring Guest Satisfaction

The Sunnyvale Hotel is operated by a major hotel management corporation. In order to ensure guest satisfaction, 300 survey forms each containing sixty-five questions are mailed to guests each month. Normally, about seventy of the forms are returned. The hotel company categorizes the guest satisfaction scores obtained into colored zones with green being the best, then clear and yellow, and red being the worst. Scores can be compared with those of equivalent hotels.

The most recent survey indicated a significant decline for the Sea Grill Restaurant with scores in the red zone. Guests' concerns were in the following areas: hostess attentiveness, spread of service, and quality of food.

Upon investigation, the director of food and beverage also realized that the name of the restaurant, "Sea Grill," was not appropriate for the type of restaurant being operated. When asked, some guests commented that "it's a bit odd to eat breakfast in a fish place."

Discussion Question

1. What would you do, as director of food and beverage, to get the guest satisfaction scores back into the clear or green zones?

Friday Evening at the Grand Hotel's Casual Restaurant

Karla Gomez is the supervisor at the Grand Hotel's casual restaurant. Karla's responsibilities include overseeing five servers and two bussers, seating guests, and taking reservations. One Friday evening, the restaurant was very busy—all twenty tables were occupied, there was a substantial wait-list, and there were people on standby. The service bar was almost full of guests and most of the seated guests in the dining area had finished their entrees or were just beginning their desserts. They were not leaving, however, in part because of cold, rainy weather outside. The guests did not seem to be in a rush to leave the restaurant, but several of the guests waiting for tables were complaining about the long wait.

Discussion Question

1. What can Karla do to solve the problem?

Summary

1. The food and beverage department division is led by the director of food and beverage, who is responsible for the efficient operation of kitchen, catering, restaurants, bars, and room service; in addition, the director has to keep up with trends and preplan for special events.
2. A hotel kitchen is the responsibility of the executive chef, who is in charge of the quality and quantity of food, organization of the kitchen and his or her sous-chefs, administrative duties, and careful calculation of financial results.
3. A hotel usually has a formal and a casual restaurant, which are either directly connected to the hotel or operated separately.
4. Bars are an important revenue source for a hotel, but they must adhere to strict guidelines to be profitable. Commensurate with its size, a hotel might have several kinds of bars, such as a lobby bar, restaurant bar, mini-bar, or even a night club.
5. The chief steward has the often unrewarded job of cleaning the kitchen, cutlery, plates, glasses, and back-stage of the hotel and is in charge of pest control and inventory.
6. Catering is subdivided into on-premise and off-premise occasions, which may include meetings, conventions, dinners, luncheons, and weddings. According to the occasion, the type of service and room set-up may vary. It involves careful planning and the interaction and cooperation of many people.
7. Room service offers the convenience of dining in the room, with quality food and beverage service, at a price acceptable to both the guest and the hotel.

Review Exercises

1. Briefly describe the challenges a food and beverage director faces on a daily basis.
2. List the measures used to determine the food and beverage department's profit and loss.
3. Explain the problems a hotel faces in making the following departments profitable: restaurants, bars, and room service.
4. Explain the importance of the catering department for a hotel and list the responsibilities of a catering sales manager.

Key Words and Concepts

Capture rate
Catering
Chefs de partie
Chief steward
Contribution margin
Director of food and beverage
Executive chef/kitchen manager
Food cost percentage
Lounges/bars
Pilferage
Pour/cost percentage
Profit
Ratios
Responsible alcoholic beverage service
Room service/minibars
Sous chefs
Stewarding

Notes

[1]Personal conversation with Evan Julian, director of food and beverage, San Diego Hilton, May 1993.

[2]Stewarding is responsible for back-of-the-house areas such as dishwashing, issuing and inventory of china, glassware, and cutlery. Stewarding duties include maintaining cleanliness in all areas.

[3]A perpetual inventory establishes a minimum inventory level at which time an order is automatically placed, avoiding shortages.

[4]Robert Selwitz, "Keeping Guests as Diners: Hotels Use a Variety of Efforts to Fill In-House Restaurants," *Hotel and Motel Management,* June 10, 1991, pp. 59–60.

[5]John Jesitus, "Hotels Take Various Approaches in Effort to Spice up Food-and-Beverage Profits," *Hotel and Motel Management,* September 7, 1992, pp. 47–48.

[6]Robert Plotkin, "Beverages: Stop Pouring Profits down the Drain," *Restaurant Hospitality,* February 1992, pp. 136–145.

[7]Ann Spiselman, "Speed and Quality in Room Service," *Hotels, 27,* 4, April 1993, p. 60.

[8]Ibid.

[9]This section draws on Spiselman, op. cit.

The Restaurant Business: Development and Classification

6

After reading and studying this chapter you should be able to do the following:

✔ Trace the history and development of the restaurant business

✔ List factors that influence restaurant concept and marketing

✔ Discuss the important elements in menu planning

✔ List the classifications of restaurants

✔ Outline the development of a restaurant chain

✔ Describe the different characteristics of chain and independent restaurants

✔ Identify some of the top chain and independent restaurants

Restaurant Development

Restaurants play an important role in society. Dining out in restaurants fulfills an important sociological need. People need not only nourishment, but also the social interaction that takes place in a restaurant setting. Restaurants are one of the few places where we use all of our senses to enjoy the experience. Our taste, sight, smell, hearing, and touch are all employed to savor the food, service, and atmosphere of the restaurant.

The successful operation of a restaurant is dependent on a number of factors. From the restaurant's operating philosophy to controls, and all the factors in between, it is not easy to succeed in operating restaurants. This chapter covers many of the factors that are necessary ingredients in the successful operation of a restaurant.

Operating Philosophy

At the heart of an enterprise is the philosophy of the owner or operator. The philosophy represents the way the company does business. It is an expression of the ethics, morals, and values by which the company operates.

Mission, Goals, and Objectives

Many companies have formal mission statements that explain their reason for being in business. Red Lobster's mission statement (Figure 6–1) is a good example of a restaurant's mission.

Restaurant Market

The market is composed of those guests who will patronize the restaurant. A prospective restaurant owner will analyze the market to determine whether sufficient demand exists in a particular market niche, such as Italian or Southern cuisines. A *niche* is a marketing term used to describe a specific share or slot of a certain market. A good indication of the size of the market can be ascertained by taking a radius of from one to five miles around the restaurant. The distance will vary according to the type and location of the restaurant. In Manhattan, it may only be a few blocks, whereas in rural West Virginia it may be a few miles. The area that falls within the radius is called the *catchment area*. The demographics of the population within the catchment area is analyzed to reveal age, number of people in various age brackets, sex, ethnicity, religion, income levels, and so on. This information is usually available from the chamber of commerce or data at the local library or real estate offices.

One yardstick used to determine the potential viability of a restaurant is to divide the number of restaurants in the catchment area by the total population. The average number of people per restaurant in the United States is about 500.

Red Lobster's mission is to provide every guest with a dining experience that exceeds expectations and ensures their return.

We serve a variety of attractive, excellent tasting food in a comfortable, inviting atmosphere.

We offer a wide range of competitive prices that provide exceptional value.

Our service is professional, knowledgeable, and friendly.

We are committed to the success of the individual, their quality of life, and to providing opportunities for recognition and professional growth and development.

We are an industry leader in providing growth and returns to our shareholders.

We are America's favorite seafood restaurant and a top choice for full-service dining.

Figure 6–1 *Mission Statement of Red Lobster Restaurants*

Perhaps this kind of saturation is one of the reasons for the high failure rate of restaurants. Obviously, each area is different; one location may have several Italian restaurants but no Southern restaurant. Therefore, a Southern restaurant would be unique in the market and, if properly positioned, may have a competitive advantage. If someone in the catchment area wanted to eat Italian food, he or she would have to choose among the various Italian restaurants. In marketing terms, the number of potential guests for the Italian restaurants would be divided by the number of Italian restaurants to determine *fair market share* (the average number of guests that would, if all other things were equal, eat at any one of the Italian restaurants). Figure 6–2a shows 1,000 potential guests. If they all decided to eat Italian in the fair market share scenario, each restaurant would receive one hundred guests. In reality, we know this does not happen—for various reasons, one restaurant becomes more popular. The number of guests that this and the other restaurants receive then is called the *actual market share*. Figure 6–2b shows an example of the actual market share that similar restaurants might receive.

Restaurant Concept

Successful restaurant concepts are created with guests in mind. All too frequently someone thinks it would be a good idea to open up a particular kind of restaurant, only to find there are insufficient guests to make it viable.

For the winners, creating and operating a restaurant business is fun—lots of people coming and going, new faces, old friends. Restaurants provide a social gathering place where employees, guests, and management can get their adrenaline flowing in positive ways. The restaurant business is exciting and

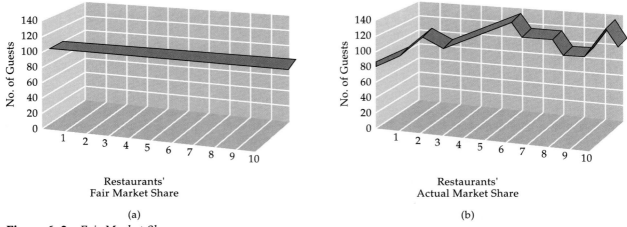

Figure 6–2 *Fair Market Share*

challenging; with the right location, food, atmosphere, and service it is possible to attract the market and make a good return on investment.

There are several examples of restaurant concepts that have endured over the past few decades. Applebee's, Chart House, Hard Rock Cafe, Olive Garden, Red Lobster, and TGI Friday's are some of the better-known U.S. chain restaurant concepts. Naturally, there are more regional and independent concepts.

The challenge is to create a restaurant concept and bring it into being, a concept that fits a definite market, a concept better suited to its market than that presented by competing restaurants.[1] Every restaurant represents a concept and projects a total impression or an image. The image appeals to a certain market—casual, formal, children, adults, ethnic, and so on. The concept should fit the location and reach out to its target market. A restaurant's concept, location, menu, and decor should intertwine.[2]

In restaurant lingo, professionals sometimes describe restaurants by the net operating percentage that the restaurant makes. TGI Friday's, for example, are usually described as 20 percent restaurants. A local restaurant may be only a 10 percent restaurant.

In order for the operation of a restaurant to be successful, the following factors need to be addressed:

✔ Mission
✔ Goals
✔ Objectives
✔ Market
✔ Concept
✔ Location
✔ Menu planning
✔ Ambiance
✔ Lease
✔ Other occupational costs

The odds in favor of being a big restaurant winner are not good. Approximately 540,000 commercial restaurants do business in the United States. Each

Corporate Profile: Planet Hollywood

Although not one of the largest restaurant chains, Planet Hollywood is undoubtedly one of the most successful and most popular restaurant companies. Robert Earl became well known for developing Great American Disaster in London during the late 1960s. At the time, it was impossible to get American food in London. After a brief, but successful, career with Hard Rock Cafe, he launched Planet Hollywood in Manhattan in 1991.

Planet Hollywood bills it-self as a theme restaurant that mixes entertainment—loud music, videos, and displays of Hollywood memorabilia—with standard fare like pizza, hamburgers, and pasta.[1] To create this show business atmosphere, Planet Hollywood's architect, David Rockwell, designed all restaurants with the idea of keeping the design fresh without overwhelming the guests with memorabilia. This creates an overall experience that is comfortable as well as exciting.

Backed by movie stars Bruce Willis, Arnold Schwarzenegger, Demi Moore, Sylvester Stallone, and Whoopi Goldberg, Earl has opened fifty-five restaurants around the world. The investment by Hollywood movie stars is indeed a great advantage for the restaurant chain. In addition to being present at every new opening, they occasionally dine at some of their restaurants. The possibility of meeting a movie celebrity, however slim it may be, is a strong force that attracts the public.

Location is also a significant factor in Planet Hollywood's success. The units are usually opened in prime locations that provide a high traffic of both tourists and residents within the catchment area. The inviting design and the well-known logo of Planet Hollywood make it extremely difficult for passersby to ignore the restaurant.

Although the main appeal of a theme restaurant like Planet Hollywood is the glamour, the excitement, and the endless distraction of Hollywood, the quality of the food served is not overlooked. Robert Earl says, "People don't eat themes—no concept in the world can succeed for long unless it also delivers great food at the right price." Beany MacGregor is the man responsible for the planning, testing, and implementation of Planet Hollywood's menu. According to MacGregor, "The first thing we tried to do was to identify who our customers would be. We wanted to be more than hamburgers and barbecue—we played with pastas, Cajun food, even California-light cuisine." The principle of matching the menu with the taste of the market resulted in some Planet Hollywood locations, among them the Beverly Hills, Paris, and New Orleans units, actually modifying their menu to accommodate the preferences of the local customers.

Unlike many restaurants, Planet Hollywood receives almost 40 percent of its sales from related merchandise. A $16 T-shirt has a pretax margin of 40 percent, nearly twice that of the average food tab of $16 per person.

Robert Earl sees potential for more than 300 restaurants worldwide. The company's new chain of sports-themed restaurants, Official All Star Cafe, features such icon investors as Andre Agassi, Ken Griffey Jr., Joe Montana, and Shaquille O'Neal. Earl's ambitious growth plans of 35 to 40 percent per year in both number of restaurants and earnings per share, may be too ambitious. Ron Paul, president of Technomic, a food industry consulting firm in Chicago, says that for that kind of growth, you need trophy locations, because you need volume on a year-round basis. However, trophy locations run out sooner or later. In 1996, about 35 percent of sales came from just four of its forty-five units—Orlando, London, New York City, and Las Vegas. The Orlando restaurant alone generates about $50 million in sales.[2] The Las Vegas Planet Hollywood is the result of a partnership with Caesars World Inc., which may be the beginning of Planet Hollywood's venture into the gaming and hotel industry, a trend that has already been seen with Hard Rock Cafe.

Diversification and the tapping of a larger market may be the key to Planet Hollywood's future success, especially in an industry that is constantly faced with shifts in consumer demands and changes in the trends people follow when choosing a theme restaurant.

[1] Reed Abelson, "At the Gate: Getting a Grip on the Value of a Glorious New Act," *New York Times*, March 10, 1996, p. PF3.
[2] Herb Greenberg, "Is This Company Really Worth $2.5 billion? Earth to Planet Hollywood," *Fortune*, December 23, 1996.

year, thousands of new ones open and thousands more close, and even more change ownership for cents on the dollar. The restaurant business is relatively easy to enter, but it is deceptively difficult to succeed in it.[3]

The restaurant concept is undoubtedly one of the major components of any successful operation. Some restaurants are looking for a concept; some concepts are searching for a restaurant.

In New York, the Restaurant Associates own and operate Rockefeller Plaza's American Festival Cafe, SeaGrill, and Savories. The Associates' latest concept is Cucina & Co., located in the Pan Am Building in New York City. Restaurant Associates plans to create an 11,000-square-foot Grand Grill multiconcept restaurant. The theme depicts the great Pan Am Clipper terminals reminiscent of the roaring twenties, with a Grand Cafe featuring a Parisian brasserie concept adjacent to the restaurant.

The Associates also have in the works a scaled-down version of Panevino, a Tuscan farmhouse concept. When asked what trends and opportunities are emerging in the industry, Restaurant Associate Nick Valenti says, "In urban locations, I'm thinking about high-quality takeout and elements of self-service in a concept. In both urban and suburban areas, it might be time to redefine the coffee shop. Stick with traditional fare but upgrade the ingredients considerably. For instance, club sandwiches should be served with fresh turkey, ripe tomatoes, and bread toasted to order."[4]

Restaurant Location

The restaurant concept must fit the location, and the location must fit the concept (see Figure 6–3). The location should appeal to the target market (expected guests). Other things being equal, prime locations cost more, so operators must either charge more for their menu items or drive sufficient volume to keep the rent/lease costs to between five and eight percent of sales.

Key location criteria include the following:

- ✔ Demographics—How many people are there in the catchment area?
- ✔ The average income of the catchment area population
- ✔ Growth or decline of the area
- ✔ Zoning, drainage, sewage, and utilities
- ✔ Convenience—How easy is it for people to get to the restaurant?
- ✔ Visibility—Can passersby see the restaurant?
- ✔ Accessibility—How accessible is the restaurant?
- ✔ Parking—Is parking required? If so, how many spaces are needed and what will it cost?
- ✔ Curbside appeal—How inviting is the restaurant?
- ✔ Location—How desirable is the neighborhood?

Several popular types of restaurant locations include the following:

- ✔ Stand-alone restaurants
- ✔ Cluster or restaurant row
- ✔ Shopping mall
- ✔ Shopping mall—free standing

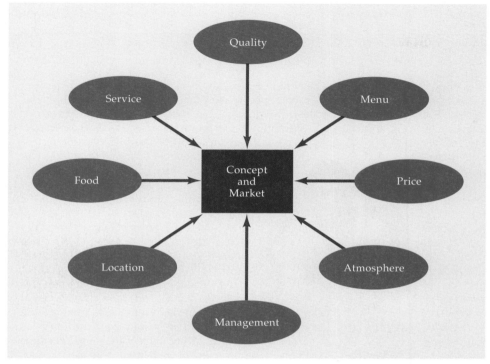

Figure 6–3 *Concept and Market* (Reprinted with permission from Donald E. Lundberg and John R. Walker, *The Restaurant from Concept to Operation.* New York: John Wiley and Sons, 1993, p. 16.)

✔ Downtown
✔ Suburban

Restaurant Ambiance

The atmosphere that a restaurant creates has both immediate conscious and subconscious effects on guests. The immediate conscious effect is how guests react to the ambiance on entering the restaurant—or even more importantly as an element in the decision-making process used in selecting a restaurant. Is it noisy? Are the tables too close? The subconscious is affected by mood, lighting, furnishings, and music; these play an important role in leaving a subtle impression on guests.

Restaurant guests are placing a greater emphasis on atmospherics (the design used to create a special atmosphere). Back in the 1970s, the majority of restaurants were quite plain. Today, atmospherics are built with the restaurant concept, which has an immediate sensory impact on customers.[5]

Perhaps the most noticeable atmospheric restaurants are those with a theme. The theme will use color, sound, lighting, decor, texture, and visual stimulation to create special effects for patrons. The chain restaurants with the highest rating in atmosphere are Planet Hollywood, Hard Rock Cafe, and Chart House.

Personal Profile:

Richard Melman and the Lettuce Entertain You Enterprises Group, Chicago

Richard Melman is a genius among restaurant operators. He is the creator of a chain of some forty eclectic restaurants in Chicago. Each is unique and authentic, be it Italian, Greek, French, Spanish, or American. Some of the restaurants are co-owned by celebrities, such as the Eccentric, co-owned by Oprah Winfrey, which describes itself as a cosmopolitan American brasserie. Its bustling, creative atmosphere is highlighted by the artwork of more than one hundred Chicago artists. The restaurant features home-cooked meals worth leaving home for: fresh seafood, pastas, steaks, chicken, salads, and homemade desserts.

Another of Melman's concepts is Papagus, an authentic Greek tavern that offers hearty Grecian delights in warm, friendly, rustic surroundings. Mezedes, a variety of bite-sized offerings, may be enjoyed with Greek wine and ouzo. The display kitchen adds an experiential atmosphere and offers specialties such as spit-roasted chicken, whole broiled red snapper, traditional braised lamb, spanikopita, and baklava.

Richard Melman's Lettuce Entertain You Enterprises Group also has other outstanding theme restaurants in the Chicago area. Scoozi recalls an artist's studio and serves Italian country cuisine; Cafe Ba-Ba-Reeba is a Spanish restaurant featuring tapas, the popular hot and cold little dishes of Spain; Un Grand Cafe, an authentic Parisian cafe,

Richard Melman

features patés, salads, fresh grilled fish, and steak, as well as daily specials; and Gino's East serves a world-famous deep-dish pizza ranked number one by *People* magazine.

Richard Melman is often described as the Steven Spielberg or Andrew Lloyd Webber of restaurants. He brought Chicago the first salad bar, the first Spanish tapas, its most popular French restaurant, and more ways to eat Italian food than Caesar ever imagined. In the past, Melman traveled extensively to Europe, where he dreamed up his most inspired restaurants—Ambria (1980), Un Grand Cafe (1981), Avanzare (1982), and Scoozi (1986). Today, he works fewer hours and delegates more. At fifty-plus, he has mellowed and his priorities have changed. Melman now concentrates on more healthful food and on being a good uncle instead of father figure to his staff. He prefers to be at home with his wife, three children, and dog. His passion is playing softball in an over-fifty league.

Richard Melman cofounded Lettuce Entertain You Enterprises in 1971. Now, twenty-plus years and thirty-six restaurants later, the company employs 3,650 and has annual revenues of $129 million. Lettuce has grown from a free-spirited den of entrepreneurs into a serious corporate player. One of Melman's strengths is his organization. Currently, eleven restaurant divisions are organized around individual partners; some of them are chefs. Each partner has total operational control of his or her restau-

Menu Planning

The menu may be the most important ingredient in the restaurant's success. The restaurant's menu must agree with the concept; the concept must be based on what the guest in the target market expects; and the menu must exceed those expectations. The type of menu will depend on the kind of restaurant being operated.

There are six main types of menus:

A la carte menus offer items that are individually priced.

Table d'hote menus offer a selection of one or more items for each course at a fixed price. This type of menu is used more frequently in hotels and in

rant; divisions report to a ten-member executive committee that includes Melman and his earliest partners.

Further expansion is being considered for Maggiano's Little Italy and the Corner Bakery, a personal favorite of Melman's. Maggiano's is based on an Italian family-style theme, with big portions, red sauce, and Frank Sinatra music. Needless to say, Maggiano's is a big hit. Interestingly, according to Lettuce's corporate chef, Russel Bry, the food is prepared for Midwestern tastes—a little less spicy than other places, especially the coasts. A concept that works well in Chicago would not transplant well to New York or Los Angeles without adjusting the taste of the food.

Over the years, Melman has stayed close to the customers by using focus groups and frequent-diner pro-

Papagus

grams. The group's training programs are rated so highly by other restaurateurs that they are keen to hire former Lettuce employees.

Melman's management style is clearly influenced by team sports. He says, "There are many similarities between running a restaurant and a team sport. However, it's not a good idea to have ten all-stars; everybody can't bat fourth. You need people with similar goals—people who want to win and play hard."[1]

The Eccentric

[1]Marilyn Alva, "Does He Still Have It?" *Restaurant Business*, 93, 4, March 1, 1994, pp. 104–111.
The author gratefully acknowledges the courtesy extended by Lettuce Entertain You Enterprises.

Europe. The advantage is the perception guests have of receiving good value.

Du jour menus list the items "of the day."

Tourist menus are used to attract tourists' attention. They frequently stress value and food that is acceptable to the tourists.

California menus are so named because, in some California restaurants, guests may order any item on the menu at any time of the day.

Cyclical menus repeat themselves over a period of time.

A menu generally consists of perhaps six to eight appetizers, two to four soups, a few salads—both as appetizers and entrees,—eight to sixteen entrees, and about four to six desserts.

The many considerations in menu planning attest to the complexity of the restaurant business. Considerations include the following:[6]

- ✔ Needs and desires of guests
- ✔ Capabilities of cooks
- ✔ Equipment capacity and layout
- ✔ Consistency and availability of menu ingredients
- ✔ Price and pricing strategy (cost and profitability)
- ✔ Nutritional value
- ✔ Contribution margin
- ✔ Accuracy in menu
- ✔ Menu analysis
- ✔ Menu design

Chain Menus

Chain menus are changing with surprising speed and creativity—and the key word is flavor. Items such as tandor chicken sandwiches, lobster pot pie, Tex-Mex egg rolls, and BLT salad have been added to the menu by one major chain. Planet Hollywood added Cajun egg rolls, the Spaghetti Warehouse added garlic cheese toast, Marie Calendar's added parmesan sprinkled mushrooms, and the House of Blues added calamari with coconut curry dipping sauce.

Casual market leader, Houlihan's, has recently introduced ten items that feature distinctive sauces. Among them are a corn cream sauce for wood-fired chicken and roasted corn pasta, and Korean-style ginger, soy, and roasted garlic for teriyaki chicken stir fry. Joe Marans, vice president of culinary development, says that with the growing popularity of ethnic food, he believes people now expect "deep flavor." So his best-selling New Orleans BBQ shrimp are seasoned with cracked, black pepper and a proprietary Louisiana spice, then pan-seared and finished with blackened voodoo beer and homemade Worcestershire sauce.

In the sandwich segment, the speed and convenience of wraps has boosted sales. A wrap is a large, usually gourmet-flavored, flour tortilla with a wide choice of fillings. A *Restaurant Business* magazine survey shows the following samplers:

- ✔ Bakers Square—spicy chicken pita
- ✔ Chevy's—Texas BBQ wrap
- ✔ Shari's—spicy turkey burger
- ✔ Pizzeria Uno—buffalo turkey roll-up
- ✔ Mozzarella's—black bean vegetarian burger

Au Bon Pain of Boston is rolling out a line of eight new sourdough bagels designed to boost breakfast sales.

Salad items include Cheesecake Factory's tuna salad San Tropez, while Dave and Buster's has added a chicken fajita salad.

In the entrees section, traditional fare is making room for specialty items, however, comfort food remains popular. Outback Steakhouse, for example, has added the outback rack, a 14 oz. rack of lamb served with Australian cabernet sauce. Red Lobster added hickory-planked salmon and Chart House, orange basil salmon. This is done to retain customer's interest.

Needs and Desires of Guests

In planning a menu, the needs and desires of the guests are what is important—not what the owner, chef, or manager thinks. If it is determined that there is a niche in the market for a particular kind of restaurant, then the menu must harmonize with the theme of the restaurant.

The Olive Garden restaurants are a good example of a national chain that has developed rapidly over the past few years. The concept has been positioned and defined as middle of the road with a broad-based appeal. During the concept development phase, several focus groups were asked their opinions on topics from dishes to decor. The result has been extremely successful.

Several other restaurants have become successful by focusing on the needs and desires of the guest. Among them are Hard Rock Cafe, TGI Friday's, Red Lobster, Applebee's, and so on.

Capabilities of Cooks

The capabilities of the cooks must also harmonize with the menu and concept. An appropriate level of expertise must be employed to match the peak demands and culinary expertise expected by the guests. The length and complexity of the menu and the number of guests to be served are both factors in determining the extent of the cooks' capabilities.

The equipment capacity and layout will have an impact on the menu and the efficiency with which the cooks can produce the food. Some restaurants have several fried or cold items on the appetizer menu simply to avoid use of the stoves and ovens, which will be needed for the entrees. A similar situation occurs with desserts; by avoiding the use of the equipment needed for the entrees, it makes it easier for the cooks to produce the volume of meals required during peak periods.

One of the best examples of effective utilization of menu and equipment is Chinese restaurants. At the beginning of many Chinese restaurant menus, there are combination dinners. The combination dinners include several courses for a fixed price. Operators of Chinese restaurants explain that about 60 to 70 percent of guests order those combinations. This helps the cooks because they can prepare for the orders and the food is produced quickly, which pleases the guests. It would create havoc if everyone ordered a la carte items because the kitchen and the cooks could not handle the volume in this way.

Equipment Capacity and Layout

All restaurant menus should be developed with regard to the capacity and layout of the equipment. Anyone who has worked in a busy kitchen on a Friday or Saturday night and been "slammed" will realize that part of the problem may have been too ambitious a menu (too many items requiring extensive preparation and the use of too much equipment).

If the restaurant is already in existence, it may be costly to alter the kitchen. Operators generally find it easier to alter the menu to fit the equipment. The important thing is to match the menu with the equipment and production scheduling. A menu can be created to use some equipment for appetizers; for this one reason, the appetizer selections on the menu often include one or two cold cuts, possibly a couple of salads, but mostly some deep fried items or soups. This keeps the stove and grill areas free for the entrees. The desserts, if they are not brought in, are mostly made in advance and served cold or heated in the microwave.

Other considerations include the following:

✔ The projected volume of sales for each menu item
✔ Is the menu fixed or does it change with the seasons?
✔ Menu size. Large menus may call for a greater variety of equipment.
✔ Speed of service desired. Fast service may call for equipment of larger capacity.
✔ Nutritional awareness[7]

Most chefs are sufficiently adaptable to be able to prepare quality meals with the equipment provided. Some may prepare a more detailed mise en place,[8] and others will go further to partially cook items so that they can be furnished to order. Of course, there is always the old standby—the daily special—that can take the pressure off the production line.

Consistency and Availability of Menu Ingredients

In the United States, most ingredients are available year round. However, at certain times of the year, some items become more expensive. This is because they are out of season—in economic terms, the demand exceeds the supply so the price goes up. An example of this would be if a storm in the Gulf of Mexico disrupts the supply of fresh fish and shellfish and causes an increase in price. To offset this kind of situation, some operators print their menus daily. Others may purchase a quantity of frozen items when the prices are low.

Price and Pricing Strategy

The target market and concept will, to a large extent, determine the menu price ranges. An example might be a neighborhood restaurant where the appetizers are priced from $3.25 to $6.95 and entrees are in the $6.95 to $11.95 price range. The selling price of each item must be acceptable to the market and profitable to the restaurateur. Factors that go into this decision include the following:

✔ What is the competition charging for a similar item?
✔ What is the item's food cost?
✔ What is the cost of labor that goes into the item?
✔ What other costs must be covered?
✔ What profit is expected by the operator?
✔ What is the contribution margin of the item?[9]

Figure 6–4 illustrates the factors that influence a restaurant's menu prices.

There are two main ways to price menus. A comparative approach analyzes the price ranges of the competition and determines the price range for appetizers, entrees, and desserts. The second method is to cost the individual dish item

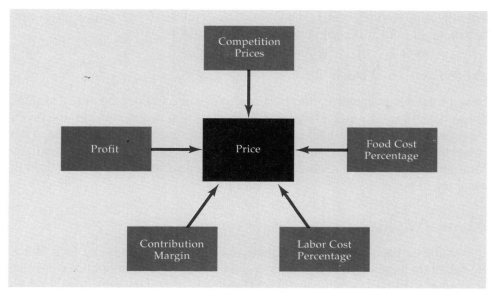

Figure 6–4 *Factors That Influence a Restaurant's Menu Prices*

on the menu and multiply it by the ratio amount necessary to achieve the desired food cost percentage. For example, to achieve a 30 percent food cost for an item priced at $6.95 on the menu, the food cost would have to be $2.09. Beverage items are priced the same way. This method will result in the same expected food cost percentage for each item. It would be great if we lived in such a perfect world. The problem is that if some items were priced out according to a 30 percent food cost they might appear to be overpriced according to customers' perceptions. For example, some of the more expensive meat and fish would price out at $18 to $21 when the restaurant would prefer to keep entree prices under $15. In order to balance this, restaurants lower the margin on the more expensive meat and fish items—as long as there are only one or two of them—and raise the price on some of the other items, such as soup, salad, chicken, and pasta. This approach is called the weighted average, whereby the factors of food cost percentage, contribution margin, and sales volume are weighted.

Nutritional Value

A more health-conscious customer has prompted most restaurant operators to make changes not only to the menu selections but also to the preparation methods. Restaurant operators are using more chicken, fish, seafood, and pasta items on the menus today compared with a few years ago. Beef is now more lean than ever before. All of these items are being prepared in more healthful ways such as broiling, poaching, braising, casseroling, or rotisserieing instead of frying.

Increasingly, restaurants are publishing the nutritional value of their food. McDonald's has taken a leadership role in this. Other restaurants are utilizing a heart-healthy symbol to signify that the menu item is suitable for guests with concerns about heart-healthy eating. Many restaurants are changing the oil used from the saturated fat, which is high in cholesterol, to 100 percent vegetable oil or canola oil, which is cholesterol free.

Accuracy in Menu

Laws prohibit misrepresentation of items being sold. In the case of restaurants, the so-called truth-in-menu laws refer to the fact that descriptions on the menu must be accurate. Prime beef must be prime cut, not some other grade, fresh vegetables must be fresh, not frozen, and Maine lobster had better actually come from Maine. Some restaurants have received sizable fines for violations of accuracy in menu.

Menu Analysis

One of the earliest approaches to menu analysis was developed by Jack Miller. He called the best-selling items *winners;* they not only sold more but were also at a lower food cost percentage. In 1982, Michael Kasavana and Donald Smith developed menu engineering, in which the best items are called *stars*—those that have the highest contribution margin and the highest sales. Later, David Pavesic suggested that a combination of three variables—food cost percentage, contribution margin, and sales volume—should be used.

Another key variable in menu analysis is labor costs. A menu item may take several hours to prepare, and it may be difficult to precisely calculate the time a cook spends in preparation of the dish. Operators add the total food and labor cost together to determine prime cost, which should not exceed about 60 to 65 percent of sales. The remaining 35 to 40 percent is for overhead and profit.

Menu Design and Layout

Basic menus can be recited by the server. Casual menus are sometimes written on a chalk or similar type board. Quick-service menus are often illuminated above the order counter. More formal menus are generally single page, or folded with three or more pages. Some describe the restaurant and type of food offered; most have beverage suggestions and a wine selection. The more up-scale American-Continental restaurants have a separate wine list.

Some menus are more distinctive than others, with pictures of the items or at least enticing descriptions of the food. Research indicates that there is a focal point at the center of the right hand page; this is the spot in which to place the star or signature item.[9]

Classifications of Restaurants

There is no single definition of the various classifications of restaurants, perhaps because it is an evolving business. Most experts would agree, however, that there are two main categories: full-service and specialty. Other categories in-

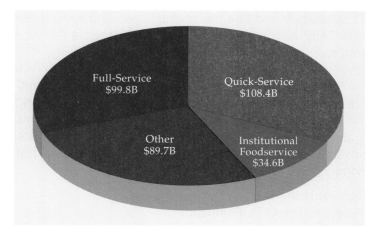

Figure 6–5 *Foodservice Industry Sales*

clude such designations as quick-service, ethnic, dinner house, occasion, ca-
sual, and so on. Some restaurants may even fall into more than one category.
For instance, a restaurant could be both quick-service and ethnic (Taco Bell).
Another restaurant can be called specialty and dinner house (Chart House).

The National Restaurant Association's figures indicate that Americans are spending an increasing number of food dollars away from home in various foodservice
operations. Americans eat out about 200 times a year, or about 4 times a week.
More than 50 percent of all consumers visit a restaurant on their birthday,[10] thereby
making it the most popular day for eating out. Mother's Day and Valentine's Day
are the second and third most popular days, respectively. The most popular meal
eaten away from home is lunch, which brings in approximately 50 percent of fast-
food restaurant sales. Figure 6–5 illustrates the foodservice industry sales by segments: full-service, quick-service, institutional, and other.

Full-Service Restaurants

A full-service restaurant is one where a good selection of menu items is offered,
generally at least fifteen or more different entrees cooked to order, with nearly
all the food being made on the premises from scratch using raw or fresh ingredients. Full-service restaurants may be formal or casual and may be further categorized by price, decor/atmosphere, level of formality, and menu. Most full-
service restaurants may be cross-referenced into other categories, as mentioned
previously. Many of these restaurants serve haute cuisine (pronounced *hote*),
which is a French term meaning elegant dining or *high food*. Many of the fine
restaurants in the United States are based on French or northern Italian cuisine,
which, together with fine Chinese cuisine, are considered by many western connoisseurs to be the finest in the world.

Most full-service restaurants are independently owned and operated by an
entrepreneur or a partnership. These restaurants are in almost every neighborhood. Today, with value-conscious customers expecting more for their
money, it is becoming increasingly more difficult to make a profit in this segment of the business because of strong competition from other restaurants.

Some companies, such as Marriott and Stouffer's, who began in the restaurant business, have since sold their restaurant chains because they could not yield the profit margin that management and investors expected.

Nation's Restaurant News (NRN) Fine Dining Hall of Fame, which was launched in 1980, now has more than 150 restaurants. Most of them are full-service, independent restaurants. These restaurants are selected by the NRN's editors and included on the basis of excellence in food quality, service, innovation, and staff training and motivation. Over the years, many of America's finest independent restaurants have been honored. Among the inductees into the Hall of Fame are the following:

Berkeley, CA—Chez Panisse
Los Angeles, CA—Spago, The Grill, Campanile
San Francisco, CA—L'Etoile, Doros, La Bourgogne
St. Helena, CA—Terra
Greenwich, CT—Restaurant Jean-Louis
Orlando, FL—The Citrus Club
Tampa, FL—Bern's Steak House, Columbia
Arlington Hills, IL—Le Titi de Paris
Chicago, IL—Morton's, Jimmy's Place, Ambia, Le Perroquet, Arun's
New Orleans, LA—K-Paul's
Boston, MA—Anthony's Pier 4, L'Espalier
Kansas City, MO—The American Restaurant
St. Louis, MO—Anthony's
New York, NY—Lettuce, Four Seasons, The Quilted Giraffe, Shunlee Palace, Café des Artistes, Tommy Toy's Parioli Romanissimo, Le Bernardin, Aureole
Durham, NC—Magnolia Grill
Cincinnati, OH—Maisonette
Philadelphia, PA—Le Bec-Fin, Fountain Restaurant
Dallas, TX—The Mansion on Turtle Creek, South Street Café, Zodiac
Houston, TX—Rotisserie for Beef and Bird, Café Annie
San Antonio, TX—Restaurant Biga
Williamsburg, VA—The Trellis
Seattle, WA—Campagne
Washington, DC—Germaine's, I Ricchi, Galileo

It is interesting to notice how many of these have a French influence in their name. In the United States, there are a number of restaurant cities, including New York, Chicago, Los Angeles, New Orleans, San Francisco, Boston, Atlanta, Houston, and Denver. Each of these cities has an example of a restaurateur extraordinaire.

In recent years, fine dining has become more fun. At places like Osteria del Circo in New York, operators are looking for guests who want spectacular meals without the fuss. Marco Maccioni, son of Sirio Maccioni of the famed Le Cirque, says that the sons did not want to simply clone Le Cirque. Thus, the brothers turned to a circus theme for its ambiance. For the menu, they sought inspiration from Mama's home cooking—pizza, pasta, and comfortable, braised dishes.

Tavern on the Green
(Courtesy Tavern on the
Green.)

Many cities have independent fine-dining restaurants that pursue those who are not content with wings and deep-fried cheese. Chefs are therefore making approachable, yet provocative food; each course is expertly prepared and may be served with wine. After dinner, guests head for the smoking room to enjoy fine cigars and single-malt scotches.

The top independent restaurant in terms of sales is the Tavern on the Green in New York, which opened in 1976. It has sales of more than $26 million from 1,000 seats—including banquets with an average dinner check of $43.50—and serves 545,000 people a year.[11] Now that's cooking!

Other restaurants of interest are operated by celebrity chefs like Wolfgang Puck, co-owner of Spago and Chinois in Los Angeles, and Alice Waters of Chez Panisse in Berkeley, California. Both have done much to inspire a new generation of talented chefs. Alice Waters has been a role model for many female chefs and has received numerous awards and published several cookbooks, including one for children.

The level of service in full-service restaurants is generally high, with a hostess or host to greet and seat patrons. Captains and food servers advise guests of special items and assist with the description and selection of dishes during order taking. If there is no separate sommelier (wine waiter), the captain or food server may offer a description of the wine that will complement the meal and assist with the order taking. Some upscale or luxury full-service restaurants have table-side cooking and French service from a gueridon cart.[12]

The decor of a full-service restaurant is generally compatible with the overall ambiance and theme that the restaurant is seeking to create. These elements of food, service, and decor create a memorable experience for the restaurant guest.

There is no national full-service luxury restaurant chain, possibly due to the following factors:

✔ Upscale full-service restaurants are not only labor intensive, but they also require a greater degree of skill to operate. The more sophisticated operation makes for a high labor cost.

✔ Only a small percentage of the population can afford the high prices that these restaurants need to charge by reason of their expensive location, decor, and labor. The restaurant is likely to be located in the high-rent district and employ a highly-skilled chef, and kitchen and service personnel who add to the labor costs. The luxurious furnishings and appointments of the restaurant may easily cost several million dollars. It takes more than a few dinners to pay for all these costs.

✔ The logistics of a national chain may prove difficult or costly to manage. Overhead costs may outweigh savings of economy of scale.

✔ Economies of scale are not as easily reaped with such a sophisticated product—a freshly prepared, high-quality meal.

✔ Consistency and quality are very difficult to maintain for such a sophisticated clientele.

✔ There is limited market appeal. This type of restaurant is more likely to succeed in major cities such as New York, Los Angeles, Boston, Chicago, New Orleans, Houston, Atlanta, and Philadelphia. There are a number of regional or greater metropolitan restaurants, each with a few locations in a city. There is an obvious benefit in both purchasing for and marketing a cluster of restaurants. In fact, most national chains have adopted the cluster concept as it increases customer awareness and builds traffic (customers).

The owner-operators of the upscale, white tablecloth restaurants have had more than their fair share of bad fortune in the past few years. First came the reduction in the tax deductibility for business entertainment from 100 percent to 80 percent, which then dropped to 50 percent. This reduced the so-called "business lunch". A general decline in the consumption of alcohol also affected the success of fine-dining establishments. In October 1987 the Wall Street stock market plunged. This forced the street-smart restaurateurs to reexamine every aspect of their business.

Success stories in such changing[13] times are hard to find. However, one savvy restaurateur even managed to make a profit with sales of $1.1 million in 1990, whereas he had experienced a loss with sales of $2 million in 1987. This was achieved using the following survival tactics:

✔ Renegotiating the restaurant's lease from $24,000 to $12,000 a month

✔ Trimming payroll, starting at the top, from an annual payroll of $675,000 in May of 1989 to $200,000 in May of 1991—and it's still dropping

✔ Using the same menu for lunch and dinner. This streamlined the mise en place—for example, the saucier (sauce chef) could come in the morning and prepare all of the sauces for the entire day. The special at lunch was always the special at dinner.

✔ Simplifying menu terminology to speed service

✔ Changing menu price structure

✔ Building up private-banquet business

✔ Controlling cost. In 1986, food cost was 32 percent of sales, and labor cost was 34 percent of sales; in 1991, food cost was 27 percent of sales, and labor cost was 20 percent of sales.

These tactics are necessary for survival in the fiercely competitive restaurant business.

The eagerly anticipated reopening of the famed New York restaurant Le Cirque 2000, gave critics plenty to rave about. Sirio Maccioni opened the original Le Cirque in the Mayfair Hotel in 1974 and employed an army of chefs who evolved into entrepreneurs. During those years, Le Cirque became a major contributor to the American appreciation of fine French dining, garnering award after award.

Le Cirque is credited with introducing Americans to dishes that would later become standard fare of upscale restaurants. Among such dishes are potato-crusted bars, crème brûlée, white truffles, and pasta primavera. Signature dishes at Le Cirque 2000 include codfish scented with Szechwan pepper, garnished with a casserole of Swiss chard and beans; cassolette of spring vegetables with chopped black truffles; and turbot grilled on a bed of dried fennel and garnished with tender vegetables. These items are offered along with classic French standards such as bouillabaisse and pot-au-feu.[14]

Specialty Restaurants

Under this general heading come fast-food or quick-service, family, ethnic, theme, casual dining, and dinner house restaurants. Be aware that some restaurants fall into more than one category, ethnic (Italian) and full-service like the Olive Garden, or specialty (seafood) and full-service, like Red Lobster.

Quick–Service/Fast–Food

The quick-service sector is the one that really drives the industry. With sales of $111 billion, it is slightly ahead of the full-service segment by dollar volume. Recently, the home-meal replacement and fast casual concepts have gained momentum. Boston Market is a leader in both sectors and has recently sped up its service and cut customers' wait time in half.

Quick-service or fast-food restaurants offer limited menus featuring food such as hamburgers, fries, hot dogs, chicken (in all forms), tacos, burritos, gyros, teriyaki bowls, various finger foods, and other items for the convenience of people on the go. Customers order their food at a counter under a brightly lit menu featuring color photographs of food items. Customers are even encouraged to

Pizza Hut (Photo Courtesy Pizza Hut.)

clear their own trays, which helps reduce costs. The following are examples of the different types of quick-service/fast-food restaurants:

Hamburger—McDonald's, Burger King, Wendy's
Pizza—Pizza Hut, Domino's, Godfather's
Steak—Bonanza, Ponderosa
Seafood—Long John Silver's
Chicken—KFC, Church's, Boston Market, Kenny Roger's, Popeye's
Sandwich—Subway
Mexican—Taco Bell, El Torito

Figure 6–6 shows the top one hundred market shares by restaurant segment.

In some of the world's major cities, where space is expensive, stand-up restaurants open where busy office workers can eat a quick meal. Also found in many major cities is "$1 Chinese Fast Food (no MSG)," where patrons select menu items and receive small portions for one dollar. This is relatively quick and easy for the kitchen staff, because they can prepare a large serving of a particular dish, put it on low heat, and portion it out as necessary. For the customers, it is fast and affordable because they can have a taste of three or four different dishes for a cost of $3 or $4 with rice and noodles usually included free.

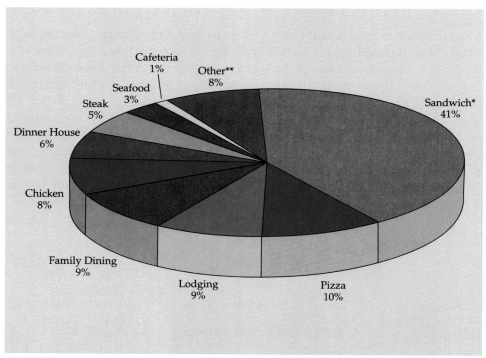

*Includes the hamburger section
**Includes sweets/snacks, retail, c-store, and multiconcept

Figure 6–6 *Total Sales for the Fiscal Year July 1, 1996–June 30, 1997 by segment in percentage* (Source: Kimberly D. Lowe and Erin Nicholas, "Chaos in a Crowded Market," *Restaurant and Institutions, 107,* 17, July 15, 1997).

In an attempt to raise flat sales figures, more quick-service restaurant (QSR) chains are using cobranding at stores and nontraditional locations, including highway plazas and shopping centers. It is hoped that the traffic-building combos will increase sales among the separate brands, such as Carl's Jr. and Green Burrito, as well as sibling concepts like Triarc Co.'s Arby's, Zu Zu, P.T. Noodles, and T.J. Cinnamon brands.

Many QSR chains are targeting international growth, mostly in the larger cities in a variety of countries.

Hamburger

The world's greatest fast-food success story is undoubtedly McDonald's. Back in the 1950s, Ray Kroc was selling soda fountains. He received an order from Mr. McDonald for two soda fountains. Ray Kroc was so interested in finding out why the McDonald brothers' restaurant needed two machines (everyone else ordered one) that he went out to the restaurant. There he saw the now-familiar golden arches and the hamburger restaurant. Ray persuaded the McDonalds to let him franchise their operation. Billions of burgers later, the reason for the success may be summarized as follows: quality, speed, cleanliness, service, and value. This has been achieved by systemizing the production process and by staying close to the original concept—keeping a limited menu, advertising heavily, being innovative with new menu items, maintaining product quality, and being consistent.

McDonald's is the giant of the entire quick-service/fast-food segment with worldwide sales of $31.8 billion. This total is amazing because it is more than the next three megachains combined—Burger King ($9.01 billion), KFC ($8.2 billion), and Pizza Hut ($7.5 billion).[15] McDonald's even has individual product items that are not the traditional burger—for example, chicken McNuggets and burritos as well as salads and fish, which all aim to broaden customer appeal.

Customer appeal has also been broadened by the introduction of breakfast and by targeting not only kids but also seniors. Innovative menu introductions have helped stimulate an increase in per-store traffic.

In recent years, because traditional markets have become saturated, McDonald's has adopted a strategy of expanding overseas. It is embarking on a rapid expansion in the world's most populous nation, China, developing 300 restaurants by the year 2000. The reason for this expansion in China is a rapidly developing middle class with a growing appetite for Western culture and food. McDonald's is now in eighty-five countries and has a potential audience of 3.2 billion people. Of the company's roughly 18,000 restaurants, some 6,400 are outside of the United States.

It is interesting to note that of the estimated $31.8 billion worldwide sales, about $15 billion are from outside of the United States, and about 50 percent of total profits come from outside of the United States.[16] More than two-thirds of new restaurants added by McDonald's are outside of the United States. McDonald's also seeks out nontraditional locations in the U.S. market, such as on military bases or smaller-sized units in the high-rent districts.

Table 6–1	Top Ten Hamburger Chains
Chain	**Sales for fiscal year July 1, 1996–June 30, 1997 ($ million)**
1. McDonald's	$31,812.0
2. Burger King	9,010.0
3. Wendy's	4,700.0
4. Hardee's	4,085.0
5. Jack in the Box	1,229.0
6. Sonic Drive-ins	1,012.7
7. Carl's Jr.	648.0
8. Whataburger	443.0
9. White Castle	351.5
10. Checker's Drive-Ins	328.0

Source: Kimberly D. Lowe and Erin Nicholas, "Chaos in a Crowded Market," *Restaurant and Institutions, 107,* 17, July 15, 1997.

McDonald's is taking another step toward being the most convenient food-service operation in the world by striking deals with gasoline companies Chevron, U.S. Petroleum Star Enterprise, and Mobil Oil Corporation to codevelop sites.

It is very difficult to obtain a McDonald's franchise in the United States because they have virtually saturated the primary markets. Carl's Jr., a California-based chain of 583 units has a franchising fee of $35,000, with a royalty fee of four percent and an advertising annuity of four percent. It often costs between $800,000 and $1 million to open a major brand fast-food restaurant. Franchises for lesser-known chains are available for less money.

Each of the major hamburger restaurant chains has a unique positioning strategy to attract their target markets. Burger King hamburgers are flame broiled, Wendy's uses fresh patties.

Fuddruckers is a restaurant chain that describes itself as the "Cadillac of Burgers." Other gourmet burger restaurants may offer larger burgers with more side dishes to choose from, and they generally have decor that would attract the nonteenage market. Some of these restaurants have beer and wine licenses. Some smaller regional chains are succeeding in gaining market share from the big-three burger chains because they provide an excellent burger at a reasonable price. In-N-Out Burger and Rally's are good examples of this. The top ten hamburger chains are listed in Table 6–1.

Pizza

The pizza segment continues to grow. By some estimates it is at least a $20 billion market,[17] with much of the growth fueled by the convenience of delivery. There are four main chains: Pizza Hut, Domino's, Godfather's, and Little Caesar's. Godfather's "makes pizza the way it was meant to be." They are also noted for their no wait lunch buffet and their cinnamon-streusal or cherry pie

Corporate Profile: Boston Market

Boston Chicken, Inc., franchises and operates Boston Market foodservice stores that specialize in fresh, convenient meals featuring homestyle entrees, sandwiches, fresh vegetables, salads, and side dishes, including mashed potatoes made from scratch. Boston Market stores combine the freshness and quality of traditional home cooking with convenience and value, and offer innovative meal solutions to today's consumers.

The company's history began in 1991 with a partnership formed by Saad Nadhir, Scott Beck, and Jeffry Shearer. They began to make a series of investments in Boston Chicken and one year later, after the partnership acquired a controlling interest, the company was traded on NASDAQ under the symbol BOST. Revenues increased and by 1994, Boston Chicken celebrated the opening of its 500th store.

The name changed to Boston Market the following year and began serving ham, turkey, and meat loaf. Moreover with the new name, the company entered the holiday market, offering whole and half hams plus special banquet-sized containers of its side dishes.

Boston Market experienced an amazing year in 1996, in which it achieved profitability. After the launching of the Boston Carver sandwiches, lunch business increased to more than 40 percent of sales. Furthermore, its strategies have also helped establish other great brands including Einstein/Noah Bagel Corp. (ENBC), which Boston Market owns and plans to add between 300 and 350 stores per year for the next several years.

In June of 1997, due to disappointing financial results, Boston Market streamlined their organizations. Area developers were formed to handle administrative duties, allowing for a reduction of staff at the company's support center.

The company has now created a customized system that it hopes will provide the world's first choice for quick, quality meals. Boston Market has set its sights to accomplish more than ever before. It plans to reach new heights in store performance, to provide its customers with the best possible service, and to take its "brands where no brands have gone before."

---

dessert pizzas. They offer a number of family combos at special prices that include drinks and a variety of pizzas and desserts. Their jumbo sampler includes four pizzas in one! There are also several smaller regional chains. Pizza Hut, with system-wide sales of $7.5 billion, has broken into the delivery part of the business over which, until recently, Domino's had a virtual monopoly. Little Caesar's, with 4,600 units and total sales of $2.1 billion, built a pizza empire on the perceived value of two pizzas for the price of one. Pizza Hut has now developed system-wide delivery units that also offer two pizzas at a reduced price. A Little Caesar's franchise fee is $20,000, with the cost to develop a store running between $120,000 and $160,000.

In response to the success of Pizza Hut's Stuffed Crust Pizza, Domino's highlights their Ultimate Deep Dish Pizza and their new Pesto Crust Pizza. They are currently stressing the quality of their advertising. With twelve toppings to choose from, people can have fun designing their own pizza.

Chicken

Chicken has always been popular and will likely remain so because it is relatively cheap to produce and it is readily available and adaptable to a variety of preparations. It also is perceived as a healthier alternative to burgers.

Kentucky Fried Chicken (KFC), with a worldwide total of more than 10,000 units and annual sales of more than $8.2 billion, dominates the chicken segment. Even though KFC is a market leader, with more than 5,100 units in the United States alone, the company continues to explore new ways to get its products to consumers. More than 350 units now offer home delivery, and in many cities, KFC is teaming up with sister restaurant Taco Bell, selling products from both chains in one convenient location. KFC continues to build menu variety as it focuses on providing complete meals to families, with new products such as Tender Roast® chicken pieces, Chunky Chicken Pot Pie, and Colonel's Crispy Strips.

Church's Chicken, the 1,333-unit division of AFC Enterprises formerly America's Favorite Chicken Company, is the second largest chicken chain. It offers a simple formula consisting of a value menu featuring Southern-style chicken, spicy chicken wings, okra, corn on the cob, coleslaw, biscuits, and other items.

Under the guidance of Hala Moddelmog, president, Church's has focused on becoming a low-cost provider and the fastest to market. To give customers the value they expect day in and day out, she says that it is necessary to have unit economies in order. Systemwide, Church's now registers 35.8 percent in food costs and 27.9 percent labor costs.[18]

Popeye's is now the third-largest chain in the chicken segment with 1,062 units. It is owned by AFC, the same parent company as Church's. Popeye's has a New Orleans-inspired "spicy chicken" chain operating more than 300 restaurants in Texas and Louisiana that is expanding into eleven markets around the country. The chain hopes to increase average-unit sales to $1 million.

There are a number of up-and-coming regional chains, such as El Pollo Loco, of Irvine, California. They focus on a marinated, flame-broiled chicken that is a unique, high-quality product. Kenny Rogers and Cluckers are also expanding rotisserie chains.

KFC Restaurant and Rotisserie Gold, a Recent Popular Addition to Their Menu (Photos Courtesy KFC.)

Steak

The steak restaurant segment is quite buoyant in spite of nutritional concerns. The upscale steak dinner houses, like Morton's of Chicago, Ruth Chris's, and Houston's continue to attract the expense account and "occasion" diners. Some restaurants are adding additional value-priced items like chicken and fish to their

Corporate Profile: Outback Steakhouse

The founders of Outback Steakhouse have proven that unconventional methods can lead to profitable results. Such methods include opening solely for dinner, sacrificing dining-room seats for back-of-the-house efficiency, limiting servers to three tables each, and handing ten percent of cash flow to the restaurants' general managers.

March 1988 saw the opening of the first Outback Steakhouse. Outback's founders, Chris Sullivan, Robert Basham, and Senior Vice-President Tim Gannon, know plenty about the philosophy "No rules, just right" because they have lived it since day one. Even the timing of their venture to launch a casual steak place came when many pundits were pronouncing red meat consumption dead in America.

The chain went public in 1990 and has since created a track record of strong earnings. In 1992, Outback posted the strongest sales growth in the casual-steakhouse sector (77.9 percent), as well as the fastest unit growth (71.8 percent). In 1993, its food cost was 39 percent of sales, versus 36 percent or less for most restaurant chains. It was evident that the three founders were piloting one of the country's hottest restaurant concepts. The trio found themselves with 230 restaurants, instead of the five they originally envisioned.

Robert Basham, cofounder, president, and chief operating officer at Outback Steakhouse, was given the Operator of the Year award at MUFSO '96 (Multi-Unit Foodservice Operators Conference). He has helped expand the chain, a

pioneer in the steak house of the 1990s, to more than 325 restaurants with some of the highest sales per unit in the industry in spite the fact that it only serves dinner.

Perhaps the strongest indication of what this company is about lies in its corporate structure, or lack thereof. Despite its rapid growth, the company has no public relations department, no human resources department, and no recruiting apparatus. In addition, the Outback Steakhouse headquarters is very different from that of a typical restaurant company. There is no lavish tower—only modest office space in an average suburban complex. Instead of settling into a conservative chair and browsing through a magazine-lined coffee table (as is the case in most reception areas), at Outback you must belly up to an actual bar, brass foot rail and all, to announce your arrival.

Also, Outback's dining experience—large, highly seasoned portions of food for moderate prices—is so in tune with today's dining experience that patrons in many of its restaurants experience hour-long dinner waits seven nights a week. The friendly service is notable, from the host who opens the door and greets guests, to the well-trained servers, who casually sit down next to patrons in the booths and explain the house specialties featured on the menu.

Using such tactics and their "No rules, just right" philosophy, they have accomplished two main goals: discipline and solid growth. Good profits and excellent marketing potentials show just how successful the business has become.

menus in order to attract more customers. Steak restaurant operators admit that they are not expecting to see the same customer every week, but hopefully every two or three weeks. The Chart House chain is careful to market their menu as including seafood and chicken, but steak is at the heart of the business, with 60 percent of sales from red meat.[19]

Ponderosa, with 566 units, and Bonanza, with 156 units, have sales of $773 million together and are owned and operated by Metromedia Steak House, Inc. They are both family concepts featuring counter service and food bars. These restaurants have also added items to their menu in order to broaden customer appeal. Some of these items are an expansion of the Grand Buffet to include Mexican food items like chimichangas, tamales, make-your-own burritos, barbecued ribs, and chicken.

Other chains in this segment include Outback Steakhouse, which is actually the number one volume steak sales restaurant, with sales of $1.07 billion. Stewart Anderson's Black Angus, Golden Corral, Western Sizzlin', and Ryan's Family Steak Houses all have sales of more than $250 million each. In fact, chains have the biggest stake in the segment.

Seafood

Red Lobster is widely regarded as the national chain of excellence in the seafood segment. The corporate profile of Red Lobster later in this chapter gives an indication of not only the corporation's success, but also the reasons for that success.

Seafood continues to be popular with consumers because of health concerns. A number of chains have introduced more baked and broiled items and dropped some of the fried ones. The seafood franchising segment is dominated by four chains—Red Lobster with 729 units, Long John Silver with 1,461 units, Captain D's with 598 units, and Landry's Seafood House with 44 units. There are, in addition, several regional chains such as Skipper's, a West Coast chain of 220 units based in Bellevue, Washington.

Red Lobster Food (Photo Courtesy Red Lobster.)

Corporate Profile: Red Lobster

In 1968, a restaurant entrepreneur took a gamble on a new seafood restaurant concept in Lakeland, Florida. He was already in his mid-fifties, but Bill Darden decided to roll the dice at a time when most other men his age were looking toward retirement.

The gamble paid off—more than Darden could ever have imagined. His single seafood restaurant—Red Lobster—has since grown to become the largest seafood restaurant company in North America, with more than 800 restaurants in forty-nine states and Canada.

Darden's restaurant career began in the 1930s in a tiny southern Georgia town called Waycross. It was there that nineteen-year-old Darden operated a small lunch counter called The Green Frog, where he served as manager, night cook, waiter, and counter server.

As he saved money from The Green Frog, he began to acquire other restaurants in Florida, Georgia, and South Carolina. In 1963, Darden and his partners bought an Orlando landmark, Gary's Duck Inn, a popular seafood restaurant.

It was so popular that Darden began to think about expanding the concept—creating a no-frills seafood restaurant that offered fast, efficient service. He collected several investors, hired an ad agency, and, as they say, the rest is history.

One constant in Red Lobster's twenty-five years of consistent growth and success has been change. Keeping pace with the ever-changing expectations of the dining-out public, North America's largest full-service seafood restaurant company continues to look for new ways to assure quality and value for its guests.

Innovative menu additions, enhanced service, and new, contemporary decor are recent examples of Red Lobster's commitment to not only meet, but also exceed, guest expectations.

This year, Red Lobster expects to serve more than 80 million pounds of seafood to more than 150 million guests. With over 729 restaurants in the United States and more than fifty in Canada, the company achieved sales in excess of $1.9 billion in fiscal year 1996.

"The Red Lobster concept is designed to offer quality seafood at moderate prices in a contemporary, nautical

setting," says Red Lobster president Jefferey J. O'Hara. "Our commitment to quality, value and service for our guests has resulted in 25 years of consistent growth." All Red Lobster restaurants are company-owned and -operated, offering comfortable and efficient table service in an informal family atmosphere. Red Lobster menus feature a broad selection of shellfish and daily fresh fish entrees, in addition to beef, chicken, and seafood-steak combination platters.

The original restaurant in Lakeland, Florida, was such an immediate success that it was necessary to enlarge and remodel it within the first month of operation. Two years later, in 1970, Red Lobster's five restaurants attracted the attention of General Mills, which purchased the chain and provided the necessary resources for rapid nationwide expansion.

A Commitment to Quality

An important contributor to this successful climb is an uncompromising commitment to quality. "Through our rigorous inspection systems . . . from the seafood purchased directly from the world's best commercial fisherman to the food served in the restaurant, Red Lobster assures quality in purchasing, distribution and restaurant operations," O'Hara says. The Red Lobster quality assurance program is recognized as a foodservice industry leader. The program includes strict purchasing standards and inspections at various critical points. Ongoing laboratory testing of products before shipment to restaurants and quality control training for managers of each restaurant assure that quality is a priority—"from sea to table."

Additionally, in the United States, voluntary seafood inspection programs administered by the United States Department of Commerce (U.S.D.C.) are a further test of quality assurance for the restaurant chain. All Red Lobster seafood carries the U.S.D.C. and/or Canadian seafood inspection approval.

"We believe our success is the result of the strength of our original seafood concept, our commitment to quality, the job our employees consistently perform daily, and a dynamic menu that meets seafood lovers' changing tastes."

Pancake

Pancakes alone are not a sufficient attraction to sustain a restaurant operation. Therefore, each of the major franchised chains has added new menu items to increase customer interest and satisfaction.

The major force in this segment is the International House of Pancakes (IHOP), with 729 units. Other major companies in this segment are Country Kitchen, a division of Minneapolis-based Carlson Companies, with 253 units, and Village Inn, the 206-unit, Denver-based subsidiary of Vicorp.

Each of the pancake chains is reacting to the health-conscious customer by offering egg substitutes and a near cholesterol-free pancake. Pancake franchises cost approximately $50,000 for the franchise fee, a four to five percent annual royalty, and a three percent advertising fee.

Sandwich Restaurants

Indicative of America's obsession with the quick and convenient, sandwiches have achieved star status. Recently, menu debuts in the sandwich segment have outpaced all others. Classics, like melts and club sandwiches, have returned with a vengeance—but now there are also wraps.

Au Bon Pain of Boston is currently rolling out a line of eight new sourdough bagels designed to boost breakfast sales and keep regulars engaged. The bagels, which include such signature flavors as Asiago Cheese and Wild Blueberry, are also available as a sandwich option. Recently, they also introduced a line of pita-based wrap sandwiches.

A sandwich restaurant is a popular way for a young entrepreneur to enter the restaurant business. The leader in this segment is Subway, which operates 8,400 units. Cofounder Fred Deluca parlayed an initial investment of $1,000 into one of the largest and fastest-growing chains in the world. Franchise fees are $10,000 with a second store fee of $2,500. Average unit sales are about $270,000 annually, with yearly costs of about $75,000.

The Subway strategy is to invest half of the chain's advertising dollars in national advertising. Franchise owners pay 2.5 percent of sales to the marketing fund. As with other chains, Subway is attempting to widen its core eighteen- to thirty-four-year-old customer base by adding Kids Packs and Value 4-inch Round sandwiches aimed at teens and women. Sandwich restaurants stress the health value of their restaurants.

Family Restaurants

Family restaurants evolved from the coffee shop style of restaurant. In this segment, most restaurants are individually or family operated. Family restaurants are generally located in or with easy access to the suburbs. Most offer an informal setting with a simple menu and service designed to please all of the family. Some of these restaurants offer alcoholic beverages, which mostly consist of beer, wine, and perhaps a cocktail special. Usually, there is a hostess/cashier standing near the entrance to greet and seat guests while food servers take the

Corporate Profile: Au Bon Pain

In 1976, Au Bon Pain was founded as a demonstration bakery by a French oven manufacturer, Pavailler. One year later, with a keen sense for discerning the taste and trend in American culture and recognizing them as opportunities for a thriving business, Louis Kane purchased Au Bon Pain. He later merged his passion for involvement in entrepreneurial ventures with Ron Shaich's passion for strategic evolution. They became partners in 1981 creating a new company, Au Bon Pain Co., Inc. They set up a pilot facility at the company's Prudential Center location that concentrated on producing frozen dough products that could be fresh baked in each bakery cafe. Sales increased by 40 percent and the number of customers increased to 35,000 per week.

Au Bon Pain opened its first bakery cart at Logan Airport in 1982. This effort represented one of the first introductions of branded food in airports and initiated a trend that is now the dominant force in airport food service. Twelve months later, Au Bon Pain was the first in the

country to recognize the potential in expanding from a croissant and bread bakery to a French bakery cafe. The company added sandwiches and coffee to its existing line of bread and croissants. In addition, customer seats and booths were added to the stores' interiors. As a result of these internal improvements, sales climbed dramatically. A few years later, in 1986, the grilled chicken sandwich was introduced, and it soon became the number one sandwich at Au Bon Pain.

Au Bon Pain began buying back its franchised units in 1987, and four years later, it opened its one-hundredth store. In the two years that followed, it opened one-hundred more bakery cafes and added to the product line. Au Bon Pain International also opened franchise operations in the Philippines and Indonesia and, in 1997, added cafes in Thailand, Brazil, and Argentina.

Au Bon Pain's success lies in its philosophy—to "be able to dance." In this case, Au Bon Pain officials define "dance" as the ability to recognize the needs of their customers and to change the strategic direction of their company to meet those needs. By applying this concept, Au Bon Pain Co., Inc.'s goal is to become the dominant bakery cafe operator, both domestically and internationally. They are striving for increased customer service and, industry-defining reputation. Au Bon Pain also hopes to expand to more than 1,000 units within the next ten years through its four growth vehicles: Au Bon Pain business unit, Saint Louis Bread business unit, international and trade channels, and manufacturing service.

Applebee's

orders and bring the plated food from the kitchen. Some family restaurants have incorporated salad and dessert bars to offer more variety and increase the average check.

The lines separating the various restaurants and chains in the family segment are blurring as operators upscale their concepts. Flagstar Co.'s acquisition of Coco's and Carrow's family restaurant brands have created the high-end niche of family dining—somewhere between traditional coffee shops and the casual dining segment. The value-oriented operator in the family dining segment is Denny's, also owned by Flagstar. The more upscale family concepts include Perkins, Marie Callender's, and Cracker Barrel, all of which are sometimes referred to as the "relaxed" segment. These chains tend to have higher check averages than do traditional and value-oriented family chains, and compete not only with them, but also with moderately priced, casual-themed operators, such as Applebee's and TGI Friday's.

Karen Brennan, vice president of marketing for the Coco's concept, says that people's use of restaurants is very different from five years ago. Consumers are thinking in terms of "meal solutions." The operators in this segment are seeking to capitalize on two trends affecting the industry as a whole—the tendency of families to dine out together more often and the quest among adults for higher quality, more flavorful food offerings. Cracker Barrel derives 45 percent of its restaurant sales from the dinner "daypart" (the dinner menu is served throughout most of the day), while only about 20 percent comes from breakfast. The average check is just a little more than $6, almost $1 more than Denny's. In TV advertising, Cracker Barrel promotes the dinner daypart menu items, including a shrimp platter, a roast-pork dish, and a turkey dinner.[20]

Ethnic Restaurants

The majority of ethnic restaurants are independently owned and operated. The owners and their families provide something different for the adventurous diner or a taste of home for those of the same ethnic background as the restaurant. The traditional ethnic restaurants sprang up to cater to the taste of the various immigrant groups—Italian, Chinese, and so on.

Perhaps the fastest growing segment of ethnic restaurants in the United States, popularity-wise, is Mexican. Mexican food has a heavy representation in the southwestern states, although, because of near-market saturation, the chains are spreading east.

Taco Bell is the Mexican quick-service market leader with a 60 percent share. This PepsiCo., Fortune 500 company has achieved this incredible result with a value-pricing policy that has increased traffic in all units. Currently, there are 6,867 units with sales of $4.4 billion.

The next biggest chain in the Mexican food segment, in terms of sales, is Chi-Chi's. Chi-Chi's 184 units have total sales of $294 million. The third largest quick-service chain is Del Taco Inc. of Costa Mesa, California, with 300 restaurants and sales of $235 million. El Torito is fourth largest with 104 units producing $229.4 million in sales. These Mexican-food chains can offer a variety of items on a value menu, starting with 49 cents.

There are a great variety of ethnic restaurants in our major cities, and their popularity is increasing. For example, in 1985 in San Diego, America's sixth largest city, there were no Thai restaurants. Today there are twenty-two, in addition to new Afghan and Ethiopian restaurants.

Casual Dining and Dinner House Restaurants

As implied, casual dining is relaxed and could include restaurants from several classifications: chain or independent, ethnic, or theme. Hard Rock Cafe, TGI Friday's, The Olive Garden, Houston's, and Red Lobster are good examples of casual dining.

Houston's is a leader in the casual restaurant segment with about $5.5 million in average per-unit sales in its 35 restaurants. The menu is limited to about forty items and focuses on American cuisine, with a $10 average per-person ticket for lunch and $16 to $18 for dinner. While encouraging local individuality in its restaurants and maintaining exceptional executive and unit general manager stability, it succeeds with no franchising and virtually no advertising.[21]

Over the past few years, the trend in dinner house restaurants has been toward more casual dining. This trend merely reflects the mode of society. Dinner house restaurants have become fun places to let off steam. There are a variety

Chart House (Courtesy Chart House Restaurants.)

Table 6–2	Top Fifteen Dinner House Restaurant Chains
Chain	**Sales for fiscal year July 1, 1996–June 30, 1997 ($ million)**
1. Applebee's	$1,540.0
2. TGI Friday's	1,145.2
3. Chili's	1,104.0
4. Ruby Tuesday	546.0
5. Bennigan's	448.0
6. Hooters	325.0
7. Red Robin	293.6
8. The Ground Round	285.9
9. Houlihan's	241.6
10. Planet Hollywood	222.5
11. Hard Rock Cafe	216.0
12. The Black-Eyed Pea	189.6
13. Houston's	177.8
14. O'Charley's	163.8
15. Chart House	160.6

Source: Kimberly D. Lowe and Erin Nicholas, "Chaos in a Crowded Market," *Restaurant and Institutions, 107,* 17, July 15, 1997.

of restaurant chains that call themselves *dinner house restaurants.* Some of them could even fit into the theme category. Table 6–2 lists some of the better-known dinner house chains.

Many dinner house restaurants have a casual, eclectic decor that may promote a theme. Chart House, for example, is a steak and seafood chain that has a nautical theme.

TGI Friday's is an American bistro dinner house with a full menu and a decor of bric-a-brac that contributes to the fun atmosphere. TGI Friday's is a chain that has been in operation for more than twenty years, so the concept has stood the

TGI Friday's (Courtesy TGI Friday's.)

test of time. TGI Friday's is featured in Chapter 7, "Restaurant Operations," as a corporation of excellence.

A recent *Restaurants and Institutions* magazine survey indicated that the following are America's favorite chains in various categories. Their respective scores, out of a possible five points, are also shown.

Burgers	1. In-N-Out Burger	3.7
	2. Wendy's	3.58
Pizza	1. Papa John's	3.57
	2. Pizza Hut	3.47
Chicken	1. Kenny Rogers Roaster	3.61
	2. Chick-fil-A	3.58
Steak houses	1. Morton's of Chicago	3.93
	2. Outback Steakhouse	3.85
Dinner houses	1. Chart House	3.93
	2. Cheesecake Factory	3.80
	3. Olive Garden	3.76
Seafood	1. Red Lobster	3.71
	2. Legal Sea Foods	3.71

One interesting finding of the survey was the difference between male and female respondents' rankings of restaurants. For instance, Chart House was the number one choice of females, whereas it was ranked number eight by men. Similarly, Morton's of Chicago was ranked number one by males, but number twenty-one by females.

Many chains are making moves toward "high-end casual"—a segment that retains the informality of casual dining, but with prices and food quality resembling that of fine dining. To take advantage of this kind of opportunity, some restaurant companies are buying other chains' concepts and refining them. In other cases, they are developing a concept in-house, with an eye toward targeting a specific price point. Brinker International trend-watcher Lane Cardwell says there is evidence that the casual dining segment is "maturing." This is also known as increased segmentation.

Whatever it is called, high-end, casual dining is potentially uncreative. According to the National Restaurant Association, food costs averaged 27 percent at full-service restaurants with a typical tab of $10 or more, versus 29 percent at full-service eateries with average checks below $10. Also, higher-margin beverage sales were 64 percent greater at more expensive restaurants. The higher checks help leverage the fixed and variable costs to yield greater profit margins, provided guests don't balk at the higher check averages. The question is how many times a week, or a month, a customer will pay $20+ per person for a meal—no matter how much value they're getting.

Wally Dodin, CEO of Friday's Hospitality Worldwide, says that people are willing to pay more for a unique experience. Consequently, Friday's opened the first of its pricier Italianni's restaurants in 1994 and plans to have 200 units by the year 2000. Chart House, one of the pioneers of this segment, decided to sell its popular lower-check Islands chain in order to concentrate on the higher-check core concept. They have also engaged the services of Rich Melman to help stimulate customer counts. The major success story in this segment is Outback Steakhouse, the steak chain that made a $20 average check profitable at more than 260 units nationally.

Theme Restaurants

Many theme restaurants are a combination of a sophisticated specialty and several other types of restaurants. They generally serve a limited menu but aim to wow the guest by the total experience. Of the many popular theme restaurants, two stand out. The first highlights the nostalgia of the 1950s, as done in the T-Bird and Corvette diners. These restaurants serve all-American food such as the perennial meat loaf in a fun atmosphere that is a throw-back to the seemingly more carefree 1950s. The food servers appear in short polka-dot skirts with gym shoes and bobby socks. They will probably be chewing bubble gum; if you fill up on the main course and decline the dessert offerings, you are likely to receive an off-beat reply like, "Thank God, because my feet are killing me."

The second popular theme restaurant is the dinner house category; among some of the better-known national and regional chains are TGI Friday's, Houlihan's, and Bennigan's. These are casual American bistro-type restaurants that combine a lively atmosphere created in part by assorted bric-a-brac to decorate the various ledges and walls. These restaurants have remained popular over the past twenty years. In a prime location, they can do extremely well.

People are attracted to theme restaurants because they offer a total experience and a social meeting place. This is achieved through decoration and atmosphere and allows the restaurant to offer a limited menu that blends with the theme. Throughout the United States and the world, there are numerous theme restaurants that stand out for one reason or another. Among them are decors featuring airplanes, railway, dining cars, rock and roll, 1960s nostalgia, and many others.

Celebrity Restaurants

Celebrity-owned restaurants have been growing in popularity. Some celebrities, such as Wolfgang Puck, came from a culinary background, while others, like Naomi Campbell, Claudia Schiffer, and Elle Macpherson (owners of the Fashion Café), did not. A number of sports celebrities also have restaurants. Among

Spago's

Corporate Profile: Fashion Café

The challenge of creating the Fashion Café Collection was to combine the intellectual appreciation of fashion with visual, stimulating displays. The nature of the collection in each location is dictated by the city and country. Local and foreign cultures interpret fashion differently, including everything from popular to local high culture.

The advent of the super model has brought a new-found focus upon the industry. Entertainment influences are, and will continue to be, a key element of fashion. Media plays a vital role as a "mood meter." Through cinema,

television, and specialty channels such as MTV, the media allows centuries of fashion to be viewed in mere minutes. These influences provide the strongest, visual marker of what is happening in fashion today. Fashion Café combines these factors, creating a unique crossroad between everyday living and glamorous runways.

Fashion Café super model partners Claudia Schiffer, Elle Macpherson, Naomi Campbell, along with Jacqueline Nims (director of acquisitions/curator) and Tommaso Buti (president and CEO), invite their customers into the glamorous world of fashion with a series of daily fashion shows. The fashion shows allow patrons to view the creations of some of the world's top designers, as well as those of hot, new designers.

Fashion Café also has a flavorful menu that includes an international selection of appetizers, luscious salads, sizzling pizzas, fresh pastas, grilled sandwiches, and scrumptious desserts.

them are Michael Jordan, Dan Marino, Walter Payton, Junior Seau, and Wayne Gretzky. Television and movie stars have also gotten into the act. Oprah Winfrey has been part owner of The Eccentric in Chicago for a number of years. Dustin Hoffman and Henry Winkler are investors in Campanile, a popular Los Angeles restaurant. Dive, in Century City (Los Angeles), is owned by Steven Spielberg; House of Blues, by Denzel Washington, Georgia, and Dan Ackroyd. Musicians Kenny Rogers and Gloria Estefan are also restaurant owners.

Celebrity restaurants generally have an extra zing to them—a winning combination of design, atmosphere, food, and perhaps the thrill of an occasional visit by the owner(s). For example, Fashion Café, in New York, invites the guest to literally step through the lens of a camera into the glamorous world of fashion. Guests are seated in the Milan, Paris, or New York rooms, where they are entertained with daily fashion shows.

Trends in Restaurant Development

✔ Demographics: As the baby boomers move into middle age, a startling statistic will emerge in the year 2000. Thirty-five to fifty-four-year-olds (the age group with the highest income) will make up almost one-third of the American population—as the forty-five to fifty-four-year-old bracket increases by an unprecedented 46 percent from 1990. Simply put, the largest demographic group will have the most money.

✔ Branding: Restaurant operators are using the power of branding, both in terms of brand name recognition from a franchising viewpoint and in the products utilized.

✔ Alternative outlets: Increased competition from "c-stores" and home meal replacement outlets.

✔ Globalization: Continued transnational development.

✔ Continued diversification within the various dining segments.

✔ More twin and multiple locations.

✔ More points of service, e.g., Taco Bell at gas stations.

✔ More hypertheme restaurants.

✔ Chains vs. independents

Evaluating the Weaknesses of a Restaurant

In groups, evaluate a restaurant and write out a list of weaknesses. Use the headings outlined in the restaurant chapters. Then, for each of the weaknesses, decide on what actions you would take to exceed guest expectations.

Restaurant concept

Create a restaurant concept and, using the headings outlined in the chapter, discuss the main elements.

Summary

1. Restaurants offer the possibility of excellent food and social interaction. In general, restaurants strive to surpass an operating philosophy that includes quality food, good value, and gracious service.

2. In order to succeed, a restaurant needs the right location, food, atmosphere, and service to attract a substantial market. The concept of a restaurant has to fit the market it is trying to attract.

3. The location of a restaurant has to match factors such as convenience, neighborhood, parking, visibility, and demographics. Typical types of locations are downtown, suburban, shopping mall, cluster, or stand alones.

4. The menu and pricing of a restaurant must match the market it wants to attract, the capabilities of the cooks, and the existing kitchen equipment.

5. The two main categories of restaurants are full service and specialty. Further distinctions can be made: quick-service, ethnic, dinner house, occasion, and casual. In general, most restaurants fall into more than one category.

Review Exercises

1. What is understood by the term *catchment area*, and why is it essential for the success of a restaurant to concentrate on a certain market?
2. Explain why it is important that the location of a restaurant matches its concept.
3. The menu is another very important part of a restaurant. Explain the following terms: *table d'hote, accuracy in menu,* and *equipment capacity.*
4. Describe the two main ways to price a menu.
5. Explain why there is no full-service luxury restaurant chain. List tactics used by full-service restaurant owners to increase profitability.
6. Explain why there is no single definition of the various classifications of restaurants; give examples.

Key Words and Concepts

Actual market share
Casual dining
Classification of restaurants
Contribution margin
Dinner house restaurants
Ethnic restaurants
Fair market share
Food cost percentage
Full-service restaurants
Haute cuisine
Independent restaurants
Market segment
Quick-service restaurants
Restaurant concept
Specialty restaurants
Theme restaurants
Weighted average

Notes

[1] Donald E. Lundberg and John R. Walker, *The Restaurant from Concept to Operation,* 2nd ed. New York: John Wiley and Sons, 1993, p. 12.
[2] Ibid.
[3] Ibid.
[4] This section draws on Jeff Weinstein and Brenda McCarthy, "Concept Creators," *Restaurants and Institutions, 103,* 15, June 15, 1993, pp. 34–59.
[5] Robert C. Lewis and Richard E. Chambers, *Marketing Leadership in Hospitality: Foundations and Practices.* New York: Van Nostrand Reinhold, 1990, pp. 339–340.
[6] Lundberg and Walker, op. cit., p. 63.
[7] Lundberg and Walker, op. cit., p. 208.
[8] French for *everything in place.* It means all the preparation that goes into cooking before the actual cooking starts.
[9] Lundberg and Walker, op. cit., p. 65.
[10] Rocco M. Angelo and Andrew N. Vladimir, *Hospitality Today: An Introduction.* East Lansing, Mich.: The Educational Institute of the American Hotel and Motel Association, 1991, p. 139.
[11] "R & I Top Independents," *Restaurants and Institutions, 102,* 10, April 1992, p. 90.
[12] A wheelable cart that is used to add flair to table-side service. It is also used for flambé dishes.
[13] Paul Fumkin, "Prunelle Thrives Despite Tough N.Y. Obstacles," *Nations Restaurant News, 25,* 20, May 20, 1991, p. 80.
[14] Milford Prewitt, "Maccioni Says Le Cirque 2000 Remains a Work in Progress," *Nation's Restaurant News, 31,* 25, June 23, 1997, pp. 3, 6.
[15] Kimberly D. Lowe & Erin Nicholas, "Cuaos in a Crowded Market," *Restaurant & Institutions,* 107, 17, July 15, 1997.
[16] McDonald's Annual Report, 1997.
[17] Ibid.
[18] Ron Ruggles, "Church's: Taking Low-Cost Dining to New Heights," *Nation's Restaurant News,* 31, 30, August 3, 1997.
[19] "Market Share Report," *Restaurant Business, 91,* 9, June 10, 1992, p. 156.
[20] Mark Hamstra, "When Segments Collide: Family Restaurants Blaze Casual Trails," *Nation's Restaurant News, 31,* 9, March 3, 1997.
[21] Charles Bernstein, "Chains, Champions, and Contenders," *Restaurants and Institutions, 107,* 3, February 1, 1997.

Restaurant Operations

7

After reading and studying this chapter you should be able to do the following:

✔ Apply the forecasting technique used in the chapter to measure expected volume of business

✔ Describe the key points in purchasing, receiving, storing, and issuing

✔ Explain the important aspects of food production

✔ Name and describe the various types of services

✔ Explain the difference between controllable expenses and fixed costs

✔ Explain the components of an income statement and operating ratios

✔ Describe the important aspects of a control system for a restaurant operation

✔ Outline the functional areas and tasks of a foodservice/restaurant manager

Front of the House

Restaurant operations are generally divided between what is commonly called front of the house and back of the house. A sample organization chart shows the differences between the front and back of the house areas in Figure 7–1.

The restaurant is run by the general manager, or restaurant manager. Depending upon the size and sales volume of the restaurant, there may be more managers with special responsibilities such as kitchen manager, bar manager, and dining room manager. These managers are usually cross-trained in order to relieve each other.

In the front of the house, restaurant operation begins with creating and maintaining what is called "curbside appeal," or keeping the restaurant looking attractive and welcoming. Ray Kroc, of McDonald's, once spent a couple of hours in a good suit with one of his restaurant managers cleaning up the parking lot of one of his restaurants. Word soon got around to the other stores that management begins in the parking lot and ends in the bathrooms. Most restaurant chains have checklists that each manager uses. In the front of the house, the parking lot, including the flower gardens, need to be maintained in good order. As guests approach the restaurant, hostesses may hold the door open and welcome them to the restaurant. At Mike Hurst's 15th Street Fisheries restaurant in Ft. Lauderdale, hostesses welcome the guests by assuring them that "we're glad you're here!"

Once inside, the hostess, or as TGI Friday's calls them, "smiling people greeters" (SPGs), greet guests appropriately and, if seating is available, escorts them to a table. If there is a wait, the hostess will take the guests' names and ask for their table preference.

Aside from greeting the guests, one of the critical functions of the hostess is to rotate arriving guests among the sections or stations. This ensures an even and timely distribution of guests—otherwise one section may get overloaded.

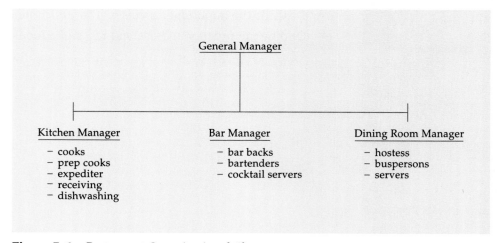

Figure 7–1 *Restaurant Organizational Chart*

Guests are sometimes asked to wait a few minutes even if tables are available. This is done to help spread the kitchen's work load.

The hostesses maintain a book, or chart, showing the sections and tables, that they use to keep track of which tables are occupied. Hostesses escort guests to the tables, present menus, and may explain special sales promotions. Some may also remove excess covers from the table.

In some restaurants, servers are allocated a certain number of tables, which may vary depending upon the size of the tables and the volume of the restaurant. Normally, five is the maximum. In other restaurants, servers rotate within their section to cover three or four tables.

The server introduces him/herself, offers a variety of beverages and/or specials, or invites guests to select from the menu. This is known as suggestive selling. The server then takes the entree orders. Often, when taking orders, the server begins at a designated point and takes the orders clockwise from that point. In this way, the server will automatically know which person is having a particular dish. When the entrees are ready, the server brings them to the table. He or she checks a few minutes later to see if everything is to the guests' liking and perhaps asks if they would like another beverage. Good servers are also encouraged, when possible, to prebus tables.

Busers and servers may clear the entree plates, while servers suggestively sell desserts by describing, recommending, or showing the desserts. Coffee and after-dinner cocktails are also offered. Suggestions for steps to take in table service include the following:

✔ Greet the guests
✔ Introduce and suggestively sell beverages
✔ Suggest appetizers
✔ Take orders
✔ Check to see everything is to the guests' liking within two bites of the entrees
✔ Ask if the guests would like another drink
✔ Bring out dessert tray and suggest after-dinner drinks and coffee

In addition to the seven steps of the table service, servers are expected to be NCO—neat, clean, and organized—and to help ensure that hot food is served hot, and cold food is served cold.

For example, during the lunch hour, servers may be scheduled to start at 11:00 A.M. The opening group of two or three people is joined by the closing group of the same number at around 11:45 P.M. If the restaurant is quiet, servers may be phased out early. When the closing group comes in, there is a quick shift meeting, or "alley rally". This provides an opportunity to review recent sales figures, discuss any promotions, and acknowledge any items that are "86'ed"—the restaurant term for a menu item that is not available. Recognition is also given to the servers during the meetings, serving as morale boosters.

Restaurant Forecasting

Most businesses, including restaurants, operate by formulating a budget that projects sales and costs for a year on a weekly and monthly basis. Financial viability is predicated on sales, and sales budgets are forecasts of expected business.

Forecasting restaurant sales has two components: guest counts or covers and the average guest check. Guest counts or covers are the number of guests patronizing the restaurant over a given time period—a week, month, or year. To forecast the number of guests for a year, the year is divided into 12, 28 and one 29-day accounting periods. The accounting periods then are broken down into four, seven-day weeks.

In terms of number of guests, Mondays usually are quiet; business gradually builds to Friday, which is often the busiest day. Friday, Saturday, and Sunday frequently provide up to 50 percent of revenue.

The average guest check is calculated by dividing total sales by the number of guests. Most restaurants keep such figures for each meal. The number of guests forecast for each day is multiplied by the amount of the average food and beverage check for each meal to calculate the total forecast sales. Each day, actual totals are compared with the forecasts. Four weekly forecasts are combined to form one accounting period; the thirteen accounting periods, when totaled, become the annual total.

Forecasting is used not only to calculate sales projections but also for predicting staffing levels and labor cost percentages. Much depends on the accuracy of forecasting. Once sales figures are determined, all expenditures, fixed and variable, have to be deducted to calculate profit or loss.[1]

Service

More than ever, what American diners really want to order when eating out is a side of good service. All too often, it is not on the menu. With increased competition, however, bad service may be going the way of Beef Wellington in American restaurants. Just as American cuisine came of age in the 1970s and 1980s, service is showing signs of maturing in the 1990s.

A new American service has emerged. A less formal—yet professional—approach is preferred by the 1990s restaurant guests. The restaurants' commitment to service is evidenced by the fact that most have increased training for new employees. For example, at Splendido in San Francisco's Embarcadero, the amount of time new servers spend in training has increased from forty to one hundred hours.

Servers are not merely order takers; they are the salespeople of the restaurant. A server who is undereducated about the menu can seriously hurt business. One would not be likely to buy a car from a salesperson who knew nothing about the car; likewise, customers feel uneasy ordering with an unknowledgeable waiter. Getting the waitstaff familiar with the menu can be a difficult task. Karen MacNeil, a restaurant service consultant and director of the New York Professional Service School, suggests two strategies: first, start from scratch and assume all servers know nothing about food; second, make learning fun—teach no more than three menu items a day and tell stories and use images to help things stick in servers' memories. It also is a good idea for the chef to coach the servers.[2]

POSITION TITLE: *Assistant Manager*
REPORTS TO: *Manager*

POSITION OVERVIEW:

Under the general supervision of the manager, subject to the Service Policy and Procedure Manual, assures constantly and consistently the creation of maximal guest satisfaction and dining pleasure.

RESPONSIBILITIES AND DUTIES:

A. Planning and organizing
  1. Studies past sales experience records, confers with manager, keeps alert to holidays and special events, and so on; forecasts loads and prepares work schedules for service employees in advance to meet requirements.
  2. Observes guest reactions and confers frequently with servers to determine guest satisfactions, dissatisfactions, relative popularity of menu items, and so on and reports such information with recommendations to the manager.
  3. Observes daily the condition of all physical facilities and equipment in the dining room, making recommendations to the manager for correction and improvements needed.
  4. Anticipates all material needs and supplies and assures availability of same.
  5. Inspects, plans, and assures that all personnel, facilities, and materials are in complete readiness to provide excellent service before each meal period.
  6. Anticipates employment needs, recommending to the manager plans for recruitment and selection to meet needs as they arise.
  7. Discusses menu changes with servers in advance to assure full understanding of new items.
  8. Conducts meetings of service employees at appropriate times.
  9. Defines and explains clearly for servers and buspersons their responsibilities for relationships
     ✓ with each other
     ✓ with guests
     ✓ with the hostess/host
     ✓ with the manager
     ✓ with the cashier
     ✓ with the kitchen personnel

B. Coordinating
  1. Ensures that servers are fully informed as to all menu items—how they are prepared, what they contain, number of ounces per portion.
  2. Periodically discusses and reviews with employees company objectives, and guest and personnel policies.

  3. Keeps manager informed at all times about service activities, progress, and major problems.

C. Supervising
  1. Actively participates in employment of new servers and buspersons, suggests recruitment sources, studies applications, checks references, and conducts interviews.
  2. Following an orientation outline, introduces new employees to the restaurant, restaurant policies, and fellow employees.
  3. Using a training plan, trains new employees and current employees in need of additional training.
  4. Promptly corrects any deviations from established service standards.
  5. Counsels employees on job issues and personal problems.
  6. Follows established policy in making station assignments for servers.
  7. Establishes, with approval of manager, standards of conduct, grooming, personal hygiene, and dress.
  8. Prepares, in consultation and with approval of the manager, applied standards of performance for servers and buspersons.
  9. Recommends deserving employees for promotion, and outstanding performers for special recognition and award.
  10. Strives at all times through the practice of good human relations and leadership to establish esprit de corps—teamwork, unity of effort, and individual and group pride.
  11. Remains constantly alert to the entire dining room situation—is sensitive to any deviation or problem and assists quickly and quietly in its correction, elleviating guests' complaints.
  12. Greets and seats guests cordially and courteously, to assure a sincere welcome and to express a genuine interest in their dining pleasure.

D. Controlling
  1. Controls performance, conduct, dress, hygiene, sanitation, and personal appearance of employees according to established policies, standards, and procedures.
  2. Studies all evidence of waste of time and materials, and makes recommendations for preventing further waste.

E. Other
  1. In emergency situations, may serve guests, act as cashier, or perform specifically assigned duties of the manager.
  2. Personifies graciousness and offers hospitality to guests and employees by showing "we're glad you're here" and "we're proud to serve you."

[238]   *Restaurant Operations*

Suggestive Selling

Suggestive selling can be a potent weapon in the effort to increase food and beverage sales. Many restaurateurs cannot think of a better, more effective, and easier way to boost profit margins. Servers report that most guests are not offended or uncomfortable with suggestive selling techniques. In fact, customers may feel special that the server is in tune with their needs and desires. It may be that the server suggests something to the guest that he or she has never considered before. The object here is to turn servers into sellers. Guests will almost certainly be receptive to suggestions from competent servers.

On a hot day, for example, servers can suggest frozen margaritas or daiquiris before going on to describe the drink specials. Likewise, servers who suggest a bottle of Mondavi Fumé Blanc to complement a fish dish or a Mondavi Pinot Noir or Cabernet Sauvignon to go with red meat are likely to increase their restaurant's beverage sales.

Upselling takes place when a guest orders a "well" drink like a vodka and tonic. In this case, the server asks if the guests would like a Stoli and tonic. (Stoli is short for Stolichnaya, a popular brand of vodka.)

The following are a few suggestions to change a restaurant's attitude toward suggestive selling:

1. Train servers as commissioned salespeople
2. Provide incentives and feedback
3. Teach servers to suggest pairings
4. Hire the sales type
5. Create students of food and wine
6. Encourage servers to upsell
7. Promote ear-grabbing phrasing
8. Recognize the unspoken suggestions
9. Incorporate role playing
10. Draw the line between sell and solicit[3]

Types of Restaurant Service

French Service

This form of service is generally reserved for haute cuisine (elegant) restaurants and complements an elegant ambiance. The food is attractively arranged on platters and presented to guests, after which the preparation of the food is completed on a gueridon table beside the guests' seats. A gueridon is a trolley-like table with a gas burner for table-side cooking. This is the most impressive and expensive form of service.

French service is conducted by an elaborate and formal staff comprised of the following:

- Maitre d'hotel: Restaurant manager
- Chef de rang: Station server in charge of service for approximately four tables. Greets guests, describes and takes menu orders, supervises service, and completes the preparation of some dishes on the gueridon and carves, slices, or debones dishes for guests.

Personal Profile: Herman Cain

Herman Cain, president and chief executive officer of Godfather's Pizza, Inc., is a living example of leadership and management successfully combined in one person. He was born in Atlanta, Georgia, to a humble family, yet rich in spirit. His mother's Bible was a leading light throughout his life and career, and his father's optimism and sacrifices instilled in him the values and the principles that guided him from rural poverty to the crest of corporate America.

Cain has always been seeking challenges that could satisfy his profound need for accomplishments and achievement. He graduated from Morehouse College with a degree in mathematics, and later earned a master's degree in computer science while working as a mathematician for the Navy. However, government service did not seem to offer many entrepreneurial opportunities. Cain's competitive spirit led him to seek more challenges with Coca-Cola.

In 1977, Cain began his experience in the foodservice industry, when he joined the Pillsbury Company. His exceptional abilities, both in terms of management, creativity, and, above all, hard work, were soon rewarded. Cain's career was well on its way to the top when, in only five years, at the age of thirty-four, he became vice president of corporate systems and services. Although such a position was the fulfillment of Cain's dream, as well as of his father's, Cain was not satisfied. He felt he was bound to achieve and move further beyond the limits.

After his many accomplishments with Pillsbury, he found himself hungering for new challenges and opportunities. At the age of thirty-six, Cain resigned his senior position and made a stunning move. He wanted to learn the restaurant business from the bottom up, and he accomplished this by tackling such tasks as broiling burgers at Burger King.

After only nine months, he had moved from being a trainee flipping burgers to regional vice president of the Philadelphia market. His next formidable accomplishment was the ultimate open door to today's success. He transformed his region from the worst performing area in Burger King's system to the best, which undoubtedly caught the attention of Pillsbury executives. The offer he received from Pillsbury was the ultimate challenge, one that a man with Cain's personality and skills could not refuse. His mission was to take over the presidency of a floundering pizza chain, Godfather's Pizza, and return it

Herman Cain

to profitability. Cain's dynamism, enthusiasm, and endless energy had finally found a way to be fully employed. In fact, Cain renewed Godfather's Pizza, breathing new life into a restaurant concept that had already been declared by many as terminated.

Within twelve months, the chain regained profitability. Two years later, Cain achieved corporate ownership, buying the chain from Pillsbury. Cain's success lies in a perfect combination of management and leadership skills. As a manager, he made use of his analytical abilities to diagnose the situation, make strategic plans, and develop tactics to return Godfather's Pizza to profitability. He capitalized on every opportunity.

Cain realized that Godfather's goal was not to be a direct competitor to the industry's leaders—Pizza Hut and Domino's—but that he had to place a sharp focus on what the chain could do best—produce consistent quality products and maintain high standards of service, the driving force in any restaurant concept. A newly assembled management team helped him implement effectively the strategic actions designed to return the company to prosperity.

Cain's enthusiasm and leadership skills were transmitted to all segments of the company. Cain is a tremendously inspirational figure; his voice is one of those that cannot be ignored. It demands and obtains attention. He speaks powerfully and with a convincing self-confidence. "I'm a firm believer that we are put on this earth to make a difference," Cain said.

Cain is now president and CEO of the National Restaurant Association (NRA) and chairman of the board of the 520-unit Godfather's Pizza chain. Herman Cain, nicknamed "The Hermanator," aims to make the NRA one of the most potent political powers in Washington. Outlining his vision and mission for the NRA, Cain states three initiatives:

1. To represent the NRA as a political force in Washington.

2. To provide more education for members, primarily through the Educational Foundation of the NRA.

3. To buff the image of the restaurant industry, promoting it as more than just a provider of jobs. "It is a $320 billion gold mine of opportunity, a vehicle to achieve the American dream."[1]

[1]Patricia B. Dailey, *Restaurants and Institutions, 107,* 14, June 1, 1992, p. 58.

French Service

   ✔ Demi chef de rang: Assistant station server, assists the chef de rang, takes beverage orders, and serves food

   ✔ Commis de rang: Food server in training. Assists the demi chef de rang with serving of water, bread, and butter; serving and clearing of plates; taking orders to the kitchen; and bringing the food into the restaurant

Russian Service

With Russian service the food is cooked in the kitchen, cut, placed onto a serving dish, and beautifully garnished. The dish then is presented to the guests and served individually by lifting the food onto the guest's plate with a serving spoon and fork. Russian service can be used at a banquet or a dinner party, where the servers may wear white gloves.

Russian Service

American Service

This is a simplified version of Russian service techniques. The food is prepared and dished onto individual plates in the kitchen, carried into the dining room, and served to guests. This method of service is more popular because it is quicker and guests receive the food hot and beautifully presented by the chef.[4]

At Posterio, servers are invited to attend a one-and one-half-hour wine class in the restaurant; about three-quarters of the forty-member staff routinely benefit from this additional training. The best employees are also rewarded with monthly prizes and with semiannual and annual prizes, which range from $100 cash, a limousine ride, dinner at Posterio, or a night's lodging at the Prescott Hotel to a week in Hawaii. Servers at other San Francisco restaurants role play the various elements of service such as greeting and seating guests, suggestive selling, correct methods of service, and guest relations to ensure a positive dining experience. A good food server in a top restaurant in many cities can earn about $40,000 a year.

Good servers quickly learn to gauge the guests' satisfaction levels and to be sensitive to guests' needs; for example, they check to ensure guests have everything they need as their entree is placed before them. Even better, they anticipate guests' needs. For example, if the guest had used the entree knife to eat the appetizer, then a clean one should automatically be placed to the guest's right side. In other words, the guest should not receive the entree and then realize he or she needs another knife.

Another example of good service is when the server does not have to ask everyone at the table who is eating what. The server should either remember or do a seating plan so that the correct dishes are automatically placed in front of guests.

Danny Meyer, owner of New York City's celebrated Union Square Cafe and recipient of both the Restaurant of the Year and Outstanding Service Awards from the James Beard Foundation, gives each of the restaurant's ninety-five employees—from busperson to chef—a $600 annual allowance ($50 each a month) to eat in the restaurant and critique the experience.

At the critically acclaimed Inn at Little Washington in Washington, Virginia, servers are required to gauge the mood of every table and jot a number (one to ten) and sometimes a description ("elated, grumpy, or edgy") on each ticket. Anything below a seven requires a diagnosis. Servers and kitchen staff work together to try to elevate the number to at least a nine by the time dessert is ordered.

The Commander's Palace in New Orleans uses an elaborate system of color-coded tickets and hand signals in the dining room to ensure that everyone walks away a billboard for the restaurant. For example, when the maitre'd touches the corner of his eye as he ushers guests to a table, it is a signal to the staff to take a good look, this is someone you should remember.

People are all impressed most by the use of their own names. Recognition of this kind is music to the ear and the ego. In upscale restaurants, guests' names are remembered by taking names from the reservation book and writing them on the meal check. This not only impresses the host and her or his guests, it may also increase the tip considerably.[5]

Back of the House

The back of the house is generally run by the kitchen manager and refers to all the areas that guests do not normally come in contact with. This includes purchasing, receiving, storing/issuing, food production, stewarding, budgeting, accounting, and control.

One of the most important aspects to running a successful restaurant is having a strong back-of-the-house operation, particularly in the kitchen. The kitchen is the backbone of every full-service restaurant, thus it must be well managed and organized. Some of the main considerations in efficiently operating the back of the house include staffing, scheduling, training, food-cost analysis, production, management involvement, management follow-up, and employee recognition. Figure 7–2 describes a day in the life of James Lorenz, kitchen manager of TGI Friday's restaurant in Lafayette, Louisiana.

Food Production

Planning, organizing, and producing food of a consistently high quality is no easy task. The kitchen manager, cook, or chef begins the production process by determining the expected volume of business for the next few days. The same period's sales from the previous year will give a good indication of the expected volume and the breakdown of the number of sales of each menu item. As described earlier, ordering and receiving will have already been done for the day's production schedule.

The kitchen manager checks the head line cook's order, which will bring the prep (preparation) area up to the par stock of prepared items. Most of the prep work is done in the early part of the morning and afternoon. Taking advantage of slower times allows the line cooks to do the final preparation just prior to and during the actual meal service.

The kitchen layout is set up according to the business projected as well as the menu design. Most full-service restaurants have similar layouts and designs for their kitchens. The layout consists of the back door area, walk-ins, the freezer, dry storage, prep line, salad bar, cooking line, expediter, dessert station, and service bar area.

The cooking line is the most important part of the kitchen layout. It might consist of a broiler station, window station, fry station, salad station, saute station, and pizza station—just a few of the intricate parts that go into the set-up of the back of the house. The size of the kitchen and its equipment are all designed according to the sales forecast for the restaurant.

The kitchen will also be set up according to what the customers prefer and order most frequently. For example, if guests eat more broiled or sauteed items, the size of the broiler and saute must be larger to cope with the demand.

Teamwork, a prerequisite for success in all areas of the hospitality and tourism industry, is especially important in the kitchen. Due to the hectic pace,

A Day in the Life of a TGI Friday's Kitchen Manager
James Lorenz, Kitchen Manager TGI Friday's, Lafayette, Louisiana

7:00 A.M.: Arrive. Check the work of cleaning crew (such as clogs in burners, stoves/ovens, etc.) for total cleanliness

7:15–7:40: Set production levels for all stations (broiler/hot sauce/expediter, cold sauce, vegetable preparation, baker preparation, line preparation: saute/noodles, pantry, fry/seafood portioning)

8:00: The first cooks begin arriving; greet them and allocate production sheets with priority items circled

9:00: On a good day, the produce arrives at 9:00 A.M. Check for quality, quantity, accuracy (making sure the prices match the quotation sheet), and that the produce is stored properly

9:30–11:00: Follow up on production. The saute cook, who is last to come in, arrives. He or she is the closing person for the morning shift.
- ✔ Follow up on cleanliness, recipe adherence, production accuracy
- ✔ Check the stations to ensure the storage of prepped items (e.g., plastic draining inserts under poultry and seafood), the shelf life of products, general cleanliness, and that what is in the station is prepared correctly (e.g., turkey diced to the right size and portioned and dated correctly)

James Lorenz

10:45: Final check of the line and production to ensure readiness. Did everyone prepare enough?

11:00–2:30: All hands on deck. Jump on the first ticket. Pretoast buns for burgers and hold in heated drawers. Precook some chicken breasts for salads. Monitor lunch until 2:30 P.M.
- ✔ Be responsible for cleanliness
- ✔ Determine who needs to get off the clock
- ✔ Decide what production is left for the remainder of the day
- ✔ Focus on changing over the line, change the food pan inserts (bar-be-que sauce, etc.)

2:30–3:15: Complete changeover of the line and check the stocking for the P.M. crew
- ✔ Final prep portioning
- ✔ Check the dishwasher area and prep line for cleanliness
- ✔ Check that the product is replaced in the store walk-in or refrigerator
- ✔ Reorganize the produce walk-in. Check the storage of food, labels, and day dots, lids on
- ✔ Thank the A.M. crew and send them home

4:00–4:15: Welcome the P.M. crew
- ✔ Place produce order (as a double check, ask the P.M. crew what they might need)

5:00: Hand over to P.M. manager

Figure 7–2 *A Day in the Life of a TGI Friday's Kitchen Manager*

pressure builds, and unless each member of the team excels, the result will be food that is delayed, not up to standard, or both.

While organization and performance standards are necessary, it is helping each other with the prepping and the cooking that makes for teamwork. "It's just like a relay race; we can't afford to drop the baton," says Amy Lu, kitchen manager of China Coast restaurant in Los Angeles. Teamwork in the back of the house is like an orchestra playing in tune, each player adding to the harmony.

Another example of organization and teamwork is TGI Friday's five rules of control for running a kitchen:

1. Order it well
2. Receive it well
3. Store it well
4. Make it to the recipe
5. Don't let it die in the window

It is amazing to see a kitchen line being overloaded, yet everyone is gratified when the team succeeds in preparing and serving quality food on time.

Kitchen/Food Production

Staffing and Scheduling

Practicing proper staffing is absolutely crucial for the successful running of a kitchen. It is important to have enough employees on the schedule to enable the restaurant, as a whole, to handle the volume on any given shift. Often it is better to overstaff the kitchen, rather than understaff it, for two reasons. First, it is much easier to send an employee home than it is to call someone in. Second, having extra employees on hand allows for cross-training and development, which is becoming a widely used method.

Problems can also be eliminated if a manpower plan is created, for example, to set levels for staffing needs. These levels should be adjusted according to sales trends on a monthly basis.

Also crucial to the smooth running of the kitchen is having a competent staff. This means putting the best cooks in the appropriate stations on the line, which will assist in the speed of service, the food quality, and the quality of the operations.

Training and Development

Implementing a comprehensive training program is vital in the kitchen, due to a high turnover rate. Trainers should, of course, be qualified and experienced in the kitchen. Often, the most competent chefs are used to train new hires. Such trainings are usually done on-the-job and may include study material. Some restaurants may even require new hires to complete a written test, evaluating the skills acquired through the training process.

Ensuring adequate training is necessary because the success of the business lies in the hands of the trainer and the trainee. If employees are properly trained when they begin their employment, little time and money will need to be spent on correcting errors. Thorough training also helps in retaining employees for longer periods of time.

Training, however, does not stop after passing a test. Developing the skills of all the employees is critical to the growth and success of the kitchen and, ultimately, the restaurant. A development program may consist of delegating duties or projects to the staff, allowing them to expand their horizons within the kitchen and the restaurant business. Such duties include projections of sales, inventory, ordering, schedule writing, and training.

This will help management get feedback on the running of the kitchen and on how well the development program works in their particular operation. Also, this allows for internal growth and promotion.

Production Procedures

Production in the kitchen is key to the success of a restaurant since it relates directly to the recipes on the menu and how much product is on hand to produce the menu. Thus, controlling the production process is crucial. To undertake such a task, production control sheets are created for each station, for example, broiler, saute, fry, pantry, window, prep, dish, and dessert. With the control sheets, levels are set up for each day according to sales.

The first step in creating the production sheets is to count the products on hand for each station. Once the production levels are determined, the amount of product required to reach the level for each recipe is decided. Once these calculations are completed, the sheets are handed to the cooks. It is important to make these calculations before the cooks arrive, considering the amount of prep time that is needed in order to produce before business is actually conducted. For instance, if a restaurant is open only for lunch and dinner, enough product should be on hand by 11:00 A.M. to ensure that the cooks are prepared to handle the lunch crowd.

When determining production, par levels should be changed weekly according to sales trends. This will help control and minimize waste levels. Waste is a large contributor to food cost, therefore the kitchen should determine the product levels necessary to make it through only one day. Products have a particular shelf life, and if the kitchen overproduces and does not sell the product within its shelf life, it must be thrown away. More importantly, this practice allows for the freshest product to reach the customers on a daily basis.

After the lunch rush, the kitchen checks to see how much product was sold and how much is left for the night shift. (Running out of a product is unacceptable and should not happen. If proper production procedures are followed, a restaurant will not have to "86" anything on the menu.) After all production is completed on all stations, the cooks may be checked out. It is essential to check out the cooks and hold them accountable for production levels. If they are not checked out, they will slide on their production, negatively impacting the restaurant and the customer.

The use of production sheets is critical, as well, in controlling how the cooks use the products, since production plays a key role in food cost. Every recipe has a particular "spec" (specification) to follow. When one deviates from the recipe, quality goes down, consistency is lost, and food cost goes up. That is why it is important follow the recipe at all times.

Management Involvement

As in any business, management involvement is vital to the success of a restaurant. Management should know firsthand what is going on in the back of the house. It is also important that they be on the line, assisting the staff in the preparation of the menu and in the other operations of the kitchen, just as they should be helping when things are rushed. When management is visible to the staff, they are prone to do what they need to be doing at all times, and food quality is more apparent and consistent. Managers should constantly be walking and talking food cost, cleanliness, sanitation, and quality. This shows the staff how serious and committed they are to the successful running of the back of the house.

As management spends more time in the kitchen, more knowledge is gained, more confidence is acquired and more respect is earned. Employee-management interaction produces a sense of stability and a strong work ethic among employees, resulting in higher morale and promoting a positive working environment.

Management Follow-Up

To ensure that policies and standards are being upheld, management follow-up should happen on a continual basis. This is especially important when cooks are held accountable to specifications and production, and when other staff members are given duties to perform. Without follow-up, the restaurant may fold.

Employee Recognition

Employee recognition is an extremely important aspect of back-of-the-house management. Recognizing employees for their efforts creates a positive work environment that motivates the staff to excel and to ultimately produce consistently better-quality food for the guests.

Recognition can take many different forms, from personally commending a staff person for his or her efforts to recognizing a person in a group setting. By recognizing employees, management can make an immediate impact on the quality of operations. This can be a great tool for building sales, as well as assisting in the overall success of the restaurant.

Purchasing

Purchasing for restaurants involves procuring the products and services that the restaurant needs in order to serve its guests. Restaurant operators set up purchasing systems that determine the following:

- ✔ Standards for each item (product specification)
- ✔ Systems that minimize effort and maximize control of theft and losses from other sources
- ✔ The amount of each item that should be on hand (par stock and reorder point)
- ✔ Who will do the buying and keep the purchasing system in motion
- ✔ Who will do the receiving, storage, and issuing of items[6]

It is desirable for restaurants to establish standards for each product, called *product specification.* When ordering meat, for example, the cut, weight, size, percentage of fat content, and number of days aged are all factors that are specified by the purchaser.

Establishing systems that minimize effort and maximize control of theft may be done by computer or manually. However, merely computerizing a system does not make it theft-proof. Instead, employing honest workers is a top priority because temptation is everywhere in the restaurant industry.

An efficient and effective system establishes a stock level that must be on hand at all times. This is called a par stock. If the stock on hand falls below a specified reorder point, the computer system automatically reorders a predetermined quantity of the item.

In identifying who will do the buying, it is most important to separate task and responsibility between the person placing the order and the person receiving the goods. This avoids possible theft. The best way to avoid losses is to have the chef prepare the order, the manager or the manager's designee place the order, and a third person responsible for the stores receive the goods together with the chef (or the chef's designee).

Commercial (for-profit) restaurant and foodservice operators who are part of a chain may have the menu items and order specifications determined at the corporate office. This saves the unit manager from having to order individually; specialists at the corporate office cannot only develop the menu but also the specifications for the ingredients to ensure consistency. Both chain and independent restaurants and foodservice operators use similar prepurchase functions:

✔ Plan menus
✔ Determine quality and quantity needed to produce menus
✔ Determine inventory stock levels
✔ Identify items to purchase by subtracting stock levels from the quantity required to produce menus
✔ Write specifications and develop market orders for purchases

Professor Stefanelli at the University of Nevada, Las Vegas, suggests a formal and an informal method of purchasing that includes the following steps.[7]

Formal	*Informal*
Develop purchase order	Develop purchase order
Establish bid schedule	Quote price
Issue invitation to bid	Select vendor and place order
Tabulate and evaluate bids	
Award contract and issue delivery order	
Inspect/receive deliveries, inventory stores, and record transactions in inventory	Receive and inspect deliveries, store, and record transaction
Evaluate and follow up	Evaluate and follow up
Issue food supplies for food production and service	Issue food supplies for food production and service

The formal method is generally used by chain restaurant operators and the informal one by independent restaurant operators.

A purchase order comes as a result of the product specification. As it sounds, a purchase order is an order to purchase a certain quantity of an item at a specific price. Many restaurants develop purchase orders for items they need on a regular basis. These then are sent to suppliers for quotations, and samples are sent in for product evaluations. For example, canned items have varying amounts of liquid. Normally, it is the drained weight of the product that matters to the restaurant operator. After comparing samples from several vendors, the operator can choose the supplier that best suits the restaurant's needs.

Receiving

When placing an order, the restaurant operator specifies the day and time (for example, Friday, 10:00 A.M. to 12:00 noon) for the delivery to be made. This prevents deliveries from being made at inconvenient times.

Receiving is a point of control in the restaurant operation. The purpose of receiving is to ensure the quantity, quality, and price is exactly as ordered. The quantity and quality relate to the order specification and the standardized recipe. Depending on the restaurant and the type of food and beverage control system, some perishable items are issued directly to the kitchen, and most of the nonperishable items go into storage.

Storing/Issuing

Control of the stores is often a problem. Records must be kept of all items going into or out of the stores. If more than one person has access to the stores, it is difficult to know where to attach responsibility in case of losses.

Items should only be issued from the stores on an authorized requisition signed by the appropriate person. One restaurateur who has been in business for many years issues stores to the kitchen on a daily basis. No inventory is kept in the production area and there is no access to the stores. To some, this may be overdoing control, but it is hard to fault the results: a good food cost percentage. All items that enter the stores should have a date stamp and be rotated using the first in–first out (FIFO) system.

First in–first out is a simple but effective system of ensuring stock rotation. This is achieved by placing the most recent purchases, in rotation, behind previous purchases. Failure to do this can result in spoilage.

Budgeting

Budgeting costs fall into two categories: fixed and variable. Fixed costs are constant no matter the volume of business. Fixed costs are rent/lease payments, interest, and depreciation. Variable costs fluctuate with the volume of business. Variable costs include controllable expenses such as payroll, benefits, direct operating expense, music and entertainment, marketing and promotion, energy and utility, administrative, and repairs and maintenance.

Regardless of sales fluctuations, variable or controllable expenses vary in some controllable proportion to sales. For example, if a restaurant is open on a Monday it must have a host, server, cook, dishwasher, and so on. The volume of business and sales total may be $750. However, on Friday that sales total might be $2,250 with just a few more staff. The controllable costs increased only slightly in proportion to the sales, and the fixed costs did not change (see Table 7–1).

Restaurant Accounting

In order to operate any business efficiently and effectively, it is necessary to determine the mission, goals, and objectives. One of the most important goals in

Table 7-1 Controllable Costs versus Fixed Costs in Terms of Sales

	Restaurant A Monday		Restaurant A Friday	
Sales				
Food	$600	75.0%	$1800.	75.0%
Beverage	150	25.0	450	25.0
Total Sales	$750	100.0	$2,250	100.0
Cost of Sales				
Food	198	26.0	540	30.0
Beverage	37.50	25.0	112.50	25.0
Total Cost of Sales	235.50		652.50	
Gross Profit	514.50		1,597.50	
Controllable expenses				
Salaries and wages	$195	26.0%	$472.50	21.0%
Employee benefits	30	4.0	90	4.0
Direct operating expense	45	6.0	90	4.0
Music	7.50	1.0	7.50	1.0
Marketing	30	4.0	30	4.0
Energy and utility	22.50	3.0	67.50	3.0
Administrative/general	30	4.0	90	4.0
Repairs and maintenance	15	2.0	45	2.0
Total Controllable Expenses	375.00		892.50	
Rent and Other Occupation Costs				
Income before interest, depreciation, and taxes				
Interest				
Depreciation				
Total				
Net income before taxes				
Taxes				
Net income				

any enterprise is a fair return on investment, otherwise known as profit. In addition, accounting for the income and expenditures is a necessary part of any business enterprise. The restaurant industry has adopted a uniform system of accounts.

The uniform system of accounts for restaurants (USAR) outlines a standard classification and presentation of operating results. The system allows for easy comparison among restaurants because each expense item has the same schedule number.

Balance Sheet

A balance sheet for a restaurant, or any business, reflects how the assets and liabilities relate to the owner's equity at a particular moment in time. The balance sheet is mainly used by owners and investors to verify the financial health of the organization. Financial health may be defined in several ways, for example, liquidity, which means having a sufficient amount of cash available to pay bills when they are due, and debt leverage, which is the percentage of a company's assets owned by outside interests (liabilities).

Restaurants are one of the few, fortunate types of businesses to operate on a cash basis for income receivables. There are no outstanding accounts receivable because all sales are in cash—even credit cards are treated as cash because of their prompt payment. Normally, restaurants invest significant funds in assets, such as equipment, furniture, and building (if they own it). The balance sheet will reflect how much of the cost of these assets has been paid for, and is thus owned by the company (owner's equity), and how much is still due to outsiders (liability). Furthermore, the balance sheet will show the extent to which the company has depreciated these assets, thus providing owners and investors with an indication of potential future costs to repair or replace existing assets.

Operating or Income Statement

From an operational perspective, the most important financial document is the operating statement. Once a sales forecast has been completed, the costs of servicing those sales are budgeted on an income statement. Table 7–2 shows an example of an income statement for a hypothetical restaurant.

The income statement, which is for a month or a year, begins with the food and beverage sales. From this total the cost of food and beverage is deducted; the remaining total is gross profit. To this amount any other income is added (e.g., cigarettes, vending machines, outside catering, and telephone income). The next heading is controllable expenses, which includes salaries, wages, employee benefits, direct operating expenses (telephone, insurance, accounting and legal fees, office supplies, paper, china, glass, cutlery, menus, landscaping, and so on), music and entertainment, marketing, energy and utility, administrative and general, repairs and maintenance. The total of this group is called total controllable expenses. Rent and other occupation costs are then deducted from the total, leaving income before interest, depreciation, and taxes. Interest and depreciation are deducted leaving a total of net income before taxes. From this amount income taxes are paid leaving the remainder as net income.

Managing the money to the bottom line requires careful scrutiny of all key results, beginning with the big ticket controllable items like labor costs, food costs, and beverages, on down to related controllables. Additionally, management may wish to compare several income statements representing operations over a number of different periods. The ideal method for comparing is to compute every component of each income statement as a percentage of its total sales. Then compare one period's percentage to another to determine if any significant trends are developing. For example, a manager could compare labor as a percent of total sales over several months, or years, to assess the impact of rising labor rates on the bottom line.

Table 7–2 Sample Income Statement

	Amount	Percentage
Sales		
Food		
Beverage		
Others		
Total sales	_____	100
Cost of Sales		
Food		
Beverage		
Others		
Total cost of sales	_____	
Gross profit	_____	
Controllable Expenses	_____	
Salaries and wages		
Employee benefits		
Direct operating expenses*		
Music and entertainment		
Marketing		
Energy and utility		
Administrative and general		
Repairs and maintenance		
Total controllable expenses	_____	
Rent and other occupation costs		
Income before interest, depreciation, and taxes		
Interest		
Depreciation		
Net income before taxes		
Income taxes	_____	
Net Income	_____	

*Telephone, insurance, legal, accounting, paper, glass, china, linens, office supplies, landscaping, cleaning supplies, etc.

Operating Ratios

Operating ratios are industry norms that are applicable to each segment of the industry. Experienced restaurant operators rely on these operating ratios to indicate the restaurant's degree of success. Several ratios are good barometers of a restaurant's degree of success. Among the better known ratios are the following:

- ✔ Food cost percentage
- ✔ Contribution margin
- ✔ Labor cost percentage
- ✔ Prime cost
- ✔ Beverage cost percentage

Food Cost Percentage

The basic food cost percentage, for which the formula is cost/sales × 100 = the food cost percentage, is calculated on a daily, weekly, or monthly basis. The procedure works in the following manner:

1. An inventory is taken of all the food and the purchase price of that food. This is called the *opening inventory*.
2. The purchases are totaled for the period and added to the opening inventory.
3. The closing inventory (the inventory at the close of the week or period for which the food cost percentage is being calculated) and returns, spoilage, complimentary meals, and transfers to other departments are also deducted from the opening inventory plus purchases.
4. This figure is the cost of goods sold. The cost of goods sold is divided by the total sales. The resulting figure is the food cost percentage.

The following example illustrates the procedure:

Food Sales	$3,000
Opening Inventory	1,000
Add Purchases	500
	1,500
Less Spoilage and Complimentary Meals	100
Less Closing Inventory	500
Cost of Goods Sold	$900

$$\frac{\text{Food Cost (\$900)}}{\text{Sales (\$3,000)}} \times 100 = 30\% \text{ Food Cost Percentage}$$

The food cost percentage calculations become slightly more complicated when the cost of staff meals, management meals and entertaining (complimentary meals), and guest food returned are all properly calculated.

Food cost percentage has long been used as a yardstick for measuring the skill of the chef, cooks, and management to achieve a predetermined food cost percentage—usually 28 to 32 percent for a full-service restaurant and a little higher for a high-volume, fast-food restaurant.

Controlling food costs begins with cost-effective purchasing systems, a controlled storage and issuing system, and strict control of the food production and sales. The best way to visualize a food cost control system is to think of the food as money. Consider a $100 bill arriving at the back door: If the wrong people get their hands on that money, it does not reach the guest or the bottom line.

Contribution Margin

More recently, attention has focused not only on the food cost percentage but also on the contribution margin. The contribution margin is the amount that a menu item contributes to the gross profit, or the difference between the cost of the item and its sales price. Some menu items contribute more than others; therefore, restaurant operators focus more attention on the items that produce a higher contribution margin. It works like this:

The cost of the chicken dish is $2.00 and its selling price is $9.95, which leaves a contribution margin of $7.95. The fish, which costs a little more at $3.25 sells for $12.75 and leaves a contribution of $9.50. The pasta cost price of $1.50 and selling price of $8.95 leave a contribution margin of $7.45. Under this scenario it would be better for the restaurants to sell more fish because each plate will yield $1.55 more than if chicken were sold.

Labor Cost Percentage

Labor costs are the highest single cost factor in staffing a restaurant. Fast-food restaurants have the lowest labor costs (about 16 to 18 percent) with family and ethnic restaurants at about 22 to 26 percent, and upscale full-service restaurants at about 30 to 35 percent.

Prime Cost

Combined food and labor costs are known as prime cost. In order to allow for a reasonable return on investment, prime cost should not go above 60 to 65 percent of sales.

There are various methods of control, beginning with effective scheduling based on the expected volume of business. In reality, because of the high cost of labor, today's restaurateurs manage by the minute. Once a rush is over, the effective manager thanks employees for doing a great job and looks forward to seeing them again. This may appear to be micromanagement, but an analysis of restaurant operations does not leave any alternatives.[8]

Beverage Cost Percentage

The beverage cost percentage is calculated like the food cost percentage. The method used most often is to first determine the unit cost and then mark up by the required percentage to arrive at the selling price. This is rounded up or down to a convenient figure. The actual beverage cost percentage is then compared with the anticipated cost percentage; any discrepancy is investigated.

The National Restaurant Association publishes guidelines for restaurant operations. These valuable documents help provide a guide for operators to use when comparing their restaurants with other similar establishments. If the costs go above the budgeted or expected levels, then management must investigate and take corrective action.

Therefore, if we are operating a casual Italian restaurant, industry comparisons would show the following:

Labor costs at 20 to 24 percent of sales
Food costs at 28 to 32 percent of food sales
Beverage costs at 18 to 24 percent of beverage sales

Lease and Controllable Expenses

Lease Costs

Successful restaurant operators will ensure that the restaurant's lease does not cost more than five to eight percent of sales. Some chain restaurants will search

Corporate Profile: TGI Friday's

In the spring of 1965, Alan Stillman, a New York perfume salesman, opened a restaurant located at First Avenue and 63rd Street. The restaurant boasted striped awnings, a blue exterior, and yellow supergraphics reading TGI Friday's. Inside were wooden floors covered with sawdust, Tiffany-style lamps, bentwood chairs, red-and-white tablecloths, and a bar area complete with brass rails and stained glass.

TGI Friday's was an immediate success. The restaurant on Manhattan's upper east side became the meeting place for single adults. In fact, *Newsweek* and the *Saturday Evening Post* called the opening of TGI Friday's "the dawn of the singles' age."

In 1971, franchisee Dan Scoggin opened a TGI Friday's in Dallas and in four other sites around the country. The success was instant; thus, began the company that is TGI Friday's today.

By 1975, there were ten TGI Friday's in eight states, but the great success that the company had seen was starting to diminish. Dan Scoggin began a country-wide tour to visit each restaurant; he talked with employees, managers, and customers to isolate the roots of successes and failures. This was the critical turning point for the company. The focus shifted from being just another restaurant chain to giving guests exactly what they wanted. The theories and philosophies Scoggin developed are the principles by which TGI Friday's now does business.

TGI Friday's goal was to create a comfortable, relaxing environment where guests could enjoy food and drink. Stained glass windows, wooden airplane propellers, racing sculls, and metal advertising signs comprised the elegant clutter that greeted guests when they entered a TGI Friday's. Nothing was left to chance. Music, lights, air conditioning, decor, and housekeeping were all designed to keep guests comfortable. Employees were encouraged to display their own personalities and to treat customers as they would guests in their own homes.

As guests demanded more, TGI Friday's provided more—soon becoming the industry leader in menu and drink selection. The menu expanded from a slate chalkboard to an award-winning collection of items representing every taste and mood.

TGI Friday's also became the industry leader in innovation—creating the now-famous potato skins and popularizing fried zucchini. This was the first restaurant chain to offer stone ground whole wheat bread, avocados, bean sprouts, and Mexican appetizers across the country. As guests' tastes continued to change, TGI Friday's introduced pasta dishes, fettuccine, brunch items, and croissant sandwiches.

America owes the popularization of frozen and ice cream drinks to TGI Friday's, where smooth, alcoholic and nonalcoholic drinks were made with fresh fruit, juices, ice cream, and yogurt. These recipes were so precise that TGI Friday's drink glasses were scientifically designed for the correct ratio of each ingredient. These specially designed glasses have since become popular throughout the industry.

Through the years, TGI Friday's success has been phenomenal. More than 200 restaurants have opened in the United States and abroad, with average gross revenues of $3.5 million per year at each location, the highest per-unit sales volume of any national chain.

TGI Friday's is now privately owned by Carlson Companies, Inc., of Minneapolis—one of the largest privately held companies in the country. Today, TGI Friday's has come to be known as a casual restaurant where family and friends meet for great food, fun, and conversation. Everyone looks forward to Friday's!

What does it take to be successful in the restaurant business, and what does it take to be a leader? The answers to these questions are crucial to success as a restaurant company. The essentials of success in business are as follows:

1. Treat everyone with respect for their dignity
2. Treat all customers as if they are honored guests in your home
3. Remember that all problems result from either poor hiring, lack of training, unclear performance expectations, or accepting less than excellence
4. Remember that management tools are methods, not objectives

As you can see, these are principles to guide decision making as opposed to step-by-step actions. However, I would submit that if these principles are not followed, then actions have very short-term effects. And if you do choose to follow them, they form a base on which you can easily decide which specific actions are necessary in any given situation.

The basics of leadership are as follows:

1. Hire the right people
2. Train everyone thoroughly and completely
3. Be sure that everyone clearly understands the performance expectations
4. Accept only excellence

Here we are dealing with the very basics of how to provide strong, clear leadership. However, once again we are talking about only the minimum requirements, not all the qualities necessary to be a good leader. Individual success and that of the company, TGI Friday's Inc., is predicated on understanding and following the essentials of success in business and the basics of leadership. Whether you are an hourly employee or a manager, it is critical that you manage your part of the business using these philosophies.

One of the things that makes TGI Friday's unique is our philosophies and theories. These are principles that each employee understands to ensure we all stay focused on the same goals. TGI Friday's philosophies and theories were first conceived in the mid-1970s. They are used to solve existing problems and enable us to be proactive to problems we have experienced in the past.

The Guest Focus

At most companies, it appears that senior management runs the company. The employees consider senior management to be the most important people with whom they interact. As a result, decisions are made in an effort to please senior management, and decisions that affect people lower in the hierarchy are viewed as less important. TGI Friday's success is dependent on inverting the typical management pyramid. Guests are the most important element in the organization; immediately following them are the employees who are closest to the guests—those people who have the greatest impact on the guests' experience. The livelihood of each employee depends on one group of people: guests. It is critical we determine what guests' needs are and fill those needs. To the extent that we accomplish this objective, the needs of each person in our pyramid will be fulfilled. Every decision at TGI Friday's is made with guests in mind.

The "Five Easy Pieces Theory" stresses TGI Friday's deep concern for our guests' satisfaction. We will always cheerfully go out of our way to serve a quality product prepared to individual tastes. In the movie titled Five Easy Pieces, the star, Jack Nicholson, goes to a restaurant and orders a side order of whole wheat toast. The waitress makes it clear that they do not serve whole wheat toast. Nicholson notes on the menu that the chicken salad sandwich comes on whole wheat bread. The annoyed waitress points to a sign in the restaurant that reads "No substitutions" and

"We reserve the right to refuse service to anyone." Jack Nicholson orders a chicken salad sandwich on whole wheat toast, but tells the waitress to hold the mayo, hold the lettuce, hold the chicken salad, and just bring him the whole wheat toast. Unwisely, she asks where she should hold the chicken salad. Nicholson sarcastically responds, "Between your knees!" On that note, he leaves, a very dissatisfied guest. Our managers and employees are responsible for honoring any guest request within realistic possibilities. Many managers take a guest's request even further and get them exactly what they want—even if the ingredients are not in the restaurant.

The "Triangle Theory" explains the need to balance and expand upon the goals of the guest, employee, and company, and maximize the results to each. Managers make many decisions and must always consider the effect of those decisions on all three sides of the triangle—the guest, the employee, and the company. Some decisions can cause one side of the triangle to prosper (temporarily) at the expense of the other two. For example, if a company overprices its menu items, it can greatly improve the bottom line. However, guests will object to being cheated and will not return. This will ultimately result in lower staffing and will eventually kill the company. Management's responsibility is to balance the results among the three sides so all sides thrive. But this is only the first step. To grow and expand the business, decisions must be made that maximize or expand all three sides of the triangle at the same time.

These are just a few of the philosophies and theories on which TGI Friday's is based. It is important that we educate our people and that we are all guided by the same principles.

Benefits

Starting compensation for managers is an individual issue, based on background and experience. In addition to a competitive base salary, TGI Friday's also offers a bonus based on sales and/or profits to all restaurant employees, including general managers, kitchen managers, assistant general managers, and other managers. Management staffing is designed to meet volume needs and may number four to seven per store. Management generally works a five-day work week.

TGI Friday's offers a complete benefits program for both hourly and management personnel. Among its features are health and dental coverage (dependent coverage is also available), vision care, life insurance, paid vacations, disability coverage, credit union, education assistance program, and a profit-sharing plan that allows employees to share in the success of the company. At TGI Friday's Inc., they also believe that recognizing employees for their outstanding effort is their opportunity to acknowledge and reinforce the behavior they want to encourage.

Chris Yubanks is the general manager of a TGI Friday's in San Diego. The typical day for Chris is a long and challenging experience. Chris usually arrives at about 7:00 A.M. and usually works until 6:00 or 7:00 P.M. Chris does routine paperwork on a daily basis; however, no day is the same as another in the restaurant business.

TGI Friday's is one of the more successful restaurant concepts in the industry today. Management is taken very seriously in this restaurant. A typical day for Chris goes as follows:

✔ Chris usually works from 7 A.M. to 6 P.M.; however, leaving at 7:00 or 8:00 P.M. is not uncommon. He is scheduled to work five days a week, but sometimes this is not the case. If a manager calls in sick or there is a major problem at the restaurant, Chris must be there to cover the shift.

✔ The first thing Chris does in the morning is turn off the alarm. Next, he checks the sales from the previous day and compares them to the previous week's numbers as well as the previous year's.

✔ The next step is to boot up the computer. Chris runs the daily reports and counts the bank in the restaurant. If all of the drawers are correct and the store bank is correct, then Chris can do the daily walk around. This is done to check the cleanliness of the restaurant as well as to see if anything is needed to open.

✔ Following this, the produce usually arrives and is checked off accordingly.

✔ Then Chris checks for proper staffing for the day. If all employees have shown up for their shifts, then production is issued to the back of the house as well as opening duties to the front of the house.

✔ The final step prior to opening is having the employee meeting. This meeting is used to let the servers know what the daily specials are and which food and drinks to push, and provides a general pumping up for the employees.

✔ After all of the opening procedures are done, the restaurant is ready to open for business.

✔ Now it is 11:30 and time to open the doors of the restaurant. Chris's job is simple—all he does for the remainder of the day is run the shift. Chris does this by constantly checking on the tables to make sure all of the guests are satisfied. When the guests are not satisfied, then Chris fixes the problem according to the guests' liking.

✔ After lunch, Chris counts out all of the employees cash drawers, cleans up the front of the house, and gets things ready for the closing manager. When the closing manager arrives at 4:30 P.M., the store bank is counted over to him or her. If the bank is correct, Chris and the closing manager go over the numbers for the day and discuss the closing shift.

Expectations of the General Manager

The expectations of the general manager are different in each restaurant; however, there are certain commonalities as well. Some of these commonalities are as follows:

✔ General managers answer directly to the owner, or to regional directors for major corporations.

✔ General managers are expected to run good numbers for the periods. The numbers analyzed are food cost, la-

for months or even years before they find the right location at the right price. Most leases are triple net, which means that the lessee must pay for all alterations, insurance, utilities, and possible commercial fees (e.g., landscaping or parking upkeep, security, etc.).

The best lease is for the longest time period with options for renewal and a sublease clause. The sublease clause is important because if the restaurant is not successful, the owner is still liable to pay the lease. With the sublease clause the owner may sublease the space to another restaurant operator or any other business.

bor cost, beverage cost. These areas are controlled in order to produce sufficient profit for the restaurant.

✔ General managers promote good morale and teamwork in the restaurant. Having a positive environment in the restaurant is of utmost importance. This will not only keep the employees happy, but it will also contribute to providing better service to the guests.

Duties and Responsibilities

The general manager of a restaurant is directly in charge of all of the operations in the restaurant. General managers are also in charge of the floor managers, kitchen manager, and all of the remaining employees in the restaurant.

The general manager should always check on the floor managers to ensure that all policies and regulations are being met. This will keep operations running smoothly.

Another important duty is to organize and control the staffing of the restaurant. The floor managers usually write the employee schedule; however, the general manager is still directly responsible for proper staffing for the period. This will help keep labor costs to about 20 percent of sales. The general manager is also in charge of conducting employee reviews and training.

Qualifications for a General Manager

To be hired as a general manager, the following qualifications are necessary:

✔ The general manager should be very knowledgeable in the restaurant business.

✔ He or she should have previously worked all the stations in a restaurant and be very familiar with them.

✔ The general manager should be able to get along with all people, be fair with all employees, and not discriminate.

✔ Having a degree is not the most important thing in becoming a general manager. However, a degree is very useful in moving up the ladder in a company to regional manager, regional director, and so on.

Budgeted Costs in a Restaurant

Running a good pace in the restaurant is of absolute importance. Every restaurant has different numbers to make. The following numbers came from a TGI Friday's-type restaurant. These numbers reflect their goals versus actual numbers run for a given week.

	GOAL	ACTUAL	VARIANCE
Food Cost	27.0	27.2	+.2
Labor Cost	19.9	20.8	+.9
Beverage Cost	19.0	18.2	−.8

As can be seen, the TGI Friday's did well with the beverage cost; however, the food cost and the labor cost are two areas to focus on for the upcoming week.

Making good percentages for the restaurant is the most important focus, simply because this is where the restaurant makes or does not make a profit. When the general manager runs good numbers, then he or she will receive a large bonus check for contributing to the profit of the restaurant. This is why it is so important to focus on these three key areas.

Scheduling the Restaurant

Appropriate scheduling plays a key role in the success of the restaurant. For one thing, overscheduling and underscheduling have a direct effect on the labor cost. If there are too many employees working on a shift for the business acquired, then the labor cost will be high. In contrast, if there are not enough employees working, then the service will suffer and overtime will increase the labor cost.

Many leases are quoted at a dollar rate per square foot per month. Depending on the location, rates may range from $1.25 per square foot up to as much as $8.00 per square foot.

Some restaurants pay a combination of a flat amount based on the square footage and a percentage of sales. This helps protect the restaurant operator in the slower months and gives the landlord a bit extra during the good months.

Once a lease contract is signed, it is very difficult to renegotiate even a part of it. Only in dire circumstances is it possible to renegotiate lease contracts. The governing factor in determining lease rates is the marketplace. The marketplace is the supply and demand. If there is strong demand for space, then rates will increase. However, with a high vacancy rate, rates will be driven down by the owners in an effort to rent space and gain income.

Controllable Expenses

Controllable expenses are all the expenses over which management and ownership has control. They include salaries and wages (payroll) and related benefits; direct operating expenses such as music and entertainment; marketing, including sales, advertising, public relations, and promotions; heat, light, and power; administrative and general expenses; and repairs and maintenance. The total of all controllable expenses is deducted from the gross profit. Rent and other occupation costs are then deducted to arrive at the income before interest, depreciation, and taxes. Once these are deducted, the net profit remains.

Successful restaurant operators are constantly monitoring their controllable expenses. The largest controllable expense is payroll. Because payroll is about 24 to 28 percent of a restaurant's sales, managers constantly monitor their employees, not by the hour but by the minute. Bobby Hays, general manager of the Chart House Restaurant in Solana Beach, California, says that he feels the pulse of the restaurant and then begins to send people home. Every dollar that Bobby and managers like him can save goes directly to the bottom line and becomes profit.

The actual sales results are compared with the budgeted amounts—ideally with percentages—and variances investigated. Most chain restaurant operators monitor the key result areas of sales and labor costs on a daily basis. Food and beverage costs are also monitored closely, generally on a weekly basis.

Controls

Every dollar earned must be watched all the way to the bank, and every dollar spent must be analyzed to see if it is really necessary. Control provides information to management for operational decision-making purposes.

Industry experts describe the following losses resulting from a lack of controls:

- ✔ The food service industry loses approximately $20 billion a year to theft and cash mishandling.
- ✔ One out of every three employees will steal if given the opportunity. This includes theft of cash, merchandise, and time.
- ✔ Approximately five percent to eight percent of gross sales is lost to internal theft.
- ✔ Thirty-five percent of all restaurants fail because of theft.
- ✔ Seventy-five percent of all missing inventory is from theft.
- ✔ Seventy-three percent of job applications are falsified.
- ✔ The majority of employees caught stealing have worked for an operation for an average of five to seven years.

Fred Del Marva, chairman and CEO of Food and Beverage Investigations, loss management investigators in Novato, California, offers the following advice to reduce back-of-the-house theft.[9]

- ✔ Conduct frequent inventories
- ✔ Distribute receiving responsibilities

- ✔ Establish a par stock
- ✔ Refuse off-peak-hour deliveries
- ✔ Use insider accounting
- ✔ Designate an employee entry/exit
- ✔ Discourage duffel bags/reserve the right to search bags
- ✔ Oversee trash disposal

Another industry expert has the following suggestion: "Owners and managers could take expensive marketing plans that are designed to increase sales by 25 percent and toss them out the window if they would just make a minimal effort to control theft," says Francis D'Addario, director of loss prevention for Hardee's food systems, Rocky Mount, North Carolina. Many operators are reluctant to crack down on theft because they simply do not want to play cop. Other operators just refuse to believe they are being cheated because they trust their long-time employees. Spotting theft is a job in itself. A variance of more than half a percent in food cost should be considered odd enough to check out. An unusual food cost variance can mean cash is going out the front door or food is going out the back.[10]

Most restaurants rely on point-of-sale (POS) systems. These systems, such as a server's hand-held ordering device that automatically prints up the order in the kitchen or bar, have improved service efficiency. However, there is a cost involved and restaurant operators need to carefully select point-of-sale systems that are appropriate for their restaurants.

Buying a POS system for a restaurant can be a major investment. It is imperative that managers get the most value for their dollars. *Restaurants and Institutions* magazine surveyed a panel of experts from companies that use POS systems who suggested the following guidelines:

1. Buy from a reliable vendor
2. Decide what you need before buying
3. Don't get carried away with technology
4. Look for a computer company that knows restaurants
5. Buy standard software packages
6. Look for an adaptable piece of equipment
7. Try to use generic hardware
8. Find a system that simultaneously runs several programs
9. Consider quick credit card verification
10. Insist on a twenty-four-hour hot line
11. User-friendly systems can pay off
12. Avoid downtime with a dual disk system
13. Find a system that helps control labor costs[11]

Foodservice Manager Job Analysis

The National Restaurant Association (NRA) has formulated an analysis of the foodservice manager's job by functional areas and tasks, which follows a natural sequence of functional areas from human resources to sanitation and safety.

Human Resource Management

Recruiting/Training
1. Recruit new employees by seeking referrals
2. Recruit new employees by advertising
3. Recruit new employees by seeking help from district manager/supervisors
4. Interview applicants for employment

Orientation/Training
1. Conduct on-site orientation for new employees
2. Explain employee benefits and compensation programs
3. Plan training programs for employees
4. Conduct on-site training for employees
5. Evaluate progress of employees during training
6. Supervise on-site training of employees that is conducted by another manager, employee leader, trainer, and so on
7. Conduct payroll sign up
8. Complete reports or other written documentation on successful completion of training by employees

Scheduling for Shifts
1. Review employee work schedule for shift
2. Determine staffing needs for each shift
3. Make work assignments for dining room, kitchen staff, and maintenance person(s)
4. Make changes to employee work schedule
5. Assign employees to work stations to optimize employee effectiveness
6. Call in, reassign, or send home employees in reaction to sales and other needs
7. Approve requests for schedule changes, vacation, days off, and so on

Supervision and Employee Development
1. Observe employees and give immediate feedback on unsatisfactory employee performance
2. Observe employees and give immediate feedback on satisfactory employee performance
3. Discuss unsatisfactory performance with an employee
4. Develop and deliver incentive for above-satisfactory performance of employees
5. Observe employee behavior for compliance with safety and security
6. Counsel employees on work-related problems
7. Counsel employees on nonwork-related problems
8. Talk with employees who have frequent absences
9. Observe employees to assure compliance with fair labor standards and equal opportunity guidelines
10. Discipline employees by issuing oral and/or written warnings for poor performance

11. Conduct employee and staff meetings
12. Identify and develop candidates for management programs
13. Put results of observation of employee performance in writing
14. Develop action plans for employees to help them in their performance
15. Authorize promotion and/or wage increases for staff
16. Terminate employment of an employee for unsatisfactory performance

Financial Management

Accounting
1. Authorize payment on vendor invoices
2. Verify payroll
3. Count cash drawers
4. Prepare bank deposits
5. Assist in establishment audits by management or outside auditors
6. Balance cash at end of shift
7. Analyze profit and loss reports for establishment

Cost Control
1. Discuss factors that impact profitability with district manager/supervisor
2. Check establishment figures for sales, labor costs, waste, inventory, and so on

Administrative Management

Scheduling/Coordinating
1. Establish objectives for shift based on needs of establishment
2. Coordinate work performed by different shifts, for example, clean up, routine maintenance, and so on
3. Complete special projects assigned by district manager/supervisor
4. Complete shift readiness checklist

Planning
1. Develop and implement action plans to meet financial goals
2. Attend off-site workshops and training sessions

Communication
1. Communicate with management team by reading and making entries in daily communication log
2. Prepare written reports on cleanliness, food quality, personnel, inventory, sales, food waste, labor costs, and so on
3. Review reports prepared by other establishment managers
4. Review memos, reports, and letters from company headquarters/main office
5. Inform district manager/supervisor of problems or developments that affect operation and performance of the establishment
6. Initiate and answer correspondence with company, vendors, and so on
7. File correspondence, reports, personnel records, and so on

Marketing Management

1. Create and execute local establishment marketing activities
2. Develop opportunities for the establishment to provide community services
3. Carry out special product promotions

Operations Management

Facility Maintenance

1. Conduct routine maintenance checks on facility and equipment
2. Direct routine maintenance checks on facility and equipment
3. Repair or supervise the repair of equipment
4. Review establishment evaluations with district manager/supervisor
5. Authorize the repair of equipment by outside contractor
6. Recommend upgrades in facility and equipment

Food and Beverage Operations Management

1. Direct activities for opening establishment
2. Direct activities for closing establishment
3. Talk with other managers at beginning and end of shift to relay information about ongoing problems and activities
4. Count, verify, and report inventory
5. Receive, inspect, and verify vendor deliveries
6. Check stock levels and submit orders as necessary
7. Talk with vendors concerning quality of product delivered
8. Interview vendors who wish to sell products to establishment
9. Check finished product quality and act to correct problems
10. Work as expediter to get meals served effectively
11. Inspect dining area, kitchen, rest rooms, food lockers, storage, and parking lot
12. Check daily reports for indications of internal theft
13. Instruct employees regarding the control of waste, portion sizes, and so on
14. Prepare forecast for daily or shift food preparation

Service

1. Receive and record table reservations
2. Greet familiar customers by name
3. Seat customers
4. Talk with customers while they are dining
5. Monitor service times and procedures in the dining area
6. Observe customers being served in order to correct problems
7. Ask customers about quality of service
8. Ask customers about quality of the food product
9. Listen to and resolve customer complaints
10. Authorize complimentary meals or beverages
11. Write letters in response to customer complaints
12. Telephone customers in response to customer complaints
13. Secure and return items left by customers

Sanitation and Safety

1. Accompany local officials on health inspections on premise
2. Administer first aid to employees and customers
3. Submit accident, incident, and OSHA reports
4. Report incidents to police
5. Observe employee behavior and establishment conditions for compliance with safety and security procedures

Trends in Restaurant Operations

✔ More flavorful food
✔ Increased take-out meals, especially at lunch
✔ Food safety
✔ Guests becoming more sophisticated and needing more things to excite them
✔ More food court restaurants in malls, movie theater complexes, and colleges and universities where guests line up (similar to a cafeteria), select their food (which a server places on a tray), and pay a cashier
✔ Steak houses are becoming more popular
✔ With more restaurants in each segment, the segments are splitting into upper, middle, and lower tiers
✔ Twin and multirestaurant locations
✔ Quick-service restaurants (QSRs) in convenience stores (c-stores)
✔ Difficulty in finding good employees

Short Staffed in the Kitchen

Sally is the general manager of one of the best restaurants in town, known as The Pub. As usual, at 6:00 P.M. on a Friday night, there is a forty-five-minute wait. The kitchen is overloaded and they are running behind in check times, the time that elapses between the kitchen getting the order and the guest receiving his or her meal. This is critical, especially if a complaint is received because a guest has waited too long for a meal to be served.

Sally is waiting for her two head line cooks to come in for the closing shift. It is now 6:15 P.M. and she receives phone calls from both of them. Unfortunately, they are both sick with the flu and are not able to come to work.

As she gets off the phone, the hostess tells Sally that a party of fifty is scheduled to arrive at 7:30 P.M. Sally is concerned, knowing that they are currently running a six person line with only four cooks. The productivity is very high, but they are running extremely long check times. How can Sally handle the situation?

Discussion Questions

1. How would you handle the short-staffing issue?
2. What measures would you take to get the appropriate cooks in to work as soon as possible?
3. What would you do to ensure a smooth, successful transition for the party of fifty?

4. How would you manipulate your floor plan to provide great service for the party of fifty?
5. How would you immediately make an impact on the long check times?
6. What should you do to ensure that all the guests in the restaurant are happy?

Shortage in Stock

It is Friday morning at 9:30 at The Pub. Product is scheduled to be delivered at 10:00. Sally specifically ordered an exceptional amount of food for the upcoming weekend because she is projecting it to be a busy holiday weekend. Sally receives a phone call at 10:30 from J&G groceries, stating that they cannot deliver the product until 10:00 A.M. on Saturday morning. She explains to the driver that it is crucial that she receives the product as soon as possible. He apologizes, however it is impossible to have delivery made until Saturday morning.

By 1:00 P.M., they are beginning to run out of product, including absolute necessities such as steaks, chicken, fish, and produce. The guests are getting frustrated because the staff are beginning to 86 a great deal of product. In addition, if they do not begin production for the P.M. shift soon, they will be in deep trouble.

On Friday nights, The Pub does in excess of $12,000 in sales. However, if the problem is not immediately alleviated, the restaurant will lose many guests and a great amount of profits.

Discussion Questions

1. What immediate measures would you take to resolve the problem?
2. How would you produce the appropriate product as soon as possible?
3. Who should you call first, if anyone, to alleviate the problem?
4. What can you do to always have enough product on hand?
5. Is it important to have a back-up plan for a situation like this? If so, what would it be?

Summary

1. Most restaurants forecast a budget on a weekly and monthly basis that projects sales and costs for a year in consideration of guest counts and the average guest check.
2. In order to operate a restaurant, products need to be purchased, received, and properly stored.
3. Food production is determined by the expected business for the next few days. The kitchen layout is designed according to the sales forecasted.
4. Good service is very important. A distinction is made among Russian, American, and French service. In addition to taking orders, servers act as salespersons for the restaurant.

5. Budgeting costs are divided into fixed costs (such as lease or rent) and variable costs, which include controllable expenses such as salaries, entertainment, and promotion.
6. Accounting for the income and expenditures is necessary in order to gain a profit. Measures of accounting are the uniform system of accounts for restaurants, a balance sheet, and an income statement.
7. Restaurant operators rely on ratios such as food cost percentage, contribution margin, labor cost percentage, and prime cost to indicate the restaurant's degree of success.

8. The point-of-sales system is one form of control that restaurants use to protect themselves from theft.
9. The front of the house deals with the part of the restaurant having direct contact with guests. In other words, what the guests see—grounds maintenance, hosts/hostesses, dining and bar areas, bartenders, busers, etc.

10. The back of the house is generally run by the kitchen manager and refers to all areas guests normally do not come in contact with. This includes: purchasing, receiving, storing/issuing, food production, stewarding, budgeting, accounting, and control.

Review Exercises

1. Briefly describe the two components of restaurant forecasting.
2. Explain the key points in purchasing, receiving, and storing.
3. Why is the kitchen layout an important aspect of food production?
4. Explain the purpose of suggestive selling. What characteristics make up a good server?
5. Accounting is important in order to determine the profitability of a restaurant. Briefly describe the following terms:

a. controllable expenses
b. uniform system of accounts
c. prime cost

6. What is the point-of-sales system, and why is a control system important for a restaurant operation?
7. What are the differences between the back of the house and the front of the house?
8. What steps must one take in preparing production sheets?

Key Words and Concepts

Average guest check
Back of the house
Balance sheet profit
Beverage cost percentage
Budgeting
Contribution margin
Control
Controllable expenses

First in—first out
Fixed costs
Food cost percentage
Front of the house
Gross profit
Income statement
Kichen manager
Labor cost percentage

Menu
Operating ratios
Par stock
Prime cost
Product specification
Production control sheets
Purchasing
Receiving

Reorder point
Restaurant accounting
Restaurant forecasting
Uniform system of accounts
Variable costs

Notes

[1]This section draws on Donald E. Lundberg and John R. Walker, *The Restaurant from Concept to Operation.* New York: John Wiley and Sons, 1993, pp. 86–87.
[2]This section draws on Beth Lorenzini, "Turn Servers into Menu Masters, " *Restaurants and Institutions, 103,* 6, March 1, 1993, pp. 93–100.
[3]This section draws on Pat DiDomenico, "The Power of Suggestions: Turn Servers into Sellers," *Restaurants USA, 13,* 2, February 1993, pp. 20–23.
[4]T. Suji, *Professional Restaurant Service.* New York: John Wiley and Sons, 1992, p. 14.
[5]This section draws on Tom Sietseima, "Restaurants Trying Harder to Please," *San Francisco Chronicle,* July 14, 1993, p. A-1.

[6]This section draws on Donald E. Lundberg and John R. Walker, *The Restaurant from Concept to Operation.* New York: John Wiley and Sons, 1993, p. 275.
[7]Ibid.
[8]Personal conversation with Bobby Hays, general manager, Chart House Restaurant, Solana Beach, California, January 1994.
[9]Personal conversation with Fred Del Marva, May 1994.
[10]This section draws on Beth Lorenzini, "The Secure Restaurant," *Restaurants and Institutions, 102,* 25, October 21, 1992, pp. 84–102.
[11]This section draws from Jeff Weinstein, "13 Things You Need to Know Before Buying a POS System," *Restaurants and Institutions, 103,* 3, February 1, 1993, pp. 131–134.

Managed Services

8

After reading and studying this chapter you should be able to do the following:

✔ Outline the different managed services segments

✔ Describe the five factors that distinguish managed services operations from commercial ones

✔ Explain the need for and trends in elementary and secondary school food service

✔ Describe the complexities in college and university foodservice

✔ Identify characteristics and trends in health care, business, and industry foodservice

Overview

Managed services consists of all foodservice operations that are classified as not-for-profit and includes the following segments:

- ✔ Airlines
- ✔ Military
- ✔ Elementary and secondary schools
- ✔ Colleges and universities
- ✔ Health care facilities
- ✔ Business and industry

Several features distinguish managed services operations from commercial ones:

1. In a restaurant, the challenge is to please the guest. In managed services, it is necessary to meet both the needs of the guest and the client (i.e., the institution itself).
2. In some operations, the guests are a captive clientele. These guests may be eating at the foodservice operation only once or on a daily basis.
3. Many managed operations are housed in host organizations that do not have foodservice as their primary business.
4. Most managed services operations produce food in large-quantity batches for service and consumption within fixed time periods. (For example, batch cooking means to produce a batch of food to serve at 11:30 A.M., another batch to serve at 12:15 P.M., and a third batch to serve at 12:45 P.M., rather than putting out all of the food for the whole lunch period at 11:30 A.M. This gives the guests who come to eat later in the serving period as good a quality meal as those who came to eat earlier.
5. The volume of business is more consistent and therefore easier to cater. Because it is easier to predict the number of meals and portion sizes, it is easier to plan, organize, produce, and serve meals; therefore, the atmosphere is less hurried than that of a restaurant. Weekends tend to be quieter than weekdays in managed services and, overall, the hours and benefits may be better than those of commercial restaurants.

Airlines

In-Flight Foodservice

Fred Martin, president of Dobbs International, believes—rightfully—that food has become a major competitive factor with the airlines. Airlines constantly are striving to be more efficient, demanding better food at the same or lower costs. Airlines may either provide meals from their own in-flight business or have the

Food being Prepared, Loaded, and Served on an Aircraft (Courtesy Dobbs International.)

service provided by a contractor. In-flight food may be prepared in a factory mode at a facility close to but outside of the airport. In these cases, the food is prepared and packaged; it then is transported to the departure gates for the appropriate flights. Once the food is loaded onto the aircraft, flight attendants take over serving the food and beverages to passengers.

In-flight foodservice is a complex logistical operation: The food must be able to withstand the transport conditions and the extended hot or cold holding period from the time it is prepared until the time it is served. If a food item is to be served hot, it must be able to rethermalize well on the plate. In addition, the meal needs to look appealing, be tasty, and be able to fit with the limited space available.[1] Finally, all food and beverage items must be delivered on time and correctly to each departing aircraft.

Caterair International is the largest in-flight caterer with 1.5 billion in sales. The company was founded in 1990 after an employee-leveraged buyout from Marriott Corporation. Marriott had been a pioneer in in-flight catering, but the corporation made a strategic decision to focus its resources on areas in which the return on investment was greater.

Dobbs International, based in Phoenix, Arizona, is the third largest in-flight caterer in its segment, with sales of $500 million. However, Dobbs is recognized as the quality service leader in airline catering.

Another major player in the in-flight food service market is Sky Chefs, headquartered in Dallas, Texas. Sky Chefs was part of American Airlines, but was sold in a strategic move to reduce debt and to allow the airline to focus on its core business.

The industry is experiencing a period of considerable growth, which has led these companies to seek new ventures. In 1993, for example, Dobbs International purchased fifteen of United Airlines' flight kitchens, which increased the company's volume by 61 percent. Sky Chefs reached a marketing agreement with Lufthansa, thus further expanding the company's operations in Europe.

The in-flight foodservice management operators plan the menus, develop the product specifications, and arrange the purchasing contracts. They also are involved with galley, design, development of in-flight service procedures, and equipment logistics.[2]

Each airline has a representative who oversees one or more locations and checks on the quality, quantity, and delivery times of all food and beverage items. Airlines regard in-flight foodservice as an expense that needs to be controlled. The cost for the average in-flight meal is just over $6.00. The cost had been higher, but in order to trim costs, many airlines now offer snacks instead of meals on a number of short flights and flights that do not span main meal times. Some airlines try to stand out by offering superior food and beverages in hopes of attracting more passengers. Others reduce or eliminate foodservice as a strategic decision to support lower fares. Generally, international flights have better-quality food and beverage service.

On board, each aircraft has two or three categories of service, usually coach, business, and first class. First- and business-class passengers usually receive free beverages and upgraded meal items and service. These meals may consist of items like fresh salmon or filet mignon. Figure 8–1 shows an in-flight menu.

AMERICAN FLAGSHIP SERVICE

TO START
An assortment of warm mixed Nuts
to accompany your preferred Cocktail or Beverage

APPETIZER
Basil-cured Salmon
Served with Tomato Caper Relish, Lemon and a Crouton

THE SALAD CART
A zesty Caesar Salad with Romaine Lettuce, Croutons,
Parmesan Cheese and Caesar Dressing
Anchovies are available for those who wish

ENTREES
CHATEAUBRIAND
Chateaubriand served with a fresh Herb and Cabernet Sauvignon Sauce,
offered with Mashed New Potatoes and Carrots seasoned with Thyme

GRILLED CHICKEN WITH FETTUCCINE
Breast of Chicken presented over Fettuccine tossed with Pesto,
Bacon, Tomato and enhanced by a Four Cheese Sauce

PACIFIC PRAWNS WITH THAI CURRY SAUCE
Jumbo Prawns served on a spicy Thai Curry Sauce, presented with
Jasmine Pineapple Rice and Black Bean and Mango Relish

BREAD BASKET
Sourdough and Multigrain Rolls

THE DESSERT CART
ICE CREAM SUNDAE
Häagen-Dazs Vanilla Ice Cream with a choice of Hot Fudge,
Butterscotch or seasonal Fruit Toppings and fresh Whipped Cream

FRUIT AND CHEESE
A sampler of Cheese
complemented by fresh Fruit and Crackers

PRIOR TO ARRIVAL
Pecan Chocolate Chip Cookies, freshly baked on board

Figure 8–1 *In-Flight Menu* (Courtesy American Airlines.)

Pizza Hut at an Airport
(Courtesy Pizza Hut.)

On international flights, the per-passenger food cost ranges from about $10.32 for Northwest Airlines to $37.10 for American Airlines.[3]

A number of smaller regional and local foodservice operators contract to a variety of airlines at hundreds of airports. Most airports have caterers or foodservice contractors who compete for airline contracts. With several international and U.S. airlines all using U.S. airports, each airline must decide whether to use its own foodservice (if it has one) or to contract with one of several independent operators.

Airport Foodservice

Foodservice at most airports is operated by management companies like ARA-MARK Leisure Services or Host International (a division of Marriott Corporation). More recently, airports have begun to use branded concepts, whereby a Pizza Hut or other branded restaurant is located in the airport.

Military

Military foodservice is a large and important component of managed services. There are about 1.8 million soldiers, sailors, and aviators in active duty in the United States. Even with the military downsizing, foodservice sales top $6 billion. Base closings have prompted many military foodservice organizations to rediscuss services and concepts in order to better meet the needs of their personnel. In particular, it was noticed that the food delivery methods needed considerable adjustment. In fact, complaints by the operators focused on excessively long times for orders, delayed delivery, and poor product and inventory control. The Department of Defense thus introduced direct vendor delivery, which proved to be a satisfactory choice. On the whole, reports indicate excellent service and product.

Recent trends in military foodservice call for services such as officers' clubs to be contracted out to foodservice management companies. This change has reduced military costs because many of the officers' clubs lost money. The clubs now have moved the emphasis from fine dining to a more casual approach with family appeal. Many clubs are renovating their base concept even further, restyling according to theme concepts, such as sports or country-western, for example. Other cost-saving measures include menu management, such as the use of a single menu for lunch and dinner (guests seldom eat both meals at the clubs). With proper plating techniques and portion size manipulation, a single menu can be created for lunch and dinner, meaning one inventory for both meals and less stock in general. To make this technique work successfully, the menu features several choices for appetizers, entrees, and desserts.

Another trend is the testing of prepared foods that can be reheated and served without much labor. Technological advances mean that field troops do not eat out of tin cans anymore; instead, they receive their food portions in plastic-and-foil pouches called MREs, or meals ready-to-eat. Today, mobile field kitchens can be run by just two people, and bulk food supplies have been replaced by preportioned, precooked food packed in trays, which then are reheated in boiling water.

Feeding military personnel includes feeding troops and officers in clubs, dining halls, and military hospitals, as well as in the field. As both the budget and the numbers of personnel decrease, the military is downsizing by consolidating responsibilities. With fewer people to cook for, fewer cooks are required.

A model for such downsizing is the U.S. Marine Corps. Since 1986, the marines have been contracting out foodservice. With smaller numbers, they could not afford to take a marine away from training to work in the dining facilities without affecting military operations.

In addition, fast-food restaurants like McDonald's and Burger King have opened on well over 200 bases; they are now installing Express Way kiosks on more bases.[4] The fast-food restaurants on base offer further alternatives for military personnel on the move.

One problem that may arise as a result of the downsizing and contracting out of military foodservice is that it is not likely that McDonald's could set up on the front line in a combat situation. The military will still have to do their own foodservice when it comes to mobilization.

Elementary and Secondary Schools

The United States government enacted the National School Lunch Act in 1946 in response to concern about malnourishment in military recruits.[5] The rationale was that if students received good meals, the military would have healthier recruits. In addition, such a program would make use of the surplus food that farmers produced.

Today, about 25 million children are fed breakfast or lunch—or both—each day in approximately 87,000 schools, at a cost of about $6 billion annually.

Many concerns currently face school foodservice. One major challenge is to balance salability with good nutrition. Apart from cost and nutritional value, the broader social issue of the universal free meal arises. Proponents of the program maintain that better nourished children have a better attention span, are less likely to be absent from school, and will stay in school longer. Offering free meals to all students also removes the poor kid stigma from school lunch. Detractors from the universal program say that if we learned anything from the social programs that were implemented during the 1960s, it was that throwing money at problems is not always the answer. Although these detractors believe conceptually in a universal program, they do not believe that it will solve the hunger problems in America.

Both sides agree that there is serious concern about what young students are eating. The recent news about the fat and cholesterol in the popcorn served at movie theaters shocked many adults. More shocking, though, is what school children are eating, as one recent survey illustrates.[6] A U.S. Department of Agriculture survey found that school lunches, on average, exceeded dietary guidelines for fat by 25 percent, for saturated fat by 50 percent, and for sodium by 85 percent. Equally shocking is the percentage of children who eat one serving or less of fruits and vegetables each day (not counting french fries), as shown in Figure 8–2.

The preparation and service of school foodservice meals varies. Some schools have on-site kitchens where the food is prepared, and dining rooms where the food is served. Many large school districts operate a central commissary that prepares the meals and then distributes them among the schools in that district. A third option is for schools to purchase ready-to-serve meals that require only assembly at the school.

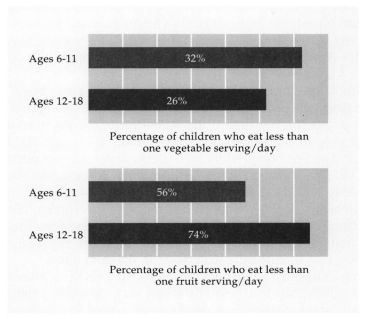

Figure 8–2 *Children and the Servings of Fruit and Vegetables They Eat* (Source: National Cancer Institute).

Schools may decide to participate in the national school lunch program (NSLP) or operate on their own. In reality, most schools have little choice because participating in the program means that federal funding is provided in the amount of approximately $1.75 per meal per student.

Meeting dietary guidelines is also an important issue. Much work has gone into establishing the nutritional requirements for children. It is difficult to achieve a balance between healthy food and costs, taking children's eating habits into account. Under the national school lunch program regulations, students must eat from what is commonly known as the type A menu. All of the items in the type A menu must be offered to all children at every meal. The children have to select a minimum of three of the five meal components in order for the school to qualify for funding. However, USDA regulations have established limits on the amount of fat and saturated fat that can be offered. Fat should not exceed 30 percent of calories per week, and saturated fat was cut down to 10 percent of calories per week. Figure 8–3 illustrates school lunch menus and Figure 8–4 shows the school lunch menu pattern requirements.

The government-funded NSLP, which pays $4.7 billion per year for the meals given or sold at a discount to schoolchildren, is a huge potential market for fast-food chains. Chains are extremely eager to penetrate into the elementary and secondary school markets, even if it means a decrease in revenues. "We do reduce the price of our product, and we do make less margin than in our normal operations," says Joy Wallace, national sales director/nontraditional sales for Pizza Hut. However, they believe that it is to their benefit to introduce Pizza Hut to young people very early—in other words, the aim is to build brand loyalty. As a matter of fact, in Duluth, Minnesota, James Bruner, foodservice director for the city schools, was forced into offering branded pizza in several junior high and high schools. The local principals, hungry for new revenue, began offering Little Caesar's in direct competition to the cafeteria's frozen pizzas.

Taco Bell is in nearly 3,000 schools, Pizza Hut in 4,500, Subway in 650; Domino's, McDonald's, Arby's, and others are well established in the market as well.

Philadelphia schools fulfill nutritional requirements and also bring brand-name food to school: Domino's prepares pizzas to the school district's specifications at a cost that is much lower than if the school made the pizza from scratch or bought it frozen. At Broward County high schools in Florida, Pizza Hut, Domino's, or a local pizzeria (depending on students' vote) delivers pizza twice a week. Two other days a week, Subway delivers sandwiches; again, the cost is lower than making similar sandwiches at school.[7]

San Juan Capistrano high school in California has gone one step further. The high school is a franchisee of Taco Bell, KFC, and Pizza Hut. Foodservice director Bill Caldwell says that this has created a win-win situation: Students get the food they like and also gain valuable work experience in the restaurants.[8]

Despite the positives, although it is not hard to convince the children, chains need to convince the adults. Much debate has arisen as to whether chains should enter the schools or not. Many parents feel that the school environment should provide a standard example of what sound nutrition should be, and they believe that with fast food as an option, that will not be the case.

WINTER ELEMENTARY LUNCH PORTION GUIDE
January 2 – April 17, 1995

DATE	MONDAY	TUESDAY	WEDNESDAY	THURSDAY	FRIDAY
Jan 2 Jan 30 Feb 27 Mar 27	1717 Bean & Cheese Burrito (1) 139 Green Beans (#16) 29 Chilled Fruit Cup (#16) 693 Milk (1)	648 Chicken Nuggets (4 ea) 118 Catsup (1 tbsp) 651 Celery Sticks (1 oz) 96 Ranch Dip (#40) 979 WW Bread & Butter (1 sl) 40 Orange Wedges (2 ea) 693 Milk (1)	406 (Turkey) Ham w/Melted Mozzarella on Bun (1) 229 French Fries (7/#) 118 Catsup (1 Tbsp) 253 Apple Wedges (2 ea) 693 Milk (1)	188 Party Pizza (12/sh) 381 Mixed Green Salad w/ (#12) 1117 Ranch Dressing (#30) 1343 Golden State Cookie (1) 693 Milk	650 Cheese Quesadilla (1) 181 Spanish Rice (#12) 651 Celery Sticks (1 oz) 1219 Jello w/Pears (#12) 693 Milk (1)
Jan 9 Feb 6 Mar 6 Apr 13	712 Corn Dog (1) 118 Catsup (2 Tbsp) 372 Mustard (1 Tbsp) 652 Potato Rounds (7/#) 521 Carrot Sticks (1 oz) 693 Milk (1)	1802 Stuffed Potato (1 ea) 381 Mixed Green Salad w/ (#12) 1117 Ranch Dressing 979 WW Bread w/Butter (1 sl) 29 Chilled Fruit Cup (#16) 693 Milk (1)	812 Spaghetti w/Pork and Turkey (#8) 1191 WW Dinner Roll (32/pan) 85 Creamy Coleslaw (#12) 269 Chilled Peaches (#16) 693 Milk (1) *	462 Cheese Pizza (1) 92 Corn (#16) 31 Gingerbread (50/pan) 693 Milk (1)	1370 Tostada Boat (1) 253 Apple Wedges (2 ea) 693 Milk (1)
Jan 16 Feb 13 Mar 13	418 Char Patty on WW Bun (1) 333 Shredded Lettuce (#16) 229 French Fries (7/#) 118 Catsup (2 Tbsp) 269 Chilled Peaches (#16) 693 Milk (1)	1779 Seafood Salad Sandwich (1) 746 Carrot Coins (1 oz) 96 Ranch Dip (#40) 1652 Brownie (80/pan) 693 Milk (1)	587 Ham & Cheese Roll-up (Pork) (1) 652 Potato Rounds (7/#) 118 Catsup (1 Tbsp) 29 Chilled Fruit Cup (#16) 693 Milk (1) *	1793 Pizza Bagel (1 ea) 1273 Celery Pieces (1 oz) 96 Ranch Dip (#40) 1304 Trail Mix (#12) 693 Milk (1)	1717 Bean & Cheese Burrito (1) 381 Mixed Green Salad w/ (#12) 1117 Ranch Dressing 40 Orange Wedges (2 ea) 693 Milk (1)
Jan 23 Feb 20 Mar 20	538 Turkey Hot Dog (1) 118 Catsup (1 Tbsp) 372 Mustard (1 Tbsp) 521 Carrot Sticks (1 oz) 273 Chilled Pineapple (#16) 693 Milk (1)	691 Turkey & Gravy (#8) 173 Whipped Potatoes (#8) 1714 Bernies Breadsticks (60/pan) 40 Orange Wedges (2 ea) 693 Milk (1)	1805 Salisbury Steak (1 ea) 92 Niblet Corn (#16) 605 Nutribun (40/pan) 1395 Kiwi Wedge (2 ea) 693 Milk (1)	686 Sausage Pizza (Pork) (1 ea) 139 Green Beans (#16) 130 Cherry Jello Dessert (2 ea) 693 Milk (1) *	403 Grilled Cheese Sandwich (12/sh) 652 Potato Rounds (#16) 118 Catsup (#12) 179 Pear Wedges (2 ea) 693 Milk (1)

LUNCH

F254

HOLIDAYS: Monday, January 2 - Use Monday's menu on Tuesday, January 3
Tuesday, January 3 - Use Tuesday's menu on Wednesday, January 4
Monday, January 16 - Use Monday's menu on Wednesday, January 18: Delete #333 Shredded Lettuce
Tuesday, January 17 - Staff Development Day
Friday, February 17 - Omit Friday's menu
Monday, February 20 - Use Monday's menu on Tuesday, February 21: Delete #521 Carrot Sticks; add #183 Cowboy Beans #16

Figure 8–3   *Sample Elementary School Lunch Menu*

275

School Lunch Patterns
For Various Age/Grade Groups

USDA recommends, but does not require, that you adjust portions by age/grade group to better meet the food and nutritional needs of children according to their ages. If you adjust portions, Groups I–IV are minimum requirements for the age/grade groups specified. If you do not adjust portions, the Group IV portions are the portions to serve all children.

			Minimum Quantities			Recommended Quantities[2]
	COMPONENTS	Preschool		Grades K-3	Grades 4-12[1]	Grades 7-12
		Ages 1-2 (Group I)	Ages 3-4 (Group II)	Ages 5-8 (Group III)	Age 9 & over (Group IV)	Ages 12 & over (Group V)
SPECIFIC REQUIREMENTS — • Must be served in the main dish or the main dish and only one other menu item. • Vegetable protein products, cheese alternate products, and enriched macaroni with fortified protein may be used to meet part of the meat/meat alternate requirement. Fact sheets on each of these alternate foods give detailed instructions for use.	**Meat or Meat Alternate** — A serving of one of the following or a combination to give an equivalent quantity:					
	Lean meat, poultry, or fish (edible portion as served)	1 oz	1-1/2 oz	1-1/2 oz	2 oz	3 oz
	Cheese	1 oz	1-1/2 oz	1-1/2 oz	2 oz	3 oz
	Large egg(s)	1/2	3/4	3/4	1	1-1/2
	Cooked dry beans or peas	1/4 cup	3/8 cup	3/8 cup	1/2 cup	3/4 cup
	Peanut butter or other nut or seed butters	2 Tbsp	3 Tbsp	3 Tbsp	4 Tbsp	6 Tbsp
	Peanuts, soy nuts, tree nuts, or seeds, as listed in program guidance, meet no more than 50% of the requirement and must be combined in the meal with at least 50% of other meat or meat alternate. (1 oz of nut/seeds=1 oz of cooked lean meat, poultry, or fish.)	1/2 oz=50%	3/4 oz=50%	3/4 oz=50%	1 oz=50%	1-1/2 oz=50%
Vegetables and/or Fruits — • No more than one-half of the total requirement may be met with full-strength fruit or vegetable juice. • Cooked dry beans or peas may be used as a meat alternate or as a vegetable but not as both in the same meal.	Two or more servings of vegetables or fruits or both to total	1/2 cup	1/2 cup	1/2 cup	3/4 cup	3/4 cup
Servings of bread or Bread Alternate — • At least 1/2 serving of bread or an equivalent quantity of bread alternate for Group I, and 1 serving for Groups II-V, must be served daily. • Enriched macaroni with fortified protein may be used as a meat alternate or as a bread alternate but not as both in the same meal. NOTE: Food Buying Guide for Child Nutrition Programs, PA-1331 (1984) provides the information for the minimum weight of a serving.	A serving is: • 1 slice of whole-grain or enriched bread • A whole-grain or enriched biscuit, roll, muffin, etc. • 1/2 cup of cooked whole-grain or enriched rice, macaroni, noodles, whole-grain or enriched pasta products, or other cereal grains such as bulgur or corn grits • A combination or any of the above	5 per week	8 per week	8 per week	8 per week	10 per week
Milk — The following forms of milk must be offered: • Whole milk • Unflavored lowfat milk NOTE: This requirement does not prohibit offering other milk, such as flavored milk or skim milk, along with the above.	A serving of fluid milk	3/4 cup (6 fl oz)	3/4 cup (6 fl oz)	1/2 pint (8 fl oz)	1/2 pint (8 fl oz)	1/2 pint (8 fl oz)

[1]Group IV is highlighted because it is the one meal pattern which will satisfy all requirements if no portion size adjustments are made.

[2]Group V specifies recommended, not required, quantities for students 12 years and older. These students may request smaller portions, but not smaller than those specified in Group IV.

Figure 8–4 *School Lunch Menu Pattern Requirements* (U.S. Department of Agriculture, National School Lunch Program.)

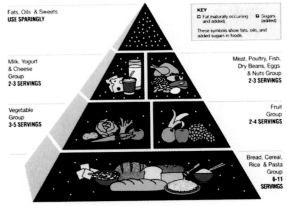

Food Guide Pyramid
A Guide to Daily Food Choices

Figure 8–5 *Food Pyramid* (U.S. Department of Agriculture and U.S. Department of Health and Human Services.)

At a recent school lunch challenge at the American Culinary Federation (ACF) Conference, chefs from around the country developed nutritious menus geared to wean children away from junk food to healthy foods. An 80-cent limit on the cost of raw ingredients was placed on the eleven finalists. Innovation and taste, as well as healthfulness, were the main criteria used to evaluate the winning entry: turkey taco salad, sausage pizza bagel, and stuffed potatoes.

Professional chefs are now working with the Department of Agriculture's Food and Consumer Services to develop healthful recipes and menus with increased appeal but without an increase in cost.[9]

Nutrition Education Programs

Nutrition education is now a required part of the nation's school lunch program. As a result of this program, children are learning to improve their eating habits, which, it is hoped, will continue for the rest of their lives. To support the program, nutritional education materials are used to decorate the dining room halls and tables. Perhaps the best example of this is the food pyramid developed by the Food and Nutrition Service of the U.S. Department of Agriculture. Figure 8–5 shows this food pyramid, which shows what to eat each day for a healthy diet.

Colleges and Universities

College and university foodservice operations are complex and diverse. Among the various constituents of foodservice management are residence halls, cafeterias/student unions, faculty clubs, convenience stores, administrative catering, and outside catering.

On-campus dining is a challenge for foodservice managers because the clientele lives on campus and eats most of its meals at the campus dining facility. Students, staff, and faculty may quickly become bored with the sameness of the

Personal Profile: Manuel Lorenzo

Manuel Lorenzo is a supervisor for Marriott Food Services and arrives at United States International University (USIU) to begin his shift at 9:00 A.M. Manuel's first duty is to check the catering board where he will find a list of scheduled catering events for the day. Manuel then plans the food preparation and starts gathering the necessary equipment.

By 10:00 A.M., Manuel goes around to all the foodservice outlets that are open during the night hours and collects money and receipts. The cash must then be immediately transported to the bank for deposit. The figures must also be entered into the company computer.

After Manuel completes handling the money, he talks with Sheri Henderson, the director of foodservices at USIU. She keeps him abreast of information for the day. This is the time any problems or concerns can be addressed. At 11:00 A.M., Manuel walks around to make sure the cafeteria is ready to serve lunch. Manuel supervises the lunch operation until it ends at 1:30. After lunch, Manuel continues working on catering functions and makes sure everything flows and is ready for dinner.

Before Manuel leaves for the day, he must check to see that all catering vehicles are tanked and running properly. Then, the storerooms must be cleaned and orga-

Manuel Lorenzo

nized. Sheri will also have a list of projects for Manuel to complete. These tasks usually consist of maintaining sanitation standards. Last, Manuel checks staffing levels for the rest of the week and deals with basic human resource functions.

Manuel sees time management as one of the major challenges of his career. Events are constantly pending, and he has only a very limited amount of time to plan, organize, and carry out those functions. Manuel contends that the only way to be successful, in this respect, is to be highly organized. Also, Manuel says that success requires one to be a "people-person." This skill helps him deal with employees effectively and helps him understand the people he serves, so that he can serve them better.

Keeping the customer satisfied is another challenge for Manuel. University foodservice operations have the unique and difficult task of keeping long-term boarding residents happy with food quality. Manuel solves this problem by serving a wide variety of entrees, yet keeping consistent with daily staples.

Each catering event is different because of the variety in food served. With each new function, Manuel learns something about food and/or culture. Manuel admits that this is one of the most interesting, exciting, and rewarding aspects of his job.

surroundings and menu offerings. Most campus dining is cafeteria style and offers cyclical menus that rotate on a predetermined schedule.

However, a college foodservice manager does have some advantages when compared with a restaurant manager. Budgeting is made easier because the on-campus students have already paid for their meals and their numbers are easy to forecast. When the payment is guaranteed and the guest count is predictable, planning and organizing staffing levels and food quantities is relatively easy and should ensure a reasonable profit margin. For instance, the daily rate is the amount of money required per day from each person to pay for the foodservice. Thus, if food service expenses for one semester of ninety-eight days amount to $650,000 for an operation with 1,000 students eating, the daily rate will be

$$\frac{\$650,000 \div 98 \text{ (days)}}{1000} = \$6.63$$

College Foodservice
(Courtesy ARAMARK.)

College foodservice operations now offer a variety of meal plans for students. Under the old board plan, when students paid one fee for all meals each day—whether they ate them or not—the foodservice operator literally made a profit from the students who did not actually eat the meals they had paid for. More typically now, students match their payments to the number of meals eaten: Monday–Friday, breakfast, lunch, dinner; dinner only; and prepaid credit cards that allow a student to use the card at any campus outlet and have the value of the food and beverage items deducted from his or her credit balance.

Leaders of the National Associations of College Auxiliary Services (NACAS), who represent 1,200 member institutes, have noticed that on-campus services and activities are undergoing continuous change. The environment has become a critical part of policy and implementation that transcends parochial interests for those that best meet the needs of the institution and, ultimately, its students.

The driving forces of change on campuses are the advent and growth of branded concepts, privatization, campus cards, and computer use.

Student Unions

The college student union offers a variety of managed services that caters to the needs of a diverse student body. Among the services offered are cafeteria food-service, beverage services, branded quick-service restaurants, and take-out food-service.

The cafeteria foodservice operation is often the "happening" place in the student union where students meet to socialize as well as to eat and drink. The cafeteria is generally open for breakfast, lunch, and dinner. Depending on the volume of business, the cafeteria may be closed during the nonmeal periods and weekends, and the cafeteria menu may or may not be the same as the residence foodservice facility. Offering a menu with a good price value is crucial to the successful operation of a campus cafeteria.

On campuses at which alcoholic beverage service is permitted, beverage services mainly focus on some form of a student pub where beer and perhaps wine and spirits may be offered. Not to be outdone, the faculty will undoubtedly have a lounge that also offers alcoholic beverages. Other beverages may be served at various outlets such as a food court or convenience store. Campus beverage service provides opportunities for foodservice operators to enhance profits.

In addition, many college campuses have welcomed branded, quick-service restaurants as a convenient way to satisfy the needs of a community on the go. Such an approach offers a win-win situation for colleges. The experience and brand recognition of chain restaurants like Pizza Hut, McDonald's, Subway, and Wendy's attract customers; the restaurants pay a fee, either to the foodservice management company or the university directly. Obviously, there is a danger that the quick-service restaurant may attract customers that the cafeteria might then lose, but competition tends to be good for all concerned.

Take-out foodservice is another convenience for the campus community. At times, students—and staff—do not want to prepare meals and are thankful for the opportunity to take meals with them. And, it is not just during examination time that students, friends, and staff have a need for the take-out option. For example, tailgate parties prior to football and basketball games or concerts and other recreational/sporting events allow entrepreneurial foodservice operators to increase revenue and profits.

The type of contract that a managed services operator signs varies depending on the size of the account. If the account is small, a fee generally is charged. With larger accounts, operators contract for a set percentage (usually about five percent) or a combination of a percentage and a bonus split.

Figure 8–6 shows a typical college menu for the dining hall where students usually eat on campus.

Responsibilities in Managed Services

A foodservice manager's responsibilities in a small or midsize operation are frequently more extensive than those of managers of the larger operations. This is because larger units have more people to whom to delegate certain functions, such as human resources. For example, following are some of the responsibilities that the foodservice manager in a small or midsize operation might have in addition to strictly foodservice responsibilities:

Employee Relations
- ✔ Business vs. personal needs, family problems
- ✔ Rewards/recognition
- ✔ Drug alcohol abuse/prevention
- ✔ Positive work environment
- ✔ Coaching/facilitating vs. directing

Human Resource Management
- ✔ Recruitment/training/evaluating
- ✔ Wage/salary administration
- ✔ Benefits administration
- ✔ Compliance with federal/state laws/EEO/Senate Bill 198
- ✔ Harassment/OSHA
- ✔ Disciplinary actions/terminations
- ✔ Unemployment/wrongful disclosure

Figure 8–6 *Sample College Menu* (Courtesy Marriott Foodservice Management.)

Financial/Budgeting

- ✔ Project budgets
- ✔ Actual vs. budget monitoring (weekly)
- ✔ Controlling food cost, labor, expenses, and so on
- ✔ Record keeping requirements/audit
- ✔ Monitoring accounts payable/receivable
- ✔ Billing/collecting
- ✔ Compliance to contracts
- ✔ Cash procedures/banking

Corporate Profile: ARAMARK

In the 1950s, Dave Davidson and Bill Fishman, both in the vending business, realized that they shared the same dreams and hopes of turning vending into a service and combining it with foodservice. The two entrepreneurs joined forces to become the first truly national vending and foodservice company. Automatic Retailers of America (ARA) was born in 1959. Fishman and Davidson had the management skills, the capital, and the expertise to expand. And this they did—ARAMARK is the world's leading provider of quality managed services. It operates in all fifty states and in eleven foreign countries, offering a very diversified and broad range of services to businesses of all sizes, and to thousands of universities, hospitals, and municipal, state, and federal government facilities. Every day, they serve more than 15 million people at more than 500,000 locations worldwide.

ARAMARK's emphasis on the quality of service management was evident from the very beginning of its operations. ARAMARK entered new markets by researching the best-managed local companies, acquiring them, and persuading key managers to stay with the company.

The company's vision, in fact, states that ARAMARK is "a company where the best people want to work." Customers recommend ARAMARK to others because they constantly exceed expectations. In this case, success is measured in the growth of the company, its earnings, and its employees themselves. This is one fundamental constant in ARAMARK's early success: It grew its business by focusing on growing its management. The company's guiding principles reaffirm such a concept:

"Because we succeed through performance, we encourage the entrepreneur in each of us, and work always to improve our service.

"Because we thrive on growth, we seek new markets and new opportunities, and we innovate to get and keep new customers."

With the 1961 acquisition of Slater System, Inc., the largest foodservice business in the country, ARAMARK began the diversification process, and has continued since to amplify the portfolio of services it now offers. The focus on management skills at every level, especially the local one, gave ARAMARK an invaluable resource. In fact, with every acquisition, local managers were encouraged and rewarded for becoming multiskilled entrepreneurs. This approach to outsourcing is, put more simply, the ability of the company to take the best management skills and apply them to all the lines of business the company uses to diversify.

Among ARAMARK operations are the following:

Food, leisure, and support services. The company provides food, specialized refreshments, dietary services, and operation support to businesses, educational facilities, government, and medical institutions. ARAMARK also manages food, lodging, hospitality, and support services at national parks and other recreational facilities that serve the general public.

Health and education services: ARAMARK provides specialized management services for hospitals and medical services. It also specializes in providing early-childhood and school-age education services.

Uniform services: The company is America's largest provider of uniform services and work apparel for virtually all types of institutions.

Magazine and book services: ARAMARK is the leading wholesale distributor of magazines, newspapers, and books.

ARAMARK successfully manages the diversity of segment concepts under the guideline of one single purpose: to be the world leader in managed services. With annual revenues in excess of $5 billion, the company is among the market leaders in all of its businesses, and it is in an ideal position for further market growth. Joseph Neubauer, chairman and CEO, realizes this:

"I am energized by the bright prospects for the journey ahead. . . . I can't wait to get started."

Adapted courtesy of ARAMARK.

Safety Administration
- ✔ Equipment training/orientation
- ✔ Controlling workers compensation
- ✔ Monthly inspections/audits (federal/state/OSHA requirements/Senate Bill 198)

Safety Budget
- ✔ Work on the expensive injuries

Food Production/Service
- ✔ Menu/recipe development
- ✔ Menu mix vs. competition
- ✔ Food waste/leftovers utilization
- ✔ Production records
- ✔ Production control
- ✔ Presentation/merchandising

Sanitation/FBI Prevention
- ✔ FBI (food-borne illness) prevention
- ✔ Sanitation/cleaning schedule
- ✔ Proper food handling/storage
- ✔ Daily prevention/monitoring
- ✔ Monthly inspection
- ✔ Health department compliance

Purchasing/Recruiting
- ✔ Ordering/receiving/storage
- ✔ Food and beverage specifications/quality
- ✔ Inventory control
- ✔ Vendor relation/problems

Staff Training/Development
- ✔ On-the-job vs. structured
- ✔ Safety/sanitation/food handling and so on
- ✔ Food preparation/presentation

A sample operating statement is shown in Figure 8–7. It shows a monthly statement for a college foodservice operation.

Health Care Facilities

Health care managed services operations are remarkably complex because of the necessity of meeting the diverse needs of a delicate clientele. Health care managed services are provided to hospital patients, long-term care and assisted-living residents, visitors, and employees. The service is given by tray, cafeteria, dining room, coffee shop, catering, and vending.

The challenge of health care managed services is to provide many special meal requirements to patients with very specific dietary requirements. Determining

DESCRIPTION		%	STUDENT UNION	%	TOTAL	%
SALES						
FOOD REGULAR	$ 951,178				951,178	
FOOD SPECIAL FUNCTIONS	40,000				40,000	
PIZZA HUT EXPRESS			$ 100,000		100,000	
BANQUET & CATERING	200,000				200,000	
CONFERENCE	160,000				160,000	
BEER			80,000		80,000	
SNACK BAR			300,000		30,000	
A LA CARTE CAFE	60,000				60,000	
** TOTAL SALES	$1,411,178		$ 480,000	100.0%	$1,891,178	100.0%
PRODUCT COST						
BAKED GOODS	$ 9,420		$ 4,700		$ 14,120	
BEVERAGE	10,000		8,000		18,000	
MILK & ICE CREAM	11,982		2,819		14,801	
GROCERIES	131,000		49,420		180,420	
FROZEN FOOD	76,045		37,221		113,266	
MEAT SEAFOOD, EGGS & CHEESE	129,017		48,000		177,017	
PRODUCE	65,500		26,000		91,500	
MISCELLANEOUS					0	
COLD DRINK	0		0		0	
** TOTAL PRODUCT COST	$ 432,964		$ 176,160	36.7%	$ 609,124	32.2%
LABOR COST						
WAGES	$ 581,000		$ 154,000		$ 735,000	
LABOR—OTHER EMPLOYEES	101,500		545,000		156,000	
BENEFITS + PAYROLL TAXES	124,794		50,657		175,451	
MANAGEMENT BENEFITS	58,320		6,000		64,320	
WAGE ACCRUALS	0				0	
** TOTAL LABOR COST	$ 865,614		$ 265,157	55.2%	$1,130,771	59.8%
FOOD OPERATING COST- CONTROLLABLE	$ 24,000		$ 6,000		$ 30,000	
CLEANING SUPPLIES	9,000		46,000		55,000	
PAPER SUPPLIES					0	
EQUIPMENT RENTAL					0	
GUEST SUPPLIES	4,500		2,500		7,000	
PROMOTIONS	35,000		5,000		40,000	
SMALL EQUIPMENT					0	
BUSINESS DUES & MEMBERSHIP	3,000				3,000	
VEHICLE EXPENSE	3,600		700		4,300	
TELEPHONE	$ 17,000		$ 5,000		$ 22,000	

Figure 8–7 *Sample Operating Statement*

which meals need to go to which patients and ensuring that they reach their destinations employs especially challenging logistics. In addition to the patients, health care employees need to enjoy a nutritious meal in pleasant surroundings in a limited time (usually thirty minutes). Because employees typically work five days in a row, care must be taken to keep changing the area and the menu using themes and specials that maintain interest.

The main focus of hospital foodservice is the tray line. Once all of the requirements for special meals have been prepared by a registered dietician, the line is set up and color coded for the various diets. The line begins with the tray, a mat, cutlery, napkin, salt and pepper, and perhaps a flower. As the tray moves along the line, various menu items are added according to the color code for the particular patient's diet. Naturally, each tray is double- and triple-checked, first at the end of the tray line and then on the hospital floor. The line generally goes floor by floor at a rate of about five trays a minute; at this rate, a large hospital

DESCRIPTION		%	STUDENT UNION	%	TOTAL	%
LAUNDRY & UNIFORMS					0	
MAINTENANCE & REPAIRS	$ 1,200		$ 200		$ 1,400	
FLOWERS	10,000		4,000		140,000	
TRAINING					0	
SPECIAL SERVICES	18,000		3,000		21,000	
MISCELLANEOUS						
** TOTAL CONTROLLABLE SUPPLIES	$ 125,300	8.9%	$ 72,400	15.1%	$ 197,700	10.5%
OPERATING COSTS- NONCONTROLLABLE						
AMORTIZATION & DEPRECIATION	$ 13,500		$ 7,000		$ 20,500	
INSURANCE	55,717		14,768		70,485	
MISCELLANEOUS EXPENSE	12,400		4,100		16,500	
ASSET RETIREMENTS					0	
RENT/COMMISSIONS	48,000		40,000		88,000	
PIZZA HUT ROYALTIES			7,000		7,000	
PIZZA HUT —						
LICENSING MARKETING			7,000		7,000	
TAXES, LICENSE & FEES	5,000		500		5,500	
VEHICLE —						
DEPRECIATION & EXPENSE	4,000				4,000	
ADMINISTRATION & SUPERVISION						
** TOTAL NONCONTROLLABLE COST	$ 138,617	9.8%	$ 80,368	16.7%	$ 218,985	11.6%
** TOTAL COST OF OPERATIONS	$1,562,495	110.7%	$ 594,085	123.8%	$2,156,580	114.0%
EXCESS OR (DEFICIT)	(151,317)	(10.7%)	(114,085%)	(23.8)	(265,402)	(14.0%)
PARTICIPATION-CONTRACTOR						
*** NET EXCESS OR (DEFICIT)						
STATISTICS						
CUSTOMER COUNT						
HOURS WORKED						
AVERAGE FOOD- SALES/CUSTOMER						

Figure 8–7   *(continued)*

with 600 beds can be served within a couple of hours. This is time-consuming for the employees, because three meals a day represent up to six hours of line time. Clearly, health care foodservice is very labor intensive, with labor accounting for about 55 to 66 percent of operating dollars. In an effort to keep costs down, many operators have increased the number of help-yourself food stations, buffets, salads, desserts, and topping bars.

Patient counts and lengths of stay are declining, which emphasizes the importance of finding new ways of generating revenues. According to 1994's ten largest self-operated hospitals, one of the basic service areas, the cafeteria, is generating the biggest revenue-producing opportunities.[10]

Hospital foodservice has evolved to the point where the need for new revenue sources has changed the traditional patient and nonpatient meal-service ratios at many institutions. This situation was imposed by the federal government when it narrowed the treatment-reimbursement criteria; originally

Health Care Foodservice
(Courtesy ARAMARK.)

66 percent of a typical acute-care facility's foodservice budget went toward patients' meals, with the remainder allocated for feeding the employees and visitors. In the past few years, as cash sales have become more important, the 66/33 percent ratio has reversed.

Ever resourceful, managers of health care operations, like Dolly Strenko of Southwestern General Hospital in Middleburg Heights, Ohio, have created such concepts as a medical mall with a retail pharmacy; flower and gift shops; boutique; a retail bakery, with an exhibition conveyor oven; and a 112-seat restaurant deli with take-out services for adjacent medical offices and outside catering for weddings, bar mitzvahs, and other functions. Dolly has also been instrumental in elevating culinary standards, the result of hiring an executive chef who was a graduate of the Culinary Institute of America.

Experts agree that because economic pressures will increase, foodservice managers will need to use a more high-tech approach, incorporating labor-saving sous-vide and cook-chill methods. This segment of the industry, which currently is dominated by self-operated managed services, will continue to see contract specialists, such as Monson Custom management, Marriott, and ARAMARK Services, increase their market share at the expense of self-operated health care managed services. One reason for this is that the larger contract companies have the economy of scale and a more sophisticated approach to quantity purchasing, menu management, and operating systems that help to reduce food and labor costs. A skilled independent foodservice operator has the advantage of being able to introduce changes immediately without having to support layers of regional and corporate employees.

Dolly Strenko

Another trend in health care managed services is the arrival of the major quick-service chains. McDonald's, Pizza Hut Express, Burger King, and Dunkin Donuts are just a few of the large companies that have joined forces with the contract managed services operators. Using branded quick-service leaders is a win-win situation for both the contract foodservice operator and the quick-service chain. As one operator put it, "The new McDonald's can be a training facility for future employees—in effect, a potential resource for our staff needs. Our union scale of $7.22 per hour could entice some 'cross-overs.' The branded image also helps the overall retail side of the foodservice operation."

The chains benefit from long-term leases at very attractive rates compared with a restaurant site. Chains assess the staff size and patient and visitor count to determine the size of unit to install. Thus far, they have found that weekday lunches and dinners are good, but the numbers on weekends are disappointing.

In contrast, several hospitals are entering the pizza-delivery business: They hook up phone and fax ordering lines, and they hire part-time employees to deliver pizzas made on the premises. This ties in with the increasing emphasis on customer service. Patients' meals now feature "comfort foods," based on the concept that the simpler the food is, the better. Hence, the resurgence of meat loaf, pot pies, meat and potatoes, and tuna salad, which contributes to customer satisfaction, and makes them feel at home and comfortable.

Business and Industry

Business and industry (B&I) managed services is one of the most dynamic segments of the managed services industry. In recent years, B&I foodservice has improved its image by becoming more colorful, with menus as interesting as commercial restaurants.

There are important terms to understand in B&I foodservice.[11]

1. *Contractors:* Companies that operate foodservice for the client on a contractual basis. Most corporations contract with managed services companies because they are in manufacturing or some other service industry. Therefore, they engage professional managed services corporations to run their employee dining facilities. Contract managed services operators have one main advantage over self-operators: They do not have to give as high a compensation and benefit package as the corporation itself.
2. *Self-operators:* Companies that operate their own foodservice operations. In some cases, this is done because it is easier to control one's own operation; for example, it is easier to make changes to comply with special nutritional or other dietary requests.
3. *Liaison personnel:* A liaison is responsible for translating corporate philosophy to the contractor and for overseeing the contractor to make certain that he or she abides by the terms of the contract.

Contractors have approximately 80 percent of the B&I market. The remaining 20 percent is self-operated, but the trend is for more foodservice operations to be contracted out. The size of the B&I sector is approximately 30,000 units. In order to adapt to corporate downsizing and relocations, the B&I segment has offered foodservice in smaller units rather than huge full-sized cafeterias. Another trend is the necessity for B&I foodservice to break even or, in some cases, make a profit. An interesting twist is the emergence of multitenant buildings, the occupants of which may all use a central facility. However, in today's turbulent business environment, there is a high vacancy rate in commercial office space. This translates into fewer guests for B&I operators in multitenant office buildings. As a result, some office buildings have leased space to commercial branded restaurants.

B&I managed services operators have responded to requests from corporate employees to offer more than the standard fast-food items of pizza and hamburgers; they want healthier foods offered, such as make-your-own sandwiches, salad bars, fresh fruit stations, and ethnic foods.

Most B&I managed services operators offer a number of types of service. The type of service is determined by the resources available: money, space, time, and expertise. Usually these resources are quite limited, which means that most operations use some form of cafeteria service.

B&I foodservice may be characterized in the following ways:

1. Full-service cafeteria with either straight line, scatter, or mobile systems
2. Limited-service cafeterias offering parts of the full-service cafeteria, fast-food service, cart and mobile service, fewer dining rooms, and executive dining rooms

Business and Industry Foodservice (Courtesy ARAMARK.)

Trends in Managed Services

✔ College and university foodservice managers face increasing challenges. *Restaurants and Institutions* magazine asked several managers to identify some of those challenges. In general, managers mentioned trying to balance rising costs with tighter dollars. Bill Rigan, foodservice center manager at Oklahoma State University, Stillwater, pointed out two main challenges: a reduction of revenues from board-plan sales combined with increased costs such as food and utilities. He dealt with these challenges by recognizing that inasmuch as he could not change the utilities or hourly rates for employees, he would have to maximize purchasing potential. He also made optimal usage of from "scratch" cooking, convenience foods, and more efficient labor scheduling.

✔ Martha Willis, foodservice director at Tennessee Technological University, Cookesville, sees declining enrollment and a reduction in state funding as challenges. This translates to a cutback in services and more pressure to produce a bigger bottom line. Martha intends to achieve this by filling vacant full-time positions with part-time and student employees. The savings made by not paying full-time employee benefits can amount to 30 percent of a person's wage.

✔ Increased use of campus cards

✔ Increased use of food-to-go, for instance before sporting events

✔ Increase use of carts at vantage points

✔ Dueling demands for foodservice managers—from students who want more freshly prepared foods in convenient locations and from administrators who want more revenue from existing sources

✔ 24-hour foodservice

✔ Increased business in health care and nursing homes

✔ Proliferation of branded concepts in all segments of managed services, including military, school and college, business and industry, health care, and airport

✔ Development of home meal replacement options in each segment of the managed services sector, as a way to increase revenue

---

Chaos in the Kitchen

Jane is the foodservice director at an on-campus dining service that feeds 800 students per meal for breakfast, lunch, and dinner. Jane arrives at her office at 7:00 A.M. (half an hour before breakfast begins) only to find many problems.

After listening to her phone messages, she finds that her breakfast cashier and one of her two breakfast dishroom employees have called in sick. The cashier position is essential and the second dishroom person is necessary at 8:15 A.M. when the students leave to go to their 8:30 A.M. classes.

Shortly after listening to the messages, the executive chef tells Jane that one of their two walk-in refrigerators is not working properly, thus some of the food is above the safe temperature of 40°F.

The lead salad person later comes to her, saying that one of the three ice machines is not working. Hence, there will not be enough ice to ice down the salad bars and to use for cold beverages at lunch.

Lastly, the catering supervisor tells Jane that he has just found out that there was a misunderstanding with the bakery that supplies their upscale desserts. The desserts were requested by the president of the university for a luncheon he is having that day, however because the employee at the bakery wrote the wrong delivery date, the desserts would not be delivered. This will cause the president to be angry.

Discussion Questions

1. How should Jane handle being short a cashier and a dishroom person at breakfast?
2. What should Jane do with the food in the defective refrigerator? Should the food that is measured to be above 40°F be saved?
3. What are Jane's options concerning the ice shortage?
4. How should Jane handle the president's function, knowing that the requested desserts have not been delivered?
5. If the special dessert cannot be purchased in time, how should the catering supervisor approach this situation with the president's office?
6. What can be done to assure that mistakes, such as the one made by the bakery employee, do not happen again?

Gas Leak

The kitchen at a major corporation's managed service business account includes several gas and electric stoves, ovens, broilers, steamers, bar-be-ques, etc. On average, the kitchen serves 500 lunches. At 10:15 A.M., on a Tuesday in December, a gas leak prompts the gas company to cut off the gas supply.

Discussion Questions

1. What can be done to offer the best possible lunch food and service?

Summary

1. Managed services operations have a nonprofit orientation and include segments such as airlines, military, schools and colleges, health care facilities, and businesses.

2. Quality food has become a major competitive factor among airlines, which either provide meals from their own in-flight business or have it prepared by a contractor, such as Caterair or Sky Chefs.

3. Service to the military includes feeding troops and officers in clubs, dining halls, and hospitals as well as out in the field. Direct vendor delivery, menu management, prepared foods, and fastfood chains directly on the base have met new trends in military foodservice.

4. Schools are either equipped with on-site kitchens and dining rooms or receive food from a central commissary. They try to balance salability with good nutrition. Today, nutrition education is a required subject in school.

5. College and university managed services operations include residence halls, cafeterias, student unions, faculty clubs, convenience stores, and catering.

6. The responsibilities of a foodservice manager are very complex. He or she is in charge of employee relations, human resource management, budgeting, safety administration, sanitation, and inventory.

7. Health care managed services operations need to provide numerous special meals to patients with very specific dietary requirements and nutritious meals in a limited time period for employees. The main areas of concern for health care managed services operations are tray lines and help-yourself food stations.

8. Business and industry managed services operations either operate with a full-service cafeteria or limited-service cafeteria. The type of service is determined by money, space, and time available.

Review Exercises

1. What are managed services operations?
2. List and explain features that distinguish managed services operations from commercial ones.
3. Describe the issues that schools are currently facing concerning school food service.
4. Explain the term *national school lunch program* (NSLP).
5. Identify recent trends in college food service management.
6. What are the pros and cons concerning fast-food chains on campus?
7. Briefly explain the complex challenges for health care managed services operations.

Key Words and Concepts

Airline
Batch cooking
Board plan
Business
Colleges and universities

Commercial foodservice
Dietary guidelines
Elementary and secondary schools
Health care

In-flight meal costs
Managed services
Military
National school lunch program

Nutrition education programs
Tray line

Notes

[1]A. McCool, F. L. Smith, and D. L. Tucker, *Dimensions of Noncommercial Foodservice Management*. New York: Van Nostrand Reinhold, 1994, p. 278.
[2]Ibid., p. 281.
[3]Ibid., p. 282.
[4]*Restaurant Business, 104,* 21, September 20, 1992, p. 118.
[5]Susie Stephensen, "School Lunch: One Correct Answer? Or Multiple Choice?" *Restaurants and Institutions,* September 1, 1993, p. 114.
[6]*U.S. News and World Report, 116,* 8, May 9, 1994, p. 18.
[7]"Schools," *Restaurants and Institutions, 103,* 20, August 15, 1993, p. 44.
[8]Jeff Weinstein, "Free-Flow Style Star in Kitchen Design Award," *Restaurants and Institutions, 104,* 21, September 1, 1993, p. 120.
[9]"School Lunch Challenge: Nutritious Food," *Restaurants and Institutions, 102,* 23, October 1, 1994, p. 29.
[10]Personal conversation with Dolly Strenko, November 1994.
[11]Philip S. Cooke. In Joan B. Bakos and Guy E. Karrick (eds.), *Dining in Corporate America: Handbook of NonCommercial Management.* Rockville, Md.: Aspen Publishers, 1989, p. xvii.

Beverages

9

After reading and studying this chapter you should be able to do the following:

✔ List the types of spirits and how they are made
✔ Describe the wine-making process and the major wine-growing regions of the world
✔ Suggest appropriate pairing of wine with foods
✔ Distinguish various types of beer
✔ Outline the history of coffee
✔ Explain a restaurant's liability in terms of serving alcoholic beverages

Serving beverages is traditional throughout the world. According to his or her culture, a person might welcome a visitor with coffee or tea—or bourbon. Beverages are generally categorized into two main groups: alcoholic and nonalcoholic. Alcoholic beverages are further categorized as wines, beer, and spirits. Figure 9–1 depicts these three categories.

Wines

Wine is the fermented juice of freshly gathered ripe grapes. Wine may also be made from other sugar-containing fruits, such as blackberries, cherries, or elderberries. In this chapter, however, we will confine our discussion to grape wines. Wine may be classified first by color: red, white, or rose. Wines are further classified as light beverage wines, still, sparkling wines, fortified wines, and aromatic wines.

Light Beverage Wines

White, red, or rose table wines are light beverage wines; such table wines may come from a variety of growing regions around the world. In the United States, the premium wines are named after the grape variety, such as chardonnay and cabernet sauvignon. This proved so successful that Europeans are now also naming their wines after the grape variety and their region of origin, such as Pouilly Fuisse and Chablis.

Sparkling Wines

Champagne, sparkling white wine, and sparkling rose wine are called the *sparkling wines*. Sparkling wines sparkle because they contain carbon dioxide. The carbon dioxide may be either naturally produced or mechanically infused

Wine	Beer	Spirits
Still	Top fermenting	Grapes/fruit
Natural	Lager	Grains
Fortified	Bottom fermenting	Cactus
Aromatic	Ale	Sugar cane/
Sparkling	Stout	Molasses
	Lager	
	Pilsner	
	Porter	

Figure 9–1 *Alcoholic Beverages*

into the wine. The best-known sparkling wine is champagne, which has become synonymous with celebrations and happiness.

Champagne became the drink of fashion in France and England in the seventeenth century. Originating in the Champagne region of France, the wine owed its unique sparkling quality to a second fermentation—originally unintentional—in the bottle itself. This process became known as *methode champenoise*.

The Benedictine monk, Dom Perignon (1638–1715), was the cellar master for the Abbaye Hautvilliers—and an exceptional wine connoisseur. He was the first to experiment with blending different wines to achieve the so-called *cuvee* (the basis of champagne production). He also revolutionized wine by retaining the resulting carbon dioxide in the bottles. Dom Perignon's methods were refined throughout the centuries and led to the modern method used in champagne production.

Champagne may, by law, only come from the Champagne region of France. Sparkling wines from other countries have *methode champenoise* written on their labels to designate that a similar method was used to make that particular sparkling wine.

Understanding the Label

The taste of the finished champagne depends ultimately on the level of sugar content, as follows:

Name	%/lt.	Taste
Extra Brut	0–1.5%	especially dry
Brut	1.5%	very dry
Extra Dry	1.2–2%	dry, semidry
Sec	2–3%	semidry, semisweet
Demi-Sec	3–5%	sweet
Doux	5+%	very sweet

Handling and Serving Champagne

Champagne should be stored horizontally at a temperature between fifty and fifty-five degrees Fahrenheit. However, it should be served at a temperature between forty-three and forty-seven degrees Fahrenheit. This is best achieved by placing the bottle in an ice bucket.

When serving champagne, there are some recommended steps to take to achieve the best results, as listed below.

1. If the bottle is presented in a champagne cooler, it should be placed upright in the cooler, with fine ice tightly packed around the bottle.
2. The bottle should be wrapped in a cloth napkin. Remove the foil or metal capsule to a point just below the wire, which holds the cork securely.
3. Hold the bottle firmly in one hand at a forty-five degree angle. Unwind and remove the wiring. With a clean napkin, wipe the neck of the bottle and around the cork.
4. With the other hand, grasp the cork so that it will not fly out. Twist the bottle and ease the cork out.
5. When the cork is out, retain the bottle at an angle for about five seconds. The gas will rush out and carry with it some of the champagne if the bottle is held upright.
6. Champagne should be served in two motions: pour until the froth almost reaches the brim of the glass. Stop and wait for the foam to subside. Then finish filling the glass to about three-quarters full.

Do's and Don'ts of Champagne

Do's:	Dark, cool cellars
	Consistent temperature
	Clean champagne flutes
Don'ts:	Artificial light
	Rapid chilling in the freezer
	Frosted glasses
	Cocktail glasses (this allows the bouquet to evaporate)

Figure 9–2   *Understanding Champagne Labels*

Fortified Wines

Sherries, ports, madeiras, and marsalas are fortified wines, meaning that they have had brandy or wine alcohol added to them. The brandy or wine alcohol imparts a unique taste and increases the alcohol content to about 20 percent. Most fortified wines are sweeter than regular wines. Each of the groups of fortified wines have several subgroups with a myriad tastes and aromas.

Aromatic Wines

Vermouths and aperitifs are aromatic wines. Aromatized wines are fortified and flavored with herbs, roots, flowers, and barks. These wines may be sweet or dry. Aromatic wines are also known as aperitifs, which generally are consumed before meals as digestive stimulants. Among the better known brands of aperitif wines are Dubonnet Red (sweet), Dubonnet White (dry), Vermouth Red (sweet), Vermouth White (dry), Byrrh (sweet), Lillet (sweet), Punt e mes (dry), St. Raphael Red (sweet), and St. Raphael White (dry).

The History of Wine

Wine has been produced for centuries. The ancient Egyptians and Babylonians recorded the fermentation process. The very first records about wine making date back about 7,000 years. The Greeks received the vine from the Egyptians and later the Romans contributed to the popularization of wine in Europe by planting vines in the territories they conquered.

The wine produced during these times was not the cabernet or chardonnay of today. The wines of yesteryear were drunk when they were young and likely to be highly acidic and crude. To help offset these deficiencies, people added different spices and honey, which made the wine at least palatable. To this day, some Greek and German wines have flavoring added.

The making of good wine is dependent on the quality of the grape variety, type of soil, climate, preparation of vineyards, and method of wine making. Thousands of grape varieties exist, thriving in a variety of soil and climatic conditions. Different plants thrive on clay, chalky, gravelly, or sandy soil. The most important wine-making grape variety is the Vitis Vinifera, which yields cabernet sauvignon, gamay, pinot noir, pinot chardonnay, and Riesling. Figure 9–3 tells an interesting story about wine.

The Making of Wine

Wine is made in six steps: crushing, fermenting, racking, maturing, filtering, and bottling (see Figure 9–4). Grapes are harvested in the autumn, after they have been scientifically tested for maturity, acidity, and sugar concentration. The freshly harvested grapes are taken to pressing houses where the grapes are destemmed and crushed. The juice that is extracted from the grapes is called *must*.

The second step of the process is the fermentation of the must, a natural phenomenon caused by yeasts on the skin of the grapes. Additional yeasts also are

In Europe, during the Middle Ages, it was considered a good thing to make a pilgrimage to Rome once in a lifetime. There is a delightful story of a German bishop who liked his wine and food so much that he sent a servant to seek out the best tavern. (The tavern door was to be marked est, meaning it is.) Est was painted on the best tavern door in the town they would reach that evening. After traveling across Germany and into northern Italy, the bishop's group came across a tavern door with Est! Est! Est! painted on it. Well, the bishop liked the wine and food at that tavern so much he never actually made it to Rome.

Figure 9–3   *Est! Est! Est!*

added either environmentally or by formula. When exposed to air in the proper environment, the yeast multiplies. Yeast converts the sugar in the grapes to ethyl alcohol, until little or no sugar remains in the wine. The degree of sweetness or dryness in the wine can be controlled at the end of the fermentation process by adding alcohol, removing the yeast by filtration, or adding sulphur dioxide.

Red wine gains its color during the fermentation process from the coloring pigments of the red grape skins, which are put back into the must.

After fermentation has ceased, the wine is transferred to racking containers, where it settles before being poured into oak barrels or large stainless steel containers for the maturing process. Some of the better wines are aged in oak barrels, from which they acquire additional flavor and character during the barrel aging. Throughout the aging process, red wine extracts tannin from the wood, which gives longevity to the wine. Some white wine and most red wine is barrel aged for periods ranging from months to more than two years. Other white

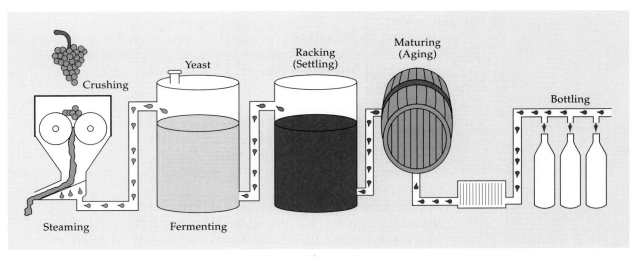

Figure 9–4   *The Wine-Making Process*

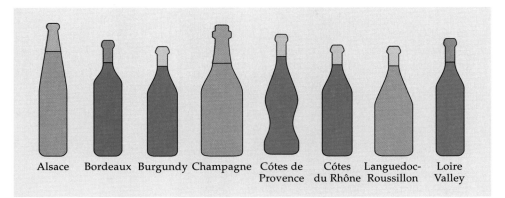

Alsace　Bordeaux　Burgundy　Champagne　Côtes de　Côtes　Languedoc-　Loire
Provence　du Rhône　Roussillon　Valley

Figure 9–5　*Wine Bottles*

wines that are kept in stainless steel containers are crisp, with a youthful flavor; they are bottled after a few months for immediate consumption.

After maturing, the wine is filtered to help stabilize it and remove any solid particles still in the wine. This process is called *fining*. The wine is then *clarified* by adding either egg white or bentonite, which sinks to the bottom of the vat. The wine then is bottled.

Fine vintage wines are best drunk at their peak, which may be a few years— or decades—away. Red wines generally take a few more years to reach their peak than do white wines. In Europe, where the climate is more variable, the good years are rated as vintage. The judgment of experts determines the relative merits of each wine-growing district and awards merit points on a scale of one to ten. The bottle shapes used are shown in Figure 9–5.

Matching Wine with Food

The combination of food and wine is one of life's great pleasures. We eat every day, so a gourmet will seek out not only exotic foods and vintage wines, but also simple food that is well prepared and accompanied by an unpretentious, but quality wine.

Over the years, traditions have developed a how-to approach to the marrying of wines and food. Generally speaking, the following traditions apply:

- ✔ White wine is best served with white meat (chicken, pork, or veal), shellfish, and fish.
- ✔ Red wine is best served with red meat (beef, lamb, duck, or game).
- ✔ The heavier the food, the heavier and more robust the wine should be.
- ✔ Champagne can be served throughout the meal.
- ✔ Port and red wine go well with cheese.
- ✔ Dessert wines best complement desserts and fresh fruits that are not highly acidic.
- ✔ When a dish is cooked with wine, it is best served with that wine.
- ✔ Regional food is best complemented by wines of the region.
- ✔ Wines should never accompany salads with vinegar dressings, chocolate dishes, or curries; the tastes will clash or be overpowering.
- ✔ Sweet wines should be served with foods that are not too sweet.

Red Wines		
Cabernet Sauvignon	Medium Dry	Lamb, Pasta with red sauce, Red meat, Cheese
Zinfandel	Medium	Lamb, Pasta with red sauce, Red meat, Cheese
Pinot Noir	Medium	Poultry, Pork, Lamb, Red meat, Pasta with red sauce
White Wines		
Chardonnay	Medium Dry	Poultry, Pork, Seafood, Pasta with white sauce, Cheese
Sauvignon Blanc	Medium Dry	Poultry, Pork, Seafood, Pasta with white sauce, Cheese
Johannisberg Riesling	Medium Sweet	Poultry, Pork, Seafood, Pasta with white sauce, Cheese
Semillon-Chardonnay	Medium Dry	Poultry, Pork, Seafood, Pasta with white sauce, Cheese

Figure 9–6   *Matching Wine with Food*

Figure 9–6 matches some of the better known varietal wines with food.

Food and wine are described by texture and flavor. Textures are the qualities in food and wine that we feel in the mouth, such as softness, smoothness, roundness, richness, thickness, thinness, creaminess, chewiness, oiliness, harshness, silkiness, coarseness, and so on. Textures correspond to sensations of touch and temperature, which can be easy to identify—for example, hot, cold, rough, smooth, thick, or thin. Regarding the marrying of food and wine, light food with light wine is always a reliable combination. Rich food with rich wine can be wonderful as long as the match is not too rich. The two most important qualities to consider when choosing the appropriate wine are richness and lightness.

Flavors are food and wine elements perceived by the olfactory nerve as fruity, minty, herbal, nutty, cheesy, smoky, flowery, earthy, and so on. A person often determines flavors by using the nose as well as the tongue. The combination of texture and flavor is what makes food and wine a pleasure to enjoy; a good match between the food and wine can make occasions even more memorable. Figure 9–7 suggests the steps to be taken in wine tasting.

Wine Tasting

Many restaurants have recently introduced wine tastings as special marketing events to promote the restaurant itself, or a particular type or label of wine. Wine tasting is more than just a process—it is an artful ritual. Wine offers a threefold sensory appeal: color, aroma, and taste. Wine tasting, thus, consists of three essential steps.

1. Hold the glass to the light. The color of the wine gives the first indication of the wine's body. The deeper the color, the fuller the wine will be. Generally, wines should be clear and brilliant.
2. Smell the wine. Hold the glass between the middle and the ring finger in a "cup-like" fashion and gently roll the glass. This will bring the aroma and the bouquet of the wine to the edge of the glass. The bouquet should be pleasant. This will tell much about what the taste will be.
3. Finally, taste the wine by rolling the wine around the mouth and by sucking in a little air—this helps release the complexities of the flavors.

Figure 9–7   *Wine Tasting*

Major Wine-Growing Regions of Europe and North America

Europe

Germany, Italy, Spain, Portugal, and France are the main European wine-producing countries. Germany is noted for the outstanding Riesling wines from the Rhine and Moselle river valleys. Italy produces the world-famous Chianti. Spain makes good wine, but is best known for sherry. Portugal also makes good wine, but is better known for its port.

France is the most notable of the European countries, producing not only the finest wines but also champagne and cognac. The two most famous wine-producing areas in France are the Bordeaux and Burgundy regions. The vineyards, villages, and towns are steeped in the history of centuries devoted to the production of the finest quality wines. They represent some of the most beautiful countryside in Europe and are well worth visiting.

In France, wine is named after the village in which the wine is produced. In recent years, the name of the grape variety is also used. The name of the wine grower is also important; because the quality may vary, reputation understandably is very important. A vineyard might also include a chateau in which wine is made.

Within the Bordeaux region, wine growing is divided into five major districts: Medoc, Graves, St. Emilion, Pomerol, and Sauternes. The wine from each of these districts has its own characteristics.

There are several other well-known wine producing regions of France, such as the Loire Valley, Alsace, and Cotes du Rhone. French people regard wine as an important part of their culture and heritage.

United States

In California, viticulture began in 1769 when Junipero Serra, a Spanish friar, began to produce wine for the missions he started. At one time the French considered California wines to be inferior. However, California is blessed with a near perfect climate and excellent vine-growing soil. In the United States, the name of the grape variety is used to name the wine, not the village or chateau

Burgundy Vineyard

Napa Valley

used by the French. The better known varietal white wines in the United States are chardonnay, sauvignon blanc, Riesling, and chenin blanc; varietal red wines are cabernet sauvignon, pinot noir, merlot, and zinfandel.

California viticulture areas are generally divided into three regions:

1. North and central coastal region
2. Great central valley region
3. Southern California region

The north and central coastal region produces the best wines in California. A high degree of use of mechanical methods allows for efficient, large-scale production of quality wines. The two best-known areas within this region are the Napa and Sonoma valleys. The wines of the Napa and Sonoma valleys resemble those of Bordeaux and Burgundy. In recent years, the wines from the Napa and Sonoma valleys have rivaled and even exceeded the French and other European wines. The chardonnays and cabernets are particularly outstanding.

The Napa and Sonoma valleys are the symbols as well as the centers of the top-quality wine industry in California. The better-known wineries of California include those shown in Figure 9–8.

Several other states and Canadian provinces provide quality wines. New York, Oregon, and Washington are the other major U.S. wine-producing states. In Canada, the best wineries are in British Columbia's Okanagan Valley and southern Ontario's Niagara peninsula. Both of these regions produce excellent wines.

Wine also is produced in many other temperate parts of the world, most notably Australia, New Zealand, Chile, Argentina, and South Africa. Figure 9–9 shows that there may be a connection between wine and health.

Napa Valley

Diamond Creek
Inglenook
Heitz
Krug
Louis Martini
Moet & Chandon
Robert Mondavi
Stag's Leap
Sterling

Sonoma Valley

Chateau St. Jean
Clos du Bois
De Loach
Dry Creek
Gundlach Bundschu
Iron Horse
Kenwood
Preston
Sebastiani

South of San Francisco

Concannon
Paul Masson
Mirassou
Ridge
Calloway
Thornton

Figure 9–8 *Better-Known California Wineries*

Personal Profile: Robert Mondavi

Since its founding in 1966, the Robert Mondavi Winery has established itself as one of the world's top wineries. Robert Mondavi, now in his eighties, still continues his activity as wine's foremost spokesperson, having greatly contributed to the wine industry throughout his successful life.

Robert Mondavi was born in 1913 to an Italian couple who had emigrated from the Marche region of Italy in 1910. His father, Cesare, became involved in shipping California wine grapes to fellow Italians. Extremely pleased with California, Cesare Mondavi decided to move to the Napa Valley and set up a firm that shipped fruit east. Robert Mondavi grew up among wines and vines and remained in his father's business.

Robert Mondavi

Robert began by improving the family enterprise, adding to it the management, production, and marketing skills he learned at Stanford University, from which he graduated in 1936. Robert acknowledged the great business potential of the Napa Valley in the broader context of the California wine industry. What the firm needed was to be upgraded with innovations in technology, to keep up with the changes in the overall business environment.

Mondavi had an ambitious dream that was realized when the Charles Krug Winery was offered for sale in 1943. The facility was purchased, and Robert knew that the strategy for success included well-planned marketing as well as the crucial wine-making expertise that the family already had.

Mondavi understood also the importance of the introduction of innovative processes that could place the winery in a competitive position. From the 1950s to the 1960s, he performed many experiments and introduced pivotal innovations. For example, Robert popularized new styles of wine, such as the chenin blanc, which was previously known as white pinot and was not doing well in the market. Mondavi changed the fermentation, turning it into a sweeter, more delicious wine. The name was also changed, and sales increased fourfold the following year.

Similarly, he noticed that the sauvignon blanc was a slow-selling wine. He began producing it in a drier style, called it fume blanc, and turned it into an immediate success. Although the winery's operations were successful, Mondavi was still looking for a missing link to the chain. A trip to Europe, designed to study the finest wineries' techniques, convinced him to adopt a new, smaller type of barrel to age the wine, which he believed added a "wonderful dimension to the finished product."

In 1966, Robert Mondavi opened the Robert Mondavi Winery, which represented the fulfillment of the family's vision to build a facility that would allow them to produce truly world-class wines. In fact, since its establishment, the winery has led the industry, standing as an example of continuous research and innovation in wine making, as well as a "monument to persistence in the pursuit of excellence."

Throughout the years of operation, the original vision remained constant: to produce the best wines that were the perfect accompaniments to food and to provide the public with proper education about the product. As a matter of fact, the Robert Mondavi Winery sponsors several educational programs, such as seminars on viticulture, a totally comprehensive tour program in the Napa Valley wineries, and the great chefs program.

All of the family members are actively involved in the operation of the winery, united and guided by a shared determination to continue the winery's tradition of excellence.

A glass of wine may be beneficial to health. This perspective was featured in the CBS news magazine program "60 Minutes," which focused on a phenomenon called the French paradox. The French eat 30 percent more fat than Americans, smoke more, and exercise less, yet they suffer fewer heart attacks—about one-third as many as Americans. Ironically, the French drink more wine than people of any other nationality—about 75 liters per person a year. Research indicates that wine attacks platelets, which are the smallest of the blood cells and which cause the blood to clot, preventing excess bleeding. However, platelets also cling to the rough, fatty deposits on arterial walls, clogging and finally blocking arteries and causing heart attacks. Wine's flushing effect removes platelets from the artery wall. Needless to say, after the "60 Minutes" program was broadcast, sales of wine, particularly red wine, in the United States increased dramatically.

Figure 9–9   *Wine and Health*

Beer

Beer is a brewed and fermented beverage made from malted barley and other starchy cereals, and flavored with hops. Beer is a generic term, embracing all brewed malt beverages with a low alcohol content, varying from 4 to 16 percent.[1] The term *beer* includes the following:

- ✔ Lager, the beverage that is normally referred to as beer, is a clear light-bodied refreshing beer.
- ✔ Ale is fuller bodied and more bitter than lager.
- ✔ Stout is a dark ale with a sweet, strong, malt flavor.
- ✔ Pilsner is not really a beer. The term *pilsner* means that the beer is made in the style of the famous beer brewed in Pilsen, Bohemia.

The Brewing Process

Beer is brewed from water, malt, yeast, and hops. The brewing process begins with water, an important ingredient in the making of beer. The mineral content and purity of the water largely determine the quality of the final product. Water accounts for 85 to 89 percent of the finished beer.

Next, grain is added in the form of malt, which is barley that has been ground to a course grit. The grain is germinated, producing an enzyme that converts starch into fermentable sugar.

The yeast is the fermenting agent. Breweries typically have their own cultured yeasts, which, to a large extent, determine the type and taste of the beer. See Figure 9–10 for a description of the brewing process.

Mashing is the term for grinding the malt and screening out any bits of dirt. The malt then goes through a hopper into a mash tub, which is a large stainless steel or copper container. Here the water and grains are mixed and heated.

The liquid is now called *wort* and is filtered through a mash filter or lauter tub. This liquid then flows into a brewing kettle, where hops are added and the mixture is boiled for several hours. After the brewing operation, the hop wort is filtered through the hop separator or hop jack. The filtered liquid then is

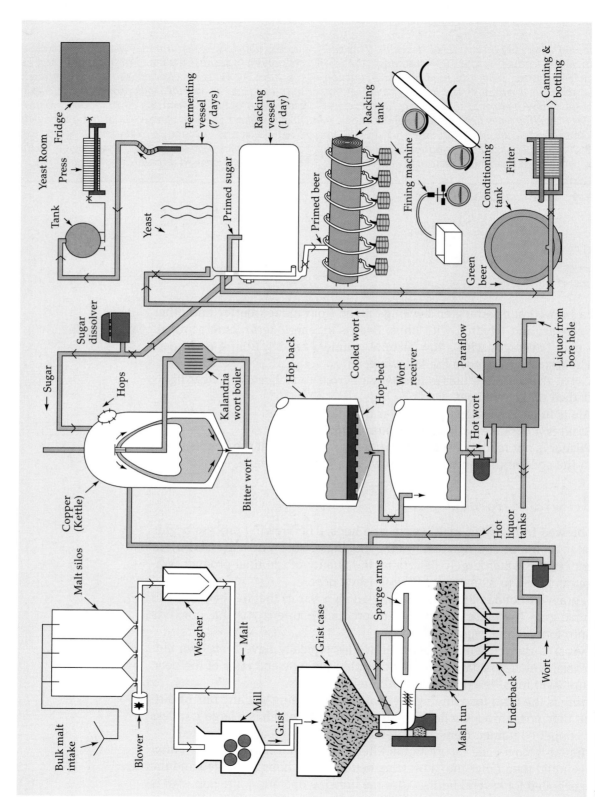

Figure 9-10 *The Beer-Making Process*

Table 9–1   Top U.S. and Canadian Brewers

U.S. BREWERS

Company	Percent of Market
Anheuser-Busch	48.8
Miller	22.8
Coors	10.7
Stroh	6.4
Heileman	4.4
Other	6.9

Greg W. Prince, "All They Wanna Do Is Sell Some Beer," *Beverage World*, March 1995, 1587, vol. 114, p. 82.

CANADIAN BREWERS

Company	Percent of Market
Molson	50.0
Labatt	44.0
U.S. Imports	3.0
Others	3.0

Wall Street Journal, March 16, 1993, p. B4.

pumped through a wort cooler and flows into a fermenting vat where pure-culture yeast is added for fermentation.[2] The brew is aged for a few days prior to being barreled for draught beer or pasteurized for bottled or canned beer. Table 9–1 shows the major U.S. and Canadian brewers.

Spirits

A spirit or liquor is made from a liquid that has been fermented and distilled. Consequently, a spirit has a high percentage of alcohol, gauged in the United States by its proof content. *Proof* is equal to twice the percentage of alcohol in the beverage; therefore, a spirit that is 80 proof is 40 percent alcohol. Spirits traditionally are enjoyed before or after a meal, rather than with the meal. Many spirits can be consumed straight or neat, or they may be enjoyed with water, soda water, juices, or cocktail mixes.

Fermentation of spirits takes place by the action of yeast on sugar-containing substances, such as grain or fruit. Distilled drinks are made from a fermented liquid that has been put through a distillation process (see Figure 9–11).

Whiskys

Among the better known spirits is whiskey, which is a generic name for the spirit first distilled in Scotland and Ireland centuries ago. The word *whiskey*

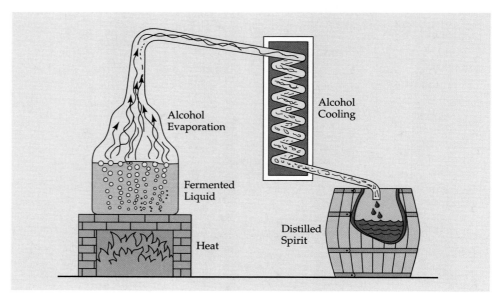

Figure 9–11   *Distillation Process*

comes from the Celtic word *visgebaugh* meaning *water of life*. Whiskey is made from a fermented mash of grain to which malt, in the form of barley, is added. The barley contains an enzyme called diastase that converts starch to sugars. After fermentation, the liquid is distilled. Spirits naturally are white or pale in color, but raw whiskey is stored in oak barrels that have been charred (burnt). This gives whiskey its caramel color. The whiskey is stored for a period of time, up to a maximum of twelve to fifteen years. However, several good whiskeys reach the market after three to five years. Most whiskeys are blended to produce a flavor and quality that is characteristic of the brand. Not surprisingly, the blending process at each distillery is a closely guarded secret. There are four distinct whiskey types that have gained a worldwide acknowledgment throughout the centuries: Scotch whisky, Irish whisky, bourbon whisky, and Canadian whisky.

Scotch Whisky

Scotch whisky, or Scotch, has been distilled in Scotland for centuries and has been a distinctive part of the Scots' way of life. From its origins in remote and romantic Highland glens, scotch whisky has become a popular and international drink, its flavor appreciated throughout the world. Scotch became popular in the United States during the days of Prohibition (1919 to 1933) when it was smuggled into the country from Canada. It is produced like other whiskeys, except that the malt is dried in special kilns that give it a smoky flavor. Only whisky made with this process can be called Scotch whisky. Some of the better-known quality blended Scotch whiskys are Chivas Regal and Johnnie Walker Black Label.[3]

Irish Whisky

Irish whiskey is produced from malted, or unmalted barley, corn, rye, and other grains. The malt is not dried like the Scotch whisky, which gives Irish whiskey a milder character, yet an excellent flavor. Two well-known Irish whiskeys are Old Bushmill's Black Bush and Jameson's 1780.[4]

Bourbon Whisky

Liquor was introduced in America by the first settlers, who used it as a medicine. Bourbon has a peculiar history. In colonial times in New England, rum was the most popular distilled spirit. After the break with Britain, settlers of Scottish and Irish background predominated. They were mostly grain farmers and distillers, producing whiskey for barter. When George Washington levied a tax on this whiskey, the farmers moved south and continued their whiskey production. However, the rye crop failed, so they decided to mix corn, particularly abundant in Kentucky, with the remaining rye. The result was delightful. This experiment occurred in Bourbon County; hence the name of the new product.

Bourbon whiskey is produced mainly from corn; other grains are also used, but they are of secondary importance. The distillation processes are similar to those of other types of whiskey. Charred barrels provide bourbon with its distinctive taste. It is curious to note that barrels can only be used once in the United States to age liquor. Aging, therefore, occurs in new barrels after each distillation process. Bourbon may be aged up to six years to improve its mellowness. Among the better-known bourbon whiskeys are Jack Daniels, Makers Mark, and George Dickle.

Canadian Whisky

Like bourbon, Canadian whiskey is produced mainly from corn. It is characterized by a delicate flavor that nonetheless pleases the taste. Canadian whiskey must be at least four years old before it can be bottled and marketed. It is distilled at 70 to 90 percent alcohol by volume. Among the better-known Canadian whiskeys are Seagrams and Canadian Club.

White Spirits

Gin, rum, vodka, and tequila are the most common of the spirits that are called *white spirits*. Gin, first known as Geneva, is a neutral spirit made from juniper berries. Although gin originated in Holland, it was in London that the word *Geneva* was shortened to gin, and almost anything was used to make it. Often gin was made in the bathtub in the morning and sold in hole-in-the-wall dramshops all over London at night. Obviously, the quality left a lot to be desired, but the poor drank it to the point of national disaster.[5] Gin also was widely produced in the United States during the Prohibition. In fact, the habit of mixing something else with it led to the creation of the cocktail. Over the years, gin

Corporate Profile: The Seagram Company, Ltd.

In simpler times, consumers met around a market square to make their purchases. In our century, the process has grown infinitely more complex. The challenge for Seagram and its customers is to continue developing channels of trade for the consumer's ultimate benefit, enhancing choice convenience, and service. That is why we take time to understand our customers' business and make our technologies fit theirs . . . why we maintain the flexibility to create strategies for individual customers.[1]

The Seagram Company, Ltd. is a leading global producer and marketer of distilled spirits, wines, coolers, fruit juices, and mixers. The company operates worldwide through two major units: The Seagram Spirits and Wine Group and The Seagram Beverage Group. The Seagram Spirits and Wine Group, the company's largest operating unit, produces, markets, and distributes more than 230 brands of distilled spirits and 195 brands of wines, champagnes, ports, and sherries. Some of Seagram's best-known names, such as Chivas Regal Premium Scotch whisky, Martell cognac, and Mumm champagne, are sold throughout the world, and others are produced primarily for sale in specific markets. The company operates on a global scale: Spirits and wines are produced by the group at facilities located in twenty-two countries in North America, South America, Europe, and Australia. Regardless of this sweepingly broad scale, the sale of Seagram spirits and wines to its customers is far from a mass operation. The company focuses on cultivating individual and personalized contact with its customers, either directly or through representatives of the company. This well-organized network of "ambassadors" (wholesalers or distributors) extends Seagram's reach to the public and allows for a closer interaction between the company and its clients.

This strong focus on customers gives Seagram's a truly competitive advantage in the industry. The close interaction has been further emphasized with the adoption of an electronic data interchange (EDI) system, which provides direct, paperless exchange of order information with the customers.

In addition to this state-of-the-art technology, Seagram's business success is attributable to other remarkable factors, such as differentiation of product lines and effective exploitation of business areas that represent a future potential. The company believes that the wide range of the Spirit and Wine Group's product portfolio, and the broad diversity of its geographic markets, reduce Seagram's vulnerability to changes in the industry's environment, such as consumers' preferences, social trends, and economic conditions.

Recent emphasis of product development, in fact, has resulted in the introduction of several new brands in 1993. In the Scotch whisky category, for example, the increased portfolio of brands has allowed the company to compete at a premium level.

Just as the creation of new brands represents an investment in the company's future, the expansion into new geographies gives Seagram's a valid and broad base for future growth. In particular, the company is devoting a great deal of attention to China, which is considered to be the single most important market opportunity of the decade. Seagram has captured a significant share of this potential market by expanding its operations and increasing its presence. Infrastructures and facilities are being established and particular emphasis is placed on strengthening business relationships with its customers.

Seagram's shows a great deal of diversity in its channels of trade. The concentration on penetrating individual hotels and restaurants has proven to be particularly effective. Spirit and wine selections offered at fine hotels and restaurants set an influential standard of taste and brand perception. Seagram's brands have obtained a strong, worldwide predominance in this segment; the all-over presence of Seagram's on wine and cocktail lists greatly influences consumers' home consumption. In order to guarantee a continuity to this process, Seagram's must nurture each individual relationship with future hosts over time. To this end, the company is working with major hotels and catering schools today to reach the great sommeliers and chefs of tomorrow.

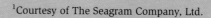

[1]Courtesy of The Seagram Company, Ltd.

became the foundation of many popular cocktails (e.g., martini, gin and tonic, gin and juice, and Tom Collins).

Rum can be light or dark in color. Light rum is distilled from the fermented juice of sugarcane, and dark rum is distilled from molasses. Rum comes mainly from the Caribbean Islands of Barbados (Mount Gay), Puerto Rico (Bacardi), and Jamaica (Myers). Rums are mostly used in mixed frozen and specialty drinks such as rum and Coke, rum punches, daiquiris, and piña coladas.

Tequila is distilled from the agave tequilana (a type of cactus), which is called *mezcal* in Mexico. Official Mexican regulations require that tequila be made in the area around the town of Tequila, because the soil contains volcanic ash, which is especially suitable for growing the blue agave cactus. Tequila may be white, silver, or golden in color. The white is shipped unaged, silver is aged up to three years, and golden is aged in oak from two to four years. Tequila is mainly used in the popular margarita cocktail or in the tequila sunrise made popular in a song by the Eagles rock group.

Vodka can be made from many sources, including barley, corn, wheat, rye, or potatoes. Because it lacks color, odor, and flavor, vodka generally is combined with juices or other mixers whose flavors will predominate.

Other Spirits

Brandy is distilled from wine in a fashion similar to that of other spirits. American brandy comes primarily from California, where it is made in column stills and aged in white-oak barrels for at least two years. The best-known American brandies are made by Christian Brothers and Ernest and Julio Gallo. Their brandies are smooth and fruity with a touch of sweetness. The best brandies are served as after-dinner drinks, and ordinary brandies are used in the well for mixed drinks.

Cognac is regarded by connoisseurs as the best brandy in the world. It is only made in the Cognac region of France, where the chalky soil and humid climate combine with special distillation techniques to produce the finest brandy. Only brandy from this region may be called *cognac.* Most cognac is aged in oak casks from two to four years or more.

Because cognacs are blends of brandies of various ages, no age is allowed on the label; instead, letters signify the relative age and quality:

VSOP	=	very superior old pale
VVSOP	=	very, very superior old pale
E	=	extra or special
F	=	fine
X	=	extra
VS	=	very special
VO	=	very old
VVO	=	very, very old
XO	=	extra old

Brandies labeled as *VSOP* must be aged at least four years. All others must be aged in wood at least five years. Five years then, is the age of the youngest cognac in a blend; usually several others of older age are added to lend taste, bouquet, and finesse. About 75 percent of the cognac shipped to Canada and the United States is produced by four companies: Courvoisier, Hennessy, Martell, and Remy Martin.

Cocktails

The first cocktails originated in England during the Victorian Era, but it wasn't until the 1920s and 1930s that cocktails became popular.

Cocktails are usually drinks made by mixing two or more ingredients (wines, liquors, fruit juices), resulting in a blend that is pleasant to the palate, with no single ingredient overpowering the others. Cocktails are mixed by stirring, shaking, or blending. The mixing technique is particularly important to achieve the perfect cocktail. Cocktails are commonly divided into two categories according to volume: short drinks (up to 3.5 ounces) and tall drinks (generally up to 8.5 ounces).

The secret of a good cocktail lies in several factors:

- ✔ The balance of the ingredients
- ✔ The quality of the ingredients. As a general rule, cocktails should be made from a maximum of three ingredients
- ✔ The skill of the bartender. The bartender's experience, knowledge, and inspiration are key factors in a perfect cocktail

A good bartender should understand the effect and the "timing" of a cocktail. It is not a coincidence that many cocktails are categorized by when they are best served. There are aperitifs, digestifs, corpse-revivers, pick-me-ups, etc. Cocktails can stimulate an appetite or provide the perfect conclusion to a fine meal.

Nonalcoholic Beverages

Nonalcoholic beverages are increasing in popularity. The 1990s have seen a radical shift from the free love 1960s and the singles bars of the 1970s and early 1980s. People are, in general, more cautious about the consumption of alcohol. Lifestyles have become healthier, and organizations like MADD (Mothers Against Drunk Driving) have raised the social conscience about responsible alcohol consumption. Overall consumption of alcohol has decreased in recent years, with spirits declining the most.

The healthful 1990s have seen the introduction of several new beverages to the nonalcoholic list.

Nonalcoholic Beer

Guinness, Anheuser-Busch, and Miller, along with many other brewers, have developed beer products that have the same appearance as regular beer, but have a lower calorie content and approximately 95–99% of the alcohol removed, either after processing or after fermentation. The taste, therefore, is somewhat different from regular beer.

Coffee

Coffee is the drink of the present. People who used to frequent bars are patronizing coffee houses. Sales of specialty coffees exceed $3 billion. The Specialty Coffee Association of America estimates that there are more than 2,500 coffee cafes nationwide and another 3,000 espresso bars.[6]

Coffee first came from Ethiopia and Mocha, which is in the Yemen Republic. Legends say that Kaldi, a young Abyssinian goatherd, accustomed to his sleepy goats, noticed that after chewing certain berries, the goats began to prance about excitedly. He tried the berries himself, forgot his troubles, lost his heavy heart, and became the happiest person in "happy Arabia." A monk from a nearby monastery surprised Kaldi in this state, decided to try the berries too and invited the brothers to join him. They all felt more alert that night during prayers![7]

In the Middle Ages, coffee found its way to Europe via Turkey, but not without some objections. In Italy, priests appealed to Pope Clement VIII to have the use of coffee forbidden among Christians. Satan, they said, had forbidden his followers, the infidel Moslems, the use of wine because it was used in the Holy Communion and had given them instead his "hellish black brew." Apparently the pope liked the drink, for his reply was, "Why, this Satan's drink is so delicious that it would be a pity to let the infidels have exclusive use of it." So his Holiness decided to baptize the drink, after which it quickly became the social beverage of Europe's middle and upper classes.[8]

In 1637, the first European coffeehouse opened in England; within thirty years, coffee houses had replaced taverns as the island's social, commercial, and political melting pots.[9] The coffee houses were nicknamed *penny universities,* where any topic could be discussed and learned for the price of a pot of coffee. The men of the period not only discussed business but actually conducted business. Banks, newspapers, and the Lloyd's of London Insurance Company began at Edward Lloyd's coffeehouse.

Coffeehouses were also popular in Europe. In Paris, Cafe Procope, which opened in 1689 and still operates today, has been the meeting place of many a famous artist and philosopher, including Rousseau and Voltaire (who are reputed to have drunk forty cups of coffee a day).

Bernini's Coffeehouse, La Jolla, California

The Dutch introduced coffee to the United States during the colonial period. Coffeehouses soon became the haunts of the revolutionary activists plotting against King George of England and his tea tax. John Adams and Paul Revere planned the Boston Tea Party and the fight for freedom at a coffeehouse. This helped established coffee as the traditional democratic drink of Americans.

Brazil produces more than 30 percent of the world's coffee, most of which goes into canned and instant coffee. Coffee connoisseurs recommend beans by name, such as arabica and robusta beans. In Indonesia, coffee is named for the island on which it grows; the best is from Java and is rich and spicy with a full-bodied flavor. Yemen, the country in which coffee was discovered, names its best coffee for the port of Mocha. Its fragrant, creamy brew has a rich, almost chocolatey aftertaste. Coffee beans are frequently blended by the merchants who roast them; one of the best blends, mocha java, is the result of blending these two fine coffees.

Coffee may be roasted from light to dark according to preference. Light roasts are generally used in canned and institutional roasts, and medium is the all-purpose roast most people prefer. Medium beans are medium brown in color, and their surface is dry. Although this brew may have snappy, acidic qualities, its flavor tends to be flat. Full, high, or Viennese roast is the roast preferred by specialty stores, where balance is achieved between sweetness and sharpness. Dark roasts have a fancy rich flavor, with espresso the darkest of all roasts. Its almost black beans have shiny, oily surfaces. All of the acidic qualities and specific coffee flavor are gone from espresso, but its pungent flavor is a favorite of espresso lovers.

Decaffeinating coffee removes the caffeine with either a solvent or water process. In contrast, many specialty coffees have things added. Among the better-known specialty coffees are café au lait or caffe latte. In these cases, milk is steamed until it becomes frothy and is poured into the cup together with the coffee. Cappuccino is made by adding steamed hot milk to an espresso, which may then be sprinkled with powdered chocolate and cinnamon.[10]

Tea

Tea is a beverage made by steeping in boiling water the leaves of the tea plant, an evergreen shrub, or a small tree native to Asia. Tea is consumed as either a hot or cold beverage by approximately half of the world's population, yet it is second to coffee in commercial importance because most of the world's tea crop is consumed in the tea-growing regions. Tea leaves contain one to three percent caffeine. This means that weight for weight, tea leaves have more than twice as much caffeine as coffee beans. However, a cup of coffee generally has more caffeine than a cup of tea because one pound of tea leaves makes 250 to 300 cups of tea whereas one pound of coffee makes only 40 cups.

The following list shows where the different types of tea originate:

China—Oolong, Orange pekoe
India—Darjeeling, Assams, Dooars
Indonesia—Java, Sumatra

Carbonated Soft Drinks

Coca-Cola and Pepsi have long dominated the carbonated soft drink market. In the early 1970's, Diet Coke and Diet Pepsi were introduced and quickly gained in popularity. The diet colas now command about a ten-percent market share. Caffeine-free colas offer an alternative, but they have not, as yet, become as popular as diet colas.

Inasmuch as U.S. market sales tend to be flat now, companies are expanding internationally. Indeed, as much as 80 percent of Coca-Cola's profits come from international sales.[11]

Juices

Popular juice flavors include orange, cranberry, grapefruit, mango, papaya, and apple. Nonalcoholic versions of popular cocktails made with juices have been popular for years and are known as virgin cocktails.

Juice bars have established themselves as places for quick, healthy drinks. Lately, "smart drinks" that are supposed to boost energy and improve concentration have become popular. The smart drinks are made up of a blend of juices, herbs, amino acids, caffeine, and sugar, and are sold under names such as Energy Plasma Blast and IQ Booster.

Other drinks have jumped on the healthy-drink bandwagon, playing on the consumer's desire to drink something refreshing, light, and healthful. Often, these drinks are fruit flavored, giving the consumer the impression of drinking something healthier than sugar-filled sodas. Unfortunately, these drinks usually just add the flavor of the fruit and rarely have any nutritional value whatsoever.

Also, some drinks are created by mixing different fruit flavors to arrive at new, exotic flavors such as Passion-Kiwi-Strawberry and Mango-Banana Delight. Some examples of such drinks are Snapple and Tropicana Twister.

Sport enthusiasts also find drinks available in stores that professional athletes use and advertise. These specially formulated *isotonic beverages* help the body regain the vital fluids and minerals that are lost during heavy physical exertion. The National Football League sponsors Gatorade and encourages its use among its athletes. The appeal of being able to drink what the professionals drink is undoubtedly one of the major reasons for the success of Gatorade's sales and marketing. Other brands of isotonic beverages include Powerade and All Sport, which is sponsored by the National Collegiate Athletics Association.

Bottled Water

Bottled water was popular in Europe years ago when it was not safe to drink tap water. In North America, the increased popularity of bottled water has coincided with the trend toward healthier lifestyles.

In the 1980s, it was chic to be seen drinking Perrier (a sparkling water) or some other imported bottled water. Perrier, which comes from France, lost market share a few years ago when an employee tampered with the product. Now the market leader is Evian (a spring water), which is also French. Domestic bottled water is equally as good as imported and is now available in various flavors that offer the consumer a greater selection.

Bottled waters are available as sparkling, mineral, and spring waters. Bottled water is a refreshing, clean-tasting, low-calorie beverage that will likely increase in popularity as a beverage on its own or to accompany another beverage such as wine or whiskey.

Bars and Beverage Management

From an operating perspective, bar and beverage management follows much the same sequence as does food management, as shown in the following list:

- Forecasting
- Determining what to order
- Selecting the supplier
- Placing the order
- Receiving the order
- Storing
- Issuing
- Serving
- Accounting
- Controlling

Bar Setup

Whether a bar is part of a larger operation (restaurant) or is a business in its own right, the physical setup of the bar is critical to its overall effectiveness. There is a need to design the area in such a way that it is not only pleasing to the eye but is also conducive to a smooth and efficient operation. This means that bar "stations," where drinks are filled, are located in strategic spots, and that each station has everything it needs to respond to most, if not all, requests. All *well liquors* should be easily accessible, with popular call brands not too far out of reach. The brands that are less likely to be ordered (and more likely to be high priced) can be farther away from the stations. The most obvious place for the high-priced, premium brands is the back bar, a place of high visibility. Anyone sitting at the bar will be looking directly at it, thus offering the customers a chance to view the bar's choices.

As for beer coolers, their location depends on the relative importance of beer to the establishment. In many places, beer is kept in coolers under the bar or below the back bar, and sample bottles or signs are displayed for customers. However, in many places beer is their biggest seller, and they may offer numerous brands from around the world. In such places, other setups may be used, such as stand-up coolers with glass doors so that customers can easily see all the varieties available. This is also true for draft beers.

Inventory Control

A good system of internal control accomplishes four broad objectives: it safeguards the company's assets, provides reliable accounting records, promotes operating efficiency, and encourages adherence to management policies.

Management philosophy and operating methods determine the extent and success of inventory and cash control. However, it involves more than establishing policies and procedures. Training is also important to ensure that employees treat inventory as cash and that they handle it as if it were their own money. Management's example will be followed by employees. If employees sense a lax management style, they may be tempted to steal. No control system can guarantee the prevention of theft completely. However, the better the control system, the less likely it is that there will be a loss.[12]

In order to operate profitably, a beverage operation manager needs to establish what the expected results will be. For example, if a bottle of gin contains twenty-five one-ounce measures, it would be reasonable to expect twenty-five times the selling price in revenue. When this is multiplied for each bottle, the total revenue can be determined and compared to the actual revenue.

One of the critical areas of bar management is the design, installation, and implementation of a system to control possible theft of the bar's beverage inventory. Theft may occur in a number of ways including giving away drinks, overpouring alcohol, mischarging for drinks, selling a call liquor at a well price, and outright stealing of bar beverages by employees. As is the case with the food operations, there is an anticipated profit margin based on the ratio of sales generated to related beverage costs. Bar management must be able to account for any discrepancies between expected and actual profit margins.

All inventory control systems require an actual physical count of the existing inventory that may be done on a weekly or monthly basis, depending on the needs of the management. This physical count is based on "units." For liquor and wine, the unit is a bottle, either .750 or 1.0 liter; for bottled beer, the unit is a case of twenty-four bottles; and for draft beer, the unit is a keg. The results of the most current physical count are then compared to the prior period's physical count to determine the actual amount of beverage inventory consumed during the period. This physical amount is translated into a cost or dollar figure by multiplying the amount consumed for each item times its respective cost per unit. The total cost for all beverages consumed is compared to the sales it generated to result in a profit margin that is compared to the expected margin.

Management should design forms that can be used to account for all types of liquor, beer, and wine available at the bar. The listing of the items should follow their actual physical setup within the bar to facilitate easy accounting of the inventory. The forms should also have columns where amounts of each inventory item can be noted. A traditional way to account for the amount of liquor in a bottle is by using the "10" count, where the level of each bottle is marked by tenths, thus a half-full bottle of well vodka would be marked on the form as a ".5." Similarly, for kegs of draft beer, a breakdown of 25 percent, 50 percent, 75 percent, and 100 percent may be used to determine its physical count.

Personnel Procedures

Another key component of internal control is having procedures in place for screening and hiring bar personnel. Employees must be experienced in bartending and cocktail serving and also must be honest, since they have access to the bar's beverage inventory and its cash.

Bar managers may also implement several other procedures to control inventory and reduce the likelihood of employee theft. One popular method is the use of "spotters," who are hired to act like normal bar customers, but are actually observing the bartenders and/or cocktailers for inappropriate behavior, such as not taking money from customers or overpouring. Another method for checking bar personnel is to perform a "bank switch" in the middle of the shift. In some cases, employees steal from the company by taking money from customers without ringing it up on the register. They keep the extra money in the cash drawer until the end of the shift when they are cashing out, at which point they retrieve the stolen funds. In order to do a bank switch, the manager must "z-out" a bartender's cash register, take the cash drawer, and replace it with a new bank. The manager then counts the money in the drawer, subtracts the starting bank, and compares that figure to the one on the register's tape. If there is a significant surplus of funds, it is highly likely that the employee is stealing. If there is less than what is indicated on the tape, the employee may be honest but careless when giving change or hitting the buttons on the register. Either way, there is a potential for loss.

Restaurant and Hotel Bars

In restaurants, the bar is often used as a holding area to allow guests to enjoy a cocktail or aperitif before sitting down to dinner. This allows the restaurant to space out the guests' orders so that the kitchen can cope more effectively; it also increases beverage sales. The profit margin from beverages is higher than the food profit margin.

In some restaurants, the bar is the focal point or main feature. Guests feel drawn to having a beverage because the atmosphere and layout of the restaurant encourages them to have a drink. Beverages generally account for about 25 to 30 percent of total sales. Many restaurants used to have a higher percentage of beverage sales, but the trend toward responsible consumption of alcoholic beverages has influenced people to decrease their consumption.

Bars carry a range of each spirit, beginning with the "well" package. The well package is the least expensive pouring brand that the bar uses when guests simply ask for a "Scotch and water." The "call" package is the group of spirits that the bar offers to guests who are likely to ask for a particular name brand. For example, guests may call for Johnnie Walker Red Label. An example of a premium Scotch is Johnnie Walker Black Label, and a super premium Scotch is Chivas Regal.

A popular method of costing each of the spirits poured is calculated according to the following example:

With quantity purchasing discounts, a well-brand bottle of vodka might cost $5.00. A bottle yields twenty-five one-ounce shots, each sold for $2.50; this means that the $5.00 bottle brings in $62.50.

The profit margins produced by bars may be categorized as follows:

Liquor Pouring Cost % (approx.)	12
Beer	25
Wine	38

When combined, the sales mix may have an average pouring cost of 16 to 20 percent.

Most bars operate on some form of par stock level, which means that for every spirit bottle in use, there is a minimum par stock level of one, two, or more bottles available as a backup. As soon as the stock level falls to a level below the par level, more is automatically purchased.

Night Clubs

There are several types of night clubs. In big cities, some cater to the upscale crowd that goes to clubs to see and be seen. These clubs have bars and may have live or recorded music. Some clubs feature a single type of music; other clubs feature rock 'n roll one night, soul the next, and rhythm and blues or reggae the following night. These clubs charge an entrance fee and a higher price for drinks than restaurants. However, the night club business is fickle; what is in one year may be out the next.

Microbreweries

In recent years, the advent of microbreweries and brewpubs (a combination brewery and pub or restaurant that brews its own fresh beer on-site to meet the taste of local customers) has changed the trend of homogenization that had characterized the brewing industry since the 1950s. Microbreweries are defined as craft breweries that produce up to 15,000 barrels (or 30,000 kegs) of beer a year. The North American microbrewery industry trend began in 1995, reviving the concept of small breweries serving fresh, all malt beer. Although regional breweries, microbreweries, and brewpubs account for only a small part of the North American brewing industry in terms of total beer production (less than three percent), they have an extremely high growth rate.

One of the reasons for the success of microbreweries and brewpubs is the wide variety of styles and flavors of beer they produce. On one hand, this educates the public about beer styles that have been out of production for decades and, on the other hand, helps brewpubs and restaurants meet the individual tastes and preferences of their local clientele.

Starting a brewpub is a fairly expensive venture. Although brewing systems come in a wide range of configurations, the cost of the equipment ranges from $200,000 to $800,000. Costs are affected by factors such as annual production capacity, beer types, and packaging. The investment in microbreweries and brew-

Corporate Profile: Starbucks Coffee Company

Operations

Starbucks Coffee Company is the leading retailer, roaster, and brand of specialty coffee in North America. More than 5 million people visit Starbucks stores each week. In addition to its more than 1,400 retail locations, the company supplies fine dining, foodservice, travel, and hotel accounts with coffee and coffee-making equipment and operates a national mail-order division.

On October 25, 1995, Starbucks Coffee International Inc., a wholly-owned subsidiary of Starbucks Coffee Company, signed an agreement with SAZABY Inc., a Japanese retailer and restaurateur. This joint-venture partnership, called Starbucks Coffee Japan, Ltd., will primarily develop Starbucks retail locations in Japan. Its first Starbucks location in Tokyo opened on August 2, 1996, and an additional ten to twelve locations are planned for Tokyo metropolitan areas during the next eighteen months.

In August 1996, Starbucks Coffee International announced plans to enter two additional Pacific Rim markets. Starbucks signed an agreement forming a joint-venture partnership that will develop Starbucks retail locations in Hawaii. Coffee Partners Hawaii opened its first store in Honolulu at Kahala Mall on December 12, 1996. Approximately thirty locations will follow during the next three to four years.

The company entered Singapore, its first country in Southeast Asia, through a licensing agreement with Bonstar Pte. Ltd. The first retail location opened on December 14, 1996. Approximately ten Starbucks locations are scheduled to open in Singapore during the next twelve to fifteen months.

Locations

Starbucks currently has multiple locations in thirty states. Starbucks also operates internationally in Alberta, British Columbia, and Ontario, Canada; Tokyo and Singapore.

In addition, Starbucks has about one-hundred licensed locations that serve customers in unique areas such as airports, university campuses, hospitals, and business dining facilities. Marriott Management Services operates most of these locations.

Starbucks and ARAMARK Corp. formed a relationship in February 1996. This arrangement includes an agreement to put licensed operations at various locations operated by ARAMARK. The first licensed location opened at the University of New Mexico in July 1996.

Specialty Sales and Marketing

Starbucks Coffee Company and U.S. Office Products announced an agreement in October 1996 to distribute Starbucks fresh roasted coffee and related products through U.S. Office Products extensive North American distributorship.

In November 1995, Starbucks announced a strategic alliance with United Airlines and is now the exclusive supplier of coffee on every United flight.

In addition, Specialty Sales and Marketing supplies coffee to the health care, business and industry, college and university, and hotel and resort segments of the food service industry; to many fine restaurants throughout North America; and to companies such as Costco, Nordstrom, Barnes & Noble, Inc., ITT/Sheraton Hotels, Westin Hotels, Star Markets, Meijer, Sodexho, Guckenheimer, and Horizon Airlines.

Product Line

Starbucks roasts more than thirty varieties of the world's finest arabica coffee beans. The company's retail locations also feature a variety of espresso beverages and locally made fresh pastries. Starbucks specialty merchandise includes Starbucks private-label espresso makers, mugs, plunger pots, grinders, storage jars, water filters, thermal carafes, and coffee makers. An extensive selection of packaged goods, including unique confections, gift baskets, and coffee-related items are available in stores, through mail order, and through a site in the Marketplace section of America Online.

In spring 1995, Starbucks introduced Frappuccino® blended beverages, a line of low-fat, creamy, iced coffee drinks. This product launch was the most successful in Starbucks history. In January 1996, the North American Coffee Partnership between Starbucks New Venture Company, a wholly-owned subsidiary of Starbucks Corporation, and Pepsi Cola announced plans to market a bottled version of Frappuccino®. The product, a low-fat, creamy blend of Starbucks brewed coffee and milk, is currently being distributed on a national basis and is available in grocery stores and in many Starbucks retail locations.

A long-term joint venture between Starbucks Coffee and Breyer's Grand Ice Cream was announced on October 31, 1995. The joint venture, designed to dish up a premium line of coffee ice creams, began national distribution of five different flavors to leading grocery stores in April 1996. By July 1996, Starbucks had become the number one brand of coffee ice cream in the United States. Currently, ice cream lovers can choose from eight delectable flavors or two ice cream bars.

In March 1995, Starbucks and Capitol Records joined forces to produce Blue Note Blend, a compact disc featuring classic jazz recordings. It was played in Starbucks locations and was the first item to be sold to customers both over the counter and by mail order. The album was so successful that the company has subsequently released several other CDs, covering a wide range of tastes and moods, including Chicago blues, rhythm and blues, legendary female vocalists, an eclectic mix from the late 1960s and early 1970s, jazz, and opera.

Community Involvement

Starbucks contributes to a variety of organizations that benefit AIDS research, child welfare, environmental awareness, literacy, and the arts. The company encourages its partners (employees) to take an active role in their own neighborhoods.

In order to support philanthropic organizations in the communities where Starbucks operates, it established the Starbucks Foundation in 1997. The foundation, launched with an initial contribution from Howard Schultz, Starbucks chairman and CEO, of $500,000, will be supported by donations from Starbucks Coffee Company and Schultz's earnings from *Pour Your Heart into It: How Starbucks Built a Company One Cup at a Time*, a book authored by Schultz and released in September 1997.

Starbucks is the leading corporate sponsor of the international relief and development organization, CARE, with an annual corporate contribution of $100,000 in addition to a $2 contribution for every CARE coffee sampler sold.

Recognition

Starbucks has received numerous awards for quality innovation, service and giving. The following list includes a selection of the numerous awards Starbucks has won.

✔ "The Stafford Award for Corporate Leadership" in recognition of the company's sensitive reuse of older spaces within cities—*Scenic America*—May 13, 1997

✔ "Best Neighborhood Coffee Bar"—*Evening* Magazine's Best of the Northwest edition—April 21, 1997

✔ "Living and Giving Award" for significant contributions made in support of diabetes research—Juvenile Diabetes Foundation of Greater Seattle—March 22, 1997

✔ "Best Coffee"—Reader's Choice—*Northwest Palate*—January/February 1997

✔ Frappuccino® blended beverage recognized as one of "The Best New Products" of 1996—*Business Week*—January 13, 1997

✔ 1997 Consumer Enhancement and Development Award of Excellence—Coopers and Lybrand Consulting—January 1997

✔ One of the "Top 10 Growth Companies," "Top 10 Growth Chains" and "Top 10 Stock Performers" of 1996—*Nation's Restaurant News*—December 23, 1996

✔ 25th Anniversary Promotion recognized as one of the "Top Ten Promotions of 1996"—*Promo*—December 1996

✔ Bottled Frappuccino® Coffee Drink recognized as one of the "Top Ten New Products of 1996"—*Food Processing*—November 1996

✔ 1996 Most Customer-Sensitive Award for Customer Service for a chain restaurant—Knowledge Exchange—August 1996

✔ 1996 Corporate Conscience Award for International Human Rights—Council on Economic Priorities—June 4, 1996

✔ 1996 International Humanitarian Award—CARE—May 10, 1996

✔ 1996 American Business Ethics Award—American Society of Chartered Life Underwriters and Chartered Financial Consultants—March 7, 1996

✔ "Change Maker of the Year"—*Restaurants & Institutions*—December 1995

✔ One of "America's 100 Fastest Growing Companies"—*Fortune Magazine*—1992 through 1996

✔ Business Enterprise Trust Award for innovative benefits plan—December 6, 1994

La Jolla Brewing Co.

pubs is well justified by the enormous potential for returns. To quote the *Wall Street Journal,* "With profit margins as high as 70%, a $250,000 microbrewery can triple the bottom line for a 200-seat restaurant and pay for itself in two years."

Microbreweries can produce a wide variety of ales, lagers, and other beers, the quality of which depends largely on the quality of the raw materials and the skill of the brewer.

Sports Bars

Sports bars have always been popular, but have become more so with the decline of disco and singles bars. They are a place people relax in the sporting atmosphere, so bar/restaurants like Trophies in San Diego or Characters at Marriott hotels have become popular "watering holes." Satellite television coverage of the top sporting events helps sports bars to draw crowds.

Coffee Shops

Another fairly recent trend in the beverage industry in the United States and Canada is the establishment of coffeehouses, or coffee shops.

Coffeehouses originally were created based on the model of Italian bars, which reflected the deeply rooted espresso tradition in Italy. The winning concept of Italian bars lies in the ambiance they create, which is suitable for conversation of a personal, social, and business nature. A talk over a cup of coffee with soft background music and maybe a pastry is a typical scenario for Italians. Much of the same concept was re-created in the United States and Canada, where there was a niche in the beverage industry that was yet to be acknowledged and filled. The original concept was modified, however, to include a much wider variety of beverages and styles of coffee to meet the tastes of their consumers, who have a tendency to prefer a greater selection of products. Consequently, the typical espresso/cappuccino offered by Italian bars has been expanded in North America to include items such as iced mocha, iced cappuccino, and so forth.

Students as well as businesspeople find coffeehouses a place to relax, discuss, socialize, and study. The success of coffee houses is reflected in the es-

CyberCafe

tablishment of chains, such as Starbucks, as well as family-owned, independent shops.

Cyber cafes are a recent trend in the coffeehouse sector. Cyber cafes offer the use of computers, with Internet capability, for about $6 per hour. Guests can enjoy coffee, snacks, or even a meal while on-line. Reasonable rates allow regular guests to have e-mail addresses.

Liquor Liability and the Law

Owners, managers, bartenders, and servers may be liable under the law if they serve alcohol to minors or to persons who are intoxicated. The extent of the liability can be very severe. The legislation that governs the sale of alcoholic beverages is called dram shop legislation. The dram shop laws, or civil damage acts, were enacted in the 1850s and dictated that owners and operators of drinking establishments are liable for injuries caused by intoxicated customers.[13]

Some states have reverted back to the eighteenth century common law, removing liability from vendors except in cases involving minors. Nonetheless, most people recognize that as a society, we are faced with major problems of underage drinking and drunk driving.

To combat underage drinking in restaurants, bars, and lounges, a major brewery distributed a booklet showing the authentic design and layout of each state's drivers license. Trade associations, like the National Restaurant Association and the American Hotel and Motel Association, have, together with other major corporations, produced a number of preventive measures and programs aimed at responsible alcohol beverage service. The major thrust of these initiatives is awareness programs and mandatory training programs like TIPS (training for intervention procedures by servers) that promote responsible alcohol service. TIPS is sponsored by the National Restaurant Association and is a certification program that teaches participants about alcohol and its effects on people, the common signs of intoxication, and how to help customers avoid drinking too much.

Consider this war story: The author once worked at an old hotel that had seven bars, and as an aspiring assistant manager, one of his duties was to take stock of the bars and calculate the beverage cost percentage.

Next morning, when outside auditors came to do the quarterly inventory control, they noticed that some of the bottles in the banquet bar were filled above the normal level in the neck of the bottle, but they weren't sure whether this was the normal "topping up" of the end of one bottle to the next or something else. A check of the alcoholic proof of the bottles showed that the gin and vodka had been diluted. Now the question was, who did it?

In recent weeks, the assistant managers' beverage cost percentages for each of the seven bars had shown varying results. First, one bar was up, then two weeks later, it was down. This was the case in each of the seven bars, even though the bottles all had the hotel's stamp on them and new bottles had only been issued when empty ones were returned.

In an attempt to find out what was happening, the general manager questioned each of the six assistant managers and concluded that several people were involved. He brought in a team of special investigators who took turns spending nights at strategic locations, such as behind a large sofa in the lounge that pro-

vided a good view of one bar and in an office with a peephole into another office. It was not long before one of the bell captains appeared with a fishing pole that he inserted through the wrought iron gate of the associates entrance to the historic bar. He managed to snag a bottle and bring it back through the gate. He then removed some of the spirits, diluted the bottle with a liquid, and returned it to the bar. Although the investigators were tempted to apprehend the bell captain, they decided to wait and see if anyone else was involved. Sure enough, the next night, another bar was tampered with in a similar fashion. This time, however, a senior assistant manager and a restaurant associate were involved. Again, no action was taken until the general manager could be consulted. This time, the police were called and, together, they questioned the senior assistant manager and the other two associates.

It turned out that a casino had recently opened near the hotel and several associates had lost large sums of money gambling. They had promised to repay the casino owner with spirits stolen from the hotel. The police then raided the casino and found some spirit bottles with the hotel's stamp on them. With this evidence, the casino owner, the hotel senior assistant manager, and the associates were prosecuted and convicted.

Figure 9–12   *Controlling Inventory*

Other programs include designated drivers, who only drink nonalcoholic beverages to ensure that friends return home safely. Some operators give free nonalcoholic beverages to the designated driver as a courtesy.

One positive outcome of the responsible alcohol service programs for operators is a reduction in the insurance premiums and legal fees that had skyrocketed in previous years.

Trends in the Beverage Industry

- ✔ The comeback of cocktails
- ✔ Designer bottled water
- ✔ Microbreweries
- ✔ More wine consumption
- ✔ Increase in coffeehouses and coffee intake

Hiring Bar Personnel

As bar manager of a popular local night club, it is your responsibility to interview and hire all bar personnel. One of your friends asks you for a job as a bartender. Since he has experience, you decide to help him out and give him a regular shift. During the next few weeks, you notice that the overall sales for his shifts are down slightly from previous weeks with other bartenders. You suspect he may be stealing from you.

Discussion Questions

1. What are your alternatives for determining whether or not your friend is, in fact, stealing?
2. If you determine that he has been stealing, how do you handle it?

Java Coffee House

Michelle Wong is manager of the Java Coffee House at a busy location on Union Street in San Francisco. Michelle says that there are several challenges in operating a busy coffeehouse, such as training staff to handle unusual circumstances. For example, one guest consumed a cup of coffee and ate two-thirds of a piece of cake and then said he didn't like the cake.

Another problem is suppliers who quote good prices to get her business and then, two weeks later, raise the price of some of the items.

Michelle says that the young employees she has at the Java Coffee House are her greatest challenge of all. According to Michelle, there are four kinds of employees—lazy; good, but not responsible; those who steal; and great ones who are no trouble.

Discussion Questions

1. What are some suggestions for training staff to handle unusual circumstances?
2. How do you ensure that suppliers are delivering the product at the price quoted?
3. What do you do with lazy employees?
4. What do you do with irresponsible employees?
5. How do you deal with employees who steal?

Summary

1. Beverages are categorized into alcoholic and nonalcoholic beverages. Alcoholic beverages are further categorized into spirits, fortified wines, wines, and beer.
2. Spirits have a high percentage of alcohol and are served before or after a meal. Fermentation and distillation are parts of their processing. The most popular white spirits are rum, gin, vodka, and tequila.
3. Wine is the fermented juice of ripe grapes. It is classified as red, white, and rose, and we distinguish between light beverage wines, sparkling wines, and aromatic wines.
4. The six steps in making wine are crushing, fermenting, racking, maturing, filtering, and boiling. France, Germany, Italy, Spain, and Portugal are the main European wine-producing areas, and California is the main American wine-producing area.
5. Beer is a brewed and fermented beverage made from malt. Different types of beer include ale, stout, lager, and pilsner.
6. Today people have become more health conscious about consumption of alcohol; nonalcoholic beverages such as coffee, tea, soft drinks, juices, and bottled water are increasing in popularity.
7. Beverages make up 20 to 30 percent of total sales in a restaurant, but managers are liable if they serve alcohol to minors. Programs such as designated driver and TIPS, and serving virgin cocktails have increased.

Review Exercises

1. What are spirits? Explain the process of fermentation and distillation and the origin of Scotch whisky and brandy.
2. What is the difference between fortified and aromatic wines? In what combination is it suggested to serve food and wine and why?
3. Describe the brewing process of beer. What is the difference between a stout and a pilsner?
4. Why have nonalcoholic drinks increased in popularity and what difficulties do bar managers face when serving alcohol?
5. Describe the origin of coffee.
6. Describe the proper procedure for handling and serving champagne.
7. Describe the origin of cocktails. What constitutes a cocktail?
8. Describe a typical bar setup.

Key Words and Concepts

Alcohol	Dram shop legislation	Microbreweries	TIPS
Aperitif	Fermenting	Must	Vintage
Beer, malt, hops, and yeast	Fortified wines	Prohibition	Wines
Champagne	Inventory Control	Sparkling wines	

Notes

[1]H. J. Grossman, *Grossman's Guide to Wines, Spirits, and Beers.* New York: Charles Scribner's Sons, 1955, p. 293.

[2]*Encyclopedia Americana,* 1991, p. 452.

[3]Michael M. Coltman, *Beverage Management.* New York: Van Nostrand Reinhold, 1989, p. 160.

[4]Ibid.

[5]C. Katsigris and M. Porter, *The Bar and Beverage Book,* 2nd ed. New York: John Wiley and Sons, 1991, p. 139.

[6]*Food Arts, 6,* 10, December 1993, p. 54.

[7]Claudia Roden, *Coffee.* Middlesex, England: Penguin Books, 1987, p. 20.

[8]Ibid.

[9]This section draws on Sara Perry, *The Complete Coffee Book.* San Francisco: Chronicle Books, 1991, p. 8.

[10]Ibid.

[11]Coca-Cola's 1993 annual report.

[12]Belverd E. Needles, Jr., Henry R. Anderson, James C. Caldwell, and Sherry K. Mills, *Principles of Accounting,* 6th ed. Boston: Houghton Mifflin Company, 1996, p. 318.

[13]Gerald D. Robin, "Alcohol Service Liability: What the Courts Are Saying," *The Cornell Hotel and Restaurant Administration Quarterly, 31,* 1, February 1991, p. 102.

Recreation and Leisure

10

After reading and studying this chapter you should be able to do the following:

✔ Discuss the relationship of recreation and leisure to wellness

✔ Explain the origins and extent of government-sponsored recreation

✔ Distinguish between commercial and noncommercial recreation

✔ Name and describe various types of recreational clubs

Recreational activities include all kinds of sports, both team and individual. Baseball, softball, football, basketball, volleyball, tennis, swimming, jogging, skiing, hiking, aerobics, rock climbing, and camping are all active forms of recreation. Passive recreational activities include reading, fishing, playing and listening to music, gardening, playing computer games, and watching television or movies.

Recreation is an integral part of the nation's total social, economic, natural resource, and urban environment. It is a basic component of individual and social behavior and aspiration.[1]

Recreation, Leisure, and Wellness

As postindustrial society has become more complex, life has become more stressed. The need to develop the wholeness of the person has become increasingly important. Compared to a generation ago, the stress levels of business executives are much higher. The term *burnout*—and indeed, the word *stress*—have only become a part of our everyday vocabulary in recent years. Recreation is all about creating a balance, a harmony in life that will maintain wellness and wholeness.

Recreation allows people to have fun together and to form lasting relationships built on the experiences they have enjoyed together. This recreational process is called *bonding*. Bonding is hard to describe, yet the experience of increased interpersonal feeling for friends or business associates as a result of a recreational pursuit is common. These relationships result in personal growth and development.

The word *recreation* is defined in the dictionary as "the process of giving new life to something, of restoring something."[2]

Recreation is synonymous with lifestyle and the development of a positive attitude. An example of this is the increased feeling of well-being experienced after a recreational activity. Some people make the mistake of trying to pursue happiness as a personal goal. It is not enough for a person to say, "I want to be happy; therefore, I will recreate." Nathaniel Hawthorne wrote in the mid-nineteenth century: "Happiness in this world, when it comes, comes inciden-

Biking, Swimming, Hiking

tally. Make it the object of pursuit, and it leads us on a wild goose chase, and it is never attained. Follow some other object, and very possibly we may find that we have caught happiness without dreaming of it."[3]

Recreation is a process that seeks to establish a milieu conducive to the discovery and development of characteristics that can lead to happiness. Happiness and well-being, therefore, are incidental outcomes of recreation. Thus, happiness may be enhanced by the pursuit of recreational activities.

The setting of personal recreational goals is equally as important as any other business or personal goal. These goals might include running a mile in under six minutes or maintaining a baseball batting average above .300. The fact that a person sets and strives to achieve goals requires personal organization. This helps improve the quality of life.

Leisure is best described as time free from work, or discretionary time. Some recreation professionals use the words leisure and recreation interchangeably, while others define leisure as the "productive," "creative," or "contemplative" use of free time.

History shows again and again a direct link between leisure and the advancement of civilization. Hard work alone leaves no time for becoming civilized. Ironically, however, the opportunity to be at leisure is the direct result of increased technological and productivity advancements.

Government–Sponsored Recreation

Various levels of government are intertwined, yet distinct, in their parks, recreation, and leisure services. The founding fathers of America said it best when they affirmed the right to life, liberty, and the pursuit of happiness in the Declaration of Independence. The general welfare clause of the Constitution has become a legal basis for federal action affecting leisure pursuits.[4]

Government raises revenue from income taxes, sales taxes, and property taxes. Additionally, government raises special revenue from recreation-related activities such as automobile and recreational vehicles, boats, motor fuels, transient occupancy taxes (TOT) on hotel accommodations, state lotteries, and others.

New York Marathon

The monies are distributed among the various recreation- and leisure-related organizations at the federal, state/provincial, city, and town levels. Recreation and leisure activities are extremely varied, ranging from cultural pursuits like museums, arts and crafts, music, theater, and dance to sports (individual and team), outdoor recreation, amusement parks, theme parks, community centers, playgrounds, libraries, and gardens.

A number of demographic factors affect participation in recreational activities: personality, sex, age, health, cultural background, upbringing, education, environment, occupation, and social contacts.[5]

Perceptions and attitudes play a major role in determining whether or not individuals participate in recreation, and if so, how much they enjoy their experiences. People's perceptions and attitudes are products of the total environment. All of the stimuli received throughout life mold an individual's outlook and feelings. These stimuli, in turn, are controlled by the person's demographics.[6] In the end, people select recreational pursuits based on their interests and capabilities.

Recreation professionals face a number of policy and legal concepts,[7] among them the following:

- Comprehensive recreation planning
- Land classification systems
- Federal revenue sharing
- Acquisition- and development-funding programs
- Land-use planning and zoning
- State and local financing
- Off-road vehicle impacts and policy
- Use of easements for recreation
- Designation of areas (such as wilderness, wild and scenic rivers, national trails, nature preserves)
- Differences in purposes and resources (of the numerous local, state/provincial, and federal agencies that control more than one-third of the nation's land, much of which is used for recreation)

National Parks in the United States

National Parks are the best idea we ever had. Absolutely American, absolutely democratic, they reflect us at our best rather than our worst.
—WALLACE STEGNER, 1983

The prevailing image of a national park is one of grand natural playgrounds, such as Yellowstone National Park; but there is much more to it than that. The United States has designated 367 national park units throughout the country, comprising a rich diversity of places and settings.

The National Parks Service was founded in 1916 by Congress to conserve park resources and to provide for their use by the public in order to leave them unimpaired for the enjoyment of future generations.

In addition to the better known parks such as Yellowstone and Yosemite, the Parks Service also manages many other heritage attractions, including the Freedom Trail in Boston, Independence Hall in Philadelphia, the Antietam National Battlefield in Sharpsburg, Maryland, and the U.S.S. Arizona Memorial at Pearl Harbor in Hawaii. The Parks Service is also charged with caring for myriad cultural artifacts, including ancient pottery, sailing vessels, colonial-period clothing, and Civil War documents.

> *There is nothing so American as our National Parks . . . the fundamental idea behind the parks . . . is that the country belongs to the people.*
> —Franklin D. Roosevelt

The ever-expanding mandate of the Parks Service also calls for understanding and preserving the environment. It monitors the ecosystem from the Arctic tundra to coral atolls, to researches the air and water quality around the nation, and participates in global studies on acid rain, climate change, and biological diversity.

The idea of preserving exceptional lands for public use as national parks arose after the Civil War when America's receding wilderness left unique national resources vulnerable to exploitation. Recent years have seen phenomenal growth in the system, with three new areas created in the last twenty years. These include new kinds of parks, such as urban recreational areas, free-flowing rivers, long-distance trails, and historic sites honoring our nation's social achievements. The system's current roster of 367 areas covers more than 80 million

Yellowstone National Park
(Courtesy Yellowstone National Park.)

acres of land, with individual areas ranging in size from the 13-million-acre Wrangell-St. Elias National Park and Preserve in Alaska to the Thaddeus Kosciuszko National Memorial (a Philadelphia row house commemorating a hero of the American Revolution), which covers two one-hundredths of an acre.

More than 272 million visitors go to the parks each year and take advantage of the full range of services and programs. The focus once placed on preserving the scenery of the most natural parks has shifted as the system has grown and changed. Today emphasis is placed on preserving the vitality of each park's ecosystem and on the protection of unique or endangered plant and animal species.[8]

National Parks in Canada

Canada has twenty-nine large national parks and more than twenty national historical parks and sites. Banff National Park, known for the world's most beautiful mountain peaks, was the first park of the system, founded in 1885. Jasper, Kootenay, Yoho Glacier, and Mt. Revelstoke national parks, several provincial parks, and the extensive Rocky Mountain Forest Reserve combine to make an immense complex of public lands along the spine of the spectacularly scenic Rocky Mountains of Alberta and British Columbia. These parks are accessed by the Canadian Pacific Railway, the Trans-Canada Highway, and small aircraft.[9]

Jasper Lodge and Park

The Canadian National Parks Act states that "The parks are hereby dedicated to the people of Canada for their benefit, education, and enjoyment—and shall be maintained and made use of, so as to leave them unimpaired for the enjoyment of future generations."

The Canadian parks have highly developed tourist service islands (such as the town of Banff), well-appointed lodges and chalets, ski resorts, sports centers, and retreats, mostly natural in character. The largest of Canada's—and perhaps the world's—national parks is Wood Buffalo in Alberta and the Northwest Territories. Its 4,481,000 hectares (17,300 square miles) serve as home to the world's largest herd of bison that are roaming wild. The park is not developed for the public, but serves strictly as a wildlife preserve.

In Canada, recreation programming became a serious concern of the government after World War II. Provincial responsibility for recreation comes under several headings: outdoor activities, sports and physical recreation, arts and culture, social activities, tourism, and travel. Within each category, the government may have differing levels of responsibility: primary, in which a department or agency is required to provide a given service; secondary, in which an agency specifically is permitted (although not required) to provide a service; and tertiary, in which an agency performs a recreation function because it is related to another primary responsibility.[10]

In the past few decades, the federal government of Canada, in response to perceived needs, has created activities themes. During the 1950s, it was physical fitness; in the 1960s, it was youth; and in the 1970s, it was cultural and multicultural expression. The 1980s and 1990s have brought a combination of previous programs, with family themes.

Public Recreation and Parks Agencies

During the early part of the nineteenth century in the United States, the parks movement expanded rapidly as a responsibility of government and voluntary organizations. By the early 1900s, fourteen cities had made provisions for supervised play facilities, and the playground movement gained momentum.

Public Golf Course

Public Basketball Court

Private initiative and financial support were instrumental in convincing city government to provide tax dollars to build and maintain new play areas.

About the same time, municipal parks were created in a number of cities. Boston established the first metropolitan park system in 1892. In 1898, the New England Association of Park Superintendents (predecessor of the American Institute of Park Executives) was established to bring together park superintendents and promote their professional concerns.

Increasingly, the concept that city governments should provide recreation facilities, programs, and services became widely accepted. Golf courses, swimming pools, bathing beaches, picnic areas, winter sports facilities, game fields, and playgrounds were constructed.

Commercial Recreation

Recreation management came of age in the 1920s and 1930s, when recreation and social programs were offered as a community service. Colleges and universities began offering degree programs. Both public and private sector recreation management has grown rapidly since 1950.

Commercial recreation has been defined as "recreation for which the consumer pays and for which the supplier expects to make a profit."[11] Commercial recreation includes theme parks, attractions, and clubs.

Theme Parks

Visiting theme parks has always been a favorite tourist activity. Theme parks create an atmosphere of another place and time, and usually concentrate on one dominant theme around which architecture, landscaping, costumed personnel, rides, shows, foodservices, and merchandise are coordinated.[12]

Theme parks and attractions vary according to theme, which might be historical, cultural, geographical, and so on. Some parks and attractions focus on a single theme, like the marine zoological Sea World parks. Other parks and attractions focus on multiple themes, like King's Island in Ohio, a family entertainment center divided into six theme areas: International Street, October First, River-Town, Hanna-Barbera Land, Coney Mall, and Wild Animal Habitat. Another example is Great America in California, a hundred-acre family entertainment center that evokes North America's past in five themes: Home Town Square, Yukon Territory, Yankee Harbor, Country Fair, and Orleans Place.[13]

Clubs

Private clubs are places where only members gather for social, recreational, professional, or fraternal reasons. Many of today's clubs are adaptations of their predecessors, mostly from England and Scotland. For example, the North American Country Club is largely patterned after the Royal and Ancient Golf Club of St. Andrews, Scotland, founded in 1758, and recognized as the birthplace of golf.

Personal and Corporate Profile: Walt Disney

A Man with a Vision and a Dream That He Was Able to Turn into Reality

To all who come to this happy place: Welcome! Disneyland is your land; here, age relives fond memories of the past, and here youth may savor the challenge and promise of the future.

Disneyland is dedicated to the hard facts that have created America, with the hope that it will be a source of joy and inspiration to all the world.

—DISNEYLAND DEDICATION PLAQUE,
July 17, 1955

In 1923, at the age of twenty-one, Walt Disney arrived in Los Angeles from Kansas City to start a new business. The first endeavor of Walt Disney and his brother Roy was a series of "shorts" called *Alice Comedies*, which featured a child actress playing with animated characters. Realizing that something new was needed to capture the audience, Walt Disney conjured up the concept of a mouse. In 1927, Disney began a series called *Oswald the Lucky Rabbit.* It was well received by the public, but Disney lost the rights due to a dispute with his distributor.

Mickey and Minnie Mouse first appeared in *Steamboat Willie,* which also incorporated music and sound, on November 18, 1928. Huge audiences were ecstatic about the Disney Brothers, who became overnight successes.

During the next few years, Walt and Roy made many Mickey Mouse films, which earned them enough to develop other projects, including full-length motion pictures in Technicolor. Their first film was *Snow White and the Seven Dwarfs,* which opened in 1937. The success of *Snow White* led to other hits: *Pinocchio* and *Fantasia* in 1940, *Dumbo* in 1941, *Bambi* in 1942, and *Saludos Amigos* in 1943. Disney also was successful with live-action films such as *The Reluctant Dragon, Song of the South,* and *20,000 Leagues Under the Sea.* In 1954, Disney entered the television revolution with the Disney television series; in 1955, "The Mickey Mouse Club" debuted on the ABC network.

Walt Disney said that Disneyland really began when his two daughters were very young. Saturday was always daddy's day, and he would take them to the merry-go-

Cinderella Castle.© Disney Enterprises, Inc.

round and sit on a bench eating peanuts while they rode. Sitting there, he felt that there should be some kind of a family park where parents and children could have fun together.[1]

Walt's original dream was not easy to bring to reality. During the bleak war years, not only was much of his overseas market closed, but the steady stream of income that paid for innovation dried up. However, even during the bleak years, Walt never gave up. Instead, he was excited to learn of the public's interest in movie studios and the possibility of opening the studios to allow the public to visit the birthplace of Snow White, Pinocchio, and other Disney characters.

Gradually the concept of Disneyland came into focus. The clincher was Walt's fascination with trains and his need for a new home with a large yard for the train. Walt had to negotiate with more than 300 bankers before he could raise the capital necessary to open Disneyland. He never gave up. Disney later wrote, "I could never convince the financiers that Disneyland was feasible, because dreams offer too little collateral."[2]

Disneyland had its growing pains—larger-than-expected opening day crowds, long lines at the popular rides, and a cash flow that was so tight that the cashiers had to rush the admission money to the bank in order to make payroll. Fortunately, since those early days, Disneyland and the Disney characters have become a part of not only Walt Disney, but also of the American dream.

By the early 1960s, Walt had turned most of his attention from film to real estate. Because he was upset when cheap motels and souvenir shops popped up around Disneyland, for his next venture, Walt Disney World, he bought 27,500 acres around the park. The center of Walt Disney World was to be the Experimental Prototype Community of Tomorrow (Epcot). Regrettably, Epcot and Walt Disney World were his dying dreams, as Walt Disney succumbed to cancer in 1966.

The ensuing years have given Disney phenomenal successes with Epcot Center movies, a TV station, The Disney Channel, Disney stores, and Disney-MGM Studios theme park. In April 1992, EuroDisneyland, now Disneyland Paris, opened near Paris. In 1994, his Royal Highness, Prince Al Waleed Bin Talal Bin Abdula of Saudi Arabia, purchased 25 percent of the EuroDisneyland Paris Resort.

The Tokyo Disneyland continues to be successful; since its opening in 1983, about 140 million people have spent an average of $85 per visit (compared with $60 at Disneyland and $70 at Walt Disney World).

The Walt Disney Co. had revenues of $10.1 billion in 1994 with movies like *The Lion King,* which netted more than $1 billion.

Both Walt Disney World and Disneyland have excellent college programs that enable selected students to work during the summer months in a variety of hotel, foodservice, and related park positions. Disney has also introduced a faculty internship that allows faculty to intern in a similar variety of positions.

Walt Disney World is composed of three major theme parks: Magic Kingdom, Epcot, and Disney-MGM Studios, with more than one hundred attractions, twenty-two resort hotels themed to faraway lands, spectacular nighttime entertainment, and vast shopping, dining, and recreation facilities that cover thousands of acres in this tropical paradise.

The Walt Disney World includes twenty-five lighted tennis courts, ninety-nine holes of championship golf, marinas, swimming pools, jogging and bike trails, water skiing, and motor boating. The resort also offers a unique zoological park and bird sanctuary on Discovery Island in the middle of Bay Lake that is alive with birds, monkeys, and alligators; 226 restaurants, lounges, and food courts; a nightclub metropolis to please nearly any musical palate; a starry-eyed tribute to 1930s Hollywood; and even bass fishing. Walt Disney World is always full of new surprises: It now features the world's most unusual water adventure park, a "snow-covered" mountain with a ski-resort theme called Blizzard Beach.

Three new Disney hotels are architecturally exciting and more affordable than ever. The fun-filled Disney's All-Star Sports Resort and Disney's colorful All-Star Music Resort are categorized as value-class hotels. The newly opened Disney's Wilderness Lodge is the park's jewel, with its impressive tall-timber atrium-lobby and rooms built around a Rocky Mountain geyser pool.

For nighttime fun, there is Planet Hollywood's newest entertainment restaurant (opened in December 1994) near Pleasure Island nightclubs. In all, the park has a cast of 37,000 hosts, hostesses, and entertainers famous for their warm smiles and commitment to making every night an especially good one for Disney guests.

There is more to enjoy than ever in ExtraTERRORestrial Alien Encounter, developed in collaboration with George Lucas, and Transportarium in New Tomorrow-land. Already open are Fantasyland's Legend of The Lion King; Epcot's INNOVENTIONS; the mind-blowing 3-D adventure, Honey, I Shrunk the Audience, in Future World; and, at the Disney-MGM Studios, the ultimate thriller, The Twilight Zone Tower of Terror™.

Magic Kingdom

The heart of Walt Disney World and its first famous theme park is the Magic Kingdom, the "happiest land on earth," where "age relives fond memories" and "youth may savor the challenge and promise of the future." It is a giant theatrical stage where guests become part of exciting Disney adventures. It is also the home of Mickey Mouse, Snow White, Peter Pan, Tom Sawyer, Davy Crockett, and the Swiss Family Robinson.

More than forty major shows and ride-through attractions, not to mention shops and unique dining facilities, fill its seven lands of imagination. Each land carries out its theme in fascinating detail—architecture, transportation, music, costumes, dining, shopping, and entertainment are designed to create a total atmosphere where guests can leave the ordinary world behind. The seven lands include the following:

Main Street, USA—Turn-of-the-century charm with horsedrawn streetcars, horseless carriages, Penny Arcade, and grand-circle tour on Walt Disney World Steam Railroad

Adventureland—Explore with Pirates of the Caribbean, wild animal Jungle Cruise, Swiss Family Treehouse, Tropical Serenade by birds, flowers, and tikis

Frontierland—Thrills on Splash Mountain and Big Thunder Mountain Railroad, musical fun in Country Bear Jamboree, Shooting Gallery, Tom Sawyer Island caves and raft rides

Liberty Square—Steamboating on the Rivers of America, mystery in the Haunted Mansion, whooping it up in Diamond Horseshoe Saloon, viewing the impressive Hall of Presidents with the addition of President Bill Clinton in a speaking role

Fantasyland—Cinderella Castle is the gateway to the new Legend of The Lion King plus Peter Pan's Flight, newly enhanced Snow White's Adventure, Mr. Toad's Wild Ride, Flying Dumbo, Alice's Mad Tea Party, musical cruise with doll-like dancers in It's a Small World, Cinderella's Golden Carousel, and Skyway cable car to Tomorrowland

Mickey's Toontown Fair—Mickey's House, Grandma Duck's Farm, Mickey's Treehouse playground, and private photo session in Mickey's Dressing Room

New Tomorrowland—Sci-Fi city of the future, new frightening Alien Encounter, Transportarium time machine travels in Circle-Vision 360, new whirling Astro-

Orbiter, speedy Space Mountain, new production of Carousel of Progress, Grand Prix Raceway, elevated Transit tour, new Disney Character show on Tomorrowland Stage

Epcot

Epcot is a unique, permanent, and ever-changing world's fair with two major themes: Future World and World Showcase. Highlights include Illumi-Nations, a nightly spectacle of fireworks, fountains, lasers, and classical music.

Future World shows an amazing exposition of technology for the near future for home, work, and play in IN-NOVENTIONS. The newest consumer products are continually added. Major pavilions exploring past, present, and future are shown in the Spaceship Earth story of communications. The Universe of Energy giant dinosaurs help explain the origin and future of energy. There are also the Wonders of Life with spectacular Body Wars, Cranium Command and other medical health subjects, the World of Motion exploring transportation, Journey into Imagination, The Land with spectacular agricultural research and environmental growing areas, and The Living Seas, the world's largest indoor ocean with thousands of tropical sea creatures.

Around The World Showcase Lagoon are pavilions where guests can see world-famous landmarks, and sample the native foods, entertainment, and culture of eleven nations:

Mexico—Mexico's fiesta plaza and boat trip on El Rio Del Tiempo plus San Angel Inn for authentic Mexican cuisine

Norway—Thrilling Viking boat journey and Restaurant Akershus

China—Wonders of China Circle-Vision 360 film tour from the Great Wall to the Yangtze River plus Nine Dragons Restaurant

Germany—Authentic Biergarten restaurant

Italy—St. Mark's Square street players and L'Originale Alfredo di Roma Ristorante

United States—The American Adventure's stirring historical drama

Japan—Re-creating an Imperial Palace plus Teppanyaki Dining Rooms

Morocco—Morocco's palatial Restaurant Marrakesh

France—Impressions de France film tour of the French countryside, Chefs de France and Bistro de Paris restaurant

United Kingdom—Shakespearean street players plus Rose & Crown Pub

Canada—Halifax to Vancouver Circle-Vision 360 tour.

Each showcase has additional snack facilities and a variety of shops featuring arts, crafts, and merchandise from each nation.

Disney-MGM Studios

With fifty major shows, shops, restaurants, ride-through adventures, and backstage tours, the Disney-MGM Studios combines real working motion picture, animation, and television studios with exciting movie attractions. The newest adventure in the Sunset Boulevard theater district is the Twilight Zone™ Tower of Terror, with a stunning thirteen-story elevator fall. The famous Chinese Theater on Hollywood Boulevard houses The Great Movie Ride.

Other major attractions include a Backstage Studio Tour of production facilities, Catastrophe Canyon, and New York Street; a tour of Walt Disney Animation Studios, Florida; exciting shows at Indiana Jones™ Epic Stunt Spectacular and Jim Henson's Muppet* Vision 3-D; plus a thrilling space flight on Star Tours.

Especially entertaining for movie and TV fans are the SuperStar Television and Monster Sound Show, where audience members take part in performances. Favorite Disney films become entertaining stage presentations in the Voyage of the Little Mermaid theater and in Beauty and the Beast, a live, twenty-five-minute musical revue at Theater of the Stars. The best restaurants include the Hollywood Brown Derby, 1950s Prime Time Cafe, Sci-Fi Dine-In Theater, Mama Melrose's Ristorante Italiano, and the Studio Commissary.

All this—and much more—is what helps make Walt Disney World the most popular destination resort in the world. Since its opening in 1971, more than 500 million guests, including kings and celebrities from around the world and all six U.S. presidents in office since the opening, have visited the parks. What causes the most comment from guests is the cleanliness, the friendliness of its cast, and the unbelievable attention to detail—a blend of showmanship and imagination that provides an endless variety of adventure and enjoyment.

Sunny beaches, exciting new adventures, a fabulous resort, and outdoor recreation facilities make a Walt Disney World excursion in Florida the ultimate dream vacation. There is a special Disney magic that frees guests from everyday cares to enjoy this unique world of fantasy, fun, thrills, and relaxation. There is something special for every age and every taste.[3]

[1]Randy Bright, *Disneyland: Inside Story.* New York: Abrams, 1987, p. 33.
[2]Ibid, p. 34.
[3]Pamela S. Weiers, "Escape to Disney's Fun and Sunshine Now," *The New York Times* Advertising supplement, February 5, 1995.

Club management is similar in many ways to hotel management. Managers are responsible for forecasting, planning, budgeting, human resource development, food and beverage facility management, and maintenance. The main differences between club management and hotel management is that with clubs, the guests feel as if they are the owners (in many cases they are), and frequently behave as if they are the owners. Their emotional attachment is stronger than that of hotel guests who do not use hotels with the same frequency that members use clubs. Another difference is that most clubs do not offer sleeping accommodations.

Club members pay an initiation fee to belong to the club and annual membership dues thereafter. Some clubs also charge a set utilization fee, usually related to food and beverages, which is charged whether or not those services are used. There are approximately 14,000 private clubs in America,[14] including both country clubs and city clubs.

The Club Manager's Association of America (CMAA) is the professional organization to which many of the club managers of the 6,000 private country clubs belong.[15] The association aims to keep managers abreast of current practices and procedures. The professional guidelines that club managers set for themselves include the following:

- Club managers shall be judicious in their relationships with club members, aware of the need to maintain a line of professional demarcation between manager and the club membership.
- Club managers shall set an example by their demeanor and behavior that employees can use as a guide in their conduct with club members and guests.
- Club managers shall serve the community in every way possible.
- Club managers shall pursue their quest for knowledge through educational seminars and meetings that will improve their ability to manage their clubs.
- Club managers shall actively partipicate in local and national association meetings and activities.
- Club managers shall be above reproach. There can be no half measure of integrity in their obligations to their clubs, their employees, their club members, or in their dealings with purveyors.
- Club managers shall be ready at all times to offer assistance to their associates, their club officials, and all others engaged in the maintenance and conduct of their club operations.
- Club managers shall not be deterred from compliance with the law as it applies to their clubs.[16]

Figure 10–1 is a sample job description for a club general manager, and Figure 10–2 lists the club management competencies.

Club Management Structure

The internal management structure of a club is governed by a constitution and bylaws. These establish election procedures, officer positions, a board of directors, and standing committees. Guidance and direction also are provided for each office and committee and how it will function.[17]

I. **Position:** General Manager

II. **Related Titles:** Club Manager; Club House Manager

III. **Job Summary:** Serves as chief operating officer of the club; manages all aspects of the club including its activities and the relationships between the club and its board of directors, members, guests, employees, community, government, and industry; coordinates and administers the club's policies as defined by its board of directors. Develops operating policies and procedures and directs the work of all department managers. Implements and monitors the budget, monitors the quality of the club's products and services, and ensures maximum member and guest satisfaction. Secures and protects the club's assets, including facilities and equipment

IV. **Job Tasks (Duties):**

1. Implements general policies established by the board of directors; directs their administration and execution
2. Plans, develops, and approves specific operational policies, programs, procedures, and methods in concert with general policies
3. Coordinates the development of the club's long-range and annual (business) plans
4. Develops, maintains, and administers a sound organizational plan; initiates improvements as necessary
5. Establishes a basic personnel policy; initiates and monitors policies relating to personnel actions and training and professional development programs
6. Maintains membership with the Club Managers Association of America and other professional associations. Attends conferences, workshops, and meetings to keep abreast of current information and developments in the field
7. Coordinates development of operating and capital budgets according to the budget calendar; monitors monthly and other financial statements for the club; takes effective corrective action as required
8. Coordinates and serves as ex-officio member of appropriate club committees
9. Welcomes new club members; meets and greets all club members as practical during their visits to the club

10. Provides advice and recommendations to the president and committees about construction, alterations, maintenance, materials, supplies, equipment, and services not provided in approved plans and/or budgets
11. Consistently ensures that the club is operated in accordance with all applicable local, state, and federal laws
12. Oversees the care and maintenance of all the club's physical assets and facilities
13. Coordinates the marketing and membership relations programs to promote the club's services and facilities to potential and present members
14. Ensures the highest standards for food, beverage, sports and recreation, entertainment, and other club services
15. Establishes and monitors compliance with purchasing policies and procedures
16. Reviews and initiates programs to provide members with a variety of popular events
17. Analyzes financial statements, manages cash flow, and establishes controls to safeguard funds; reviews income and costs relative to goals; takes corrective action as necessary
18. Works with subordinate department heads to schedule, supervise, and direct the work of all club employees
19. Attends meetings of the club's executive committee and board of directors
20. Participates in outside activities that are judged as appropriate and approved by the board of directors to enhance the prestige of the club; broadens the scope of the club's operation by fulfilling the public obligations of the club as a participating member of the community

V. **Reports to:** Club President and Board of Directors

VI. **Supervises:** Assistant General Manager (Club House Manager); Food and Beverage Director; Controller; Membership Director; Director of Human Resources; Director of Purchasing; Golf Professional (Director of Golf); Golf Course Superintendent; Tennis Professional; Athletic Director; Executive Secretary

Courtesy: Club Managers Association of America

Figure 10–1 *Job Description, Club Manager*

The members elect the officers and directors of the club. The officers represent the membership by establishing policies by which the club will operate. Many clubs and other organizations maintain continuity by having a succession of officers: from secretary to vice president, president, and board of directors. The person elected president is the person the membership feels is the most qualified person to lead the club for that year. Regardless of who is elected president, the club manager must be able to work with that person and the other officers.

Private Club Management
History of Private Clubs
Types of Private Clubs
Membership Types
Bylaws
Policy Formulation
Board Relations
Chief Operating Officer Concept
Committees
Club Job Descriptions
Career Development
Golf Operations Management
Golf Course Management
Tennis Operations Management
Swimming Pool Management
Yacht Facilities Management
Fitness Center Management
Locker Room Management
Other Recreational Activities

Food and Beverage Operations
Sanitation
Menu Development
Nutrition
Pricing Concepts
Ordering/Receiving/Controls/Inventory
Food and Beverage Trends
Quality Service
Creativity in Theme Functions
Design and Equipment
Food and Beverage Personnel
Wine List Development

***Accounting and Finance
    in the Private Club***
Accounting and Finance Principles
Uniform System of Accounts
Financial Analysis
Budgeting
Cash Flow Forecasting
Compensation and Benefit
    Administration
Financing Capital Projects
Audits
Internal Revenue Service
Computers
Business Office Organization
Long-Range Financial Planning

Human and Professional Resources
Employee Relations
Management Styles
Organizational Development
Balancing Job and Family
    Responsibilities
Time Management
Stress Management
Labor Issues
Leadership vs. Management

Building and Facilities Management
Preventive Maintenance
Insurance and Risk Management
Clubhouse Remodeling and
    Renovation

Contractors
Energy and Water Resource
    Management
Housekeeping
Security
Laundry
Lodging Operations

***External and Governmental
    Influences***
Legislative Influences
Regulatory Agencies
Economic Theory
Labor Law
Internal Revenue Service
Privacy
Club Law
Liquor Liability
Labor Unions

Management and Marketing
Communication Skills
Marketing Through In-House
    Publications
Professional Image and Dress
Effective Negotiation
Member Contact Skills
Working with the Media
Marketing Strategies in a Private
    Club Environment

Courtesy: Club Managers Association of
America

Figure 10–2   *Club Management Competencies*

The president presides at all official meetings and is a leader in policy making.[18] The vice president will, in the absence of the president, perform the presidential duties. If the club has more than one vice president, then the title *first, second, third,* and so on may be used. Alternatively, vice presidents may be assigned to chair certain functions, such as membership. Vice presidents usually chair one or more committees.

The treasurer obviously must have some financial/accounting background because an integral part of his or her duties is to give advice on financial matters such as employing external auditors, preparing budgets, and installing control systems.

The secretary records the minutes of meetings and takes care of club-related correspondence. This position can be combined with that of treasurer, in which case the position is titled *secretary-treasurer.* The secretary may also serve on or chair certain committees.

Committees play an important part in the club's activities. If the committees are effective, the operation of the club is more efficient. The term of committee

Country Club (Photo courtesy of the Club Managers Association.)

membership is specified, and committee meetings are conducted in accordance with Robert's Rules of Order, which are procedural guidelines on the correct way to conduct meetings. Typical committees include the following: house, membership, finance/budget, entertainment, sports, special/ad hoc, and so on.

Country Clubs

A country club offers recreational facilities; the focus generally is on golf, but tennis and swimming are frequently included. Occasionally, other activities, such as horseback riding, pool rooms, card rooms, aerobic facilities, and other activities are also provided for the members' enjoyment.

Nearly all country clubs have one or more lounges and restaurants, and most have banquet facilities. Members and their guests enjoy these services and can be billed monthly. The banquet facilities are used for formal and informal parties, dinners, dances, weddings, and so on by members and their personal guests. Some country clubs charge what might seem to be an excessive amount for the initiation fee in order to maintain exclusivity—as much as $250,000 in some cases.

Country clubs have two or more types of membership. Full membership enables members to use all of the facilities all of the time. Social membership only allows members to use the social facilities: lounges, bars, restaurants, and so on and perhaps the pool and tennis courts. Other forms of membership can include weekday and weekend memberships.

A few years ago, country clubs were often considered to be bastions of a social elite. Although that description still may be somewhat true, today there are numerous examples of new clubs that have opened without the "stuffy" waiting list and "what's-your-pedigree?" approach to would-be members. Additionally, at the newer clubs, the cost of initiation and membership may be considerably less than at some of the more-established clubs.

City Clubs

City clubs are predominantly business oriented; they vary in size, location, type of facility, and services offered. Some of the older, established clubs own their own buildings, and others lease space. Clubs exist to cater to the wants and needs of members. Clubs in the city fall into the following categories:

- ✔ Professional
- ✔ Social
- ✔ Athletic
- ✔ Dining
- ✔ University
- ✔ Military
- ✔ Yachting
- ✔ Fraternal
- ✔ Proprietary

Personal Profile: Sally Burns Rambo

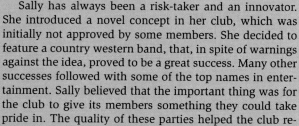

A Giver of the First Order

General Manager
Lakewood Country Club Dallas
Voted 1991 Club Manager of the Year

After graduating from high school at sixteen, Sally Burns Rambo began her professional career working in a bank. The actual launch in the business environment came when she began to work at the local newspaper. Her talent earned her a promotion to office manager. Working as office manager gave her an opportunity to become well known in the community. This led to her being offered a club's office manager position by the Eastern Hills Country Club members.

During the first six months that she worked at the club, two club managers were fired, so leaders of the club persuaded Sally to serve as interim manager until someone else was appointed. However, nobody else was ever appointed for that position, and Sally was the general manager of the club for the next twenty-one years.

Her talents and skills were not forgotten after her retirement. In fact, she was again persuaded to manage a club that was in serious decline. Sally recalls that she regretted taking this position for about four months, because the club was in extremely bad condition. But she accepted the challenge with enormous determination: "You've never been a quitter and you're not going to quit now," she told herself. By improving the quality of food and service, she made Lakewood a fun place to be. Members and guests enjoyed themselves and looked forward to visiting the club.

Sally has always been a risk-taker and an innovator. She introduced a novel concept in her club, which was initially not approved by some members. She decided to feature a country western band, that, in spite of warnings against the idea, proved to be a great success. Many other successes followed with some of the top names in entertainment. Sally believed that the important thing was for the club to give its members something they could take pride in. The quality of these parties helped the club regain membership. Sally is a hands-on manager who makes sure all details are attended to. She adds that "you make your money on member-sponsored parties" and "you have to get your business volume that way rather than through regular dining room business because most members will not dine at the club every day."

Key ingredients in Sally's success include her continually educating herself, and her caring enthusiasm to staffing. "Hire the right people, pay them well, let them show what they know, and they will make you look good." Sally has a staff of 102 full-time employees, serving 1,400 members, including families—up from less than 400 when she took over as manager.

Sally is a firm believer in dedication and hard work. In fact, she often works twelve hours a day and she never drinks on the job![1]

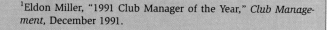

Professional clubs, as the name implies, are clubs for people in the same profession. The National Press Club in Washington, D.C., the Lawyer's Club in New York City, and the Friars Club for actors and other theatrical people in Manhattan are good examples.

Social clubs allow members to enjoy one another's company; members represent many different professions, yet they have similar socioeconomic backgrounds. Social clubs are modeled after the famous men's social clubs in London, such as Boodle's, St. James's, and White's. At these clubs, it is considered bad form to discuss business. Therefore, conversation and social interaction is focused on companionship or entertainment unrelated to business.

The oldest social club in America is thought to be the Fish House in Philadelphia, founded in 1832. To ensure that the Fish House would always be socially oriented rather than business oriented, it was formed as a men's cooking club with each member taking turns preparing meals for the membership.[19]

Other social clubs exist in several major cities. The common denominator is that they all have upscale food and beverage offerings and have club managers to manage them.

Athletic clubs give city workers and residents an opportunity to work out, swim, play squash and/or racquetball, and so on. Some of the downtown athletic clubs provide tennis courts and running tracks on the roof. Athletic clubs also have lounges, bars, and restaurants at which members may relax and interact socially. Some athletic clubs also have meeting rooms and even sleeping accommodations.

Dining clubs are generally located in large city office buildings. Memberships are often given as an inducement to tenants who lease space in the office building. These clubs are always open for lunch and occasionally for dinner.

University clubs are private clubs for alumni. With a few exceptions, they are for one university's alumni. University clubs are generally located in the high-rent district and offer a variety of facilities and attractions focusing on food and beverage service.

Military clubs cater to both NCOs (noncommissioned officers) and enlisted officers. Military clubs offer similar facilities as other clubs for recreation and entertainment, and food and beverage offerings. Military clubs are located on base and have in recent years given over their club management to civilians.

Yacht clubs provide members with moorage slips, where their boats are kept secure. In addition to moorage facilities, yacht clubs have lounge, bar, and dining facilities similar to other clubs. Yacht clubs are based on a sailing theme and attract members with various backgrounds who have sailing as one of their common interests.

Fraternal clubs include many special organizations such as the Veterans of Foreign Wars, Elks, and Shriners. These organizations foster camaraderie and often assist charitable causes. They generally are less elaborate than other clubs, but have bars and banquet rooms that can be used for various activities.

Proprietary clubs operate on a for-profit basis. They are owned by corporations or individuals; people wanting to become members purchase a membership, not a share in the club. Proprietary clubs became popular with the real estate boom in the 1970s and 1980s. As new housing developments were planned, clubs were included in several of the projects. Households paid a small initiation fee and monthly dues between $30 and $50, allowing the whole family to participate in a wide variety of recreational activities.

Clearly, the opportunities for recreation and leisure abound. The goal must be to achieve a harmony between work and leisure activities and to become truly professional in both giving and receiving these services. The next few years will see a substantial increase in the leisure and recreational industries.

Noncommercial Recreation

Noncommercial recreation includes voluntary organizations, campus, armed forces, and employee recreations as well as recreation for special populations.

Voluntary Organizations

Voluntary organizations are nongovernmental, nonprofit agencies, serving the public-at-large or selected elements with multiservice programs that often include a substantial element of recreational opportunity. The best-known voluntary organizations include the Boy Scouts, Girl Scouts, YMCA, YWCA, and YM-YWHA.

In the early 1900s, YMCAs began to offer sporting facilities and programs. The Ys, though nonprofit, were pioneers in basketball, swimming, and weight training. Later, commercial health clubs also began to evolve, offering men's and women's exercise on alternating days. As the sports and fitness movement grew, clubs became oriented toward special interests. Now, clubs can be classified as follows: figure salons, health clubs, body-building gyms, tennis clubs, racquetball centers, or multipurpose clubs.[20]

A multipurpose club has more exclusive recreation programs than a health club. Leagues, tournaments, and classes are common for racquet sports, and most clubs offer several types of fitness classes. Some innovative clubs offer automatic bank tellers, stock market quote services, computer matching for tennis competition, auto detailing, laundry and dry cleaning services, and wine-cellar storage.

Club revenue comes from membership fees, user fees, guest fees, food and beverage sales, facility rental, and so on. Human resources accounts for about 66 percent of expenses at most clubs.

It is amazing to realize that in the center of a city, there may be several voluntary organizations, each serving a particular segment of the population. Richard Kraus writes that a study of the city of Toronto that examined various land uses and leisure programs in the city's core found the following organizations: a Boy's Club, a Mission, the Center of the Metropolitan Association for the Retarded, a Catholic settlement house, a day care center, an Indian center, a YM-YWHA, a service center for working people, a Chinese center, a Ukrainian center, and several other organizations meeting special needs and interests. These were all in addition to public parks, recreation areas, and nineteen churches.

Campus, Armed Forces, and Employee Recreation

Campus Recreation

North America's colleges and universities provide a major setting for organized leisure and recreational programs with services involving millions of participants each year. The programs include involvement by campus recreation offices, intramural departments, student unions, residence staffs, or other sponsors. The activities have heavy components of the following types: competitive sports and games; outdoor recreation trips and events; cultural programs such as music, drama, dance, and films; and leisure-oriented activities.[21]

The various recreational activities help in maintaining good morale on campus. Some use recreational activities such as sports or orchestras or theater companies as a means of gaining alumni support. Students look for an exciting and interesting social life. For this reason, colleges and universities offer a wide range of recreational and social activities that may vary from campus to campus.

Armed Forces Recreation

It is the official policy of the Department of Defense to provide a well-rounded morale, welfare, and recreational program for the physical, social, and mental well-being of its personnel. Each of the services sponsors recreational activities under the auspices of the Morale, Welfare, and Recreation Program (MWR), which reports to the Office of the Assistant Secretary of Defense for Manpower, Reserve Affairs, and Logistics. MWR activities are provided to all military personnel and civilian employees at all installations.

MWR programs include the following types of activities:

- Sports, including self-directed, competitive, instructional, and spectator programs
- Motion pictures
- Service clubs and entertainment
- Crafts and hobbies
- Youth activities for children of military families
- Special interest groups such as aero, automotive, motorcycle, and power boat clubs, as well as hiking, skydiving, and rod and gun clubs
- Rest centers and recreation areas
- Open dining facilities
- Libraries

Recreation is perceived as an important part of the employee benefits package for military personnel, along with the G.I. Bill, medical services, commissaries, and exchanges.

Employee Recreation

Business and industry have realized the importance of promoting employee efficiency. Human resource experts have found that workers who spend their free time at constructive recreational activities have less absenteeism resulting from emotional tension, illness, excessive use of alcohol, and so on. Employee recreation programs may also be an incentive for a prospective employee to join a company.

In the United States and Canada, almost all of the leading corporations have an employee recreation and wellness program. Some companies include recreation activities in their team-building and management-development programs.

Recreation for Special Populations

Recreation for special populations involves professionals and organizations who serve groups such as the mentally ill, mentally retarded, or physically challenged. In recent years, there has been increased recognition of the need to provide recreational programs for special populations. These programs, developed for each of the special population groups, use therapeutic recreation as a form of treatment.

One of the sports programs for people with disabilities that has received considerable attention in recent years is the Special Olympics, an international program of physical fitness, sports training, and athletic competition for children and adults with mental retardation. The program is unique because it accommodates competitors at all ability levels by assigning participants to competition divisions based on both age and actual performance.[22]

Today, the Special Olympics serves more than 1 million individuals in the United States and more than seventy other countries. Among the official sports are track and field events, swimming, diving, gymnastics, ice skating, basketball, volleyball, soccer, softball, floor hockey, poly hockey, bowling, Frisbee disk, downhill skiing, cross-country skiing, and wheelchair events. The National Parks and Recreation Association and numerous state and local agencies and societies work closely with Special Olympics in promoting programs and sponsoring competitions.[23]

Trends in Recreation and Leisure

- ✔ An increase in all fitness activities
- ✔ An increase in personal leisure time devoted to computer activities
- ✔ A serge in travel and tourism
- ✔ In addition to a continuation of traditional recreation and leisure activities, special programs targeted toward "at-risk" youths and "latch key" children are also being developed
- ✔ Several additional products in the commercial sector
- ✔ Additional learning and adventure opportunities for the elderly, such as Elderhostel

Service Proposal for Guests

You recently joined the front desk of a nice resort hotel in New England and your hotel manager has complimented you on your guest service ability. She has asked you to develop a walking/jogging trail for the guests.

Discussion Question

1. What would be some of the key elements to consider in developing a proposal for your hotel guests?

Overpopulation of National Parks

Our national parks are under serious threat from a number of sources including congestion resulting from overvisitation, consequent environmental degradation, and pollution.

There are too many people and too many vehicles in the most popular national parks. Many bring their city lifestyle, leaving garbage lying around, listening to loud music, and leaving the trails.

Discussion Question

1. List the recommendations you have for the park superintendents to help save the parks.

Summary

1. Recreation is free time that people use to restore, rest, and relax their minds and bodies. Recreational activities can be passive or active, an individual or a group activity.
2. Recreational activities range from cultural pursuits such as museums or theaters, to sports or outdoor recreation such as amusement parks, community centers, playgrounds, and libraries. These services involve various levels of government.
3. National parks preserve exceptional lands for public use, emphasizing the protection of their ecosystems and endangered plant and animal species and honoring historical sites. Two of the best known of the current 367 parks in the United States include Yellowstone and Yosemite national parks.
4. Today, city governments are increasingly expected to provide recreational facilities such as golf courses, swimming pools, picnic areas, and playgrounds as a community service.
5. Commercial recreation—for example, theme parks, clubs, and attractions—involves a profit for the supplier of the recreational activity.

6. Clubs are places where members gather for social, recreational, professional, or fraternal reasons. There are many different types of clubs such as country clubs or city clubs, according to the interests they represent to their members.

7. Noncommercial recreation includes governmental and nonprofit agencies, such as voluntary organizations, campus, armed forces, employee recreation, and recreation for special populations such as the physically challenged.

Review Exercises

1. Define recreation and its importance to human wellness. What factors affect an individual's decision to participate in recreational activities?
2. Describe the origin of government-sponsored recreation in consideration of the origin and purpose of national parks.
3. Briefly describe the difference between commercial and noncommercial recreation.
4. Briefly explain the purpose of a theme park and the purpose of clubs.
5. Explain the concept of recreation for special populations.

Key Words and Concepts

Clubs
Commercial recreation
Government-sponsored recreation
Leisure
National parks
National Parks Service
Noncommercial recreation
Recreation
Recreation for special populations
Theme parks
Voluntary organizations
Wellness

Notes

[1] Douglas M. Knudson, *Outdoor Recreation.* New York: Macmillan, 1980, p. 1.
[2] Bruno Hans Geba, *Being at Leisure, Playing at Life: A Guide to Health and Joyful Living.* La Mesa, California: Leisure Science Systems International, 1985, p. 19.
[3] Ibid., p. 66.
[4] Janet R. MacClean, J. Peterson, and D. Martin, *Recreation and Leisure: The Changing Scene,* 4th ed. New York: John Wiley and Sons, 1985, p. 72.
[5] Michael Chubb and Holly R. Chubb, *One Third of Our Time: An Introduction to Recreation Behavior and Resources.* New York: John Wiley and Sons, 1981, p. 191.
[6] Ibid.
[7] Knudson, op. cit., pp. 7–8.
[8] This section draws on information supplied by the National Parks Service.
[9] Knudson, op. cit., p. 261.
[10] Richard Kraus, *Recreation and Leisure in Modern Society,* 3rd ed. Glenview, Ill.: Scott, Foresman, 1984, pp. 159–160.
[11] MacLean, op. cit., p. 220.
[12] Ady Milman, "Theme Parks and Recreation," *VNR's Encyclopedia of Hospitality and Tourism.* New York: Van Nostrand Reinhold, 1993, p. 934.
[13] Other prominent theme parks and attractions are Knott's Berry Farm, Universal Studios, and Six Flags over America.
[14] Richard Martin, "Tradition Gives Way to Reform," *Nation's Restaurant News, 23,* 4, January 23, 1989, p. F-7.
[15] Personal interview with Joe Purdue, Club Managers Association of America, January 1995.
[16] Ted E. White, *Club Operations and Management.* Boston: CBI Publishing, 1979, pp. 6–7.
[17] Ibid., p. 17.

[18]Ibid.

[19]Stephen Birmingham, *America's Secret Aristocracy.* New York: Berkeley Books, 1990, p. 209.

[20]John C. Crossley and Lynn M. Jamieson, *Introduction to Commercial Recreation.* Champaign, Ill.: Sagamore Publishing, 1988, p. 248.

[21]Kraus, op. cit., p. 213.

[22]Richard Kraus and John Shank, *Therapeutic Recreation Service: Principles and Practices,* 4th ed. Dubuque, Iowa: Wm. C. Brown, 1983, p. 143.

[23]Ibid.

The Gaming Entertainment Industry

11

After reading and studying this chapter you should be able to do the following:

✔ Outline the history of the gaming entertainment industry
✔ Describe the various activities related to gaming entertainment
✔ Explain how gaming entertainment is converging with other aspects of the hospitality business
✔ List the most popular games on the casino floor
✔ Discuss the controversies surrounding the gaming entertainment industry

One of the most significant developments in the hospitality industry during the past two decades has been the astounding growth of the casino industry and its convergence with the lodging and hospitality industries. What has emerged from this development is an entirely new arena of hospitality known as the gaming entertainment industry. With its rapid expansion in North America and throughout the world, new opportunities have been created for hospitality careers. This chapter explores the gaming entertainment industry and details exciting developments yet to come in this dynamic and controversial segment of the hospitality business.

Gaming Entertainment Defined

The gaming industry includes a whole range of activities including casinos (both land-based and riverboats), card rooms, charitable games, lottery operated games, and wagering on greyhound and horse races. The gaming industry as a whole is larger than most people can believe. Over five hundred billion dollars (that is right, almost a half-trillion dollars), is wagered, or bet, on games or races every year. This total amount bet is what is called the "handle" in the gaming industry, and is often a misunderstood concept. When a customer places a bet in any type of gaming activity, sometimes they win and sometimes they lose. The total amount of all bets is the "handle," and the net amount of spending by the customer is termed "win" by the gaming industry. Annual industry win, some forty-eight million dollars, is much lower than industry handle, and represents actual consumer spending for gaming activities. Casinos account for about half of the U.S. gaming win, with lotteries following close behind. Lotteries and casinos together make up around 85 percent of consumer spending in the gaming industry.[1]

For the purposes of this chapter, the term *gaming entertainment* refers to one subset of the gaming industry, namely the casino industry. What used to be known as the casino business is now known as gaming entertainment. The dramatic growth of this part of the hospitality business has brought with it significant changes in how businesses in this industry operate and what they offer their guests. The changes have been so great that a new name needed to be created to accurately describe all of the amenities this industry provides.

What is the difference between gambling and gaming then? Gambling is playing a game of risk for the thrill of the "action" and the chance of making money. True gamblers spend a great deal of time learning and understanding a favorite game of risk and enjoying its subtle attributes, and they find an enjoyable challenge in trying to "beat the house" or win more than they lose from a casino. A gambler has little interest in anything other than the casino floor and the games it offers. It is true that the 60 million visitors who come to Las Vegas and Atlantic City, and the hundreds of thousands who frequent casino operations in twenty-six states, love the green felt tables, the whirling roulette wheels, the feel of the chips, and the thrill of the game. The rows of colorful slot machines sounding out musical tones and flashing lights, the distant sounds of someone hitting a jackpot, and bells ringing and guests shouting creates an environment of excitement and anticipation that can only be found on the casino floor.

Not long ago, the presence of a slot machine or a blackjack table was all that was needed to bring in the visitors. However, with the rapid spread of casinos throughout North America, this is no longer true. The competitive nature of the casino business has created a bigger, better product to meet the needs of their guests. As Steve Wynn, Mirage Resorts CEO, puts it, now the casino floor is "a thing which people pass on their way to visit the things that really matter to them." The product that has evolved over the past decade is what is called gaming entertainment.

Gaming entertainment offers games of risk only as part of a total package of entertainment and leisure time activities. Gaming entertainment serves a customer base of "social gamblers," customers who play a game of risk as a form of entertainment and a social activity, combining gambling with many other activities during their visit. Social gamblers, by this definition, are interested in many of the amenities of the gaming entertainment operation and take part in many diverse activities during a stay. Gaming entertainment refers to the casino gaming business and all of its aspects, including hotel operations, entertainment offerings, retail shopping, recreational activities, and other types of operations in addition to wagering on the gaming floor. The heart of gaming entertainment is what Glen Schaeffer, president of Circus Circus, has dubbed the "entertainment megastore" with thousands of rooms; dynamic, interesting, exterior architecture; nongaming attractions—that is, a building someone can design a vacation around, with 100,000 square feet or more of casino at its core. Schaeffer has said this product "is to tourism what the Pentium chip is to technology," a dynamic new tourism product that serves as a destination attraction. Gaming entertainment is the business of hospitality and entertainment with a core strength in casino gaming, also known as the global hospitality-gaming-entertainment market.

According to this definition, a gaming entertainment business always has a casino floor area that offers various games of risk and that serves as the focal point for marketing to and attracting guests. Next in importance to the guests is high-quality food and beverage operations. Gaming entertainment is one of the last hospitality concepts to support the full-service, table-side gourmet restaurant, in addition to the lavish buffet offerings that many casino locations offer. The number of foodservice concepts is wide and diverse—from signature restaurants featuring famous chefs, to ethnic offerings, to quick-service, franchised outlets. The gaming entertainment industry offers unlimited career opportunities in restaurant management and the culinary arts that were unheard of just a decade ago.

Gaming entertainment also goes hand-in-hand with the lodging industry, because hotel rooms are part of the package. Full-service hotels are part and parcel of gaming entertainment. Rooms, food and beverage, convention services, banquet facilities, health spas, recreation, and other typical hotel amenities support gaming entertainment. Most of the largest and most complex hotels in the world are found in gaming entertainment venues, a number of which are described in detail later in this chapter.

So far we have discussed gaming entertainment as a place to gamble on the casino floor, eat and drink, have a place to sleep and relax, and maybe do some business. But gaming entertainment offers much more. The entertainment offerings range from live performances by the most famous entertainers to production shows that use the latest high-tech wizardry. Gaming entertainment encompasses theme parks and thrill rides, museums, and cultural centers. The most popular gaming entertainment destinations are designed around a central theme that includes the architecture and the operations.[2]

Unlike its predecessor, the casino business, the gaming entertainment business has numerous revenue-generating activities. Gaming revenue is produced from casino win, or the money guests spend on the casino floor. The odds of any casino game favor the house, some more than others. Casino win is the cost of gambling to guests, who often win over the house in the short run, and are therefore willing to place bets and try their luck.

Nongaming revenue comes from sources that are not related to wagering on the casino floor. As the gaming entertainment concept continues to emphasize activities other than gambling, nongaming revenue is increasing in importance. Gaming revenues for Las Vegas, as a percentage of total revenues, have been declining for the past twenty years and now make up just slightly more than half of total revenues. Hotel room revenues in Las Vegas make up about 20 percent of total revenues and other nongaming revenues make up 11 percent of total revenue. This is what gaming entertainment is truly about—hospitality and entertainment based on the attraction of a casino.

What forms does gaming entertainment take? The megaresorts of Las Vegas and Atlantic City garner the most publicity as the meccas of the gaming entertainment industry. However, there are smaller properties throughout Nevada and other casino based businesses in twenty-six states and seven Canadian provinces. These casinos take the form of commercially operated businesses, both privately and publicly held. Some are land-based, meaning the casinos are housed in regular buildings. Others are riverboats that cruise up and down a river, or barges that are moored in water and do not cruise, called dockside casinos. Casinos are also operated by Native American tribes on their reservations and tribal lands. These are land-based casinos and are often as complex as any operation in Las Vegas. Gaming entertainment is also popular on cruise ships as part of the cruise vacation product or on what is called cruises to nowhere, where gaming and entertainment on board the ship are the main attraction.

There is strong support for gaming in the marketplace as an entertainment activity. Thirty-two percent of U.S. households gamble in casinos, an increase of 11 million households since earlier in the decade. U.S. households make 176 million visits annually to casinos. According to market research, more than 90 percent of U.S. adults say casino entertainment is acceptable for themselves or others. Sixty-two percent of U.S. adults say casino entertainment is acceptable for anyone, and 30 percent say it is acceptable for others but not themselves. Only eight percent of Americans say casino entertainment is not acceptable for anyone.[3]

The demographic makeup of the typical gaming entertainment guest has remained consistent during the past several years. In comparison to the average

American, casino players tend to have higher levels of income and education and are more likely to hold white-collar jobs. The customer profile of Las Vegas has gotten younger, and people who spend money want a total entertainment experience. Gaming entertainment operators are becoming more retail-driven and try to bring people in with a new hotel, magic shop, exclusive restaurants, or other shops. And guests have responded to these efforts. According to the latest Las Vegas Visitor Profile Study, the average visitor to Las Vegas stays 3.7 nights, budgets $580 for gambling, and spends $58 per night on lodging, $111 on food and drink, $38 on local transportation, $63 on shopping, $27 on shows, and another $7 on sightseeing. The average bet among those who play table games is usually a little more than $12.

Knowing the customers and their preferences is becoming critical in the gaming entertainment business. For example, Harrah's Entertainment, aiming to become America's first national-brand casino, created a Total Gold players' card. Gamblers accumulate points for their computer-monitored play. The card is then used to dispense cash back to players or vouchers good for complimentary rewards at any of its thirteen U.S. casinos. Most casino companies have similar players' clubs that operate like the airlines' frequent-flier programs. But Harrah's Entertainment Inc. became the first gaming entertainment chain to "comp," or redeem, those points systemwide. For instance, players can earn cash-value points gambling in Kansas City and then cash them in toward the price of a hotel room at Harrah's Las Vegas casino. Harrah's believes that linking the Total Gold card to a computer database of its estimated 6 million customers nationwide elevates the gaming entertainment firm to a new level of marketing sophistication.

Historical Review of Gaming Entertainment

Las Vegas—the name alone summons images of millions of neon lights, elaborate shows, outrageous performers, and bustling casinos, where millions are won and lost every night. Las Vegas is all of that, but much more. This city represents the American dream. A dusty watering hole less than seventy years ago, it has been transformed into one of the most elaborate cities in the world and one of the hottest vacation spots for the entire family. Las Vegas is second only to Walt Disney World as the favorite vacation destination in the United States.

The gaming entertainment business has its roots in Las Vegas. From the early 1940s until 1978, Las Vegas had a monopoly on the casino business, not the gaming entertainment business. Casinos had no hotel rooms, entertainment, or other amenities. The hotels that existed were just a place to sleep when a guest was not on the casino floor. This was the era when a slot machine or a blackjack table was enough to attract guests to the operation. Regulatory reforms of casino gaming, such as the development of centralized gaming control by powerful regulatory agencies, were an important development during these early years. These include the Gaming Control Board and Nevada Gaming Commission. There were strict rules established as to who and what must be licensed.

A number of state-run lotteries were established during the 1960s when states began to realize that large revenues could be gained from lottery gaming. In the mid-1970s, a federal Commission on the Review of the National Policy Toward Gambling issued a report affirming that the legalization and control of gambling activity is a matter for the jurisdiction of state governments. The legal status of gaming is not the same as other businesses. Gaming is said to be a "privileged" business. Those who conduct most common types of businesses have a "right" to do so. There is no "right" to conduct a gaming business. The states have broad authority to regulate gaming. To exercise the full extent of this power, however, the legislature must exercise it by granting broad power to regulatory authorities.

Casino gambling, seen as a desperate remedy for Atlantic City's severe economic situation at the time, was approved by a voter referendum in a statewide ballot in November 1976.[4] Following the referendum, casino gambling was legalized in the state of New Jersey by the Casino Control Act. The state looked to the casino hotel industry to invest capital, create jobs, pay taxes, and attract tourists, thus revitalizing the economy and creating a financial environment in which urban redevelopment could occur. The Act initiated a number of fees and taxes specific to the casino hotel business that would provide revenues to support regulatory costs, to fund social services for the disabled and the elderly throughout the state, and to provide investment funds for the redevelopment of Atlantic City. The Casino Control Act created the Casino Control Commission, whose purpose was not only to ensure the success and integrity of the Atlantic City casino industry, but also to carry out the objective of reversing the city's economic fortunes.

Sensing that the objectives of the Casino Control Act were being fulfilled in New Jersey, and wanting similar benefits for their state, but not wanting land-based casino gambling, Iowa legalized riverboat casinos thirteen years later. They were followed in rapid succession by Illinois, Mississippi, Louisiana, Missouri, and Indiana. Most recently, Michigan voters approved three land-based casinos for Detroit. With the spread of the casino industry throughout the United States and Canada, the competitive nature of the industry began to create a need for what is now known as gaming entertainment with the addition of noncasino attractions. Gaming entertainment is, therefore, a natural evolution of the casino industry.

Native American Gaming

In *California* v. *Cabazon Band of Mission Indians et al.* (1987), the Supreme Court decided 6–3 that once a state has legalized any form of gambling, the Native Americans in that state have the right to offer and self-regulate the same games, without government restrictions. The state of California and the county of Riverside had sought to impose local and state regulations on card and bingo clubs operated by the Cabazon and Morongo Bands of Mission Indians. These court decisions were unequivocal in their recognition of the rights of tribes with regard to certain gaming activities.

Congress, which some observers say was alarmed by the prospect of tribal gaming going out of control, responded to these court decisions by passing the *Indian Gaming Regulatory Act of 1988* (IGRA). The IGRA provides a framework by which games are conducted to protect both the tribes and the general public. For example, the IGRA outlines criteria for approval of casino management contracts entered into by tribes and establishes civil penalties for violation of its provisions. The act clearly is a compromise as it balances the rights of sovereign tribal nations to conduct gaming activities with the rights of the federal and state governments to regulate activities within their borders.

The three objectives of the IGRA were to (a) provide a statutory basis for the operation of gaming by Native American tribes as a means of promoting tribal economic development, self-sufficiency, and strong tribal governments; (b) provide a statutory basis for the regulation of gaming by a Native American tribe adequate to shield it from organized crime and other corrupting influences; and (c) establish an independent regulatory authority the National Indian Gaming Commission (NIGC), for governing gaming activity on Native American lands.

IGRA defines three different kinds, or "classes," of Native American gaming activities: (a) Class I gaming, consisting of social games played solely for prizes of minimum value or traditional forms of Native American gaming; (b) Class II gaming, consisting of bingo, games similar to bingo, and card games explicitly authorized by the laws of the state; and (c) Class III gaming, consisting of all forms of gaming that are neither Class I nor Class II gaming, and therefore including most of what are considered casino games.

The significance of the definition of Class III gaming activity is that it defines the games that (a) must be located in a state that permits such gaming for any purpose by any person, organization, or entity and (b) are conducted in conformance with a compact that states are required to negotiate "in good faith" with the tribes.

While the federal gaming law precludes state taxation, the tribes in several states have made voluntary payments and also negotiated payments to state governments under certain circumstances. Often tribes give local governments voluntary payments in recognition of services the tribe receives, and some pay revenues in exchange for permission to maintain a casino gambling monopoly in a state. In Michigan, Connecticut, and Louisiana, tribes have agreed to make payments to the state as part of their comprehensive compacts for casino gambling. In almost all the states, the tribes make payments to the state for state costs incurred in the process of regulation of the casinos as provided for in the negotiated agreements.

Gambling on Native American lands account for more than 11 percent of all the winnings from gambling in the United States. Approximately one dollar out of every four lost by players to casinos is lost at Native American casinos. There are 281 gaming facilities on reservation lands in thirty-two states, and Native American gaming has been the fastest growing sector of casino gaming in the United States. Additional Native American gaming is conducted by the First Nations Bands of Canada.

National Gambling Impact Study Commission

The need for better research concerning the controversies over casino entertainment, and gaming in general, has been recognized. The U.S. federal government has realized that gaming has become a major industry, but without a good understanding of its effect on the economy and society. On August 3, 1996, the National Gambling Impact and Policy Commission Act became a reality "when President Clinton signed the act into law. This act established a nine-member federal commission whose task is to conduct a two-year "comprehensive legal and factual study of the social and economic impacts of gambling in the United States." The commission, which will have the authority to hold hearings, administer oaths, hear testimony, receive evidence, employ an executive director and staff, and contract with outside research organizations, will focus on the following six distinct areas of concern:

✔ Review existing federal, state, local, and Native American tribal government policies and practices with respect to the legalization, or prohibition, of gambling, including a review of the costs of such policies and practices

✔ Study the relationship between gambling and crime, analyzing existing reinforcement and regulatory practices that seek to address such a relationship

✔ Assess pathological, or problem gambling, including its impact on individuals, families, businesses, social institutions, and the economy

✔ Review the general impact of gambling on society, including the role of advertising and the impact of gambling on depressed economic areas

✔ Assess the extent to which gambling provides revenue to government and the extent to which alternative revenue sources exist

✔ Study the interstate and international effects of gambling by electronic means, including the use of interactive technologies and the Internet

Size and Scope of Gaming Entertainment

The number of publicly traded gaming entertainment companies has recently tripled to a total of forty-five, with a market capitalization of $30 billion. Gaming entertainment is now big business.

Why is the gaming/entertainment industry growing so quickly? Basically, because people like to wager, and historically, there has been more demand than supply for wagering opportunities. As public acceptance of legalized gaming has grown, and state and local governments have permitted gaming entertainment establishments to open, supply is beginning to meet demand.

The gaming entertainment industry pays more than 2 billion dollars per year in gambling privilege taxes to state governments. Casino development has been credited with revitalizing economies through new capital investment, job creation, new tax revenue, and increased tourism. A 1996 study of the gaming entertainment industry by the Arthur Andersen consulting firm resulted in the following comments:

The casino gaming industry is clearly an important provider of jobs, wages and taxes to the U.S. economy. The jobs created are well paying which match the national average wage and exceed average wages of several other industries. In addition, the number of jobs created for every $1 million in reported revenues is significantly higher than several high-growth and other more ma-ture industries analyzed for purposes of comparison in this study. Unlike many other major U.S. industries that rely on foreign labor, casino gaming hires its employees principally from within the U.S. Furthermore, the casino gaming industry creates additional jobs in a number of domestic supplier businesses. These secondary impacts further ripple through the economy, ultimately im-pacting all industries across the length and breadth of the country.[5]

Casino gaming relies more heavily than most industries on domestic labor and domestic suppliers. Casino operations are relatively labor intensive, thus they create more direct jobs than those in other industries. For every $1 mil-lion in revenues, the casino gaming industry creates 13 direct jobs, far ex-ceeding the numbers created by other industries such as the soft drink, cellu-lar phone services, video cassette sales and rentals, and cable television services industries. In fact, it is the spending by casino employees, as opposed to spend-ing by new tourists drawn to a region by a casino, that accounts for a large percentage of casino's positive impacts on overall consumer spending.[6]

Casino gaming has created more than 700,000 direct and indirect jobs with wages of approximately $21 billion. When unemployment is high and an area is in economic despair, casinos create jobs. Atlantic City created 40,000 jobs and evened out seasonality of employment in that economy.

Casino gaming companies pay an average of 12 percent of total revenues in taxes. Casino gaming companies contribute to federal, state, and local govern-ments through gaming-related and other taxes. Direct taxes include property, federal/state income, and construction sales and use taxes, which all industries pay, and gaming taxes, which are levied only on the gaming industry at rates ranging from 6.25 percent to 20 percent of gaming revenues.

Although casino gaming companies pay a particularly high percent of their total revenues, federal taxes represent less than 18 percent of the total tax bur-den, with the remainder being paid at the state and local levels. Gaming taxes, by far the largest tax paid by the industry, are often specifically designated by state and local governments for expenditure on such things as infrastructure im-provements, education, and benefits for the elderly and disabled.

The casino entertainment industry, a relatively new part of the hospitality business, has some controversial elements to it. The majority of people find a visit to a casino enjoyable and entertaining and have no objections to gaming entertainment businesses. However, others have strong objections to casino gaming based on their moral beliefs, or opinions, that there are social costs as-sociated with gaming entertainment operations. Although the moral beliefs of others can never be questioned, the social costs of casino entertainment should be reviewed. The two major concerns associated with casino entertainment are the impact on crime, both organized crime and street crime, and the impact on gambling addictions as a result of the spread of casino entertainment.

Organized Crime and Casinos

The common assumption that casinos increase crime is partially grounded in stereotypes from the early years of the industry. There was an irrefutable con-nection between organized crime and several participants in the commercial casino industry during the first two decades of its existence in Nevada. However, confusion persists in the minds of many about the present structure of casino ownership and the character of casino regulation. Links to organized crime, which have some historical relevance, are not substantiated by current research. Experience has taught us that issues of political corruption and organized crime are more likely to be by-products of illegal gambling than of well-regulated legal commercial gaming. This reality, along with the corporatization of commercial gaming industries and the professionalization of regulatory bodies, has undermined the crime argument against gambling.

Casino operators have proven they can, with proper controls, manage their business with integrity. In this way, they have overcome the stigma attached to casino gaming, ensuring that their industry has become part of the hospitality/entertainment sector. Regulatory and enforcement agencies must be well funded and professionally organized to carry out complicated background investigations, regulation, and enforcement. These activities can be extremely expensive. For example, the budget for the New Jersey Division of Gaming Enforcement is more than $36 million while the budget for New Jersey's Casino Control Commission is nearly $26 million.

Since the early 1970s, the ownership of casinos in America has predominantly shifted to publicly held companies whose shares are traded on the major stock exchanges. For example, the five largest in terms of annual revenue (Caesars World, Circus Circus Enterprises, Hilton, Mirage, and Harrah's Entertainment) are all traded on the New York Stock Exchange. Of the next fourteen largest casino companies, four are traded on the NYSE, two on the AMEX, and eight on NASDAQ. As publicly traded entities, these companies are answerable to the Securities and Exchange Commission, as well as to the gaming commissions in their respective states and to local law enforcement. The largest of these companies are in the portfolios of major institutional investors such as Prudential Insurance Co., Kemper Financial Services, First Interstate Bancorp, and the Oppenheimer Group.

Casino entertainment is one of the most tightly regulated industries in the United States. Nevada employs 372 regulators at a cost of $19 million, while New Jersey employs 650 regulators at a cost of $50 million. These costs are paid for by the casino industry through regulatory fees.[7]

Organizations that supply labor and goods to the casino hotel industry have had a different history. In 1991, after lengthy investigations, Atlantic City's local chapter of the Hotel Employees and Restaurant Employees International Union was forced to accept the appointment of a federal monitor with broad disciplinary and oversight powers. Union officials found to have ties to organized crime were removed from office. In 1995, the national office of the same union was also taken over by a federal overseer.

Street Crime and Casinos

With the opening of casinos in Atlantic City in 1978, and despite a strengthened police force, the growth in the crime index of Atlantic City began to exceed that of the state as a whole. As casinos opened, crime rates began to rise. Between 1977 and 1984, total violent crimes increased by more than 116 percent. In 1977, before the first casino opened, the Atlantic City Metropolitan Statistical Area (MSA) ranked fiftieth among the nation's 257 MSAs in per capita violent and property crime. In 1981, the Atlantic City MSA was ranked first. Overall, from 1977 to 1990, the crime rate in that city rose by an incredible 230 percent. This was more than 25 times the single-digit growth rate of 9 percent reported from the remainder of the state of New Jersey and has required the city to increase its police department's budget by 300 percent. The Atlantic City experience is often cited by those who contend that casinos promote street crime.

Uniform crime statistics fail to take into account the dramatic influx of visitors to Atlantic City. Conventional crime-rate statistics are based on resident populations. Atlantic City has so many visitors that its actual population is always considerably higher than what is used to compute crime rates. The consequence of using crime rate statistics based on resident populations, and not adjusted for extremely high counts of visitors, is an artificial inflation of those rates. Typically, when the number of tourists is accounted for, the crime rate in casino jurisdictions is not significantly different from other noncasino metropolitan areas that entertain a large number of tourists and other visitors.

Gambling Addictions

The American Psychiatric Association defines pathological gambling as a chronic and progressive failure to resist impulses to gamble, and gambling behavior that compromises, disrupts, or damages personal, family, or vocational pursuits. While the terms pathological and compulsive are technically not synonymous, professionals and laypersons use them interchangeably.

While pathological gambling does not involve the use of a substance, research conducted by numerous scholars has noted a similarity with other addictive behaviors. For example, pathological gamblers state that they seek action as well as money, or a means of escaping from problems—an aroused, euphoric state comparable to the high derived from cocaine or other drugs. Action means excitement, thrills and tension—"when the adrenaline is flowing." The desire to remain in action is so intense that many gamblers will go for days without sleeping, without eating, and even without going to the bathroom. Pathological gamblers, like alcoholics and drug addicts, are preoccupied with seeking out gambling; they gamble longer than intended and with more money than intended.

Pathological gambling was originally recognized in the International Classification of Disease of the World Health Organization in 1979, and in the Diagnostic and Statistical Manual (DSM) of the American Psychiatric Association in 1980. The DSM is currently in its fourth revision (DSM-IV) and represents the most recent clinical definition of pathological gambling. The DSM-IV criteria provide guidelines for mental health professionals to diagnose patients. Of the ten diagnostic criteria, a pathological gambler meets five or more.

The phenomenon of pathological gambling is a very personal one. It is the extent to which gambling interferes with one's life, one's job, one's family, or some aspect of daily living, that determines whether one has a gambling problem. It is only indirectly related to the amount of money one wagers and the type of gambling activity in which it is wagered. None of the diagnostic criteria measures the amount of money that is gambled or the form of the gambling activity. The depth of despair to which a pathological gambler may fall can be truly disturbing. The most effective means of dealing with the problem is joining a chapter of Gamblers Anonymous (GA). Research of GA members shows an involvement in white-collar crimes such as embezzlement and insurance fraud, which are difficult to quantify.

Lifetime prevalence rates for pathological gambling range from 0.1 percent to 2.7 percent. The studies that have measured current prevalence rates for pathological gambling show that the illness is confined to between 0.5 percent and 1.2 percent of the population. Those who have some problems with gambling abuse, but are not yet pathological, are scored as "problem gamblers," with lifetime prevalence rates of less than one-half of one percent.

Casino proponents argue that the type of clientele that are attracted to casino operations are less likely to become compulsive gamblers, while casino opponents maintain that an increased accessibility to any form of gambling increases the incidence of compulsive gambling. At the least, there appears to be some relationship between casinos and compulsive gambling, and there appears to be little disagreement on this point.

Progressive casino entertainment companies show a high degree of social responsibility toward dealing with the problem of underage and pathological gambling. A benchmark study on proactive programs to deal with gambling addictions within the casino entertainment industry is found in the Responsible Gaming Resource Guide published by the American Gaming Association.[8] The programs discussed within this publication include (a) an acknowledgment, through mission statements and policy guidelines, that no form of gambling is free of compulsive gambling and that compulsive gambling is a significant mental health problem; (b) an acknowledgment of the responsibility to actively prevent underage people from gambling at the facility, especially because research has found high rates of compulsive gambling among teenagers; (c) the provision of educational information for employees and customers concerning the signs and symptoms of compulsive gambling and where help is available; (d) the training of supervisory personnel to identify and intervene with compulsive gamblers; (e) the creation of an internal structure such as a job position or a committee that examines, on an on-going basis, issues related to compulsive gambling; and (f) the acknowledgment of the responsibility to provide some financial support to qualified professional organizations to conduct education/information research and/or treatment programs in the community relating to compulsive gambling.

The phenomenon of gambling addiction is one that the casino entertainment industry takes seriously. With the rapid growth of the gaming industry in general, and the casino entertainment specifically, research into the causes of gambling addiction and effective treatment is only now beginning. The National Center for Responsible Gambling is a nonprofit research and education foundation created by the members of the American Gaming Association. The center is funding gambling addiction research and programs through which comprehensive education, prevention, and assistance treatment strategies can be developed and implemented.

Key Players in the Industry

The leading participants in the gaming entertainment business are Mirage Resorts, Harrah's Entertainment, Hilton Hotels Corporation, ITT Corporation, Circus Circus, and MGM Grand. They all have diverse property portfolios and solid business practices and are well respected by Wall Street.

Mirage Resorts operates casinos primarily in Las Vegas. The company's Mirage property is a tropical-themed casino and hotel that features a volcano erupting at regular intervals. Its Treasure Island casino and hotel has a pirate theme, highlighted by live sea battles between a pirate ship and a British frigate. Other Las Vegas casino/hotel properties include the Golden Nugget (located in downtown Las Vegas) and the Monte Carlo (50 percent owned through a joint venture with Circus Circus). The company is spending well over $1.5 billion on the construction of its Bellagio property on the Las Vegas Strip, a massive facility the company wants to bill as the most luxurious casino property in Las Vegas.

Harrah's Entertainment operates casinos in major gaming markets throughout the United States. Its casinos are located in Reno, Lake Tahoe, Las Vegas, and Laughlin, Nevada; and in Atlantic City, New Jersey. One of the most geographically diverse casino companies, it also operates riverboat and dockside casinos in Illinois, Louisiana, Missouri, and Mississippi; and Native American reservation casinos in Arizona and Washington. In all, the company operates more than 700,000 square feet of gaming space. Although Harrah's also operates nearly 6,500 hotel rooms and more than 50 restaurants, it derives nearly 80 percent of its revenues from its casinos. Harrah's Entertainment, Inc. is the Premier Name in Casino Entertainment. The Harrah's brand was born in Reno, Nevada, in the late 1930s and has since grown to become the largest casino entertainment company in North America. Harrah's history is a rich combination of casino expertise and quality, which was launched in northern Nevada and expanded across the continent. Today, Harrah's is a $1.5 billion dollar company, publicly traded on the New York Stock Exchange. The gaming division of the former Promus Companies is now a separate, publicly traded company, with seventeen properties in nine states and one foreign country, and 23,000 employees.

Hilton owns, manages, and/or franchises more than 220 hotels around the world. Hilton, with its $3-billion purchase of Bally Entertainment, is the nation's largest gambling business. U.S. gaming operations include three casino hotels in Las Vegas, two in Atlantic City, two in Reno, and one in Laughlin; a riverboat casino in New Orleans; and interest in a Canadian casino.

Formerly a superconglomerate involved in everything from white bread to Chilean politics, ITT Corp. is focused on the hospitality, gambling, and information services industries. It owns the Sheraton chain, with more than 400 hotels, and the three Caesar's World hotel/casinos. ITT's business information services include ITT World Directories, which produces telephone directories in

Personal Profile: Stephen A. Wynn

Chairman and CEO of Mirage Resorts, Las Vegas

Hotels magazine selected Stephen Wynn as the ninth independent hotelier of the world for playing a major role in transforming Las Vegas from a gambling venue for adults into a multidimensional resort destination for the whole family and also for managing the Mirage, one of the world's best-run megahotels.

The $750 million, 3,000-room Mirage resort casino changed the face of Las Vegas. Mirage has fine gourmet restaurants, a huge lagoonlike pool, an atrium filled with palm trees, a children's game arcade and, of course, a first-rate casino.

Wynn also operates Treasure Island, the midcasino hotel, which beckons tourists inside every night with a sign featuring a smiling pirate. Treasure Island has free street-side mock battles nightly, complete with cannon fire and a sinking ship. When the show is over, many in the crowd walk over the dock into the thirty-six-story hotel's casino, seven restaurants, and retail shops. The hotel has a pool, spa, game arcade, showrooms, convention center, and two wedding chapels—with built-in video cameras.

Steve also runs two other casino-hotels: the 2,000-room Golden Nugget in downtown Vegas and the 300-room Golden Nugget in Laughlin, Nevada. With close to 8,200 rooms, Mirage, Inc., is ranked number sixty-one among the world's largest hotel chains.

Steve has 18,000 highly motivated employees who keep guestrooms, casinos, and other attractions impeccable, according to industry analysts. The Mirage properties are exceptional, drawing a commanding share of a demanding market with an exceptionally high company-wide occupancy.

Wynn began his career in Vegas at age twenty-five with a degree in English literature from the University of Pennsylvania. In a very short time, he became an executive and part owner of the Frontier Hotel. He owned and operated a Nevada wine-importing company from 1969 to 1972. He then turned a real estate deal into a profit, which allowed him to begin a major investment in Golden Nugget in 1972. (The Golden Nugget was renamed the Mirage in 1991.)

Stephen A. Wynn

In 1973, Wynn acquired control of the company, which, at the time, had no rooms. In 1980, he opened the $140 million Golden Nugget/Atlantic City, which he sold to Bally Corporation for $400 million in 1987. That year, Wynn started building the Mirage.

Stephen Wynn's latest adventure is the $1.4 billion, 3,500-room Bellagio, opened in 1998. Bellagio features a $35 million water show in a man-made lake, a $77 million water-themed show produced by Cirque du Soleil, and shopping provided by Armani, Tiffany, Gucci, and Channel. He also invested $60 million in art for the new Bellagio Resort because he wants to attract art lovers and other chic people who are looking for more than a prizefight. In addition, Wynn has plans for a $500 million-plus resort in Biloxi, Mississippi, and another resort in Atlantic City, New Jersey.

Wynn is confident that both his projects and Las Vegas will continue to thrive. This can be seen through the numbers tracking the performance of Mirage Resort, Inc. The following information compares the third quarter statistics of 1996 and 1997.

Mirage Resorts, Inc.
For the Periods Ended September 30

	Three Months	
	1997	1996
Net revenues*	$369,153	$338,552
Company-wide table games win percentage	25.5%	19.2%
Company-wide occupancy of standard guest rooms	98.7%	99.2%
Average standard guest room rate**	$86	$88

*Dollars in thousands, except room rate amounts.
**Cash rate (i.e., excluding complimentary accommodations) at the company's Las Vegas hotels.
Source: Mirage Resorts, Inc.

seven countries, and ITT Educational Services (83 percent-owned), which offers vocational and technical training. The company has agreed to be bought by the much smaller Starwood Lodging, a real estate investment trust, following a takeover battle instigated by Hilton Hotels' unsolicited offer for ITT.

ITT purchased Caesars World Inc. in 1994, including Caesars Palace in Las Vegas, Caesars Tahoe, Caesars Atlantic City and other operations, thereby merging the lodging and gaming entertainment businesses.

Circus Circus is betting its hotels and casinos will be big winners. Named for its carnival-themed Circus Circus Hotel, the company owns or operates casinos and hotels in three states. The company owns nine casino/hotels in Nevada, including the Circus Circus, Excalibur, and Luxor in Las Vegas; 50 percent stakes in three casino/hotels in Las Vegas, Reno, and Elgin, Illinois; and two casino-only operations in Las Vegas and Tunica, Mississippi. It also operates a casino for another owner in Las Vegas. The company is continuing to build gambling resorts for middle-income families and is developing a mile-long strip at the south end of the Las Vegas strip with hotels, casinos, a retail complex, and entertainment facilities.

MGM Grand prides itself on operating the world's largest hotel/casino. The MGM Grand Hotel, located on 113 acres along the Las Vegas strip, has more than 5,000 rooms and a 171,500-square-foot casino with some 3,700 slot machines, about 160 table games, some 50 shops, a theme park, and a special-events center featuring acts such as Neil Diamond and Luther Vandross. Across the strip is the 2,000-room New York-New York Hotel and Casino, MGM Grand's 50 percent joint venture with Primadonna Resorts. MGM Grand also runs a hotel/casino in northern Australia that caters to Asian gamblers. The company has agreed to develop casinos in Atlantic City, New Jersey, and South Africa. Kirk Kerkorian owns a 61.6 percent share of MGM Grand.

Two other gaming entertainment companies, Boyd Gaming and Grand Casinos, Inc. are expanding rapidly into markets across the United States.

Boyd Gaming operates ten gaming and hotel facilities in four states. The company's six Las Vegas properties are The Stardust Resort and Casino, Sam's Town Hotel and Gambling Hall, the Eldorado Casino, the Joker's Wild Casino, the California Hotel and Casino, and the Fremont Hotel and Casino. Outside Nevada, Boyd operates the Sam's Town Hotel and Gambling Hall, a dockside gaming and entertainment complex in Tunica County, Mississippi; Sam's Town Casino, a Kansas City, Missouri, casino complex; and the Silver Star Hotel and Casino, a land-based gaming and entertainment facility owned by the Choctaw Indians.

Grand Casinos, Inc. is a casino entertainment company that develops, constructs, and manages land-based and dockside casinos in emerging gaming markets. Grand Casinos, Inc. has been a publicly traded company since 1991 and is listed on the New York Stock Exchange under the trading symbol GND. The company currently owns and operates the three largest casino hotel resorts in the state of Mississippi, manages two land-based casinos in Louisiana, and manages two casino hotel resorts in Minnesota.

Exciting Gaming Entertainment Projects

The Mirage megaresort at the heart of the Las Vegas strip has a volcano that erupts every few minutes and a tropical rain forest with soaring palms and sparkling waterfalls. Guests checking into the hotel face a giant aquarium where live sharks swim. The pool is a tropical paradise of waterfalls and connected lagoons. The property contains a European shopping boulevard and a wide variety of themed food and beverage operations. There is meeting and convention space for up to 5,000 attendees. The showroom is the home of the famous magic and illusions of Siegfried & Roy and their white tigers. The resort is also the home of a family of Atlantic bottlenose dolphins.

Station Casino Kansas City is one of the largest floating casino operations in the world. The 140,000-square-foot, two-barge casino is home to 3,000 slot machines and 190 table games. In addition to the casino, the facility includes twelve restaurants, eleven lounges, a 200-room hotel, a 1,400-seat special events arena, a microbrewery, an arcade, a child-care center, and an eighteen-screen movie theater. The attractions at Station Casino are coordinated through a Victorian theme, including a cobblestone street that winds through a re-creation of Victorian-era Kansas City, complete with antiques and a hand-painted sky.

New York New York in Las Vegas is an eye-catching property with twelve hotel towers, each a replica of a Manhattan skyscraper. There is a Coney Island-style amusement area, a casino that feels like Central Park at dusk, a food court designed to simulate a Little Italy neighborhood, a 300-foot-long replica of the Brooklyn Bridge, and a 150-foot-tall model of the Statue of Liberty at the front of the resort. The property is jointly owned by MGM Grand and Primadonna Resorts.

Star Trek: The Experience attraction and outer-space themed SpaceQuest casino located in the Las Vegas Hilton is a $70 million joint venture of Hilton Corp. and the Paramount Parks Division of Viacom International Inc. The project targets

The famous aquarium behind the front desk at the Mirage in Las Vegas

baby boomers and Generation X customers interested in science fiction and space-related entertainment. The SpaceQuest, separate from the main casino, simulates a ride aboard a space station. Television screens create an illusion of space flight. Gaming equipment unique to the 20,000-square-foot SpaceQuest casino includes slot machines activated by breaking a light beam.

Wild Wild West Casino at Bally's Park Place in Atlantic City, New Jersey, is the city's first highly themed, entertainment-oriented, technologically advanced casino entertainment product. The casino has an 1880s frontier mining town, mountain scapes, model trains, animatronic characters, and colorful storefronts. There is a fifty-foot-high canyon with waterfalls, a talking gold prospector, and a wisecracking vulture perched on a twelve-foot-high cactus.

The Masquerade Village at the Rio Hotel & Casino in Las Vegas is a Tuscany village themed retail area with twenty stores and six restaurants, including a wine cellar tasting room. Its Masquerade Show in the Sky features five themed floats suspended from the ceiling that parade above the casino via an overhead track. Costumed entertainers and musicians perform from atop the floats and from other posts inside the casino during free shows throughout the day. Guests are invited to ride on the floats and participate in the shows.

Luxor Las Vegas, operated by Circus Circus, was constructed as a thirty-story pyramid and houses the world's largest atrium, measuring 29 million cubic feet. It also features a beam of light emanating from its peak that is so intense it can be seen as far away as Los Angeles, California. The 4,500 rooms are appointed in Egyptian architecture. The lobby area includes a life-sized replica of the great Temple of Ramses II and large Egyptian murals. The resort includes a museum containing reproductions of the items found in King Tutankhamen's tomb, which was discovered in 1922 by Howard Carter. The items are positioned exactly as they were found, according to records maintained by the Carter expedition. The

The registration area of the Luxor Las Vegas megaresort, with its Egyptian antiquity theme. The lobby is at the base of a thirty-story pyramid with the largest atrium in the world

Guests can observe the beer-making process at the Monte Carlo Pub & Brewery located in the Monte Carlo Resort & Casino in Las Vegas. Note the catwalk above is part of a function area used by the property for reception and cocktail parties to view the brewpub operations

resort also has a Theater of Time, the site of an IMAX 3D theater using the IMAX Personal Sound Environment headset, an advanced liquid crystal display technology for three-dimensional viewing.

Grand Casino Tunica, with the largest dockside casino between Las Vegas and Atlantic City, is located in Tunica County, Mississippi, just south of Memphis. The three-story, 140,000-square-foot gaming area is unlike any in the area. With more than 3,000 slot machines and 108 table games, guests can enjoy the atmosphere of the San Francisco Gold Rush, the New Orleans Mardi Gras, the Great American West of the 1870s, or an 1890s Mississippi riverboat town. Six restaurants, two entertainment lounges, a Kids Quest, a Grand Arcade, and a luxury hotel are located on this 2,000-acre site. There are plans to develop it into a premier destination resort.

The Monte Carlo Pub & Brewery, located in the Monte Carlo Resort & Casino in Las Vegas, is one of the largest brewpubs in the United States. Six different styles of Monte Carlo-labeled beer are regularly produced, including a light beer, an India pale ale, and an American-style, unfiltered wheat ale. The pub also features a traditional Irish stout, a rich amber ale, and a regular brewer's special. Gourmet, brick-oven pizzas and sausage platters, and a full line of salads and sandwiches are on the menu. Huge copper beer barrels and antique furnishings add to the brewpub's atmosphere. The hotel offers a meeting room and function area from which guests can get a bird's-eye view of the entire operation. The brewpub also features an outdoor patio that overlooks the lavish 21,000-square-foot Monte Carlo pool area, which includes a wave pool and an easy river ride.

Treasure Island megaresort's entrance is across a long wooden bridge that traverses the waters of Buccaneer Bay. Every ninety minutes each evening, cannon and musket fire are exchanged in a dramatic pyrotechnic battle between the pirate ship *Hispañiola* and the British frigate HMS *Britannia* in the middle of the bay. The showroom in this property is home to the world-famous performance troupe Cirque du Soleil, and features an unusual circus act with no animals but an overabundance of imagination.

Forum Shops at Caesars Palace draws an estimated 50,000 people a day and makes an average of $1,200 per square foot, far above the industry norm of $400.

The pirate battle in front of the Treasure Island megaresort. Thousands of guests to Las Vegas watch this show every ninety minutes in front of the hotel entrance

The Roman streetscape themed, half-million-square-foot retail area features the Festival Fountain Plaza, which incorporates animatronic statues of gods, such as Bacchus, Apollo, and Venus, with a fountain and light show. Another main feature is the Atlantic attraction, a fountain featuring animatronic figures that come to life during the Lost City of Atlantis laser light show that includes fire and other special effects. The backdrop for this attraction is a 50,000-gallon aquarium that can support 650 fish from 25 fish families. The Race for Atlantis ride uses a giant screen IMAX 3-D motion simulator, the first of its kind to combine IMAX's large format film making with 3-D computer animation, sound engineering, and motion simulation. The result is a multisensory experience that takes riders on an exhilarating chariot race through the legendary kingdom of Atlantis. Upscale retailers include Christian Dior, Versace, Niketown, a Virgin Megastore, and Wolfgang Puck's Spago restaurant. The FAO Schwarz store is the company's largest and features a 46-foot animatronic Trojan Horse.

Fremont Street Experience consists of a four-block long pedestrian mall light and sound show with sky parades that take place every two hours. A canopy known

The Fremont Street Experience in the downtown area of Las Vegas consists of a four-block long pedestrian mall light and sound show, with sky parades that take place every two hours

as a space frame, which is really a giant video-quality animation screen, covers the entire area. The light shows are broadcast on 2 million-plus light bulbs from end to end that can produce 40,000 shades of color. There is virtually no image, animated or actual, that cannot be produced. The clarity and depth are close to movie quality. Digital sound accompaniments come from a 54,000-watt sound system pumped through clusters of exposed speakers, forty in each block.

Foxwoods Resort Casino, near Ledyard, Connecticut, only a several-hour drive from New York City, is one of the largest gaming entertainment operations in the world. It is owned and managed by the Mashantucket Pequot Tribal Nation. There are two full-service hotels, restaurants and lounges, retail stores, amusement rides, and a museum and research center supporting the Pequot community.

Newest Projects of Gaming Entertainment

Bellagio is a megaresort soon to appear on the Las Vegas strip at a cost of more than $1.5 billion dollars, which is more than the initial construction cost of Disneyworld. The 3,000-room hotel is fronted with a nine-acre lake featuring 2,200 fountains that perform a choreographed water dance several times each evening. The lobby includes an art gallery containing $150 million in fine art, including works by Picasso, Renoir, and Rembrandt. The signature showroom is home to a $70-million creation by Cirque du Soleil performed on a stage submerged in water, and a 15,000-square-foot conservatory featuring a massive flower display with classical gardens and European fountains and pools.

ITT Caesars Riverboat at Bridgeport, Indiana, will be located on the Indiana side of the Ohio River, just west of Louisville, Kentucky. The vessel will be 450-feet long and 104-feet wide, with more than 80,000 square feet of casino space on four decks. The casino will carry 3,000 slot machines and 150 table games. The site of the new riverboat megaresort is a 232-acre tract of riverfront property that

The Bellagio in Las Vegas, a 3,000-room Mediterranean themed resort named after the Italian city on Lake Como. Steve Wynn, CEO of Mirage Resorts, promises that this hotel is "the most romantic hotel in the world."

includes a 500-room convention-style Sheraton hotel, upscale shopping mall, sports arena, IMAX theater, Magical Empire, attractions, and an eighteen-hole golf course. The terminal for the riverboat is 130,000 square feet and houses four restaurants and an adjacent children's theme park. To facilitate visits from Louisville across the river, the company is developing a "Caesars Chariots" gondola system that will transport customers up and over the Ohio River in sky cars. The people mover will carry 1,000 persons per hour.

The MGM Grand, a 5,000-room megaresort in Las Vegas, will be themed out as the "City of Entertainment." An area called the Studio Walk will resemble a Hollywood sound stage and feature a number of Hollywood landmarks, five restaurants, a food court, six retail stores, and a nightclub. The entrance to the resort is graced by a "liquid gold," six-story lion entry, fronting 80-foot entertainment walls that run multimedia and light shows continuously.

The Beau Rivage megaresort is the most magnificent resort on the Mississippi Gulf Coast and, perhaps, in the entire Southeast. This 32-story, 1,780-room resort, with its stately oak-tree-lined entrance, cascading fountains, lush formal gardens, and fragrant magnolias, graces acres of white sand beach overlooking the Gulf. As the newest Mirage Resorts property, Beau Rivage features twelve distinctive restaurants, an 85,000-square-foot casino, a 1,500-seat showroom, an elegantly appointed spa and salon, a shopping esplanade, and a 30,000-square-foot conference and convention center for banquets and business meetings, all under one roof.

Hilton Hotel Paris Casino Resort is a $700 million, 3,000-room operation inspired by the prominent landmarks of Paris, France, a city that draws about one-third as many visitors annually as Las Vegas. The project includes a half-sized, fifty-story replica of France's Eiffel Tower and an 85,000-square-foot casino. It has 130,000 square feet of casino space, a half-acre health spa, and a retail complex supplied by several French companies. An existing monorail that links the MGM Grand Hotel and Bally's Las Vegas (owned by Hilton) stops at a replica of a Paris Metro Station.

Las Vegas Sand's Venetian resort, casino, and convention complex is the largest megaresort ever planned. The $2 billion project includes 6,000 suites, each with 700 square feet of space, including sunken living rooms, two-line phones, and in-room fax machines. Inspired by the canals, bridges, and ancient architecture of Venice, Italy, the property includes a 1,200-foot replica of Venice's Grand Canal, which fronts 150 stores. The Venetian has two casinos of 100,000 square feet each.

The MGM Grand Detroit megaresort is planned as an art-deco complex constructed in downtown Detroit. In addition to a spacious 100,000-square-foot gaming area with 40-foot-high ceilings, the complex plans include a 36-story, 800-room hotel designed to be the Midwest's premier resort hotel; a diverse array of signature restaurant and retail facilities; a state-of-the-art, five-screen cineplex movie theater; approximately 70,000 square feet of convention, ballroom, and meeting facilities; a 1,200-seat showroom theater; and a climate-controlled parking garage.

Le Jardin is Atlantic City's newest megaresort with 2,000 rooms and three acres of vaulted glass atriums. Lush horticultural gardens change with the seasons. It will be springtime 365 days a year, taking the seasonality out of the Atlantic City gaming entertainment market.

Careers in Gaming Entertainment

Careers in the gaming entertainment industry are unlimited. Students of the industry who understand the multidisciplinary needs of the business find five initial career tracks in hotel operations, food and beverage operations, casino operations, retail, and entertainment operations.

Hotel Operations

The career opportunities in gaming entertainment hotel operations are much like the career opportunities in the full-service hotel industry, with the exception that food and beverage can be a division of its own and not part of hotel operations. The rooms and guest services departments offer the most opportunities for students of hospitality management. As gaming entertainment properties have hotels that are much larger than nongaming hotels, department heads have a larger number of supervisors reporting to them and more responsibilities. Reservations, front desk, housekeeping, valet parking, and guest services can all be very large departments with many employees.

Food and Beverage Operations

Gaming entertainment has a foundation of high-quality food and beverage service in a wide variety of styles and concepts. Some of the best foodservice operations in the hospitality industry are found in gaming entertainment operations. There are many career opportunities in restaurant management and the culinary arts. As with hotel operations, gaming entertainment properties are typically very large and contain numerous food and beverage outlets, including a number of restaurants, hotel room service, banquets and conventions, and retail outlets. Many establishments support gourmet, high-end signature restaurants. It is not unusual to find many more executive-level management positions in both front- and back-of-the-house food and beverage operations in gaming entertainment operations than in nongaming properties.

Casino Operations

Casino operations jobs fall into five functional areas. Gaming operations staff include slot machine technicians (approximately one technician for forty machines), table-game dealers (approximately four dealers for each table game), and table-game supervisors. Casino service staff includes security, purchasing,

Personal Profile: Stacy L. Burns

Following a Career in Gaming Entertainment

After her third year attending Purdue University's Restaurant, Hotel, Institutional, and Tourism Management program, Stacy took a summer internship with the Showboat Hotel and Casino in Atlantic City, New Jersey, in 1992. She rotated through all departments in hotel operations for the 800-room, full-service casino hotel, and developed working experience in line positions including PBX reservations, front desk, housekeeping, environmental services, linen, uniforms, and bell desk. As part of her internship, Stacy supervised shifts in PBX, housekeeping, environmental services, front desk, and valet. After her internship was completed, Stacy decided to accept full-time employment with the Showboat and assumed a position as kitchen manager in the casino's buffet operation. She supervised every aspect of food preparation and display in a 650-seat buffet room. After two years with Showboat, Stacy returned to Purdue and earned her bachelor of science degree.

Stacy L. Burns

Following graduation, Stacy decided to follow a career in gaming entertainment. Hired by the Sands Hotel and Casino in 1995 as assistant manager for room service and food court operations, Stacy was responsible for the day-to-day activities of a $5-million-per-year room service operation and a four-unit food court outlet. She was also part of the opening team for a state-of-the-art, Hollywood themed, 400-seat buffet operation.

In 1996, Stacy joined the opening team for the riverboat casino operations of Ameristar Casino in Council Bluffs, Iowa, as front office manager. She was responsible for the initial installation of property management hardware and software including call accounting, PBX, and all point-of-sale systems used throughout the hotel and food and beverage operations. Stacy developed standard operating procedures and hired and trained employees in a number of departments including PBX, reservations, guest services, valet, front desk, and gift shop departments.

Stacy moved to Las Vegas at the end of 1996 to take a position as guest service manager with Harrah's Entertainment Inc. flagship property on the strip in Las Vegas. She became responsible for managing front desk operations and front services, with specific attention to bell desk, valet, and limousines for the casino megaresort. Stacy had full responsibility for the redesign of new facilities in a major property renovation. She worked with architects and engineers to redesign the bell desk, baggage room, valet, Porte Cochere, and front desk areas. One of her tasks was to complete spec-out and purchase two limousines at a cost of $70,000 each.

Early in 1998, she was promoted to a hotel manager position at the Lake Tahoe Harrah's in Reno, Nevada. Stacy's career path is typical of a focused and energetic student of the industry who is willing to work hard and learn new responsibilities with each new position.

and maintenance and facilities engineers. Marketing staff includes public relations, market research, and advertising professionals. Human resources staffs includes employee relations, compensation, staffing, and training specialists. Finance and administration staff includes lawyers, accounts payable, audit, payroll, and income control specialists.[9]

While there was little organized dealer training as recently as a decade ago, the explosive growth of the gaming industry has increased the need for trained dealers skilled at working a variety of table games including blackjack, craps, roulette, poker, and baccarat. Now, through the use of text books and videotapes combined with hands-on training at a mock casino, future dealers learn the techniques and fine points of dealing at classes offered by both colleges and private schools.

Retail Operations

The increased emphasis on nongaming sources of revenues in gaming entertainment business demands an expertise in all phases of retail operations, from store design and layout to product selection, merchandising, and sales control. Negotiating with concession subcontractors may also be a part of the overall retail activities. Retail operations often support the overall theme of the property and can often be a major source of revenue; however, retail management careers are often an overlooked career path in the gaming entertainment industry.

Entertainment Operations

Because of the increased competition, gaming entertainment companies are creating bigger and better production shows to turn their properties into destination attractions. Some production shows have climbed into the $30–40 million range and require professional entertainment staffs to produce and manage them. Gaming entertainment properties often present live entertainment of all sorts, with headline acts drawing huge audiences. For example, at the MGM Grand, there are three entertainment showcases. These include the 15,000-seat Grand Arena, used for professional boxing matches and for stars like Tina Turner; the smaller 1,700-seat theater that houses an elaborate production show called EFX; and a 700-seat theater that plays host to lesser stars like Tom Jones and Rodney Dangerfield.

As a result of this emphasis on entertainment, there exists career opportunities for those interested in stage and theater production, lighting and box office management, and talent management and booking.

Trends in the Gaming Entertainment Industry

- ✔ Gaming entertainment is depending less on casino revenue and more on room, food and beverage, retail, and entertainment revenue for its profitability and growth
- ✔ The gaming entertainment industry and lodging industry are converging as hotel room inventory is rapidly expanding in gaming entertainment properties
- ✔ Gaming entertainment, along with the gaming industry as a whole, will continue to be scrutinized by government and public policy makers as to the net economic and social impact of its activities
- ✔ As the gaming entertainment industry becomes more competitive, exceptional service quality will become an increasingly important competitive advantage for success
- ✔ The gaming entertainment industry will continue to provide management opportunities for careers in the hospitality business

VIP

A frequent guest of the casino makes a last-minute decision to travel to your property for a weekend stay. The guest enjoys gaming as a leisure activity and is one of the casino's better customers. When he arrives at the casino, he is usually met by a casino host and treated as a very important person due to his level of wagering at the blackjack tables. This guest is worth approximately $50,000 in casino win per year to the hotel. Due to his last-minute arrangements, however, the guest cannot notify a casino host that he is on his way to the hotel. Upon arriving, he finds a very busy registration desk. He must wait in line for twenty minutes, and when he tries to check in, he is told that the hotel is full. The front desk clerk acts impatient when the guest says that he is a frequent customer. In a fit of frustration, the would-be guest leaves the hotel and makes a mental note that all casinos have similar odds at the blackjack table and maybe another property will give him the respect he deserves.

Discussion Question

1. What systems, or procedures, could you institute to make sure this type of oversight does not happen in your property?

Negotiating with Convention Groups

Your convention sales department receives a call from a trip director for a large convention group. The group will use many function rooms for meetings during the day and will generate a substantial amount of convention services revenue. Likewise, their food and beverage needs are quite elaborate and will be great for the food and beverage department budget. However, the group is very sensitive concerning room price and is willing to negotiate the time of week for their three-night stay.

Discussion Question

1. What are the considerations that a gaming entertainment property must take into account when determining room rates for convention groups?

Summary

1. The casino industry has developed into a new business called gaming entertainment with the introduction of full-service hotels, retail, and entertainment offerings.
2. In order to operate gaming entertainment businesses, it is necessary to understand the relationship between the casino and other departments in the operation.
3. Gaming entertainment is strictly regulated by state governments, and the integrity developed over time by these regulations is necessary for the survival of the industry.
4. Pathological gambling does not affect a large percentage of the population, but all gaming industry operators and employees should be aware of the phenomenon.
5. Nongaming revenue is increasing as a percentage of total revenue of gaming entertainment businesses.
6. Native American gaming entertainment businesses are a means for economic self-development by tribal people.

Review Exercises

1. Briefly describe the history of legalized gaming in the United States.
2. What defines a gaming entertainment business?
3. Explain the attraction of gaming entertainment to the destination of a tourist.
4. List the various games that typically exist on the casino floor.
5. Why is it necessary for strict regulations to be in force on the casino floor?
6. How are hotel operations in a gaming entertainment business different from hotel operations in a nongaming environment?

Key Words and Concepts

Baccarat	Chips	Hard count	Odds
Bet	Gaming	Drop	Poker
Big 6	Gambling	Hold	Roulette
Blackjack	Gross gaming win	Keno	Slot machine
Cage	Handle	Marker	Soft count
Casino			

Notes

[1] E.M. Cristainsen, "The United States 1996 Gross Annual Wager," Supplement to *International Gaming and Wagering Business*, 18, 1997.

[2] V.H. Eade and R.H. Eade, *Introduction to the Casino Entertainment Industry.* Upper Saddle River, New Jersey: Prentice Hall, 1997.

[3]Harrah's Casinos. Harrah's Survey of U.S. Casino Entertainment. Harrah's Entertainment, Inc., Memphis, Tennessee, 1996.

[4]C.G. Braunlich, "Lessons from the Atlantic City Casino Experience," *Journal of Travel Research, 34,* 3, pp. 46–56.

[5]Arthur Andersen, *Economic Impacts of Casino Gaming in the United States*, Volume 1: Macro Study, American Gaming Association, 1996.

[6]Arthur Andersen, *Economic Impacts of Casino Gaming in the United States*, Volume 2: Micro Study, American Gaming Association, 1997.

[7]International Gaming Institute (University of Las Vegas, Nevada), *The Gaming Industry: Introduction and Perspectives.* New York: John Wiley, 1996.

[8]C.G. Braunlich and M.A. Steinberg, *Resource Guide for Responsible Gaming Programs*, American Gaming Association, 1996.

[9]K. Hashimoto, S. Fried Kline, and G.G. Fenich, *Casino Management.* Dubuque, Iowa: Kendall/Hunt, 1995.

Meetings, Conventions, and Expositions

12

After reading and studying this chapter you should be able to do the following:

✔ Name the main hospitality industry associations

✔ Describe the various types of meetings

✔ Explain the difference between meetings, expositions, and conventions

✔ Describe the role of a meeting planner

✔ Explain the primary responsibilities of a convention and visitors bureau or authority

✔ List the steps in event management

Historical Review

People have gathered to attend meetings, conventions, and expositions since ancient times, mainly for social, sporting, political, or religious purposes. As cities became regional centers, the size and frequency of such activities increased, and various groups and associations set up regular expositions.

Associations go back many centuries to the Middle Ages and before. The guilds in Europe were created during the Middle Ages to secure proper wages and maintain work standards. Associations began in the United States at the beginning of the eighteenth century, when the Rhode Island candle makers organized themselves.

Today, according to the American Society of Association Executives (ASAE), in the United States, about 6,000 associations operate at the national level, and a hundred thousand more function at the regional, state, and local levels. The association business is big business. Associations spend about $53.5 billion holding 215,000 meetings and conventions that attract approximately 22.6 million attendees (see Figure 12–1).

The hospitality and tourism industry itself consists of a number of associations, including the following:

- ✔ The American Hotel and Motel Association
- ✔ The National Restaurant Association
- ✔ The International Association of Convention and Visitors Bureaus
- ✔ Hotel Sales and Marketing Association
- ✔ Meeting Planners Association
- ✔ Association for Convention Operation Management
- ✔ Club Managers Association
- ✔ Professional Convention Management Association

In reality, associations are the only independent political force for industries like hospitality, offering the following benefits:[1]

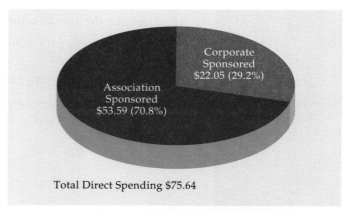

Total Direct Spending $75.64

Figure 12–1 *The Conventions Market*

✔ Governmental/political voice
✔ Marketing avenues
✔ Education
✔ Member services
✔ Networking

Thousands of associations hold annual conventions at various locations across North America and the rest of the world. Some associations alternate their venues from east to central to west; others meet at fixed locations such as the National Restaurant Association (NRA) show in Chicago or the American Hotel and Motel Association (AH&MA) convention and show in New York.

As Figure 12–1 indicates, professional and trade associations hold 70 percent of the conventions market, totaling $75 billion a year.[2]

Types of Meetings

Meetings are conferences, workshops, seminars, or other events designed to bring people together for the purpose of exchanging information.[3] Meetings can take any one of the following forms:

Clinic: A workshop-type educational experience in which attendees learn by doing. A clinic usually involves small groups interacting with each other on an individual basis.

Forum: An assembly for the discussion of common concerns. Usually experts in a given field take opposite sides of an issue in a panel discussion, with liberal opportunity for audience participation.

Seminar: A lecture and a dialogue that allow participants to share experiences in a particular field. A seminar is guided by an expert discussion leader, and usually thirty or fewer persons participate.

Symposium: An event at which a particular subject is discussed by experts and opinions are gathered.

Workshop: A small group led by a facilitator or trainer. It generally includes exercises to enhance skills or develop knowledge in a specific topic.

Meetings are mostly organized by corporations; associations; or social, military, educational, religious, and fraternal groups (SMERF). The reasons for having a meeting can range from the presentation of a new sales plan to a total quality management workshop. The purpose of meetings is to affect behavior. For example, as a result of attending a meeting, a person should know or be able to do certain things. Some outcomes are very specific; others may be less so. For instance, if a meeting were called to brainstorm new ideas, the outcome might be less concrete than for other types of meetings. The number of people attending a meeting can vary.

Successful meetings require a great deal of careful planning and organization. In San Francisco, a major convention city, convention delegates spend approximately $300 per day,[4] almost twice that of vacation travelers. Figure 12–2 shows convention delegates' spending in San Francisco in 1993.

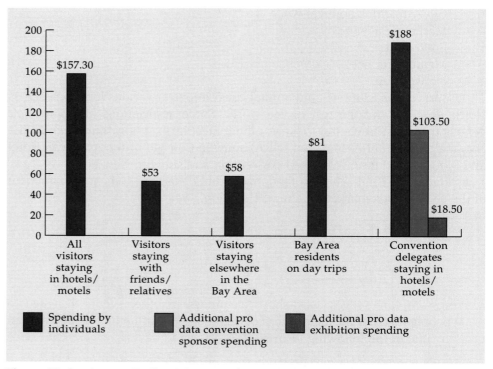

Figure 12–2 *Average Daily Visitor Spending in San Francisco* (Reprinted with permission from the *San Francisco Examiner.* August 28, 1994, p. B2.)

Meetings are set up according to the wishes of the client. The three main types of meeting setups are theater style, classroom style, and boardroom. Theater style generally is intended for a large audience that does not need to make a lot of notes or refer to documents. This style usually consists of a raised platform and a lectern from which a presenter addresses the audience. Classroom setups are used when the meeting format is more instructional and participants need to take detailed notes or refer to documents. A workshop-type meeting often uses this format. Boardroom setups are made for small numbers of people. The meeting takes place around one block rectangular table.

Expositions are events designed to bring together purveyors of products, equipment, and services in an environment in which they can demonstrate their products and services to a group of attendees at a convention or trade show.[5] Exhibitors are an essential component of the industry because they pay to exhibit their products to the attendees. Exhibitors interact with attendees with the intention of making sales or establishing contacts and leads for follow up. Expositions can take up several hundred thousand square feet of space, divided into booths for individual manufacturers or their representatives. In the hospitality industry, the two largest expositions are the AH&MA's annual New York show (held in November at the Javits Center) and the NRA's Annual Exposition held every May in Chicago. Both events are well worth attending.

NRA Show (Photos courtesy of the National Restaurant Association.)

Conventions are generally larger meetings with some form of exposition or trade show included. A number of associations have one or more conventions per year. These conventions raise a large part of the association's budget. A typical convention follows a format like this:

✔ Welcome/registration
✔ Introduction of president
✔ President's welcome speech, opening the convention
✔ First keynote address by a featured speaker
✔ Exposition booths open (equipment manufacturers and trade suppliers)
✔ Several workshops or presentations on specific topics
✔ Luncheon
✔ More workshops and presentations
✔ Demonstrations of special topics (e.g., culinary arts for a hospitality convention)
✔ Vendors' private receptions
✔ Dinner
✔ Convention center closes

Figure 12–3 shows a convention event profile for a trade show.

Conventions are not always held in convention centers; in fact, the majority are held in large hotels over a three- to five-day period. The headquarters hotel is usually the one in which most of the activity takes place. Function space is allocated for registration, the convention, expositions, meals, and so on.

Associations used to be viewed as groups that held annual meetings and conventions with speeches, entertainment, an educational program, and social events. They have changed in activity and perception.

Key Players in the Industry

The need to hold face-to-face meetings and attend conventions has grown into a multibillion dollar industry. Many major and some smaller cities have convention centers with nearby hotels and restaurants.

San Diego
Convention Center Corporation
EVENT PROFILE

EVENT STATISTICS

Event Name:	/6/San Diego Apartment Association Trade Show	ID:	9506059
Sales Person:	Joy Peacock	Initial Contact:	8/3/1994
Event Manager:	Trish A. Stiles	Move In Date:	6/22/1995
ConVis Contact:		Move In Day:	Thursday
Food Person:		Move In Time:	6:01 am
Event Tech.:		First Event Date:	6/23/1995
Event Attend.:		First Event Day:	Friday
Nature of Event:	LT Local Trade Show	Start Show Time:	6:01 am
Event Parameter:	60 San Diego Convention Center	End Show Time:	11:59 pm
Business Type 1:	41 Association	# of Event Days:	1
Business Type 2:	91 LOCAL	Move Out Date:	6/23/1995
Booking Status:	D Definite	Move Out Day:	Friday
Rate Schedule:	III Public Show, Meetings and Location	Out Time:	11:59 pm
Open to Public:	No	Date Confirmed:	8/3/1994
Number Sessions:	1	Attend per Sesn:	3000
Event Sold By:	F Facility (SDCCC)	Tot Room Nights:	15
Abbrev. Name:	/6/Apartment Assn	Public Release:	Yes
Est Bill Amount:	Rent - 6,060.00 Equip –	0.00 Food –	0.00
Last Changed On:	8/20/94 in: Comment Maintenance	By – Joy Peacock	

This Event has been in the facility before

CLIENT INFORMATION

Company: San Diego Apartment Assn, a non-profit Corporation
Contact Name: Ms. Leslie Cloud, Sales and Marketing Coord.
1011 Camino Del Rio South, Suite 200, San Diego, CA 92108   ID: SDAA
Telephone Number: (619) 297-1000
Fax Number: (619) 294-4510
Alternate Number: (619) 294-4510

Company: San Diego Apartment Assn, a non-profit Corporation
Alt Contact Name: Ms. Pamela A. Trimble, Finance & Operations Director
1011 Camino Del Rio South, Suite 200, San Diego, 92108
Telephone Number: (619) 297-1000
Fax Number: (619) 297-4510

EVENT LOCATIONS

ROOM	MOVE IN	IN USE	ED	MOVE OUT	BS	SEAT	RATE	EST. RENT	ATTEND
A	6/22/95 6:01 am	6/23/95	1	6/23/95 11:59 pm	D	E	III	6,060.00	5000
AS	6/22/95 6:01 am	6/23/95	1	6/23/95 11:59 pm	D	E	III	0.00	10
R01	6/22/95 6:01 am	6/23/95	1	6/23/95 11:59 pm	D	T	III	0.00	450
R02	6/22/95 6:01 am	6/23/95	1	6/23/95 11:59 pm	D	T	III	0.00	350
R03	6/22/95 6:01 am	6/23/95	1	6/23/95 11:59 pm	D	T	III	0.00	280
R04	6/22/95 6:01 am	6/23/95	1	6/23/95 11:59 pm	D	T	III	0.00	280
R05	6/22/95 6:01 am	6/23/95	1	6/23/95 11:59 pm	D	T	III	0.00	460

FOOD SERVICES

ROOM	DATE	TIME	BS ATTEND	EST. COST FOOD SERVICE

There are No Food Services booked for this event

Figure 12–3   *Convention Program* (Courtesy of the San Diego Convention Center.)

8/29/1994
16:15:28

San Diego
Convention Center Corporation
EVENT PROFILE

Page: 2
9506059

EVENT EQUIPMENT/SERVICES

ROOM   MOVE IN   INUSE   ED MOVE OUT   QUANTITY EQUIPMENT
There is No Equipment booked for this event

FOLLOW-UP/CHECKLIST ITEMS

FOLLOW-UP	DATE	ITEM	COMPLETED DATE	ASSIGN TO
	9/26/94	C DUE/date contracted		Vincent R. Magana
	8/22/94	c from sales	8/23/94	Sonia Michel
	8/22/94	c to licensee	8/23/94	Sonia Michel
	8/22/94	date c 1st printed	8/22/94	Sonia Michel

EVENT COMMENTS

8/3/94–JMP–This is a very strong hold for this group. CAD is pursuing a release of Hall A from Group Health and then this will be confirmed on a first option. Also holding an alternate date in April until this is released. All other rooms are clear.

200 BOOTHS – have used Carden in the past.
This is a trade show for the Apartment industry — products and services needed to keep a rental property in shape. Use Rooms 1–5 as seminar rooms. Trish has been the Event Coordinator for '93 – '94.

8/18/94 - JMP-CAD has been able to clear Hall A on a first option for move-in on 22nd from Group Health. Made definite and requested Sonia produce a contract. NOTE TO SONIA: Contract should be signed and mailed to alternate contact Pam Trimble. Meeting logistics only will go through Leslie. Note to housekeeping: we did the cleaning for the 1994 show.

LICENSE AGREEMENT REQUEST

EVENT COMMENTS

Requested:	Saturday, 08/20/94, 2:56 pm
License #:	9506059
Sales Person:	JMP
Nature of Event:	Local Trade
Full Legal Name of Licensee:	Yes
Insurance Y/N:	Yes
Deposit Schedule:	50-50
Special Arrangements or Directions:	Contract should be signed and sent to alternate contact Pam Trimble. Leslie is responsible for meeting logistics only.
Gross Revenues F/B Revenue:	$1000 concessions
In House A/V Revenue:	$600
Security Revenue:	$200
Telecom. Revenue:	$220

(Below, identify MI/MO or event days and attendance for each event).
Other business in Center: GROUP HEALTH, definite, Hall B-1 (m/o 22nd), 3000ppl; ALCOHOLICS ANON, definite, Hall B, move-in; SECURITY EXPO, tentative, Hall C (m/i 22nd, show 23rd), 6600ppl; ENTRP. EXPO, contracted, Ballroom (m/i 23rd), 2000ppl.

Figure 12–3   *(continued)*

Personal Profile: Carol C. Wallace

President and CEO, San Diego Convention Center Corporation

Carol grew up in a single-parent household in Cincinnati, Ohio. Her mother was an excellent role model who shared her experiences with Carol, stressing education and a strong work ethic. Carol began work at age thirteen selling penny candy, and ever since has aspired to be the best that she can be.

The road to achieving this goal began by completing her education. After graduating from Ohio State University with a degree in English and journalism, Carol intended to go to graduate school and become a teacher. It was while she was working at the university that she began to plan meetings. This led to involvement with the Ohio Lung Association in a public relations capacity. Carol not only planned meetings but also special events, like the 1973 Run for Life and Breath, and the first statewide "Go Cold Turkey" no-smoking campaigns.

Carol was invited to speak about the success of these events at a national conference in Dallas. She found the resultant career challenge that she was offered in Dallas too tempting to pass up; besides, she adds, the 80-degree weather was much better than the 30-degree weather she had left in Ohio! In 1976, she began working in the Public Affairs Department, Office of Special Events planning meetings. In 1980, Carol noticed a career announcement for the Dallas Convention Center, which was looking for an entry-level convention services representative. She applied, was accepted, and began working at what was then the fifth largest convention center in the United States. Carol says that this was like being an intern in a hospital where you worked hard to support the senior staff.

After two years at the Dallas Convention Center, Carol spoke with her manager about career prospects and was soon promoted to assistant manager of the facility. In 1989, Carol was recruited by an executive search firm to become the opening executive director of the Denver Convention Complex. Carol recalls that the opportunity of opening a new convention complex allowed her to develop personally, as she was responsible for hiring a com-

Carol Wallace

plex staff and for a successful inauguration. Carol had gone quite a long way from her beginnings in Ohio. But, there was still more to come. In 1991, Carol was again approached by an executive recruiter, who offered to move her to San Diego's new convention center. Carol's performance at the San Diego Convention Center has been very successful, thus continuing her outstanding career journey.

Carol's day is mainly taken up with meetings, such as the following:

✔ Meetings with staff deal with the renovation of the concourse and civic theater, which are both run by the convention center

✔ Meetings with the foodservice operations staff: the concourse outlets are run by the center

✔ Meetings with City Hall, necessary for the planning and preparation for the Republican National Convention

✔ Meetings with the architects about the center's expansion

✔ Meetings with meeting planners who are considering San Diego as a site for their clients' events

Carol also has to travel in order to represent the center and the city at the major meeting planners conventions. Carol's philosophy is that a job is not a mere 8 to 5 routine: "If the job is not done, then stay until it is." Her focus is not, "I'm doing this because I want to be successful"—success will come as a result of doing excellent work. A story illustrating this happened in Dallas one Saturday—a day that Carol was not usually in the office. Just as Carol was about to leave, she got a call from a man, whose flight had been delayed three hours, requesting a tour of the center. After giving the man a comprehensive tour, her boss received a call on Monday morning from the same man. Apparently, he was the big decision maker for a major convention that they had been trying to book for months. Yes, you guessed, Carol had impressed him so much he booked the convention.

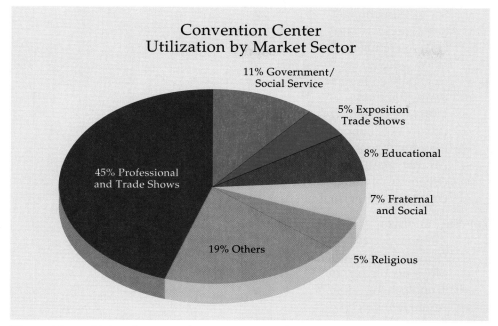

Figure 12–4 *Major Players in the Convention Industry*

The major players in the convention industry are convention and visitors' bureau (CVBs) meeting planners and their clients, the convention centers, specialized services, and exhibitions. The wheel diagram in Figure 12–4 shows the number of different people and organizations involved with meetings, conventions, and expositions.

Meeting Planners

Meeting planners may be independent contractors who contract out their services to both associations and corporations as the need arises or they may be full-time employees of corporations or associations. In either case, meeting planners have interesting careers. According to the International Convention Management Association (ICMA), about 212,000 full- and part-time meeting planners work in the United States.

The professional meeting planner not only makes hotel and meeting bookings but also plans the meeting down to the last minute, always remembering to check to ensure that the services contracted for have been delivered. In recent years, the technical aspects of audiovisual and simultaneous translation equipment have added to the complexity of meeting planning.

The meeting planner's role varies from meeting to meeting, but may include some or all of the following activities:[6]

Premeeting Activities
- ✔ Plan meeting agenda
- ✔ Establish meeting objectives
- ✔ Predict attendance

- ✔ Set meeting budget
- ✔ Select meeting site
- ✔ Select meeting facility
- ✔ Select hotel(s)
- ✔ Negotiate contracts
- ✔ Plan exhibition
- ✔ Prepare exhibitor correspondence and packet
- ✔ Create marketing plan
- ✔ Plan travel to and from site
- ✔ Arrange ground transportation
- ✔ Organize shipping
- ✔ Organize audiovisual needs

On-site activities
- ✔ Conduct pre-event briefing
- ✔ Prepare executive plan
- ✔ Move people in/out
- ✔ Troubleshoot
- ✔ Approve invoices

Postmeeting Activities
- ✔ Debrief
- ✔ Evaluate
- ✔ Provide recognition and appreciation
- ✔ Arrange shipping
- ✔ Plan for next year

The meeting planner has several critical interactions with hotels, including negotiating the room blocks and rates. Escorting clients on site inspections gives the hotel an opportunity to show their level of facilities and service. The most important interaction is normally with the catering/banquet/conference department associates; especially the services manager, maitre d', and captains; these frontline associates can make or break a meeting. For example, meeting planners often send boxes of meeting materials to hotels expecting the hotel to automatically know which meeting they are for. On more than one occasion,

Meeting Planner at Site Inspection

they have ended up in the hotel's main storeroom, much to the consternation of the meeting planner.

Fortunately for most meeting planners, once they have taken care of a meeting one year, subsequent years typically are very similar.

Convention centers and hotels provide meeting space and accommodations as well as food and beverage facilities and service. The convention center and a hotel team from each hotel capable of handling the meeting will attempt to impress the meeting planner. The hotel sales executive will send particulars of the hotel's meeting space and a selection of banquet menus and invite the meeting planner for a site inspection. During the site inspection, the meeting planner is shown all facets of the hotel, including the meeting rooms, guest-sleeping rooms, the food and beverage outlets, and any special facility that may interest the planner or the client.

Convention and Visitors Bureaus (CVB)

Convention and visitors bureaus (CVBs) are a major player in the meetings, conventions, and expositions market. The International Association of Conventions and Visitors Bureaus (IACVB) describes a CVB as a not-for-profit umbrella organization that represents an urban area that tries to solicit business- or pleasure-seeking visitors.

The convention and visitors bureau comprises a number of visitor industry organizations representing the various industry sectors:

- ✔ Transportation
- ✔ Hotels and motels
- ✔ Restaurants
- ✔ Attractions
- ✔ Suppliers

The bureau represents these local businesses by acting as the sales team for the city. A bureau has four primary responsibilities:

1. To encourage groups to hold meetings, conventions, and trade shows in the area it represents
2. To assist those groups with meeting preparations and to lend support throughout the meeting
3. To encourage tourists to partake of the historic, cultural, and recreational opportunities the city or area has to offer
4. To develop and promote the image of the community it represents[7]

The outcome of these four responsibilities is for the cities' tourist industry to increase revenues. Bureaus compete for business at trade shows, where interested visitor industry groups gather to do business. For example, a tour wholesaler who is promoting a tour will need to link up with hotels, restaurants, and attractions in order to package a vacation. Similarly, meeting planners are able to consider several locations and hotels by visiting a trade show. Bureaus generate leads (prospective clients) from a variety of sources. One source, associations, have national/international offices in major cities like Washington, D.C. (so that they can lobby the government), New York, Chicago, and San Francisco.

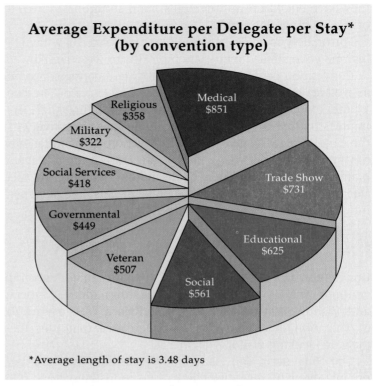

Figure 12–5 *Average Expenditure per Delegate per Stay* (Reprinted with permission from *Hotel and Motel Management, 209,* 3, February 22, 1994, p. 6. Copyright by Advanstar Communications, Inc.)

A number of bureaus have offices or representatives in these cities or a sales team who will make follow-up visits to the leads generated at trade shows. Alternatively, they will make cold calls on potential prospects such as major associations, corporations, and incentive houses. The sales manager will invite the meeting, convention, or exposition organizer to make a familiarization (FAM) trip to do a site inspection. The bureau assesses the needs of the client and organizes transportation, hotel accommodations, restaurants, and attractions accordingly. The bureau then lets the individual properties and other organizations make their own proposals to the client. Figure 12–5 shows the average expenditure per delegate per stay by the convention type; Figure 12–6 shows the breakdown of delegate expenditures per stay; and Figure 12–7 indicates the percentage of each item of expenditure.

Convention Centers

Convention centers are huge facilities where meetings and expositions are held. Parking, information services, business centers, and food and beverage facilities are all included in the centers.

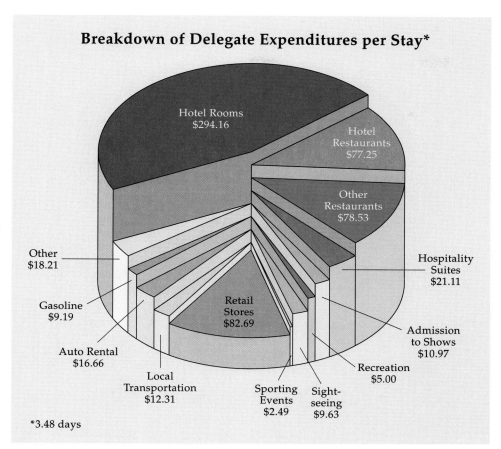

Breakdown of Delegate Expenditures per Stay*

Hotel Rooms
$294.16

Hotel
Restaurants
$77.25

Other
Restaurants
$78.53

Hospitality
Suites
$21.11

Other
$18.21

Gasoline
$9.19

Retail
Stores
$82.69

Admission
to Shows
$10.97

Auto Rental
$16.66

Recreation
$5.00

Local
Transportation
$12.31

Sporting
Events
$2.49

Sight-
seeing
$9.63

*3.48 days

Figure 12–6 *Breakdown of Delegate Expenditure per Stay* (Reprinted with permission from *Hotel and Motel Management, 209,* 3, February 22, 1994, p. 6. Copyright by Advanstar Communications, Inc.)

Jacob K. Javits Convention Center in New York City

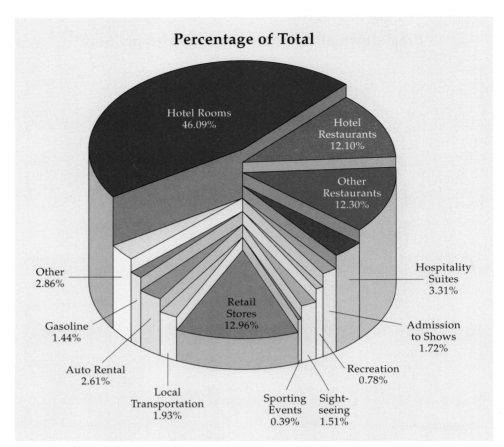

Figure 12–7 *Percentage of Delegate Expenditure per Item* (Reprinted with permission from *Hotel and Motel Management, 209,* 3, February 22, 1994, p. 6. Copyright by Advanstar Communications, Inc.)

Usually convention centers are corporations owned by county, city, or state governments and operated by a board of appointed representatives from the various groups having a vested interest in the successful operation of the center. The board appoints a president or general manager to run the center according to a predetermined mission, and goals and objectives.

Convention centers have a variety of exposition and meeting rooms to accommodate both large and small events. The centers generate revenue from the rental of space, which frequently is divided into booths (one booth is about 100 square feet). Large exhibits may take several booths' space. Additional revenue is generated by the sale of food and beverages, concession stand rentals, and vending machines. Many centers also have their own subcontractors to handle staging, construction, lighting, audiovisual, electrical, and communications.

In addition to the megaconvention centers, a number of prominent centers also contribute to the local, state, and national economies. One good example is the Rhode Island Convention Center. The $82-million center, representing the second-largest public works project in the state's history, is located in the heart of downtown Providence, adjacent to the 14,500-seat Providence Civic Center.

Corporate Profile:

Las Vegas Convention and Visitors Authority (LVCVA)

The LVCVA is one of the top convention and visitors bureaus, charged with the following mission: "To attract to the Las Vegas area a steadily increasing number of visitors to support the hotel and motel room inventory in Clark County."[1]

During the 1994 financial year, the Las Vegas Convention and Visitors Authority hosted more than 290 conventions attended by more than 1 million delegates. The LVCVA is organized in the following way: State law establishes the number, appointment, and terms of the authority's board of directors. A twelve-member board provides guidance and establishes policies to accomplish the LVCVA mission.

Seven members are elected officials of the county, and each represents one of the incorporated cities therein; the remaining five members are nominated by the Las Vegas Chamber of Commerce and represent different segments of the industry. The board is one of the most successful public/private partnerships in the country. Under the presidency of Manuel J. Cortez, the Las Vegas Convention and Visitors Authority and its board of directors have received numerous awards, among them the following:

World Travel Awards

✔ World's Leading Tourist and Convention Board

✔ World's Leading Conference and Convention Center

✔ World's Leading Gaming Destination

✔ Top North American Tourist and Convention Board

The Las Vegas Convention and Visitors Authority's organizational structure is shown above. The board of directors employs a president (executive) to serve as chief executive officer. Other members of the executive staff are vice president marketing, vice president operations, and vice president facilities. The marketing division's first priority is to increase the number of visitors to Las Vegas and southern Nevada. The division is composed of

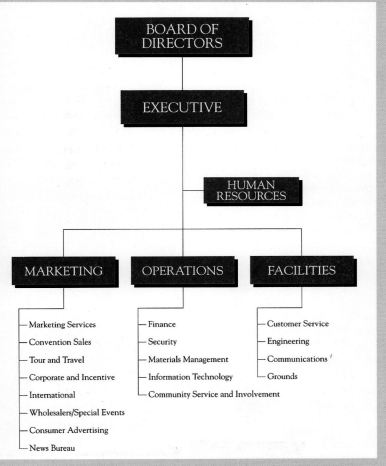

Organizational Chart, Las Vegas Convention and Visitors Authority (Courtesy of The Las Vegas Convention and Visitors Authority.)

eight teams that specialize in various market segments to increase the number of visitors and convention attendance. The teams are also shown above.

The marketing services team is responsible for providing visitor services including research, registration, convention housing, hotel/motel reservations, and visitor information. The research team tracks the dynamics of the Las Vegas and Clark County tourism marketplace, along with the competitive gaming and tourism environment. The registration department coordinates and provides temporary help for conventions and trade shows being held in Las Vegas. The housing division receives and processes hotel and motel housing forms from convention and trade show delegates, forwarding the reservations to participating hotels daily. The reservations department operates toll-free telephone lines, transferring the calls of travel agents, tourists, conventioneers, and special event attendees to hotels and motels within a requested location and price range.

Five visitor centers operate in Jean, Boulder City, Mesquite, Laughlin, and Las Vegas seven days a week and serve more than 38,000 visitors a month. A brochure room supports the visitor centers by answering thousands of telephone calls and letters requesting a variety of information on Las Vegas including recreation, weddings, entertainment, and special events. The staff sends out posters, brochures, and other information.

The convention sales team coordinates convention sales efforts at the Authority and contributes to the success of convention sales citywide by providing sales leads to the hotels. Sales managers travel throughout the United States and the world, meeting with association meeting planners to sell the benefits of holding conventions in Las Vegas. Members of the team also attend numerous conventions and trade shows where they host or sponsor special events and functions to entice conventions and trade shows to Las Vegas.

With a market share of 88 percent of leisure travelers visiting Las Vegas, travel promotion is vital to the LVCVA. The tour and travel team is responsible for positioning Las Vegas as a complete and affordable destination, and the preeminent gaming and entertainment capital of the world. Because 39 percent of all leisure travelers use a travel agent, the tour and travel team aggressively markets Las Vegas with travel agents.

Familiarization trips for travel agents are conducted by team members to generate enthusiasm and excitement around Las Vegas bookings. Travel agent presentations are also scheduled in both primary and selected secondary airline market cities. Similar events are also scheduled for Laughlin, which also advertises a 1-800 number for tourism information.

The corporate and incentive markets are traditionally considered the high end of the travel industry. These buyers are extremely sophisticated and value-conscious, and are looking for the highest quality facilities and amenities. Corporate and incentive team members attend various trade shows throughout the United States and Canada, as well as selected cities in Europe and Asia, promoting Las Vegas as a complete, value-oriented, flexible, and accessible resort destination for corporate meetings.

With increases in visitation from almost every country, the LVCVA's international team is charged with maintaining a high profile in the international marketplace, positioning Las Vegas and southern Nevada as the preferred destination and the gateway to the West. Team members travel throughout the world from the Pacific Rim countries of Japan, Korea, and Taiwan to the European countries of Germany, Switzerland, France, and Austria, as well as Canada and South America. Team sales executives provide information, brochures, and sales material in foreign languages emphasizing Las Vegas as a world-class, full-service resort destination.

The team also serves on an air service task force through McCarran International Airport and provides a steady flow of current information to key airline executives seeking support for nonstop service to Las Vegas when considering new destinations. In November 1994, the LVCVA, in partnership with McCarran International Airport, welcomed the first regularly scheduled international nonstop flight to Las Vegas. Condor Airlines' inaugural flight from Cologne, Germany, to Las Vegas is an example of the work of the joint air service task force.

Since 1992, wholesale travel has been one of the fastest-growing segments of the Las Vegas tourism market. During the past three years, the wholesale market has increased more than 75 percent, and the wholesaler team positions Las Vegas as a destination without limits on the variety of packages and activities that can be arranged. To provide education on the variety of activities offered by Las Vegas, the wholesaler team plans and implements several annual familiarization tours for wholesalers.

Annual Special Events

✔ Las Vegas Senior Classic

✔ Las Vegas Invitational

✔ National Finals Rodeo

✔ Big League Weekend

✔ Las Vegas Bowl

✔ Laughlin River Days

✔ Laughlin River Flight

✔ Laughlin Rodeo Days

In recent years, special event planners have also showed increased interest in Las Vegas and Laughlin as event destinations. Team members travel to several special event trade shows and conferences to maximize the opportunities for special events to be held in Las Vegas. The team works in cooperation with Las Vegas Events and the Laughlin Marketing Partners to aggressively pursue events that provide television exposure and draw large numbers of participants, spectators, and visitors.

Las Vegas Territory Matching Grant Funds

The Las Vegas Territory grants program provides funding for the advertising and promotion of special events in rural Clark County to attract visitors to the outlying areas. These events create a more enhanced vacation experience and provide a variety of additional activities for the Las Vegas visitor. Some examples are Boulder City Art in the Park, Henderson Industrial Days, Mesquite Arts Festival, NLV Parade of Many Cultures, and Mt. Charleston Festival in the Pines.

Travelers responded to the new advertising theme—"A World of Excitement in One Amazing Place"—and the Las Vegas tourism and convention business continues to flourish despite a slow-growing domestic travel demand and increased competition last year. Although many destinations report flat visitor volume, Las Vegas is experiencing double-digit increases.

The advertising team is responsible for developing the general marketing strategy that provides a blueprint for the development of specific marketing initiatives, advertisements, and public relations efforts. These strategies are incorporated into each division of the marketing department.

During fiscal year 1993, the Las Vegas News Bureau became a part of the LVCVA. The news bureau provides information about Las Vegas and southern Nevada through direct contact with national and international freelance journalists and working members of print and broadcast media. The bureau also maintains a complete photographic collection of Las Vegas, depicting the resort and entertainment growth of the area over a period of almost fifty years.

The operations department provides administrative support services to the marketing and facilities divisions, as well as security for the entire authority. Activities within operations are shown above.

```
                      /Finance
                      /Security
OPERATIONS —— Materials Management
                      /Information Technology
                      /Community Service and Involvement
```

Activities within Operations Department

Finance

The finance division maintains a general accounting system for the authority to ensure accountability in compliance with legal provisions and in accordance with generally accepted accounting principles. Finance is composed of financial services, accounting, and payroll activities. Additional responsibilities include the preparation of the authority's annual financial report (CAFR) and the annual budget. The CAFR has received the Government Finance Officers Association (GFOA) Excellence in Financial Reporting Award from 1985 through 1994. The budget has also been honored by GFOA, receiving the Distinguished Budget Presentation award from 1990 through 1994.

Materials Management

Materials management supports the marketing, operations, and facilities divisions by providing for purchasing of materials, services, and goods needed to meet its goals and objectives. Materials management is responsible for the storage and distribution of various supply items through an extensive warehousing program, as well as through printing and mail distribution.

Security

The security division provides protection of authority property, equipment, employees, and convention attendees twenty-four hours a day, 365 days a year, and also oversees paid parking and fire safety functions. The team patrols both the convention center and Cashman Field properties, and is trained in first aid assistance. Several officers have been recognized by the authority board and convention organizations for providing lifesaving measures to convention attendees.

Information Technology

The information technology division (ITD) is responsible for efficiently and effectively meeting the automation and information needs of the authority. ITD sustains a staff of technically competent professionals to design, maintain, implement, and operate the systems necessary to support the goals of the authority.

Rental Waiver Program

The LVCVA successfully runs an annual rental waiver program that provides $100,000 in grant money for in-kind use of Cashman Field facilities and equipment. Dozens of legitimate, registered Nevada nonprofit groups use the facility each year, transforming Cashman Field into a virtual civic center.

The LVCVA's research division tracks trends and statistics that give an accurate picture of the tremendous growth in southern Nevada from 1984 through 1994. The LVCVA's unique structure—housing both the building management and marketing teams within the same organization—has produced significant operational efficien-cies and resulted in the optimal use of facilities. The figure included here provides an indication of the LVCVA's success in marketing the destination.

Funding for the bureau comes mainly from the transient occupancy tax (TOT). This is a tax on hotel accommodations that the city charges all visitors. The amount of the tax varies from about 10 percent to 19.25 percent. Over a year, this adds up to millions of dollars. Only a part of the TOT tax goes to the CVB; most of it goes into the city's general fund or to fund specific projects. The balance of the bureau's budget comes from members fees and promotions.[1]

---

[1]The author gratefully acknowledges that this section draws on information given by the Las Vegas Convention and Visitors Authority.

Providence Convention Center (Courtesy Providence R.I. Convention Center.)

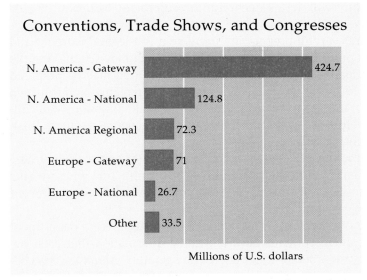

Figure 12–8 *Average Convention Center Income from Delegate Spending* (Courtesy of San Diego Convention Center.)

The 365,000-square foot center offers a 100,000-square-foot main exhibit hall, a 20,000-square-foot ballroom, eighteen meeting rooms, and a full-service kitchen that can produce 5,000 meals per day. The exhibit hall divides into four separate halls, and the facility features its own telephone system, allowing individualized billing. A special rotunda function room at the front of the building features glass walls that offer a panoramic view of downtown Providence for receptions of up to 365 people. Extensive use of glass on the facade of the center provides ample natural light throughout the entrance and prefunction areas.

A convention center can draw millions of new dollars into the economy of the city in which it is located. Figure 12–8 shows the average center income from delegate spending at conventions, trade shows, and congresses held at North American gateway cities, North American national/regional cities, European gateway cities, European national cities, and other cities.

Event Management

The larger convention center events are planned years in advance. As stated earlier, the convention and visitors bureau is usually responsible for the booking of conventions more than eighteen months ahead. Obviously, both the convention and visitors bureau and the convention center marketing and sales teams work closely with each other. Once the booking becomes definite, the senior event manager assigns an event manager to work with the client throughout the sequence of pre-event, event, and postevent.

The booking manager is critical to the success of the event by booking the correct space and working with the organizers to help them save money by allocating only the space really needed and allowing the client to begin setting up on time. A contract is written based on the event profile. The event profile stipulates in writing all of the client's requirements and gives relevant information, such as which company will act as decorator subcontractor to install carpets and set up the booths.

The contract requires careful preparation because it is a legal document and will guarantee certain provisions. For example, the contract may specify that the booths may only be cleaned by center personnel or that food may be prepared for samples only, not for retail. After the contract has been signed and returned by the client, the event manager will from time to time make follow-up calls until about six months before the event when arrangements such as security, business services, and catering will be finalized.

The event manager is the key contact between the center and the client. She or he will help the client by introducing approved subcontractors who are able to provide essential services. Figure 12–9 shows a job description for an event manager.

Two weeks prior to the event an event document is distributed to department heads. The event document contains all the detailed information that each department needs to know in order for the event to run smoothly. About ten days before the event, a WAG meeting (week at a glance) is held. The WAG meeting is one of the most important meetings at the convention center because it provides an opportunity to avoid problems—like two event groups arriving at the same time or additional security for concerts or politicians. About this same time, a preconvention or pre-expo meeting is held with expo managers and their contractors—shuttle bus managers, registration operators, exhibit floor managers, and so on.

Once the setup begins, service contractors marshall the eighteen-wheeler trucks to unload the exhibits by using radio phones to call the trucks from a nearby depot. When the exhibits are in place, the exposition opens and the public is admitted. Figure 12–10 shows an event document for the Sixth International Boat Show at the San Diego Convention Center. It gives information regarding the exact amount of space allocated, the contact person, and the schedule of events.

Specialized Services

A number of companies offer specialized services such as transportation, entertainment, audiovisual, escorts and tour guides, convention setup, and destination management.

Trends in Conventions, Meetings, and Expositions

- ✓ *Globalization/international participation:* More people are going abroad to attend meetings.
- ✓ *The cloning of shows:* Some international shows do not travel very well (i.e., agricultural machinery). Thus, organizations such as Bleinheim or Reed Exposition Group lift components and create shows in other countries.
- ✓ *Competition:* Competitiveness has increased among all destinations. Convention centers will expand and new centers will come on line.
- ✓ *Technology:* The industry needs to be more sophisticated. The need for fiber optics is present everywhere.
- ✓ Shows are growing at a rate of five to ten percent per year.

SAN DIEGO CONVENTION CENTER

EVENT MANAGER

DEFINITION

Under moderate direction from the services manager, plans, directs, and supervises assigned events and represents services manager on assigned shifts.

KEY RESPONSIBILITIES

- Plans, coordinates, and supervises all phases of the events to include set ups, move ins and outs, and the activities themselves
- Prepares and disseminates set-up information to the proper departments well in advance of the activity, and ensures complete readiness of the facilities
- Responsible for arranging for all services needed by the tenant
- Coordinates facility staffing needs with appropriate departments
- Acts as a consultant to tenants and the liaison between in-house contractors and tenants
- Preserves facility's physical plant and ensures a safe environment by reviewing tenants plans; requests and makes certain they comply with facility, state, county, and city rules and regulations
- Prepares accounting paperwork of tenant charges, approves final billings, and assists with collection of same
- Resolves complaints, including operational problems and difficulties
- Assists in conducting surveys, gathering statistical information, and working on special projects as assigned by services manager
- Conducts tours of the facilities.

MINIMUM REQUIREMENTS

- Bachelor's degree in hospitality management, business, or recreational management from a fully accredited university or college, plus two (2) years of experience in coordinating major conventions and trade shows
- Combination of related education/training and additional experience may substitute for bachelor's degree
- An excellent ability to manage both fiscal and human resources
- Knowledge in public relations; oral and written communications
- Experienced with audiovisual equipment

225 Broadway, Suite 710 • San Diego, CA 92102 • (619) 239-1989
FAX (619) 239-2030
Operated by the San Diego Convention Center Corporation

Figure 12–9 *Job Description for an Event Manager* (Courtesy of San Diego Convention Center.)

EVENT DOCUMENT
REVISED COPY
/6/SAN DIEGO INTERNATIONAL BOAT SHOW
Monday, January 2, 1995 – Monday, January 9, 1995

SPACE: Combined Exhibit Halls AB, Hall A - How Manager's Office, Box Office by Hall A, Hall B –
Show Manager's Office, Mezzanine Room 12, Mezzanine Room 13, Mezzanine Rooms 14 A&B, AND
Mezzanine Rooms 15 A&B

CONTACT: Mr. Jeff Hancock
National Marine Manufacturers Association, Inc.
4901 Morena Blvd.
Suite 901
San Diego, CA 92117
Telephone Number: (619) 274-9924
Fax Number: (619) 274-6760
Decorator Co.:   Greyhound Exposition Services
Sales Person: Denise Simenstad
Event Manager: Jane Krause
Event Tech.:   Sylvia A. Harrison

SCHEDULE OF EVENTS:

Monday, January 2, 1995
5:00 am – 6:00 pm   Combined Exhibit Halls AB
Service contractor move in GES,
Andy Quintena

Tuesday, January 3, 1995
8:00 am – 6:00 pm   Combined Exhibit Halls AB
Service contractor move in GES,
Andy Quintena

12:00 pm – 6:00 pm   Combined Exhibit Halls AB
Exhibitor move in

Wednesday, January 4, 1995
8:00 am – 6:00 pm   Combined Exhibit Halls AB
Exhibitor move in
Est. attendance: 300

Thursday, January 5, 1995
8:00 am – 12:00 pm   Combined Exhibit Halls AB
Exhibitor final move in

11:30 am – 8:30 pm   Box Office by Hall A
OPEN: Ticket prices, Adults $6, Children 12 & under $

Figure 12–10 *Event Document, International Boat Show* (Courtesy of the San Diego
Convention Center.)

Double-Booked

The convention bureau in a large and popular convention destination has jurisdiction over the convention center. A seasoned convention sales manager, who has worked for the bureau for seven years and produces more sales than any other sales manager, has rebooked a 2,000-person group for a three-day exposition in the convention center. The exposition is to take place two years from the booking date.

The client has a fifteen-year history of holding conventions, meetings, and expositions in this convention center and has always used the bureau to contract all space and services for them. In fact, the sales manager handling the account has worked with the client for seven of the fifteen years. The bureau considers this client a "preferred customer."

The convention group meeting planner also appears in a magazine ad giving a testimony of praise for the convention bureau, this particular sales manager, and the city as a destination for conventions.

Shortly after the meeting planner rebooks this convention with the bureau, the bureau changes sales administration personnel, not once, but three times. This creates a challenge for the sales managers in terms of producing contracts, client files, and event profiles, and in the recording and distribution of information. The preferred customer who rebooked has a contract, purchase orders for vendor services, a move in and setup agenda, and an event profile, all supplied by the sales manager. The sales manager has copies of these documents as well. The two hotels where the group will be staying also have contracts for the VIP group.

As is the nature of this particular bureau, other sales managers have been booking and contracting space for the same time period as the group that rebooked. In fact, the exhibit hall has been double booked, as have the break-out rooms for seminars, workshops, and food and beverage service. The groups that were contracted later are all first-time users of the facility.

This situation remains undetected until ten days prior to the groups' arrival. It is brought to the attention of the bureau and the convention center only when the sales manager distributes a memo to schedule a pre-con meeting with the meeting planner and all convention center staff.

Due to the administrative personnel changes, necessary information was not disseminated to key departments and key personnel. The convention center was never notified that space had been contracted for the preferred customer. The preferred customer has been told about this potentially catastrophic situation. Now there is a major dilemma to rectify.

Discussion Questions

1. Ultimately, who is responsible for decision making with regard to this situation?
2. What steps should be taken to remedy this situation?

3. Are there fair and ethical procedures to follow in order to provide space for the preferred customer? If so, what are they?
4. What measures, if any, should be taken in handling the seasoned sales manager?
5. What leverage does the meeting planner have to secure this and future business with the bureau?
6. List five ramifications if the preferred customer is denied space and usage of the convention center.
7. How can this situation be avoided in the future?

Not Enough Space

Denise is the sales manager of a large convention center. A client has requested an exhibition that would not only bring excellent revenue but is an annual event that several other convention centers would like to host.

Exhibitions typically take one or two days to set up, with three or four days of exhibition, and one day to break down. There are professional organizations that handle each part of the setup and breakdown.

When Denise checks the space available on the days requested for the exhibition, she notices that another exhibition is blocking a part of the space needed by her client.

Discussion Question

1. What can Denise do to get this exhibition to use the convention center without inconveniencing either exhibition too much?

Summary

1. Conventions, meetings, and expositions serve social, political, sporting, or religious purposes. Associations offer benefits such as a political voice, education, marketing avenues, member services, and networking.
2. Meetings are events designed to bring people together for the purpose of exchanging information. Typical forms of meetings are conferences, workshops, seminars, forums, and symposiums.
3. Expositions bring together purveyors of products, equipment, and services in an environment in which they can demonstrate their products. Conventions are meetings that include some form of exposition or trade show.
4. Meeting planners contract out their services to associations and corporations. Their responsibilities include premeeting, on-site, and postmeeting activities.

5. The convention and visitors bureaus are nonprofit organizations that assess the needs of the client and organize transportation, hotel accommodations, restaurants, and attractions.
6. Convention centers are huge facilities, usually owned by the government, where meetings and expositions are held. Events at convention centers require a lot of planning ahead and careful event management. A contract based on the event profile and an event document are parts of effective management.

Review Exercises

1. What are associations and what is their purpose?
2. Explain the term SMERF.
3. Describe the main types of meeting setups.
4. What are a workshop and a seminar?
5. Explain the difference between an exposition and a convention.
6. What is a convention center?
7. List the duties of CVBs.
8. Conventions require careful planning. Explain the purpose of an event profile and an event document.
9. Discuss the different promotional tools, how they relate to each other, and their relationship to the marketing mix.

Key Words and Concepts

Associations
Boardroom style
Classroom style
Clinic
Convention
Convention centers

Convention and visitors
    bureaus
Exposition
Familiarization trip
Forum

Incentive market
Meeting
Meeting planner
Seminar
Site inspection

Symposium
Theater style
Trade show
Workshop

Notes

[1] John Hogan, *Lodging*, December 1993.
[2] From Deloitte and Touche, Convention Liaison Council, as quoted in *USA Today*, April 5, 1994.
[3] Rhonda J. Montgomery and Sandra K. Strick, *Meetings, Conventions, and Expositions: An Introduction to the Industry*. New York: Van Nostrand Reinhold, 1995, p. 13.
[4] Wendy Tanaka, "Convention Attendees Spend More," *San Francisco Examiner*, August 28, 1994, p. B2.

[5] Deny G. Rutherford, *Introduction to the Conventions, Expositions, and Meeting Industry*. New York: Van Nostrand Reinhold, 1990, p. 44.
[6] Montgomery and Strick, op. cit., pp. 171–172.
[7] Montgomery and Strick, op. cit., p. 19.

Marketing, Human Resources, and Culture

13

After reading and studying this chapter you should be able to do the following:

- ✔ Discuss the importance of environmental scanning as it relates to marketing and sales
- ✔ List and explain each of the steps in the marketing process
- ✔ Show how a competitor analysis is conducted
- ✔ Explain the term *product life cycle*
- ✔ State the difference between marketing and sales
- ✔ List and explain the steps in human resources management and development processes
- ✔ Describe culture and ethnic diversity

Each segment of the hospitality industry uses the services of the marketing, sales, and human resources departments.

Marketing

Marketing and sales are critically important to the success of hospitality organizations. Without guests, there is no need for frontline employees or anyone else for that matter! Marketing is all about finding out what guests' wants and needs are and providing them at a reasonable cost and profit.

Marketing begins with a corporate philosophy and a mission, but the philosophy and mission should not just hang on an office wall. It should be practiced every day by everyone. Peter Drucker, highly respected management guru, says that the only valid definition of business purpose is to create customers. In the hospitality industry, we would quickly add "and keep them coming back." Creating a customer means finding a product or service that a number of people want or need. When Kemmons Wilson began Holiday Inns, he was successful because he fulfilled a need that many families and businesspeople had: a quality lodging experience at a value. Ray Kroc is another example of giving the American public what they wanted. Through McDonald's quick-service restaurants, he met the need for food on the run.

Alastair Morrison identifies eleven characteristics of marketing or customer orientation.[1]

1. Customer needs are the first priority.
   - Answering customer needs produces more satisfied customers.
   - All departments, managers, and staff share a common goal.
2. Understanding customers and their needs is a constant concern and research activity.
   - Knowing customers and their needs increases the ability to satisfy these needs.
3. Marketing research is an ongoing activity that should be assigned a very high priority.
   - Changes in customer needs and characteristics are identified.
   - Viability of new services and products are determined.
4. Frequent reviews are made of strengths and weaknesses relative to competitors.
   - Strengths are accentuated and weaknesses addressed.
5. The value of long-term planning is fully appreciated.
   - Changes in customer needs are anticipated and acted on; marketing opportunities are realized.
6. Customers' perceptions of the organization are known.
   - Services, products, and promotions are designed to match the customers' image.
7. Interdepartmental cooperation is valued and encouraged.
   - Increased cooperation leads to better services and greater customer satisfaction.

8. Cooperation with complementary organizations is recognized as worthwhile.
    ✔ Increased cooperation generates greater customer satisfaction.
9. Change is seen as inevitable and not as being unnecessary.
    ✔ Adaptations to change are made smoothly and are not resisted.
10. The scope of business or activities is broadly set.
    ✔ Opportunities that serve customers more comprehensively, or those that tap into related fields, are capitalized upon.
11. Measurement and evaluation of marketing activities is frequent.
    ✔ Effective marketing programs or tactics are repeated or enhanced; ineffective ones are dropped.
    ✔ Marketing expenditures and human resources are used effectively.

Large corporations and small independent hospitality operators both go through similar decision-making processes to seek out new market opportunities and to increase market share in existing markets.

Environmental Analysis

Before the first decisions about marketing can be made, it is advisable to gain background information on topics such as environmental analysis. Environmental analysis means studying the economic, social, political, and technological influences that could affect the hospitality business. Figure 13–1 illustrates the environmental scanning process.

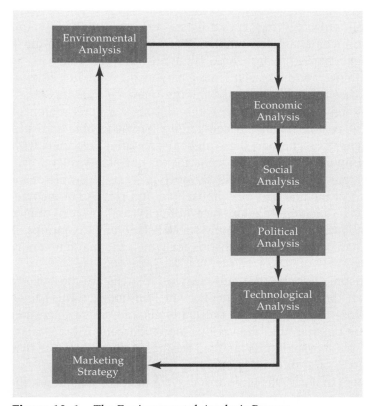

Figure 13–1 *The Environmental Analysis Process*

Economic Impacts

The economy can affect hospitality corporations in a macro way (the big picture) or in a micro way (the local picture). In a macro sense, interest rates affect the cost of borrowing money, and exchange rates affect the number of tourists visiting specific destinations. Some economists suggest that the economy goes through cycles. We can all agree that the mid-1980s seemed like boom times compared to the recession of the early 1990s. As a result, people today are more value conscious, which is why the economy segment of the lodging industry has grown in recent years.

The importance of environmental analysis should not be underestimated. The knack of being at the right place at the right time may be luck for some, but it is a carefully calculated move for others. There are many good examples of hospitality leaders who saw the environment changing and with it the wants, needs, and expectations of guests: Ray Kroc, with quick-service restaurants; Richard Melman, with table dining; Robert Hazard, with hotels; and Herb Kelleher, with the airline business, were all trailblazers with one thing in common—the ability to scan the environment and be leaders in the path of progress by developing products and services that anticipated and provided for peoples' wants and needs.

To many who come across a good idea, it may seem like common sense to exploit an opportunity. Still, many corporations are struggling today because they have not done a good environmental scan.

Social Analysis

A survey of our social landscape reveals that lifestyles in the 1990s are more hectic. With more two-income families, additional stresses are placed on those families who must juggle parenting and work. Higher divorce rates have led to more single-parent families and increased female careerism. A greater emphasis on fitness and wellness has led to more of a grazing approach to eating. Food-service trends are definitely toward healthier eating. In this and other sectors of the hospitality industry, customers have become more knowledgeable and, as a consequence, have higher expectations; these higher expectations, coupled with a quest for value, add up to ever-changing scenarios for hospitality operators.

Demographics are a part of social analysis. Demographics are a profile of society in a given area and include age, sex, household and per capita income, family size, occupation, education, religion, race/ethnicity, and national origin. Demographic information is used by marketing specialists to identify groups of people with similar characteristics and problems for which the marketers may develop a solution.

We all know that people living in the more expensive areas are more likely to go on a cruise than those in the low-income neighborhoods. Cruise lines therefore know to whom to send promotional materials and which television and radio programs are popular with the various target markets. A target market, just as it sounds, is a market that is targeted for the product or service that a company is planning to offer or already offers.

In general, consumers in the 1990s have developed a taste for instant gratification. People are taking more vacations, but shorter ones, to destinations that are closer to home. Lifestyles have become more casual; hence, the increase in casual-theme restaurants. As a nation, approximately 30 percent of our food dollar is eaten away from home.

Political Analysis

Both federal and state legislators and judiciary affect the hospitality industry in a number of ways: employment legislation, minimum wage, health care, taxes on benefit packages, the tax deduction of business meals dropping to 50 percent from 80 percent, and city-wide no-smoking ordinances. Much may also depend on the political party in control.

Technological Analysis

Since labor is the single highest cost in the hospitality business, any technology that leads to greater efficiency is worth investigating. In all sectors of the industry, technological advances are benefiting guests and businesses alike. Consider how much safer a guest feels with an electromagnetic room door opener than a key. The key was easy to duplicate, but the plastic card becomes invalid as soon as the guest checks out. In restaurants, hand-held remote ordering devices have helped speed up service to guests from both the bar and kitchen. Computers are now able to store hundreds of menus and, at the push of a button, calculate the amount of ingredients for a recipe for any number of guests. Some can even make out purchase orders as well.

The benefit of environmental scanning is to focus the attention of the top management prior to formulating the next steps in the marketing process, namely, the following:

- ✔ Marketing planning
- ✔ Market assessment
- ✔ Market demand
- ✔ Competitive analysis
- ✔ Positioning
- ✔ Marketing goals and objectives
- ✔ Marketing mix
- ✔ Action plan based on the Ps (place, product, price, promotion)
- ✔ Performance evaluation
- ✔ Budget vs. actual
- ✔ Investigate variance
- ✔ Take corrective actions

Figure 13–2 illustrates the elements of marketing planning.

Market Assessment

Market assessment simply tries to determine if there is a need for a product or service in the market and to assess its potential. This is done by examining the existing market, its size, demographics, key players, customers' wants and needs, and general conditions and trends.

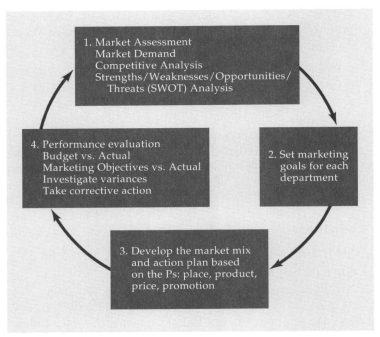

Figure 13–2 *Marketing Planning*

Market Demand

Market demand is not always so easy to quantify. However, by doing our best to gather all available information we can guesstimate the demand for a particular product or service.

Within the hospitality industry, there is obviously considerable variation among the different components: travel and tourism, lodging, foodservice, leisure, and recreation. To assess the market for Amtrak or a discount airline, it would be necessary to consider peoples' travel habits: Who are the potential users, how many are there, and where are they located?

For a lodging company that might want to determine the number of female business travelers, information is available from organizations like the American Hotel and Motel Association or consultants and research organizations such as Pannel Kerr Forster. Some surveys have indicated that approximately 40 percent of all business travel is by females. Therefore, we can deduce that if there were 10,000 hotel rooms in a city center and if they were, on average, 70 percent occupied with a 40 percent business (versus conventions and family) mix there would be

$$10,000 \times .7 \times .4 = 2,800 \text{ women business travelers visiting that city}$$

Competitor Analysis

Analyzing the competitions' strengths and weaknesses will help us determine which strategies to use in the marketing action plan. All hospitality businesses

| | | Competitors | | | | | |
Benefit	Our Operation	1	2	3	4	5	6

Figure 13–3 *Comparison Matrix*

have competitors. The competition may be across the street or across the country or the world. Usually in the lodging, restaurant, and foodservice sectors, the competition is close; for example, most people going to New Orleans for Mardi Gras will stay at a hotel in the city. The question is which one. Similarly, guests selecting restaurants and foodservice establishments will usually choose one within a given radius of about ten miles—give or take a few miles. Therefore, most restaurants realize that their competition is either other restaurants of a similar nature or those within a similar price range; in some cases, such as quick-service restaurants, the competition may also be convenience stores, or even take-out meals.

Competition may be farther away when it comes to destination vacation spots. A family living in St. Louis may want a winter vacation in Mexico, but may also consider the Caribbean, Hawaii, Florida, or southern California.

For the purpose of comparison with competitors, marketers make a matrix of the important elements. In each case, the elements may be selected by the marketing person, owner/operators, and top management/department heads. Figure 13–3 shows a comparison matrix form. The appropriate elements are listed in the left-hand column under the heading of benefit. Then, our operation is compared with others using a 1–10 or 1–100 scoring system and/or written comments.

One of the benefits of a comparison matrix is that it helps to focus attention on where our operations are better or worse compared to the competition. Obviously, some elements are beyond owner's and management's control. For example, you cannot move a hotel or restaurant over a few blocks because you don't like its current location.

The elements that are controllable are those that are given the greatest attention; service and quality of food are good examples. Another benefit of a comparison matrix is to identify the market segments that we and the competition are best suited to serve. An example of this is Hyatt Hotels and Resorts introducing Camp Hyatt in order to attract families at a time when their usual business guests are not using the hotels much. By targeting regular Hyatt hotel business guests, Camp Hyatt has been successful in offering a benefit and a service to a specific target market.

Positioning

Positioning means to occupy a specific place in the market and project that position to the target market. In the process of doing the competitive analysis of the strengths and weakness of the competition, it usually becomes apparent which position a corporation or independent hospitality business should occupy and project. Some companies are deliberately adopting the new concept of positioning in several market segments. Marriott and Choice Hotels are good examples.

Because McDonald's is so strong in the children's market, Wendy's and Burger King position themselves as more adult quick-service burger restaurants. Motel 6 operations position themselves as the least expensive national chain where guests will receive a clean comfortable room for about $26. Positioning statements help get the message across to the target market (e.g., "Did somebody say McDonald's?").

Marketing Goals and Objectives

Setting marketing goals gives a measure by which progress toward the goals can be monitored. Goals are set for the total enterprise and for each department. An example of a marketing goal for a hotel might be to increase weekend occupancy from 43.2 percent to 48.2 percent by a specified date. Another could be to increase the average daily rate from $76 to $80. Other goals target each market segment, such as corporate meetings and conventions, sport, leisure, and so on. Goals are set for each of the hospitality operations' units or departments. Campus foodservice managers would set sales goals for outside catering, satellite restaurants, tailgate parties, and so on.

Objectives are the how-to tactics used in order to meet or exceed the goals. Using the preceding examples, management would plan and organize specific activities that would result in a five percent increase in weekend occupancy. Objectives must be planned for each goal.

Marketing Mix

The *marketing mix* is the term used to focus on the pertinent Ps: place, product, price, promotion, partnership, packaging, programming, and people.

Place means the location, which is extremely important for hospitality businesses. The expression "In business, the three most important things are location, location, location!" stresses that importance. Hotels, motels, restaurants, tourist attractions, and destinations to a large extent either thrive or perish based on their location.

The only problem is that owners and managers must, if they have a prime location, produce the revenue to keep the mortgage or lease payments to a certain percentage of total sales. In a restaurant, for example, operators aim to keep mortgage or lease payments to about six to eight percent of sales in order to allow an appropriate amount to cover other costs and produce a reasonable profit.

The *product* must suit the wants and needs of the target market. The product is positioned to meet those wants and needs as a result of the previous steps in

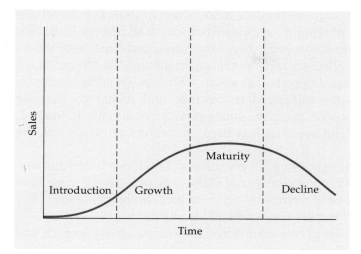

Figure 13–4 *Product Life Cycle*

the marketing process. Additionally, surveys and focus groups (small groups that are a representative sample of the target market) provide feedback on the extent to which the product meets their wants and needs.

A great example of ensuring that the product suits the needs of the target market was Marriott's development of Courtyard Inns, which they developed after extensive research on what their target market wanted. They constructed prototype rooms on which focus groups were invited to comment. This careful product development led to the launch of a very successful new type of lodging concept.

All products and services are at some stage in the product life cycle, just as humans go through the life cycle from birth/introduction, growth, maturity, and declining period. Figure 13–4 shows the stages in the product life cycle. An example of a product that was introduced a few years ago and had a very quick growth rate, an early maturity, and rapid decline was the disco. To a large extent, sports bars and coffeehouses have taken over.

Price plays an important role in purchasing decisions, as we all know from experience. Most guests are price sensitive—as the old expression says, there is no loyalty that $.25 won't change. In other words, if the fast-food restaurant across the street offers the same product for $.25 less, then (other things being equal) they will get the business.

Obviously, things like value are closely linked with price. People will only purchase a particular product or service if they perceive that it is a good value—hence the value-meal packs and real-meal deals. The closer price is to value, the more likely the guest will be satisfied and will return.

In recent years, pricing in the hospitality industry has had an interesting effect on consumer behavior. In the early 1980s, hospitality enterprises increased prices and found that guests kept coming. Many businesses were liberal with expense accounts that enabled executives to stay in better hotels and entertain clients in expensive restaurants.

At that time these costs were all tax deductible. Then, in 1986, tax deductions of business expenses for restaurant meals were reduced to 80 percent (they subsequently were reduced to 50 percent). These measures, combined with the recession, had a profound effect on restaurants, especially upscale restaurants.

Quite naturally, business dropped off as guests who were spending money on dining traded down to the midpriced restaurants, and midpriced clientele moved into the quick-service segment. Quick-service restaurants flourished, and convenience stores and supermarkets began to put delicatessens into the stores.

Price also played a part in the surge of economy and midprice hotels and motels that have come on-line in recent years. Guests resisted paying more than what they considered to be a reasonable price for hotel accommodations. The fact that the luxury hotel market was overbuilt also helped.

Price may be determined in two main ways: the comparative approach and the cost-plus approach. The comparative approach assesses what other similar operations are charging for the same or similar service/product. The cost-plus approach means that all the costs are accounted for and a selling price is determined after an amount for profit is allocated. As you can likely already determine, both methods have advantages and disadvantages.

Promotion, which includes the techniques for communicating information about the products/services available, is the most highly visible element of the marketing mix. The most important promotional tools are advertising, personal selling, sales promotion, and public relations.

Advertising is any form of paid, nonpersonal communication used by an identified sponsor to persuade or inform certain audiences about a product.[2] For example, a restaurant advertises in a local newspaper, on the radio, or on television, to reach its target market. Other forms of advertising include magazines and billboards.

Personal selling in the hospitality industry can take the form of sales blitzes or "upselling" in restaurants, or at the front desks of hotels.

Sales promotions offer inducements to buyers. In the hospitality industry, they include free gifts, such as when a quick-service restaurant gives away a toy. Promotions may also include coupons. Most newspapers or *Penny Saver*s have restaurant coupons, and the entertainment guide may offer discount coupons for hotel rooms and even airline transportation. These sales promotions usually seek to boost sales during slow periods.

Public relations (PR) includes all communications aimed at increasing good will in the user communities. PR seeks to build a positive image of the organization and its products. Ronald McDonald Houses are a famous example of public relations. Other examples include sponsorship of local organizations and events, and providing scholarships.

Partnerships occur when two or more hospitality/tourism organizations come together, providing an overall marketing campaign. They include related marketing programs and cooperative advertising, which is when two or more companies are mentioned on the same advertisement. An example of this would be the American Airlines, Citibank, Visa Card.

Publicity is also about the organization's communication with the public. However, it is not paid for by the organization. It is free and, therefore, not controlled by the organization. This can be good or bad, as in the case of Jack in the Box and the E. coli bacteria outbreak. On the other hand, consideration should be taken of the goodwill created by organizations participating in charity events.

Packaging is when organizations combine two or more items or activities, such as fly-drive-hotel-attractions visits, and sell them as a group. Another very successful form of packaging is the convenient McDonald's Happy Meal concept. Although different from the previous example, it nonetheless appeals to a particular market segment.

Programming is when a company like Hyatt offers Camp Hyatt to families with children. A complete program of events is planned so that parents and children may, if they wish, do separate activities. Club Med also programs some of its locations for specific activities like snorkeling, sailing, tennis, and so forth. Some of these are for families, and some only for adults.

In the hospitality and tourism industry, *people* are an important part of the marketing mix—one airplane is much like the next, but it is the "people service" that makes the difference. Radisson Hotel's "Yes I Can" program was based on customer research and proved successful because employees really cared and wanted to make a difference.

Performance Evaluation

Evaluating the actual operations against expected performance is ongoing and lets an organization see how well it has done compared with how well it said it would do. Providing performance feedback enables management to plan future marketing strategies. If expected and actual performance vary, then the discrepancy is examined and alternative strategies are developed. Having established the results and the reasons for any variances, the final step in the marketing process is to take the necessary corrective action to achieve the company's goals.

Director of Marketing and Sales Meeting

Personal Profile: Carroll R. Armstrong

President and CEO, Baltimore Convention and Visitors Bureau

Twenty-five years ago, Carroll R. Armstrong was well on his way to becoming a successful jazz musician when he changed careers. Since that time, his career has progressed to his present position of marketing director at the San Diego Convention Center. Carroll has been a force in the success in four major convention centers. A colleague describes Carroll as the number one convention center marketing professional in the country. However, his biggest challenge was opening the San Diego Convention Center.

In 1987, when Carroll arrived in San Diego, he looked at the existing convention centers. Carroll concluded that if San Diego was to be successful, the center must compete for business in several markets; in addition to the traditional convention center markets, two nontraditional convention center markets, incentive business and the corporate markets, were increasingly important. These additional market segments would help maximize the property and create additional revenue.

In the 1980s, many of the convention centers operated in an institutional mode. Because they were state or city owned, they were expected to lose money. The challenge of the San Diego Convention Center was that it could not open and operate in the same way as others did. The convention center would have to be more economically self-

Carroll R. Armstrong

sufficient. The center would have to be the pump primer and operate like any other business.

The philosophy that Carroll created was that the center would operate like a fine hotel. Whereas many other centers contract out their foodservice and consequently have mediocre reputations, the San Diego Convention Center's catering has white-glove "Escoffier" food preparation and service. Carroll realized that the me-generation wants service with style, and, if they are getting value, they will pay the few extra costs.

The strategy of differentiating the center by service has been successful because the center has won the meeting planners' choice award from *Meeting News Magazine.* This recognizes that one of the major goals of the convention center is to run the center like a first-class hotel, so that delegates can walk from the hotels to the convention center without noticing any difference. To achieve this, the center has uniformed doorpersons and concierge-like, guest-relations staff to answer questions and offer suggestions about everything from a meeting room location to city-wide entertainment. Additionally, guest-service guides stand near elevators to direct attendees to appropriate rooms taking those who spend the most.

In 1996, in recognition of his expertise and leadership Carroll was appointed president of the Baltimore Convention and Visitors Bureau.

Sales

Sales is an important part of marketing. The difference between marketing and sales is that with marketing, the focus is on the guest. With sales the focus is on the product or service for sale.

More people have the title *sales manager* or *account executive* than *marketing director.* The sales department is responsible for making sales to guests in the target market. Sales can be to new accounts or existing ones. Each sales department is organized in a way that best suits the organization. Some companies have national—even international—sales offices in addition to unit sales departments. The sales team may then be split up according to the various target markets: association, corporate, catering, and so on, and by region—Northeast, Midwest, West, and so on. The sales team maintains account files with follow-up ticklers. It also prospects for new business by making cold calls on potential clients (usually by telephone) or in the form of a sales blitz, whereby the team will cover given areas of a city and pound the pavement. In a sales blitz, the team asks companies about their accommodations and restaurant needs and which hotels and restaurants they currently use; the team also obtains the names of the people responsible for booking hotels and restaurants so that they may be invited to the hotel for a personal tour (usually including lunch). During the tour, the sales account executive quantifies the demand and type of accommodations or meals required and the number of room nights per month or restaurant meals in order to be able to quote competitive rates.

Each member of the sales team has a quota of dollar sales to achieve. Therefore, sales professionals guard their clients very carefully. Making a sale and influencing the guest to become a repeat guest is vital in today's competitive marketplace. About 80 percent of a hotel's and some restaurants' business comes from about 20 percent of the guests.

Human Resources Management

It is precisely because the hospitality industry offers intangible services and products that human resources management is so critical to the success of the organization. One hotel restaurant or tourism enterprise is often much the same as the other; what makes the difference is service and professionalism.

As we already know, the hospitality industry is the largest in the world, employing some 70 million people. No other industry has as much frontline guest contact between employees and guests—especially entry-level employees. Employment ranges from entry-level positions to specialized positions, supervisory positions, and managerial/executive positions. Human resources is all about attracting, selecting, orienting, training, developing, and evaluating the performance of an organization's most important resources, the human ones.

In addition to these activities, several other functions are part of the human resources process, including job descriptions, job specifications, advertising, payroll and benefits, grievances, and ensuring conformance to federal and state or provincial legislation.

The complexity of human resources management and development in the hospitality industry is increased by the fact that many unskilled workers are employed for entry-level positions, often with little or no training. Also, there is enormous and increasing cultural diversity within the industry. Figure 13–5 shows the human resources management and development process.

Each segment of the hospitality industry follows the human resources functions. In this section, we will examine them sequentially. The business and economic conditions of recent years necessitated what has been called reengineering, downsizing, or right-sizing.

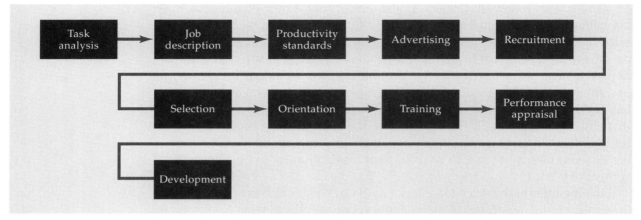

Figure 13–5 *Human Resources Management and Development Process*

Task Analysis

Because human resource or labor costs are the highest single cost of being in business, it has become necessary to examine each task of each employee to determine its outcome on the guest experience. A good example of analyzing a task from a guest's viewpoint is to start when a guest arrives at a hotel. Traditionally, one person acted as a greeter/doorperson and took the guest's luggage; that person gave the luggage to a bellperson, who in turn transported it to the front desk. After the guest had registered, it was quite possible that another bellperson transported the guest's luggage to the assigned room. This not only involved the guest interacting with three or four different individuals, but it also annoyed the guest because of the amount of tipping involved.

Ordinarily, task and job analysis examines the tasks necessary to perform the job; when approved and listed, these tasks become the job description. An example is that the job description of a hotel doorperson would include greeting an arriving automobile, opening the passenger or driver door, welcoming the guests to the hotel, offering to remove the guests' luggage from the car, transporting it to the front desk (or holding it on the cart) while the guests register, and then escorting the guests and transporting the luggage to the allocated room. Some innovative hotels have cross-trained their employees to the point that the person who greets guests outside the hotel actually rooms the guests by handling the check in, allocating the room, and then escorting the guests. This means that the guests only come in contact with one or two employees. The program has been extremely well received by guests.

Job Description

A job description is a detailed description of the activities and outcomes expected of the person performing the job (see Figure 5–1). The job description is important because it can become a legal document. Some cases have come before the courts and administrative agencies in which employees who were dismissed have sued the former employer, claiming that they did not know or were not properly informed of the duties required.

Today, many companies have employees sign their job descriptions to avoid any confusion or misunderstandings about their job and its responsibilities. The job description specifies the knowledge, qualifications, and skills necessary to do the job successfully. Job descriptions can be used as good performance measurement tools.

Productivity Standards

With today's high labor costs, increasing employee productivity has become a major issue. Productivity standards may be established for each position within the organization. They are determined by measuring or timing how long it takes to do a given task. Departments then are staffed according to forecasted demand, whether restaurant covers, hotel occupancy, or attendance at a theme park.

Employee productivity is measured in dollar terms by dividing sales by labor costs. If sales totaled $46,325 and labor costs were $9,265, productivity would be measured as a factor of five. This means that for every dollar in labor costs, $5 in sales was generated. Another way of expressing employee productivity is to divide sales by the number of employees, to arrive at the sales generated per employee.

Other measures of productivity might be the number of covers served by a foodservice employee or the number of guests checked in by a front-desk agent.

Recruitment and Selection

Recruitment and selection is the process of finding the most suitable employee for the available position. The process begins with announcing the vacancy; sometimes this is done first within the organization, then outside. Applications are received from a variety of sources:

- ✔ Internal promotion
- ✔ Employee referrals
- ✔ Applicant files
- ✔ Transfers within the company
- ✔ Advertising
- ✔ Colleges and universities
- ✔ Government-sponsored employment services

Application forms and resumés are accepted and screened by the human resources department. Many companies require applicants to come to the property and personally fill out the application form. The human resources department then reviews the application form and resumé for accuracy and to ensure that the prospective employee is legally entitled to work in the country. It is advisable to do extensive background checks, although most previous employers will, for legal reasons, generally only give the beginning and ending dates of employment. See Figure 13–6 for a description of the recruitment and selection process.

Applicants are invited to attend an interview with the employment manager. This is a general screening interview to determine that the applicant is suitable

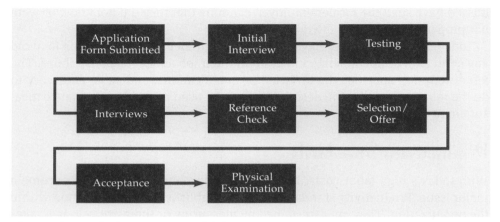

Figure 13–6 *The Recruitment and Selection Process*

for employment in a general way. Employment managers look for dress, mannerisms, attentiveness, attitude, and interest; they also ask questions that encourage the applicant to answer in some detail. This necessitates asking open-ended questions such as "What did you like most and least about your last job?" Questions like this invite the applicant to open up. The two-way exchange of information allows the prospective employee to ask or learn about the job and the corporation. Assuming the applicant makes a favorable impression, she or he will be invited for a second interview with the department head. The interview with the department head will assess the candidate's ability to do the job and his or her interpersonal suitability to join the department team.

Selection means to select the most suitably qualified candidate for the available position. Providing candidates meet the minimum requirements stated in the job specification, then the best individual may be selected from the qualified applicants. Part of the selection process might involve tests (personality, aptitude, skill, psychological) to ensure that candidates possess the requisite interpersonal skills or knowledge to do the job. In addition, some companies, as a condition of employment, require new employees to take a drug-screening test.

Assuming the reference and background checks are positive, a formal offer is made in writing to the prospective employee. The offer outlines the terms and

Human Resources Manager
Checking References

conditions of employment and has a date by which the offer must be accepted. The last step in the recruitment and selection process is a medical examination. The medical examination acts as a precaution for both the employee and the corporation.

Orientation

Either prior to beginning or during the first few days of employment, new hires are required to attend an orientation session. At the orientation, new employees learn details about the corporation's history and about compensation and benefits. Safety and fire prevention are also introduced as well as the property's service philosophy. Department heads and the general manager usually introduce themselves to the new employees and wish them well in their new positions.

Training

Training in many organizations is an ongoing activity that is conducted by a training department, a training manager, or by line management or specially selected individuals within each department. The first step in establishing a training program is to identify training needs and then set training objectives. Because the training must be geared toward guest expectations, training often focuses on areas where current service falls short of guest expectations.

There are five main types of employee training: apprentice, simulation, certification, on-the-job, and off-the-job. Apprentice training is given to people who are new to a particular job. The training is specially designed to teach participants the correct way to do a particular task. This often follows the "tell me, show me, let me do it" routine.

Simulation training simulates the actual workplace. For example, there are specially prepared simulation exercises for travel agents on the Sabre and Apollo airline reservation systems. Once the trainee has reached the required level of proficiency, she or he then is allowed to do real ticketing.

Certification training enables individuals to gain corporate or professional certification by attaining passing scores on practical or theoretical tests. These tests are generally job specific and are helpful in motivating employees to develop in a professional manner. The Culinary Federation of America operates a certification program, as does the National Restaurant Association and the American Hotel and Motel Association.

On-the-job training (OJT) helps maintain standards by having managers, supervisors, trainers, or fellow employees coach individuals in the most effective way to do the required work. OJT allows the trainee to quickly learn the best way to do the work based on the experience of trial and error. New hotel housekeepers may work with an experienced employee for a few days to learn the preferred way to do rooms.

Off-the-job training is done away from the workplace and is usually used for nontechnical training, such as effective communications, team-building, motivation, and leadership. These topics often are handled by outside experts. These training methods help individuals to quickly learn the job and to improve their performance in doing the work. Some interesting anonymous industry comments heard in training sessions include the following:

- ✔ People in the organization are a reflection of the leadership.
- ✔ We don't run restaurants, we manage associations.
- ✔ We hire cheerleaders.
- ✔ What do you do to get your employees to smile? SMILE! I'm lucky if they don't look as if they are in pain!!
- ✔ We are hiring people today that we wouldn't have let in as customers a few years ago.
- ✔ You can teach nice people, but you can't teach people to be nice.
- ✔ You achieve what you inspect, not what you expect.

Performance Appraisal

The purpose of performance appraisal is to compare an employee's actual performance to preestablished standards as described in the job description. Performance appraisal has been viewed by the industry as positive as well as negative. The positive attributes of performance appraisal include giving feedback to employees, building the appraisal into a personal development plan, establishing a rationale for promotion and wage/salary increases, and helping to establish objectives for training programs.

Some of the negative aspects of performance reviews include the following:

- ✔ Too many appraisals expect the immediate supervisor to take sole responsibility for doing the appraisal.
- ✔ Managers often do a poor job of giving feedback to employees.
- ✔ Managers save up incidents to dump on employees at evaluation times.
- ✔ Managers are biased in their appraisals.
- ✔ Managers may be either too hard or too soft on employees.
- ✔ Too many employees are not aware of the performance criteria that they will be evaluated against.

Another major difficulty with most performance appraisal systems is that the judgments involved are frequently subjective, relating primarily to personality traits or observations that cannot be verified. Three common distortions in performance appraisals include the following:

- ✔ Recent behavior influence. An evaluator's judgment may be influenced by the employee's recent behavior (good or bad). It is important to guard against giving recent behavior greater emphasis in the appraisal.
- ✔ The halo effect. The halo effect occurs when a supervisor is overly concerned with one particular aspect of the overall job, such as punctuality. If an employee is punctual, he or she will likely receive a better evaluation than one who is occasionally late even if his or her productivity is somewhat less.
- ✔ Like-me syndrome. We all tend to like people who are similar to ourselves; naturally, there is a tendency to give a better appraisal to those employees who are most like ourselves.

There is an inherent weakness in all appraisals. Any system by which a superior rates a subordinate is likely to cause resentment in the person being rated or anxiety in the rater. The basic answer to the anxiety problem is to develop a

Job Analysis	Describes the job and personal requirements for a particular job.
Performance Standards	States expected performance.
Performance Appraisal	Appraises the level of employee performance and compares each element to standards.

Figure 13–7 *Linkages among Job Analysis, Job Description, and Performance Appraisal*

supportive social system aimed at reducing individual anxiety and thus freeing up energies for constructive purposes. The supportive system includes help from peers and supervisors that will make the employee feel more positive toward the experience and offer a real chance for improvement.

One of the best analogies about managerial feedback to employees was given by Dr. Ken Blanchard in *The One Minute Manager,* who said that there is no such thing as an unmotivated person. An unmotivated employee may be a superstar at the local bowling alley. But imagine that, as Fred rolls the ball down the alley, a supervisor stands there and says "You only knocked down seven pins; why didn't you knock them all down?" Then, to make matters worse, the manager places a curtain in front of the pins so that Fred will not know what to aim for or how well he bowled. Finally, the supervisor removes both the curtain and the pins. When Fred is asked to bowl again, he replies, "I can't; I don't have anything to aim at!" This is analogous to the many people who work for organizations without knowing job performance expectations and the criterion for appraisal.

Performance appraisals make the link between performance standards and organizational goals. Another critical element is the linkage between the job analysis, job description, and appraisal form. Figure 13–7 shows the importance of the linkage among job analysis, job description, and performance appraisal.

Performance appraisals need to be fair, equal, and nondiscriminatory. Performance—not personality—needs to be judged. Although there are a variety of ways to judge employee performance, the graphic scale is the most widely used rating scale. Such scales generally have either five or seven numbers (see Figure 13–8). An alternative format is shown in Figure 13–9.

The biggest advantage of the graphic rating scale is that it saves time for the person completing it, time that should be spent on other things.

Self-appraisal is a form of appraisal that lets employees evaluate their own performance. This may then become the basis of discussion with the supervisor/manager. It also complements an MBO (Management by Objective) program as it enables employees to have a say in setting their own objectives. Obviously, the supervisor/manager will also complete an appraisal form and sit down to compare notes with the employee.

Developmental appraisal is a progressive appraisal technique, aimed at helping the employee to develop and to improve in the performance of his or her duties. A specific employee development plan will stipulate the kind of development that will help the employee to improve performance. An example of this form is shown in Figure 13–10.

The important thing to remember when considering performance appraisal and the law is that managers must run a tight ship. Appraisals must not only be

Appearance

Neat and in good taste	Neat but occasionally not in good taste	Sometimes careless	Untidy	Not suitable for the job
1	2	3	4	5

Ability to Learn

Learns with exceptional rapidity	Grasps instructions readily	Average ability to learn new things	Somewhat slow in learning	Limited in new duties
1	2	3	4	5

Figure 13–8 *Graphic Rating Scales*

Accuracy

1. ( ) Rarely makes mistakes
2. ( ) Above average
3. ( ) Average
4. ( ) Below average
5. ( ) Highly inaccurate

Figure 13–9 *Performance Appraisal Checklist*

fair but must also be seen to be fair. This means that when appraisals are used as a criteria for promotion (or in extreme circumstances, the release of an employee), the appraisal system must withstand careful scrutiny. It only takes one disgruntled employee to file a grievance with the Equal Employment Opportunity Commission for a substantial amount of management time and money to be spent. Even if the company were to win the case it would still lose money. Team appraisals are becoming popular because most people don't want to let the team down, so each member encourages others to excel.

Compensation

Compensation is the term used to describe what most people call a paycheck. Actually, however, compensation is more than a paycheck; it is the total reward system, consisting of established policies and procedures to govern the compensation package. The compensation package includes wages, salaries, and benefits. The term *wages* is generally used with hourly employees, and the term *salaries* usually is used for employees who work for a set rate of pay. Compensation and benefits can amount to 25 to 39 percent of payroll, making them the highest single cost factor in the hospitality industry.

The Fair Labor Standards Act (FLSA) requires industries to distinguish not between management and nonmanagement, but between exempt and nonexempt

MBO – DEVELOPMENTAL TYPE APPRAISAL FORM

Priority Urgency	Duties	Performance Expectations	Performance Appraisal				
			Far Below Standard	Below Standard	Meets Standard	Above Standard	Well Above Standard

EMPLOYEE DEVELOPMENT PLAN:

1. What kind of development will help improve performance?
   (_____) a. on-the-job training
   (_____) b. training course
   (_____) c. self-development
   (_____) d.

2. How will this developmental training be arranged? _____
   _____
   _____

3. How long will it take? _____
   _____
   _____

Figure 13–10 *MBO/Development Appraisal Form*

employees. Exempt employees are those who fall under section 13 (a) (1) of the federal minimum wage law. Exempt employees are not paid overtime because they are performing managerial supervisory duties a minimum of 60 percent of their work time. Nonexempt employees are paid overtime for any hours worked beyond the thirty-five or forty-hour work week.

Appropriate levels of compensation are set once the job is evaluated for skill levels, responsibility, competencies, knowledge, and working conditions. Frequently, a range is set, with increments allowing for progression after a specified time. Jobs then are graded and priced, taking into account items such as tips or service charges.

Some companies offer bonuses or other incentives based on achieving certain results; others have instituted employee stock ownership plans (ESOP). The idea of employee ownership of a company is not new, but it does improve commitment and performance, as does the concept of profit sharing.

Over the years, various legislative acts have been enacted that have affected hospitality human resources. The Fair Labor Standards Act (1938 and as amended) is a broad federal statute that covers the following:

- ✔ Federal minimum wage law
- ✔ Employee meals and meal credit
- ✔ Equal pay
- ✔ Child labor
- ✔ Overtime
- ✔ Tips, tip credits, and tip-pooling procedures
- ✔ Uniforms and uniform maintenance
- ✔ Record keeping
- ✔ Exempt versus nonexempt employees

The Equal Pay Act of 1963 prohibits companies from paying different salaries on the basis of sex. The Civil Rights Act of 1964 went further and established the Equal Employment Opportunity Commission (EEOC). This act makes it unlawful to discriminate with respect to hiring, compensating, working conditions, privileges, or terms of employment. In 1967, the Age Discrimination Act was passed, prohibiting employment discrimination against those over forty years of age.

Employee safety has become significantly more important because of the large increase in workers' compensation claims. This increase has resulted in large increases in insurance premiums. Employers have been forced to pay special attention to employee safety, including the use and handling of dangerous chemicals.

Employee Assistance Programs (EAP) have been instituted at many progressive companies. Employees who have problems may request help (assistance) in confidence, without losing their jobs. The emphasis of most EAPs is on prevention and on intervening before a crisis stage is reached.

Employee Development

Employee development is a natural progression from appraisal. A development plan is made by the employee and his or her supervisor. The plan will outline the development activity and indicate when the development will take place. In well-run corporations, employee development is ongoing; it may take the form of in-house training or workshops and seminars on specific topics.

Certification is an excellent form of employee development because it validates a person's ability to do an excellent job and become more professional. Certification can be internal or external. Internal certification occurs when a company has stipulated certain criteria associated with a position (such as knowing the menu, being able to describe each item, and so on). External certification occurs when an employee takes courses toward a professional designation, such as the National Restaurant Association's Foodservice Management Professional (FMP).

Corporate Profile:

Marriott International, Inc./Host Marriott Corporation

Marriott International became a public company in October 1993, when Marriott Corporation split into two separate companies. Marriott International manages lodging and service businesses. It has operations in fifty states and twenty-four countries, with approximately 170,000 employees. It has annual sales of about $8 billion.

Host Marriott Corporation focuses on two basic businesses—real estate ownership and airport and tollroad concessions. Host Marriott has operations or properties in thirty-eight states and six countries, with approximately 23,000 employees. The company has annual sales of about $1.3 billion, with significant operating cash flow.

ator of timeshare projects (71,000 interval owners at 31 resorts). In total, the group manages or franchises over 1,200 hotels with approximately 229,000 rooms.

The service group has three principal divisions. Marriott Management Services provides food and facilities management for business, education, and health care clients, with more than 3,000 accounts. Marriott Senior Living Services manages communities offering independent and assisted living for older Americans. Marriott Distribution Services provides food and related products to the company's operations and external clients through eleven distribution centers. J. W. Marriott, Jr., is chairman, president, and chief executive officer of Marriott International.

Marriott International, Inc.

"We are committed to being the best lodging and management services company in the world by treating employees in ways that create extraordinary customer service and shareholder value."
—Mission statement

Marriott International owns the trademarks, trade names, and reservation and franchise systems that were formerly owned by Marriott Corporation. The new company has two operating groups. Their divisions are leaders in their respective businesses and enjoy strong customer preference.

The Lodging Group is composed of Marriott's eight hotel management divisions: Marriott Hotels and Resorts, managing or franchising full-service hotels (316 hotels); Courtyard, the company's moderately priced lodging division (296 hotels); Residence Inns, the leader in the extended-stay segment (224 hotels); Fairfield Inn, Marriott's economy lodging division (284 hotels); TownePlace Suites, the newest moderately priced lodging product designed for the extended-stay traveler (the first opened in 1997); Ritz-Carlton, the premier hotel brand in the luxury segment (33 hotels); Renaissance Hotels and Resorts, providing upscale, full-service accommodations for business, group, and resort travelers (71 hotels); and Marriott Vacation Club International, a premier developer and oper-

Host Marriott Corporation

The leading operator of airport and tollroad food, beverage, and merchandise concessions, Host Marriott expanded in 1992 by acquiring the airport operations of Dobbs Houses, Inc. Host Marriott now serves approximately seventy-five airports, primarily in the United States, with some concessions in Australia, New Zealand, and Pakistan. The company also operates ninety-three food and merchandise units on fourteen U.S. tollroads and has concessions at forty-two sports and entertainment attractions. Host is a licensee of seventeen major nationally branded food and merchandise concepts.

The company owns 130 Marriott lodging properties (including two hotels now under construction) and fourteen retirement communities, located in thirty-three states and three countries that are managed under long-term agreements with Marriott International, Inc. Host Marriott or its subsidiaries act as general or limited partners in a number of Marriott lodging partnerships, and own certain parcels of land.

Host Marriott's lodging portfolio includes twenty-eight full-service hotels, among them the San Francisco Marriott and the New York Marriott Marquis; fifty-four Courtyard hotels (moderate price segment); eighteen Residence Inn properties (extended-stay segment); and thirty Fairfield Inn properties (economy segment). Richard E. Marriott is chairman of Host Marriott.

Employee Retention

Employee retention is the exact opposite of employee turnover. Whether it is called retention or turnover, the subject is still a major concern for the hospitality industry, in general, and human resources directors, in particular.

It is frustrating for management to spend time and effort on employees who go through the employment process only to leave a short time later. Retention is expressed as a percentage; if a department has one hundred employees on January 1 and sixty-three stay through the year, then the retention rate is 63 percent. This means that thirty-seven people left the organization and had to be replaced. Experts estimate that the turnover of one hourly position per week costs between $150,000 and $213,000 per year.[3]

Peter Yu, president of Richfield Hotel Management, estimated that the entire industry loses $1.8 billion per year because of employee turnover. Each turnover costs Richfield about $1,400. Richfield has a 35 to 40 percent retention rate, which has improved by 10 percent since beginning an employee-maintenance program; the next goal is to achieve 50 percent retention.[4]

To reduce losses, Ritz-Carlton intensified its employee-selection process. Then the company encouraged employees' input in creating their work environment. Within a few years, the company lowered its turnover rate from 90 percent to 30 percent. Ritz-Carlton aspires to maintain a 20 percent turnover rate.[5]

Equal Employment Opportunity (EEO)

Equal employment opportunity is the legal right of all individuals to be considered for employment and promotion on the basis of their ability and merit. The intent of this legislation is to prevent discrimination against applicants for the reasons given in the Civil Rights Act. The EEOC is the organization that individuals may turn to if they feel that they have been discriminated against. If it agrees, the commission will file charges against individuals or organizations.

Americans with Disabilities Act (ADA)

The ADA has two components: Employment and Public Accommodations. The ADA prohibits discrimination against persons with disabilities and stipulates that employers must make "readily achievable" modifications to their premises and to the work practices and working conditions for the disabled. Existing facilities need not be retrofitted to provide full accessibility. However, barrier removal that is readily achievable and easily completed without significant difficulty or expense is required in all existing buildings.

Harassment

Employers are responsible for creating and maintaining a working environment that is pleasant, and for avoiding hostile, offensive, intimidating, or discriminatory conduct or statements. In other words, the workplace must be kept free from all forms of harassment, including those based on sex, race, religious choice, ethnic background, and age. Sexual harassment, in particular, has occurred frequently during the past few years. Although very controversial in its identification and definition, sexual harassment does include unwanted sexual advances, requests for sexual favors, and verbal or physical actions of a sexual nature. It is important to note that an offensive environment does not need to involve a request for sexual favors. An offensive environment also may be created by lewd jokes or comments, displaying explicit or sexually suggestive material, or hands-on behavior.

In order to handle such an issue in an appropriate manner, the management should take the following actions:

1. Establish a sexual harassment policy that defines clearly what will not be tolerated and states the penalties for violation.
2. React promptly to reports with even-handed, thorough investigation.
3. Keep all instances confidential.
4. Keep appropriate documentation and decide on the appropriate disciplinary action.

Culture

Culture is a learned behavior. Someone who lives in the United States learns from its culture a unique set of beliefs, values, attitudes, habits, customs, traditions, and other forms of behavior. Besides other cultures like African, Asian, Latino, European, and American, there are cultural variations, such as African-American, Asian-American, Hispanic-American, European-American, and French-Canadian, for example. These cultural variations are a blend of cultures.

Culture influences the way people behave, and there are many differences among the various cultures. For instance, American culture is more individualistic than the Asian or Latin cultures. Consider also the differences between the genders in these cultures. America's multicultural society gives us an opportunity to learn from one another instead of simply thinking "my way is best." It is best to be aware of and respect the culture of others and try to harmonize with it; otherwise, misunderstanding might occur.

Multicultural management recognizes cultural differences among employees that are attributable to membership in distinct ethnic groups. Multicultural management is an approach to managing the workplace that allows for differences in values arising from gender, economic level, and age, as well as ethnic group. In today's hospitality industry, it is necessary for managers—and, indeed, all employees—to have a cross-cultural awareness and an understanding of ethnic identity. Cultural barriers in hospitality workplaces do exist, therefore it is important to understand ethnic diversity, minorities, and how to train ethnic groups in order to understand the various cultural aspects in our hospitality workplace.

Cultural Barriers

Culture can be manifested in many ways, such as style of dress, language, food, gestures, manners, and so on. Although many individuals have difficulty dealing with foreign customs and language, these are relatively easy components, because they are visible and comprehensible. It is much harder to detect and to deal with values, assumptions, and perceptions.

Adjusting to another culture can be particularly frustrating if one comes from a low-context culture and has to operate in a high-context culture. A low-context culture is one in which the bulk of information, intentions, and meanings are conveyed in words and sentences; context, therefore, plays a smaller role. High-context cultures are those in which the context is of great importance and what is behind the words is as important as the words themselves.

The North American and North European cultures are low-context cultures. Information and intentions are expressed in words and sentences in the clearest possible manner. The prevailing culture in Japan is a high-context culture; not only does what is said count, but how it is said, who said it, and when. What was not said is also significant, as are the pauses, the silences, and the tone. In high-context cultures, reading between the lines and interpreting the meaning behind the words is of utmost importance; the words themselves have different meanings and do not always convey true intentions to an outsider. For example, the Japanese rarely use the word *no;* instead, they use a host of substitutes that may not convey their true intention to the Western ear. Similarly, when Japanese use affirmative statements, they do not assign the same meaning to them as we do.

Language

Language can be another barrier to cultural understanding. Even when people use the same language, misunderstandings and misinterpretations occur. The same words and symbols have different meanings to individuals from different cultural backgrounds.

Ethnic Diversity

Ethnic diversity refers to accepting all people regardless of appearances or mannerisms. Cultural diversity enriches the workplace. America's ethnic diversity is growing. By the year 2000, the work force is expected to consist of Hispanics, 29 percent; African-Americans, 18 percent; and Asian-Americans, 11 percent.[6] These core groups will be the backbone of the hospitality industry. The growth projected for the Asian and Hispanic populations in the United States will, in the twenty-first century, mean that one quarter to one-third of all workplaces will belong to racial or ethnic minority groups.[7]

Personal Cultural Barriers

We too often approach others from our own cultural perspective and expect them to be like us. We react when people respond or behave in a way that is "different." These behaviors may lead to stereotyping—always expecting certain groups to behave in certain ways. A bad experience with one person does not mean that all experiences with others from that culture will be bad. Preconceived negative attitudes about certain groups is called *prejudice.*

Ideally, the managers of tomorrow will welcome the ethnic diversity that they are bound to encounter, and they will have a personal desire to learn more about cultures and environments different from their own. But even those employers who don't see cultural pluralism as an extension of the practices of American democracy realize that they must be prepared to function effectively as hospitality managers in a pluralistic environment. Culture has a profound impact on the attitudes, priorities, and behavior of individuals and groups. To be able to interact with people from different cultures is vital in order to understand their values, norms, and priorities.

Hospitality managers have a responsibility to develop and recognize the realities facing the hospitality industry in the next ten to fifteen years. Ethnic and cultural diversity is a large part of that reality.

Trends in Marketing, Human Resources, and Culture

- ✔ Human resources directors becoming marketing-oriented in order to attract and retain the best possible employees
- ✔ Human resources directors becoming more proactive in employment and staffing
- ✔ Use of the Internet for posting vacancies and e-mail for applications
- ✔ Use of more behavioral, structured interviews
- ✔ Relationship marketing, including keeping track of guests, sending birthday cards, etc.
- ✔ Partnering, such as a Subway store at a gas station, twin restaurant locations, or cooperative advertising (i.e., American Express and Delta Airlines)
- ✔ Direct marketing with databases of mailing lists
- ✔ Use of the Internet for communicating information and for reservations

---

Cooperation

The executive housekeeper of the Lattuca Inn has repeatedly complained to you about Bernise, a long-time housekeeper at the hotel. As the human resources manager, you feel obliged to confront Bernise about ignoring her boss. Bernise says she does not like the executive housekeeper and, after speaking with her, she still refuses to cooperate.

Recently, Bernise was asked to present a voucher for her lunches. Reports have come in from the employee cafeteria showing that she still will not cooperate.

Discussion Question

1. As human resources manager, what should you do?

Too Much of a Good Thing

Schrock's Pub and Steak House in Little Doe, Montana, is a booming success and has been for more than thirty years. Once the only establishment in Little Doe, Schrock's is now facing competition from other independent restaurant/bars and a few large, national chains along the lines of Chili's and Applebee's.

Schrock and his sons, proprietors of Schrock's after purchasing the pub from Ken Crocker prior to World War II, saw the effect that the new competition was having on overall sales and revenue. They realized that while they were unable to compete on price, they could indeed compete in other areas such as menu offerings and ambiance. Through strict controls on cost, both in the kitchen and in the bar, they were able to remain competitive. Whereas in the past, a dish was prepared at the whim and attitude of the cook, to the delight of the patrons, all recipes were now standardized. Under the new kitchen controls, food cost to sales were lowered and each item's contribution margin increased. The same type of controls were instituted in the bar with similar results.

All was well with Schrock's Pub until Jay, the grandson of Jacob, returned home from the university, where he majored in hospitality/restaurant management. When the elder Schrock sat down with Jay to review the business prior to Jay's becoming assistant general manager, Jay noted that Schrock's seemed to be holding onto its usual customer base. Sales were relatively flat and overall profit, while not as good as prechain competition days, was okay. Jay noticed and pointed out to the elder Schrock that since all the new controls were put into effect, consumer complaints were increasing. The complaints centered around the portion size and lack of bite in the bar drinks. Obviously, the clientele, although loyal, were expressing some dissatisfaction when they compared the new Schrock's to the old. Further research found that customers did not think that the service was as personal as it used to be. For example, everyone knew John Reigal did not particularly like the taste of vodka, but Al the bartender was no longer able to tailor John's drinks due to the new control system. Similar stories about the lack of responsiveness of the waitstaff were forthcoming from an informal focus group.

The family then began to discuss the merits of standardization that had keep Schrock's afloat as opposed to the less conventional approach that made Schrock's a success in the early years. The discussion swirled around issues of efficiency, empowerment, control, and competitive edge.

The Schrock's have contracted you, a senior associate at Norman Hotel and Restaurants Inc., an international consulting firm, to assist in bettering Schrock's Pub.

Discussion Question

1. How would you advise them?

The Forum Takes Wing

In August of 1994, Steve Departe, former chef at the exclusive Broodmoore Country Club, and his wife Alice Cable opened The Forum, a classic European restaurant in a small suburb of a large, midwestern city.

Given their experience, including Alice's family's having a successful chain of pizza shops, the Forum opened to great acclaim. The local newspaper's restaurant critic gave it four out of five forks. The critic especially praised the level of service, the atmosphere, and the appetizers and entrees. The food was of top quality and prepared fresh with great flair. The waitstaff was pulled from various area restaurants and country clubs and thus, had a great deal of experience and knowledge of foodservice.

Not only did The Forum receive good press, it also enjoyed good word-of-mouth recommendations. For a town and metro area accustomed to midwestern fare—steak, chops, ribs, chicken, and so forth—The Forum was a success.

The Forum also contained a lounge to handle the waiting crowds. In keeping with chef Departe's vision, it had an extensive selection of premium wines for both the lounge and dining room. Also true to his vision, beer selection was limited to a few imports and only the top domestic brand. The liquor selection was not spectacular, but offered a great deal more variety than many other local restaurants and stand-alone lounges.

The dining room, especially on the weekends, was full. It was not very large, seating only eighty-five customers. Reservations were a must for Friday and Saturday, however Sunday was usually the slowest day. The weekdays were often very slow, but the rush during the weekend evened out the week. The average check per diner was about $16.50 on the weekends. This represented an average contribution margin of almost $6.00. Food cost to sales ranged from 43.1 to 47.3 percent. A separate analysis of the lounge showed a contribution margin of almost $4.00 per person and food and beverage cost to sales ratio of only 27 percent.

When chef Departe became aware of the results, he did some research on the surrounding proprietors and friends in the industry. He concluded that his food cost to sales ratio was too high. He also noticed the abundance of sports bars in the area and their relatively low food cost to sales ratio and high contribution margins.

During the summer of 1995 and fall of 1996, chef Departe expanded his lounge business to include a few inexpensive bar items such as chicken wings and onion rings. He also extended the selection of beers available. Chef Departe eventually gave the lounge a sports theme, taking advantage of the local baseball team being in the playoffs and the new football expansion team. He installed two large-screen televisions for the fans and ran "munchie" and dinner specials during televised events of the home team. The results astounded chef Departe, as his lounge total sales climbed and his margin increased. By December 1996, The Forum had been redesigned and reopened as The Arena, a premier sports bar specializing in hot wings and fried mushrooms.

Much to the dismay of chef Departe, the results did not mirror his lounge's initial success. Within a month, his total revenues were 40 percent below the previous year. His staff of trained, expert servers were let go and replaced with fewer and less well trained college students.

Discussion Questions

1. What do you think went wrong with the running of the restaurant?
2. How would you advise chef Departe and his wife as far as changing the concept of the restaurant is concerned?
3. What marketing strategies would you use to bring in customers and keep the contribution margins high and the food cost to sales ratio low?
4. How would you handle the situation?

Summary

1. Marketing and human resources are specialized departments that serve other departments of the hospitality industry.
2. The main purpose of marketing is to create customers. It includes environmental, social, political, technological, and competitive analysis. Place, product, price, promotion, packaging, programming, and people altogether make up the marketing mix of hospitality.
3. Efficient, guest-focused employees are important for the success of an industry. Applicants have to go through a recruitment and selection process, orientation, and careful training.
4. Employees are evaluated by performance appraisals. In order for an appraisal to be fair there has to be a close link between job analysis, job description, and the appraisal.
5. Every hospitality industry is required to comply with the Equal Employment Opportunity Commission, to make modifications to the workplace and its practices to accommodate disabled workers and keep the workplace free of all forms of harassment.
6. As America's ethnic diversity is growing, management needs to recognize cultural differences. In this sense it is essential to avoid stereotyping and to consider differences such as language, values, and perceptions.

Review Exercises

1. What is meant by the term *market assessment?* In this context explain the purpose of environmental analysis.
2. Explain the purpose of competitive analysis and explain the terms *comparison matrix* and *positioning.*
3. Describe the importance of price and product and list two ways used to determine price.
4. What is the difference between marketing and sales?
5. Briefly explain the process of employee selection.
6. Name and describe positive and negative effects of performance evaluation, in consideration of the like-me syndrome and halo effect.
7. Define culture and its impact on the hospitality industry in today's pluralistic environment.

Key Words and Concepts

Age Discrimination Act	Equal employment opportunity	Lifestyles	Political analysis
Americans with Disabilities Act	Equal Employment Opportunity Commission	Market demand	Positioning
Civil Rights Act	Equal Pay Act	Market share	Productivity standards
Comparison matrix	Exempt and nonexempt employees	Marketing action plan	Product life cycle
Compensation	Expense accounts	Marketing goals and objectives	Recruitment
Competitive analysis	Fair Labor Standards Act	Marketing mix	Selection
Corporate philosophy	Focus groups	Orientation	Social analysis
Culture	Harassment	Performance appraisal	Target markets
Demographics	Job description	Performance evaluation	Task analysis
Economic analysis		Place, product, price, and promotion	Technological analysis
Environmental analysis			Training

Notes

[1] Alastair M. Morrison, *Hospitality and Travel Marketing*, Albany, N.Y.: Delmar, 1989, p. 14.

[2] Ricky W. Griffin and Ronald J. Ebert, *Business*, 4th ed. Upper Saddle River, New Jersey: Prentice-Hall, p. 455.

[3] Timothy N. Troy, "Hospitality Associations Waging War in Minnesota," *Hotel and Motel Management, 208*, 15, September 6, 1993, p. 6.

[4] Ibid.

[5] Ibid.

[6] Dennis Law, "Making Diversity Work," *Restaurants and Institutions, 104*, 2, January 15, 1994, p. 84.

[7] Ibid.

Leadership and Management

After reading and studying this chapter you should be able to do the following:

✔ Distinguish the characteristics and attributes of leaders
✔ Define leadership
✔ Distinguish between transactional and transformational leadership
✔ Differentiate between leadership and management
✔ Define ethics and apply the importance of ethical behaviors to the hospitality industry

Leadership

Fascination with leadership goes back many centuries. Lately, however, it has come into prominence as the hospitality, tourism, and other industries strive for perfection in the delivery of services and products in an increasingly competitive environment. Leaders can and do make a difference.

Few tasks or goals can be accomplished by one person working alone. For this reason, society has many organizations. Few groups, however, can accomplish much without an individual who acts as leader. The leader can and often does have a significant influence on the group and its direction.

Characteristics of Leaders

Leaders can be identified by certain characteristics. For example, the *U.S. Guidebook for Marines* lists the following traits:

- ✔ Bearing
- ✔ Courage
- ✔ Decisiveness
- ✔ Dependability
- ✔ Endurance
- ✔ Enthusiasm
- ✔ Initiative
- ✔ Integrity
- ✔ Judgment
- ✔ Justice
- ✔ Knowledge
- ✔ Loyalty
- ✔ Tact
- ✔ Unselfishness

A Marine officer will likely add that what is most important is integrity. Integrity has been described as doing something right even though no one may be aware of it.

In addition to the leadership traits, there are also identifiable practices common to leaders.[1]

1. Challenge the process: active, not passive; search for opportunities; experiment and take risks
2. Inspire a shared vision: create a vision; envision the future; enlist others
3. Enable others to act: not alone; foster collaboration; strengthen others
4. Model the way: plan; set examples; plan small wins
5. Encourage the heart: share the passion; recognize individual contributions; celebrate accomplishments

Definitions of Leadership

Because of the complexities of leadership, different types of leadership, and individual perceptions of leaders, leadership has several definitions. Many definitions share commonalities, but there are also differences. In terms of hospitality leadership, the following definition is appropriate: Leading is the process by which a person with vision is able to influence the activities and outcomes of others in a desired way.

Leaders know what they want and why they want it—and they are able to communicate it to others and gain their cooperation and support.

Leadership theory and practice has evolved over time to a point where current practitioners may be identified as transactional or transformational leaders.

Transactional Leadership

Transactional leadership is viewed as a process by which a leader is able to bring about desired actions from others by using certain behaviors, rewards, or incentives. In essence, an exchange or transaction takes place between leader and follower.[2] Figure 14–1 shows the transactional model of leadership.

This concept illustrates the coming together of the leader, the situation, and the followers. A hotel general manager who pressures the food and beverage director to achieve certain goals in exchange for a bonus is an example of transactional leadership.

Transformational Leadership

Leadership involves looking for ways to bring about longer-term, higher-order changes in follower behavior.[3] This brings us to transformational leadership. The term *transformational leadership* is used to describe the process of eliciting performance above and beyond normal expectations.[4] A transformational leader is one who inspires others to reach beyond themselves and do more than

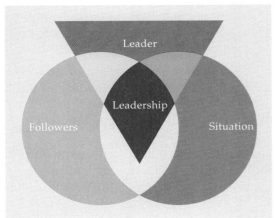

Figure 14–1 *Transactional Model of Leadership* (Warren Bennis, *On Becoming a Leader,* Reading, Mass.: Addison-Wesley, p. 45.)

Corporate Profile: Health Fitness Dynamics, Inc.

HFD was founded in 1977 by Judith Singer. According to Dr. Singer, it was "originally a health fitness promotion company that worked with major corporations and government agencies to help them develop wellness programs." Today, however, HFD specializes in the design, development, marketing, and management of health spas.

Singer single-handedly operated the facility until 1981, when she moved to Florida to become the ladies' spa director at a well-known Florida spa. At this time, Health Fitness Dynamic became an inactive company. Soon after moving to Florida, Singer attended a convention where she met Patricia Mortenson. Dr. Singer offered Mortenson the job of fitness supervisor at the spa where she was employed. Two years later, in 1983, they decided to leave the spa and incorporate HFD in Florida. HFD became the first full-service health spa consulting company in the United States.

Due to its uniqueness, Singer and Mortenson faced some challenges getting started, but their forward-thinking and accurate predictions allowed them to succeed in their endeavor. The owners believed that "the future would bring about a heightened awareness of spas . . . and, therefore, an increase in their numbers and usage." They had the foresight to realize an unmet need

Patricia Mortenson

Judith Singer

and were, therefore, in a position to assume a valuable role in the growth of the health spa industry. Still, Singer and Mortenson faced formidable challenges such as that of educating their clients on how to market and manage spas as profit centers and how to distinguish between "destination" and "amenity" spas.

In 1985, HFD developed a proprietary software package to aid their clients in planning spa facilities. According to Singer and Mortenson, "it has proven to be a significant asset in helping our clients make sound business decisions and has also helped to educate many developers, resort owners and operators, architects, interior designers, etc." HFD has also designed and implemented systems of operations that enhance "not only the guest experience, but also the marketing potential of the spa." HFD strives to maintain the utmost in service. Its credo is providing maximum client contact and keeping their service fresh and personalized. Health Fitness Dynamics, Inc. also serves its clients by offering them the opportunity to work with their extensive network of resource people.

Judith Singer and Patricia Mortenson are truly respected ladies in the fields of service and hospitality. Together, they have pioneered a new frontier in the tourism world and, more importantly, have done so successfully.

they originally thought possible; this is accomplished by raising their commitment to a shared vision of the future.[5]

Transformational leaders have a hands-on philosophy, not in terms of performing the day-to-day tasks of subordinates, but in developing and encouraging their followers individually.[6] Transformational leadership involves three important factors:

1. Charisma
2. Individual consideration
3. Intellectual stimulation

Examples of Leadership Excellence

Dr. Martin Luther King, Jr., was one of the most charismatic transformational leaders in history. King dedicated his life to achieving rights for all citizens by nonviolent methods. His dream of how society could be was shared by millions of Americans. In 1964 Dr. King won the Nobel Peace Prize.

Martin Luther King, Jr.

In the hospitality and tourism industry, one of the outstanding transformational leaders is Wayne Calloway, former CEO of Pepsico. He had a vision that Pepsico could become the best consumer products company in the world. He envisioned a day when pizza, tacos, and chicken would be as convenient and easy to get as a bag of potato chips. With this vision, Calloway set about changing the way the company's Pizza Hut, Taco Bell, and KFC chains offer their services to the public. Now Pizza Hut's delivery and carry-out services earn twice what the eat-in restaurants do, and vendors at football stadiums, basketball arenas, school cafeterias, and airport shops sell Pizza Hut pizza.[7]

Another transformational leader is Herb Kelleher, president and CEO of Southwest Airlines. He is able to inspire his followers to pursue his corporate vision and reach beyond themselves to give Southwest Airlines that something extra that sets it apart from its competitors.

Wayne Calloway

Kelleher recognizes that the company does not exist merely for the gratification of its employees; he knows that Southwest Airlines must perform and be profitable. However, he believes strongly that exceptional performance can best be attained by valuing individuals for themselves. Passengers who fly Southwest may see Herb Kelleher; he travels frequently and is likely to be found serving drinks, fluffing pillows, or just wandering up and down the aisle talking to passengers. The success of Southwest and the enthusiasm of its employees indicate that Herb Kelleher has achieved his goal of weaving together individual and corporate interests so that all members of the Southwest family benefit. Kelleher proves that transformational behavior (visioning, valuing, articulating, inspiring, empowering, and continually communicating) can be practiced by leaders in all types and at all levels of an organization.[8]

Another great leader in the restaurant industry was Ray Kroc of McDonald's, whose actions tell the tale. Consider the following example of how Ray Kroc instilled his vision of cleanliness:

On his way back to the office from an important lunch at the best place in town, Ray Kroc asked his driver to pass through several McDonald's parking lots. In one parking lot, he spotted paper littering the parking area. He went to the nearest pay phone, called the office, got the name of the store manager, and called him to offer help in picking up the trash. Both Ray Kroc, the owner of the McDonald's chain in his expensive business suit, and the young manager of the store met in the parking lot and got on their hands and knees to pick up the paper.

This anecdote has been told thousands of times within the McDonald's system to emphasize the importance of the vision of cleanliness.

In their fascinating book entitled *Lessons in Leadership: Perspectives for Hospitality Industry Success,* Bill Fisher, president and COO of the American Hotel

Personal Profile: Herb Kelleher

Herb Kelleher, CEO of Southwest Airlines, is the living embodiment of the phrase *one of a kind.* With his charismatic personality, he is a person who leaves a distinctive mark on whatever he does.

Since the birth of Southwest Airlines in 1971 as a tiny Texas commuter airline with four airplanes, Herb Kelleher—simply Herb to even his most distant acquaintances—has nurtured Southwest Airlines into the eighth largest airline, with revenues of $1.2 billion a year. The company has been profitable every year since 1973. When other carriers lost billions or were struggling with bankruptcy during the early 1990s, Southwest was the only company that remained consistently profitable—a record unmatched in the U.S. airline industry—cheerfully pursuing its growth plans by buying more planes, expanding into new cities, and hiring personnel. Southwest is also a model of efficiency: It is an eleven-time winner of the U.S. Department of Transportation's Triple Crown, a monthly citation for the best on-time performance, fewest lost bags, and fewest overall complaints. Now that it is once again a time of prosperity, Kelleher's operation, based on flights covering relatively short distances for prices that are sometimes

Herb Kelleher and a Southwest Airplane

shockingly low, is likely to experience rapid growth and become even more of a leading power.

One of the keys to this success lies in the company's mission. Southwest Airlines aims at providing cheap, simple, and focused airline service. Kelleher devoted enormous attention to thousands of small decisions, all designed to achieve simplicity. Among these small but tremendously strategic decisions were the removal of closets at the front of the planes, to improve passengers' speed in boarding and departing; and no onboard food, except snacks, which is justified by the short distances the flights cover on average (about 375 miles). Southwest also refused the computerized reservation system used by travel agents. Nearly half of all Southwest tickets are sold directly to customers, saving about $30 million annually. There is no assigned seating, no first-class seating, no baggage transfer. Planes have been standardized: Southwest only operates one type of aircraft, the 737, which simplifies flight crew training and maintenance personnel training.

These relatively minor privations have their positive counterpart in the fact that Southwest ground crew can turn around a plane at the gate in about fifteen minutes!

and Motel Association, and Charles Bernstein, editor of *Nation's Restaurant News,* interviewed more than one-hundred industry leaders and asked each to respond in an up-close-and-personal manner to some excellent questions. Some of their answers follow.

"Experience is a hard teacher. It gives the test first, and then you learn the lesson." Richard P. Mayer, former chairman and CEO of Kentucky Fried Chicken and president of General Foods Corporation, says that the key traits and factors that he looks for in assessing talent include the following:

- ✔ Established personal goals
- ✔ The drive and ambition to attain those goals, tempered and strengthened with integrity
- ✔ Proven analytical and communications skills
- ✔ Superior interpersonal capabilities
- ✔ A sense of humor
- ✔ An awareness and appreciation of the world beyond her or his business specialty

Bill Fisher, President and COO, the American Hotel and Motel Association

The airline's customers especially appreciate its low fares and on-time schedules.

Who is behind all this? The airline's success is credited to Kelleher's unorthodox personality and entrepreneurial management style. Born and raised in New Jersey, he was the son of the general manager of Campbell Soups Inc. He began to show leadership qualities as student body president both in high school and in college. From his original idea of becoming a journalist, Kelleher shifted his goal to the practice of law. By the mid-1960s, he was successfully practicing in San Antonio, Texas, his wife's hometown. However, he was always seeking the possibility of starting a venture of his own. The big chance came in 1966, when a banker client, Rolling King, suggested that Texas needed a short-haul commuter airline. That was the trigger: Southwest was born in 1971.

Steve Lewing, a Gruntal & Co. analyst, describes Kelleher as "brilliant, charming, cunning and tough."[1] He is, indeed, a unique character. He is a man characterized by a strong sense of humor, who has appeared in public dressed as Elvis and the Easter Bunny, who "has carved an antic public persona out of his affection for cigarettes, bourbon, and bawdy stories."[2]

The CEO, like all great leaders, never stepped into an ivory tower. He is directly supervising his business, personally approving expenses over $1,000. His outstanding hands-on efforts also lead to unusually good labor-management relations, on the basis of the motto "People are the most important of resources." In fact, he has managed to establish very strongly that old bond of loyalty between employees and their company that may have disappeared elsewhere in the American corporate environment.

He represents some sort of a father figure to his employees, as well as the jester, the "Lord of Ha-Ha." This personal feature is, and must be, reflected in his personnel: "What we are looking for, first and foremost, is a sense of humor," says Kelleher, "and then people who have to excel to satisfy themselves."[3] The effort that he gets out of his employees makes the real difference. Unlike workers at most other carriers, Southwest employees are willing to pitch in whenever needed. For example, a reservation clerk in Dallas took a call from an anxious customer who was putting his eighty-eight-year-old mother aboard a flight to St. Louis. The woman was quite frail, the fellow explained, and he wasn't quite sure she could handle the change of planes in Tulsa. "No sweat," replied the clerk, "I'll fly with her as far as Tulsa and make sure she gets safely on the St. Louis flight."

Kelleher's outstanding leadership ability is also shown in his long-term thinking. He has gathered a top-rank team of potential successors, which will guarantee the airline's future prosperity. However, Kelleher will be hard to replace. He is the leader who inspires, the amiable uncle to refer to, the cheerleader who motivates, the clown who makes it fun.

[1] Kenneth Labich, "Is Herb Kelleher America's Best CEO?" *Fortune, 129,* 9, May 2, 1994, p. 52.
[2] Ibid.
[3] Ibid.

✔ Receptivity to ideas (no matter the source)
✔ A genuine, deep commitment to the growth and profitability of the business[9]

Ferdinand Metz, certified master chef and president of the Culinary Institute of America, believes the essence of success is to possess exemplary leadership qualities—"being a fair manager, an inspiring motivator, and most of all, a diplomat when dealing with people." These leadership qualities alone, however, do not ensure success. A good deal of expertise in the field is also needed. This knowledge, combined with personal qualities, will allow you to make a significant contribution to your chosen profession.[10]

James Irwin is president and CEO of Emco Foodservice Systems, a major food service distribution firm headquartered in Pittsburgh, Pennsylvania, and a member of the Food Service Distribution Hall of Fame. He commented that "many people are not willing to pay the price for success, yet do not realize the rewards far outweigh the costs. Many people follow a path of 'least resistance' that limits their ability to exercise their full potential." He suggested that "success is exceptional performance and achievement on a consistent basis over a period of time," and "a successful person will lead with an authority earned by integrity and not compromise ethics or morals for financial gain or position."[11]

The essence of success has as many meanings as there are people to ponder it. One concept of success is to couple one's personal and family interests, dreams, and aspirations with a business or professional career that complement and fortify each other.

Another aspect of leadership is the ability to motivate others in a hospitality working environment; decision making is also essential. These are discussed later in the chapter.

Isadore Sharp is the founder, president, and chief executive officer of the Four Seasons-Regent Hotels and Resorts. Sharp was named Canada's outstanding CEO of the year. He was chosen from a blue-chip list of Canadian executives as the business leader who best exemplifies excellence in corporate achievement, leadership, vision, innovation, and global competitiveness. In just thirty years, Sharp built his business from a single hotel on Jarvis Street in downtown Toronto to the world's largest luxury hotel and resort operation, with forty-three hotels in seventeen countries.

Isadore Sharp, Chairman of the Board, Four Seasons-Regent Hotels and Resorts

Issy Sharp, as he is known, has the ability to conceive a vision of what is possible, the business acumen to plan for success, and the unique gift to inspire others to help carry the dream through to reality. Sharp was an architect working with his father in a two-man construction company when he chose to develop a property in Toronto into an elegant, hospitable home-away-from-home for business or leisure travelers.

Since opening that first hotel, Four Seasons has grown into a top international luxury hotel chain. Sharp credits his staff for the Four Seasons' success. Isadore Sharp also plays a key role in the community; not only is he a director of several corporations, but he also has a special affinity for activities that support cancer research because he lost a young son to the disease. He initiated the corporate sponsorship for the Terry Fox Marathon of Hope and continues to direct the annual run, which has been tagged as the largest fund-raising event in the world, having raised some $35 million by the spring of 1993.[12]

John E. Martin, former president and CEO of Taco Bell Corporations, took over in 1983, when Taco Bell was a regional chain suffering from an identity crisis. However, since 1989, its total system sales have quadrupled to $2.6 billion and total units have tripled to roughly 3,300. Taco Bell has built a commanding 70-percent share in the Mexican-style quick-service restaurant category. In recent years, sales and profits have risen dramatically; by 2001, the goal is to reach 10,000 points of distribution and $30 billion in sales. Martin's vision was to have the Taco Bell brand being sold not only in restaurants, but also in such nontraditional venues as carts, kiosks, hospitals, schools, airports, and even supermarkets.

John E. Martin, former President and CEO of Taco Bell and Current Chairman and CEO of Newriders

Martin improved the image of the industry by putting more dignity into it and making real careers for people. He simplified the restaurants, making the manager more self-sufficient, and increased incentives. Unit general managers have the authority to hire their own assistants, schedule labor, authorize many purchases, and make many other decisions that previously needed an area supervisor's sign-off.

Personal Profile: Linda Novey

Linda Novey, of Linda Novey Enterprises in Sarasota, Florida, is a modern success story. Known as Ms. Hospitality, Linda is recognized as an international consultant and lecturer in areas of total quality management, customer service, motivation, marketing, and competitive analysis. She was the first female appointee to the development board for Chase Development Corporation and one of the first women to sit on the national board of directors for S.C.O.R.E..

She completed her college degree one class at a time while taking care of her three daughters. In order to finance the opening of her company in 1982, she was forced to take out a mortgage on her home. Ms. Novey certainly did not get where she is today by not being a risk-taker!

Since then, her company has expanded to include more than 800 clients, some of which include hotels such as the Ritz-Carlton Hotels and Resorts Worldwide; Marriott Hotels and Resorts; Omni International Hotels and Resorts; Four Seasons Hotels, Canada; Rockresorts, Hawaii; The Oriental Hotel in Bangkok, Thailand; and Holiday Inns International Division. She also serves nonhospitality corporations such as Neiman Marcus Inc.; Florida's Division of Tourism; the University of South Florida; Queen Margaret College in Edinburgh, Scotland; The International Association of Les Clefs d'Or in Zurich, Switzerland; and Business Travel Associations in Georgia, Florida, and New York.

Linda Novey

Linda and her employees help companies to improve their customer relations through an anonymous service audit known as the Novey Report. According to Linda, industry experts from her company spend three or four days at a given hotel, resort, or company. During this time, they evaluate the facility's performance. Two weeks later, a comprehensive report is presented to the company's department of customer relations, indicating areas that need improvement in management-employee relations and employee-customer service relations. It is up to the client to improve upon these aspects.

Linda Novey also acts as a motivational speaker. Besides hosting motivational seminars for hotels, resorts, and nonhospitality corporations, she has also delivered key lectures at various universities and colleges in America and Europe.

According to Ms. Novey, "Smiles, sales, and showmanship are the keys to success in the service industry." Her motto has certainly proven true, as can be seen by 98 percent of her business coming from repeat clients. With such an optimistic motto, a sense of adventure, and savvy business skills, there is reason to predict a bright and prosperous future for Linda Novey Enterprises in the year 2000 and beyond.

The TACO system—total automation of company operations—saves managers up to fifteen hours per week, allowing them more time to interact with customers and to train employees. The system even provides the manager with a daily profit-and-loss statement to keep track of targets.

Martin had other innovative ideas, such as using a machine that can make 1,200 tacos per hour, and preparing and distributing high-quality food products made outside the restaurants to reduce kitchen space and labor.

"It's ridiculous to think that a restaurant system must be thousands of little factories across the country all doing the same repetitive process," he says.[13]

Van E. Eure's foodservice career began as a teenager, waiting tables at The Angus Barn, known to loyal patrons as North Carolina's "Beefeater's Haven." The Angus Barn was established in 1960 by her father, Thad Eure, Jr., and his partner, Charlie Winston. After college, Eure taught high school English and

Van E. Eure

Student Glimpse: Michael R. Thorpe

The Leader of the Future Will Be a Holistic One

Michael R. Thorpe, who has just successfully completed his studies, earning a Bachelor of Science Degree in Hotel and Restaurant Management at the United States International University, is an outstanding example of the leadership skills that can be acquired throughout the school and college career.

Mike's leadership abilities developed from an early age, with his involvement in the Boy Scouts of America. Looking back at that memorable time, Mike recognizes how important it is for a leader to be a good role model. He emphasizes the fact that it is necessary to make a sharp distinction between "good" leaders and "bad" leaders, thus establishing a learning process that is based on the identification of both "shoulds" (positive examples, experiences, activities, skills) and "should-nots" (mistakes, negative attitudes). Michael's experience with the Boy Scouts was one that provided him with fundamental values and skills, which were acknowledged when he achieved the rank of Eagle Scout.

Michael R. Thorpe

In high school as well as in college, Mike's leadership skills were progressively developed and utilized. He believes that the key to learning is involvement. In fact, he always took part in school activities, also emphasizing the importance of maintaining a broad horizon of interests. In particular, Michael chose to actively participate in a variety of extracurricular activities, including academic, service-oriented, and sports organizations. He stresses the belief that there is a strict correlation among such fields that shapes the overall personality of the leader. "The leader of the future will be a holistic one," Mike says.

Michael's involvement in academic organizations, such as the student body government council; in sports, as the captain of the football team and vice president of the football club; and in service-oriented enterprises, such as the Hosteur's Society HRTM Club, to which he was elected president, helped him develop the necessary skills for high-quality interaction with people. He learned that a good leader is someone who is able to gather a group of individuals and coordinate each single talent, skill, propensity, and personality into a successful team, joining forces in the pursuit of one common goal. Each member of the team must be fulfilled in his or her need for belonging, personal satisfaction, recognition, and so on. In order to accomplish this task, Mike understood that a leader must also be extremely respectful of each individual's personal life, needs, problems, cultural background, and diversity—setting aside personal likes and dislikes. Diversity also provides an opportunity for the leader to learn from the people he or she guides, an opportunity that every leader must have the humility and willingness to pursue.

In Mike's words, the leader must act as a "glue" that unites people, and the organizer who finds the "right place" for each individual, a place in which he or she will be able to excel, and perform at his or her full potential.

Work experience throughout his college career has also taught Mike that workers will function at their best in a work environment that is appealing and challenging, and that provides them with the right tools—in terms of knowledge, motivation, rewards, climate—to produce the optimal outcome.

In order to achieve such results, Michael excludes, as much as possible, the carrot-on-a-stick approach. He feels that such a method is a superficial remedy that doesn't get to the root of the problem—and thus doesn't solve it—and doesn't consider that a leader deals with human beings intrinsically characterized by a distinct intelligence and personality. Furthermore, when dealing with subordinates' failures or mistakes, Michael prefers to approach the person(s) in question from his or her point of view, trying to understand what the cause of the inefficiency might be, and at the same time performing a thorough self-analysis in order to establish whether that person's poor performance is determined by his own possible leadership mistake.

Mike greatly respects a leader who creates a sense of cooperation, community, and teamwork. Just like in a family, the leader should step down from an intolerable ivory tower, and be open to each member of the team, to listen and be willing to help with possible personal problems, emphasizing the importance of open communication. And, just like in a family, the leader must be the caring parent who can also progressively impose discipline and obtain the results expected depending on the members' potential.

Mike understands the role of a father, as he has a three-year-old who represents, among other things, the ultimate challenge for leadership. "While workers' livelihood does depend on the employer/leader."

elementary school in Kenya, Africa, for five years; in 1982, she returned to the United States to join her father in the restaurant business. In 1984, she was promoted to senior dining room manager and, following the death of her father in 1988, she took over the operation of the restaurant with her mother, Alice Eure. Today, the restaurant has a seating capacity of 600 and employs 180 people.

Eure's professional and civic activities include the following: member, Knights of the Vine; member, La Chaine des Rotisseurs; board member, North Carolina Citizens of Business and Industry; board member, Public Service Company of North Carolina; board member, Theatre in the Park; member, The Fifty Group (a local networking organization of top executives); and member, The Foundation of Hope (for research and treatment of mental illness, founded by Thad Eure, Jr.). In 1991, Eure was named Master Lady by the Raleigh chapter of Knights of the Vine and was awarded the Mondail Medal of Honor by the National Chaine des Rotisseurs.

The Distinction between Leadership and Management

Leadership is an ageless topic; it has been described as a social influence process that can occur in nearly any interaction among people. Leadership has a broader scope than management, which came in vogue about one hundred years ago with its more narrow focus on accomplishing organizational goals. Modern management was invented, in a sense, to help the new railroads, steel mills, and auto companies achieve what legendary entrepreneurs envisioned. Without such management, these complex enterprises tended to become chaotic in ways that threatened their very existence.[14]

Managing is the formal process in which organizational objectives are achieved through the efforts of subordinates. *Leading* is the process by which a person with vision is able to influence the behavior of others in some desired way. Although managers have power by virtue of the positions they hold, organizations seek managers who are leaders by virtue of their personalities, their experience, and so on.

The differences between management and leadership can be illustrated as follows:[15]

Manager	*Leader*
administers	innovates
is a copy	is an original
maintains	develops
focuses on systems and structure	focuses on people
relies on control	inspires trust
has a short-range view	has a long-range perspective
asks how and when	asks what and why
has an eye on the bottom line	has an eye on the horizon

initiates	originates
accepts the status quo	challenges it
does things right	does the right thing

Leadership focuses on style and ideals, whereas management focuses on the method and process. Leadership does not produce consistency and order, as the word itself implies; it produces movement.[16]

The leadership challenge is about leading people, not merely managing them. Leadership begins where management ends, where the systems of rewards and punishments, control and scrutiny, give way to innovation, individual character, and the courage of convictions.[17]

Markets, customers, technology, and competitors continually change. The active leader anticipates these changes and strategically adapts the organization to continue to prosper in the following ways:

1. Repositioning products/services to build a competitive advantage
2. Recruiting talented people to execute the new strategies
3. Establishing organizational resources that tightly focus on new strategies[18]

The most effective leaders share a number of skills, and these skills are always related to dealing with employees. The following suggestions outline an approach to becoming a hotel leader rather than just a manager:

✔ Be decisive—Hotel managers are confronted with dozens of decisions every day. Obviously, you should use your best judgment to resolve those decisions that come to roost at your doorstep. As a boss, make the decisions that best meet both your objectives and your ethics, and then make your decisions known.

✔ Follow through—Never promise what you can't deliver, and never build false hopes among your employees. Once expectations are dashed, respect for and the reputation of the boss are shot.

✔ Select the best—A boss, good or bad, is carried forward by the work of his or her subordinates. One key to being a good boss is to hire the people who have the best potential to do what you need them to do. Take the time and effort to screen, interview, and assess the people who have not only the skills that you require, but also the needed values.

✔ Empower employees—Give people the authority to interact with the customer. The more people feel important, the better they work.

✔ Enhance career development—Good bosses recognize that most of their people want to improve themselves. However, career development is a two-edged sword: If we take the initiative to train and develop our people properly, then the competition is likely to hire them. The only way a boss can prevent the loss of productive workers looking for career development is to provide opportunities for growth within the organization.

✔ Seek support—Our industry is changing daily, from the type of services we offer to the ways we offer them. Depending on how we integrate change into the workplace, people can either resist it or support it. As a boss, involve people in any change that affects them.

Corporate Profile: Carlson Companies

One of America's recent corporate hospitality success stories is Carlson Companies, Inc. In 1938, entrepreneur Curtis Carlson with an idea, a mail drop, $50 in borrowed capital, and trading stamps founded the Gold Bond Trading Stamp Company, in Minneapolis. Carlson marketed the trading stamp concept from local to regional and finally to national markets in Super Valu food stores.

In the late 1960s, Carlson and several other partners collectively bought a 50-percent interest in the Radisson Hotel in downtown Minneapolis; within two years, he bought out all the other partners. Carlson took the hotel chain to twenty-two hotels in twenty-three years, but freely admits that he was not smart enough to expand by franchising. As explained to him by former president of Carlson Hospitality Group, Juergen Bartels, it was not necessary to put down your own money in order to expand a successful hotel company; it could be done by franchising. As a result there are now more than 340 Radisson hotels and more are being added, especially in eastern Europe.

The Carlson Hospitality Group also includes about 400 TGI Friday's restaurants in eight countries; Country Lodging, a limited-service hotel with country-style charm at thirty-five locations in the United States and Canada; and Country Kitchen, a family-style restaurant chain with 253 locations in three countries.

Before Carlson ever heard of TGI Friday's, he ran Haberdashery restaurants in the Minneapolis area. Although

Curtis Carlson

moderately successful, this restaurant never took off. Later came Country Kitchen. Carlson was initially approached when the company operated fewer than ten restaurants; he liked the name but thought that the profit potential was small. Ironically, a few years later, he bought the chain, which by then was much larger. Carlson explained that the sales were there, but they were not making money. He said, "I thought it was a case of poor accounting or management. So I thought I was smart enough to take those restaurants, but then we bought it and never made any money either!" Today, however, the chain, which is all franchised, is doing well.

The 1990s are providing an interesting challenge for Carlson: how to change from owner-operator to a management company and maintain quality standards with rapid growth. With a philosophy that "No one should be last," aggressive goals and guidelines are set annually and underperforming managers and franchisees are regularly weeded out.[2] "The basics here are growth and providing quality, and those that can't provide both are gone."

Carlson Hospitality now lends its lodging and foodservice expertise via management contracts, joint ventures, or "O.P.M."—other people's money.

[1]This section draws on Bill Carlino, "Carlson Cos," *Nation's Restaurant News, 27,* 13, March 29, 1993, pp. 43–84.
[2]Ibid.

✔ Don't have all the answers—Bosses who don't admit a lack of knowledge or expertise, who don't find good people and rely on them, and who feel they have all the answers will not go very far up the ladder.

✔ Don't be tough-minded, hard-nosed, and abrasive—These characteristics scare people into performing for the short run, but after a while the adrenalin is replaced with subtle resistance. If you want to manage for the long term, you have to motivate people on their terms, not yours, which means you have to be receptive to dealing with employees as people.

✓ Don't play politics—Some managers mortgage the future to look good now. Knowing the right people and earning favors is one way to promote your future, but at the point at which your reliance on politics becomes obvious and excessive, you become a liability to your company.

✓ Don't shoot the messenger—If you get bad news once, just shooting the messenger will give you bad news again.

There is no big secret to being a good boss. It all comes back to the relationship between you and the people who work for you. In other words, treat others as you would want to be treated.[19]

Management

Managers forecast, plan, organize, make decisions, communicate, motivate, and control the efforts of a group to accomplish predetermined goals. Management establishes the direction that the organization will take. Sometimes this is done with the help of employees or outside consultants, such as marketing research specialists. Managers obtain the necessary resources for the tasks to be accomplished and they supervise and monitor group and individual progress toward goal accomplishment.

Top managers, such as presidents and chief executive officers who are responsible for the entire company, tend to focus most of their time on strategic planning and the organization mission. They also spend time on organizing and controlling the activities of the corporation. Most top managers do not get involved in the day-to-day aspects of the operation. These duties and responsibilities fall to middle and supervisory management. In hospitality lingo, one would not expect Bill Marriott to pull a shift behind the bar at the local Marriott hotel. Although capable, his time and expertise are used in shaping the company's future. Thus, although the head bartender and Bill Marriott may be considered management, they require slightly different skills to be effective and efficient managers.

Managerial Skills

In addition to the management functions of forecasting, planning, organizing, communicating, motivating, and controlling, there are other major skill areas: conceptual, human, and technical.

Conceptual skills enable top managers to view the corporation as a complete entity and yet understand how it is split into departments to achieve specific goals. Conceptual skills allow a top manager to view the entire corporation, especially the interdependence of the various departments.

Managers need to lead, influence, communicate, supervise, coach, and evaluate employees' performances. This necessitates a high level of interpersonal human skills. The ability to build teams and work with others is a human skill that successful managers need to cultivate.

Managers are required to have the technical skills to understand and use techniques, methods, equipment, and procedures. These skills are more important for use in lower levels of management. As a manager rises through the

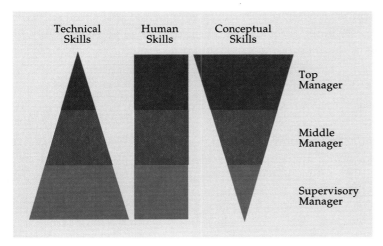

Figure 14–2 *Management Skill Areas*

ranks, the need for technical skills decreases and the need for conceptual skills increases (see Figure 14–2).

Before identifying the key management functions, we need to first realize the critical importance of the corporate philosophy, culture, and values, and the corporation's mission, goals, and objectives.

Corporate Philosophy

The definition of corporate philosophy is changing from one of managers planning, organizing, implementing, and measuring to that of managers counseling associates, giving them the resources, and helping them to think for themselves. The outcome is a more participative management style, which results in associate empowerment, increased productivity, and guest and employee satisfaction. Corporate philosophy has strong links to quality leadership and the total quality management (TQM) process.

Corporate philosophy embraces the values of the organization: These include ethics, morals, fairness, and equality. The new paradigm in corporate American hospitality is the shift in emphasis from the production aspect of our business to the focus on the guest-related services. The philosophy of "whatever it takes" is winning over "it's not my job." Innovation and creativity are winning over "that's the way we've always done it." Successful organizations are those who are able to impart their corporate philosophies to employees and guests alike— Disney Corporation is a good example of a corporation that has a permeating corporate philosophy.

There is no set formula for a corporate philosophy. However, to be truly effective, a corporate philosophy must be unique to the organization. Common denominators of a successful corporate philosophy include the following:

1. A clear statement of purpose
2. A definition of the responsibilities of the business
3. Adherence to principles ahead of profits

The most important element in maintaining an organization's image is the practice of making corporate philosophy part of the daily lives of the people involved. Keeping the philosophy alive begins at the top and is conveyed to every level, so that people at the bottom are committed and involved.

Corporate Culture

Corporate culture is the overall style or feel of a company. A company's culture governs how people relate to one another and their jobs. It can be summed up with the phrase, "This is how we do things around here." The casual image of the Chart House restaurant chain is a definite part of their corporate culture. However, don't be fooled—their managers may appear casual, but they are very professional. Each of the major corporations has a culture, some more pronounced than others. It is a good idea to align yourself with a corporation that blends with your culture, values, and style.

Mission Statement

A mission statement is a short statement of the central purposes, strategies, and values of a company. Essentially, a corporation's mission statement should answer the question, "What business are we in?" A good mission statement will go beyond the obvious and include the corporation's purpose, values, and strategies (see Figure 14–3).

Goal

A goal is a specific target to be met. In a hotel, for example, one of the goals might be to increase occupancy from 80 to 85 percent. Another might be to maintain the average daily rate (ADR) at $78. Goals may be written for each department on a variety of topics from alcohol awareness training to reducing employee turnover. Today, most corporations involve their employees in goal setting. This not only ties in with total quality management, but also encourages employees to buy into the process and increases the likelihood that goals may even be exceeded.

Mission Statement

The Ritz-Carlton, Laguna Niguel, will be recognized internationally as the leading five-star, five-diamond resort hotel in North America. We will be unique in combining the genuine warmth and vitality of southern California with the traditional setting found in the finest hotels of Europe.

Every guest will feel that he or she is our most important guest. They will find us easy to do business with, and will be impressed by our uncompromising, consistent service and our ability to anticipate and fulfill even their unexpressed wishes. They will appreciate our creative, sophisticated, world-class cuisine and services. Our versatile entertainment will enhance our elegant, relaxing atmosphere. In addition, our guests will enjoy the unparalleled beauty of our location along with the museum-quality art collection.

Our employees will be proud of their association with the hotel and will be an integral part of our success. They will see the Ritz-Carlton as the best hotel to work in, a place where they can grow personally and professionally. Our staff will remain committed to continuously improving and refining our facilities and service.

The owners and the corporate office will be proud of the hotel, and will have confidence in us. They will see us as a source of qualified managers for new hotels. The owners and the corporate office will be committed to helping us refine the facility's quality and improve its profitability, in partnership with the executive committee.

The community will also be proud of the hotel, and will see it as a cooperative, involved business resident of the county.

Figure 14–3 *Mission Statement, Ritz-Carlton, Laguna Niguel* (Courtesy Ritz-Carlton, Laguna Niguel.)

Objectives

Objectives are the actions that are needed to accomplish the goal. Using the hotel occupancy example, the objective will state how the goal will be met. The objective then identifies the specific actions necessary to produce the desired result. In order for the hotel to increase the occupancy from 80 to 85 percent, specific actions might include the following:

✔ Conduct a travel agent sales blitz in key feeder cities
✔ Host ten travel agents' familiarization (FAM) tours
✔ Direct mail a number of American Express, Visa, MasterCard, and Discover card holders, and so on

Once the corporate philosophy, culture, mission, goals, and objectives are finalized, the management functions will have guidance and direction to help steer the organization to success.

Key Management Functions

The key management functions are forecasting, planning, organizing, decision making, communicating, motivating, and controlling. These management functions are not conducted in isolation; rather they are interdependent and frequently happen simultaneously, or at least overlap.

Forecasting

This is the first of the management functions and involves a forecast of expected business volumes. In hotel terms, that means occupancy percentages and in restaurants, the number of covers. Similarly, in institutional foodservice, as close an estimate of guests as possible is needed in order for management to plan effectively to cater for everyone. Forecasting is important because either over- or under-forecasting will cause the subsequent functions of management to be planned on slightly inaccurate assumptions.

Restaurant managers forecast the number of covers for a given night by taking several variables into account, including the following:

The time of year—Summer, fall, winter, spring (to allow for seasonal fluctuations).

The day of week—Demand is different on each night of the week, with Friday generally being the busiest.

Expected weather—Fine weather may increase demand whereas foul weather may decrease it.

Advance reservations—Any reservations already made become the starting point for the count of the expected number of covers.

Forecasting takes various factors into account, evaluates them, and produces a calculated guess as to how much business can be expected. Because it is the first management function, it is important to do it accurately because those that follow are based on the forecast of business.

The majority of the products and services offered in the hospitality industry are perishable. The value of hotel rooms or prepared food items perish if they are not

A Sales Director and the Sales Team Going over the Sales Forecast (Courtesy the Pan Pacific Hotel, San Diego, CA.)

sold within a certain period of time. A restaurant manager and chef will forecast how many guests to expect for the next week, then order food and schedule employees. Hotels publish weekly and fourteen-day forecasts to enable all the departments to gauge the volume of business for their outlets and allocate resources accordingly. Restaurants, foodservice management, and travel and tourism organizations all make similar projections to forecast the expected business volume.

Planning

There are two main types of planning: long-range or strategic, and short-range or tactical. Long-range, strategic planning is the process of determining the major objectives of an organization along with the policies and strategies that will govern the acquisition, use, and disposition of the resources that are necessary to achieve those objectives. Strategic plans are made for five years or more into the future. Tactical plans are made for up to one year.

An example of strategic hospitality planning for a restaurant chain would be as follows: Do we modify or change our concept? Kentucky Fried Chicken made a strategic move when they changed their name to KFC. This downplays the fact that the chicken is fried, a method of cooking that is not well received by the more health-conscious population of the 1990s. Strategic planning also assesses the opportunities and alternatives for expansion into international markets.

In tourism terms, a country or a destination would make a master plan of how they would reach the predetermined goals of increasing the number of tourists, encouraging them to stay longer and spend more, and exceeding tourists' expectations of a quality visit.

Hospitality corporations make long-range plans in areas ranging from human resources development to financial plans, and from hospitality renovation to the operation of their franchise division.

The more senior a manager, the longer the planning horizon is. A corporate manager at the top of an organization is primarily occupied with the company's vision, mission, organizational objectives, and major policy areas. Middle-level managers' planning responsibilities focus on translating the objectives of the organization into goals for the frontline managers and supervisors. Frontline managers are involved in scheduling employees and developing and executing plans to achieve the organizational goals.

Tactical plans have a shorter time frame and narrower scope than strategic plans. A tactical plan is concerned with what the lower levels of management and employees must do to achieve the strategic goals.

Operational plans provide managers with a step-by-step approach to accomplish her or his goals. The overall purpose of planning is to have the entire organization moving harmoniously toward the goals.

There are seven steps in organizational planning:

1. Setting objectives—This first step in planning decides the expected outcomes—goals/objectives. The goals should be specific, measurable, and achievable.
2. Analyzing and evaluating the environment—This involves analyzing political, economic, social, and other trends that may affect the corporation.

The level and intensity of turbulence is evaluated in relation to the organization's present position and the resources available to achieve goals.

3. Determining alternatives—This involves developing courses of action that are available to a manager to reach a goal. Input may be requested from all levels of the organization. Group work is normally better than individual input.

4. Evaluating alternatives—This calls for making a list of advantages and disadvantages of each alternative. Among the factors to be considered are resources and effects on the organization.

5. Selecting the best solution—This analysis of the various alternatives should result in determining one course of action that is better than the others. It may, however, involve combining two or more alternatives.

6. Implementing the plan—Once the optimum solution is decided on, the manager needs to decide the following:

    Who will do what?
    By when?
    What resources are required?
    At what benefit?
    At what cost?
    What reporting procedures will there be?
    What authority will be granted to achieve the goals?

7. Controlling and evaluating results—Once the plan is implemented, it is necessary to monitor progress toward goal accomplishment.

Organizing

Once the vision, mission, goals, objectives, and plans for the company have been agreed on, the work necessary to complete those tasks must be organized. Organizing is the process of arranging the resources of the corporation in such a way that activities systematically contribute to the corporation's goals. The purpose of organizing is to give each person a specific task and to ensure that these tasks are coordinated.[20]

Most corporations are made up of two organizations: a formal one and an informal one. The formal organization is the one depicted by the corporate organizational chart. It shows the authority, responsibility, and chains of command.

The informal organization is the "shadow organization" that emerges as people interact with one another on the job. It reflects the way "things really get done around here."[21]

In recent years, corporations have been down-sizing or right-sizing their management and organizational structures. Most hospitality operations are organized according to the best way of serving the guest. Most of the segments that make up the hospitality industry have similar organizational structures, including kitchens, restaurants, hotels, airlines, cruise lines, and others.

Decision Making

Centralized decision making means that decisions are made at the corporate level. In a centralized corporation, most decisions are channeled down the chain of command from the top managers. Lower-level employees simply follow policies and procedures. Marriott is an example of a centralized company. However, even centralized corporations have adopted initiatives such as TQM and empowerment, which have given more leeway to the frontline employees to do whatever it takes to satisfy the guest.

Decentralized decision making is the extent to which the decision making is spread throughout the organization. Managers at every level are empowered to make decisions. The more decisions that are made at lower levels, the more decentralized an organization is said to be.

Span of control or span of management refers to the number of people that one manager can effectively manage. There is no set limit on the number of people that a manager can supervise because it depends on the type of organization (centralized versus decentralized) and the degree of its sophistication in terms of efficiency and effectiveness. The trend today is for the span of control to increase to twelve or more. Previously, management theorists had suggested a comfortable maximum span of control of six to eight subordinates. The reasons for increasing the span of control are to remain competitive by reducing costs, to increase efficiency by allowing a greater say in the operation by all levels of employees, and to increase the amount of available computerized information.

The success of all organizations, whether they are large multinational corporations or sole proprietorships, depends on the quality of decision making. Beginning with a mission, goals, and objectives, the success of all organizations depends on decision making.

There are two main types of decisions: programmed decisions and nonprogrammed decisions. A programmed decision recurs on a regular basis—for example, when the number of New York steaks goes below a specified number, an order for more is automatically placed. Programmed decisions generally become a standard operating procedure (SOP).

A nonprogrammed decision is nonrecurring and made necessary by unusual circumstances, such as which computer hardware and software a restaurant should install, or whether to expand by franchising or by company-owned restaurants. These are unique decision situations that will not likely recur for several years.

The more sophisticated a company is, the more programmed decisions are made. Many large corporations have policy and procedure manuals to guide managerial and supervisory decision making. Nonprogrammed decisions call for greater analysis, innovation, and problem-solving skills.

Decision makers follow a process of eight major steps:

1. Identification and definition of problem
2. Identification of decision criteria
3. Allocation of weights to criteria
4. Development of alternatives
5. Analysis of alternatives
6. Selection of alternative
7. Installation of alternative
8. Evaluation of decision effectiveness

Figure 14–4 illustrates the decision-making process.

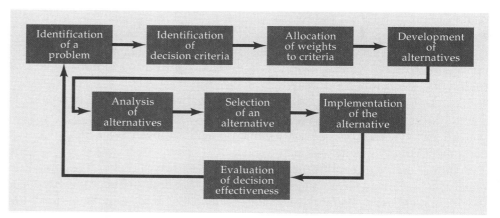

Figure 14–4 *Eight-Step Decision-Making Process* (Stephen P. Robbins, *Management,* 3d ed. Englewood Cliffs, N.J.: Prentice Hall, 1991, p. 153.)

Step 1: Identification and Definition of Problem

A problem exists when there is a discrepancy between current and desired results. The decision-making process begins with identifying and defining the problem(s). It is not always easy to identify the problem because other issues may muddy the waters. To illustrate the point, there is an interesting story of a maximum security prison warden who was about to retire after a distinguished career. One day, an associate reported to him that the pass keys for the section in which the hard-core prisoners were housed were missing. This presented the warden with a dilemma: If he reported the missing keys to his supervisors, his exemplary career would be tarnished—indeed, disciplinary action against him might be taken. The real problem, however, is not the loss of the keys or how to find the keys; it is containing the hard-core prisoners who might escape.

In a hotel setting, problem situations can be identified with respect to guest check in. In some of the larger city-center, convention-oriented hotels, there are frequently long lines of guests waiting to check into the hotel. Defining this problem is best done by writing a problem statement, that is, the problem is that it takes too long for guests to register, or guests do not like waiting to register. Once the problem has been accurately stated, it becomes easier to move to the next step in the decision-making process.

Herb Kelleher, president of Southwest Airlines, made the decision to remove the closets at the front of Southwest planes. This was in response to a problem: It took too long to turn around the planes. To be competitive and successful, it is necessary to reduce the turn-around time in order to squeeze more flights into each day. The situation that caused or contributed to the turn-around problem was that the first people on the plane typically went to the closets first and then grabbed the nearest seats. On landing, the departing passengers were held up while the people in the front rows rummaged through the closets for their bags. The airline now turns around about 85 percent of its flights in fifteen minutes or less and is one of the most profitable airlines, with a remarkable 16 percent average return on equity over the past several years.[22]

Table 14–1 Criteria and Weight in Restaurant Selection	
How much do we want to spend?	10
What type of food would we prefer?	8
How much time do we have?	6
How is the food quality?	9
How is the atmosphere?	6
How is the service?	7
How convenient is parking?	6
How is the restaurant's reputation?	6
How far do we want to go to a restaurant?	7

Step 2: Identification of Decision Criteria

Once the problem has been identified and defined, it is necessary to determine the criteria relevant to the decision. Suppose the problem is that we are hungry; then the decision criteria might be the following:

1. What type of food would we prefer?
2. How much time do we have?
3. How much do we want to spend?
4. How convenient is parking?
5. What is the restaurant's reputation?
6. How is the food quality?
7. How is the service?
8. How is the atmosphere?

These criteria are developed by the group who would like to eat out at a restaurant. Criteria that are not identified are usually treated as unimportant.

Step 3: Allocation of Weights to Criteria

To the decision makers, the decision criteria all have differing levels of importance. For instance, is the expected cost of the meal more important than the atmosphere? If so, a higher weight should be attached to that criterion.

One method used to weigh the criteria is to give the most important criterion a weight of ten and then score the others according to their relative importance. In the meal example, the cost of the meal might receive a weight of ten, whereas the atmosphere might be awarded a weight of six. Table 14–1 lists a sample of criteria and weights for restaurant selection.

Step 4: Development of Alternatives

In developing alternatives, decision makers list the viable alternatives that could resolve the problem. No attempt is made to evaluate these alternatives, only to list them. Using the restaurant scenario, the alternatives are shown in Figure 14–5.

Step 5: Analysis of Alternatives

The alternatives are analyzed using the criteria and weights established in steps two and three. Figure 14–6 shows the values placed on each of the alternatives by the group. (It does not show the weighted values.)

KFC

Taco Bell

Pizza Hut

McDonald's

Applebee's

The Olive Garden

Wendy's

Figure 14–5 *Restaurant Alternatives*

	KFC	Taco Bell	Pizza Hut	McDonald's	Applebee's	Olive Garden	Wendy's
Price	9	10	10	10	7	7	9
Type of food	7	8	9	8	8	9	9
How much time	9	9	7	10	7	6	10
Quality of food	7	7	8	7	8	8	8
Atmosphere	7	7	8	7	9	9	7
Service	6	6	7	7	8	9	7
Convenient parking	10	10	10	9	10	10	10
Restaurant reputation	8	8	8	7	8	9	8
How far away	8	8	8	10	7	7	8
Total	71	73	75	76	72	74	75

Figure 14–6 *Analysis of Alternatives*

	KFC	Taco Bell	Pizza Hut	McDonald's	Applebee's	Olive Garden	Wendy's
Price	90	100	100	100	70	70	90
Type of food	56	64	72	64	64	72	72
How much time	54	54	42	60	42	36	60
Quality of food	63	63	72	63	72	72	72
Atmosphere	42	42	48	42	54	54	42
Service	42	42	49	49	56	63	49
Convenient parking	60	60	60	56	60	60	60
Restaurant reputation	48	48	48	42	48	54	48
How far away	56	56	56	70	49	49	56
Total	511	529	547	546	515	530	549

Figure 14–7 *Weighted Values Analysis*

The weighted values of the group's decision about which restaurant to go to are shown in Figure 14–7.

Once the weighted values are totaled we can see that Pizza Hut and Wendy's are the restaurants with the highest scores. Notice how these are not the restaurants with the highest scores before the weighted values were included.

Step 6: Selection of Alternative

The sixth step involves the selection of the best alternative. Once the weighted scores for each alternative have been totaled, it will become obvious which is the best alternative.

Step 7: Installation of Alternative

Installing the alternative means to put the decision into action. Sometimes good decisions fail because they are not put into action.

Step 8: Evaluation of Decision Effectiveness

The final step in the decision loop is to evaluate the effectiveness of the decision. As a result of the decision, did we achieve the goals we set? If the decision was not effective, then we must find out why the desired results were not attained. This would mean going back to step one. If the decision was effective, then no action, other than recording the outcome, needs to be taken.

Communicating

Communication is the oil that lubricates all the other management functions of forecasting, planning, organizing, motivating, and controlling. Additionally, because managers spend a high percentage of their time communicating, this makes the communication function doubly important. Managers interact with others throughout the day by the following means:

✔ Telephone
✔ Mail/fax
✔ Memos and other internal/external written communication
✔ Personal face to face meetings

The simplest method of communication involves a sender, a message, and a receiver. However, merely sending a message cannot ensure that the message will be received and understood correctly.

Several factors can distort the communication process, ranging from noise interference to poor listening skills and inappropriate tuning. The middle of a busy lunch service is not the time to be asking the chef a question or bothering her or him with some communication about the company's policy on sick-pay benefits.

Face-to-face tends to be the best means of communication. The instant feedback provides both sender and receiver with a better understanding of the communication. In contrast, one-way communication does not allow the receiver to respond or check the intended meaning and find out what action he or she should take.

Some of the barriers to effective interpersonal communication are the following.[23]

✔ Hearing what we expect to hear
✔ Ignoring information that conflicts with what we think we know
✔ Evaluating the source
✔ Differing perceptions
✔ Words that mean different things to different people
✔ Inconsistent nonverbal signals
✔ Effects of emotions
✔ Noise

Effective communicators use techniques to improve the communication process, such as the following:

✔ Being sensitive to the receiver's world
✔ Being aware of symbolic meanings
✔ Using clear, direct, simple language
✔ Moving from defensive to supportive communication
✔ Understanding the relationship between two parties
✔ Being aware of the level of trust

Grapevine/Informal Communication

Most organizations have informal communication channels known as *grapevines*. Informal communication can both help and hinder effective communication.

Informal communication with staff can help develop trust and commitment. The people who have the best understanding of the jobs are the employees who are doing the jobs. Therefore, by communicating with the staff informally, the following benefits may be gained.[24]

- ✔ Identify potential problems
- ✔ Gain staff commitment to organization
- ✔ Gather information to use in decision making and planning

Some ideas suggested for effective informal communication include the following:[25]

- ✔ Do not be a stranger—Walk around the department and make yourself accessible to your staff
- ✔ Use employees' names when talking with them so that they feel recognized and respected
- ✔ Keep your staff informed—If you keep them updated on what is going on in your department and at your property, they are more likely to keep you informed as well
- ✔ Maintain an open-door policy, and be sure that your employees know about it
- ✔ Be sure your employees know that you want, value, and need their ideas
- ✔ Listen noncritically and objectively to employees' concerns and contributions
- ✔ Do not react emotionally or critically when someone brings you bad news
- ✔ Use good listening skills—An employee won't talk if no one is listening
- ✔ Never miss an opportunity to compliment an employee for a quality contribution.

Informal communication is a powerful tool that sometimes is overlooked. If used properly, valuable information will be provided, relationships and commitment will be developed, and a positive working environment will be created, thereby strengthening the communication links throughout the entire organization.[26]

Motivating

Motivation is the art or process of initiating and sustaining behavior toward certain goals. Motivation is all about inspiring someone to do something because he or she wants to do it, not because someone says to do it. As the American and Canadian hospitality and tourism industries have right-sized the organizational structure by reducing the number of levels of management, there is an increasing need for motivation. One hotel general manager, Steve Pelzer, said that his biggest problem was how to motivate employees. This section will help you understand your own motivation and influence that of those you will lead in the future.

The following motivational theories have been suggested by scholars and experts on motivation:

- ✔ Intrinsic and extrinsic theories
- ✔ Vicarious theories
- ✔ Content theories
- ✔ Process theories
- ✔ Goal-setting theories

Intrinsic and Extrinsic Motivation

Intrinsic and extrinsic motivation refer to the source of a person's motivation. Intrinsic motivation relates to the internal stimuli or need that occurs within us and causes us to be motivated. An example is the good feelings that occur when a task has been done well. Extrinsic motivation is caused by external stimuli. Being praised by a colleague is an example of extrinsic motivation.

Vicarious Motivation

Vicarious motivation relates to our seeing another person rewarded or punished; we perceive that we will receive similar treatment for similar actions. We naturally want to please so when we see another person receiving compliments for their actions the positive motivational effect is likely to rub off on us.

Content Theories

There is no single cause of motivation; instead, several factors may influence a person's desire to do things. Some suggest that motivation is linked to need satisfaction. This is closely related to the need–drive goal cycle, in which motivation occurs when a need within us initiates a drive toward a certain goal. For example, if a foodservice manager who seeks recognition (a need) meets certain goals, she or he will receive a bonus (a goal). The individual may work long hours (a drive) in order to accomplish the goal. Once the goal has been achieved, the need will be temporarily satisfied, and the behavior will subside until the need is reactivated. One of the interesting aspects of motivation is that different people have different needs.

One of the significant content theories of motivation is Maslow's hierarchy of needs. Maslow's theory has influenced motivational techniques for many years. The theory suggests that there are five basic needs or motives common to adults:

1. Physiological needs: Necessities for life, including food, air, and fluids, all of which are essential to our physical existence
2. Safety needs: The security and assurance that our physiological needs will be met in the future
3. Love and belonging needs: Social needs such as the need for affection or the need for acceptance by others
4. Esteem needs: The needs of self-respect and respect from others
5. Self-actualization needs: The need for self-fulfillment; the need to reach one's potential[27]

Figure 14–8 shows Maslow's five needs together with examples of how each might be satisfied in an organizational setting.

Although Maslow's theory was first proposed in 1943, it is still widely and highly regarded as having a significant influence on management and employee motivation.

Another widely accepted and influential theory of motivation is Frederick Herzberg's explanation of motivator and hygiene factors. While studying managers in the work environment, psychologist Frederick Herzberg concluded that two separate and distinct sets of factors influenced individual motivation.

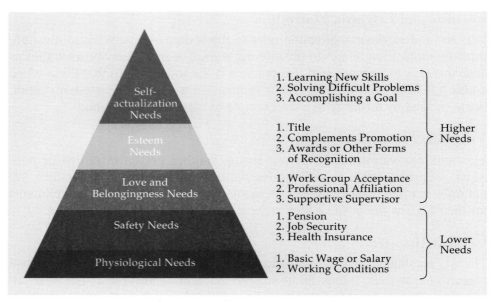

Figure 14–8 *Maslow's Needs Hierarchy in Organizational Settings* (Donald D. White and David A. Bednar, *Organizational Behavior: Understanding and Managing People at Work,* 2nd ed. Boston: Allyn and Bacon, 1991, p. 149.)

Herzberg referred to these groups of factors as satisfiers and dissatisfiers, or motivators and hygienes. Table 14–2 shows both the motivators and hygiene factors.

The main premise of Herzberg's theory is that if the hygiene factors are not met, it is unlikely that much motivation will occur, no matter how many of the motivators are met. However, once the hygiene factors have been met, significant motivation will occur once the motivator factors are present.

Process Theories

Process theories are concerned with the decision to make an effort. We process information on a certain topic and then decide the amount of effort to be used to do a particular task. There are two main process theories: expectancy theory and equity theory.

Table 14–2 Herzberg's Motivators and Hygiene Factors

Motivators	Hygienes
Work itself	Company policies and administration
Recognition	Salary
Responsibility	Working conditions
Achievement	Relationships with supervisors
Growth	Relationships with peers
Advancement	Relationships with subordinates
	Security
	Status

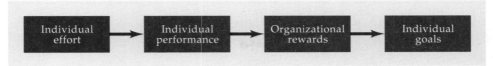

Figure 14–9 *Expectancy Model* (Stephen P. Robbins, *Management,* 3rd ed. Englewood Cliffs, N.J.: Prentice Hall, 1991, p. 440.)

The expectancy theory is based on the premise that people will put out effort equivalent to the perceived rewards. If people think they are definitely going to receive rewards, they are more likely to be motivated and give the extra effort required to achieve the goals. Bonuses utilize the expectancy theory of motivation. For example, if a foodservice manager meets or exceeds a predetermined level of profitability, she or he will receive financial, and possibly other, bonus incentives. Figure 14–9 shows a simplified version of the Expectancy Model.

Equity theory relates to the exchange of individual contributions for organizational rewards. Equity theory suggests that an individual's motivation relies on three important variables:

1. The inputs an individual perceives she or he is contributing
2. The outcomes (rewards) an individual perceives she or he is receiving
3. The way in which an individual's inputs and outcomes compare to the inputs and outcomes of another person[28]

Many of us tend to evaluate our own efforts in comparison with outcomes/rewards and then compare them to the outcomes/rewards of others doing similar activities. Our motivation will likely be affected positively or negatively by our level of satisfaction based on the comparison.

Goal-Setting Theories

Both companies and individuals are better off when they set goals. Even if they are not all reached, the results will be better than if no goals were set. As a result, many companies have included some form of goal setting as part of the reward and recognition programs.

Goal setting is a key element in management by objective (MBO). With MBO, goals are generally set by employees, not managers. Once the employees have set the individual and group/department goals, management approves the goals. Employees are far more likely to achieve and even exceed goals that they have had a part of setting than they are to achieve goals prescribed from above. Quality assurance programs and, more recently, total quality management and empowerment have contributed greatly to employee motivation.

Controlling

The purpose of control is to provide information to management for decision-making purposes. Control closes the cycle of management function by determining whether or not the corporation reached its goals. Remember that at the outset, criteria are set, and the quality levels are established. The last management function is to determine how well we have done what we said we would do.

Corporate Profile: The Ritz-Carlton Hotel Company

A Commitment to Excellence and Quality Service Worldwide

The Ritz-Carlton Hotel Company was officially organized in the summer of 1983, although the Ritz-Carlton's history and tradition long precede that date. With the purchase of The Ritz-Carlton, Boston, and the acquisition of the exclusive rights to use the name, came a rich heritage. Built in 1927, The Ritz-Carlton, Boston, has nurtured a tradition of excellence rooted in the philosophy of the celebrated hotelier, Cesar Ritz. The landmark property is the only Ritz-Carlton of that era to continuously operate since opening.

Beginning with one hotel in 1983, the company now operates thirty-one hotels worldwide (twenty-one city hotels and ten resorts) in the United States, Hong Kong, Australia, Mexico, South Korea, and Spain. Expansion in Asia includes the opening of hotels in Singapore and Osaka, Japan.

The Ritz-Carlton Hotel Company, with headquarters in Atlanta, Georgia, has built its reputation on reliable service and commitment to quality. The Ritz-Carlton mission is to provide the finest personal service and facilities, instill well-being, and fulfill even the unexpressed wishes and needs of guests. Under the charismatic leadership and insistence on high standards of Horst Schulze, president and chief operating officer of Ritz-Carlton, the company was awarded the prestigious

Horst Schulze

Malcolm Baldrige National Quality Award in 1993. The Ritz-Carlton is the only hospitality organization to have ever won this coveted honor, given by the United States Department of Commerce for quality management.

Quality planning begins with Schulze, whose commitment to excellence is apparent in the many innovations and changes he has initiated over the years. Perhaps the most significant is the launching of a comprehensive quality management program. Hallmarks of the program include participatory executive leadership, thorough information gathering, coordinated planning and execution, and a trained work force that is empowered "to move heaven and earth" to satisfy customers. Committed employees rank as the most essential element. All are schooled in the company's Gold Standards, which include a credo, motto, three steps of service, and twenty Ritz-Carlton basics. Each employee is expected to understand and adhere to these standards, which describe processes for solving problems that guests may have as well as detailed grooming, housekeeping, and safety and efficiency standards. "We are ladies and gentlemen serving ladies and gentlemen" is the motto of all Ritz-Carlton hotels, exemplifying anticipatory service provided by all staff members.

The control function provides management with the necessary information to make informed decisions about the organization's progress toward meeting the predetermined goals. Control has three main elements:

1. Establishing standards of performance
2. Measuring current performance against expected performance
3. Acting on significant variance from expected performance

Unfortunately, reality is not as simple as these three elements. Many variables—some controllable, some uncontrollable—distort the picture. All three of these main elements are interrelated with other management functions, such as planning and decision making. Both practicing executives and management theorists agree that control is a vital and necessary part of management.

To provide such service, the employee training process is the finest in the industry. To underscore the importance of maintaining quality service as the organization grows, Mr. Schulze himself conducts the employee orientation at each new hotel. The two-day orientation, however, is just the beginning. Employee indoctrination at The Ritz-Carlton Hotel Company includes one hundred additional hours of on-the-job training, daily inspections for appearance, periodic performance reviews, and, again, an unrelenting emphasis on quality. The Ritz-Carlton aims to convince employees that they are important members of an elite team always looking for ways to improve. The company also rewards exceptional performance with things like fully paid vacations. Much of the responsibility for ensuring high-quality guest services and accommodations rests with the staff. A significant example of the responsibility given to employees is the fact that each Ritz-Carlton staff member is empowered to make a decision that could cost the hotel up to $2,000. Mr. Schulze insists that it is not the amount of money that is important, but, rather, the emphasis on the corporate environment that encourages employees to make decisions and speak up. "They need to feel part of the organization and really work for the organization," Schulze says.

The company's philosophy ultimately results in high-standard properties. All Ritz-Carlton Hotels offer twenty-four-hour room service, twice-daily maid service, complimentary shoeshine, terrycloth robes in all guest rooms, a floor reserved for nonsmokers, and in-house fitness facilities. Other special features include The Ritz-Carlton Club, a private lounge offering complimentary food and beverages throughout the day and the services of a special concierge, as well as dining rooms that represent culinary excellence and top value. A highly trained concierge staff stands by to respond to additional guest needs.

The Ritz-Carlton Hotel Company also maintains a sophisticated guest recognition program designed to determine and fulfill the needs of repeat visitors by tracking their individual requests and preferences. A guest who visits The Ritz-Carlton, Atlanta, can expect the same individualized service at any Ritz-Carlton, from New York to Sidney, Australia.

Each property is designed to be a comfortable haven for travelers and a social center for the community. The architecture and art work are carefully selected to complement the hotel's environment. "We go to great lengths to capture the spirit of a hotel and its locale," says Mr. Schulze. "This creates a subtle balance and celebrates a gracious, relaxed lifestyle. The Ritz-Carlton Directory of Hotels and Resorts welcomes the guest in a promising way: "We trust you'll find The Ritz-Carlton warm, relaxed yet refined; a most comfortable home away from home."

RITZ-CARLTON is a federally registered trademark of The Ritz-Carlton Hotel Company.

Service and Total Quality Management (TQM)

The increasingly open and fiercely competitive marketplace exerts an enormous pressure on service industries to deliver superior service. Inspired by rising guest expectations and competitive necessity, many hospitality companies have jumped on the service quality bandwagon.

The Ritz-Carlton Hotel Company, winner of the 1993 Malcolm Baldrige National Quality Award, has a credo that is printed on a small laminated card that all employees must memorize or carry on their person at all times, when on duty. The reverse side of the card has the Ritz-Carlton Basics (see Figure 14–10), which are twenty steps to successful service.

The quality movement began at the turn of the century as a means of ensuring consistency among the parts produced in the different plants of a single company so that they could be used interchangeably. TQM is a participative process that empowers all levels of employees to work in groups to establish guest service expectations and determine the best way of meeting or exceeding those expectations. Notice that *guest* is the term preferred over *customer*. The inference here is that if we treat customers like guests, we are more likely to ex-

1. The credo will be known, owned, and energized by all employees.
2. Our motto is: "We are ladies and gentlemen serving ladies and gentlemen." Practice teamwork and lateral service to create a positive work environment.
3. The three steps of service shall be practiced by all employees.
4. All employees will successfully complete training certification to ensure they understand how to perform to the Ritz-Carlton standards in their positions.
5. Each employee will understand their work areas and hotel goals as established in each strategic plan.
6. All employees will know the needs of their internal and external customers (guests and employees) so that we may deliver the products and services they expect. Use guest preference pads to record specific needs.
7. Each employee will continuously identify defects throughout the hotel.
8. Any employee who receives a customer complaint owns the complaint.
9. Instant guest pacification will be ensured by all. React quickly to correct the problem immediately. Follow up with a telephone call within twenty minutes to verify the problem has been resolved to the customer's satisfaction. Do everything you possibly can to never lose a guest.
10. Guest incident action forms are used to record and communicate every incident of guest dissatisfaction. Every employee is empowered to resolve the problem and to prevent a repeat occurrence.
11. Uncompromising levels of cleanliness are the responsibility of every employee.
12. Smile—We are on stage. Always maintain positive eye contact. Use the proper vocabulary with our guests. (Use words like *good morning, certainly, I'll be happy to,* and *my pleasure.*)
13. Be an ambassador of your hotel in and outside of the work place. Always talk positively. No negative comments.
14. Escort guests rather than pointing out directions to another area of the hotel.
15. Be knowledgeable of hotel information (hours of operation, etc.) to answer guest inquiries. Always recommend the hotel's retail and food and beverage outlets prior to outside facilities.
16. Use proper telephone etiquette. Answer within three rings and with a smile. When necessary, ask the caller, "May I place you on hold?" Do not screen calls. Eliminate call transfers when possible.
17. Uniforms are to be immaculate; wear proper and safe footwear (clean and polished), and your correct name tag. Take pride and care in your personal appearance (adhering to all grooming standards).
18. Ensure all employees know their roles during emergency situations and are aware of fire and life safety response processes.
19. Notify your supervisor immediately of hazards, injuries, equipment, or assistance that you need. Practice energy conservation and proper maintenance and repair of hotel property and equipment.
20. Protecting the assets of a Ritz-Carlton hotel is the responsibility of every employee.

Figure 14–10 *The Ritz-Carlton Basics* (Courtesy The Ritz-Carlton Hotel Company.)

ceed their expectations. One successful hotelier has insisted for a long time that all employees treat guests as they would like to be treated themselves.[29]

TQM is a continuous process that works best when managers are also good leaders. A successful company will employ leader–managers who create a stimulating work environment in which guests and employees (sometimes called *internal guests* when one employee serves another, who in turn serves a guest) become an integral part of the mission by participating in goal and objective setting.

Installing TQM is exciting because once everyone becomes involved there is no way of stopping the creative ways employees will solve guest-related problems and improve service. Other benefits include cost reductions, increased guest and employee satisfaction, and, ultimately, profit. The quality leadership process has eleven key steps that are shown in Figure 14–11.

Top executives and line managers are responsible for the success of the TQM process; when they commit to ownership of the process, it will be successful. Focused commitment is the foundation of a quality service initiative, and leadership is the critical component in promoting commitment. Achieving TQM is a top down-bottom up process that must have the active commitment and participation of all employees, from the top executives down to the bottom of the

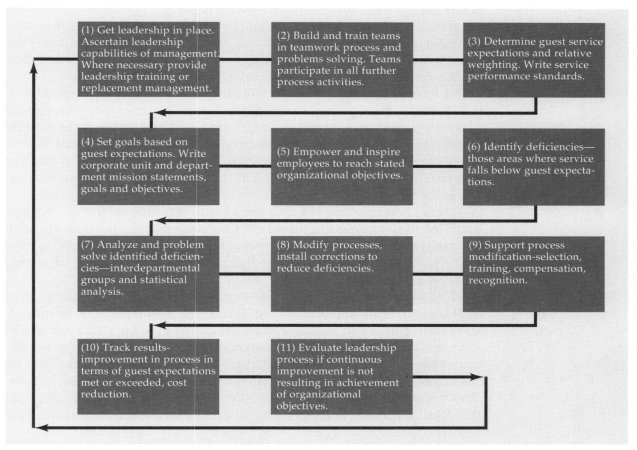

Figure 14–11 *Eleven Steps in Quality Leadership*

corporate ladder. The expression, "If you are not serving the guest, then you had better be serving someone who is" still holds true today.

The difference between TQM and quality control (QC) is that QC focuses on error detection, whereas TQM focuses on error prevention. Quality control is generally based on industrial systems and, because of this, tends to be product oriented rather than service oriented. To the guest, services are experiential; they are felt, lived through, and sensed. The moment of truth is the actual guest contact.

Ethics

Ethics is a set of moral principles and values that people use to answer questions of right and wrong. Ethics can also be defined as the study of the general nature of morals and the specific moral choices to be made by the individual in his or her relationship with others.[30]

Much individual interpretation of ethics is based on one's own value system. Where did this value system originate? What happens if one value system is different from another? Fortunately, certain universal guiding principles are agreed on by virtually all religions, cultures, and societies.[31] At the very root of all principles is that all people's rights are important and should not be violated. This belief is central to civilized societies; without it, chaos would reign.

The forward to *Ethics in Hospitality Management*, edited by Stephen S. J. Hall, Robert A. Beck professor emeritus at Cornell University, poses the age-old question: "Is overbooking rooms ethical? How does one compare the legal responsibilities of the innkeeper to the moral obligations?" He adds that to compound the situation further, what is a "fair" or "reasonable" wage? A "fair" or "reasonable" return on investment? Is it "fair" or ethical to underpay employees for the benefit of the investors?

"English Common Law left such decisions to the 'reasonable man.' A judge would ask the jury, 'Was this the act of a reasonable man?'"[32] Interestingly, what is considered ethical in one country may not be in another. For example, in some countries it is considered normal to bargain for rooms; in others, bargaining would be considered bad form.

Ethics and morals have become an integral part of hospitality decisions, from employment (equal opportunity and affirmative action) to truth in memos. Many corporations and businesses have developed a code of ethics that all employees use to make decisions. This became necessary because too many managers were making decisions without regard to the impact of such decisions on others. Hall is one of the pioneers of ethics in hospitality; each year, he organizes a scholarship for an essay on a topic related to ethics in hospitality. Hall also developed a code of ethics for the hospitality service and tourism industry:

1. We acknowledge ethics and morality as inseparable elements of doing business and will test every decision against the highest standards of honesty, legality, fairness, impunity, and conscience.

2. We will conduct ourselves personally and collectively at all times so as to bring credit to the service and tourism industry at large.

3. We will concentrate our time, energy, and resources on the improvement of our own products and services and we will not denigrate our competition in the pursuit of our own success.

4. We will treat all guests equally regardless of race, religion, nationality, creed, or sex.

5. We will deliver all standards of service and product with total consistency to every guest.

6. We will provide a totally safe and sanitary environment at all times for every guest and employee.

7. We will strive constantly, in words, actions, and deeds, to develop and maintain the highest level of trust, honesty, and understanding among guests, clients, employees, employers, and the public at large.

8. We will provide every employee at every level all of the knowledge, training, equipment, and motivation required to perform his or her tasks according to our published standards.

9. We will guarantee that every employee at every level will have the same opportunity to perform, advance, and be evaluated against the same standard as all employees engaged in the same or similar tasks.

10. We will actively and consciously work to protect and preserve our natural environment and natural resources in all that we do.

11. We will seek a fair and honest profit, no more, no less.

The saying "Do unto others as you would have them do unto you" goes back to the Bible, ancient Greek, and even ancient Chinese cultures. This is a belief that most cultures would agree is a good one to guide decisions. Forte Hotels International for many years adopted the belief of Lord Forte that we should take care of our guests as we would like to be taken care of.

Robert Hass, CEO of Levi Strauss Co., has an interesting comment on corporate ethics and value: "Companies have to wake up to the fact that they are more than a product on a shelf. They're a behavior as well."[33]

Some corporations use a statement of aspirations to define shared values that will guide both work force and corporate decisions. For example, at Levi Strauss, each employee is expected to take part in the so-called core curriculum—a series of training programs that deal with values, ethical practices, empowerment, and an appreciation of diversity.[34] The purpose is to release the enormous power of involved employees.

Ethical Dilemmas in Hospitality

In the old days, certain actions may not have been considered ethical but management often looked the other way. Following are a few scenarios that are not seen as ethical today and are against most company's ethical policies:

1. As catering manager of a large banquet operation, the flowers for the hotel are booked through your office. The account is worth $15,000 per month. The florist offers you a ten-percent discount. Do you accept this? If you accept this, with whom do you share it?

2. As purchasing agent, you are responsible for procurement of $5 million worth of perishable and nonperishable items for a major restaurant chain. In order to get your business, a supplier offers you a substantial bargain on a house. You can live in the house, which will be under another person's name, for as long as you continue to buy from this supplier. The quality of this supplier's products and services are equal to the others. What should you do with the offer?

3. An edict had recently come from the executive committee of the hotel that reservations from a certain part of the world were only to be taken through the embassy because the hotel had experienced severe problems with guests from this part of the world. On one occasion, one of the occupants of a suite had sent a servant to the park to collect wood, which they then used to make a fire in the room in order to prepare food. They wondered why bells were ringing, and why fifteen fire trucks had arrived. Now, a group of well-dressed men approach you, offer greetings, and say that their boss, a very distinguished individual, would like to stay for an indefinite period. They produce a briefcase full of $100 bills as a deposit. You decline, stating that the hotel is full, which it is not. What should have happened?

These and other ethical dilemmas are not always simply right or wrong.

There are three key categories of questions to be answered when making decisions:

1. Is it legal? Will I be violating either civil law or company policy?
2. Is it balanced? Is it fair to all concerned in the short term as well as the long term? Does it promote win-win relationships?
3. How will it make me feel about myself? Will it make me proud? Would I feel good if my decision were published in the newspaper? Would I feel good if my family knew about it?[35]

Social Responsibilities in Business

"Ethics is broadly concerned with how persons or organizations act, or should act, in relations with others."[36] The so-called breakdown of socially acceptable behavior appears to be a universal problem. Whatever the cause, this malaise has affected business, government, and society.

In recent years, society's interest in, and awareness of, social responsibility has increased enormously. For example, the "greening" of North America has led to a decrease in the use of hazardous chemicals, including some pesticides. The protection and preservation of the environment has become a major issue for most of the population.

Social responsibility, however, goes beyond doing away with nonbiodegradable fast-food containers to becoming involved in the community in which a company or one of its hospitality-tourism operations is located. This is known as giving something back to the community.

For example, consider Hilton's corporate mission (see Figure 14–12).

*T*o be recognized as the world's best first-class hotel organization, to constantly strive to improve, allowing us to prosper as a business for the benefit of our guests, our employees, and our shareholders.

Fundamental to the success of our mission are the following:

PEOPLE:

Our most important asset. Involvement, teamwork, and commitment are the values that govern our work.

PRODUCT:

Our programs, services, and facilities. They must be designed and operated to consistently provide superior quality that satisfies the needs and desires of our guests.

PROFIT:

The ultimate measure of our success—the gauge for how well and how efficiently we serve our guests. Profits are required for us to survive and grow.

With this mission come certain guiding principles:

QUALITY COMES FIRST:

The quality of our product and service must create guest satisfaction; that's our number one priority.

VALUE:

Our guests deserve quality products at a fair price. That is how to build business.

CONTINUOUS IMPROVEMENT:

Never standing on past accomplishments, but always striving—through innovation—to improve our product and service, to increase our efficiency and profitability.

TEAMWORK:

At Hilton, we are a family, working together, to get things done.

INTEGRITY:

We will never compromise our code of conduct—we will be socially responsible—we are committed to Hilton's high standards of fairness and integrity.

Figure 14–12 *Hilton's Corporate Mission* (Courtesy of Hilton Hotels Corporation, Beverly Hills, California.)

Trends in Leadership and Management

✓ Leading a more diverse group of associates
✓ An increased need for training resulting from near full employment
✓ Many entry-level employees do not have basic job skills
✓ Creating leaders out of line managers
✓ Managing salaries all the way to the bottom line
✓ Establishing individual business units to make their own profit, or subcontracting out the department

✔ Instead of keeping a person on payroll for a function that is only needed occasionally, outsourcing that service out to a specialist

✔ Cutting down on full-time employees and hiring more part-time employees to avoid paying benefits

Position Requirements

Your resort has management vacancies in the following positions:

Executive Chef
Executive Housekeeper
Front Office Manager

Write an advertisement, listing the traits you consider to be most important for these positions.

Performance Standards

Charles and Nancy both apply for the assistant front office manager position at a 300-room, upscale hotel. Charles has worked for a total of 8 years in 3 different hotels and has been with this hotel for three months as a front office associate. Initially, he had a lot of enthusiasm. Lately, however, he has been dressing a bit slovenly and his figures, cash, and reports have been off. In addition, he is occasionally "rattled" by demanding guests.

Nancy recently graduated from college, with honors, with a degree in hospitality management. While attending college, she worked part-time as a front desk associate at a budget motel. Nancy does not have a lot of experience working in a hotel, or in customer service in general, however she is quite knowledgeable from her studies and is eager to begin her career.

It appears that Charles would have been considered a prime candidate for the position, because of his extensive experience in other hotels and the knowledge he has of the hotel's culture. In view of his recent performance, however the rooms division manager will need to sit down with Charles to review his career development track.

Discussion Questions

1. What are the qualifications for the job that should be considered for both applicants?

2. How should the discussion between the rooms manager and the rooms division manager and Charles be handled? Make specific recommendations sion manager.

3. Who would be the best person for the job? Why?

Reluctant to Change

You have just been appointed assistant manager at an old, established, but busy New York restaurant. Your employees respond to your suggested changes with, "We have always done it this way before." The employees really do not know any other way of doing things.

Discussion Question

1. How should you handle this situation?

Summary

1. Leadership is defined as the process by which a person is able to influence the activities and outcomes of others in a desired way.
2. Managing is a process in which organizational goals are achieved through efforts of subordinates, whereas leading is the process of influencing the behavior of others.
3. Managers have to forecast, plan, organize, and control the efforts of a group in order to achieve goals. They need to be skilled in conceptual, human, and technical areas.
4. Every company operates according to its corporate philosophy and culture; creates a mission statement that outlines the central purposes, strategies, and values of the corporation; and strives to achieve certain goals and follow objectives in order to achieve these goals.
5. The key management functions are forecasting, organizing, decision making, planning, communicating, motivating, and controlling.
6. Forecasting considers and evaluates various factors and produces an estimate of how much business is expected.
7. Most organizations are made up of a formal and an informal organization, which plan either for long- or short-term purposes. Both types have to make programmed and nonprogrammed decisions.
8. Communications links all management functions together. Managers interact via phone, fax, memos, face-to-face, and grapevine information.
9. A manager has to be able to motivate the people he or she works with in order to achieve goals. Numerous theories of motivation exist, including intrinsic and extrinsic theories, content theories, process theories, goal-setting, and reinforcement theories.
10. In questions of employment, realistic advertising, room overbooking, and aspirations, ethics and morals have become an integral part of hospitality decisions.
11. Society's interest in social responsibility has increased and influenced hospitality in the form of recyclable fast-food containers and involvement in the community in which the hotel is located.

Review Exercises

1. Define leadership and name essential qualities of a good leader.
2. Distinguish between transactional and transformational leadership. Why is Wayne Calloway an excellent example of transformational leadership?
3. Briefly describe why Taco Bell leadership is an example of excellence.
4. Explain the difference in long- and short-term planning and list the seven steps in organizational planning.
5. Distinguish between formal and informal organization.

6. Identify the eight major steps in decision making. Why is a compnay more sophisticated when it makes more programmed decisions?

7. Define motivation and explain vicarious motivation and expectancy theory.

8. Describe the relationship among corporate philosophy, quality leadership and service, and total quality management.

9. In what ways have ethics and social awareness influenced the hotel industry?

Key Words and Concepts

Centralization
Communicating
Controlling
Corporate culture
Corporate philosophy
Decentralization
Decision making
Equity theory

Expectancy theory
Forecasting
Goal-setting theory
Herzberg's motivation and hygiene factors
Hierarchy of human needs
Human skills, conceptual skills, and technical skills

Leadership
Management
Maslow's hierarchy of needs
Mission, goals, and objectives
Motivating
Organizing

Planning
Professionalism
Situational leadership
Span of control
Total quality management
Transactional leadership
Transformational leadership

Notes

[1] James M. Kouzes and Barry Z. Posner, *The Leadership Challenge: How to Get Extraordinary Things Done in Organizations*, San Francisco: Jossey-Bass, 1987, p. 8.

[2] Donald D. White and David A. Bednar, *Organizational Behavior: Understanding and Managing People at Work*, 2nd ed. Boston: Allyn and Bacon, 1991, pp. 407–412.

[3] White and Bednar, op. cit., p. 408.

[4] H. M. Burns, *Leader*. New York: Harper and Row, 1978, p. 84.

[5] Ibid.

[6] Ibid.

[7] Patricia Sellers, "Pepsi Keeps on Going after No. 1," *Fortune, 123,* 5, March 11, 1991, pp. 62–70.

[8] White and Bednar, op. cit., p. 413.

[9] W. P. Fisher and C. Bernstein, *Lessons in Leadership: Perspectives for Hospitality Industry Success.* New York: Van Nostrand Reinhold, 1991, p. 44.

[10] Ibid., p. 35.

[11] Ibid., p. 29.

[12] This draws on Doug Caldwell, "Isadore Sharp: Outstanding CEO of the Year," *Canadian Manager,* Spring 1993, pp. 16–17.

[13] Based on James Scarpa, "Leadership Awards," *Restaurant Business, 90,* 8, May 20, 1991, p. 97.

[14] John P. Kotter, *A Force for Change: How Leadership Differs from Management.* New York: Free Press, 1990, pp. 3–4.

[15] Warren Bennis, *On Becoming a Leader.* Reading, Mass.: Addison-Wesley, p. 45.

[16] Ibid.

[17] Kouzes and Posner, op. cit., p. xvii.

[18] James A. Belasco, *Teaching the Elephant to Dance.* New York: Plume, 1991, p. 6.

[19] Charles Brewton, *Hotel and Motel Management, 207,* 6, April 6, 1992, p. 13; reprinted with permission courtesy of *Hotel and Motel Management.*

[20] Norman M. Scarborough, *Business: Gaining the Competitive Edge.* Boston: Allyn and Bacon, 1992, p. 138.

[21] Ibid., p. 158.

[22] Stephen P. Robbins, *Management,* 3d ed. Englewood Cliffs, New Jersey: Prentice-Hall, 1991, p. 153.

[23] Leonard R. Sayles and George Strauss, *Human Behavior in Organizations.* Englewood Cliffs, New Jersey: Prentice-Hall, 1966, pp. 238–246.

[24] Karen L. Seelkoff, "Nine Steps to Better Communication," *Hotels, 27,* 11, November 1993, p. 24.

[25] Ibid.

[26] Ibid.

[27] Adapted from White and Bednar, op. cit., pp. 148–149.

[28] White and Bednar, op. cit., p. 178.

[29] Personal conversation with Lord Forte, chairman of the board, Forte Hotels International, May 1971.

[30] Angelo M. Rocco and Andrew N. Vladimir, *Hospitality Today: An Introduction.* East Lansing, Mich.: The Educational Institute of the American Hotel and Motel Association, 1991, p. 390.

[31]Ibid.

[32]Stephen S. J. Hall (ed.), *Ethics in Hospitality Management: A Book of Readings.* East Lansing, Mich.: The Educational Institute of the American Hotel and Motel Association, 1992, p. 75.

[33]Jim Impoco, "Working for Mr. Clean Jeans," *U.S. News and World Report, 115,* 5, August, 2, 1993, p. 50.

[34]Ibid.

[35]Rocco and Vladimir, op. cit., p. 27.

[36]William D. Hall, *Making the Right Decisions: Ethics for Managers.* New York: John Wiley and Sons, 1993, p. 3.

Glossary

A

Actual market share   The market share that a business actually receives compared with the fair market share, which is an equal share of the market.

ADA   American with Disabilities Act.

ADR   See Average daily rate.

Agenda 21   A charter produced during the 1992 Earth Summit held in Rio de Janeiro, Brazil, which addresses issues pertaining to the environment and sustainable development and is intended to prepare the world to successfully meet the challenges in the coming century.

AHMA   American Hotel and Motel Association.

A la carte   1. A menu on which food and beverages are listed and priced individually. 2. Foods cooked to order compared with foods cooked in advance and held for later service.

Alcohol   Naturally occurring and easily synthesized compound that induces intoxication when consumed.

Allocentric   Psychological term referring to someone who enjoys varied and unfamiliar activities.

Ambiance   The combined atmosphere created by the decor, lighting, service, possible entertainment (such as background music), and so on, that enhances the dining or lodging experience.

Amenities   Features that add material comfort, convenience, or smoothness to a guest's stay. Examples include hair shampoo, an iron and ironing board in each room, in-room coffee maker, and so on.

Aperitif   A fortified wine flavored with one or more herbs and spices, usually consumed before a meal.

Apollo   Name of a commonly used airline reservation system.

Average daily rate (ADR)   One of the key operating ratios that indicate the level of a hotel's performance. The ADR is calculated by dividing the amount of dollar sales by the number of rooms sold.

Average guest check   The average amount each group spends. Mostly used in a restaurant setting.

B

Baby boomers   Anyone born in the twenty-year period from 1946 through 1965. Baby boomers represent the largest segment of the population—about eighty-one million United States residents in 1990. Baby boomers travel more frequently than their parents, and regard travel as a necessity rather than a luxury.

Back of the house   Refers to the support areas behind the scenes in a hotel or motel, including housekeeping, laundry, engineering, and food service. Also refers to individuals who operate behind the scenes to make a guest's stay pleasant and safe.

Bar mitzvah   A Jewish religious ritual and family celebration commemorating the religious adulthood of a boy on his thirteenth birthday.

Batch cooking   The cooking of food in quantities for consumption throughout a meal period. Used in noncommercial food service to avoid putting out all the food at 11:30 and having it spoil. Batches are cooked for readiness at 11:30, 12, 12:30, etc.

Bat mitzvah   A Jewish religious ritual and family celebration commemorating the religious adulthood of a girl on her thirteenth birthday.

Bed and breakfast   A rate that combines a night's accommodation with a breakfast the following day. The breakfast can be either a full or continental breakfast.

Benchmarking   A process by which an organization reassesses its traditional business practices by comparing them with the best practices of other organizations.

Beverage cost percentage   Similar to food cost percentage, except it relates to beverages.

Boardroom-style meetings   A type of meeting setup designed for a small number of participants who will sit around a rectangular table.

Bonding   A recreational process by which people form relationships built on the experiences they have enjoyed together.

Budgeting   The process of forecasting sales and costs.

C

Call package   In bar operations, it is the group of spirits that the bar offers to guests who ask for a specific name brands.

Capture rate   A term used in hotel food and beverage to describe the number of hotel guests who use the food and beverage outlets.

Catchment area   The geographical area that falls within a specific radius established to determine the size of a restaurant's market (usually 1 to 5 miles).

Catering   Part of the food and beverage division of a hotel that is responsible for arranging and planning food and beverage functions for conventions and smaller hotel groups and local banquets booked by the sales department.

Celebrity restaurants   Restaurants that are owned, or partially owned, by celebrities.

Central reservations system   Allows guests to call one phone number to reserve a room at any of the specific chain's properties.

CFA   Culinary Federation of America.

Champagne   Sparkling wine made in the Champagne district of France.

Charter of Sustainable Tourism   A result of the World Conference on Sustainable Tourism held in Spain in 1995, recognizing the objective of developing a tourism industry that meets economic expectations and environmental requirements, and respects not only the social and physical structure of the location, but also the local population.

Chef de partie (shef-de-par-tée)   Also known as station chef. Produces the menu items for a station under the direct supervision of the chef or sous chef.

CHRIE   Stands for Council on Hotel, Restaurant, and Institutional Education.

City ledger   A client whose company has established credit with a certain hotel. Charges are posted to the city ledger and accounts are sent once or twice monthly.

Class III gaming   A class of gaming created by the Indian Gaming Regulatory Act that includes most casino games. For a state to have class III gaming, casino gaming must be legalized for commercial (non-Indian) gaming operators and must be conducted in conformance with a contract, or agreement, between state governments and the tribes.

Classroom-style meetings   A type of meeting setup generally used in instructional meetings, such as workshops.

Clinic   A form of meeting whose attenders learn by doing.

Club   Association of persons with a common objective, usually jointly supported and meeting periodically.

Cold calling   A type of prospecting whereby sales representatives call on individuals or organizations and have no idea if these people will turn out to be true sales prospects.

Commercial food service   Operations that compete for customers in the open market.

Commission caps   Limits the amount of commission earned by travel agents booking airline tickets. The caps were imposed in 1995, changing commissions to $25 each way for domestic flights and reducing commissions for international flights from eleven percent to eight percent.

Comp   Short for complimentary, or the offering of hospitality services at no charge as a reward for a customer's participation in gaming activities. Complimentaries can include room nights, food, beverage, show tickets, and even transportation to and from the gaming operation.

Compensation   Remuneration including salary, wages, and benefits.

Competitor analysis An analysis of competitors' strengths and weaknesses.

Concept The elements in a food-service operation that contribute to its function as a complete and organized system serving the needs and expectations of its guests.

Concierge A uniformed employee of the hotel who has a separate desk in the lobby or on special concierge floors and answers questions, solves problems, and performs the services of a private secretary for the hotel's guests.

Contractors Companies that operate food service for the client on a contractual basis.

Contribution margin Key operating figure in menu engineering, determined by subtracting food cost from selling price as a measure of profitability.

Controller Head accountant who manages the accounting department and all financial dealings of the hotel.

Convention Generic term referring to any size of business or professional meeting held in one specific location, which usually also includes some form of trade show or exposition. Also refers to a group of delegates or members who assemble to accomplish a specific goal.

Conventions and visitors bureaus 1. Organizations responsible for promoting tourism at the regional and local level. 2. A not-for-profit umbrella organization that represents a city or urban area in soliciting and servicing all types of travelers to that city or area, whether for business, pleasure, or both.

Corporate travel agencies Also known as outplants, corporate travel agencies specialize, either partly or wholly, in handling corporate or government accounts.

Corporate travel manager Individuals employed by corporations, associations, government agencies, and other types of organizations to coordinate the organization's travel arrangements.

Covers The guest count of a restaurant.

Cuisine Food cooked and served in styles from around the world.

D

Database Organized collection of information, such as names, addresses, prices, and dates.

Demographics Statistical study of the characteristics of human populations.

Decision making The process of choosing a course of action among alternatives to solve a specific problem.

Destination Location where travelers choose to visit and spend time.

Destination-management companies Organizations in charge of developing and implementing tourism programs.

Diversity An increase in the heterogeneity of an organization through the inclusion of different ethnic groups.

DOC Director of Catering.

Dram shop legislation Includes laws and procedures that govern the legal operation of establishments that sell measured alcoholic beverages.

Du jour French expression used in menus, meaning "of the day."

E

Economics The science relating to the production, distribution, and use of goods and services.

Ecotourism Responsible travel to natural areas that conserves the environment and sustains the well-being of the local people.

EEO Equal employment opportunity.

EEOC Equal Employment Opportunity Commission.

Elastic Demand changes with economic conditions.

Employee training For many organizations, it is an ongoing activity that is conducted by a training department, a training manager, or by line management or specially selected individuals within each department.

Entremetier (awn-truh-mit-tee-háy) Vegetable chef.

Entrepreneur Individual who creates, organizes, manages, and assumes the risk of an enterprise or business.

Environmental analysis An analysis of how the uncontrollable and controllable factors will affect a hospitality and travel organization's direction and success. It is an element of situation, market, and feasibility analyses, and provides a foundation for long- and short-term marketing plans.

Equal Pay Act An act that prohibits discrimination in which employers pay men more than women for jobs requiring substantially equal skills, effort, and responsibility.

Equity theory   A theory of job motivation that emphasizes the role played by an individual's belief in the equity or fairness of rewards and punishments in determining his or her performance and satisfaction.

Ethics   A set of moral principles and values that determine what is good and what is bad. The study of the general nature of morals and the specific moral choices to be made by the individual in his or her relationship with others.

Ethnic restaurants   A restaurant featuring a particular cuisine such as Chinese, Mexican, or Italian.

European plan   An accommodation-only rate that includes no meals.

Executive committee   A committee of hotel executives from each of the major departments within the hotel generally made up of the general manager, director of rooms division, food and beverage director, marketing and sales director, human resources director, accounting and/or finance director, and engineering director.

Exempt employees   Those employees who under Section 13(a)(1) of the Federal Minimum Wage Law are not required to be paid overtime. This is because they are primarily engaged in managerial or administrative functions.

Expectancy theory   A theory that suggests employees will produce in accordance with the expected return or compensation.

Expense accounts   Accounts primarily used for entertaining purposes.

Exposition   Event held mainly for informational exchanges among trade people. Large exhibition in which the presentation is the main attraction as well as being a source of revenue for an exhibitor.

F

Fair Labor Standards Act of 1938   Established a policy for minimum wage and a maximum length of the work week.

Fair market share   A market share based on each business receiving an equal share of the market.

Familiarization (fam) trips   Free or reduced-price trip given to travel agents, travel writers, or other intermediaries to promote destinations.

Fermentation   The chemical process in which yeast acts on sugar or sugar-containing substances, such as grain or fruit, to produce alcohol and carbon dioxide.

FIFO   See First-in, first-out.

Finger foods   Appetizers and bits of foods that can be eaten without the aid of utensils.

Fining   Process by which wine that has matured is filtered to help stabilize it and remove any solid particles still in the wine.

First-in, first-out (FIFO)   The supplies that are ordered first are used first.

Fixed costs   A cost or expense for a fixed period and range of activity that does not change in total but becomes progressively smaller per unit as volume increases.

Floor supervisor   Supervises day-to-day work of room attendants at larger motels. Also called assistant housekeepers.

Focus groups   A gathering of eight to twelve people who are interviewed as a group by a facilitator.

FOM   See Front office manager.

Food cost percentage   A ratio comparing the cost of food sold to food sales, which is calculated by dividing the cost of food sold during a given period by food sales during the same period.

Forecasting   Process of estimating future events in the food service industry.

Fortified wines   Wine to which brandy or other spirits have been added to stop any further fermentation and/or to raise its alcoholic strength.

Forum   A public assembly or lecture involving audience discussion.

Franchise   Refers to 1. the authorization given by one company to another to sell its unique products and services, or 2. the name of the business format or product that is being franchised.

Franchisee   Person who purchases the right to use and/or sell the products and services of the franchiser.

Franchiser   An individual or company that licenses others to sell its products or services.

French service   Restaurant service in which one waiter (a captain) takes the order, does the tableside cooking, and brings the drinks and food and the secondary or back waiter serves bread and water, clears each course, crumbs the table, and serves the coffee.

Front office manager (FOM)   Person who manages the front office department.

Front of the house   Comprises all the areas the guests will contact, including the lobby, corridors, elevators, guest rooms, restaurants and bars, meeting rooms, and restrooms. Also refers to employees who staff these areas.

Full-service restaurants   A restaurant that 1. has more than a dozen or so main-course items on the menu, and 2. cooks to order.

G

Gaming   Wagering of money or other valuables on the outcome of a game or other event.

Gaming entertainment industry   Businesses that offer games of risk as a part of a total package of entertainment and leisure time activities including resort hotels, various food service concepts, retail shopping, theme parks, live entertainment, and recreational pursuits.

Garde manger (gar-mawn-zháy)   Pantry chef who prepares all cold appetizers, desserts, and salads.

GDP   See Gross domestic product.

General manager   Head manager in an organization. Ultimately responsible for the operation of the hospitality establishment and the supervision of its employees. Held directly accountable by the corporation or owners for the operation's level of profitability.

Grievance   A complaint filed by an employee against the employer or employer's representative.

Gross gaming revenue (GGR)   The net spending of customers on gaming. This does not include spending on non-gaming operations such as food and beverage, hotel rooms, and other retail expenditures.

Gross domestic product (GDP)   Total value of goods and services produced within a country, minus the net payments on foreign investments.

Gross operating profit   Revenues minus operating costs before taxes.

Gross operating revenue   Total payments received for goods and services.

H

Handle   Dollars wagered, or bet, often confused with "win." Whenever a customer places a bet, the handle increases by the amount of the bet. The handle is not affected by the outcome of the bet.

Hops   The dried, conical fruit of a special vine that imparts a special bitterness to beer.

Horizontal integration   Having representation in the multiple sectors of the market place. May be achieved by purchasing or developing a mid-scale hotel chain or an all-suite or economy chain, so the corporation has representation in each price range.

Hospice   An old French word meaning "to provide care/shelter for travelers." The word hospitality is derived from this word.

Hospitality   1. The cordial and generous reception of guests. 2. Wide range of businesses, each of which is dedicated to the service of people away from home.

Hotelier   Keeper, owner, or manager of the property.

Human resources manager or director   Manages the hotel's employee benefits program and monitors compliance with laws that relate to equal opportunity in hiring and promotion.

I

Illegal aliens   Individuals who move to another country illegally, without permission to enter as either immigrants or refugees. Also called undocumented workers.

Incentive travel   Marketing and management tool currently used to motivate people by offering travel rewards for achieving a specific goal.

Indian Gaming Regulatory Act   A federal act that created a statutory basis for the operation of gaming by Indian tribes in order to promote tribal economic development, self-sufficiency, and strong tribal governments.

Institutional food service   Operations that serve people who are members of particular societal institutions, such as hospitals, colleges, schools, nursing homes, the military, and industry.

J

Job description   A description of the duties and responsibilities involved with a particular job.

Joint venture   A commercial undertaking by two or more people.

K

Kitchen brigade   System of kitchen organization in which the staff is divided into specialized departments, all contributing collectively to the preparation of a meal.

L

Labor cost percentage Similar to food cost percentage, except it relates to labor.

Labor intensive Relying on a large work force to meet the needs of guests.

Lager beer The beverage that is normally referred to as beer; it is clear, light-bodied, and refreshing.

Leadership The process by which a person with vision is able to influence the activities and outcome of others in a desired way.

Leads In the convention and visitors bureaus' lingo, leads are prospective clients.

Leisure Freedom resulting from the cessation of activities, especially time free from work or duties.

Leveraged money Where loans are used to finance most of the purchase price.

Liaison personnel Workers who are responsible for translating corporate philosophy to the contractor and for overseeing the contractor to make sure he or she abides by the terms of the contract.

M

Malt Germinated barley.

Management The functions of forecasting, planning, decision making, communicating, organizing, motivating.

Management contracts A written agreement between an owner and an operator of a hotel or motor inn by which the owner employs the operator as an agent (employee) to assume full responsibility for operating and managing the property.

Marketing consortium (referral organizations) Made up of independent hotels who refer guests to each of the other members' hotels.

Marketing mix The term used to focus on the pertinent Ps: place, product, price, promotion, partnership, packaging, programming, and people.

Market niche A specific share or slot of a certain market.

Market segment Smaller, identifiable groups that can be defined using any set of characteristics, such as those found in geographic, demographic, or psy-

chographic information. Subgroups of customers who share a specific set of needs and expectations.

Mashing In the making of beer, it is the process of grinding the malt and screening out any bits of dirt.

Mash tub In the making of beer, it is a large stainless steel or copper container used to mix and heat water and grains.

Meeting Gathering of people for a common purpose.

Meeting planner Coordinates every detail of meetings and conventions.

Megaresort An extremely large gaming entertainment complex with thousands of guest rooms, a large gaming area, a number of ballrooms and breakout facilities, numerous food and beverage outlets including room service and banquet facilities, and numerous retail and recreational offerings.

Menu engineering Tool in menu planning that uses the menu as a whole, not individual items that make up the menu, as a measure of profitability.

Mise en place (miss-en-plás) French phrase meaning "everything in its place"; state of overall preparedness; having all the necessary ingredients and cooking utensils at hand and ready to use at the moment work on a dish begins.

Multiplier effect Concept that refers to new money that is brought into a community to pay for hotel rooms, restaurant meals, and so on. To some extent, it then passes into the community when the hotel or restaurant orders supplies and services, pays employees, and so on.

Mundo Maya A joint, ecotourism endeavor comprising of the countries in which the Mayan civilization was, and still is, found. These countries are Belize, El Salvador, Guatemala, Honduras, and the five Mexican states of Quitana Roo, Yucatán, Campeche, Tabasco, and Chiapas.

Must A mixture of grape pulp, skins, seeds, and stems.

N

National Center for Responsible Gaming (NCRG) The NCRG is a research and education foundation created by the gaming entertainment industry to fund gambling addiction research.

National Gambling Impact and Policy Commission Act This act established a nine-member federal commission impacts of all types of gambling in the United States.

National tourism organizations (NTOs) Organizations national governments use to promote their countries.

Networking The process of meeting with and gathering information from an ever-expanding channel of acquaintances.

Night auditing The process of verifying and balancing the guests' accounts.

NRA National Restaurant Association.

NTOs See National tourism organizations.

O

Occupancy forecast Forecast of hotels occupancy for a given period.

On-line Access to a computer via a terminal.

Operating ratios Ratios that indicate an operation's performance.

Overbooking Lodging practice of booking 10 to 15 percent more reservations than available to combat the loss of revenue resulting from guests who make reservations but who do not arrive.

P

PABS See Profit analysis by segment.

Par stock Level of stock that must be kept on hand at all times. If the stock on hand falls below this point, a computerized reorder system will automatically reorder a predetermined quantity of the item.

Pathological gambling An addiction in which there is a chronic and progressive failure to resist impulses to gamble; includes gambling behavior that comprises, disrupts, or damages personal, family, or vocational pursuits.

Performance evaluation or appraisal A meeting between a manager and one of his or her employees to 1. let the employee know how well he or she has learned to meet company standards, and 2. let managers know how well they are doing in hiring and training employees.

PMS See Property management systems.

POS See Point of sale.

Point of sale (POS) Computerized system that allows bars to set drink prices according to the specific ingredients served.

Poissionier (pwa-saw-nee-héy) Fish station chef.

Political analysis An analysis of the impact that current and pending legislation may have on the organization.

Portfolio financing The grouping of several investments with a portfolio that spreads the investment risk.

Positioning Process of establishing a distinctive place in the market (and in the minds of potential guests).

Pour-cost percentage Similar to food cost percentage, except used in beverage control.

Prime cost The cost of food sold plus payroll costs (including employee benefits). These are a restaurant's largest costs.

Privilege taxes Taxes paid by gaming companies to local, regional, and state governments for the privilege of operating a gaming business, often designated as a percentage of gross gaming revenue (GGR).

Product life cycle The stages of market acceptance of products and services.

Product specification The establishment of standards for each product, determined by the purchaser. (For example, when ordering meat, product specification will include the cut, weight, size, percentage of fat content, etc.)

Productivity standards Standards of measurement established to gauge employee productivity.

Profit analysis by segment (PABS) Using a combination of marketing information and cost analysis, this process identifies average revenues generated by different market segments and then examines the contribution margin for each of the segments considering the cost of making those sales.

Proof Figure representing liquor's alcohol content.

Property management systems (PMS) A system of storing and retrieving information on reservations, room availability, and room rates. The system may also interface with outlets (bars, restaurants, etc.) for recording guest charges.

Psychocentric Psychological term referring to a self-inhibited, nonadventuresome person.

Psychographic research Attempts to classify people's internal motives and behavior.

Q

Quick-service restaurants Restaurants that offer quick service.

R

Real Estate Investment Trust (RIET)[1]   A method that allows small investors to combine their funds and protects them from double taxation that is levied against an ordinary corporation or trust; designed to facilitate investment in real estate as a mutual fund facilitates investment in securities.

[1]*The Dictionary of Real Estate Appraisal,* American Institute of Real Estate Appraisers, Chicago, Illinois, 1984, p. 250.

Recreation   Refreshment of strength and spirits after work; a means of diversion.

Resort   Place providing recreation and entertainment, especially to vacationers.

Responsible gaming   Strategies employed by the gaming entertainment industry to mitigate pathological and underage gambling, including prevention, education and awareness programs for employees, customers, and local communities.

Rollover   To roll a booking over from one occasion to the next.

Room occupancy percentage   A key operating ratio for hotels that is calculated by finding the number of rooms occupied and dividing by rooms available.

Rules of order   Procedural guidelines regarding the correct way to conduct a meeting.

Russian service   Restaurant service in which the entree, vegetables, and starches are served from a platter onto the diner's plate by a waiter.

S

SABRE   Name of a commonly used airline reservation system.

Saucier (sauce-see-háy)   Saute cook.

Segmenting   Splitting the market with user groups that have common characteristics.

Self-operators   Companies that operate their own food service operations.

Seminar   A type of meeting that involves a lecture and a dialogue that allow participants to share experiences in a particular field.

Service encounter   Period of time in which a customer directly interacts with either personnel or the physical facilities and other visible elements of a hospitality business.

Sexual harassment   Occurs whenever any unwanted sexually oriented behavior changes an employee's working conditions and/or creates a hostile or abusive work environment.

Shoppers   People who are paid to use a bar like regular guests, except they closely watch the operation.

Social analysis   An analysis of social trends and customs used in compiling an upscale marketing plan.

Sommelier (so-mal-ee-yáy)   In a restaurant, the person with considerable wine knowledge who orders and serves wines.

Sous chef (soo-shef)   A cook who supervises food production and who reports to the executive chef; he or she is second in command of a kitchen.

Sous-vide (sou-veed)   Air-tight pouches of prepared food that can be quickly reheated.

Sparkling wine   Wine containing carbon dioxide, which provides effervescence when the wine is poured.

Spirits   Another name for distilled drinks.

Spreadsheet   Computerized version of an accountant's ledger book that not only records numeric information but also performs calculations with that information as well.

Stewarding   The department in a hotel or food-service operation responsible for the back of the house cleanliness in the food and beverage areas; the cleanliness of the china, cutlery, glassware; and the custody of related food and beverage equipment.

Symposium   A formal meeting at which several specialists deliver short addresses on a specific topic or related topics.

Suites   Combined living space with kitchen facilities, or a bedroom section with an attached parlor.

Suggestive selling   Employees suggestively sell products and services of the operation.

T

Table d'hote   French for "table of the host." During medieval times, poorer travelers had to eat with the landlord and his family in the kitchen, and they were served the "ordinary" fare at a nominal cost.

Target market   The market that the operation wants to focus on.

Taverns Establishments that serve some food but specialize in alcoholic beverages.

Technological analysis An analysis of the technological changes that may impact the company.

Technology All the uses derived from discoveries and innovations to satisfy needs; generally refers to industrial technology.

Texture Referring to food and wine, texture is the combination of the qualities in food or wine that correspond to sensations of touch and temperature, such as softness, smoothness, roundness, richness, thickness, creaminess, chewiness, oiliness, harshness, silkiness, coarseness, and so on.

Theater-style meeting setup A meeting setup usually intended for a large audience that is not likely to need to take notes or refer to documents. It generally consists of a raised platform and a lectern from which the presenter addresses the audience.

Theme parks Based on a particular setting or artistic interpretation and operate with hundreds or thousands of acres of parkland and hundreds or thousands of employees running the operation.

Theme restaurants A restaurant distinguished by its combination of decor, atmosphere, and menu.

TIPS Stands for training for intervention procedures by servers. Sponsored by the NRA, TIPS is a certification program that informs participants about alcohol and the effects of alcohol on people, the common signs of intoxication, and how to help customers avoid drinking too much.

TOs See Tourism offices.

Total Quality Management (TQM) A process of total organizational involvement in improving all aspects of the quality of product or service.

Tourism Travel for recreation or the promotion and arrangement of such travel.

Tourism offices (TOs) Organizations in charge of developing and implementing tourism programs for individual states. Also referred to as destination marketing organizations.

Tourists People who take trips of 100 miles or more and who stay at least one night away from home.

Tour operators Agencies that sell tour packages to groups of tourists and usually include an escort or guide with the tour.

TQM See Total quality management.

Trade show Event held for informational exchanges among trade people. Also called exposition.

Transactional leadership Determines what subordinates need to do to achieve objectives, classify those requirements, and help subordinates become confident they can reach their objectives.

Transformational leadership Leadership through personal vision and energy, inspiring followers, and having a major impact on the organization.

Travel and tour wholesaler Company or an individual who designs and packages tours.

Trends Prevailing tendencies or general movements.

Triple net lease A lease in which the lessee must pay for all alterations, insurance, utilities, and possible commercial fees (e.g., landscaping or parking upkeep, security, etc.).

Truth-in-menu laws Provisions that prohibit misrepresentation of items being sold. They require that the descriptions on the menu must be accurate.

Turnover rate Calculated by dividing the number of workers replaced in a given time period by the average number of employees needed to run the business.

U

Undocumented workers Individuals who move from another country illegally, without permission to enter as either immigrants or refugees. Also called illegal aliens.

Uniform system of accounts A system of accounts used in the hospitality industry whereby all accounts have the same codes and all accounting procedures are done the same way.

V

Vacation ownership Offers consumers the opportunity to purchase fully furnished vacation accommodations in a variety of forms, such as weekly intervals or points in point-based systems, for a percentage of the cost of full ownership.

Variable costs Costs that will vary according to the volume of business.

Vertical integration The ownership of or linkage with suppliers of raw materials or airlines owning hotels.

Vintage   Year in which a wine's grapes were harvested.

W

Well package   In bar operations, it is the least expensive pouring brand of drinks that the bar uses when the customers do not ask for a specific name brand.

Whiskey   A liquor distilled from a fermented mash of grain to which malt, in the form of barley, is added.

White spirits   Denomination that classifies spirits such as gin, rum, vodka and tequila.

Win   Dollars won by the gaming operation from its customers. The net spending of customers on gaming is called the win, also known as gross gaming revenue (GGR).

Wines   Fermented juice of grapes or other fruits.

Word processors   Computerized replacement for typewriters as the writing tool of choice.

Workshop   A usually brief intensive educational program, conducted by a facilitator or a trainer, designed for a relatively small group of people, that focuses especially on techniques and skills in a particular field.

Wort   In the making of beer, it is the liquid obtained after the mashing process.

Y

Yacht club   A private club located near a large body of water, whose main purpose is to provide facilities such as marinas to boat owners.

Yield management   Practice of analyzing past reservation patterns, room rates, cancellations, and no shows in an attempt to maximize profits and occupancy rates and to set the most competitive room rates.

Index

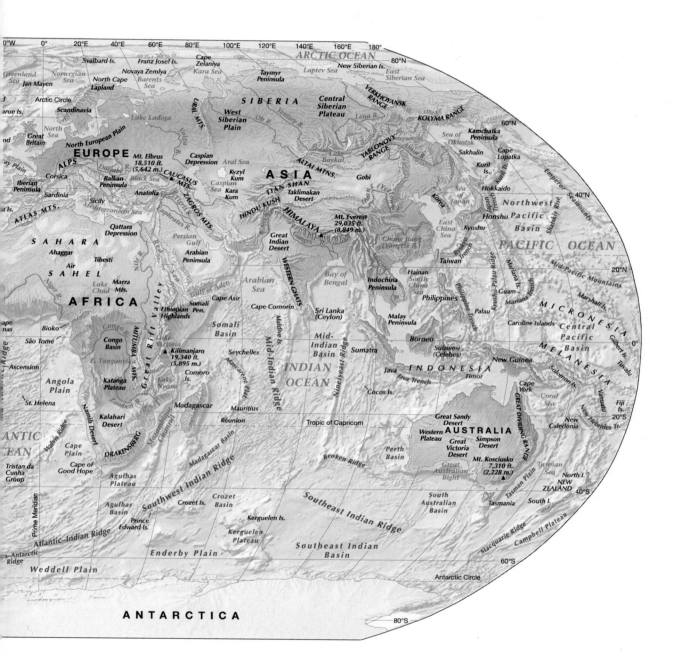

PHYSICAL GEOGRAPHY

CALIFORNIA EDITION

Taken from:

Physical Geography, A Landscape Appreciation, Ninth Edition
by Tom L. McKnight and Darrel Hess

Pearson Education

New York   Boston   San Francisco
London   Toronto   Sydney   Tokyo   Singapore   Madrid
Mexico City   Munich   Paris   Cape Town   Hong Kong   Montreal

Cover photographs courtesy of Corbis Images.
Cartographer: GeoNova

Excerpts taken from:

Physical Geography, A Landscape Appreciation, Ninth Edition
by Tom L. McKnight and Darrel Hess
Copyright © 2008, 2005, 2002, 1999, 1996, 1993, 1990, 1987, 1984
Published by Prentice Hall
Upper Saddle River, New Jersey 07458

Printed in the United States of America

10 9 8 7 6 5 4 3 2 1

2008260109

MT/JW

Pearson
Custom Publishing
is a division of

www.pearsonhighered.com

ISBN 10: 0-558-11417-2
ISBN 13: 978-0-558-11417-6

Introduction to the California Edition

It would be difficult to find another part of the world where the physical geography is as varied and interesting as here in California. Our state contains an astonishing range of environments that includes coastal beaches, high mountain peaks, wet temperate forests, and the driest of deserts.

What's Inside

In this California Edition of *Physical Geography: A Landscape Appreciation*, 9th edition, by McKnight and Hess, you'll find the textbook in its entirety, plus a collection of nine field guides that introduce the diverse physical geography of the state. Most of the field guides feature detailed "road logs" for self-guided field trips in locations around the state—including in many of our most popular national parks.

How to Use the California Edition

Throughout the textbook you'll see California map icons directing you to specific field guides, (FG1, FG2, and so on). Each field guide includes information exclusively about California, along with locator maps, photographs, textbook references, key terms, additional reading, and recommended Web sites. The pages of these guides have been perforated so that they may easily be separated from the book and taken on a field trip.

Although most of the field guides are designed to use when you venture out to see these places for yourself, they also enable "armchair travelers" to better understand the physical geography of California. The latitudes and longitudes of field guide stops are provided to aid in navigating to these locations using GPS, and also so that these locations can be studied remotely using Google Earth™ or the U.S. Geological Survey *National Map*. Instructors may find these guides useful as well when assigning independent field work projects for students.

Contributors to the California Edition

I extend my special thanks to Professors Edward Aguado, Patricia Deen, Barbara Holzman and Les Rowntree—their enthusiasm and knowledge of California is clearly revealed in their contributions to this field guide collection. Thanks also to all at Pearson Education who made this edition possible, especially to Christian Botting, Dan Kaveney, Rebecca Rinker, Meg Tiedemann, and most of all, to Senior Managing Editor, Elizabeth Kaster.

All of us hope that these field guides help you appreciate and enjoy the physical geography of the Golden State.

Darrell Hess
City College of San Francisco

Field Guides in the California Edition

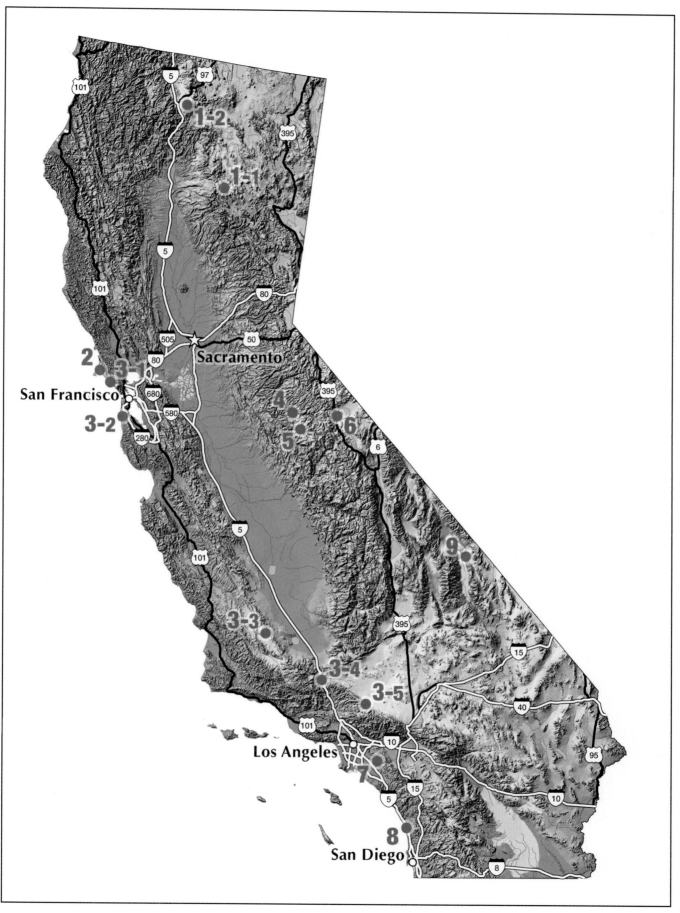

Brief Contents

Student Animations CD Contents

Contents

3

Introduction to the Atmosphere 54

4

Insolation and Temperature 74

5

Atmospheric Pressure and Wind 106

6

Atmospheric Moisture 140

7

Transient Atmospheric Flows and Disturbances 178

10

Cycles and Patterns in the Biosphere 288

11

Terrestrial Flora and Fauna 312

12

Soils 352

13

Introduction to Landform Study 386

14

The Internal Processes 412

15

Preliminaries to Erosion: Weathering and Mass Wasting 458

16

The Fluvial Processes 480

17

Solution Processes and Karst Topography 514

PEOPLE AND THE ENVIRONMENT Sinkholes in
Florida   520

18

The Topography of Arid Lands 528

PEOPLE AND THE ENVIRONMENT
Desertification   537

19

Glacial Modification of Terrain 554

20

Coastal Processes and Terrain 588

PEOPLE AND THE ENVIRONMENT The Sumatra
Earthquake and Tsunami of 2004   594
FOCUS Bleaching of Coral Reefs   607

Preface

To the Student

Welcome to *Physical Geography: A Landscape Appreciation*! In this book you'll learn about fundamental processes and patterns in the natural world—the kinds of things you can see whenever you walk outside: clouds in the sky, mountains, streams and valleys, and the plants and animals that inhabit the landscape. You'll also learn about human interactions with the natural environment—how events such as hurricanes, earthquakes, and floods affect our lives and the world around us, as well as how human activities are increasingly altering our environment.

If you opened this book expecting that the study of geography was going to be memorizing names and places on maps, you'll be surprised to find that geography is much more than that. Geographers study the location and distribution of things—tangible things such as rainfall, mountains, and trees, and less tangible things such as language, childhood nutrition, and political ideology. In short, everything that is a component of the physical or human landscape. As geographers, we look for—and try to explain—patterns in these landscapes. In this book we'll help you understand weather and climate; global patterns of water and ice; the distribution of plants, animals, and soil around the world; and the topographic development of the landscape through processes such as faulting, volcanic activity, and stream and glacial erosion. By the time you finish this book you'll understand and "appreciate" the landscape in new ways.

If you take a minute to skim through the book, you'll see some of the features that will help you learn this material:

- The book includes many diagrams, maps, and photographs. Physical geography is a visual discipline, so the figures and captions will allow you to get the most out of each chapter.

- Photographs have "locator maps" to help you learn the locations of the many places we mention in the book.

- Each chapter includes a *Learning Review* with a list of *Key Terms* and *Study Questions* to test your comprehension of major concepts.

- The alphabetical glossary at the end of the book provides definitions for all of the key terms.

- Most of the chapters include icons that direct you to the CD that accompanies the book. The animations on the CD explain important concepts in physical geography. Each animation includes a written and an audio narration to explain what you're seeing, as well as a short quiz to test your understanding.

- A reference map of physical features of the world is found inside the front cover of the book, and a reference map of the countries of the world is found inside the back cover.

To the Instructor

Physical Geography: A Landscape Appreciation presents the concepts of physical geography in a clear, readable way to help students comprehend the landscape around them. The ninth edition of the book has undergone a thorough revision, while maintaining the time-proven approach to physical geography first presented by Tom McKnight more than two decades ago.

Users of earlier editions will see that the overall sequence of chapters and topics remains the same, although material has been updated in several key areas:

- A new section on Science and Geography has been added to Chapter 1.

- An expanded section on human-induced changes in the atmosphere, including ozone depletion and air pollution, is included in Chapter 3.

- Material on the Coriolis effect has been moved to Chapter 3 so that it precedes the discussion of ocean currents in Chapter 4.

- Information about energy, electromagnetic radiation, and basic heating and cooling processes has been expanded in Chapter 4.

- El Niño and other periodic ocean-atmospheric phenomena such as the Pacific Decadal Oscillation are now covered in Chapter 5, following the explanation of the general circulation of the atmosphere and localized wind systems.

- Material on the characteristics of water and phase changes has been expanded upon and moved to the beginning of Chapter 6, where it serves as the introduction to the discussion of moisture in the atmosphere.

- A new section on measuring and understanding climate change and global warming, including the latest findings of the 2007 *Fourth Assessment Report of the Intergovernmental Panel on Climate Change*, has been incorporated into the end of Chapter 8. This new section can also stand alone for instructors wishing to discuss this material at a different point in their course.

- More extensive coverage of the movement of ocean waters—including tides and deep ocean circulation patterns—is found in Chapter 9.

- Chapters 10 and 11 on biogeography have been updated and reorganized for greater clarity.

- Chapter 13 includes an expanded section on rocks and minerals.

- More extensive coverage of the history and evidence of plate tectonics is found in Chapter 14.

- Chapter 16 on fluvial processes and Chapter 18 on the topography of arid lands have been updated and reorganized with greater emphasis on processes and landforms.

- Chapter 20 now includes expanded sections on tsunamis and human modification of shorelines.

- Key material found in "focus boxes" in previous editions has been integrated directly into the text. New, shorter focus boxes found in this edition include:

  - *The UV Index*
  - *Monitoring Earth's Radiation Budget*
  - *Measuring Sea Surface Temperature by Satellite*
  - *Forecasting El Niño*
  - *Water Vapor Satellite Images*
  - *Global Dimming*
  - *Hurricane Katrina*
  - *Hurricanes and Global Warming*
  - *Climate Change in the Arctic*
  - *Paleoclimatology at Dome C*
  - *Thawing Permafrost in Alaska*
  - *Oceans Becoming More Acidic*
  - *The Aral Sea and Lake Chad*
  - *Subsidence from Groundwater Extraction*
  - *Changing Climate Affects Bird Populations*
  - *Rainforest Loss in Brazil*
  - *Earthquake Forecasting*
  - *The Madison Valley Landslide*
  - *The Bird's-foot of the Mississippi*
  - *Disintegration of Antarctic Ice Shelves*
  - *Shrinking Alaskan Glaciers*
  - *The Sumatra Earthquake and Tsunami of 2004*
  - *Bleaching of Coral Reefs.*

The Teaching and Learning Package

- **Instructor Resource Center on DVD (IRC) (0-13-243839-9):** Everything you need where you want it. The Prentice Hall IRC saves the instructor time and effort in lecture preparation. The IRC on DVD is

well organized, and makes it easy to access all of the digital resources. Included are:

Figures—All photos and illustrations from the text in jpeg format. Animations—All animations ready for use in your lecture presentation as Power-Point™ slides or Flash files.

Lecture Power-Points—Pre-authored PowerPoint™ slides outline the concepts of each chapter with embedded art. You can use them as is for lecture, or customize them to fit your lecture needs.

TestGen—Computerized test generator that lets you view and edit test-bank questions, transfer questions to tests, and print the test in a variety of customized formats.

Personal Response System questions in Power-Point™.

Electronic files of the Instructor's Manual and Test Item File, including links to WebCT/BlackBoard test question cartridges.

- **Transparencies (0-13-179051-X):** Images and illustrations pertaining to the text's core concepts have been selected and enhanced for optimal classroom presentations. All images within the transparency pack are also available electronically on the Instructor Resource Center on DVD (0-13-24389-9).

- **MyGeographyPlace:** Available online at www.prenhall.com/mcknight, it provides a variety of exercises with instant feedback to help students master the concepts of each chapter. An access code for MyGeographyPlace is bound into the front cover of every new copy of this textbook.

- **Laboratory Manual (0-13-238113-3):** Written by Darrel Hess, the Laboratory Manual offers a comprehensive set of lab exercises to accompany any physical geography class. The Laboratory Manual is available at a discount when packaged with the text. Contact your local Prentice Hall representative for details.

- **Study Guide (0-13-230323-X):** Incorporating text and art from the text, Darrel Hess has created the essential study tool for students. Included are chapter notes, with key terms and page references, study questions, self-check exercises, and a vocabulary review. The Study Guide is available at a discount when packaged with the text; contact your local Prentice Hall representative for details.

- *Goode's World Atlas* **(0-13-612824-6):** Prentice Hall and Rand McNally are pleased to announce that Prentice Hall is now distributing *Goode's World Atlas*—the number one atlas used by college professors—to colleges and universities worldwide. *Goode's World Atlas* is the world's premiere educational atlas, and for good reason. It features nearly 250 pages of maps, from definitive physical and political maps to important thematic maps that illustrate the spatial aspects of many important topics. The current 21st edition of the atlas features fully updated content and has been vetted by an academic board comprised of some of the most trusted names in geography today. Prentice Hall offers the atlas at a dramatically reduced price with *Physical Geography: A Landscape Appreciation*. See your local Prentice Hall representative for details.

- **Instructor's Manual (0-13-224323-7):** Intended as a resource for both new and experienced instructors, the manual includes a topic and lecture outline, and suggested answers to end of chapter review questions.

- **Test Item File (0-13-238112-5):** Printed bank of test questions, a valuable complement to an instructor's own quiz/test files.

- **TestGen (0-13-243840-2):** TestGen is a computerized test generator that lets you view and edit test-bank questions, transfer questions to tests, and print the test in a variety of customized formats.

- **Answer Key to Laboratory Manual (0-13-230324-8):** Provides answers to problem sets presented in the Laboratory Manual.

Acknowledgments

Dozens of colleagues, students, and friends were helpful in the preparation of the original version of this book and its eight succeeding editions. Their assistance has been gratefully acknowledged previously. Here we acknowledge those who have provided assistance in recent years, both as reviewers of the text and as reviewers of the animations that accompany it. We are delighted to recognize their contributions.

Barbara Holzman of San Francisco State University provided a valuable critique of the material on biogeography. Stephen Stadler of Oklahoma State University and Randall Schaetzl of Michigan State University provided particular expertise in climatology and pedology, respectively, as well as furnishing broad-scale critiques of other parts of the book.

Other helpful reviews and critiques were provided by the following people:

Casey Allen, *Weber State University*

Sergei Andronikov, *Austin Peay State University*

Greg Bierly, *Indiana State University*

Mark Binkley, *Mississippi State University*

Peter Blanken, *University of Colorado*

Margaret Boorstein, *Long Island University*

James Brey, *University of Wisconsin Fox Valley*

Sean Cannon, *Brigham Young University–Idaho*

Jongnam Choi, *Western Illinois University*

Glen Conner, *Western Kentucky University*

Carlos E. Cordova, *Oklahoma State University*

Richard A. Crooker, *Kutztown University of Pennsylvania*

Mike DeVivo, *Grand Rapids Community College*

Bryan Dorsey, *Weber State University*

Don W. Duckson, Jr., *Frostburg State University*

Tracy Edwards, *Frostburg State University*

Steve Emerick, *Glendale Community College*

Michael Grossman, *Southern Illinois University—Edwardsville*

Perry J. Hardin, *Brigham Young University*

Barbara Holzman, *San Francisco State University*

Paul Hudson, *University of Texas*

Catherine Jain, *Palomar College*

Steven Jennings, *University of Colorado at Colorado Springs*

Dorleen B. Jenson, *Salt Lake Community College*

Kris Jones, *Saddleback College*

Ryan Kelly, *Lexington Community College*

Rob Kremer, *Metropolitan State College of Denver*

Steve LaDochy, *California State University*

Michael Madsen, *Brigham Young University—Idaho*

Kenneth Martis, *West Virginia University*

Thomas Orf, *Las Positas College*

Michael C. Pease, *University of New Mexico*

Stephen Podewell, *Western Michigan University*

Nick Polizzi, *Cypress College*

Robert Rohli, *Louisiana State University*

John H. Scheufler, *Mesa College*

Robert A. Sirk, *Austin Peay State University*

Timothy Warner, *West Virginia University*

Many of my colleagues at City College of San Francisco offered helpful comments and questions about material in the previous edition of this book, including Robert Manlove, Richard Neil, and Karen Noll. I especially want to thank my colleagues who provided detailed critiques of sections of the manuscript for the current edition of the book: Dack Lee, Joyce Lucas-Clark, Kathryn Pinna, Todd Rigg, Carole Toebe, and Katryn Wiese. I also extend my appreciation to my many students over the years. Their curiosity, thoughtful questions, and cheerful acceptance of my enthusiasm for geography have helped me as a teacher and as a textbook author.

An outstanding Prentice Hall team shepherded this project to fruition. Chris Rapp, Margaret Ziegler, and Jeff Howard provided expertise and help during the early stages of the project. Associate Editor Amanda Brown and Media Editor Andrew Sobel provided key initiative and support in the creation of the print and electronic supplements that complement and support the book. Thanks to all at CADRE Design, especially to Ian "E" Shakeshaft and Robert Bleeker, for their great work on the CD that accompanies this book. Copy Editor Marcia Youngman, Proofreader Michael Rossa, Project Manager Timothy Flem, Editorial Assistant Jessica Neumann, and Photo Researcher Jerry Marshall have been a pleasure to work with. Production Editor Shari Toron is the quintessential professional who brought together a wide variety of diverse elements and assembled them into the book you see here. My special gratitude goes to Publisher for Geosciences, Dan Kaveney, who guided this entire enterprise with his unfailing good humor and thoughtful creativity. He's simply the best.

Finally, it's no mystery to me why many authors acknowledge their spouse when they've finished a book: Special thanks go to my wife, Nora, for her help, understanding, and support throughout the many months I spent in front of the computer.

Darrel Hess
Earth Sciences Department
City College of San Francisco
50 Phelan Avenue
San Francisco, CA 94112
dhess@ccsf.edu

Dedication

For my brother, Roger

D.H.

About the Authors

Tom L. McKnight taught geography at UCLA from 1956 to 1993. He received his bachelor's degree in geology from Southern Methodist University in 1949, his master's degree in geography from the University of Colorado in 1951, and his Ph.D. in geography and meteorology from the University of Wisconsin in 1955. During his long academic career, Tom served as chair of the UCLA Department of Geography from 1978 to 1983, and was director of the University of California, Education Abroad Program in Australia from 1984 to 1985. Passionate about furthering the discipline of geography, he helped establish the UCLA/Community College Geography Alliance and generously funded awards for both undergraduate and graduate geography students. His many honors include the California Geographical Society's Outstanding Educator Award in 1988, and the honorary rank of Professor Emeritus upon his retirement from UCLA. In addition to *Physical Geography: A Landscape Appreciation*, his other college textbooks include *The Regional Geography of the United States and Canada; Oceania: The Geography of Australia, New Zealand, and the Pacific Islands;* and *Introduction to Geography*, with Edward F. Bergman. Tom passed away in 2004—the geographic community misses him enormously.

Darrel Hess began teaching geography at City College of San Francisco in 1990 and has served as chair of the Earth Sciences Department since 1995. After earning his bachelor's degree in geography at the University of California, Berkeley in 1978, he served for two years as a teacher in the Peace Corps on the Korean island of Cheju-do. Upon returning to the United States, he worked as a writer, photographer, and audiovisual producer. His association with Tom McKnight began as a graduate student at UCLA, where he served as one of Tom's teaching assistants. Their professional collaboration developed after Darrel graduated from UCLA with a master's degree in geography in 1990. He first wrote the Study Guide that accompanied the fourth edition of *Physical Geography: A Landscape Appreciation*, and then the Laboratory Manual that accompanied the fifth edition. Darrel has been authoring both works ever since. In 1999 Tom asked Darrel to join him as co-author of the textbook. As did Tom, Darrel greatly enjoys the outdoor world. Darrel and his wife Nora are avid hikers, campers, and scuba divers.

1
Introduction to Earth

Earth is the ancestral and, thus far, the only home of humankind. People live on the surface of Earth in a physical environment that is extraordinarily complex, extremely diverse, infinitely renewing, and yet ultimately fragile.

This habitable environment exists over almost the entire face of Earth, which means that its horizontal dimensions are vast (Figure 1-1a). Its vertical extent, however, is very limited, as Figure 1-1b shows. The great majority of all earthly life inhabits a zone less than 5 kilometers (3 miles) thick, and the total vertical extent of the life zone is about 30 kilometers (20 miles).

Geography as a Field of Learning

It is within this shallow life zone that geographers focus their interest and do their work. In fact, the word *geography* comes from the Greek words for "earth description." Geography has always been (and remains) a generalized—as opposed to a specialized—discipline. Its viewpoint is one of broad understanding. Several thousand years ago many scholars were more truly "earth describers" than anything else. However, over the centuries there has been a trend away from generalized Earth description toward more specific scholarly specializations. This narrowing of focus led to the growth of a variety of more specialized disciplines—such as geology, meteorology, economics, and biology—along with a concomitant eclipsing of geography. If "mother geography gave birth to many offshoot sciences," as some geographers have said, it is clear that these developing disciplines soon became better known than their progenitor.

It was not until the 1600s that a rekindling of interest in geography in the European world began, and it was another two centuries before there was a strong impetus given to the discipline by geographers from various countries. A prominent geographic theme that has persisted through the centuries is that geographers study how things differ from place to place—in other words, geography is the areal differentiation of Earth's surface. There is a multiplicity of "things" to be found on Earth, and nearly all of them are distributed unevenly, thus providing a spatial, or geographic, aspect to the planet.

Table 1-1 lists the kinds of things to which we are referring. These things are divided into two columns signifying the two principal branches of geography. The elements of **physical geography** are natural in origin,

and for this reason physical geography is sometimes called *environmental geography*. The elements of **cultural geography** are those of human endeavor, so this branch is sometimes referred to as *human geography*. The list of physical geography elements is essentially complete as a broad tabulation. The list of cultural geography elements, on the other hand, is merely suggestive of a much longer inventory of both material and nonmaterial features.

All the items listed in Table 1-1 are familiar to us, and this familiarity highlights another basic characteristic of geography as a field of learning: geography has no peculiar body of facts or objects of study that it can call wholly its own. The particular focus of geology is rocks, the attention of economics is fastened on economic systems, demography examines human population, and so on. Geography, however, is a very broad field of inquiry and "borrows" its objects of study from related disciplines. Geographers, too, are interested in rocks and economic systems and population, but only in certain aspects of these elements.

In simplest terms, geographers are concerned with the spatial, or distributional, aspects of the elements listed in Table 1-1. Thus, geography is both a physical science and a social science because it combines characteristics of both, effectively bridging the gap between the two. A geographer does not specialize in studying the environment as an ecologist does, or in concentrating on human social relationships as a sociologist does. Instead, geography is concerned with the environment as it provides a home for humankind, and with the way humans utilize and alter this environmental home.

Another basic characteristic of geography is its interest in interrelationships. One cannot understand the distribution of soils, for example, without knowing something of the rocks from which the soils were derived,

◁ Composite satellite image of Earth and the Moon. The Moon is shown about twice its relative size. (*NASA.*)

TABLE 1-1 The Elements of Geography	
Physical Elements	**Cultural Elements**
Rocks	Population
Landforms	Settlements
Soil	Economic activities
Flora	Transportation
Fauna	Recreation activities
Climate	Languages
Water	Religion
Minerals	Political systems
	Traditions
	And many others

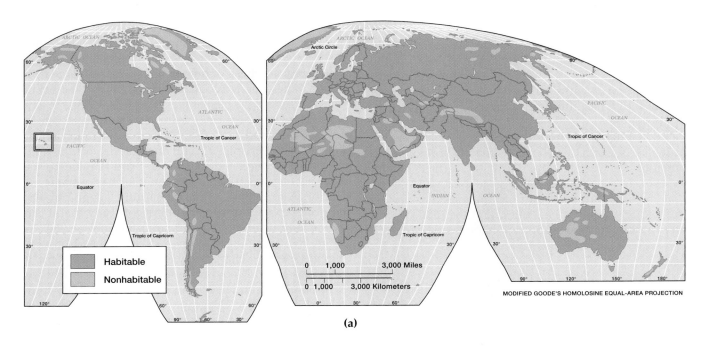

(a)

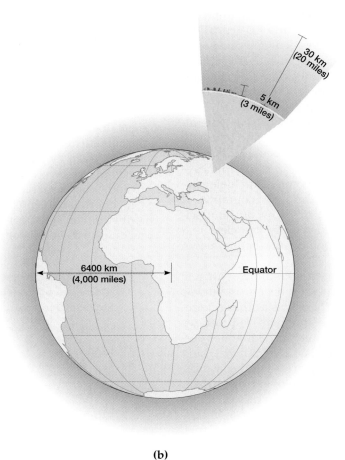

(b)

▲ **Figure 1-1** **(a)** Most of Earth's land surface is habitable, as indicated by this world map. The uninhabitable areas are too hot, too cold, too wet, too dry, or too rugged to support much human life. These uninhabitable areas include parts of the Arctic, most of Greenland, Antarctica, various mountainous regions, and several deserts. **(b)** Vertically, the habitable zone surrounding Earth is extremely restricted. The blanket of air surrounding the planet is relatively thin: It extends only to an altitude of about 30 kilometers (20 miles) and then fades into the emptiness of space. To understand the relative thinness of the atmosphere, consider that Earth's radius is 6400 kilometers (4000 miles), while the "living zone" of the air is a layer only 5 kilometers (3 miles) high. If Earth were a peach, this living zone would be thinner than its fuzz.

the slopes on which the soils developed, and the climate and vegetation under which they developed. Similarly, it is impossible to comprehend the distribution of agriculture without an understanding of climate, topography, soil, drainage, population, economic conditions, technology, historical development, and a host of other factors, both physical and cultural. Thus, the elements in Table 1-1 are enmeshed in an intricate web of interrelationships, all of which are encompassed in the discipline we call *geography*. In short, the fundamental questions of geographic inquiry are, "Why what is where and so what?"

Science and Geography

The subject matter of this book is physical geography. We shall examine the various components of the natural environment, the nature and characteristics of the physical elements of the landscape, the processes involved in their development, their distribution over Earth, and their basic interrelationships. We shall largely ignore interrelationships among the various elements of cultural geography except where they help to explain the development or contemporary distribution patterns of the physical elements, and the ways in which humans influence or alter the physical environment.

Science as a Field of Learning

Because physical geography is concerned with processes and patterns in the natural world, knowledge in physical geography is advanced through the study of science, and so it may be useful for us to begin with a few words about science in general.

Science is often described—although somewhat simplistically—as a process that follows the *scientific method*:

1. Observe phenomena that stimulate a question or problem.
2. Offer an educated guess—a *hypothesis*—about the answer.
3. Design an experiment to test the hypothesis.
4. Predict the outcome of the experiment if the hypothesis is correct, and if the hypothesis is incorrect.
5. Conduct the experiment and observe what actually happens.
6. Draw a conclusion or formulate a simple generalized "rule" based on the results of the experiment.

In practice, however, science doesn't always work through experimentation; in many fields of science, data collection through observation of a phenomenon is the basis of knowledge. In some regards science is best thought of as a process—or perhaps even as an attitude—for gaining knowledge. The scientific approach is based on observation, experimentation, logical reasoning, skepticism of unsupported conclusions, and the willingness to modify or even reject long-held ideas when new evidence contradicts them.

Although the term "scientific proof" is sometimes used by the general public, strictly speaking, science does not "prove" ideas. Instead, science works by eliminating alternative explanations—eliminating explanations that aren't supported by evidence. In fact, in order for a hypothesis to be "scientific," there must be some test or possible observation that could *disprove* it—if there is no way to disprove an idea, then that idea simply can't be supported by science.

The word "theory" is often used in everyday conversation to mean a "hunch" or conjecture. However, in science a *theory* represents the highest order of understanding for a body of information—a logical, well-tested explanation that encompasses a wide variety of facts and observations. Thus, as we will see in Chapter 14, the "theory of plate tectonics" represents an empirically supported, broadly accepted, overarching framework for understanding processes operating within Earth.

The acceptance of scientific ideas and theories is based on a preponderance of evidence, not on "belief" and not on the pronouncements of "authorities." New observations and new evidence often cause scientists to revise their conclusions and theories or those of others. Much of this self-correcting process for refining scientific knowledge takes place through peer-reviewed journal articles: Peers—that is, fellow scientists—scrutinize a scientific report for sound reasoning, appropriate data collection and solid evidence before it is published; reviewers needn't agree with the author's conclusions, but they must attempt to ensure that published articles meet rigorous standards of scholarship.

Since new evidence may prompt scientists to change their ideas, good science tends to be somewhat cautious in the conclusions that are drawn. For this reason, the findings of many scientific studies are prefaced by phrases such as "the evidence suggests," or "the results most likely show." In some cases, different scientists interpret the same data quite differently and so disagree in their conclusions. Frequently, studies find that "more research is needed." The kind of uncertainty sometimes inherent in science may lead the general public to question the conclusions of scientific studies—especially when presented with a simple, and perhaps comforting nonscientific alternative. It is, however, this very uncertainty that often compels scientists to push forward in the quest for knowledge and understanding!

In this book we present the fundamentals of physical geography as it is supported by scientific research and evidence. In some cases, we will describe how our current understanding of a phenomenon developed over time; in other cases we will point out where uncertainty remains, where there is still disagreement among scientists, or where intriguing questions still remain.

Numbers and Measurement Systems

Because so much of science is based on observation and measurable data, any thorough study of physical geography entails the use of mathematics. Although this book introduces physical geography primarily in a conceptual way without the extensive use of mathematical formulas, numbers and measurement systems are nonetheless important for us. Throughout the book, we use numbers and simple formulas to help illustrate concepts—the most obvious of which are numbers used to describe distance, size, weight, and temperature.

There are two quite different systems of measurement used around the world today—the International (or "metric") System and the English System. In the United States much of the general public is most familiar with the so-called *English System of measurement*—using measurements such as miles, pounds, and degrees Fahrenheit. Most of the rest of the world—and the entire scientific community—uses the **international system of measurement** (abbreviated **SI** from the French *Système International*)—using measurements such as kilometers, kilograms, and degrees Celsius. You have probably noticed that this book gives measurements in both SI and English units. If you're not yet familiar with both systems, with just a little effort you can learn the basic equivalents in each. Tables 1-2 and 1-3 provide some simple conversion formulas; a detailed table of equivalents between English and SI units appears in Appendix I.

Global Environmental Change

Some characteristics of the global environment are in a state of perpetual change and apparently have been throughout its existence—this is very obvious when we consider Earth's atmosphere. As with most other natural phenomena, the rate of change of the atmosphere has generally been very slow, although the effects have been profound. One has only to look at the occurrence of past ice ages to recognize that the habitability of various parts of Earth has varied remarkably through time as temperature and precipitation conditions have changed.

Throughout this book, the topic of global environmental change—both human induced and natural—will be addressed. We pay special attention to specific aspects of the accelerating impact that human activities have on the environment. For example, in the chapters on the atmosphere we discuss such issues as global warming, ozone depletion, and acid rain, while in later chapters we look at issues such as rainforest removal and coastal erosion. Rather than treat global environmental change as a separate topic, we integrate this theme throughout the book. We also supplement the main text material with short boxed essays, some of which are entitled "People and the Environment," which focus on specific cases of human interaction with the natural environment. These essays also serve to illustrate the interrelationships between various aspects of the environment, such as the relationships between changing global temperatures, changing sea level, changing quantities of polar ice, and the changing distribution of plant and animal species.

TABLE 1-2 Conversions: S.I. to English		
	Quick Approximation	Conversion Formulas
Distance:	1 centimeter = a little less than $\frac{1}{2}$"	cm × 0.394 = inches
	1 meter = a little more than 3'	m × 3.281 = feet
	1 kilometer = about $\frac{2}{3}$ mile	km × 0.621 = miles
	1 cm (centimeter) = 10 mm (millimeters)	
	1 m (meter) = 100 cm	
	1 km (kilometer) = 1000 m	
Volume:	1 liter = about 1 quart	liters × 1.057 = quarts
Mass (Weight):	1 gram = about $\frac{1}{30}$ ounce	g × 0.035 = ounces
	1 kilogram = about 2 pounds	kg × 0.205 = pounds
	1 kg (kilogram) = 1000 g (grams)	
Temperature:	1°C change = 1.8°F change	(°C × 1.8) + 32 = °F

TABLE 1-3 Conversions: English to S.I.

	Quick Approximation	Conversion Formulas
Distance:	1 inch = about $2\frac{1}{2}$ cm	inches $\times$ 2.540 = cm
	1 foot = about $\frac{1}{3}$ m	feet $\times$ 0.305 = m
	1 yard = about 1 m	yards $\times$ 0.914 = m
	1 mile = about $1\frac{1}{2}$ km	miles $\times$ 1.609 = km
	1' (foot) = 12" (inches)	
	1 yard = 3'	
	1 mile = 5280'	
Volume:	1 quart = about 1 liter	quarts $\times$ 0.946 = liters
	1 gallon = about 4 liters	gallons $\times$ 3.785 = liters
	1 gallon = 4 quarts	
Mass (Weight):	1 ounce = about 30 g	ounces $\times$ 28.350 = g
	1 pound = about $\frac{1}{2}$ kg	pounds $\times$ 0.454 = kg
	1 lb (pound) = 16 oz (ounces)	
Temperature:	1°F change = about 0.6°C change	(°F $-$ 32) $\div$ 1.8 = °C

The Environmental Spheres

Although there are billions of celestial bodies in the universe, insofar as we know the environment of our planet is different from that of all the others. This unique environment has produced a unique landscape: a combination of solids, liquids, and gases; organic and inorganic matter; a bewildering variety of life forms; and an extraordinary diversity of physical features that is not even approximated on any other known planet. In this book, our study of geography is built around an attempt to "appreciate" (i.e., understand) this unique landscape. As we proceed from chapter to chapter, the notion of landscape development and landscape modification will serve as a central theme.

For the remainder of this chapter, our attention is focused on a few broad concepts—the place of Earth in the solar system, the basic physical characteristics of this planet, and the functional relationship between Earth and its prime source of energy, the Sun. Understanding these concepts will help us comprehend the remarkable landscape we inhabit.

From the standpoint of physical geography, the surface of Earth is a complex interface where the four principal components of the environment meet and to some degree overlap and interact (Figure 1-2). The solid, inorganic portion of Earth is sometimes referred to as the **lithosphere**[1] (*litho* is Greek for "stone"), comprising the rocks of Earth's crust as well as the broken and unconsolidated particles of mineral matter that overlie the solid bedrock. The lithosphere's surface is shaped into an almost infinite variety of landforms, both on the seafloors and on the surfaces of the continents and islands.

The gaseous envelope of air that surrounds Earth is the **atmosphere** (*atmo* is Greek for "air"). It contains the complex mixture of gases needed to sustain life. Most of the atmosphere adheres closely to Earth's surface, being densest at sea level and rapidly thinning with increased altitude. It is a very dynamic sphere, kept in almost constant motion by solar energy and Earth's rotation.

The **hydrosphere** (*hydro* is Greek for "water") comprises water in all its forms. The oceans contain the vast majority of the water found on Earth and are the moisture source for most precipitation. A subcomponent of the hydrosphere is known as the **cryosphere** (*cry* comes from the Greek word for "cold")—water frozen as snow and ice.

The **biosphere** (*bio* is Greek for "life") encompasses all the parts of Earth where living organisms can exist; in its broadest and loosest sense, the term also includes the vast variety of earthly life forms (properly referred to as *biota*).

These four spheres are not four discrete and separated entities but rather are considerably intermingled. This intermingling is readily apparent when considering an ocean—a body that is clearly a major component of the hydrosphere and yet may contain a vast quantity of fish and other organic life that are

---

[1] As we will see in Chapter 13, in the context of *plate tectonics* and our study of landforms, the term "lithosphere" is used specifically to refer to large "plates" consisting of Earth's crustal and upper mantle rock.

▲ **Figure 1-2**   The physical landscape of Earth's surface is composed of four overlapping and interacting systems called *spheres*. The *atmosphere* is the air we breathe. The *hydrosphere* is the water of rivers, lakes, and oceans, the moisture in soil and air, as well as the snow and ice of the *cryosphere*. The *biosphere* is the habitat of all earthly life, as well as the life forms themselves. The *lithosphere* is the soil and bedrock that cover Earth's surface. This scene shows Wonder Lake and Mt. McKinley in Denali National Park, Alaska. *(John Warden/Tony Stone Images.)*

part of the biosphere. An even better example is soil, which is composed largely of bits of mineral matter (lithosphere) but also contains life forms (biosphere), soil moisture (hydrosphere), and air (atmosphere) in pore spaces. The four spheres can serve as important organizing concepts for the systematic study of Earth's physical geography and will be used that way in this book.

Before focusing our attention on the spheres, however, we set the stage by considering the planetary characteristics of Earth and noting the most important relationships between our planet and its basic source of energy, the Sun.

The Solar System

Solar System Formation

We live on an extensive rotating, complicated mass of mostly solid material that orbits the enormous ball of superheated gases we call the Sun. The geographer's concern with spatial relationships properly begins with the relative location of this spaceship Earth in the universe.

Earth is one of eight *planets* of our *solar system*, which also contains more than 100 *moons* revolving around the planets, an unknown number of *dwarf planets* such as Pluto, scores of *comets* ("dirty snowballs" composed of frozen liquid and gases together with small pieces of rock and metallic minerals), more than 50,000 *asteroids* (small, rocky objects, mostly less than a few kilometers in diameter), and millions of *meteoroids* (most of them the size of sand grains).

The medium-sized star we call our Sun is the central body of the solar system and makes up more than 99 percent of its total mass. The solar system is part of the Milky Way Galaxy, which consists of at least 200,000,000,000 stars arranged in a disk-shaped spiral that is 100,000 *light-years* in diameter (1 light-year equals about 9 trillion kilometers—the distance a beam of light travels over a period of one year) and 10,000 light-years thick at the center (Figure 1-3). The Milky Way Galaxy is only one of at least a billion galaxies in the universe.

▲ **Figure 1-3**   The structure of the Milky Way Galaxy. *(From Edward J. Tarbuck and Frederick K. Lutgens,* Earth Science, *11th ed., Upper Saddle River, NJ: Pearson-Prentice Hall, 2006.)*

The vastness of the universe is beyond normal comprehension. To begin to develop an understanding for astronomical distances, we might consider a reduced-scale model of the universe. If the distance between Earth and the Sun, which is about 150,000,000 kilometers (93,000,000 miles), is taken to be 2.5 centimeters (1 inch), then the distance from Earth to the nearest star would be 7.2 kilometers (4.5 miles), and the distance from Earth to the next galaxy beyond the Milky Way would become about 240,000 kilometers (150,000 miles).

The origin of Earth, and indeed of the universe, is incompletely understood. It is generally accepted that the universe began with a cosmic "explosion" called the *big bang*. The most widely held view is that the big bang took place some 13.7 billion years ago—similar to the age of the oldest known stars. The big bang began in a fraction of a second after an infinitely dense fireball started to expand away in all directions at extraordinary speeds, pushing out the fabric of space and filling the universe with the energy and matter we see today.

Our solar system apparently originated between 4.5 and 5 billion years ago when a *nebula*—huge, cold, diffuse cloud of gas and dust—began to contract inward, owing to its own gravitational collapse, forming a hot, dense *protostar* (Figure 1-4). This hot center—our Sun—was surrounded by a cold, revolving disk of gas and dust that eventually condensed and coalesced to form the planets.

All of the planets revolve around the Sun in elliptical orbits, with the Sun located at one *focus* (Figure 1-5). With the exception of the dwarf planet Pluto, whose orbit is somewhat askew, all the planetary orbits are in nearly the same plane (Figure 1-6), perhaps revealing their relationship to the formative nebular disk. The Sun rotates on its own axis from west to east, and as seen from the Sun each of the planets revolves around it from west to east. Moreover, most of the planets rotate from west to east on their own axes (Uranus rotates "sideways" with its rotational axis almost parallel to its orbital plane; Venus rotates from east to west). Generally, planets revolve more slowly and have a lower temperature as their distance from the Sun increases.

◀ **Figure 1-4**   The birth of the solar system. (1) Diffuse gas cloud, or nebula, begins to contract inward. (2) Cloud flattens into nebular disk as it spins around a central axis. (3) Particles in the outer parts of the disk collide with each other to form protoplanets. (4) Protoplanets coalesce into planets and settle into orbits around the hot center. (5) The final product: a central Sun surrounded by eight orbiting planets. (Solar system not shown in correct scale.)

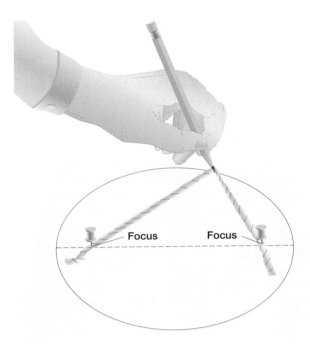

▲ **Figure 1-5** Drawing an ellipse with the help of two tacks and a string. When held taut against the string, the pencil traces out an ellipse. The closer together the tacks are placed, the less ovate (or egg shaped) the ellipse. (When the tacks are so close together that they are in the same spot, the result is a circle.) Each tack represents one focus of the ellipse.

The four inner *terrestrial planets*—Mercury, Venus, Earth, and Mars—are generally smaller, denser, less oblate (more nearly spherical), and rotate more slowly on their axes than the four outer *Jovian planets*—Jupiter, Saturn, Uranus, and Neptune. Also, the inner planets are composed principally of mineral matter and, except for airless Mercury, have diverse but relatively shallow atmospheres.

By contrast, the four Jovian planets tend to be much larger, more massive (although they are less dense), much more oblate, and they rotate more rapidly. The Jovian planets are mostly composed of gases such as hydrogen and helium—perhaps liquid near the surface, but frozen toward the interior—as well as ices of compounds such as methane and ammonia. The Jovian planets generally have atmospheres that are dense, turbulent, and relatively deep.

It was long thought that tiny Pluto was the outermost planet in the solar system. In recent years, however, a number of astronomers have discovered many other icy bodies—similar in composition to comets and Pluto itself—orbiting the Sun beyond Neptune in what is referred to as the *Kuiper Belt*. In August 2006 the International Astronomical Union decided to reclassify Pluto and other similar-size objects within the solar system as "dwarf planets." Some astronomers speculate that there may be several dozen yet to be

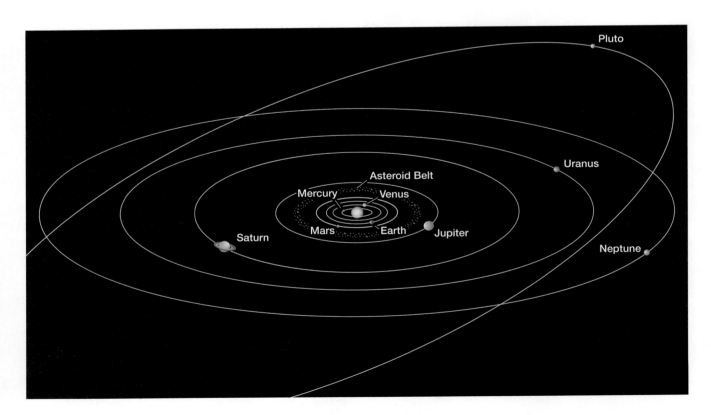

▲ **Figure 1-6** The solar system. (Not drawn to correct scale.)

discovered dwarf planets in the outer reaches of the solar system.

The Size and Shape of Earth

Is Earth large or small? The answer to this question depends on one's frame of reference. If the frame of reference is the universe, Earth is almost infinitely small. The radius of our planet is only about 6400 kilometers (4000 miles), a minute distance on the scale of the universe, whereas, for instance, the Moon is 385,000 kilometers (239,000 miles) from Earth, the Sun is 150,000,000 kilometers (93,000,000 miles) away, and the nearest star is 40,000,000,000,000 kilometers (25,000,000,000,000 miles) distant.

In a human frame of reference, however, Earth is a very impressive mass. Its highest point is more than 8800 meters (29,000 feet) above sea level, and the deepest spot in the oceans is more than 11,000 meters (36,000 feet) below sea level (Figure 1-7). The vertical

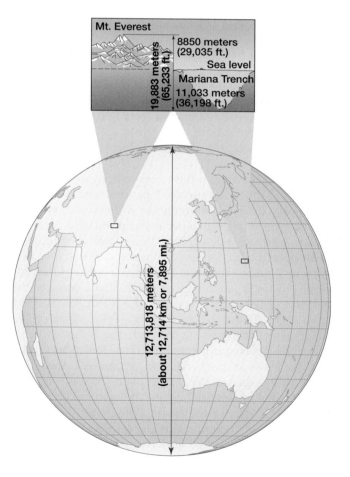

▲ **Figure 1-7** Earth's maximum relief (the difference in elevation between the highest and lowest points) is 19,883 meters (65,233 feet) or about 20 kilometers (12 miles) from the top of Mount Everest to the bottom of the Mariana Trench in the Pacific Ocean.

distance between these two extremes is about 20 kilometers (12 miles), which is minuscule when contrasted with the 12,735-kilometer (7909-mile) diameter of Earth. To illustrate this relationship, if we had a globe with a diameter the height of a 40-story building, the difference in elevation between the highest point of the continents and the lowest point in the ocean basins would be represented by the width of a single brick on top of the building.

More than 2600 years ago Greek scholars correctly reasoned Earth to have a spherical shape. About 2200 years ago, Eratosthenes, the director of the Greek library at Alexandria, calculated the circumference of Earth trigonometrically. He determined the angle of the noon Sun rays at Alexandria and at another city, Syene, measured the distance between the two localities (960 kilometers [600 miles]), and from these angular and linear distances he was able to estimate an Earth circumference of almost 43,000 kilometers (26,700 miles) which is reasonably close to the actual figure of 40,000 kilometers (24,900 miles). Some historians believe that Eratosthenes made errors in his calculations, errors that partially canceled one another and made his result more accurate than it deserved to be. Be that as it may, several other Greek scholars made independent calculations of Earth's circumference during this period, and all their results were close to reality, which indicates the antiquity of accurate knowledge of the size and shape of Earth.

Earth is almost, but not quite, spherical. The cross section revealed by a cut through the equator would be circular, but a similar cut from pole to pole would be an ellipse rather than a circle (Figure 1-8). Any rotating body has a tendency to bulge around its equator and flatten at the polar ends of its rotational axis. Although the rocks of Earth may seem quite rigid and immovable to us, they are sufficiently pliable to allow Earth to develop a bulge in its midriff. The slightly flattened polar diameter of Earth is 12,714 kilometers (7900 miles), whereas the slightly bulging equatorial diameter is 12,757 kilometers (7927 miles), a difference of only about 0.3 percent. Thus, our planet is properly described as an *oblate spheroid* rather than a true sphere.

In addition, the shape of Earth has obvious deviations from true sphericity that are the result of topographic irregularities on its surface. This surface varies in elevation from the highest mountain peak, Mount Everest, at 8850 meters (29,035 feet) above sea level, to the deepest ocean trench, the Mariana Trench of the Pacific Ocean, at 11,033 meters (36,198 feet) below sea level, a total difference in elevation of 19,883 meters (65,233 feet). Although prominent on a human scale of perception, this difference is minor on a planetary scale, as Figure 1-7 illustrates. If Earth were the size of a basketball, Mount Everest would be an imperceptible pimple no greater than 0.010 millimeter (about seven ten-thousandths of an inch), high. Similarly, the

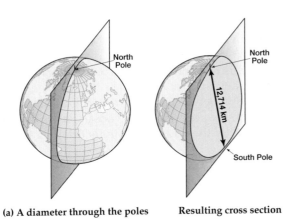

(a) A diameter through the poles   Resulting cross section

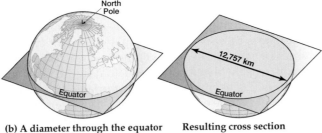

(b) A diameter through the equator   Resulting cross section

▲ **Figure 1-8** Earth is not quite a perfect sphere because its surface flattens a bit at the North Pole and the South Pole. Thus, a cross section through the poles, shown in **(a)**, has a diameter slightly less than the diameter of a cross section through the equator, shown in **(b)**. There is flattening at the poles and bulging all around the equator. However, because the bulging is evenly distributed all around the globe, it has no effect on the circular shape of the equatorial cross section.

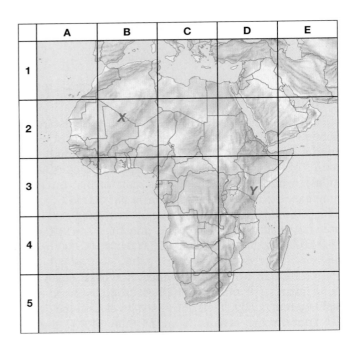

▲ **Figure 1-9** An example of a grid system. The location of point X can be described as 2B or as B2; the location of Y is 3D or D3.

Mariana Trench would be a tiny crease only 0.023 millimeter (about one-thousandth of an inch) deep. This represents a depression smaller than the thickness of a sheet of paper.

Our perception of the relative size of topographic irregularities has been further confused by three-dimensional wall maps and globes that emphasize such landforms. To portray any noticeable appearance of topographic variation, the vertical distances on such maps are usually exaggerated 8 to 20 times their actual proportional dimensions, as are many diagrams used in this book.

The variation from true sphericity, then, is exceedingly minute. For our purposes, Earth may properly be considered a sphere.

The Geographic Grid

Any understanding of the distribution of geographic features over Earth's surface requires some system of accurate location. Such a system should be capable of pinpointing with mathematical precision the position of any spot on the surface. The simplest technique for

achieving this precision is to design a grid system consisting of two sets of lines that intersect at right angles, thus permitting the location of any point on the surface to be described by the appropriate intersection, as shown in Figure 1-9. Such a rectangular grid system has been reconfigured for Earth's spherical surface, forming a geographic grid consisting of east–west and north–south lines.

If our planet were a nonrotating body, the problem of describing precise surface locations would be more formidable than it is. Imagine the difficulty of trying to describe the location of a particular point on a perfectly round, perfectly clean Ping-Pong ball. Fortunately, Earth does rotate, and we can use its rotation axis as a starting point to describe locations on Earth. Earth's rotation axis is an imaginary line that connects the points on Earth's surface called the *North Pole* and the *South Pole* (Figure 1-10). Further, if we visualize an imaginary plane passing through Earth halfway between the poles and perpendicular to the axis of rotation, we have another valuable reference feature: the **plane of the equator**. Where this plane intersects Earth's surface is the imaginary midline of Earth, called simply the **equator**. We use the North Pole, South Pole, rotational axis, and equatorial plane as natural reference features for measuring and describing locations on Earth's surface.

Great Circles Any plane that is passed through the center of a sphere bisects that sphere (divides it into two equal halves) and creates what is called a **great circle** where it intersects the surface of the sphere

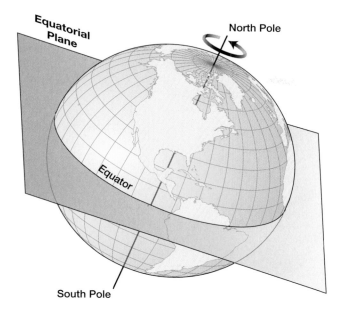

▲ **Figure 1-10** Earth spins around its rotation axis, an imaginary line that passes through the North Pole and the South Pole. An imaginary plane bisecting Earth midway between the two poles defines the equator.

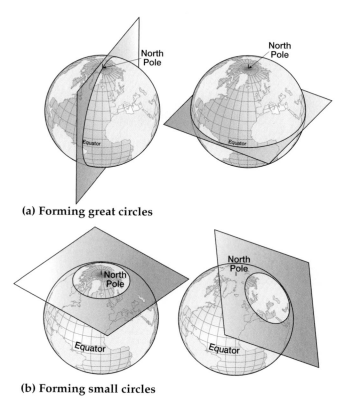

(a) Forming great circles

(b) Forming small circles

▲ **Figure 1-11** Comparison of great and small circles. **(a)** A great circle results from the intersection of Earth's surface with any plane that passes through Earth's center. **(b)** A small circle results from the intersection of Earth's surface with any plane that does not pass through Earth's center.

(Figure 1-11a). Planes passing through any other part of the sphere produce what are called *small circles* where they intersect the surface (Figure 1-11b). Great circles have two principal properties of special interest.

1. A great circle is the largest circle that can be drawn on a sphere; it represents the circumference of that sphere and divides its surface into two equal halves or hemispheres. For example, the Sun illuminates one-half of Earth at any given moment. The edge of the sunlit hemisphere, called the *circle of illumination*, is a great circle that divides Earth between a light half and a dark half.

2. Only one great circle can be drawn on a sphere to include any two given points (not diametrically opposite each other). As a consequence, the segment, or arc, of the great circle connecting those two points is always the shortest route between the points. Such routes on Earth are known as *great circle routes* (great circle routes will be discussed in more detail in Chapter 2).

The geographic grid used as the locational system for Earth is based on the principles just discussed. Furthermore, the system is closely linked with the various positions assumed by Earth in its orbit around the Sun. The grid system of Earth is referred to as a **graticule** and consists of lines of latitude and longitude.

Latitude

Latitude is a description of location expressed as an angle north or south of the equator. As shown in Figure 1-12, we can project a line from any location on Earth's surface to the center of Earth. The angle between this line and the equatorial plane is the latitude of that location.

Latitude is expressed in degrees, minutes, and seconds. There are 360 degrees (°) in a circle, 60 minutes (′) in one degree, and 60 seconds (″) in one minute. Latitude varies from 0° at the equator to 90° north at the **North Pole** and 90° south at the **South Pole**. Any position north of the equator is *north latitude*, and any position south of the equator is *south latitude* (the equator itself is simply referred to as having a latitude of 0°).

A line connecting all points of the same latitude is called a **parallel** (because it is parallel to all other lines of latitude). The equator is the parallel of 0° latitude, and it, alone of all parallels, constitutes a great circle. All other parallels are small circles—all aligned in true east–west directions on Earth's surface. Since latitude is expressed as an angle, it can be infinitely subdivided—parallels can be constructed for every degree of latitude, or even for fractions of a degree of latitude.

Although it is possible to either construct or visualize an unlimited number of parallels, seven latitudes

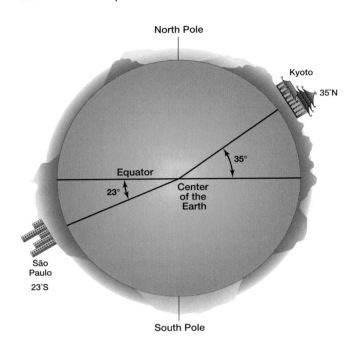

▲ **Figure 1-12**   Measuring latitude. An imaginary line from Kyoto, Japan, to Earth's center makes an angle of 35° with the equator. Therefore, Kyoto's latitude is 35° N. An imaginary line from São Paulo, Brazil, to Earth's center makes an angle of 23°, giving this South American city a latitude of 23° S.

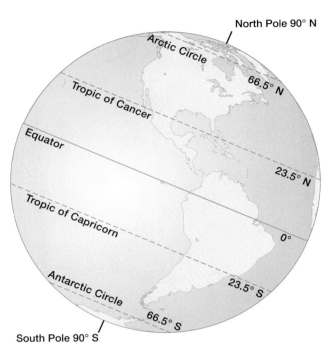

▲ **Figure 1-13**   Seven important parallels. As discussed later, these latitudes represent special points where rays from the Sun strike Earth's surface.

are of particular significance in a general study of Earth (Figure 1-13):

1. Equator, 0°
2. Tropic of Cancer, 23.5° N
3. Tropic of Capricorn, 23.5° S (see Figure 1-14)
4. Arctic Circle, 66.5° N
5. Antarctic Circle, 66.5° S
6. North Pole, 90° N
7. South Pole, 90° S

The North Pole and South Pole are of course points rather than lines, but can be thought of as infinitely small parallels. The importance of these seven parallels will be explained later in this chapter.

Regions on Earth are sometimes described as falling within general bands of latitude. The following common terms associated with latitude are used throughout this book (note that there is some overlap between several of these terms):

• **Low latitude**—generally between the equator and 30° N and S
• **Midlatitude**—between about 30° and 60° N and S
• **High latitude**—latitudes greater than about 60° N and S
• **Equatorial**—within a few degrees of the equator
• **Tropical**—within the tropics (between 23.5° N and 23.5° S)

▲ **Figure 1-14**   The Tropic of Capricorn, like all other parallels of latitude, is an imaginary line. As a significant parallel, however, its location is often commemorated by a sign. This scene is near Alice Springs in the center of Australia. *(Tom L. McKnight photo.)*

TABLE 1-4 Length of Degrees of Latitude and Longitude

Latitude (degrees)	Length of 1° of Latitude Measured along a Meridian		Length of 1° of Longitude Measured along a Parallel	
	Kilometers	Miles	Kilometers	Miles
0	110.567	68.703	111.321	69.172
10	110.605	68.726	109.641	68.129
20	110.705	68.789	104.649	65.026
30	110.857	68.883	96.488	59.956
40	111.042	68.998	85.396	53.063
50	111.239	69.121	71.698	44.552
60	111.423	69.235	55.802	34.674
70	111.572	69.328	38.188	23.729
80	111.668	69.387	19.394	12.051
90	111.699	69.407	0	0

- **Subtropical**—slightly poleward of the tropics, generally around 25–30° N and S
- **Polar**—within a few degrees of the North or South Pole

Nautical Miles Each degree of latitude on the surface of Earth covers a north–south distance of about 111 kilometers (69 miles; Table 1-4). The distance varies slightly with latitude because of the flattening of Earth at the poles. The distance measurement of a *nautical mile*—and the description of speed known as a *knot* (one nautical mile per hour)—is defined by the distance covered by one minute of latitude (1′), the equivalent of about 1.15 statute miles or about 1.85 kilometers.

Longitude

Latitude comprises one-half of Earth's grid system, the north–south component. The other half is **longitude**—an angular description of east–west location, also measured in degrees, minutes, and seconds.

Longitude is represented by imaginary lines extending from pole to pole and crossing all parallels at right angles. These lines, called **meridians**, are not parallel to one another except where they cross the equator. Any pair of meridians are farthest apart at the equator, becoming increasingly close together northward and southward and finally converging at the poles. A meridian, then, is a great semicircle that extends from one pole to the other, crossing all parallels of latitude perpendicularly and being aligned in a true north–south direction.

The distance between meridians varies significantly, but predictably. At the equator, the surface length of one degree is about the same as that of one degree of latitude. However, because meridians converge toward the poles, the distance covered by one degree of longitude decreases poleward (Table 1-4), diminishing to zero at the poles where all meridians meet at a point.

The equator is a natural baseline from which to measure latitude, but no such natural reference line exists for longitudinal measurement. Consequently, for most of recorded history, there was no accepted longitudinal baseline; each country would arbitrarily select its own "prime meridian" as the reference line for east–west measurement. Thus, the French measured from the meridian of Paris, the Italians from the meridian of Rome, and so forth. There were at least 13 prime meridians in use in the 1880s. Not until the late 1800s was standardization finally achieved.

United States and Canadian railway executives adopted a standard time system for all North American railroads in 1883, and the following year an international conference was convened in Washington, D.C., to achieve the same goal on a global scale and to agree upon a single prime meridian. After weeks of debate, the delegates (by a vote of 21 to 1, with 2 abstentions) chose the meridian passing through the Royal Observatory at Greenwich, England, just east of London, as the **prime meridian** for all longitudinal measurement (Figure 1-15). The principal argument for adopting the Greenwich meridian as the prime meridian was a practical one: More than two-thirds of the world's shipping lines already used the Greenwich meridian as a navigational base.

▲ **Figure 1-15** The prime meridian of the world, longitude 0°0′0″ at Greenwich, England, which is about 32 km (20 miles) down the river Thames from the heart of London. *(Tom L. McKnight photo)*

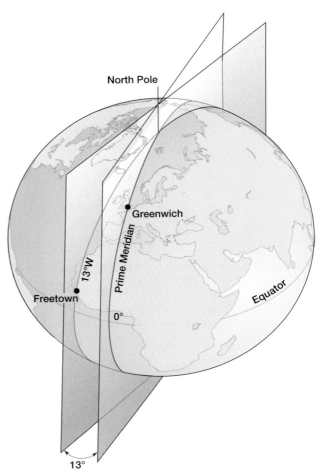

▲ **Figure 1-16** The meridians that mark longitude are defined by intersecting imaginary planes passing through the poles. Here are shown the planes for the prime meridian through Greenwich, England, and the meridian through Freetown, Sierra Leone, at 13° west longitude.

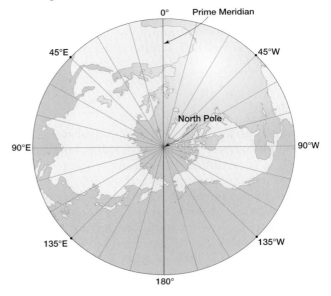

▲ **Figure 1-17** A polar view of meridians radiating from the North Pole. Think of each line as the top edge of an imaginary plane passing through both poles. All the planes are perpendicular to the plane of the page.

Thus, an imaginary north–south plane passing through Greenwich and through Earth's axis of rotation represents the plane of the prime meridian. The angle between this plane and a plane passed through any other point and the axis of Earth is a measure of longitude. For example, the angle between the Greenwich plane and a plane passing through the center of the city of Freetown (in the western African country of Sierra Leone) is 13 degrees, 15 minutes, and 12 seconds. Since the angle is formed west of the prime meridian, the longitude of Freetown is written 13°15′12″ W (Figure 1-16).

Longitude is measured both east and west of the prime meridian to a maximum of 180° in each direction. Exactly halfway around the globe from the prime meridian, in the middle of the Pacific Ocean, is the 180° meridian (Figure 1-17). All places on Earth, then, have a location that is either east longitude or west longitude, except for points exactly on the prime meridian (described simply as 0° longitude) or exactly on the 180th meridian (described as 180° longitude).

The network of intersecting parallels and meridians creates a geographic grid over the entire surface of Earth (Figure 1-18). The location of any place on Earth's surface can be described with great precision by reference to detailed latitude and longitude data.

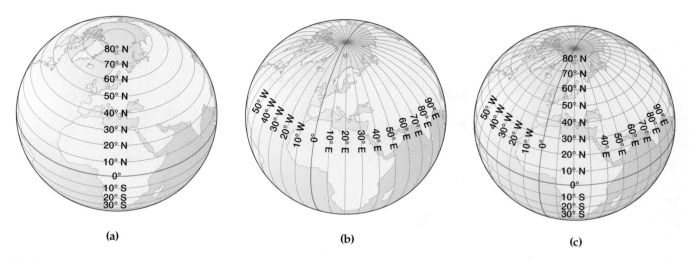

▲ **Figure 1-18** Development of the geographic grid, or graticule. **(a)** Parallels of latitude. **(b)** Meridians of longitude. **(c)** The two combined to form a complete grid system.

For example, at the 1964 World's Fair in New York City, a time capsule (a container filled with records and memorabilia of contemporary life) was buried. For reference purposes, the U.S. Coast and Geodetic Survey determined that the capsule was located at 40°28′34.089″ north latitude and 73°43′16.412″ west longitude. At some time in the future, if a hole were to be dug at the spot indicated by those coordinates, it would be within 15 cm (6 inches) of the capsule.

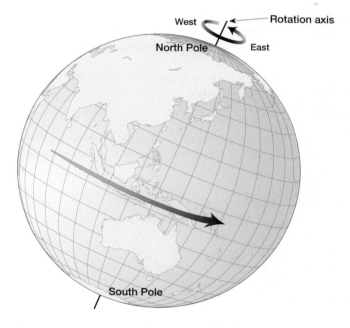

▲ **Figure 1-19** Earth rotates from west to east on a rotation axis that is tilted from the vertical.

Earth–Sun Relations

Earth–Sun Relations

Life on Earth is dependent on solar energy, therefore the functional relationship between Earth and the Sun is of vital importance. This relationship does not remain the same throughout the year because the perpetual motions of Earth continuously change the geometric perspective between the two bodies.

Earth Movements Two basic Earth movements—its daily rotation on its axis and its annual revolution around the Sun—along with the inclination and "polarity" of Earth's rotation axis, combine to change Earth's orientation to the Sun during the year and thus are of special interest to geographers.

Earth's Rotation on Its Axis

Earth rotates from west to east on its axis (Figure 1-19), a complete rotation requiring 24 hours (from the vantage point of looking down at the North Pole from space,

Earth is rotating in a counterclockwise direction). The Sun, the Moon, and the stars appear to rise in the east and set in the west—this is, of course, an illusion created by the steady eastward spin of Earth.

Rotation causes all parts of Earth's surface except the poles to move in a circle around Earth's axis. Table 1-5 shows the speed of this motion at various latitudes. Although the speed of rotation varies from place to place, it is constant at any given place. This is the reason that we experience no sense of motion. Often one can get the same impression in a modern jetliner, where a smooth flight at cruising speed is much like sitting in a comfortable living room. Only

TABLE 1-5 Speed of Rotation of Earth's Surface at Selected Latitudes		
Latitude	Kilometers per Hour	Miles per Hour
0	1669.9	1037.6
10	1642.0	1021.9
20	1569.7	975.4
30	1447.3	899.3
40	1280.9	795.9
50	1075.5	668.3
60	837.0	520.1
70	572.8	355.9
80	291.0	180.8
90	0	0

during takeoff and landing is the sense of motion quite apparent. Similarly, the motion and speed of earthly rotation would become apparent to us only if that rotation rate suddenly increased or decreased (a very unlikely event!).

Rotation has several striking effects on the physical characteristics of Earth's surface. Most important are the following:

1. The constancy of Earth's rotation in the same direction causes an apparent deflection in the flow path of both air and water currents. The deflection is to the right in the Northern Hemisphere and to the left in the Southern Hemisphere. This phenomenon is called the *Coriolis effect* and is discussed in detail in Chapter 3.

2. The rotation of Earth brings any point on the surface through the increasing and then decreasing gravitational pull of the Moon and the Sun. Although the land areas of Earth are too rigid to be significantly moved by these oscillating gravitational attractions, oceanic waters move onshore and then recede in a rhythmic pattern as a result of the interplay of earthly rotation with these gravitational forces. The rise and fall of water level constitutes the *tides*, which are discussed further in Chapter 9.

3. Undoubtedly the most important effect of earthly rotation is the *diurnal* (daily) alternation of light and darkness, as portions of Earth's surface are turned first toward and then away from the Sun. This variation in exposure to sunlight greatly influences local temperature, humidity, and wind movements. Except for the organisms that live either in caves or in the ocean deeps, all forms of life have adapted to this sequential pattern of light and darkness. We human beings fare poorly when our *circadian* (daily) *rhythms* are misaligned as the result of high-speed air travel that significantly interrupts the normal sequence of daylight and darkness. We are left with a sense of fatigue and psychological distress known as "jet lag," which can include unpleasant changes in our usual patterns of appetite and sleep.

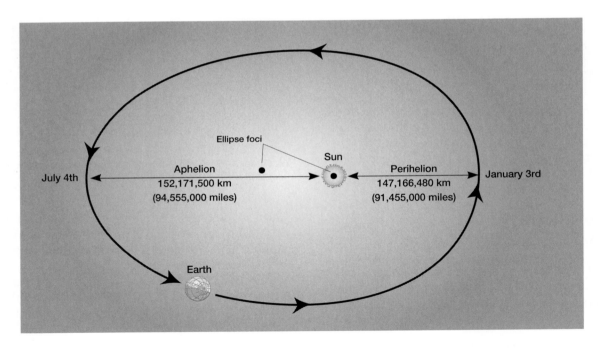

▲ **Figure 1-20**   The path Earth follows in its revolution around the Sun is an ellipse having the Sun at one focus. The line marking the shortest distance between the Sun and Earth's orbit is called the perihelion and is 147,166,480 kilometers (91,455,000 miles) long. The line marking the greatest distance between the Sun and Earth's orbit is called the aphelion and is 152,171,500 kilometers (94,555,000 miles) long. (In this diagram the elliptical shape of Earth's orbit is greatly exaggerated.)

Earth's Revolution around the Sun

Another significant Earth motion is its revolution around the Sun. Each revolution takes 365 days, 5 hours, 48 minutes, and 46 seconds, or 365.242199 days. This is known officially as the *tropical year* and for practical purposes is usually simplified to 365.25 days. (Astronomers define the year in other ways as well, but the duration is very close to that of the tropical year and need not concern us here.)

The path followed by Earth in its journey around the Sun is not a true circle but an ellipse (Figure 1-20). Because of this elliptical orbit, the Earth–Sun distance is not constant; rather, it varies from 147,166,480 kilometers (91,455,000 miles) at the closest or **perihelion** position (*peri* is from the Greek and means "around" and *helios* means "Sun") on about January 3, to 152,171,500 kilometers (94,555,000 miles) at the farthest or **aphelion** position (*ap* is from the Greek and means "away from") on about July 4. The average Earth–Sun distance is defined as one *astronomical unit* (1 AU) and is 149,597,892 kilometers (92,955,806 miles). Earth is 3.3 percent closer to the Sun during the Northern Hemisphere winter than during the Northern Hemisphere summer, an indication that the varying distance between Earth and the Sun is not an important determinant of seasonal temperature fluctuations.

While the varying distance between Earth and the Sun does not cause the change of seasons, two additional factors in the relationship of the Earth to the Sun—inclination and polarity—work together with rotation and revolution to produce the changes of seasons.

Inclination of Earth's Axis

The imaginary plane defined by the orbital path of Earth around the Sun is called the **plane of the ecliptic** (Figure 1-21). However, the plane of the ecliptic does not match the plane of the equator because Earth's rotation axis is not perpendicular to the ecliptic plane. Rather, the axis is tilted about 23.5° away from the perpendicular (Figure 1-22) and maintains this tilt throughout the year. This tilt is referred to as the **inclination of Earth's axis**.

Polarity of Earth's Axis

Not only is Earth's rotation axis inclined relative to its orbital path, no matter where Earth is in its orbit around the Sun the axis always points in the same direction relative to the stars—toward the North Star, Polaris. In other words, at any time during the year, Earth's rotation axis is parallel to its orientation at all other times.

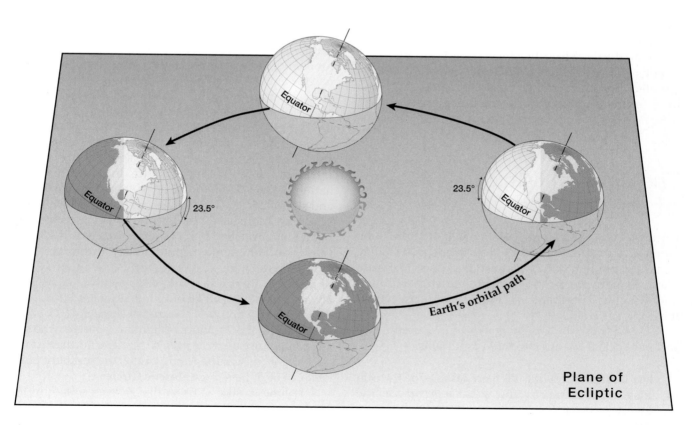

▲ **Figure 1-21** The plane of the ecliptic is the orbital plane of Earth. This imaginary plane passes through the Sun and through every point on Earth's orbit around the Sun. Because Earth's rotation axis is tilted, the plane of the ecliptic and the equatorial plane do not coincide.

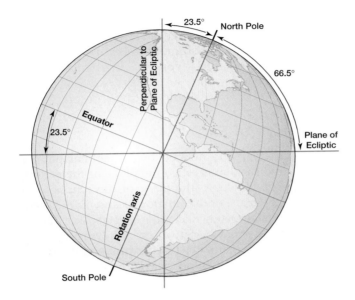

▲ **Figure 1-22** Earth's rotation axis forms an angle of 66.5° with the plane of the ecliptic, and this tilt is called the inclination of the axis. It is commonly described not in terms of this angle, however, but rather as being 23.5° from a line perpendicular to the plane of the ecliptic.

This characteristic is called the **polarity of the rotation axis** (or **parallelism**) (Figure 1-23).

The combined effects of rotation, revolution, inclination, and polarity result in the seasonal patterns experienced on Earth. Notice in Figure 1-23 that at one point in Earth's orbit, on about June 21, the North Pole is oriented most directly toward the Sun, while six months later, on about December 21, the North Pole is oriented most directly away from the Sun—this is the most fundamental feature of the annual march of the seasons.

The Annual March of the Seasons

During a year, the changing relationship of Earth to the Sun results in variations in day length and in the angle at which the Sun's rays strike the surface of Earth. These changes are most obvious in the mid- and high latitudes, but important variations take place within the tropics as well.

As we discuss the annual march of the seasons, we will pay special attention to three conditions:

1. The latitude receiving the vertical rays of the Sun (also referred to as the *subsolar point* or the *declination of the Sun*).
2. The **solar altitude** (the height of the Sun above the horizon) at different latitudes.
3. The length of day at different latitudes.

Initially, we emphasize the conditions on four special days of the year: The March equinox, the June solstice, the September equinox, and the December solstice (Figure 1-24), although the transitions between these special days are important for us as well. As we describe the change of seasons, the significance of the "seven important parallels" discussed earlier in this chapter will become clear. We begin with the June solstice.

June Solstice On the **June solstice**, which occurs on or about June 21 (the exact date varies slightly from year to year), the Earth reaches the position in its orbit where the North Pole is oriented most directly toward the Sun. On this day, the rays from the Sun at noon are striking perpendicular to the surface at the **Tropic of Cancer**, 23.5° north of the equator (Figure 1-25). Were you at the Tropic of Cancer on this day, the Sun will be directly overhead in the sky at noon (in other words, the solar altitude would be 90°). However, were you a few degrees of latitude north or south of the Tropic of Cancer, the noon sun would be a few degrees lower in the sky—the farther north or south of the Tropic of Cancer you were, the lower in the sky the noon Sun will be. The Tropic of Cancer marks the northernmost location reached by the vertical rays of the Sun in the annual cycle of Earth's revolution.

You will recall that the dividing line between the daylight half of Earth and nighttime half of Earth is known as the **circle of illumination**. The relationship of the circle of illumination to the parallels on any given day of the year determines the day length experienced at different latitudes. On the June solstice, the circle of illumination bisects the equator (Figure 1-25), so on this day the equator receives equal day and night—12 hours of daylight and 12 hours of darkness. However, as we move north of the equator, the portion of each parallel in daylight increases—in other words, as we move north of the equator, day length increases. Conversely, day length decreases as we move south of the equator.

Notice that on the June solstice, the circle of illumination reaches 23.5° to the far side of the North Pole and stops short 23.5° to the near side of the South Pole, as Figure 1-25 shows. As Earth rotates on its axis, all points north of 66.5° N (in other words, within 23.5° of the North Pole) remain continuously within the circle of illumination, thus experiencing 24 continuous hours of daylight. By contrast, all points south of 66.5° S are always outside the circle of illumination and thus have 24 continuous hours of darkness. These special parallels defining the 24 hours of light and dark on the solstice dates are called the *polar circles*. The northern polar circle, at 66.5° N, is the **Arctic Circle**; the southern polar circle, at 66.5° S, is the **Antarctic Circle**.

The June solstice is called the *summer solstice* in the Northern Hemisphere and the *winter solstice* in the Southern Hemisphere (what are commonly called the "first day of summer" and the "first day of winter" in their respective hemispheres).

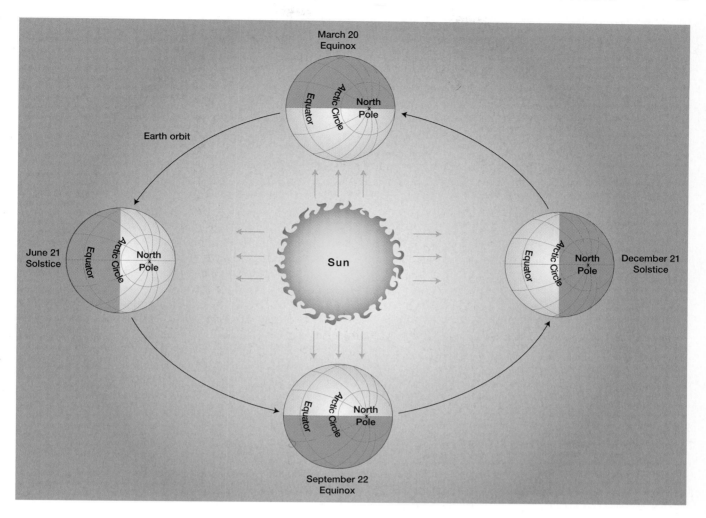

▲ **Figure 1-23**   A "top view" of the march of the seasons. Earth's rotational axis maintains polarity (points in the same direction) throughout the year. One-half of Earth is illuminated at all times during the year. Here light blue is the illuminated half and dark blue is the unilluminated half. The line between the two halves is called the circle of illumination. Note its position relative to the polar circles on June 21, date of the summer solstice in the Northern Hemisphere, and December 21, date of the winter solstice in the Northern Hemisphere.

September Equinox   Three months after the June solstice, on approximately September 22 (as with solstice dates, this date also varies slightly from year to year), Earth experiences the **September equinox**. Notice in Figure 1-26 that the vertical rays of the Sun are striking the equator. Notice also that the circle of illumination just touches both poles, bisecting all other parallels—on this day all locations on Earth experience 12 hours of daylight and 12 hours of darkness (the word "equinox" comes from the Latin, meaning "the time of equal days and equal nights"). At the equator—and only at the equator—every day of the year has 12 hours of daylight and 12 hours of darkness; all other locations have equal day and night only on an equinox.

The September equinox is called the *autumnal equinox* in the Northern Hemisphere and the *vernal equinox* in the Southern Hemisphere (and what are commonly called the "first day of fall" and the "first day of spring" in their respective hemispheres).

December Solstice   On the **December solstice**, which occurs on or about December 21, the Earth reaches the position in its orbit where the North Pole is oriented most directly away from the Sun; the vertical rays of the Sun now strike 23.5° S, the **Tropic of Capricorn** (Figure 1-27). Once again, the circle of illumination reaches to the far side of one pole and falls short on the near side of the other pole, but this time the illuminated hemispheres are reversed. Areas north of the Arctic Circle now always lie outside the circle of illumination and are thus in continuous darkness, whereas areas within the Antarctic Circle are continuously within the circle and thus in daylight for 24 hours.

Although the latitude receiving the vertical rays of the Sun has shifted 47° from June 21 to December 21,

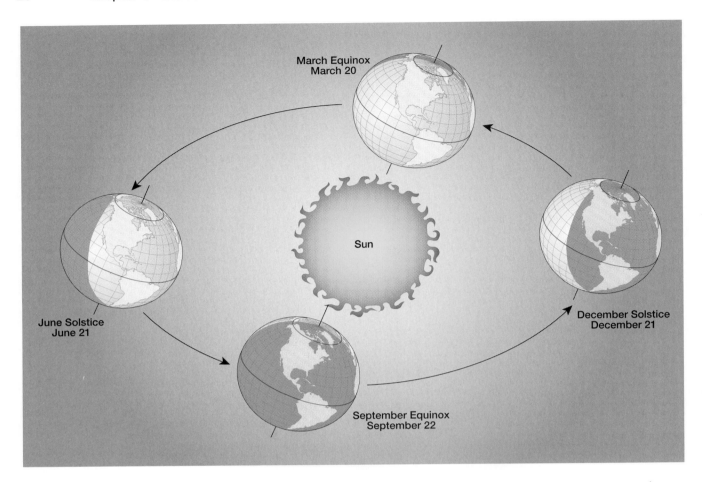

▲ **Figure 1-24**   The annual march of the seasons showing Earth–Sun relations on the June solstice, September equinox, December solstice, and March equinox.

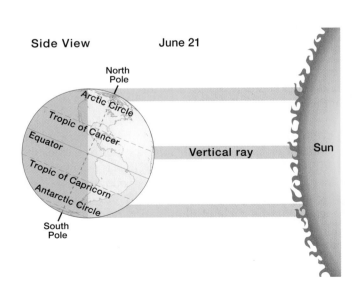

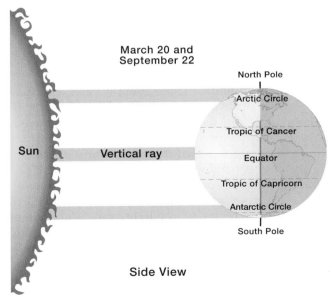

▲ **Figure 1-25**   Earth–Sun configuration during the June solstice. At this time, the Sun's noon rays strike vertically at 23.5° N latitude. During the June solstice (Northern Hemisphere summer), sunlight is concentrated in the Northern Hemisphere. Vertical rays never strike any farther north than 23.5° north latitude.

▲ **Figure 1-26**   Earth–Sun configuration during the March and September equinoxes, which usually occur on March 20 and September 22, respectively. On these two days, the noon rays of the Sun strike vertically on the equator.

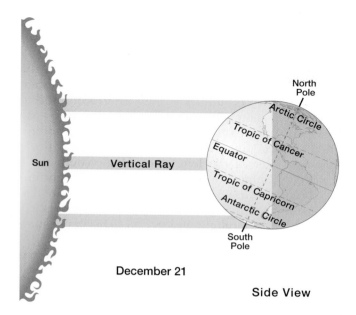

December 21

Side View

Sun

Vertical Ray

North Pole

Arctic Circle

Tropic of Cancer

Equator

Tropic of Capricorn

Antarctic Circle

South Pole

▲ **Figure 1-27** Earth–Sun configuration during the December solstice. At this time, the Sun's noon rays strike vertically at 23.5° S latitude. During the December solstice (Northern Hemisphere winter), sunlight is concentrated in the Southern Hemisphere. Vertical rays never strike any farther south than 23.5° south latitude.

the relationships between Earth and the Sun on the June solstice and the December solstice are very similar—the conditions in each hemisphere are simply reversed. The December solstice is called the *winter solstice* in the

Northern Hemisphere and the *summer solstice* in the Southern Hemisphere (what are commonly called the "first day of winter" and the "first day of summer," respectively).

March Equinox   Three months after the December solstice, on approximately March 20, Earth experiences the **March equinox**. The relationships of Earth and the Sun are virtually identical on the March equinox and the September equinox (Figure 1-26). The March equinox is called the *vernal equinox* in the Northern Hemisphere and the *autumnal equinox* in the Southern Hemisphere (what are commonly called the "first day of spring" and the "first day of fall," respectively).

Table 1-6 summarizes the conditions present during the solstices and equinoxes. The enormous variations in length of daylight and noon sun angle at different latitudes at the time of a solstice are shown in Table 1-7.

Seasonal Transitions

In the preceding discussion of the solstices and equinoxes, we mainly emphasized the conditions on just four special days of the year. It is important to understand the transitions in day length and Sun angle that take place between those days as well.

Latitude Receiving the Vertical Rays of the Sun   Following the March equinox, the vertical rays of the Sun migrate from the equator northward and strike the Tropic

Day	March Equinox	June Solstice	September Equinox	December Solstice
Latitude of vertical rays of Sun	0°	23.5° N	0°	23.5° S
Day length at Equator	12 hours	12 hours	12 hours	12 hours
Day length in midlatitudes of Northern Hemisphere	12 hours	Day length becomes longer with increasing latitude north of equator.	12 hours	Day length becomes shorter with increasing latitude north of equator.
Day length in midlatitudes of Southern Hemisphere	12 hours	Day length becomes shorter with increasing latitude south of equator.	12 hours	Day length becomes longer with increasing latitude south of equator.
24 hours of daylight	Nowhere	From Arctic Circle to North Pole	Nowhere	From Antarctic Circle to South Pole
24 hours of darkness	Nowhere	From Antarctic Circle to South Pole	Nowhere	From Arctic Circle to North Pole
Season in Northern Hemisphere	Spring	Summer	Autumn	Winter
Season in Southern Hemisphere	Autumn	Winter	Spring	Summer

TABLE 1-6 Conditions on Equinoxes and Solstices

TABLE 1-7 Day Length and Noon Sun Angle at Time of June Solstice

Latitude	Day Length	Noon Sun Angle (degrees above horizon)
90° N	24 h	23.5
80° N	24 h	33.5
70° N	24 h	43.5
60° N	18 h 53 min	53.5
50° N	16 h 23 min	63.5
40° N	15 h 01 min	73.5
30° N	14 h 05 min	83.5
20° N	13 h 21 min	86.5
10° N	12 h 43 min	76.5
0°	12 h 07 min	66.5
10° S	11 h 32 min	56.5
20° S	10 h 55 min	46.5
30° S	10 h 12 min	36.5
40° S	09 h 20 min	26.5
50° S	08 h 04 min	16.5
60° S	05 h 52 min	6.5
70° S	0	0
80° S	0	0
90° S	0	0

Source: After Robert J. List, *Smithsonian Meteorological Tables*, 6th rev. ed., Washington, D.C.: Smithsonian Institution, 1963, Table 171.

of Cancer on the June solstice (although latitudes north of the Tropic of Cancer never experience the vertical rays of the Sun, the June solstice marks the day of the year when the Sun is highest in the sky in those latitudes). After the June solstice, the vertical rays migrate south, striking the equator again on the September equinox and finally to their southernmost latitude on the December solstice (the December solstice marks the day of the year when the Sun is lowest in the sky in the Northern Hemisphere). Following the December solstice, the vertical rays migrate northward, reaching the equator once again on the March equinox.

Day Length   Only at the equator is day length constant throughout the year (virtually 12 hours of daylight every day of the year). Following the shortest day of the year in the Northern Hemisphere on the December solstice, the period of daylight gradually increases everywhere north of the equator until the longest day of the year on the June solstice. Conversely, during this period, day length diminishes for all points south of the equator.

From the June solstice until the September equinox, the pattern is reversed, with the days getting shorter in the Northern Hemisphere and longer in the Southern Hemisphere until the September equinox, when day and night are again equal all over Earth.

Following the September equinox, the days of the Northern Hemisphere continue to become shorter, and those of the Southern Hemisphere continue to lengthen. By the December solstice, the days are shortened progressively northward, reaching a minimum of no daylight north of the Arctic Circle. During this same interval, day length gets longer south of the equator, reaching a maximum of 24 hours of continuous daylight south of the Antarctic Circle. Again, this pattern is reversed following the December solstice, and periods of daylight and darkness become equalized over the entire world at the March equinox.

Overall, the annual variation in day length is the least in the tropics and greatest in the high latitudes.

Day Length in the Arctic and Antarctic   The patterns of day and night in the Arctic and Antarctic are especially intriguing. On the March equinox, the Sun rises at the North Pole and is above the horizon continuously for the next six months. Week by week, the region experiencing 24 hours of daylight extends south from the North Pole until the June solstice—when the entire region from the North Pole to the Arctic Circle experiences 24 hours of daylight. Following the June solstice, the region experiencing 24 hours of daylight diminishes week by week until the September equinox—when the Sun sets at the North Pole and remains below the horizon continuously for the next six months.

Week by week following the September equinox, the region experiencing 24 hours of darkness extends south from the North Pole until the December solstice—when the entire region from the North Pole to the Arctic Circle experiences 24 hours of darkness. Following the December solstice, the region experiencing 24 hours of darkness diminishes week by week until the March equinox—when the Sun again rises at the North Pole. In the Southern Hemisphere, these seasonal patterns are simply reversed.

Significance of Seasonal Patterns

Both day length and the angle at which the Sun's rays strike Earth are principal determinants of the amount of solar energy received at any particular latitude. As a generalization, the higher the angle at which the sunlight strikes Earth, the more effective is the resultant heating. Where the Sun's rays strike Earth perpendicularly (at a 90° angle), solar energy is concentrated onto the smallest possible surface area. Where the Sun's rays strike Earth obliquely (at an angle smaller than 90°), the same amount of energy is spread over a larger surface area—thus, the amount of energy reaching a particular surface area is significantly smaller. Day length influences patterns of solar energy receipt on Earth as well. For example, short periods of daylight in winter and long periods of daylight in summer contribute to seasonal differences in temperature in the mid- and high latitude regions of Earth.

Thus, the tropical latitudes are generally always warm because they always have high Sun angles and consistent day lengths that are close to 12 hours long. Indeed, the region between the tropic lines is the only part of Earth that experiences 90° Sun angles sometime during the year. Conversely, the polar regions are consistently cold because they always have low Sun angles—even the 24-hour days in summer do not compensate for the low angle of incidence of sunlight. Seasonal temperature differences are large in the midlatitudes because of sizable seasonal variations in Sun angles and length of day. This topic will be explored further in Chapter 4.

Telling Time

Malcolm Thomson, a Canadian authority on the physics of time, has noted that there are only three natural units of time: the *tropical year*, marked by the return of the seasons; the *lunar month*, marked by the return of the new moon; and the *day*, marked by passage of the Sun. All other units, such as the hour, minute, and second, are human-made to meet the needs of society.

In prehistoric times, the rising and setting of the Sun were probably the principal means of telling time. As civilizations developed, however, more precise timekeeping was required. Early agricultural civilizations in Egypt, Mesopotamia, India, China, and even England, as well as the Aztec and Mayan civilizations in the New World, observed the Sun and the stars to tell time and keep accurate calendars.

Local *solar noon* can be determined by watching for the moment when objects cast their shortest shadows. The Romans used sundials to tell time (Figure 1-28) and gave great importance to the noon position, which they called the *meridian*—the Sun's highest (*meri*) point of the day (*diem*). Our use of A.M. (*ante meridian*: before noon) and P.M. (*post meridian*: after noon) was derived from the Roman world.

When nearly all transportation was by foot, horse, or sailing vessel, it was difficult to compare time at different localities. In those days, each community set its own time by correcting its clocks to high noon at the moment of the shortest shadow. A central public building, such as a temple in India or a county courthouse in Kansas, usually had a large clock or loud bells to toll the hour. Periodically, this time was checked against the shortest shadow.

Standard Time

As the telegraph and railroad began to speed words and passengers between cities, the use of local solar

▲ **Figure 1-28** A typical sundial. A sundial is the oldest known device for measuring time, having been used in Babylon at least as early as 4000 years ago. The two main parts of any sundial are a horizontal face and a vertical piece of metal—called a *gnomon*—in its center. The upper edge of the gnomon must slant upward from the dial face at an angle equal to the latitude at the place where the sundial is installed. The gnomon points toward the North Pole in the Northern Hemisphere and toward the South Pole in the Southern Hemisphere. When the Sun shines on it, the gnomon casts a shadow that tells the time. As the Sun appears to move across the sky during the course of a day, the position of the shadow changes. The time shown in this photograph is about 11:00 A.M. (*Richard Kolar/Earth Scenes.*)

time created increasing problems. A cross-country rail traveler in the United States in the 1870s might have experienced as many as 24 different local time standards between the Atlantic and Pacific coasts. Eventually, the railroads stimulated the development of a standardized time system. At the 1884 International Prime Meridian Conference in Washington, D.C., countries agreed to divide the world into 24 standard time zones, each extending over 15° of longitude. The mean local solar time of the Greenwich (prime) meridian was chosen as the standard for the entire system. The prime meridian became the center of a time zone that extends 7.5° of longitude to the west and 7.5° to the east of the prime meridian. Similarly, the meridians that are multiples of 15°, both east and west of the prime meridian, were set as the central meridians for the 23 other time zones (Figure 1-29).

Although **Greenwich Mean Time (GMT)** is now referred to as **Universal Time Coordinated (UTC)**, the prime meridian is still the reference for standard time. Since it is always the same number of minutes after the hour in all standard time zones (keeping in mind that a few countries, such as Saudi Arabia, do not adhere to standard time zones), we usually need to know only the correct time at Greenwich and the number of hours that our local time zone is later or earlier than the Greenwich meridian to know exact local time. Figure 1-29 shows the number of hours later or earlier than UTC it is in each time zone of the world.

Most of the countries of the world are sufficiently small in their east–west direction so as to lie totally within a single time zone. However, large countries may encompass several zones: Russia occupies nine time zones;

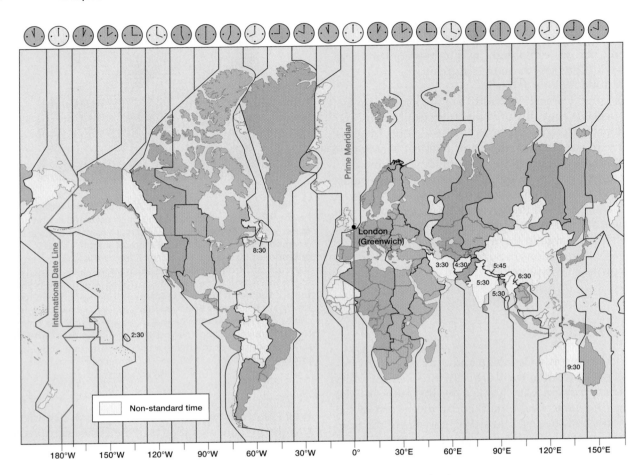

▲ **Figure 1-29** The 24 time zones of the world, each centered on meridians spaced 15° apart.

including Alaska and Hawaii, the United States spreads over six (Figure 1-30); Canada, six; and Australia, three. In international waters, time zones are defined to be exactly 7°30′ to the east and 7°30′ to the west of the central meridians. Over land areas, however, zone boundaries vary to coincide with appropriate political and economic boundaries. For example, continental Europe from Portugal to Poland shares one time zone, although longitudinally covering about 30°. At the extreme, China extends across four 15° zones, but the entire nation, at least officially, observes the time of the 120th east meridian, which is the one closest to Beijing.

In each time zone, there is a controlling meridian along which clock time is the same as Sun time (i.e., the Sun reaches its highest point in the sky at 12:00 noon). On either side of that meridian, of course, clock time does not coincide with Sun time. The deviation between the two is shown for one U.S. zone in Figure 1-31.

From the map of time zones of the United States (Figure 1-30), we can recognize a great deal of manipulation of the time zone boundaries for economic and political convenience. For example, the Central Standard Time Zone, centered on 90° W, extends all the way to 105° W (which is the central meridian of the Mountain Standard Time Zone) in Texas to keep most of that state within the same zone. By contrast,

El Paso, Texas, is officially within the Mountain Standard Time Zone in accord with its role as a major market center for southern New Mexico, which observes Mountain Standard Time. In the same vein, northwestern Indiana is in the Central Standard Time Zone with Chicago.

International Date Line

In 1519, Ferdinand Magellan set out westward from Spain, sailing for East Asia with 241 men in five ships. Three years later, the remnants of his crew (18 men in one ship) successfully completed the first circumnavigation of the globe. Although a careful log had been kept, the crew found that their calendar was one day short of the correct date. This was the first human experience with time change on a global scale, the realization of which eventually led to the establishment of the **International Date Line**.

One advantage of establishing the Greenwich meridian as the prime meridian is that its opposite arc is in the Pacific Ocean. The 180th meridian, transiting the sparsely populated mid-Pacific, was chosen as the meridian at which new days begin and old days exit from the surface of Earth. The International Date Line deviates from the 180th meridian in the Bering Sea to

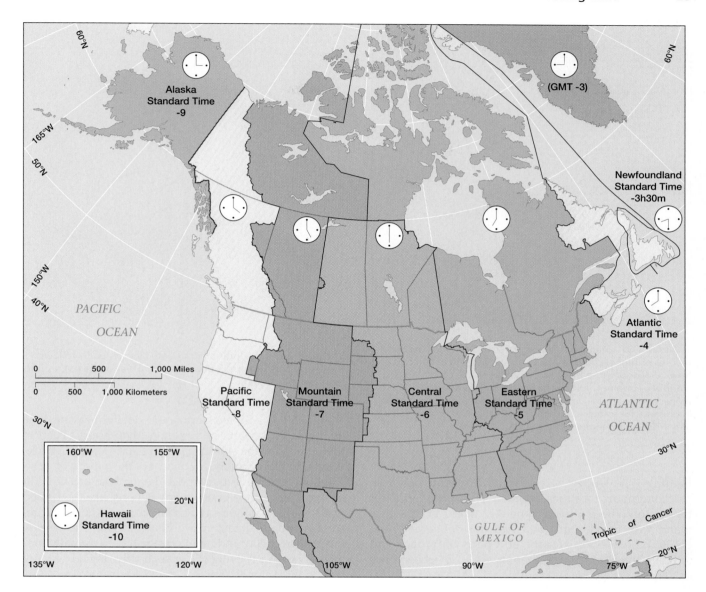

▲ **Figure 1-30** Times zones for Canada and the United States. Zone boundaries often do not follow meridians. The number in each time zone refers to the number of hours earlier than UTC.

include all of the Aleutian Islands of Alaska within the same day and again in the South Pacific to keep islands of the same group (Fiji, Tonga) within the same day (Figure 1-32). The extensive eastern displacement of the date line in the central Pacific is due to the widely scattered locations of the many islands of the country of Kiribati.

The International Date Line is in the middle of the time zone defined by the 180° meridian. Consequently, there is no time zone (i.e., hourly) change when crossing the International Date Line—there is a change only on the calendar, not on the clock. When you cross the International Date Line going from west to east, it becomes one day earlier (e.g., from January 2 to January 1); when you move across the line from east to west, it becomes one day later (e.g., from January 1 to January 2).

Except at Greenwich noon, two days exist on Earth at the same time: the more recent one (e.g., January 2),

extending from the International Date Line westward to the current position of midnight, and the older one (e.g., January 1), extending the rest of the way to the date line. A new day first appears on Earth at midnight at the International Date Line. For the next 24 hours, the new day advances westward around the world, finally covering the entire surface for one hour at the end of this period (when it is noon at the Greenwich meridian). For the next 24 hours, this day leaves Earth, one hour at a time, making its final exit 48 hours after its first appearance.

Daylight-Saving Time

To conserve energy during World War I, Germany ordered all clocks set forward by an hour. This practice allowed the citizenry to "save" an hour of daylight by shifting the daylight period into the usual evening hours, thus reducing the consumption of electricity for

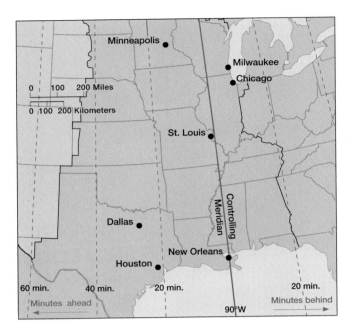

▲ **Figure 1-31** Standard clock time versus Sun time. The Sun reaches its highest point in the sky at 12:00 noon in St. Louis and New Orleans because these two cities lie on the controlling meridian. For places not on the controlling meridian, the Sun is highest in the sky at some time other than standard time noon. In Chicago, for instance, the Sun is highest in the sky at 11:50 A.M. and in Dallas it is highest in the sky at 12:28 P.M.

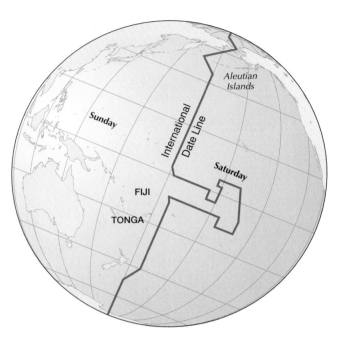

▲ **Figure 1-32** The International Date Line generally follows the 180th meridian, but it deviates around various island groups, most notably Kiribati.

lighting. The United States began a similar policy in 1918, but many localities declined to observe "summer time" until the Uniform Time Act made the practice mandatory in all states that had not deliberately exempted themselves. Hawaii, and parts of Indiana and Arizona, have exempted themselves from observance of *daylight-saving time* under this act.

Russia has adopted permanent daylight-saving time (and double daylight-saving time—two hours ahead of Sun time—in the summer). In recent years, Canada, Australia, New Zealand, and most of the nations of western Europe have also adopted daylight-saving time. In the Northern Hemisphere, many nations, like the United States, begin daylight-saving time in mid-March and resume standard time in early November. In the tropics, the lengths of day and night change little seasonally, and there is not much twilight. Consequently, daylight-saving time would offer little or no savings for tropical areas.

Chapter 1 Learning Review

Key Terms

Before answering the study questions, review the definitions of the following key terms (page references are provided for you):

Antarctic Circle (*p. 18*)
aphelion (*p. 17*)
Arctic Circle (*p. 18*)
atmosphere (*p. 5*)
biosphere (*p. 5*)
circle of illumination (*p. 18*)
cryosphere (*p. 5*)
cultural geography (*p. 1*)
December solstice (*p. 19*)
equator (*p. 10*)
graticule (*p. 11*)
great circle (*p. 10*)
Greenwich Mean Time (GMT) (*p. 23*)

hydrosphere (*p. 5*)
inclination of Earth's axis (*p. 17*)
International Date Line (*p. 24*)
international system of measurement (SI) (*p. 4*)
June solstice (*p. 18*)
latitude (*p. 11*)
lithosphere (*p. 5*)
longitude (*p. 13*)
March equinox (*p. 21*)
meridian (*p. 13*)
North Pole (*p. 11*)
parallel (*p. 11*)
perihelion (*p. 17*)

physical geography (*p. 1*)
plane of the ecliptic (*p. 17*)
plane of the equator (*p. 10*)
polarity (parallelism) of the rotation axis (*p. 18*)
prime meridian (*p. 13*)
September equinox (*p. 19*)
solar altitude (*p. 18*)
South Pole (*p. 11*)
Tropic of Cancer (*p. 18*)
Tropic of Capricorn (*p. 19*)
Universal Time Coordinated (UTC) (*p. 23*)

Study Questions for Key Concepts

After studying this chapter, you should be able to answer the following questions:

Geography as a Field of Learning (p. 1)
1. Contrast physical geography and cultural geography.

The Environmental Spheres (p. 5)
2. Identify and briefly describe the four environmental spheres.

The Solar System (p. 6)
3. In what ways do the inner and outer planets of our solar system differ from each other?

The Size and Shape of Earth (p. 9)
4. Compare the size of Earth to that of its surface features and atmosphere.
5. Is the Earth perfectly spherical? Explain.

The Geographic Grid (p. 10)
6. Define and explain the following terms associated with latitude and longitude: *parallel, meridian, equator, prime meridian.*
7. What is a *great circle*? A *small circle*? Provide examples of both.
8. Latitude ranges from _____° to _____°, while longitude ranges from _____° to _____°.
9. Using a world map or globe, estimate the latitude and longitude of both New York City and Sydney, Australia. Be sure to specify if these locations are north or south latitude, and east or west longitude.

Earth–Sun Relations (p. 15)
10. Describe and explain the four factors in Earth–Sun relations associated with the change of seasons: *rotation, revolution* around the Sun, *inclination of Earth's axis,* and *polarity of Earth's axis.*
11. Does the *plane of the ecliptic* coincide with the *plane of the equator*? Explain.
12. On which day of the year is Earth closest to the Sun? Farthest from the Sun?

The Annual March of the Seasons (p. 18)
13. Beginning with the March equinox, describe the changing latitude of the vertical rays of the Sun throughout the year.

14. For the equator, describe the relative angle of the noon Sun above the horizon (the *solar altitude*) and the length of day on the following days of the year: March equinox, June solstice, September equinox, and December solstice.
15. For the midlatitudes of the Northern Hemisphere, describe the relative angle of the noon Sun above the horizon and the length of day on the following days of the year: March equinox, June solstice, September equinox, and December solstice.
16. For the North Pole, describe the relative angle of the noon Sun above the horizon and the length of day on the following days of the year: March equinox, June solstice, September equinox, and December solstice.
17. In terms of the change of seasons, explain the significance of the *Tropic of Cancer,* the *Tropic of Capricorn,* the *Arctic Circle,* and the *Antarctic Circle.*
18. What is the longest day of the year in the Northern Hemisphere? What is the longest day of the year in the Southern Hemisphere?
19. What would be the effect on the annual march of the seasons if Earth's axis was not inclined relative to the plane of the ecliptic?

Telling Time (p. 23)
20. What happens to the hour when crossing a time zone moving from west to east?
21. What happens to the day when crossing the international date line moving from east to west?
22. Using the map of North American time zones (Figure 1-30) for reference, if it is 5:00 P.M. standard time on Thursday in New York City, what is the day and time in Los Angeles?
23. Using the map of world time zones (Figure 1-29) for reference, if it is 5:00 P.M. standard time on Thursday in New York City, what is the day and time in Rome, Italy?

Additional Resources

Books:

Blaise, Clark. *Time Lord: Sir Sanford Fleming and the Creation of Standard Time.* New York: Pantheon Books, 2000.

Gregory, K.J. *The Changing Nature of Physical Geography.* New York: Oxford University Press, 2000.

Smithson, Peter, Ken Addison, and Ken Atkinson. *Fundamentals of the Physical Environment,* 3rd ed. New York: Routledge, 2002.

Sobel, Dava. *Longitude.* New York: Walker and Company, 1995.

Internet Sites:
The Earth Observatory
http://earthobservatory.nasa.gov/
The Earth Observatory is National Aeronautics and Space Administration's (NASA's) Internet site that provides information and images of Earth.
U.S. Naval Observatory Astronomical Applications Department
http://aa.usno.navy.mil/
This site provides astronomical data such as sunrise and sunset times.

2
Portraying Earth

The surface of Earth is the focus of the geographer's interest. The enormity and complexity of this surface would be difficult to comprehend and analyze without tools and equipment to aid in systematizing and organizing the varied data. Although many kinds of tools are used in geographic studies, the most important and universal are maps because the mapping of any geographic feature is normally essential to understanding the spatial distributions and relationships of that feature. Our concern in this chapter is the usefulness of maps to geographers. In some cases, geographers deal with maps as an end in themselves, but more often than not maps serve geographers as a means to some end. This book is a case in point. It contains numerous maps of various kinds, each inserted in the book to further your understanding of some fact, concept, or relationship. In each case, the map serves as a pedagogic device to enhance learning.

This chapter outlines the positive and negative attributes of maps and other tools for portraying any portion of Earth. Our purpose in the chapter is twofold:

1. To describe the basic characteristics of maps, including their capabilities and limitations.
2. To describe the various ways a landscape can be portrayed—through map projections, globes, photographs, and remotely sensed imagery (Figure 2-1).

▲ **Figure 2-1** Earth is indeed a sphere. This is a composite of thousands of images made by the National Oceanographic and Atmospheric Administration (NOAA) series of weather satellites. *(Tom Van Sant/Geosphere Project, Santa Monica Science Photo Library/Photo Researchers, Inc.)*

The Nature of Maps

A **map** is a two-dimensional representation of Earth and the spatial distribution of selected phenomena—normally components of a landscape. In essence, a map is a scaled drawing of a portion of a landscape representing the area at a reduced scale and showing only selected data. A map serves as a surrogate (a substitute) for any surface we wish to portray or study. Although any surface can be mapped—the lunar surface, for instance, or that of Mars—all the maps we are concerned with in this book portray portions of Earth's surface.

The basic attribute of maps is their ability to show distance, direction, size, and shape in their horizontal (that is to say, two-dimensional) spatial relationships. In addition to these fundamental graphic data, most maps show other kinds of information as well. Maps nearly always have a special purpose, and that purpose is usually to show the distribution of one or more phenomena (Figure 2-2). Thus, a map may be designed to show

street patterns, the distribution of Tasmanians, the ratio of sunshine to cloud, the number of earthworms per cubic meter of soil, or any of an infinite number of other facts or combinations of facts. Because they depict graphically "what is where" and because they are often helpful in providing clues as to "why" such a distribution occurs, maps are indispensable tools for geographers.

Even so, it is important to realize that maps have their limitations. First of all, no map is perfectly accurate. Although most people understand that not everything we might read in a book, in a newspaper, or on the Internet is necessarily valid (thus the somewhat cynical adage, "Don't believe everything you read"), these same people may uncritically accept all information portrayed on a map as being true. Most people have insufficient experience with maps to view them with the same critical eye as they have for the written word. Nevertheless, the inaccuracy of maps is ubiquitous simply because it is impossible to portray the curved surface of Earth on a flat piece of paper without distortion. The extent to which this geometric impossibility becomes a problem when interpreting a map depends especially on two related variables: how much of Earth is being shown on a map (for example, these distortions are always significant on a world map, but less significant in a map showing a very limited region of Earth), and the *scale* of the map—the topic we turn to next.

◀ Terra satellite image of Florida in 2003. *(MODIS/NASA.)*

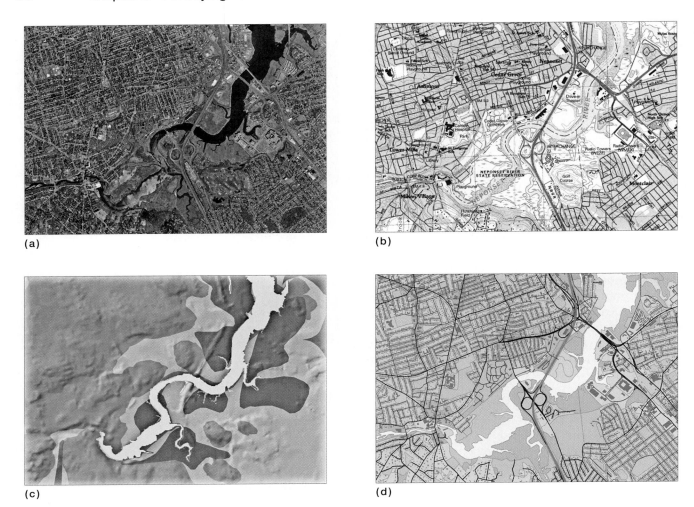

(a)

(b)

(c)

(d)

▲ **Figure 2-2**   Sampler of maps of the Boston-Quincy-Milton area in Massachusetts at an original scale of 1:25,000. **(a)** Orthophoto map. **(b)** Topographic map. **(c)** Geologic map. **(d)** Road map. *(ESRI.)*

Map Scale

A map is always smaller than the portion of Earth's surface it represents, and so any user who is to understand the areal relationships (distances or relative sizes, for example) depicted on that map must know how to use a **map scale**. The scale of a map gives the relationship between length measured on the map and the corresponding actual distance on the ground. Knowing the scale of a map makes it possible to measure distance, determine area, and compare sizes.

Scale can never be represented with perfect accuracy on a map because of the impossibility of rendering the curve of a sphere on the flatness of a sheet of paper without distortion. Therefore, a map scale cannot be constant (in other words, the same) over the entire map. If the map is of a small area, the scale is so nearly perfect that it can be accepted uncritically throughout the map. If the map represents either a large portion or Earth's entire surface, however, there may be enormous scale variations because of the significant distortions involved (such a map, for example, might need to list different scales for different latitudes). Thus, it is

important for us to understand the capabilities and recognize the limitations of different kinds of maps and maps at different scales.

Scale Types

There are several ways to portray scale on a map, but only three are widely used: the graphic method, the fractional method, and the word method (Figure 2-3).

Graphic Map Scales   A **graphic scale** uses a line marked off in graduated distances. To determine the distance between two points on Earth's surface, one measures the distance between the points on the map and compares that length with a measurement along the line of the graphic scale belonging to the map. The advantage of a graphic scale is its simplicity: you determine approximate distances on the surface of Earth by measuring them directly on the map— graphic scales are commonly used by motorists to estimate travel distances on a road map. Moreover, a graphic scale remains correct when a map is reproduced in a larger or smaller size because the

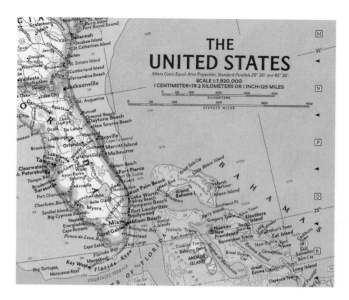

▲ **Figure 2-3** All three expressions of scale are shown on this map. Included are a fractional scale (1:7,920,000), a word scale (1 centimeter = 79.2 kilometers or 1 inch = 125 miles), and a graphic scale (shown in both miles and kilometers). *(Courtesy of National Geographic Society.)*

length of the graphic scale line is changed precisely as the map size is changed.

Fractional Map Scales   A **fractional scale** compares map distance with ground distance by proportional numbers expressed as a fraction or ratio called a **representative fraction**. For example, a common fractional scale uses the representative fraction 1/63,360, usually expressed as the ratio 1:63,360. This notation means that one unit of distance on the map represents an actual distance of 63,360 of the same units on the ground. Thus, one millimeter on the map represents an actual distance of 63,360 millimeters on the ground, while one inch on the map represents an actual distance of 63,360 inches on the ground, and so forth.

Verbal Map Scales   A **verbal scale** (or *word scale*) states in words the ratio of the map scale length to the actual distance on Earth's surface, such as "five centimeters to 10 kilometers" or "one inch to five miles." A verbal scale is simply a mathematical manipulation of the fractional scale. For example: There are 63,360 inches in one mile, so on a map with a fractional scale of 1:63,360, we can say that "one inch represents one mile."

Large and Small Map Scales

The adjectives *large* and *small* are comparative rather than absolute. In other words, scales are "large" or "small" only in comparison with other scales. A **large-scale map** is one that has a relatively large representative fraction, which means that the denominator is small. Thus, 1/10,000 is a larger value than, say, 1/1,000,000, and so a scale of 1:10,000 is large in comparison with one

of 1:1,000,000; consequently, a map at a scale of 1:10,000 is called a large-scale map. Such a map portrays only a small portion of Earth's surface but portrays it in considerable detail. For example, if this page were covered with a map having a scale of 1:10,000, it would be able to show just a small part of a single city, but that part would be rendered in great detail.

A **small-scale map** has a small representative fraction—in other words, one having a large denominator. A map having a scale of 1:10,000,000 is classified as a small-scale map. If it were covered with a map of that scale, this page would be able to portray about one-third of the United States, but only in limited detail.

Figure 2-4 compares various scales and gives some idea of what is visible with each.

Map Essentials

Maps come in an infinite variety of sizes and styles and serve a limitless diversity of purposes. Some are general reference maps—a map of the world, say, or one of the western coast of Africa. Others are *thematic maps*, which means that they show the location or distribution of particular phenomena, as shown in Figure 2-5. Regardless of type, however, every map must contain a few basic components to facilitate their use. Omission of any of these essential components decreases the clarity of the map and makes it more difficult to interpret.

Title   This should be a brief summary of the map's content or purpose. It should identify the area covered and provide some indication of content, such as "Road Map of Kenya," "River Discharge in Northern Europe," or "Seattle: Shopping Centers and Transit Lines."

Date   This should indicate the time span over which the information was collected. In addition, some maps also give the date of publication of the map. Most maps depict conditions or patterns that are temporary or even momentary. For a map to be meaningful, therefore, the reader must be informed when the data were gathered, as this information indicates how timely or out of date the map is.

Legend   Most maps use symbols, colors, shadings, or other devices to represent features or the amount, degree, or proportion of some quantity. Some symbols are self-explanatory, but it is usually necessary to include a legend box in a corner of the map to explain the symbolization.

Scale   Any map that serves as more than a pictogram must be drawn to scale, at least approximately. A graphic, verbal, or fractional scale is therefore necessary.

Direction   Direction is normally shown on a map by means of the geographic grid, with meridians running

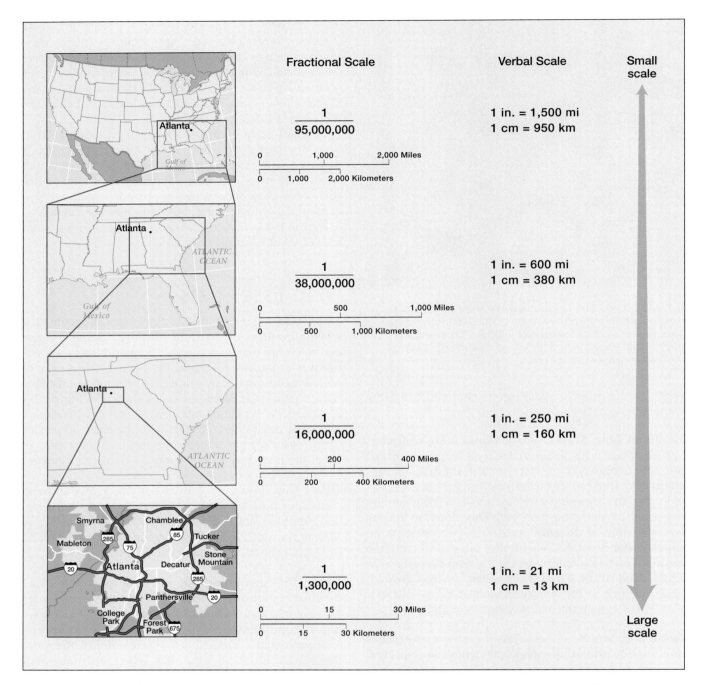

Fractional Scale	Verbal Scale	Small scale

$$\frac{1}{95,000,000}$$

1 in. = 1,500 mi
1 cm = 950 km

0   1,000   2,000 Miles

0   1,000   2,000 Kilometers

$$\frac{1}{38,000,000}$$

1 in. = 600 mi
1 cm = 380 km

0   500   1,000 Miles

0   500   1,000 Kilometers

$$\frac{1}{16,000,000}$$

1 in. = 250 mi
1 cm = 160 km

0   200   400 Miles

0   200   400 Kilometers

$$\frac{1}{1,300,000}$$

1 in. = 21 mi
1 cm = 13 km

0   15   30 Miles

0   15   30 Kilometers

Large scale

▲ **Figure 2-4** Comparisons of distance and area at various map scales. A small-scale map portrays a large part of Earth's surface but depicts only the most salient features, whereas a large-scale map shows only a small part of the surface but in considerably more detail.

north to south and parallels running east to west across the map. If no grid is shown, direction may be indicated by a straight arrow pointing northward, which is called a *north arrow*. A north arrow is aligned with the meridians and thus points toward the north geographic pole.

Location As we learned in Chapter 1, the standard system for locating places on a map is a geographic grid showing latitude and longitude by means of parallels and meridians. Other grid systems are sometimes used for specifying locations because the latitude/longitude

system, with its angular subdivisions, is cumbersome to use. These alternative systems are devised like the x- and y-coordinates of a graph. Some maps display more than one coordinate system.

Data Source For most thematic maps, it is useful to indicate the source of the data.

Projection Type On many maps, particularly small-scale ones, the type of map projection is indicated (map projections are discussed later in this chapter).

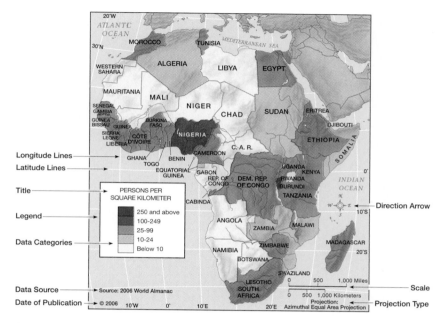

▲ **Figure 2-5**   A typical thematic map containing all the essentials.

The Role of Globes

For properly portraying the sphericity of Earth, there is no substitute for a model globe (Figure 2-6). If manufactured carefully, a globe can be an accurate representation of the shape of our planet. The only thing changed in the transition from the immensity of Earth to the manageable proportions of a model globe is size. A globe is capable of maintaining the correct geometric relationships of meridian to parallel, of equator to pole, of continents to oceans. It can show comparative distances, comparative sizes, and accurate directions. It can represent, essentially without distortion, the spatial relationships of the features of Earth's surface.

A globe is not without disadvantages, however. For one thing, only half of it can be viewed at one time, and the periphery of the visible half is not easy to see. Moreover, almost any globe must be constructed at a very small scale, which means that it is incapable of portraying much detail. The principal problem with a globe, then, is that it is too cumbersome for almost any use other than classroom study or quiet contemplation. Because maps are much more portable and versatile than globes, there are literally billions of maps in use over the world, whereas globes are extremely limited both in number and variety.

Map Projections

The challenge to the *cartographer* (mapmaker) is to try to combine the geometric exactness of a globe with the convenience of a flat map. This melding has been attempted for many centuries, and further refinements continue to be made. The fundamental problem is always the same: to transfer data from a spherical surface to a flat piece of paper with a minimum of distortion.

A **map projection** is a system whereby the spherical surface of Earth is transformed to display it on a flat surface. The basic principle of map projection is direct and simple. Imagine a transparent globe on which are drawn meridians, parallels, and continental boundaries; also imagine a light bulb in the center of this globe. A piece of paper, either held flat or rolled into some shape such as a cylinder or cone, is placed over the globe as in Figures 2-7, 2-8, and 2-9. When the bulb is lighted, all the lines on the globe are projected outward

▲ **Figure 2-6**   A model globe provides a splendid broad representation of Earth at a very small scale, but few details can be portrayed. *(1989 David Sailors/The Stock Market.)*

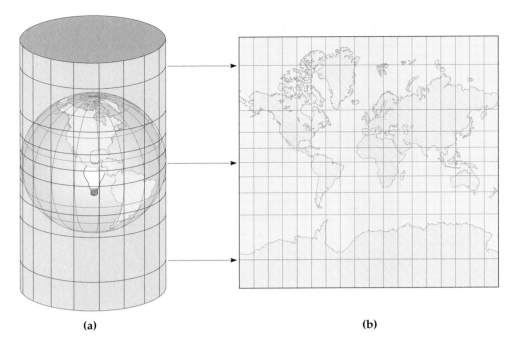

(a)   (b)

▲ **Figure 2-7   (a)** The origin of a cylindrical projection, as illustrated by a globe with a light in its center, projecting images onto an adjacent cylinder. **(b)** The resulting map is called a cylindrical projection.

onto the paper. These lines are then sketched on the paper. When the paper is laid out flat, a map projection has been produced. (Very few map projections have ever been constructed by such an actual optical projection from a globe onto a piece of paper—nearly all are derived by mathematical computation.)

Because a piece of paper cannot be closely fitted to a sphere without wrinkling or tearing, no matter how the transformation is done, data from a globe (parallels, meridians, continental boundaries, and so forth) cannot be transferred to a map without distortion of shape, relative area, distance, and/or direction. However, the cartographer can choose to control or reduce one or more of these distortions—although not all distortions

can be controlled on a single map. Cartographers often strive especially to maintain accuracy of either size or shape.

The Major Dilemma: Equivalence versus Conformality

The cartographer wants any map to portray distances and directions accurately so that the sizes and shapes shown on the map are correct. However, such perfection is impossible, and so a compromise must be struck. Which to emphasize: size or shape? Which to sacrifice: shape or size? This is one of the central problems both

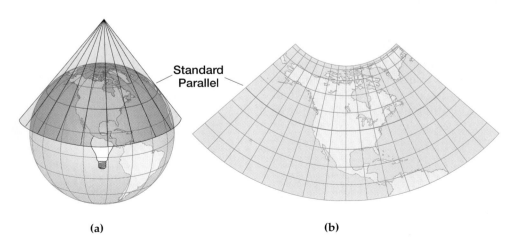

Standard Parallel

(a)   (b)

▲ **Figure 2-8   (a)** The origin of a conic projection, as illustrated by a globe with a light in its center, projecting images onto a cone. **(b)** The resulting map is called a conic projection.

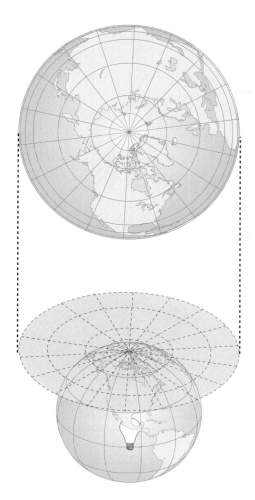

▲ **Figure 2-9** The origin of a plane projection as illustrated by a globe with a light in its center, projecting images onto an adjacent plane. The resulting map goes by various names: azimuthal projection, plane projection, or zenithal projection.

proper areal relationships. Most equivalent world maps, which are small-scale maps, therefore display disfigured shapes. For example, as Figure 2-10b shows, Greenland and Alaska are usually shown as more "squatty" than they actually are.

Conformality A **conformal projection** is one in which proper angular relationships are maintained so that the shape of something on the map is the same as its shape on Earth. It is impossible to depict true shapes for large areas such as a continent, but they can be approximated, and for small areas the true shape can be shown on a conformal map. All conformal projections have meridians and parallels crossing each other at right angles, just as they do on a globe.

The outstanding problem with conformal projections is that the size of an area must often be considerably distorted to depict the proper shape. Thus, the scale necessarily changes from one region to another. For example, a conformal map of the world normally greatly enlarges sizes in the higher latitudes. Figure 2-10a shows the conformal projection known as a *Mercator projection* (discussed in greater detail later in this chapter).

Except for maps of very small areas (in other words, large-scale maps), where both can be closely approximated, conformality and equivalence cannot be maintained on the same projection, and thus the art of mapmaking, like politics, is an art of compromise. For example, Figure 2-11 shows a *Robinson projection*, which is a compromise between equivalence and conformality that shows reasonably accurate shapes and has a reasonably constant scale, especially in the middle and lower latitudes. The Robinson projection is a popular choice as a general purpose classroom map.

As a rule of thumb, it can be stated that some projections are purely conformal, some are purely equivalent, none are both conformal and equivalent, and many are neither purely conformal nor purely equivalent but rather a compromise between the two.

in constructing and in choosing a map projection. The projection properties involved are called **equivalence** and **conformality** (Figure 2-10).

Equivalence In an **equivalent projection** (also called an **equal area projection**), the size ratio of any area on the map to the corresponding area on the ground is the same all over the map. To illustrate, suppose you have a world map before you and you place four dimes at different places (perhaps one on Brazil, one on Australia, one on Siberia, and one on South Africa). Calculate the area covered by each coin. If it is the same in all four cases, there is a good chance that the map is an equivalent projection—in other words, that there are equal areal relationships all over it.

Equivalent projections are very desirable because, with them, misleading impressions of size are avoided. (The world maps in this book are mostly equivalent projections because they are so useful in portraying distributions of the various geographic features we will be studying.) They are by no means perfect, however. Equivalence is difficult to achieve on small-scale maps because shapes must be sacrificed to maintain

Families of Map Projections

Because there is no possible way to avoid distortion completely, no map projection is perfect. More than a thousand types of map projections have been devised for one purpose or another. Most of them can be grouped into just a few families. Projections in the same family generally have similar properties and related distortion characteristics.

Cylindrical Projections

As Figure 2-7 shows, a **cylindrical projection** is obtained by mathematically "wrapping" the globe with a cylinder of paper in such a way that the paper touches

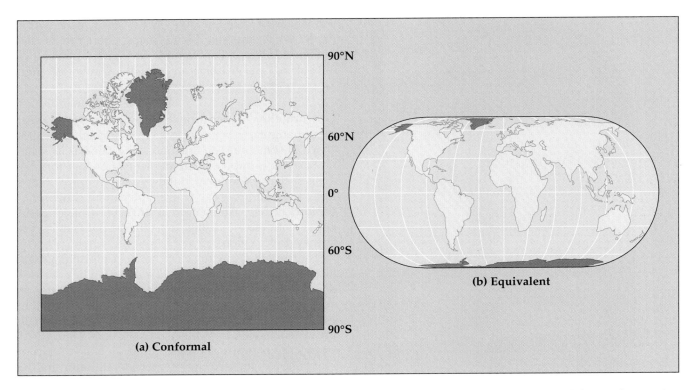

(b) Equivalent

(a) Conformal

▲ **Figure 2-10** It is particularly difficult to portray the whole world accurately on a map. Compare the sizes and shapes of Antarctica, Alaska, and Greenland in these examples. **(a)** A conformal projection (the *Mercator*) depicts accurate shapes, but the sizes are severely exaggerated. **(b)** An equivalent projection (the *Eckert*) is accurate with regard to size, but shapes are badly distorted.

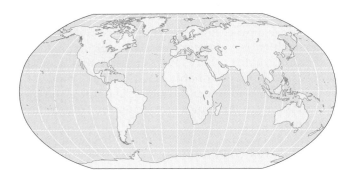

▲ **Figure 2-11** Many world maps are neither purely conformal nor purely equivalent, but a compromise between the two. One of the most popular compromises is the Robinson projection shown here.

the globe only at the globe's equator. We say that paper positioned this way is *tangent* to the globe at the equator, and the equator is called the *circle of tangency* (some cylindrical projections choose a circle of tangency other than the equator). The curved parallels and meridians of the globe then form a perfectly rectangular grid on the map. Having the equator as the tangency line produces a right-angled grid (meridians and parallels meet at right angles) on a rectangular map. There is no size distortion at the circle of tangency, but size distortion increases progressively with increasing distance from this circle, a characteristic clearly exemplified by the Mercator projection.

Mercator: The Most Famous Projection Although some map projections were devised centuries ago, there has been a continuing refining of projection techniques right up to the present day. Thus, it is remarkable that the most famous of all projections, the **Mercator projection**, originated in 1569 by a Flemish geographer and cartographer, is still in common usage today without significant modification (see Figure 2-10a).

Gerhardus Mercator produced some of the best maps and globes of his time. His place in history, however, is based largely on the fact that he developed a special-purpose projection that became inordinately popular for general-purpose use. The Mercator projection is essentially a navigational chart of the world designed to facilitate oceanic navigation.

The prime advantage of a Mercator map is that it shows *loxodromes* as straight lines. A **loxodrome**, also called a **rhumb line**, is a curve on the surface of a sphere that crosses all meridians at the same angle and represents a line of constant compass direction. A navigator first plots the shortest distance between origin and destination on a map projection in which great circles are shown as straight lines, as shown in Figure 2-12 (*great circle routes* are discussed in Chapter 1), and then transfers that route to a Mercator projection with straight-line loxodromes. This procedure allows the navigator to generally follow a great circle route by simply making periodic changes in the compass course of the airplane or ship. Today, of course, these calculations are all done by computer.

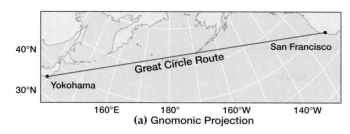

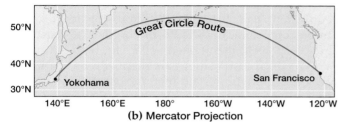

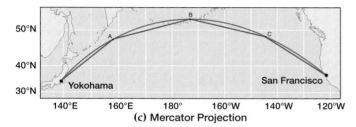

▲ **Figure 2-12** The prime virtue of the Mercator projection lies in is usefulness for straight-line navigation. **(a)** The shortest distance between two locations—here San Francisco and Yokohama—can be plotted on a *gnomonic* projection (on which great circles are shown as straight lines). **(b)** The great circle route plotted in (a) can be transferred to a Mercator projection with mathematical precision. **(c)** On the Mercator projection, straight-line loxodromes can then be substituted for the curved great circle. The loxodromes allow the navigator to maintain constant compass headings over small distances while still approximating the curve of the great circle. The navigator can plot a straight-line course from Yokohama to A, then a new straight-line course from A to B, and so on across the Pacific to San Francisco.

A Mercator map is relatively undistorted in the low latitudes. However, because this is a conformal projection, size distortion increases rapidly in the middle and high latitudes. Because the projection method causes the meridians to appear as parallel lines rather than lines that converge at the poles, there is extreme east–west distortion in the higher latitudes. And, in order to maintain conformality, Mercator compensated for the east–west stretching by spacing the parallels of latitude increasingly farther apart so that north–south stretching occurs at the same rate. This procedure allowed shapes to be approximated with reasonable accuracy, but at great expense to proper size relationships. Area is distorted by 4 times at the 60th parallel of latitude and by 36 times at the 80th parallel. If the North Pole were shown on a Mercator projection, it would be a line as long as the equator rather than a single point.

It is clear then that the Mercator projection is excellent for straight-line navigation but not for most other uses.

Despite the obvious flaws associated with areal distortion in the high latitudes, Mercator projections have been widely used in American classrooms and atlases. Indeed, several generations of American students have passed through school with their principal view of the world provided by a Mercator map. This has created many misconceptions, not the least of which is confusion about the relative sizes of high-latitude landmasses. For example, on a Mercator projection, the island of Greenland appears to be as large as or larger than Africa, Australia, and South America. In actuality, however, Africa is 14 times larger than Greenland, South America is 9 times larger, and Australia is 3.5 times larger.

The Mercator projection was devised several centuries ago for a specific purpose, and it still serves that purpose well. Its fame, however, is significantly due to its misuse.

Plane Projections

A **plane projection** (also called with an *azimuthal projection* or a *zenithal projection*) is obtained by projecting the markings of a center-lit globe onto a flat piece of paper that is tangent to the globe at some point. Such a projection is shown in Figure 2-9. The point of tangency can be any spot on the globe, but it is usually either the North or South Pole or some point on the equator. There is no distortion immediately around the point of tangency, but distortion increases progressively away from this point.

No more than one hemisphere can be displayed with any success on a plane projection. These projections may often show a view similar to the one one gets when looking at a globe in the classroom and the same view an astronaut sees from distant space (Figure 2-13). This half-view-only characteristic can be a drawback, of course, just as it is with a globe, although plane projections can be useful for focusing attention on a specific region.

Conic Projections

As Figure 2-8 shows, a **conic projection** is obtained by projecting the markings of a center-lit globe onto a cone wrapped tangent to, or intersecting, a portion of the globe. Normally the apex of the cone is positioned above a pole, which means that the circle of tangency coincides with a parallel. This parallel then becomes the principal parallel of the projection; distortion is least in its vicinity and increases progressively as one moves away from it. Consequently, conic projections are best suited for regions of east–west orientation in the middle latitudes, being particularly useful for maps of the United States, Europe, or China.

It is impractical to use conic projections for more than one-fourth of Earth's surface (a semihemisphere), and they are particularly well adapted for mapping relatively small areas, such as a state or county.

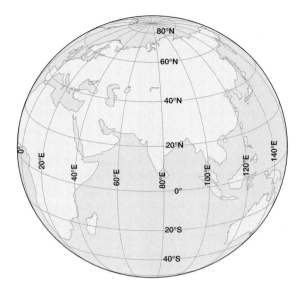

▲ **Figure 2-13**   An orthographic plane projection.

Pseudocylindrical Projections

A **pseudocylindrical projection** (also called an *elliptical* or *oval projection*) is a roughly football-shaped map, usually of the entire world (see Figures 2-10b and 2-11), although sometimes only the central section of a pseudocylindrical projection is used for maps of lesser areas.

In most pseudocylindrical projections, a central parallel (usually the equator) and a central meridian (often the prime meridian) cross at right angles in the middle of the map, which is a point of no distortion; distortion in size and shape normally increases progressively as one moves away from this point in any direction. All of the other parallels are then drawn parallel to the central one. All the other meridians are drawn so that all of them begin at a common point at the top of the oval

and end at a common point at the bottom; the result, of course, is that all meridians except the central one must be drawn as curved lines.

Interrupted Projections   One technique used with pseudocylindrical projections to minimize distortion of the continents is to "interrupt" oceanic regions— *Goode's interrupted homolosine projection* (Figure 2-14) is a popular example of this. Goode's projection is equivalent, and, although it is impossible for this map to be conformal, the shapes of continental coastlines are very well maintained, even in high latitudes. When global distributions are mapped, the continents are often more important than the oceans, and yet the oceans would occupy most of the map space in a normal projection. Hence, the projection can be interrupted in the Pacific, Atlantic, and Indian oceans and can be based on central meridians that pass through each major landmass. With no land area far from a central meridian, shape and size distortion is greatly decreased. The interruption of the projection in the oceans creates a void in the map, one that is simply filled with information not part of the map. The result is that some of the oceanic portions of the map are torn apart and otherwise distorted, but the major landmasses are shown with relatively little distortion, and the overall accuracy of the distribution pattern is enhanced. You'll see that many of the maps used in this book employ variations of Goode's interrupted projection.

Computer Cartography

Cartographers have been at work since the days of the early Egyptians, but it is only in the last half century, with the introduction of computers in the 1950s that their technology has advanced beyond manual drawing

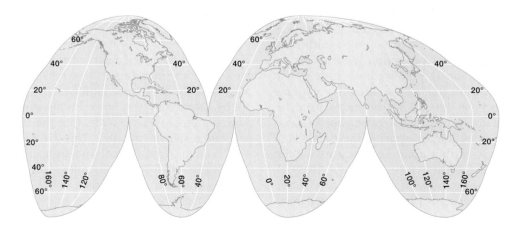

▲ **Figure 2-14**   An interrupted projection of the world. The purpose of the interruptions is to portray certain areas (usually continents) more accurately, at the expense of portions of the map (usually oceans) that are not important to the map's theme. The map shown here is a Goode's interrupted homolosine equal-area projection. A variation of this projection is used for many maps in this book.

on a piece of paper. Computers have provided incredible improvements in speed and data handling ability, and computer cartography has become a prominent high-technology field.

One of the first widely used software packages for automated cartography was *symap*, developed in 1965. It allowed the cartographer to input map boundaries along with data values. The computer then interpolated values of the mapped variable and produced a distribution map. Since then there have been remarkable improvements in desktop and mainframe computers, making possible sophisticated, high-quality maps produced via relatively inexpensive and widely available software (including *GIS* software packages, discussed later in this chapter). Not only does the computer greatly reduce the time involved in map production, it also allows the cartographer to examine alternative map layouts simply by changing details on the monitor. As an example of how computer-generated maps have improved since the days of symap, just look at any of the maps in this book; all of them were made with desktop computers.

Isolines

Geographers employ a variety of cartographic devices to display data on maps. One of the most widespread devices for portraying the spatial distribution of some phenomenon is the **isoline** (from the Greek *isos*, "equal"), which is also called by a variety of related terms, such as *isarithm*, *isogram*, *isopleth*, and *isometric line*, all of which can be considered as synonymous for our purposes. The word isoline is a generic term that refers to any line that joins points of equal value of something. More than 100 kinds of isolines have been identified by name, ranging from *isoamplitude* (used to describe radio waves) to *isovapor* (water vapor content of the air).

Some isolines represent tangible surfaces, such as the **elevation contour** lines on a topographic map (Figure 2-15). Most, however, signify such intangible features as temperature and precipitation, and some express relative values such as ratios or proportions (Figure 2-16). Only a few types of isolines are important in an introductory physical geography course:

- *Elevation contour line*—a line joining points of equal elevation (see *Focus: Topographic Maps* in this chapter and Appendix II for a description of U.S. Geological Survey topographic maps)
- *Isotherm*—a line joining points of equal temperature
- *Isobar*—a line joining points of equal atmospheric pressure
- *Isohyet*—a line joining points of equal quantities of precipitation (*hyeto* is from the Greek, meaning "rain")
- *Isogonic line*—a line joining points of equal magnetic declination

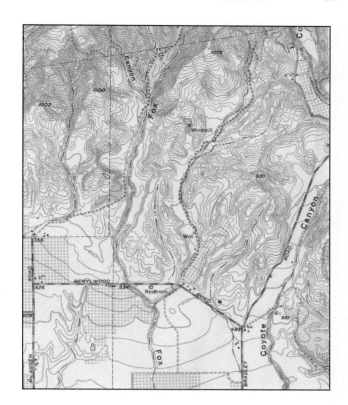

▲ **Figure 2-15**   This portion of a typical United States Geological Survey topographic map quadrangle illustrates the use of contour lines. This is a section of the Santa Paula, California, quadrangle. (The map scale is 1:62,500; the contour interval is 20 feet [7 meters].) *(U.S. Geological Survey, U.S. Department of the Interior.)*

To construct an isoline, it is always necessary to estimate values that are not available. As a simple example, Figure 2-17 illustrates the basic steps in constructing an isoline map. Each dot in Figure 2-17a represents a data collection station, and the number next to each dot is the value recorded at that station. (These data could be values of any variable—temperature, pressure, elevation above sea level, or anything else.) Suppose we want to draw isolines that connect all the points having a value of 140. These points are located by interpolating between two recorded values. For example, at the top left are points labeled 137 and 142. The 140 isoline will fall between these two points. At the bottom left, the 140 isoline will fall between the points 138 and 149. Once all of the 140-bracketing pairs have been identified, the 140 points are joined as shown in Figure 2-17b. The line is the 140 isoline. In Figure 2-17c, the interpolation process is repeated for other isolines, and in Figure 2-17d shading is added to clarify the pattern.

The basic characteristics of isolines are as follows:

1. They are always closed lines; that is, they have no ends. On a map, of course, an isoline is likely to extend beyond the edge, and when that happens, the closure is not seen. (This absence of closure is seen with all the isolines in Figure 2-17.)

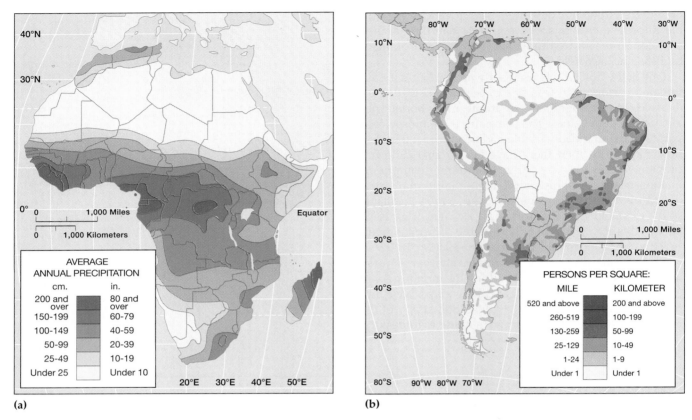

(a)

(b)

▲ **Figure 2-16** Isolines can be used to show the spatial variation of some phenomenon: **(a)** intangible features, such as in this map that shows average annual precipitation for the continent of Africa (on this map the areas between isolines have been shaded to clarify the pattern); **(b)** ratios or proportions, such as in this map that displays the population density of South America in terms of persons per square kilometer or square mile.

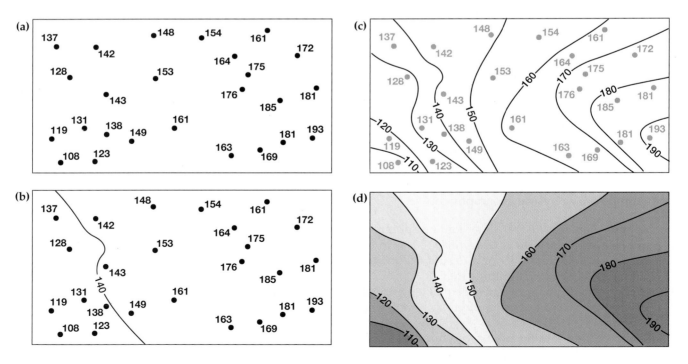

▲ **Figure 2-17** Drawing isolines. **(a)** Each dot represents a measuring station, and the number next to each dot is the quantity measured or calculated at that station. **(b)** The approximate location of one or more critical isolines (in this case the value of 140) is interpolated and drawn. **(c)** The other isolines at 10-unit intervals are interpolated and drawn. **(d)** Shading is added for clarity.

FOCUS Topographic Maps

Mapping agencies such as the U.S. Geological Survey produce many different kinds of maps. Among the most useful to geographers are topographic maps, which convey both human-built features such as roads and buildings and natural features such as rivers, glaciers, and areas of forest cover. Topographic maps also depict the topography of a landscape with elevation contour lines (Figure 2-A). From these two-dimensional maps, it is possible to envision the three-dimensional topography, making "topo" maps especially useful when studying landform patterns. A complete description of topographic map symbols and rules for interpreting elevation contour lines is found in Appendix II.

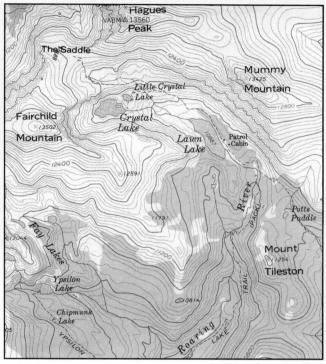

▲ **Figure 2-A**   Portrayal of terrain by means of elevation contour lines. Here is a photo of Hagues Peak and Mummy Mountain in Colorado's Rocky Mountain National Park *(Tom L. McKnight photo)* along with a standard topographic map of the same area. Where the contours are close together, the slope is steep; where the lines are far apart, the slope is gentle. (The map scale is 1:125,000; the contour interval is 80 feet [27 meters].) *(U.S. Geological Survey, U.S. Department of the Interior.)*

2. Because they represent gradations in quantity, isolines can never touch or cross one another except under rare and unusual circumstances.

3. The numerical difference between one isoline and the next is called the *interval*. Although intervals can be varied according to the wishes of the map-maker, it is normally more useful to maintain a constant interval all over a given map.

4. Isolines close together indicate a steep gradient (in other words, a rapid change); isolines far apart indicate a gentle gradient.

Edmund Halley (1656–1742), an English astronomer and cartographer (for whom Halley's Comet is named), was not the first person to use isolines, but in 1700 he produced a map that was apparently the first published map to have isolines. This map showed isogonic lines in the Atlantic Ocean. Isoline maps are now commonplace and are very useful to geographers even though an isoline is an artificial construct—that is, it does not occur in nature. For instance, an isoline map can reveal spatial relationships that might otherwise go undetected. Patterns that are too large, too abstract, or too detailed for ordinary comprehension are often significantly clarified by the use of isolines.

The Global Positioning System

The **global positioning system (GPS)** is a satellite-based system for determining accurate positions on or near Earth's surface. It was developed in the 1970s and 1980s by the U.S. Department of Defense to aid in navigating aircraft, guiding missiles, and controlling ground troops.

The system is based on a network of 24 high-altitude satellites configured so that a minimum of four are in view of any position on Earth. Each satellite continuously transmits both identification and positioning information that can be picked up by receivers on Earth (Figure 2-18). The distance between a given receiver and each member in a group of four (or more) satellites is calculated by comparing clocks stored in both units. Because four satellites are used, it is possible to calculate the three-dimensional coordinates of the receiver's position. The system already has accuracy greater than that of the best base maps. Even the simplest GPS units determine position within 10 meters (33 feet).

The first receivers were the size of a file cabinet, but continued technological improvement has reduced them to the size of a paperback book, and they are still shrinking (Figure 2-19). The cost is also diminishing rapidly: at the time of this writing, a good receiver sells for less than $100.

In 1983, President Ronald Reagan made access to the system free to the public, and astounding commercial growth has resulted. It is anticipated that eventually practically everything that moves in our society—airplane, truck, train, car, bus, ship, cell phone—will be equipped with a GPS receiver. Meanwhile, GPS has been employed in earthquake forecasting, ocean floor mapping, volcano monitoring, and a variety of mapping projects. For example, recognizing that GPS is a relatively inexpensive way of collecting data, the Federal Emergency Management Agency (FEMA) has used the system for damage assessment following such natural disasters as floods and hurricanes.

GPS technology came into its own following the World Trade Center disaster of September 11, 2001. An application was developed that enabled firefighters and other disaster workers to identify and bar code items found in the enormous heaps of rubble at Ground Zero, along with the time, date, and GPS location. Prior to this solution, it required three to five minutes to catalog each item, and workers had to guess where they were in the grid system. Handheld GPS equipment allowed workers to catalog each item in about 30 seconds, with greatly increased accuracy.

Commercial applications now far outnumber military uses of the system. The sale of GPS services brings in about $10 billion annually into the U.S. economy. What was born as a military system has become a national economic resource.

In part because of the great accuracy of even inexpensive GPS units, latitude and longitude are increasingly being reported in decimal form, such as 94°45.5′ W, rather than in its traditional form of 94°45′30″ W. Even

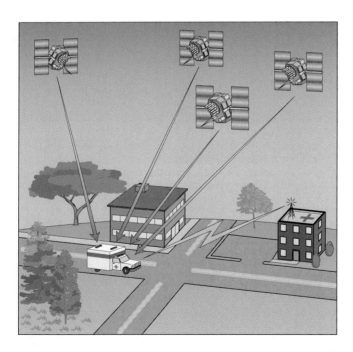

▲ **Figure 2-18** Global positioning system (GPS) satellites circling 17,700 kilometers (11,000 miles) above Earth broadcast signals that are picked up by the receiver in an ambulance and used to pinpoint the location of the ambulance at any moment. A transmitter in the ambulance then sends this location information to a dispatch center, and all other ambulances in the rescue system likewise receive and transmit their location information. Knowing the location of all ambulances at any given moment, the dispatcher is able to route the closest available vehicle to each emergency and then direct that vehicle to the nearest appropriate health facility.

▲ **Figure 2-19** A handheld GPS receiver. It receives signals sent by the network of global positioning system satellites, calculating its position anywhere in the world to within 10 meters (33 feet). *(Ken M. Johns/Photo Researchers, Inc.)*

FOCUS Stereo Aerial Photographs

The workhorse of *photogrammetry* for many years has been black-and-white vertical aerial photographs taken automatically at regular spatial intervals, where each position from which a photograph is taken is called either an *air station* or a *camera station*. The stations are usually close enough together to allow a considerable overlap in neighboring photographs. For instance, Figure 2-B is a diagram of two vertical aerial photographs being taken sequentially at camera stations 1 and 2. Because of the distance between these two points, the resulting photographs overlap by 60 percent in the direction of flight. Figure 2-C shows a sample of photographs taken in this way. When properly aligned, this overlap produces a three-dimensional appearance.

With a *stereoscope* (a binocular optical instrument) and two overlapping photographs, an observer can view an object simultaneously from two perspectives to obtain the mental impression of a three-dimensional model. Vertical distance (height) can be measured from the model, and contours can be plotted. When this information is then combined with two-dimensional measurements obtained with an interpreter's ruler of known scale, the length, breadth, and height of features can readily be ascertained.

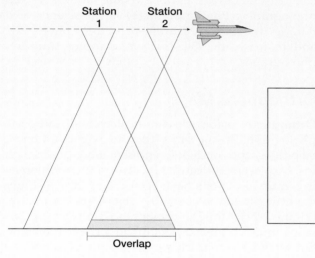

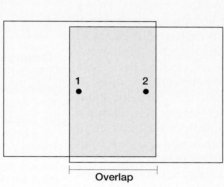

◀ **Figure 2-B** To create overlapping aerial vertical photographs, one photograph is taken when the plane is at the position labeled Station 1, and a second is taken when the plane is at the position labeled Station 2. Because of the distance between these two stations, the photographs overlap by about 60 percent.

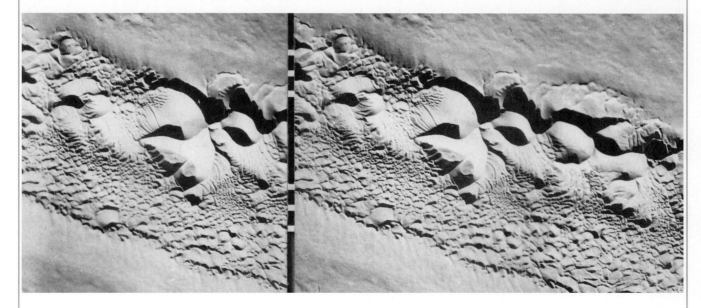

▲ **Figure 2-C** Stereo aerial photographs of star sand dunes in the Erg Er Raoui, Algeria. *(U.S. Air Force.)*

the simplest handheld GPS units can provide location co-ordinates with a resolution of 0.01′ (1/100th minute) or even 0.001′ (1/1000th minute) of latitude and longitude (for reference, a difference in latitude of 0.001′ represents a distance of less than two meters [about six feet]).

Remote Sensing

Throughout most of history, maps have been the only tools available to depict anything more than a tiny portion of Earth's surface with any degree of accuracy. However, the sophisticated technology developed in recent years permits precision recording instruments to operate from high-altitude vantage points, providing a remarkable new set of tools for the study of Earth. **Remote sensing**, broadly considered, is any measurement or acquisition of information by a recording device that is not in physical contact with the object under study—in this case, Earth's surface.

The use of satellites is revolutionizing the remote sensing industry. Since the Russians launched *Sputnik* in 1957, imaging satellites have become increasingly sophisticated and versatile. We now have hundreds of satellites from dozens of countries perched high in the atmosphere where they either are circling Earth in a "low" orbit (altitude 20,000 kilometers [12,400 miles] or less) or in a lofty *geosynchronous orbit* (usually about 36,000 kilometers [22,400 miles] high) that allows a satellite to remain over the same spot on Earth at all times. These satellites gather data and produce images that provide communications, global positioning, weather data, and a variety of other information for a plethora of commercial and military applications.

Aerial Photographs

Aerial photography was almost the only form of remote sensing used for geographic purposes until the last few decades. An **aerial photograph** is one taken from an elevated platform, such as a balloon, airplane, or rocket. The earliest aerial photographs were taken from balloons in France in 1858 and in the United States in 1860. A major problem with photographs taken from balloons—the lack of control of the platform—was overcome in the early twentieth century by the development of airplanes. By World War I (1914–1918), systematic aerial photographic coverage was possible.

Depending on the camera angle, aerial photographs are classified as either *oblique* or *vertical* (Figure 2-20). The advantage of oblique photographs, where the camera angle is less than 90°, is that features are seen from a more or less familiar point of view. The disadvantage is that, because of perspective, measurement is more difficult than on vertical photographs, which are taken with the optical axis of the camera approximately perpendicular to the surface of Earth.

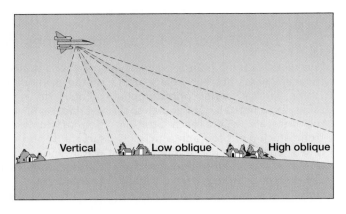

▲ **Figure 2-20**   On the basis of the angle between the camera and Earth's surface, aerial photographs are classified as vertical, low oblique, or high oblique.

Precise measurement is possible on vertical aerial photographs. **Photogrammetry** is the science of obtaining reliable measurements from photographs and, by extension, the science of mapping from aerial photographs.

Orthophoto Maps

Orthophoto maps are multicolored, distortion-free photographic image maps. They are prepared from aerial photographs or digital representations of aerial photos. Displacements caused by camera tilt or differences in terrain elevations have been removed, which gives the orthophoto the geometric characteristics of a map (Figure 2-21). Thus, an orthophoto can show the landscape in much greater detail than a conventional map but retains the map characteristic of a common scale that allows precise measurement of distances. Thus, an orthophoto map combines the image characteristics of a photo with the geometric qualities of a map. Orthophoto maps are particularly useful in flat-lying coastal areas because they can show subtle topographic detail in areas of very low relief, such as marshlands.

Color and Color Infrared Sensing

Color photogrammetry was developed slowly in the 1940s and 1950s, with many of the improvements coming as a result of the importance of color aerial photographs during World War II (1939–1945). In contrast to black-and-white images, where only a few tones can be recognized, a large number of hues can be discriminated on color photographs.

The word "color" without any modifier refers to the visible-light region of the electromagnetic spectrum (Figure 2-22) and means any of the colors seen in a rainbow. Another development of World War II, however, was *color infrared (color IR) film*, which is film sensitive to radiation in the infrared region of the spectrum. First known as "camouflage-detection" film because of its ability to discriminate living vegetation from the

▲ **Figure 2-21** Orthophoto map of Wilmington, North Carolina; original scale: 1:24,000. *(U.S. Geological Survey.)*

withering vegetation used to hide objects during the war, color IR film has become one of the most versatile tools available to the interpreter.

Because it can sense radiation beyond the visible-light region of the spectrum, color IR film is more

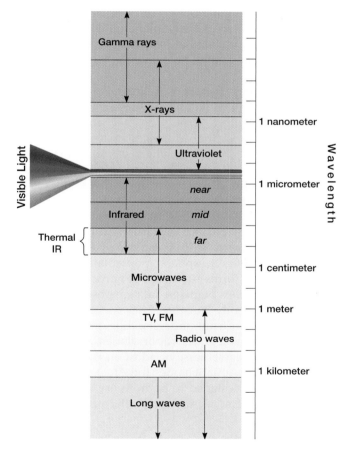

▲ **Figure 2-22** The electromagnetic spectrum. All humans can sense is radiation from the visible-light region. Conventional photography can use only a small portion of the total spectrum. Various specialized remote-sensing scanners, such as color IR film and thermal scanners, are capable of "seeing" radiation from other parts of the spectrum.

versatile than black-and-white and (visible) color films. The infrared region of the electromagnetic spectrum is divided into near, middle, and far sections relative to the visible-light region. With color IR film photographing in the near infrared, blue is filtered out and photographic infrared added. The images produced in this way, even though they are "false-color" images (e.g., living vegetation appears red), are still extremely valuable. One of the major uses of color IR imagery is to identify and evaluate vegetation (Figure 2-23).

Much of the usable portion of the near infrared cannot be detected by photographic emulsions. One result of this limitation has been the development of various optical–mechanical scanner systems that can sense far into the infrared and at the same time simulate color IR photographic imagery. Landsat satellites, described later in this chapter, have this capability.

Thermal Infrared Sensing

None of the middle or far infrared part of the electromagnetic spectrum, called the *thermal infrared* (thermal IR), can be sensed with film; as a result, special supercooled scanners are needed. Thermal scanning senses the radiant temperature of objects and may be carried out either day or night. The photographlike images produced in this process are particularly useful for showing diurnal temperature differences between land and water and between bedrock and alluvium, for studying thermal water pollution, and for detecting forest fires.

By far the greatest use of thermal IR scanning systems to date has been on meteorological satellites (for example, see *Focus: GOES Weather Satellites*, in Chapter 6). Although the spatial resolution (the size of the smallest feature that can be identified) is only on the order of a few kilometers (a few miles), it is more than sufficient to provide details that allow weather forecasting that is far more accurate and complete than has ever before been possible.

Microwave Sensing

Systems that sense wavelengths even longer than infrared ones are used in Earth sciences, including microwave radiometry, which senses radiation in the 100-micrometer to 1-meter range. Although such systems have low spatial resolution, they are particularly useful for showing subsurface characteristics such as moisture.

Multispectral Remote Sensing

Although it is still common for remote sensing systems to gather data from only one part of the electromagnetic spectrum at a time, sophisticated sensors are increasingly multispectral or *multiband* (the latter name because the various regions of the electromagnetic spectrum are sometimes called *bands*). These instruments image more

▲ **Figure 2-23**   Color infrared image of Mississippi River. Healthy vegetation is shown in red. *(NASA/Science Photo Library/Photo Researchers, Inc.)*

than one region of the electromagnetic spectrum simultaneously from precisely the same location. Thus, while traditional black-and-white photographic film is sensitive to only a narrow band of visible radiation, a satellite equipped with a multiband instrument images the surface of Earth in several spectrum regions at once, each designated for a unique application.

Landsat   The early NASA space missions (Mercury, Gemini, and Apollo) used multiband photography obtained through multicamera arrays. These imaging experiments were so successful that NASA then developed what was initially called the *Earth Resources Technology Satellite* series (ERTS) and later renamed *Landsat*. The 1970s and 1980s saw the launch of five Landsat satellites carrying a variety of sensor systems. Except for a low spatial resolution—80 meters (260 feet)—the multiband Landsat system with its continuous observation capability was nearly ideal in imagery production.

Unlike aerial photographs, which are produced on film, a Landsat image is digital and is conveyed through a matrix of numbers, with each number representing a single value for the specific pixel and band. These data are stored in the satellite, eventually transmitted to an Earth receiving station, numerically manipulated by a computer, and produced as a set of gray values and/or colors on a screen or hard-copy format (Figure 2-24).

The basic early Landsat imaging instrument was a **multispectral scanning system (MSS)**, a four-band system that gathered a set of digital numbers for each picture element (pixel) collected. One Landsat MSS image covers an area of 183-by-170 kilometers (115-by-106 miles) and includes more than 30 million pieces of data. Figure 2-25 is a typical Landsat MSS image. Landsat 4 and Landsat 5, launched in the early 1980s, carried an improved multispectral scanner known as the *thematic mapper*. Unlike the four general bands of the MSS, the seven bands of the thematic mapper are more narrowly defined—a refinement that provides improved resolution and greater imaging flexibility.

In 1999 Landsat 7 was launched. Landsat 7 carries an *enhanced thematic mapper plus* (ETM+) that provides images in eight spectral bands with a resolution of 15 meters (49 feet) in the panchromatic band (sensitive to visible and near infrared wavelengths), 30 meters (98 feet) in the six narrow bands of visible and short infrared wavelengths, and 60 meters (197 feet) in thermal infrared. A description of the primary applications for the various bands is provided in Table 2-1. As of this writing, both Landsat 5 and Landsat 7 remain in active operation.

Earth Observing System Satellites   In 1999 NASA launched the first of its *Earth Observing System (EOS)* satellites known as *Terra*. The key instrument of these satellites is the *Moderate Resolution Imagery Spectroradiometer* (MODIS), which gathers data in 36 spectral bands (Figure 2-26) and provides images covering the entire planet every one to two days. Other devices onboard Terra include the *Clouds and the Earth's Radiant Energy System* (CERES) instruments for monitoring the energy balance of Earth, and the *multiangle image spectroradiometer* (MISR) capable of distinguishing various types of atmospheric particulates, land surfaces, and cloud forms—with special processing, three-dimensional models of image data are possible.

The more recently launched EOS satellite, *Aqua*, was designed to enhance our understanding of Earth's water cycle by monitoring water vapor, clouds, precipitation, glaciers, and soil wetness. In addition to instruments such as MODIS, Aqua includes the *Atmospheric Infrared Sounder* (AIRS), designed to permit very accurate temperature measurements throughout the atmosphere.

Radar and Sonar Sensing

All the systems mentioned so far work by sensing the natural radiation emitted by or reflected from an object and are therefore characterized as *passive systems*. Another type of system, called an *active system*, has its own source of electromagnetic radiation. The most important

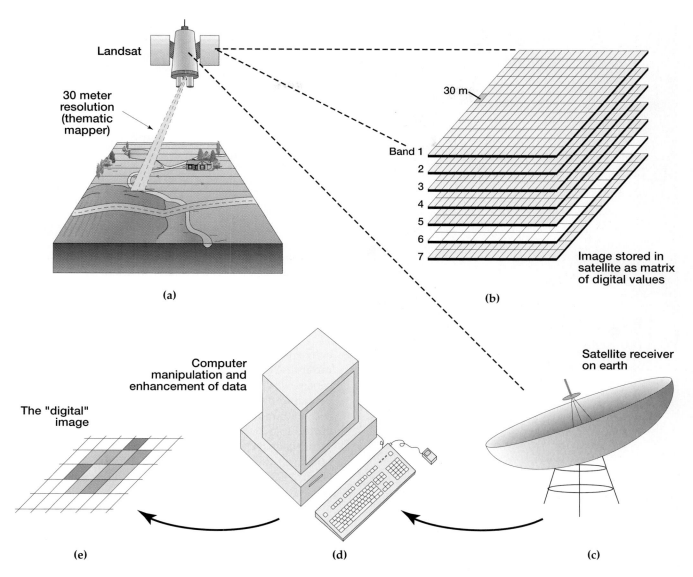

▲ **Figure 2-24**   The sequence of events that takes place as a satellite scan is converted to a digital image. *(Courtesy of Robert McMaster.)*

TABLE 2-1 Bands of the Landsat Enhanced Thematic Mapper Plus

Band Number	Bandwidth (micrometers)	Name of Spectral Region	Applications
1	0.45–0.52	Blue	Spots water penetration and vegetation
2	0.52–0.60	Green	Spots vegetation
3	0.63–0.69	Red	Spots vegetation (is sensitive to red pigments in plants)
4	0.76–0.90	Near IR	Measures biomass, analyzes soil
5	1.55–1.75	Middle IR	Detects soil moisture; excellent for hydrologic work
6	10.4–12.5	Thermal	Detects geothermal resources and vegetation stress
7	2.08–2.35	Middle IR	Analyzes geologic features
8	0.52–0.90	Panchromatic	High-resolution images

▲ **Figure 2-25** A mosaic of Landsat images showing the Iberian Peninsula and surrounding area. *(Geospace/Science Photo Library/Photo Researchers, Inc.)*

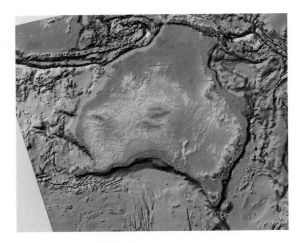

▲ **Figure 2-27** A topographic map of Australia constructed from radar data. The colors represent altitude, from gray (deep ocean) through blue, green, and yellow to red (highest). Relief features are shaded. The data for this image were gathered by the Seasat satellite. *(British Petroleum/National Remote Sensing Centre/Science Photo Library/Photo Researchers, Inc.)*

active sensing system used in the Earth sciences is **radar**, the acronym for *radio detection and ranging*. Radar senses wavelengths longer than 1 millimeter, using the principle that the time it takes for an emitted signal to reach a target and then return to the sender can be converted to distance information.

Initially, radar images were viewed only on a screen, but they are now available in photographlike form (Figure 2-27). In common with some other sensors, radar is capable of operating by day or night, but it is unique in its ability to penetrate atmospheric moisture. Thus, some wet tropical areas that could never be sensed by other systems have now been imaged by radar. Radar imagery is particularly useful for terrain analysis and meteorology. Another active remote sensing system, **sonar** (*sound navigation and ranging*), permits underwater imaging so that scientists can determine the form of that part of Earth's crust hidden by the world ocean.

Geographic Information Systems

Geographic information systems (GIS) are automated systems for the capture, storage, retrieval, analysis, and display of spatial data. They consist of computer software and hardware that act together as both a set of tools for analyzing geographic location and as a kind of information system designed specifically for spatial data. Geographic information systems are libraries of information that use maps to organize and store information. The systems allow information to be viewed and analyzed in an intuitive, visual manner. Just as an ordinary computer database management system can manipulate rows and columns of data in tabular form, a GIS allows data management using the link between tabular data and a map.

▲ **Figure 2-26** Dust blowing off the coast of Morocco over the Atlantic Ocean. The Atlas Mountains are shown on the right and the Canary Islands to the left in the true-color image taken on November 4, 2003, by the MODIS (moderate resolution imaging spectroradiometer) instrument aboard the Terra satellite. *(NASA.)*

This means that the map must be encoded into the computer, usually as numbers representing coordinates of locations at points, or as numbers forming a grid covering the mapped area. Once the data and the map are inside the GIS, the user can organize or search the data using the map, or the map using the data.

Geographic information systems developed from computer science, geography, and cartography and found their greatest initial uses in surveying, photogrammetry, computer cartography, spatial statistics, and remote sensing. So commonly are they now used in

geographical analysis that GIS has become a science of spatial analysis by itself (known as *geographic information science*), and the software has spun off a multibillion-dollar industry in spatial data and spatial information.

GIS involves specialized hardware and software that allows the users to collect, store, retrieve, reorganize, analyze, and display geographic data from the real world (Figure 2-28). An important attribute is the capability of the GIS data from different maps and sources, such as field data, map data, and remotely sensed images, to be registered together at the correct geographic

▲ **Figure 2-28** Land use on Cape Cod in 1951. Dark green shows areas of undisturbed vegetation, yellow shows areas of residential housing, and purple shows areas of industrial development. *(MassGIS.)*

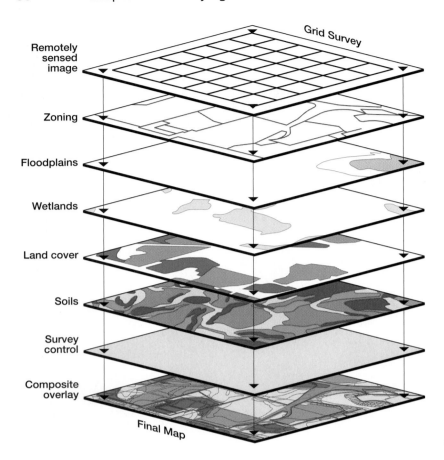

Grid Survey

Remotely sensed image

Zoning

Floodplains

Wetlands

Land cover

Soils

Survey control

Composite overlay

Final Map

◀ **Figure 2-29** Much GIS work involves layers of spatial data superimposed upon one another.

location within a common database, with a common map scale and map projection. One map layer, such as the locations of rivers, can then be cross-referenced to another, such as geology, soils, or slope.

GIS is mainly used in overlay analysis, where two or more layers of data are superimposed or integrated. GIS treats each spatially distributed variable as a particular layer in a sequence of overlays. As shown in Figure 2-29, input layers bring together such diverse elements as topography, vegetation, land use, land ownership, and land survey. Details of these various components are converted to digital data and are synthesized onto a reference map or data set.

Geographic information systems are used in a diverse array of applications concerned with geographic location. Because they provide impressive output maps and a powerful methodology for analytical studies, GIS can bring a new and more complete perspective to resource management, environmental monitoring, and environmental site assessment.

GIS technology was especially useful in the rubble pile that was Ground Zero at the World Trade Center disaster. Structural engineers assessed the situation and sent the data to the mapping operation. Infrastructure data were integrated with the building plans to provide a (three-dimensional) view underground. Thus building damage detail was mapped, as well as outage detail regarding electrical, water, gas, steam, and telephone

services. Also assessed were vehicle and pedestrian access to the area, including subway and river crossings. Change and recovery were monitored on a daily basis, as were utility outages, mass transit rerouting information, and street closures.

The Role of the Geographer

A vast array of imagery of various types and of different areas is available to the interpreter, ranging from black-and-white photographs to the output of exotic sensing systems. Many foreign governments place restrictions on coverage of their territory, but the United States has made imagery easily accessible to its own citizens and to others. For example, all images from the U.S. civilian space program (including Landsat) are unclassified and obtainable at a modest cost.

In using these images and equipment, the geographer should never lose sight of the major objective: to understand Earth better. The new imagery technology available to us is an adjunct to field study, geographic description, and maps but is not a substitute for any of these.

Certain types of imagery are useful for particular purposes; no single sensing system has universal applicability for all problems. Accordingly, each interpreter must select and obtain the best type of imagery for his or her special needs. For providing an overview of the lithosphere, for example, high-altitude space imagery has been of particular value and has led to important discoveries. This type of imagery might have limited value in detailed terrain studies, however, where large-scale color or black-and-white photographs might be more appropriate.

For studying the hydrosphere, to cite another example, images of different scales have proved useful. Satellite images of an entire hemisphere can tell us much about the water content in clouds, air masses, glaciers, and snowfields at a given time, but detailed conventional color photographs might be better for discriminating a complicated shoreline because of scale and the penetrating ability of the film. On the other hand, the biosphere and especially its vegetation are often best appreciated on color IR imagery of several scales—overall vegetation patterns on satellite images and detailed imagery down to 1:5000 for crop and forest inventory studies.

Features of human creation are generally not evident on very high-altitude imagery, but they become increasingly clear as one approaches Earth. Thus, survey patterns, transportation lines, rural settlements, and cities are best interpreted on imagery of intermediate or large scale.

Chapter 2 Learning Review

Key Terms

Before answering the study questions below, review the definitions of the following key terms (page references are provided for you):

aerial photograph *(p. 44)*
conformality (conformal projection) *(p. 35)*
conic projection *(p. 37)*
cylindrical projection *(p. 35)*
elevation contour line *(p. 39)*
equal area projection *(p. 35)*
equivalence (equivalent projection) *(p. 35)*
fractional scale *(p. 31)*
geographic information systems (GIS) *(p. 48)*

global positioning system (GPS) *(p. 41)*
graphic scale *(p. 30)*
isoline *(p. 39)*
large-scale map *(p. 31)*
loxodrome *(p. 36)*
map *(p. 29)*
map projection *(p. 33)*
map scale *(p. 30)*
Mercator projection *(p. 36)*
multispectral scanning system (MSS) *(p. 46)*

orthophoto map *(p. 44)*
photogrammetry *(p. 44)*
plane projection *(p. 37)*
pseudocylindrical projection (elliptical projection) *(p. 38)*
radar *(p. 48)*
remote sensing *(p. 44)*
representative fraction *(p. 31)*
rhumb line *(p. 36)*
small-scale map *(p. 31)*
sonar *(p. 48)*
verbal scale *(p. 31)*

Study Questions for Key Concepts

After studying this chapter, you should be able to answer the following questions:

The Nature of Maps (p. 29)
1. Why is it impossible for a map of the world to portray the Earth as accurately as can be done with a globe?

Map Scale (p. 30)
2. Describe and explain the concepts of graphic map scales, fractional map scales, and verbal map scales.
3. What is meant by a map scale of 1:10,000?
4. Explain the difference between large-scale and small-scale maps.

Map Projections (p. 33)
5. Explain the differences between an equivalent map and a conformal map.
6. Is it possible for a map to be both conformal and equivalent? Neither conformal nor equivalent?

Families of Map Projections (p. 35)
7. Briefly describe the four major families of map projections: cylindrical, plane, conic, and pseudocylindrical (elliptical).

8. Why is a Mercator projection useful as a navigation map? Why is it not ideal for use as a general purpose classroom map?
9. Why are there so many types of map projections?

Isolines (p. 39)
10. Explain the concept of an *isoline*.
11. What characteristics on maps are shown by *isotherms*, *isobars*, and *elevation contour lines*?

Remote Sensing (p. 44)
12. What are some of the applications of color IR imagery?
13. What are some of the applications of thermal IR imagery?
14. How is multispectral remote sensing different from radar sensing?

Geographic Information Systems (p. 48)
15. Distinguish between GPS and GIS.

Additional Resources

Books:

Campbell, James B. *Introduction to Remote Sensing*, 3rd ed. New York: Guilford Publications, 2002.

Clarke, Keith C. *Getting Started with Geographic Information Systems*, 4th ed. Upper Saddle River, NJ: Prentice Hall, 2003.

Longley, Paul A., Michael F. Goodchild, David J. Maguire, and David W. Rhind. *Geographic Information Systems and Science*. New York: John Wiley & Sons, 2001.

Monmonier, Mark. *How to Lie with Maps*, 2nd ed. Chicago: University of Chicago Press, 1996.

Wilford, John Noble. *The Mapmakers*, revised ed. New York: Alfred A. Knopf, 2000.

Internet Sites:
The Earth Observatory

http://earthobservatory.nasa.gov/

The Earth Observatory is National Aeronautics and Space Administration's (NASA's) Internet site that provides information and images of Earth.

Landsat

http://landsat7.usgs.gov/

The Landsat satellite program is the longest-running project for the generation of moderate-resolution images of Earth from space.

The National Map

http://www.nationalmap.usgs.gov/

The National Map is an interactive map service that provides access to a wide range of geospatial data.

Terra Satellite Images

http://terra.nasa.gov/

This site has links to images and information about the Terra satellite—the flagship satellite in the Earth Observing System (EOS).

U.S. Geological Survey

http://www.usgs.gov/

The U.S. Geological Survey home page has links to sites where topographic maps, geological maps, research papers, and publications of general interest may be viewed or purchased.

3
Introduction to the Atmosphere

Earth is different from all other known planets in a variety of ways. One of the most notable differences is the presence around our planet of an atmosphere distinctive from other planetary atmospheres. It is our atmosphere that makes life possible on Earth. The atmosphere supplies most of the oxygen that animals must have to survive, as well as the carbon dioxide needed by plants. It helps maintain a water supply, which is essential to all living things. It insulates Earth's surface against temperature extremes and thus provides a livable environment over most of the planet. It also shields Earth from much of the Sun's ultraviolet radiation, which otherwise would be fatal to most life forms.

Air, generally used as a synonym for atmosphere, is not a specific gas, but rather a mixture of gases—mainly nitrogen and oxygen. In addition, most air contains minor but varying quantities of solid and liquid particles that can be thought of as impurities. The individual particles are mostly microscopic and therefore held in suspension in the air. Most air also contains some gaseous impurities.

Pure air is invisible because the gases in it are colorless, odorless, and tasteless. Gaseous impurities, on the other hand, can often be smelled, and the air may even become visible if enough microscopic solid and liquid impurities coalesce (stick together) to form particles large enough to either reflect or scatter sunlight. Clouds, by far the most conspicuous visible features of the atmosphere, represent the coalescing of water droplets or ice crystals around microscopic particulates that act as *condensation nuclei*.

Size of Earth's Atmosphere

The atmosphere completely surrounds Earth and can be thought of as a vast ocean of air with Earth at its bottom (Figure 3-1). It is held to Earth by gravitational attraction and therefore accompanies our planet in all its celestial motions. The attachment of Earth and atmosphere is a loose one, however, and the atmosphere can therefore move on its own, doing things that the solid Earth cannot do.

Although the atmosphere extends outward at least 10,000 kilometers (6000 miles), most of its mass is concentrated at very low altitudes. More than half of the mass of the atmosphere lies below the elevation of North America's highest peak, Mount McKinley in Alaska, elevation 6.2 kilometers (3.8 miles), and more than 98 percent of it lies within 26 kilometers (16 miles) of sea level

◀ Aitutaki Lagoon in the Cook Islands. *(Getty Images, Inc.— Stone Allstock.)*

▲ **Figure 3-1** The atmosphere completely surrounds Earth in this composite satellite image; beyond is the blackness of outer space. *(Planetary Visions, Ltd./Photo Researchers, Inc.)*

(Figure 3-2). Therefore, relative to Earth's diameter of about 13,000 kilometers (8000 miles), the "ocean of air" we live in is a very shallow one.

In addition to reaching upward above Earth's surface, the atmosphere also extends slightly downward. Because

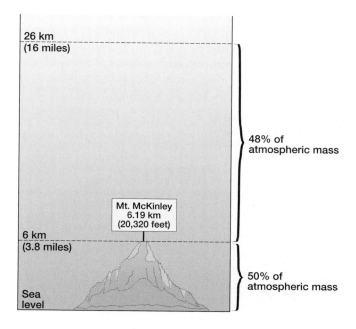

▲ **Figure 3-2** Most of the atmospheric mass is close to Earth's surface. More than half of the mass is below the elevation of Mount McKinley, North America's highest peak.

air expands to fill empty spaces, it penetrates into caves and crevices in rocks and soil. Moreover, it is dissolved in the waters of Earth and in the bloodstreams of organisms.

The atmosphere interacts with other components of the earthly environment, and it is instrumental in providing a hospitable milieu for life. Whereas we often speak of human beings as creatures of Earth, it is perhaps more accurate to consider ourselves creatures of the atmosphere. As surely as a crab crawling on the sea bottom is a resident of the ocean, a person living at the bottom of the ocean of air is a resident of the atmosphere.

Composition of the Atmosphere

The chemical composition of pure, dry air at lower elevations (elevations lower than about 80 kilometers or 50 miles) is simple and uniform, and the concentrations of the major components are basically unvarying over time. Certain minor gases and nongaseous particles vary markedly from place to place and from time to time, however, as does the amount of moisture in the air.

Permanent Gases

Nitrogen and Oxygen   The two most abundant gases in the atmosphere are *nitrogen* and *oxygen* (Figure 3-3 and Table 3-1). Nitrogen makes up more than 78 percent of the total, and oxygen makes up nearly 21 percent. Nitrogen is added to the air by the decay and burning of organic matter, volcanic eruptions, and the chemical breakdown of certain rocks, and it is removed by certain biological processes and by being washed away in rain or snow. Overall, the addition and removal of nitrogen gas are balanced, and consequently the quantity present in

Gas	Percent of Volume of Dry Air	Concentration in Parts per Million Parts of Air
Permanent gases		
Nitrogen (N_2)	78.084	
Oxygen (O_2)	20.946	
Argon (Ar)	0.934	
Neon (Ne)	0.00182	18.2
Helium (He)	0.00052	5.2
Krypton (Kr)	0.00011	1.1
Hydrogen (H_2)	0.00005	0.5
Variable gases		
Water vapor (H_2O)	0–4	
Carbon dioxide (CO_2)	0.038	380
Carbon Monoxide (CO)		Less than 100
Methane (CH_4)	0.00017	1.7
Ozone (O_3)		Less than 2
Sulfur dioxide (SO_2)		Less than 1
Nitrogen dioxide (NO_2)		Less than 0.2

TABLE 3-1 Principal Gases of Earth's Atmosphere

the air remains constant over time. Oxygen is produced by vegetation and is removed by a variety of organic and inorganic processes; its total quantity also apparently remains stable.

The remaining 1 percent of the atmosphere's volume consists mostly of the inert gas argon. These three principal atmospheric gases—nitrogen, oxygen, argon—have a minimal effect on weather and climate and therefore need no further consideration here. The trace gases neon, helium, krypton, and hydrogen also have little effect on weather and climate.

Variable Gases

Several other gases occur in sparse but highly variable quantities in the atmosphere, and their influence on weather and climate is significant.

Water Vapor   Water in the form of a gas is known as **water vapor**. Water vapor is invisible—the visible forms of water in the atmosphere, such as clouds and precipitation, consist of water in its liquid or solid form. Water vapor is most abundant in air overlying warm, moist surface areas such as tropical oceans, where water

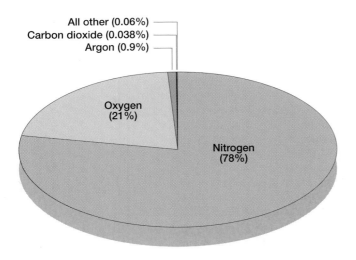

▲ **Figure 3-3**   Proportional volume of the gaseous components of the atmosphere. Nitrogen and oxygen are the dominant components.

vapor may amount to as much as 4 percent of total volume. Over deserts and in polar regions, the amount of water vapor is but a tiny fraction of 1 percent.

In the atmosphere as a whole, the total amount of water vapor remains nearly constant. Thus, its listing as a "variable gas" in Table 3-1 means variable in location, not variable in time. Water vapor has a significant effect on weather and climate in that it is the source of all clouds and precipitation; water vapor also plays important roles in a number of heating and cooling processes in the atmosphere.

Carbon Dioxide   Another important atmospheric component is **carbon dioxide** (CO_2). Like water vapor, carbon dioxide also has a significant influence on climate, primarily because of its ability to absorb infrared radiation and thereby help warm the lower atmosphere. Carbon dioxide is distributed fairly uniformly in the lower layers of the atmosphere although its concentration has been increasing steadily for the last century or so because of the increased burning of fossil fuels—the proportion of carbon dioxide in the atmosphere has been increasing at a rate of about 0.0002 percent (2 parts per million) per year and at present is about 380 parts per million. Most atmospheric scientists conclude that the increased levels of CO_2 are causing the lower atmosphere to warm up enough to produce significant, although still somewhat unpredictable, global climatic changes (the topic of "global warming" will be presented in greater detail in Chapter 4).

Ozone   Another minor but vital gas in the atmosphere is **ozone**, which is a molecule made up of three oxygen atoms (O_3) instead of the more common two oxygen atoms (O_2). For the most part, ozone is concentrated in a layer of the atmosphere called the **ozone layer**, which lies between 15 and 48 kilometers (9 and 30 miles) above Earth's surface. Ozone is an excellent absorber of ultraviolet solar radiation; it filters out enough of these rays to protect life forms from potentially deadly effects (a discussion of the recent thinning of the ozone layer follows later in this chapter).

The other variable gases listed in Table 3-1—carbon monoxide, sulfur dioxide, nitrogen oxides, and various hydrocarbons—are increasingly being introduced into the atmosphere by emission from factories and automobiles. All of them are hazardous to life and may possibly have some effect on climate. Methane, introduced into the atmosphere both naturally and through human activity, absorbs certain wavelengths of radiation and so plays a role in regulating the temperature of the atmosphere.

Particulates (Aerosols)

The larger nongaseous particles in the atmosphere are mainly liquid water and ice, which form clouds, rain, snow, sleet, and hail. There are also dust particles large enough to be visible, which are sometimes kept aloft in the turbulent atmosphere in sufficient quantity to cloud the sky (Figure 3-4), but they are too heavy to remain long in the air. Smaller particles, invisible to the naked eye, may remain suspended in the atmosphere for months or even years.

The solid and liquid particles found in the atmosphere are collectively called **particulates** or **aerosols**. They have innumerable sources, some natural and

▲ **Figure 3-4**   Dust particles sometimes cloud the sky for a short time over a limited part of Earth's surface. On some occasions, as in this scene from the central part of New South Wales, Australia, the term dust storm is very appropriate, and the visual effect is imposing, if not menacing. *(Tom L. McKnight photo.)*

some the result of human activities. Volcanic ash, wind-blown soil and pollen grains, meteor debris, smoke from wildfires, and salt spray from breaking waves are examples of particulates from natural sources. Particulates coming from human sources consist mostly of industrial and automotive emissions and smoke and soot from fires of human origin.

These tiny particles are most numerous near their places of origin—above cities, seacoasts, and active volcanoes. They may be carried great distances, however, both horizontally and vertically by the restless atmosphere. They affect weather and climate in two major ways:

1. Many are *hygroscopic* (which means they absorb water), and water vapor condenses around them as they float about. This accumulation of water vapor molecules is a critical step in cloud formation, as we shall see in Chapter 6.
2. Some either absorb or reflect sunlight, thus decreasing the amount of solar energy that reaches Earth's surface.

Vertical Structure of the Atmosphere

The next five chapters deal with atmospheric processes and their influence on climatic patterns. Our attention in these chapters will be devoted primarily to the lower portion of the atmosphere, which is the zone in which most weather phenomena occur. Even though the upper layers of the atmosphere affect the environment of Earth's surface only minimally, it is still useful to have some understanding of the total atmosphere. Therefore, we now note some general characteristics of the atmosphere in its total vertical extent, emphasizing vertical patterns of temperature, pressure, and composition.

A given layer (altitudinal zone) of the atmosphere has different names depending on the characteristic or feature under discussion. In this section, we are discussing thermal layers; later we introduce other names for these overlapping layers.

Thermal Layers

Most of us have had some personal experience with temperature variables associated with altitude. As we climb a mountain, for instance, we sense a decrease in temperature. Until about a century ago, it was generally assumed that temperature decreased with increasing altitude throughout the whole atmosphere, but now we know that such is not the case.

As shown in Figure 3-5, the vertical pattern of temperature is complex, consisting of a series of layers in which temperature alternately decreases and increases.

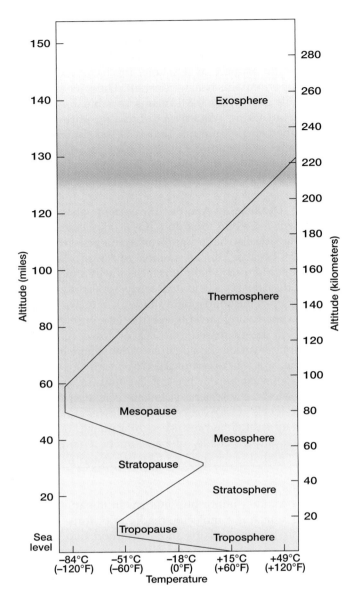

▲ **Figure 3-5** Thermal structure of the atmosphere. Air temperature decreases with increasing altitude in the troposphere and mesosphere and increases with increasing altitude in the stratosphere and thermosphere.

From the surface of Earth up, these thermal layers are called the *troposphere, stratosphere, mesosphere, thermosphere,* and *exosphere.* In addition to these five principal names, we also have special names for the top of the first three layers: *tropopause, stratopause,* and *mesopause.* We use the *-sphere* name when talking about an entire layer and the *-pause* name when our interest is either in the upper portion of a layer or in the boundary between two layers.

Troposphere   The lowest layer of the atmosphere—and the one in contact with Earth's surface—is known as the **troposphere**. The names *troposphere* and **tropopause** (the top of the troposphere) are derived from the Greek word *tropos* ("turn") and imply an overturning of the air in this zone as a result of vertical mixing and turbulence. The depth of the troposphere varies in both time and place (Figure 3-6). It is deepest over tropical regions and shallowest over the poles, deeper in summer than in winter, and varies with the passage of warm and cold air masses. On the average, the top of the troposphere (including the tropopause) is about 18 kilometers (11 miles) above sea level at the equator and about 8 kilometers (5 miles) above sea level over the poles.

Stratosphere The names **stratosphere** and **stratopause** come from the Latin *stratum* ("a cover"), implying a layered or stratified condition without vertical mixing. The stratosphere extends from an altitude of 18 kilometers (11 miles) above sea level to about 48 kilometers (30 miles).

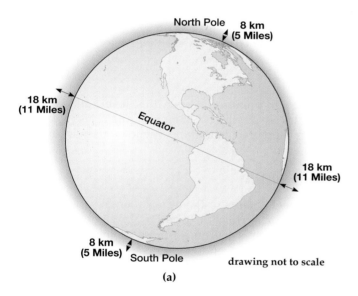

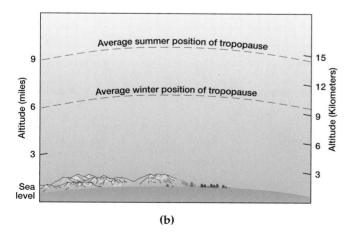

▲ **Figure 3-6** The depth of the troposphere is variable. **(a)** This thermal layer is deepest over the equator and shallowest over the poles. **(b)** It is deeper in summer than in winter. (The thickness of the atmosphere is greatly exaggerated in this drawing.)

Upper Thermal Layers The names **mesosphere** and **mesopause** are from the Greek *meso* ("middle"). The mesosphere begins at 48 kilometers (30 miles) and extends to about 80 kilometers (50 miles) above sea level. Above the mesopause is the **thermosphere** (from the Greek *therm*, meaning "heat"), which begins at an altitude of 80 kilometers (50 miles) above sea level and has no definite top. Instead it merges gradually into the region called the **exosphere**, which in turn blends into interplanetary space. Traces of atmosphere extend for literally thousands of kilometers higher. Therefore, "top of the atmosphere" is a theoretical concept rather than a reality, with no true boundary between atmosphere and outer space.

Temperature Patterns in the Atmosphere Air temperature changes with altitude (Figure 3-5). Beginning at sea level, where the average global temperature is about 15°C (59°F), temperature first decreases steadily with increasing altitude through the troposphere, reaching an average temperature of about −57°C (−71°F) at the tropopause. Temperature remains constant through the tropopause and for some distance into the stratosphere. At an altitude of about 20 kilometers (12 miles), air temperature begins increasing with increasing altitude, reaching a maximum at 48 kilometers (30 miles) at the bottom of the mesosphere, where the temperature is about −2°C (28°F). Then the temperature decreases with increasing altitude all through the mesosphere, reaching a minimum at the top of that layer at an altitude of 80 kilometers (50 miles). Temperature remains constant for several kilometers into the thermosphere and then begins to increase until, at an altitude of 200 kilometers (125 miles), it is higher than the maximum temperature in the troposphere. In the exosphere, the normal concept of temperature no longer applies.

Each "warm zone" in this temperature gradient has a specific source of heat. In the lower troposphere, the heat source is the surface of Earth itself—solar energy warms the surface of Earth, and this energy is in turn transferred through a number of different processes to the troposphere immediately above. The warm zone at the stratopause is near the top of the ozone layer, where ozone is absorbing the ultraviolet portion of sunlight and thereby warming the atmosphere. In the thermosphere, various atoms and molecules also absorb ultraviolet rays from the Sun and are thus split and heated. The "cold zones" that separate these warm zones are cold simply because they lack such sources of heat.

Although there are many interesting physical relationships in the stratosphere, mesosphere, thermosphere, and exosphere, our attention in this book is directed almost entirely to the troposphere because storms and essentially all the other phenomena we call "weather" occur here. Occasionally, however, we must consider atmospheric conditions above the troposphere—especially the ozone layer.

Pressure

Atmospheric pressure can be thought of, for simplicity's sake, as the "weight" of the overlying air. (In Chapter 5, we explore the concept of pressure in much greater detail.) The taller the column of air above an object, the greater the air pressure exerted on that object, as Figure 3-7 shows. Because air is highly compressible, the lower layers of the atmosphere are compressed by the air above, and this compression increases both the pressure exerted by the lower layers and the density of these layers. Air in the upper layers is subjected to less compression and therefore has a lower density and exerts a lower pressure.

Air pressure is normally highest at sea level and decreases rapidly with increasing altitude. The change of pressure with altitude is not constant, however. As a generalization, pressure decreases upward at a decreasing rate, as Figure 3-8 shows. Table 3-2 expresses the pressure at various altitudes as a percentage of sea-level pressure. From it we see, for instance, that at an altitude of 16 kilometers (10 miles)—a typical elevation of the tropopause—atmospheric pressure is only 10 percent of its sea-level value; this is just another way to say that most of the mass of the atmosphere is found relatively close to the ground.

One-half of all the gas molecules making up the atmosphere lie below 5.6 kilometers (3.5 miles), and 90 percent of them are concentrated in the first 16 kilometers (10 miles) above sea level (see Figure 3-2). Pressure becomes so slight in the upper layers that, above about 80 kilometers (50 miles), there is not enough to register on an ordinary barometer, the instrument used to

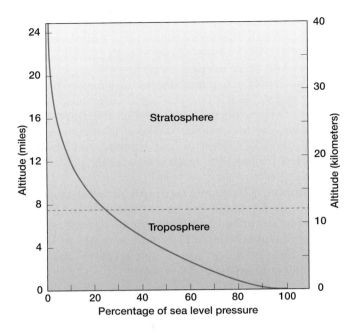

▲ **Figure 3-8**   Air pressure decreases with increasing altitude but not at a constant rate.

measure air pressure. Above this level, atmospheric molecules are so scarce that air pressure is less than that in the most perfect laboratory vacuum at sea level.

Composition

The principal gases of the atmosphere have a remarkably uniform vertical distribution throughout the lowest 80 kilometers (50 miles) or so of the atmosphere. This zone of homogenous composition is referred to as the **homosphere** (Figure 3-9). The sparser atmosphere above this zone does not display such uniformity; rather, the gases tend to be layered in accordance with their weights—molecular nitrogen (N_2) below, with atomic oxygen (O), helium (He) and hydrogen (H)

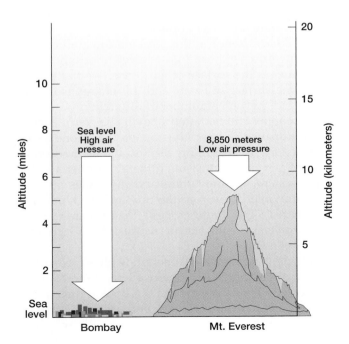

▲ **Figure 3-7**   Atmospheric pressure is highest at sea level and diminishes rapidly with increasing altitude.

TABLE 3-2 Atmospheric Pressure at Various Altitudes Expressed as a Percentage of Sea-Level Pressure

Altitude		Percentage of Sea-Level Pressure
Kilometers	Miles	
0	0	100
5.5	3.5	50
16	10	10
32	20	1
48	30	0.1
80	50	0.001
96	60	0.00001

successively above. This higher zone is called the **heterosphere**.

Water vapor also varies in its vertical distribution. Most is found near Earth's surface, with a general diminishment with increasing altitude. Over 16 kilometers (10 miles) above sea level, the temperature is so low that any moisture formerly present in the air has already frozen into ice. At these altitudes, therefore, there is rarely enough moisture to provide the raw material to make even a wisp of a cloud. If you have done any flying, you may recall the remarkable sight of a cloudless sky overhead once the plane breaks through the top of a solid cloud layer below.

Two other vertical compositional patterns are worthy of mention here.

1. The ozone layer, which, as stated above, lies between 15 and 48 kilometers (9 and 30 miles) up, is sometimes called the **ozonosphere**. Despite its name, the ozone layer is not composed primarily of ozone. It gets its name because that is where the concentration of ozone relative to other gases is at its maximum. Even in the section of the ozone layer where the ozone attains its greatest concentration, at about 25 kilometers (15 miles) above sea level, this gas only accounts for no more than about 15 parts per million of the atmosphere.

2. The *ionosphere* is a deep layer of electrically charged molecules and atoms (which are called *ions*) in the middle and upper mesosphere and

▲ **Figure 3-10**   The Aurora Borealis in the ionosphere as photographed over spruce trees in central Alaska, near Fairbanks. *(Jack Finch/Science Photo Library/Photo Researchers, Inc.)*

the lower thermosphere, between about 60 and 400 kilometers (40 and 250 miles). The ionosphere is significant because it aids long-distance communication by reflecting radio waves back to Earth. It is also known for its *auroral displays,* such as the "northern lights" (Figure 3-10) that develop when charged atomic particles from the Sun are trapped by the magnetic field of Earth near the poles. In the ionosphere, these particles "excite" the nitrogen molecules and oxygen atoms, causing them to emit light, not unlike a neon lightbulb.

These two layers are shown in Figure 3-11, and Figure 3-12 shows the vertical relationship among all the various sphere names.

Human-Induced Atmospheric Change

As world population has exploded and technology has become more sophisticated, the human race has increasingly had an unintended and uncontrolled impact on the atmosphere—an impact seen all over the globe. The human impact, in simplest terms, consists of the introduction of impurities into the atmosphere at a pace previously unknown. Although for many years a concern of atmospheric scientists, by the early part of this decade the consequences of human-induced changes in the atmosphere were receiving international attention—attention that is growing year by year.

In an address on behalf of the chairman of the Intergovernmental Panel on Climate Change (IPCC) at the Seventh Conference of Parties to the United Nations

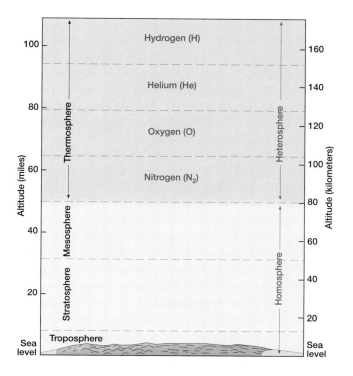

▲ **Figure 3-9**   The homosphere is a zone of uniform vertical distribution of gases. In the heterosphere, however, the distribution lacks this uniformity.

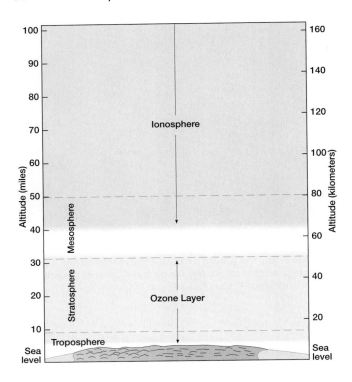

▲ **Figure 3-11** The ozone layer contains significant concentrations of ozone. The ionosphere is a deep layer of ions, which are electrically charged molecules and atoms.

Framework Convention on Climate Change held in Morocco in November 2001, Dr. Bert Metz reminded participants that:

> " ... the overwhelming majority of scientific experts, whilst recognizing that scientific uncertainties exist, nonetheless believe that human-induced climate change is already occurring [and] that future changes in climate are inevitable. ... "

Dr. Rajendra K. Pachauri, chairman of the IPCC, expressed deep concern while addressing the Twentieth Session of the IPCC in Paris in February 2003:

> Human society has necessarily to be concerned with the impacts of its actions on all elements of nature, which indeed determine the very survival of every species on this planet ... While we as human beings concern ourselves essentially with the direct effects of climate change on our lives, we need to assess with greater rigour the impacts of climate change on ecosystems, on biodiversity, on wildlife, on water and soil, because all of these would soon impact on human existence as well.

In subsequent sections of the book, we will highlight a number of aspects of human-induced atmospheric change. The first major topic of global environmental change we spotlight is the depletion of the ozone layer.

Depletion of the Ozone Layer

Ozone Depletion

As we described earlier, ozone is naturally produced in the stratosphere. It is a form of oxygen molecule consisting of three atoms of oxygen (O_3) rather than the more common two atoms (O_2). Ozone is created in the upper atmosphere by the action of ultraviolet solar radiation on *diatomic oxygen* (O_2) molecules.

Ultraviolet (UV) radiation from the Sun is divided into three bands (from longest to shortest wavelengths): *UV-A, UV-B,* and *UV-C* (radiation will be discussed in more detail in Chapter 4). In the stratosphere, under the influence of UV-C, O_2 molecules split into oxygen atoms; some of the free oxygen atoms combine with O_2 molecules to form O_3 (Figure 3-13). The natural breakdown of ozone in the stratosphere occurs when, under the influence of UV-B and UV-C, ozone breaks down into O_2 and a free oxygen atom. Through this ongoing natural process of ozone formation and breakdown, nearly all of UV-C and much of UV-B radiation is absorbed by the ozone layer. The absorption of UV radiation in this photochemical process also serves to warm this layer of the atmosphere.

About 90 percent of all atmospheric ozone is found in the stratosphere where it forms a fragile "shield" by absorbing most of the potentially dangerous ultraviolet

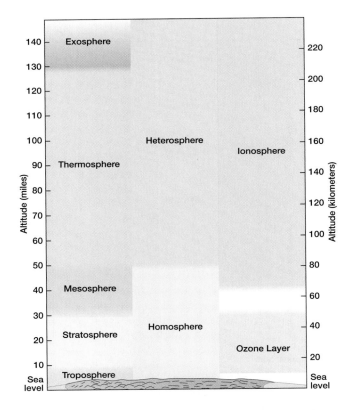

▲ **Figure 3-12** The vertical distribution pattern of the various atmospheric "spheres."

Natural Ozone Formation:

$$O_2 \xrightarrow{\text{UV-C}} O + O$$

$$O_2 + O \longrightarrow O_3$$

Natural Ozone Breakdown:

$$O_3 \xrightarrow{\text{UV-B \& UV-C}} O_2 + O$$

▲ **Figure 3-13** Ultraviolet radiation splits oxygen molecules (O_2) into free oxygen atoms (O), some of which combine with other O_2 molecules to form ozone (O_3); also under the influence of UV light, ozone naturally breaks back down into O_2 and a free oxygen atom.

radiation from the Sun (the UV-A that passes through the ozone layer is generally thought to be relatively harmless). Ultraviolet radiation is biologically destructive in many ways. Prolonged exposure to UV radiation is linked to skin cancer—both the generally curable nonmelanoma varieties as well as much more serious melanoma; it is also linked to increased risk for cataracts; it can suppress the human immune system, diminish the yield of many crops, disrupt the aquatic food chain by killing microorganisms such as phytoplankton on the ocean surface, and doubtless has other negative effects still undiscovered.

Ozone is also produced near Earth's surface in the troposphere through human activities, forming one of components of *photochemical smog* (discussed later in

this chapter). However, it has been recently observed thinning of the stratospheric ozone layer that has triggered much research and monitoring.

The "Hole" in the Ozone Layer   Although there are natural factors that can alter the ozone layer, the consensus among atmospheric scientists today is that the dramatic thinning of the ozone layer observed since the 1970s is due primarily (if not entirely) to the release of human-produced chemicals. The most problematic of these chemicals are known as **chlorofluorocarbons (CFCs)**, but other ozone-depleting substances include halons (used in some kinds of fire extinguishers) and methyl bromide (a pesticide).

CFCs are odorless, nonflammable, noncorrosive, and generally nonreactive—for this reason, scientists originally believed CFCs could not have any effect on the environment. They were widely used in refrigeration and air-conditioning (the cooling liquid Freon™ is a CFC), in foam and plastic manufacturing, and in aerosol sprays.

Although extremely stable and inert in the lower atmosphere, CFCs are broken down by ultraviolet radiation once they reach the ozonosphere. Under the influence of UV radiation, a chlorine atom is released from a CFC molecule (Figure 3-14); the chlorine atom then reacts with ozone, breaking it apart to form one chlorine monoxide (ClO) molecule and one O_2 molecule. The chlorine monoxide molecule can then react with a free atom of oxygen, forming a diatomic oxygen

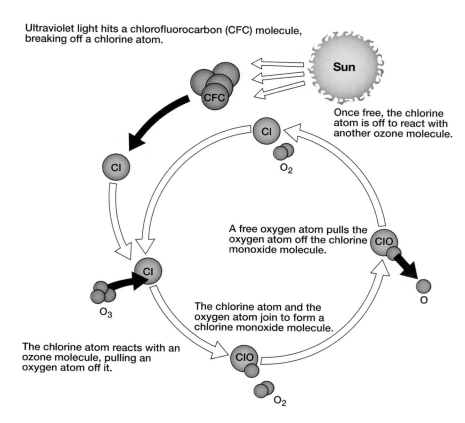

Ultraviolet light hits a chlorofluorocarbon (CFC) molecule, breaking off a chlorine atom.

Sun

Once free, the chlorine atom is off to react with another ozone molecule.

A free oxygen atom pulls the oxygen atom off the chlorine monoxide molecule.

The chlorine atom and the oxygen atom join to form a chlorine monoxide molecule.

The chlorine atom reacts with an ozone molecule, pulling an oxygen atom off it.

◀ **Figure 3-14** The destruction of ozone in the stratosphere by chlorine atoms derived from the breakdown of CFCs in the atmosphere. Chlorine atoms are unchanged by the reaction and can repeat the process. Thus a single chlorine atom can destroy tens of thousands of ozone molecules. *(After J. T. Mackenzie and L. Mackenzie,* Our Changing Planet, *Prentice Hall, Upper Saddle River, NJ, 1995.)*

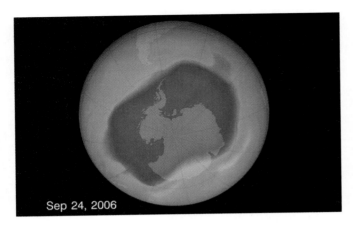

Sep 24, 2006

▲ **Figure 3-15**   The Antarctic ozone hole on September 24, 2006. The area over Antarctica, shown in dark blue and violet, has the lowest concentration of ozone. *(NASA.)*

molecule while freeing the chlorine atom to react with another ozone molecule. As many as 100,000 ozone molecules can be destroyed for every chlorine atom released.

Not only is the ozone layer thinning, in some places it has temporarily disappeared almost entirely. Monitored by a satellite instrument called *TOMS* (Total Ozone Spectrometer), the annual ebb and flow of the ozone layer has been continuously mapped since 1979 with a "hole" developing and persisting over Antarctica longer and longer each year (Figure 3-15). By the late 1980s, an ozone "hole" was found over the Arctic as well.

Why is ozone depletion more severe over the polar regions, particularly Antarctica? In part because of the extreme cooling of Antarctica during the winter, a whirling wind pattern known as the *polar vortex* develops, effectively isolating the polar air from the atmosphere in lower latitudes. Within the stratosphere, ice crystals form thin *polar stratospheric clouds* (PSC)—the presence of these clouds can dramatically accelerate the process of ozone destruction. The ice crystals in PSCs provide surfaces on which a number of reactions can take place, including the accumulation of chlorine-based molecules. With the return of sunlight in the polar spring (September in the Southern Hemisphere), UV radiation triggers the catalytic reaction, and ozone depletion begins.

The thinning of ozone over the Arctic has been generally less severe than over the Antarctic because comparable atmospheric conditions to those in Antarctica are less well developed over the North Pole.

Stratospheric ozone depletion has been correlated with increased levels of ultraviolet radiation reaching ground level in Antarctica, Australia, mountainous regions of Europe, central Canada, and New Zealand. In part because of the increased health risks posed by higher levels of UV radiation reaching the surface, a

UV Index has been established to provide the public with information about the intensity of UV radiation in an area (see the box, *"People and the Environment: The UV Index"*).

The Montreal Protocol   These discoveries were sufficiently alarming that a number of countries including the United States banned the use of CFCs in aerosol sprays in 1978. A major international treaty—the Montreal Protocol on Substances That Deplete the Ozone Layer—was promulgated in 1987 to set timetables for phasing out the production of the major ozone-depleting substances. More than 160 countries, including all major producers of ozone-depleting substances, have ratified the proposal. Following stipulations of the treaty and its more recent amendments, the industrial world has banned CFC production since 1996. Moreover, the protocol signatories pledged a fund of more than $700 million to help developing countries implement alternatives to CFCs and end their production by 2010.

Even with the Montreal Protocol fully implemented the ozone layer will not recover immediately because the reservoir of CFCs in the atmosphere may persist for 50 or 100 years. Some research suggests that improvement might be detected as soon as 2015, but other studies indicate it may be 2050 before recovery is well underway.

Air Pollution

In addition to diminishing stratospheric ozone, humans have altered the composition of the atmosphere in other ways as well, most obviously in the form of photochemical smog and other forms of air pollution within the troposphere.

The atmosphere has never been without pollutants. There are many natural sources of contaminants in the atmosphere: smoke from wildfires, ash from volcanic eruptions, windblown dust, pollen from plants, salt particles from breaking waves. Sometimes great natural events—particularly from volcanic eruptions and forest fires—have created severe localized pollution that was dispersed to affect weather patterns over large areas. Humans, however, have greatly exacerbated the pollution problem by adding to the frequency and magnitude of the release of pollutants into the air.

Smoke   Some types of air pollution are of recent origin, but others have been present for a very long time. Smoke, for example, has been recognized as a notable offender for centuries. Indeed, the burning of coal was prohibited in London by royal proclamation in the year 1300, with beheading as the penalty for anyone caught in the act! In 1661, an English royal commission wrote of the London air as "hell on earth;... this pestilential smoak which corrodes the very yron, and spoils all the moveables, leaving a soot on all things that it lights, and

PEOPLE AND THE ENVIRONMENT The UV Index

The *UV Index* was developed by the National Weather Service and the Environmental Protection Agency (EPA) to inform the public about levels of harmful ultraviolet radiation reaching the surface. The UV Index is a forecast of the next day's level of UV radiation, given on a scale of 1 to 11+, with 1 representing relatively low UV exposure risk, and levels of 8 or greater representing relatively high UV exposure risk (Figure 3-A).

The UV Index for the United States is based on forecast levels of ozone in the region, as well as the amount of cloud cover and the elevation of a city. In general, the lower the concentration of stratospheric ozone and the clearer the skies, the greater the level of harmful UV radiation that will reach the surface (Figure 3-B).

The ozone concentration data are obtained by the *SBUV/2* (Solar Backscatter Ultraviolet/2) instruments on the National Oceanic and Atmospheric Administration's (NOAA) *Polar Orbiting Environmental Satellites* and from the *TIROS Operational Vertical Sounder.*

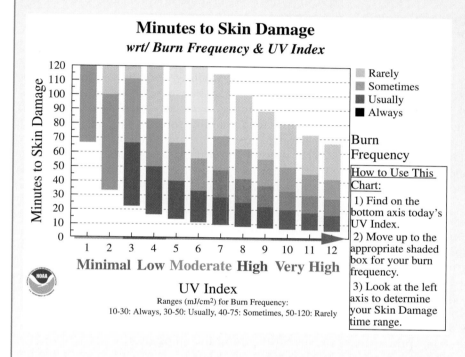

Figure 3-A   The UV Index. *(NOAA.)*

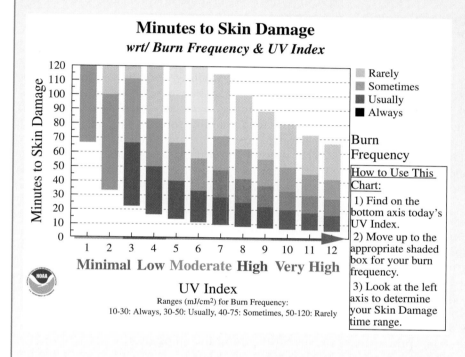

▲ **Figure 3-B**   UV Index Forecast map. *(NOAA.)*

so fatally seizing the lungs of the inhabitants, that the cough and the consumption spares no man."

With the advent of the Industrial Revolution, pollution became more widespread and intense, and by the twentieth century it was recognized as a major societal problem. Air-pollution "episodes" have often been death-dealing: 63 people killed over a five-day period in Belgium's Meuse Valley in 1930; 6000 illnesses and 20 deaths in Donora, Pennsylvania, during a week in 1948; 4000 deaths in London during a five-day ordeal in 1952. In addition to these isolated episodes, however, is the general increase in foul air over most of the world, creating a variety of health menaces and other difficulties.

By far the greatest problems are associated with cities because of the concentration of people and activities, and particularly of internal combustion engines and industrial establishments. The presence of pollutants in the air is most obviously manifest by impaired visibility due to fine particulate matter and associated water droplets. More critical, however, is the health hazard imposed by increasing concentrations of chemical impurities in the air. The principal components of air pollution in the United States are fine particulate matter, ozone, carbon monoxide, nitrogen dioxide, lead, and sulfur dioxide. Below, we describe several of these.

Sulfur Compounds   A large portion of the sulfur compounds found in the atmosphere are of natural origin, released from volcanoes or hydrothermal vents such as those in Yellowstone National Park—hydrogen sulfide (H_2S) with its familiar "rotten egg" smell is one example of this. However, especially over the last century, human activity has increased the release of sulfur compounds into the atmosphere, primarily through the burning of fossil fuels such as coal and petroleum. Sulfur is one of the minor impurities in coal and oil; when those fuels are burned, sulfur compounds such as sulfur dioxide (SO_2) are released. Sulfur dioxide itself is a lung irritant and corrosive, but it also may react in the atmosphere to produce secondary pollutants such as sulfur trioxide (SO_3) and sulfuric acid (H_2SO_4) —one of the contributors to acid rain (discussed in Chapter 6).

Nitrogen Compounds   Nitric oxide (NO) is a gas that can form in water and soil as a natural byproduct of biological processes; it generally breaks down quite quickly. However, NO may also form through combustion that takes place at high temperatures and pressures—such as in an automobile engine. Nitric oxide reacts in the atmosphere to form nitrogen dioxide (NO_2), a corrosive gas that gives some polluted air its yellow and reddish-brown color. Although NO_2 itself tends to break down quickly, it may in turn react under the influence of sunlight to form several different components of *smog.*

Photochemical Smog   A number of gases react to ultraviolet radiation in strong sunlight to produce secondary pollutants, making up what is known as **photochemical smog** (Figure 3-16). (The word "smog" was originally derived from the combination of the words *smoke* and *fog*; photochemical smog usually includes neither.) Nitrogen dioxide and hydrocarbons (also known as *volatile organic compounds* or VOC)— both of which can result from the incomplete burning of fuels such as gasoline—are major contributors to photochemical smog. Nitrogen dioxide breaks down under ultraviolet radiation to form nitric oxide, which may then react with VOC to form peroxyacetyl nitrate (PAN), which has become a significant cause of crop and forest damage in some areas.

The breakdown of NO_2 into NO also frees an oxygen atom that can react with O_2 molecules to form ozone—the main component of photochemical smog. Ozone has an acrid, biting odor that is distinctive of photochemical smog, causing damage to vegetation, corroding building materials (such as paint, rubber, plastics), and damaging sensitive tissues in humans (eyes, lungs, noses).

The state of the atmosphere is also an important determinant of the level of air pollution, especially photochemical smog. If there is considerable air movement, the pollutants can be quickly and widely dispersed. On the other hand, stagnant air allows for a rapid accumulation of pollutants. Thus, air pollution is particularly notable when anticyclonic (high-pressure) conditions prevail, with air subsiding from above and little surface wind flow. If the air is particularly stable, temperature inversions develop which function as "stability lids" that inhibit updrafts and general air movement. Almost all the cities that are persistently among the smoggiest in the world, such as Mexico City and Los Angeles, are characterized by a high frequency of temperature inversion and anticyclonic development.

▲ **Figure 3-16**   Smog over the eastern portion of the city of Santiago, Chile. (© *AFP/CORBIS.*)

Consequences of Anthropogenic Air Pollution
Although the effects of atmospheric pollutants vary, in general all forms of air pollution adversely affect lung function. Carbon monoxide, sulfur dioxide, and particulates can contribute to cardiovascular disease, while prolonged exposure to some particulates may promote lung cancer. Nitrogen oxides and sulfur dioxide are the principal contributors to acid rain. Tropospheric ozone damages crops and trees and is now the most widespread air pollutant, and it continues on a rising trend. The Environmental Protection Agency (EPA) reports that perhaps one-fifth of all hospital cases involving respiratory illness in the summer are a consequence of ozone exposure.

The atmosphere of our planet evolved over many millions of years to provide an environment suitable for life as we know it. As humans have developed technology and spread their civilization, they also have abused the atmosphere by increasing, intensifying, and diversifying the pollutants released into it. In the last few decades in the United States, there has been a downward trend in the emission of all pollutants except nitrogen oxides and ozone, largely as a result of increasingly stringent emission standards imposed by the EPA. Although significant steps are now being taken to reverse the growth of atmospheric pollution, as global population continues to expand, the pollutant load expands with it, and an ongoing effort on the part of all countries will be required to curtail the problem.

Weather and Climate

Now that we have described the composition and structure of the atmosphere, we turn more specifically to the broad set of processes operating within this ocean of air.

The vast and invisible atmospheric envelope is energized by solar radiation, stimulated by earthly motions, and affected by contact with Earth's surface. The atmosphere reacts by producing an infinite variety of conditions and phenomena known collectively as *weather*—the study of weather is known as *meteorology*. The term **weather** refers to short-run atmospheric conditions that exist for a given time in a specific area. It is the sum of temperature, humidity, cloudiness, precipitation, pressure, winds, storms, and other atmospheric variables for a short period of time. Thus, we speak of the weather of the moment or the week or the season, or perhaps even of the year or the decade.

Weather is in an almost constant state of change, sometimes in seemingly erratic fashion, yet in the long view, it is possible to generalize the variations into a composite pattern which is termed *climate*. **Climate** is the aggregate of day-to-day weather conditions over a long period of time. It encompasses not only the average characteristics, but also the variations and extremes. To describe the climate of an area requires weather information over an extended period, normally at least three decades.

Weather and climate, then, are related but not synonymous terms. The distinction between them is the difference between immediate specifics and protracted generalities. As the country philosopher once said, "Climate is what you expect; weather is what you get." Stated more sarcastically, "It is the climate that attracts people to a location, and the weather that makes them leave."

Weather and climate have direct and obvious influences on agriculture, transportation, and human life in general. Moreover, climate is a significant factor in the development of all major aspects of the physical landscape—soils, vegetation, animal life, hydrography, and topography.

Because climate and weather are generated in the atmosphere, our ultimate goal in studying the atmosphere is to understand the distribution and characteristics of climatic types over Earth. To achieve this understanding, we must consider in detail many of the processes that take place in the atmosphere. While our ultimate goal is an understanding of long-run atmospheric conditions (climate), we will spend the next four chapters gaining an appreciation for the dynamics involved in the momentary state of the atmosphere (weather).

The Elements of Weather and Climate

The atmosphere is a complex medium, and its mechanisms and processes are sometimes very complicated. Its nature, however, is generally expressed in terms of only a few variables, which are measurable. The data thus recorded provide the raw materials for understanding both temporary (weather) and long-term (climate) atmospheric conditions.

These variables can be thought of as the **elements of weather and climate**. The most important are (1) temperature, (2) moisture content, (3) pressure, and (4) wind (Table 3-3). These are the basic ingredients of weather and climate—the ones you hear about on the nightly weather report. Measuring how they vary in time and space makes it possible to decipher at least partly the complexities of weather dynamics and climatic patterns.

The Controls of Weather and Climate

Variations in the climatic elements are frequent, if not continuous, over Earth. Such variations are caused, or at least strongly influenced, by certain semipermanent attributes of our planet, which are often referred to as the **controls of weather and climate** (Table 3-3). The principal controls are briefly described in the paragraphs that follow and are explained in more detail in subsequent chapters. Although they are discussed individually here, it should be emphasized that there often is much overlap and interaction among them, with widely varying effects.

TABLE 3-3 The Elements and Controls of Weather and Climate

Elements of weather and climate	Controls of weather and climate
Temperature	Latitude
Pressure	Distribution of land and water
Wind	General circulation of the atmosphere
Moisture content	General circulation of the oceans
	Altitude
	Topographic barriers
	Storms

Latitude   We noted in Chapter 1 that the continuously changing positional relationship between the Sun and Earth brings continuously changing amounts of sunlight, and therefore of radiant energy, to different parts of Earth's surface. Thus, the basic distribution of heat over Earth is first and foremost a function of latitude, as indicated in Figure 3-17. In terms of elements and controls, we say that the control latitude strongly influences the element temperature.

Distribution of Land and Water   Probably the most fundamental distinction concerning the geography of climate is the distinction between continental climates and maritime (oceanic) climates. Oceans heat and cool more slowly and to a lesser degree than do landmasses, which means that maritime areas experience milder temperatures than continental areas in both summer and winter. For example, Seattle, Washington, and Fargo, North Dakota, are at approximately the same latitude (47° N), with Seattle on the western coast of the United States and Fargo deep in the interior. Seattle has an average January temperature of 5°C (41°F), while the January average in Fargo is −13°C (7°F). In the opposite season, Seattle has a July average temperature

of 19°C (66°F), whereas in Fargo the July average is 22°C (71°F).

Oceans are also a much more prolific source of atmospheric moisture. Thus, maritime climates are normally more humid than continental climates. The uneven distribution of continents and oceans over the world, then, is a prominent control of the elements moisture content and temperature.

General Circulation of the Atmosphere   The atmosphere is in constant motion, with flows that range from transitory local breezes to vast regional wind regimes. At the planetary scale, a semipermanent pattern of major wind and pressure systems dominates the troposphere and greatly influences most elements of weather and climate. As a simple example, most surface winds in the tropics come from the east, whereas the middle latitudes are characterized by flows that are mostly from the west, as Figure 3-18 shows.

General Circulation of the Oceans   Somewhat analogous to atmospheric movements are the motions of the oceans (Figure 3-19). Like the atmosphere, the oceans have many minor motions, but they also have a broad general pattern of currents. These currents assist in heat transfer by moving warm water poleward and cool water equatorward. Although the influence of currents on climate is much less than that of atmospheric circulation, the former is not inconsequential. For example, warm currents are found off the eastern coasts of continents, and cool currents occur off western coasts—a distinction that has a profound effect on coastal climates.

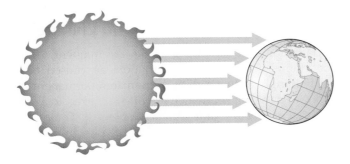

▲ **Figure 3-17**   Solar energy coming to Earth. See Figure 1-24 and the accompanying text for a review of this topic.

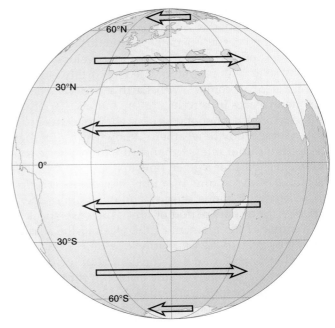

▲ **Figure 3-18**   The general circulation of the atmosphere is an important climatic control. This diagram is a highly simplified version of the actual circulation, which is discussed in Chapter 5.

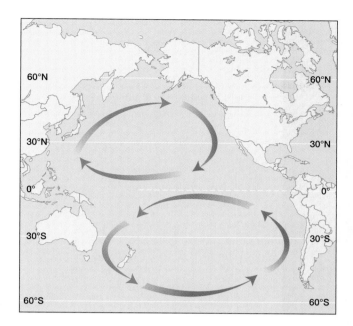

▲ **Figure 3-19** The general circulation of the oceans involves the movement of large amounts of warm water (red arrows) and cool water (blue arrows). These surface ocean currents have a significant climatic effect on neighboring landmasses.

Altitude We have already noted that three of the four weather elements—temperature, pressure, and moisture content—generally decrease upward in the troposphere and are therefore under the influence of the control altitude. This simple relationship between the three elements and the control has significant ramifications for many climatic characteristics, particularly in mountainous regions (Figure 3-20).

Topographic Barriers Mountains and large hills sometimes have prominent effects on one or more elements of climate by diverting wind flow (Figure 3-21). The side of a mountain range facing the wind (the

▲ **Figure 3-20** Increasing altitude affects many components of the environment, as indicated by the variety of natural vegetation patterns on the slopes of Blanca Peak in south-central Colorado. (*Tom L. McKnight photo.*)

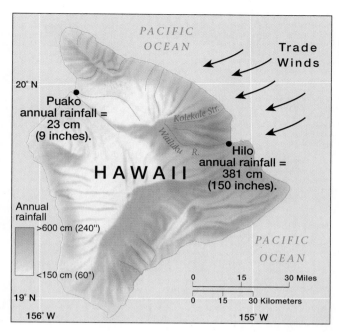

▲ **Figure 3-21** A topographic barrier as a control of climate. The difference in average annual rainfall in these two locations on the island of Hawaii is caused by the mountain range separating them. Moisture-laden trade winds coming in from the northeast drop their moisture when forced to rise by the eastern face of the mountains. The result is a very wet eastern side of the island and a very dry western side.

"windward" side), for example, is likely to have a climate vastly different from that of the sheltered ("leeward") side.

Storms Various kinds of storms occur over the world; some have very widespread distribution, whereas others are localized (Figure 3-22). Although they often result from interactions among other climate controls, all storms create specialized weather circumstances and so are considered to be a control. Indeed, some storms are prominent and frequent enough to affect not only weather but climate as well.

Before we move on to Chapter 4 to discuss temperature, the first of the elements of weather and climate, we need to consider one additional control of weather and climate—or perhaps more correctly, a control of some of the controls of weather and climate—the rotation of Earth.

The Coriolis Effect

Coriolis Effect

Everyone is familiar with the unremitting force of gravity. Its powerful pull toward the center of Earth influences all vertical motion that takes place near Earth's

◀ **Figure 3-22** A prominent storm system over the British Isles is counterpointed by localized thunderstorms over North Africa, Sicily, Italy, and Greece. *(European Space Agency/Science Photo Library/Photo Researchers, Inc., April 1992.)*

surface. Much less well known, however, because of its inconspicuous nature, is a pervasive horizontal influence on earthly motions. All things that move over the surface of Earth or in Earth's atmosphere appear to drift sideways as a result of Earth's rotation. George Hadley described this apparent deflection in the 1730s, but it was not explained quantitatively until Gaspard G. Coriolis (1792–1843), a French civil engineer and mathematician, did so a century later. The phenomenon is called the **Coriolis effect** in his honor (Figure 3-23). The Coriolis effect is frequently, and correctly, referred to as the "Coriolis force," especially when mathematically calculating its consequences. In this book we retain the more general term Coriolis effect when referring to this phenomenon.

The nature of the deflection due to the Coriolis effect can be demonstrated by imagining a rocket fired toward New York City from the North Pole. During the few minutes that the rocket is in the air, earthly rotation will have moved the target some kilometers to the east because the planet rotates from west to east. If the Coriolis effect was not included in the ballistic computation, the rocket would pass some

distance to the west of New York City (Figure 3-24). To a person standing at the launch point and looking south, the uncorrected flight path appears to deflect to the right.

This rightward deflection (in the Northern Hemisphere) applies no matter in which direction the rocket moves. If a rocket were aimed at New York City from a location on the same parallel of latitude—say, northern California—there would also be a drift to the right (as viewed by a person at the launch sight and looking east). During the time the rocket is in motion, both the California firing point and the New York target rotate eastward. Because Earth rotates, the landing point of an uncorrected flight path is southwest of New York City (Figure 3-25).

The Coriolis principle applies to any freely moving object—ball, bullet, airplane, automobile, even a person walking. For these and other short-range movements, however, the deflection is so minor and counterbalanced by other factors (such as friction, air resistance, and initial impetus) as to be insignificant. Long-range movements, on the other hand, can be significantly influenced by the Coriolis effect. The accurate firing of

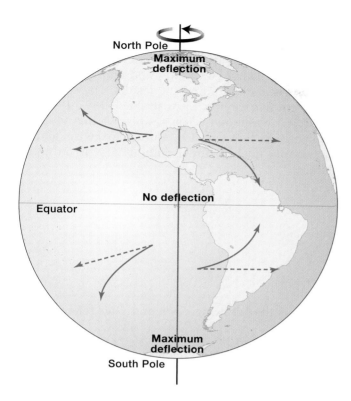

▲ **Figure 3-23** The deflection caused by the Coriolis effect is to the right in the Northern Hemisphere and to the left in the Southern Hemisphere. The dashed lines represent the planned route, and the solid lines represent actual movement.

artillery shells or launching of rockets and spacecraft requires careful compensation for the Coriolis effect if the projectiles are to reach their targets.

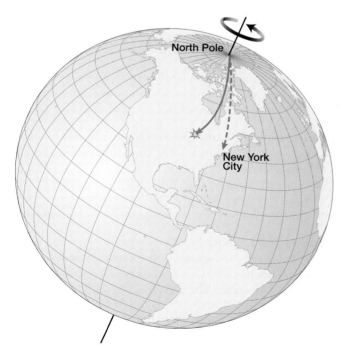

▲ **Figure 3-24** A rocket launched from the North Pole toward New York City lands to the west of the target if the Coriolis effect is not considered when the flight path is computed.

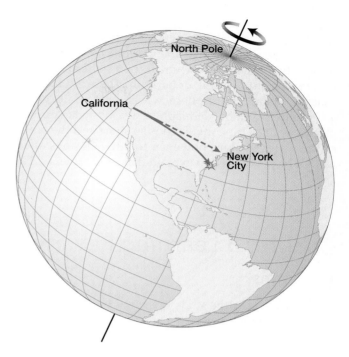

▲ **Figure 3-25** A rocket fired toward New York City and launched from a point at the same latitude in California appears to curve to the right because both firing and target points rotate to the east while the rocket is in the air.

The following are four basic points to remember:

1. Regardless of the initial direction of motion, any freely moving object appears to deflect to the right in the Northern Hemisphere and to the left in the Southern Hemisphere.
2. The apparent deflection is strongest at the poles and decreases progressively toward the equator, where there is zero deflection.
3. The Coriolis effect is proportional to the speed of the object, and so a fast-moving object is deflected more than a slower one.
4. The Coriolis effect influences direction of movement only; it has no influence on speed.

The major importance of the Coriolis effect in our study of climate involves its influence on winds and ocean currents:

1. All winds are affected by the Coriolis effect.
2. Ocean currents are also deflected by the Coriolis effect.

The latter is an important component of the dynamics of the general circulation of the oceans, with Northern Hemisphere currents trending to the right and Southern Hemisphere currents to the left. The Coriolis effect deflection is also a causative factor in the *upwelling* of cold water that takes place in subtropical latitudes where cool currents veer away from continental coastlines. The surface water that moves away from the shore is replaced by cold water rising from below.

One phenomenon that the Coriolis effect does not appear to influence is the circulation pattern of water that drains out of a sink or bathtub. There is a folk tale that Northern Hemisphere washbowls drain clockwise and Southern Hemisphere washbowls counterclockwise. The time involved is so short and the speed of the water so slow, however, that the Coriolis effect cannot be postulated to explain these movements. The characteristics of the plumbing system, the shape of the washbowl, and pure chance are more likely to determine the flow patterns. A reader can test this hypothesis, of course, by filling and emptying several washbowls and recording the results. The senior author spent five months in Australia in 1992–1993 and tested 100 washbowls. The results: 34 that emptied clockwise, 39 that emptied counterclockwise, and 27 that simply gushed down without a swirl in either pattern.

Chapter 3 Learning Review

Key Terms

Before answering the study questions below, review the definitions of the following key terms (page references are provided for you):

carbon dioxide *(p. 57)*
chlorofluorocarbons (CFCs) *(p. 63)*
climate *(p. 67)*
controls of weather and climate
 (p. 67)
Coriolis effect *(p. 70)*
elements of weather and climate
 (p. 67)
exosphere *(p. 59)*

heterosphere *(p. 61)*
homosphere *(p. 60)*
mesopause *(p. 59)*
mesosphere *(p. 59)*
ozone *(p. 57)*
ozone layer *(p. 57)*
ozonosphere *(p. 61)*
particulates (aerosols) *(p. 57)*

photochemical smog *(p. 66)*
stratopause *(p. 59)*
stratosphere *(p. 59)*
thermosphere *(p. 59)*
tropopause *(p. 58)*
troposphere *(p. 58)*
water vapor *(p. 56)*
weather *(p. 67)*

Study Questions for Key Concepts

After studying this chapter, you should be able to answer the following questions:

Size of Earth's Atmosphere (p. 55)
1. Why is the question "How deep is the atmosphere?" difficult to answer?

Composition of the Atmosphere (p. 56)
2. Describe and contrast the most important "constant" and "variable" components of the atmosphere.
3. Briefly describe some of the roles that *water vapor, carbon dioxide,* and *particulates (aerosols)* play in atmospheric processes.
4. Describe both the vertical distribution of water vapor in the atmosphere and its horizontal (geographic) distribution near Earth's surface.

Vertical Structure of the Atmosphere (p. 58)
5. Discuss the size and general temperature characteristics of the *troposphere* and *stratosphere*.
6. Describe how atmospheric pressure changes with increasing altitude.

7. In our study of physical geography, why do we concentrate primarily on the troposphere rather than on other zones of the atmosphere?

Human-Induced Atmospheric Change (p. 61)
8. What is *ozone* and why is it important in the atmosphere?
9. What is meant by the "hole in the ozone layer" and what has caused this?
10. Describe and explain the causes of *photochemical smog*.

Weather and Climate (p. 67)
11. What is the difference between *weather* and *climate*?
12. What are the four elements of weather and climate?
13. Briefly describe the seven dominant controls of weather and climate.
14. Describe the *Coriolis effect* and its cause.

Additional Resources

Books:

Cox, John D. *Storm Watchers: The Turbulent History of Weather Prediction from Franklin's Kite to El Niño.* Hoboken, NJ: John Wiley & Sons, 2002.

Graedel, T. E., and P. J. Crutzen. "The Changing Atmosphere," *Scientific American,* Vol. 259, September 1989, pp. 58–68.

Lutgens, Frederick K., and Edward J. Tarbuck. *The Atmosphere: An Introduction to Meteorology,* 9th ed. Upper Saddle River, New Jersey: Pearson-Prentice Hall, 2004.

Internet Sites:

Environmental Protection Agency (EPA)

http://www.epa.gov/

The EPA provides information about climate change, air and water pollution, ozone, acid rain, and pesticide contamination.

Intergovernmental Panel on Climate Change

http://www.ipcc.ch/

The Intergovernmental Panel on Climate Change was established to study and assess global climate change and its influence on human populations.

National Oceanic and Atmospheric Administration (NOAA)

http://www.noaa.gov/

The National Oceanic and Atmospheric Administration (NOAA) oversees a number of government agencies, including the National Weather Service. NOAA's home page provides links to sites about weather, climate, weather satellites, the oceans, and coastlines.

4
Insolation and Temperature

The temperature of the air at any time and at any place in the atmosphere is the result of the interaction among a variety of complex factors. In this chapter, our attention is focused on the energetics of the atmosphere—the important processes involved in bringing *insolation* (incoming solar radiation) to the atmosphere, in determining the extent of heating (and cooling) that takes place, and in transferring heat from one place to another. Understanding these processes will help us understand the distribution of temperature over Earth.

The Impact of Temperature on the Landscape

All organisms have certain temperature tolerances, and most are harmed by wide fluctuations in temperature. Thus, when the weather becomes particularly hot or cold, mobile organisms are likely to search for shelter, and their apparent presence in the landscape is diminished. Human beings also seek haven from temperature extremes, although they have other options (such as specialized clothing) that allow them to brave the elements. In a broader view, immoderate temperatures have a more profound effect on the landscape because both animals and plants often evolve in response to hot or cold climates. For this reason, the inventory of flora and fauna in any area of temperature extremes is likely to be determined by the capability of the various species to withstand the long-term temperature conditions. An example of such an adaptation is shown in Figure 4-1a.

Most inorganic components of the landscape also are affected by long-run temperature conditions. For example, temperature is a basic factor in soil development, and repeated fluctuations of temperature are a prominent cause of the breakdown of exposed bedrock. The human-built landscape is also influenced by temperature considerations, as demonstrated by architectural styles and building materials. An example of such influence is shown in Figure 4-1b.

Energy, Heat, and Temperature

We begin by clarifying a few terms and concepts that we will use in our discussion of atmospheric heating. In the most basic sense, the universe is made up of just

◀ Frost-covered trees along the Lower Dells, Matthiessen State Park, Illinois. *(Getty Images.)*

(a)

(b)

▲ **Figure 4-1** **(a)** A yellow-headed collared lizard in the desert of western Colorado. It strikes an erect pose to keep its belly off the hot rock. *(Rod Plank/Photo Researchers, Inc.)* **(b)** The town museum in Igloolik in Canada's Northwest Territories is built in a style that is adjusted to the cold climate. *(Robert Sememiuk/The Stock Market.)*

two kinds of "things": *matter* and *energy*. The concept of matter is fairly easy to comprehend. Matter is the "stuff" of the universe: the solids, liquids, gases—and atomic particles—from which all things are made. Matter has mass and volume; we can easily see and feel many kinds of matter. The concept of energy, on the other hand, may be more difficult to grasp.

Energy

Energy is commonly defined as the "ability to do work," but in practice, it may be better to describe what energy does rather than trying to define it. Energy refers to anything that changes the state or condition of matter. For example, it takes energy to cause something to move faster, or cause it to change direction, or cause it to break apart.

There are many forms of energy: kinetic energy, chemical energy, and radiant energy, among many others. Although energy can neither be created nor destroyed, it can, and frequently does, change from one form to another. In our discussion of the heating of the atmosphere, we will look at just a few forms of energy and the transformations between these forms.

In order to understand the heating of the atmosphere—or anything else—we first need to consider what is happening at the atomic or molecular level—a scale that we do not readily comprehend in our everyday lives. A great simplification of reality: All substances are composed of extraordinarily tiny, constantly "jiggling" *atoms*, commonly bonded together into combinations of atoms called *molecules*. The state of those substances—whether they are solid, liquid, gas, (or plasma, which is an ionized gas)—depends in part on how vigorously the molecules are jiggling back and forth in place. Because of this constant movement, the molecules in all substances possess energy. This kind of *internal energy* is a form of **kinetic energy**—the energy of movement.

The average amount of kinetic energy possessed by the molecules in a substance is closely associated with a physical property that we can often readily sense in our everyday lives: how hot or cold something is.[1] When a substance becomes warmer, it indicates that the average kinetic energy of the molecules in that substance has increased. In other words, energy has been added that has caused the molecules to jiggle back and forth more vigorously. So this brings us to several important definitions.

Temperature and Heat

Temperature is a description of the average kinetic energy of the molecules in a substance (strictly speaking, the average "back and forth" or *translational kinetic energy* of the molecules). The more vigorous the jiggling of the molecules (and therefore the greater the internal kinetic energy), the higher the temperature of a substance.

Heat refers to energy that transfers from one object or substance to another because of a difference in temperature. Sometimes the term **thermal energy** is used interchangeably with the term heat. A substance doesn't "contain" heat—heat is simply the energy that is transferred from an object with a higher temperature to an object with a lower temperature, thereby decreasing the internal energy of the hotter object and increasing the internal energy of the cooler object.

Measuring Temperature

Instruments used to measure temperature are called **thermometers**. The temperature of an object is relative

[1] In this book, the adjectives hot, cold, warm, and cool are used frequently; like other descriptive words that appear (high, low, wet, dry, fast, slow, to name a few), they are often used in a comparative sense; something is hot or cold in comparison with something else.

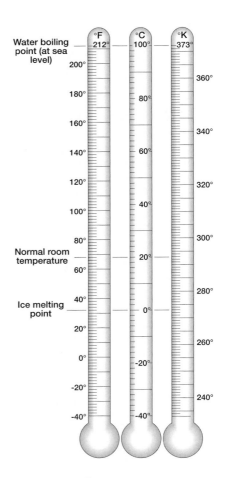

▲ **Figure 4-2** The Fahrenheit, Celsius, and Kelvin temperature scales.

to one of three temperature scales that are in concurrent use (Figure 4-2). Each permits a precise measurement, but the existence of three scales creates an unfortunate degree of confusion.

Fahrenheit Scale   The temperature scale most widely understood by the general public in the United States is the Fahrenheit scale (named after Gabriel Daniel Fahrenheit, the eighteenth-century German physicist who devised it). Public weather reports from the National Weather Service and the news media usually state temperatures in degrees Fahrenheit. The reference points on this scale are the sea-level freezing and boiling points of pure water, which are 32° and 212°, respectively. The United States is one of only a few countries that still use the Fahrenheit scale.

Celsius Scale   In most other countries, the Celsius scale (named for Anders Celsius, the eighteenth-century Swedish astronomer who devised it) is used either exclusively or predominantly. It is an accepted component of the International System of measurement (SI) because it is a decimal scale with 100 units (degrees) between the freezing and boiling points of water. The Celsius scale has long been used for scientific work in the United States and is now slowly being established

FOCUS Gathering Temperature Data

At thousands of locations (called *stations*) throughout the world, temperature data are recorded on a regular basis. These data provide important raw material for contemporary weather reports and forecasts as well as for long-run climatic analyses. Data from some stations goes back more than a century. Although an electronic temperature sensor linked to a remote computer is by far the most common way data are gathered today, in a few stations around the world the temperature indicated by a traditional liquid-filled thermometer is still recorded by a human observer (Figure 4-A).

Liquid-filled thermometers have been used for many centuries. The mercury or ethyl alcohol inside such a

▲ **Figure 4-A**   A weather instrument shelter. It is placed a short distance above the ground, is painted white so that it reflects direct sunlight, and has slatted sides to permit air circulation. *(Dr. E. R. Degginger.)*

thermometer expands when heated and contracts when cooled; the glass tube of the thermometer is calibrated at a few fixed temperatures (such as the freezing and boiling points of water), and then values between these extremes are interpolated. Among the most useful of traditional liquid-filled thermometers are minimum and maximum thermometers.

A *minimum thermometer* records the lowest temperature in a given period (Figure 4-B). In this instrument, a small glass wire shaped like a tiny dumbbell (called an *index*) is placed in the column of alcohol (which is used instead of mercury because it is transparent and allows the index to be seen). The thermometer is kept horizontal. When the temperature decreases, the alcohol contracts, and the tension in its concave surface is strong enough to drag the index down. When the temperature increases, the alcohol expands and rises in the tube. It does not pull the index with it because the concave surface does not generate enough tension in that direction. Thus, the index is left behind as clear evidence of the lowest temperature reached. After this value is read by the observer, the thermometer is reset by inverting it so that the index drops to the end of the column again.

A *maximum thermometer* has a narrow constriction in the glass tube just above the bulb. It is also kept horizontal. As the temperature rises, the mercury expands and is forced through the constriction one tiny drop at a time. When the temperature subsequently falls, however, nothing forces the mercury back through the constriction, and so the column cannot get shorter. The height of the column indicates the maximum temperature attained. The thermometer is reset by shaking or whirling it to force the mercury back into the bulb.

Data gathered at each station (whether compiled by computer or human observer) is used to calculate a number of different temperature measures. The *daily mean temperature* is calculated by averaging 24 hourly readings or is estimated from the average of the maximum and minimum. From these data can also be calculated the *daily temperature range*, which is the number of degrees difference between the highest and lowest recorded values of the 24-hour period. The *monthly mean temperature* for each station is determined by averaging the daily means for each day in the calendar month. The *annual mean temperature* represents the average of the 12 monthly means. The difference between the means of the warmest and coldest months is the *annual temperature range*.

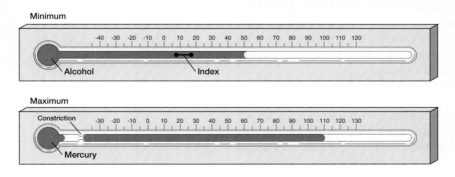

▲ **Figure 4-B**   Minimum and maximum thermometers.

to supersede the Fahrenheit scale in all usages in this country.

To convert from degrees Celsius to degrees Fahrenheit, the following formula is used:

degrees Fahrenheit = (degrees Celsius × 1.8) + 32°

To convert from degrees Fahrenheit to degrees Celsius, the formula is

degrees Celsius = (degrees Fahrenheit − 32°) ÷ 1.8

Kelvin Scale   For many scientific purposes, the Kelvin scale (named for the nineteenth-century British physicist William Thomson, also known as Lord Kelvin) has long been used because it measures what are called *absolute temperatures*, which means that the scale begins at *absolute zero*, the lowest possible temperature.[2] The scale maintains a 100-degree range between the boiling and freezing points of water. There are no negative values. Because this scale is not normally used by climatologists and meteorologists, we ignore it in this book except to compare it to the Fahrenheit and Celsius scales. On the Celsius scale, absolute zero is at −273° and so the conversion is simple:

degrees Celsius = degrees Kelvin −273°

degrees Kelvin = degrees Celsius +273°

Solar Energy

The Sun is the only significant source of energy for Earth's atmosphere. Millions of other stars radiate energy, but they are too far away to affect Earth. Energy is also released from inside Earth, primarily as radioactive decay of minerals, and energy is released on the ocean floor through hydrothermal vents, although probably not enough to influence the atmosphere significantly. Thus, the Sun supplies essentially all of the energy that drives most of the atmospheric processes. Further, we will see that it is the unequal heating of the Earth by the Sun that ultimately puts the atmosphere in motion and is responsible for the most fundamental patterns of weather and climate.

The Sun is a star of average size and average temperature, but its proximity to Earth gives it a far greater influence on our planet than that exerted by all other celestial bodies combined. The Sun is a prodigious generator of energy. In a single second, it produces more energy than the amount used by humankind since civilization began. The Sun functions as an enormous thermonuclear reactor, producing energy through

nuclear fusion—under extremely high temperatures and pressures, nuclei of hydrogen are fused together to form helium—a process that utilizes only a very small portion of the Sun's mass but provides an immense and continuous flow of energy that is dispersed in all directions.

Electromagnetic Radiation

The Sun gives off energy in the form of **electromagnetic radiation**—sometimes referred to as **radiant energy**. We have experience almost every day with many different kinds of electromagnetic radiation: visible light, microwaves, X-rays, and radio waves are all forms of electromagnetic radiation.

Electromagnetic radiation entails the flow of energy in the form of waves. These waves of energy move through space by way of rapidly oscillating electromagnetic fields. These electromagnetic fields are oscillating in the same rhythm as the vibrations of the electrical charges that form them—for example, it is the oscillation of electrons within an atom that can generate visible light. Electromagnetic radiation does not require a medium (the presence of matter) to pass through. The electromagnetic waves traverse the great voids of space in unchanging form. The waves travel outward from the Sun in straight lines at the *speed of light*—300,000 kilometers (186,000 miles) per second.

Only a tiny fraction of the Sun's radiant output is intercepted by Earth. The waves travel through space without loss of energy, but since they are diverging from a spherical body their intensity continuously diminishes with increased distance from the Sun (Figure 4-3). As a

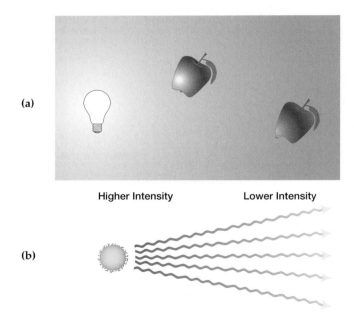

(a)

Higher Intensity   Lower Intensity

(b)

▲ **Figure 4-3   (a)** The closer apple intercepts more rays from the lightbulb and therefore is better illuminated than the farther apple. **(b)** Electromagnetic waves from the Sun spread out as they move outward from the Sun. Thus their intensity decreases as they get farther and farther from the Sun.

---

[2]In classical physics *absolute zero* is the temperature at which molecules have their *zero-point energy* (have no kinetic energy that can be given up). In quantum physics, however, the zero-point energy (lowest energy state for a system) need not be actually zero.

result of this intensity decrease and the distance separating Earth from the Sun, less than one two-billionth of total solar output reaches the outer limit of Earth's atmosphere, having traveled 150,000,000 kilometers (93,000,000 miles) in just over eight minutes. Although it consists of only a minuscule portion of total solar output, in absolute terms the amount of solar energy Earth receives is enormous: the amount received in one second is approximately equivalent to all the electric energy generated on Earth in a week.

Electromagnetic radiation can be classified on the basis of *wavelength*—the distance between the crest of one wave and the crest of the next (Figure 4-4). Collectively, electromagnetic radiation of all wavelengths comprises what is called the **electromagnetic spectrum** (Figure 4-5). Electromagnetic radiation varies enormously in wavelength—ranging from the exceedingly short wavelengths of gamma rays and X-rays (with some wavelengths less than one-billionth of a meter), to the exceedingly long wavelengths of television and radio waves (with some wavelengths measured in kilometers). For the physical geographer, however, only three areas of the spectrum are of importance:

1. **Visible light:** Wavelengths of radiation to which the human eye is sensitive make up a fairly narrow band of the electromagnetic spectrum known as **visible light**, and include wavelengths between about 0.4 and 0.7 micrometers (μm; one micrometer equals one-millionth of a meter). Visible light ranges from the shortest wavelength of radiation the human eye can sense—violet—through the progressively longer wavelengths of blue, green, yellow, orange, and finally red, the longest wavelength of radiation the human eye can see (you'll notice that this sequence of color is the same as you see in a rainbow, from inner to outer; see p. 140).

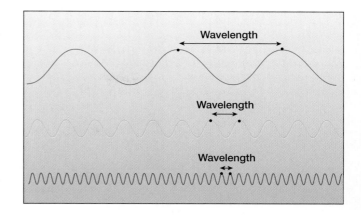

▲ **Figure 4-4** Electromagnetic waves can be of almost any length. The distance from one crest to the next is called the *wavelength*.

While visible light makes up a narrow band on the electromagnetic spectrum, approximately 47% of the total energy coming from the Sun arrives at Earth as visible light.

2. **Ultraviolet Radiation:** Wavelengths of radiation just shorter than the human eye can sense, with wavelengths from about 0.01 to 0.4 micrometers, make up the **ultraviolet (UV)** portion of the electromagnetic spectrum. The Sun is a prominent natural source of ultraviolet rays, and solar insolation reaching the top of our atmosphere contains a considerable amount (approximately 8% of the total energy coming from the Sun). However, as we saw in Chapter 3, much of the UV radiation from the Sun is absorbed by the ozone layer, and so the shortest ultraviolet wavelengths do not reach Earth's surface where they could cause considerable damage to most living organisms.

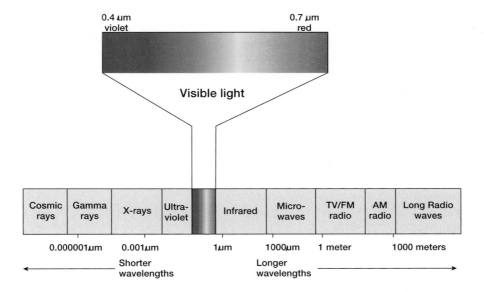

▲ **Figure 4-5** The electromagnetic spectrum.

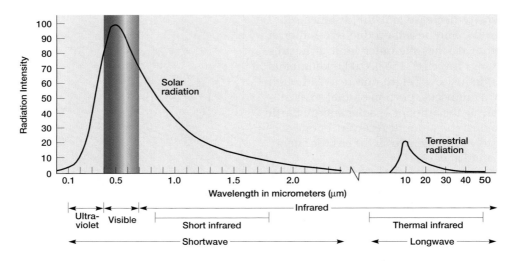

▲ **Figure 4-6**   Comparison of solar and terrestrial radiation intensity. Wavelength is in micrometers (μm).

3. **Infrared Radiation:** Wavelengths of radiation just longer than the human eye can sense make up the **infrared** (IR) portion of the electromagnetic spectrum, with wavelengths between 0.7 and about 1000 micrometers (1 millimeter). Infrared radiation ranges from the short or *near infrared* wavelengths emitted by the Sun to much longer wavelengths sometimes called **thermal infrared**. (Infrared "heat lamps" are designed to emit thermal infrared energy.) A large portion of solar energy comes to Earth as short infrared radiation (approximately 45% of the total), while radiation emitted by Earth is entirely thermal infrared.

Solar radiation is almost completely in the form of visible light, ultraviolet and short infrared radiation, which as a group is referred to as **shortwave radiation** (Figure 4-6). Radiation emitted by Earth—or **terrestrial radiation**—is entirely in the thermal infrared portion of the spectrum and is referred to as **longwave radiation**. A wavelength of about 4 micrometers is considered the boundary on the spectrum separating long waves from short ones; thus, all terrestrial radiation is longwave radiation, while virtually all solar radiation is shortwave radiation.

Insolation

The total **insolation** (*in*coming *sol*ar radi*ation*) received at the top of the atmosphere is believed to be constant when averaged over a year, although it may vary slightly over long periods of time with fluctuations in the Sun's temperature. This constant amount of incoming energy—referred to as the *solar constant*—is about 1372 watts per square meter (W/m^2). One watt is equal to 1 joule per second (a *joule* is a unit of energy equivalent to about 0.239 calories; 1 *calorie* being the amount

of heat required to raise the temperature of 1 gram of water [at 15°C] by 1°C).

The entrance of insolation into the upper atmosphere is just the beginning of a complex series of events in the atmosphere and at Earth's surface. Some of the insolation is reflected off the atmosphere back out into space, where it is lost. The remaining insolation may pass through the atmosphere, where it can be transformed either before or after reaching Earth's surface. This mixed reception of solar energy—and the resulting energy cascade that ultimately heats Earth's surface and atmosphere—are discussed after a brief digression to define our terms.

Basic Heating and Cooling Processes in the Atmosphere

Before looking at the events that occur after energy travels from the Sun to Earth, we first need to examine the physical processes involved in the movement of heat energy. Our goal is to provide practical explanations of the most important processes associated with the heating and cooling of the atmosphere. As such, in some cases we limit our discussion of a process to the aspects of direct importance to meteorology.

Radiation

Radiation—or **emission**—is the process by which electromagnetic energy is emitted from an object. All objects radiate electromagnetic energy, but hotter bodies are more potent radiators than cooler ones (Figure 4-7). In general, the hotter the object, the more intense its radiation—because the Sun is much hotter than Earth, it emits about 2 billion times more energy than Earth.

▲ **Figure 4-7**   All objects radiate electromagnetic energy, but hot objects radiate with greater intensity than cool objects.

In addition, the hotter the object, the shorter the wavelengths of that radiation. Hot bodies radiate mostly short waves, while cooler bodies radiate mostly long waves. The Sun is the ultimate "hot" body of our solar system, and so nearly all of its radiation is in the shortwave portion of the electromagnetic spectrum. Earth, on the other hand, is cooler than the Sun, so Earth emits longer wavelengths of radiant energy.

Temperature, however, is not the only control of radiation effectiveness. Objects at the same temperature may vary considerably in their radiating capability. A body that emits the maximum possible amount of radiation at all wavelengths is called a *blackbody radiator*. Both the Sun and Earth function very nearly as blackbodies, that is, as perfect radiators. They radiate with almost 100 percent efficiency for their respective temperatures. The atmosphere, on the other hand, is not as efficient a radiator as either the Sun or Earth's surface.

Absorption

Electromagnetic waves striking an object may be assimilated by that object—this process is called **absorption**. Different materials have different absorptive capabilities, with the variations depending in part on the wavelength of radiation involved. Although it is a great simplification, when electromagnetic waves strike a material, atoms or even whole molecules in that material may be forced into vibration by the *frequency* of the incoming electromagnetic waves. (Since all wavelengths of electromagnetic radiation travel at the same speed, short wavelengths of radiation arrive with a higher frequency than do longer wavelengths.) The increased vibrations of the atoms and molecules result in an increase in the internal kinetic energy of the absorbing material, and so the material becomes warmer—thus, an increase in temperature is a typical response to the absorption of electromagnetic radiation.

As a basic generalization, a good radiator is also a good absorber, and a poor radiator is a poor absorber. Mineral materials (rock, soil) are generally excellent absorbers; snow and ice are poor absorbers; water surfaces

▲ **Figure 4-8**   Most solar radiation that reaches Earth's surface is either absorbed or reflected. In this example, the white clothes of one skier reflect much of the solar energy, keeping him cool, whereas the dark clothes of the other skier absorb energy, thereby raising his temperature.

vary in their absorbing efficiency. One important distinction concerns color. Dark-colored surfaces are much more efficient absorbers of radiation in the visible portion of the spectrum than light-colored surfaces (as exemplified by the uncomfortably warm skier wearing dark clothing in Figure 4-8).

As we will see, both water vapor and carbon dioxide are efficient absorbers of certain wavelengths of radiation, while nitrogen, the most abundant gas in the atmosphere, is not.

Reflection

Reflection is the ability of an object to repel electromagnetic waves without altering either the object or the waves. When insolation is reflected by the atmosphere or the surface of Earth, it is deflected away, unchanged, in the general direction from which it came. A mirror, for example, is designed to be highly efficient in reflecting visible light.

In our context, reflection is the opposite of absorption. If the wave is reflected, it cannot be absorbed. Hence, an object that is a good absorber is a poor reflector, and vice versa (Figure 4-8). A simple example of this principle is the existence of unmelted snow on a sunny day. If it is to melt, the snow must absorb energy from the Sun. Although the air temperature may be well above freezing, the snow does not melt rapidly because its white surface reflects away a large share of the solar energy that strikes it.

Scattering

Gas molecules and particulate matter in the air can deflect light waves and redirect them in a type of reflection known as **scattering** (Figure 4-9). This deflection involves a change in the direction of the light wave, but no change in wavelength. Some of the waves are backscattered into space and thus are lost to Earth, but many of them continue through the atmosphere in altered but random directions eventually striking the surface as *diffuse radiation*.

The amount of scattering that takes place depends on the wavelength of the light as well as on the size, shape, and composition of the molecule or particulate. In general, shorter wavelengths are more readily scattered than longer ones by the gases in the atmosphere. One prominent kind of scattering, known as *Rayleigh scattering*, takes place when the shortest wavelengths of visible light—violet and blue—are scattered more easily in all directions by the gas molecules in the atmosphere than are the longer wavelengths of visible light—orange and red. This is why on a clear day the sky is blue. (The sky is blue and not violet because of the greater prevalence of blue wavelengths in solar radiation and because our eyes are less sensitive to violet light.) Were there no scattering of blue light by the atmosphere, the sky would appear black. When the sun is low in the sky, the light has passed through so much atmosphere that nearly all of the blue wavelengths have been scattered away, leaving only the longest wavelengths of visible light, orange and red—the dominant colors of light we see at sunrise and sunset (Figure 4-10).

When the atmosphere contains large quantities of larger particles, such as suspended aerosols, all wavelengths of visible light are more equally scattered (a

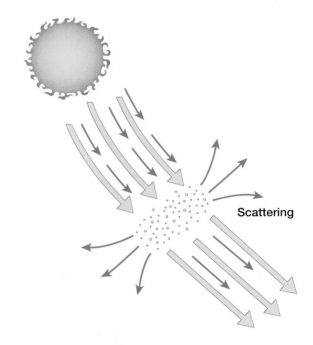

▲ **Figure 4-9**   Gas molecules and impurities in the atmosphere scatter and redirect light waves. Some waves are scattered into space and therefore lost to Earth; others are scattered but continue through the atmosphere in altered directions. There is greater scattering of blue light than the longer wavelengths of visible light.

process known as *Mie scattering*), leaving the sky looking gray rather than blue.

In terms of atmospheric heating, one of the consequences of scattering—especially Rayleigh scattering—is that the intensity of solar radiation striking the surface of Earth is less than that of the solar radiation striking the upper atmosphere because scattering redirects a portion of the insolation back out to space (Figure 4-11).

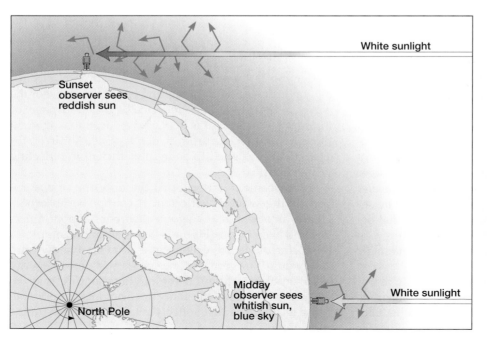

◀ **Figure 4-10**   Short wavelengths (blue and violet) of visible light are scattered more effectively than longer wavelengths. Consequently, when the Sun is overhead on a clear day, one can see blue sky in all directions because blue light was selectively scattered. At sunrise or sunset, however, the path that light must take through the atmosphere is much longer, with the result that most of the blue light is scattered out before the light waves reach Earth's surface. Thus, the Sun appears reddish in color.

◀ **Figure 4-11** The predominant colors of a sunset are orange and red, as in this scene of the Sun setting behind the Golden Gate Bridge in San Francisco. *(Darrel Hess photo.)*

Transmission

Transmission is the process whereby electromagnetic waves pass completely through a medium, as when light waves are transmitted through a pane of clear, colorless glass. There is obviously considerable variability among mediums in their capacity to transmit electromagnetic waves. Earth materials, for example, are very poor transmitters of insolation; sunlight is absorbed at the surface of rock or soil and does not penetrate at all. Water, on the other hand, transmits sunlight well: even in very murky water, light penetrates some distance below the surface, and in clear water, sunlight may illuminate to considerable depths.

The transmission ability of a medium generally depends on the wavelength of radiation. For example, glass has high transmissivity for shortwave radiation but not for longwave radiation. Heat builds up in a closed automobile left parked in the Sun because shortwave radiation is transmitted through the window glass and is absorbed by the upholstery. The longwave radiation then emitted by the interior of the car does not readily transmit out through the glass, causing the inside of the car to warm up (Figure 4-12). This is commonly called the **greenhouse effect**.[3]

The Greenhouse Effect The greenhouse effect is at work in the atmosphere (Figure 4-13). A number of gases in the atmosphere, known as **greenhouse gases**, readily transmit incoming shortwave radiation from the Sun but do not easily transmit outgoing longwave terrestrial radiation. The most important greenhouse gas is water vapor, followed by carbon dioxide. Many other trace gases such as methane also play a role, as do some kinds of clouds.

In the simplest terms, incoming shortwave solar radiation transmits through the atmosphere to Earth's

▲ **Figure 4-12** Transmission is illustrated by the shortwave insolation (sunlight) being transmitted through the car windows and into the car interior. Because glass allows transmission of only shortwave radiation, the longer waves reradiated by the heated upholstery are not able to escape through the windows. This is known as the *greenhouse effect*.

[3]The term greenhouse effect was given to this process because it was long thought that greenhouses maintained heat in the same manner—the glass roof transmitting shortwave solar energy inhibited the passage of longwave radiation out. Recently, it has been shown that this is not the full story; for example, greenhouses having windows made of rock salt, which permits equal transmission of longwaves and shortwaves, experience a heat buildup approximately as great as that of ordinary glass greenhouses. Further investigation showed that glass greenhouses maintain high temperatures largely because the warm air in the building is trapped and does not dissipate through the mixing with the cooler air outside. Thus, the term greenhouse effect is based on a misconception, and the retention of heat in the lower troposphere because of differential transmissivity for the shortwaves and longwaves should probably be called something else; "atmospheric effect" has been suggested, but greenhouse effect continues to be the customary term.

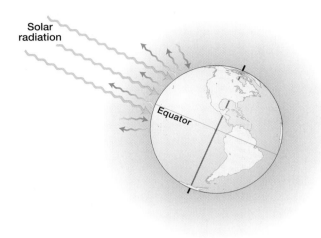

▲ **Figure 4-13** The atmosphere easily transmits shortwave radiation from the Sun but is a poor transmitter of the longer waves radiated from Earth's surface. This selective transmission causes the *greenhouse effect* in the atmosphere.

surface, where this energy is absorbed, raising the temperature of the surface. However, the longwave radiation emitted by Earth's surface is inhibited from transmitting back through the atmosphere by the greenhouse gases. Much of this outgoing terrestrial radiation is absorbed by greenhouse gases and clouds and then reradiated back toward the surface, hence delaying this energy loss to space.

The greenhouse effect is one of the most important heating processes in the troposphere. The greenhouse effect keeps Earth's surface and lower troposphere much warmer than would be the case if there were no atmosphere—without the greenhouse effect, the average temperature of Earth would be about −15°C (5°F) rather than the present average of 15°C (59°F).

While the ongoing, natural greenhouse effect in the atmosphere makes life as we know it possible, over the last century or so a significant increase in greenhouse gas concentration—especially carbon dioxide—has been measured. This increase in atmospheric carbon dioxide is closely associated with human activity, especially the burning of fossil fuels such as petroleum and coal (carbon dioxide is one of the by-products of combustion). The increase in greenhouse gas concentration has been accompanied by a slight, yet nonetheless measurable, increase in average global temperature, raising the likelihood that humans are altering the global energy balance of the atmosphere. This important issue, generally referred to as *global warming*, will be addressed in more detail at the end of this chapter after we have concluded our discussion of atmospheric heating processes and patterns.

Conduction

The movement of heat energy from one molecule to another without changes in their relative positions is called **conduction**. This process enables heat to be transferred from one part of a stationary body to another, or from one object to a second object when the two are in contact.

Conduction comes about through molecular collision, as the blown-up view in Figure 4-14 illustrates. A "hot" molecule becomes increasingly agitated as heat is added to it and collides against a cooler, calmer molecule, transferring kinetic energy to it. In this manner, the heat is passed from one place to another. When two molecules of unequal temperature are in contact with one another, heat energy transfers from the hotter to the cooler until they attain the same temperature.

The ability of different substances to conduct heat is quite variable. For example, most metals are excellent conductors, as can be demonstrated by pouring hot coffee into a metal cup and then touching your lips to the edge of the cup. The heat of the coffee is quickly conducted throughout the metal and burns the lips of the incautious drinker. In contrast, hot coffee poured

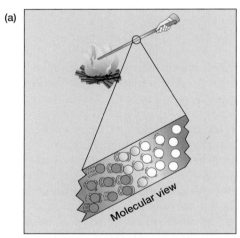

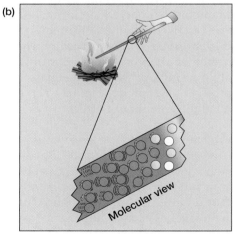

▲ **Figure 4-14** Energy is conducted from one place to another by molecular agitation. One end of the metal rod is in the flame and so becomes hot. This heat is then conducted the length of the rod and will burn the hand of the incautious rod-holder.

into a ceramic cup heats the cup very slowly because such earthy material is a poor conductor.

Earth's land surface warms up rapidly during the day because it is a good absorber of incoming shortwave radiation, and some of that warmth is transferred away from the surface by conduction. A small part is conducted deeper underground, but not much, because Earth materials are not good conductors. Another portion of this absorbed heat is transferred to the lowest portion of the atmosphere by conduction from the ground surface. Air, however, is a poor conductor, and so only the air layer touching the ground is heated very much (perhaps a layer just a few millimeters thick). Physical movement of the air is required to spread the heat around.

Moist air is a slightly more efficient conductor than dry air. If you are outdoors on a winter day, you will stay warmer if there is little moisture in the air.

Convection

In the process of **convection**, heat is transferred from one point to another by the predominately vertical circulation of a fluid, such as air or water. Convection involves movement of the heated molecules from one place to another. (Do not confuse the movement of molecules from one place to another in the process of *convection* with the back-and-forth vibratory movement and molecular collisions associated with *conduction*—in convection, the molecules physically move away from the heat source; in conduction, they do not.)

If your room is heated by a "radiator" (Figure 4-15), you have taken advantage of convection. The heated air immediately above the radiator rises because the heating has caused it to expand and therefore become less dense than the nearby air. Surrounding air then moves in to fill the void left by the rising warm air. In turn, cooler air from above descends to replace that which has moved in from the side, and a cellular circulation is established—up, out, down, and in.

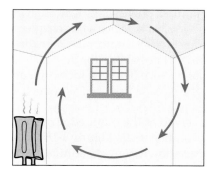

▲ **Figure 4-15** A "radiator" in a closed room sets up a convective circulation system. Air warmed by the radiator rises, and cooler air flows toward the radiator to replace the heated air that has risen.

A similar convective pattern frequently develops in the atmosphere. Unequal heating (for a variety of reasons) may cause a parcel of surface air to become warmer than the surrounding air, and thus the warm air will rise. The heated air expands and moves upward in the direction of lower pressure. The cooler surrounding air then moves in toward the heat source, and air from above sinks down to replace that which has moved in from the sides, thus establishing a convective circulation system, also called a **convection cell**. The prominent elements of the system are an updraft of warm air and a downdraft of air after it has cooled. Convection is common in each hemisphere during its summer and throughout the year in the tropics.

Advection

When the dominant direction of heat transfer in a moving fluid is horizontal, the term **advection** is applied. In the atmosphere, wind may transfer warm or cool air horizontally from one place to another through the process of advection. As we will see in the following chapter, some wind systems develop as part of large atmospheric convection cells: the horizontal component of air movement within such a convection cell is properly called advection.

Adiabatic Cooling and Warming

Whenever air ascends or descends, its temperature changes. This invariable result of vertical movement is due to the variation in pressure. When air rises, it expands because there is less air above it, and so less pressure is exerted on it (Figures 4-16a and b). When air descends, it is compressed because there is more air above it, and so more pressure is exerted on it (Figures 4-16c and d).

Expansion: Adiabatic Cooling The expansion that occurs in rising air is a cooling process even though no heat is lost. As air rises and expands, the molecules spread through a greater volume of space and this requires energy. As the molecules spread farther away from each other their frequency of collision decreases, resulting in a decrease in temperature. This is called **adiabatic cooling**—cooling by expansion (*adiabatic* means without the gain or loss of heat). In the atmosphere, any time air rises, it cools adiabatically.

Compression: Adiabatic Warming Conversely, when air descends, it must become warmer. The descent causes compression as the air comes under increasing pressure. The molecules draw closer together and collide more frequently. The result is an increase in temperature even though no heat is added from external

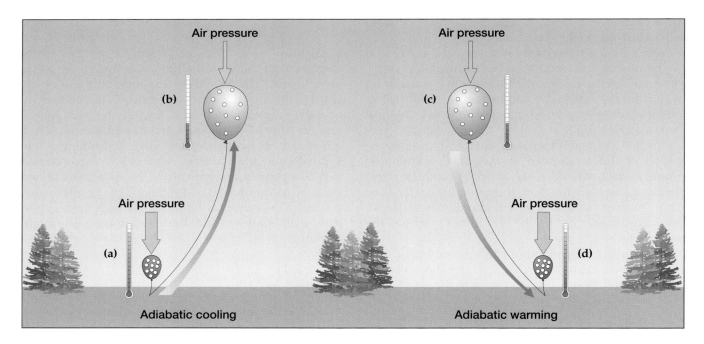

▲ **Figure 4-16**   As the thermometers next to the balloons indicate (a, b), rising air cools adiabatically due to expansion and (c, d) descending air warms adiabatically due to compression. No heat transfer is involved in either process.

sources. This is called **adiabatic warming**—warming by compression. In the atmosphere, any time air descends it warms adiabatically.

As we will see in Chapter 6, adiabatic cooling of rising air is one of the most important processes involved in cloud development and precipitation, while the adiabatic warming of descending air has just the opposite effect.

Latent Heat

The physical state of water in the atmosphere frequently changes—ice changes to liquid water, liquid water changes to water vapor, and so forth. Depending on the process, these *phase changes* involve either the storage or release of energy known as **latent heat** (*latent* is from the Latin, "lying hidden"). The two most common phase changes are **evaporation**, in which liquid water is converted to gaseous water vapor, and **condensation**, in which gaseous water vapor is converted to liquid water. During the process of evaporation, latent heat energy is stored and so evaporation is, in effect, a cooling process. On the other hand, during condensation latent heat energy is released and so condensation is, in effect, a warming process.

As we will explore more fully in Chapters 6 and 7, a great deal of energy is transferred from one place to another in the atmosphere in the form of water vapor. Energy that is stored in one location through evaporation can be released as heat in another location far away. We will also see that many storms, such as hurricanes, are fueled by the release of latent heat.

The Heating of the Atmosphere

Atmospheric Energy Balance

We now turn to the specifics of atmospheric heating. What happens to solar radiation when it enters Earth's atmosphere? How is it received and distributed? What are the dynamics of converting electromagnetic radiation to atmospheric heat?

In the long run, there is a balance between the total amount of insolation received by Earth and its atmosphere on one hand, and the total amount of radiation returned to space on the other (Figure 4-17). (As we suggested earlier, humans are likely altering the energy balance of the atmosphere slightly through global warming, to be discussed at the end of this chapter. For the purposes of understanding atmospheric heating processes, we will ignore that possibility for the moment.)

The annual balance between incoming and outgoing radiation is the *global energy budget*, which can be illustrated by using 100 "units" of energy to represent total insolation received at the outer edge of the atmosphere and tracing its dispersal (Figure 4-18). Keep in mind that the values shown here are annual averages for the entire globe and do not apply to any specific location.

Most of the insolation that enters the atmosphere does not heat it directly. About 31 units of total insolation are reflected (or scattered) back into space by the atmosphere and the surface; this radiation that is

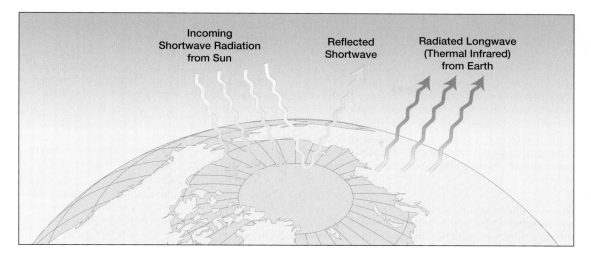

▲ **Figure 4-17**   The big picture: Earth's energy budget in simplified form. Incoming shortwave radiation and outgoing longwave radiation are in a long-term balance.

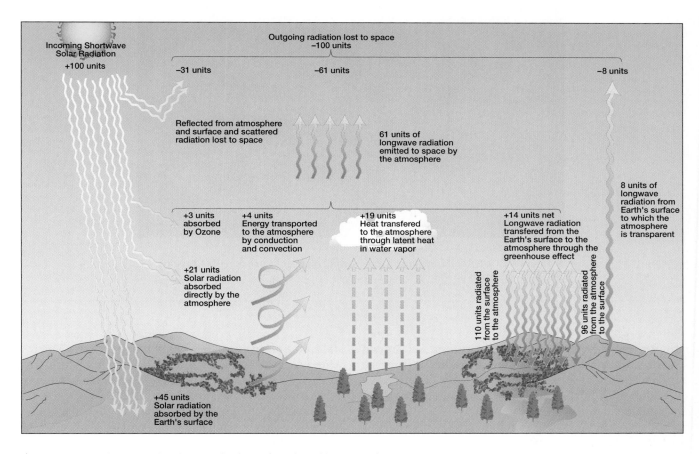

▲ **Figure 4-18**   The generalized energy budget of Earth and its atmosphere.

bounced back into space is called Earth's **albedo.** (Albedo is the reflectivity of an object. The higher the albedo value, the more radiation the object reflects.) About 45 units of the insolation pass on through the atmosphere to Earth's surface, leaving only 24 units to heat the atmosphere directly, 3 of them heating the ozone layer and 21 heating the rest of the atmosphere.

Terrestrial longwave radiation emitted from Earth's surface to the atmosphere amounts to about 110 units. This is possible because the atmosphere's greenhouse effect absorbs large amounts of energy and reradiates it back to Earth. In effect, the surface heats the lower atmosphere and in turn the lower atmosphere reheats the surface. The sequence of radiation between Earth and

FOCUS Monitoring Earth's Radiation Budget

Earth's radiation budget is monitored on an ongoing basis by several permanently orbiting satellites. Sensors on board the satellites detect both reflected shortwave radiation and emitted longwave radiation in several wavelength bands to gather information about Earth's surface and atmosphere.

One of the most important instruments used is the *Advanced Very High Resolution Radiometer* (AVHRR), first carried onboard TIROS-N launched in October of 1978. A much more advanced instrument, the AVHRR/3,

was first carried onboard NOAA-15, launched in May of 1998. NOAA-15 is one of the satellites operated by the National Oceanographic and Atmospheric Administration (NOAA). NOAA-15 is one of several *Polar Orbiting Environmental Satellites* (POES), each making about 14 orbits a day. Polar orbits allow these satellites to provide complete global coverage four times each day. Data gathered from the POES is used to monitor weather and ocean conditions, as well as to provide a database for climate change research.

Earth's radiation budget is monitored day and night using the AVHRR/3 instrument. Figure 4-C shows outgoing longwave radiation at night in watts per square meter. Notice the very high emission of longwave radiation from the subtropical and midlatitude desert regions in the southwestern United States, northern Africa, and eastern central Eurasia. The clear nighttime skies and the generally low water vapor content of the air permit significant transmission of longwave radiation away from the surface into space.

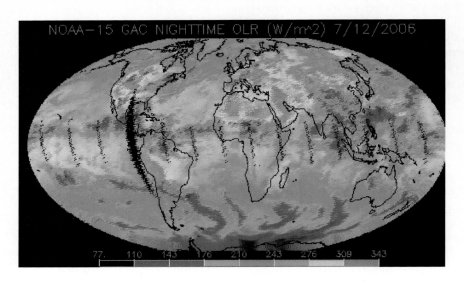

▲ **Figure 4-C**   NOAA-15 satellite image showing nighttime emission of outgoing longwave radiation (in W/m²). *(Source: NOAA.)*

atmosphere continues indefinitely. In terms of annual balance, for every 110 units of energy radiated from the surface to the atmosphere, about 96 units of longwave radiation are returned to Earth. Thus the atmosphere receives a net gain of 14 units.

Some of the longwave radiation emitted by Earth's surface, however, is transmitted directly through the atmosphere without being absorbed by the greenhouse gases. Approximately 8 units of energy in the form of longwave radiation with wavelengths between about 8 and 12 micrometers transmit through what is called the *atmospheric window*—a range of wavelengths of infrared radiation that isn't strongly absorbed by any atmospheric component.

Another important method of energy transfer from the surface to the atmosphere is the transport of latent heat in water vapor. About three-fourths of all sunshine

falls on a water surface when it reaches Earth. Much of this energy is utilized in evaporating moisture from oceans, lakes, and other bodies of water. Thus, the energy is passed into the atmosphere as latent heat stored in the resulting water vapor; it will be released subsequently when condensation takes place. This amounts to about 19 units in the heat budget equation. Another 4 units of energy are conducted from Earth's surface back into the atmosphere, where it is dispersed by convection.

For the most part, then, the atmosphere is heated by the surface of Earth, although the Sun is the original source of the energy. Thus, there is an intimate link between troposphere temperatures and Earth surface conditions. The air temperature at any given time represents the balance between insolation and terrestrial radiation.

This complicated sequence of atmospheric heating has many ramifications. One of the most striking is that the atmosphere is heated mostly from below rather than from above. The result is a troposphere in which cold air overlies warm air. This "unstable" situation (explored further in Chapter 6) creates an environment of almost constant convective activity and vertical mixing. If the atmosphere were heated directly from the Sun, producing warm air at the top and cold air near Earth's surface, the situation would be stable, essentially without vertical air movements. The result would be a troposphere that is largely motionless, apart from the effects of Earth's rotation.

Variations in Heating by Latitude and Season

 FG9

The radiation budget we have been discussing is broadly generalized. There are, however, many latitudinal and vertical imbalances in this budget, and these are among the most fundamental causes of weather and climate variations. In essence, we can trace a causal continuum wherein radiation differences lead to temperature differences that lead to air-density differences that lead to pressure differences that lead to wind differences that often lead to moisture differences. It has already been noted that world weather and climate differences are fundamentally caused by the unequal heating of Earth and its atmosphere. This unequal heating is the result of latitudinal and seasonal variations in how much energy is received by Earth.

Latitudinal and Seasonal Differences

There are only a few basic reasons for the unequal heating of different latitudinal zones.

Angle of Incidence   The angle at which rays from the Sun strike Earth's surface is called the **angle of incidence**. This angle is measured from a line drawn tangent to the surface, as Figure 4-19 shows. By this definition, a ray striking Earth's surface vertically, when the Sun is directly overhead, has an angle of incidence of 90°, a ray striking the surface at a slant has an angle of incidence smaller than 90°, and for a ray striking Earth tangent to the surface the angle of incidence is zero.

Because Earth's surface is curved and because the positional relationship between Earth and the Sun is always changing, the angle of incidence is also always changing. This changing angle is the primary determinant of the intensity of solar radiation received at any spot on Earth. If a ray strikes Earth's surface vertically, the energy is concentrated in a small area; if the ray strikes Earth obliquely, the energy is spread out over a larger portion of the surface. The more nearly perpendicular the ray (in other words, the closer to 90° the angle of incidence), the smaller the surface area heated by a given amount of insolation and the more effective the heating. The yellow areas on the globe's surface indicate the comparative spread of rays. It is clear that, considering the year as a whole, the insolation received by high-latitude regions is much less intense than that received by tropical areas (Figure 4-20).

Atmospheric Obstruction   We have already noted that clouds, particulate matter, and gas molecules in the atmosphere may absorb, reflect, or scatter insolation. The result is a reduction in the intensity of the energy received at Earth's surface. On the average, sunlight received at Earth's surface is only about half as strong as it is at the top of Earth's atmosphere.

This weakening effect varies from time to time and from place to place depending on two factors: the

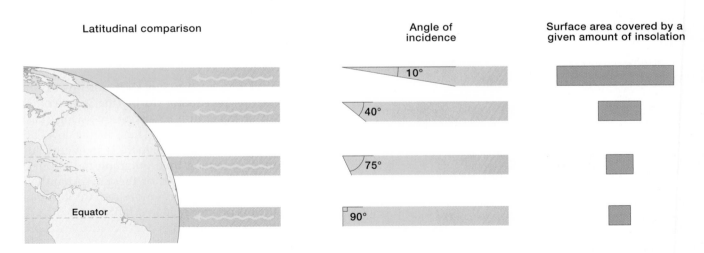

▲ **Figure 4-19**   The angle at which solar rays hit Earth's surface varies with latitude. The higher the angle, the more concentrated the energy and therefore the more effective the heating. The day shown in this diagram is the March/September equinox.

◀ **Figure 4-20** The noontime Sun is very low in the sky during winter in the high latitudes. This is a November scene at the village of Mesters Vig in Greenland, at about 70° north latitude. *(Simon Fraser/Science Photo Library/Photo Researchers, Inc.)*

amount of atmosphere the radiation has to pass through, as shown in Figure 4-21, and the transparency of that atmosphere (Figure 4-22). The distance a ray of sunlight travels through the atmosphere (commonly referred to as *path length*) is determined by the angle of incidence. A high-angle ray (in other words, a nearly perpendicular ray) traverses a shorter course through the atmosphere than a low-angle one. A tangent ray (one having an incidence angle of zero) must pass through nearly 20 times as much atmosphere as a vertical ray (one striking Earth at a 90° angle).

The effect of atmospheric obstruction on the distribution of solar energy at Earth's surface is to reinforce

the pattern established by the varying angle of incidence. Solar radiation is more depleted of energy in the high latitudes than in the low latitudes. Thus, there are smaller losses of energy in the tropical atmosphere than in the polar atmosphere—however, as we will see, this general pattern is complicated by patterns of cloud cover.

Day Length The duration of sunlight is another important factor in explaining latitudinal inequalities in heating. Longer days allow more insolation to be received and thus more heat to be absorbed. In tropical regions, this factor is relatively unimportant because the number of hours between sunrise and sunset does not vary significantly from one month to another; at the equator, of course, daylight and darkness are equal in length (12 hours each) every day of the year. In middle and high latitudes, however, there are pronounced seasonal variations in day length. The conspicuous buildup of heat in summer in these regions is largely a consequence of the long hours of daylight, and the winter cold is a manifestation of limited insolation being received because of the short days.

Latitudinal Radiation Balance

As the vertical rays of the Sun shift northward and southward across the equator during the course of the year, the belt of maximum solar energy swings back and forth through the tropics. Thus, in the low latitudes, to about 28° N and 33° S, there is an energy surplus, with more incoming than outgoing radiation. In the latitudes north and south of these two parallels, there is an energy deficit, with more radiant loss than gain. The surplus of energy in low latitudes is directly related to the consistently high angle of incidence, and the energy deficit in high latitudes is associated with low angles.

Figure 4-23 shows the distribution of average daily insolation at the surface around the world for December

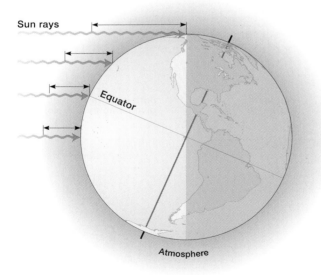

▲ **Figure 4-21** Atmospheric obstruction of sunlight. Low-angle rays must pass through more atmosphere than high-angle rays; thus, the former are subject to more depletion through reflection, scattering, and absorption. The day shown in this diagram is the December solstice.

▲ **Figure 4-22** Sunrise on the island of Nauru in the central Pacific. Clouds and haze deplete the amount of insolation that reaches Earth's surface. *(Tom L. McKnight photo.)*

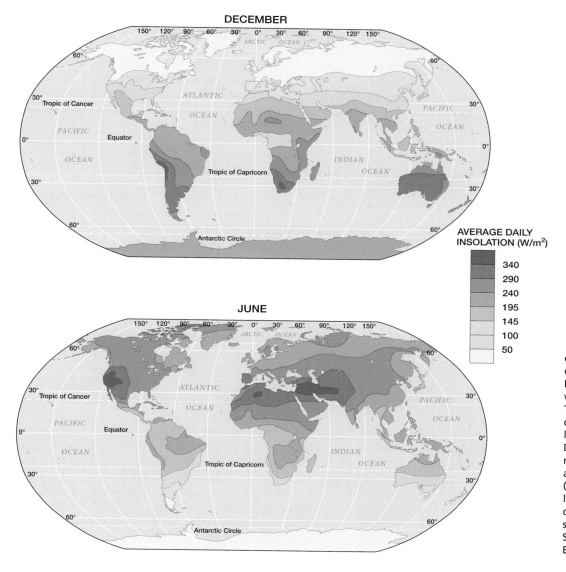

AVERAGE DAILY
INSOLATION (W/m²)

340
290
240
195
145
100
50

◀ **Figure 4-23** World distribution of average daily insolation for December and June in watts per square meter. The pattern is determined mainly by latitude (note the low December levels in northern areas) and amount of cloudiness (note the high June levels in such cloud-free desert areas as the southwestern United States and southern Eurasia).

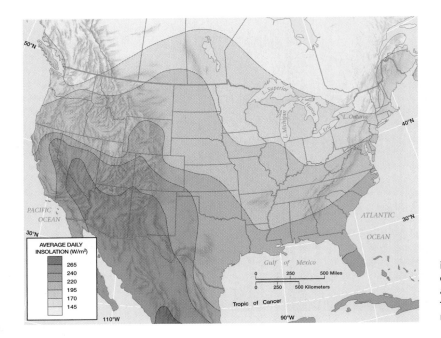

Figure 4-24 Average annual daily insolation in watts per square meter received in the 48 conterminous states and adjacent parts of Canada and Mexico. The sunny southwestern areas receive the most radiation; the cloudy northeastern and northwestern areas receive the least.

and June, and Figure 4-24 shows the annual average annual daily insolation for the United States and parts of Canada and Mexico. The maps show the average daily insolation received in watts per square meter W/m²; 1 watt = 0.239 calories per second). The variations are largely latitudinal, as is to be expected. The principal interruptions to the simple latitudinal pattern are based on the presence or absence of frequent cloud cover, where insolation is reflected, diffused, and scattered. In Figure 4-24, for example, it can be seen that insolation is greatest in the southwestern United States, where clouds are consistently sparse and is least in the northwestern and northeastern corners of the country, where cloud cover is frequent.

Despite the variable pattern shown on the maps, there is a long-term balance between incoming and outgoing radiation for the Earth–atmosphere complex as a whole; in other words, the net radiation balance for Earth is zero. The mechanisms for exchanging heat between the surplus and deficit regions involve the general circulation patterns of the atmosphere and oceans, which are discussed later in the book.

Land and Water Contrasts

As we've seen, the atmosphere is heated mainly by heat reradiated and transferred from Earth's surface rather than by heat directly received from the Sun; thus, the heating of Earth's surface is a primary control of the heating of the air above it. To comprehend variations in air temperatures, it is useful to understand how different kinds of surfaces react to solar energy. There is considerable variation in the absorbing and reflecting capabilities

of the almost limitless kinds of surfaces found on Earth—soil, water, grass, trees, cement, rooftops, and so forth. Their varying receptivity to insolation in turn causes differences in the temperature of the overlying air.

By far the most significant contrasts are those between land and water surfaces. The generalization is that land heats and cools faster and to a greater degree than water (Figure 4-25).

Heating

A land surface heats up more rapidly and reaches a higher temperature than a comparable water surface subject to the same insolation. In essence, a thin layer of land is heated to relatively high temperatures, whereas a thick layer of water is heated more slowly to moderate temperatures. There are several significant reasons for this difference.

1. **Specific Heat:** Water has a higher **specific heat** than land. Specific heat is the amount of energy required to raise the temperature of 1 gram of a substance by 1°C. The specific heat of water is about five times as great as that of land, which means that water can absorb much more solar energy without its temperature increasing.
2. **Transmission:** Sun rays penetrate water more deeply than they do land; that is, water is a better transmitter of radiation than land. Thus, in water solar energy is absorbed through a much greater volume of matter, and maximum temperatures remain considerably lower than they do on land, where the heat is concentrated at the surface and maximum temperatures can be much higher.

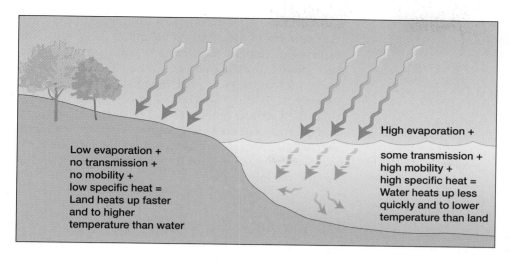

Low evaporation +
no transmission +
no mobility +
low specific heat =
Land heats up faster
and to higher
temperature than water

High evaporation +

some transmission +
high mobility +
high specific heat =
Water heats up less
quickly and to lower
temperature than land

◄ **Figure 4-25** Some contrasting characteristics of the heating of land and water.

3. **Mobility:** Water is highly mobile, and so turbulent mixing and ocean currents disperse the heat both broadly and deeply. Land, of course, is essentially immobile, and so heat is dispersed only by conduction (and land is a relatively poor conductor of heat).

4. **Evaporative Cooling:** The unlimited availability of moisture on a water surface means that evaporation is much more prevalent than on a land surface. The latent heat needed for this evaporation is drawn from the water and its immediate surroundings, causing a drop in temperature. Thus, the cooling effect of evaporation slows down any heat buildup on a water surface.

Cooling

When both are overlain by air at the same temperature, a land surface cools more rapidly and to a lower temperature than a water surface. During winter, the shallow, heated layer of land radiates its heat away quickly. Water loses its heat more gradually because the heat

has been stored deeply and is brought only slowly to the surface for radiation. As the surface water cools, it sinks and is replaced by warmer water from below. The entire water body must be cooled before the surface temperatures decrease significantly.

Implications

The significance of these contrasts between land and water heating and cooling rates is that both the hottest and coldest areas of Earth are found in the interiors of continents, distant from the influence of oceans. In the study of the atmosphere, probably no single geographic relationship is more important than the distinction between continental and maritime climates. A continental climate experiences greater seasonal extremes of temperature—hotter in summer, colder in winter—than a maritime climate.

These differences are shown in Figure 4-26, which portrays average monthly temperatures for San Diego and Dallas. These two cities are at approximately the

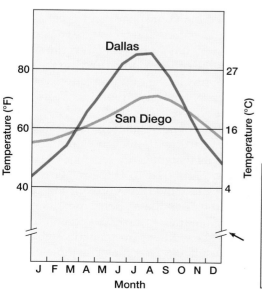

Dallas
Latitude: 32° 51' N
Annual average temperature: 18°C (65°F)

San Diego
Latitude: 32° 44' N
Annual average temperature: 17°C (63°F)

◄ **Figure 4-26** Annual temperature curves for San Diego, California, and Dallas, Texas. Although both have similar average annual temperatures, they have very different annual temperature regimes. In both summer and winter, San Diego, situated on the coast, experiences milder temperatures than inland Dallas.

TABLE 4-1 Average Annual Temperature Range by Latitude, in Degrees Celsius

Latitude	Northern Hemisphere	Southern Hemisphere
0	0	0
15	3	4
30	13	7
45	23	6
60	30	11
75	32	26
90	40	31

Source: From Frederick K. Lutgens and Edward J. Tarbuck, *The Atmosphere: An Introduction to Meteorology*, 9th ed. (Upper Saddle River, NJ: Pearson-Prentice Hall, 2004), p. 71. Used by permission of Prentice Hall.

same latitude and experience almost identical lengths of day and angles of incidence. Although their annual average temperatures are almost the same, the monthly averages vary significantly. Dallas, in the interior of the continent, experiences notably warmer summers and cooler winters than San Diego, which enjoys the moderating influence of an adjacent ocean.

The oceans, in a sense, act as great reservoirs of heat. In summer they absorb heat and store it. In winter they give off heat and warm the air. Thus, they function as a sort of global thermostatically controlled heat source, moderating temperature extremes.

The ameliorating influence of the oceans can also be demonstrated, on a totally different scale, by comparing latitudinal temperature variations in the Northern Hemisphere with those in the Southern Hemisphere. The Northern Hemisphere is often thought of as a land hemisphere because 39 percent of its area is land surface; the Southern Hemisphere is a water hemisphere, with only 19 percent of its area as land. Table 4-1 shows the *average annual temperature range* (difference in average temperature of the coldest and warmest months) for comparable parallels in each hemisphere. It is obvious that the land hemisphere has greater extremes.

Mechanisms of Heat Transfer

If there were no mechanisms for moving heat poleward in both hemispheres, the tropics would become progressively warmer until the amount of heat energy absorbed equaled the amount radiated from Earth's surface and the high latitudes would become progressively colder. Such temperature trends do not occur because there is a persistent shifting of warmth toward the high latitudes and the consequent cooling of the

low latitudes. This shifting is accomplished by circulation patterns in the atmosphere and in the oceans. The broad-scale or planetary circulation of these two mediums moderates the buildup of heat in equatorial regions and the loss of heat in polar regions, thereby making both those latitudinal zones more habitable than they would otherwise be. Both the atmosphere and oceans act as enormous thermal engines, with their latitudinal imbalance of heat driving the currents of air and water, which in turn transfer heat and somewhat modify the imbalance.

Atmospheric Circulation

Of the two mechanisms of global heat transfer, by far the more important is the general circulation of the atmosphere. Air moves in an almost infinite number of ways, but there is a broad planetary circulation pattern that serves as a general framework for moving warm air poleward and cool air equatorward. Some 75 to 80 percent of all horizontal heat transfer is accomplished by atmospheric circulation.

Our discussion of atmospheric circulation is withheld until Chapter 5, following consideration of some fundamentals concerning pressure and wind.

Oceanic Circulation

  Ocean Circulation Patterns

Winds disturb the surface of the sea with swells and waves, but winds also can propel large bodies of water. These sometimes become currents. Surface water can flow at about 1 percent to 2 percent of wind speed, meaning that water in a surface current might travel some tens or even hundreds of kilometers in a day.

There is a close relationship between the general circulation patterns of the atmosphere and oceans. Various kinds of oceanic water movements are categorized as **ocean currents**, and it is air blowing over the surface of the water that is the principal force driving the major surface ocean currents. In the other direction, the heat energy stored in the oceans has important effects on atmospheric circulation.

For our purposes in understanding heat transfer by the oceans, we are concerned primarily with the broad-scale surface currents that make up the general circulation of the oceans (Figure 4-27). These major currents respond to changes in wind direction, but they are so broad and ponderous that the response time normally amounts to many months. In essence, ocean currents reflect average wind conditions over a period of several years, with the result that the major components of oceanic circulation are closely related to major components of atmospheric circulation. (We discuss the wind

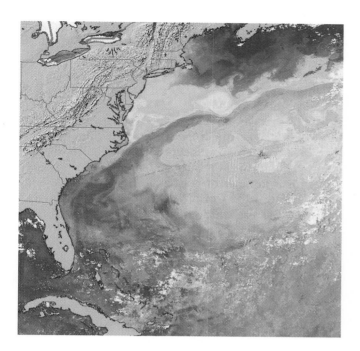

▲ **Figure 4-27**   Multi-pass satellite image showing the Gulf Stream off the east coast of North America. Red represents relatively high water temperature while blue represents relatively low water temperatures. Several vertical and horizontal bands are not actual temperature features but are caused by incomplete satellite data. *(NOAA.)*

patterns responsible for ocean current movement in Chapter 5.)

The Basic Pattern   All the oceans of the world are interconnected. Because of the location of landmasses and the pattern of atmospheric circulation, however, it is convenient to visualize five relatively separate ocean basins—North Pacific, South Pacific, North Atlantic, South Atlantic, and South Indian. Within each of these basins, there is a similar pattern of surface current flow based on a general similarity of prevailing wind patterns.

Despite variations based on the size and shape of the various ocean basins and on the season of the year, a single simple pattern of surface currents is characteristic of all the basins (Figure 4-28). It consists of a series of enormous elliptical loops elongated east–west and centered approximately at 30° of latitude (except in the Indian Ocean, where it is centered on the equator). These loops, called **subtropical gyres**, flow clockwise in the Northern Hemisphere and counterclockwise in the Southern Hemisphere.

On the equatorward side of each subtropical gyre is the *Equatorial Current*, which moves steadily toward the west. The two equatorial currents have an average position 5° to 10° north or south of the equator and are separated by the *Equatorial Countercurrent*, which is an east-moving flow approximately along the equator in each ocean. The equatorial currents feed the Equatorial Countercurrent near its western margin in each basin. Water from the Equatorial Countercurrent in turn drifts poleward to feed the Equatorial Current near the eastern end of its path.

Near the western margin of each ocean basin, the general current curves poleward. As these currents approach the poleward margins of the ocean basins, they curve east; as they reach the eastern edges of the basins they curve back toward the equator, producing an incompletely closed loop in each basin.

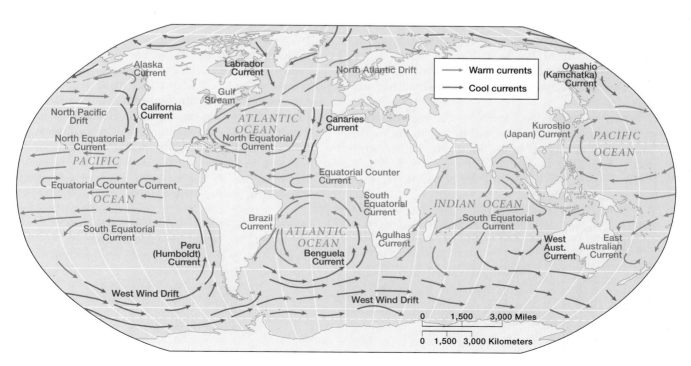

▲ **Figure 4-28**   The major surface ocean currents.

The movement of these currents, although impelled by the wind, is also influenced by the deflective force of Earth's rotation—the Coriolis effect (discussed in Chapter 3). The Coriolis effect dictates that the ocean currents are deflected to the right in the Northern Hemisphere and to the left in the Southern Hemisphere. A glance at the basic pattern shows that the current movement around the gyres responds precisely to the Coriolis effect.

Northern and Southern Variations   In the two Northern Hemisphere basins—North Pacific and North Atlantic—the bordering continents lie so close together at the poleward basin margin that the bulk of the current flow is prevented from entering the Arctic Ocean. This effect is more pronounced in the Pacific than in the Atlantic. The North Pacific has very limited flow northward between Asia and North America, whereas in the North Atlantic a larger proportion of the flow escapes northward between Greenland and Europe.

In the Southern Hemisphere, the continents are far apart. Thus, the poleward segments of the gyres in the South Pacific, South Atlantic, and South Indian oceans are connected as one continuous flow in the uninterrupted belt of ocean that extends around the world in the vicinity of latitude 60° S (Figure 4-28). This circumpolar flow is called the *West Wind Drift*.

Current Temperatures   Of utmost importance to our understanding of latitudinal heat transfer are the temperatures of the various currents. Each major current can be characterized as *warm* or *cool* relative to the surrounding water at that latitude. The generalized temperature characteristics are as follows:

1. Low-latitude currents (Equatorial Current, Equatorial Countercurrent) have warm water.
2. Poleward-moving currents on the western sides of ocean basins carry warm water toward higher latitudes.
3. Northern components of the Northern Hemisphere gyres carry warm water toward the north and east.
4. Southern components of the Southern Hemisphere gyres (generally combined into the West Wind Drift) are strongly influenced by Antarctic waters and are essentially cool.
5. Equatorward-moving currents on the eastern sides of ocean basins carry cool water toward the equator.

In summary, from the perspective of the margins of the continents, the general circulation of the oceans is a poleward flow of warm tropical water along the east coasts of continents and an equatorward movement of cool high-latitude water along the west coasts of continents.

Western Intensification   In addition to differences in temperature, the poleward moving warm currents off the east coast of continents tend to be narrower, deeper, and faster than the equatorward moving cool currents flowing off the west coast of continents. This phenomenon is called *western intensification* because it occurs on the western side of the subtropical gyres (in other words, it occurs in the currents flowing poleward off the east coasts of continents in the midlatitudes). This intensification of poleward moving warm currents arises for a number of reasons, including the Coriolis effect. Because the Coriolis effect is greater in higher latitudes, the eastward moving high-latitude current flow is deflected back toward the equator more strongly than the westward moving equatorial current flow is deflected toward the poles. This means that cool water is slowly flowing back toward the equator across much of the eastward-moving high latitude currents, whereas the poleward-flowing warm currents are confined to a fairly narrow zone off the east coasts of continents.

Rounding Out the Pattern   Three other aspects of oceanic circulation are influential in heat transfer:

1. The northwestern portions of Northern Hemisphere ocean basins receive an influx of cool water from the Arctic Ocean (Figure 4-29). A prominent cool current from the vicinity of Greenland comes southward along the Canadian coast, and a smaller flow of cold water issues from the Bering Sea southward along the coast of Siberia to Japan.
2. Wherever an equatorward-flowing cool current pulls away from a subtropical western coast, a pronounced and persistent **upwelling** of cold water occurs. For example, if winds along the west coast of a Northern Hemisphere continent are blowing from the north or northwest, the Coriolis effect will deflect some of the surface water away from the coast. As surface water pulls away from the coast, it will be replaced with water from deeper below. Upwelling brings nutrient-rich water to the surface, making west-coast marine ecosystems highly productive. The upwelling also brings colder water to the surface, generally decreasing the surface temperature of the already cool equatorward moving currents off the western coast of continents. Upwelling is most striking off South America but is also notable off North America, northwestern Africa, and southwestern Africa. It is much less developed off the coast of western Australia.
3. In addition to the surface ocean currents we've just described, there is a deep ocean circulation pattern—sometimes called the *global conveyor belt circulation*—that influences global climate in subtle, but nonetheless important ways. The deep ocean conveyor belt circulation is discussed in greater detail in Chapter 9.

FOCUS Measuring Sea Surface Temperature by Satellite

Sea surface temperature (SST) is one of the most important influences of weather and climate. The SST influences not only the temperature of air masses that originate over ocean areas (and so the weather of continental areas over which these air masses may pass), but also the intensity of storms such as hurricanes. Regular monitoring of SST helps scientists anticipate the onset of El Niño and La Niña events (discussed in Chapter 5) and provides important information about long-term changes to Earth's environment.

Before the development of advanced weather satellites, much of the information about sea surface temperatures came from ships or buoys at sea, leaving large gaps in coverage. Today, a number of satellites regularly monitor SST around the world. For example, the AVHRR (Advanced Very High Resolution Radiometer) onboard NOAA's *Polar Orbiting Environmental Satellites* provides SST data by detecting thermal infrared radiation emitted from the ocean surface (Figure 4-D). Correlation of this remotely sensed data with actual surface temperature measurements has increased the accuracy of global SST estimates in recent years, especially with an interpolation formula known as the *Reynolds Optimally Interpolated (OI) Sea Surface Temperature*. Global OI SSTs are calculated on a weekly basis, making this information an invaluable tool for meteorologists, climatologists, and oceanographers alike.

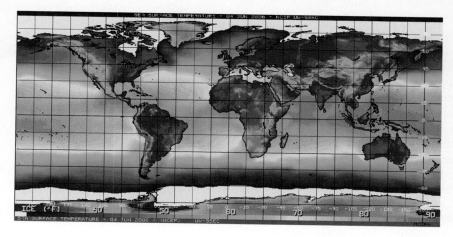

▲ **Figure 4-D**   Global sea surface temperature in June 2006 derived from data gathered from the five-channel AVHRR on NOAA Polar Orbiting Environmental Satellites. *(National Centers for Environmental Prediction/NOAA.)*

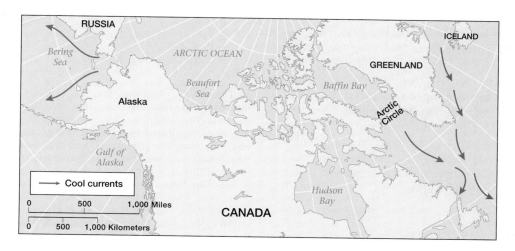

▲ **Figure 4-29**   Cold-water movements in ocean basins of the Northern Hemisphere.

Vertical Temperature Patterns

As we study the geography of weather and climate most of our attention is directed to the horizontal dimension; in other words, we are concerned with the spatial distribution of phenomena over the surface of Earth. From time to time, however, we must focus on vertical patterns or processes because of their influence on surface features. This statement is particularly pertinent with regard to the atmosphere.

Environmental Lapse Rate

Temperature change with increasing altitude within the troposphere is relatively predictable. As we learned in Chapter 3, throughout the troposphere, under typical conditions, there is a general decrease in temperature with increasing altitude (Figure 4-30a). However, there are many exceptions to this general statement. Indeed, the rate of vertical temperature decline can vary according to season, time of day, amount of cloud cover, and a host of other factors. In some cases, there is even an opposite trend, with the temperature increasing upward for a limited distance.

The observed trend of vertical temperature change in the atmosphere is described by the **environmental lapse rate**. Determining the lapse rate of a column of air involves measuring air temperature at various elevations. Then a graph of temperature as a function of height is drawn to produce a temperature profile of that air column. When measuring such a lapse-rate temperature change, only the thermometer is moved; the air is at rest. If the air is moving vertically, expansion or compression will cause an adiabatic temperature change—such adiabatic lapse rates are explored more fully in Chapter 6.

Average Lapse Rate

Although the rate at which temperature decreases with height is variable, particularly in the lowest few hundred meters of the troposphere, the average rate of temperature change is about 6.5°C per 1000 meters (3.6°F per 1000 feet). This is called the **average lapse rate**, or normal vertical temperature gradient within the troposphere. The average lapse rate tells us that if a thermometer measures the temperature 1000 meters above a previous measurement, the reading will be, on the average, 6.5°C cooler; conversely, if a second measurement is made 1000 meters lower than the first, the temperature will be about 6.5°C warmer.

Temperature Inversions

The most prominent exception to an average lapse-rate condition is a **temperature inversion**, a situation in which temperature in the troposphere increases, rather

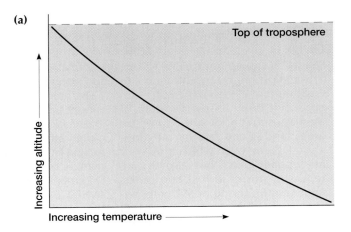

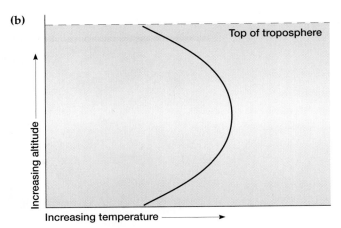

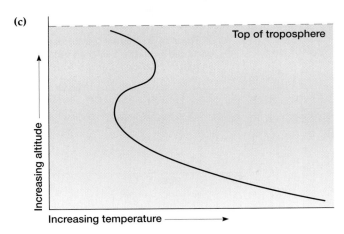

▲ **Figure 4-30**   A comparison of normal and inverted lapse rates. **(a)** Tropospheric temperature normally decreases with increasing altitude. **(b)** In a surface inversion, temperature increases with increasing altitude from ground level to some distance above the ground. **(c)** In an upper-air inversion, temperature first decreases with increasing altitude as in a normal lapse rate, but then at some altitude well below the tropopause begins to increase with increasing altitude.

than decreases, with increasing altitude. Inversions are relatively common in the troposphere but are usually of brief duration and restricted depth. They can occur near Earth's surface, as in Figure 4-30b, or at higher levels, as in Figure 4-30c.

Inversions influence weather and climate. As we shall see in Chapter 6, an inversion inhibits vertical air movements and greatly diminishes the possibility of precipitation. Inversions also contribute significantly to increased air pollution because they create stagnant air conditions that greatly limit the natural upward dispersal of urban-industrial pollutants (Figure 4-31).

Surface Inversions The most readily recognizable inversions are those found at ground level. These are usually classified as *radiation inversions* because they result from rapid radiational cooling. They occur typically on a long, cold winter night when a land surface (an efficient radiator) rapidly emits longwave radiation into a clear, calm sky. The ground is soon colder than the air above it and so now cools the air by conduction. In a relatively short time, the lowest few hundred meters of the troposphere become colder than the air above and a temperature inversion is in effect. Radiational inversions are primarily winter phenomena because there is only a short daylight period for incoming solar heating and a long night for radiational cooling. They are therefore much more prevalent in high latitudes than elsewhere.

An inverted surface temperature gradient can also be the result of an *advectional inversion*, in which there is a horizontal inflow of cold air into an area. This condition commonly is produced by cool maritime air blowing into a coastal locale. Advectional inversions are usually short-lived (typically overnight) and shallow. They may occur at any time of year, depending on the location of the relatively cold surface and on wind movement.

Another type of surface inversion results when cooler air slides down a slope into a valley, thereby displacing slightly warmer air. This fairly common occurrence during winter in some midlatitude regions is called a *cold-air-drainage inversion*.

Upper-Air Inversions Temperature inversions well above the ground surface nearly always are the result of air sinking from above. These *subsidence inversions* are usually associated with high-pressure conditions, which are particularly characteristic of subtropical latitudes throughout the year and of Northern Hemisphere continents in winter. A subsidence inversion can be fairly deep (sometimes several thousand meters), and its base is usually a few hundred meters above the ground, as low-level turbulence prevents it from sinking lower.

Global Temperature Patterns

The goal of this and the four succeeding chapters is to examine the world distribution pattern of climate. With the preceding pages as background, we now turn our attention to the worldwide distribution of temperature, the first of the four climate elements.

Maps of global temperature patterns display seasonal extremes rather than annual averages. January and July are the months of lowest and highest temperatures for most places on Earth, and so maps portraying the average temperatures of these two months provide a simple but meaningful expression of thermal conditions in winter and summer (Figures 4-32 and 4-33). Temperature distribution is shown by means of **isotherms**, lines joining points of equal temperature. Temperature maps are based on monthly averages, which are based on daily averages; the maps do not show the maximum daytime heating or the maximum nighttime cooling. Although the maps are on a very small scale, they permit a broad understanding of temperature patterns for the world.

Prominent Controls of Temperature

Gross patterns of temperature are controlled largely by four factors—altitude, latitude, land–water contrasts, and ocean currents.

Altitude Because temperature responds sharply to altitudinal changes, it would be misleading to plot actual temperatures on a temperature map, since high-altitude stations would almost always be colder than low-altitude stations. The complexity introduced by hills and mountains would make the map more complicated and difficult to comprehend. Consequently, the data for most maps displaying world temperature patterns are modified by reducing the temperature to what it would be if the station were at sea level. This is done most simply by using the average lapse rate, a method that produces artificial temperature values but eliminates the complication of terrain differences. Maps plotted in this way are useful in showing world patterns, but they are not satisfactory for indicating actual temperatures for locations that are not close to sea level.

▲ **Figure 4-31** Downtown Los Angeles on a "mild" smog day. The top of the inversion is visible where the mountains rise above the smog layer. *(Joan Clemons photo.)*

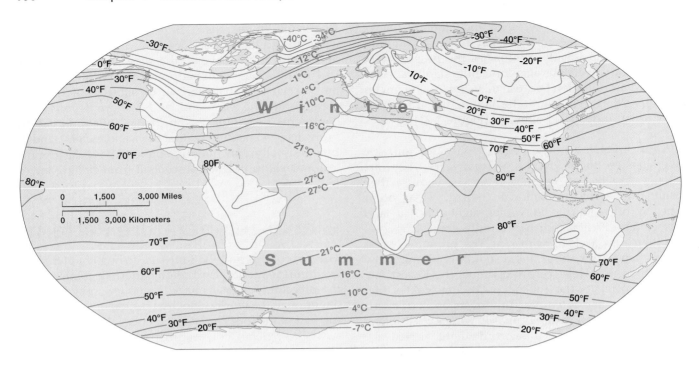

▲ **Figure 4-32**   Average January sea-level temperatures.

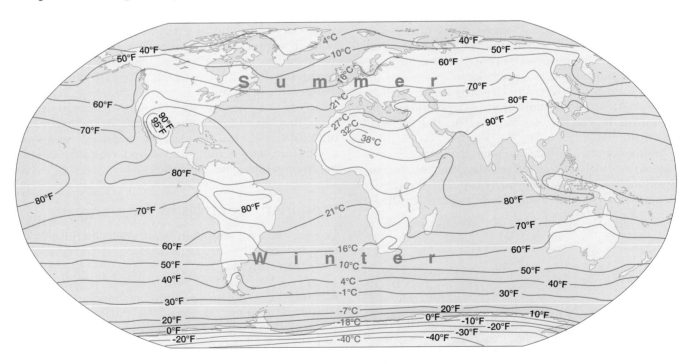

▲ **Figure 4-33**   Average July sea-level temperatures.

Latitude   Clearly the most conspicuous feature of any world temperature map is the general east–west trend of the isotherms, roughly following the parallels of latitude. If Earth had a uniform surface and did not rotate, the isotherms would probably coincide exactly with parallels, showing a progressive decrease of temperature poleward from the equator. However,

Earth does rotate, and it has ocean waters that circulate and land that varies in elevation. Consequently, there is no precise temperature correlation with latitude. Nevertheless, the fundamental cause of temperature variation the world over is insolation, which is governed primarily by latitude, and the general temperature patterns reflect latitudinal control.

Land–Water Contrasts The different heating and cooling characteristics of land and water are also reflected conspicuously on a temperature map. Summer temperatures are higher over the continents than over the oceans, as shown by the poleward curvature of the isotherms over continents in the respective hemispheres (July in the Northern Hemisphere, January in the Southern Hemisphere). Winter temperatures are lower over the continents than over the oceans; the isotherms bend equatorward over continents in this season (January in the Northern Hemisphere, July in the Southern Hemisphere). Thus, in both seasons, isotherms make greater north–south shifts over land than over water.

Another manifestation of the land–water contrast is the regularity of the isothermal pattern in the midlatitudes of the Southern Hemisphere, in contrast to the situation in the Northern Hemisphere. There is very little land in these Southern Hemisphere latitudes, and so contrasting surface characteristics are absent.

Ocean Currents Some of the most obvious bends in the isotherms occur in near-coastal areas of the oceans, where prominent warm or cool currents reinforce the isothermal curves caused by land–water contrasts. Cool currents deflect isotherms equatorward, whereas warm currents deflect them poleward. Cool currents produce the greatest isothermal bends in the warm season: Note the January situation off the western coast of South America and the southwestern coast of Africa or the July conditions off the western coast of North America. Warm currents have their most prominent effects in the cool season: witness the isothermal pattern in the North Atlantic Ocean in January.

Seasonal Patterns

Apart from the general east–west trend of the isotherms, probably the most conspicuous feature of Figures 4-32 and 4-33 is the latitudinal shift of the isotherms from one map to the other. The isotherms follow the changing balance of insolation during the course of the year, moving northward from January to July and returning southward from July to January. Note, for example, the 10°C (50°F) isotherm in southernmost South America: in January (midsummer), it is positioned at the southern tip of the continent, whereas in July (midwinter), it is shifted considerably to the north. This isothermal shift is much more pronounced in high latitudes than in low and also much more pronounced over the continents than over the oceans. Thus, tropical areas, particularly tropical oceans, show relatively small displacement of the isotherms from January to July, whereas over middle- and high-latitude landmasses, an isotherm may migrate northward or southward more than 4000 kilometers (2500 miles)—some 14° of latitude—as illustrated in Figure 4-34.

Isotherms are also more tightly packed in winter. This close line spacing indicates that the temperature gradient (rate of temperature change with horizontal distance) is steeper in winter than in summer, which in turn reflects the greater contrast in radiation balance in winter. The temperature gradient is also steeper over continents than over oceans.

The coldest places on Earth are over landmasses in the higher latitudes. During July, the polar region of Antarctica is the dominant area of coldness. In January, the coldest temperatures occur many hundreds of kilometers south of the North Pole, in subarctic

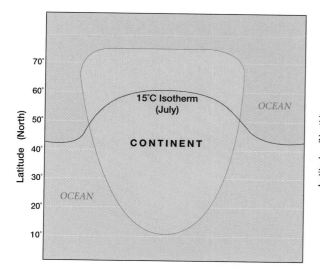
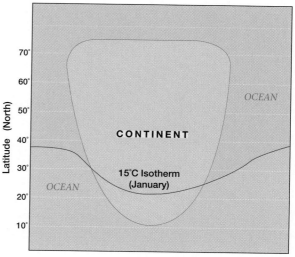

▲ **Figure 4-34** Idealized seasonal migration of the 15°C (59°F) isotherm over a hypothetical Northern Hemisphere continent. The latitudinal shift is greatest over the interior of the continent and least over the adjacent oceans. For example, over the western ocean, the isotherm moves only from latitude 38° N in January to 42° N in July, but over the continent the change is from 22° N in January all the way to 60° N in July. The isotherm can be thought of as separating the warmer region in the south (shaded in orange) from the colder region in the north (shaded in blue).

portions of Siberia, Canada, and Greenland. The principle of greater cooling of land than water is clearly demonstrated.

The highest temperatures also are found over the continents. The locations of the warmest areas in summer, however, are not equatorial. Rather, they are in subtropical latitudes, where descending air maintains clear skies most of the time, allowing for almost uninterrupted insolation. Frequent cloudiness precludes such a condition in the equatorial zone. Thus, the highest July temperatures occur in northern Africa and in the southwestern portions of Asia and North America, whereas the principal areas of January heat are in subtropical parts of Australia, southern Africa, and South America.

Average annual temperatures are highest in equatorial regions, however, because these regions experience so little winter cooling. Subtropical locations cool substantially on winter nights, and so their annual average temperatures are lower. The ice-covered portions of the Earth—Antarctica and Greenland—remain quite cold throughout the year.

Annual Temperature Range

Another map useful in understanding the global pattern of air temperature is one that portrays the average annual range of temperatures (Figure 4-35). **Average annual temperature range** is the difference between the average temperatures of the warmest and coldest months (normally July and January). The data are portrayed on the map by isolines that resemble isotherms.

Enormous seasonal variations in temperature occur in the interiors of high-latitude continents, and continental areas in general experience much greater ranges than do equivalent oceanic latitudes. At the other extreme, the average temperature fluctuates only slightly from season to season in the tropics, particularly over tropical oceans.

Global Warming and the Greenhouse Effect

 Global Warming

As we described earlier in this chapter, the "natural" greenhouse effect has been part of the basis of life on Earth since the early atmosphere formed. Without it, our planet would be a frozen mass, perhaps 30°C (54°F) colder than it is today. Over the last three decades, the greenhouse effect has received considerable attention from the media and the general public. Data gathered from surface weather stations, ships, buoys, balloons, satellites, ice cores, and other paleoclimatological sources indicate that the climate of Earth is becoming warmer. This warming trend has become known to the public as **global warming**.

Over the twentieth century, average global temperatures increased by about 0.6°C (1°F)—in the last quarter of the twentieth century alone temperatures increased 0.2–0.3°C (0.4°F). This temperature increase over the

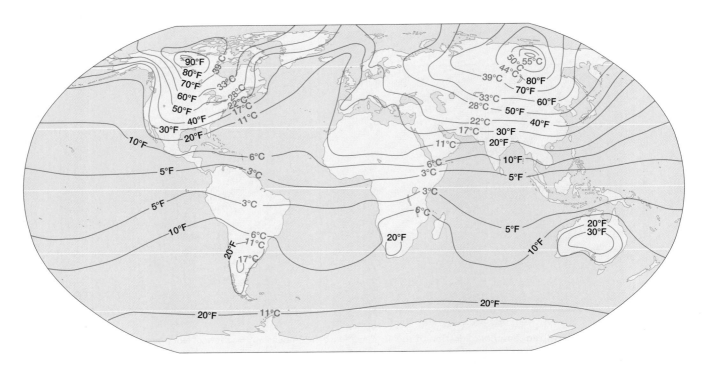

▲ **Figure 4-35**   The world pattern of average annual temperature range. The largest ranges occur in the interior of high-latitude landmasses.

Global Mean Temperature over Land & Ocean

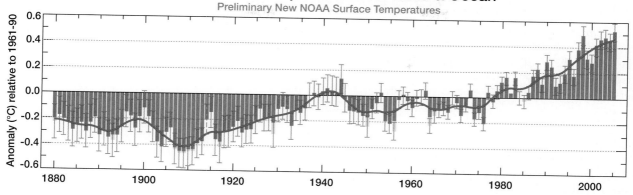

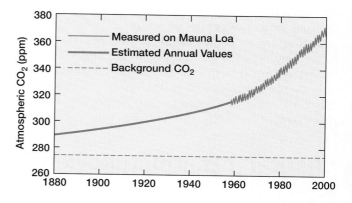

▲ **Figure 4-36**   Global Mean Temperature over Land and Ocean, 1880–2005. *(Source: National Climate Data Center/NOAA.)*

last 100 years is apparently greater than that of any other century in at least the last 1000 years, and the rate of temperature increase over the last three decades may be greater than at any time in several hundred thousand years. The 1990s are likely to have been the warmest decade of the last millennium, and the current decade is on its way to be warmer still. Since direct instrument measurements of Earth's temperature only go back a few centuries, past temperature patterns are calculated using proxy measures—such as data deciphered from polar ice cores—there is a margin of error in these figures, however, the evidence clearly points toward a warming trend (Figure 4-36).

The "culprit" in global warming appears to be a human-enhanced greenhouse effect. Since the industrial era began in the mid 1700s, human activities have increased the concentrations of greenhouse gases—such as carbon dioxide, methane, tropospheric ozone, and chlorofluorocarbons in the atmosphere. As greenhouse gas concentrations in the atmosphere increase, more terrestrial radiation is retained in the lower atmosphere, thereby raising global temperatures.

Carbon dioxide (CO_2) is thought to be responsible for about 64 percent of the human-enhanced greenhouse effect. CO_2 concentrations have been rising steadily since the Industrial Revolution began in the mid-1700s (Figure 4-37). Carbon dioxide is a principal by-product of combustion of anything containing carbon, such as coal and petroleum. World consumption of fossil fuels has been increasing at a rate of 2.0–2.5 percent per year in recent decades. Since 1750, carbon dioxide levels in the atmosphere have increased by more than 30 percent. The latest paleoclimatological data indicates that the current concentration of CO_2 in the atmosphere of nearly 380 ppm is greater than at any time in the last 650,000 years, and that the current rate of increase is greater than at any time in the last 20 millennia.

Many other greenhouse gases have been added to the atmosphere by human activity. Methane—produced by grazing livestock and rice paddies and a by-product

▲ **Figure 4-37**   Change in atmospheric carbon dioxide concentration from 1880–2000. *(After Michael Collier and Robert Webb,* Floods, Droughts, and Climate Change, *Tucson: University of Arizona Press, 2002.)*

of the combustion of wood, natural gas, coal, and oil—has more than doubled since 1750. Nitrous oxide—which comes from chemical fertilizers and automobile emissions—has increased by 17 percent since 1750. Chlorofluorocarbons (CFCs) are synthetic chemicals that were widely used as refrigerants and as propellants in spray cans until quite recently (see Chapter 3 for a discussion of another consequence of CFCs in the atmosphere—ozone depletion). Many of these gases, and others, are being released into the atmosphere at accelerating rates.

The increase in greenhouse gas concentrations, especially carbon dioxide, correlates well with the observed increase in global temperature: as CO_2 has increased, so have average global temperatures (Figure 4-38).

It is well known that climate undergoes frequent natural fluctuations, becoming warmer or colder regardless of human activities. There is, however, an increasing body of evidence that indicates that *anthropogenic* (human-induced) factors are responsible for the recent temperature increases. The Intergovernmental Panel on Climate Change (IPCC) is the most important international organization of atmospheric scientists and policy analysts assessing global climate change. The conclusion of the *Third Assessment Report of the IPCC* in 2001 was that

> The Earth's climate system has demonstrably changed on both global and regional scales since the pre-industrial era ... There is new and stronger evidence that most of the warming observed over the last 50 years is attributable to human activities.

Evidence of the influence of human activity on climate that has been gathered over the last few years made the *Fourth Assessment Report* from the IPCC, released in 2007, even more emphatic in its findings.

The observed changes in climate are not uniform around the world, and predictions of some of the consequences of increased levels of greenhouse gases are still subject to vigorous debate among scientists. Because both the causes and implications of global warming are so complicated—due especially to the many feedback loops involved in climate systems—the preceding description of global warming serves only as our introduction to the topic. In subsequent chapters, after increasing our understanding of processes of weather and climate, we will further

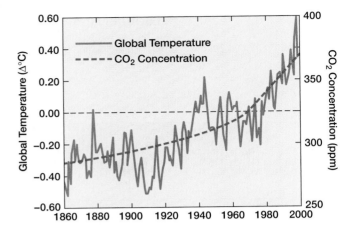

▲ **Figure 4-38**   The relationship between atmospheric carbon dioxide concentration and mean global temperature. (*After Michael Collier and Robert Webb*, Floods, Droughts, and Climate Change, *Tucson: University of Arizona Press, 2002.*)

explore both the natural and anthropogenic aspects of global environmental change, including global warming, in much greater detail.

Chapter 4 Learning Review

Key Terms

Before answering the study questions below, review the definitions of the following key terms (page references are provided for you):

absorption *(p. 81)*
adiabatic cooling *(p. 85)*
adiabatic warming *(p. 86)*
advection *(p. 85)*
albedo *(p. 87)*
angle of incidence *(p. 89)*
average annual temperature range *(p. 102)*
average lapse rate *(p. 98)*
condensation *(p. 86)*
conduction *(p. 84)*
convection *(p. 85)*
convection cell *(p. 85)*
electromagnetic radiation *(p. 78)*
electromagnetic spectrum *(p. 79)*
energy *(p. 75)*

environmental lapse rate *(p. 98)*
evaporation *(p. 86)*
global warming *(p. 102)*
greenhouse effect *(p. 83)*
greenhouse gases *(p. 83)*
heat *(p. 76)*
infrared radiation *(p. 80)*
insolation *(p. 80)*
isotherm *(p. 99)*
kinetic energy *(p. 76)*
latent heat *(p. 86)*
longwave radiation *(p. 80)*
ocean current *(p. 94)*
radiant energy *(p. 78)*
radiation (emission) *(p. 80)*
reflection *(p. 81)*

scattering *(p. 82)*
shortwave radiation *(p. 80)*
specific heat *(p. 92)*
subtropical gyres *(p. 95)*
temperature *(p. 76)*
temperature inversion *(p. 98)*
terrestrial radiation *(p. 80)*
thermal energy *(p. 76)*
thermal infrared radiation *(p. 80)*
thermometer *(p. 76)*
transmission *(p. 83)*
ultraviolet (UV) radiation *(p. 79)*
upwelling *(p. 96)*
visible light *(p. 79)*

Study Questions for Key Concepts

After studying this chapter, you should be able to answer the following questions:

Energy, Heat and Temperature (p. 75)

1. What is the difference between *heat* (or *thermal energy*) and *temperature*?
2. What is the relationship between the temperature of a substance and its internal kinetic energy?

Solar Energy (p. 78)

3. Describe and contrast the portions of the electromagnetic spectrum referred to as *shortwave radiation* and *longwave radiation*.
4. What is *insolation*?

Basic Heating and Cooling Processes in the Atmosphere (p. 80)

5. What is the difference between *absorption* and *reflection*? Between *absorption* and *transmission*?
6. What generally happens to the temperature of an object as a response to the absorption of electromagnetic radiation?
7. How is *scattering* different from *reflection*?
8. Why is the sky blue? Why are sunsets orange and red?
9. Describe and explain the *greenhouse effect* in the atmosphere, noting the two most important natural *greenhouse gases*.
10. What is the difference between *conduction* and *convection*?
11. How and why does *conduction* influence the temperature of air above a warm surface? Above a cold surface?
12. What role does convection play in heating the troposphere?
13. What happens to the temperature of rising air? Of descending air? Why?
14. Why do we say that *evaporation* is a cooling process and *condensation* a warming process?

The Heating of the Atmosphere (p. 86)

15. Briefly describe how the troposphere is heated by the Sun.
16. What is *albedo*?
17. Why does temperature generally decrease with increasing altitude in the troposphere?
18. "The atmosphere is mostly heated by the Earth rather than the Sun." Comment on the validity of this statement.

Variations in Heating by Latitude and Season (p. 89)

19. Explain the reasons for the unequal heating (by latitude) of the Earth by the Sun.
20. Why are there greater seasonal temperature differences in the high latitudes than in the tropics?

Land and Water Contrasts (p. 92)

21. Explain why land heats and cools faster and more than water.

Mechanisms of Heat Transfer (p. 94)

22. What are the two dominant mechanisms of heat transfer around the world?
23. How would global temperature patterns be different without this heat transfer?
24. What is the relative temperature of the ocean current flowing along the west coast of a continent in the midlatitudes? Along the east coast of a continent?
25. Describe the basic pattern of ocean currents around the margins of a major ocean basin (including the relative temperature of each current—either "cool" or "warm"). You should be able to sketch the direction of movement and note the relative temperature of major ocean currents on a blank map of an ocean basin.

Vertical Temperature Patterns (p. 98)

26. Describe the *average lapse rate* in the troposphere.
27. What is a *temperature inversion*?
28. What is the difference between a *radiational inversion* and an *advectional inversion*?

Global Temperature Patterns (p. 99)

29. What is an *isotherm*?
30. Using the isotherm maps of average January and July sea level temperature (Figures 4-32 and 4-33) describe the influence of latitude, season, land–water contrasts, and ocean currents on global temperature patterns. For example, explain why the following isotherms vary in latitude across the maps:
    - January −1°C (30°F) isotherm in the Northern Hemisphere
    - July 21°C (70°F) isotherm in the Northern Hemisphere
31. Where in the world do we find the greatest *average annual temperature ranges* and where do we find the smallest average annual temperature ranges? Why?

Global Warming and the Greenhouse Effect (p. 102)

32. How might humans be enhancing the natural greenhouse effect?

Additional Resources

Books:

Aguado, Edward, and James E. Burt. *Understanding Weather and Climate*, 4th ed. Upper Saddle River, NJ: Prentice Hall, 2007.

Drake, Frances. *Global Warming: The Science of Climatic Change*. New York: Oxford University Press, 2000.

Leggett, Jeremy. *The Carbon War: Global Warming and the End of the Oil Era*. New York: Routledge, 2001.

Internet Sites:

Intergovernmental Panel on Climate Change
http://www.ipcc.ch/
The Intergovernmental Panel on Climate Change was established to study and assess global climate change and its influence on human populations.

National Weather Service
http://www.nws.noaa.gov/
This site provides links to local National Weather Service offices, as well as to other sites that offer current weather forecasts, weather maps, information on storm conditions, and satellite images.

Unisys Weather
http://weather.unisys.com/
This site is a good source for current weather maps and weather forecasts for the United States.

5
Atmospheric Pressure and Wind

To the layperson, atmospheric pressure is the most difficult climate element to comprehend. The other three—temperature, wind, and moisture—are more readily understood because our bodies are much more sensitive to them. We can "feel" heat, air movement, and humidity, and we are quick to recognize variations in these elements. Pressure, on the other hand, is a phenomenon of which we are usually unaware; its variations are considerably less noticeable to our senses. Pressure usually impinges on our sensitivity only when we experience rapid vertical movement, as in an elevator or an airplane because of the difference in pressure inside and outside our ears, which is sometimes relieved only by "popping" them.

Despite its inconspicuousness, pressure is an important feature of the atmosphere. It is tied closely to the other weather elements, acting on them and responding to them. Pressure has an intimate relationship with wind: spatial variations in pressure are responsible for air movements. Hence, pressure and wind are often discussed together, as is done in this chapter.

The Impact of Pressure and Wind on the Landscape

The influence of atmospheric pressure on the landscape is significant but indirect; this influence is manifested mostly by wind and temperature as these two elements respond to pressure changes. The impact of wind is more direct and explicit than the impact of temperature because wind has the energy to transport solid particles in the air and thus has a visible component to its activity. Vegetation may bend in the wind and loose material of whatever kind may be shifted from one place to another. The results are nearly always short-run and temporary, however, and usually have no lasting effect on the landscape except at the time of a severe storm. Nevertheless, pressure and wind are major elements of weather and climate, and their interaction with other atmospheric components and processes cannot be overestimated.

The Nature of Atmospheric Pressure

Gas molecules, unlike those of a solid or liquid, are not strongly bound to one another. Instead, they are in continuous motion, colliding frequently with one another

◄ Winds from Hurricane Dennis on Cayman Brac, Cayman Islands. (*Alamy Images.*)

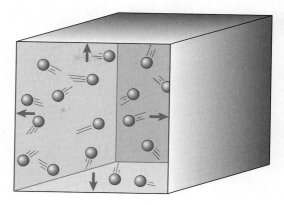

▲ **Figure 5-1** Gas molecules are always in motion. In this closed container, they bounce around, colliding with one another and with the walls of the container. These collisions give rise to the pressure exerted by the gas.

and with any surfaces to which they are exposed. Consider a container in which a gas is confined, as in Figure 5-1. The molecules of the gas zoom around inside the container and collide again and again with the walls. The *pressure* of the gas is defined as the force the gas exerts on some specified area of the container walls.

The atmosphere is made up of gases, of course, and so **atmospheric pressure** is the force exerted by the gas molecules on some area of Earth's surface or on any other body, including yours. At sea level, the pressure exerted by the atmosphere is slightly more than 1 kilogram per square centimeter (about 14.7 pounds per square inch). This value drops with increasing altitude because the farther away you get from Earth and its gravitational pull, the fewer gas molecules are present in the atmosphere.

The atmosphere exerts pressure on every solid or liquid surface it touches. The pressure is omnidirectional, which means it is exerted equally in all directions—up, down, sideways, and obliquely. In other words, atmospheric pressure is not simply a "weight" from above. This means that every square centimeter of any exposed surface—animal, vegetable, or mineral—at sea level is subjected to that much pressure (Figure 5-2). We are not sensitive to this ever-present burden of pressure because our bodies contain solids and liquids that are not significantly compressed and air spaces that are at the same pressure as the surrounding atmosphere; in other words, there is an exact balance between outward pressure and inward pressure.

Factors Influencing Atmospheric Pressure

The pressure of a gas is proportional to its density and temperature. This relationship can be explained by

▲ **Figure 5-2** The empty plastic bottle on the left was opened and then sealed tightly at an elevation of 3030 meters (9945 feet); when brought down to sea level the surrounding higher atmospheric pressure partially collapses the bottle. The bottle on the right contains air at sea level pressure. *(Darrel Hess photo.)*

several equations collectively referred to as the *ideal gas law.* The cause-and-effect association, however, is complex. Variations in any one of the three variables can cause variations in the other two. In this section, we examine how pressure varies with density, temperature, and the ways in which vertical movement of air influences surface atmospheric pressure.

Density and Pressure   Density is the mass of matter in a unit volume. For example, if you have a 10-kilogram cube of material with edge lengths of 1 meter, the density of that material is 10 kilograms per cubic meter ($10\,kg/m^3$). The density of solid material is the same on Earth or the moon or in space, that of liquids varies very slightly from one place to another, and that of gases varies greatly with location. Gas density changes so easily because a gas expands as far as the environmental pressure will allow. If you have 10 kg of gas in a container that has a volume of 1 cubic meter, the gas density is $10\,kg/m^3$. If you then transfer all the gas to a container having a volume of 5 cubic meters, the gas expands to fill the larger volume. There are the same number of gas molecules that were in the smaller container (in other words, the same mass), but they are now spread out over a volume five times as large. Therefore, the gas density in the larger container is only $2\,kg/m^3$ (10 kg divided by 5 cubic meters).

The density of a gas is proportional to the pressure on it. The reverse of this statement is also true: the pressure a gas exerts is proportional to its density. The denser the gas, the greater the pressure it exerts.

The atmosphere is held to Earth by the force of gravity which prevents the gaseous molecules from escaping into space. At lower altitudes, the gas molecules of the atmosphere are packed more densely together (Figure 5-3). Because the density is higher, there are

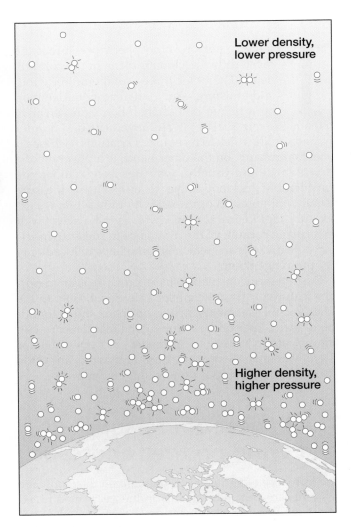

Lower density, lower pressure

Higher density, higher pressure

▲ **Figure 5-3** In the upper atmosphere, gas molecules are far apart and collide with each other infrequently, a condition that produces relatively low pressure. In the lower atmosphere, the molecules are closer together, and there are many more collisions, a condition that produces high pressure.

more molecular collisions and therefore higher pressure at lower altitudes. At higher altitudes, the air is less dense and there is a corresponding decrease in pressure. At any level in the atmosphere, then, the pressure is directly proportional to the air density at that altitude.

Temperature and Pressure   If air is heated, as we noted in the preceding chapter, the molecules become more agitated and their speed increases. This increase in speed produces a greater force to their collisions and results in higher pressure. Therefore, if other conditions remain the same (in particular, if volume is held constant), an increase in the temperature of a gas produces an increase in pressure, and a decrease in temperature produces a decrease in pressure. Knowing this, you might conclude that the air pressure will be high on warm days and low on cold days. Such is not usually the case, however: warm weather is generally associated with low atmospheric pressure and cool weather with high atmospheric pressure. While this seems contradictory, recall that we made the qualifying statement "if other conditions remain the same" in describing how temperature and pressure are related. When air is heated and no control is kept on its volume, it expands, which decreases its density. Thus, the increase in temperature may be accompanied by a decrease in pressure caused by the decrease in density.

Dynamic Influences on Air Pressure Surface air pressure may also be influenced by "dynamic" factors. In other words, air pressure may be influenced by the movement of the air—especially the vertical movement of air associated with different rates of air convergence and divergence at the surface and in the upper troposphere. As a generalization, descending air tends to be associated with relatively high pressure at the surface, while rising air tends to be associated with relatively low pressure at the surface.

In short, atmospheric pressure is affected by differences in air density, air temperature, and air movement; and the relationship among these variables is complex. It is important for us to be alert to these linkages, but it is often difficult to predict how a change in one variable will influence the others in a specific instance. Nevertheless, some useful generalizations about the factors associated with areas of high pressure and low pressure near the surface can be made:

- Strongly descending air is often associated with high pressure at the surface—a **dynamic high**.
- Very cold surface conditions are often associated with high pressure at the surface—a **thermal high**.
- Strongly rising air is often associated with low pressure at the surface—a **dynamic low**.
- Very warm surface conditions are often associated with relatively low pressure at the surface—a **thermal low**.

Surface pressure conditions often can be traced to one of these factors being dominant.

Mapping Pressure with Isobars

Atmospheric pressure is measured with instruments called **barometers**. The first liquid-filled barometers date back to the 1600s, and measurement scales based on the height of a column of mercury are still in use (average sea-level pressure using a mercury barometer is 760 millimeters or 29.92 inches). Today, however, one of the most common units of measure for atmospheric pressure is the **millibar**. The millibar (mb) is an expression of force per surface area. One millibar is defined as 1000 dynes per square centimeter (one dyne is the force required to accelerate 1 gram of a mass 1 centimeter

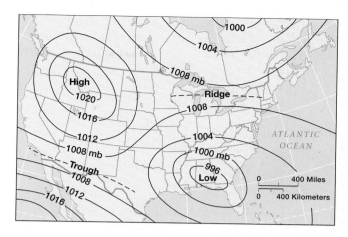

▲ **Figure 5-4**   Isobars are lines connecting points of equal atmospheric pressure. When they have been sketched on a weather map, it is easy to determine the location of high-pressure and low-pressure centers. This simplified weather map shows pressure in millibars.

per second per second).[1] Average sea-level pressure is 1013.25 millibars. In many countries air pressure is described with the *kilopascal* (kPa; 1 kPa = 10 mb).

Once pressure in millibars is plotted on a weather map, it is then possible to draw isolines of equal pressure called **isobars**, as shown in Figure 5-4. The pattern of the isobars reveals the horizontal distribution of pressure in the region under consideration. Prominent on such maps are roughly circular or oval areas characterized as being either "high pressure" or "low pressure." These **highs** and **lows** represent relative conditions—pressure that is higher or lower than that of the surrounding areas. In a similar way, a **ridge** is an elongated area of relatively high pressure, while a **trough** is an elongated area of relatively low pressure. It is important to keep the relative nature of pressure measurement in mind. For example, a pressure reading of 1005 millibars could be either "high" or "low" depending on the pressure of the surrounding areas.

On most maps of air pressure, actual pressure readings are adjusted to represent pressures at a common elevation, usually sea level. This is done because pressure decreases rapidly with increasing altitude, and consequently significant variations in pressure readings are likely at different weather stations simply because of differences in elevation.

As with other types of isolines, the relative closeness of isobars indicates the horizontal rate of pressure change, or **pressure gradient**. The pressure gradient can be thought of as representing the "steepness" of the

---

[1]In the definition of a dyne the term "per second per second" may seem strange. However, in this case we are describing the force required to *accelerate* a mass, in other words, the force required to change its speed or direction. Thus, the dyne describes the rate of change, not the speed.

pressure "slope" (or more correctly, the abruptness of the pressure change over a distance), a characteristic that has a direct influence on wind, the topic to which we turn next.

The Nature of Wind

Development of Wind Patterns

The atmosphere is virtually always in motion. Air is free to move in any direction, its specific movements being shaped by a variety of factors. Some airflow is lackadaisical and brief; some is strong and persistent. Atmospheric motions often involve both horizontal and vertical displacement. **Wind** refers to horizontal air movement; it has been characterized as "air in a hurry." Instead of being called wind, small-scale vertical motions are normally referred to as *updrafts* and *downdrafts;* large-scale vertical motions are *ascents* and *subsidences;* the term wind is applied only to horizontal movements. Although both vertical and horizontal motions are important in the atmosphere, much more air is involved in horizontal movements than in vertical.

Direction of Movement

Insolation is the ultimate cause of wind because all winds originate from the same basic sequence of events: unequal heating of different parts of Earth's surface brings about temperature gradients that generate pressure gradients, and these pressure gradients set air into motion. Winds represent nature's attempt to even out the uneven distribution of air pressure over Earth.

Air generally flows from areas of high pressure to areas of low pressure. If Earth did not rotate and if there were no friction, that is precisely what would happen—a direct movement of air from a high-pressure region to a low-pressure region. However, rotation and friction both exist, and so this general statement is usually not completely accurate. The direction of wind movement is determined principally by the interaction of three factors: pressure gradient, the Coriolis effect, and friction.

Pressure Gradient If there is higher pressure on one side of a parcel of air than on the other, the air will begin to move from the higher pressure toward the lower pressure, as shown in Figure 5-5. If you visualize a high-pressure area as a pressure "hill" and a low-pressure area as a pressure "valley," it is not difficult to imagine air flowing "down" the pressure gradient in the same manner that water flows down a hill (keep in

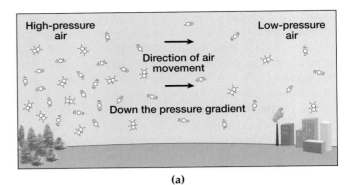

(a)

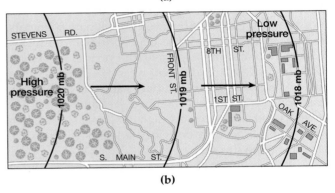

(b)

▲ **Figure 5-5** **(a)** A parcel of air bordered by high-pressure air on one side and low-pressure air on the other moves toward the low-pressure area. We say this movement is "down the pressure gradient." **(b)** If pressure gradient were the only force involved, air would flow perpendicular to the isobars.

mind that these terms are metaphorical—air isn't necessarily actually flowing downhill).

The *pressure-gradient force* acts at right angles to the isobars in the direction of the lower pressure. If there were no other factors to consider, that is the way the air would move, crossing the isobars at 90° (Figure 5-6a). However, such a flow rarely occurs in the atmosphere.

The Coriolis Effect Because Earth rotates, any object moving freely near Earth's surface appears to deflect to the right in the Northern Hemisphere and to the left in the Southern Hemisphere. The Coriolis effect has an important influence on the direction of wind flow (for a review of the Coriolis effect see Chapter 3). The Coriolis effect deflection acts at 90° from the direction of movement—to the right in the Northern Hemisphere and to the left in the Southern Hemisphere. There is an eternal battle, then, between the pressure-gradient force moving air from high toward low pressure and the deflection of the Coriolis effect 90° from its pressure-gradient path: the Coriolis effect keeps the wind from flowing directly down a pressure gradient, while the pressure gradient force prevents the Coriolis effect from turning the wind back up the pressure slope. Where these two factors are in balance—as is usually the case in the upper atmosphere—wind moves parallel to the isobars and is called a **geostrophic wind**[2] (Figure 5-6b).

Most winds in the atmosphere are geostrophic or nearly geostrophic in that they flow nearly parallel to the isobars. Only near the ground is there another significant factor—friction—to further complicate the situation.

Friction   In the lowest portions of the troposphere, a third force influences wind direction—*friction*. The frictional drag of Earth's surface slows wind movement and so the influence of the Coriolis effect is reduced (you will recall that more rapidly moving objects are deflected more by the Coriolis effect than are slowly moving objects). Instead of blowing perpendicular to the isobars (in response to the pressure gradient) or parallel to them (where pressure gradient force and the Coriolis effect are in balance), the wind takes an intermediate course between the two and crosses the isobars at some angle between 0° and 90° (Figure 5-6c). In essence, friction reduces wind speed, which in turn reduces the Coriolis effect deflection—thus, although the Coriolis effect does introduce a deflection to the right (in the Northern Hemisphere) the pressure gradient "wins the battle" and air flows into an area of low pressure and away from an area of high pressure.

As a general rule, the frictional influence is greatest near Earth's surface and diminishes progressively upward (Figure 5-7). Thus, the angle of wind flow across the isobars is greatest (closest to 90°) at low altitudes and becomes smaller at increasing elevations. The **friction layer** of the atmosphere extends to only about 1000 meters (approximately 3300 feet) above the ground. Higher than that, most winds follow a geostrophic or near-geostrophic course.

(a) Pressure Gradient Force only:

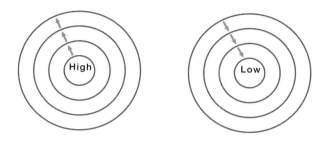

(b) Upper Atmosphere—Pressure Gradient Force and Coriolis Effect:

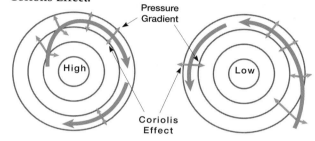

(c) Lower Atmosphere—Pressure Gradient Force, Coriolis Effect, and Friction:

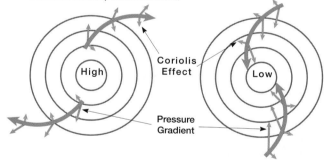

▲ **Figure 5-6**   The direction of wind flow is determined by a combination of three factors. **(a)** If the pressure gradient force were the only factor influencing wind direction, air would flow down the pressure gradient away from high pressure and toward low pressure, crossing the isobars at right angles. **(b)** In the upper atmosphere (above about 1000 m/3300 ft), an approximate balance develops between the pressure gradient force and the Coriolis effect deflection, resulting in geostrophic wind blowing parallel to the isobars; wind circulates clockwise around a high and counterclockwise around a low in the Northern Hemisphere. **(c)** In the lower atmosphere, friction slows the wind (which results in less Coriolis effect deflection), and so wind diverges clockwise out of a high and converges counterclockwise into a low in the Northern Hemisphere.

Cyclones and Anticyclones

    FG7

    Cyclones and Anticyclones

Distinct and predictable wind-flow patterns develop around all high-pressure and low-pressure centers—

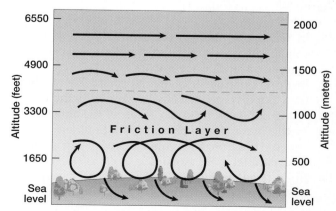

▲ **Figure 5-7**   A vertical cross section of the atmosphere to show wind movement. Near Earth's surface, friction causes wind flow to be turbulent and irregular. At higher altitudes, where there is less friction, the lines of wind flow are much straighter.

---

[2]Strictly speaking, geostrophic wind is only found in areas where the isobars are parallel and straight; the term *gradient wind* is a more general term used to describe wind flowing parallel to the isobars. In this book we use the term geostrophic to mean all wind blowing parallel to the isobars.

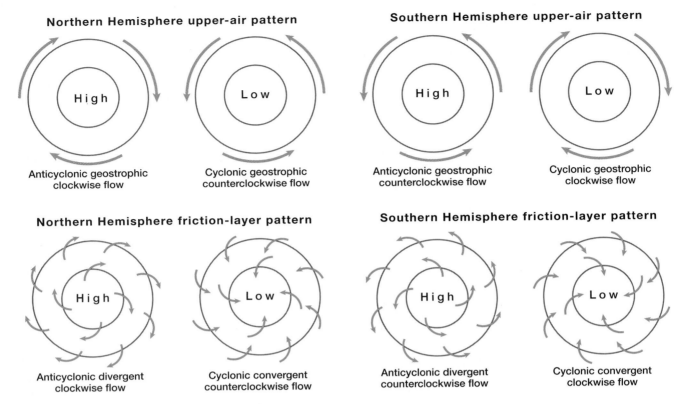

Figure 5-8   The eight basic patterns of air circulation around pressure cells.

patterns determined by the pressure gradient, Coriolis effect, and friction. A total of eight circulation patterns are possible: four in the Northern Hemisphere and four in the Southern Hemisphere. Within each hemisphere there are two patterns associated with high pressure centers and two patterns associated with low pressure centers, as shown in Figure 5-8.

High-Pressure Circulation Patterns   A high-pressure center is known as an **anticyclone**, and the flow of air associated with it is described as being *anticyclonic.* The four patterns of anticyclonic circulation, shown in Figure 5-8, are as follows:

1. In the upper atmosphere of the Northern Hemisphere, the winds move clockwise in a geostrophic manner parallel to the isobars.
2. In the friction layer of the Northern Hemisphere, there is a divergent clockwise flow, with the air spiraling out away from the center of the anticyclone.
3. In the upper atmosphere of the Southern Hemisphere, there is a counterclockwise, geostrophic flow parallel to the isobars.
4. In the friction layer of the Southern Hemisphere, the pattern is a mirror image of the Northern Hemisphere case. The air diverges in a counterclockwise pattern.

Low-Pressure Circulation Patterns   Low-pressure centers are called **cyclones**, and the associated wind movement is said to be *cyclonic.* As with anticyclones,

Northern Hemisphere cyclonic circulations are mirror images of their Southern Hemisphere counterparts:

1. In the upper atmosphere of the Northern Hemisphere, air moves counterclockwise in a geostrophic pattern parallel to the isobars.
2. In the friction layer of the Northern Hemisphere, a converging counterclockwise flow exists.
3. In the upper atmosphere of the Southern Hemisphere, there is clockwise, geostrophic flow paralleling the isobars.
4. In the friction layer of the Southern Hemisphere, the winds converge in a clockwise spiral.

Cyclonic patterns in the lower troposphere may at first glance appear to be misleading because the arrows seem to defy the Coriolis effect—in the Northern Hemisphere, the arrows seem to bend to the left, whereas we know that the Coriolis deflection is to the right. Remember, however, that wind patterns are the balance of several different forces acting in different directions: As air begins to flow down the pressure gradient into a low, the Coriolis effect does indeed deflect wind to the right—and this introduces the counterclockwise flow in the Northern Hemisphere (see Figure 5-6c and the animation *Development of Wind Patterns*).

Thus, large-scale winds do not blow from high pressure to low. Indeed, whether the wind is geostrophic or not, there is always high pressure on one side and low pressure on the other.

PEOPLE AND THE ENVIRONMENT Wind Energy

As the production of electricity from the burning of fossil fuels becomes increasingly costly—and with rising concern about increasing levels of greenhouse gases—more attention is being paid to the harnessing of energy from sunlight, tides, and wind. They are particularly attractive resources because they are free, renewable, clean, and virtually unlimited. The problem is to devise the technology to harness them economically.

Until quite recently, most windmills were relatively small structures used to pump water and drive electric generators. Within the last 25 years, however, much attention has been paid to the development of large-scale electricity generation by *wind farms,* a concentration of thousands of giant wind turbines all connected to an electrical grid.

If a wind turbine is to produce energy, there must be steady wind, not too strong or too weak. A slight breeze will not turn the blades, and a powerful gust might severely damage the machine. In a steady wind of 15 to 20 knots, large wind turbines can convert about one-third of the available wind energy to electricity. Their efficiency generally increases with greater wind speed and with large blade size. The available energy is proportional to the cube of the wind speed. Thus a

20-knot wind can provide eight times more energy than a wind of 10 knots.

Wind farms are creatures of the 1980s; none existed prior to about 1982. The U.S. Congress enacted research and development legislation in 1980, and the U.S. Department of Energy infused a modest amount of developmental money (about $40 million per year in the 1980s) into the industry. Various states, particularly California, provided some financing and tax incentives. As a result, some major corporations, a few utility companies, and many small new firms have developed and installed turbines. Worldwide, wind-generated electricity capacity today is more than 10 times greater than it was just 15 years ago, with the greatest increases taking place in Europe—especially Germany and Spain.

For many years California led the United States in wind power development, due in part to generous tax credits and to the availability of undeveloped land in windy locales. There were fewer than 200 turbines in the state in 1982, but today there are more than 13,000, with a total power generation capacity of more than 2300 megawatts. Wind turbines in California are mostly concentrated in three locations: Altamont Pass, about 80 kilometers (50 miles) east of San

Francisco (Figure 5-A); San Gorgonio Pass, 160 kilometers (100 miles) east of Los Angeles; and Tehachapi Pass, 80 kilometers (50 miles) southeast of Bakersfield. In addition, there are half a dozen smaller wind farms elsewhere in the state. The combined output of these machines meets about 1.5 percent of the state's total electricity demand.

Generating electricity from wind turbines is an appealing activity because it does not deplete any resources or create pollution and, unlike solar energy, is not restricted to daytime use. Moreover, it usually does not interfere with other forms of land use; for example, most California wind farms are in pastoral areas, and cattle have no problem grazing among the windmills.

By the late 1990s the expansion of California's wind energy program was, at least for the time being, leveling off. However, wind-generated electricity capacity has been expanding rapidly in other states and by 2006 Texas had surpassed California in terms of total generation capacity. Improved technology has been lowering the cost of wind-generated power, making it likely that the growth of the wind energy industry will continue in the future.

◄ **Figure 5-A** Wind turbines in the Altamont Pass, California, wind farm. (*Darrel Hess photo.*)

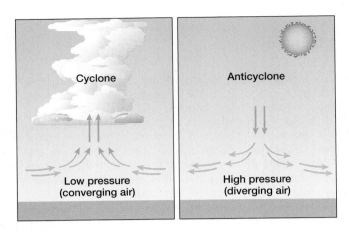

▲ **Figure 5-9** In a cyclone (low-pressure cell), air converges and rises. In an anticyclone (high-pressure cell), air descends and diverges.

Vertical Movement within Cyclones and Anticyclones

A prominent vertical component of air movement is also associated with pressure centers. As Figure 5-9 shows, air descends in anticyclones and rises in cyclones. Such motions are particularly notable in the lower troposphere. The anticyclonic pattern can be visualized as upper air sinking down into the center of the high and then diverging near the ground surface. Opposite conditions prevail in a low-pressure center, with the air converging horizontally into the cyclone and then rising. Notice in Figure 5-9 that cyclones and rising air are associated with clouds, while anticyclones and descending air are associated with clear conditions—the reasons for this will be explained in Chapter 6.

Wind Speed

Thus far, we have been considering the direction of wind movement and paying little attention to speed. Although some complications are introduced by inertia and other factors, it is accurate to say that the speed of wind flow is determined primarily by the pressure gradient. If the gradient is steep, the air moves swiftly; if the gradient is gentle, movement is slow. This relationship can be portrayed in the simple diagram of Figure 5-10. The closeness of the isobars indicates the steepness of the pressure gradient.

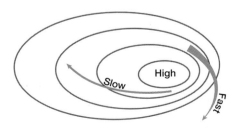

▲ **Figure 5-10** Wind speed is determined by the pressure gradient, which is indicated by the spacing of isobars. Where isobars are close together, the pressure gradient is steep and wind speed is high; where isobars are far apart, the pressure gradient is gentle and wind speed is low.

Over most of the world most of the time, surface winds are relatively gentle. As Figure 5-11 shows, for instance, annual average wind speed in North America is generally between 6 and 12 knots.[3] Cape Dennison in Antarctica holds the dubious distinction of being the windiest place on Earth, with an annual average wind speed of 38 knots. The most persistent winds are usually in coastal areas or high mountains.

Vertical Variations in Pressure and Wind

Although the main topic of this chapter is the horizontal distribution of pressure and wind, it is worthwhile to note major features of the vertical pattern as well.

Atmospheric pressure, with only minor localized exceptions, decreases rapidly with height (Table 5-1). The pressure change is most rapid at lower altitudes, the rate of decrease diminishing significantly above about 3 kilometers (10,000 feet). Prominent surface pressure centers (anticyclones and cyclones) often "lean" with height, which is to say that they are not absolutely vertical in orientation.

Wind speed is quite variable from one altitude to another and from time to time, usually increasing with height. Winds tend to move faster above the friction layer. As we shall see in subsequent sections, the very strongest tropospheric winds are usually found at intermediate levels in what are called *jet streams* or in violent storms near Earth's surface.

The General Circulation of the Atmosphere

Global Atmospheric Circulation

Earth's atmosphere is an extraordinarily dynamic medium. It is constantly in motion, responding to the various forces described previously as well as to a variety of more localized conditions. Some atmospheric motions are broadscale and sweeping; others are minute and momentary. Most important to an understanding of geography is the general pattern of circulation, which involves major semipermanent conditions of both wind and pressure. This circulation is the principal mechanism for both longitudinal and latitudinal heat transfer and is exceeded only by the global pattern of insolation as a determinant of world climates.

---

[3]Recall that a *knot* is a unit of speed equivalent to 1 nautical mile per hour. A nautical mile is a bit longer than a "statute" mile, the former being equal to 6076 feet or 1852 meters and the latter being equal to 5280 feet or 1609 meters. A knot is also equivalent to 1.85 km/hr (1.15 statute miles per hour).

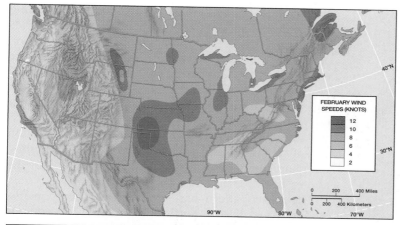

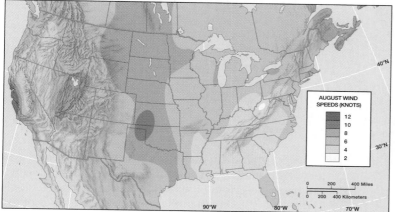

◀ **Figure 5-11** Average North American wind speeds in February and August. Wind speed tends to be higher in winter than in summer because pressure changes are more abrupt and storms are more frequent in winter than in summer. The Great Plains tend to have the highest speed winds in all seasons. The strong coastal winds in California during summer largely result from heating in the interior Central Valley (such *sea breezes* are discussed later in this chapter).

TABLE 5-1 How Atmospheric Pressure Varies with Altitude

Altitude		
Kilometers	Miles	Pressure (millibars)
18	11	75.6
16	10	104
14	8.7	142
12	7.4	194
10	6.2	265
9.0	5.6	308
8.0	5.0	356
7.0	4.3	411
6.0	3.7	472
5.0	3.1	540
4.0	2.5	617
3.5	2.2	658
3.0	1.9	701
2.5	1.6	747
2.0	1.2	795
1.5	0.9	846
1.0	0.6	899
0.5	0.3	955
0	0	1013

If Earth were a nonrotating sphere of uniform surface, we could expect a very simple circulation pattern (Figure 5-12). The greater amount of insolational heating in the equatorial region would produce a girdle of low pressure around the world, and radiational cooling at the poles would develop a cap of high pressure in those areas. Surface winds in the Northern Hemisphere would flow directly down the pressure gradient from north to south, whereas those in the Southern Hemisphere would follow a similar gradient from south to north. Air would rise at the equator in a large convection cell and flow toward the poles (south to north in the Northern Hemisphere and north to south in the Southern Hemisphere), where it would subside into the polar highs.

Earth does rotate, however, and in addition has an extremely varied surface. Consequently, the broadscale circulation pattern of the atmosphere is much more complex than that shown in Figure 5-12. Apparently only the tropical regions have a complete vertical convective circulation cell. Similar cells have been postulated for the middle and high latitudes, but observations indicate that the midlatitude and high-latitude cells either do not exist or are weakly and sporadically developed. The low-latitude cells—one north and one south of the equator—can be thought of as gigantic convection systems (Figure 5-13). These two prominent tropical circulations are called **Hadley cells**, after George Hadley (1685–1768), an English meteorologist who first

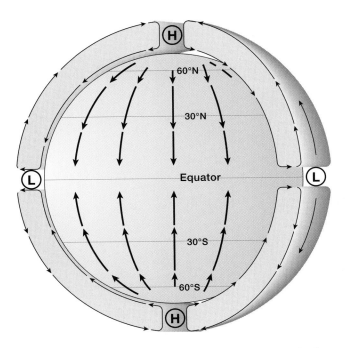

▲ **Figure 5-12** Wind circulation patterns would be simple if Earth's surface were uniform (no distinction between continents and oceans) and if the planet did not rotate. High pressure at the poles and low pressure at the equator would produce northerly surface winds in the Northern Hemisphere and southerly surface winds in the Southern Hemisphere.

conceived the idea of enormous convective circulation cells in 1735.

Around the world in equatorial latitudes, warm air rises, producing a region of relative low pressure at the surface. This air ascends to great heights, mostly in thunderstorm updrafts. By the time this air reaches the upper troposphere at elevations of about 15 kilometers (50,000 feet), it has cooled. The air then spreads north and south and moves poleward, eventually descending at latitudes of about 30° N and S, where it forms bands of high pressure at the surface (Figure 5-14). One portion of the air diverging from these surface high-pressure zones flows toward the poles, while another portion flows back toward the equator—where the Northern and Southern Hemisphere components converge and the warm air rises again.

Although the Hadley cell model is a simplification of reality, it is a useful starting point for understanding the main components of the general circulation of the atmosphere.

The basic pattern has seven surface components, which are replicated north and south of the equator (Figures 5-15 and 5-16). From pole to equator, they are:

1. Polar high
2. Polar easterlies
3. Polar front (Subpolar low)
4. Westerlies
5. Subtropical high
6. Trade winds
7. Intertropical convergence zone

Tropospheric circulation is essentially a closed system, with neither a beginning nor an end, and so we can begin describing it almost anywhere. It seems logical, however, to begin in the subtropical latitudes of the five major ocean basins because these areas serve as the "source" of the major surface winds of the planet.

Subtropical Highs

Each ocean basin has a large semipermanent high-pressure cell centered at about 30° of latitude called a **subtropical high (STH)** (Figure 5-17). These gigantic

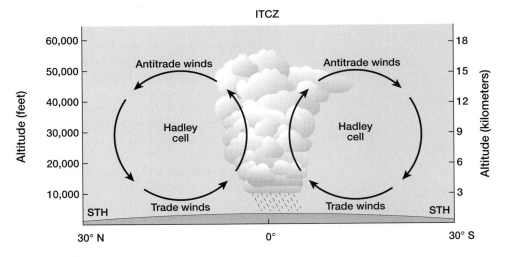

▲ **Figure 5-13** Distinct cells of vertical circulation occur in tropical latitudes; they are called Hadley cells. The equatorial air rises to some 12 to 15 kilometers (40,000 or 50,000 feet) before spreading poleward. The vertical dimension of the Hadley cells is considerably exaggerated in this idealized diagram.

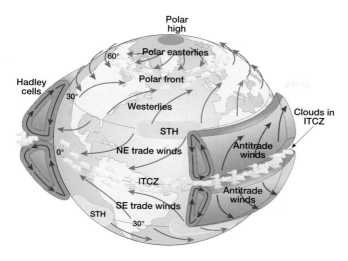

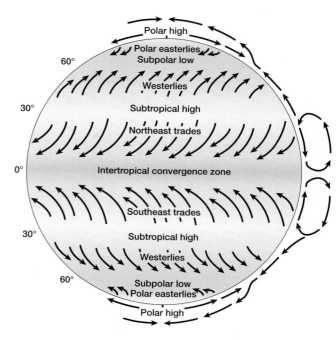

▲ **Figure 5-14**   Idealized global circulation. Rising air of the ITCZ in the Hadley cell is deflected aloft and forms westerly Antitrades, while surface winds diverging from the STH form easterly trade winds. The upper atmosphere flow of the westerlies is shown with faint blue arrows. (Vertical dimension exaggerated considerably.)

▲ **Figure 5-15**   The seven surface components of the general circulation of the atmosphere, disregarding the effect of landmasses. (The vertical component is considerably exaggerated and the upper atmosphere flow over the midlatitudes is omitted.)

anticyclones, with an average diameter of perhaps 3200 kilometers (2000 miles), develop from the descending air of the Hadley cells. They are usually elongated east–west and tend to be centered in the eastern portions of a basin (in other words, just off the west coasts of continents). Their latitudinal positions vary from time to time, shifting a few degrees poleward in summer and a few degrees equatorward in winter.

The STHs are so persistent that most have been given a proper name (such as the Azores High in the North Atlantic and the Hawaiian High in the North Pacific). From a global standpoint, the STHs represent intensified cells of high pressure (and subsiding air) in two general ridges of high pressure that extend around the world in these latitudes, one in each hemisphere. The high-pressure ridges are significantly broken up over the continents, especially in summer when inland temperatures produce lower air pressure, but the STHs normally persist over the ocean basins throughout the year because temperatures and pressures there remain essentially constant. Associated with these high-pressure cells is a general subsidence of air from higher altitudes in the form of a broadscale, gentle downdraft. A permanent feature of the STHs is a subsidence temperature inversion that covers wide areas in the subtropics.

Within an STH, the weather is nearly always clear, warm, and calm. We shall see in the next chapter that subsiding air is totally inimical to the development of clouds or the production of rain. Instead, these areas are characterized by warm, subtropical sunshine. Thus, it comes as no surprise that these anticyclonic, subsiding-air regions coincide with most of the world's major deserts.

Subtropical highs are also characterized by an absence of wind: in the center of an STH air is primarily subsiding; horizontal air movement and divergence begins toward the edges. These regions are sometimes called the **horse latitudes**, presumably because sixteenth- and seventeenth-century sailing ships were sometimes becalmed there and their cargos of horses were thrown overboard to conserve drinking water.

The air circulation pattern around an STH is anticyclonic: divergent clockwise in the Northern Hemisphere and counterclockwise in the Southern Hemisphere. In essence, the STHs can be thought of as gigantic wind wheels whirling in the lower troposphere, fed with air sinking down from above and spinning off winds horizontally in all directions (Figure 5-18). The winds are not dispersed uniformly around an STH, however; instead, they are concentrated on the northern and southern sides. Wind flow is less pronounced on the eastern and western sides of an STH because of the high-pressure ridge in those latitudes.

Although the global flow of air is essentially a closed circulation from a viewpoint at Earth's surface, the STHs can be thought of as the source of two of the world's three major surface wind systems: the trade winds and the westerlies.

Trade Winds

Issuing from the equatorward sides of the STHs and diverging toward the west and toward the equator is the major wind system of the tropics—the **trade**

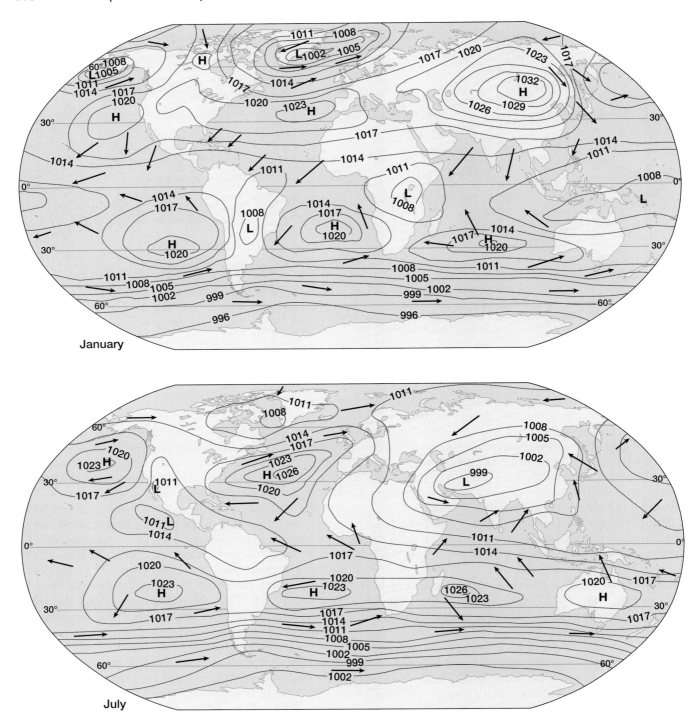

▲ **Figure 5-16** Average atmospheric pressure and wind direction in January and July. Pressure is reduced to sea-level values and shown in millibars. Arrows indicate generalized surface wind movements.

winds. These winds cover most of Earth between about latitude 25° N and latitude 25° S (see Figure 5-18). They are particularly prominent over oceans but tend to be significantly interrupted and modified over land-masses. Because of the vastness of Earth in tropical latitudes and because most of this expanse is oceanic, the trade winds dominate more of the globe than any other wind system.

The trade winds are predominantly easterly; that is, they generally flow toward the west (winds are named for the direction from which they blow; an *easterly* wind blows from east to west, a *westerly* wind blows from the west, and so forth). There is also a latitudinal component to their movement, however. In the Northern Hemisphere, they usually come from the north-east (and are sometimes called the *northeast trades*);

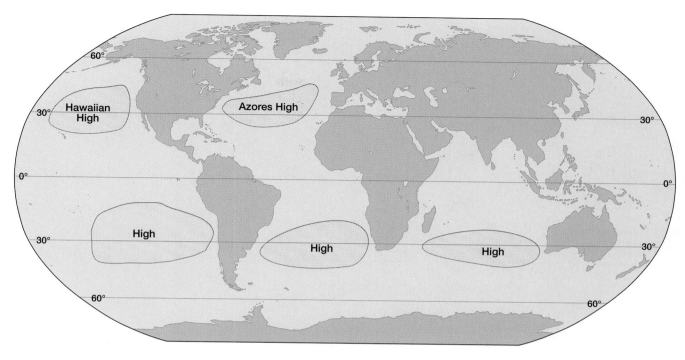

▲ **Figure 5-17**   The subtropical highs, also called the *horse latitudes*.

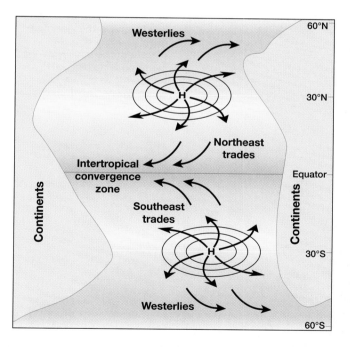

▲ **Figure 5-18**   The air that descends and diverges out of the subtropical highs is the source of the surface trade winds and westerlies.

south of the equator, they are from the southeast (the *southeast trades*). There are exceptions to this general pattern, especially over the Indian Ocean, where westerly winds sometimes prevail, but for the most part there is easterly flow above the tropical oceans.

Indeed, the trade winds are by far the most "reliable" of all winds. They are extremely consistent in both direction and speed, as Figure 5-19 shows. They blow most of the time in the same direction at the same speed, day and night, summer and winter (Figure 5-20). This steadiness is reflected in their name: trade winds really means "winds of commerce." Mariners of the sixteenth century recognized early that the quickest and most reliable route for their sailing vessels from Europe to America lay in the belt of northeasterly winds of the southern part of the North Atlantic Ocean. Similarly, the trade winds were used by Spanish galleons in the Pacific Ocean, and the name became applied generally to these tropical easterly winds.

The trades originate as warming, drying winds capable of holding an enormous amount of moisture. As they blow across the tropical oceans, they evaporate vast quantities of moisture and therefore have a tremendous potential for storminess and precipitation. They do not release the moisture, however, unless forced to do so by being uplifted by a topographic barrier or some sort of pressure disturbance (the reasons for this will be explained in Chapter 6). Low-lying islands in the trade-wind zone are often desert islands because the moisture-laden winds pass over them without dropping any rain. If there is even a slight topographic irregularity, however, the air that is forced to rise may release abundant precipitation (Figure 5-21). Some of the wettest places in the world are windward slopes in the trade winds, such as in Hawaii (see Figure 3-21).

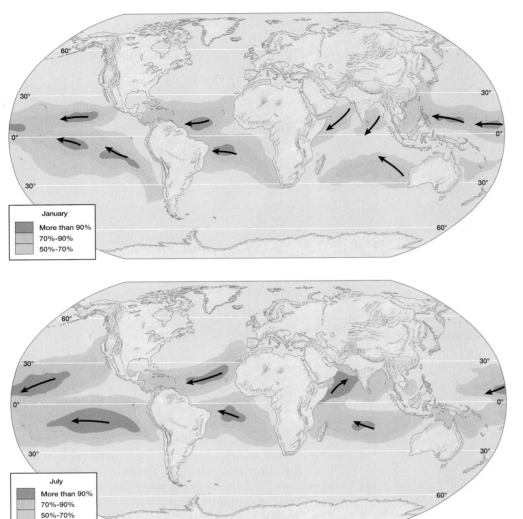

◀ **Figure 5-19** The trade winds are by far the most consistent of the major wind systems. These maps show their frequency of consistency for the midseason months of January and July. In the orange areas, for instance, the wind blows in the indicated direction more than 90 percent of the time. Note the monsoon wind reversal in southern Asia during July, which will be discussed later in this chapter.

▲ **Figure 5-20** Tropical coastal areas often experience the ceaseless movement of the trades. This breezy scene is at Cairns on the northeastern coast of Queensland, Australia. *(Tom L. McKnight photo.)*

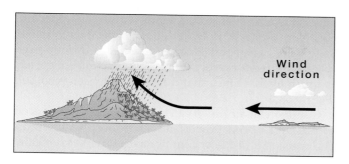

▲ **Figure 5-21** Trade winds are usually heavily laden with moisture, but they do not produce clouds and rain unless forced to rise. Thus, they may blow across a low-lying island with little or no visible effect. An island of greater elevation, however, causes the air to rise up the side of the mountain, and the result is usually a heavy rain.

Intertropical Convergence Zone

The northeast and southeast trades come together in the general vicinity of the equator, although the latitudinal position shifts seasonally northward and southward following the Sun. This shift is greater over land than over sea because the land heats more. The zone where the air from the Northern Hemisphere and Southern Hemisphere meet is usually called the **intertropical convergence zone**, or simply the **ITCZ**, but it is also referred to as the **doldrums** (this last name is attributed to the fact that sailing ships were often becalmed in these latitudes).

The ITCZ is a zone of convergence and weak horizontal airflow characterized by feeble and erratic winds. It is a globe-girdling zone of low pressure associated with high rainfall, instability, and rising air in the Hadley cells (see Figure 5-14). It is not a region of continuously ascending air, however. Almost all the rising air of the tropics ascends in the updrafts that occur in thunderstorms in the ITCZ, and these updrafts pump an enormous amount of sensible heat and latent heat of condensation into the upper troposphere, where much of it spreads poleward.

The ITCZ often appears as a well-defined, relatively narrow cloud band over the oceans (Figure 5-22). Over continents, however, it is likely to be more diffused and indistinct, although thunderstorm activity is common.

The Westerlies

The Jet Stream and Rossby Waves

The fourth component of the general atmospheric circulation is represented by the arrows that issue from the poleward sides of the STHs in Figure 5-18. This is the great wind system of the midlatitudes, commonly called the **westerlies**. These winds flow basically from west to east around the world in the latitudinal zone between about 30° and 60° both north and south of the equator. Because the globe is smaller at these latitudes than in the tropics, the westerlies are less extensive than the trades; nevertheless, they cover much of Earth.

Near the surface, the westerlies are much less constant and persistent than the trades, which is to say that in the midlatitudes surface winds do not always

◀ **Figure 5-22** A well-defined band of clouds marks the ITCZ over equatorial Africa in this infrared satellite image (darker shades of gray indicate higher surface temperatures). Note the generally clear skies off the west coasts of northern and southern Africa, corresponding to the areas of the subtropical highs, and the cloudiness and storms in the band of westerlies in the midlatitudes. *(Courtesy of the Naval Research Laboratory.)*

flow from the west but may come from almost any point of the compass. Near the surface there are interruptions and modifications of the westerly flow, which can be likened to eddies and countercurrents in a river. These interruptions are caused by surface friction, by topographic barriers, and especially by migratory pressure systems, which produce airflow that is not westerly.

Jet Streams Although the surface westerlies are somewhat variable, the geostrophic winds aloft, however, blow very prominently from the west. Moreover, there are two remarkable "cores" of high-speed winds in each hemisphere called **jet streams**: one called the *polar front jet stream* (or simply the *polar jet stream*) and the other called the *subtropical jet stream*, at high altitudes in the westerlies (Figure 5-23). The belt of the westerlies can therefore be thought of as a meandering river of air moving generally from west to east around the world in the midlatitudes, with the jet streams as its fast-moving cores.

The polar front jet stream, which usually occupies a position 9 to 12 kilometers (30,000 to 40,000 feet) high, is not centered in the band of the westerlies; it is displaced poleward, as Figure 5-23 shows (the name comes from its location near the *polar front*). This jet stream is a feature of the upper troposphere located over the area of greatest horizontal temperature gradient—that is, cold just poleward and warm just equatorward.

A jet stream is not always the sharply defined narrow ribbon of wind as often portrayed on weather maps;

rather it is a zone of strong winds within the upper troposphere westerly flow. Jet stream speed is variable. Sixty knots is generally considered as the minimum speed required for recognition as a jet stream, but speeds as much as five times that number have been recorded (Figure 5-24).

Commercial air travel can be significantly influenced by the high-speed flow of upper tropospheric winds. The cruising altitude of commercial jetliners is typically 9 to 12 kilometers (30,000 to 40,000 feet)—a typical elevation for the polar front jet stream. It generally takes longer to fly from east to west across the United States than it does to fly from west to east. When traveling from the east, a "headwind" is likely to impede progress, while traveling from the west, a "tailwind" may reduce travel time.

Rossby Waves The polar front jet stream shifts its latitudinal position with some frequency, and this change has considerable influence on the path of the westerlies. Although the basic direction of movement is west to east, frequently sweeping undulations develop in the westerlies and produce a meandering jet stream path that wanders widely north and south (Figure 5-25). These curves are very large and are generally referred to as long waves or **Rossby waves** (after the Chicago meteorologist C. G. Rossby, who first explained their nature). At any given time, there are usually from three to six Rossby waves in the westerlies of each hemisphere. These waves can be thought of as

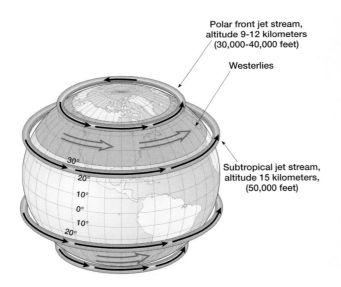

▲ **Figure 5-23** Neither jet stream is centered in the band of the westerlies. The polar front jet stream is closer to the poleward boundary, and the subtropical jet stream is closer to the equatorward boundary of this wind system. The two jet streams are not at the same altitude; the subtropical jet stream is at a higher altitude than the polar front jet stream.

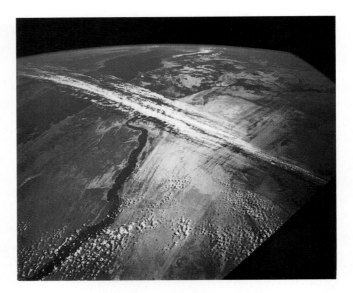

▲ **Figure 5-24** A jet stream sometimes generates a distinctive cloud pattern that is conspicuous evidence of its presence, as in this photograph taken over the Nile Valley and Red Sea. Equatorward of the axis of the jet there is a tendency for air to rise, a condition that can produce thin clouds. Poleward of the axis, the air is clear. *(NASA/Headquarters.)*

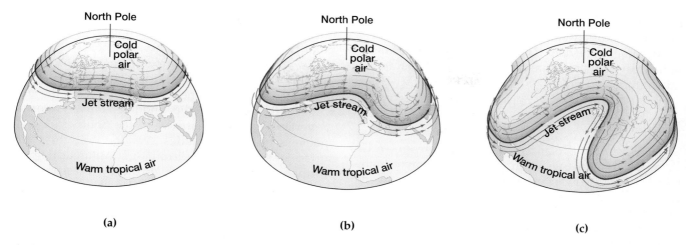

(a)   **(b)**   **(c)**

▲ **Figure 5-25**   Rossby waves as part of the general flow (particularly the upper-air flow) of the westerlies. **(a)** When there are few waves and their amplitude (north–south component of movement) is small, cold air usually remains poleward of warm air. **(b)** This distribution pattern begins to change as the Rossby waves grow. **(c)** When the waves have great amplitude, cold air pushes equatorward and warm air moves poleward.

separating cold polar air from warmer tropical air. When the polar front jet stream path is more directly west–east, there is a *zonal flow* pattern in the weather, with cold air poleward of warm air. However, when the jet stream begins to oscillate and the Rossby waves develop significant amplitude (which means a prominent north–south component of movement) there is a *meridional flow*: cold air is brought equatorward and warm air moves poleward, bringing frequent and severe weather changes to the midlatitudes.

The subtropical jet stream is usually located at high altitudes—just below the tropopause, as Figure 5-26a shows—over the poleward margin of the subsiding air of the STH. It has less influence on surface weather patterns because there is less temperature contrast in the associated air streams. Sometimes, however, the polar front jet and the subtropical jet merge as shown in Figure 5-26b to produce a broad belt of high-speed winds in the upper troposphere—a condition that can intensify the weather

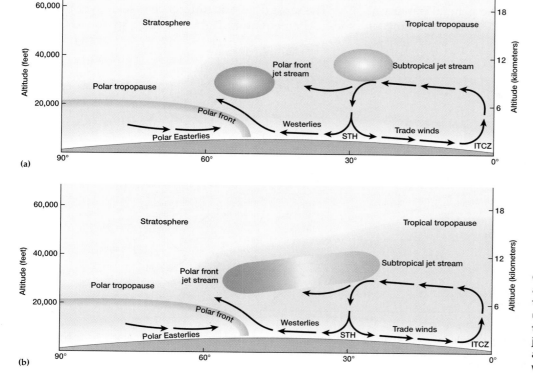

◀ **Figure 5-26   (a)** A vertical cross section of the atmosphere cut perpendicular to the jet streams, showing the usual relative positions of the two jet streams. **(b)** The two jet streams sometimes merge, and the result is intensified weather conditions.

conditions associated with either zonal or meridional flow of the Rossby waves.

All things considered, no other portion of Earth experiences such short-run variability of weather as the midlatitudes.

Polar Highs

Situated over both polar regions are high-pressure cells called **polar highs** (see Figure 5-14). The Antarctic high, which forms over an extensive, high-elevation, very cold continent, is strong, persistent, and almost a permanent feature above the Antarctic continent. The Arctic high is much less pronounced and more transitory, particularly in winter. It tends to form over northern continental areas rather than over the Arctic Ocean. Air movement associated with these cells is typically anticyclonic. Air from above sinks down into the high and diverges horizontally near the surface, clockwise in the Northern Hemisphere and counterclockwise in the Southern Hemisphere, forming the third of the world's wind systems, the polar easterlies.

Polar Easterlies

The third broad-scale global wind system occupies most of the area between the polar highs and about 60° of latitude (Figure 5-27). The winds move generally from east to west and are called the **polar easterlies**. They are typically cold and dry but quite variable.

Polar Front

The final surface component of the general pattern of atmospheric circulation is a zone of low pressure at about 50° to 60° of latitude in both Northern and Southern hemispheres. The zone is commonly called the **polar front**, although it is sometimes most clearly visible by the presence of semipermanent zones of low pressure called the **subpolar lows**. The polar front is a meeting ground and zone of conflict between the cold winds of the polar easterlies and the relatively warmer westerlies. The subpolar low of the Southern Hemisphere is nearly continuous over the uniform ocean surface of the cold seas surrounding Antarctica. In the Northern Hemisphere, however, the low-pressure zone is discontinuous, being interrupted by the continents. It is much more prominent in winter than in summer and is best developed over the northernmost reaches of the Pacific and Atlantic oceans, forming the Aleutian Low and the Icelandic Low respectively.

The polar front area is characterized by rising air, widespread cloudiness, precipitation, and generally unsettled or stormy weather conditions (Figure 5-28). Many of the migratory storms that travel with the westerlies have their origin in the conflict zone of the polar front.

Vertical Patterns of the General Circulation

As we have seen, over tropical regions, between the equator and 20° to 25° of latitude, surface winds generally blow from the east. In the midlatitudes, the surface winds are generally westerly, while in the highest latitudes, surface winds are again easterly. In the upper elevations of the troposphere, however, the wind patterns are somewhat different from the surface winds (Figure 5-29).

The most dramatic difference is seen over the tropics. After equatorial air has risen in the ITCZ, the

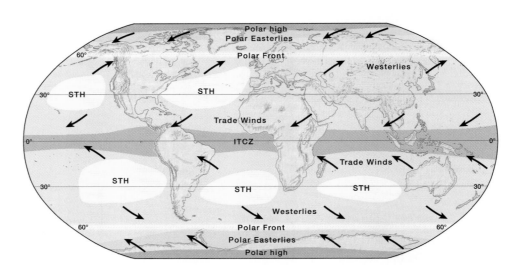

▲ **Figure 5-27**   Map showing the generalized locations of the seven components of the general circulation patterns of the atmosphere. (In this map projection, the areal extent of the high-latitude components—polar high, polar easterlies, polar front—is considerably exaggerated.)

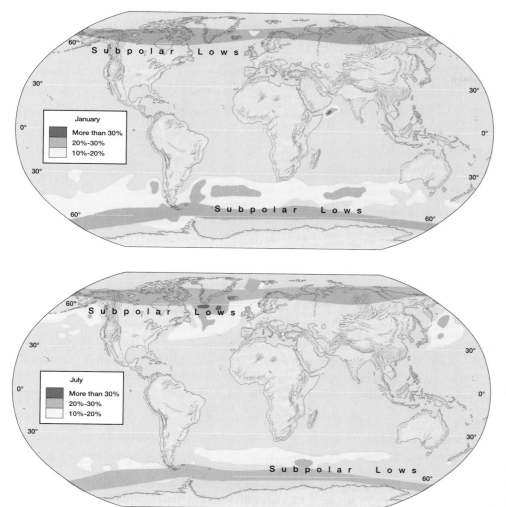

◀ **Figure 5-28** Frequency of gale-force winds over the oceans in January and July. It is clear from this map that the strongest oceanic winds are associated with activities along the polar front of the subpolar lows.

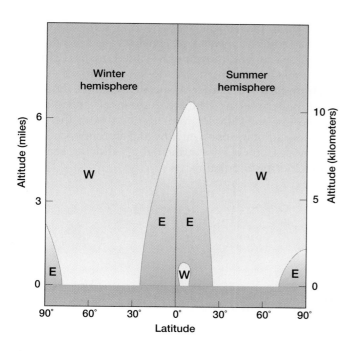

▲ **Figure 5-29** A generalized cross section through the troposphere, showing the horizontal component of air movement. (Legend: E = easterly winds; W = westerly winds.)

high-elevation poleward flow of air in the Hadley cell is deflected by the Coriolis effect (see Figure 5-14). This results in upper-elevation winds blowing from the southwest in the Northern Hemisphere and from the northwest in the Southern Hemisphere in the **antitrade winds**. This flow eventually becomes more westerly and encompasses the subtropical jet stream. Thus, at the surface within the tropics, winds are generally from the east, while high above the antitrade winds are blowing from the west.

Modifications of the General Circulation

There are many variations to the pattern discussed on the preceding pages, and all features of the general circulation may appear in altered form, much different from the idealized description. Indeed, components sometimes disappear from sizable parts of the atmosphere where they are expected to exist. Even the troposphere sometimes "disappears" (for example, during a

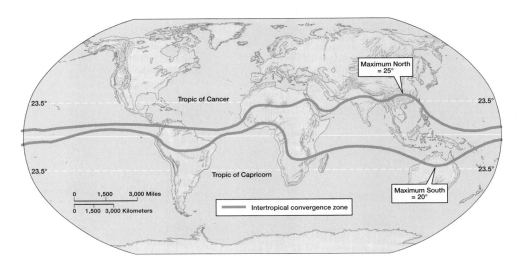

▲ **Figure 5-30** Typical maximum poleward positions of the intertropical convergence zone at its seasonal extremes. The greatest variation in location is associated with monsoon activity in Asia and Australia.

high-latitude winter with very cold surface temperatures, the atmospheric temperature may steadily increase with height into the stratosphere; in such cases the tropopause cannot be identified). Nevertheless, the generalized pattern of global wind and pressure systems comprises the seven components described above. To understand how real-world weather and climate differ from this general picture, it is necessary to discuss two important modifications of the generalized scheme.

Seasonal Variations in Location

Seasonal Pressure and Precipitation Patterns

The seven surface components of the general circulation shift latitudinally with the changing seasons. When sunlight, and therefore surface heating, is concentrated in the Northern Hemisphere (Northern Hemisphere summer), all components are displaced northward; during the opposite season (Southern Hemisphere summer), everything is shifted southward. The displacement is greatest in the low latitudes and least in the polar regions. The ITCZ, for example, can be found as much as 25° north of the equator in July and 20° south of the equator in January (Figure 5-30), while the polar highs experience little or no latitudinal displacement from season to season.

Weather is affected by shifts in the general circulation components only minimally in equatorial and polar regions, but the effects can be quite significant in the midlatitudes and their fringes. For example, as we will see in Chapter 8, regions of *mediterranean climate,* which are centered at about 35° of latitude, have warm, rainless summers while under the influence of the STH;

in winter, however, the belt of the westerlies shifts equatorward, bringing changeable and frequently stormy weather to these regions. Also, as we will see, the shift of the ITCZ is closely tied to seasonal rainfall patterns in large areas within the tropics.

Monsoons

By far the most significant disturbance of the pattern of general circulation is the development of **monsoons** in certain parts of the world, particularly southern and eastern Asia (Figure 5-31). The word monsoon is derived from the Arabic *mawsim* (meaning "season") and has come to mean a seasonal reversal of winds, a general sea-to-land movement—called **onshore flow**—in summer and a general land-to-sea movement—called **offshore flow**—in winter. Associated with the monsoon wind pattern is a distinctive seasonal precipitation regime—heavy summer rains derived from the moist maritime air of the onshore flow and a pronounced winter dry season when continental air moving seaward dominates the circulation.

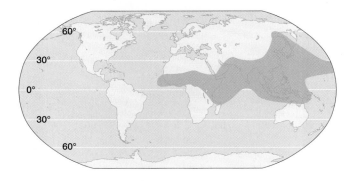

▲ **Figure 5-31** The principal monsoon areas of the world.

It would be convenient to explain monsoon circulation simply on the basis of the unequal heating of continents and oceans. A strong thermal (in other words, heat-produced) low pressure cell generated over a continental landmass in summer attracts oceanic air onshore; similarly, a prominent thermal anticyclone in winter over a continent produces an offshore circulation. It is clear that these thermally induced pressure differences contribute to monsoon development (see Figure 5-16), but they are not the whole story.

Monsoon winds essentially represent unusually large latitudinal migrations of the trade winds associated with the large seasonal shifts of the ITCZ over southeastern Eurasia. The Himalayas evidently also play a role—this significant topographic barrier allows greater winter temperature contrasts between South Asia and the interior of the continent to the north, and this in turn may influence the location and persistence of the subtropical jet stream in this region.

It is difficult to overestimate the importance of monsoon circulation to humankind. More than half of the world's population inhabits the regions in which climates are largely controlled by monsoons. Moreover, these are generally regions in which the majority of the populace depends on agriculture for its livelihood. Their lives are intricately bound up with the reality of monsoon rains, which are essential for both food production and cash crops (Figure 5-32). The failure, or even late arrival, of monsoon moisture inevitably causes widespread hunger and economic disaster.

Although the causes are complex, the characteristics of monsoons are well known, and it is possible to describe the monsoon patterns with some precision. There are two major monsoon systems (one in South Asia and the other in East Asia), two minor systems (in Australia and West Africa), and several other regions where monsoon tendencies develop (especially in Central America and the southeastern United States).

The most notable environmental event each year in South Asia is the annual burst of the summer monsoon, illustrated in Figure 5-33a. In this first of the two major monsoon systems, prominent onshore winds spiral in from the Indian Ocean, bringing life-giving rains to the parched subcontinent. In winter, South Asia is dominated by outblowing dry air diverging generally from the northeast. This flow is not very different from normal northeast trades except for its low moisture content.

Turning to the second of the two major monsoon systems, we see that winter is the more prominent season in the East Asian monsoon system, which primarily affects China, Korea, and Japan and is illustrated in Figure 5-33b. A strong outflow of dry continental air, largely from the northwest, is associated with anticyclonic circulation around the massive thermal high-pressure cell over western Eurasia called the Siberian High. The onshore flow of maritime air in summer is not as notable as that in South Asia, but it does bring southerly and southeasterly winds, as well as considerable moisture, to the region.

▲ **Figure 5-32** Flooding caused by summer monsoon rains in Dhaka, Bangladesh. *(Chip Hires/Gamma-Liaison, Inc.)*

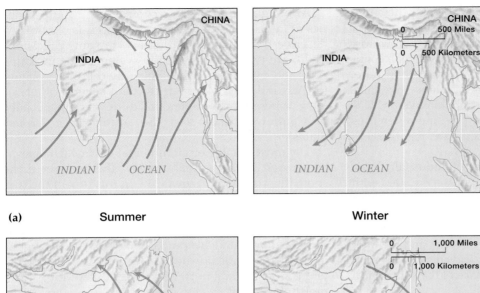

(a)   Summer   Winter

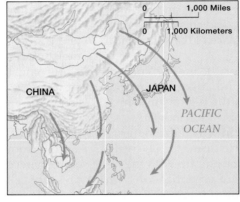

(b)   Summer   Winter

◀ **Figure 5-33** The two major monsoon systems. **(a)** The South Asian monsoon is characterized by a strong onshore flow in summer and a somewhat less pronounced offshore flow in winter. **(b)** In East Asia, the outblowing winter monsoon is stronger than the inblowing summer monsoon.

In one of the two minor systems, the northern quarter of the Australian continent experiences a distinct monsoon circulation, with onshore flow from the north during the height of the Australian summer (December through March) and dry, southerly, offshore flow during most of the rest of the year. This system is illustrated in Figure 5-34a.

The south-facing coast of West Africa is dominated within about 650 kilometers (400 miles) of the coast by the second minor monsoonal circulation. This system is shown in Figure 5-34b. Moist oceanic air flows onshore from the south and southwest during summer, and dry, northerly, continental flow prevails in the opposite season.

Localized Wind Systems

The preceding sections have dealt with only the broad-scale wind systems that make up the global circulation and influence the climatic pattern of the world. There are many kinds of lesser winds, however, that are of considerable significance to weather and climate at a more localized scale. Such winds are the result of local pressure gradients that develop in response to

topographic configurations in the immediate area, sometimes in conjunction with broad-scale circulation conditions.

Sea and Land Breezes

A common local wind system along tropical coastlines and to a lesser extent during the summer in midlatitude coastal areas is the cycle of **sea breezes** during the day and **land breezes** at night (Figure 5-35). (As is usual with winds, the name tells the direction from which the wind comes. A sea breeze blows from sea to land, and a land breeze blows from land to sea.) This is essentially a convectional circulation caused by the differential heating of land and water surfaces. The land warms up rapidly during the day, heating the air above by conduction and reradiation. This heating causes the air to expand and rise, creating low pressure that attracts surface breezes from over the adjacent water body. Because the onshore flow is relatively cool and moist, it holds down daytime temperatures in the coastal zone and provides moisture for afternoon showers. Sea breezes are sometimes strong, but they rarely are influential for more than 15 to 30 kilometers (10 to 20 miles) inland.

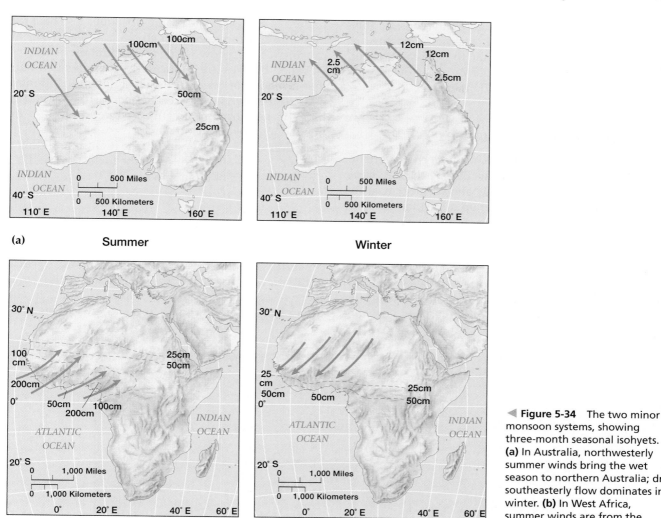

(a)   Summer   Winter

(b)   Summer   Winter

◀ **Figure 5-34** The two minor monsoon systems, showing three-month seasonal isohyets. **(a)** In Australia, northwesterly summer winds bring the wet season to northern Australia; dry southeasterly flow dominates in winter. **(b)** In West Africa, summer winds are from the southwest and winter winds are from the northeast.

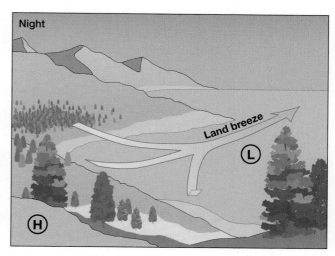

▲ **Figure 5-35** In a typical sea–land breeze cycle, diurnal heating over the land produces relatively low pressure there, and this low-pressure center attracts an onshore flow of air from the sea. Later, nocturnal cooling over the land causes high air pressure there, a condition that creates an offshore flow of air.

The reverse flow at night is normally considerably weaker than the daytime wind. The land and the air above it cool more quickly than the adjacent water body, producing relatively higher pressure over land. Thus, air flows offshore in a land breeze.

Valley and Mountain Breezes

Another notable daily cycle of airflow is characteristic of many hill and mountain areas. During the day, conduction and reradiation from the land surface cause air near the mountain slopes to heat up more than air over the valley floor (Figure 5-36). The heated air rises, creating a low-pressure area, and then cooler air from the valley floor flows upslope from the high-pressure area to the low-pressure area. This upslope flow is called a **valley breeze**. The rising air often causes clouds to form around the peaks, and afternoon showers are common in the high country as a result. After dark, the

pattern is reversed. The mountain slopes lose heat rapidly through radiation, which chills the adjacent air, causing it to slip downslope as a **mountain breeze**.

Valley breezes are particularly prominent in summer, when solar heating is most intense. Mountain breezes are often weakly developed in summer and are likely to be more prominent in winter. Indeed, a frequent winter phenomenon in areas of even gentle slope is air drainage, which is simply the nighttime sliding of cold air downslope to collect in the lowest spots; this is a modified form of mountain breeze.

Katabatic Winds

Related to simple air drainage is the more general and powerful spilling of air downslope in the form of **katabatic winds** (from the Greek *katabatik,* which means "descending"). These winds originate in cold upland areas and cascade toward lower elevations

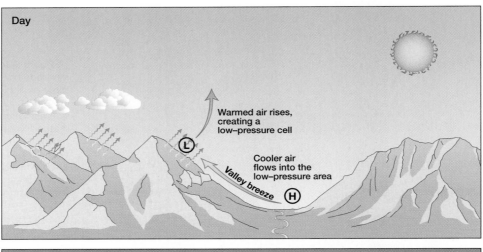

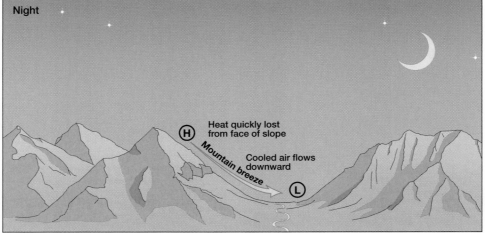

▲ **Figure 5-36** Daytime heating of the mountain slopes causes the air above the slopes to warm and rise, creating lower air pressure than over the valley. Cooler valley air then flows along the pressure gradient (in other words, up the mountain slope) in what is called a valley breeze. At night, the slopes radiate their heat away and as a result the air just above them cools. This cooler, denser air flows down into the valley in what is called a mountain breeze.

under the influence of gravity; they are sometimes referred to as *gravity-flow winds.* The air in them is dense and cold, and although warmed adiabatically as it descends, it is usually colder than the air it displaces in its downslope flow.

Katabatic winds are particularly common in Greenland and Antarctica, especially where they come whipping off the edge of the high, cold ice sheets. Sometimes a katabatic wind will become channeled through a narrow valley where it may develop high speed and considerable destructive power. An infamous example of this phenomenon is the *mistral,* which sometimes surges down France's Rhône Valley from the Alps to the Mediterranean Sea. Similar winds are called *bora* in the Adriatic region and *taku* in southeastern Alaska.

Foehn/Chinook Winds

Another downslope wind is called a **foehn** (pronounced as in fern but with a silent "r") in the Alps, and a **chinook** in the Rocky Mountains. It originates only when a steep pressure gradient develops with high pressure on the windward side of a mountain and a low-pressure trough on the leeward side. Air moves down the pressure gradient, which means from the windward side to the leeward side, as shown in Figure 5-37. The downflowing air on the leeward side is dry and relatively warm: it has lost its moisture through precipitation on the windward side, and it is warm relative to the air on the windward side because it contains all the latent heat of condensation given up by the condensing of the snow or rain that fell at the peak. As the wind blows down the leeward slope, it is further warmed adiabatically, and so it arrives at the base of the range as a warming, drying wind. It can produce a remarkable rise of temperature leeward of the mountains in just a few minutes. It is known along the Rocky Mountains front as a "snow-eater" because

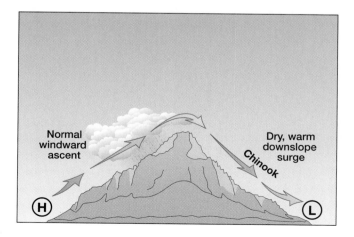

▲ **Figure 5-37**   A chinook is a rapid downslope movement of relatively warm air. It is caused by a pressure gradient on the two faces of a mountain.

it not only melts the snow rapidly but also quickly dries the resulting mud.

Santa Ana Winds   Similar winds in California, known as **Santa Ana winds**, develop when a cell of high pressure persists over the interior of the western United States for several days. The wind diverges clockwise out of the high, bringing dry, warm northerly or easterly winds to the coast (instead of the more typical cool, moist air from the westerlies). The Santa Anas are noted for high speed, high temperature, and extreme dryness. Their presence provides ideal conditions for wildfires. Virtually every year they make headlines by fanning large brush fires that destroy dozens of homes in late summer and fall and occasionally in spring.

El Niño–Southern Oscillation

   El Niño

One of the basic tenets of physical geography is the interrelatedness of the various elements of the environment. Nowhere is environmental interrelatedness shown better than at the air–ocean interface—that vast horizontal surface that marks the meeting of atmosphere and hydrosphere over 70 percent of Earth. These two great fluid systems interact in intricate and often perplexing fashion so that cause and effect become almost meaningless concepts. Thus far in our look at weather and climate, we have introduced patterns of temperature, ocean circulation, wind, and pressure without fully exploring important feedback mechanisms that are a part of such interactions. Nor have we explored the complexity introduced by cyclical variations in oceanic and atmospheric patterns, occurring over periods of years or even decades.

A prize example of this interrelatedness and complexity is **El Niño**, an episodic atmospheric and oceanic phenomenon of the equatorial Pacific Ocean, particularly prominent along the west coast of South America. During an El Niño event, abnormally warm water appears at the surface of the ocean off the west coast of South America, replacing the cold, nutrient-rich water that usually prevails. Once thought to be a local phenomenon, we now know that El Niño is associated with changes in pressure, wind, precipitation, and ocean conditions over large regions of Earth. During a strong El Niño event, productive Pacific fisheries off South America are disrupted and heavy rains come to some regions of the world while drought comes to others.

A slight periodic warming of Pacific coastal waters has been noticed by South American fishermen for many generations. It typically occurs around Christmastime—hence the name *El Niño* (Spanish for "the boy" in reference to the Christ child). Every three to seven years, however, the warming of the ocean is much greater, and fishing is likely to be much poorer. Historical records have documented the effects of El Niño for several hundred years, with archeological and paleoclimatological evidence pushing the record back several thousand years.

It was not until the major 1982–1983 event, however, that El Niño received worldwide attention (Figure 5-38). Over a period of several months, there were crippling droughts in Australia, India, Indonesia, the Philippines, Mexico, Central America, and southern Africa; devastating floods in the western and southeastern United States, Cuba, and northwestern South America; destructive tropical cyclones in parts of the Pacific (such as in Tahiti and Hawaii) where they are normally rare; and a vast sweep of ocean water as much as 8°C (14°F) above normal stretched over 13,000 kilometers (8000 miles) of the equatorial Pacific, causing massive dieoffs of fish, seabirds, and coral. Directly attributable to these events were more than 1500 human deaths, damage estimated at nearly $9 billion, and vast ecological changes.

In 1997–1998, another strong El Niño cycle took place. This time worldwide property damage exceeded $30 billion, at least 2100 people died, and tens of thousands of people were displaced. There were severe blizzards in the Midwest, devastating tornadoes in the southeastern United States, and much higher than average rainfall in California. So what happens during El Niño that causes such widespread changes in the weather?

Normal Pattern

To understand El Niño, we begin with a description of the normal conditions in the Pacific Ocean basin (Figure 5-39a). As we saw in Chapter 4, usually the waters off the west coast of South America are cool. The wind and pressure patterns in this region are dominated by the persistent subtropical high (STH) associated with the subsiding air of the Hadley cell circulation (see Figure 5-18). As the trade winds diverge from the STH, they flow from east to west across the Pacific—this tropical airflow drags surface ocean water westward across the Pacific basin in the warm Equatorial Current (introduced in Chapter 4; see Figure 4-28). As surface water pulls away from the coast of South America, an upwelling of cold, nutrient-rich ocean water rises into the already cool Peru current. This combination of cool water and high pressure result in relatively dry conditions along much of the west coast of South America.

In contrast to the cold water and high pressure near South America, in a normal year on the other side of the Pacific Ocean near Indonesia things are quite different. The trade winds and the equatorial current pile up warm water, raising sea level in the Indonesian region as much as 60 centimeters (about 2 feet) higher than near South America, turning the tropical western Pacific into an immense storehouse of energy and moisture. Warm water and persistent low pressure prevail around northern Australia and Indonesia; local convective thunderstorms develop in the intertropical convergence

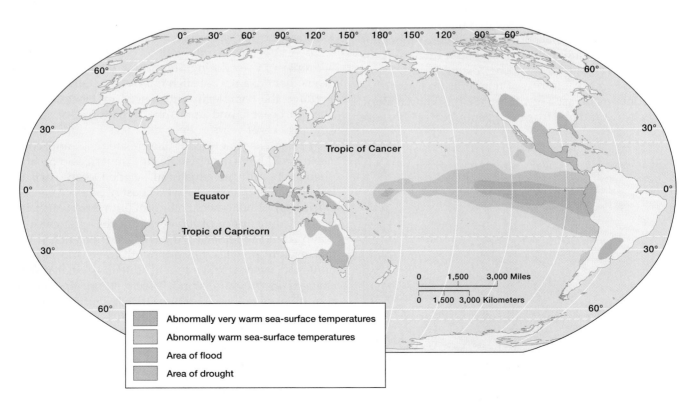

▲ **Figure 5-38** Some major weather events associated with El Niño during its 1982–1983 outbreak. Abnormally warm ocean water in the eastern equatorial Pacific is the most readily recognizable characteristic.

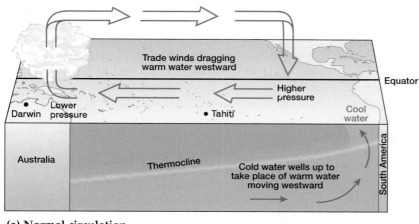

(a) Normal circulation

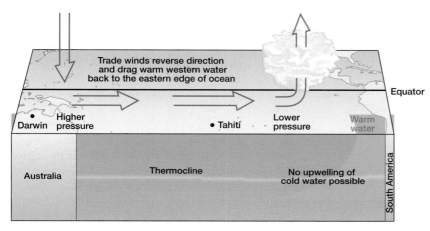

(b) Circulation during El Niño

◀ **Figure 5-39** **(a)** Normal conditions in the South Pacific. **(b)** These conditions either weaken or reverse during an El Niño event.

zone (ITCZ), producing high annual rainfall in this region of the world. After this air rises in the ITCZ, it begins to flow poleward but is deflected by the Coriolis effect into the upper-atmosphere westerly *antitrade winds;* some of this air flow aloft eventually subsides into the STH on the other side of the Pacific (see Figure 5-14). This general circuit of air flow is called the **Walker Circulation**, after the British meteorologist Gilbert Walker (1868–1958) who first described these circumstances. (Although Figure 5-39 shows the Walker Circulation as a closed convection cell, recent studies suggest that this is probably too simplistic—while the upper atmosphere is generally flowing from west to east, a closed "loop" of air flow probably doesn't exist.)

El Niño Pattern

Every few years, the normal pressure patterns in the Pacific change (Figure 5-39b). High pressure develops over northern Australia and low pressure develops to the east near Tahiti. This "seesaw" of pressure is known as the **Southern Oscillation**. It was first recognized by Gilbert Walker in the first decade of the twentieth century. Walker had become director of the Meteorological Service in

colonial India in 1903, where a search was underway for a method to predict the monsoon—when the life-giving South Asian monsoon failed to develop, drought and famine ravaged India. In the global meteorological records, Walker thought that he saw a pattern: in most years pressure is low over northern Australia (specifically, Darwin, Australia) and high over Tahiti, and in these years, the monsoon usually comes as expected. However, in some years pressure is high in Darwin and low in Tahiti, and in these years the monsoon would often—but not always—fail. As it turned out, Walker's observed correlation between the monsoons in India and the Southern Oscillation of pressure was not reliable enough to predict the monsoons. However, by the 1960s meteorologists recognized a connection between Walker's Southern Oscillation and the occurrence of strong El Niño warming near South America. This overall coupled ocean–atmosphere pattern is now known as the **El Niño-Southern Oscillation** or simply **ENSO**.

While no two ENSO events are alike, we can describe a typical El Niño cycle: for many months before the onset of an El Niño, the trade winds pile up warm water in the western Pacific near Indonesia. A bulge of warm equatorial water perhaps 25 centimeters (10 inches) high then begins to move to the east across the Pacific toward South America. Such slowly moving bulges of warm water are known as *Kelvin waves*. A Kelvin wave might take two or three months to arrive off the coast of South America (Figure 5-40). The bulge of warm water in a Kelvin wave spreads out little as it moves across the ocean since the Coriolis effect effectively funnels the eastward-moving water toward the equator in both hemispheres.

When the Kelvin wave arrives at South America, sea level rises as the warm water pools. The usual high pressure in the subtropics has weakened; upwelling no longer brings cold water to the surface, so ocean temperature rises still further—an El Niño is underway. By this time the trade winds have weakened or even reversed directions and started to flow from the west—blowing moist air into the deserts of coastal Peru. The **thermocline** boundary between near-surface and cold deep ocean waters lowers. Pressure increases over Indonesia and the most active portion of the ITCZ in the Pacific shifts from the now-cooler western Pacific, toward the now-warmer central and eastern Pacific basin. Drought strikes northern Australia and Indonesia; the South Asian monsoon may fail or develop weakly. The subtropical jet stream over the eastern Pacific shifts its path, guiding winter storms into the southwestern United States—California and Arizona experience more powerful winter storms than usual, resulting in high precipitation and flooding.

La Niña

Adding to the complexity is a more-recently recognized component of the ENSO cycle, **La Niña**. In some ways,

La Niña is simply the opposite of El Niño: the waters off South America become unusually cool; the trade winds are stronger than usual; the waters off Indonesia are unusually warm; the southwestern United States is drier than usual while Southeast Asia and northern Australia are wetter. However, La Niña conditions are not as prominent or as predictable as those of El Niño.

Causes of ENSO

So which comes first with the onset of an El Niño event—the change in ocean temperature or the change in pressure and wind? The "trigger" of an ENSO event is not clear since atmospheric pressure and wind patterns are tied together with the ocean in a complex feedback loop with no clear starting point: if atmospheric pressure changes, wind changes; when wind changes, ocean currents and ocean temperature may change; when ocean temperature changes, atmospheric pressure changes—and that in turn may change wind patterns still more. In short, the causes of ENSO are not fully understood.

Not only are the causes of ENSO elusive, even the effects are not completely predictable. For example, while a strong El Niño generally brings high precipitation to the southwestern United States, a mild or moderate El Niño might bring either drought or floods. Further, although we can generalize that during a strong El Niño floods are more likely in California than in La Niña years (8 of the 10 wettest years between 1950 and 1982 were during El Niño events), floods can happen in any year, no matter what ENSO is doing. In other words, El Niño might "open the storm door"

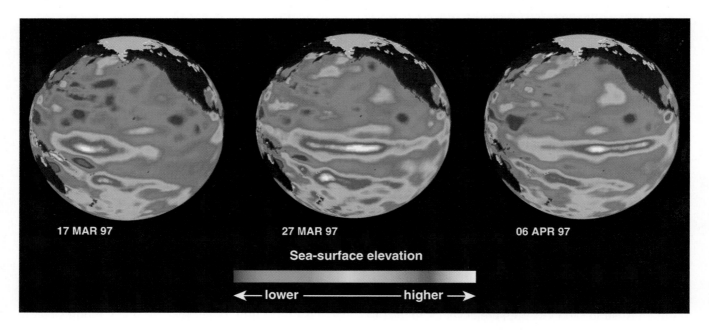

17 MAR 97 **27 MAR 97** **06 APR 97**

Sea-surface elevation

⟵ lower ————— higher ⟶

▲ **Figure 5-40** Progress of a Kelvin wave during the 1997–1998 El Niño. These satellite images from the California Institute of Technology, Jet Propulsion Laboratory, show the bulge of warm water in a Kelvin wave slowly moving across the equatorial Pacific Ocean during the 1997–1998 El Niño. *(From U.S. Geological Survey Fact Sheet 175–1999,* El Niño Sea-Level Rise Wreaks Havoc in California's San Francisco Bay Region, *1999.)*

PEOPLE AND THE ENVIRONMENT Forecasting El Niño

Since the powerful El Niño of 1982–1983 caught large populations unprepared, a concerted multinational effort has been undertaken to understand El Niño and its teleconnections. Part of this effort included anchoring some 70 instrument buoys in the tropical eastern Pacific Ocean in the *Tropical Atmosphere/Ocean Array* (TAO/TRITON array) to monitor ocean and atmospheric conditions—especially sea surface temperature and wind direction (Figure 5-B). By 1994, sufficient data had been gathered to begin to develop computer models to predict the onset of an El Niño event several months in advance.

These efforts were rewarded in 1997: by that spring, the TAO/TRITON buoys were recording a surge of

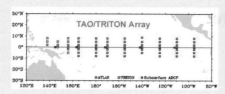

▲ **Figure 5-B** The TAO/TRITON Array of instrument buoys in the tropical Pacific Ocean. *(NOAA.)*

warm water moving to the east across the equatorial Pacific, replacing the normally cool water off the west coast of South America (Figures 5-C and 5-D). Months in advance of its arrival, the onset of the 1997–1998 El Niño was announced by the Climate Prediction Center of National

Oceanic and Atmospheric Administration (NOAA), and preparations were made for the series of powerful storms that eventually struck southwestern North America that winter. Even with this forewarning, the 1997–1998 El Niño resulted in billions of dollars of damage and is blamed for the deaths of thousands of people around the world.

The TAO/TRITON array has become an indispensable tool for the study of El Niño and its companion phenomenon, La Niña (Figure 5-E), as well as the atmospheric and oceanic conditions in the tropical Pacific in general. Scientists don't fully understand all aspects of El Niño, but the greatly improved forecasting tools should prevent the public from being taken by surprise again.

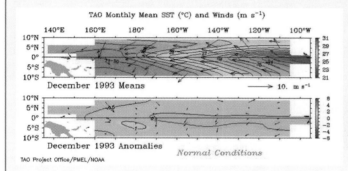

◀ **Figure 5-C** Normal conditions in the tropical Pacific Ocean in December 1993; sea surface temperature and wind measured by the TAO/TRITON Array. *(NOAA.)*

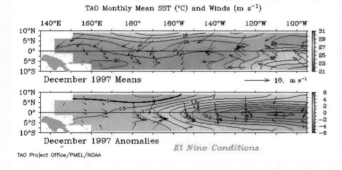

◀ **Figure 5-D** El Niño conditions in the tropical Pacific Ocean in December 1997; sea surface temperature and wind measured by the TAO/TRITON Array. *(NOAA.)*

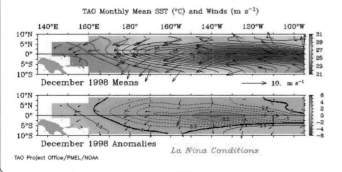

◀ **Figure 5-E** La Niña conditions in the tropical Pacific Ocean in December 1998; sea surface temperature and wind measured by the TAO/TRITON Array. *(NOAA.)*

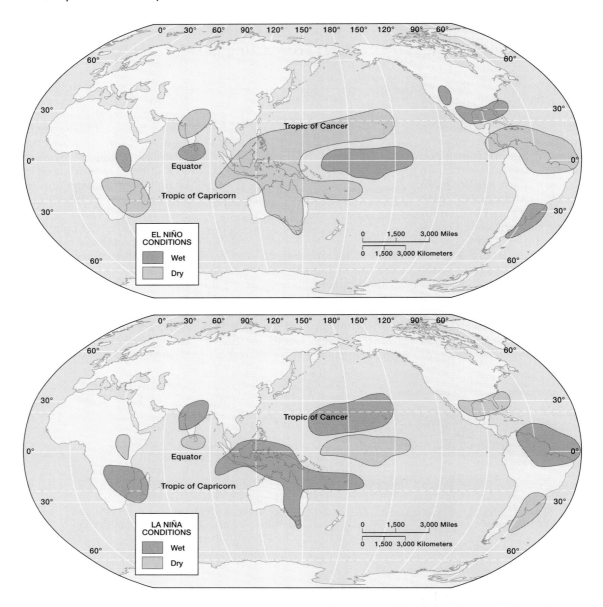

▲ **Figure 5-41** Generalized precipitation patterns during **(a)** El Niño conditions and **(b)** La Niña conditions. *(After Michael Collier and Robert Webb,* Floods, Droughts, and Climate Change, *University of Arizona Press, Tucson 2002.)*

every few years, but there is no guarantee that the storms will actually come.

Teleconnections

As more has been learned about ENSO over the last few decades, its connections with oceanic and atmospheric conditions inside and outside the Pacific basin are increasingly being recognized (Figure 5-41). Drought in Brazil; cold winters in the southeastern United States; high temperatures in the Sahel; a weak monsoon in India; tornadoes in Florida; fewer hurricanes in the North Atlantic—all seem to correlate quite well with a strong El Niño event. Such coupling of weather and oceanic events in one part of the world with those in another are termed **teleconnections**.

Adding to the complexity of these teleconnections is growing evidence that long-term ENSO patterns may be influenced by other ocean–atmosphere cycles, such as the *Pacific Decadal Oscillation* (discussed below).

Over the last century, there have been perhaps 23 significant El Niños and 15 La Niñas—occurring on average once every three or four years. It appears that El Niños have been becoming more frequent and progressively warmer in recent decades—the 1997–1998 event was probably the strongest El Niño of the last 200 years, and it developed more rapidly than any in the last 40 years—although the reasons for this are not yet clear. There is speculation that global warming may be influencing the intensity of the El Niño cycle, but a clear connection has not yet been found.

Over the last 25 years, great strides have been taken toward forecasting El Niño events months in advance—largely because of better satellite monitoring of ocean conditions and the establishment of the TAO/TRITON array of oceanic buoys in the tropical Pacific (see box on "Forecasting El Niño"). While there is much left to be learned, a clearer understanding of cause and effect, of countercause and countereffect of ENSO, is gradually emerging.

Other Multi-Year Atmospheric and Oceanic Cycles

El Niño is the best known multi-year atmospheric/oceanic cycle, although a number of other cyclical patterns have now been recognized.

Pacific Decadal Oscillation

The *Pacific Decadal Oscillation* (PDO) is a long-term pattern of sea surface temperature change between the northern/west tropical and eastern tropical Pacific Ocean. Approximately every 20 to 30 years the sea surface temperatures in these zones abruptly shift. From the late 1940s to late 1970s, the northern/west tropical Pacific was relatively warm while the eastern tropical Pacific was relatively cool (the PDO "negative" or "cool" phase); from the late 1970s through the mid-1990s, this pattern switched, with cooler sea surface temperatures in the northern/west tropical Pacific and warmer conditions in the east tropical Pacific (the PDO "positive" or "warm" phase; Figure 5-42). In the late 1990s the switch back to the negative phase was underway, but by the early 2000s it wasn't clear if this negative phase was going to be short-lived.

Although the causes of the PDO are not well understood, the pattern of relatively warm and relatively cool ocean water seems to influence the location of the jet stream (and so storm tracks across North America)

as well as the intensity of El Niño events. For example, when the PDO is in a positive phase with warmer water in the eastern tropical Pacific, the influence of El Niño on regional weather patterns appears to be more significant.

The North Atlantic Oscillation and the Arctic Oscillation

In the North Atlantic Ocean basin two related but somewhat irregular multi-year cycles of pressure, wind patterns, and temperature exist: the *North Atlantic Oscillation* and the *Arctic Oscillation*.

The *North Atlantic Oscillation* (NAO) is an irregular "seesaw" of pressure differences between two regional components of the general atmospheric circulation in the North Atlantic Ocean basin: the Icelandic Low and the subtropical high (the Azores High). In the "positive" phase of the NAO, a greater pressure gradient exists between the Icelandic Low and the Azores High (in other words, the Low exhibits lower than usual pressure, while the High exhibits higher than usual pressure). During such a positive phase, winter storms tend to take a more northerly track across the Atlantic, bringing mild, wet winters to Europe and the eastern United States but colder, drier conditions in Greenland.

In the "negative" phase of the NAO, both the Icelandic Low and the Azores High are weaker. During such a negative phase, winter storms tend to bring higher than average precipitation to the Mediterranean and colder winters in northern Europe and the eastern United States, while Greenland experiences milder conditions.

The *Arctic Oscillation* alternates between warm and cold phases that are closely associated with the NAO. During the Arctic Oscillation "warm" phase (associated with the NAO positive phase), the polar high is weaker, so cold air masses don't move as far south and sea surface temperatures tend to be warmer in Arctic waters—although Greenland tends to be colder than usual. During the Arctic Oscillation "cold" phase (associated with the NAO negative phase), the polar high is strengthened, bringing cold air masses farther south

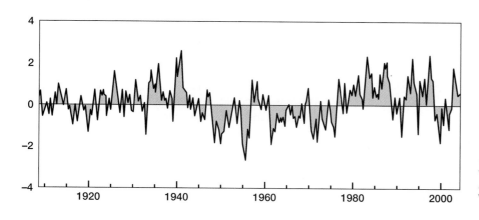

◀ **Figure 5-42** Pacific decadal oscillation index. Positive values indicate warm water in the eastern tropical Pacific, while negative values indicate relatively cool water in the same area. *(After Aguado, Edward and James E. Burt,* Understanding Weather and Climate, *4th ed., 2007.)*

and leaving Arctic waters colder—although Greenland tends to be warmer than usual.

As with El Niño and the Pacific Decadal Oscillation, the causes of the North Atlantic Oscillation and the Arctic Oscillation are not well understood. Nor are all of the possible teleconnections between atmospheric and oceanic cycles in the North Atlantic and other parts of the world.

Chapter 5 Learning Review

Key Terms

Before answering the study questions below, review the definitions of the following key terms (page references are provided for you):

anticyclone *(p. 112)*
antitrade winds *(p. 125)*
atmospheric pressure *(p. 107)*
barometer *(p. 109)*
chinook *(p. 131)*
cyclone *(p. 112)*
doldrums *(p. 121)*
dynamic high *(p. 109)*
dynamic low *(p. 109)*
El Niño *(p. 131)*
ENSO (El Niño–Southern Oscillation) *(p. 133)*
foehn *(p. 131)*
friction layer *(p. 111)*
geostrophic wind *(p. 111)*
Hadley cells *(p. 115)*
high *(p. 109)*
horse latitudes *(p. 117)*

intertropical convergence zone (ITCZ) *(p. 121)*
isobar *(p. 109)*
jet stream *(p. 122)*
katabatic winds *(p. 130)*
land breeze *(p. 128)*
La Niña *(p. 134)*
low *(p. 109)*
millibar *(p. 109)*
monsoon *(p. 126)*
mountain breeze *(p. 130)*
offshore flow *(p. 126)*
onshore flow *(p. 126)*
polar easterlies *(p. 124)*
polar front *(p. 124)*
polar high *(p. 124)*
pressure gradient *(p. 109)*
ridge *(p. 109)*

Rossby waves *(p. 122)*
Santa Ana winds *(p. 131)*
sea breeze *(p. 128)*
Southern Oscillation *(p. 133)*
subpolar lows *(p. 124)*
subtropical high (STH) *(p. 116)*
teleconnection *(p. 136)*
thermal high *(p. 109)*
thermal low *(p. 109)*
thermocline *(p. 134)*
trade winds *(p. 117)*
trough *(p. 109)*
valley breeze *(p. 130)*
Walker Circulation *(p. 133)*
westerlies *(p. 121)*
wind *(p. 110)*

Study Questions for Key Concepts

After studying this chapter, you should be able to answer the following questions:

The Nature of Atmospheric Pressure (p. 107)

1. What generally happens to atmospheric pressure with increasing altitude?
2. Explain how atmospheric pressure is related to air density and air temperature.
3. What factors generally cause *low atmospheric pressure* and *high atmospheric pressure* cells near the surface?
4. Is rising air more commonly associated with low or high pressure at the surface? Is descending air more commonly associated with low or high pressure at the surface?
5. What is a millibar? An isobar?
6. When referring to air pressure, what is a *ridge* and what is a *trough*?

The Nature of Wind (p. 110)

7. Why don't winds simply flow down a pressure gradient?
8. How and why are surface ("friction layer") winds different from upper-atmosphere *geostrophic* winds?

9. Describe and explain the pattern of wind flow in the Northern Hemisphere around:
   • a surface high
   • a surface low
   • an upper atmosphere high
   • an upper atmosphere low
   (You should be able to sketch in wind direction on isobar maps of highs and lows near the surface and in the upper atmosphere for both the Northern and Southern Hemispheres.)
10. What is the reason for the difference in wind flow patterns in the Northern Hemisphere and the Southern Hemisphere?
11. What is a *cyclone*? An *anticyclone*?
12. Describe the pattern of vertical air movement within a cyclone and an anticyclone.
13. Describe the relationship between the "steepness" of a *pressure gradient* and the speed of the wind along that pressure gradient: describe the general wind

speed associated with a gentle (gradual) pressure gradient and a steep (abrupt) pressure gradient.

Vertical Variations in Pressure and Wind (p. 114)

14. Does atmospheric pressure always decrease with increasing height? Explain.
15. Why are upper-air winds usually faster than surface winds?

The General Circulation of the Atmosphere (p. 114)

16. What are the *Hadley Cells,* and what generally causes them?
17. Describe the general location and characteristics of the following atmospheric circulation components:
    - *intertropical convergence zone (ITCZ)*
    - *trade winds*
    - *subtropical highs*
    - *westerlies*

    You should be able to sketch in the location of these four components on a blank map of an ocean basin.
18. Discuss the characteristic weather associated with the ITCZ and the characteristic weather associated with subtropical highs.
19. Why do trade winds cover such a large part of the globe?
20. Describe the general location and characteristics of the *jet streams* of the westerlies.

21. What are *Rossby waves*?
22. Briefly describe the location and general characteristics of the high-latitude components of the general circulation patterns of the atmosphere:
    - *polar front* (subpolar lows)
    - *polar easterlies*
    - *polar highs*
23. Differentiate between trade winds and *antitrade* winds.

Modifications of the General Circulation (p. 125)

24. Describe and explain the seasonal shifts of the general circulation patterns; especially note the significance of the seasonal shifts of the ITCZ and the subtropical highs.
25. Describe and explain the South Asian *monsoon.*

Localized Wind Systems (p. 128)

26. Explain the origin of *land–sea breezes.*
27. In what ways are *sea breezes* and *valley breezes* similar?

El Niño–Southern Oscillation (p. 131)

28. What is the *Walker Circulation*?
29. Contrast the oceanic and atmospheric conditions in the tropical Pacific Ocean basin during an *El Niño* event with those of a normal pattern.

Additional Resources

Books:

Collier, Michael and Robert Webb. *Floods, Droughts, and Climate Change.* Tucson: University of Arizona Press, 2002.

Harman, Jay R. *Synoptic Climatology of the Westerlies: Process and Patterns.* Washington, DC: Association of American Geographers, 1991.

Nash, J. Madeline. *El Niño: Unlocking the Secrets of the Master Weather-Maker.* New York: Warner Books, 2002.

Ramage, C. S. *Monsoon Meteorology.* New York: Academic Press, 1971.

Internet Sites:
National Oceanic and Atmospheric Administration (NOAA)

http://www.noaa.gov/

The National Oceanic and Atmospheric Administration (NOAA) oversees a number of government agencies, including the National Weather Service. NOAA's home page provides links to sites about weather, climate, weather satellites, the oceans, and coastlines.

National Undersea Research Program

http://www.noaa.gov/ocean.html

This site has information about current ocean conditions and current marine research.

6
Atmospheric Moisture

The fourth element of weather and climate is moisture. Although it might seem that we all are familiar with water, most atmospheric moisture occurs not as liquid water but rather as water vapor, which is much less conspicuous and much less familiar. One of the most distinctive attributes of water is that it occurs in the atmosphere in three physical states, as Figure 6-1 shows: solid (snow, hail, sleet, ice), liquid (rain, water droplets), and gas (water vapor). Of the three states, the gas state is the most important insofar as the dynamics of the atmosphere are concerned.

The Impact of Atmospheric Moisture on the Landscape

When the atmosphere contains enough moisture, water vapor may condense to form haze, fog, cloud, rain, sleet, hail, or snow, producing a skyscape that is both visible and tangible.

Precipitation produces dramatic short-run changes in the landscape whenever rain puddles form, streams and rivers flood, or snow and ice blanket the ground. The long-term effect of atmospheric moisture is even more fundamental. Water vapor stores energy that can galvanize the atmosphere into action. Rainfall and snowmelt in soil and rock are an integral part of weathering and erosion. In addition, the presence or absence of precipitation is critical to the survival of almost all forms of terrestrial vegetation.

The Nature of Water: Commonplace but Unique

Water is the most widespread substance on the surface of Earth, occupying more than 70 percent of the surface area of the planet. Water is also perhaps the most distinctive substance found on Earth: pure water has no color, no taste, and no smell. It turns to a solid at 0°C (32°F) and boils at sea level at 100°C (212°F). The density of liquid water at 4°C is 1 gram per cubic centimeter (1 g/cm^3), while the density of ice is only 0.92 g/cm^3—meaning that the solid form of water actually floats in the liquid form. It has a very high heat capacity and is an extremely good solvent. It has the ability to move upward into narrow openings. Water set the stage for the evolution of life and is still an essential ingredient of all life today.

Before we look specifically at the role of water in weather and climate, we must get to know the water molecule itself better—the characteristics of the water molecule help explain many of water's unique properties. What we learn about the nature of water over the next few pages will help us understand many processes discussed in the remaining chapters of the book.

(a)

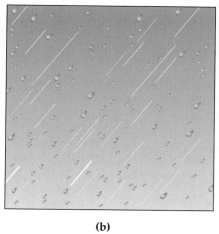
(b)

(c)

▲ **Figure 6-1** Water can exist in any one of three physical states in the atmosphere. **(a)** When the temperature is below freezing, water exists in the solid state we know as ice. **(b)** When the temperature is above freezing, water may exist in the familiar liquid state. **(c)** Moisture also exists in the gaseous state as water vapor. Water vapor is invisible, as indicated by the empty area between the tip of the spout and the beginning of the steam cloud. The heat of the stove causes the liquid water in the kettle to boil and become water vapor. This vapor issues from the spout and quickly cools back into tiny liquid drops that we see as the steam cloud.

◄ Rainbow over Absaroka Mountains near Livingston, Montana. *(The Stock Connection.)*

The Water Molecule

As we discussed in earlier chapters, the fundamental building blocks of matter are *atoms*. Atoms are almost incomprehensibly small—there are about 100,000,000,000,000,000,000,000 atoms in a thimble filled with 1 gram of water. Atoms themselves are composed of still smaller *subatomic particles*: positively charged *protons* and neutrally charged *neutrons* in the *nucleus* of the atom, surrounded by negatively charged *electrons*.[1] The whirling electrons are held by electrical attraction to the protons in "shells" surrounding the nucleus of the atom. In many atoms the number of electrons, protons, and neutrons are normally equal—for example, an atom of the *element* oxygen typically has eight protons and eight electrons, along with eight electrically neutral neutrons.[2]

Two or more atoms can be held together to form a *molecule* by bonding. There are many different types of bonds in nature. Inside the water molecule two atoms

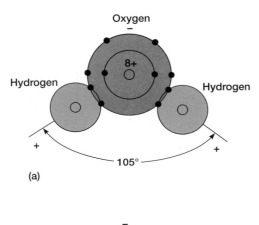

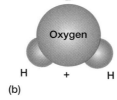

▲ **Figure 6-2**   A water molecule is made up of two hydrogen atoms and one oxygen atom. **(a)** Covalent bonds hold the hydrogen atoms and oxygen atom together. **(b)** The oxygen side of the molecule has a slight negative charge while the hydrogen side has a slight positive change. *(After Trujillo and Thurman, Essentials of Oceanography, 8th ed., Upper Saddle River, NJ: Pearson-Prentice Hall, 2005.)*

---

[1] Although it was once thought that the smallest particles of matter were electrons, protons, and neutrons, we know now that some subatomic particles themselves are made of still smaller particles such as *quarks*.

[2] Atoms with a large number of protons will usually have a greater number of neutrons than protons. The number of neutrons can and do vary, without affecting the chemical behavior of the atom—atoms of an element with identical numbers of protons but different numbers of neutrons are called *isotopes*. If the number of electrons is different from the number of protons, the neutral atom becomes an electrically charged *ion*.

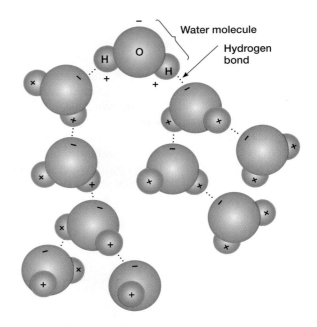

▲ **Figure 6-3**   Hydrogen bonds form between water molecules because the negatively charged oxygen side of one molecule is attracted to the positively charged hydrogen side of another molecule. *(After Trujillo and Thurman, Essentials of Oceanography, 8th ed., Upper Saddle River, NJ: Pearson-Prentice Hall, 2005.)*

of hydrogen and one atom of oxygen (H_2O) are held together by *covalent bonds*, in which the oxygen and hydrogen atoms share electrons (some of the electrons move between energy shells of both atoms; Figure 6-2). Because of the shape of the electron shells around the oxygen, the resulting structure of a water molecule is such that the hydrogen atoms are not opposite one another, but rather are on the same side of the molecule (separated by an angle of 105°). As a consequence of this geometry, a water molecule has electrical *polarity*: the oxygen side of the molecule has a slight negative charge, while the hydrogen side has a slight positive charge.

It is the weak electrical polarity of the molecules that gives water many of its interesting properties. For example, water molecules tend to orient themselves toward each other so that the negatively charged oxygen side of one molecule is next to the positively charged hydrogen side of another molecule. This attraction forms a **hydrogen bond** between adjacent water molecules (Figure 6-3). Although hydrogen bonds are relatively weak (compared with the covalent bonds that hold together the atoms in an individual water molecule), it does mean that water molecules tend to "stick" to each other (when molecules of the same substance stick together it is called *cohesion*).

Properties of Water

One of the most striking properties of water is its liquidity at the temperatures found at most places on

Earth's surface. The liquidity of water greatly enhances its versatility as an active agent in the atmosphere, lithosphere, and biosphere.

Most substances contract as they get colder no matter what the change in temperature. When freshwater becomes colder, however, it contracts only until it reaches 4°C (39°F) and then expands (as much as 9 percent) as it cools from 4°C to its freezing point of 0°C (32°F). As water is cooled from 4°C to its freezing point, water molecules begin to form hexagonal structures, held together by hydrogen bonding. When frozen, water is made entirely of these structures—hexagonal snowflakes reflect the internal structure of these ice crystals. As we will see in Chapter 15, this expansion can break apart rocks and so is an important process of *weathering* (the disintegration of rock exposed to the atmosphere). Because water expands as it approaches freezing, ice is less dense than liquid water. As a result, ice floats on and near the surface of water. If it were denser than water, ice would sink to the bottom of lakes and oceans, where melting would be virtually impossible, and eventually many water bodies would become ice choked. In fact, because freshwater becomes less dense as it approaches its freezing point, water that is ready to freeze rises to the tops of lakes, and hence all lakes freeze from the top down. (Note: the expansion of liquid water is not a factor for ocean water because the high salinity prevents the hexagonal structures from forming until the water is completely frozen.)

Because of its electrical polarity, liquid water molecules tend to stick together, giving water extremely high **surface tension**—a thin "skin" of molecules forms on the surface of liquid water causing it to "bead" (Figure 6-4). Some insects use the stickiness of water to stride atop the surface of a body of water (the weight of the insect spread over the surface area of the water is less than the force of the hydrogen bonds sticking the water together). Later in this chapter we'll see that surface tension influences the way that water droplets grow within a cloud.

In addition, water molecules "stick" easily to many other substances—a characteristic known as *adhesion*. Surface tension combined with adhesion allows water to climb upward in narrow openings. Confined in this way, water can sometimes climb upward for many centimeters or even meters, in an action called **capillarity**. Capillarity enables water to circulate upward through rock cracks, soil, and the roots and stems of plants.

Water can dissolve almost any substance and it is sometimes referred to as the "universal solvent." Because water molecules are polar, they not only are attracted to each other but to other polar chemical compounds as well. Water molecules attach themselves quickly to the ions that constitute the outer layers of solid materials and in some cases can overcome the strength of those bonds, tearing the ions out of the solid and eventually dissolving the material. As a result, water in nature is nearly always impure, by which we mean that it contains various other chemicals in addition to its hydrogen and oxygen atoms. As water moves through the atmosphere, on the surface of Earth, and in soil, rocks, plants, and animals, it carries with it a remarkable diversity of dissolved minerals and nutrients as well as tiny solid particles in suspension.

Another environmentally important characteristic of water is its great heat capacity. As we saw in Chapter 4, *specific heat* (or *specific heat capacity*) is defined as the amount of energy required to raise the temperature of 1 gram of a substance (at 15°C) by 1 degree Celsius. When water is warmed, it can absorb an enormous amount of energy with only a small increase in temperature. Water's specific heat (1 calorie/gram) is exceeded by that of no other common substance except ammonia. The high heat capacity is a consequence of the relatively large amount of kinetic energy required to overcome the hydrogen bonds between water molecules. The practical result, as we saw in Chapter 4, is that bodies of water are very slow to warm up during the day or in summer, and very slow to cool off during the night or in winter. Thus, water bodies have a moderating effect on the temperature of the overlying atmosphere by serving as reservoirs of warmth during winter and having a cooling influence in summer.

Phase Changes of Water

Phase Changes of Water

Water of Earth is found naturally in three states: as a liquid, as a solid, and as a gas. The great majority of the world's moisture is in the form of liquid water, which can be converted to the gaseous form (water vapor) by

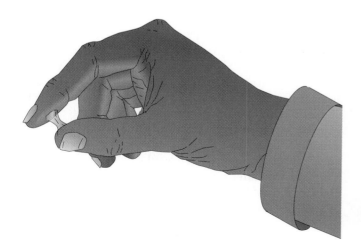

▲ **Figure 6-4**   A steady-handed person can hold a drop of water between two fingers because the attraction of one water molecule for another provides the water with strong surface tension.

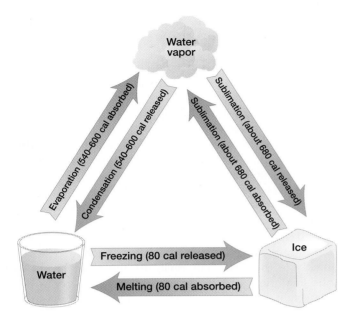

▲ **Figure 6-5** Phase changes of water are accompanied by the exchange of latent heat. The arrows indicate gain or loss of latent heat. The values given for heat absorbed or released during evaporation/condensation and sublimation are for one gram of water.

evaporation or to the solid form (ice) by freezing. Water vapor can be converted to liquid water by **condensation** or directly to ice by **sublimation**. (Sublimation is the process whereby a substance converts either from the gaseous state directly to the solid state, or from the solid state directly to the gaseous state without ever passing through the liquid state.)[3] Ice can be converted to liquid water by melting or to water vapor by sublimation. In each of these *phase changes,* there is an exchange of *latent heat* energy, a concept we first introduced in Chapter 4 (Figure 6-5). An understanding of phase changes and latent heat are central to understanding several atmospheric processes we will describe later in this chapter.

Latent Heat If you insert a thermometer into a pan of cool water on your stove, and then add heat to the water by turning on the burner, you will notice an interesting pattern of temperature change: at first, the temperature of the water will increase, as you might expect. However, once the water begins to boil, the temperature of the water will not increase above 100°C (212°F; at sea level)—even if you turn up the flame on your stove! This result is just one of several important observations we can make about water as it changes states.

Figure 6-6 is a temperature chart showing the amount of energy (in calories) required to melt a one-gram block of ice and then convert it to water vapor (recall that 1 *calorie* is the amount of heat required to increase the temperature of 1 gram of water by 1°C). In this example, we begin with our block of ice at a temperature of −40°C. As heat is added, the temperature of the ice increases quickly; only 20 calories of heat are needed to increase the temperature of the ice to its melting point of 0°C. Once the ice begins to melt, it absorbs 80 calories of heat per gram, but the temperature does not increase above 0°C until all of the ice has melted. We then add another 100 calories of heat to increase the temperature of the liquid water from 0°C to 100°C, its boiling point at sea level. Once the water is boiling, it absorbs 540 calories per gram, but once again, the temperature does not increase above 100°C until all of the liquid water is converted to water vapor.

Even as heat is added, the temperature of water does not increase while it is undergoing a phase change. Here's why: in order for ice to melt, energy must be added to "agitate" water molecules enough to break some of the hydrogen bonds that are holding these molecules together as ice crystals—the energy added does not increase the temperature of the ice but instead increases the internal structural energy of water molecules so that they can break free to become liquid.[4] The energy required to melt ice is called the *latent heat of melting.* The opposite is also true: When water freezes, the liquid water molecules must give up some of their internal structural energy in order to revert to a less agitated condition in which ice can form. The energy released as water freezes is called the *latent heat of fusion.* For each gram of ice, 80 calories of heat are absorbed when ice melts, and 80 calories of heat are released when water freezes.

In a similar way, energy must be added to agitate liquid water molecules enough for them to escape into the surrounding air as water vapor—the energy added doesn't increase the temperature of the liquid water, but instead increases the internal structural energy of water molecules so that they can break free to become vapor. The energy required to vaporize liquid water is called the **latent heat of vaporization**. And, once again, the opposite is also true: when water vapor condenses back to liquid water, the highly agitated water vapor molecules must give up some of their internal structural energy in order to revert to a less agitated liquid state. The energy released during condensation is called the **latent heat of condensation**. For each gram of liquid water at a temperature of 100°C, 540

---

[3] Sometimes the term *sublimation* is restricted to a description of the phase change from a solid state directly to a gaseous state, and *deposition* used to describe the phase change from a gaseous state directly to a solid state. In this book, as is common practice, we use the term sublimation for both.

[4] It may be helpful to think of *latent heat* as the energy used to break or form the bonds (the rearrangement of the structure between two phases), while *specific heat* is the energy used to raise the temperature (the "speed" of the molecules in one phase).

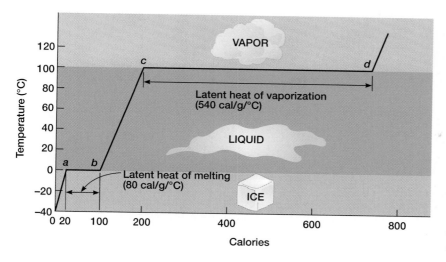

◀ **Figure 6-6** The energy input (in calories) and the associated temperature changes as one gram of ice is melted and then converted to water vapor. The latent heat of vaporization is much greater than the latent heat of melting. *(After Trujillo and Thurman,* Essentials of Oceanography, *8th ed., Upper Saddle River, NJ: Pearson-Prentice Hall, 2005.)*

calories of heat are absorbed as water vaporizes, and 540 calories of heat are released when water vapor condenses.

The value for the latent heat of vaporization given above refers to circumstances in which water is boiling. *Boiling* occurs when vaporization takes place beneath the surface of the liquid water—not just at the surface. In nature, however, most water vapor is added to the atmosphere through simple *evaporation* off the surface of water bodies at temperatures below 100°C. In this case, the energy required for evaporation is greater than when water is boiling. The **latent heat of evaporation** ranges from 540 calories to about 600 calories depending on the temperature of the water (it is approximately 585 calories when the liquid water is at a temperature of 20°C [68°F]).

Notice in Figure 6-5 that about seven times more heat is needed to evaporate one gram of liquid water than is needed to melt one gram of ice. Notice also that when sublimation takes place, the latent heat exchange is simply the total of the solid-liquid and liquid-gas exchanges.

Importance of Latent Heat in the Atmosphere The significance of the exchange of latent heat during phase changes—especially between liquid water and water vapor—is straightforward. Whenever evaporation takes place, energy is removed from the liquid in order to vaporize some of the water, and so the temperature of the remaining liquid is reduced. Because latent heat energy is "stored" in water vapor during evaporation, evaporation is, in effect, a cooling process. The effect of such *evaporative cooling* is experienced when a swimmer leaves a swimming pool on a dry, warm day. The dripping wet body immediately loses moisture through evaporation to the surrounding air, and the skin feels the resulting drop in temperature.

Conversely, because latent heat energy must be released during condensation, condensation is, in effect, a warming process. Water vapor represents a "reservoir"

of heat—whenever and wherever condensation takes place, this heat is added back to the atmosphere. As we will begin to see later in this chapter, the release of latent heat during condensation plays important roles in the stability of the atmosphere and in the power of many storms.

Water Vapor and the Hydrologic Cycle

Although the vast majority of water on Earth is in liquid form—and although the ultimate goal of this chapter is to understand the development of clouds and precipitation—for the moment we will direct our attention to water vapor, the source of moisture for clouds and precipitation.

Water vapor is a colorless, odorless, tasteless, invisible gas that mixes freely with the other gases of the atmosphere. We are likely to become aware of water vapor when humidity is high because the air feels sticky, clothes feel damp, and our skin feels clammy, or when humidity is low because our lips chap and our hair won't behave. Water vapor is a minor constituent of the atmosphere, with the amount present being quite variable from place to place and from time to time. It is virtually absent in some places but constitutes as much as 4 percent of the total atmospheric volume in others. Essentially, water vapor is restricted to the lower troposphere. More than half of all water vapor is found within 1.5 kilometers (about 1 mile) of Earth's surface, and only a tiny fraction exists above 6 kilometers (about 4 miles).

The Hydrologic Cycle

The widespread distribution of water vapor in the atmosphere reflects the ease with which moisture can

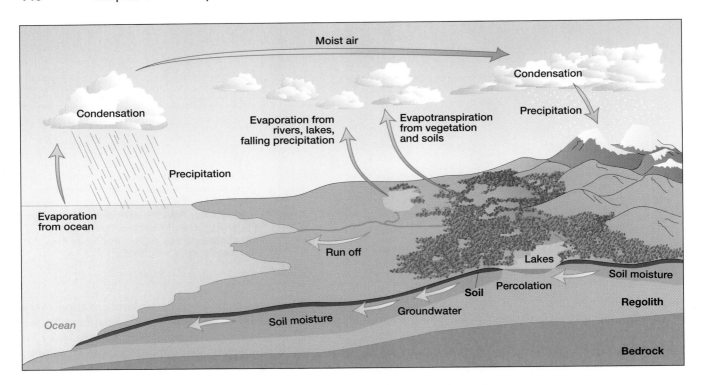

▲ **Figure 6-7**   The hydrologic cycle is a continuous interchange of moisture between the atmosphere and Earth.

change from one state to another at the pressures and temperatures found in the lower troposphere. Moisture can leave Earth's surface as a gas and return as a liquid or solid. Indeed, there is a continuous interchange of moisture between Earth and the atmosphere (Figure 6-7). This unending circulation of our planet's water supply is referred to as the **hydrologic cycle**, and its essential feature is that liquid water (primarily from the oceans) evaporates into the air, condenses to the liquid (or solid) state, and returns to Earth as some form of precipitation. The movement of moisture through the cycle is intricately related to many atmospheric phenomena and is an important determinant of climate because of its role in rainfall distribution and temperature modification. We will discuss the complete hydrologic cycle in greater detail in Chapter 9.

Next we turn specifically to the process that puts water vapor into the atmosphere—evaporation.

Evaporation

In our description of phase changes and the evaporation process above, we simplified things a bit. As it turns out, both evaporation and condensation may be taking place at the same time. Strictly speaking, water vapor is added to the air when the rate of evaporation exceeds the rate of condensation, in other words, there is *net evaporation* (Figure 6-8). The rate of evaporation from a water surface, and therefore net evaporation, depends on three factors: the temperature (of both air

and water), the amount of water vapor already in the air, and whether the air is still or moving.

Rates of Evaporation

The water molecules in warm water are more agitated than those in cool water; thus, there tends to be more evaporation from warm water than from cold.

Warm air also promotes evaporation. Just as high water temperature produces more agitation in the molecules of liquid water, so high air temperature produces more agitation in the molecules of all the gases making up the air. The more "energetic" gas molecules in warm air may collide with the liquid water surface and impart enough kinetic energy for some of the liquid water molecules to break their hydrogen bonds and enter the air above as vapor.

Water molecules cannot keep vaporizing and entering the air without limit, however. As we learned in Chapter 5, each gas in the atmosphere exerts pressure. Total atmospheric pressure is simply the sum of the pressures exerted by all of the individual gases in the atmosphere. The pressure exerted by water vapor is called the **vapor pressure**. At any given temperature, there is a maximum vapor pressure that water molecules can exert. The higher the temperature, the higher the maximum vapor pressure (in other words, there can be more water vapor in warm air than in cold air). When water molecules in the air are exerting the maximum possible vapor pressure at a given temperature, the air is *saturated* with water vapor—at this point, the

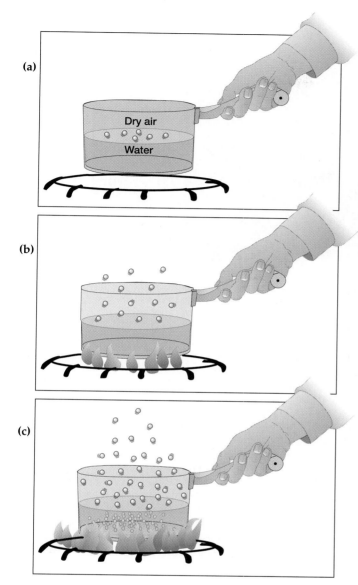

If the air overlying a water surface is almost saturated with water vapor, the rate of evaporation is about the same as the rate of condensation, and so very little further evaporation can take place. If the air remains calm and the temperature doesn't change, there is no net evaporation. If the air is in motion, however, through windiness and/or turbulence, the water vapor molecules in it are dispersed more widely. This dispersing of water vapor molecules originally in the air at the air–water interface means that air is now further from saturation and so the rate of evaporation increases.

To summarize, the rate of evaporation from a water surface is determined by the temperature of the water, the temperature of the air, and the degree of windiness. Higher temperatures, greater windiness, and drier air lead to greater net evaporation.

Evapotranspiration

Although most of the water that evaporates into the air comes from bodies of water, a relatively small amount comes from the land. This evaporation from land has two sources: (1) soil and other inanimate surfaces, and (2) plants. The amount of moisture that evaporates from soil is relatively minor, and thus most of the land-derived moisture present in the air comes from plants. The process whereby plants give up moisture through their leaves is called *transpiration,* and so the combined process of water vapor entering the air from land sources is called **evapotranspiration**. Thus, the water vapor in the atmosphere was added through evaporation from bodies of water and evapotranspiration from land surfaces.

Whether a given land location is wet or dry depends on the rates of evapotranspiration and precipitation. To analyze these rates, we need to know about a concept called *potential evapotranspiration.* This is the amount of evapotranspiration that would occur if the ground at the location in question were sopping wet all the time. To determine a value for the potential evapotranspiration at any location, data on temperature, vegetation, and soil characteristics at that location are added to the actual evapotranspiration value in a formula that results in an estimate of the maximum evapotranspiration that could result under local environmental conditions if the moisture were available.

In locations where the precipitation rate exceeds the potential evapotranspiration rate, a water surplus accumulates in the ground. In many parts of the world, however, there is no groundwater surplus, except locally and/or temporarily, because the potential evapotranspiration rate is higher than the precipitation rate. Where potential evapotranspiration exceeds actual precipitation, there is no water available for storage in soil and in plants; dry soil and brown vegetation are the result.

▲ **Figure 6-8** Evaporation involves the escape of water molecules from a liquid surface into the air as water vapor. It can take place at any temperature, but high temperatures increase the energy of the molecules in the liquid and therefore accelerate the rate of evaporation. **(a)** With the burner off, some molecules break free from the surface as water vapor, whereas some return from the air to the liquid surface. **(b)** As the water temperature rises, all of the molecules become more agitated, and so more of the water molecules break free from the surface as water vapor than return to the liquid surface from the air. **(c)** Continued heating increases molecular activity so much that the air may become saturated with water vapor.

rate of evaporation and the rate of condensation are the same. If this maximum vapor pressure is exceeded, more water vapor molecules will leave the air through condensation than are added to the air through evaporation—net condensation will take place until the rates of evaporation and condensation are again matched and the air again has its maximum vapor pressure.

FOCUS GOES Weather Satellites

The satellite images commonly seen on television weather reports come from a pair of satellites known as GOES, or *Geostationary Operational Environmental Satellites*. The GOES satellites are operated by the National Oceanic and Atmospheric Administration (NOAA) and have become essential tools for weather forecasting. The two GOES satellites are geostationary, orbiting at a distance of 35,800 kilometers (22,300 miles) in fixed locations relative to the surface of Earth below. GOES-East orbits above the equator in South America (75° W), where it can see the conterminous United States, as well as much of the north and south Atlantic Ocean. GOES-West orbits above the equator in the Pacific (135° W), where it can see most of the Pacific Ocean from Alaska to New Zealand.

The primary instruments onboard the GOES satellites are the *Sounder* and the *Imager*. The sounder provides information about vertical temperature and moisture variations within the atmosphere, as well as data about ozone distribution. The imager has sensors to detect both radiant and reflected electromagnetic energy in several different bands of wavelengths. The intensity of radiation in each wavelength band is measured, recorded, and then transmitted down to the surface, where the images are processed. The GOES satellites send back several images each hour, allowing time-lapse satellite "movie" loops to be produced. Up-to-date GOES satellite images are now readily available to the public through many Internet sites (e.g., www.noaa.gov).

Satellite images showing visible light as well those showing various bands of infrared wavelengths are useful in weather forecasting since each provides different kinds of information about Earth's surface and the atmosphere. Visible light satellite images show sunlight that has been reflected off the surface of Earth or by clouds in the atmosphere (Figure 6-A). The brightness of a surface depends both on its *albedo* (reflectance) and the angle of the light striking it. The brightest (high albedo) surfaces in visible light are typically the tops of clouds and snow or ice-covered surfaces. The darkest

▲ **Figure 6-A**   GOES-West visible light satellite image showing a midlatitude cyclone approaching the west coast of North America. *(Courtesy of Naval Research Laboratory, Marine Meteorology Division.)*

(low albedo) surfaces are typically land areas (especially unvegetated land surfaces), and the oceans—which are usually the darkest surfaces seen on visible light satellite images.

The infrared images of Earth and its atmosphere are produced by the GOES satellites day and night and are among the most widely used in meteorology. Infrared images show the longwave ("thermal infrared") radiation that has been emitted by the surface of the Earth or by clouds in the atmosphere (Figure 6-B). Warm objects emit more longwave radiation than cold objects, and so infrared images show us, in effect, differences in temperature. Differences in infrared intensity are repro-

duced on black-and-white satellite images so that cooler surfaces (those emitting relatively little longwave radiation) are shown in white, while warmer surfaces are shown in black. It is also common to assign colors to different intensities of infrared radiation. In infrared images, the tops of high clouds are easy to distinguish from low clouds and fog. The tops of high clouds, such as massive cumulonimbus clouds, are much colder than low clouds and fog, and so will appear brighter (white) on infrared images. Low clouds and fog tend to have similar temperatures to that of the surface, and so will appear as nearly the same shade of gray as the surface below.

▲ **Figure 6-B**   GOES-West infrared satellite image taken at the same time as Figure 6-A. *(Courtesy of Naval Research Laboratory, Marine Meteorology Division.)*

Measures of Humidity

The amount of water vapor in the air is referred to as **humidity**. It can be measured and expressed in a number of ways, each useful for certain purposes.

Absolute Humidity

One direct measure of the water vapor content of air is **absolute humidity**—the mass of water vapor in a given volume of air. Absolute humidity is normally expressed in grams of water vapor per cubic meter of air (1 gram is approximately 0.035 ounces, and 1 cubic meter is about 35 cubic feet). For example, if a cubic meter of air contains 12 grams of water vapor, the absolute humidity would be 12 g/m^3. The maximum possible absolute humidity for a parcel of air is limited by the temperature: cold air has a small maximum absolute humidity while warm air has a great maximum absolute humidity (Figure 6-9).

If the volume of air changes (as happens when air expands or compresses as it moves vertically), the value of the absolute humidity also changes even though there is no change in the total amount of water vapor present. For this reason, absolute humidity is generally not used to describe moisture in air that is rising or descending.

Specific Humidity

The mass of water vapor in a given mass of air is called the **specific humidity** and is usually expressed in grams of water vapor per kilogram of air (for comparison one cubic meter of air at sea level has a mass of about 1.4 kg at room temperature). For example, if a kilogram of air contains 15 grams of water vapor, the specific humidity is 15 g/kg.

Specific humidity changes only as the quantity of water vapor varies; it is not affected by variations in air volume in the way that absolute humidity is. Specific humidity is particularly useful in studying the characteristics and movements of air masses (discussed in Chapter 7).

Vapor Pressure

As we saw earlier, the contribution of water vapor to the total pressure of the atmosphere is called the *vapor pressure*. Vapor pressure can be expressed in the same way as total atmospheric pressure, in millibars. The maximum possible vapor pressure at a given temperature is called the **saturation vapor pressure**. Notice in Figure 6-10 that at a temperature of 10°C (50°F) the saturation vapor pressure is a little over 10 mb, while at 30°C (86°F) the saturation vapor pressure is about 40 mb—illustrating again that warm air has the potential to contain much more water vapor than cold air.

Absolute humidity, specific humidity, and vapor pressure are all ways of expressing the actual amount of water vapor in the air—and as such, are indications of the quantity of water that could be extracted by condensation and precipitation. However, before we discuss condensation and precipitation, we need to introduce the important concept of *relative humidity*.

Relative Humidity

The most familiar of humidity measures is **relative humidity**. Unlike absolute humidity, specific humidity, and vapor pressure, relative humidity is not a direct measure of the actual water vapor content of the air. Rather, relative humidity describes how close the air is to saturation with water vapor.

Relative humidity is a ratio (expressed as a percentage) that compares the actual amount of water vapor in the air to the water vapor *capacity* of the air. **Capacity** is the maximum amount of water vapor that can be in the air at a given temperature.[5] As we've seen in Figures 6-9 and 6-10, cold air has a low water vapor capacity, while warm air has a high water vapor capacity. (In popular terms, it is sometimes said that warm air can "hold" more water vapor than cold air, but this is somewhat

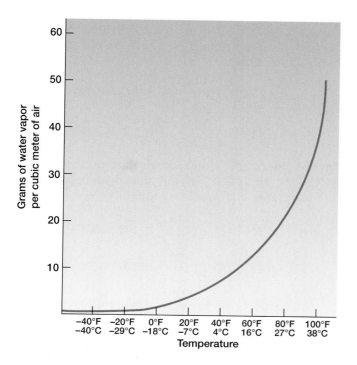

▲ **Figure 6-9**   Saturation absolute humidity (in g/m^3). The maximum amount of water vapor in a given volume of air increases as the temperature increases.

---

[5] Depending on the measure of actual water vapor content being used, capacity is also called the *saturation absolute humidity*, *saturation specific humidity*, or *saturation vapor pressure*.

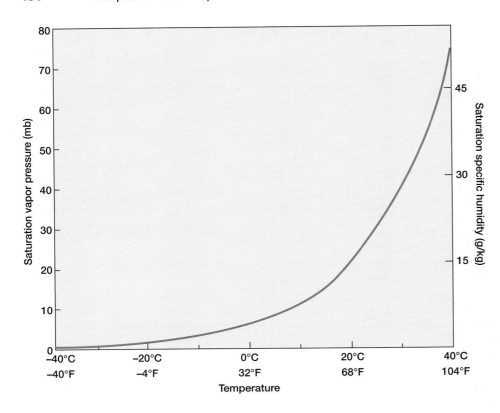

◀ **Figure 6-10** Saturation vapor pressure (in millibars) and saturation specific humidity (in grams per kilogram). As temperature increases, the water vapor capacity of the air increases. *(After Aguado and Burt, Understanding Weather and Climate, 4th ed., Upper Saddle River, NJ: Pearson Prentice Hall, 2007.)*

misleading. The air doesn't actually hold water vapor as if it were in a sponge. Water vapor is simply one of the gaseous components of the atmosphere. The water vapor capacity of the air is determined by the temperature, which determines the rate of vaporization of water.)

Relative humidity is calculated with a simple formula:

$$\text{Relative humidity} = \frac{\text{Actual water vapor in air}}{\text{Capacity}} \times 100$$

For example, suppose that a kilogram of air contains 10 grams of water vapor (in other words, the specific humidity is 10 g/kg). If the temperature is 25°C (77°F), the capacity of the air is about 20 g/kg (see Figure 6-10), and so the relative humidity is

$$\frac{10 \text{ g}}{20 \text{ g}} \times 100 = 50\%$$

A relative humidity of 50% means that the air contains half of the maximum possible water vapor at that temperature. In other words, the air is 50 percent of the way to saturation.

Relative humidity changes if either the water vapor content or the water vapor capacity of the air changes. If, in our example above, 5 grams of water vapor are added to the air through evaporation while the temperature remains constant (so keeping the capacity unchanged), relative humidity will increase:

$$\frac{15 \text{ g}}{20 \text{ g}} \times 100 = 75\%$$

Conversely, if water vapor is removed from the air by condensation or dispersal, the relative humidity can decrease.

Relative humidity will also change when the temperature changes—even if the actual amount of water vapor in the air remains the same. Again, beginning with our initial example above, if the temperature increases from 25°C (77°F) to 33°C (91°F), the water vapor capacity increases from 20 to 30 grams, and so relative humidity decreases:

$$\text{at 25°C (77°F): } \frac{10 \text{ g}}{20 \text{ g}} \times 100 = 50\%$$

$$\text{at 33°C (91°F): } \frac{10 \text{ g}}{30 \text{ g}} \times 100 = 33\%$$

On the other hand, if the temperature decreases from 25°C (77°F) to 14°C (57°F), the capacity decreases from 20 to 10 grams, and so relative humidity increases:

$$\text{at 25°C (77°F): } \frac{10 \text{ g}}{20 \text{ g}} \times 100 = 50\%$$

$$\text{at 20°C (68°F): } \frac{10 \text{ g}}{15 \text{ g}} \times 100 = 67\%$$

$$\text{at 14°C (57°F): } \frac{10 \text{ g}}{10 \text{ g}} \times 100 = 100\%$$

Notice that the air can be brought to saturation (100% relative humidity) simply through a decrease in temperature—no water vapor has been added. As we will see, the most common way that air is brought to the point of saturation and condensation is through cooling.

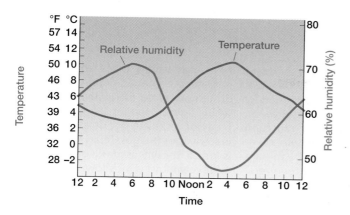

▲ **Figure 6-11** Typically there is an inverse relationship between temperature and relative humidity on any given day. As the temperature rises, the relative humidity decreases. Thus, relative humidity tends to be lowest in midafternoon and highest just before dawn.

Temperature–Relative Humidity Relationship The relationship between temperature and relative humidity is one of the most important in all of meteorology: as temperature increases, relative humidity decreases; as temperature decreases, relative humidity increases (at least until condensation begins). This inverse relationship is portrayed in Figure 6-11, which demonstrates the fluctuation in temperature and relative humidity during a typical day (assuming no variation in the amount of water vapor in the air). In the early morning, the temperature is low and the relative humidity is high—because the air's water vapor capacity is low. As the air warms up during the day, the relative humidity declines—because the warm air has a higher water vapor capacity than cool air. With the approach of evening, air temperature decreases, the air's water vapor capacity diminishes, and relative humidity increases.

See Appendix III for a description of how relative humidity can be determined using a simple instrument known as a *psychrometer*.

Related Humidity Concepts

Two other concepts related to relative humidity are useful in a study of physical geography: *dew point temperature* and *sensible temperature*.

Dew Point Temperature As we have seen, when air is cooled the water vapor capacity decreases and relative humidity increases. Cooling can bring formerly unsaturated air to the saturation point. The temperature at which saturation is reached is called the **dew point temperature**, or simply the **dew point**. The dew point temperature varies with the moisture content of the air. In our example above, we saw that air containing 10 grams of water vapor per kilogram of air reaches its dew point when chilled to about 14°C (57°F); air containing 20 grams of water vapor per kilogram of air reaches its dew point at about 25°C (77°F).

Although dew point is expressed as a temperature, in practice it becomes one of the most useful ways of describing the actual water vapor content of a parcel of air. For example, if a parcel of air has a dew point temperature of 14°C (57°F), then we know that the specific humidity of the parcel is 10 g/kg; if the dew point of the parcel is 25°C (77°C), then the specific humidity must be 20 g/kg.

Sensible Temperature The term **sensible temperature** refers to the temperature as it feels to a person's body. It involves not only the actual air temperature but also other atmospheric conditions, particularly relative humidity and wind, that influence our perception of heat and cold.

On a warm, humid day, the air seems hotter than the thermometer indicates, and the sensible temperature is said to be high. This is because the air is near saturation, and so perspiration on the human skin does not evaporate readily. Thus, there is little evaporative cooling and the air seems warmer than it actually is. On a warm, dry day, evaporative cooling is effective, and thus the air seems cooler than it actually is; in this case, we say that the sensible temperature is low.

On a cold, humid day, the coldness seems more piercing because body heat is conducted away more rapidly in damp air; the sensible temperature is again described as low. On a cold, dry day, body heat is not conducted away as fast. The temperature seems warmer than it actually is, and we say that the sensible temperature is relatively high.

The amount of wind movement also affects sensible temperature, primarily by its influence on evaporation and the convecting away of body heat. This is especially true when the air temperature is below the freezing point of water—on windy cold days the wind may lower the apparent temperature significantly. See Appendix III for a description of the *heat index* and *wind chill*.

Condensation

Condensation is the opposite of evaporation. It is the process whereby water vapor is converted to liquid water. In other words, it is a change in state from gas to liquid. In order for condensation to take place, the air must be saturated. In theory, this saturated state can come about through the addition of water vapor to the air, but in practice it is usually the result of the air being cooled to a temperature below the dew point.

Saturation alone is not enough to cause condensation, however. Surface tension makes it virtually impossible to grow droplets of pure water. Because surface tension inhibits an increase in surface area, it makes it very difficult for additional water molecules to enter a droplet. (On the other hand, molecules can

FOCUS Water Vapor Satellite Images

Although water vapor in the atmosphere is invisible to the human eye, sensors onboard weather satellites can detect water vapor by measuring selected wavelengths of electromagnetic radiation. Satellite *water vapor images* show regions of dry air and moist air in the atmosphere—even if these areas are cloud free and so won't show clearly on conventional visible light or infrared weather satellite images (Figures 6-C, 6-D, and 6-E).

Recall from Chapter 4 that the "atmospheric window" is a portion of the longwave band of electromagnetic spectrum (between about 8 and 12 micrometers [μm]) for which the atmosphere is nearly transparent. In other words, longwave radiation emitted by Earth's surface or from clouds with wavelengths between 8 and 12 μm is not readily absorbed by greenhouse gases such as water vapor. However, wavelengths of radiation outside the atmospheric window—specifically 6.7 μm and 7.3 μm—are prominently absorbed and then reradiated by water vapor.

By detecting the wavelengths of infrared radiation emitted by water vapor, scientists have a way to estimate the quantity of water vapor in the atmosphere: We infer that regions with high emission of infrared radiation at 6.7 μm and 7.3 μm contain relatively large amounts of water vapor, while regions with low emission of those wavelengths contain relatively small amounts of water vapor.

In gray-scale ("black and white") water vapor images, darker shades of gray show areas of relatively dry air, while lighter shades of gray show areas of relatively moist air. In color water vapor images, relatively dry air is often shown as dark blue, while relatively moist air is shown in shades of orange and red.

Because water vapor images detect infrared emission from water vapor in the middle and upper troposphere (above about 4500 meters [15,000 feet]), in addition to providing information about the moisture content of the atmosphere, these images also provide information about wind movement in the upper atmosphere, especially when time-sequence "movie loops" are used.

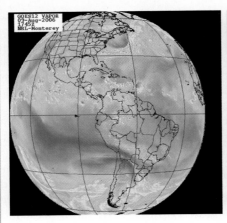

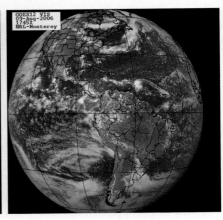

▲ **Figure 6-C** Water vapor satellite image of North and South America taken by NOAA's GOES-East satellite. Note the relatively dry areas (shown in dark blue) behind a cold front in the Atlantic just east of the United States and off the west coast of South America. The small patch of very moist air (shown in orange) just east of the Lesser Antilles Islands in the Caribbean is a developing tropical storm. *(Courtesy of Naval Research Laboratory, Marine Meteorology Division.)*

▲ **Figure 6-D** Infrared satellite image taken at the same time as Figure 6-C. *(Courtesy of Naval Research Laboratory, Marine Meteorology Division.)*

▲ **Figure 6-E** Visible light satellite image taken at the same time as Figure 6-C. *(Courtesy of Naval Research Laboratory, Marine Meteorology Division.)*

easily leave a small droplet by evaporation, thereby decreasing its area.) Thus, it is necessary to have a surface on which condensation can take place. If no such surface is available, no condensation occurs. In such a situation, the air becomes **supersaturated** (has a relative humidity greater than 100%) if cooling continues.

Normally, plenty of surfaces are available for condensation. At ground level, availability of a surface is obviously no problem. In the air above the ground, there is also usually an abundance of "surfaces," as represented by tiny particles of dust, smoke, salt, pollen, bacteria, and other compounds. Most of these various particles are microscopic and therefore invisible to the naked eye (Figure 6-12). They are most concentrated over cities, seacoasts, and volcanoes, which are the source of much particulate matter but are present in lesser amounts throughout the troposphere. They are referred to as *hygroscopic particles* or **condensation nuclei**, and they serve as collection centers for water molecules during condensation.

As soon as the air temperature cools to the dew point, water vapor molecules begin to condense around condensation nuclei. The droplets grow rapidly as more and more water vapor molecules stick to them, and as they become larger, they bump into one another and coalesce as the colliding droplets stick together. Continued growth can make them large enough to be visible, forming haze or cloud particles. The diminutive size of these particles can be appreciated by realizing that a single raindrop may contain a million or more condensation nuclei plus all their associated moisture.

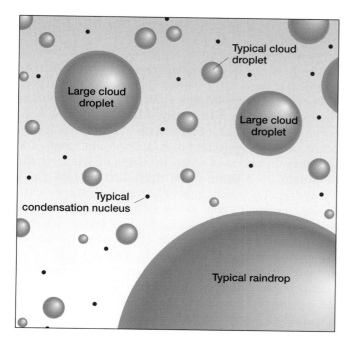

▲ **Figure 6-12** Comparative sizes of condensation nuclei and condensation particles. Condensation nuclei can be particles of dust, smoke, salt, pollen, bacteria, or any other microscopic matter found in the air.

Clouds often may be composed of liquid water droplets even when their temperature is below freezing. Although water in large quantity freezes at 0°C (32°F), if it is dispersed as fine droplets, it can remain in liquid form at temperatures as cold as −40°C (−40°F). Water that persists in liquid form at temperatures below freezing is said to be *supercooled*. **Supercooled water** droplets are important to condensation because they promote the growth of ice particles in cold clouds by freezing around them or by evaporating into vapor from which water molecules are readily added to the ice crystals.

Adiabatic Processes

 Adiabatic Processes and Atmospheric Stability

One of the most significant facts in physical geography is that the only way in which large masses of air can be cooled to the dew point temperature is by expansion as the air masses rise. Thus, the only prominent mechanism for the development of clouds and the production of rain is adiabatic cooling. As we noted in Chapter 4, when air rises, its pressure decreases, and so it expands and cools adiabatically.

As a parcel of unsaturated air rises, it cools at the relatively steady rate of 10°C per 1000 meters (5.5°F per 1000 feet). This is known as the **dry adiabatic rate** (also called the *dry adiabatic lapse rate*). (The term is a misnomer: the air is not necessarily "dry"; it is simply unsaturated.) If the air mass rises high enough, it cools to the dew point temperature, condensation begins, and clouds form. The altitude at which this occurs is known as the **lifting condensation level** (LCL). Under normal circumstances, the LCL is clearly visible as the base of the clouds that form (Figure 6-13).

As soon as condensation begins, latent heat is released (this heat was stored originally as the latent heat of evaporation). If the air continues to rise, cooling due to expansion continues but release of the latent heat counteracts some of the adiabatic cooling and slackens the rate of cooling. This diminished rate of cooling is called the **saturated adiabatic rate** (also called the *saturated adiabatic lapse rate* or *moist adiabatic rate*; Figure 6-14) and depends on temperature and pressure but averages about 6°C per 1000 meters (3.3°F per 1000 feet).

Adiabatic warming occurs when air descends. Typically, descending air will warm at the dry adiabatic rate of 10°C/1000 meters (5.5°C/1000 feet).[6] The increasing

---

[6] Although descending air typically warms following the dry adiabatic rate, there is a circumstance when this may not be the case. If air descends through a cloud, some water droplets may evaporate and the evaporative cooling will counteract some of the adiabatic warming. As a result, such descending air can warm at a rate close to the saturated adiabatic rate. As soon as evaporation of water droplets ceases, this descending air will warm following the dry adiabatic rate.

▲ **Figure 6-13** The flat bottoms of these massive cumulonimbus clouds represent the lifting condensation level. The summer skyscape in this view is from central Namibia. *(Tom L. McKnight photo.)*

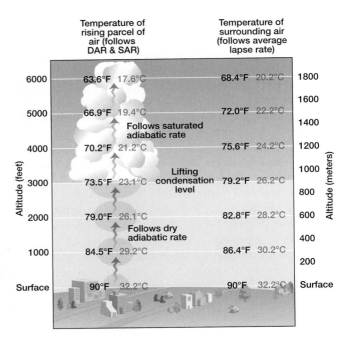

▲ **Figure 6-15** A hypothetical comparison of lapse rates. The column of temperatures on the right represents the vertical temperature gradient of the surrounding air through which a parcel of air (shown at left) is rising and cooling adiabatically. The temperature change of the nonrising air at the right is generalized as the average lapse rate (6.5°C per 1000 meters; 3.6°F per 1000 feet). On the left, the rising air first cools at the dry adiabatic rate (DAR 10°C per 1000 meters; 5.5°F per 1000 feet). Above the lifting condensation level, where condensation begins to take place, the air continues to rise but the rate of cooling is reduced to the saturated adiabatic rate (SAR 6°C per 1000 meters; 3.3°F per 1000 feet).

temperature of descending air increases the water vapor capacity of the air and thus causes saturated air to become unsaturated. In short, this why descending air does not make clouds.

In any consideration of adiabatic temperature changes, remember that we are dealing with air that is rising or descending. The adiabatic rates are not to be confused with the *average lapse rate* (or *environmental lapse rate*) described in Chapter 4, which pertains to still air (Figure 6-15).

Some of the implications of adiabatic temperature changes can be seen in Figure 6-16, showing the temperature changes associated with a hypothetical parcel of air moving up and over a mountain range. The parcel is unsaturated when it begins to rise over the mountain, so it cools at the dry adiabatic rate. Once the lifting condensation level is reached, the air continues to rise and cool at the saturated adiabatic rate as condensation forms a cloud. Once the air reaches the summit, it begins to descend down the lee side of the mountain (in this example, the moisture condensed out of the rising air was left as precipitation or clouds on the windward side of the mountain, and as the air descends, no evaporation takes place). The descending air warms at the dry adiabatic rate, so by the time the air has reached sea level again, it is significantly warmer and significantly drier (in both relative and absolute terms) than when it started out. We will see that this circumstance is one way in which deserts are formed.

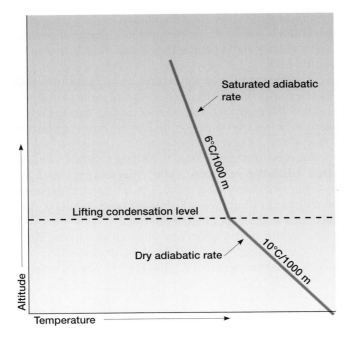

▲ **Figure 6-14** Unsaturated rising air cools at the dry adiabatic rate. Above the lifting condensation level, rising saturated air cools at the saturated adiabatic rate.

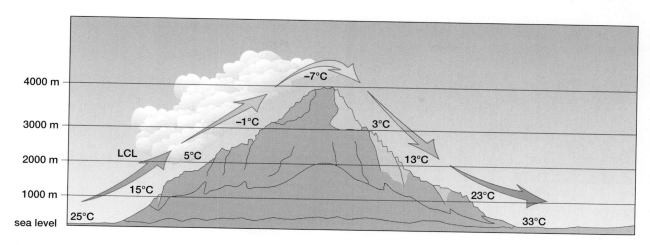

▲ **Figure 6-16** Temperature changes in a hypothetical parcel of air passing over a 4000 meter (13,100 foot) high mountain (assuming no evaporation as the air descends down the lee side of the mountain). The lifting condensation level (LCL) of the parcel is 2000 meters, the dry adiabatic rate is 10°C/1000 m, and the saturated adiabatic rate is 6°C/1000 m. Notice that because of the release of latent heat during condensation on the windward side of the mountain, by the time the air has descended back down to sea level on the leeward side, it is warmer than before it started up the windward side.

Clouds

Clouds are collections of minute droplets of water or tiny crystals of ice. They are the visible expression of condensation and provide perceptible evidence of other things happening in the atmosphere. They provide at a glance some understanding of the present weather and are often harbingers of things to come. At any given time, about 50 percent of Earth is covered by clouds, the basic importance of which is that they are the source of precipitation. Not all clouds precipitate, but all precipitation comes from clouds.

Clouds are also important because of their influence on radiant energy. They receive both insolation from above and terrestrial radiation from below, and then they may absorb, reflect, scatter, or reradiate this energy. Thus understanding the function of clouds in the global energy budget is important, and clouds must be taken into account when trying to anticipate the causes or consequences of climate change.

Classifying Clouds

Although clouds occur in an almost infinite variety of shapes and sizes, certain general forms recur commonly. Moreover, the various cloud forms are normally found only at certain generalized altitudes, and it is on the basis of these two factors—form and altitude—that clouds are classified (Table 6-1).

Cloud Form The international classification scheme for clouds recognizes three forms (Figure 6-17).

1. *Cirriform* clouds (Latin *cirrus*, "a lock of hair") are thin and wispy and composed of ice crystals rather than water droplets.
2. *Stratiform* clouds (Latin *stratus*, "spread out") appear as grayish sheets that cover most or all of the sky, rarely being broken up into individual cloud units.
3. *Cumuliform* clouds (Latin *cumulus*, "mass" or "pile") are massive and rounded, usually with a flat base and limited horizontal extent but often billowing upward to great heights.

TABLE 6-1 The International Classification Scheme for Clouds

Family	Type	Form	Characteristics
High	Cirrus	Cirriform	
	Cirrocumulus	Cirriform	Thin, white, icy
	Cirrostratus	Cirriform	
Middle	Altocumulus	Cumuliform	Layered or puffy; made of liquid water
	Altostratus	Stratiform	
Low	Stratus	Stratiform	General overcast
	Stratocumulus	Stratiform	
	Nimbostratus	Stratiform	
Vertical	Cumulus	Cumuliform	Tall, narrow, puffy
	Cumulonimbus	Cumuliform	

(a)

(b)

(c)

◀ **Figure 6-17** **(a)** The classic cirrus clouds referred to as "mares' tails" because of their shape. *(Joyce Photographics/Photo Researchers, Inc.)* **(b)** A low stratus cloud overcast near Needles, Utah. *(Claudia Parks/The Stock Market.)* **(c)** Cumulus clouds over wheat field near Palouse, Washington. *(Jim Corwin/Photo Researchers, Inc.)*

These three cloud forms are subclassified into 10 types based on shape (Figure 6-18). The types overlap, and cloud development frequently is in a state of change, so that one type may evolve into another. Three of the 10 types are purely of one form, and these are called **cirrus clouds**, **stratus clouds**, and **cumulus clouds**. The other 7 types are combinations of these 3. Cirrocumulus clouds, for example, have the wispiness of cirrus clouds and the puffiness of cumulus clouds.

Precipitation comes from clouds that have "nimb" in their name, specifically *nimbostratus* or *cumulonimbus*. Normally these types develop from other types; that is, cumulonimbus clouds develop from cumulus clouds, and nimbostratus clouds develop from stratus clouds.

Cloud Families As the final detail of the international classification scheme, the 10 cloud types are divided into four families on the basis of altitude.

1. *High clouds* are generally found above 6 kilometers (20,000 feet). Because of the small amount of water vapor and low temperature at such altitudes, these clouds are thin, white, and composed of ice crystals. Included in this family are *cirrus*, *cirrocumulus*, and *cirrostratus*. These high clouds often are harbingers of an approaching weather system or storm.

2. *Middle clouds* normally occur between about 2 and 6 kilometers (6500 and 20,000 feet). They may be either stratiform or cumuliform and are composed of liquid water. Included types are *altocumulus* and *altostratus*. The puffy altocumulus clouds usually indicate settled weather conditions, whereas the lengthy altostratus are often associated with changing weather.

3. *Low clouds* usually are below 2 kilometers (6500 feet). They sometimes occur as individual clouds but more often appear as a general overcast. Low cloud types include *stratus*, *stratocumulus*, and *nimbostratus*. These low clouds often are widespread and are associated with somber skies and drizzly rain.

4. A fourth family, *clouds of vertical development*, grows upward from low bases to heights of as much as 15 kilometers (60,000 feet). Their horizontal spread is usually very restricted. They indicate very active vertical movements in the air. The relevant types are *cumulus*, which usually indicate fair weather, and **cumulonimbus**, which are storm clouds.

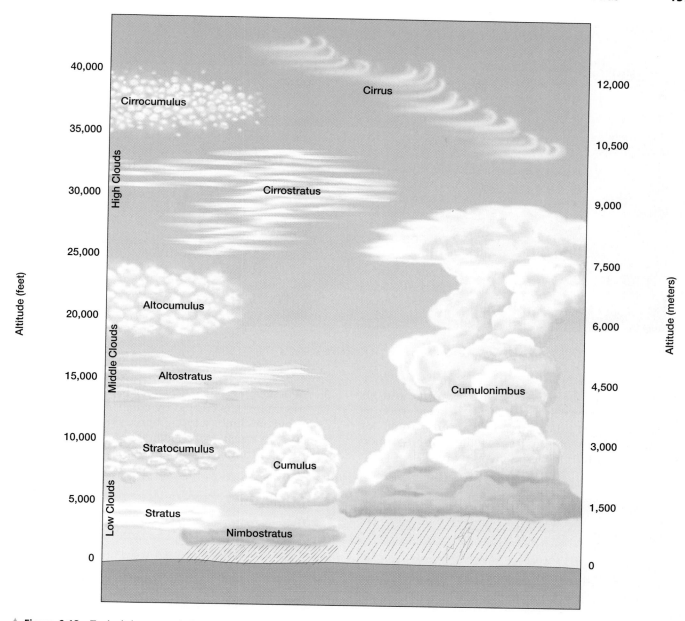

▲ **Figure 6-18** Typical shapes and altitudes of the 10 principal cloud types.

Fog

From a global standpoint, fogs represent a minor form of condensation. Their importance to humans is disproportionately high, however, because they can hinder visibility enough to make surface transportation hazardous or even impossible (Figure 6-19). **Fog** is simply a cloud on the ground. There is no physical difference between a cloud and fog, but there are important differences in how each forms. Most clouds develop as a result of adiabatic cooling in rising air, but only rarely is uplift involved in fog formation. Instead, most fogs are formed either when air at Earth's surface cools to below its dew point or when enough water vapor is added to the air to saturate it.

There are four generally recognized types of fog (Figure 6-20):

1. A *radiation fog* results when the ground loses heat through radiation, usually at night. The heat radiated away from the ground passes through the lowest layer of air and into higher areas. The air closest to the ground cools as heat flows conductively from it to the relatively cool ground, and fog condenses in the cooled air at the dew point.

▲ **Figure 6-19**   An advection fog enveloping the harbor at Ketchikan, Alaska. *(Tom L. McKnight photo.)*

2. An *advection fog* develops when warm, moist air moves horizontally over a cold surface, such as snow-covered ground or a cold ocean current. Air moving from sea to land is the most common source of advection fogs.

3. An *upslope fog*, or *orographic fog* (from the Greek *oro*, "mountain"), is created by adiabatic cooling when humid air climbs a topographic slope.

4. An *evaporation fog* results when water vapor is added to cold air that is already near saturation.

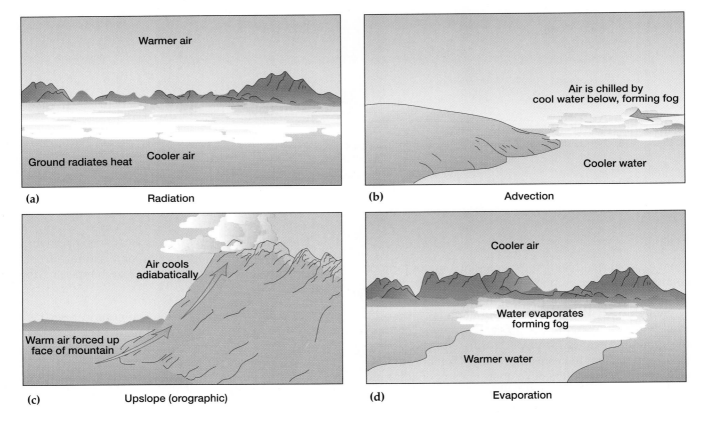

▲ **Figure 6-20**   The four principal types of fog: **(a)** radiation, **(b)** advection, **(c)** upslope (orographic), **(d)** evaporation.

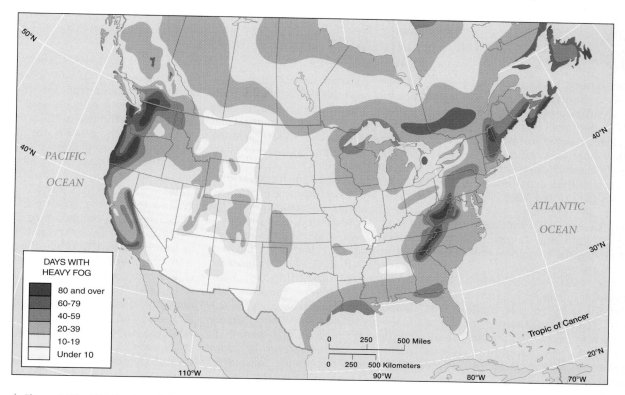

▲ **Figure 6-21** Distribution of fog in the United States and Southern Canada.

As can be seen in Figure 6-21, areas of heavy fog in North America are mostly coastal. The western-mountain and Appalachian fogs are mostly radiation fogs. Areas of minimal fog are in the Southwest, Mexico, and the Great Plains in both the United States and Canada, where available atmospheric moisture is limited and winds are strong.

Dew

Dew also originates from terrestrial radiation. Nighttime radiation cools objects (grass, pavement, automobiles, or whatever) at Earth's surface, and the adjacent air is in turn cooled by conduction. If the air is cooled enough to reach saturation, tiny beads of water collect on the cold surface of the object. If the temperature is below freezing, ice crystals (*white frost*) rather than water droplets are formed (Figure 6-22).

The Buoyancy of Air

Because most condensation and precipitation are the result of rising air, conditions that promote or hinder upward movements in the troposphere are obviously of great importance to weather and climate. Depending on how buoyant it is, air rises more freely and extensively under some circumstances than under others. Therefore, the concept of air buoyancy is one of the most significant in physical geography.

Atmospheric Stability

The tendency of any object to rise in a fluid is called the *buoyancy* of that object. For the present discussion, you should picture a given parcel of air (one having imaginary boundaries) as being an "object" and the surrounding air as being the fluid. As with other gases (and liquids, too), an air parcel tends to seek its own level. This means that a parcel of air moves vertically until it reaches a level at which the surrounding air is of equal density. Said another way, if a parcel of air is warmer, and thus less dense, than the surrounding air, it tends to rise. If a parcel is cooler, and therefore denser, than the surrounding air, it tends either to sink or at least resist uplift. Thus, we say that warm air is more buoyant than cool air.[7]

If a parcel of air resists upward vertical movement, it is said to be **stable** (Figure 6-23). If stable air is forced to rise, perhaps by coming up against a mountain slope, it does so only as long as the force is applied. Once the force is removed, the air sinks back to its former position. In other words, stable air is nonbuoyant. When unstable air comes up against the same mountain, it continues to rise once it has passed the peak.

---

[7] Water vapor content may also slightly influence air buoyancy. Because water vapor molecules have a lower molecular weight than nitrogen molecules (N_2) or oxygen molecules (O_2), when air has a high water vapor content, heavier N_2 and O_2 molecules have been displaced by lighter H_2O molecules and so such moist air is just slightly "lighter" than dry air. Overall, however, air temperature is by far the most important determinant of air buoyancy.

PEOPLE AND THE ENVIRONMENT Global Dimming

Atmospheric particulates have long been recognized to be an influence on weather and climate. As early as 1783, Benjamin Franklin proposed that the massive volcanic eruption of Laki fissure in Iceland was responsible for the many months of unusually frigid weather experienced in parts of Europe. By the 1980s, ice core research in Greenland was revealing signs that in years following the release of ash and sulfuric acid from large volcanic eruptions, global temperatures were lower.

The 1991 eruption of Mount Pinatubo in the Philippines allowed climatologists to test models that predicted the influence of large quantities of particulates in the atmosphere. The eruption released about 20 million tons of sulfate aerosols and lowered global temperatures by approximately 0.5°C (0.9°F) for about one year, closely matching model predictions.

Anthropogenic particulates have also been recognized as an influence on weather. By the 1950s, it was known that clouds could be artificially "seeded" with silver iodide smoke to increase condensation and perhaps increase precipitation. In terms of increasing precipitation, such *cloud seeding* had limited success, but it raised the concern that unintended human-produced air pollution could possibly promote cloud formation. By the late 1980s, satellite images were showing clouds persisting over oceanic shipping lanes: the sulfate aerosols from ship smokestacks were in effect "seeding" clouds.

Project INDOEX, a multinational study led by atmospheric scientist Veerabhadran Ramanathan in the 1990s, showed that the plume of sulfates, smoke particles, and other anthropogenic aerosols blowing over the Indian Ocean was blocking sunlight and promoting cloud formation, effectively reducing the amount of sunlight reaching the surface by 10 percent. Other studies confirmed that human-generated pollutants were increasing cloud cover and reducing the amount of solar radiation reaching the surface. By the later part of the twentieth century, data from several different research projects suggested that radiation reaching the surface had decreased by about 9 percent in Antarctica, 10 percent in parts of the United States, 22 percent in Israel, and nearly 30 percent in parts of Russia. By the early years of this decade, this phenomenon had become known as "global dimming." In short, it appears that human-released aerosols are increasing cloud cover and thereby acting to cool the surface and lower troposphere.

Some atmospheric scientists had long suspected that the "contrails" (condensation trails) from jet airliners might locally alter the atmospheric energy budget slightly (Figure 6-F). Condensation trails develop when water vapor in jet exhaust cools in the supersaturated cold air of the upper troposphere. These human-made clouds can reflect radiation when they are thick (acting much like a reflective cover of stratus clouds), but after some time they may turn into a wispier cover of cirrus-like clouds that absorb outgoing longwave radiation and so act as "warming" clouds.

Estimating the specific effects of contrails on lower troposphere temperatures proved difficult since there are few opportunities to study the atmosphere when contrails are absent from the sky—until September 11, 2001. The grounding of all commercial airline traffic over the United States in the three days following 9/11 showed that in the absence of contrails, the daily temperature range across the country increased sharply by more than 1°C (2°F)—the days were hotter and the nights were colder without contrails to absorb longwave radiation at night (which normally leads to higher nighttime temperatures) and reflect incoming radiation during the day (which normally leads to lower daytime temperatures). Overall, contrails are not seen by most atmospheric scientists to be a major contributor to global dimming. However, the measurable effect of contrails on local temperatures highlights the significance of human-produced clouds to the energy budget of Earth.

The *Aqua* satellite was launched by NASA in 2002. The satellite carries instruments that can measure the consequences of human-released "dimming" pollutants on Earth's energy budget. NASA's James Hansen reports that while human-enhanced greenhouse effect has, in effect, retained an additional 2.6 to 3.0 watts per square meter (W/m^2) of energy, global dimming has reduced the energy received by about 1.5 W/m^2. In other words, perhaps half of the warming caused by human greenhouse gas emissions has been counteracted by cooling caused by human aerosol pollution. This raises a paradoxical concern for atmospheric scientists: if human-produced global dimming has been masking some of the effects of global warming, if we continue our efforts to reduce atmospheric pollutants that also cause dimming, we'll face higher temperatures from global warming.

▲ **Figure 6-F**   Contrails over northwestern Europe on April 25, 2004; MODIS image taken by the Terra satellite. (*NASA.*)

(a)

(b)

▲ **Figure 6-22**   **(a)** Dewdrops on a wild daisy. *(Lawrence Pringle/Photo Researchers, Inc.)* **(b)** White frost emphasizes the delicate lacework of a spider web in Yellowstone Park's Hayden Valley. *(Tom L. McKnight photo.)*

In the atmosphere, high stability is promoted when cold air is beneath warm air, a condition most frequently observed during a temperature inversion. With colder, denser air below warmer, lighter air, upward movement is unlikely. A cold winter night is typically a highly stable situation, although high stability can also occur in the daytime. Because it does not rise, and therefore stays at an essentially constant pressure and volume, highly stable air obviously provides little opportunity for adiabatic cooling unless there is some sort of forced uplift. Highly stable air is normally not associated with cloud formation and precipitation.

Air is said to be **unstable** if it either rises without any external force other than the buoyant force or continues to rise after such an external force has ceased to function. In other words, unstable air is buoyant. When a mass of air is heated enough so that it is warmer than the surrounding air, it becomes unstable. This is a typical condition on a warm summer afternoon (Figure 6-24). The unstable air rises until it reaches an altitude where the surrounding air has similar temperature and density, which is referred to as the *equilibrium level*. While ascending, it will be cooled adiabatically. In this situation, clouds are likely to form.

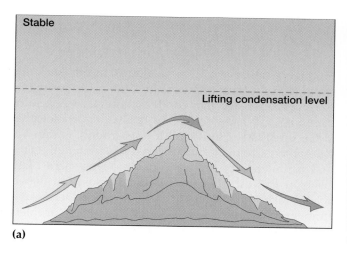

(a)

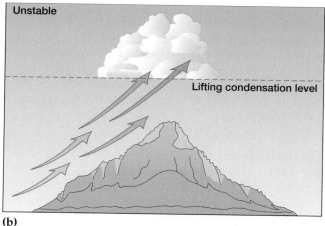

(b)

▲ **Figure 6-23**   **(a)** As stable air blows over a mountain, it rises only as long as it is forced to do so by the mountain slope. On the leeward side, it moves downslope. **(b)** When unstable air is forced up a mountain slope, it is likely to continue rising of its own accord until it reaches surrounding air of similar temperature and density; if it rises to the lifting condensation level, clouds form.

▲ **Figure 6-24** On a summer day, the air just above the blacktop surface gets warmer than the air above the grass. This unstable warmer air rises until it reaches an altitude where the surrounding air has similar temperature and density.

There is an intermediate condition, called *conditional instability*, between absolute stability and absolute instability. An air parcel is conditionally unstable when the environmental lapse rate is somewhere between the dry and saturated adiabatic rates. Near the surface, such a parcel of air is the same temperature or cooler than the surrounding air and so acts like stable air. If forced to rise above the lifting condensation level, however, the release of latent heat during condensation may provide enough buoyancy to make the parcel unstable. It then behaves the way unstable air does, rising until it reaches an altitude where the surrounding air has density and temperature similar to its own.

Determining Air Stability

The various degrees of air stability, from highly stable to unstable, are related to the lapse rate of the surrounding air (the *environmental lapse rate*) and the dry and saturated adiabatic rates followed by a moving parcel of air (Figure 6-25). An accurate determination of the stability of any mass of air depends on temperature measurements, but a rough indication can often be obtained simply by observing the state of the sky (primarily the cloud forms).

Determination of Stability via Temperature and Lapse Rate The temperature of the rising air can be compared with the temperature of surrounding nonrising air by a series of thermometer readings at different elevations. The rising air cools (at least initially) at the dry adiabatic rate of 10°C per 1000 meters (5.5°F per 1000 feet). The environmental lapse rate of the surrounding (nonrising) air depends on many things and may be different from the dry adiabatic rate.

For example, if the environmental lapse rate of the surrounding air is less than the dry adiabatic rate of the rising air, as in Figure 6-25a, at every elevation the rising air is cooler than the surrounding air and therefore stable. Under such conditions, the air rises only when forced to do so. Once the lifting force is removed, the air ceases to rise and will actually sink.

On the other hand, if the environmental lapse rate of the surrounding air is greater than the dry adiabatic rate of the rising air, at every elevation the rising air is warmer than the air around it and it is unstable. The unstable air rises until it reaches an elevation where the surrounding air is of similar temperature and density (Figure 6-25b).

The situation may become more complicated after the rising air is cooled to its dew point temperature at the lifting condensation level. Once condensation begins, latent heat is released. This situation increases the tendency toward instability and reinforces the rising trend (Figure 6-25c).

Visual Determination of Stability The cloud pattern in the sky is often indicative of air stability. Unstable air is associated with distinct updrafts, which are likely to produce vertical clouds (Figure 6-26). Thus, the presence of cumulus clouds suggests instability, and a towering cumulonimbus cloud is an indicator of pronounced instability. Horizontally developed clouds, most notably stratiform, are characteristic of stable air that has been forced to rise, and a cloudless sky may be an indicator of stable air that is immobile.

Regardless of stability conditions, no clouds form unless the air is cooled to the dew point temperature—unstable rising air will not produce any clouds if the dew point of the rising air is not reached. Thus the mere absence of clouds is not certain evidence of stability; it is only an indication.

The general features of stable and unstable air are summarized in Table 6-2.

Precipitation

All **precipitation** originates in clouds, but most clouds do not yield precipitation. Exhaustive experiments have demonstrated that condensation alone is insufficient to produce raindrops. The tiny water droplets that make up clouds cannot fall to the ground as rain because their size makes them very buoyant and the normal turbulence of the atmosphere keeps them aloft. Even in still air, their fall would be so slow that it would take many days for them to reach the ground from even a low cloud. Besides that, most droplets would evaporate in the drier air below the cloud before they made a good start downward.

Despite these difficulties, rain and other forms of precipitation are commonplace in the troposphere. What is it, then, that produces precipitation in its various forms?

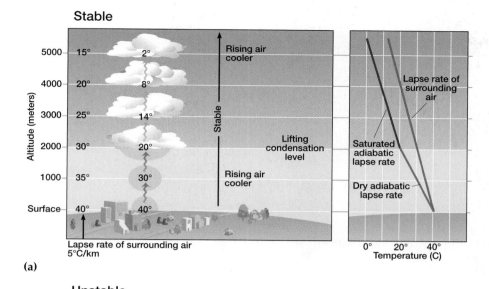

(a)

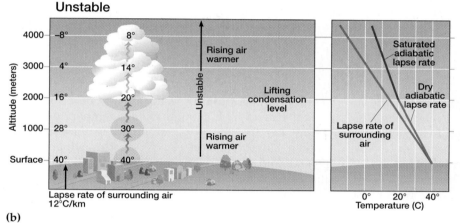

(b)

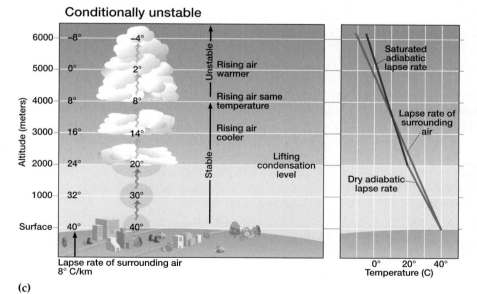

(c)

◀ **Figure 6-25** In these drawings, the lapse rate of surrounding air shows the temperature of the atmosphere at different elevations, whereas the dry adiabatic rate (DAR) and the saturated adiabatic rate (SAR) show the temperature of a rising parcel of air. At any given elevation, if the rising parcel of air is warmer than the surrounding air, the parcel will be unstable; if the rising parcel of air is the same temperature or cooler than the surrounding air, the parcel will be stable and will rise only if forced to do so. In these examples, the DAR is given to be 10°C/1000 m, the SAR is given to be 6°C/1000 m, and the lifting condensation level is given to be 2000 meters (2 km). Notice that the lapse rate of the surrounding air (the environmental lapse rate) is different in each of the examples. **(a)** At all elevations, the rising parcel of air is cooler than the surrounding air, so the parcel is stable and will rise only if forced. **(b)** At all elevations, the rising parcel of air is warmer than the surrounding air, so the parcel is unstable and will rise because of its buoyancy. **(c)** In this example, the rising parcel of air is cooler than the surrounding air and is stable up to an elevation of 4000 meters; above that elevation, the release of latent heat during condensation warms the rising air enough to make it unstable—thus the rising air is conditionally unstable.

The Processes

An average-sized raindrop contains several million times as much water as the average-sized water droplet found in any cloud. Consequently, great multitudes of droplets must join together to form a drop large enough

to overcome both turbulence and evaporation and thus be able to fall to Earth under the influence of gravity.

Two mechanisms are believed to be principally responsible for producing precipitation particles: (1) collision and coalescence of water droplets, and (2) ice-crystal formation.

▲ **Figure 6-26** Multiple cumulus clouds in the foreground with a cumulonimbus developing an anvil top in the background—indications of unstable atmospheric conditions. This is a localized thunderstorm near Wiluna, Western Australia. *(Tom L. McKnight photo.)*

Collision/Coalescence In many cases, particularly in the tropics, cloud temperatures are greater than 0°C (32°F); these are known as *warm clouds*. In such clouds, rain is produced by the collision and coalescing (merging) of water droplets. Condensation alone cannot yield rain because it produces lots of small droplets but no large drops. Thus, tiny condensation droplets must coalesce into drops large enough to fall as precipitation. Different-sized water droplets fall through a cloud at different speeds. Larger ones fall faster, overtaking and often coalescing with smaller ones, which are swept along in the descent (Figure 6-27). This sequence of events favors the continued growth of the larger particles.

Not all collisions result in coalescence, however. The air displaced around a falling large drop can push very tiny droplets out of its path. In addition, there is evidence to suggest that differences in the electrical charges of droplets may influence coalescence as well.

Collision/coalescence is the process most responsible for precipitation in the tropics, and it also produces some of the precipitation in the middle latitudes.

Ice-Crystal Formation Many clouds or portions of clouds extend high enough to have temperatures well below the freezing point of liquid water (these are known as *cold* or *cool clouds*). In this situation, ice crystals and supercooled water droplets often coexist in the cloud. These two types of particles are in direct "competition" for the water vapor that is not yet condensed. There is lower saturation vapor pressure around the ice crystals than around liquid water droplets—this means that if the air around a liquid water droplet is saturated (100% relative humidity), that same air is supersaturated around an ice crystal. Thus, the ice crystals attract most of the water vapor, and the liquid water droplets, in turn, evaporate to replenish the diminishing supply of vapor, as shown in Figure 6-28. Therefore, the ice crystals grow at the expense of the water droplets until the crystals are large enough to fall. As they descend through the lower, warmer portions of the cloud, they pick up more moisture and become still larger. They may then either precipitate from the cloud as snowflakes or melt and precipitate as raindrops.

TABLE 6-2 Characteristics of Stable and Unstable Air	
Stable Air	**Unstable Air**
Nonbuoyant; remains immobile unless forced to rise	Buoyant; rises without outside force
If clouds develop, tend to be stratiform or cirriform	If clouds develop, tend to be cumuliform
If precipitation occurs, tends to be drizzly	If precipitation occurs, tends to be showery

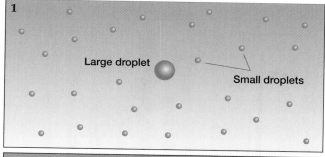

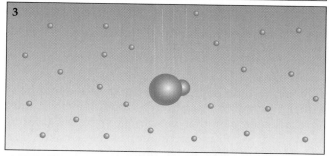

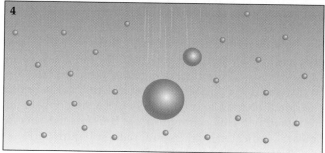

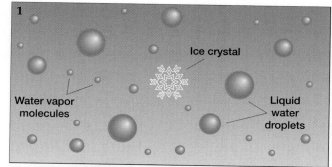

▲ **Figure 6-28** Precipitation by means of ice-crystal formation in clouds (the Bergeron process). Ice crystals grow by attracting water vapor to themselves, causing the liquid water droplets that make up the cloud to evaporate to replenish the water vapor supply. The process of growing ice crystals and shrinking cloud droplets may continue until the ice crystals are large and heavy enough to fall. (Particle sizes are greatly exaggerated.)

▲ **Figure 6-27** Raindrops forming by collision and coalescence. Large droplets fall more rapidly than small ones, coalescing with some and sweeping others along in their descending path. As droplets become larger during descent, they sometimes break apart.

Precipitation by ice-crystal formation was first proposed by the Swedish meteorologist Tor Bergeron more than half a century ago. It is now known as the *Bergeron process* and is believed to account for the majority of precipitation outside of tropical regions.

Forms of Precipitation

Several forms of precipitation can result from the processes just described depending on air temperature and turbulence.

Rain By far the most common and widespread form of precipitation is **rain**, which consists of drops of liquid water. Most rain is the result of condensation and precipitation in ascending air that has a temperature above freezing, but some results from the thawing of ice crystals as they descend through warmer air (Figure 6-29).

Meteorologists often make a distinction among "rain," which goes on for a relatively long time; *showers*, which are relatively brief and involve large drops; and *drizzle*, which consists of very small drops and usually lasts for some time.

Snow The general name given to solid precipitation in the form of ice crystals, small pellets, or flakes is **snow**. It is formed when water vapor is converted directly to ice without an intermediate liquid stage.

▲ **Figure 6-30** Enormous hailstones gathered by geographer Bob Solomon in his backyard in Sydney, Australia, after an intense hailstorm in September 1999. The average hailstone in this collection weighed 85 grams (3 ounces) and had a diameter of 8 cm (3 inches). *(Photo courtesy of Robert Solomon.)*

▲ **Figure 6-29** A towering cumulonimbus cloud produces a small but intense thunderstorm over the desert of southern Arizona near Tombstone. *(Photo courtesy of Linda O'Hirok.)*

However, the water vapor may have evaporated from supercooled liquid cloud droplets inside cold clouds.

Sleet In the United States, *sleet* refers to small raindrops that freeze during descent and reach the ground as small pellets of ice. In other countries, the term is often applied to a mixture of rain and snow.

Glaze *Glaze* is rain that turns to ice the instant it collides with a solid object. Raindrops fall through a shallow layer of subfreezing air near the ground. Although the drops do not freeze in the air (in other words, they do not turn to sleet), they become supercooled while in this cold layer and are instantly converted to an icy surface when they alight. The result can be a thick coating of ice that makes both pedestrian and vehicular travel hazardous as well as breaks tree limbs and transmission lines.

Hail The precipitation form with the most complex origin is **hail**, which consists of either small pellets or larger lumps of ice (Figure 6-30). Hailstones are usually composed of roughly concentric layers of clear and cloudy ice. The cloudy portions contain numerous tiny air bubbles among small crystals of ice, whereas the clear parts are made up of large ice crystals.

Hail is produced in cumulonimbus clouds as a result of great instability and strong vertical air currents (updrafts and downdrafts) (Figure 6-31). Because highly unstable air is needed in order for it to form, hail tends

to be more common in summer than in the middle of winter. For hail to form from a cloud, the cloud must have a lower part that is warmer than the freezing point of 0°C (32°F) and an upper part that is colder than this. Updrafts carry water droplets from the above-freezing layer or small ice particles from the lowest part of the below-freezing layer upward, where they grow by collecting moisture from supercooled cloud droplets. When the particles become too large to be supported in the air, they fall, gathering more moisture on the way down. If they encounter a sufficiently strong updraft, they may be carried skyward again, only to fall another time. This sequence may be repeated several times, as indicated by the spiral path in Figure 6-31.

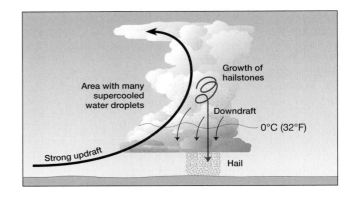

▲ **Figure 6-31** Hail is produced in cumulonimbus clouds that are partly at a temperature above the freezing point of water and partly at a temperature below the freezing point of water. The curved and spiral arrows indicate paths a hailstone takes as it is forming. *(After John Oliver,* Climatology: Selected Applications. *V. H. Winston and Sons, New York, 1981, p. 140.)*

A hailstone normally continues to grow whether it is rising or falling in the below-freezing layer, providing it passes through portions of the cloud that contain supercooled droplets. If there is considerable supercooled moisture available, the hailstone, which is ice, becomes surrounded by a wet layer that freezes relatively slowly, producing large ice crystals and forcing the air out of the water. The result is clear-ice rings. If there is a more limited supply of supercooled droplets, the water may freeze almost instantly around the hailstone. This fast freezing produces small crystals with tiny air bubbles trapped among them, forming opaque rings of ice.

Hailstones may be formed in a single descent and still consist of concentric shells of varying degrees of opaqueness. In this case, the layering is apparently due to variations in the rate of accumulation of supercooled droplets, with the accumulation rate based on differences in the amount of supercooled water in various parts of the descent path.

The eventual size of a hailstone depends on the amount of supercooled water in the cloud, the strength of the updrafts, and the total length (up, down, and sideways) of the path taken by the stone through the cloud. The largest known hailstone, which fell in Kansas in 1970, weighed 766 grams (1.67 pounds).

Atmospheric Lifting and Precipitation

The role of rising air and adiabatic cooling has been stressed in this chapter. Only through these events can any significant amount of precipitation originate. It remains for us to consider the causes of rising air. There are four principal types of atmospheric lifting. One type is spontaneous, and the other three require the presence of some external force. More often than not, however, the various types operate in conjunction.

Convective Lifting

Because of unequal heating of different surface areas, a parcel of air near the ground may be warmed by conduction more than the air around it. The density of the heated air is reduced as the air expands, and so the parcel rises toward a lower-density layer, in a typical **convective lifting** situation, as shown in Figure 6-32a. The pressure of the unstable air decreases as the air rises, and so it cools adiabatically to the dew point temperature. Condensation begins and a cumulus cloud forms. With the proper humidity, temperature, and stability

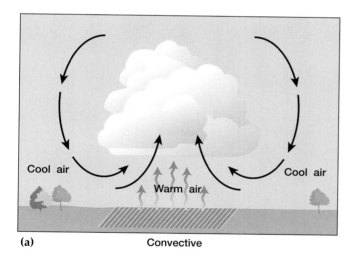
(a) Convective

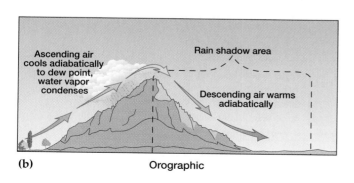
(b) Orographic

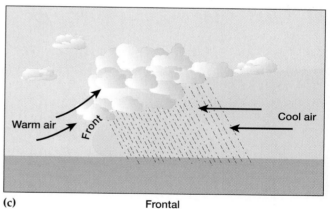
(c) Frontal

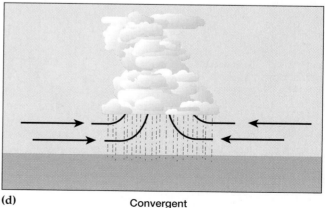
(d) Convergent

▲ **Figure 6-32** The four basic types of atmospheric lifting and precipitation: **(a)** convective, **(b)** orographic, **(c)** frontal, **(d)** convergent.

conditions, the cloud is likely to grow into a towering cumulonimbus thunderhead, with a downpour of showery raindrops and/or hailstones accompanied sometimes by lightning and thunder.

An individual convective cell is likely to cover only a small horizontal area, although sometimes multiple cells are formed very close to each other, close enough to form a much larger cell. *Convective precipitation* is typically showery, with large raindrops falling fast and furiously but only for a short duration. It is particularly associated with the warm parts of the world and warm seasons.

In addition to the spontaneous uplift just described, various kinds of forced uplift, such as air moving over a mountain range, can trigger formation of a convective cell if the air tends toward instability. Thus convective uplift often accompanies other kinds of uplift.

Orographic Lifting

Topographic barriers that block the path of horizontal air movements are likely to cause large masses of air to travel upslope, as Figure 6-32b shows. This kind of forced ascent from **orographic lifting** can produce

orographic precipitation if the ascending air is cooled to the dew point. As we learned above, if significant instability has been triggered by the upslope motion, the air keeps rising when it reaches the top of the slope and the precipitation continues. More often, however, the air descends the leeward side of the barrier. As soon as it begins to move downslope, adiabatic cooling is replaced by adiabatic warming and condensation and precipitation ceases. Thus the windward slope of the barrier is the wet side, the leeward slope is the dry side, and the term **rain shadow** is applied to both the leeward slope and the area beyond as far as the drying influence extends (Figure 6-33).

Orographic precipitation can occur at any latitude, any season, any time of day. The only requisite conditions are a topographic barrier and moist air to move over it. Orographic precipitation is likely to be prolonged because there is a relatively steady upslope flow of air.

Frontal Lifting

When unlike air masses meet, they do not mix. Rather, a zone of discontinuity called a *front* is established between them, and the warmer air rises over the cooler

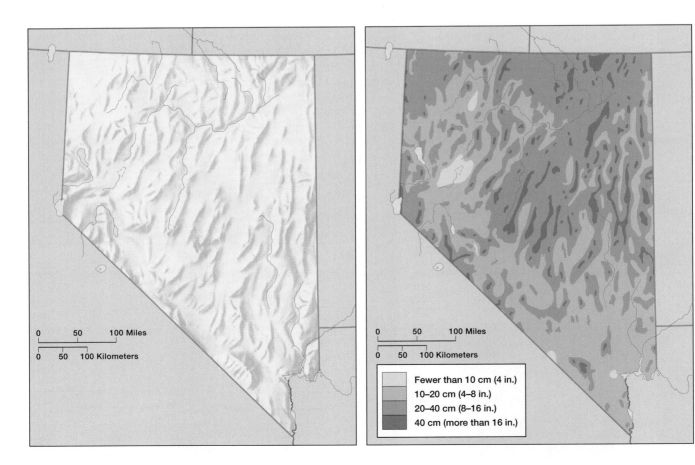

▲ **Figure 6-33** Comparison of annual precipitation and topography in Nevada. Where there are mountains, the air is forced to rise and there is more precipitation. Where there are basins, there is less precipitation. The relationship is simple, straightforward, and typical of mountainous environments.

air, as shown in Figure 6-32c. As the warmer air is forced to rise, it may be cooled to the dew point with resulting clouds and precipitation. Precipitation that results from such **frontal lifting** is referred to as *frontal precipitation*. We shall discuss frontal precipitation in greater detail in the next chapter. It tends to be widespread and protracted, but it is also frequently associated with convective showers.

Frontal activity is most characteristic of the midlatitudes, and so frontal precipitation is particularly notable in those regions, which are meeting grounds of cold polar air and warm tropical air. It is less significant in the high latitudes and rare in the tropics because those regions contain air masses that tend to be like one another.

Convergent Lifting

Less common than the other three types, but nevertheless significant in some situations, is **convergent lifting** and the accompanying *convergent precipitation*, illustrated in Figure 6-32d. Whenever air converges, the result is a general uplift because of the crowding. This forced uplift enhances instability and is likely to produce showery precipitation. It is frequently associated with cyclonic storm systems and is particularly characteristic of the low latitudes. It is common, for example, in the intertropical convergence zone (ITCZ) (discussed in Chapter 5) and is notable in such tropical disturbances as hurricanes and easterly waves.

Global Distribution of Precipitation

Seasonal Pressure and Precipitation Patterns

The most important geographic aspect of atmospheric moisture is the spatial distribution of precipitation. The broad-scale zonal pattern is based on latitude, but many other factors are involved and the overall pattern is complex. This section of the chapter focuses on a series of maps that illustrate worldwide and U.S. precipitation distribution. A major cartographic device used on these maps is the **isohyet,** a line joining points of equal quantities of precipitation.

Average Annual Precipitation

The amount of precipitation on any part of Earth's surface is determined by the nature of the air mass involved and the degree to which that air is uplifted. The humidity, temperature, and stability of the air mass are mostly dependent on where the air originated (over land or water, in high or low latitudes) and on the trajectory it

has followed. The amount of uplifting and whether that uplifting takes place are determined largely by zonal pressure patterns, topographic barriers, storms, and other atmospheric disturbances.

The most conspicuous feature of the worldwide annual precipitation pattern is that the tropical latitudes contain most of the wettest areas (Figure 6-34). The warm easterly trade winds are capable of carrying enormous amounts of moisture, and where they are forced to rise, very heavy rainfall is usually produced. Equatorial regions particularly reflect these conditions, as warm, moist, unstable air is uplifted in the ITCZ, where warm ocean water easily vaporizes. Considerable precipitation also results where trade winds are forced to rise by topographic obstacles. As the trades are easterly winds, it is the eastern coasts of tropical landmasses—for example, the east coast of Central America, northeastern South America, and Madagascar—where this orographic effect is most pronounced. Where the normal trade-wind pattern is modified by monsoons, the onshore trade-wind flow may reverse direction. Thus, the wet areas on the western coast of southeastern Asia, India, and what is called the Guinea Coast of West Africa are caused by the onshore flow of southwesterly winds that are nothing more than trade winds diverted from a "normal" pattern by the South Asian and West African monsoons.

The only other regions of high annual precipitation shown on the world map are narrow zones along the western coasts of North and South America between 40° and 60° of latitude. These areas reflect a combination of frequent onshore westerly airflow, considerable storminess, and mountain barriers running perpendicular to the direction of the prevailing westerly winds. The presence of these north–south mountain ranges near the coast restricts the precipitation to a relatively small area and creates a pronounced rain shadow effect to the east of the ranges.

The principal regions of sparse annual precipitation on the world map are found in three types of locations.

1. Dry lands are most prominent on the western sides of continents in subtropical latitudes (centered at 25° or 30°). High-pressure conditions dominate at these latitudes, particularly on the western sides of continents, which are closer to the normal positions of the subtropical high-pressure cells. High pressure means sinking air, which is not conducive to condensation and precipitation. The presence of cool ocean currents also contributes to the atmospheric stability and dryness of these regions. These dry zones are most extensive in North Africa and Australia primarily because of the blocking effect of landmasses or highlands to the east. (The presence of such landmasses prevents moisture from coming in from that direction.)

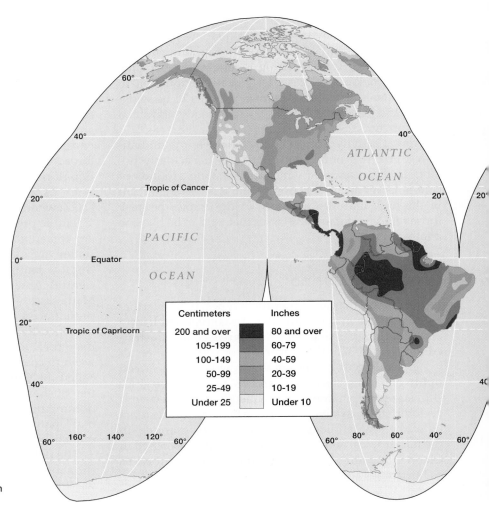

▶ **Figure 6-34** Average annual precipitation over the land areas of the world.

2. Dry regions in the midlatitudes are most extensive in central and southwestern Asia, but they also occur in western North America and southeastern South America. In each case, the dryness is due to lack of access for moist air masses. In the Asian situation, this lack of access is essentially a function of distance from any ocean where onshore airflow might occur. In North and South America, there are rain shadow situations in regions of predominantly westerly airflow.

3. In the high latitudes, there is not much precipitation anywhere. Water surfaces are scarce and cold, and so little opportunity exists for moisture to evaporate into the air. As a result, polar air masses have low absolute humidities and precipitation is slight. These regions are referred to accurately as cold deserts.

One further generalization on precipitation distribution is the contrast between continental margins and interiors. Because coastal regions are much closer to moisture sources, they usually receive more precipitation than interior regions.

Seasonal Precipitation Patterns

A geographic understanding of climate requires knowledge of seasonal as well as annual precipitation patterns. Over most of the globe, the amount of precipitation received in summer is considerably different from the amount received in winter. This variation is most pronounced over continental interiors, where strong summer heating at the surface induces greater instability and the potential for greater convective activity. Thus, in interior areas, most of the year's precipitation occurs during summer months, and winter is generally a time of anticyclonic conditions with diverging airflow.

Coastal areas often have a more balanced seasonal precipitation regime, which is again a reflection of their nearness to moisture sources.

Maps of average January and July precipitation provide a reliable indication of winter and summer

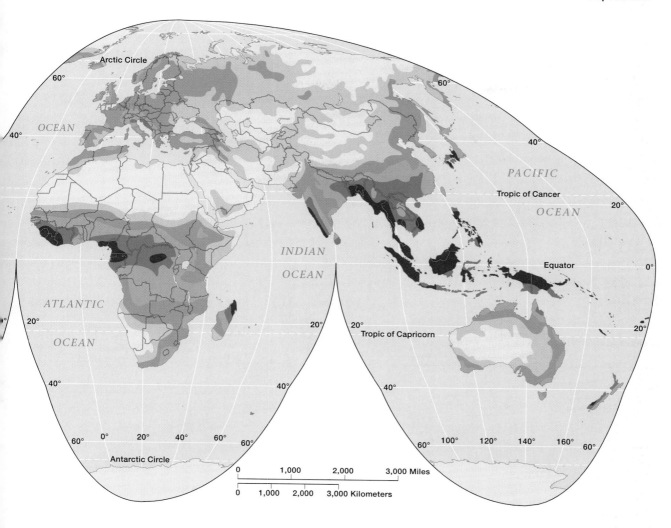

rain–snow conditions (Figure 6-35). Prominent generalizations that can be derived from the maps include the following.

1. The seasonal shifting of major pressure and wind systems, a shifting that follows the Sun (northward in July and southward in January), is mirrored in the displacement of wet and dry zones. This is seen most clearly in tropical regions, where the heavy rainfall belt of the ITCZ clearly migrates north and south in different seasons.

2. Summer is the time of maximum precipitation over most of the world. Northern Hemisphere regions experience heaviest rainfall in July, and Southern Hemisphere locations receive most precipitation in January. The only important exceptions to this generalization occur in relatively narrow zones along western coasts between about 35° and 60° of latitude, as illustrated for the United States in Figure 6-36. The same abnormal trend occurs in South America, New Zealand, and southernmost Australia. These regions experience the summer dryness associated with the seasonal shift of the STH.

3. The most conspicuous variation in seasonal precipitation is found, predictably, in monsoon regions (principally southern and eastern Asia, northern Australia, and West Africa), where summer tends to be very wet and winter is generally dry.

Precipitation Variability

The maps considered thus far all portray average conditions. The data on which they are based were gathered over decades, and thus the maps represent abstraction rather than reality. In any given year or any given season, the amount of precipitation may or may not be similar to the long-term average.

Precipitation variability is the expected departure from average precipitation in any given year, expressed as a percentage above or below average. For example, a precipitation variability of 20 percent means that a location expects to receive either 20 percent more or 20 percent less precipitation than average in any given year. If

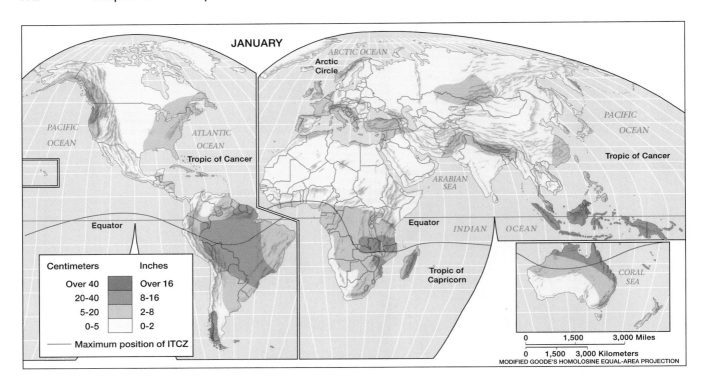

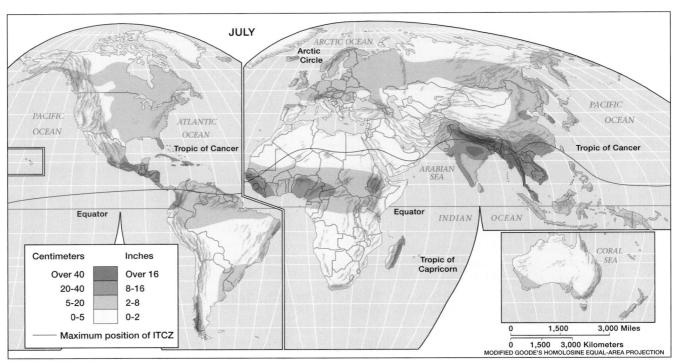

▲ **Figure 6-35**   Average January and July precipitation over the land areas of the world. The red line marks the typical maximum poleward position of the intertropical convergence zone (ITCZ).

a location has a long-term average annual precipitation of 50 cm (20″) and has a precipitation variability of 20%, the "normal" rainfall for a year would be either 40 cm (16″) or 60 cm (24″)—in the long run, the average comes out to 50 cm (20″).

Figure 6-37 reveals that regions of normally heavy precipitation experience the least variability and normally dry regions experience the most. Said another

way, dry regions experience great fluctuations in precipitation from one year to the next.

Acid Rain

One of the most vexing and perplexing environmental problems since the latter part of the twentieth century has been the rapidly increasing intensity, magnitude,

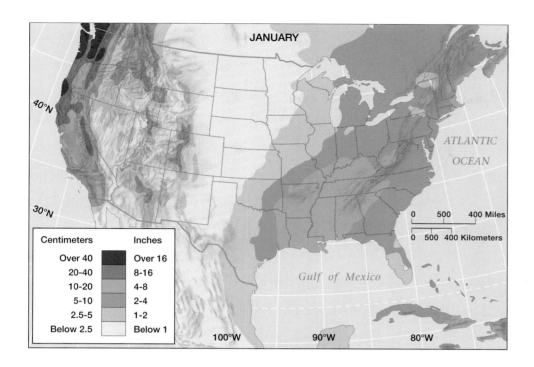

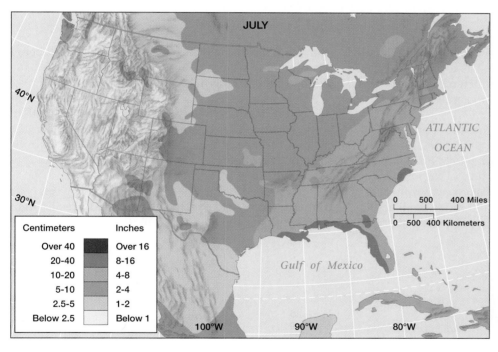

Figure 6-36 Average January and July precipitation in the United States. Winter precipitation is heaviest in the Pacific Northwest; summer rainfall is greatest in the Southeast.

and extent of **acid rain**—more generally called *acid precipitation* or *acid deposition*. This term refers to the deposition of either wet or dry acidic materials from the atmosphere on Earth's surface. Although most conspicuously associated with rainfall, the pollutants may fall to Earth with snow, sleet, hail, or fog or in the dry form of gases or particulate matter.

Sulfuric and nitric acids are the principal culprits recognized thus far. Evidence indicates that the principal human-induced sources are sulfur dioxide (SO_2) emissions from smokestacks (particularly electric utility companies in the United States, the smelting of metal ores in Canada), and nitrogen oxides (NO_x) from

motor vehicle exhaust. These and other emissions of sulfur and nitrogen compounds are expelled into the air, where they may be wafted hundreds or even thousands of kilometers by winds. During this time they may mix with atmospheric moisture to form the sulfuric and nitric acids that are precipitated sooner or later.

Acidity is measured on a *pH scale* based on the relative concentration of hydrogen ions (Figure 6-38). The scale ranges from 0 to 14, where the lower end represents extreme *acidity* (battery acid has a pH of 1) and the upper end extreme *alkalinity*. (Alkalinity is the opposite of acidity; a substance that is very acidic can also be characterized as being of very low alkalinity, and a

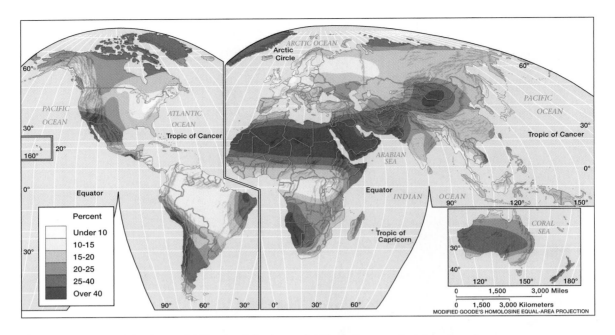

▲ **Figure 6-37** Precipitation variability. Precipitation variability is the expected departure from average precipitation in any given year. Dry regions (such as northern Africa, the Arabian peninsula, southwestern Africa, central Asia, and much of Australia) experience greater variability than humid areas (such as the eastern United States, northern South America, central Africa, and western Europe).

highly alkaline substance has very low acidity. The alkaline chemical lye, for instance, has a pH of 13.) The pH scale is a logarithmic scale, which means that a difference of one whole number on the scale reflects a 10-fold change in absolute values.

Rainfall in clean, dust-free air has a pH of about 5.6. Thus any precipitation that has a pH value of less than 5.6 is considered to be acid precipitation. Normal rain is slightly acidic (because slight amounts of carbon dioxide dissolve in rain drops to form *carbonic acid*, a mild acid), but acid rain can be as much as 100 times more acidic. Increasingly, precipitation with a pH of less than 4.5

(the level below which most fish perish) is being recorded. For example, around Washington D.C., the average pH of rain is 4.2 to 4.4 (Figure 6-39).

Many parts of Earth's surface have naturally alkaline soil or bedrock that neutralizes acid precipitation. Soils developed from limestone, for example, contain calcium carbonate, which can neutralize acid. Granitic soils, on the other hand, have no neutralizing component (Figure 6-40).

Damage from Acid Precipitation Acid precipitation is known to be a major hazard to the environment. The

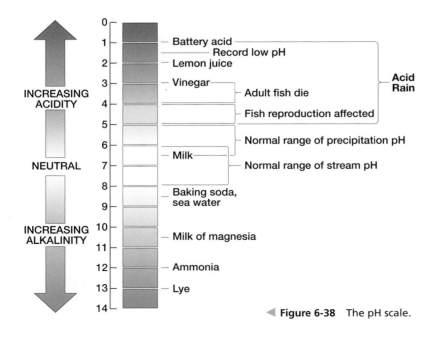

◀ **Figure 6-38** The pH scale.

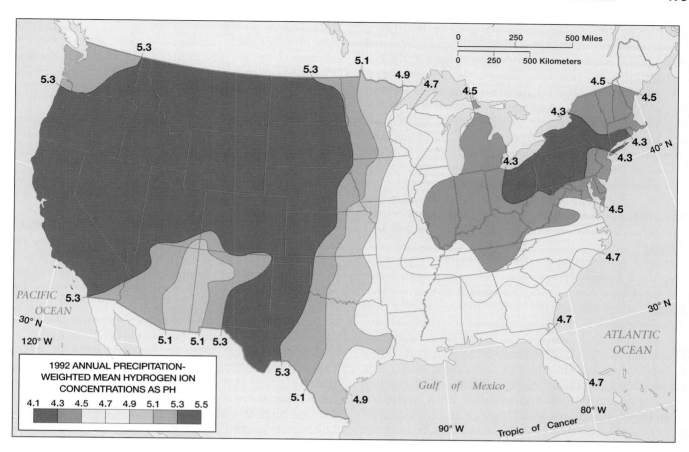

▲ **Figure 6-39**   Map showing acidity of rain in the conterminous United States. *(From Elaine McGee,* Acid Rain and Our Nation's Capital, *U.S. Geological Survey Publication 1995–394–904.)*

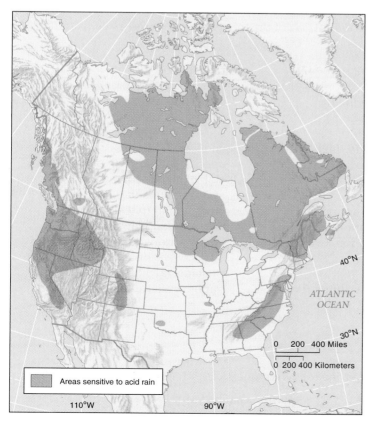

◀ **Figure 6-40**   Areas in the United States and Canada particularly sensitive to acid rain because of a scarcity of natural buffers.

most conspicuous damage is being done to aquatic ecosystems. Several hundred lakes in the eastern United States and Canada became biological deserts in the last quarter century, primarily due to acid rain. Forest diebacks are currently taking place on every continent except Antarctica. In some parts of eastern and central Europe, 30 to 50 percent of the forests have been affected or killed by acid rain. Even buildings and monuments are being destroyed; acid deposition has caused more erosion on the marble Parthenon in Athens in the last 30 years than in the previous 30 centuries.

One of the great complexities of the situation is that much of the pollution is deposited at great distances from its source. Downwind locations receive unwanted acid deposition from upwind origins. Thus Scandinavians and Germans complain about British pollution; Canadians blame U.S. sources; New Englanders accuse the Midwest.

One of the thorniest issues in North American international relations has been the Canadian dissatisfaction with the approach of the U.S. government in the 1980s toward mitigation of acid rain. Acid rain has been viewed by Canadians as a grave environmental concern, and it is believed that about half the acid rain falling on Canada comes from U.S. sources, particularly older coal-burning power plants in the Ohio and Tennessee River valleys.

In the United States, significant progress toward reducing emissions that cause acid rain has been made since Title IV of the 1990 Clean Air Act Amendments was implemented, creating the Acid Rain Program monitored by the Environmental Protection Agency (EPA). The program requires major reductions in SO_2 and NO_x, especially from coal-burning electricity-generating plants that annually produce about 70 percent of SO_2 emissions and 20 percent of NO_x emissions in the United States. The program has been quite successful. The EPA reports that by 2004, SO_2 emission had dropped more than 40 percent from 1980 levels and NO_x emissions have been reduced significantly as well, leading to reduced levels of acid rain in some regions of the country.

In 1991, Canada and the United States signed the bilateral Air Quality Agreement that addressed the issue of acid rain and transboundary air pollution. With full implementation of the agreement in 2010, SO_2 emissions should be reduced to 50 percent of their 1980 levels. In 2000, the United States and Canada signed Annex 3 to the Agreement, with the goal of reducing emission of both NO_x and volatile organic compounds (VOC) as well.

Acid rain is now clearly in the public consciousness. Progress is being made toward reducing the emissions that cause acid rain, but a sustained effort is still needed. Although the costs of reducing the acid rain problem are high, it is clear that the costs of not doing so will be exponentially greater.

Chapter 6 Learning Review

Key Terms

Before answering the study questions below, review the definitions of the following key terms (page references are provided for you):

absolute humidity *(p. 149)*
acid rain (acid deposition) *(p. 173)*
capacity *(p. 149)*
capillarity *(p. 143)*
cirrus clouds *(p. 156)*
condensation *(p. 144)*
condensation nuclei *(p. 153)*
convective lifting *(p. 167)*
convergent lifting *(p. 169)*
cumulonimbus clouds *(p. 156)*
cumulus clouds *(p. 156)*
dew *(p. 159)*
dew point (dew point temperature) *(p. 151)*
dry adiabatic rate *(p. 153)*
evaporation *(p. 144)*

evapotranspiration *(p. 147)*
fog *(p. 157)*
frontal lifting *(p. 169)*
hail *(p. 166)*
humidity *(p. 149)*
hydrogen bond *(p. 142)*
hydrologic cycle *(p. 146)*
isohyet *(p. 169)*
latent heat of condensation *(p. 144)*
latent heat of evaporation *(p. 145)*
latent heat of vaporization *(p. 144)*
lifting condensation level *(p. 153)*
orographic lifting *(p. 168)*
precipitation *(p. 162)*
precipitation variability *(p. 171)*
rain *(p. 165)*

rain shadow *(p. 168)*
relative humidity *(p. 149)*
saturated adiabatic rate *(p. 153)*
saturation vapor pressure *(p. 149)*
sensible temperature *(p. 151)*
snow *(p. 165)*
specific humidity *(p. 149)*
stable (air) *(p. 159)*
stratus clouds *(p. 156)*
sublimation *(p. 144)*
supercooled water *(p. 153)*
supersaturated (air) *(p. 153)*
surface tension *(p. 143)*
unstable (air) *(p. 161)*
vapor pressure *(p. 146)*

Study Questions for Key Concepts

After studying this chapter, you should be able to answer the following questions:

The Nature of Water: Commonplace but Unique (p. 141)

1. What is a *hydrogen bond* between water molecules?

2. Describe what happens to the density of water as it freezes.

3. What is meant by *surface tension* of water?

Phase Changes of Water (p. 143)
4. How do phase changes of water entail the exchange of heat? (In other words, explain *latent heat*.)
5. Why is evaporation a "cooling" process? Why is condensation a "warming" process?

Evaporation (p. 146)
6. Describe the conditions associated with relatively high rates of evaporation, and the conditions associated with relatively low rates of evaporation.
7. What is *evapotranspiration*?

Measures of Humidity (p. 149)
8. What is *absolute humidity*? *Specific humidity*?
9. What is meant by *saturation vapor pressure*?
10. What determines the water vapor "capacity" of air?
11. Describe and explain what is meant when we say that the *relative humidity* of the air is 50 percent.
12. What happens to the relative humidity of a parcel of air when the temperature decreases? Why?
13. What happens to the relative humidity of a parcel of air when the temperature increases? Why?
14. What is the *dew point* temperature?
15. Explain *sensible temperature*.

Condensation (p. 151)
16. Under what circumstances can air become *super-saturated*?
17. Explain the role of *condensation nuclei* to the condensation process.
18. How is it possible for air to become *supercooled*?

Adiabatic Processes (p. 153)
19. Which cooling process in the atmosphere is responsible for the formation of most clouds (and nearly all clouds that produce precipitation)?
20. What happens to the relative humidity of an unsaturated parcel of air as it rises? Why?
21. What is the relationship of the dew point temperature of a parcel of air to its *lifting condensation level*?
22. Why does a rising parcel of unsaturated air cool more rapidly than a rising parcel of saturated air (in which condensation is taking place)? In other words, explain why there is a *dry adiabatic rate* and a *saturated adiabatic rate*.
23. Why doesn't descending air form clouds?

Clouds (p. 155)
24. Describe the three main forms of clouds.
25. Identify the four families of clouds.
26. Describe the four principal types of fogs.

The Buoyancy of Air (p. 159)
27. What is the difference between *stable air* and *unstable air*?
28. What conditions make a parcel of air unstable?
29. Why might the stability of a rising parcel of air change above the lifting condensation level?
30. Are *stratus* clouds associated with stable or unstable air? Are *cumulus* clouds associated with stable or unstable air?

Precipitation (p. 162)
31. How is hail related to atmospheric instability?

Atmospheric Lifting and Precipitation (p. 167)
32. Describe the four main lifting mechanisms of air.
33. What is a *rain shadow* and why does one form? In your answer, explain the role of adiabatic temperature changes, as well as changes in both the relative humidity and the actual water vapor content of the air, in the formation of rain shadows.

Global Distribution of Precipitation (p. 169)
34. Using the global map of average annual precipitation (Figure 6-34), explain the causes of:
   - Wet regions within the tropics
   - Wet regions along the west coasts of continents in the midlatitudes (between about 40 and 60° N and S)
   - Dry regions along the west coasts of continents in the subtropics (at about 20 to 30° N and S)
   - Dry areas within the midlatitudes
35. Using the maps of average January and July precipitation (Figure 6-35) contrast and explain the seasonal rainfall patterns in central Africa.
36. What is meant by the term *precipitation variability*?
37. What is the general relationship of precipitation variability to average annual precipitation?

Acid Rain (p. 172)
38. What are some of the circumstances that cause *acid rain*?

Additional Resources

Books:
Aguado, Edward, and James E. Burt. *Understanding Weather and Climate*, 4th ed. Upper Saddle River, NJ: Pearson-Prentice Hall, 2007.
Hamblyn, Richard. *The Invention of Clouds: How an Amateur Meteorologist Forged the Language of the Skies*. New York: Farrar, Straus and Giroux, 2001.
Ludlum, David M. *The Audubon Society Field Guide to North American Weather*. New York: Alfred A. Knopf, 1991.
Park, Chris. *Acid Rain*. New York: Methuen, 1988.

Internet Sites:
Naval Research Laboratory
http://www.nrlmry.navy.mil/sat_products.html
The Naval Research Laboratory (NRL) provides a wide range of current satellite images and satellite images with weather map overlays. The NRL also maintains an extensive archive of past satellite images of tropical cyclones.

Water Resources of the United States
http://water.usgs.gov/
This site has links to data and information about water quality, acid rain, and streamflow.

7
Transient Atmospheric Flows and Disturbances

In Chapter 5 we explored the general circulation of the atmosphere, mainly the broad-scale wind and pressure systems of the troposphere. Now we sharpen our focus a bit.

Over most of Earth, particularly in the midlatitudes, day-to-day weather conditions are accompanied by phenomena that are more limited than general circulation phenomena in both magnitude and permanence. These more limited phenomena involve the flow of air masses as well as a variety of atmospheric disturbances usually referred to as *storms*. Both flows and disturbances are secondary features of the general circulation of the atmosphere. They move in with the general circulation as migratory entities that persist for a relatively short time before dissipating.

Air masses and storms, then, are transient and temporary, but in some parts of the world they are so frequent and dominating that their interactions are major determinants of weather and, to a lesser extent, climate.

The Impact of Storms on the Landscape

Storms are usually very dramatic phenomena. Under ordinary nonstormy conditions, the atmosphere tends to be quietly inconspicuous, but storms bring excitement. The combination of expansive clouds, swirling winds, and abundant precipitation—often accompanied by thunder and lightning—that characterizes many storms makes us acutely aware of the awesome power latent in the gaseous environment we inhabit.

Even the mildest atmospheric disturbance is likely to influence our immediate activities, as when, for example, we seek shelter from wind or rain. The landscape may be significantly transformed in the short run, particularly if the storm is a violent one. Flooded streets, windblown trees, and darkened skies are prominent examples of the changes that occur.

The long-run impact of storms on the landscape is often equally notable. Damage varies with the intensity of the disturbance, but such things as uprooted trees, accelerated erosion, flooded valleys, destroyed buildings, and decimated crops are likely to result. Most storms also have a positive long-term effect on the landscape, however, as they promote diversity in the vegetative cover, increase the size of lakes and ponds,

◀ Thunderstorm over Canyonlands National Park, Utah. *(Getty Images Inc.—Stone Allstock.)*

and stimulate plant growth via the moisture they add to the ground.

Air Masses

Although the troposphere is a continuous body of mixed gases that surrounds the planet, it is by no means a uniform blanket of air. Instead, it is composed of many large, variable parcels of air that are distinct from one another. Such parcels are referred to as **air masses**.

Characteristics

To be distinguishable, an air mass must meet three requirements:

1. It must be large. A typical air mass is more than 1600 kilometers (1000 miles) across and several kilometers deep (Figure 7-1).
2. It must have uniform properties in the horizontal dimension. This means that at any given altitude in the mass, its physical characteristics—primarily temperature, humidity, and stability—are relatively homogeneous. As an example, this homogeneity is shown for temperature in Figure 7-1.
3. It must be a recognizable entity and travel as one. Thus, it must be distinct from the surrounding air, and when it moves, it must retain its original characteristics and not be torn apart by differences in airflow.

Origin

An air mass develops its characteristics by remaining over a uniform land or sea surface long enough to acquire the temperature/humidity/stability characteristics of the surface. The stagnation needs to last for only a few days if the underlying surface has prominent temperature and moisture characteristics. For the air to stagnate, it needs to be relatively stable. Highly unstable air does not form a true air mass because it is constantly moving upward, away from the surface whose characteristics it is to acquire. Most air masses, then, form in areas with anticyclonic conditions.

The formation of air masses is normally associated with what are called *source regions:* regions of Earth's surface that are particularly well suited to generate air masses. Such regions must be extensive, physically uniform, and associated with air that is stationary or anticyclonic. Ideal source regions are ocean surfaces and

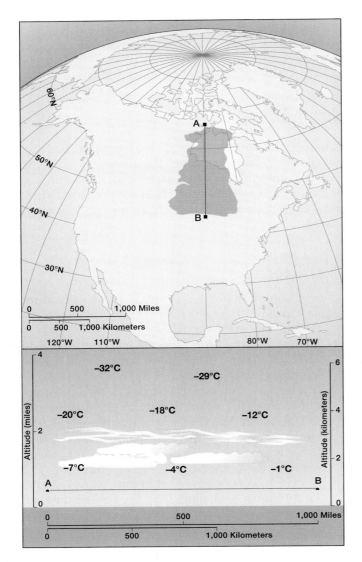

▲ Figure 7-1 A schematic representation of a large air mass developed over central Canada. The cross section along line AB shows temperatures for various parts of the air mass. The general uniformity of temperatures in the horizontal dimension is clear.

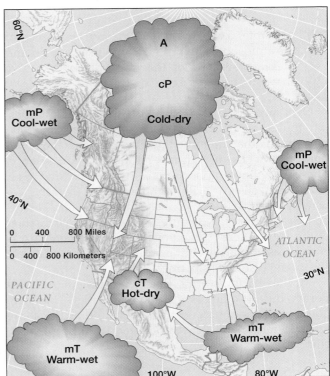

▲ Figure 7-2 Major air masses that affect North America and their generalized paths. (For an explanation of the air-mass codes A, cP, mP, cT, and mT, see Table 7-1.)

extensive flat land areas that have a uniform covering of snow, forest, or desert.

Figure 7-2 portrays the principal recognized source regions for air masses that affect North America. Warm-air masses can form in any season over the waters of the southern North Atlantic, the Gulf of Mexico/Caribbean Sea, and the southern North Pacific and in summer over the deserts of the southwestern United States and northwestern Mexico. Cold-air masses develop over the northern portions of the Atlantic and Pacific oceans and over the snow-covered lands of north-central Canada.

It may well be that the concept of source regions is of more theoretical value than actual value. A broader view, one subscribed to by many atmospheric scientists, holds that air masses can originate almost anywhere in

the low or high latitudes but rarely in the midlatitudes due to the prevailing westerlies where persistent wind would prevent air mass formation (Figure 7-3).

Classification

Air masses are classified on the basis of source region. The latitude of the source region correlates directly with the temperature of the air mass, and the nature of the surface strongly influences the humidity content of the air mass. Thus, a low-latitude air mass is warm or hot; a high-latitude one is cool or cold. If the air mass develops over a continental surface, it is likely to be dry; if it originates over an ocean, it is usually moist.

A one- or two-letter code is generally used to identify air masses. Although some authorities recognize other categories, the basic classification is sixfold, as shown in Table 7-1.

Movement and Modification

Some air masses remain in their source region for long periods, even indefinitely. In such cases, the weather associated with the air mass persists with little variation. Our interest, however, is in masses that leave their source region and move into other regions, particularly into the midlatitudes.

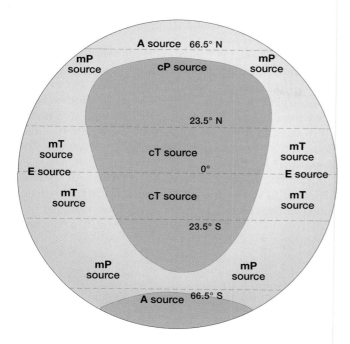

▲ **Figure 7-3** Schematic world map of air-mass source regions. Continents are shown in green and oceans in blue. The tropics and subtropics are important source regions as are the high latitudes. Air masses do not originate in the middle latitudes except under unusual circumstances.

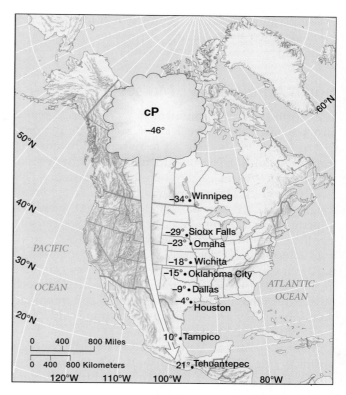

▲ **Figure 7-4** An example of temperatures resulting from a strong midwinter outburst of cP air from Canada. All temperatures are in degrees Celsius.

When an air mass departs from its source region, its structure begins to change, owing in part to thermal modification (heating or cooling from below), in part to dynamic modification (uplift, subsidence, convergence, turbulence), and perhaps also in part to addition or subtraction of moisture.

Once it leaves its source area, an air mass modifies the weather of the regions into which it moves: it takes source-region characteristics into other regions. A classic example of this modification is displayed in Figure 7-4, which diagrams a situation that may occur one or more times every winter. A midwinter outburst of continental polar (cP) air from northern Canada sweeps down across the central part of North America. With a source-region temperature of −46°C(−50°F) around Great Bear Lake, the air mass has warmed to −34°C (−30°F) by the time it reaches Winnipeg, Manitoba, and it continues to warm as it moves southward.

Throughout its southward course, the air mass becomes warmer, but it also brings some of the coldest weather that each of these places will receive all winter. Thus, the air mass is modified, but it also modifies the weather in all regions it passes through. (In summer, cP air is much less well developed and prominent, but occasionally it provides cooling relief to portions of eastern and central North America.)

TABLE 7-1 Simplified Classification of Air Masses			
Type	Code	Source Regions	Source-Region Properties
Arctic/Antarctic	A	Antarctica, Arctic Ocean and fringes, and Greenland	Very cold, very dry, very stable
Continental polar	cP	High-latitude plains of Eurasia and North America	Cold, dry, very stable
Maritime polar	mP	Oceans in vicinity of 50°–60° latitude	Cold, moist, relatively unstable
Continental tropical	cT	Low-latitude deserts	Hot, very dry, unstable
Maritime tropical	mT	Tropical and subtropical oceans	Warm, moist, of variable stability
Equatorial	E	Oceans near the equator	Warm, very moist, unstable

Temperature, of course, is only one of the characteristics modified by a moving air mass. There are also modifications in humidity and stability.

North American Air Masses

The North American continent is a prominent area of air-mass interaction. The lack of mountains trending east to west permits polar air to sweep southward and tropical air to flow northward unhindered by terrain, particularly over the eastern two-thirds of the continent (see Figure 7-2). Major north–south trending mountain ranges in the western part of the continent, however, impede the movement of the Pacific air masses, causing significant modification of their characteristics.

Continental polar air masses develop in central and northern Canada, and *Arctic* (A) air masses originate farther north. These two masses are similar to each other except that the latter is even colder and drier than the former. They are dominant features in winter with their cold, dry, stable nature.

Maritime polar (mP) air that affects North America normally originates as cold, dry, cP air and then moves off the land. Once over water, this air either stagnates or else moves slowly over the North Pacific or North Atlantic, acquiring its mP characteristics only in its low-altitude portion. Consequently, the lower layers are cool, moist, and relatively unstable, whereas conditions at higher altitudes in the air mass may be cold, dry, and stable. Pacific mP air normally brings widespread cloudiness and heavy precipitation to the mountainous coastal regions, but it is often severely modified in crossing the western ranges. By the time it reaches the interior of the continent, it has moderate temperatures and clear skies. In summer, the ocean is colder than the land, and so Pacific mP air produces fog and low stratus clouds along the coast but takes no distinctive weather conditions to the interior.

Air masses that develop over the North Atlantic are also cool, moist, and unstable. Except for occasional incursions into the mid-Atlantic coastal region, however, Atlantic mP air does not affect North America because the prevailing circulation of the atmosphere is westerly.

Maritime tropical (mT) air from the Atlantic/Caribbean/Gulf of Mexico is warm, moist, and unstable. It strongly influences weather and climate east of the Rockies in the United States, southern Canada, and much of Mexico, serving as the principal precipitation source in this broad region. It is more prevalent and extensive in summer than in winter, bringing periods of uncomfortable humid heat.

Pacific mT air originates over water in areas of anticyclonic subsidence, and so it is cooler, drier, and more stable than Atlantic mT air. The influence of the former is felt only in the southwestern United States and northwestern Mexico, where in winter this air produces some coastal fog and occasional moderate orographic rainfall if forced to ascend mountain slopes. It is also the source of some summer rains in the southwestern interior.

Continental tropical (cT) air is relatively unimportant in North America because its source region is not extensive and consists of varied terrain. There is no winter air-mass genesis in this northern Mexico/southwestern U.S. source region, but in summer hot, very dry, unstable cT air develops. It surges into the southern Great Plains area on occasion, bringing heat waves and drought conditions.

Equatorial (E) air affects North America only in association with hurricanes. It is similar to mT air except that E air provides an even more copious source of rain than does mT air because of high humidity and much instability.

Fronts

Cold Fronts and Warm Fronts

When unlike air masses meet, they do not mix readily; instead, a boundary zone called a **front** develops between them (Figure 7-5). A front should not be thought of as a simple two-dimensional boundary surface or an extensive zone of gradual transition. Rather, it consists of a relatively narrow but nevertheless three-dimensional zone of discontinuity within which the properties of the air change rapidly. A typical front is several kilometers or even tens of kilometers wide.

The frontal concept was developed by Norwegian meteorologists during World War I, and the term front was coined because these scientists considered the clash between unlike air masses to be analogous to a confrontation between opposing armies along a battle front. As the more "aggressive" air mass advances at the expense of the other, there is some mixing of the two within the frontal zone, but for the most part the air masses retain their separate identities as one is displaced by the other. Thus, the basic significance of a front is that it functions as a barrier between two air masses, preventing their mingling except in the narrow transition zone.

Because the most conspicuous difference between air masses is usually temperature, a front usually separates warm air from cool air. At any given altitude or at any given latitude, there is warm air on one side of the front and cool air on the other, with a fairly abrupt temperature gradient through the front. Air masses may also have different densities, humidity levels, and stability, of course. Frequently all these factors have a steep gradient through the front.

An important attribute of fronts is that they "lean" or slope upward from the surface, as Figure 7-5 shows. The slope of a front allows air to be uplifted and adiabatic cooling to take place. Indeed, fronts lean so much

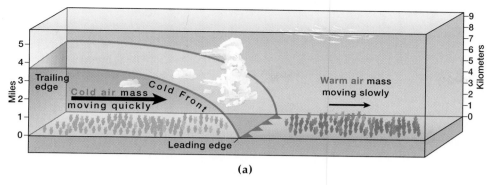

(a)

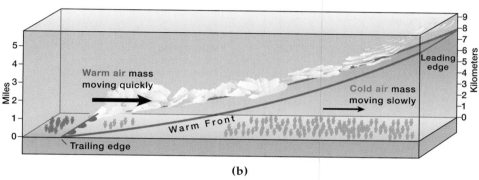

(b)

◀ **Figure 7-5** When unlike air masses come together, a front is formed. A front always slopes so that warmer air overlies cooler air. **(a)** When a cold-air mass is actively underriding a warm-air mass, a cold front is formed. **(b)** When a warm-air mass is actively overriding a cold-air mass, a warm front results. (In these diagrams, the vertical scale has been exaggerated.)

that they are much closer to horizontal than vertical. The normal slope of a front varies between 1:50 and 1:300, with an average of 1:150. This last ratio, for instance, means that 150 kilometers away from the surface position of the front, the front is at a height of only 1 kilometer above the ground. Because of this very low angle of slope (less than 1°), the steepness shown in most vertical diagrams of fronts is greatly exaggerated. A front always slopes so that warmer air overlies cooler air, which means that a *cold front* leans "backward" so that its lower altitude part (the "leading edge" in Figure 7-5a) precedes its higher altitude ("trailing edge") part, whereas a *warm front* leans "forward" so that the higher altitude part of the front (the "leading" edge in Figure 7-5b) is ahead of the lower altitude part ("trailing edge").

In some cases, a front remains stationary for a few hours or even a few days. More commonly, however, it is in more or less constant motion, shifting the position of the boundary between the air masses but maintaining its function as a barrier between them. Usually one air mass is displacing the other; thus, the front advances in the direction dictated by the movement of the more active air mass. Regardless of which air mass is advancing, it is always the warmer that rises over the cooler. The warmer, lighter air is inevitably forced aloft, and the cooler, denser mass functions as a wedge on which the lifting occurs.

Warm Fronts

A front formed by advancing warm air is called a **warm front**. Its slope is gentle, averaging about 1:200.

The warm air ascends over retreating cool air, with the temperature of the warm air decreasing adiabatically as the air rises. The usual result is clouds and precipitation. Because the frontal uplift is very gradual, clouds form slowly and there is not much turbulence. High-flying cirrus clouds may signal the approaching front many hours before it arrives. As the front comes closer to where the first cirrus clouds formed, the clouds become lower, thicker, and more extensive, typically developing into altocumulus or altostratus. Precipitation usually occurs broadly; it is likely to be protracted and gentle, without much convective activity. If the rising air is inherently unstable, however, precipitation can be showery and even violent. As illustrated in Figure 7-6, most precipitation falls ahead of the ground-level position of the moving front. The ground-level position of a warm front is portrayed on a weather map either by a red line (if color is used) or (more typically) by a solid black line along which black semicircles are located at regular intervals, with the semicircles extending in the direction toward which the front is moving (Figure 7-7).

Cold Fronts

A front formed by advancing cold air is called a **cold front**. Because there is friction between the ground surface and the lowest portion of the front, the advance of the lower portion is slowed relative to the upper portion. As a result, a cold front tends to become steeper as it moves forward and usually develops a protruding "nose" a few hundred meters above the ground (Figure 7-8). The average cold front is twice as steep as

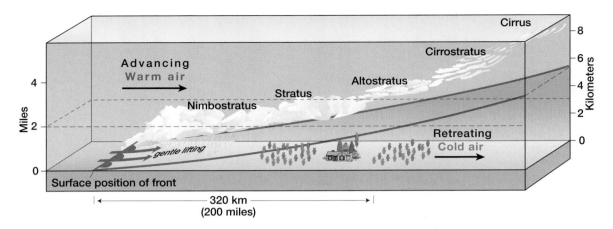

▲ **Figure 7-6**   Along a warm front, warm air rises above cooler air. Often widespread cloudiness and precipitation develop along and in advance of the ground-level position of the front. Higher and less dense clouds are often dozens or hundreds of kilometers ahead of the ground-level position of the front. (In this diagram, the vertical scale has been exaggerated.)

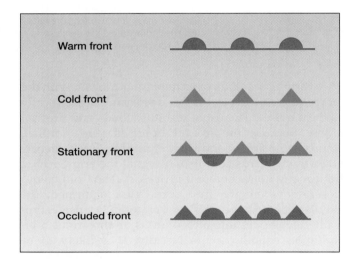

▲ **Figure 7-7**   Weather map symbols for fronts.

the average warm front, as Figure 7-5 indicates. Moreover, cold fronts normally move faster than warm fronts, this difference represented by the black arrows of different lengths in Figure 7-5. This combination of steeper slope and faster advance leads to rapid lifting of the warm air ahead of the cold front. The rapid lifting often makes the warm air very unstable, and the result is blustery and violent weather along the cold front. Vertically developed clouds are common, with considerable turbulence and showery precipitation. Both clouds and precipitation tend to be concentrated along and immediately behind the ground-level position of the front. Precipitation is usually of higher intensity but shorter duration than that associated with a warm front.

On a weather map, the ground-level position of a cold front is shown either by a blue line or a solid black line studded at intervals with solid triangles that extend

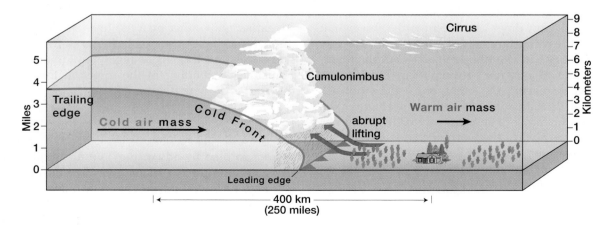

▲ **Figure 7-8**   As a cold front advances, the warm air ahead of it is forced upward by the cold air behind the front. This displacement often creates cloudiness and relatively heavy precipitation along and immediately behind the ground-level position of the front. (In this diagram, the vertical scale has been exaggerated.)

in the direction toward which the front is moving (see Figure 7-7).

Stationary Fronts

When neither air mass displaces the other, their common boundary is called a **stationary front.** It is difficult to generalize about the weather along such a front, but often gently rising warm air produces limited precipitation similar to that along a warm front. As Figure 7-7 shows, stationary fronts are portrayed on a weather map by a combination of warm and cold front symbols.

Occluded Fronts

A fourth type of front, called an *occluded front*, is formed when a cold front overtakes a warm front. The development of occluded fronts is discussed later in this chapter.

Atmospheric Disturbances

We now turn our attention to the various kinds of atmospheric disturbances that occur within the general circulation. Most of these disturbances involve unsettled and even violent atmospheric conditions and are referred to as *storms*. Some, however, produce calm, clear, quiet weather that is quite the opposite of stormy. The following are common characteristics of atmospheric disturbances in general:

1. They are smaller than the components of the general circulation, although they are extremely variable in size.
2. They are migratory and transient.
3. They have a relatively brief duration, persisting for only a few minutes, a few hours, or a few days.
4. They produce characteristic and relatively predictable weather conditions.

Midlatitude Disturbances The middle latitudes are the principal battleground of tropospheric phenomena: where polar and tropical air masses meet and come into conflict, where most fronts occur, and where weather is most dynamic and changeable from season to season and from day to day. Many kinds of atmospheric disturbances are associated with the midlatitudes, but two of these—*midlatitude cyclones* and *midlatitude anticyclones*—are much more important than the others because of their size and prevalence.

Tropical Disturbances The low latitudes are characterized by monotony—the same weather day after day, week after week, month after month. Almost the only breaks are provided by transient atmospheric disturbances, of which by far the most significant are *tropical cyclones* (known as *hurricanes* when they intensify), but also less dramatic disturbances known as *easterly waves*.

Localized Severe Weather Other localized atmospheric disturbances occur in many parts of the world. Short-lived but sometimes severe atmospheric disturbances such as *thunderstorms* and *tornadoes* often develop in conjunction with other kinds of storms.

Midlatitude Cyclones

Midlatitude Cyclones

Probably most significant of all atmospheric disturbances are **midlatitude cyclones**. Throughout the midlatitudes, they dominate weather maps, are basically responsible for most day-to-day weather changes, and bring precipitation to much of the populated portions of the planet. Consisting of large, migratory low-pressure systems, they are usually called *depressions* in Europe and sometimes referred to as either *lows, wave cyclones,* or *extratropical cyclones* in the United States.

Midlatitude cyclones are associated primarily with air-mass convergence and conflict in regions between about 35° and 70° of latitude. Thus, they are found almost entirely within the band of westerly winds. Their general path of movement is toward the east, which explains why weather forecasting in the midlatitudes is essentially a west-facing vocation.

Because each midlatitude cyclone differs from all others in greater or lesser detail, any description must be a general one only. The discussions that follow, then, pertain to "typical" or idealized conditions. Moreover, these conditions are presented as Northern Hemisphere phenomena. For the Southern Hemisphere, the patterns of isobars, fronts, and wind flow should be visualized as mirror images of the Northern Hemisphere patterns.

Characteristics

A typical mature midlatitude cyclone has a diameter of 1600 kilometers (1000 miles) or so. It is essentially a vast cell of low-pressure air, with ground-level pressure in the center typically between 990 and 1000 millibars. The system (shown by closed isobars on a weather map, as in Figure 7-9a) usually tends toward an oval shape, with the long axis trending northeast–southwest. Often a clear-cut pressure trough extends southwesterly from the center.

Midlatitude cyclones have a converging counterclockwise circulation pattern in the Northern Hemisphere. This wind flow pattern attracts cool air from

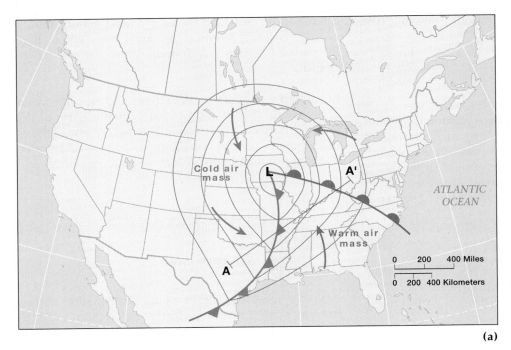

(a)

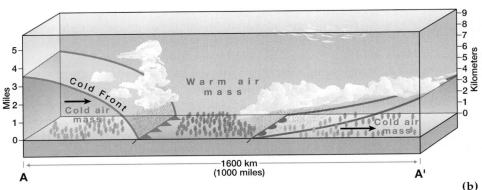

(b)

�◀ **Figure 7-9**   A map **(a)** and a cross section **(b)** of a typical mature midlatitude cyclone. In the Northern Hemisphere, there is usually a cold front trailing to the southwest and a warm front extending toward the east. Arrows in (b) indicate the direction of frontal movement.

the north and warm air from the south. The convergence of these unlike air masses characteristically creates two fronts: a cold front that extends to the southwest from the center of the cyclone and runs along the pressure trough extending from the center of the storm, and a warm front extending eastward from the center and running along another, usually weaker, pressure trough. These two fronts divide the cyclone into a *cool sector* north and west of the center and a *warm sector* to the south and east. At ground level, the cool sector is the larger of the two, but aloft the warm sector is more extensive. This size relationship exists because both fronts lean over the cool air. Thus, the cold front slopes upward toward the northwest, and the warm front slopes upward toward the northeast, as Figure 7-9b shows.

Clouds and precipitation develop in the zones within a midlatitude cyclone where air is rising. Because warm air rises along both fronts, the typical result is two zones of cloudiness and precipitation that overlap

around the center of the storm (where air is rising in the center of the low pressure cell) and extend outward in the general direction of the fronts. Along and immediately behind the ground-level position of the cold front (the steeper of the two fronts), a band of cumuliform clouds usually yields showery precipitation. The air rising more gently along the more gradual slope of the warm front produces a more extensive expanse of horizontally developed clouds, perhaps with widespread, protracted, low-intensity precipitation (Figure 7-10). In both cases, most of the precipitation originates in the warm air rising above the fronts and falls down through the front to reach the ground in the cool sector.

This precipitation pattern does not mean that all of the cool sector has unsettled weather and that the warm sector experiences clear conditions throughout. Although most frontal precipitation falls within the cool sector, the general area to the north, northwest, and west of the center of the cyclone is frequently cloudless as soon as the cold front has moved on. Thus,

◀ **Figure 7-10** A large midlatitude cyclone centered near Lake Michigan. The band of clouds extending down across the southern states to the west marks the cold front. *(SeaWiFS Project, NASA/Goddard Space Flight Center/ORBIMAGE.)*

much of the cool sector is typified by clear, cold, stable air. In contrast, the air of the warm sector is often moist and tending toward instability, and so thermal convection and surface-wind convergence may produce sporadic thunderstorms. Also, sometimes one or more *squall lines* of intense thunderstorms develop in the warm sector in advance of the cold front.

Weather Changes with the Passing of a Front

When a front passes through a region, abrupt weather changes normally occur. For example, with the passage of a cold front (see Figures 7-8 and 7-9), we note the following:

1. The temperature decreases sharply.
2. Winds shift from southerly ahead of the front to northwesterly following it (in the Northern Hemisphere).
3. The front is in a pressure trough, so pressure falls as the front approaches and rises after it passes.
4. Generally clear skies are replaced by cloudiness and precipitation at the front.

Similar changes, although of lesser magnitude, occur with the passage of a warm front.

Movements

Midlatitude cyclones are essentially transient features, on the move throughout their existence. There are four kinds of movement involved (Figure 7-11):

1. The whole system moves as a major disturbance in the westerlies, traversing the middle latitudes generally from west to east. The rate of movement averages 32 to 48 kilometers (20 to 30 miles) per hour, which means that the storm can cross the United States in some three to four days. It typically moves faster in winter than in summer.
2. The system has a cyclonic wind circulation, with air generally converging counterclockwise from all sides in the Northern Hemisphere.
3. The cold front normally advances faster than the storm is moving. Thus, it swings counterclockwise around its pivot in the center, increasingly moving into and displacing the warm sector.
4. The warm front usually advances more slowly than the storm. This difference in speed causes the front to lag behind and has the effect of seeming to swing clockwise in the direction of the advancing cold front. (This is only an apparent motion, however. In reality, the warm front is moving west to east, just like every other part of the system.)

The route of a cyclone is likely to be undulating and erratic, although it moves generally from west to east, often in association with the path of the jet stream.

Life Cycle

Cyclogenesis A typical midlatitude cyclone develops from origin to maturity in three to six days and from maturity to dissipation in about the same length of time. Most begin as "waves" (hence the alternative name *wave cyclone*) along the polar front, which as we saw in Chapter 5 is the contact zone between the relatively cold air of the polar easterlies and the relatively warm air of the westerlies. The opposing air flows normally have a relatively smooth linear motion on either side of the polar front (Figure 7-12a). On occasion, however, the smooth frontal surface may be

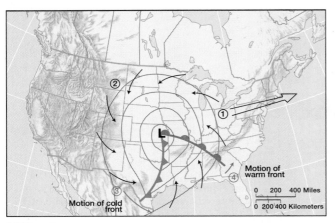

(a) Day 1

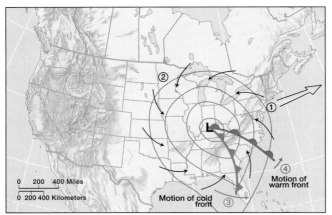

(b) Day 2

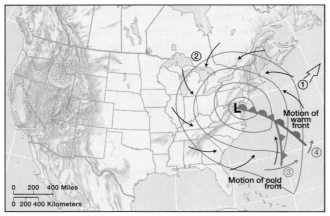

(c) Day 3

▲ **Figure 7-11** **(a)** Four varieties of motion occur in a typical midlatitude cyclone: (1) The entire system moves west to east in the general flow of the westerlies; (2) there is cyclonic counterclockwise airflow; (3) the cold front advances; (4) the warm front advances. **(b and c)** Days 2 and 3: because the cold front is traveling faster than the warm front, the distance between the two decreases over time. On day 3, the storm has started to occlude.

distorted into a wave shape (Figure 7-12b). Various ground factors—such as topographic irregularities, temperature contrasts between sea and land, or the

influence of ocean currents—can apparently initiate a wave along the front, but it is believed that the most common cause of *cyclogenesis* (the birth of cyclones) is upper troposphere conditions in the vicinity of the polar front jet stream.

There appears to be a close relationship between upper-level airflow and ground-level disturbances. When the upper airflow is *zonal*—by which we mean relatively straight from west to east—ground-level cyclonic activity is unlikely. When winds aloft behave as shown in Figure 7-13, meandering north to south (this pattern is called *meridional airflow*), large waves of alternating pressure troughs and ridges are formed and cyclonic activity at ground level is intensified. As seen in Figure 7-13, most midlatitude cyclones are centered below the polar front jet stream axis and downstream from an upper-level pressure trough.

A cyclone is unlikely to develop at ground level unless there is divergence above it. In other words, the convergence of air near the ground must be supported by divergence aloft. Such divergence can be related to changes in either speed or direction of the wind flow, but it nearly always involves broad north-to-south meanders in the Rossby waves and the jet stream (Figure 7-14).

Cyclogenesis also occurs on the leeward side of mountains. A low-pressure area drifting with the westerlies becomes weaker when it crosses a mountain range. As it ascends the range, the column of air compresses and spreads, slowing down its counterclockwise spin. When descending the leeward side, the air column stretches vertically and contracts horizontally. This change in shape causes it to spin faster and may initiate cyclonic development even if it were not a full-fledged cyclone before. This chain of events happens with some frequency in winter on the eastern flanks of the Rocky Mountains, particularly in Colorado, and with lesser frequency on the eastern side of the Appalachian Mountains, in North Carolina and Virginia. Cyclones formed in this way typically move toward the east and northeast and often bring heavy rain or snowstorms to the northeastern United States and southeastern Canada.

Occlusion   Ultimately, the storm dissipates because the cold front overtakes the warm front. As the two fronts come closer and closer together (Figure 7-12c-e), the warm sector at the ground is increasingly displaced, forcing more and more warm air aloft. When the cold front catches up with the warm front, warm air is no longer in contact with Earth's surface and an **occluded front** is formed (Figure 7-15). This **occlusion** process usually results in a short period of intensified precipitation and wind until eventually all the warm sector is forced aloft and the ground-level low-pressure center is surrounded on all sides by cool air. This sequence of events weakens the pressure gradient and shuts off the storm's energy and air lifting mechanism so that it dies out (Figure 7-12f).

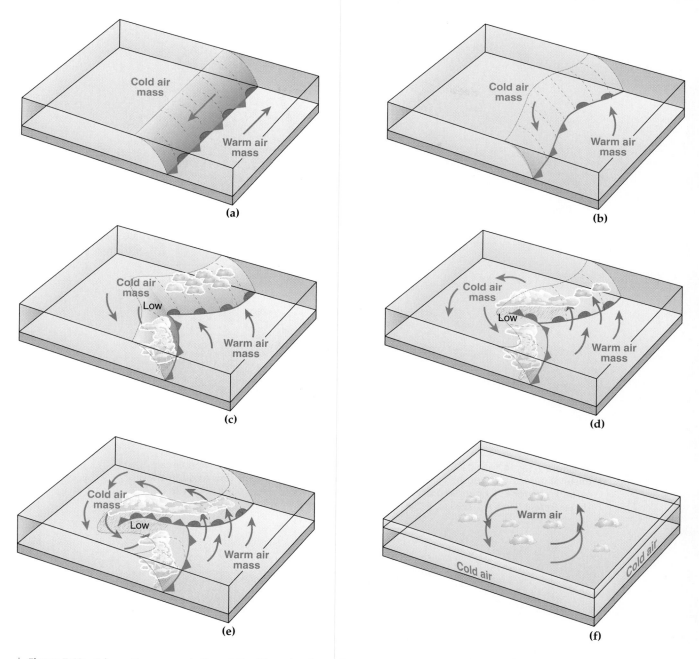

▲ **Figure 7-12** Schematic representation of the life cycle of a midlatitude cyclone. **(a)** Front develops. **(b)** Wave appears along front. **(c)** Cyclonic circulation is well developed. **(d)** Occlusion begins. **(e)** Occluded front is fully developed. **(f)** Cyclone dissipates. *(After Edward J. Tarbuck and Frederick K. Lutgens, The Atmosphere, 7th ed., Prentice Hall, Upper Saddle River, NJ, 1998, p. 363.)*

Occurrence and Distribution

At any given time, from 6 to 15 midlatitude cyclones exist in the Northern Hemisphere midlatitudes, and an equal number in the Southern Hemisphere. They occur at scattered but irregular intervals throughout the zone of the westerlies.

In each hemisphere, these migratory disturbances are more numerous, better developed, and faster moving in winter than in summer. They also follow much more equatorward tracks in winter. In the Southern Hemisphere, the Antarctic continent provides a prominent year-round source of cold air, and so vigorous cyclones are almost as numerous in summer as in winter. The summer storms are farther poleward than their winter cousins, however, and are mostly over the Southern Ocean. Thus, they have little effect on land areas.

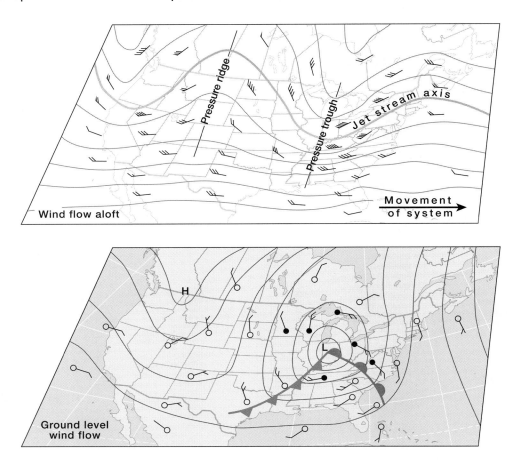

▲ **Figure 7-13**   A typical winter situation in which the upper-level airflow is meridional (meanders north and south), creating standing waves aloft and cyclonic flow at ground level. *(After Frederick K. Lutgens and Edward J. Tarbuck,* The Atmosphere, *7th ed., Prentice Hall, Upper Saddle River, NJ, 1998, p. 248.)*

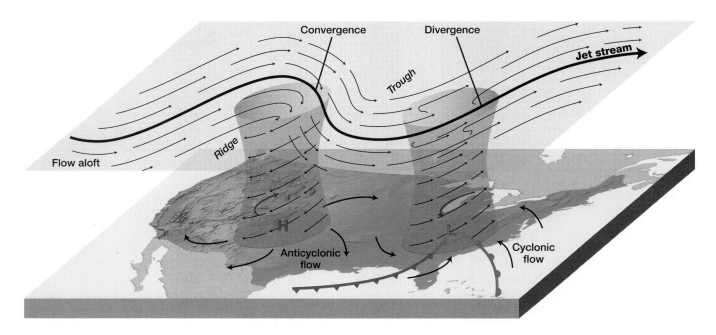

▲ **Figure 7-14**   An idealized depiction of how convergence and divergence aloft support anticyclonic and cyclonic circulation at ground level. *(After Frederick K. Lutgens and Edward J. Tarbuck,* The Atmosphere, *9th ed., Upper Saddle River, NJ: Prentice Hall, 2004.)*

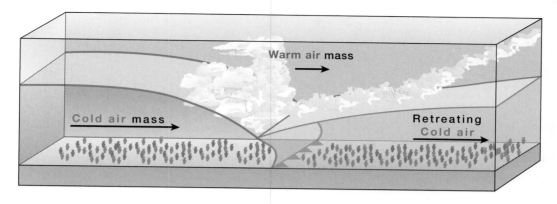

▲ **Figure 7-15** An occluded front develops when the leading edge of a cold front catches up with the trailing edge of a warm front, lifting all of the warm air off the ground.

Midlatitude Anticyclones

Another major disturbance in the general flow of the westerlies is the **midlatitude anticyclone**, frequently referred to simply as a *high* (H). This is an extensive, migratory high-pressure cell of the midlatitudes (Figure 7-16). Typically it is larger than a midlatitude cyclone and generally moves west to east with the westerlies.

Characteristics

As with any other high-pressure center, a midlatitude anticyclone has air converging into it from above, subsiding, and diverging at the surface, clockwise in the Northern Hemisphere and counterclockwise in the Southern Hemisphere. No air-mass conflict or surface convergence is involved, and so anticyclones contain no fronts (the fronts shown in Figure 7-16 are outside the high-pressure system). The weather is clear and dry with little or no opportunity for cloud

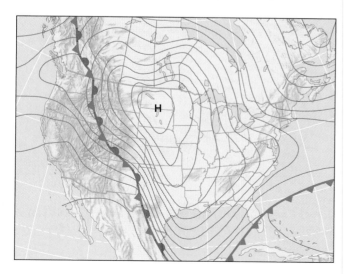

▲ **Figure 7-16** A typical well-developed midlatitude anticyclone centered over the Dakotas. Both fronts shown here are considered to be outside the high-pressure system.

formation. Wind movement is very limited near the center of an anticyclone but increases progressively outward. Particularly along the eastern margin (the leading edge) of the system, there may be strong winds. In winter, anticyclones are characterized by very low temperatures.

Anticyclones move toward the east either at the same rate as or a little slower than midlatitude cyclones. Unlike cyclones, however, anticyclones are occasionally prone to stagnate and remain over the same region for several days. This stalling brings clear, stable, dry weather to the affected region, which enhances the likelihood that air pollutants will become concentrated. Such stagnation may block the eastward movement of cyclonic storms, causing protracted precipitation in some other region while the anticyclonic region remains dry.

Relationships of Cyclones and Anticyclones

Midlatitude cyclones and anticyclones alternate with one another in irregular sequence around the world in the midlatitudes (Figure 7-17). Each can occur independently of the other, but there is often a functional relationship between them. This relationship can be seen when an anticyclone closely follows a cyclone, as diagrammed in Figure 7-18. The winds diverging from the eastern margin of the high fit into the flow of air converging into the western side of the low. It is easy to visualize the anticyclone as a polar air mass having the cold front of the cyclone as its leading edge.

Minor Tropical Disturbances: Easterly Waves

An **easterly wave** is a long but weak migratory, low-pressure system that may occur almost anywhere between 5° and 30° of latitude (Figure 7-19). They are a common kind of *tropical disturbance,* usually consisting

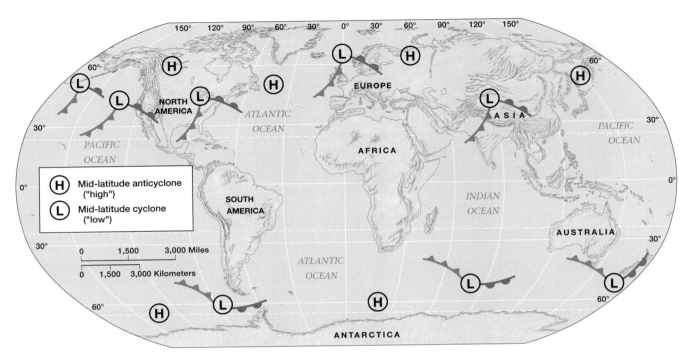

▲ **Figure 7-17** At any given time, the midlatitudes are dotted with midlatitude cyclones and anticyclones. This map depicts a hypothetical situation in January. Note the orientation of fronts in the Southern Hemisphere storms.

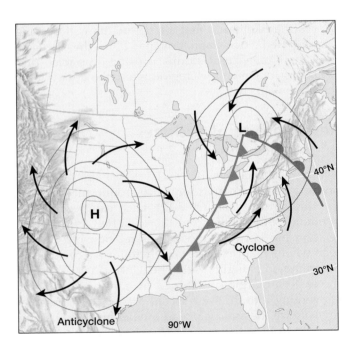

▲ **Figure 7-18** Midlatitude cyclones and anticyclones often occur in juxtaposition in the middle latitudes.

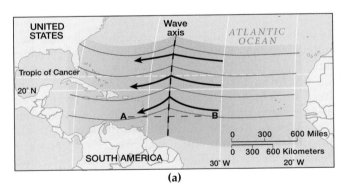

(a)

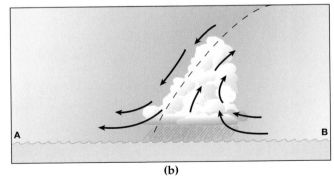

(b)

▲ **Figure 7-19** Diagrammatic map view **(a)** and cross section **(b)** of an easterly wave. The arrows indicate general direction of airflow.

of a band of small thunderstorms with little or no cyclonic rotation. Easterly waves are usually several hundred kilometers long and nearly always oriented north–south. They drift slowly westward in the flow of the trade winds, bringing characteristic weather with them. Ahead of the wave is fair weather with divergent airflow. Behind the wave, convergent conditions prevail, with moist air being uplifted to yield convective thunderstorms and sometimes widespread cloudiness. There is little or no temperature change with the passage of easterly waves.

Most of the easterly waves that move across the North Atlantic originate over North Africa, then move out over the Atlantic in the trade winds. The vast majority of easterly waves weaken and die out over the ocean, but a small percentage intensify into more powerful tropical cyclones—our next topic.

Major Tropical Disturbances: Hurricanes

Hurricanes

Tropical cyclones are intense, low-pressure disturbances that develop in the tropics and occasionally move poleward into the midlatitudes. Intense tropical cyclones are known by different names in different parts of the world: **hurricanes** in North and Central America, *typhoons* in the western North Pacific, *baguios* in the Philippines, and simply *cyclones* in the Indian Ocean and Australia. Hurricanes are considerably smaller than midlatitude cyclones, typically having a

diameter of between 160 and 1000 kilometers (100 and 600 miles; Figure 7-20).

Tropical cyclones develop from incipient low-pressure perturbations in trade-wind flow, generally called *tropical disturbances* by the U.S. National Weather Service. About 100 of these are identified each year over the tropical North Atlantic, but only a few strengthen into hurricanes. Three categories of tropical disturbances are recognized on the basis of wind speed:

1. A **tropical depression** has wind speeds of less than 33 knots (61 kilometers or 38 miles per hour), but has developed a closed wind circulation pattern.
2. A **tropical storm** has winds between 34 and 63 knots (63 and 117 kilometers or 39 and 73 miles per hour).
3. A hurricane has winds greater than 64 knots (119 kilometers or 74 miles per hour).

When a tropical depression's winds reach a speed of 34 knots (the threshold for it to be classed as a *tropical storm*), it is assigned a name from an alphabetical list that is prepared in advance. Each of the three U.S. tropical storm tracking centers—at Miami, Honolulu, and Guam—keeps a separate list of names for storms originating in their area (after a few years, hurricane and typhoon names are used again unless the storm was especially notable—such as Katrina and Andrew—in which case the name is retired from the list). The Miami center names and tracks tropical storms in the Atlantic,

▲ **Figure 7-20** Satellite image of Hurricane Katrina at 9:15 A.M. eastern time on August 29, 2005. *(NOAA.)*

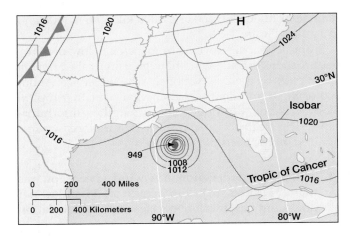

▲ **Figure 7-21** Simplified weather map of Hurricane Andrew on August 25, 1992. The isobars show a very steep gradient around the low-pressure center. *(After National Weather Service.)*

Caribbean, and the Pacific as far as 140° west longitude. The Honolulu center is responsible for storms between that meridian and the International Date Line. The Joint Typhoon Warning Center on Guam takes over in the area west of the date line.

Characteristics

Hurricanes (as we generally refer to tropical cyclones in this chapter) consist of prominent low-pressure centers that are essentially circular, with a steep pressure gradient outward from the center (Figure 7-21). As a result, strong winds spiral inward. Winds must reach a speed of 64 knots for the storm to be officially classified as a hurricane, although winds in a well-developed hurricane often double that speed and occasionally triple it.

The converging cyclonic wind pattern of a hurricane pulls in warm, moist air—the "fuel" that powers the storm. As warm, water vapor-laden air spirals into the storm, it rises in intense updrafts within towering cumulonimbus clouds. As the air rises it cools adiabatically, bringing the air to saturation; condensation releases vast amounts of liquid water that builds up the huge clouds and feeds the heavy rain. Condensation also releases latent heat. It is the release of latent heat that powers and strengthens a storm by increasing the instability of the air: in a short period of time and in a relatively small area, a hurricane releases an enormous amount of energy into the atmosphere. An average mature hurricane releases in one day approximately as much energy as

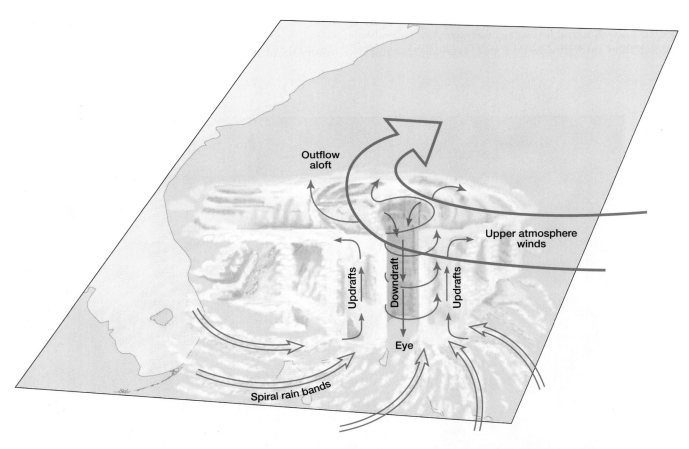

▲ **Figure 7-22** An idealized cross section through a well-developed hurricane. Air spirals into the storm horizontally and rises rapidly to produce towering cumulus and cumulonimbus clouds that yield torrential rainfall. In the center of the storm is the eye, where air movement is downward.

generated by all electric utility plants in the United States in one year.

Eye of a Hurricane   A remarkable feature of a well-developed hurricane is the nonstormy **eye** in the center of the storm (Figure 7-22). The winds do not converge to a central point, but rather reach their highest speed at the **eye wall**, which is the edge of the eye. The eye has a diameter from 16 to 40 kilometers (10 to 25 miles) and is a singular area of calmness in the maelstrom that whirls around it.

The weather pattern within a hurricane is relatively symmetrical around the eye. Bands of dense cumulus and cumulonimbus clouds (called *spiral rain bands*) curve in from the edge of the storm to the eye wall, producing heavy rain that generally increases in intensity inward. Updrafts are common throughout the hurricane—except in the eye—becoming most prominent around the eye wall. Near the top of the storm, air diverges clockwise out into the upper troposphere, except in the eye, where a downdraft inhibits cloud formation.

The clouds of the eye wall tower to heights that may exceed 16 kilometers (10 miles). Within the eye, there is no rain and almost no low clouds; scattered high clouds may part to let in intermittent sunlight. The wall of thunderstorms circling the eye is sometimes surrounded by a new wall of thunderstorms. The inner wall disintegrates and is replaced by the outer wall. The process, called *eye-wall replacement,* usually lasts less than 24 hours and tends to weaken the storm.

Origin

Hurricanes form only over warm oceans in the tropics (the ocean water temperature generally needs to be at least 26.5°C [80°F] to a depth of 50 meters [160 feet] or more), and at least a few degrees north or south of the equator (Figure 7-23). Because the Coriolis effect is so minimal near the equator, no hurricane has ever been observed to form within 3° of it, no hurricane has ever been known to cross it, and the appearance of hurricanes closer than some 8° or 10° of the equator is very rare. More than 80 percent originate in or just on the poleward side of the intertropical convergence zone.

The exact mechanism of formation is not completely understood, but hurricanes always develop out of a preexisting disturbance in the tropical troposphere. Easterly waves, discussed earlier, provide low-level convergence and lifting that catalyze the development of many hurricanes. Even so, fewer than 10 percent of all easterly waves grow into hurricanes. Hurricanes can evolve only when there is no significant **wind shear** with height (*wind shear* refers to a significant change in wind direction or wind speed with increasing elevation), which implies that temperatures at low altitudes are reasonably uniform over a wide area.

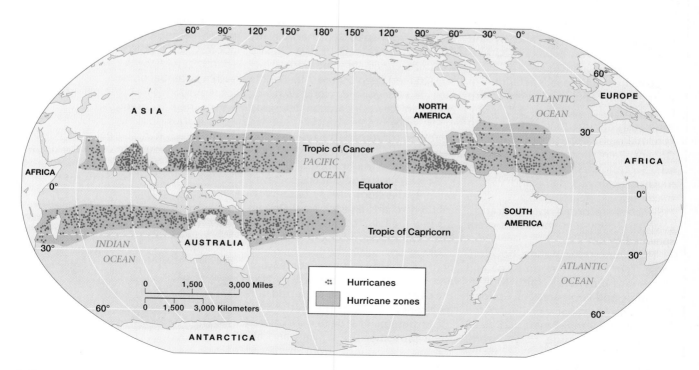

▲ **Figure 7-23**   Location of origin points of hurricanes over a 19-year period. *(After W. M. Gray, "Tropical Cyclone Genesis," Atmospheric Science Paper 234, Department of Atmospheric Science, Colorado State University, Fort Collins, 1975.)*

PEOPLE AND THE ENVIRONMENT Hurricane Katrina

On August 23, 2005, the 12th tropical depression of the season developed in the southeastern Bahamas. By the next day, the depression had strengthened and was named Tropical Storm Katrina. The storm moved slowly to the northwest, strengthening into a category 1 hurricane just a few hours before making landfall in south Florida on August 25th with winds gusting to 78 knots (145 kph; 90 mph). As Katrina moved westward over Florida, it left more than 40 centimeters (16 inches) of rain in Perrine, Florida.

Although weakened by its passage over land, Katrina quickly intensified again as it moved out over the warm waters of the Gulf of Mexico. For the next two days, Katrina gained strength, becoming a category 5 storm on the 28th with winds of more than 150 knots (275 kph; 170 mph), and a central pressure of 902 mb (the 6th lowest of any recorded Atlantic storm; the lowest on record was Hurricane Wilma two months later that year, with a pressure of 882 mb). By the time Katrina made landfall on the Gulf Coast just southeast of New Orleans on the morning of August 29th, it had weakened slightly to a strong category 3 storm. By the evening of August 29, Katrina had weakened to tropical storm strength and by the next day had been downgraded to a tropical depression (Figure 7-A).

Sustained wind speeds at landfall in southeastern Louisiana were more than 108 knots (200 kph; 125 mph); wind gusts of more than 87 knots (160 kph; 100 mph) were recorded in New Orleans. Rainfall storm totals exceeded 25 centimeters (10 inches) along much of Katrina's path, and with a maximum of nearly 38 centimeters (15 inches) recorded in Big Branch, Louisiana. Sixty-two tornadoes were spawned by Katrina.

The greatest devastation, however, came from Katrina's storm surge and flooding from heavy rain. Mobile, Alabama, and large areas of Gulfport and Biloxi, Mississippi, were inundated by Katrina's 8.0 to 8.5 meter (26 to 28 foot) high storm surge. New Orleans, although spared from a direct hit by the storm (the eye passed just east of the city), was first flooded beginning

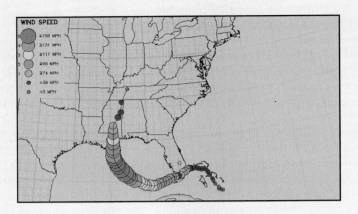

▲ **Figure 7-A**   Path of Hurricane Katrina from August 23 to August 30, 2005. Wind speed is indicated by colored dots. *(© 2005 Ray Sterner and Steve Babin, Johns Hopkins University Applied Physics Laboratory.)*

at about 7:00 A.M. A 3.0 to 3.6 meter (10 to 12 foot) storm surge rolled up the Intercoastal Waterway from the Gulf into the city's Industrial Canal, overtopping and scouring levees and flooding the eastern parts of the city. About three hours later—after some news agencies had reported that New Orleans had luckily escaped the worst destruction of Katrina—a second flood hit the city when the London Avenue and 17th Street Canals failed, sending water pouring into the central parts of the city from Lake Pontchartrain. By August 31, 80 percent of New Orleans was underwater—in some places 6 meters (20 feet) deep (Figure 7-B). For the next few days, the world watched events in New Orleans on television while government officials seemed unable to coordinate the rescue effort needed to help the thousands of people trapped in the flooded city.

So why was New Orleans so devastated by this storm? Many factors contributed to this disaster. New Orleans sits in a shallow "bowl" alongside the Mississippi River. Draining this once swampy area over the last few hundred years has led to soil compaction and subsidence that has left parts of the city below sea level, protected only by a series of levees. The wetlands of the Mississippi River delta once offered some protection by slowing and absorbing the punch from hurricane storm surges, but flood control efforts upstream have changed the sediment

load of the river and over the last few decades these protective marshlands on the lower delta have been sinking and eroding away, now offering little protection from storms. Finally, the levees themselves were inadequate, not being designed to handle such an enormous surge of water.

The loss of life from Hurricane Katrina may never be known with certainty, but is likely to have been more than 1200. More than a year later, tens of thousands of survivors were still displaced—especially citizens from the poorest parts of New Orleans. Some scientists had been warning about such a potential disaster for years, and local authorities were pressing for financial help to strengthen the levees. Even if those planned measures had been taken, it isn't clear if it would have been enough to avert the disaster in New Orleans.

▲ **Figure 7-B**   Floodwaters from Hurricane Katrina in New Orleans on September 1, 2005. *(AP.)*

Movement

Hurricanes occur in a half-dozen low-latitude regions. They are most common in the North Pacific basin, originating largely in two areas: east of the Philippines and west of southern Mexico and Central America. The third most notable region of hurricane development is in the west-central portion of the North Atlantic basin, extending into the Caribbean Sea and Gulf of Mexico. These ferocious storms are also found in the western portion of the South Pacific and all across the South Indian Ocean, as well as in the North Indian Ocean both east and west of the Indian peninsula. They are very rare in the South Atlantic and in the southeastern part of the Pacific, apparently because the water is too cold and because high pressure dominates. The strongest and largest hurricanes are typically those of the China Sea; only a few storms in other parts of the world have attained the size and intensity of the large East Asian "super" typhoons.

Once formed, hurricanes follow irregular tracks within the general flow of the trade winds. A specific path is very difficult to predict many days in advance, but the general pattern of movement is highly predictable. Roughly one-third of all hurricanes travel east to west without much latitudinal change. The rest, however, begin on an east–west path and then curve prominently poleward, where they either dissipate over the adjacent continent or become enmeshed in the general flow of the midlatitude westerlies (Figure 7-24). Hurricanes sometimes survive (with diminished intensity) off the east coasts of continents in the midlatitudes because of the warm ocean currents there; hurricanes do not survive in the midlatitudes off the west coasts of continents because of the cool ocean currents there.

In one region—the southwestern Pacific Ocean north and northeast of New Zealand—there is a marked variation from this general flow pattern. Hurricanes in this part of the Pacific usually move erratically from northwest to southeast. Therefore, when they strike an island such as Fiji or Tonga, they approach from the west, a situation not replicated anywhere else in the world at such a low latitude. These seemingly aberrant tracks apparently result from the simple fact that the tropospheric westerlies extend quite far equatorward in the Southwest Pacific, and hurricanes there are basically steered by the general circulation pattern.

Whatever their trajectory, hurricanes do not last long. The average hurricane exists for only about a week, with four weeks as the maximum duration. The longer-lived hurricanes are those that remain over tropical oceans. As soon as a hurricane leaves the ocean and moves over land, it begins to die because its energy source (warm, moist air) is cut off. If it stays over the ocean but moves into the midlatitudes, it dies as it penetrates the cooler environment. It is not unusual for a tropical hurricane that moves into the midlatitudes to diminish in intensity but grow in areal size until it develops into a midlatitude cyclone that travels with the westerlies.

In most regions, there is a marked seasonality to hurricanes (Figure 7-25). They are largely restricted to late summer and fall presumably because this is the time that ocean temperatures are highest and the

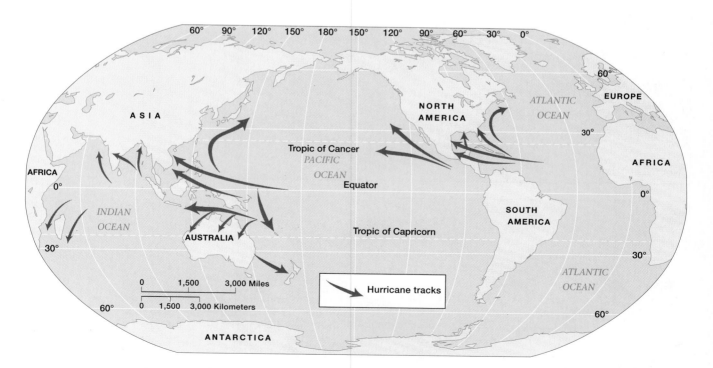

▲ **Figure 7-24**   Major generalized hurricane tracks.

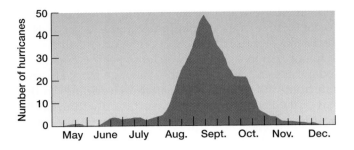

▲ **Figure 7-25** Seasonality of North Atlantic-Caribbean hurricanes over a nine-year period. Fall is hurricane season, with a prominent maximum in September.

intertropical convergence zone is shifted farthest poleward.

Damage and Destruction

Hurricanes are known for their destructive capabilities. Some of the destruction comes from high winds and torrential rain, and in some cases, tornadoes are spawned by a hurricane. However, the overwhelming cause of damage and loss of life is the flooding brought by high seas. The low pressure in the center of the storm allows the ocean surface to bulge as much as 1 meter (3 feet). To this is added a **storm surge** of wind-driven water as much as 7.5 meters (25 feet) above normal tide level when the hurricane pounds into a shoreline. Thus, a low-lying coastal area can be severely inundated, and 90 percent of hurricane-related deaths are drownings (Figure 7-26).

The greatest hurricane disaster in U.S. history occurred in 1900 when Galveston Island, Texas, was overwhelmed by a 6-meter (20-foot) storm surge that killed as many as 8000 people, nearly one-sixth of Galveston's population. In other regions, hurricane devastation has been much greater. The flat deltas of the Ganges and Brahmaputra rivers in Bangladesh have been subjected to enormous losses of human life from Indian Ocean cyclones: 300,000 deaths in 1737, another 300,000 in 1876, another 500,000 in 1970, and 175,000 in 1991. Most of the damage along the Gulf coast of the United States in August 2005 from Hurricane Katrina was caused by an eight-meter high (26 foot) storm surge (Figure 7-27).

Although the amount of damage caused by a hurricane depends in part on the physical configuration of the landscape and the population size and density of the affected area, storm strength is the most important factor. In the United States, the **Saffir-Simpson Hurricane Scale** has been established to rank the relative intensity of hurricanes, ranging from 1 to 5, with 5 being the most severe (Table 7-2).

Destruction and tragedy are not the only legacies of hurricanes, however. Such regions as northwestern Mexico, northern Australia, and southeastern Asia rely on tropical storms for much of their water supply. Hurricane-induced rainfall is often a critical source of moisture for agriculture. Although crops within the immediate path of the storm may be devastated by winds and flooding, a much more extensive area may be nurtured by the life-giving rains.

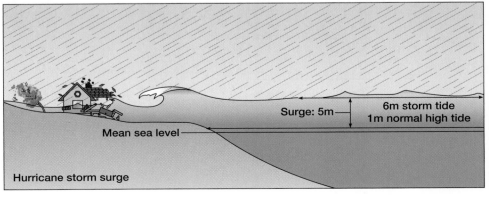

◄ **Figure 7-26** When a hurricane storm surge accompanies a normal high tide, the torrent can overwhelm a coastal area.

PEOPLE AND THE ENVIRONMENT Hurricanes and Global Warming

The 2005 hurricane season in the North Atlantic was the most active on record, with 28 named storms (Figure 7-C). Three of the most powerful hurricanes ever measured in terms of minimum atmospheric pressure in the eye occurred that year: Katrina, Rita, and Wilma (Figure 7-D; Table 7-A). Given the connection between high ocean temperature and hurricane formation in general—as well as mounting evidence that global warming is slightly increasing sea surface temperatures—an obvious question to ask is whether or not the increase in hurricane activity is tied to global warming?

Over the last 10 years or so, there has been a general increase in the annual number of hurricanes in the North Atlantic. However, many meteorologists think that this increase in frequency is simply part of a multidecadal cycle of hurricane activity that has been well documented since the early 1900s. Known as the *Atlantic Multi-Decadal Signal,* the pattern includes such factors as higher sea surface temperatures (SST), lower vertical wind shear, and an expanded upper-level westward flow of the atmosphere off North Africa. Although the underlying causes of all the components of the Atlantic Multi-Decadal Signal are not completely understood, the recent upswing in hurricane frequency can

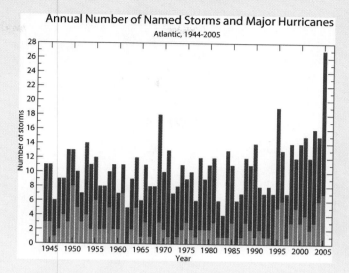

▲ **Figure 7-C**   Annual number of named tropical storms and major hurricanes in North Atlantic basin from 1944 to 2005. Category 3 or higher storms are shown in red. *(NOAA.)*

likely be explained without tying it to global warming. Meteorologists at NOAA's Climate Prediction Center have generally been forecasting a higher-than-average number of North Atlantic tropical storms since the early part of this decade.

On the other hand, recent studies of hurricane intensity suggest there may be a connection between global warming and the observed increase in the number of powerful North Atlantic hurricanes over the last decade.

Some climate models show a relationship between the potential intensity of hurricanes and higher SSTs. The recent trend toward a greater annual occurrence of Category 3 or higher hurricanes is consistent with those predictions. Some meteorologists think that the evidence is strong enough to conclude that there is a connection between global warming, higher SSTs, and an increased frequency of powerful hurricanes in the North Atlantic. For other atmospheric scientists, however, there simply isn't enough data yet to come to that conclusion.

TABLE 7-A The 10 Most Intense Hurricanes (based on lowest central pressure) in the North Atlantic Basin from 1851 to 2005.

Hurricane	Year	Minimum Pressure
Hurricane Wilma	2005	882 mb
Hurricane Gilbert	1988	888 mb
The Labor Day Hurricane	1935	892 mb
Hurricane Rita	2005	895 mb
Hurricane Allen	1980	899 mb
Hurricane Katrina	2005	902 mb
Hurricane Camille	1969	905 mb
Hurricane Mitch	1998	905 mb
Hurricane Ivan	2004	910 mb
Hurricane Janet	1955	914 mb

Source: NOAA

▲ **Figure 7-D**   Hurricane Wilma, the strongest North Atlantic hurricane ever recorded, as it approached Mexico's Yucatan Peninsula on October 20, 2005. *(NOAA.)*

◀ **Figure 7-27**   Large casino barge washed across highway 90 in Biloxi, Mississippi, by the storm surge of Hurricane Katrina in August 2005. *(AP.)*

TABLE 7-2 Saffir-Simpson Hurricane Scale

Category	Central Pressure (millibars)	Wind Speed Kilometers per Hour	Wind Speed Miles per Hour	Storm Surge (meters)	Damage
1	>979	119–153	74–95	1.2–2.5	Minimal
2	965–979	154–177	96–110	1.6–2.4	Moderate
3	945–964	178–209	111–130	2.5–3.6	Extensive
4	920–944	210–250	131–155	3.7–5.4	Extreme
5	<920	>250	>155	>5.4	Catastrophic

Localized Severe Weather

Several kinds of smaller atmospheric disturbances are common in various parts of the world. Some are locally of great significance, and some are destructive. All occur at a much more localized scale than do tropical cyclones and midlatitude cyclones, although *thunderstorms* and *tornadoes* may be associated with both kinds of larger storms.

Thunderstorms

FG9

A **thunderstorm**, defined as a violent convective storm accompanied by thunder and lightning, is usually localized and short-lived. It is always associated with vertical air motion, considerable humidity, and instability, a combination that produces a towering cumulonimbus cloud and (nearly always) showery precipitation.

Thunderstorms sometimes occur as individual clouds, produced by nothing more complicated than thermal convection; such developments are commonplace in the tropics and during summer in much of the midlatitudes. Thunderstorms are also frequently found in conjunction with other kinds of storms, however, or are associated with other mechanisms that can trigger unstable uplift. Thus thunderstorms often accompany hurricanes, tornadoes, fronts (especially cold fronts) in midlatitude cyclones, and orographic lifting that may produce unstable buoyancy.

The uplift, by whatever mechanism, of warm, moist air must release enough latent heat of condensation to sustain the continued rise of the air. In the early stage of thunderstorm formation (Figure 7-28), called the *cumulus stage*, updrafts prevail and the cloud grows. Above the freezing level, supercooled water droplets and ice crystals coalesce: when they become too large to be supported by the updrafts, they fall. These falling particles drag air with them, initiating a downdraft. When the downdraft with its accompanying precipitation leaves the bottom of the cloud, the thunderstorm enters the *mature stage*, in which updrafts and downdrafts coexist as the cloud continues to enlarge. The mature stage is the most active time, with heavy rain often accompanied by hail, blustery winds,

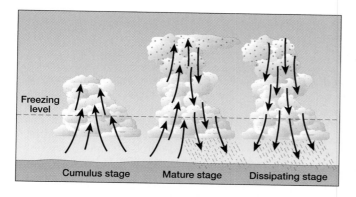

▲ **Figure 7-28** Sequential development of a thunderstorm cell.

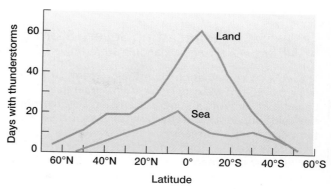

▲ **Figure 7-29** Average number of days per year with thunderstorms, as generalized by latitude. Most thunderstorms are in the tropics. Land areas experience many more thunderstorms than ocean areas because land warms up much more in summer.

lightning, thunder, and the growth of an anvil top composed of ice crystals on the massive cumulonimbus cloud. Eventually downdrafts dominate and the *dissipating stage* is reached, with light rain ending and turbulence ceasing.

Thunderstorms are most common where there are high temperatures, high humidity, and high instability, a combination typical of the intertropical convergence zone. There is a general decrease in thunderstorm frequency away from the equator, and they are virtually unknown poleward of 60° of latitude (Figure 7-29). There is much greater frequency of thunderstorms over

land than water because summer temperatures are higher over land and most thunderstorms occur in the summer. In the interior of the United States in spring and summer, severe thunderstorms frequently produce hail (Figure 7-30) and are occasionally associated with tornadoes (discussed later in this chapter).

Lightning   At any given moment some 2000 thunderstorms exist over the Earth. These storms produce about 6000 flashes of **lightning** every minute, or more

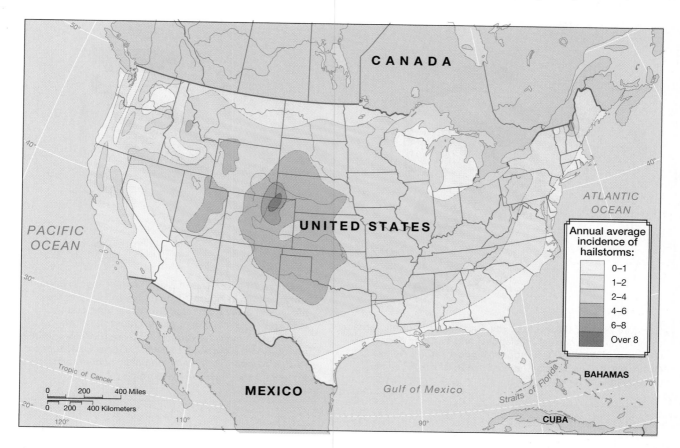

▲ **Figure 7-30** Average number of hailstorms in the United States. (*After Edward Aguado and James E. Burt,* Understanding Weather and Climate, *4th ed., Upper Saddle River, NJ: Pearson-Prentice Hall, 2007.*)

FOCUS Forecasting Severe Storms with NEXRAD
Stephen Stadler, Oklahoma State University

The volatile combination of mT air from the Gulf of Mexico, cP air from Canada, cT air from the desert, and the cold, dry southwesterly flow of the polar front jet stream makes the Oklahoma sky the world's most prolific breeder of tornadoes. New technology, such as NEXRAD, now in place in Oklahoma allows for improved identification of the atmospheric conditions that spawn severe thunderstorms and tornadoes.

NEXRAD (for *next-generation radar*) can dissect the internal workings of a severe thunderstorm and thereby determine its severity. The operating principle on which the system works is the *Doppler effect,* familiar to anyone who has ever been stopped at a railroad track as a train crosses a road. As the train approaches, the pitch of its whistle seems to get higher and higher. After the train passes, the whistle pitch seems to get lower and lower as the train gets farther and farther away. In reality, the whistle always has the same pitch; the apparent change depends on whether the sound source is approaching or receding from the listener.

Electromagnetic waves (light waves, radio waves, microwaves, and so forth) are also subject to the Doppler effect. NEXRAD transmits microwaves through the atmosphere toward a target storm. Raindrops, ice crystals, and hail reflect some of the microwaves back to the NEXRAD site, and how much of the transmitted signal is reflected gives an estimate of the intensity of the storm.

Figure 7-E shows a NEXRAD reflectivity display of severe thunderstorms in northern Oklahoma and southern Kansas, the type of information also obtainable from any conventional radar system. However, tornado funnels are usually only a few hundred meters across, and it is rare that radar can detect them using reflectivity alone. NEXRAD enjoys an advantage over conventional radar in that NEXRAD can detect motion toward and away from the radar site to within 3 kilometers (2 miles) per hour. Figure 7-F is a display of the same storms as shown by Figure 7-E but using NEXRAD's motion-detection capability. In Figure 7-F, notice the southern portion of the large storm at the center. Light green, indicating wind movement in excess of 50 knots away from the radar site, and light orange, indicating wind movement in excess of 50 knots toward the site, exist side by side. This is a strong counterclockwise rotation that is the hallmark of a mesocyclone. A radar operator would issue a tornado warning based on this display.

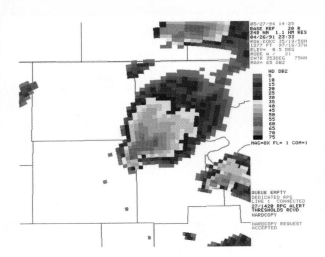

▲ **Figure 7-E**   NEXRAD reflectivity display of springtime tornadic thunderstorms in northern Oklahoma and southern Kansas. *(Courtesy of WSR88-D Operational Support Facility, Norman, Oklahoma; originally published in* Bulletin of the American Meteorological Society.*)*

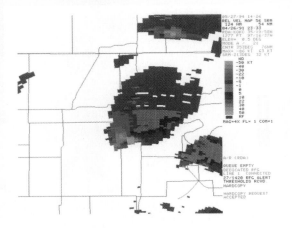

▲ **Figure 7-F**   NEXRAD display of radial velocity in the storms shown in Figure 7-E. Light green indicates rapid movement away from radar site, while light orange indicates rapid movement toward radar site—this combination indicates counterclockwise rotation within a mesocyclone. *(Courtesy of WSR88-D Operational Support Facility, Norman, Oklahoma; originally published in* Bulletin of the American Meteorological Society.*)*

▲ **Figure 7-31** Lightning over Tucson, Arizona. *(A. and J. Verkaik/CORBIS.)*

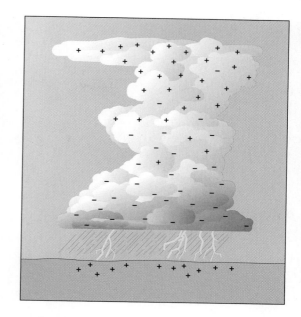

▲ **Figure 7-32** Typical arrangement of electrical charges in a thunderstorm cloud. Positively charged particles are mostly high in the cloud, whereas negatively charged particles tend to be concentrated near the base.

than 8.5 million lightning bolts daily. A lightning flash heats the air along its path to as much as 10,000°C (18,000°F), and can develop 100,000 times the amperage used in household electricity (Figure 7-31).

With such frequency and power, lightning clearly poses a significant potential danger for humanity. In the United States, on average about 65 deaths are blamed on lightning annually. The most dangerous places to be during a lightning storm are under a tree, in a boat, on a tractor, and playing golf. However, two out of three people struck by lightning in this country are not killed. It is a massive but brief shock, and quick first aid (mouth-to-mouth resuscitation and cardiopulmonary resuscitation) can save most victims.

The sequence of events that leads to lightning discharge is known, but the exact mechanism of electrification is not completely understood. Development of a large cumulonimbus cloud causes a separation of electrical charges. Updrafts carrying positively charged water droplets or crystals rise in the icy upper layers of the cloud while falling ice pellets gather negative charges and transport them downward (Figure 7-32). The growing negative charge in the lower part of the cloud attracts a growing positive charge on the Earth's surface immediately below. The contrast between the two (cloud base and ground surface) builds to tens of millions of volts before the insulating barrier of air that separates the charges is overcome.

Finally, a finger of negative current flicks down from the cloud and meets a positive charge darting upward from the ground. This makes an electrical connection of ionized air from cloud to ground, and a surge of electrical power strikes downward as the first lightning flash. Other flashes may follow in relatively quick succession, until all or most of the negative charges have been drained out of the cloud base.

In addition to such ground-to-cloud discharges, less spectacular but more frequent lightning is exchanged between adjacent clouds or between the upper and lower portions of the same cloud.

The abrupt heating occasioned by a lightning bolt produces instantaneous expansion of the air, which creates a shock wave that becomes a sound wave that we hear as **thunder**. The lightning and thunder occur simultaneously, but we perceive them at different times. Lightning is seen at essentially the instant it occurs because its image travels at the speed of light. Thunder, however, travels at the much slower speed of sound. Thus, it is possible to estimate the distance of a lightning bolt by timing the interval between sight and sound: A three-second delay means the lightning strike was about one kilometer away; a 5-second interval indicates that the lightning flash was about a mile away. Rumbling thunder is indicative of a long lightning trace some distance away, with one portion being nearer than another to the hearer. If no thunder can be heard, the lightning is far away—probably more than 20 kilometers (a dozen miles).

◀ **Figure 7-33** A tornado moves across a field in Texas toward a country road. *(Warren Faidley photo, ImageState/International Stock Photography Ltd.)*

Tornadoes

Tornadoes

Although very small and localized, the **tornado** is one of the most destructive of all atmospheric disturbances. It is the most intense vortex in nature: a deep low-pressure cell surrounded by a violently whirling cylinder of wind (Figure 7-33). These are tiny storms, generally less than 400 meters (a quarter of a mile) in diameter, but they have the most extreme pressure gradients known—as much as a 100-millibar difference from the center of the tornado to the air immediately outside the funnel. This extreme pressure difference produces winds of extraordinary speed. Maximum wind speed estimates range up to 480 kilometers (300 miles) per hour. Air sucked into the vortex also rises at an inordinately fast rate. Such a storm clearly has the capability of transporting a little girl to the land of Oz!

Tornadoes usually originate a few hundred meters above the ground, the rotating vortex becoming visible when upswept water vapor condenses into a **funnel cloud**. The tornado advances along an irregular track that generally extends from southwest to northeast in the United States. Sometimes the funnel sweeps along the ground, devastating everything in its path, but its trajectory is usually twisting and dodging and includes frequent intervals in which the funnel lifts completely off the ground and then touches down again nearby. Most tornadoes have damage paths 50 meters (about 150 feet) wide, move at about 48 kilometers (30 miles) per hour, and last for only a few minutes. Extremely destructive ones may be over 1.5 km (1 mile) wide, travel at 95 kilometers (60 miles) per hour, and may be on the ground for more than an hour, with maximum longevity recorded at about eight hours.

The strength of a tornado is commonly described using the **Fujita tornado intensity scale** (Table 7-3).[1] About two-thirds of all tornadoes in the United States are classed as "weak," 30 percent are classed as "destructive," and 2 percent are classed as "violent." The average annual death toll from violent tornadoes in the United States is 60.

[1]The Enhanced F-scale for tornado damage is an update of the original F-scale. It is based on estimates of 3-second gust wind speeds as determined by the observed damage from a tornado. The Enhanced F-scale will be implemented in the United States beginning in 2007.

FOCUS Forecasting Severe Storms with the Oklahoma Mesonetwork
Stephen Stadler, Oklahoma State University

The Oklahoma Mesonetwork—or *Mesonet*—is a system of more than 110 solar-powered automated weather stations that radio readings every 15 minutes. Before the Mesonetwork was in place, there were only a dozen hourly reporting stations in Oklahoma with considerable distance between them. The Mesonetwork is the most extensive state weather network in the United States and presents forecasters with new possibilities in short-term forecasting.

Tornado-generating thunderstorms frequently occur along a *dryline*, the boundary between mT and cT air and a zone in which surface air streams are forced to converge and lift. The dryline can generate some of the largest tornadic thunderstorms on Earth. Therefore, its exact position is critical in forecasting where storms will begin. The Mesonetwork, with its average spacing of 30 kilometers (18 miles) between stations, gives forecasters a precise view of dryline location. Figure 7-G

shows a dryline in western Oklahoma. Note the relatively high dew point temperatures east of the line in the mT air and the higher air temperatures and lower dew point temperatures in the cT air west of the line. The wind data show air streams are converging and, by implication, rising along the dryline. In this situation, severe thunderstorms are most likely just to the east of the dryline.

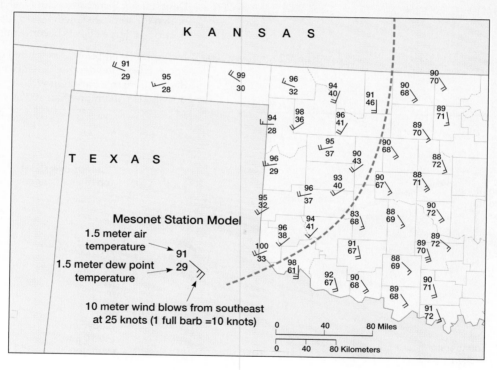

▲ **Figure 7-G** Oklahoma Mesonetwork depiction of a dryline that could generate severe storms. *(Courtesy of Oklahoma Mesonetwork Project.)*

The dark, twisting funnel of a tornado contains not only cloud but also sucked-in dust and debris. Damage is caused largely by the strong winds, flying debris, and swirling updraft, although the abrupt drop in pressure when the center of the storm passes over a closed building may be a minor factor.

Formation As with many other storms, the exact mechanism of tornado formation is not well understood. They may develop in the warm, moist, unstable air associated with a midlatitude cyclone, such as along a squall line that precedes a rapidly advancing cold front

or along the cold front itself. Virtually all tornadoes are generated by severe thunderstorms. The basic requirement is vertical wind shear—a significant change in wind speed or direction from the bottom to the top of the storm. On a tornado day, low-level winds are southerly and jet stream winds are southwesterly, and this difference in direction causes turbulence on the boundary between the two systems. The conventional updrafts that become thunderstorms reach several kilometers up into the atmosphere, and the wind shear can cause air to roll along a horizontal axis (Figure 7-34). Strong updrafts in such a rapidly maturing *supercell*

TABLE 7-3 Fujita Tornado Intensity Scale and Enhanced F Scale

Fujita Scale			Enhanced F Scale			Expected Level of Damage
F Number	kph	mph	EF Scale	3-second gust kph	3-second gust mph	
F0	<116	<72	0	105–137	65–85	Light: Broken tree branches; uprooted small trees; billboards and chimneys damaged.
F1	116–180	72–112	1	138–177	86–110	Moderate: Roof surfaces peeled off; mobile homes overturned or pushed off their foundations.
F2	181–253	113–157	2	178–217	111–135	Considerable: Mobile homes destroyed; roofs blown off wooden-frame houses; uprooted large trees; light objects become "missiles."
F3	254–332	158–206	3	218–266	136–165	Severe: Trains derailed or overturned; walls and roofs torn off from well-constructed houses; heavy cars thrown off ground.
F4	333–419	207–260	4	267–322	166–200	Devastating: Structures with weak foundations blown for some distance; well-built houses destroyed; large objects become missiles.
F5	>419	>260	5	Over 322	Over 200	Incredible: Well-built houses lifted off foundations and carried considerable distance before complete destruction; tree bark removed; automobile-sized missiles carried more than 100 meters.

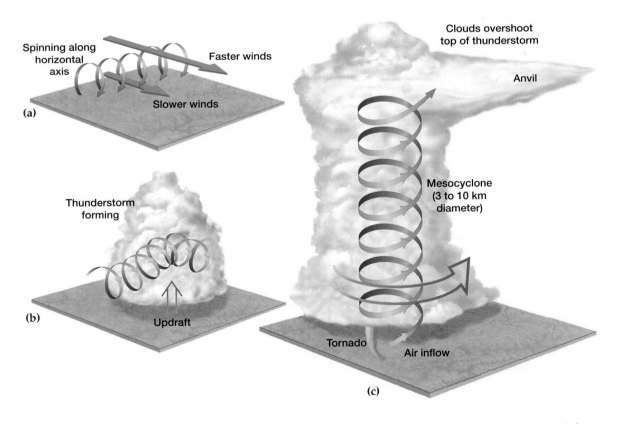

▲ **Figure 7-34** The formation of a mesocyclone often precedes tornado formation. **(a)** Winds are stronger aloft than at the surface (called *speed wind shear*), producing a rolling motion about a horizontal axis. **(b)** Strong thunderstorm updrafts tilt the horizontally rotating air to a nearly vertical alignment. **(c)** The mesocyclone, a vertical cylinder of rotating air, is established. If a tornado develops it will descend from a slowly rotating wall cloud in the lower portion of the mesocyclone. *(After Frederick K. Lutgens and Edward J. Tarbuck,* The Atmosphere, *7th ed., Prentice Hall: Upper Saddle River, NJ, 1998.)*

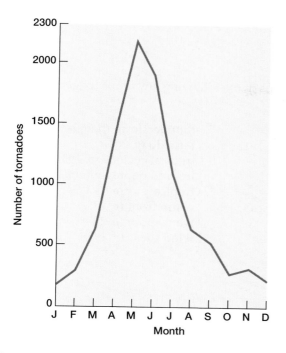

▲ **Figure 7-35** Seasonality of tornadoes in the United States.

thunderstorm may then tilt this rotating air vertically, developing into a **mesocyclone**, with a diameter of 3 to 10 kilometers (2 to 6 miles). About half of all mesocyclones formed result in a tornado.

Spring and early summer are favorable for tornado development because of the considerable air-mass contrast present in the midlatitudes at that time; a tornado can form in any month, however (Figure 7-35). Most occur in midafternoon, at the time of maximum heating.

Tornadoes do occur in the middle latitudes and subtropics, but more than 90 percent are reported in the United States, where about 1000 are sighted each year (Figure 7-36). Such concentration in a single area presumably reflects optimum environmental conditions, with the relatively flat terrain of the central and southeastern United States providing an unhindered zone of interaction between prolific source regions for Canadian cP and Gulf mT air masses. Although between 800 and 1200 tornadoes are recorded annually in the United States, the actual total may be considerably higher than that because many small tornadoes that occur briefly in uninhabited areas are not reported.

True tornadoes are apparently restricted to land areas. Similar-appearing funnels over the ocean, called **waterspouts**, have a lesser pressure gradient, gentler winds, and reduced destructive capability.

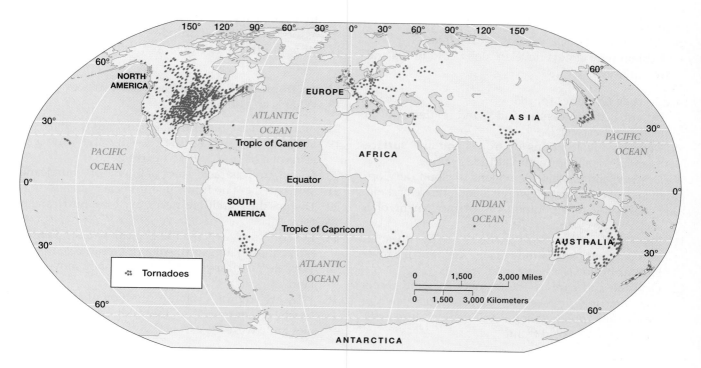

▲ **Figure 7-36** Anticipated distribution of tornadoes over the world in any given five-year period.

Chapter 7 Learning Review

Key Terms

Before answering the study questions below, review the definitions of the following key terms (page references are provided for you):

air mass *(p. 179)*
cold front *(p. 183)*
easterly wave *(p. 191)*
eye (of a hurricane) *(p. 195)*
eye wall *(p. 195)*
front *(p. 182)*
Fujita tornado intensity scale *(p. 204)*
funnel cloud *(p. 204)*
hurricane *(p. 193)*
lightning *(p. 201)*

mesocyclone *(p. 207)*
midlatitude anticyclone *(p. 191)*
midlatitude cyclone *(p. 185)*
occluded front *(p. 188)*
occlusion *(p. 188)*
Saffir-Simpson Hurricane Scale *(p. 198)*
stationary front *(p. 185)*
storm surge *(p. 198)*
thunder *(p. 203)*

thunderstorm *(p. 200)*
tornado *(p. 204)*
tropical cyclone *(p. 193)*
tropical depression *(p. 193)*
tropical storm *(p. 193)*
warm front *(p. 183)*
waterspout *(p. 207)*
wind shear *(p. 195)*

Study Questions for Key Concepts

After studying this chapter, you should be able to answer the following questions:

Air Masses (p. 179)
1. What is an *air mass,* and what conditions are necessary for one to form?
2. What regions of Earth are least likely to produce air masses? Why?
3. Why is an air mass unlikely to form over the Rocky Mountains of North America?
4. Why are maritime polar air (mP) masses from the Atlantic Ocean less important to the United States than mP air masses from the Pacific Ocean?

Fronts (p. 182)
5. What is a *cold front?* What is a *warm front?*
6. Explain why clouds develop along cold fronts and warm fronts.

Midlatitude Cyclones (p. 185)
7. Describe the pressure and wind patterns of a *midlatitude cyclone.*
8. Describe the locations of fronts and the surface "sectors" of a mature midlatitude cyclone.
9. Describe and explain the regions of cloud development and precipitation within a midlatitude cyclone.
10. Discuss the four components of movement of a midlatitude cyclone.
11. Explain the process of *occlusion.* Why does an *occluded front* usually indicate the "death" of a midlatitude cyclone?
12. Describe and explain the changes in wind direction, atmospheric pressure, sky conditions (such as clouds and precipitation), and temperature with the passing of a cold front.

13. Discuss the origin of midlatitude cyclones. What is the relationship between upper-level airflow and the formation of surface disturbances in the midlatitudes?
14. What parts of the world are most affected by midlatitude cyclones?

Midlatitude Anticyclones (p. 191)
15. Describe the pressure pattern, wind direction, and general weather associated with a *midlatitude anticyclone.*
16. In what ways are midlatitude anticyclones often associated with midlatitude cyclones?
17. Why are there no fronts in a midlatitude anticyclone?

Minor Tropical Disturbances: Easterly Waves (p. 191)
18. What is an *easterly wave?*

Major Tropical Disturbances: Hurricanes (p. 193)
19. Describe and explain the pressure and wind patterns of a *tropical cyclone* (hurricane).
20. Discuss the characteristics of the *eye* of a hurricane.
21. Why are there no fronts in a tropical cyclone?
22. Discuss the conditions necessary for a hurricane to form?
23. Describe and explain the typical paths taken by hurricanes in the North Atlantic Ocean basin.
24. Why do hurricanes weaken when they move over land?
25. Why are tropical cyclones common along the east coasts of continents in the midlatitudes, but not along the west coasts?

26. What is a hurricane *storm surge,* and what causes one?
27. Do hurricanes have any beneficial effects? Explain.

Localized Severe Weather (p. 200)
28. Discuss the general sequence of *thunderstorm* development and dissipation.
29. Why are thunderstorms more common over land than over water?

30. Describe the wind and pressure characteristics of a *tornado.*
31. Discuss the general formation of a tornado from a *supercell thunderstorm* and *mesocyclone.*

Additional Resources

Books:

Davies, Pete. *Inside the Hurricane.* New York: Henry Holt and Company, 2000.

Kessler, Edwin, ed. *The Thunderstorm in Human Affairs.* Norman: University of Oklahoma Press, 1988.

Larson, Erik. *Isaac's Storm: A Man, A Time, and the Deadliest Hurricane in History.* New York: Crown Publishers, 1999.

Monmonier, Mark. *Air Apparent: How Meteorologists Learned to Map, Predict, and Dramatize Weather.* Chicago: University of Chicago Press, 1999.

Internet Sites:

Daily Weather Maps of the National Weather Service
http://www.hpc.ncep.noaa.gov/dwm/dwm.shtml

The Daily Weather maps provide detailed surface and upper atmosphere weather maps on a week-to-week basis.

Geostationary Satellite Server
http://www.goes.noaa.gov/

This site is a good source of the latest images from the GOES weather satellites.

National Storm Prediction Center
http://www.spc.noaa.gov/

The Storm Prediction Center provides forecasts and information about tornadoes and severe thunderstorms.

National Hurricane Center
http://www.nhc.noaa.gov/

The Tropical Prediction Center of the National Hurricane Center furnishes up-to-date information, storm warnings, and current satellite images of active hurricanes.

Naval Research Laboratory
http://www.nrlmry.navy.mil/sat_products.html

The Naval Research Laboratory (NRL) provides a wide range of current satellite images and satellite images with weather map overlays. The NRL also maintains an extensive archive of past satellite images of tropical cyclones.

8
Climatic Zones and Types

The basic goal of the geographic study of climate, as with the geographic study of anything else, is to understand its spatial characteristics—its distribution over Earth. Such understanding is exceedingly difficult to achieve for climate, however, because so many variables are involved. It is relatively easy to describe and even to map the distribution of such uncomplicated phenomena as giraffes, voting patterns, and a host of other concrete entities or simple relationships. Climate, however, is a result of a number of elements that are, for the most part, continuously and independently variable.

Temperature, for instance, is one of the simplest climatic elements, and yet in this textbook more than 40 maps and diagrams are used to convey various temperature patterns around the world. Although temperatures can be measured precisely, some form of abstraction is necessary for tabulation and analysis. Most widely used is the arithmetic mean (average). For some purposes, however, the most probable temperature or some expression of temperature variation (e.g., standard deviation) is more useful, and for still other purposes extremes are more important than averages. The point at issue is that climate involves almost continuous variation, not only of temperature but also a host of other factors. Thus, a satisfactory synthesis of all these data involves a great deal of generalization and subjectivity.

Climate Classification

To cope with the great diversity of information encompassed by the concept of climate, the most meaningful climatic characteristics must be selected and some systematic way must be found to classify them. Classifiers generally have chosen temperature and precipitation as the most significant and understandable features of climate, as well as the most available, and that is the method we follow in this chapter.

The Purpose of Classifying Climates

In this book, we have a clear-cut and straightforward requirement: we need a classification scheme that is useful as a learning tool. Specifically, we need a device to simplify, organize, and generalize a vast array of data into a comprehensible system that helps us understand the distribution of climates over Earth.

◀ Snowstorm in Boston, Massachusetts. *(Lawrence Jackson/AP.)*

Suppose a geography student in Georgia is asked to describe the climate of southeastern China. The student may at first be bewildered by such an assignment. However, a world map portraying the distribution of climate types will show the student that southeastern China has the same climate as the southeastern United States (see Figure 8-4). Thus, the student's familiarity with the home climate in Georgia provides a basis for understanding the general characteristics of the climate of southeastern China.

Early Classification Schemes

The earliest known climatic classification scheme originated with the ancient Greeks, perhaps 2200 years ago. Although the "known world" was very small at that time, Greek scholars were aware of the shape and approximate size of Earth. They knew that at the southern limit of their world, along the Nile River and the southern coast of the Mediterranean, the climate was much hotter and drier than on the islands and northern coast of that sea. At the other end of the world known to the Greeks, along the Danube River and the northern coast of the Black Sea, things were much colder, especially in winter. So the Greeks spoke of three climatic zones: the *Temperate Zone* of the midlatitudes, in which they lived (Athens is at 38° N latitude); the *Torrid Zone* of the tropics to the south, and the *Frigid Zone* to the north. Because they knew that Earth is a sphere, they suggested that the Southern Hemisphere has similar Temperate and Frigid zones, making five in all.

For many centuries, this classification scheme was handed down from scholar to scholar. Gradually these five climatic zones were confused with, and eventually their climates ascribed to, the five astronomical zones of the Earth, bounded by the Tropics of Cancer and Capricorn and the Arctic and Antarctic circles (Figure 8-1). This revision put the equatorial rainy zone in with the hot arid region in the Torrid Zone, extended the Temperate Zone to include much of what the Greeks had called Frigid, and moved the Frigid Zone poleward to the polar circles. This simplistic but unrealistic classification scheme persisted for more than a thousand years and was finally discarded only in the twentieth century.

Today we generally recognize five basic climate zones in the world: *equatorial warm-wet, tropical hot-dry, subtropical warm temperate, midlatitude cool temperate,* and *high-latitude cold* (Figure 8-2). The equatorial and tropical zones are differentiated by rainfall amount and frequency. The two temperate zones differ primarily in whether summer or winter is the dominant season (in Atlanta, for instance, houses are designed to be cool in summer, whereas in Minneapolis keeping warm

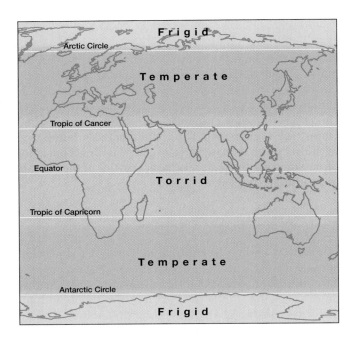

▲ **Figure 8-1** The original Greek climate classification scheme was expanded and correlated with Earth's five astronomical zones to depict a world comprising five climate zones.

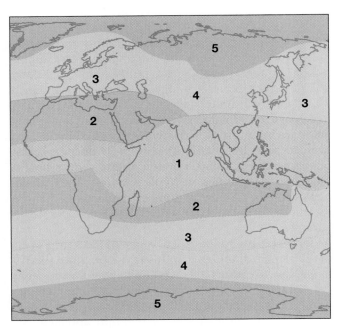

▲ **Figure 8-2** The major climatic zones of the Old World, as recognized today: (1) equatorial warm-wet, (2) tropical hot-dry, (3) subtropical warm temperate, (4) midlatitude cool temperate, (5) high-latitude cold.

in winter is more important; thus, summer is the dominant season in the former, and winter is the dominant season in the latter). The cold zone has hardly any summer—not enough to grow important crops. Climatologists have refined this five-zone scheme by subdividing these general zones into specific climate types, sometimes looking to natural vegetation distribution as an important indicator of climate.

The Köppen Climate Classification System

Classification schemes having the greatest pedagogic value share three important attributes:

1. They are relatively simple to comprehend and to use.
2. They show some sort of orderly pattern over the world.
3. They give some indication of zone genesis.

The **Köppen climate classification system** meets these criteria reasonably well and is by far the most widely used climatic classification system. Wladimir Köppen (1846–1940) was a Russian-born German climatologist who was also an amateur botanist. The first version of his scheme appeared in 1918, and he continued to modify and refine it for the rest of his life, the last version being published in 1936. The Köppen system uses a numerical basis of classification (temperature and precipitation averages), with many zone boundaries determined by the climatic conditions associated with vegetation patterns.

The system uses as a database only the average annual and average monthly values of temperature and precipitation, combined and compared in a variety of ways. Consequently, the necessary statistics are commonly tabulated and easily acquired. Data for any location (called a *station*) on Earth can be used to determine the precise classification of that place, and the areal extent of any recognized climatic type can be determined and mapped. This means that the classification system is functional at both the specific and the general level.

Köppen defined four of his five major climatic groups primarily by temperature characteristics, the fifth (the B group) on the basis of moisture. He then subdivided each group into types according to various temperature and precipitation relationships. One of the system's distinctive features is a symbolic nomenclature consisting of a combination of letters to designate the various climatic types, with each letter having a precisely defined meaning (Figure 8-3 and Table 8-1).

The Köppen system has been widely used, although often modified, and its terminology has been even more widely adopted. There are some deficiencies in the system, however, as in any other climatic classification scheme. Köppen himself was unsatisfied with his last version and did not consider it a finished product. Thus, many geographers and climatologists have used the Köppen system as a springboard to devise systems of their own or to modify the "final" Köppen classification.

The Modified Köppen System

The system of climatic classification used in this book is a *modified Köppen system*. It encompasses the basic design of the Köppen system but with a variety of minor modifications. Some of these modifications follow the

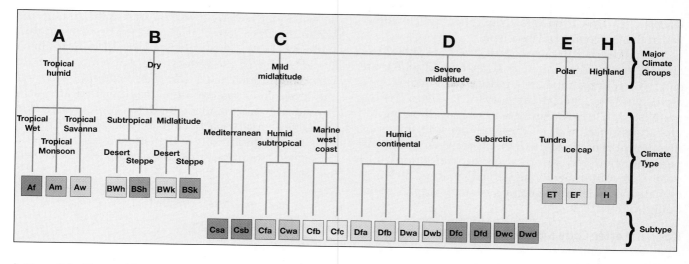

▲ **Figure 8-3** The modified Köppen climatic classification.

TABLE 8-1 Climate Types of the Modified Köppen Classification System

Major Group	Climate Type	Letter Code	General Characteristics
A–Tropical Humid Climates	Tropical Wet	Af	Rain throughout year
	Tropical Savanna	Aw	Winter (low-Sun) dry season
	Tropical Monsoon	Am	Short dry season; heavy rains in other months
B–Dry Climates	Subtropical Desert	BWh	Low-latitude (hot) desert
	Subtropical Steppe	BSh	Low-latitude (hot) semiarid
	Midlatitude Desert	BWk	Midlatitude (cold) desert
	Midlatitude Steppe	BSk	Midlatitude (cold) semiarid
C–Mild Midlatitude Climates	Mediterranean	Csa	Dry, hot summer
		Csb	Dry, warm summer
	Humid Subtropical	Cfa	No dry season; hot summer
		Cwa	Dry winter; hot summer
	Marine West Coast	Cfb	No dry season; warm summer
		Cfc	No dry season; cool summer
D–Severe Midlatitude Climates	Humid Continental	Dfa	Severe winter; no dry season; hot summer
		Dfb	Severe winter; no dry season; warm summer
		Dwa	Severe winter; dry winter; hot summer
		Dwb	Severe winter; dry winter; warm summer
	Subarctic	Dfc	Severe winter; no dry season; cool summer
		Dfd	Very cold winter; no dry season
		Dwc	Dry winter; cool summer
		Dwd	Dry winter, very cold winter
E–Polar Climates	Tundra	ET	Polar tundra with no true summer
	Ice Cap	EF	Polar ice cap
H–Highland Climates		H	High elevation climates

lead of Glen Trewartha, late geographer and climatologist at the University of Wisconsin.

The modified Köppen system describes five major climate groups (groups A, B, C, D, and E) which are subdivided into a total of 14 individual climate types, along with the special category of *highland* (H) climate (see Table 8-1). Figure 8-4 is a map showing the global distribution of all these climates. In this book no attempt is made to distinguish between pure Köppen and modified Köppen system definitions: our goal is to comprehend the general pattern of world climate, not to learn a specific system or nitpick about boundaries.

Köppen Letter Code System In the modified Köppen system, each climate type is designated by a descriptive name and by a series of letters defined by specific temperature and/or precipitation values. The first letter designates the major climate group; the second letter usually describes precipitation patterns, while the third letter (if any) describes temperature patterns. Table 8-2 provides a general description of the meaning of the letters (see Appendix V for the exact definitions used for classification). Although the letter code system seems complicated at first, it provides a shorthand method for summarizing key characteristics of each climate. For example, if we look for the definitions of the letters in *Csa*, one of the letter code combinations for a *mediterranean climate*, we see that:

C = *mild midlatitude climate*

s = *summer dry season*

a = *hot summers*

As we'll see later in this chapter, that is a very good synopsis of this climate.

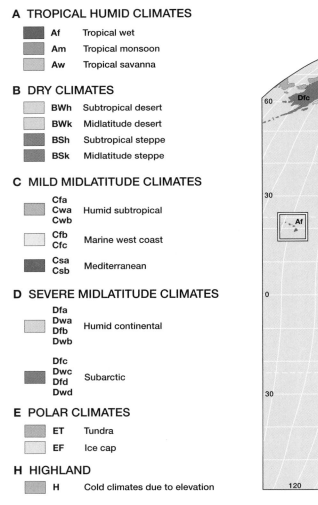

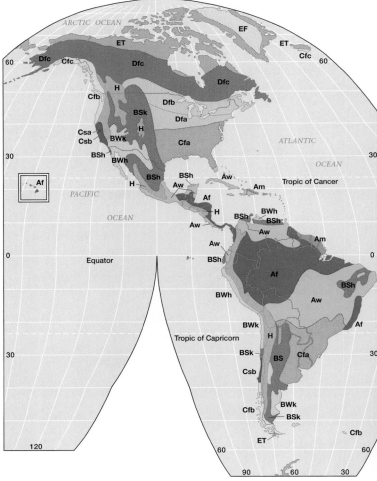

▲ **Figure 8-4** Climatic regions over land areas (modified Köppen system).

Climographs

Probably the most useful tool in a general study of world climatic classification is a simple graphic representation of monthly temperature and precipitation for a specific weather station. Such a graph is called a **climograph** (or *climatic diagram*); a typical one is shown in Figure 8-5. The customary climograph has 12 columns, one for each month, with a temperature scale on the left side and a precipitation scale on the right. Average monthly temperatures are connected by a curved line in the upper portion of the diagram, and average monthly precipitation is represented by bars extending upward from the bottom.

The value of a climograph is twofold: (1) it displays precise details of important aspects of the climate of a specific place, and (2) it can be used to classify the climate of that place.

World Distribution of Major Climate Types

Seasonal Pressure and Precipitation Patterns

Most of the remainder of this chapter is devoted to a discussion of climatic types. Our attention is focused primarily on three questions:

1. Where are the various climate types located?
2. What are the characteristics of each climate?
3. What are the main controls of these climates?

As we begin our look at climates of the world—a seemingly daunting task at first glance—keep in mind that few new concepts are introduced in this section.

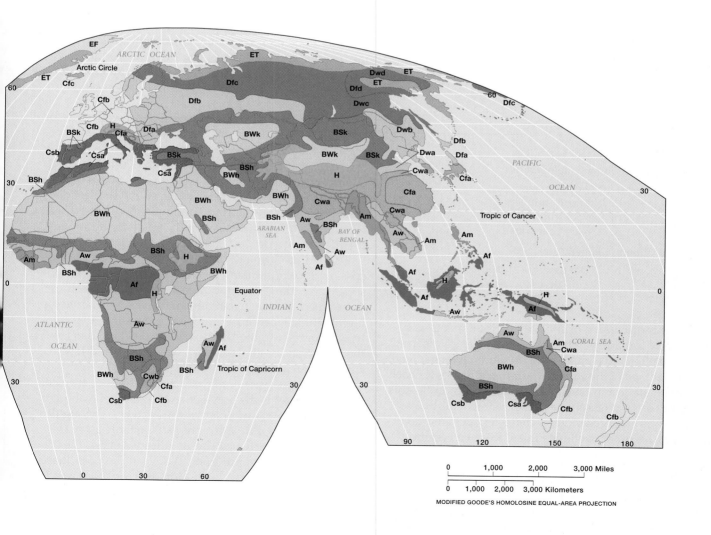

MODIFIED GOODE'S HOMOLOSINE EQUAL-AREA PROJECTION

TABLE 8-2 Generalized Description of the Letter Codes of the Modified Köppen Climate Classification System

First Letters: Major climate group

A	Tropical Humid	low latitude; warm and wet
B	Dry	evaporation exceeds precipitation
C	Mild Midlatitude	mild winters, warm or hot summers
D	Severe Midlatitude	severe, cold winters
E	Polar	very high latitude, cold climates
H	Highland	high mountains; elevation is dominant control

Second Letters:

A, C, and D Climate Precipitation

f	wet all year
m	monsoonal precipitation pattern (very wet summer)
w	winter dry season
s	summer dry season

B Climate Precipitation

W	desert
S	steppe

E Climate Temperature

T	tundra
F	ice cap

Third Letters:

C and D Climates Temperature

a	hot summers
b	warm summers
c	cool summers
d	very cold winters

B Climate Temperature

h	hot desert or steppe
k	cold desert or steppe

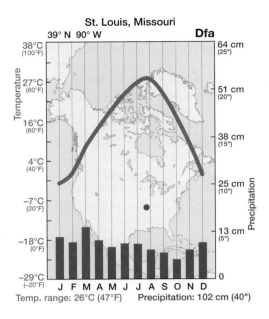

▲ **Figure 8-5** A typical climograph.

Rather, this discussion of climate distribution lets us systematically organize what we have already learned about weather and climate from previous chapters. Also, take advantage of the climate "summary" tables for each major climate group (such as Table 8-3 on p. 217)—this series of tables concisely describes the general location, temperature and precipitation characteristics, and dominant controls for each climate in the Köppen system.

Tropical Humid Climates (Group A)

The tropical humid climates occupy almost all the land area of Earth within some 15–20° of the equator in both the Northern and Southern Hemispheres

(Figure 8-6). This globe-girdling belt of A climates is interrupted slightly here and there by mountains or small regions of aridity, but it dominates the equatorial regions and extends poleward to beyond the 25° parallel in some windward coastal lowlands. The fundamental character of the A climates is molded by their latitudinal location.

The A climates are noted not so much for warmth as for lack of coldness. These are the only truly winterless climates of the world. They are characterized by moderately high temperatures throughout the year, as is to be expected from their near-equatorial location. The Sun is high in the sky every day of the year, and even the shortest days are not appreciably shorter than the longest ones. These are climates of perpetual warmth (interestingly though, they do not experience the world's highest temperatures).

The words "winter" and "summer" are used in discussing tropical climates, though, as in the "winter monsoon" and the "summer monsoon"—in this context, these adjectives mean that time of the year when mid- or high latitude locations are indeed cold or hot. Alternately, we can refer to the "high-Sun season" (summer) and the "low-Sun season" (winter), where high and low are strictly relative terms.

The second typifying characteristic of the tropical humid climates is the prevalence of moisture. Although not universally rainy, much of the A zone is among the wettest in the world. Warm, moist, unstable air masses frequent the oceans of these latitudes, and the intertropical convergence zone (ITCZ) influences these regions for much of the year. Moreover, onshore winds and thermal convection are commonplace phenomena. Thus, the A group has not only abundant sources of moisture, but also abundant mechanisms for uplift.

TABLE 8-3 Summary of A Climates: Tropical Humid

Type	Location	Temperature	Precipitation	Dominant Controls of Climate
Tropical Wet (Af)	Within 5–10° of equator; farther poleward on eastern coasts	Warm all year; very small ATR; small DTR; high sensible temperature	No dry season; 152–254 cm (60–100 in.) annually; many thunderstorms	Latitude; ITCZ trade wind convergence; onshore wind flow
Tropical savanna (Aw)	Fringing Af between 25° N and S	Warm to hot all year; moderate ATR and DTR	Distinct wet and dry seasons; 90–180 cm (35–70 in.) annually	Seasonal shifting of tropical wind and pressure belts, especially ITCZ
Tropical monsoon (Am)	Windward tropical coasts of Asia, Central and South America, Guinea coast of Africa	Similar to Af with slightly larger ATR; hottest weather just before summer monsoon	Very heavy in summer; short winter dry season; 254–508 cm (100–200 in.) annually	Seasonal wind direction reversal associated with ITCZ movement; jet stream fluctuation; continental pressure changes

All A climates lie within about 25° of the equator, with the vast majority within 20°. All are winterless, with no monthly average temperature below 18°C (64°F). All are always very humid and have high rainfall totals. ATR = annual temperature range; DTR = daily temperature range.

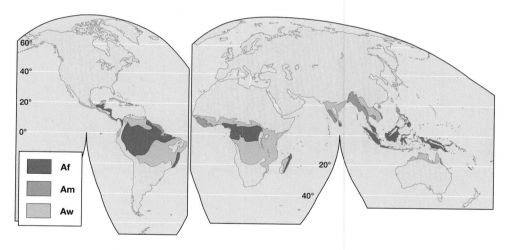

◀ **Figure 8-6**   Distribution of A climates.

High humidity and considerable rainfall are expectable results. Table 8-3 summarizes A group characteristics.

The tropical humid climates are classified into three types on the basis of annual rainfall. The **tropical wet** has abundant rainfall every month of the year. The **tropical savanna** is characterized by a low-Sun dry season and a prominent but not extraordinary high-Sun wet season. The **tropical monsoon** has a dry season and a distinct very rainy high-Sun wet season.

Tropical Wet Climate (Af)   Tropical wet climates are predominantly equatorial, found in an east–west sprawl astride the equator and extending some 5–10° poleward on either side (Figure 8-6). In some eastern-coast locations, they may extend as much as 25° away from the equator. The largest areas of Af climate occur in the upper

Amazon basin of South America, the northern Congo (Zaire) basin of Africa, and the islands of the East Indies.

The single most descriptive word that can be applied to the tropical wet climate is monotonous because it is a seasonless climate, with endless repetition of the same weather day after day after day. Warmth prevails, with every month having an average temperature close to 27°C (80°F), as Figure 8-7 shows. The terms *summer* and *winter* do not really apply because the *average annual temperature range* (the difference between the average temperatures of the coolest and warmest months) is minuscule, typically only 1 or 1.5°C (2 or 3°F) and only rarely over 4°C (7°F), by far the smallest annual temperature range of any climatic type. This seasonless condition in Af regions has given rise to the saying, "Night is the winter of the tropics."

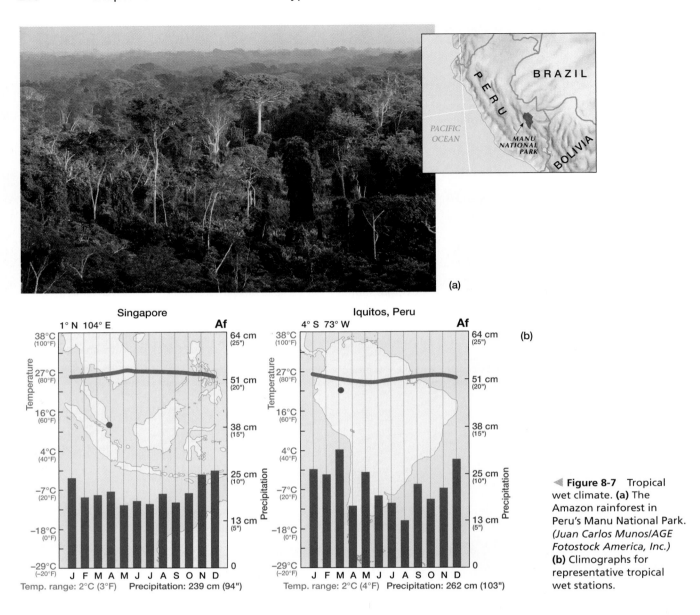

(a)

(b)

◀ **Figure 8-7** Tropical
wet climate. **(a)** The
Amazon rainforest in
Peru's Manu National Park.
*(Juan Carlos Munos/AGE
Fotostock America, Inc.)*
(b) Climographs for
representative tropical
wet stations.

Daily temperature variations are somewhat greater than annual ones, although still not impressive. This is one of the few climates in which the *average daily temperature range* exceeds the average annual temperature range (Figure 8-8). On a typical afternoon, the temperature rises to the low 30s °C (high 80s °F), dropping to the low 20s °C (middle or low 70s °F) in the coolest period just before dawn. The temperature rarely extends much into the mid-30s °C, (90s °F), even on the hottest days, and it's equally unusual to have much cooling at night.

Regardless of the thermometer reading, however, the weather feels warm in this climate because high humidity makes for high sensible temperatures, except perhaps where a sea breeze blows. Both absolute and relative humidity are high, and rain can be expected just about every day—sometimes twice or three times a day (Figure 8-9). Rainfall is of the unstable, showery

variety, usually coming from convective thunderstorms that yield heavy rain for a short time. A typical morning dawns bright and clear. Cumulus clouds build up in the forenoon and develop into cumulonimbus thunderheads, producing a furious convectional rainstorm in early afternoon. Then the clouds usually disperse so that by late afternoon there is a partly cloudy sky and a glorious sunset. The clouds often recur at night to create a nocturnal thunderstorm, followed by dispersal once again. The next day dawns bright and clear, and the sequence repeats.

Each month receives several centimeters of rain, and the annual total normally is between 150 and 250 centimeters, (60 and 100 inches), although in some locations it is considerably greater. Yearly rainfall in the Af climate is exceeded by that of only one other type of climate (tropical monsoon).

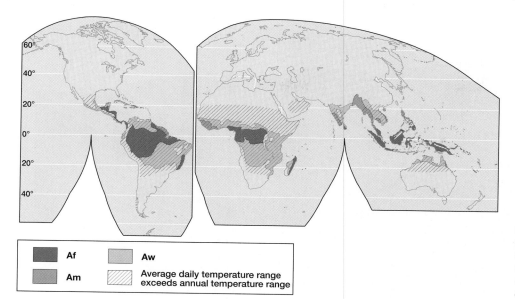

◀ **Figure 8-8** Land portions of the world where the average daily temperature range exceeds the average annual temperature range. This characteristic is typical of A climates but rare in other climates.

Why these climatic conditions occur where they do is relatively straightforward. The principal climatic control is latitude. A Sun high in the sky throughout the year makes for relatively uniform insolation through the year, and so there is little opportunity for seasonal temperature variation. This extensive heating produces considerable thermal convection, which accounts for a portion of the raininess. More important, the influence of the ITCZ for most or all of the year leads to widespread uplift of warm, humid, unstable air. Persistent onshore winds along trade-wind (i.e., east-facing) coasts provide a consistent source of moisture and add another mechanism for precipitation—orographic ascent. Indeed, the maximum poleward extent of Af climate is found along such trade-wind coasts, as in Central America and Madagascar. Interior areas, however, typically lack a great deal of wind—a consequence of the persistent influence of the ITCZ and its ongoing convective updrafts (you'll recall that the latitudes around the equator are sometimes referred to as the "doldrums" because of the lack of horizontal air movement).

Tropical Savanna Climate (Aw) The most extensive of the A climates, the tropical savanna, generally lies both to the north and south of the Af (Figure 8-4). It is widespread in Africa to the east of the tropical wet region, extending poleward to about latitudes 30° S and 10° N. It occurs broadly in South America and southern Asia and to a lesser extent in northern Australia, Central America, and the Caribbean islands.

The distinctive characteristic of the Aw climate is its clear-cut seasonal alternation of wet and dry periods (Figure 8-10). This characteristic is explained by the fact that Aw climates lie between the unstable, converging air of the ITCZ (which dominates the Af climates) on their equatorial side and stable, anticyclonic air of the subtropical high on their poleward side. As the global wind and pressure systems shift latitudinally with the Sun over the course of a year, Aw regions experience significant contrasts in weather. During the low-Sun season (winter), all wind and air-pressure systems shift toward the opposite hemisphere so that savanna regions are dominated by subtropical high-pressure conditions of subsiding and diverging air which produce dry weather and clear skies. In summer, the systems shift in the opposite direction, bringing the ITCZ and its wet tropical weather patterns into the Aw region (these seasonal precipitation patterns are clearly seen in Figure 6-35 in Chapter 6). The poleward limits of Aw climate are approximately equivalent to the poleward maximum migration of the ITCZ (Figure 8-11).

Annual rainfall totals in the tropical savanna climate are generally less than in the other two A climates, as Table 8-3 shows; typical Aw annual averages are between 90 and 180 centimeters (35 and 70 inches). The high-Sun season is conspicuously wet, with one to four months

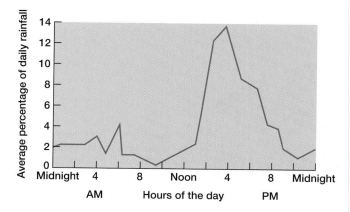

▲ **Figure 8-9** A typical daily pattern of rainfall in an Af climate. This example, from Malaysia, shows a heavy concentration in midafternoon with a small secondary peak at or shortly before dawn.

(a)

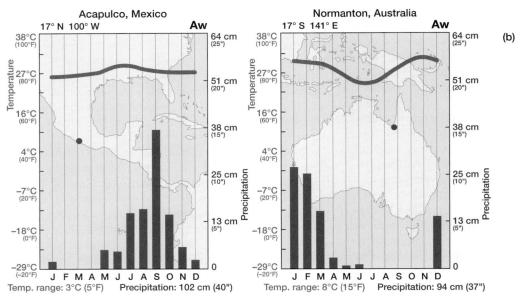

(b)

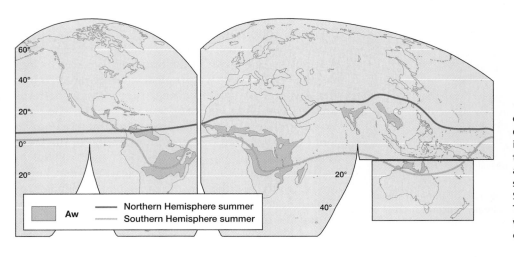

Figure 8-10 Tropical savanna climate. **(a)** Tall savanna grassland at the end of the wet season in Masai Mara National Reserve in Kenya. *(Michele Burgess/Corbis/ Stock Market.)* **(b)** Climographs for representative tropical savanna stations.

Figure 8-11 The intertropical convergence zone migrates widely during the year. The red line shows its typical northern boundary in the Northern Hemisphere summer, and the orange line indicates its southern boundary in the Southern Hemisphere summer. These lines coincide approximately with the poleward limits of Aw climate.

receiving at least 25 centimeters (10 inches) of rain. The low-Sun season, on the other hand, is distinctly a time of drought, sometimes with three or four rainless months.

Average annual temperatures in Aw regions are about the same as in Af regions, but with a somewhat greater month-to-month variation in the former. Winter is a little cooler and summer a little hotter than in Af regions, giving an annual temperature range generally between 3 and 8°C (5 and 15°F). The hottest time of the year is likely to be in late spring just before the onset of the summer rains.

Many tropical savanna climate areas can be thought of as having three seasons rather than two. The wet season is much like the wet season anywhere else in the tropics, with high sensible temperatures, muggy air, and frequent convective showers. The early part of the dry season is a period of clearing skies and slight cooling. The later part of the dry season is a time of fire: wildfires, fueled by the desiccated grass and shrubs, are common almost every year during this season.

Tropical Monsoon Climate (Am) The tropical monsoon climate is most extensive on the windward (west-facing) coasts of southeastern Asia (primarily India, Myanmar [formerly Burma], and Thailand), but it also occurs in more restricted coastal regions of western Africa, northeastern South America, the Philippines, northeastern Australia, and some islands of the East Indies (Figure 8-12a).

The distinctiveness of the Am climate is shown primarily in its rainfall pattern (Figure 8-12b). During the high-Sun season, an enormous amount of rain falls in association with the "summer" monsoon. It is not unusual to have more than 75 centimeters (30 inches) of

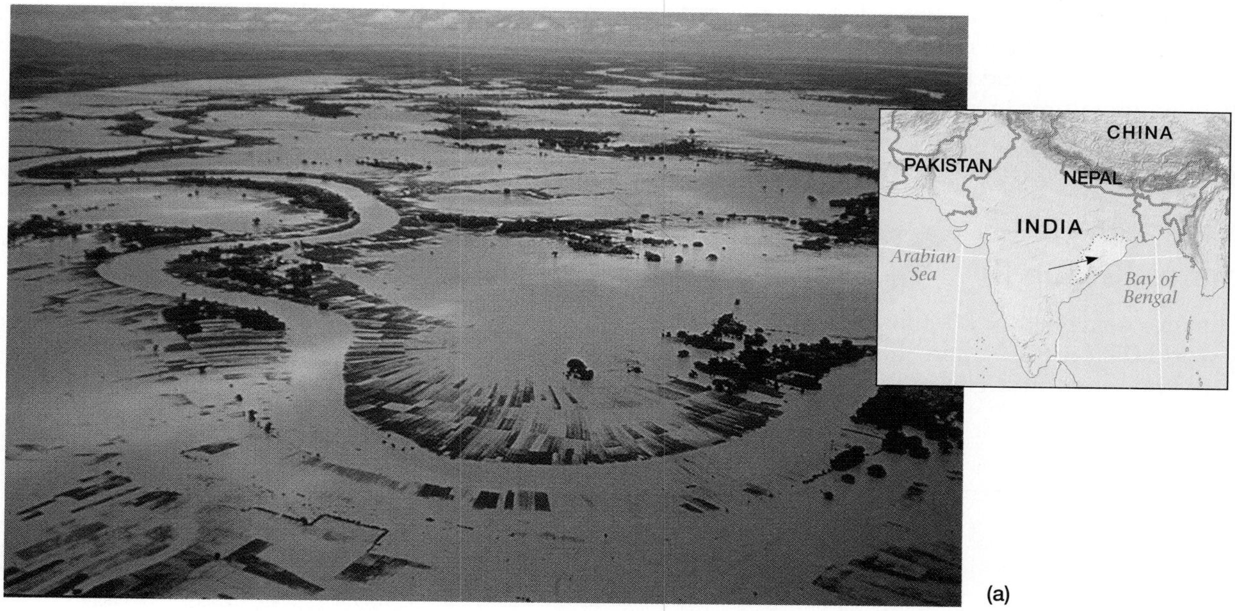

(a)

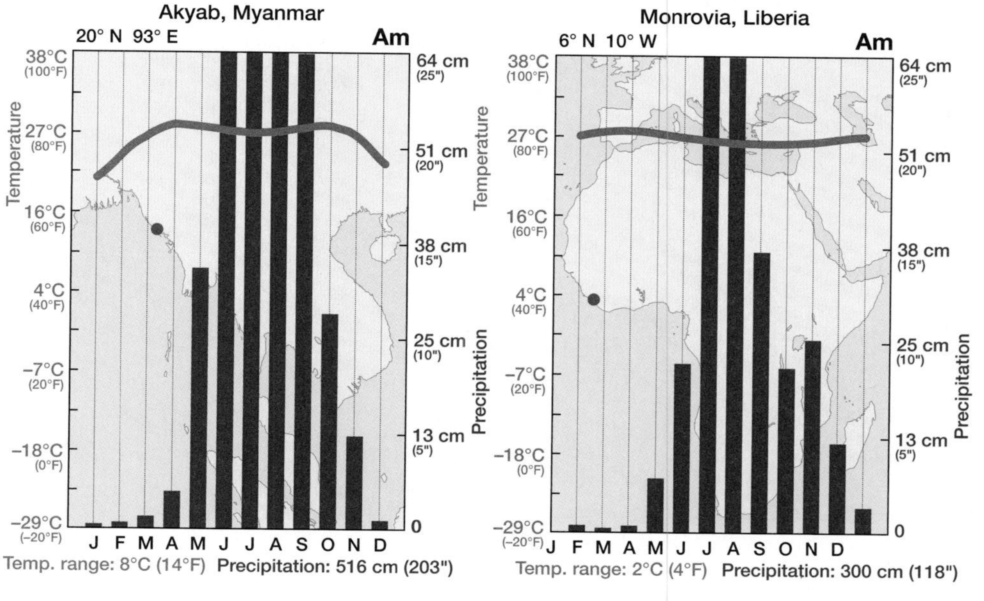

(b)

Figure 8-12 Tropical monsoon climate. **(a)** Monsoon floods inundate the landscape in the Indian state of Orissa. *(Brian Blake/John Hillelson Agency.)* **(b)** Climographs for representative tropical monsoon stations.

rain in each of two or three months. The annual total for a typical Am station is between 250 and 500 centimeters (100 and 200 inches). An extreme example is Cherrapunji (in the Khasi hills of Assam in eastern India), which has an annual average of 1065 centimeters (425 inches). Cherrapunji has been inundated with 210 centimeters (84 inches) in three days, with 930 centimeters (366 inches) in one month, and with a memorable 2647 centimeters (1042 inches) in its record year (Figure 8-13).

During the low-Sun season, Am climates are dominated by offshore winds. The "winter" monsoon during this season produces little precipitation: from one to four months may record less than 6 centimeters (2.5 inches) per month, and one or two months may be rainless.

A lesser distinction of the Am climate is its annual temperature curve. Although the annual temperature range may be only slightly greater than in a tropical wet climate, the highest Am temperatures normally occur in late spring prior to the onset of the summer monsoon. The heavy cloud cover of the wet monsoon period shields out some of the insolation, resulting in slightly lower temperatures in summer than in spring. Apart from these monsoonal modifications, the climatic characteristics of Af and Am locations are similar.

Dry Climates (Group B) FG9

The dry climates cover about 30 percent of the land area of the world (Figure 8-14), more than any other climatic zone. Although at first glance their distribution

pattern appears erratic and complex, it actually has a considerable degree of predictability.

The arid regions of the world develop either as a result of the lack of air uplift necessary for cloud formation, or from the lack of moisture in the air—in some cases, both. The largest expanses of dry areas are in subtropical latitudes, especially in the western and central portions of continents where subsidence associated with subtropical high-pressure cells suppresses upward vertical motion; high-altitude temperature inversions often develop, further inhibiting the likelihood of updrafts and adiabatic cooling. Cool ocean currents serve to increase atmospheric stability in west coast locations, and subsidence in the lee of mountain barriers extends the region's dryness in some subtropical locations. Desert conditions also occur over extensive ocean areas, and it is quite reasonable to refer to marine deserts.

In the midlatitudes, particularly in central Asia, arid climates are found in areas that are cut off from sources of surface moisture either by great distances or by their position in the rain shadow of topographic barriers.

The concept of dry climate is a complex one because it involves the balance between precipitation and evapotranspiration and so depends not only on rainfall but also on temperature. Generally, higher temperature engenders greater potential evapotranspiration, and so hot regions can receive more precipitation than cool regions and yet be classified as dry.

As Table 8-1 and Figure 8-4 show, the two main categories of B climates are *desert* and *steppe*. Deserts are extremely arid, while steppes are semiarid. Normally

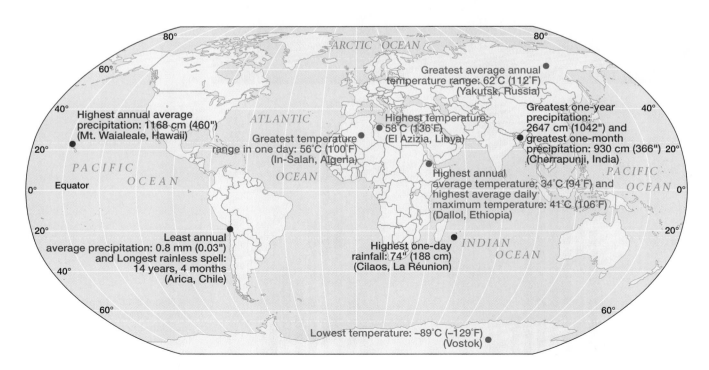

▲ **Figure 8-13** Locations of some extreme weather records.

the deserts of the world are large core areas of aridity surrounded by a transitional fringe of steppe that is slightly less dry. The two B climates are further classified based on temperature into "hot" **subtropical desert** and **subtropical steppe**, and "cold" **midlatitude desert** and **midlatitude steppe**. Our discussion here focuses on the deserts because they represent the epitome of dry conditions—the arid extreme. Most of what is stated about deserts applies to steppes but in modified intensity. Table 8-4 gives an overview of all the B climates.

Subtropical Desert Climate (BWh) In both the Northern and Southern Hemispheres, subtropical deserts lie either in or very near the band of the subtropical highs (Figure 8-15). Arid conditions reach to the western coasts of all continents in these latitudes

in part due to the added stability provided by cool ocean currents. Subsidence is weaker on the western sides of the subtropical highs, with the result that, except in North Africa, which is sheltered from oceanic influence by the Arabian peninsula, the aridity does not extend to the eastern coast of any continent in these latitudes (Figure 8-16). Climographs for two typical BWh locations are shown in Figure 8-16b.

The enormous expanse of BWh climate in North Africa (the Sahara) and southwestern Asia (the Arabian Desert) represents more desert area than is found in the rest of the world combined. Such an extensive development is explained by the year-round presence of anticyclonic conditions and the remoteness from any upwind source of moisture. The adjacency of Eurasia makes Africa a continent without an eastern coast

TABLE 8-4 Summary of B Climates: Dry

Type	Location	Temperature	Precipitation	Dominant Controls of Climate
Subtropical desert (BWh)	Centered at latitudes 25–30° on western sides of continents, extending into interiors; most extensive in northern Africa and southwestern Asia	Very hot summers, relatively mild winters; enormous DTR, moderate ATR	Rainfall scarce, (typically less than 30 cm [12 in.]) unreliable, intense; little cloudiness	Subsidence from subtropical highs; cool ocean currents; rain shadow of mountains
Subtropical steppe (BSh)	Fringing BWh except on west	Similar to BWh but more moderate	Semiarid	Similar to BWh
Midlatitude desert (BWk)	Central Asia; western interior of United States; Patagonia	Hot summers, cold winters; very large ATR, large DTR	Meager (typically less than 25 cm, [10 in.]) erratic, mostly showery; some winter snow	Distant from sources of moisture; some rain shadow effects
Midlatitude steppe (BSk)	Peripheral to BWk; transitional to more humid climates	Similar to BWk but slightly more moderate	Semiarid; some winter snow	Similar to BWk

B climates are widespread in the subtropics where they are associated with anticyclonic conditions. In the midlatitudes they occur in extreme continental locations that are remote from sources of moisture. Deserts are arid, steppes are semiarid, and evaporation exceeds precipitation in both.

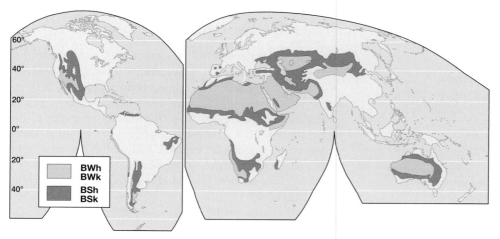

■	BWh BWk
■	BSh BSk

◀ **Figure 8-14** Distribution of B climates.

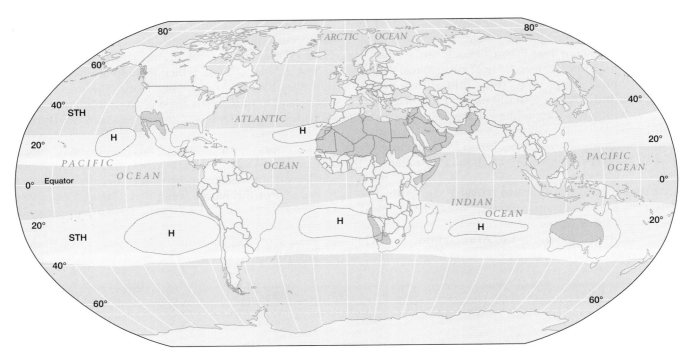

▲ **Figure 8-15**   The coincidence of the subtropical high-pressure zones and BWh climates is striking.

north of 10° N latitude, and so the BWh climate extends from coast to coast in northern Africa. This climate is also expansive in Australia (50 percent of the continental area) because the mountains that parallel the eastern coast of that continent are just high enough to prevent Pacific winds from penetrating; most of Australia is in the rain shadow of those eastern highlands.

Subtropical deserts have a much more restricted longitudinal extent in southwest Africa, South America, and North America, but they are elongated latitudinally along the coast because of the presence of cold offshore waters which chill the overlying air and inhibit precipitation. The greatest elongation occurs along the western side of South America, where the Atacama Desert is not only the "longest" but also the driest of the dry lands. The Atacama is sandwiched in a "double" rain shadow position (Figure 8-17): moist winds from the east are kept out of this region by one of the world's great mountain ranges (the Andes), and Pacific air is thoroughly chilled and stabilized as it passes over the world's most prominent cold current (the Peru or "Humboldt").

The distinctive climatic characteristic of deserts is lack of moisture, and three adjectives are particularly applicable to precipitation conditions in subtropical deserts: scarce, unreliable, intense.

1. *Scarce*—Subtropical deserts are among the most nearly rainless regions on Earth. According to unofficial records, some have experienced several consecutive years without a single drop of moisture falling from the sky. Most BWh regions, however, are not totally without precipitation. Annual totals of between 5 and 20 centimeters (2 and 8 inches) are characteristic, and some places receive as much as 38 centimeters (15 inches).

2. *Unreliable*—An important climatic axiom is that the less the mean annual precipitation, the greater its variability (see Figure 6-37 in Chapter 6). The very concept of an "average" yearly rainfall in a BWh location is misleading because of year-to-year fluctuations. Yuma, Arizona, for example, has a long-term average rainfall of 7.6 centimeters (3.0 inches), but over a two decade period it has received as little as 1.3 centimeters (0.5 inch) and as much as 18 centimeters (7 inches) in a given year. In short, percentage deviation from the norm tends to be very high in BWh climates.

3. *Intense*—Most precipitation in these regions falls in vigorous convective showers that are localized and of short duration. Thus, the rare rains may bring brief floods to regions that have been bereft of surface moisture for months.

Temperatures in BWh regions also have certain distinctive characteristics. The combination of low-latitude location and lack of cloudiness permits a great deal of insolation to reach the surface. Summers are interminably long and blisteringly hot, with monthly averages in the middle to high 30s °C (high 90s °F)—significantly hotter than most equatorial regions. Midwinter months have average temperatures in the high teens °C (60s °F), which gives moderate annual temperature ranges of 8° to 14°C (15–25°F).

Daily temperature ranges, on the other hand, are sometimes astounding. Summer days are so hot that the

(a)

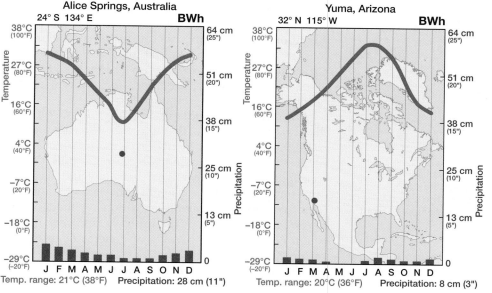

(b)

Alice Springs, Australia
24° S 134° E   **BWh**
Temp. range: 21°C (38°F)   Precipitation: 28 cm (11")

Yuma, Arizona
32° N 115° W   **BWh**
Temp. range: 20°C (36°F)   Precipitation: 8 cm (3")

◀ **Figure 8-16** Subtropical desert climate. **(a)** A subtropical desert landscape sometimes contains an abundance of sand. This scene is from central Namibia. *(Tom L. McKnight photo.)* **(b)** Climographs for representative subtropical desert stations.

nights do not have time to cool off significantly, but during the transition seasons of spring and fall, a 28°C (50°F) fluctuation between the heat of the afternoon and the cool of the following dawn is not unusual—generally clear skies and low water vapor content permit rapid nocturnal cooling from unimpeded longwave radiation transmission through the atmosphere.

Subtropical deserts often experience considerable windiness during daylight, but the air is usually calm at night. The daytime winds are apparently related to rapid daytime heating and strong convective activity, which accelerates surface currents. The persistent winds are largely unimpeded by soil and vegetation, with the result that a great deal of dust and sand is frequently carried along.

Specialized and unusual temperature conditions prevail along western coasts in subtropical deserts

(Figure 8-18). The cold waters offshore (the result of cool currents and *upwelling* of cold deeper ocean water) chill any air that moves across them. This cooling produces high relative humidity as well as frequent fog and low stratus clouds. Precipitation almost never results from this advective cooling, however, and the influence normally extends only a few kilometers inland. The immediate coastal region, however, is characterized by such abnormal desert conditions as relatively low summer temperatures (typical hot-month averages in the low 20s °C or low 70s °F), continuously high relative humidity, and greatly reduced annual and daily temperature ranges, as indicated by a comparison of Figures 8-16b and 8-19.

Subtropical Steppe Climate (BSh)   The BSh climates characteristically surround the BWh climates (except

▲ **Figure 8-17** The Atacama Desert is in a "double" rain shadow: The Andes Mountains to the east block the movement of moist air from the Atlantic, and the cold Peru (Humboldt) Current to the west inhibits the flow of moist Pacific air inland.

on the western side), the former separating the latter from the more humid climates beyond. Temperature and precipitation conditions are not significantly unlike those just described for BWh regions except that the extremes are more muted in the steppes (Figure 8-20). Thus, rainfall is somewhat greater and more reliable,

and temperatures are slightly moderated. Moreover, the meager precipitation tends to have a seasonal concentration. On the equatorward side of the desert, rain occurs in the high-Sun season; on the poleward side, it is concentrated in the low-Sun season.

Midlatitude Desert Climate (BWk) The BWk climates occur primarily in the deep interiors of continents, where they are either far removed geographically or blocked from oceanic influence by mountain ranges (Figure 8-4). The largest expanse of midlatitude dry climates, in central Asia, is both distant from any ocean and protected by massive mountains on the south from any contact with the South Asian summer monsoon. In North America, high mountains closely parallel the western coast and moist maritime air from the Gulf of Mexico affects the eastern half of the continent; as a result, the dry climates are displaced well to the west (Figure 8-21). The only other significant BWk region is in southern South America, where the desert reaches all the way to the eastern coast of Patagonia (southern Argentina). This anomalous situation has developed because the continent is so narrow in these latitudes that all of it lies in the rain shadow of the Andes to the west and the cool Falkland Current to the east. Climographs for two typical BWk locations are shown in Figure 8-21b.

Precipitation in midlatitude (BWk) deserts is much like that of subtropical (BWh) deserts—meager and erratic. Differences lie in two aspects: seasonality and intensity. Most BWk regions receive the bulk of their precipitation in summer, when warming and instability are common. Winter is usually dominated by low temperatures and anticyclonic conditions. Although most BWk precipitation is of the unstable, showery variety, there are also some periods of general overcast and protracted drizzle.

The principal climatic differences between midlatitude and subtropical deserts are in temperature, especially winter temperature (see Figure 8-21a), with BWk regions having severely cold winters. The average cold-month temperature is normally below freezing,

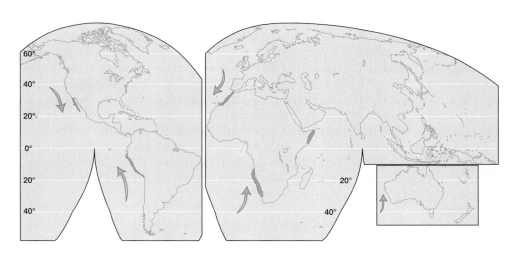

◀ **Figure 8-18** Cool, foggy west coast deserts are found along coasts paralleled by cool ocean currents and cold upwellings. Such deserts are mostly in subtropical west coast locations, with two exceptions: They are absent from the western coast of Australia, and they occur on the eastern coast of the "horn" of Africa (Somalia).

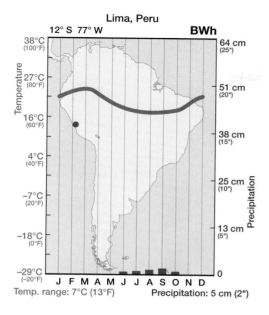

▲ **Figure 8-19** Climograph for a cool west coast desert station.

and some BWk stations have six months with below-freezing averages. This cold produces average annual temperatures that are much lower than in BWh regions and greatly increases the annual temperature range; variations exceeding 28°C (50°F) between January and July average temperatures are not uncommon.

Midlatitude Steppe Climate (BSk) As in the subtropics, midlatitude steppes generally occupy transitional positions between deserts and humid climates. Typically midlatitude steppes have more precipitation than midlatitude deserts and lesser temperature extremes. Figure 8-22 presents typical BSk climographs. In western North America, the steppe climate is much more extensive in area than is

the desert, so that the desert-core-and-steppe-fringe model is not followed exactly. Semiarid conditions are broadly prevalent; only in the interior southwest of the United States is the climate sufficiently arid to be classified as desert.

Mild Midlatitude Climates (Group C)

The middle latitudes exhibit great short-run weather variability. Seasonal contrasts are also marked in these latitudes, which lack both the constant heat of the tropics and the almost-continuous cold of the polar regions. The midlatitudes are a region of air-mass contrast, with frequent alternating incursions of tropical and polar air producing more convergence than anywhere else except at the equator. This air-mass conflict creates a kaleidoscope of atmospheric disturbances and weather changes. The seasonal rhythm of temperature is usually more prominent than that of precipitation. Whereas in the tropics the seasons are characterized as wet and dry, in the midlatitudes they are clearly summer and winter.

The mild midlatitude climates (Group C climates) occupy the equatorward margin of the middle latitudes, occasionally extending into the subtropics and being elongated poleward in some western coastal areas (Figure 8-23). They constitute a transition between warmer tropical climates and severe midlatitude climates.

Summers in the C climates are long and usually hot; winters are short and relatively mild. These zones, in contrast to the A climate zones, experience occasional winter frosts and therefore do not have a year-round *growing season*. Precipitation is highly variable in the C climates, with regard to both total amount and seasonal distribution. Year-round moisture deficiency is not characteristic, but there are sometimes pronounced seasonal moisture deficiencies.

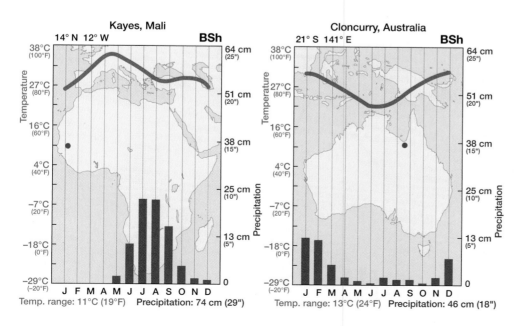

◄ **Figure 8-20** Climographs for representative subtropical steppe stations.

(a)

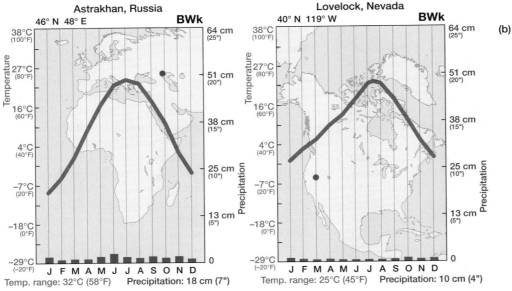

Astrakhan, Russia
46° N 48° E   **BWk**
Temp. range: 32°C (58°F)   Precipitation: 18 cm (7")

Lovelock, Nevada
40° N 119° W   **BWk**
Temp. range: 25°C (45°F)   Precipitation: 10 cm (4")

◀ **Figure 8-21** Midlatitude desert climate. **(a)** Midlatitude deserts are characterized by cold winters. Here a fresh snowfall covers such typical desert plants as creosote bush and yucca near Kingman in northwestern Arizona. *(Tom L. McKnight photo.)* **(b)** Climographs for representative midlatitude desert stations.

(b)

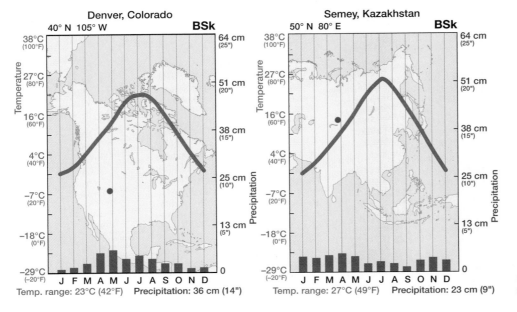

Denver, Colorado
40° N 105° W   **BSk**
Temp. range: 23°C (42°F)   Precipitation: 36 cm (14")

Semey, Kazakhstan
50° N 80° E   **BSk**
Temp. range: 27°C (49°F)   Precipitation: 23 cm (9")

◀ **Figure 8-22** Climographs for representative midlatitude steppe stations.

The C climates are subdivided into three types primarily on the basis of precipitation seasonality and secondarily on the basis of summer temperatures: **mediterranean, humid subtropical**, and **marine west coast**. Table 8-5 presents an overview.

Mediterranean Climate (Csa, Csb) The two Cs climates are sometimes referred to as *dry summer subtropical,* but the more widely used designation is *mediterranean.* (The proper terminology is without capitalization because it is a generic term for a type of climate; Mediterranean with the capital M refers to a specific region around the Mediterranean Sea.)

Cs climates are found on the western side of continents centered at about latitudes 35° N and 35° S. With one exception, all mediterranean regions are small, being restricted mostly to coastal areas either by interior mountains or by limited landmasses. These small regions are in central and southern California (Figure 8-24), central Chile, the southern tip of Africa, and the two southwestern "corners" of Australia. The only extensive area of mediterranean climate is around the borderlands of the Mediterranean Sea.

Cs climates have three distinctive characteristics:

1. The modest annual precipitation falls in winter, summers being virtually rainless.

TABLE 8-5 Summary of C Climates: Mild Midlatitude

Type	Location	Temperature	Precipitation	Dominant Controls of Climate
Mediterranean (Csa, Csb)	Centered at 35° latitude on western sides of continents, limited east–west extent except in Mediterranean Sea area	Warm/hot summers; mild winters; year-round mildness in coastal areas	Moderate (38–64 cm [15–25 in.]) annually, nearly all in winter; much sunshine, some coastal fog	STH subsidence and stability in summer; westerly winds and cyclonic storms in winter
Humid subtropical (Cfa, Cwa)	Centered at 30° latitude on eastern sides of continents; considerable east–west extent	Summers warm/hot, sultry; winters mild to cold	Abundant (100–150 cm [40–60 in.] annually), mostly rain; summer maxima but no true dry season	Westerly winds and storms in winter; moist onshore flow in summer; monsoons in Asia
Marine west coast (Cfb, Cfc)	Latitudes 40–60° on western sides of continents; limited inland extent except in Europe	Very mild winters for the latitude; generally mild summers; moderate ATR	Moderate to abundant, mostly in winter; many days with rain; much cloudiness	Westerly flow and oceanic influence year-round

C climates occupy the equatorward margin of the middle latitudes but may extend considerably poleward along western coasts. Summers are long and usually hot; winters are short and relatively mild; precipitation conditions are varied.

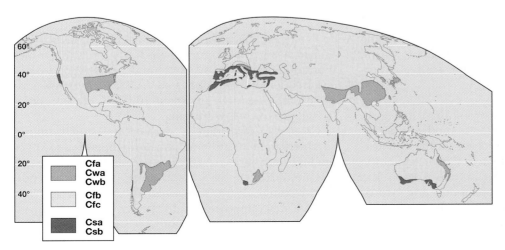

◀ **Figure 8-23** Distribution of C climates.

(a)

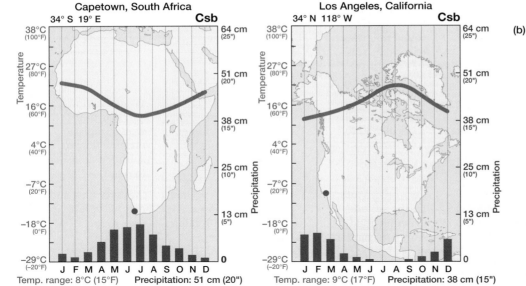

(b)

Capetown, South Africa
34° S 19° E   **Csb**
Temp. range: 8°C (15°F)   Precipitation: 51 cm (20")

Los Angeles, California
34° N 118° W   **Csb**
Temp. range: 9°C (17°F)   Precipitation: 38 cm (15")

◀ **Figure 8-24** Mediterranean climate. **(a)** An open oak woodland is a typical mediterranean landscape in southern California. *(Tom L. McKnight photo.)* **(b)** Climographs for representative mediterranean stations.

2. Winter temperatures are unusually mild for the midlatitudes, and summers vary from hot to warm.
3. Clear skies and abundant sunshine are typical especially in summer.

Two representative locations are shown in Figure 8-24b. Average annual precipitation is modest ranging from about 38 centimeters (15 inches) on the equatorward margin to about 64 centimeters (25 inches) at the poleward margin. The midwinter rainfall is from 8 to 13 centimeters (3 to 5 inches) per month, and two or three midsummer months are totally dry. Only one other climatic type, marine west coast, has such a concentration of precipitation in winter (Figure 8-25).

Most mediterranean climate is classified as Csa, which means that summers are hot, with midsummer monthly averages between 24 and 29°C (75 and 85°F) and frequent maxima above 38°C (100°F). Average cold-month temperatures are about 10°C (50°F), with occasional minima below freezing.

Coastal mediterranean areas have much milder summers than inland mediterranean areas as a result of sea breezes; these coastal climates are classified as Csb (Figure 8-26). In the coastal areas, the average hot-month temperature is between 16 and 21°C (60 and 70°F). Csb winters are slightly milder than Csa winters, the former having cold-month averages of about 13°C (55°F). Csb regions also have higher humidity, frequent

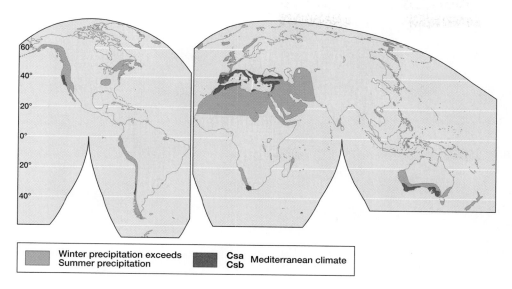

◀ **Figure 8-25** Lands that have precipitation maxima in winter rather than in summer are mostly associated with mediterranean and marine west coast climates and regions adjacent to them.

Winter precipitation exceeds Summer precipitation

Csa Csb   Mediterranean climate

nocturnal coastal advection fog, and occasional low stratus overcast.

The genesis of mediterranean climates is clear-cut. In summer, these regions are dominated by dry, stable, subsiding air from the eastern portions of subtropical highs (STHs). In winter, the wind and pressure belts shift equatorward, and mediterranean regions come under the influence of the westerlies with their migratory midlatitude cyclones and associated fronts. Almost all precipitation comes from these cyclonic storms, except for occasional tropical influences in California.

Humid Subtropical Climate (Cfa, Cwa) Whereas mediterranean climates are found on the western side of continents, humid subtropical climates are found on the eastern side of continents at about the same latitude. The humid subtropical climate covers a more

extensive area both latitudinally and longitudinally than the mediterranean (see Figure 8-23). In some places, it reaches equatorward to almost 15° of latitude and extends poleward to about 40°. Its east–west extent is greatest in North America, Asia, and South America (Figure 8-27).

The humid subtropical climates differ from mediterranean climates in several important respects:

1. Summer temperatures in humid subtropical regions are generally warm to hot, with the highest monthly averages between 24 and 27°C (75 and 80°F). This is not dissimilar to the situation in Cs climates, but the humid subtropical regions are characterized by much higher humidity in summer, and so sensible temperatures are higher. Cfa days tend to be hot and sultry, and often night brings little relief.

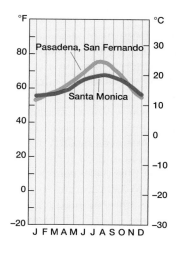

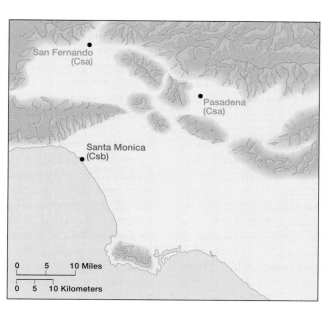

◀ **Figure 8-26** There are often significant temperature differences between coastal and inland mediterranean areas. This climograph shows the annual temperature curves for three stations in Southern California: Santa Monica (a coastal station; Csb climate) and Pasadena and San Fernando (inland stations having exactly the same average temperature for each month; Csa climate). The physiographic map shows the topographic and coastal relationships of the three stations.

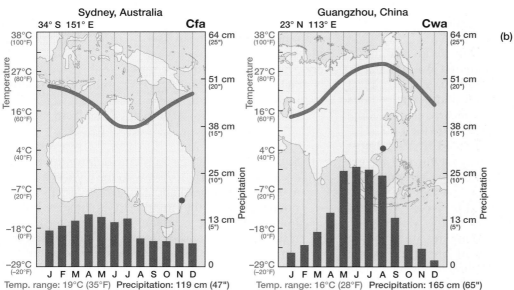

(a)

(b)

▲ **Figure 8-27** Humid subtropical climate. **(a)** The landscape of the humid subtropics, in its natural condition, is largely forested. This view of pine trees and "yellow" soil is in southern Mississippi, near Moss Point. (*Tom L. McKnight photo.*) **(b)** Climographs for representative humid subtropical stations.

2. Precipitation in humid subtropical regions tends to have a summer maximum.

3. Winter temperatures in Cfa regions are mild on the average, but winter is punctuated by cold waves that bring severe weather for a few days at a time.

Minimum temperatures can be 6–12°C (10–20°F) lower in the humid subtropics than in mediterranean regions, which means that killing frosts occur much more frequently in the former, especially in North America and Asia. The importance of this fact can be shown by agricultural adjustments. For example, the northernmost limit of commercial citrus production in the eastern United States (Florida, a Cfa climate) is at about 29° N latitude, but in the western United States (California, a Cs climate) it is at 38° N latitude, 1000 kilometers (625 miles) farther north (Figure 8-28).

The mild-summer characteristics of mediterranean (Csb) coasts have no counterpart in the humid subtropical regions in part because mediterranean climates are all adjacent to cool currents, whereas warm currents wash the humid subtropical coasts.

Annual precipitation is generally abundant and in some places copious, with a general decrease inland from east to west (Figure 8-29). Averages mostly are between 100 and 150 centimeters (40 and 60 inches), although some locations record as little as 75 centimeters (30 inches) and some receive up to 250 centimeters (100 inches). Summer is usually the time of precipitation maxima, associated with onshore flow and frequent convection. Winter is a time of diminished precipitation, but it is not really a dry season except in China, where winter monsoon conditions dominate. The rain and occasional snow of winter are the result of midlatitude cyclones passing through the region. In the North

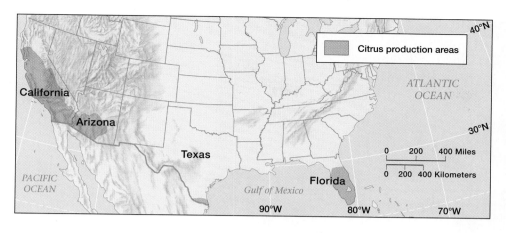

 ◀ **Figure 8-28** Distribution of citrus production in the conterminous United States. Winter cold spells prohibit commercial citrus growing north of central Florida in the eastern United States; the lack of severe freezes in much of California allows citrus to be grown much farther north. (*After U.S. Census of Agriculture, 1992.*)

American and Asian coastal areas, a late summer-autumn bulge in the precipitation curve is due to rainfall from tropical cyclones. Figure 8-27b shows two typical climographs for the humid subtropical climate.

To understand the controls of humid subtropical climates, it is again useful to make a comparison with mediterranean regions since both generally lie in the same latitude. During winter, westerly winds bring midlatitude cyclones and precipitation to both regions. In summer, however, in mediterranean regions along west coasts the poleward migration of the subtropical high and relatively cool ocean water stabilizes the atmosphere bringing dry weather, while on the eastern side of continents, where humid subtropical climates are found, no such stability exists—summer rain comes from the onshore flow of maritime air and frequent convective uplift, as well as the influence of tropical cyclones.

Marine West Coast Climate (Cfb, Cfc)   As the name implies, marine west coast climates are situated on the

western side of continents between about 40° and 65°; this is a windward location in the band of the westerlies. Only in the Southern Hemisphere, where landmasses are small in these latitudes (e.g., New Zealand, southeast Australia, and southernmost South America), does this oceanic climate extend across to eastern coasts (Figure 8-30).

The most extensive area of marine west coast climate is in western and central Europe, where the maritime influence can be carried some distance inland without hindrance from topographic barriers. The North American region is much more restricted interiorward by the presence of formidable mountain ranges that run perpendicular to the direction of onshore flow.

The dominant climate control for these regions is straightforward: persistent maritime influence from the onshore flow of the westerlies off the relatively cool west coast ocean waters throughout the year. This air current creates an extraordinarily temperate climate considering the latitude: lack of extreme temperatures, consistently high humidity, much cloudiness, and a high proportion of days with some precipitation. In contrast, mediterranean climates equatorward of Cfb regions come under greater influence of the subtropical high in summer, bringing clear, dry conditions during that time of year.

Two typical Cfb climographs are shown in Figure 8-30b. The oceanic influence ameliorates temperatures most of the time; this moderation is particularly noticeable when the daily and seasonal maxima and minima are considered. Isotherms tend to parallel the coastline rather than following their "normal" east–west paths. Indeed, temperatures on a western coast in these latitudes decrease poleward less than half as fast as on an eastern coast. Average hot-month temperatures are generally between 16 and 21°C (60 and 70°F), with cold months averaging between 2 and 7°C (35 and 45°F). There are occasionally very hot days (Seattle has recorded a temperature of 37°C or 98°F and Paris has reached 38°C or 100°F), but prolonged heat waves are rare. Similarly, very cold days occur on occasion, but low temperatures rarely persist. Frosts are relatively

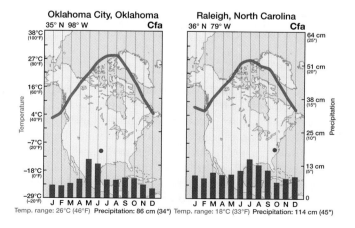

▲ **Figure 8-29** Annual precipitation in Cfa regions generally decreases from east to west, or interiorward into a continent. Raleigh, North Carolina, 240 kilometers (150 miles) from the Atlantic coast, receives 114 centimeters (45 inches) of precipitation annually, whereas Oklahoma City, 1760 kilometers (1100 miles) from the coast, receives only 86 centimeters (34 inches).

(a)

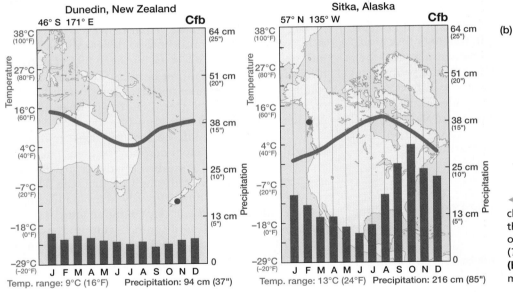

(b)

Dunedin, New Zealand
46° S 171° E   **Cfb**

Temp. range: 9°C (16°F)   Precipitation: 94 cm (37")

Sitka, Alaska
57° N 135° W   **Cfb**

Temp. range: 13°C (24°F)   Precipitation: 216 cm (85")

◀ **Figure 8-30**   Marine west coast climate. **(a)** Big trees dominate this marine west coast landscape on Canada's Vancouver Island. (*Tom L. McKnight photo.*) **(b)** Climographs for representative marine west coast stations.

infrequent except in interior European locations. London, for example, at 52° N latitude, experiences freezing temperatures on fewer than half the nights in January. There is also an abnormally long growing season for the latitude; around Seattle, for instance, the growing season is a month longer than that around Atlanta, a city lying 14° of latitude farther equatorward.

Marine west coast climates are among the wettest of the middle latitudes, although the total amount of Cfb/Cfc precipitation is not remarkable except in upland areas. Some localities receive as little as 50 centimeters (20 inches), but a range of between 75 and 125 centimeters (30 and 50 inches) is more typical. Much higher totals are recorded on exposed slopes, reaching 250 to 375 centimeters (100 to 150 inches) in some places. Snow is

uncommon in the lowlands, but higher, west-facing slopes receive some of the heaviest snowfalls in the world.

Perhaps more important to an understanding of the character of the marine west coast climate than total precipitation is *precipitation frequency*. Rainfall probability and reliability are high, but intensity is low. Drizzly frontal precipitation is characteristic. Humidity is high, with much cloudiness. Seattle, for example, receives only 43 percent of the total possible sunshine each year, in contrast to 70 percent in Los Angeles, and London has experienced as many as 72 consecutive days with rain. (Is it any wonder that the umbrella is that city's civic symbol?) Indeed, some places on the western coast of New Zealand's South Island have recorded 325 rainy days in a single year.

Severe Midlatitude Climates (Group D)

The severe midlatitude climates occur only in the Northern Hemisphere (Figure 8-31) because the Southern Hemisphere has limited landmasses at the appropriate latitudes—between 40° and 70°. This climatic group extends broadly across North America (encompassing the northeastern United States and much of Canada and Alaska) and Eurasia (from eastern Europe through most of Russia to the Pacific Ocean).

Continentality, by which is meant remoteness from oceans, is a keynote in the D climates. Landmasses are broader at these latitudes than anywhere else in the world. Even though these climates extend to the eastern coasts of the two continents, they experience little maritime influence because the general atmospheric circulation is westerly, bringing air from the interior of the continents to the east coasts.

The most conspicuous result of continental dominance of D climates is broad annual temperature fluctuation. These climates have four clearly recognizable seasons: a long, cold winter, a relatively short summer that varies from warm to hot, and transition periods in spring and fall. Annual temperature ranges are very large, particularly at more northerly locations where winters are most severe. Precipitation is moderate, although throughout the D climates it exceeds the potential evapotranspiration. Summer is the time of precipitation maximum, but winter is by no means completely dry, and snow cover lasts for many weeks or months.

The severe midlatitude climates are subdivided into two types on the basis of temperature. The **humid continental** type has long, warm summers, while the **subarctic** type is characterized by short summers and very cold winters. Table 8-6 summarizes the D climates.

Humid Continental Climate (Dfa, Dfb, Dwa, Dwb)

The latitudinal range of humid continental climate in North America and Asia is between 35° and 55° (Figure 8-32). The European region spreads from 35° to 60° in central Europe and tapers easterly through Russia and into Siberia. Figure 8-32b shows some typical climographs.

TABLE 8-6 Summary of D Climates: Severe Midlatitude

Type	Location	Temperature	Precipitation	Dominant Controls of Climate
Humid continental (Dfa, Dfb, Dwa, Dwb)	Northern Hemisphere only; latitudes 35–55° on eastern sides of continents	Warm/hot summers; cold winters; much day-to-day variation; large ATR	Moderate to abundant (50–125 cm [20–50 in.] annually); with summer maxima; diminishes interior-ward and poleward	Westerly winds and storms, especially in winter; monsoons in Asia
Subarctic (Dfc, Dfd, Dwc, Dwd)	Northern Hemisphere only, latitudes 50–70° across North America and Eurasia	Long, dark, very cold winters; brief, mild summers; enormous ATR	Meager (13–50 cm [5–20 in.] annually), with summer maxima; light snow in winter but little melting	Pronounced continentality; westerlies and cyclonic storms alternating with prominent anticyclonic conditions

D climates occur only in the broad Northern Hemisphere landmasses between about 50 and 70° of latitude. Winters are long, dark, and unremittingly cold; summers are short and mild. Precipitation is meager, but evaporation is small.

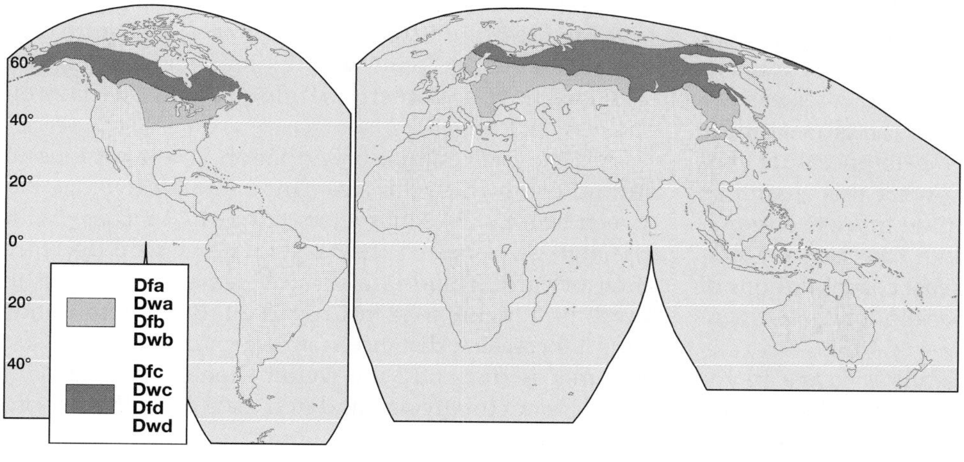

Figure 8-31 Distribution of D climates.

(a)

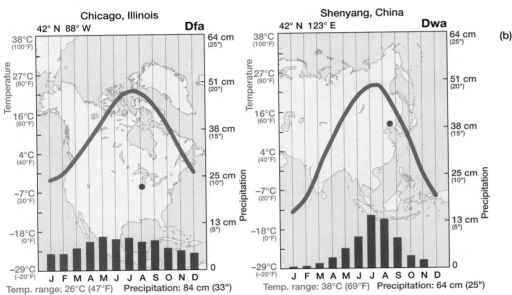

(b)

Chicago, Illinois
42° N 88° W **Dfa**
Temp. range: 26°C (47°F) Precipitation: 84 cm (33")

Shenyang, China
42° N 123° E **Dwa**
Temp. range: 38°C (69°F) Precipitation: 64 cm (25")

◀ **Figure 8-32** Humid continental climate. **(a)** The barren look of winter in a humid continental climate. This open woodland of deciduous trees is near Detroit in southern Michigan. (*Tom L. McKnight photo.*) **(b)** Climographs for representative humid continental stations.

This climatic type is dominated by the westerly wind belt throughout the year, which means that there are frequent weather changes associated with the passage of migratory pressure systems, especially in winter. Variability, then, both seasonal and daily, is a prominent characteristic. Although large areas of humid continental climate are located along the coastlines of eastern North America and Eurasia—at much the same latitude as marine west coast climates—the temperature pattern is continental. The explanation for this is simple: while westerly winds bring maritime influence to marine west coast locations throughout the year, westerly winds bring continental air to the east coast locations of humid continental climates—especially cold continental air masses during winter.

Hot-month temperatures generally average in the mid-20s °C (mid-70s °F), and so summers are as warm as those of the humid subtropical climate to the south,

although summer is shorter. The average cold-month temperature is usually between −12° and −4°C (10 and 25°F), with from one to five months averaging below freezing. Winter temperatures decrease rapidly northward in the humid continental climates, as Figure 8-33 shows, and the growing season diminishes from about 200 days on the southern margin to about 100 days on the northern edge.

Despite their name, precipitation is not copious in humid continental climates. Annual totals average between 50 and 100 centimeters (20 and 40 inches), with the highest values on the coast and a general decrease interiorward. There is also a decrease from south to north (see Figure 6-36 in Chapter 6). Both these trends reflect increasing distance from warm moist air masses. Summer is distinctly the wetter time of the year, but winter is not totally dry, and in coastal areas the seasonal variation is muted. Summer rain is mostly convective

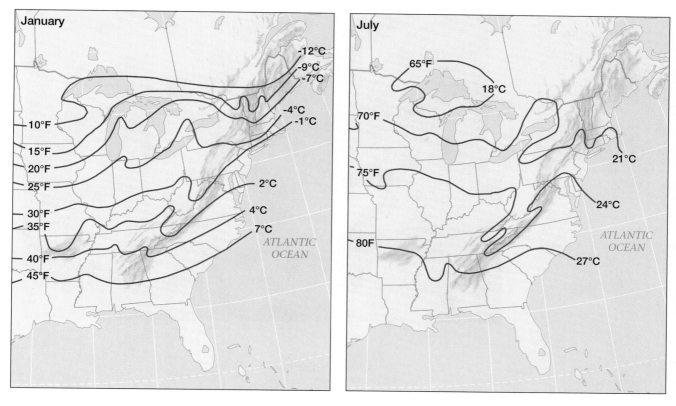

▲ **Figure 8-33** North–south temperature variation in the midlatitudes is much sharper in winter than in summer. These maps of the eastern United States show a very steep north–south temperature gradient in January (left), with a more gradual gradient in July (right).

or monsoon in origin. Winter precipitation is associated with midlatitude cyclones, and much of it falls as snow. During a typical winter, snow covers the ground for only two or three weeks in the southern part of these regions, but for as long as eight months in the northern portions (Figure 8-34).

Day-to-day variability and dramatic changes are prominent features of the weather pattern. These are regions of cold waves, heat waves, blizzards, thunderstorms, tornadoes, and other dynamic atmospheric phenomena.

Subarctic Climate (Dfc, Dfd, Dwc, Dwd) The subarctic climate occupies the higher midlatitudes generally between 50° and 70°. As Figure 8-4 shows, this climate occurs as two vast, uninterrupted expanses across the broad northern landmasses: from western Alaska across Canada to Newfoundland and across Eurasia from Scandinavia to easternmost Siberia (Figure 8-35). The name *boreal* (which means "northern" and comes from Boreas, mythological Greek god of the north wind) is sometimes applied to this climatic type in Canada; in Eurasia it is often called *taiga,* after the Russian name for the forest in the region where this climate occurs. Figure 8-35b shows some typical climographs.

The keyword in the subarctic climate is "winter," which is long, dark, and bitterly cold. In most places, ice

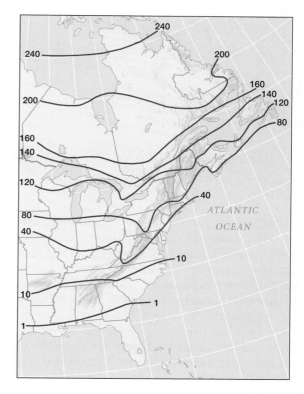

▲ **Figure 8-34** The average duration of snow cover in eastern North America including the Dfa region. The numbers on the isolines represent the average annual number of days with a snow cover of 2.5 centimeters (1 inch) or more.

(a)

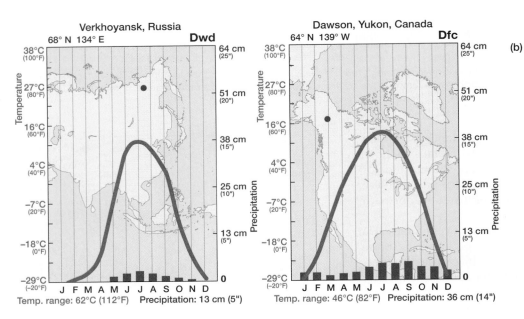

(b)

Figure 8-35 Subarctic climate. **(a)** Trees, rocks, and water are the principal landscape elements in the subarctic climate. This scene shows the Rushing River in western Ontario, Canada. (*Tom L. McKnight photo.*) **(b)** Climographs for representative subarctic stations.

begins to form on the lakes in September or October and doesn't thaw until May or later. For six or seven months, the average temperature is below freezing, and the coldest months have averages below −38°C (−36°F). The world's coldest temperatures, apart from the Antarctic and Greenland ice caps, are found in the subarctic climate; the records are −68°C (−90°F) in Siberia and −62°C (−82°F) in Alaska.

Summer warms up remarkably despite its short duration. Although the intensity of the sunlight is low (because of the small angle of incidence), summer days are very long and nights are too short to permit much radiational cooling. Average hot-month temperatures are typically in the midteens or low 20s °C, (high 50s or low 60s °F), but occasional frosts may occur in any month.

Annual temperature ranges in this climate are the largest in the world. Variations from average hot-month to average cool-month temperatures frequently exceed 45°C (80°F) and in some places are more than 50°C (100°F). The absolute annual temperature variation (fluctuation from the very coldest to the very hottest ever recorded) sometimes reaches unbelievable magnitude—especially in deep inland locations; the world record is −68°C to +37°C (−90°F to +98°F), a range of 105°C (188°F) in Verkhoyansk, Siberia.

Spring and fall are brief transition seasons that slip by rapidly, usually in April/May and September/October. Summer is short, and winter is dominant.

Precipitation is usually meager in the subarctic climates. Annual totals range from only 13 centimeters

(5 inches) to about 50 centimeters (20 inches), with the higher values occurring in coastal areas. The low temperatures allow for little moisture in the air, and anticyclonic conditions predominate. Despite these sparse totals, the evaporation rate is low and the soil is frozen for much of the year so that moisture is adequate to support a forest. Summer is the wet season, and most precipitation comes from scattered convective showers. Winter experiences only light snowfalls (except near the coasts), which may accumulate to depths of 60 to 90 centimeters (2 or 3 feet). The snow that falls in October is likely to still be on the ground in May because little melts over the winter. Thus, a continuous thin snow cover exists for many months despite the sparseness of actual snowfall.

Polar Climates (Group E)

Being farthest from the equator, as Figure 8-36 shows, the polar climates are remote from low latitude solar heating and receive inadequate insolation for any significant warming. By definition, no month has an average temperature of more than 10°C (50°F) in a polar climate. If the wet tropics represent conditions of monotonous heat, the polar climates are known for their enduring cold. They have the coldest summers and the lowest annual and absolute temperatures in the world. They are also extraordinarily dry, but evaporation is so minuscule that the group as a whole is classified as non-arid.

The two types of polar climates are distinguished by summer temperature. The **tundra** climate has at least one month with an average temperature exceeding the freezing point. The **ice cap** climate does not. Table 8-7 summarizes the E climates.

Tundra Climate (ET) The name *tundra* originally referred to the low, ground-hugging vegetation of high-latitude and high-altitude regions, but the term has been adopted to refer to the climate of the high-latitude regions as well. The generally accepted equatorward edge of the tundra climate is the 10°C

TABLE 8-7 Summary of E Climates: Polar

Type	Location	Temperature	Precipitation	Dominant Controls of Climate
Tundra (ET)	Fringes of Arctic Ocean; small coastal areas in Antarctica	Long, cold, dark winters; brief, cool summers; large ATR, small DTR	Very sparse (less than 25 cm [10 in.] annually), mostly snow	Latitude; distance from sources of heat and moisture; extreme seasonal contrasts in sunlight/darkness
Ice cap (EF)	Antarctica and Greenland	Long, dark, windy, bitterly cold winters; cold windy summers; large ATR, small DTR	Very sparse (less than 13 cm [5 in.] annually), all snow	Latitude; distance from sources of heat and moisture; extreme seasonal contrasts in sunlight/darkness; polar anticyclones

E climates are found in Antarctica, Greenland, various Arctic islands, and the Arctic fringes of North America and Eurasia. They are lands of enduring cold; no month has an average temperature of more than 10°C (50°F), and most are much colder than that. Precipitation is scanty, but the evaporation rate is extremely low. Strong winds are common.

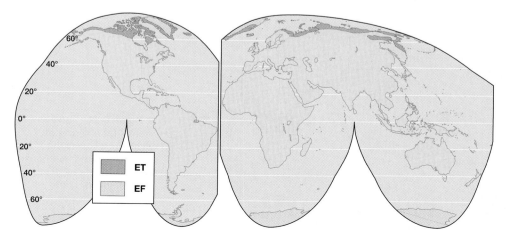

Figure 8-36 Distribution of E climates.

(50°F) isotherm for the average temperature of the warmest month. This same isotherm corresponds approximately with the poleward limit of trees so that the boundary between D and E climates (in other words, the equatorward boundary of the tundra climate) is the "treeline."

At the poleward margin, the ET climate is bounded by the isotherm of 0°C (32°F) for the warmest month, which approximately coincides with the extreme limit for growth of any plant cover. More than for any other climatic type, the delimitation of the tundra climate demonstrates Köppen's contention that climate is best delimited in terms of plant communities (Figure 8-37). Figure 8-37b shows typical climographs for a tundra climate.

Long, cold, dark winters and brief, cool summers characterize the tundra. Only one to four months

experience average temperatures above freezing, and the average hot-month temperature is between 4 and 10°C (in the 40s °F). Freezing temperatures can occur at any time, and frosts are likely every night except in midsummer. Although an ET winter is bitterly cold, it is not as severe as in the subarctic climate farther south because the ET climate is less continental. Coastal stations in the tundra often have cold-month average temperatures of only about −18°C (0°F), whereas an inland ET location is more likely to average −32°C or −35° (−25°F or −30°F). Annual temperature ranges are fairly large, commonly between 22 and 33°C (40 and 60°F). Daily temperature ranges are small because the Sun is above the horizon for most of the time in summer and below the horizon for most of the time in winter; thus nocturnal cooling is limited in

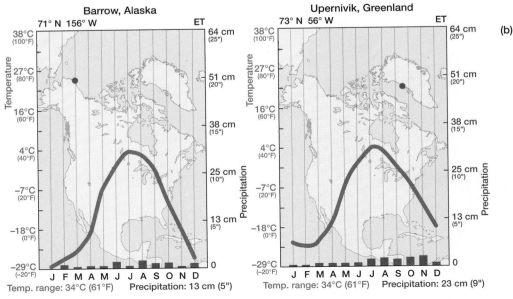

(a)

(b)

◀ **Figure 8-37** Tundra climate. **(a)** A carpet of wildflowers covers the tundra in this summer scene near Nome, Alaska. (*Fred Bruemmer/DRK Photo.*) **(b)** Climographs for representative tundra stations.

PEOPLE AND THE ENVIRONMENT Climate Change in the Arctic

Although signs of global warming have been observed in many parts of the world, among the most dramatic indications have come from the polar regions. During the last 50 years, average temperatures in the Arctic have been increasing at about twice the rate as in lower latitudes. For example, in western Canada and Alaska, winter temperatures are perhaps 3°C (5°F) higher today than they were just 50 years ago. The consequences of these rising temperatures include the retreat of glaciers, melting of permafrost, diminishing thickness and extent of sea ice, and changing distributions of both flora and fauna.

In terms of annual averages, the extent of sea ice has decreased by almost 1,000,000 square kilometers (386,000 square miles) since 1975—an 8 percent decrease. The decline has been even greater when summer sea-ice cover—known as *perennial sea ice*—is measured: the amount of sea ice at the end of summer is about 20 percent less than it was 30 years ago. The summer retreat of sea ice in September 2005 was the greatest ever measured since regular satellite monitoring of the ice pack was started in 1979 (Figures 8-A and 8-B).

The retreat of the Arctic sea ice pack due to higher global temperatures leads to a feedback loop in the climate system: As the cover of sea ice diminishes there is less reflectance of insolation and more absorption by the relatively dark ocean surface now exposed to sunlight—which leads to higher ocean temperatures which in turn leads to more melting of the ice pack. Some computer models suggest that at the present rate of greenhouse gases concentration increase in the atmosphere—and the associated expected temperature increase—it is possible that the summer Arctic sea ice cover could actually disappear by the end of this century.

▲ **Figure 8-A**   Satellite image composite showing minimum extent of Arctic sea ice in 1979. *(NASA.)*

▲ **Figure 8-B**   Satellite image composite showing minimum extent of Arctic sea ice in 2005. *(NASA.)*

The Greenland Ice Sheet covers nearly all of Greenland. As temperatures have increased over the last few decades, the extent of the seasonal melting of the ice sheet has expanded significantly. The area of the ice sheet that exhibits summer surface melting and *melt pond* formation has grown by more than 15 percent since 1979. As meltwater seeps down into the ice sheet, it tends to increase the melting of ice and may be leading to more rapid movement of the ice over the bedrock below. The annual loss of ice through direct melting and the more rapid flow of outlet glaciers into the ocean more than doubled between 1996 and 2005—from about 90 cubic kilometers (about 22 cubic miles) a year in 1996 to about 224 cubic kilometers (about 54 cubic miles) per year in 2005. In 2006, data analyzed by a University of Texas team indicated that the ice sheet was melting at a rate three times greater than just five years earlier.

The loss of ice from Greenland's ice sheets is not uniform. It is greatest in the south, while in the north the ice sheet appears to be growing, most likely due to higher precipitation—another possible consequence of changing climate patterns in the Arctic.

Over the last few decades, global sea level has been rising by about 2 mm per year. This rise in sea level is a result of the melting of glaciers in the Arctic and elsewhere in the world as well as from the thermal expansion of water as the ocean becomes warmer. Were the Greenland Ice Sheet to completely melt, global sea level would rise by nearly 7 meters (23 feet). The increase in freshwater entering the ocean has other ramifications as well: the decrease in salinity can potentially alter the deep ocean *global conveyer-belt circulation* (discussed in more detail in Chapter 9), and this in turn could change the exchange of heat between the tropics and high latitudes.

Concern about habitat loss in the Arctic has also been growing among scientists. For example, as the extent of sea ice diminishes decade by decade, the iconic polar bear faces difficult circumstances. Polar bears regularly hunt for seal pups and other prey on the sea ice during the summer, but because the sea ice is breaking up earlier than in the past, the polar bears are facing increasingly challenging times. As a likely consequence of diminishing hunting opportunities, polar bears around western Hudson Bay in Canada now weigh about 15 percent less than they did 30 years ago.

summer, and daytime warming is almost nonexistent in winter.

Moisture availability is very restricted in ET regions despite the proximity of an ocean. The air is simply too cold to hold much moisture, and so the absolute humidity is almost always very low. Moreover, anticyclonic conditions are common, with little uplift to encourage condensation. Annual total precipitation is generally less than 25 centimeters (10 inches), but is somewhat greater in eastern Arctic Canada. Generally, more precipitation falls in the warm season than in winter, although the total amount in any month is small, and the month-to-month variation is minor. Winter snow is often dry and granular; it appears to be more than it actually is because there is no melting and because winds swirl it horizontally even when no snow

is falling. Radiation fogs are fairly common throughout ET regions, and sea fogs are sometimes prevalent for days along the coast.

Ice Cap Climate (EF) The most severe of Earth's climates is restricted to Greenland (all but the coastal fringe) and most of Antarctica, the combined extent of these two regions amounting to more than 9 percent of the world's land area (Figure 8-38). The EF climate is one of perpetual frost where vegetation cannot grow, and the landscape consists of a permanent cover of ice and snow. Figure 8-38b shows typical climographs.

The extraordinary severity of EF temperatures is emphasized by the fact that both Antarctica and Greenland are ice plateaus, so that relatively high altitude is added to high latitude as a thermal factor. All months

(a)

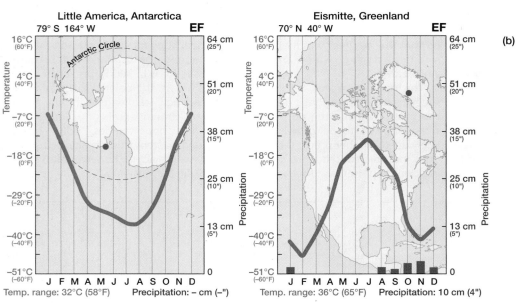

(b)

Little America, Antarctica
79° S 164° W   EF
Temp. range: 32°C (58°F)   Precipitation: – cm (–")

Eismitte, Greenland
70° N 40° W   EF
Temp. range: 36°C (65°F)   Precipitation: 10 cm (4")

◀ **Figure 8-38** Ice cap climate. **(a)** The infinite bleakness of an ice cap can be imagined in this view of scientists at work on the Ross Ice Shelf of Antarctica. (*Maria Stenzel/National Geographic Society.*) **(b)** Climographs for representative ice cap stations. (Note that the temperature scales are different from those of the other climographs in the chapter; note also that the climograph for Eismitte, Greenland is based on incomplete data.)

have average temperatures below freezing, and in the most extreme locations the average temperature of the warmest month is below −18°C (0°F). Cold-month temperatures average between −34 and −51°C (−30° and −60°F), and extremes well below −73°C (−100°F) have been recorded at interior Antarctic weather stations.

The air is chilled so intensely from the underlying ice that strong surface temperature inversions prevail most of the time. Heavy, cold air often flows downslope as a vigorous katabatic wind. A characteristic feature of the ice cap climate, particularly in Antarctica, is strong winds and blowing snow.

Precipitation is very limited. These regions are polar deserts; most places receive less than 13 centimeters (5 inches) of moisture annually. The air is too dry and too stable, with too little likelihood of uplift, to permit much precipitation. Evaporation, of course, is minimal, and so an actual moisture surplus may be added to the ice.

Highland Climate (Group H)

FG1
FG4

Highland climate is not defined in the same sense as all the others we have just studied. Climatic conditions in mountainous areas have almost infinite variations from place to place, and many of the differences extend over very limited horizontal distances. Köppen did not recognize highland climate as a separate group, but most of the researchers who have modified his system have added such a category. Highland climates are delimited in this book to identify relatively high uplands (mountains and plateaus) having complex local climate variation in small areas (Figure 8-39).

The climate of any highland location is usually closely related to that of the adjacent lowland, particularly with regard to seasonality of precipitation. Some aspects of highland climate, however, differ significantly from those of the surrounding lowlands. With highland climates, latitude becomes less important as a climatic control than altitude and exposure. The critical climatic controls on a mountain slope are usually

relative elevation and angle of exposure to Sun and wind (Figure 8-40).

Altitude variations influence all four elements of weather and climate. As we learned in Chapter 4, a vertical temperature gradient of about 6.5°C/1000 meters (3.6°F/1000 feet) generally prevails. Atmospheric pressure also decreases rapidly with increased elevation. Air movement is less predictable in highland areas, but it tends to be brisk and abrupt, with many local wind systems. Precipitation is characteristically heavier in highlands than in surrounding lowlands, so that the mountains usually stand out as moist islands on a rainfall map (Figure 8-41; also see Figure 6-33).

Altitude is more significant than latitude in determining climate in highland areas, so that a pattern of *vertical zonation* is usually present. The steep vertical gradients of climatic change are expressed as horizontal bands along the slopes. An increase of a few hundred meters in elevation may be equivalent to a journey of several hundred kilometers poleward insofar as temperature and related environmental characteristics are concerned. Vertical zonation is particularly prominent in tropical highlands (Figure 8-42).

Exposure—whether a slope, peak, or valley faces windward or leeward—has a profound influence on climate. Ascending air on a windward face brings a strong likelihood of heavy precipitation, whereas a leeward location is sheltered from moisture or has predominantly downslope wind movement with limited opportunity for precipitation. The angle of exposure to sunlight is also a significant factor in determining climate, especially outside the tropics. Slopes that face equatorward receive direct sunlight, which makes them warm and dry (through more rapid evapotranspiration); adjacent slopes facing poleward may be much cooler and moister simply because of a smaller angle of solar incidence and more shading. Similarly, west-facing slopes receive direct sunlight in the hot afternoon, but east-facing slopes are sunlit during the cooler morning hours.

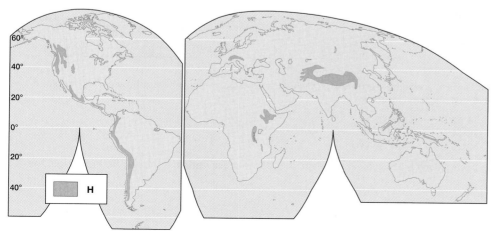

◀ **Figure 8-39** Distribution of H climate.

▲ **Figure 8-40**   Mountain climates are quite variable because of changes in altitude and exposure. This is a summer scene near Rainy Pass in the North Cascade Mountains of Washington. *(Tom L. McKnight photo.)*

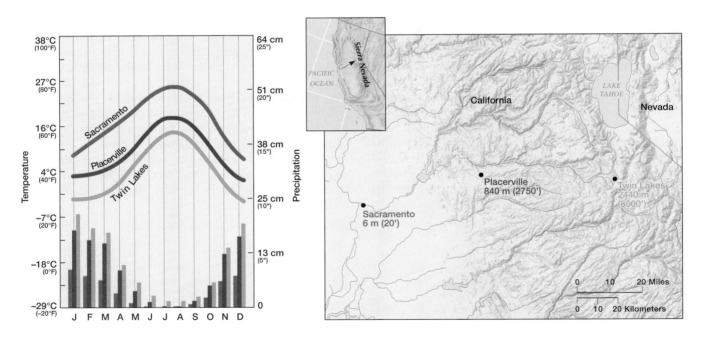

▲ **Figure 8-41**   This figure contrasts the California weather records of a lowland station (Sacramento) with those of two highland localities (Placerville and Twin Lakes) at about the same latitude.

Twin Lakes	2440 m (8000′)	38°42′N	120°02′W
Placerville	840 m (2750′)	38°44′N	120°44′W
Sacramento	6 m (20′)	38°35′N	121°30′W

With increasing elevation, we see the expected decrease in temperature and increase in precipitation, although all three retain the characteristic summer dry regime.

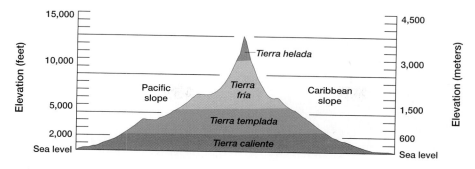

▲ **Figure 8-42** Vertical climate zonation is particularly noticeable in tropical mountainous areas. This diagram idealizes the situation at about 15° N latitude in Guatemala and southern Mexico. *Tierra caliente* ("hot land") is a zone of high temperatures, dense vegetation, and tropical agriculture. *Tierra templada* ("temperate land") is an intermediate zone of slopes and plateaus and temperatures most persons would find comfortable. *Tierra fria* ("cold land") is characterized by warm days and cold nights, and its agriculture is limited to hardy crops. *Tierra helada* ("frozen land") is a zone of cold weather throughout the year.

Changeability is perhaps the single most conspicuous characteristic of highland climate. The thin, dry air permits rapid influx of insolation by day and rapid loss of radiant energy at night, and so daily temperature ranges are very large, with frequent and rapid oscillation between freeze and thaw. Daytime upslope winds and convection cause rapid cloud development and abrupt storminess. Travelers in highland areas are well advised to be prepared for sudden changes from hot to cold, from wet to dry, from clear to cloudy, from quiet to windy, and vice versa (Figure 8-43).

Global Patterns Idealized

It should be clear by now that there is a fairly predictable global pattern of climatic types based primarily on latitude, position on a continent, and the general circulation of the atmosphere and oceans. Figure 8-44 summarizes the idealized distribution of the mild (A, B, and C) climates along the west coasts of continents, where the distribution pattern is slightly more regular than along the east coasts.

▲ **Figure 8-43** Snow often accumulates to a considerable depth in mountainous regions in winter. Here a snowblower is clearing a parking lot near Bear Lake in Colorado's Rocky Mountain National Park. *(Tom L. McKnight photo.)*

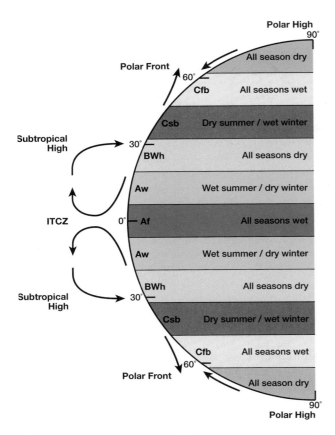

▲ Figure 8-44 Idealized seasonal precipitation patterns and climates along the west coast of continents. Note that the progressions north and south of the equator are mirror images. Much of this pattern is due to the seasonal shifts of the ITCZ and the subtropical highs.

A more general model of the climate distribution on a hypothetical continent is shown in Figure 8-45. The model portrays the idealized distribution of five of the six groups and most of the types and subtypes; highland climate is not included because its location is determined solely by topography. Groups A, C, D, and E are defined by temperature, which means that their boundaries are strongly latitudinal because they are determined by insolation. The B group is defined by moisture conditions, and its distribution cuts across those of the thermally defined groups. Such a model is a predictive tool. One can state, with some degree of assurance, that at a particular latitude and a general location on a continent, a certain climate is likely to occur. Moreover, the locations of the climatic types relative to one another can be understood more clearly when they are all shown together this way.

Climatic Distribution in Africa: A Practically Perfect Pattern

The real world holds many refinements and modifications to the idealized global pattern, of course, but the "hypothetical continent" model shows the general alignments with considerable validity. This can be seen clearly at the continental scale when we look at the distribution of climate types in Africa (Figure 8-46).

In the center of the continent is a hot, wet core region (Af), and at the proper subtropical latitudes are two hot, dry core regions (BWh). Between these precipitation extremes are the two expected transition climates

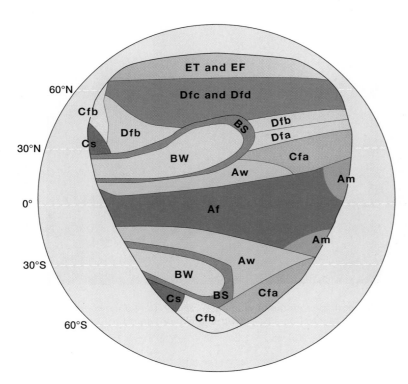

◄ Figure 8-45 The presumed arrangement of Köppen climatic types on a large hypothetical continent.

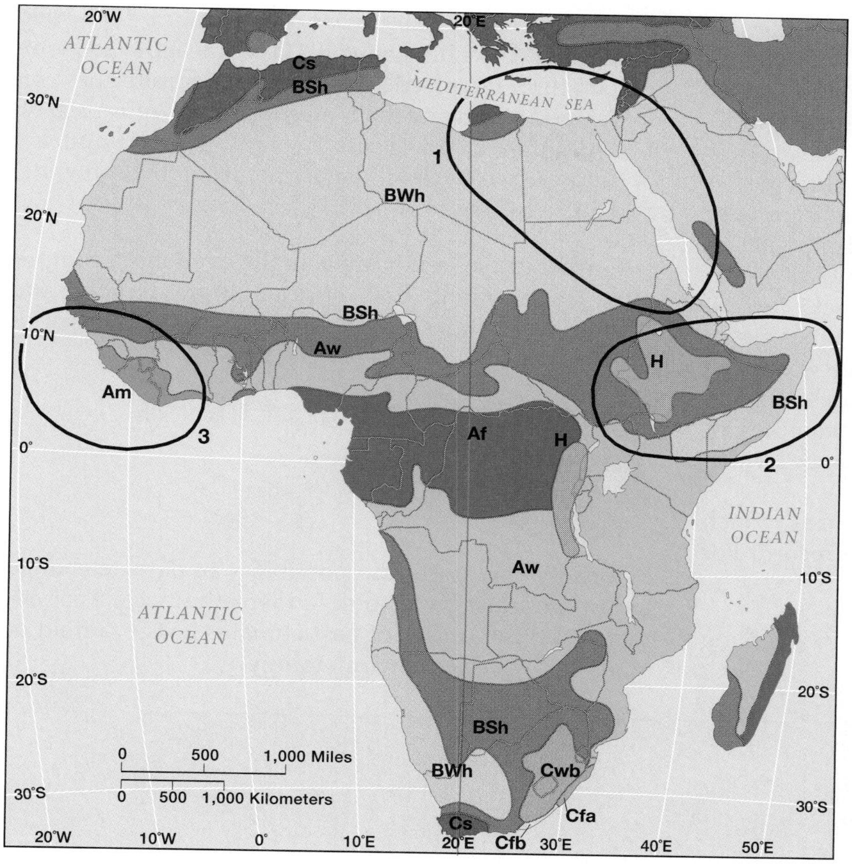

Figure 8-46 The climatic regions of Africa. The pattern is mostly regular and "normal." The three black ovals mark the principal exceptions to that normality: (1) a greatly expanded area of B climate in the northeast; (2) an unusual and complex climatic pattern in East Africa; and (3) monsoon development along the Guinea coast of West Africa.

(Aw and BSh), and north and south of the BWh deserts the transition (BSh) again occurs, leading into the moister C climates of the middle latitudes. It is a practically perfect pattern through the A climates and the subtropical B climates into the fringe of the C climates on the poleward extremities of the continent.

The inevitable anomalies, for the most part, can be explained fairly easily.

1. Most striking is the vast extent of dry climate in North Africa. The expectation is for desert to extend from the western coast for a considerable distance inland, but in this case it carries all the way to the eastern border of the continent. Desert covers the entire continent because the Eurasian landmass immediately to the northeast of Africa excludes maritime air and preserves the characteristic of continentality clear across North Africa.
2. The distribution of climatic types in the eastern equatorial portion, from about latitudes 10° N to 10° S, is quite different from what might be expected. The expected Af climate is replaced by Aw, H, BSh, and BWh. This anomaly is due in part to the higher elevations of most of East Africa, which produce the lower temperatures typical of a highland zone, and in part to the airflow pattern along the coast north of about 5° S latitude. Influenced by the South Asian monsoon, winds blow parallel to this coast (northeasterly in winter and southwesterly in summer) throughout the year, which means that maritime air is rarely carried inland and dryness prevails.
3. The climate along the western Guinea Coast is Am rather than the expected Af or Aw. Although the full story of monsoon origin is not clear, there is a definite seasonal reversal of wind flow in this region, with maritime southwesterlies bringing a heavy summer rainy season and dry northeasterlies dominating for the remainder of the year.

Global Climate Change

So far in this chapter, we have discussed global climate patterns as we observe them today. Although it has been useful for us to learn the fundamentals of weather and climate by first studying such "constant" circumstances, a thorough understanding of the atmosphere requires us now to explore how patterns can change over time. In earlier chapters we discussed several cyclical and episodic events, such as El Niño and the Pacific Decadal Oscillation, as well as human-influenced changes to the atmosphere, such as the depletion of the ozone layer and increased greenhouse gas concentrations.

For the remainder of this chapter, we look more specifically at climate change. We especially want to address questions first raised in Chapter 4: is human activity causing global climate change, and if so, what are the likely long-term consequences? In providing a thoughtful answer to these questions, we will look at how climate change is recognized, what kinds of factors may lead to climate change, and what evidence indicates that climate is currently changing.

As we first saw in Chapter 3, within any climate system there is expected fluctuation in weather from year to year. The random variation in weather from year to year can be thought of as the background "noise" in the long-term climate record. Within the climate record, however, other kinds of variation may be present: episodic events and natural cycles of change with periods ranging from a few years to many decades (El Niño and the Pacific Decadal Oscillation are examples of this), as well as long-term global climate change (which can also exhibit cycles of its own).

The time scale of observations influences which kinds of patterns stand out in the climate record. For example, in the case of global temperature:

- Over the last 70 million years, a clear global cooling trend is visible (Figure 8-47a).

- Over the last 150,000 years, temperature fluctuated significantly until about 10,000 years ago when temperature increased sharply; temperature has remained warm and fairly steady since. (Figure 8-47b).
- Over the last 150 years a warming trend appears underway—a clear departure from the previous 850 years (Figure 8-47c).

Further, these trends are actually even more complicated than might first appear: these temperature changes weren't necessarily uniform around the world.

Determining Climates of the Past

 End of the Last Ice Age

Before we can assess the possibility of climate change today, we must have some understanding of past climates and the causes of past climate change, a field of study known as **paleoclimatology**.

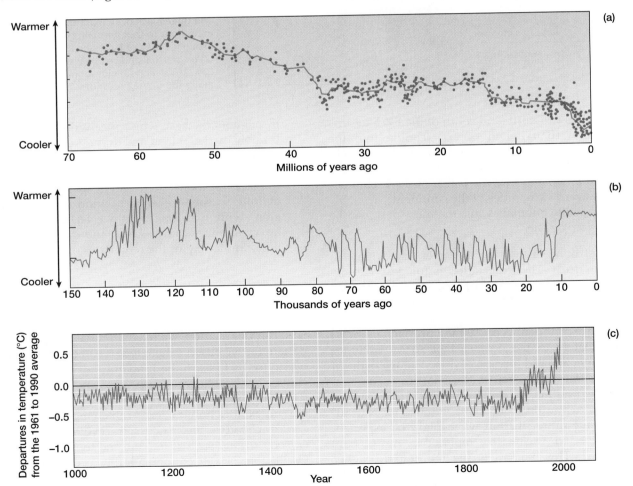

▲ **Figure 8-47** Global temperature change at three different time scales. **(a)** 70 million years ago to present (derived from ice volume and ocean temperature proxy measures). **(b)** 150,000 years ago to present (derived from North Atlantic Ocean proxy measures). **(c)** 1000 years ago to present (derived from proxy measures and the historical record after 1900). *(After Edward Aguado and James E. Burt,* Understanding Weather and Climate, *4th ed., Upper Saddle River, NJ: Pearson-Prentice Hall, 2007, and Frederick K. Lutgens and Edward J. Tarbuck,* The Atmosphere, *9th ed., Upper Saddle River, NJ: Pearson-Prentice Hall, 2004.)*

Detailed instrument records of weather go back only a few hundred years, so it is necessary to use *proxy* measures of climate to reconstruct conditions in the past. Information about past climate can come from many different sources: tree rings, ice cores, oceanic sediments, coral reefs, relic soils, and pollen, among others. No single method for determining past climate conditions is ideal—each has its own strengths and weaknesses. However, by correlating the results achieved with one method with those from another, paleoclimatologists have been able to construct a detailed history of Earth's climate.

Dendrochronology   Most trees growing in temperate areas increase trunk diameter by adding one concentric *tree ring* for each year of growth. By counting the number of rings, the age of a tree may be determined. Tree rings also provide information about climate: during years when the growing conditions are favorable (such as mild temperatures and/or ample precipitation), tree rings tend to be wider than in years when the growing conditions are harsher.

Both living and dead trees can be used in **dendrochronology** (the study of past events and past climate through the analysis of tree rings). Small cores are taken so that living trees are not harmed, and fallen trees, buried trunks, and timber from archeological sites all may be used to extend tree ring chronology. By comparing and correlating the tree ring patterns of many trees in an area, dendrochronologists can not only determine the age of the trees, but can establish dates for catastrophic events such as floods and fires that have killed trees, as well as identify periods of drought and lower or higher temperatures.

Oxygen Isotope Analysis of Oceanic Sediments   In the nucleus of many atoms the number of protons and neutrons is the same. For example, the normal oxygen atom contains 8 protons and 8 neutrons, giving it an atomic weight of 16 (^{16}O or "oxygen 16"). However, a small number of oxygen atoms have 2 extra neutrons, giving these atoms an atomic weight of 18 (^{18}O). ^{16}O and ^{18}O are known as **isotopes** of oxygen. Both isotopes of oxygen can be found in common molecules such as water (H_2O) and calcium carbonate ($CaCO_3$).

The ratio of $^{18}O/^{16}O$ in the molecules of substances such as water and calcium carbonate can actually tell us something about the environment in which those molecules formed. Because they contain the lighter oxygen isotope, water molecules with ^{16}O evaporate more easily than those with ^{18}O, and so precipitation such as rain and snow tends to be relatively rich in ^{16}O. During an ice age, great quantities of ^{16}O are locked up in glacial ice on the continents, leaving a greater concentration of ^{18}O in the oceans; during a warmer, interglacial period, the glacial ice melts, returning ^{16}O to the oceans.

Ocean floor sediments provide a record of the changing $^{18}O/^{16}O$ ratio in seawater over periods of thousands of years. A number of common marine microorganisms, such as *foraminifera*, excrete shells or exoskeletons of calcium carbonate, and the remains of these organisms build up layer upon layer on the ocean floor. By comparing the $^{18}O/^{16}O$ ratio of the calcium carbonate in these layers of sediment, scientists can determine when periods of glaciation took place. If the $^{18}O/^{16}O$ ratio in the calcium carbonate is high (in other words, relatively high amounts of ^{18}O are present), we can infer those organisms were living during a glacial period; if the $^{18}O/^{16}O$ ratio is low, we can infer those organisms were living during an interglacial period.

Ice Cores   The $^{18}O/^{16}O$ ratio can also give us climate information through the analysis of ice cores. By drilling down into glaciers, a record of snowfall going back thousands of years may be obtained in some locations (Figure 8-48). Such ice cores offer several kinds of information about past conditions. A greater number of water molecules with ^{18}O evaporate from

▲ **Figure 8-48**   Scientists in Antarctica drilling an ice core as part of the EPICA project (European Project for Ice Coring in Antarctica). (*British Antarctic Survey.*)

FOCUS Paleoclimatology at Dome C, Antarctica

Ice cores have yielded a long and detailed proxy record of Earth's past climate. Oxygen isotope analysis, trapped air bubbles, and atmospheric aerosol deposits within the layers of ice have offered information about past temperature and greenhouse gas concentrations, as well as cataclysmic events such as major volcanic eruptions. Of all the locations where ice cores have been extracted from glacial ice, the most significant is probably Dome C in Antarctica.

Dome C is located about 1750 kilometers (1080 miles) from the South Pole at a latitude of 75° S and a longitude 123°E—this is where the Antarctic ice cap is at its thickest (Figure 8-C). The coring has been undertaken by the *European Project for Ice Coring in Antarctica* (EPICA). A multinational team of scientists has extracted a continuous 10 centimeter- (4 inch-) diameter ice core record to a depth of more than 3 kilometers (2 miles) (Figure 8-D). So far, the analysis has provided climate and atmospheric composition data back 740,000 years—far longer than any other ice core—providing climate information on two more glacial/interglacial cycles than have previous ice cores. When EPICA at Dome C is complete, the climate record might well extend back over 950,000 years.

▲ **Figure 8-C**   Map of Antarctica showing the location of EPICA Dome C.

▲ **Figure 8-D**   EPICA scientists at Dome C in Antarctica removing a core from the barrel of an ice core drill. *(British Antarctic Survey.)*

So far the Dome C climate record shows that the present concentration of CO_2 in the atmosphere is about 27 percent greater than at any time in the last 650,000 years, and that increases and decreases in global temperature are closely correlated with changes in CO_2 concentration—with temperatures high when CO_2 concentrations are high, and vice versa. Further, the findings at Dome C closely match the proxy climate record derived from the oxygen isotope analysis of the calcium carbonate in *foraminifera* (tiny marine creatures) found in oceanic sediments, adding to the scientists' confidence in the soundness of the Dome C data.

Among the most interesting findings of the ice core analysis are from a period between about 400,000 and 650,000 years ago. Two of the warm interglacial periods that occurred during this time span were relatively mild compared to the interglacial periods of the last 400,000 years. Further, carbon dioxide and methane concentrations were lower during those two earlier interglacial periods than during more recent interglacials. This data helps climatologists judge the "sensitivity" of the climate to increased levels of greenhouse gases—which can in turn lead to better computer model predictions of future climate.

the oceans when temperatures are high than when temperatures are low, thus the $^{18}O/^{16}O$ ratio found in a layer of ice serves as a "thermometer" for the climate at the time that snow fell. Oxygen isotope analysis of ice cores has become one of the most important ways scientists have been able to construct a record of past global temperature—a record that now goes back more than 700,000 years.

Ice cores also provide direct information about the composition of the atmosphere in the past. As snow accumulates and is compacted into glacial ice, air bubbles from the atmosphere become frozen into the ice. These tiny air bubbles deep in glaciers are preserved samples of the atmosphere in the past, allowing direct measurements of the concentration of CO_2 and other gases to be made.

Ice core analysis shows a close relationship between greenhouse gas concentration (especially carbon dioxide and methane) and temperature over the past 650,000 years. Lower concentrations of greenhouse gases are present during glacial episodes, while higher concentrations of greenhouses gases are present during interglacial warm periods.[1]

Pollen Analysis   Another important method used for determining past climates comes from the field of *palynology*, or *pollen analysis*. Air-borne pollen from trees and other plants can be preserved in sediment layers on lake bottoms and in bogs. Cores of these sediment layers are taken and analyzed.

---

[1]Interestingly, some recent evidence shows that it may be several hundred years after temperature increases before greenhouse gas concentrations increase—this suggests that in the past an increase in greenhouse gas concentration may not have always been the trigger for a temperature increase; rather, greenhouse gas concentrations (at least initially) began to increase as a consequence of warmer conditions.

Radiocarbon dating of material in each layer provides an estimate of the age of organic material younger than about 50,000 years. Radiocarbon dating works by comparing the ratio of two isotopes of carbon found in organic material: radioactive ^{14}C decays over time at a known rate into the more common "daughter" isotope ^{12}C, so the $^{14}C/^{12}C$ ratio serves as indication of how long ago the plant or animal material was alive. With the age of a sediment layer known, palynologists look at the types of pollen present to determine which plants and trees were living at the time that layer was forming. Since plant species change as the environment changes—some species are better adapted for colder conditions, for example—the prevalence of one plant community over another acts as a proxy for the climate of the time.

Causes of Long-Term Climate Change

Orbital Variations and Climate Change

A quick glance back to Chapter 4 and the diagram showing Earth's solar radiation budget (Figure 4-18) will remind you of the many variables that influence patterns of temperature: the quantity of incoming solar radiation, the albedo of the atmosphere and surface, the concentration of greenhouse gases, the transport of energy through oceanic and atmospheric circulation, and many others. A change in any one of those variables has the potential to change temperature, wind, pressure, and moisture patterns.

Not surprisingly then, a number of mechanisms are likely to have had a role in past climate change and may be operating in the present day as well. Although by no means a comprehensive description, in the following sections we describe several kinds of mechanisms of climate change.

Volcanic Activity and Meteor Impacts Large quantities of particulates ejected into the atmosphere by volcanic eruptions can alter global temperatures. Fine volcanic ash and other aerosols can reach the stratosphere, where they may circle the globe for years, blocking incoming solar radiation and lowering temperature. For example, the 1991 eruption of Mount Pinatubo in the Philippines increased aerosol concentrations (especially sulfur dioxide) in the atmosphere enough to lower global temperatures by about 0.5°C (0.9°F) for the next year.

Large asteroid or meteorite impacts also can eject enough dust into the atmosphere to significantly alter global climate. It is now widely accepted by scientists that the impact of a 10-kilometer wide asteroid 65 million years ago was perhaps the single most important factor that led to the extinction of the dinosaurs.

Fluctuations in Solar Output A link between past climates and variations in the energy output of the Sun has been pursued by scientists for many decades.

For example, some researchers have looked for a relationship between climate and sunspot activity. *Sunspots* appear as dark spots on the surface of the Sun. They are slightly cooler regions of the Sun's photosphere and are associated with intense magnetic storms on the surface of the Sun, as well as the ejection of charged particles (some of the charged particles reach the Earth as part of the *solar wind* where they produce auroral displays in the upper atmosphere; see Figure 3-10).

Some scientists have noted that several past climate events, such as the *Little Ice Age*—a period of unusually cold weather from about 1400 to 1850—corresponded with a period of greatly reduced sunspot activity between 1645 and 1715 (known as the *Maunder Minimum*). Correlations between precipitation patterns and the well-documented 11-year cycle of sunspot activity have also been suggested.

Although some of the relationships between sunspot cycles and climate appear at first to be strong statistically, most scientists remain unconvinced—in part because there is no clear physical mechanism that can explain how periods of greater or few sunspots can influence climate.

Variations in Earth–Sun Relations As we saw in Chapter 1, the change of seasons is largely a consequence of the changing orientation of Earth's rotational axis to the Sun during the year (see Figure 1-24). You'll recall that we said that Earth's axis maintains an inclination of 23.5° at all times, that Earth's axis always points toward the North Star Polaris, and that Earth is closest to the Sun on January 3rd. As it turns out, all of those aspects of Earth-Sun relations change over periods of thousands of years in a series of predictable, well-documented cycles:

- The inclination of Earth's axis, or *obliquity*, varies from 22.1° to 24.5° in a cycle lasting about 41,000 years. When there is greater inclination, seasonal variation between the low latitudes and high latitudes tends to be greater; when there is less inclination, seasonal contrasts are less significant.
- The "shape" of Earth's elliptical orbit, or *eccentricity*, varies in a series of cycles of lasting about 100,000 years. Sometimes Earth's orbit is nearly circular, while at other times the orbit is much more elliptical, thus influencing the distance between the Earth and Sun. The present difference in distance between the Earth and Sun at aphelion and perihelion is about 3 percent (about a 5,000,000 kilometer difference), but over the last 600,000 years or so, the difference has varied from 1 percent to 11 percent. The greater the difference

in distance, the greater the difference in insolation at various points in Earth's orbit.

- Earth's axis "wobbles" like a spinning top, and so over time it points in different directions relative to the stars in a 25,800-year cycle called *precession*. Precession alters the timing of the seasons relative to Earth's position in its orbit around the Sun.

As these long-term cycles "overlap" there are periods of time when significantly less radiation reaches Earth surface (especially in the high latitudes), and periods of time when there are greater or smaller seasonal contrasts. For example, during periods when there is less "seasonality"—in other words, when there are smaller contrasts between winter and summer—more snow can accumulate in high latitudes due to greater snowfall from milder winters and less melting will take place due to lower summer temperatures.

These cycles are known as **Milankovitch cycles**, after Milutin Milankovitch, an early twentieth century Yugoslavian astronomer. Milankovitch looked at the combined effects of these cycles and concluded that they were responsible for an approximately 100,000-year cycle of insolation variation that has taken Earth into and out of periods of glaciation over the last few millions of years. Although his ideas were mostly rejected by other scientists during his lifetime, recent paleoclimatological work has shown that cyclical variation in Earth–Sun relations is one key to the timing of glacial and interglacial events.

However, these astronomical cycles present some problems as well—for example, the effects of precession that produce cooler conditions in one hemisphere should produce warmer conditions in the other, but this does not appear to be the case. Other factors certainly play a part in the onset and end of glacial periods.

Greenhouse Gases Concentration   As we first saw in Chapter 4, greenhouse gases, such as carbon dioxide, methane, and water vapor, play an important role in regulating the temperature of the troposphere. It is also well known—most notably through ice core analysis—that past fluctuations in global temperature have been accompanied by fluctuations in greenhouse gas concentration—warmer periods in the past are associated with higher concentrations of gases such as CO_2, while cooler periods associated with lower concentrations of CO_2.

While the cause and effect relationship between increased greenhouse gases and increased temperatures might seem clear, a number of important feedback mechanisms add to the complexity.

Feedback Mechanisms   Sea ice and continental ice sheets have high albedos—in other words, these surfaces reflect much of the shortwave radiation that strikes them (Figure 8-49). If global climate were to

▲ **Figure 8-49**   Sea ice off the east coast of Greenland during the summer thaw. *(Simon Fraser/Science Photo Library.)*

cool, ice would expand and this would in turn reflect more incoming radiation, which would lead to more cooling—which in turn would lead to greater still expansion of ice; this is known as a *positive feedback mechanism*. On the other hand, if climate were to warm, this would reduce the ice cover, which would reduce the albedo and therefore increase absorption by the surface, which would lead to higher temperatures and therefore still less ice cover—another positive feedback mechanism.

One of the most complicated series of feedback mechanisms associated with climate change has to do with water vapor. As climate warms, evaporation increases—so increasing the concentration of water vapor in the atmosphere. As we've learned, water vapor is one of the key greenhouse gases, so as warming increases evaporation, the greater concentrations of water vapor in the atmosphere will lead to still more warming—another positive feedback mechanism. However, here is where things become complicated.

An increase in water vapor would also likely lead to increased cloud cover. Clouds can act as efficient reflectors of solar radiation (so leading to cooling), as well as efficient absorbers of terrestrial radiation (and so contributing to warming). In other words, increased cloud cover can lead to both cooling and warming!

The net effect—cooling or warming—evidently depends on the type of clouds that form. For example, a deep layer of cumulus clouds does not increase albedo as much as it increases absorption of longwave radiation from the surface—thus leading to warming. On the other hand, the expansion of stratus cloud cover increases albedo more than it increases longwave absorption—thus leading to cooling. The effects of clouds remain one of the great complications when modeling future climate change.

The Roles of the Ocean   Many important variables in climate change involve the oceans. The oceans absorb a great deal of CO_2 from the atmosphere—some estimates suggest that the oceans have absorbed one-third to one-half of the carbon that human activities have released into the atmosphere since the industrial revolution. Once in the ocean, marine plants and animals remove carbon from the ocean water through photosynthesis and the extraction of calcium carbonate to form shells and exoskeletons. Much of this carbon is eventually deposited in sediment layers on the ocean floor. In addition, vast quantities of carbon in the form of *methane hydrates* (a kind of ice made from methane and water) are found in some oceanic sediments. Should these methane hydrates be disturbed and the trapped methane (a greenhouse gas) released into the atmosphere, a sudden increase in atmospheric temperature could result (some evidence suggests that this actually happened about 55 million years ago, resulting in a prominent warming period in Earth's history). Finally, the oceans obviously play an important role in transferring heat from low latitudes to high latitudes. Should patterns of ocean circulation change, climate can be significantly altered (this possibility is considered in Chapter 9).

Climate Models

How do atmospheric scientists predict what climate will be like in the future? Predictions of future temperature and precipitation patterns are mostly the product of sophisticated computer simulations known as **general circulation models** (GCMs). In short, a GCM is a mathematical model of Earth's climate system. In such a computer-simulated world, assumptions are made about many parameters: the amount of radiation striking the surface, the extent of cloud cover, variations in ocean temperature, changes in wind and pressure patterns, changes in greenhouse gas concentration, variations in surface albedo, as well as many others.

Before trying to predict future climates, a GCM must pass several "tests." First, the GCM must be able to simulate present atmospheric processes and climate—in other words, it must reliably replicate processes and patterns in the present-day atmosphere. Next, the GCM must be able to simulate past climate change, so data on past climate conditions are input into the program and the simulation is run "forward" to the present day. If the model can't "predict" what has actually happened to climate, adjustments must be made to the program. The model can then be run forward to make predictions about future climate. A common scenario for GCMs is to predict the future climate assuming a doubling of CO_2 levels by the year 2050.

Because of the enormous complexities of the atmosphere, different GCMs use different assumptions about how the atmosphere works, and so each GCM will come up with different predictions about the future. Figure 8-50 shows the future global temperature predictions of three GCMs, assuming a doubling of atmospheric carbon dioxide levels—all three predict a 4°C or greater increase in the mid- and high latitudes of the Northern Hemisphere.

Evidence of Current Global Warming

The paleoclimatological record provides the backdrop with which we can compare both the rate and the magnitude of climate change over the last century. As we saw in Chapter 4, the Intergovernmental Panel on Climate Change (IPCC) is the most authoritative international body providing information about climate change to global leaders. In describing evidence of climate change over the last century, *Climate Change 2007: The Physical Science Basis* in the Fourth Assessment Report of the IPCC released in February 2007 states that:

> Warming of the climate system is unequivocal, as is now evident from observations of increases in global average air and ocean temperatures, widespread melting of snow and ice, and rising global mean sea level.

The report further notes that:

- Between the period 1850–1899 and the period 2001–2005 global average temperature increased by 0.76°C (1.37°F), with estimates ranging from 0.57–0.95°C (1.03–1.71°F). Figure 8-51 shows the temperature anomalies, or departure from average, from 1880 to 2005 for the atmosphere as a whole, over the oceans and over land.
- Based on instrument data of temperature since 1850, 11 of the 12 warmest years on record occurred between 1995 and 2006.
- Over the last 50 years average global temperature has been increasing at a rate of about 0.13°C (0.23°F) per decade, almost twice the rate of the twentieth century as a whole. Average temperatures in the Northern Hemisphere during this time period are likely (greater than 66% probability) to be higher than at any time in at least 1300 years.
- Data since 1961 shows that global ocean temperature has increased to depths of at least 3000 meters (9800 feet), and that 80% of the heat added to the global climate system has been absorbed by the oceans.
- In part because of thermal expansion of seawater, global sea level has been rising. During the twentieth century, the estimated total global sea level rise was 0.17 meters (6.7 inches). The average rate of global sea level rise between 1961 and 2003 was

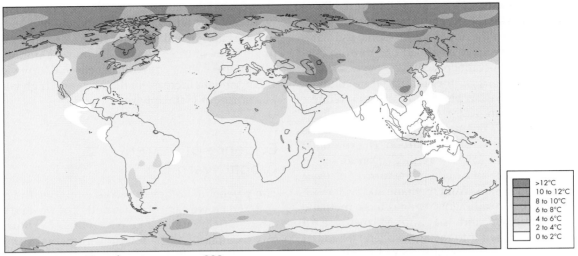

(a) DJF $2xCO_2 - 1xCO_2$ surface air temperature: CCC

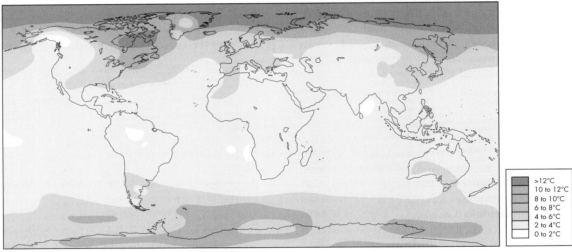

(b) DJF $2xCO_2 - 1xCO_2$ surface air temperature: GFHI

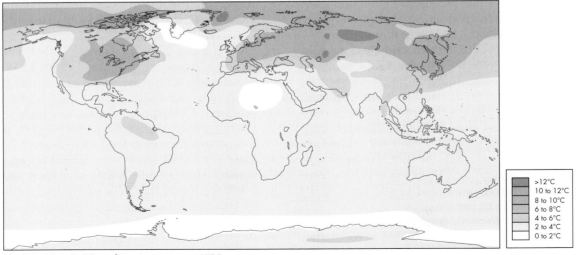

(c) DJF $2xCO_2 - 1xCO_2$ surface air temperature: UKHI

▲ **Figure 8-50**   Temperature changes in December, January, and February as predicted by three different General Circulation Models assuming a doubling of atmospheric CO_2. *(After Aguado and Burt,* Understanding Weather and Climate, *4th ed., 2007.)*

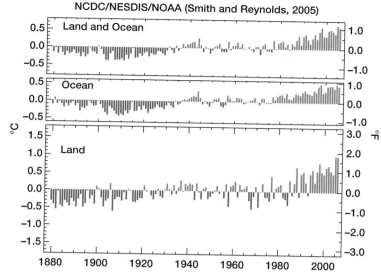

June Global Surface Mean Temp Anomalies

NCDC/NESDIS/NOAA (Smith and Reynolds, 2005)

◀ **Figure 8-51** Temperature anomalies of global air temperature during last 150 years: over Earth's entire surface, over oceans, and over land. *(National Climatic Data Center, NOAA.)*

about 1.8 mm (0.07 inches) per year, although between 1993 and 2003 the rate had increased to about 3.1 mm (0.12 inches) per year; it is not clear if this recent higher rate represents a long-term trend.

- In the Arctic, over the last 100 years average temperatures have been increasing at almost twice the global rate, although in this region there is high observed variability from decade to decade.
- Since 1978, data from satellites shows that average summer sea ice in the Arctic has been decreasing at a rate of about 7.4% per decade (at the end of the summer of 2005, the extent of Arctic sea ice was the smallest measured since regular satellite monitoring of the ice pack began in 1979). Sea ice around Antarctica has shown great annual variation and local changes, but no statistically significant average trend has been observed.
- Ice caps and glaciers decreased in both hemispheres, contributing to sea level rise; the flow speed of some Greenland and Antarctic outlet glaciers has increased.
- Since 1980, temperatures at the top of the permafrost layer have increased by as much as 3°C (5.4°F), and since 1900 the extent of seasonally frozen ground has been reduced by about 7%.
- Observations indicate that there has been an increase in the number of intense tropical cyclones in the North Atlantic Ocean basin since 1970, and this is correlated with an increase in sea surface temperatures in the tropics.
- The average amount of water vapor in the atmosphere over both land and ocean areas has increased since the 1980s, consistent with the higher water vapor capacity of warmer air.
- Between 1900 and 2005 statistically significant increases in average precipitation were observed in parts of North America, South America, Central and Northern Asia, and Northern Europe, while decreases in average precipitation were observed in Southern Africa, South Asia, around the Mediterranean, and in the Sahel; since the 1970s, longer and more intense droughts have been observed over wide areas.

These observed increases in global temperature and the secondary effects of this warming correlate very closely with an increase in greenhouse gas concentrations tied to human activity. The IPCC concludes that concentrations of carbon dioxide, the most important anthropogenic greenhouse gas, increased from a pre-industrial level of about 280 parts per million (ppm) to 379 ppm by 2005. Methane, another key anthropogenic greenhouse gas, increased in concentration from a pre-industrial level of about 715 parts per billion (ppb) to about 1774 ppb by 2005. Recently analyzed ice core data from Dome C in Antarctica shows that the current concentrations of both carbon dioxide and methane in the atmosphere are higher than at any time in the last 650,000 years. Further, the rate of carbon dioxide increase over the last 30 years may be as much as 100 times greater than at any other time in the past 650,000 years. It is likely that this increase in greenhouse gases would have caused more warming than that observed if not offset by slight cooling from anthropogenic and volcanic aerosols.

So, is it possible that the changes in climate observed over the last century have natural causes and are not the result of anthropogenic increases in greenhouses gases? While scientists must always leave open that possibility, the consensus of atmospheric scientists is that the observed changes in global climate over the last century cannot be explained through natural causes alone.

It may be instructive to provide several examples of the findings of the scientific community about global warming. The American Geophysical Union (AGU), an international organization of research scientists, concludes that:

> Human activities are increasingly altering the Earth's climate. These effects add to natural influences that have been present over Earth's history. Scientific evidence strongly indicates that natural influences cannot explain the rapid increase in global near-surface temperatures observed during the second half of the 20th century…Atmospheric carbon dioxide concentrations have increased since the mid-1700s through fossil fuel burning and changes in land use, with more than 80% of this increase occurring since 1900. Moreover, research indicates that increased levels of carbon dioxide will remain in the atmosphere for hundreds to thousands of years. It is virtually certain that increasing atmospheric concentrations of carbon dioxide and other greenhouse gases will cause global surface climate to be warmer.
>
> (Source: American Geophysical Union, *Human Impacts on Climate*, adopted by AGU Council in December 2003)

The *Fourth Assessment Report* of the IPCC released in 2007 concludes that:

> Most of the observed increase in globally averaged temperatures since the mid-20th century is *very likely* [greater than 90% probability] due to the observed increase in anthropogenic greenhouse gas concentrations…Discernible human influences now extend to other aspects of climate, including ocean warming, continental-average temperatures, temperature extremes and wind patterns.

The IPCC report further states that:

> The understanding of anthropogenic warming and cooling influences on climate has improved since the Third Assessment Report (TAR) [in 2001], leading to *very high confidence* [a 9 out of 10 chance] that the globally averaged net effect of human activities since 1750 has been one of warming…

In assessing the credibility of these statements and the quality of science behind them, keep in mind that the IPCC reports are the result of work of hundreds of specialists; the conclusions of the report are refereed by a separate group of reviewers, and the final edited work approved by the delegates of more than 100 countries. Because the IPCC's reports are consensus views, the agreed-upon conclusions often involve compromise on the part of scientists. Climate change researcher and biologist, Tim Flannery, has described the IPCC report conclusions as "lowest-common-denominator science" and that the conclusions "carry great weight…precisely because they represent a consensus view."[2]

---

[2]Flannery, Tim. *The Weather Makers: How Man is Changing the Climate and What it Means for Life on Earth.* New York: Atlantic Monthly Press, 2005, p. 246.

Consequences of Global Warming

While the consensus of atmospheric scientists is that human activity is indeed altering global climate, predicting the extent of future climate change and its consequences are less certain. The IPCC's *Fourth Assessment Report* of 2007 concludes that it is *likely* [a greater than 66% probability] that global climate "sensitivity" to a doubling of pre-industrial carbon dioxide levels will be a temperature increase of 2.0 to 4.5°C (3.6 to 8.1°F), with a best estimate of about 3.0°C (5.4°F).

However, projections of the temperature increase expected by the middle or end of this century are more complicated to calculate: in addition to the great complexity of the global climate system itself is uncertainty about how levels of greenhouse gases will actually change in coming decades. Several different emission scenarios were modeled by the IPCC. The various scenarios were based on different rates of global population increase, different rates of fossil fuel use, different rates of per capita economic growth around the world, among other factors. The findings of the IPCC in the *Fourth Assessment Report* include:

- Over the next two decades climate will warm at a rate of about 0.2°C (0.4°F) per decade.
- If greenhouse gas emissions continue at or above the present rates, the changes in global climate during this century will very likely be (more than 90% probability) greater than the observed changes during the twentieth century.
- The best estimates of the global temperature increase by the year 2099 for the six emissions scenarios studied for the *Fourth Assessment Report* range from a low of 1.8°C (3.3°F) to a high of 4.0°C (7.2°F). The accompanying rise in sea level from thermal expansion and increased rates of ice flow from Antarctica and Greenland under these scenarios ranges from about 0.18 meters (7.1 inches) to 0.59 meters (23.2 inches) by the end of this century, but there is uncertainty in these estimates. Even a modest increase in sea level, however, will cause widespread retreat of shorelines, inundating many heavily populated coastal areas and increasing vulnerability to storms such as hurricanes.
- Warming is expected to be greatest over land and in high northern latitudes, and least over the Southern Ocean; snow cover on land is expected to diminish.
- Sea ice is projected to diminish in the Arctic and Antarctic in all emission scenarios, with summer sea ice disappearing in the Arctic by the end of this century in some scenarios.
- It is likely that tropical cyclones will become more intense in association with projected increases in sea surface temperatures; the storm tracks of mid-latitude cyclones are projected to move poleward.
- Precipitation is very likely to increase in high latitudes and likely to decrease in most subtropical areas over land.

- It is very likely (greater than 90% probability) that heat waves, heavy precipitation events, and hot extremes will occur more frequently.

Among the most troubling findings of the IPCC is that global temperatures are projected to continue increasing and sea level to continue rising for several centuries even if the concentrations of greenhouse gases are stabilized. Such ongoing increases in temperature and sea level could continue for perhaps 1000 years because of the very long time required for carbon dioxide to be removed from the atmosphere.

What can be done to ameliorate the situation? The bottom line is to reduce carbon dioxide emissions, particularly from smokestacks and internal combustion engines. The United States makes up only about 5% of the world's population but is the leading producer of greenhouse gases in the world (nearly one-quarter of the world total); China ranks a close second. Developing countries are increasing emission output as they attempt to build their own industrial infrastructures. Addressing the obvious economic needs of developing nations while attempting to curb carbon dioxide emissions presents a painful dilemma: These nations argue that industrialized nations created the problem and now want the developing countries to forego the benefits of industrialization in order to protect the atmosphere.

The participants in the Kyoto Protocol to the United Nations Framework Convention on Climate Change in 1997 agreed that all emitters of carbon dioxide (the top six are the United States, China, Russia, Japan, Germany, and India) would cut greenhouse gas emissions by an average of 5 percent below 1990 levels by the year 2012. More than 150 countries have ratified the agreement.

Even if the goals of carbon dioxide reduction specified under the Kyoto Protocol are achieved, according to current estimates, the reductions will not be enough to avoid most of the anticipated changes in global climate and environment described above. Indeed, it is estimated that eliminating the observed warming trend would require a decrease of at least 50 percent in burning fossil fuels—a goal much more difficult to achieve than the very modest reductions specified by the Kyoto Protocol. For this reason, many policy makers now advocate that in addition to working toward reducing greenhouse gas emissions, we also need to prepare for the environmental changes that seem inevitable in a warmer world.

The United States has yet to sign on to the Kyoto Protocol (as of early 2007) primarily because some government leaders fear that the economic cost to the country would be too high. A counterargument made by many scientists, and increasingly by both political and business leaders, is that the long-term cost of *not* addressing global warming will likely be even higher.

Chapter 8 Learning Review

Key Terms

Before answering the study questions below, review the definitions of the following key terms (page references are provided for you):

climograph *(p. 215)*
dendrochronology *(p. 249)*
general circulation models (GCMs) *(p. 253)*
highland climate *(p. 243)*
humid continental (climate) *(p. 235)*
humid subtropical (climate) *(p. 229)*
ice cap (climate) *(p. 239)*
isotopes *(p. 249)*

Köppen climate classification system *(p. 212)*
marine west coast (climate) *(p. 229)*
mediterranean (climate) *(p. 229)*
midlatitude desert (climate) *(p. 223)*
midlatitude steppe (climate) *(p. 223)*
Milankovitch cycles *(p. 252)*
paleoclimatology *(p. 248)*
subarctic (climate) *(p. 235)*

subtropical desert (climate) *(p. 223)*
subtropical steppe (climate) *(p. 223)*
tropical monsoon (climate) *(p. 217)*
tropical savanna (climate) *(p. 217)*
tropical wet (climate) *(p. 217)*
tundra (climate) *(p. 239)*

Study Questions for Key Concepts

After studying this chapter, you should be able to answer the following questions:

The Köppen Climate Classification System (p. 212)

1. Explain the basic concept of the *Köppen climate classification system.*
2. In the Köppen climate classification letter code system, what information is given by the first letter, the second letter, and the third letter?
3. What information is conveyed in a *climograph?*

World Distribution of Major Climate Types (p. 215)

4. Briefly describe the major climate groups of the Köppen climate classification system: A, B, C, D, E, and H.
5. Describe the general location, temperature characteristics, precipitation characteristics, and main controls of the following 10 climate types. You

should also be able to recognize these climates from a climograph:

- Af   Tropical wet
- Aw   Tropical savanna
- Am   Tropical monsoon
- BWh   Subtropical desert
- BWk   Midlatitude desert
- Cs   Mediterranean
- Cfa   Humid subtropical
- Cfb   Marine west coast
- Dfa   Humid continental
- Dfc   Subarctic

6. Why do Af (tropical wet) climates receive rain all year while Aw (tropical savanna) climates receive rain only in the summer?

7. What are the main differences in controls of BWh (subtropical desert) and BWk (midlatitude desert) climates?

8. Why are subtropical desert (BWh) climates generally hotter in summer than tropical humid (A) climates?

9. Why are dry climates usually displaced toward the western sides of continents?

10. Why are dry climates much more extensive in North Africa than in any other subtropical location?

11. Why do Cs (mediterranean) climates have dry summers and wet winters?

12. What causes the relatively mild temperatures of marine west coast climates?

13. What is meant by the phrase "continentality is a keynote in D climates"?

14. Although both cities are coastal, New York City has a continental climate while Seattle, Washington, has a maritime climate. Why?

15. Why do subarctic (Dfc) climates have such a wide annual temperature range?

16. Why are polar climates so dry?

Global Climate Change (p. 247)

17. How can tree rings provide information about past climate?

18. What kind of information about past climate can be learned from ice core analysis?

19. What are *Milankovitch cycles* and in what ways might they influence climate?

20. Describe and explain at least one feedback mechanism that would further increase global temperatures once a warming trend has started.

21. Why do some types of clouds tend to cool the surface of Earth, while other types of clouds tend to warm the surface?

22. What roles do the oceans play in influencing the carbon dioxide concentrations in the atmosphere?

Additional Resources

Books:

Barry, R. G. *Mountain Weather and Climate,* 2nd ed. New York: Routledge, 1992.

Flannery, Tim. *The Weather Makers: How Man Is Changing the Climate and What It Means for Life on Earth.* New York: Atlantic Monthly Press, 2005.

Kolbert, Elizabeth. *Field Notes from a Catastrophe: Man, Nature and Climate Change.* New York: Bloomsbury, 2006.

Internet Sites:

Intergovernmental Panel on Climate Change
http://www.ipcc.ch/

The Intergovernmental Panel on Climate Change was established to study and assess global climate change and its influence on human populations.

National Climatic Data Center
http://www.ncdc.noaa.gov/

The National Climatic Data Center is a good site to begin a search for climate records for locations around the world. Start with the links to the Regional Climate Centers, where you can retrieve historical summaries of climate data for hundreds of cities across the United States.

National Geophysical Data Center
http://www.ngdc.noaa.gov/

The National Geophysical Data Center is a great starting point for finding information about glaciology, marine geology, paleoclimatology, solar–terrestrial physics, and geophysics.

National Oceanic and Atmospheric Administration (NOAA)
http://www.noaa.gov/

The National Oceanic and Atmospheric Administration (NOAA) oversees a number of government agencies, including the National Weather Service. NOAA's home page provides links to sites about weather, climate, weather satellites, the oceans, and coastlines.

9
The Hydrosphere

The hydrosphere is at once the most pervasive and the least well defined of the four "spheres" of Earth's physical environment. It includes the surface water in oceans, lakes, rivers, and swamps; all underground water; frozen water in the form of ice, snow, and high-cloud crystals; water vapor in the atmosphere; and the moisture temporarily stored in plants and animals.

The hydrosphere overlaps significantly with the other three spheres. Liquid water, ice, and even water vapor occur in the soil and rocks of the lithosphere. Water vapor and cloud particles composed of liquid water and ice are important constituents of the lower portion of the atmosphere, and water is a critical component of every living organism of the biosphere. Life is impossible without water; every living thing depends on it. Watery solutions in living organisms dissolve or disperse nutrients for nourishment. Most waste products are carried away in solutions. Indeed, the total mass of every living thing is more than half water, the proportion ranging from about 60 percent for some animals to more than 95 percent for some plants.

It is through moisture, then, that the interrelationships of the four spheres are most conspicuous and pervasive. In Chapter 6 we introduced many of the physical properties of water. In this chapter, we will examine the geography of water in much greater detail.

The Hydrologic Cycle

Hydrologic Cycle

This unique substance, water, essential to life and finite in amount, is distributed very unevenly on, in, and above Earth. The great bulk of all moisture, more than 99 percent, is in storage—in oceans, lakes, and streams, locked up as glacial ice, or held in rocks below Earth's surface (Figure 9-1). Water frozen as ice in glaciers and continental ice sheets represents about three-fourths of all of the freshwater on the planet.

The proportional amount of moisture in these various storage reservoirs is relatively constant over thousands of years. Only during an "ice age" is there a notable change in these components: during periods of glaciation, the volume of the oceans becomes smaller as the ice sheets grow and the level of atmospheric water vapor diminishes; then during deglaciation, the ice melts, the volume of the oceans increases as the meltwater flows into them, and there is an increase in atmospheric water vapor.

The remaining small fraction—less than 1 percent—of Earth's total moisture is involved in an almost continuous sequence of movement and change, the effects of which are absolutely critical to life on this planet. This tiny portion of Earth's water supply moves from one storage area to another—from ocean to air, from air to ground, and so on—in the **hydrologic cycle**. We first introduced the hydrologic cycle in Chapter 6. In the present chapter, we examine the complexities of this cycle in more detail.

The hydrologic cycle can be viewed as a series of storage areas interconnected by various transfer processes, in which there is a ceaseless interchange of moisture in terms of both its geographic location and its physical state (Figure 9-2). Liquid water on Earth's surface evaporates to become water vapor in the atmosphere. That vapor then condenses and precipitates, either as liquid water or as ice, back onto the surface. This precipitated water then runs off into storage areas and later evaporates into the atmosphere once again. As this is a closed, circular system, we can begin the discussion at any point. It is perhaps clearest to start with the movement of moisture from Earth's surface into the atmosphere.

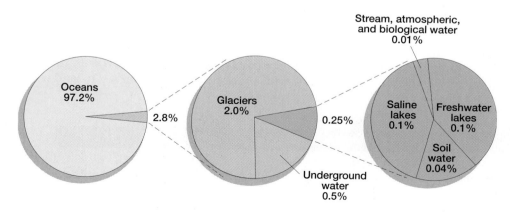

◄ **Figure 9-1** Moisture inventory of Earth.

◄ Lake Murphysboro State Park, Illinois. *(Getty Images/Dennis Flaherty.)*

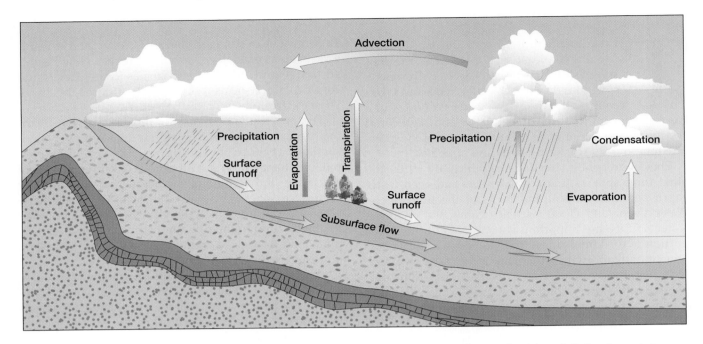

▲ **Figure 9-2**   The hydrologic cycle. The two major components are evaporation from surface to air and precipitation from air to surface. Other important elements of the cycle include transpiration of moisture from vegetation to atmosphere, surface runoff and subsurface flow of water from land to sea, condensation of water vapor to form clouds from which precipitation may fall, and advection of moisture from one place to another.

Surface-to-Air Water Movement

Most of the moisture that enters the atmosphere from Earth's surface does so through evaporation. (Transpiration is the source of the remainder.) The oceans, of course, are the principal source of water for evaporation. They occupy 71 percent of Earth's surface, have unlimited moisture available for ready evaporation, and are extensive in low latitudes, where considerable heat and wind movement facilitate evaporation. As a result, an estimated 86 percent of all evaporated moisture is derived from ocean surfaces (Table 9-1). (The 14 percent that comes from land surfaces includes the twin processes of evaporation and transpiration.)

Water vapor from evaporation remains in the atmosphere a relatively short time—usually only a few hours or days. During that interval, however, it may move a considerable distance, either vertically through convection or horizontally through advection driven by wind currents.

Air-to-Surface Water Movement

Sooner or later, water vapor in the atmosphere condenses to liquid water or sublimates to ice to form cloud particles. As we saw in Chapter 6, under the proper circumstances clouds may drop precipitation in the form of rain, snow, sleet, or hail. As Table 9-1 shows, 78 percent of this precipitation falls into the oceans and 22 percent falls onto land.

Over several years, total worldwide precipitation is approximately equal to total worldwide evaporation/ transpiration. Although precipitation and evaporation/ transpiration balance in time, they do not balance in place: evaporation exceeds precipitation over the oceans, whereas the opposite is true over the continents. This imbalance is explained by the advection of moist maritime air onto land areas, so that there is less moisture available for precipitation over the ocean.

Except for coastal spray and storm waves, the only route by which moisture moves from sea to land is via the atmosphere.

TABLE 9-1 Comparison of Moisture Balance of Continents and Oceans

	Percentage of Total World Surface Area	Percentage of Total World Precipitation Received	Percentage of Total World Evaporation/Transpiration That Occurs from the Surface
Oceans	71	78	86
Continents	29	22	14

Movement on and beneath Earth's Surface

Looking at Table 9-1, you may wonder why the oceans do not dry up and the continents become flooded, there being 8 percent more water leaving the ocean than precipitating back into it and 8 percent more water falling on land than evaporating off it. The reason such drying up and flooding do not take place is **runoff**, that portion of Earth's circulating moisture that moves in the liquid state from land to sea.

The 78 percent of total global precipitation that falls on the ocean is simply incorporated immediately into the water already there; the 22 percent that falls on land goes through a more complicated series of events. Rain falling on a land surface collects on that surface, runs off if the surface is a slope, or infiltrates the ground. Any water that pools on the surface eventually either evaporates or sinks into the ground, runoff water eventually ends up in the ocean, and infiltrated water is either stored temporarily as soil moisture or percolates farther down to become part of the underground water supply. Much of the soil moisture eventually evaporates or transpires back into the atmosphere, and much of the underground water eventually reappears at the surface via springs. Then sooner or later, and in one way or another, most of the water that reaches the surface evaporates again, and the rest is incorporated into streams and rivers and becomes runoff flowing into the oceans. This runoff water from continents to oceans amounts to 8 percent of all moisture circulating in the global hydrologic cycle. It is this runoff that balances the excess of precipitation over evaporation taking place on the continents and that keeps the oceans from drying up and the land from flooding.

Residence Times

Although the hydrologic cycle is a closed system and is believed to have an unvarying total capacity, there is enormous variation in the cycling of individual molecules of water. A particular molecule of water may be stored in oceans and deep lakes, or as glacial ice, for thousands of years without moving through the cycle, and one trapped in rocks buried deep beneath Earth's surface may be excluded from the cycle for hundreds of thousands of years.

However, whatever water is moving through the cycle is in almost continuous motion (Figure 9-3). Runoff water can travel hundreds of kilometers to the sea in only a few days, and moisture evaporated into the atmosphere may remain there for only a few minutes or hours before it is precipitated back to Earth. Indeed, at any given moment, the atmosphere contains only a few days' potential precipitation.

▲ **Figure 9-3**   Oregon's Lake Trillium with morning fog. Moisture constantly moves through the hydrologic cycle through evaporation, condensation, precipitation, and runoff. *(© Craig Tuttle/CORBIS.)*

The Oceans

Despite the facts that most of Earth's surface is oceanic and that the vast majority of all water is in the oceans (see Figure 9-1), our knowledge of the seas was fairly limited until recently. The ocean is a hostile environment for most air-breathing creatures, including humans. Thus, only with great care can humans venture beneath the sea's surface, and only within the last five decades or so has sophisticated equipment been available to catalog and measure details of the maritime environment.

How Many Oceans?

From the broadest viewpoint, there is but one ocean. This "world ocean" has a surface area of 360 million square kilometers (139 million square miles) and contains 1.32 billion cubic kilometers (317 million cubic miles) of salt water. It spreads over almost three-fourths of Earth's surface, interrupted here and there by continents and islands. Although tens of thousands of bits of land protrude above the blue waters, the world ocean is so vast that half a dozen continent-sized portions of it are totally devoid of islands, without a single piece of land breaking the surface of the water. It is one or more

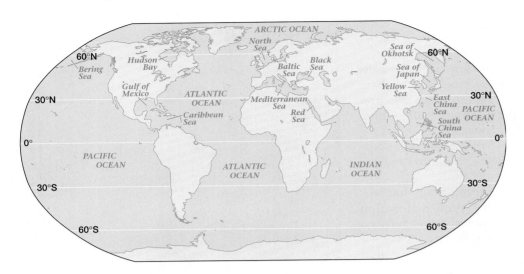

◀ **Figure 9-4** The four principal oceans and the major seas of the world.

of these large expanses of water we are usually referring to when we use the term *ocean*.

In generally accepted usage, the world ocean is divided into four principal parts—the Pacific, Atlantic, Indian, and Arctic oceans (Figure 9-4). (Some people refer to the waters around Antarctica as the *Antarctic Ocean* or the *Great Southern Ocean,* but this distinction is not generally accepted.) The boundaries of the four oceans are not everywhere precise, and around some of their margins are partly landlocked smaller bodies of water called *seas, gulfs, bays,* and other related terms. Most of these smaller bodies can be considered as portions of one of the major oceans, although a few are so narrowly connected (Black Sea, Mediterranean Sea, Hudson Bay) to a named ocean as to deserve separate consideration, as Figure 9-4 and Table 9-2 show. This

TABLE 9-2 Oceans and Major Seas of the World

	Approximate Surface Area		Percentage of Water Present on Earth*
	Square Miles	Square Kilometers	
Pacific Ocean	64,186,000	166,884,000	46
Atlantic Ocean	31,862,000	82,841,000	23
Indian Ocean	28,350,000	73,710,000	20
Arctic Ocean	5,427,000	14,110,000	4
South China Sea	1,150,000	2,990,000	—
Caribbean Sea	971,000	2,525,000	—
Mediterranean Sea	969,000	2,519,000	—
Bering Sea	875,000	2,275,000	—
Gulf of Mexico	600,000	1,560,000	—
Sea of Okhotsk	550,000	1,430,000	—
East China Sea	480,000	1,248,000	—
Sea of Japan	405,000	1,053,000	—
Hudson Bay	318,000	827,000	—
North Sea	222,000	577,000	—
Yellow Sea	220,000	572,000	—
Black Sea	190,000	494,000	—
Red Sea	175,000	455,000	—
Baltic Sea	160,000	416,000	—

*Values are omitted for the 14 seas because of their minimal size relative to the size of the world's oceans.

nomenclature is further clouded by the term *sea*, which is used sometimes synonymously with *ocean*, sometimes to denote a specific smaller body of water around the edge of an ocean, and occasionally to denote an inland body of water.

The *Pacific Ocean* (Figure 9-5a) is twice as large as any other body of water on Earth. Five of the seven continents are on its fringes. It occupies about one-third of the total area of Earth, more than all the world's land surfaces combined. It contains the greatest average depth of any ocean as well as the deepest known oceanic trenches. Although the Pacific extends almost to the Arctic Circle in the north and a few degrees beyond the Antarctic Circle in the south, it is largely a tropical ocean. Its greatest girth is in equatorial regions; almost one-half of the 38,500-kilometer (24,000-mile) length of the equator is in the Pacific. The character of this ocean often belies its tranquil name, for it houses some of the most disastrous of all storms (typhoons) and many of the world's major volcanoes are either in it or around its edge.

The *Atlantic Ocean* is slightly less than half the size of the Pacific (Figure 9-5b). Its latitudinal extent is roughly the same as that of the Pacific, but its east–west spread is only about half as great. Its average depth is also only a little less than that of the Pacific.

The *Indian Ocean* (Figure 9-5c) is a little smaller than the Atlantic, and its average depth is slightly less than that of the Atlantic. Nine-tenths of its area is south of the equator.

The *Arctic Ocean* (Figure 9-5d) is much smaller and shallower than the other three. It is connected to the Pacific by a relatively narrow passageway between Alaska and Siberia, but it has a broad and indefinite connection with the Atlantic between North America and Europe.

Characteristics of Ocean Waters

Wherever they are found, the waters of the world ocean have many similar characteristics, but they also show significant differences from place to place. The differences are particularly notable in the surface layers, down to a depth of about 100 meters (about 350 feet).

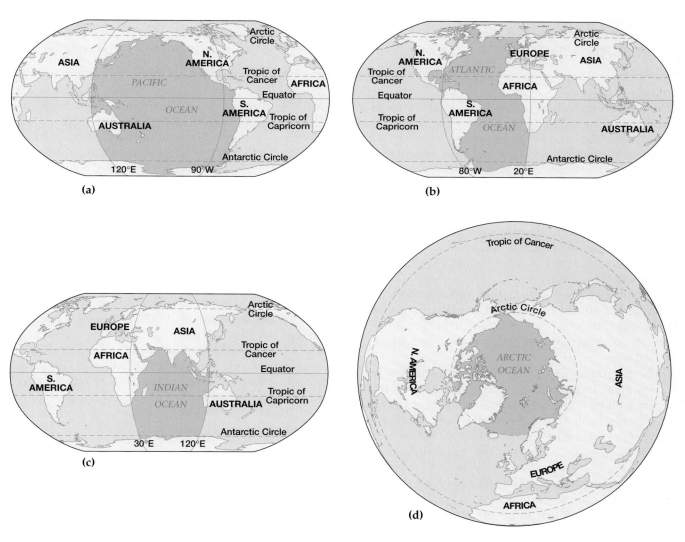

▲ **Figure 9-5** The four major parts of the world ocean: **(a)** the Pacific Ocean, **(b)** the Atlantic Ocean, **(c)** the Indian Ocean, **(d)** the Arctic Ocean.

PEOPLE AND THE ENVIRONMENT Oceans Becoming More Acidic

The oceans absorb carbon dioxide from the atmosphere. Perhaps one-third of the excess CO_2 released into the air each year by human activity has been absorbed by the oceans. When CO_2 is taken in by the ocean, it forms *carbonic acid* (H_2CO_3), a weak acid. Research now suggests that as a result of the great quantities of CO_2 absorbed since the beginning of the industrial revolution, the ocean is becoming more acidic.

Currently, ocean water is slightly alkaline, with a pH of 8.1 (see Chapter 6 for a description of the pH scale). Although still alkaline, this value is estimated to be about 0.1 lower—in other words more acidic—than it was in the preindustrial era. Given the current rate of fossil fuel use and continued absorption of CO_2 by the oceans, the pH of ocean water could drop to 7.7 by the end of this century.

The consequences of a slightly more acidic ocean are not completely known, but it is likely that it will affect the growth of organisms such as coral polyps and microscopic creatures such as *foraminifera* (Figure 9-A) that build their shells or exoskeletons from calcium carbonate ($CaCO_3$) extracted from seawater. As the oceans become more acidic, there are fewer calcium ions in seawater and so the growth of calcium carbonate shells is inhibited. It is not clear if these creatures will be able to adapt to the changing chemistry of the ocean.

Since foraminifera are at the bottom of the oceanic food web, among the potentially important consequences of a decline in their numbers would be the loss of food for a number of fish, such as mackerel and salmon. If the increased acidity of the oceans reduces the growth of coral

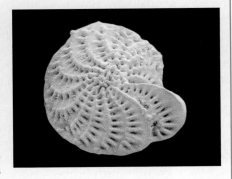

▲ **Figure 9-A**   Scanning electron microscope image of *Elphidium crispum*, one of many kinds of single-celled foraminifera, magnified approximately 80 times. (*Photo Researchers, Inc.*)

polyps, coral reefs—already under stress worldwide from higher temperatures—might possibly degrade even further (a more complete discussion of coral reefs is found in Chapter 20).

Chemical Composition   Seawater contains dissolved minerals, which make up about 3.5 percent of its total mass. Almost all known elements are found to some extent in seawater, but by far the most important are sodium (Na) and chlorine (Cl), which form sodium chloride (NaCl)—the common salt we know as table salt. (In the language of chemistry, "salts" are substances that result when a base neutralizes an acid. For instance, sodium chloride is formed when the base sodium hydroxide [NaOH] neutralizes hydrochloric acid [HCl].)

The **salinity** of seawater is a measure of the concentration of dissolved salts, which are mostly sodium chloride but also include salts containing magnesium, sulfur, calcium, and potassium. The average salinity of seawater is about 35 parts per thousand, or 3.5 percent of total mass.

The geographic distribution of surface salinity varies. At any given location on the ocean surface, the salinity depends on how much evaporation is taking place and how much fresh water (primarily from rainfall and stream discharge) is being added. Where the evaporation rate is high, so is salinity; where the inflow of fresh water is high, salinity is low. Typically the lowest salinities are found where rainfall is heavy and near the mouths of major rivers. Salinity is highest in partly landlocked seas in dry, hot regions because here the evaporation rate is high and stream discharge is minimal. As a general pattern, salinity is low in equatorial regions because of heavy rainfall, cloudiness,

and humidity, all of which inhibit evaporation, and also because of considerable river discharge. Salinity rises to a general maximum in the subtropics, where precipitation is low and evaporation extensive, and decreases to a general minimum in the polar regions, where evaporation is minimal and there is considerable inflow of fresh water from rivers and ice caps.

Temperature   As is to be expected, surface seawater temperatures generally decrease with increasing latitude. The temperature often exceeds 26°C (80°F) in equatorial locations and decreases to −2°C (28°F), the average freezing point for seawater, in Arctic and Antarctic seas. (Dissolved salts lower the freezing point of the water from the 0°C (32°F) of pure water.) The western sides of oceans are nearly always warmer than the eastern margins because of the movement of major ocean currents (see Figure 4-28 in Chapter 4). This pattern of warmer western parts is due to the contrasting effects of poleward-moving warm currents on the west side of ocean basins and equatorward-moving cool currents on the east side of ocean basins.

Density   Seawater density varies with temperature, degree of salinity, and depth. High temperature produces low density, and high salinity produces high density. Deep water has high density because of low temperature and because of the pressure of the overlying water.

Surface layers of seawater tend to contract and sink in cold regions, whereas in warmer areas deeper waters tend to rise to the surface. Surface currents also affect this situation, particularly by producing an upwelling of colder, denser water in some localities.

Movement of Ocean Waters

The liquidity of the ocean permits it to be in continuous motion, and this motion can be grouped under three headings: waves, currents, and tides. The movement of almost anything over the surface—wind, a boat, a swimmer—can set surface water into motion. The ocean surface is almost always ridged with swells and waves, therefore, and below the surface there is the less conspicuous restlessness of currents. Disturbances in that part of Earth's crust that underlies ocean water can also trigger significant movements in the water, and the gravitational attraction of nearby heavenly bodies causes the greatest movements of all: the tides.

Waves consist mostly of a change in the shape of the ocean surface, with little displacement of water. Currents involve a considerable displacement of water, particularly horizontally, but also vertically and obliquely. By far the greatest vertical movements of ocean waters are due to tides.

Tides

Tides

On the shores of the world ocean, almost everywhere, the sea level fluctuates regularly. For about six hours each day, the water rises, and then for about six hours it falls. These rhythmic oscillations have continued unabated, day and night, winter and summer, for eons. **Tides** are essentially bulges in the sea surface in some places that are compensated by "sinks" in the surface at other places. Thus, tides are primarily vertical motions of the water. In shallow-water areas around the margins of the oceans, however, the vertical oscillations of the tides may produce significant horizontal water movements as well.

Causes of Tides It is a law of physics that every object in the universe exerts an attractive gravitational force on every other body. Thus, Earth exerts an attractive force on the Moon, and the Moon exerts an attractive force on Earth. The same is true for Earth and the Sun. It is the gravitational attraction between the Moon and Earth, and between the Sun and Earth, that cause tides.

The strength of the force of gravity is inversely proportional to the square of the distance between the two bodies, and so, the Sun being 150,000,000 kilometers (93,000,000 miles) from Earth and the Moon 385,000 kilometers (239,000 miles), the Moon produces a greater percentage of Earth's tides than does the Sun. The lunar tides are about twice as strong as the solar tides. To keep things simple, let us first discuss lunar tides alone, ignoring solar tides for the moment.

Gravitational attraction pulls ocean water toward the Moon. There is more gravitational attraction on the side of Earth facing the Moon than on the opposite side of Earth—where the inward or *centripetal force* needed to keep Earth in its orbit is slightly greater. The difference in forces slightly elongates the shape of the global ocean, so that two bulges of ocean water develop—one on the side of Earth facing the Moon and the other on the opposite side of Earth. As Earth rotates, coastlines move into and out of these bulges, producing simultaneous tides on the opposite sides of Earth and low tides halfway between.

As Earth rotates eastward, the tidal progression appears to move westward. The tides rise and fall twice in the interval between two "rising" Moons, an interval that is about 50 minutes longer than a 24-hour day. The combination of Earth's rotation and the Moon's revolution around Earth means that Earth makes about 12° more than a full rotation between each rising of the Moon. Thus, two complete tidal cycles have a duration of about 24 hours and 50 minutes. This means that on all oceanic coastlines there are normally two high tides and two low tides about every 25 hours.

The magnitude of tidal fluctuation is quite variable in time and place, but the sequence of the cycle is generally similar everywhere. From its lowest point, the water rises gradually for about 6 hours and 13 minutes, so that there is an actual movement of water toward the coast in what is called a **flood tide**. At the end of the flooding period, the maximum water level, *high tide*, is reached. Soon the water level begins to drop, and for the next 6 hours and 13 minutes there is a gradual movement of water away from the coast, this movement being called an **ebb tide**. When the minimum water level (*low tide*) is reached, the cycle begins again.

Monthly Tidal Cycle The vertical difference in elevation between high and low tide is called the **tidal range**. Changes in the relative positions of Earth, Moon, and Sun induce periodic variations in tidal ranges, as shown in Figure 9-6. The greatest range (in other words, the highest tide) occurs when the three bodies are positioned in a straight line, which usually occurs twice a month near the times of the full and new Moons. When thus aligned, the joint gravitational pull of the Sun and Moon is along the same line, so that the combined pull is at a maximum. This is true both when the Moon is between Earth and the Sun and when Earth is between the Moon and Sun. In either case, this is a time of higher than usual tides, called **spring tides**. (The name has nothing to do with the season; think of water "springing" up to a very high level.)

When the Sun and Moon are located at right angles to one another with respect to Earth, their individual gravitational pulls are diminished because they are now pulling at right angles to each other. This right-angle

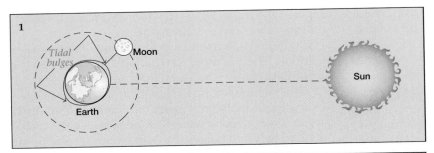

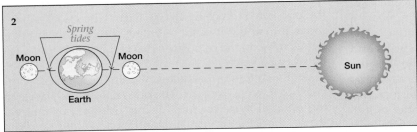

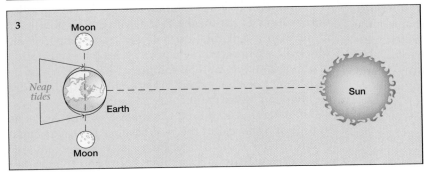

◄ Figure 9-6 Juxtaposition of the Sun, Moon, and Earth accounts for variations in Earth's tidal range. The three basic positional relationships are illustrated here. (1) When the Moon and Sun are neither aligned nor at right angles to each other, we have normal levels of high tides on both sides of Earth. (2) When the Sun, Earth, and Moon are positioned along the same line, *spring tides* (the highest high tides) are produced. (3) When the line joining Earth and the Moon forms a right angle, with the line joining Earth and the Sun, *neap tides* (the lowest high tides) result.

pulling results in a lower than normal tidal range called a **neap tide**. The Sun–Moon alignment that causes neap tides generally takes place twice a month at about the time of first quarter and third quarter moons.

Tidal range is also affected by the Moon's nearness to Earth. The Moon follows an elliptical orbit in its revolution around Earth, the nearest point (called *perigee*) being about 50,000 kilometers (31,200 miles), or 12 percent, closer than the farthest point (*apogee*). During perigee, tidal ranges are greater than during apogee.

Global Variations in Tidal Range Tidal range fluctuates all over the world at the same times of the month. There are, however, enormous variations in range along different coastlines (Figure 9-7). Midocean islands may experience tides of only one meter (3 feet) or less, whereas continental seacoasts have greater tidal ranges, the amplitude being greatly influenced by the shape of the coastline and the configuration of the sea bottom beneath coastal waters. Along most coasts, there is a moderate tidal range of 1.5–3 meters (5–10 feet). Some partly landlocked seas, such as the Mediterranean, have almost negligible tides. Other places, such as the northwestern coast of Australia, experience enormous tides of 10 meters (35 feet) or so.

The greatest tidal range is found at the upper end of the Bay of Fundy in eastern Canada (Figure 9-8), where

a 15-meter (50-foot) water-level fluctuation twice a day is not uncommon, and a wall of seawater—called a **tidal bore**—several centimeters to more than a meter in height rushes up the Petitcodiac River in New Brunswick for many kilometers (Figure 9-9).

Tidal variation is exceedingly small in inland bodies of water. Even the largest lakes usually experience a tidal rise and fall of no more than 5 centimeters (2 inches). Effectively, then, tides are important only in the world ocean, and they are normally noticeable only around its shorelines.

Currents

Ocean Circulation Patterns

As we learned in Chapter 4, the world ocean contains a variety of currents that shift vast quantities of water both horizontally and vertically. Surface currents are caused primarily by wind flow, while other currents are set in motion by contrasts in temperature and salinity. All currents are likely to be influenced by the size and shape of the particular ocean, the configuration and depth of the sea bottom, and the Coriolis effect. Some currents involve subsidence of surface waters

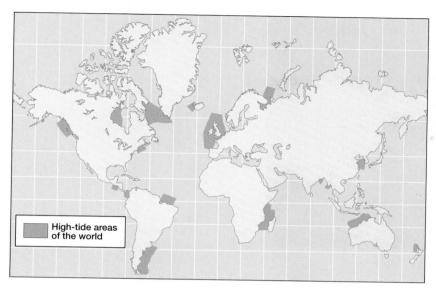

◀ **Figure 9-7** Areas with tidal ranges exceeding 4 meters (13 feet). The pattern is not a predictable one as it depends on a variety of unrelated factors, particularly shoreline and seabottom configuration. (*After J. L. Davies, Geographical Variation in Coastal Development, 2nd ed., New York: Longman, 1980, p. 179.*)

downward; other vertical flows bring an upwelling of deeper water to the surface.

Geographically speaking, the most prominent currents are the major horizontal flows that make up the general circulation of the various oceans. The dominant surface currents introduced in Chapter 4 are generally referred to as *subtropical gyres* (see Figure 4-28). They are set up by the action of the dominant surface wind systems in the tropics and midlatitudes: the trade winds and the westerlies.

Deep Ocean Circulation In addition to the major surface ocean currents, there is an important system of deep ocean circulation as well. This circulation of deep ocean water occurs because of differences in water density that arise from differences in salinity and temperature. For this reason, this water movement is sometimes referred to as **thermohaline circulation**. Ocean water will become denser, and thus sink, if its salinity increases or its temperature decreases. This

happens predominantly in high-latitude ocean areas where the water is cold and salinity increases when sea ice develops (the dissolved salts are not taken up in the ice when water freezes, so increasing the salinity of the remaining water).

The combination of deep ocean water movement through thermohaline circulation, along with influences from surface ocean currents, establishes an overall **global conveyer-belt circulation** pattern (Figure 9-10). Beginning in the North Atlantic, cold, dense water sinks and slowly flows deep below the surface to the south, where it eventually joins the eastward moving deep, cold, high salinity water circulating around Antarctica. Some of this deep water eventually flows north into the Indian and Pacific Oceans, where it rises to form a shallow, warm current that flows back to the North Atlantic Ocean, where it sinks and begins its long journey once again. These deep ocean currents might travel only 15 kilometers (9 miles) in a year—thus requiring many centuries to complete a single circuit.

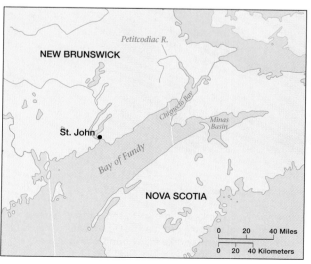

◀ **Figure 9-8** The world's maximum tides are in the Bay of Fundy, where ocean water moves long distances up many of the coastal rivers twice a day.

◀ **Figure 9-9** A tidal bore moving up the Petitcodiac River in New Brunswick, Canada. *(J. H. Robinson/Photo Researchers, Inc.)*

Recent research suggests that a connection exists between the global conveyer-belt circulation and global climate. For example, if global climate becomes warmer, the freshwater runoff from the melting of Greenland's glaciers could form a pool of lower density water in the North Atlantic—and this lower density surface water could disrupt the downwelling of water in the North Atlantic, altering the redistribution of heat around the world.

Waves

To the casual observer, the most conspicuous motion of the ocean is provided by waves. Most of the sea surface is in a state of constant agitation, with wave crests and troughs bobbing up and down most of the time. Moreover, around the margin of the ocean, waves of one size or another lap, break, or pound on the shore in endless procession.

Most of this movement is like running in place from the water's point of view, with little forward progress. Waves in the open ocean are mostly just shapes, and the movement of a wave across the sea surface is a movement of form rather than of substance or, to say the same thing another way, of energy rather than matter. Individual water particles make only small oscillating movements. Only when a wave "breaks" does any significant shifting of

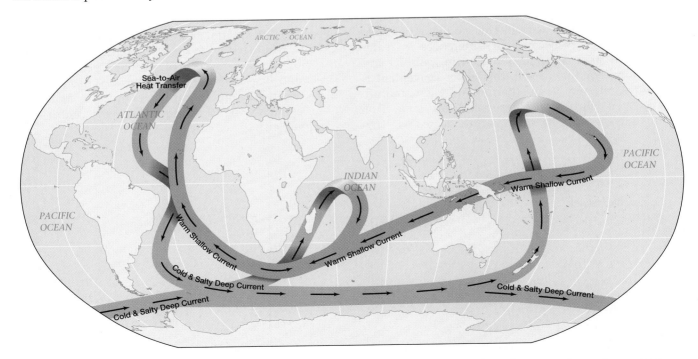

▲ **Figure 9-10** Global conveyor-belt circulation. In the North Atlantic Ocean warm water sinks and moves to the south as a deep subsurface flow. It joins cold deep water near Antarctica, eventually moving into the Indian and North Pacific Ocean where the water rises slowly, eventually flowing back into the North Atlantic where it again sinks. One circuit may take many hundreds of years. *(After: Trujillo and Thurman,* Essentials of Oceanography, *8th ed., Upper Saddle River, NJ: Pearson-Prentice Hall, 2005.)*

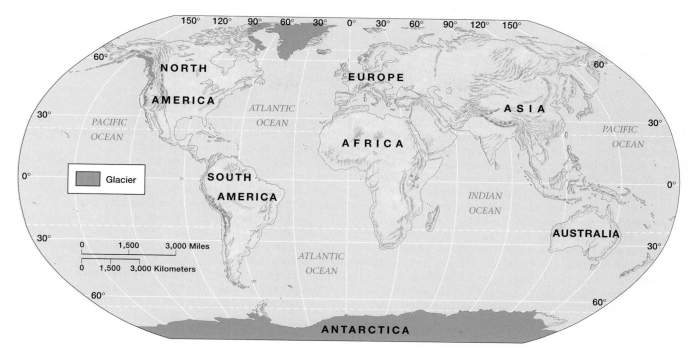

▲ **Figure 9-11**   Glacial ice covers about 10 percent of Earth's surface. This ice is confined primarily to Antarctica and Greenland, with small amounts also found at high elevations in the Canadian Rockies, Andes, Alps, and Himalayas.

water take place. Waves are discussed in detail in Chapter 20.

Permanent Ice— The Cryosphere

Second only to the world ocean as a storage reservoir for moisture is the solid portion of the hydrosphere— the ice of the world, or *cryosphere*—as we learn from a glance back at Figure 9-1. Although minuscule in comparison with the amount of water in the oceans, the moisture content of ice at any given time is more than twice as large as the combined total of all other types of storage (underground water, surface waters, soil moisture, atmospheric moisture, and biological water).

The ice portion of the hydrosphere is divided between ice on land and ice floating in the ocean, with the land portion being the larger. Ice on land is found as alpine glaciers, ice sheets, and ice caps, all of which are studied in Chapter 19. Approximately 10 percent of the land surface of Earth is covered by ice (Figure 9-11). It is estimated that there is enough water locked up in this ice to feed all the rivers of the world at their present rate of flow for nearly 900 years.

Oceanic ice has various names, depending on size:

- **Ice pack:** An extensive and cohesive mass of floating ice

- **Ice shelf:** A massive portion of a continental ice sheet that projects out over the sea

- **Ice floe:** A large, flattish mass of ice that breaks off from larger ice bodies and floats independently

- **Iceberg:** A chunk of floating ice that breaks off from an ice shelf or glacier (Figure 9-12)

▲ **Figure 9-12**   Iceberg above and below the water line. *(Getty Images, Inc.—Image Bank.)*

PEOPLE AND THE ENVIRONMENT Thawing Permafrost in Alaska

In locations such as the region around the city of Fairbanks in central Alaska, permanently frozen soil or *permafrost* is widespread just below the surface. During the summer, only the upper 30 to 100 centimeters (12 to 40 inches) of soil thaws in what is called the *active layer;* below that is a layer of permanently frozen ground perhaps 50 meters (165 feet) thick. Much of the permafrost found in the high latitude areas of the world has been frozen for at least the last few thousands of years, but as a response to higher average temperatures, it is beginning to thaw. In just the last 30 years, a warming trend has been observed, bringing the ground temperature in some areas above the melting point of the permafrost (Figure 9-B).

For many people used to living in temperate environments, it might seem that having the ground thaw wouldn't be a problem, but such is not the case. As permafrost thaws, it may soften the soil and cause roads and pipelines to deform. In areas with poor surface drainage, the degradation of permafrost can lead to what is called *wet thermokarst* conditions, where the surface subsides and the ground becomes oversaturated with water. In some cases, unpaved roads become impassible. In the last three decades, the number of days that the Alaska Department of Natural Resources permits oil exploration activity in areas of tundra has been cut in half due to the increasingly soft ground.

As formerly frozen soils thaw, it will likely lead to an increase in the activity of microorganisms in the soil. This could in turn increase the rate of decomposition of organic matter long sequestered in the frozen ground. As this organic matter is decomposed by microorganisms, carbon dioxide or methane can be released, perhaps contributing to increasing greenhouse gas concentrations in the atmosphere.

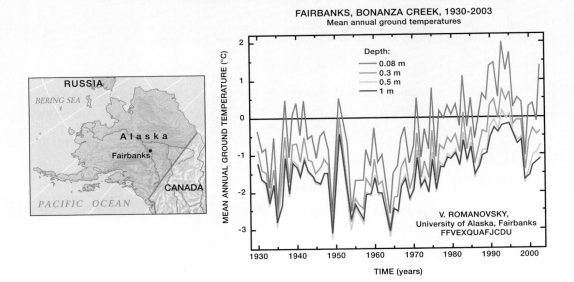

▲ **Figure 9-B** Mean annual ground temperatures at Bonanza Creek, Fairbanks, Alaska from 1930 to 2003. *(NOAA/Vladimir E. Romanovsky, University of Alaska, Fairbanks.)*

Despite the fact that some oceanic ice freezes directly from seawater, all forms of oceanic ice are composed entirely of fresh water because the salts present in the seawater in its liquid state are never taken up into the ice crystals when that water freezes.

The largest ice pack covers most of the surface of the Arctic Ocean (Figure 9-13); on the other side of the globe, an ice pack fringes most of the Antarctic continent (Figure 9-14). Both of these packs become greatly enlarged during their respective winters, their areas being essentially doubled by increased freezing around their margins.

There are a few small ice shelves in the Arctic, mostly around Greenland; but several gigantic shelves are attached to the Antarctic ice sheet, most notably the Ross ice shelf of some 100,000 square kilometers (40,000 square miles). Some Antarctic ice floes are enormous; the largest ever observed was 10 times as large as the state of Rhode Island.

Over the last decade, because of increasing temperatures, formerly stable ice shelves in Antarctica have broken apart. Since the early 1990s as much as 8000 square kilometers (over 3000 square miles) of Antarctic ice shelves have disintegrated. In 2002, the

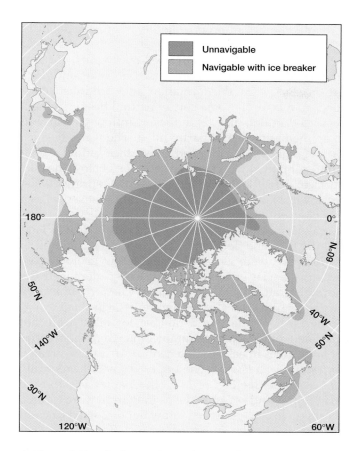

▲ **Figure 9-13** The largest ice pack on Earth covers most of the Arctic Ocean, making that body of water essentially unnavigable. Powerful icebreaker ships allow passage from the Atlantic to the Pacific via this northern route, the fabled "Northwest Passage" of early European explorers. In the last 30 years the Arctic ice pack has diminished by more than 10 percent from the extent shown here.

Larsen-B ice shelf on the Antarctic Peninsula disintegrated in less than a month, and the much larger Larsen-C shelf just to the south is showing signs that its mass is being reduced because of increasing water temperatures below it. (See Chapter 19 for further discussion of changes in glaciers and ice sheets around the world.)

Permafrost

A relatively small proportion of the world's ice occurs beneath the land surface as ground ice. This type of ice occurs only in areas where the temperature is continuously below the freezing point, and so it is restricted to high-latitude and high-elevation regions (Figure 9-15). Most permanent ground ice is **permafrost**, which is permanently frozen subsoil. It is widespread in northern Canada, Alaska, and Siberia and found in small patches in many high mountain areas. Some ground ice is aggregated as veins of frozen water, but most of it develops as ice crystals in the spaces between soil particles.

As a response to increasing temperatures, areas of permafrost in many parts of the world are showing signs of thawing. As the ground thaws, buildings, roads, pipelines, and airport runways are increasingly destabilized, and transportation and business are likely to be disrupted as a consequence.

Surface Waters

Surface waters represent only about 0.25 percent of the world's total moisture supply (Figure 9-1), but from the human viewpoint they are of incalculable value. Lakes, swamps, and marshes abound in many parts of the world, and all but the driest parts of the continents are seamed by rivers and streams.

Lakes

Lakes have been called "wide places in rivers." In even simpler terms, a **lake** is a body of water surrounded by land. No minimum or maximum size is attached to this definition, although the word *pond* is often used to designate a very small lake. Well over 90 percent of the

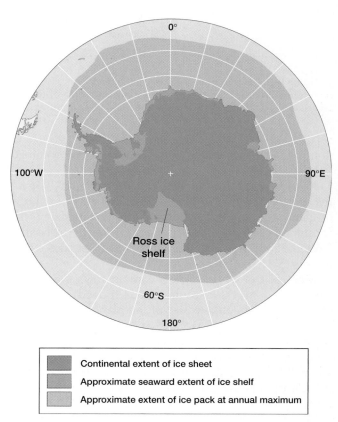

▲ **Figure 9-14** Maximum extent of ice in Antarctica today. The ice sheet covers land, and the ice shelf and ice pack are oceanic ice. As is true in the Arctic, over the last three decades the extent of sea ice around Antarctica has diminished from that shown here.

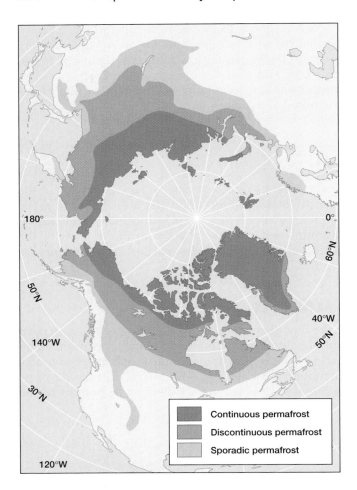

▲ **Figure 9-15** Extent of permafrost in the Northern Hemisphere. All the high-latitude land areas and some of the adjacent midlatitude land areas are underlain by permafrost.

(map legend)
Continuous permafrost
Discontinuous permafrost
Sporadic permafrost

nonfrozen surface water of the continents is contained in lakes.

Lake Baykal (often spelled Baikal) in Siberia is by far the world's largest freshwater lake in terms of volume of water, containing considerably more water than the combined contents of all five Great Lakes in the central United States. It is also the world's deepest lake—1742 meters (5715 feet) deep.

Most of the world's lakes contain fresh water, but some of the largest lakes are saline. Indeed, more than 40 percent of the lake water of the planet is salty, with the lake we call the Caspian Sea containing more than three quarters of the total volume of all the world's nonoceanic saline water. (In contrast, Utah's famous Great Salt Lake contains less than 1/2500 the volume of the Caspian.) Any lake that has no natural drainage outlet, either as a surface stream or as a sustained subsurface flow, will become saline.

Most small salt lakes and some large ones are *ephemeral*, which means that they contain water only sporadically and are dry much of the time because they are in dry regions with insufficient inflow to maintain them on a permanent basis. We will discuss ephemeral lakes in desert regions in greater detail in Chapter 18.

Most lakes are fed and drained by streams, but lake genesis is usually due to other factors. Two conditions are necessary for the formation and continued existence of a lake: (1) some sort of natural basin having a restricted outlet, and (2) sufficient inflow of water to keep the basin at least partly filled. The water balance of most lakes is maintained by surface inflow, sometimes combined with springs and seeps below the lake surface. A few lakes are fed entirely by springs. Most freshwater lakes have only one stream that serves as a drainage outlet.

Lakes are distributed very unevenly over the land (Figure 9-16 and Table 9-3). They are very common in regions that were glaciated in the recent geologic past because glacial erosion and deposition deranged the normal drainage patterns and created innumerable basins (Figure 9-17; also see Figure 19-28 in Chapter 19). Some parts of the world notable for lakes were not glaciated, however. For example, the remarkable series of large lakes in eastern and central Africa was created by faulting as Earth's crust spread apart tectonically (for example, see Figure 14-13 in Chapter 14); and the many thousands of small lakes in Florida were formed by sinkhole collapse when rainwater dissolved calcium carbonate from the limestone bedrock (for example, see Figure 17-A in Chapter 17).

Most lakes are relatively temporary features of the landscape. Few have been in existence for more than a few thousand years, a time interval that is momentary in the grand scale of geologic time. Inflowing streams bring sediment to fill lakes up; outflowing streams cut channels progressively deeper to drain them; and as the lake becomes shallower, a continuous increase in plant growth accelerates the infilling. Thus, the destiny of most lakes is to disappear naturally.

Human Alteration of Natural Lakes Human activity also plays a part in the disappearance of lakes. For example, the diversion of streams flowing into California's Mono Lake (to the east of Yosemite National Park) has reduced its volume by one-half since the 1940s. More dramatically, the diversion of rivers flowing into the Aral Sea (Figure 9-18)—the fourth largest lake in the world in 1960—has caused this lake to shrink to one-quarter of its original size over the last few decades.

Reservoirs One of the most notable things people have done to alter the natural landscape is to produce artificial lakes, or *reservoirs*. Such lakes have been created largely by the construction of dams, ranging from small earth mounds heaped across a gully to immense concrete structures blocking the world's major rivers (Figure 9-19, p. 278). Some reservoirs are as large as medium-sized natural lakes.

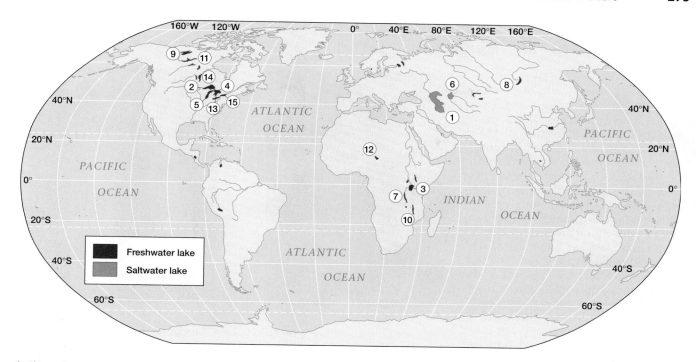

▲ **Figure 9-16**   Large lakes of the world: (1) Caspian Sea; (2) Lake Superior; (3) Lake Victoria; (4) Lake Huron; (5) Lake Michigan; (6) Aral Sea (now reduced in size from that shown here); (7) Lake Tanganyika; (8) Lake Baykal; (9) Great Bear Lake; (10) Lake Malawi; (11) Great Slave Lake; (12) Lake Chad (now reduced in size from that shown here); (13) Lake Erie; (14) Lake Winnipeg; (15) Lake Ontario.

Reservoirs are constructed for a number of different reasons, including controlling floods, ensuring a stable agricultural or municipal water supply, and for the generation of hydroelectric power—frequently for all of these reasons. The creation of artificial lakes has had immense ecological and economic consequences, not all of them foreseen at the time of construction. In addition to the obvious loss of the land that has been inundated by the waters of the reservoir, downstream ecosystems may be altered by restricted stream flows; and in some locations rapid sedimentation may restrict the useful life of a reservoir. In Chapter 16, we will consider the implications of flood control through the use of dams and river levees.

Swamps and Marshes

Closely related to lakes but less numerous and containing a much smaller volume of water are swamps and

TABLE 9-3 The World's Largest Lakes Ranked by Surface Area

Rank	Name	Continent	Area Square Miles	Area Square Kilometers	Water
1	Caspian Sea	Asia	143,250	372,450	Salt
2	Lake Superior	North America	31,700	82,420	Fresh
3	Lake Victoria	Africa	26,700	69,400	Fresh
4	Lake Huron	North America	23,000	59,800	Fresh
5	Lake Michigan	North America	22,300	58,000	Fresh
6	Lake Tanganyika	Africa	12,650	33,000	Fresh
7	Lake Baykal	Asia	12,200	31,700	Fresh
8	Great Bear Lake	North America	12,100	31,500	Fresh
9	Lake Malawi	Africa	11,550	30,000	Fresh
10	Great Slave Lake	North America	11,300	29,400	Fresh

FOCUS The Aral Sea and Lake Chad

Two of the largest lakes in the world—the Aral Sea on the Uzbekistan–Kazakhstan border and Lake Chad in central Africa—have been reduced to just a fraction of their former sizes over the last half century, but for largely different reasons.

The Aral Sea was once the world's fourth largest lake in terms of surface area, but beginning in the 1960s, irrigation projects designed to boost agricultural production in Soviet Central Asia cut off much of the water flowing into the lake. The sea is now only about 25 percent of its original size (Figure 9-C). The once viable commercial fishing industry is gone, and winds now carry away a cloud of choking clay and salt dust lifted from the exposed lake bottom. The sea has split into several pieces. Recent reengineering of the Syr Darya River delta should allow the northern remnant of the Aral Sea to remain near its present size, but the southern remnants are likely to disappear completely within a couple of decades.

Forty years ago, Lake Chad was one of the largest lakes in Africa, but

▲ **Figure 9-C** The Aral Sea in 1973 and in 2004. *(Images courtesy of the United Nations Environmental Programme,* One Plant, Many People *Atlas.)*

ongoing drought has reduced it to about 10 percent of its original size (Figure 9-D). Nearly all of the lake's water comes from the Chari River flowing into the lake from the south. The lake is shallow and surrounded by an extensive wetlands area—once the second largest in Africa. Because the lake is shallow, it responds quite quickly to changes in inflow. Although water diversion projects along the Chari River have contributed to the reduction of Lake Chad, climate change in the region is likely responsible for most of its ongoing decline.

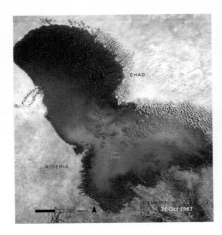
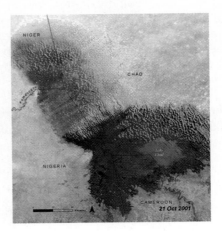

▲ **Figure 9-D** Lake Chad in 1963 and 2001. *(Images courtesy of the United Nations Environmental Programme,* One Plant, Many People *Atlas.)*

▲ **Figure 9-17** Glaciation is responsible for the formation of St. Mary Lake in Montana's Glacier National Park. *(Tom L. McKnight photo.)*

▲ **Figure 9-18** In 1960, the Aral Sea was the world's fourth largest lake. However, as irrigation needs have forced farmers to drain more and more water from the rivers feeding the Aral, its volume has decreased by more than two-thirds in the last 40 years. Where fish once swam, camels now wander over the floor of the "sea." If present trends continue, the Aral may cease to exist. *(Gerd Ludwig/National Geographic Society.)*

▲ **Figure 9-19** One of the largest reservoirs in the West is Lake Mead, behind Hoover Dam on the Nevada–Arizona border. *(Lowell Georgia/Photo Researchers, Inc.)*

marshes, flattish places that are submerged in water at least part of the time but are shallow enough to permit the growth of water-tolerant plants (Figure 9-20). The conceptual distinction between the terms is that a **swamp** has a plant growth that is dominantly trees, whereas a **marsh** is vegetated primarily with grasses and rushes. Both are usually associated with coastal plains, broad river valleys, or recently glaciated areas. Sometimes they represent an intermediate stage in the infilling of a lake.

Rivers and Streams

Although containing only a small proportion of the world's water at any given time, rivers and streams are an extremely dynamic component of the hydrologic cycle. (Although the terms are basically interchangeable,

in common usage a *stream* is smaller than a *river.* Geographers, however, call any flowing water a stream, no matter what its size.) Streams provide the means by which the land surface drains and by which water, sediment, and dissolved chemicals are moved ever seaward. The occurrence of rivers and streams is closely, but not absolutely, related to precipitation patterns. Humid lands have many rivers and streams, most of which flow year-round; dry lands have few, almost all of which are ephemeral (which means they dry up for part of the year).

Tables 9-4 and 9-5 list the world's longest and largest rivers, and Figure 9-21 on p. 280 shows the drainage basins feeding them. (A *drainage basin* is all the land area drained by a river and its tributaries.) A mere two dozen great rivers produce one-half of the total stream discharge of the world. The mighty Amazon yields nearly 20 percent of the world total, 4.5 times the discharge of the second-ranking river, the Congo (Zaire). Indeed, the discharge of the Amazon is three times as great as the total combined discharge of all rivers in the United States. The Mississippi is North America's largest river by far, with a drainage basin that encompasses about 40 percent of the total area of the 48 conterminous states and a flow that amounts to about one-third of the total discharge from all other rivers of the nation.

We will explore the ways in which streams shape the landscape of the continents in Chapter 16.

▲ **Figure 9-20** Marshes are particularly numerous along the poorly drained South Atlantic and Gulf of Mexico coasts of the United States. This is Loxahatchee Marsh in Florida. *(Mark E. Gibson/The Stock Market.)*

TABLE 9-4 The World's Longest Rivers

Rank	Name	Continent	Empties Into	Length Kilometers	Length Miles
1	Nile	Africa	Mediterranean Sea	6600	4130
2	Amazon	South America	Atlantic Ocean	6200	3900
3	Missouri-Mississippi	North America	Gulf of Mexico	6000	3740
4	Yangtze	Asia	East China Sea	5450	3400
5	Ob-Irtysh	Asia	Kara Sea	5450	3400
6	Hwang Ho	Asia	Yellow Sea	4650	2900
7	Amur	Asia	Tartar Strait	4500	2800
8	Congo (Zaire)	Africa	Atlantic Ocean	4300	2700
9	Lena	Asia	Laptev Sea	4300	2700
10	Mackenzie	North America	Beaufort Sea	4200	2635
11	Mekong	Asia	South China Sea	4150	2600
12	Niger	Africa	Gulf of Guinea	4150	2600
13	Yenisy	Asia	Kara Sea	4000	2500
14	Paraná	South America	Atlantic Ocean	3900	2450
15	Volga	Europe	Caspian Sea	3700	2300

TABLE 9-5 The World's Largest Rivers Ranked by Average Discharge and Drainage Area

Name	Continent	Average Discharge (cubic meters per second)	Rank by Discharge Volume	Drainage Area (Square kilometers)	Rank by Drainage Area
Amazon	South America	175,000	1	5,800,000	1
Congo (Zaire)	Africa	40,000	2	4,000,000	2
Yangtze	Asia	22,000	3	1,900,000	9
Brahmaputra	Asia	20,000	4	935,000	20
Ganges	Asia	19,000	5	1,060,000	18
Yenisy	Asia	17,000	6	2,600,000	5
Mississippi	North America	17,000	7	3,200,000	3
Orinoco	South America	17,000	8	880,000	24
Lena	Asia	15,500	9	2,510,000	6
Paraná	South America	15,000	10	2,200,000	8
St. Lawrence	North America	14,000	11	1,300,000	14
Irrawaddy	Asia	13,600	12	430,000	35
Ob	Asia	12,500	13	2,500,000	7
Mekong	Asia	11,000	14	800,000	26
Tocantins	South America	10,000	15	910,000	23

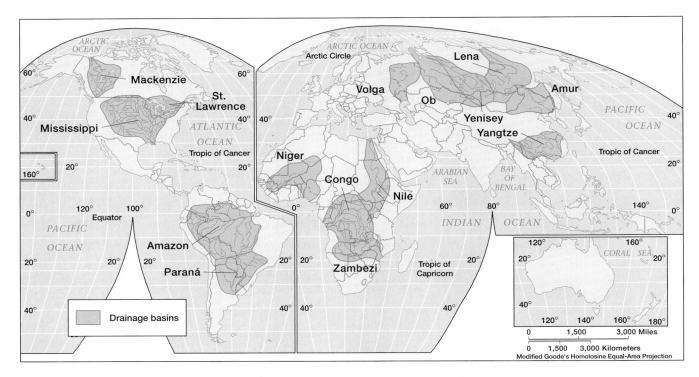

▲ **Figure 9-21**   The world's largest drainage basins are scattered over the four largest continents in all latitudes.

Underground Water

1. The Water Table
2. Groundwater Cone of Depression

Beneath the land surface is another important component of the hydrosphere—underground water. As Figure 9-1 shows, the total amount of underground water is about 2.5 times that contained in lakes and streams. Moreover, underground water is much more widely distributed than surface water. Whereas lakes and rivers are found only in restricted locations, underground water is almost ubiquitous, occurring beneath the land surface throughout the world. Its quantity is sometimes limited, its quality is sometimes poor, and its occurrence is sometimes at great depth, but almost anywhere on Earth one can dig deep enough and find water.

More than half of the world's underground water is found within 800 meters (about half a mile) of the surface. Below that depth, the amount of water generally decreases gradually and erratically. Although water has been found at depths below 10 kilometers (6 miles), it is almost immobilized because the pressure exerted by overlying rocks is so great and openings are so few and small.

Almost all underground water comes originally from above. Its source is precipitation that either percolates directly into the soil or else seeps downward eventually from lakes and streams.

Once the moisture gets underground, any one of several things can happen to it depending largely on the nature of the soil and rocks it infiltrates. The quantity of water that can be held in subsurface material (rock or soil) depends on the **porosity** of the material, which is the percentage of the total volume of the material that consists of voids (pore spaces or cracks) that can fill with water. The more porous a material is, the greater the amount of open space it contains and the more water it can hold.

Porosity is not the only factor affecting underground water flow. If water is to move through rock or soil, the pores must be connected to one another and be large enough for the water to move through them. The ability to transmit underground water (as opposed to just hold it, as in the definition of porosity) is termed **permeability**, and this property of subsurface matter is determined by the size of pores and by their degree of interconnectedness. The water moves by twisting and turning through these small, interconnected openings. The smaller and less connected the pore spaces, the less permeable the material and the slower the water moves.

The rate at which water moves through rock depends on both porosity and permeability. For example, clay is usually of high porosity because it has a great many **interstices** (openings) among the minute flakes that make up the clay, but it generally has low permeability because the interstices are so tiny that the force of molecular attraction binds the water to the clay flakes and holds it in place. Thus, clay is typically very porous but relatively impermeable and consequently can trap large amounts of water and keep it from draining.

Underground water is stored in, and moves slowly through, moderately to highly permeable rocks called **aquifers** (from the Latin, *aqua,* "water," and *ferre,* "to bear"). The rate of movement of the water varies with the situation. In some aquifers, the flow rate is only a few centimeters a day; in others, it may be several hundred meters per day. A "rapid" rate of flow would be 12 to 15 meters (40 to 50 feet) per day.

Impermeable materials composed of components such as clay or very dense rock, which hinder or prevent water movement, are called **aquicludes** (Figure 9-22).

The general distribution of underground water can probably best be understood by visualizing a vertical subsurface cross section. Usually at least three and often four *hydrologic zones* are arranged one below another. From top to bottom, these layers are called the *zone of aeration,* the *zone of saturation,* the *zone of confined water,* and the *waterless zone.*

Zone of Aeration

The topmost band, the **zone of aeration**, is a mixture of solids, water, and air. Its depth can be quite variable, from a few centimeters to hundreds of meters. The interstices in this zone are filled partly with water and partly with air. The amount of water fluctuates considerably with time. After a rain, the pore spaces may be saturated with water, but the water may drain away rapidly. Some of the water evaporates, but much is absorbed by plants, which later return it to the atmosphere by transpiration. Water that molecular attraction cannot hold seeps downward into the next zone.

Zone of Saturation

Immediately below the zone of aeration is the **zone of saturation**, in which all pore spaces in the soil and cracks in the rocks are fully saturated with water. The moisture in this zone is called **groundwater**; it seeps slowly through the ground following the pull of gravity and guided by rock structure. The top of the saturated zone is referred to as the **water table**. The orientation and slope of the water table usually conform roughly to the slope of the land surface above, nearly always approaching closer to the surface in valley bottoms and being more distant from it beneath a ridge or hill. Where the water table intersects Earth's surface, water flows out. A lake, swamp, marsh, or permanent stream is almost always an indication that the water table reaches the surface there. In humid regions, the water table is higher than in arid regions, which means that

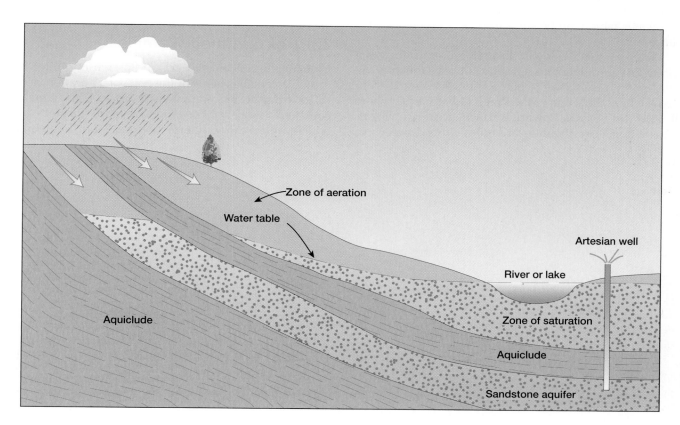

▲ **Figure 9-22**   An aquifer is a rock structure that is permeable and/or porous enough to hold water, whereas an aquiclude has a structure that is too dense to allow water to penetrate it.

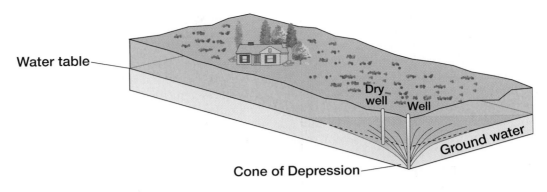

Water table

Dry well

Well

Ground water

Cone of Depression

▲ **Figure 9-23**   If water is withdrawn from a well faster than it can be replenished, a cone of depression will develop. This can effectively lower the water table over a large area. Nearby shallow wells may run dry because they lie above the lowered water table.

the zone of saturation is nearer the surface in humid regions. Some desert areas have no saturated zone at all.

Sometimes a localized zone of saturation develops above an aquiclude, and this configuration forms a *perched water table.*

A well dug into the zone of saturation fills with water up to the level of the water table. When water is taken from the well faster than it can flow in from the saturated rock, the water table drops in the immediate vicinity of the well in the approximate shape of an inverted cone. This striking feature is called a **cone of depression** (Figure 9-23). If many wells are withdrawing water faster than it is being replenished naturally, the water table may be significantly depressed over a large area.

Water percolates slowly through the saturated zone along tiny parallel paths. Gravity supplies much of the energy for groundwater percolation, leading it from areas where the water table is high toward areas where it is lower—that is, toward surface streams or lakes. Percolation flow channels are not always downward,

however. Often the flow follows a curving path and then turns upward (against the force of gravity) to enter the stream or lake from below. This trajectory is possible because saturated-zone water at any given height is under greater pressure beneath a hill than beneath a stream valley. Thus, the water moves toward points where the pressure is least.

The lower limit of the zone of saturation is marked by the absence of pore spaces and therefore the absence of water. This boundary may be a single layer of impermeable rock, or it may simply be that the increasing depth has created so much pressure that no pore spaces exist in any rocks at that level.

Zone of Confined Water

In many, but not most, parts of the world, a third hydrologic zone lies beneath the zone of saturation, separated from it by impermeable rock. This **zone of confined water** contains one or more aquifers into which water can infiltrate (Figure 9-24). Sometimes

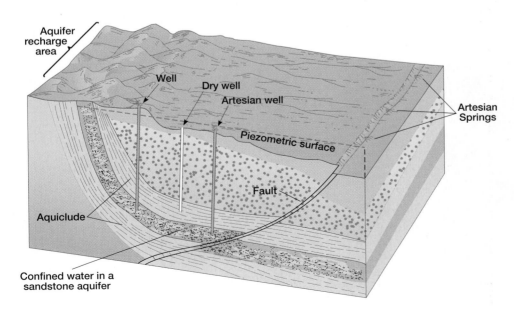

Aquifer recharge area

Well

Dry well

Artesian well

Piezometric surface

Artesian Springs

Fault

Aquiclude

Confined water in a sandstone aquifer

◀ **Figure 9-24**   An artesian system. Surface water penetrates the aquifer in the recharge area and infiltrates downward. It is confined to the aquifer by impermeable strata (aquicludes) above and below. If a well is dug through the upper aquiclude into the aquifer, the confining pressure forces the water to rise in the well. In an artesian well, the pressure forces the water to the surface; in a subartesian well, the water is forced only part way to the surface and must be pumped the rest of the way.

aquifers alternate with impermeable layers (aquicludes). Water cannot penetrate an aquifer in this deep zone by infiltration from above because of the impermeable barrier, and so any water the zone contains must have percolated along the aquifer from a more distant area where no aquiclude interfered. Characteristically, then, an aquifer in the confined water zone is a sloping or dipping layer that reaches to, or almost to, the surface at some location, where it can absorb infiltrating water. The water works its way down the sloping aquifer from the catchment area, building up considerable pressure in its confined situation.

If a well is drilled from the surface down into the confined aquifer, which may be at considerable depth, the confining pressure forces water to rise in the well. The elevation to which the water rises is known as the **piezometric surface**. In some cases, the pressure is enough to allow the water to rise above the ground, as shown in Figure 9-25. This free flow of water is called an **artesian well**. If the confining pressure is sufficient to push the water only partway to the surface and it must be pumped the rest of the way, the well is **subartesian**.

Unlike the distribution of groundwater, which is closely related to precipitation, the distribution of confined water is quite erratic over the world. Confined water underlies many arid or semiarid regions that are poor in surface water or groundwater, thus providing a critical resource for these dry lands.

Waterless Zone

At some depth below the surface, there is no water because the overlying pressure increases the density of the rock and so there are no pores. This **waterless zone** generally begins several kilometers beneath the land surface.

Groundwater Mining

In most parts of the world where groundwater occurs, it has been accumulating for a long time. Rainfall and snowmelt seep and percolate downward into aquifers, where the water may be stored for decades or centuries or millennia. Only in recent years have most of these aquifers been discovered and tapped by humans. They represent valuable sources of water that can supplement surface water resources. Underground water has been particularly utilized by farmers to irrigate in areas that contain insufficient surface water.

The accumulation of underground water is tediously slow. Its use by humans, however, can be distressingly rapid. In many parts of the U.S. Southwest, for example, the recharge (replenishment) rate averages only 0.5 centimeter (0.2 inch) per year, but it is not uncommon for a farmer to pump 75 centimeters (30 inches) per year. Thus, yearly pumpage is equivalent to 150 years' recharge. This rate of groundwater use can be likened to mining because a finite resource is being removed with no hope of replenishment. For this reason, the water in some aquifers is referred to as "fossil water." Almost everywhere in the world that underground water is being utilized on a large scale, the water table is dropping steadily and often precipitously.

The Ogallala Aquifer A classic example of groundwater mining is seen in the southern and central

▲ **Figure 9-25** An artesian well in Australia's Great Artesian Basin, the largest and most productive source of confined water in the world. This scene shows the Pilliga Bore in northwestern New South Wales. *(Tom L. McKnight photo.)*

PEOPLE AND THE ENVIRONMENT Subsidence from Groundwater Extraction

One of the consequences of prolonged groundwater extraction can be the compaction of sediments in an aquifer. If groundwater is extracted at a much greater rate than it is being recharged, not only will the water table drop, but the surface of land itself can subside. The list of regions where land subsidence due to groundwater pumping has been measured is long: California's San Joaquin Valley, the Houston-Galveston area of Texas and areas near Baton Rouge in Louisiana, among others.

Las Vegas, Nevada, is also experiencing substantial subsidence from groundwater extraction. Since the 1950s the land surface in the Las Vegas Valley has subsided by as much as 2 meters (about 6 feet). From 1992 to 1997 alone, some areas in the valley subsided 20 centimeters (8 inches) (Figure 9-E). As a result of the subsidence, fissures have developed on the surface and well casings have been damaged.

New technology permits the monitoring of ground subsidence from space using *Satellite Interferometric Synthetic Aperture Radar* (InSAR). Over a period of time, radar signals from a satellite are bounced off the ground from the same location overhead. By measuring the difference in distance over a period of months or years, ground subsidence or uplift can be measured with a resolution of 5 to 10 millimeters (1/4 to 1/2 inch). Maps showing the relative change in ground level are called *interferograms.*

Such InSAR interferograms have enabled scientists to not only monitor changes in ground level, but also to recognize new faults (breaks in a rock structure along which there has been movement). Faults may be revealed in interferograms because in some locations ground subsidence is at least partly controlled by the orientation of subsurface fault planes.

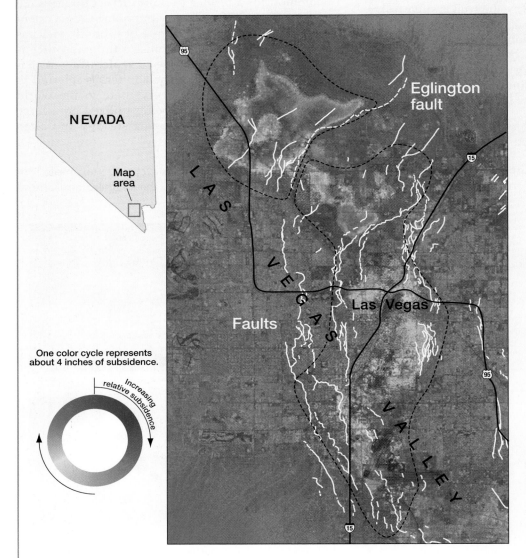

One color cycle represents about 4 inches of subsidence.

◀ **Figure 9-E**   InSAR-derived maps showing ground subsidence due to groundwater pumping in the Las Vegas Valley between April 1992 and December 1997. (*From USGS Fact Sheet 165-00,* Land Subsidence in the United States, *2000.*)

parts of the Great Plains, where the largest U.S. aquifer, the Ogallala or High Plains Aquifer, underlies 585,000 square kilometers (225,000 square miles) of eight states. The Ogallala formation consists of a series of limey and sandy layers that function as a gigantic underground reservoir ranging in thickness from a few centimeters in parts of Texas to more than 300 meters (1000 feet) under the Nebraska Sandhills (Figure 9-26). Water has been accumulating in this aquifer for some 30,000 years. At the midpoint of the twentieth century, it was estimated to contain 1.4 billion acre-feet (1.7 quadrillion liters or 456 trillion gallons) of water, an amount roughly equivalent to the volume of one of the larger Great Lakes.

Farmers began to tap the Ogallala in the early 1930s. Before the end of that decade, the water table was already dropping. After World War II, the development of high-capacity pumps, sophisticated sprinklers, and other technological innovations encouraged the rapid expansion of irrigation based on Ogallala water. Water use in the region has almost quintupled since 1950. The results of this accelerated usage have been spectacular. Above ground, there has been a rapid spread of high-yield farming into areas never before cultivated (especially in Nebraska) and a phenomenal increase in irrigated crops in all eight Ogallala states. Beneath the surface, however, the water table is sinking ever deeper. Farmers who once obtained water from 15-meter (50-foot) wells now must bore to 45 or 75 meters (150 or 250 feet), and as the price of energy skyrockets, the cost of pumping increases operating expenses enormously. Some 170,000 wells tap the Ogallala; many are already played out, and most of the rest must be deepened annually.

Anguish over this continuously deteriorating situation is widespread. Some farmers are shifting to crops that require less water. Others are adopting water- and energy-conserving measures that range from a simple decision to irrigate less frequently to the installation of sophisticated machinery that uses water in the most efficient fashion. Many farmers have faced or will soon face the prospect of abandoning irrigation entirely. During the next four decades, it is estimated that 2 million hectares (5 million acres) now irrigated will revert to dry-land production. Other farmers concentrate on high-value crops before it is too late, hoping to make a large profit and then get out of farming.

Water conservation is further complicated by the obvious fact that groundwater is no respecter of property boundaries. A farmer who is very conservative in his or her water use must face the reality that less careful neighbors are pumping from the same aquifer and that their profligacy may seriously diminish the water available to everyone.

The situation varies from place to place. The Nebraska Sandhills have the most favorable conditions. The aquifer is deepest there, previous water use was minimal, and there is a relatively rapid recharge rate. Indeed, for the 13-county area that makes up the bulk of the Sandhills, withdrawal averages only about 10 percent of recharge, a remarkable situation. In contrast, the 13 counties of southwestern Kansas have a withdrawal rate more than 20 times the recharge rate—a clearly unsustainable situation.

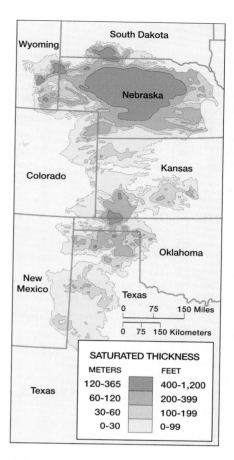

▲ **Figure 9-26** The Ogallala or High Plains Aquifer. Darker areas indicate greater thickness of the water-bearing strata.

Chapter 9 Learning Review

Key Terms

Before answering the study questions, review the definitions of the following key terms (page references are provided for you):

aquicludes *(p. 281)*

aquifers *(p. 281)*

artesian well *(p. 283)*

cone of depression *(p. 282)*

ebb tide *(p. 267)*

flood tide *(p. 267)*

global conveyer-belt circulation
  (p. 269)
groundwater (p. 281)
hydrologic cycle (p. 261)
iceberg (p. 271)
ice floe (p. 271)
ice pack (p. 271)
ice shelf (p. 271)
interstices (p. 280)
lake (p. 273)

marsh (p. 278)
neap tide (p. 268)
permafrost (p. 273)
permeability (p. 280)
piezometric surface (p. 283)
porosity (p. 280)
runoff (p. 263)
salinity (p. 266)
spring tide (p. 267)
subartesian (well) (p. 283)

swamp (p. 278)
thermohaline circulation (p. 269)
tidal bore (p. 268)
tidal range (p. 267)
tides (p. 267)
waterless zone (p. 283)
water table (p. 281)
zone of aeration (p. 281)
zone of confined water (p. 282)
zone of saturation (p. 281)

Study Questions for Key Concepts

After studying this chapter, you should be able to answer the following questions:

The Hydrologic Cycle (p. 261)
1. Where is most of the world's fresh water found?
2. Explain the role of evaporation in the *hydrologic cycle.*
3. What is the relationship between transpiration and evaporation?
4. Describe the roles of advection and runoff in the hydrologic cycle.
5. In what part of the hydrologic cycle is water most likely to stay for a very short time? A very long time? Why?

The Oceans (p. 263)
6. "How many oceans are there?" Why is this a difficult question to answer?
7. Is the Pacific Ocean significantly different from other oceans? Explain.
8. Why does salinity vary in different parts of the world ocean?

Movement of Ocean Waters (p. 267)
9. Why do most oceanic areas experience two high tides and two low tides each day?
10. Distinguish between *flood tide* and *ebb tide.*

11. Describe and explain *spring tides* and *neap tides.*
12. What is a *tidal bore?*
13. Explain the *global conveyor belt circulation.*

Permanent Ice—The Cryosphere (p. 271)
14. Why does all sea ice consist of freshwater?
15. Describe the characteristics and global distribution of *permafrost.*

Surface Waters (p. 273)
16. Why are lakes considered to be "temporary" features of the landscape?
17. Distinguish among a *lake,* a *swamp,* and a *marsh.*

Underground Water (p. 280)
18. Explain the characteristics of an *aquifer.*
19. Explain the concept of a *water table.*
20. Describe and explain the cause of a *cone of depression.*
21. Under what circumstances can a *zone of confined water* develop?
22. Distinguish between an *artesian well* and a *subartesian well.*
23. Why is the water from some aquifers referred to as *fossil water?*

Additional Resources

Books:

Leopold, L. B. *Water: A Primer.* San Francisco: W. H. Freeman, 1974.

Leslie, Jacques. *Deep Water: The Epic Struggle over Dams, Displaced People, and the Environment.* New York: Farrar, Straus and Giroux, 2005.

Opie, John. *Ogallala: Water for a Dry Land,* 2nd ed. Lincoln: University of Nebraska Press, 2000.

Internet Sites:

National Undersea Research Program

http://www.noaa.gov/ocean.html

This site has information about current ocean conditions and current marine research.

NOAA Arctic Theme Page

http://www.arctic.noaa.gov/

NOAA provides current information and data about the Arctic region of Earth.

Water Resources of the United States

http://water.usgs.gov/

This site has links to data and information about water quality, acid rain, and stream flow.

10
Cycles and Patterns in the Biosphere

Of the four principal components of our earthly environment, the biosphere has the boundaries that are hardest to pin down. The atmosphere consists of the envelope of air that surrounds the planet, the lithosphere is the solid portion, and the hydrosphere encompasses the various forms of water. These three spheres are distinct from one another and easy to visualize. The biosphere, on the other hand, impinges spatially on the other three. It consists of the incredibly numerous and diverse array of organisms—plants and animals—that populate our planet. Most of these organisms exist at the interface between atmosphere and lithosphere, but some live largely or entirely within the hydrosphere or the lithosphere, and others move relatively freely from one sphere to another.

The Impact of Plants and Animals on the Landscape

Originally, vegetation grew in profusion over most of the land surface of the planet. Today, native plants are still widespread in parts of the world sparsely populated by humans, as Figure 10-1a shows. However, much of the vegetation in populated areas has been removed, and much that persists has been adulterated and modified by human introduction of crops, weeds, and ornamental plants (Figure 10-1b). Native animal life is much less apparent in the landscape than plant life and is often more conspicuous by sound (especially birds and insects) than by sight. Still we should keep in mind that wildlife usually is shy and reclusive, and its absence may be more apparent than real. Moreover, most species of animals are tiny and therefore less noticeable in our normal scale of vision.

Both plants and animals interact with other components of the natural landscape (such as soil, landforms, and water) and sometimes become important influences in the development and evolution of these components.

The Geographic Approach to the Study of Organisms

Even the simplest living organism is an extraordinarily complex entity. When a student sets out to learn about

an organism—be it alga or anteater, tulip or turtle—she or he embarks on a complicated quest for knowledge. An organism differs in many ways from other aspects of the environment, but most significantly in that it is alive and its survival depends on an enormously intricate set of life processes.

To learn about even a single organism is a truly Herculean task. It is much easier to understand a cloud than a chrysanthemum, simpler to comprehend a moraine than a moose, less difficult to perceive a tornado than a tarantula. If our goal as geographers were a complete understanding of the world's organisms, we would need at least the life span of a Methuselah. As beneficial as such knowledge would be, however, a student of geography can be a bit less ambitious. With organisms, as with every other feature of the world, the geographer must focus on certain aspects rather than on a complete comprehension of the whole.

The geographic viewpoint is that of broad understanding, whether we are dealing with plants and animals or with anything else. This does not mean that we ignore the individual organism; rather it means that we seek generalizations and patterns and assess their overall significance. Here, as elsewhere, the geographer is interested in distributions and relationships. A major part of geography's distinctiveness is that it is an integrative discipline that studies phenomena from a broad-scale viewpoint. **Biogeography**, then, is the study of the distribution patterns of plants and animals, and how these patterns change over time.

The Search for a Meaningful Classification Scheme

When a geographer studies any set of phenomena, he or she attempts to group individual members of the set in some meaningful fashion. In some cases, the geographer borrows classification schemes from specialists in other disciplines. Often, however, schemes devised for other purposes are not particularly useful for geographic studies, and the geographer must develop different ones.

The systematic study of plants and animals is primarily the domain of the biologist, and many biological classification schemes have been devised. By far the most significant and widely used is the *binomial* (two-name) system originally developed by the Swedish botanist Carolus Linnaeus in the eighteenth century. This system focuses primarily on the morphology (structure and form) of organisms and groups them on the basis of structural similarity (see Appendix VI). The Linnaean scheme is generally useful for geographers, but it has certain shortcomings that preclude its total acceptance. Its principal disadvantage for geographic use is that it is based entirely on anatomic similarities,

▲ **Figure 10-1** (a) Many parts of Earth are still covered with native vegetation, with little or no human impact in evidence. This forested scene is near Marlinton, West Virginia. *(Tom L. McKnight photo)* (b) A small natural pothole of wetland remains, but most of the natural vegetation in this scene has been displaced by crops. This is wheat country in the Canadian province of Alberta. *(Bates Littlehales/Animals Animals/Earth Scenes.)*

whereas geographers are more interested in distribution patterns and habitat preferences.

It would be nice to be able to say that geographers have come up with a more appropriate classification scheme, but such is not the case, nor is a universally accepted geographic classification of organisms ever likely to be developed. Too many subjective decisions would have to be made, making widespread agreement on any scheme very unlikely.

Seeking Pertinent Patterns

Among the life forms of our planet are perhaps 600,000 species of plants and more than twice that many species of animals. With such an overwhelming diversity of organisms, how can we study their distributions and relationships in any meaningful manner? A logical approach is to decide on some generalizing procedures and useful groupings and then consider the patterns that emerge.

The term **biota** refers to the total complex of plant and animal life. The basic subdivision of biota separates **flora**, or plants, from **fauna**, or animals. In this book, we recognize a further fundamental distinction—between oceanic biota and terrestrial (living on land; *terrenus* is Latin for "earth") biota.

The inhabitants of the oceans are generally divided into three groups—*plankton* (floating plants and animals), *nekton* (animals such as fish and marine mammals that swim freely), and *benthos* (animals and plants that live on or in the ocean bottom). Although these marine life forms are fascinating, and despite the fact that 70 percent of Earth's surface is oceanic, in this book we pay scant attention to oceanic biota primarily because of constraints of time and space. The terrestrial biota will be our primary focus of interest for most of our study of the biosphere.

We begin our study of biogeography with a look at the broadest patterns and cycles in the biosphere—biogeochemical cycles.

Biogeochemical Cycles

The web of life comprises a great variety of organisms coexisting in a diversity of associations. Processes and interactions within the biosphere are exceedingly intricate. Organisms survive only through a bewildering complex of systemic flows of energy, water, and nutrients. These flows are different in different parts of the world, in different seasons of the year, and under various local circumstances (Figure 10-2).

It is generally believed that, for the last billion years or so, Earth's atmosphere and hydrosphere have been composed of approximately the same balance of chemical components we live with today. This constancy implies a planetwide condition in which the various chemical elements have been maintained by cyclic passage through the tissues of plants and animals—first absorbed by an organism and then returned to the air/water/soil through decomposition. These grand cycles—collectively called *biogeochemical cycles*—which sustain all life on our planet, have continued for millennia, at rates and scales almost too vast to conceptualize. In recent years, however, the rapid growth of the human population and the accompanying ever-accelerating rate at which we consume Earth resources have had a deleterious effect on every one of these cycles. Not all of the damage is yet irreparable, but the threat that such disruption will produce irreversible harm to the biosphere is increasing.

Although we describe biogeochemical cycles separately in the subsections below, you will see that many of these cycles are closely interrelated. It is appropriate, then, for us to begin with the most fundamental of these cycles—the flow of energy through the biosphere.

▲ **Figure 10-2** Organisms survive in the biosphere through a complex of systemic flows of energy, water, and nutrients. These wildflowers are in Mount Rainier National Park, Washington. *(© Craig Tuttle/CORBIS.)*

The Flow of Energy

1. Net Primary Productivity
2. Biological Productivity in Midlatitude Oceans

The Sun is the basic energy source on which nearly all life ultimately depends (forms of life utilizing geochemical energy from hydrothermal vents on the ocean floor are a well-known exception). Solar energy can ignite life processes in the biosphere through *photosynthesis*, the production of organic matter by chlorophyll-containing plants and bacteria.

Only about 0.1 percent of the solar energy that reaches Earth is fixed in photosynthesis. More than half of that total is used immediately in the plant's own *respiration*, and the remainder is temporarily stored. Eventually this remainder enters a *food chain*. An increasing proportion of this energy, however, is being diverted to the direct support of one species—*Homo sapiens*.

If the biosphere is to function properly, its components must be recycled continually. In other words, after one organism uses a component, that component must be converted, at the expense of some energy, to a reusable form. For some components, this conversion can be accomplished in less than a decade; for others, it may require hundreds of millions of years.

Solar energy is of course fundamental to life on Earth. Although readily absorbed by some substances, this energy is also readily reradiated. Thus, it is difficult to store and easy to lose. Happily, most places on Earth receive a daily renewal of the supply.

Photosynthesis and Respiration   The biosphere is a temporary recipient of a small fraction of the solar energy that reaches Earth, which is "fixed" (made stable) by green plants through the process of **photosynthesis** (Figure 10-3). The key to photosynthesis is a light-sensitive pigment known as *chlorophyll* that is found within the *chloroplasts* of leaf cells. Chlorophyll absorbs certain wavelengths of visible light, while prominently reflecting green light (this is why leaves look green).

In the presence of sunlight and chlorophyll a photochemical reaction takes carbon dioxide from the air and combines it with water to form the energy-rich *carbohydrate* compounds we know as sugars and releases molecular oxygen. In this process, the energy from sunlight is stored as chemical energy in the sugars. In simplified form, the chemical equation for photosynthesis is

$$CO_2 + H_2O \xrightarrow{\text{light}} \text{carbohydrates} + O_2$$

In turn, plants can use simple sugars to build more complex carbohydrates, such as starches.

The stored chemical energy in the form of carbohydrates is utilized in the biosphere primarily in two ways: some of the stored energy cycles through the biosphere when animals eat either the photosynthesizing plants or other animals that have eaten plants. The other portion of the stored energy in carbohydrates is consumed directly by the plant itself in a process known as **plant respiration**. In the process of respiration, the stored energy in carbohydrates is *oxidized*, releasing water, carbon dioxide, and heat energy. The simplified chemical equation for plant respiration is

$$\text{Carbohydrates} + O_2 \rightarrow CO_2 + H_2O + \text{energy (heat)}$$

Net Primary Productivity   Plant growth depends on a surplus of carbohydrate production. *Net photosynthesis* is the difference between the amount of carbohydrate produced in photosynthesis and that lost in plant respiration. **Net primary productivity** describes the net photosynthesis of a plant community over a period of one year, usually measured in the amount of fixed carbon per unit area (kilograms of carbon per square meter per year). Net primary productivity is, in effect, a measure of the amount of chemical energy stored in a plant community and is reflected in the dry weight of organic material, or **biomass**, of that community.

Net primary productivity varies widely from environment to environment around the world. It tends to be highest on land within the tropics where both high

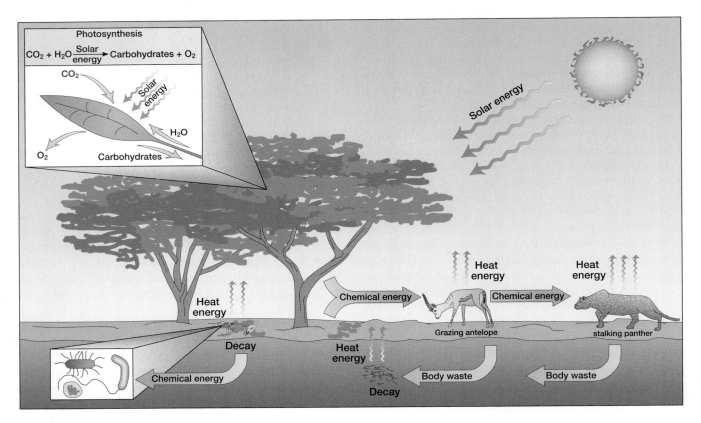

▲ **Figure 10-3**   Energy flow in the terrestrial biosphere. Plants use solar energy in photosynthesis, storing that energy in the sugar molecules they manufacture. Grazing and browsing animals then acquire that energy when they eat the plants. Other animals eat the grazers/browsers and thereby acquire some of the energy originally in the plants. Body wastes from all the animals, the bodies of the animals once they die, and dead plant matter that has fallen to the ground all return energy to the soil. As all this waste and dead matter decays, it gives off energy in the form of heat. Thus, the energy originally produced in nuclear reactions in the Sun ends up as random heat energy in the universe.

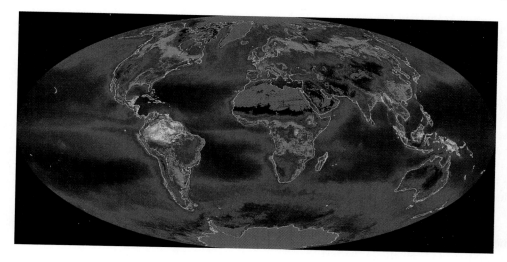

◄ **Figure 10-4** Annual net primary productivity. This composite satellite image shows net primary productivity ($kg/m^2/year$) based on the rate at which plants absorb carbon dioxide out of the air. The areas of highest annual average productivity are shown in yellow and red; areas of progressively lower productivity are shown in green, blue, and purple. *(NASA.)*

precipitation and high insolation are available for plant growth but generally diminishes poleward, especially in extremely arid and extremely cold environments (Figure 10-4). In the oceans, productivity is strongly influenced by the nutrient content of the water. For example, off the west coasts of continents in the midlatitudes, the upwelling of cold, nutrient-rich water results in high net primary productivity (Figure 10-5).

The carbohydrates incorporated into plant tissue are in turn consumed by animals or decomposed by microorganisms. Plant-eating animals convert some of the

consumed carbohydrates back to carbon dioxide and exhale it into the air (animal respiration); the remainder is decomposed by microorganisms after the animal dies. The carbohydrates acted upon by microorganisms are ultimately oxidized into carbon dioxide and returned to the atmosphere (soil respiration).

The Hydrologic Cycle

The most abundant single substance in the biosphere, by far, is water. It is the medium of life processes and the source of their hydrogen. Most organisms contain considerably more water in their mass than anything else, as Table 10-1 shows. Every living thing depends on keeping its water supply within a narrow range. For example, humans can survive without food for 2 months or more, but they can live without water for only about a week.

All living things require water to carry out their life processes. Watery solutions dissolve nutrients and carry them to all parts of an organism. Through chemical reactions that take place in a watery solution, the organism converts nutrients to energy or to materials it needs to grow or to repair itself. In addition, the organism needs water to carry away waste products.

There are two ways in which water is found in the biosphere: (1) *in residence,* with its hydrogen chemically bound into plant and animal tissues; and (2) *in transit,*

▲ **Figure 10-5** Net primary productivity around the North Atlantic Ocean basin is reflected in the density of chlorophyll. Red and dark green indicate the highest density of chlorophyll in this image from NASA's Nimbus-7 satellite; notice the high marine productivity in the region of coastal upwelling off northwest Africa. *(Photo Researchers, Inc.)*

TABLE 10-1 Water Content in Some Plants and Animals

Organism	Percentage Water In Body Mass
Human	65
Elephant	70
Earthworm	80
Ear of corn	70
Tomato	95

as part of the transpiration–respiration stream. As we learned in Chapter 9, the movement of water from one sphere to another is called the *hydrologic cycle* (see Figure 9-2).

The Carbon Cycle

Carbon is one of the basic elements of life and a part of all living things. The biosphere contains a complex mixture of carbon compounds, more than half a million in total. These compounds are in continuous states of creation, transformation, and decomposition.

The main components of the **carbon cycle** entail the transfer of carbon from carbon dioxide to living matter and then back again to carbon dioxide (Figure 10-6). This conversion is initiated when carbon dioxide from the atmosphere is photosynthesized into carbohydrate compounds (*assimilation*), as shown in the photosynthesis equation we learned earlier. In turn, respiration by plants and soil returns carbon to the atmosphere in the form of carbon dioxide. This is a true cycle or, more precisely, a complex of interlocking cycles; carbon moves constantly from the inorganic reservoir to the living system and back again. A similar cycle takes place in the ocean.

The carbon cycle operates relatively rapidly (the time measured in years or centuries), but only a small proportion (thought to be less than 1 percent) of the total quantity of carbon on or near Earth's surface is part of the cycle at any given moment. The overwhelming bulk of near-surface carbon has been concentrated over millions of years in geologic deposits—such as coal, petroleum, and carbonate rocks—composed of dead organic matter that accumulated mostly on sea bottoms and was subsequently buried. Carbon from this reservoir is normally incorporated into the cycle very gradually, mostly by normal rock weathering. In the last century and a half, however, humans have added considerable carbon dioxide to the atmosphere by extracting and burning fossil fuels (coal, oil, natural gas) containing carbon fixed by photosynthesis many millions of years ago. This rapid acceleration of the rate at which carbon is freed and converted to carbon dioxide is likely to have far-reaching effects on both the biosphere and atmosphere. For example, global warming from increasing concentrations of carbon dioxide in the atmosphere may lead to changes in the natural distribution patterns of both plants and animals.

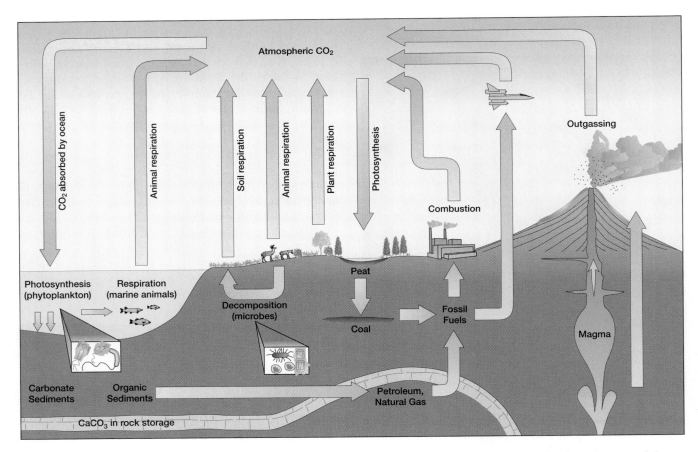

▲ **Figure 10-6** The carbon cycle. Carbon from the carbon dioxide in the atmosphere is used by plants to make the carbon-containing sugars formed during photosynthesis. Through various paths, these compounds are eventually again converted to carbon dioxide and returned to the atmosphere.

The Oxygen Cycle

Oxygen is a building block in most organic molecules and consequently makes up a significant proportion of the atoms in living matter.

Although our atmosphere is now rich in oxygen, it was not always so. Earth's earliest atmosphere was oxygen poor; indeed, in the early days of life on this planet, about 3.4 billion years ago, oxygen was poisonous to living cells. Evolving life had to develop mechanisms to neutralize or, better still, exploit its poisonous presence. This exploitation was so successful that most life now cannot function without oxygen.

The oxygen now in the atmosphere is largely a by-product of plant life, as the equation for photosynthesis shows. Thus, once life could sustain itself in the presence of high amounts of oxygen in the air, primitive plants made possible the evolution of higher plants and animals by providing molecular oxygen for their metabolism.

The **oxygen cycle** (Figure 10-7) is extremely complicated and is summarized only briefly here. Oxygen occurs in many chemical forms and is released into the atmosphere in a variety of ways. Most of the oxygen in the atmosphere is molecular oxygen (O_2) produced when plants decompose water molecules in photosynthesis. Some atmospheric oxygen is bound up in water molecules that came from evaporation or plant transpiration, and some is bound up in the carbon dioxide released during animal respiration. Much of this carbon dioxide and water is eventually recycled through the biosphere via photosynthesis.

Other sources of oxygen for the oxygen cycle include atmospheric ozone, oxygen involved in the oxidative weathering of rocks, oxygen stored in and sometimes released from carbonate rocks, and various other processes, including some (such as the burning of fossil fuels) that are human induced.

The Nitrogen Cycle

Although nitrogen gas is an apparently inexhaustible component of the atmosphere (air is about 78 percent N_2), only certain species of soil bacteria and blue-green algae can use this essential nutrient in its gaseous form.

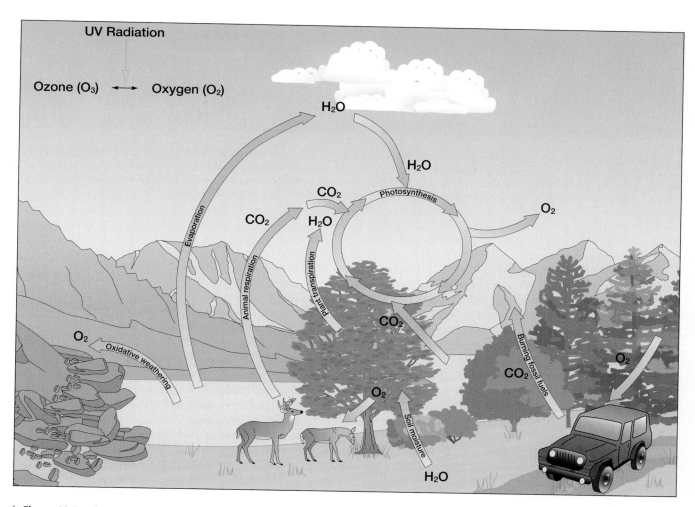

▲ **Figure 10-7**   The oxygen cycle. Molecular oxygen is essential for almost all forms of life. It is made available to the air through a variety of processes and is recycled in a variety of ways.

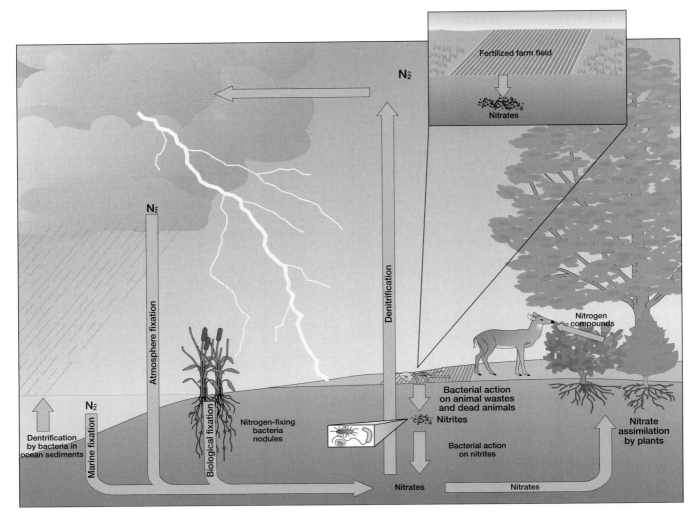

▲ **Figure 10-8** The nitrogen cycle. Atmospheric nitrogen is fixed into nitrates in various ways, and the nitrates are then assimilated by green plants, some of which are eaten by animals. Dead plant and animal materials, as well as animal wastes, contain various nitrogen compounds, and these compounds are acted on by bacteria so that nitrites are produced. The nitrites are then converted by other bacteria to nitrates, and thus the cycle continues. Still other bacteria denitrify some of the nitrates, releasing free nitrogen into the air again.

For the vast majority of living organisms, atmospheric nitrogen is usable only after it has been converted to nitrogen compounds (*nitrates*) that can be used by plants (Figure 10-8). This conversion process is called **nitrogen fixation**, and the overall process is called the **nitrogen cycle**. Some nitrogen is fixed in the atmosphere by lightning and cosmic radiation, and some is fixed in the ocean by marine organisms, but the amount involved in these processes is minimal. It is nitrogen fixation by soil microorganisms and associated plant root nodules that provides most of the usable nitrogen for Earth's biosphere.

Once atmospheric nitrogen has been fixed into an available form (nitrates), it is assimilated by green plants, some of which are eaten by animals. The animals then excrete nitrogenous wastes in their urine. These wastes, as well as the dead animal and plant material, are attacked by bacteria, and *nitrite* compounds

are released as a further waste product. Other bacteria convert the nitrites to nitrates, making them available again to green plants. Still other bacteria convert some of the nitrates to nitrogen gas in a process called **denitrification**, and the gas becomes part of the atmosphere. This atmospheric nitrogen is then carried by rain back to Earth, where it enters the soil–plant portion of the cycle once more.

Human activities have produced a major modification in the natural nitrogen cycle. The synthetic manufacture of nitrogenous fertilizers and widespread introduction of nitrogen-fixing crops (such as alfalfa, clover, and soybeans) have significantly changed the balance between fixation and denitrification. The short-term result has been an excessive accumulation of nitrogen compounds in many lakes and streams. This buildup of nitrogen depletes the oxygen supply of the water and upsets the natural balance.

Other Mineral Cycles

Although carbon, oxygen, and nitrogen—along with hydrogen—are the principal chemical components of the biosphere, many other minerals are critical nutrients for plants and animals. Most notable among these trace minerals are phosphorus, sulfur, and calcium, but more than a dozen others are occasionally significant.

Some nutrients are cycled along gaseous pathways, which primarily involve an interchange between biota and the atmosphere–ocean environment, as we just saw in the carbon, oxygen, and nitrogen cycles. Other nutrients follow sedimentary pathways, which involve interchange between biota and the Earth–ocean environment. Elements with sedimentary cycles include calcium, phosphorus, sulfur, copper, and zinc.

In a typical sedimentary cycle, the element is weathered from bedrock into the soil. Some of it is then washed downslope with surface runoff or percolated into the groundwater supply. Much of it reaches the ocean, where it may be deposited in the next round of sedimentary rock formation. Some, however, is ingested by aquatic organisms and later released into the cycle again through waste products and dead organisms.

In general, the amounts of biotic nutrients available on Earth are finite. These nutrients move over and over through cycles that are extremely variable from place to place; increasingly, some of these cycles have either been damaged or modified by human interference.

Food Chains

The unending flows of energy, water, and nutrients through the biosphere are channeled in significant part by direct passage from one organism to another in pathways referred to as *food chains*. A **food chain** is a simple concept, as Figure 10-9 shows: Organism A is eaten by Organism B, which thereby absorbs A's energy and nutrients; Organism B is eaten by Organism C, with similar results; Organism C is eaten by D; and so on.

In nature, however, the matter of who eats whom may be extraordinarily complex, with a bewildering number of interlaced strands. Therefore, "chain" probably is a misleading word in this context because it implies an orderly linkage of equivalent units. It is more accurate to think of this energy transfer process as a "web" with interconnected parts or links. Each link acts as an energy transformer that ingests some of the energy of the preceding link, uses some of that energy for its own sustenance, and then passes some of the balance on to the next link.

The fundamental units in any food chain are the **producers**—the *autotrophs*, or "self-feeders"—in other words, plants. Plants fix carbon and effectively store solar energy through photosynthesis. The plants may then be eaten by the *consumers*, or *heterotrophs*. Plant-eating animals are called *herbivores* (*herba* is Latin for "plant"; *vorare*, "to devour"), which are referred to as **primary consumers**. The herbivores then become food for other animals, *carnivores* (*carne*, is Latin for "meat"), which are referred to as **secondary consumers** or *predators*. There may be many levels of secondary consumers in a food chain, as Figure 10-9 shows.

A food chain can also be conceptualized as a **food pyramid** because the number of energy-storing organisms is much, much larger than the number of primary consumers; the number of primary consumers is larger than the number of secondary consumers; and so on up the pyramid (Figure 10-10). There are usually several

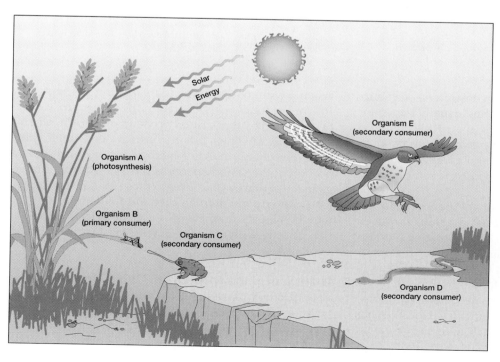

▲ **Figure 10-9** A simple food chain.

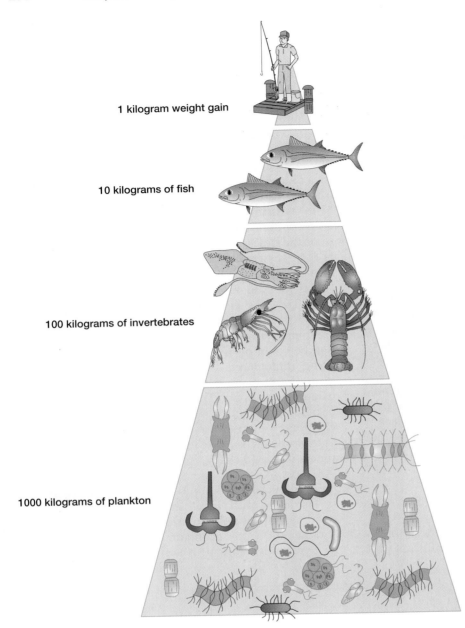

1 kilogram weight gain

10 kilograms of fish

100 kilograms of invertebrates

1000 kilograms of plankton

◀ **Figure 10-10**   A food pyramid. It takes 1000 kilograms (about 1 ton) of plankton (microscopic marine plants and animals) to provide a 1-kilogram (2-pound) weight gain for a human. *(Adapted from* Life Nature Library/Ecology, *drawing by Otto van Eersel, New York: Time-Life Books, 1963, p. 37.)*

levels of carnivorous secondary consumers, each succeeding level consisting of fewer and usually larger animals. The final consumers at the top of the pyramid are usually the largest and most powerful predators in the area (Figure 10-11). We say that organisms share the same *trophic level* when they consume the same general types of food in a food pyramid.

The consumers at the apex of the pyramid do not constitute the final link in the food chain, however. When they die, they are fed on by scavenging animals and by tiny (mostly microscopic) organisms that function as **decomposers**, returning the nutrients to the soil to be recycled into yet another food pyramid.

So why are so many producers needed to support so few top predators in a food pyramid? The answer has to do with the relative inefficiency with which stored energy is transferred from one trophic level to the next.

When a primary consumer eats a plant, perhaps only 10% of the total energy stored in the plant can be effectively stored by that primary consumer. In turn, when a secondary consumer eats the primary consumer, there is further energy transfer inefficiency. In short, only a portion of the stored energy is transferred from the organisms of one trophic level to those in the next trophic level. (In terms of human diet and food supply, this is why it is much more energy efficient to feed a population directly with grains than with meat from grain-fed animals.)

Pollutants in the Food Chain   While stored energy is not efficiently passed on from one organism to the next in a food chain, some chemical pollutants can be. An increasing concern is evidence that some chemical pollutants can become concentrated within a food

▲ **Figure 10-11**   A lynx pouncing on a snowshoe hare in a Montana forest. *(Alan Carey/Photo Researchers, Inc.)*

chain—a process referred to as *biological amplification.* For example, while some chemical pesticides released into the air, water, or soil degrade relatively quickly into harmless substances, others, such as DDT, are quite stable and may become concentrated in the fatty tissues of organisms at higher levels of a food chain. The concentration of chemical pesticides, as well as the concentration of some heavy metals such as mercury and lead, have resulted in harmful effects and even death in the animal (and human) consumers at the top of the food chain.

Natural Distributions

The most basic studies of organisms made by geographers are usually concerned with distribution. Here we are concerned with such questions as, "What is the range of a certain species or group of plants/animals?" "What are the reasons behind this distribution pattern?" and "What is the significance of the distribution?"

Here we begin our discussion of factors influencing distribution patterns in the biosphere at the most fundamental level. The natural distribution of any species or group of organisms is determined by four conditions: evolutionary development, migration/dispersal, reproductive success, and extinction.

Evolutionary Development

The Darwinian theory of natural selection, sometimes referred to as "survival of the fittest," explains the origin of any species as a normal process of descent, with modification, from parent forms. The progeny best adapted to the struggle for existence survive to produce viable offspring, whereas those less well adapted perish. This long, slow, and essentially endless process accounts for the development of all organisms.

To understand the distribution of any species or *genus* (a closely related group of organisms), therefore, we begin with a consideration of where it evolved. In some cases, there was a very localized beginning for a genus; in other cases, similar evolutionary development at several scattered localities led to the same genus. Unfortunately, the evidence on which case applies in a given situation is not always clear. As an example of these two extremes, consider the contrast in apparent origin of two important groups of plants—*acacias* and *eucalypts* (Figures 10-12 and 10-13). Acacias are an extensive genus of shrubs and low-growing trees represented by numerous species found in low-latitude portions of every continent that extends into the tropics or subtropics. Eucalypts, on the other hand, are a genus of trees native only to Australia and a few adjacent islands. Acacias apparently evolved prior to the separation of the continents and are now present throughout the southern hemisphere, while the genus Eucalyptus evolved after the Australian continent was isolated and only occurs naturally in Australia. (We will discuss the changing locations of the continents over geologic time when we introduce the theory of plate tectonics in Chapter 14.)

Migration/Dispersal

Throughout the millennia of Earth's history, organisms have always moved from one place to another. Animals

▲ **Figure 10-12**   Hundreds of species of acacias grow in semiarid and subhumid portions of the tropics. This scene from central Kenya shows acacias in tree form, although lower shrub forms are more common. *(Tom L. McKnight photo.)*

possess active mechanisms for locomotion—legs, wings, fins, and so on—and their possibilities for migration are obvious. Plants are also mobile, however. Although most individual plants become rooted and therefore fixed in location for most of their life, there is much opportunity for passive migration, particularly in the seed stage. Wind, water, and animals are the principal natural mechanisms of seed dispersal.

The contemporary distribution pattern of many organisms is often the result of natural migration or dispersal from an original center(s) of development. Among thousands of examples that could be used to illustrate this process are the following:

1. **Coconut Palms:** The coconut palm (*Cocos nucifera*) is believed to have originated in southeastern Asia and adjacent Melanesian islands. It is now extraordinarily widespread along the coasts of tropical continents and islands all over the world. Most of this dispersal apparently has come about because

▲ **Figure 10-13**   The original forests of Australia were composed almost entirely of species of eucalyptus. This scene is in eastern New South Wales, near Eden. *(Tom L. McKnight photo.)*

PEOPLE AND THE ENVIRONMENT Changing Climate Affects Bird Populations

Over the last decade, scientists have documented changes in a number of animal populations that appear to be tied to global warming. Bird populations can be especially sensitive indicators of climate change because many species of birds have specific environmental requirements for feeding, nesting, and migration. Further, since birds are generally quite mobile, a bird population may respond fairly quickly to local environmental changes.

Data suggests that higher global temperatures are already having an effect on some bird populations. The National Audubon Society's annual Christmas Bird Count has gathered information about bird populations for many years. Data from the Christmas Bird Count shows that in warmer years, most bird species do not fly as far south for the winter as they do in cooler years; in warmer years, birds may also spend their summers farther north.

A changing climate may also be affecting the timing of bird migrations. Research has shown that several species of birds that migrate north into Michigan are arriving two or three weeks earlier in the spring than they did 45 years ago. Birds in some locations are nesting earlier because plants are blooming sooner—which results in an earlier proliferation of insects on which the birds feed. The British Trust for Ornithology reports that 20 out of 65 species of birds they studied are laying eggs nine days sooner today than they did just 35 years ago.

Although some bird species may be able to adjust to a warming climate by altering their migration patterns—shifting their ranges north in the

▲ **Figure 10-A** Adult male bobolink, *Dolichonyx oryzivorus.* (© B. Henry/VIREO.)

Northern Hemisphere, for example—this may not actually occur in some cases. New evidence suggests that habitats may respond to climate change in different ways. Forest communities in North America may not simply shift north of their present locations in response to a warmer climate. Instead, individual plant and animal species within that forest community may respond differently to climate change, perhaps leaving both a dislocated and an altered habitat for birds and other creatures.

One of the earliest studies of the potential effects of global warming on bird populations in North America looked at the songbird the bobolink (Figure 10-A). Bobolinks have an extraordinarily long migration—a round trip of about 20,000 kilometers (12,400 miles). In summer, they nest in meadows and fields in southern Canada, New England, and south of the Great Lakes to Idaho. In the Northern Hemisphere winter they fly south to the grasslands of northern Argentina, Paraguay and southwestern Brazil. A study in the mid-1990s modeled the relationship between the distribution of boblinks and climate. The study concluded that with the projected climate and vegetation changes associated with a doubling of atmospheric CO_2, the bobolink might not be able to nest south of the Great Lakes, depriving this region of one of its most beloved songbirds.

coconuts, the large hard-shelled seeds of the plant, can float in the ocean for months or years without losing their fertility. Thus, they wash up on beaches throughout the world and colonize successfully if environmental conditions are right (Figure 10-14). This natural dispersion was significantly augmented by human help in the Atlantic region, particularly by the deliberate transport of coconuts from the Indian and Pacific Ocean areas to the West Indies.

2. **Cattle Egrets:** The cattle egret (*Bubulcus ibis*) apparently originated in southern Asia, but during the last few centuries has spread to other warm areas of the world, particularly Africa (Figure 10-15). In recent decades, a change in land use in South America has caused a dramatic expansion in the cattle egret's range. At least as early as the nineteenth century, some cattle egrets crossed the Atlantic from West Africa to Brazil, but they were unable to find suitable ecological conditions and

▲ **Figure 10-14** Coconuts have a worldwide distribution in tropical coastal areas, in part because the nut can float long distances and then take root if it finds a favorable environment. This sprouting example is from the island of Vanua Levu in Fiji. *(Tom L. McKnight photo.)*

thus did not become established. The twentieth-century introduction of extensive cattle raising in tropical South America apparently provided the missing ingredient, and egrets quickly adapted to the newly suitable habitat. Their descendants spread northward throughout the subtropics and are now common inhabitants of the Gulf coastal plain in the southeastern United States, are well established in California, and occur as far north as southeastern Canada. Also within the twentieth century, cattle egrets dispersed at the other end of their "normal" range to enter northern Australia and spread across that continent.

Reproductive Success

A key factor in the continued survival of any biotic population is reproductive success. Poor reproductive success can come about for a number of reasons—heavy predation (a fox eats quail eggs from a nest); climatic change (heavy-furred animals perishing in a climate that was once cold but has warmed up for some reason or other); failure of food supply (a string of unusually cold winters keeps plants from setting seed); and so on.

Changing environmental conditions are also likely to favor one group over another, as when warming

waters on the fringes of the Arctic Ocean allowed cods to expand their range at the expense of several other types of fishes. Thus, reproductive success is usually the limiting factor that allows one competing population to flourish while another languishes (Figure 10-16).

Extinction FG5

The range of a species can be diminished by the dying out of some or all of the population. The history of the biosphere is replete with examples of such range diminution, varying from minor adjustments in a small area to extinction over the entire planet. Evolution is a continuing process. No species is likely to be a permanent inhabitant of Earth, and during the period of its ascendancy there is apt to be a great deal of distributional variation within a species, part of which is caused by local die-offs.

Plant Succession One of the simplest and most localized examples of this process is **plant succession**, in which one type of vegetation is replaced naturally by another. Plant succession is a normal occurrence in a host of situations; a very common one involves the infilling of a lake (Figure 10-17). As the lake gradually fills with sediments and organic debris, the aquatic plants at the bottom are slowly choked out while the sedges, reeds, and mosses of the shallow edge waters become more numerous and extensive. Continued infilling further diminishes the aquatic habitat and allows for the increasing encroachment of low-growing land plants such as grasses and shrubs. As the process continues, trees move in to colonize the site, replacing the grasses and shrubs and completing the transition from lake to marsh to meadow to forest.

A similar series of local animal replacements would accompany the plant succession because of the significant habitat changes. Lake animals would be replaced by marsh animals, which in turn would be replaced by meadow and forest animals.

Plant succession is not to be confused with true extinction. Extinction is permanent, but species succession is not. Although a particular plant species may not be growing at a given time in a given location, it may reappear quickly if environmental conditions change and if there is an available seed source. Extinction means a species is extinct over the entire world, eliminated forever from the landscape. Extinction has taken place many times in Earth's history. Indeed, it is estimated that half a billion species have become extinct during the several-billion-year life of our planet. Probably the most dramatic example is the disappearance of the dinosaurs about 65 million years ago. For many millions of years, those gigantic reptiles were the dominant life forms of our planet, and yet in a relatively short period of geologic time they were all wiped out. The reasons behind their extermination are imperfectly

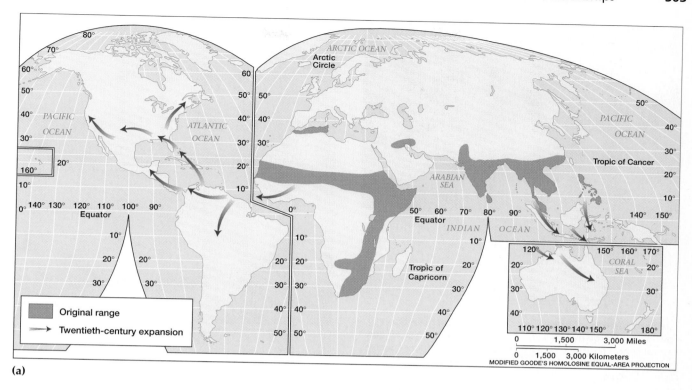

(a)

▲ **Figure 10-15**   Natural dispersal of an organism. (a) During the twentieth century, cattle egrets expanded from their Asian–African range into new habitats in the Americas and Australia. (b) Cattle egrets have found a happy home among the cattle herds of Texas. *(Alan D. Carey/Photo Researchers, Inc.)*

(b)

understood (evidently due in large part to the environmental changes associated with a catastrophic asteroid impact), but the fact remains that there have been innumerable such natural extinctions of entire species in the history of the world.

As we will discuss in Chapter 11, human activities are currently leading to the extinctions of plant and animal species at an alarming rate, primarily through the destruction of natural habitat.

Environmental Relationships

The survival of plants and animals depends on an intimate and sometimes precarious set of relationships with other elements of the environment. The details of these relationships vary with different species, but we can generalize about many of them. They can be discussed at various scales of generalization. However, you must remember that a generalization that is true at one scale may be quite invalid at another. For example, if we are considering global or continental patterns of biotic distribution, we are concerned primarily with gross generalizations that deal with average conditions, seasonal characteristics, latitudinal extent, zonal winds, and other broad-scale factors. If our interest is instead a small area, such as an individual valley or a single hillside, we are more concerned with such localized environmental factors as degree of slope, direction of exposure, and permeability of topsoil.

Whatever the scale, there are nearly always exceptions to the generalizations, and the smaller the scale, the more numerous the exceptions. (Remember that a

▲ **Figure 10-16** Once nearly exterminated, American bison now occur in large numbers in areas of suitable habitat. Under natural conditions they have a high level of reproductive success. This scene is in Elk Island National Park in western Canada. *(Tom L. McKnight photo.)*

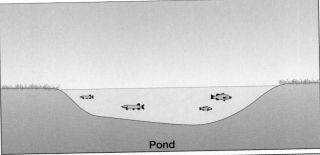

Pond

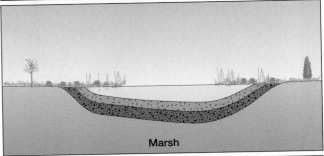

Marsh

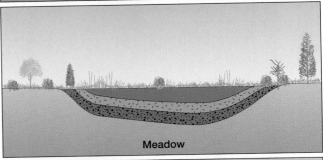

Meadow

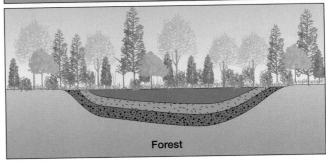

Forest

▲ **Figure 10-17** A simple example of plant succession: infilling of a small lake. Over time, successional colonization by different plant associations changes the area from pond to marsh to meadow to forest.

small-scale map shows a relatively large portion of Earth's surface, and a large-scale map shows a relatively small portion.) Thus, in a region that is generally humid, there are probably many localized sites that are extremely dry, such as cliffs or sand dunes. In even a very dry desert, there are likely to be several places that are always damp, such as an oasis or a spring.

Throughout the following discussion of environmental relationships, keep in mind that both *intraspecific competition* (among members of the same species) and *interspecific competition* (among members of different species) are at work. Both plants and animals compete with one another as they seek light, water, nutrients, and shelter in a dynamic environment. The term **limiting factor** is often used to describe the variable that is most important in determining the survival of an organism.

The Influence of Climate

At almost any scale, the most prominent environmental constraints on biota are exerted by various climatic factors.

Light No green plant can survive without light. We have already discussed the basic process—photosynthesis—whereby plants produce stored chemical energy; this process is activated by light. It is essentially for this reason that photosynthetic vegetation is absent from deeper ocean areas, where light does not penetrate.

Light can have a significant effect on plant shape, as Figure 10-18 shows. In places where the amount of light is restricted, such as in a dense forest, trees are likely to be very tall but have limited lateral growth. In areas that have less dense vegetation, more light is available, and as a result trees are likely to be expansive in lateral spread but truncated vertically.

Another important light relationship involves how much light an organism receives during any 24-hour period. This relationship is called **photoperiodism**. Except in the immediate vicinity of the equator, the seasonal variation in the photoperiod becomes greater with increasing latitude. Fluctuation in the photoperiod

▲ **Figure 10-18**   In an open stand (left), there is abundant light all around the tree and it responds by broad lateral growth rather than vertical growth. Under crowded conditions (right), less light reaches the tree and it elongates upward rather than spreading laterally.

stimulates seasonal behavior—such as flowering, leaf fall, mating, and migration—in both plants and animals.

Moisture   The broad distribution patterns of the biota are governed more significantly by the availability of moisture than by any other single environmental factor. A prominent trend throughout biotic evolution has been the adaptation of plants and animals to either excesses or deficiencies in moisture availability (Figure 10-19). The availability of water is not wholly dependent on climate—precipitation versus evaporation—but it is very largely determined by these atmospheric dynamics.

Temperature   The temperature of the air and the soil is also important to biotic distribution patterns. Fewer species of both plants and animals can survive in cold regions than in areas of more moderate temperatures. Plants, in particular, have a limited tolerance for low temperatures because they are continuously exposed to the weather, and they experience tissue damage and other physical disruption when their cellular water freezes. Animals in some instances are able to avoid the bitterest cold by moving around to seek shelter. Even so, the cold-weather areas of high latitudes and high elevations have a limited variety of animals and plants.

Wind   The influence of wind on biotic distributions is more limited than that of the other climatic factors. Where winds are persistent, however, they often serve as a constraint. The principal negative effect of wind is that it causes excessive drying by increasing evaporation from exposed surfaces, thus causing a moisture deficiency (Figure 10-20). In cold regions, wind escalates the rate at which animals lose body heat.

The sheer physical force of wind can also be influential: A strong wind can uproot trees, modify plant forms, and increase the heat intensity of wildfires. On the positive side, wind sometimes aids in the dispersal of biota by carrying pollen, seeds, lightweight organisms, and flying creatures.

Edaphic Influences

Soil characteristics, known as **edaphic factors** (from *edaphos*, Greek for "ground" or "soil"), also influence

▲ **Figure 10-19**   Even the most stressful environments often contain distinctive and conspicuous plants. These large cacti—organ pipe on the left and saguaro on the right—prosper in the parched Sonoran desert along the Arizona–Mexico border. (*Tom L. McKnight photo.*)

▲ **Figure 10-20**   Some plants are remarkably adaptable to environmental stress. In this timberline scene from north-central Colorado, there is no question about the prevailing wind direction. Persistent wind from the right has so desiccated this subalpine fir that only branches growing toward the left survive. This preferred growth direction places the trunk of the tree between them and the wind. *(Tom L. McKnight photo.)*

biotic distributions. These factors are direct and immediate in their effect on flora but usually indirect in their effect on fauna. Soil is a major component of the habitat of any vegetation, of course, and its characteristics significantly affect rooting capabilities and nutrient supply. Especially significant are soil texture, soil structure, humus content, chemical composition, and the relative abundance of soil organisms.

Topographic Influences

In global distribution patterns of plants and animals, general topographic characteristics are the most important factor affecting distribution. For example, the assemblage of plants and animals in a plains region is very different from that in a mountainous region. At a more localized scale, the factors of slope and drainage are likely to be significant, primarily the steepness of the slope, its orientation with regard to sunlight, and the porosity of the soil on the slope.

Wildfire

Most environmental factors that affect the distribution of plants and animals are passive, and their influences are slow and gradual. Occasionally, however, abrupt and catastrophic events, such as floods, earthquakes, volcanic eruptions, landslides, insect infestations, and droughts, also play a significant role. By far the most important of these is wildfire (Figure 10-21). In almost all portions of the continents, except for the always-wet regions where fire simply cannot start and the always-dry

▲ **Figure 10-21**   Wildfires are commonplace in many parts of the world. This ground fire in the Top End of the Northern Territory of Australia is almost an annual occurrence under natural conditions. *(Tom L. McKnight photo.)*

PEOPLE AND THE ENVIRONMENT Wildfires in Yellowstone

During the summer of 1988, Yellowstone National Park experienced the most devastating wildfires within human memory. Beginning in late June, 13 major fires burned out of control within a burn perimeter that covered nearly half of the park's 880,000 hectares (2.2 million acres). On a single day (August 20), more area was torched than had burned in any previous decade since the park was created in 1872.

The park's fire-management policy, in place since 1976, decreed that human-caused fires were to be suppressed, but natural fires were to be left alone unless they threatened human life, private property, or significant natural resources. The theory behind this let-burn policy is that the ecosystem contained in any large national park should be allowed to function naturally and remain as pristine as possible, both in appearance and in process. Natural processes—drought, flood, insect infestation, wildfire, and so forth—should not be interfered with. During the 11 years prior to 1988 that this policy had been in effect, 235 nature-caused fires had been allowed to burn, with the largest destroying only 3,000 hectares (7400 acres).

However, the summer of 1988 was unique: rainless, hot, and windy. Regardless of the fire-management policy, Yellowstone was ripe for conflagration in 1988. Eight of the 13 major fires were caused by humans, and attempts to suppress these were made from the outset. The other five were not fought until late July, at which time an all-out effort at suppression was begun. This prodigious effort was largely ineffectual. The horrendous weather conditions produced firestorms that were totally uncontrollable. About 400,000 hectares (1 million acres) was affected by the fires, and it is thought that firefighters "saved" less than 800 hectares (2000 acres), although some buildings (most notably Old Faithful Inn) were spared because of the suppression efforts.

Indeed, suppression often caused more harm than benefit. A burned forest may return to its original condition in 100 years, but a bulldozer scar made in creating a fireline may persist for ten times that long. In any case, on September 11, six millimeters (a quarter inch) of rain and snow fell and accomplished what the firefighters could not: the fires were quenched (Figure 10-B).

The Yellowstone fires received massive media attention. The American public mourned the "devastation" of its most famous national park. The National Park Service was excoriated for its "shortsighted" fire-management policy, and political repercussions were widespread.

Certainly, the conflagration produced negative results. Large expanses of forest and grassland were killed, and thousands of small animals undoubtedly died. However, the body count of large animals was fewer than 400, mostly elk (of which there are more than 30,000 in the park). This is not a significantly larger total than the number of road-killed animals in Yellowstone in an average summer. Tourism dropped about 10 percent in July, 30 percent in August, and 75 percent during the first three weeks of September. Most important locations were briefly evacuated, and the entire park was closed to visitors for only two days.

On balance, however, the positive results of the fires far outweigh the negative ones. Habitat diversity was greatly enhanced. Much of Yellowstone was covered only with an old-growth lodgepole pine forest, but one result of the massive, uneven burning of 1988 is a mosaic of vegetation that has been missing for a long time.

The fires are an overall boon to the ecosystem. Many of Yellowstone's coniferous trees reproduce by means of cones that require great heat before they can open and drop their seeds. Fires are necessary to recycle bound-up nutrients. Since the fires, this nutrient fix has been particularly manifested by a vigorous growth of grasses, herbs, and shrubs (Figure 10-C) which invigorate the entire food web.

▲ **Figure 10-B**   Firefighter mopping up some of the last remnants of Yellowstone's fires in 1988. *(Tom L. McKnight photo.)*

▲ **Figure 10-C**   This photograph was taken from the same spot as Figure 10-B, five years after the fires. The vegetation of the forest floor has regrown thoroughly. It will take much longer for the trees to regenerate. *(Tom L. McKnight photo.)*

regions where there is an insufficiency of combustible vegetation, uncontrolled natural fires have occurred with surprising frequency. Fires generally result in complete or partial devastation of the plant life and the killing or driving away of all or most of the animals. These results, of course, are only temporary; sooner or later, vegetation sprouts and animals return. At least in the short run, however, the composition of the biota is changed, and if the fires occur with sufficient frequency the change may be more than temporary.

Wildfire can be very helpful to the seeding or sprouting of certain plants and the maintenance of certain plant interactions. In some cases, grasslands are sustained by relatively frequent natural fires, which inhibit the encroachment of tree seedlings. Moreover, many plant species, particularly certain trees such as the giant sequoia and the southern yellow pine, scatter their seeds only after the heat of a fire has caused the cones or other types of seedpods to open.

Environmental Correlations: Example of Selva

One of the most important themes in physical geography is the intertwining relationships of the various components of the environment. Time after time we note situations in which one aspect of the environment affects another—sometimes conspicuously, sometimes subtly. In terms of broad distribution patterns, climate, vegetation, and soil have a particularly close correlation. Before we go on to discuss some of the details of biogeographical patterns in the following chapter, it may be helpful to provide an example of some of these correlations by examining the distribution of tropical rainforest.

On any map showing the world distribution of major plant associations, one of the conspicuous units is the *selva*, or *tropical rainforest*. A vast extent of selva exists in northern South America (primarily within the watershed of the Amazon River), central Africa (mostly within the watershed of the Congo [Zaire] River), and the East Indies, with more limited patches in Central America, Colombia, West Africa, Madagascar, Southeast Asia, and northeastern Australia (Figure 10-22).

Climate A general explanation of this distribution pattern is simple. With very limited exceptions, the tropical rainforest occurs wherever relatively abundant precipitation and uniformly warm temperatures occur throughout the year, especially in areas of *tropical wet* (Af) climate (described in Chapter 8). It is tempting to state that the tropical wet climate "creates" the conditions necessary for tropical rainforest, but the cause-and-effect relationship is not that simple—for example, transpiration from the local vegetation is very much a part of the hydrologic cycle in tropical rainforest regions.

Flora Because of the high temperatures and high humidity, regions having a tropical wet climate are normally covered with natural vegetation that is unexcelled in luxuriance and variety. Tropical rainforest is a broadleaf evergreen forest with numerous tree species. Many of the trees are very tall, and their intertwining tops form an essentially continuous canopy that prohibits sunlight from shining on the forest floor. Often shorter trees form a second and even a third partial canopy at lower elevations. Most of the trees are smooth barked and have no low limbs, although there is a profusion of vines and hanging plants that entangle

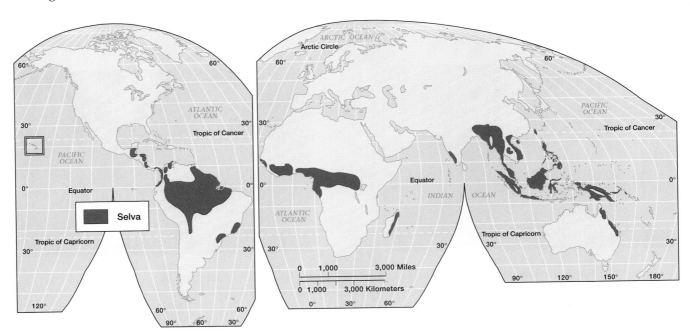

▲ **Figure 10-22** World distribution of tropical rainforest, or *selva*.

impenetrable tangle of bushes, shrubs, vines, and small trees is called a *jungle.*

Fauna   Regions of tropical rainforest are the realm of flyers, crawlers, creepers, and climbers. Larger species, particularly hoofed animals, are not common. Birds and monkeys inhabit the forest canopy often in great quantity and diversity. Snakes and lizards are common both on the forest floor and in the trees. Rodents are sometimes numerous at ground level, but the sparser population of larger mammals is typically secretive and nocturnal. Aquatic life, particularly fish and amphibians, is usually abundant. Invertebrates, especially insects and arthropods, are characteristically superabundant.

Soil   The copious, warm, year-round rains provide an almost continuous infiltration of water downward, with the result that soils are usually deep but highly leached and infertile. Leaves, twigs, flowers, and branches frequently fall from the trees to the ground, where they are rapidly decomposed by the abundant earthworms, ants, bacteria, and microfauna of the soil. The accumulated litter is continuously incorporated into the soil, where some of the nutrients are taken up by plants and the remainder are carried away by the infiltrating water. *Laterization* (rapid weathering of mineral matter and speedy decomposition of organic matter) is the principal soil-forming process; it produces a thin layer of fertile topsoil that is rapidly used by plants and a deep subsoil that is largely an infertile mixture of such insoluble constituents as iron, aluminum, and magnesium compounds. These minerals typically impart a reddish color to the soil. River floodplains tend to develop soils of higher fertility because of flood-time deposition of silt.

Hydrography   The abundance of runoff water on the surface feeds well-established drainage systems. There is usually a dense network of streams, most of which carry both a great deal of water and a heavy load of sediment. Lakes are not common because there is enough erosion to drain them naturally. Where the land is very flat, swamps sometimes develop through inadequate drainage and the rapid growth of vegetation.

In the next chapter, we will explore many other correlations among the patterns in the biosphere, lithosphere, atmosphere, and hydrosphere.

▲ **Figure 10-23**   A tropical rainforest scene in Ecuador. *(Darrel Hess photo.)*

the trunks and dangle from higher limbs (Figure 10-23). The dimly lit forest floor is relatively clear of growth because lack of sunlight inhibits survival of bushes and shrubs. Where much sunlight reaches the ground, as along the edge of a clearing or banks of a stream, a maze of undergrowth can prosper. This sometimes

Chapter 10 Learning Review

Key Terms

Before answering the study questions, review the definitions of the following key terms (page references are provided for you):

biogeography *(p. 289)*
biomass *(p. 292)*

biota *(p. 291)*
carbon cycle *(p. 294)*

decomposers *(p. 298)*
denitrification *(p. 296)*

edaphic factors *(p. 305)*
fauna *(p. 291)*
flora *(p. 291)*
food chain *(p. 297)*
food pyramid *(p. 297)*
limiting factor *(p. 304)*

net primary productivity *(p. 292)*
nitrogen cycle *(p. 296)*
nitrogen fixation *(p. 296)*
oxygen cycle *(p. 295)*
photoperiodism *(p. 304)*
photosynthesis *(p. 292)*

plant respiration *(p. 292)*
plant succession *(p. 302)*
primary consumers *(p. 297)*
producers *(p. 297)*
secondary consumers *(p. 297)*

Study Questions for Key Concepts

After studying this chapter, you should be able to answer the following questions:

Biogeochemical Cycles (p. 291)
1. What is the primary source of energy for the biosphere?
2. How is solar energy "stored" in the biosphere?
3. Describe and explain the process of *photosynthesis.*
4. Describe and explain the process of *plant respiration.*
5. What is meant by *net primary productivity*?
6. What is the relationship of *biomass* to net primary productivity?
7. Describe the basic steps in the *carbon cycle.*
8. Most of the carbon at or near Earth's surface is not involved in any short-term cycling. Explain.
9. What is the primary source of carbon that humans have added to the atmosphere?
10. What is the importance of photosynthesis to the flow of energy, water, oxygen, and carbon through the biosphere?

11. Why is it difficult to integrate nitrogen gas from the atmosphere into the nitrogen cycle of the biosphere?
12. Explain the differences between *nitrogen fixation* and *denitrification.*

Food Chains (p. 297)
13. What is the relationship of a *food chain* to a *food pyramid*?
14. Explain the roles of *producers, consumers,* and *decomposers* in the food chain.
15. What is the difference between *primary consumers* and *secondary consumers*?
16. Looking at Figure 10-10, explain why it takes 1000 kilograms of plankton to produce only 10 kilograms of fish.

Natural Distributions (p. 299)

17. Describe one mechanism through which plant seeds can be dispersed over great distances.
18. Explain the concept of *plant succession.*

Environmental Relationships (p. 303)

19. What is meant by the term *limiting factor?*

20. Explain how both photosynthesis and *photoperiodism* are dependent on sunlight.
21. Why are trees in dense forests likely to be tall with narrow tops?
22. What are the beneficial effects of wildfire?

Additional Resources

Books:

Hengeveld, R. *Dynamic Biogeography.* New York: Cambridge University Press, 1990.

Quammen, David. *The Song of the Dodo: Island Biogeography in an Age of Extinctions.* New York: Scribner, 1996.

Internet Sites:

The Earth Observatory

http://earthobservatory.nasa.gov/

The Earth Observatory is National Aeronautics and Space Administration's (NASA's) Internet site that provides information and images of Earth.

U.S. Fish and Wildlife Service

http://www.fws.gov/

This site provides information about environmental quality, endangered species, and habitat conservation in the United States.

USGS Biological Resources

http://biology.usgs.gov/

This web site offers information about U.S. Geological Survey projects monitoring ecosystems and wildlife.

11
Terrestrial Flora and Fauna

Having considered fundamental patterns and processes in the biosphere in the previous chapter, we now turn more specifically to the geographical distribution of plants and animals. We begin with some concepts to help us study groups of organisms.

Ecosystems and Biomes

In our search for organizing principles that help us comprehend the biosphere, two concepts are of particular value—*ecosystem* and *biome*.

Ecosystem: A Concept for All Scales

The term **ecosystem** is a contraction of the phrase *ecological system*. An ecosystem includes all the organisms in a given area, but it is more than simply a community of plants and animals existing together. The ecosystem concept encompasses the totality of interactions among the organisms and between the organisms and the nonliving portion of the environment in the area under consideration. The nonliving portion of the environment includes soil, rocks, water, sunlight, and atmosphere, but it can essentially be considered as nutrients and energy.

An ecosystem, then, is fundamentally an association of plants and animals along with the surrounding nonliving environment and all the interactions in which the organisms take part. The concept is built around the flow of energy among the various components of the ecosystem, which is the essential determinant of how a biological community functions (Figure 11-1).

This functional, ecosystemic concept is very attractive as an organizing principle for the geographic study of the biosphere. It must be approached with caution, however, because of the various scales at which it can be applied. There is an almost infinite variety in the magnitude of ecosystems we might study. At one extreme of scale, for example, we can conceive of a global ecosystem that encompasses the entire biosphere; at the other end of the scale might be the ecosystem of a fallen log, the underside of a rock, or even a drop of water.

If we are going to identify and understand broad distributional patterns in the biosphere, we must focus only on ecosystems that can be recognized at a useful scale.

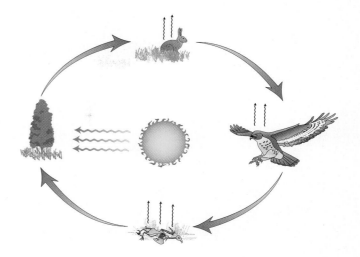

▲ **Figure 11-1** The flow of energy in a simple ecosystem. Energy from the Sun is trapped by the grass during photosynthesis. The grass is then eaten by a rabbit, which is eaten by a hawk, which then dies. The energy originally contained in the photosynthetic products made by the grass passes through stages during which it is bound up in the body molecules of the rabbit and the hawk but ultimately becomes heat energy lost from the live animals and from the decaying dead matter.

Biome: A Scale for All Biogeographers

Among terrestrial ecosystems, the type that provides the most appropriate scale for understanding world distribution patterns is called a **biome**, defined as any large, recognizable assemblage of plants and animals in functional interaction with its environment. A biome is usually identified and named on the basis of its dominant vegetation, which normally constitutes the bulk of the biomass (the total weight of all organisms—plant and animal) in the biome, as well as being the most obvious and conspicuous visible component of the landscape.

There is no universally recognized classification system of the world's terrestrial biomes, but scholars commonly accept 10 major types:

- Tropical rainforest
- Tropical deciduous forest
- Tropical scrub
- Tropical savanna
- Desert
- Mediterranean woodland and shrub
- Midlatitude grassland
- Midlatitude deciduous forest
- Boreal forest
- Tundra (Arctic and alpine)

A biome comprises much more than merely the plant association that gives it its name. A variety of

◀ Migrating wildebeest, *Connochaetes taurinus*, crossing the Mara River in the Masai Mara Reserve, Kenya. *(Minden Pictures.)*

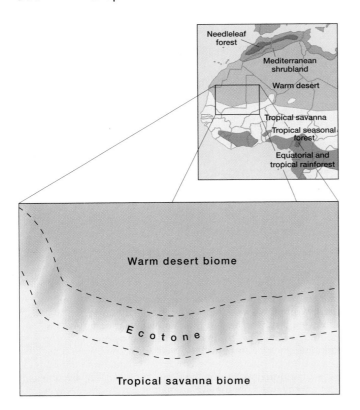

▲ **Figure 11-2** A hypothetical boundary between two biomes of the world. The irregular boundary between the two shows much interfingering, or interdigitation. This transition zone is called an ecotone.

other kinds of vegetation usually grows among, under, and occasionally over the dominant plants. Diverse animal species also occupy the area. Often, as we saw in Chapter 10, significant and even predictable relationships exist between the biota (particularly the flora) of a biome and the associated climate and soil types.

On any map showing the major biome types of the world (such as Figure 11-25 later in this chapter), the regional boundaries are somewhat arbitrary. Biomes do not occupy sharply defined areas in nature, no matter how sharp the demarcations may appear on a map. Normally the communities merge more or less imperceptibly with one another through **ecotones**—transition zones of competition in which the typical species of one biome intermingle with those of another (Figure 11-2).

Before we describe the flora and fauna of the world's terrestrial biomes, we need to say something about plants and animals themselves.

Terrestrial Flora

The natural vegetation of the land surfaces of Earth is of interest to the geographer for three reasons:

1. Over much of the planet, the terrestrial (land-dwelling) flora is the most significant visual component of the landscape. Plants often grow in such profusion that they mask all other elements of the environment. Topography, soils, animal life, and even water surfaces are often obscured or obliterated by plants. Only in areas of rugged terrain, harsh climate, or significant human activities are plants not likely to dominate the landscape.

2. Vegetation is a sensitive indicator of other environmental attributes. Floristic characteristics typically reflect subtle variations in sunlight, temperature, precipitation, evaporation, drainage, slope, soil conditions, and other natural parameters. Moreover, the influence of vegetation on soil, animal life, and microclimatic characteristics is frequently pervasive.

3. Vegetation often has a prominent and tangible influence on human settlement and activities. In some cases, it is a barrier or hindrance to human endeavor; in other instances, it provides an important resource to be exploited or developed.

Characteristics of Plants

Despite the fragile appearance of many plants, most varieties are remarkably hardy. Although exposed to the elements and without any ability to seek shelter, plants are capable of surviving the harshest environmental circumstances. They survive, and often flourish, in the wettest, driest, hottest, coldest, and windiest places on Earth. Much of their survival potential is based on a subsurface root system that is capable of sustaining life despite whatever may happen to the above-surface portion of the organism.

The survival capability of a species also depends in part on its reproductive mechanism. Plants that endure seasonal climatic fluctuations from year to year are called **perennials**, whereas those that perish during times of climatic stress (such as winter) but leave behind a reservoir of seeds to germinate during the next favorable period are called **annuals**.

Plant life varies remarkably in form, from microscopic algae to gigantic trees. Most plants, however, have common characteristics—roots to gather nutrients and moisture and anchor the plant; stems and/or branches for support and for nutrient transportation from roots to leaves; leaves to absorb and convert solar energy for sustenance and to exchange gases and transpire water; and reproductive organs for regeneration.

Floristic Terminology

To continue our consideration of plants, we need a specialized vocabulary. Here are some of the terms used in the discussion.

First of all, plants can be divided into two categories: those that reproduce through *spores* and those that reproduce through *seeds.* The former include two major groups:

1. *Bryophytes* include the true mosses, peat mosses, and liverworts. Presumably they have never in geologic history been very dominant among plant communities, except in localized situations.
2. *Pteridophytes* are ferns, horsetails, and club mosses (which are not true mosses). During much of geologic history, great forests of tree ferns, giant horsetails, and tall club mosses dominated continental vegetation, but they are less dominant today.

Plants that reproduce by means of seeds are encompassed in two broad groups:

1. The more primitive of the two groups, the **gymnosperms** (naked seeds), carry their seeds in cones, and when the cones open, the seeds fall out. (For this reason, gymnosperms are sometimes called **conifers**.) Gymnosperms were largely dominant in the geologic past; today the only large surviving gymnosperms are cone-bearing trees such as pines.
2. **Angiosperms** (vessel seeds) are the flowering plants. Their seeds are encased in some sort of protective body, such as a fruit, nut, or pod. Trees, shrubs, grasses, crops, weeds, and garden flowers are angiosperms. Along with a few conifers, they have dominated the vegetation of the planet for the last 50 or 60 million years.

Several other terms are commonly used to describe vegetation, as summarized in Figure 11-3. Their definitions are not always precise, but their meanings generally are clear.

1. One fundamental distinction is made on the basis of stem or trunk composition. **Woody plants** have stems composed of hard fibrous material, whereas **herbaceous plants** have soft stems. Woody plants are mostly trees and shrubs; herbaceous plants are mostly grasses, forbs, and lichens.
2. With trees, whether or not a plant loses its leaves sometime during the year is an important distinguishing characteristic. An **evergreen tree** is one that sheds its leaves on a sporadic or successive basis but always appears to be fully leaved. A **deciduous tree** is one that experiences an annual period in which all leaves die and usually fall from the tree, due to either a cold season or a dry season.
3. Trees are also often described in terms of leaf shapes. **Broadleaf trees** have leaves that are flat and expansive in shape, whereas **needleleaf trees** are adorned with thin slivers of tough, leathery, waxy needles rather than typical leaves. Almost all needleleaf trees are evergreen, and the great

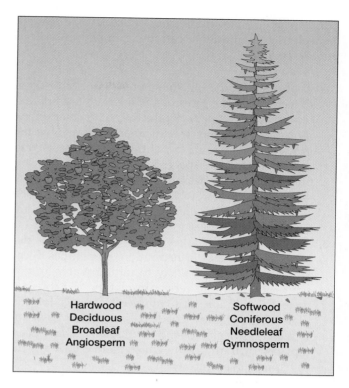

▲ **Figure 11-3** Terminology used in describing plants. Although the terminology is somewhat confusing, there are conspicuous differences between hardwood (angiosperm) and softwood (gymnosperm) trees. The most obvious difference is in general appearance.

majority of all broadleaf trees are deciduous, except in the rainy tropics, where everything is evergreen.

4. *Hardwood* and *softwood* are two of the most unsatisfactory terms in biogeography, but they are widely used in everyday parlance so we must not ignore them. Hardwoods are angiosperm trees that are usually broad leaved and deciduous. Their wood has a relatively complicated structure, but it is not always hard. Softwoods are gymnosperms; nearly all are needleleaf evergreens. Their wood has a simple cellular structure, but it is not always soft.

Environmental Adaptations

Despite the hardiness of most plants, there are definite tolerance limits that govern their survival, distribution, and dispersal. During hundreds of millions of years of development, plants have evolved a variety of protective mechanisms to shield against harsh environmental conditions and to enlarge their tolerance limits. Two prominent adaptations to environmental stress are *xerophytic* and *hygrophytic* adaptations.

Xerophytic Adaptations   The descriptive term for plants that are structurally adapted to withstand protracted dry conditions is *xerophytic* (*xero* is Greek for "dry"; *phyt-* comes from *phuto-*, Greek for "plant"). **Xerophytic adaptations** can be grouped into four general types:

1. Roots are modified in shape or size to enable them to seek widely for moisture. Sometimes taproots extend to extraordinary depths to reach subterranean moisture. Also, root modification may involve the growth of a large number of thin hairlike rootlets to penetrate tiny pore spaces in soil (Figure 11-4).

2. Stems are sometimes modified into fleshy, spongy structures that can store moisture. Plants with such fleshy stems are called *succulents;* most cacti are prominent examples.

3. Leaf modification takes many forms; all are designed to decrease transpiration. Sometimes a leaf surface is hard and waxy to inhibit water loss or white and shiny to reflect insolation and thus reduce evaporation. Still more effective is for the plant to have either tiny leaves or no leaves at all. In many types of dry-land shrubs, leaves have been replaced by thorns, from which there is virtually no transpiration (Figure 11-5).

▲ **Figure 11-5**   Cacti lack leaves, but instead have thorns from which there is no water loss through transpiration. *(Darrel Hess photo.)*

4. Perhaps the most remarkable floristic adaptation to aridity is not structural but involves the plant's reproductive cycle. Many xerophytic plants lie dormant for years without perishing. When rain eventually arrives, these plants promptly initiate and pass through an entire annual cycle of germination, flowering, fruiting, and seed dispersal in only a few days, then lapse into dormancy again if the drought resumes.

Hygrophytic Adaptations   Some plants are particularly suited to a wet terrestrial environment. Distinction is sometimes made between **hydrophytes** (species living more or less permanently immersed in water, such as the water lilies in Figure 11-6a) and **hygrophytes** (moisture-loving plants that generally require frequent soakings with water, as do many ferns, mosses, and rushes), but both groups are often identified by the latter term.

Hygrophytes are likely to have extensive root systems to anchor them in the soft ground, and hygrophytic trees often develop a widened, flaring trunk near the ground to provide better support (Figure 11-6b). Many hygrophytic plants that grow in standing or moving water have weak, pliable stems that can withstand the ebb and flow of currents rather than standing erect against them; the buoyancy of the water, rather than the stem, provides support for the plant.

The Critical Role of Competition

As important as climatic, edaphic, and other environmental characteristics are to plant survival, a particular species will not necessarily occupy an area just because all these conditions are favorable. Plants are just as competitive as animals or used-car salespersons. Of the dozens of plant species that might be suitable for an area, only one or a few are likely to survive.

This is not to say that all plants are mutually competitive; indeed, thousands of ecologic niches can be

▲ **Figure 11-4**   Desert plants have evolved various mechanisms for survival in an arid climate. Some plants produce a long taproot that penetrates deeply in search of the water table. More common are plants that have no deep roots but rather have myriad small roots and rootlets that seek any moisture available near the surface.

plants but more commonly at their spatial groupings. Over most land surfaces, the natural vegetation occurs in considerable variety, but regardless of species diversity, plant associations can usually be classified on the basis of dominant members, dominant appearance, or both.

The Inevitability of Change In considering the major vegetational associations, we should remember that the floristic pattern of Earth is impermanent. The plant cover that exists at any given time and place may be in a state of constant change or may be relatively stable for millennia before experiencing significant changes. Sooner or later, however, change is inevitable. Sometimes the change is slow and orderly, as when a lake is filled in, as described earlier, or when there is a long-term trend toward different climatic conditions over a broad area. On occasion, however, the change is abrupt and chaotic, as in the case of a wildfire.

At some time in Earth's history, all parts of the present landmasses were newly created and therefore unvegetated. Such new land is first occupied temporarily by some plant association that soon gives way to another and then another and another. Many complicated changes occur until some sort of floristic stability is attained. Each succeeding association alters the local environment, making possible the establishment of the next association. The general sequential trend is toward taller plants and greater stability in species composition. The longer plant succession continues, the more slowly change takes place because more advanced associations usually contain species that live a relatively long time.

Eventually a plant association of constant composition comes into being. In other words, a point is reached where change is no longer noticeable, and each succeeding generation of the association is much like its predecessor. This stable association is generally referred to as the **climax vegetation**, and the various associations leading up to it are called *seral stages*.

The implication of the term climax vegetation is that the dominant plants of a climax association have demonstrated that, of all possibilities for that particular situation, they can compete the most successfully. Thus, they represent the optimal floristic cover for that environmental context. The climax vegetation presumably persists unchanged for an indefinite period until the next environmental disturbance. The climax vegetation is, then, an association in equilibrium with prevailing environmental conditions. When these conditions change, the climax stage is disturbed and another succession sequence is initiated.

Identifying and Mapping Associations The geographer attempting to recognize spatial groupings of plants faces some significant difficulties. Plant associations that are similar in appearance and in environmental relationships can occur in widely

▲ **Figure 11-6** Some types of plants flourish in a totally aqueous environment. **(a)** These lily pads virtually cover the surface of a bay of Cold Lake, on the Alberta–Saskatchewan border in western Canada. *(Tom L. McKnight photo.)* **(b)** Many hygrophytic trees, such as these cypress in Louisiana, have wide, flaring trunks near the ground to provide firmer footing in the wet environment. *(Eastcott/Momatiuk/Photo Researchers, Inc.)*

occupied without impinging on one another. However, most plants draw their nutrients from the same soil and their energy from the same Sun, and what one plant obtains cannot be used by another.

Spatial Groupings of Plants

A geographer trying to understand the floristic characteristics of the environment sometimes looks at individual

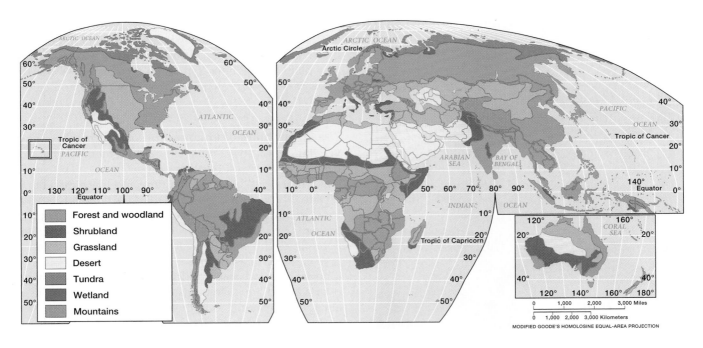

▲ **Figure 11-7** The major natural vegetation associations.

separated localities and are likely to contain totally different species. At the other extreme, exceedingly different plant associations can often be detected within a very small area. As the geographer tries to identify patterns and recognize relationships, generalization invariably is needed. This generalization must accommodate gradations, ecotones, interdigitations, and other irregularities. When associations are portrayed on maps, therefore, their boundaries represent approximations in nearly all cases.

Another special problem facing the student who would learn about Earth's environment is that in many areas the natural vegetation has been completely removed or replaced through human interference. Forests have been cut, crops planted, pastures seeded, and urban areas paved. Over extensive areas of Earth's surface, therefore, climax vegetation is the exception rather than the rule. Most world maps that purport to show natural vegetation ignore human interference and are actually maps of theoretical natural vegetation, in which the mapmaker makes assumptions about what the natural vegetation would be if it had not been modified by human activity.

The Major Floristic Associations There are many ways to classify plant associations. For broad geographical purposes, emphasis is usually placed on the structure and appearance of the dominant plants. The major associations generally recognized (Figure 11-7) include the following:

1. **Forests** consist of trees growing so close together that their individual leaf canopies generally overlap. This means that the ground is largely in shade,

a condition that usually precludes the development of much undergrowth. Forests require considerable annual precipitation and can survive in widely varying temperature zones. Except where moisture is inadequate or the growing season very short, forests are likely to become the climax vegetation association in any area.

Trees depend so much on the availability of moisture primarily because, unlike other plants, they must have a mechanism for transporting mineral nutrients a relatively great distance from the place of acquisition (roots) to the place of need (leaves). Such transport can take place only in a dilute solution; therefore much water is needed by trees throughout the growing season. Other plant forms can flourish in areas of relatively high precipitation, but they rarely become dominant because they are shaded out by trees.

2. **Woodlands** are tree-dominated plant associations in which the trees are spaced more widely apart than in forests and do not have interlacing canopies (Figure 11-8). Ground cover may be either dense or sparse, but it is not inhibited by lack of sunlight. Woodland environments are generally drier than forest environments.

3. **Shrublands** are plant associations dominated by relatively short woody plants generally called *shrubs* or *bushes*. Shrubs take a variety of forms, but most have several stems branching near the ground and a leafy foliage that begins very close to ground level. Trees and grasses may be interspersed with the shrubs but are less prominent in the landscape. Shrublands have a wide latitudinal range, but they are generally restricted to semiarid or arid locales.

▲ **Figure 11-8**   A piñon–juniper woodland scene in central Arizona. *(C. Prescott-Allen/Earth Scenes.)*

4. **Grasslands** may contain scattered trees and shrubs, but the landscape is dominated by grasses and forbs (broadleaf herbaceous plants). Prominent types of grassland include *savanna,* low-latitude grassland characterized by tall grasses; *prairie,* midlatitude grassland characterized by tall grasses; and *steppe,* midlatitude grassland characterized by short grasses and bunchgrasses. Grasslands are associated with semiarid and subhumid climates.

5. **Deserts** are typified by widely scattered plants with much bare ground interspersed. Desert is actually a climatic term, and desert areas may have a great variety of vegetation, including grasses, succulent herbs, shrubs, and straggly trees (Figure 11-9). Some extensive desert areas comprise loose sand, bare rock, or extensive gravel, with virtually no plant growth.

6. **Tundra,** as we noted in Chapter 8, consists of a complex mix of very low plants, including grasses,

▲ **Figure 11-9**   Some deserts contain an abundance of plants, but they are usually spindly and always xerophytic. This scene is near Phoenix, Arizona. *(Tom L. McKnight photo.)*

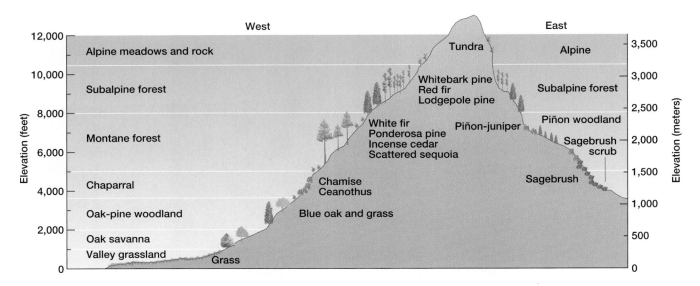

▲ **Figure 11-10** A west–east profile of California's Sierra Nevada, indicating the principal vegetation at different elevations on the western (wet) and eastern (dry) sides of the range.

forbs, dwarf shrubs, mosses, and lichens, but no trees. Tundra occurs only in the perennially cold climates of high latitudes or high altitudes.

7. **Wetlands** have a much more limited geographic extent than the associations described above. They are characterized by shallow standing water all or most of the year, with vegetation rising above the water level. The most widely distributed wetlands are swamps (with trees as the dominant plant forms) and marshes (with grasses and other herbaceous plants dominant) (for example, see Figure 11-6).

Vertical Zonation In Chapter 8, we learned that mountainous areas often have a distinct pattern of **vertical zonation** in vegetation patterns (Figure 11-10). Significant elevational changes in short horizontal distances cause various plant associations to exist in relatively narrow zones on mountain slopes. This zonation is largely due to the effects of elevation on temperature and precipitation (Figure 11-11).

The essential implication is that elevation changes are the counterpart of latitude changes; in other words, to travel from sea level to the top of a tall tropical peak

▲ **Figure 11-11** Vertical zonation of vegetation patterns on the east slope of the Sierra Nevada in California. Sagebrush in the lowest elevations gives way to piñon woodland and pockets of subalpine forest in higher elevations; above the treeline alpine tundra is found. The high peak in the center is Mount Whitney. *(Darrel Hess photo.)*

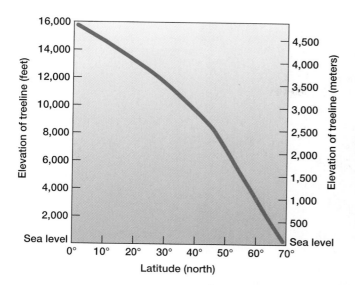

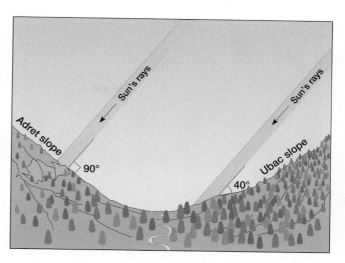

▲ **Figure 11-12**   Treeline elevation varies with latitude. This graph for the Northern Hemisphere shows that trees cease to grow at an elevation of about 5000 meters (16,000 feet) in the equatorial Andes of South America but at only 3000 meters (10,000 feet) at 40° N latitude in Colorado. At 70° N latitude in northern Canada, the treeline is at sea level.

▲ **Figure 11-13**   A typical adret–ubac situation. The noon Sun rays strike the adret slope at approximately a 90° angle, a condition that results in maximum heating. The same rays strike the ubac slope at approximately a 40° angle, with the result that the heating is spread over a large area and is therefore less intense.

is roughly equivalent environmentally to a horizontal journey from the equator to the Arctic. This elevation–latitude relationship is shown most clearly by how the elevation of the upper **treeline** (the elevation above which trees are unable to survive) varies with latitude (Figure 11-12).

An interesting detail of vertical zonation is that the elevation–latitude graph for the Southern Hemisphere is different from that of the Northern Hemisphere. For example, between latitudes 35° S and 40° S in Australia and New Zealand, the treeline is below 1800 meters (6000 feet); at comparable latitudes in North America, the treeline is nearly twice as high. The reason for this significant discrepancy is not completely understood.

Treeline variation represents only one facet of the broader design of vertical zonation in vegetation patterns. All vegetation zones are displaced downward with increasing distance from the equator. This principle accounts for the significant vegetational complexity found in all mountainous areas.

Local Variations   Each major vegetation association extends over a large area of Earth's surface. Within a given association, however, there are also significant local variations caused by a variety of local environmental conditions, as illustrated by the following two examples:

1. **Exposure to sunlight.** The direction in which a sloped surface faces is often a critical determinant of vegetation composition, as illustrated by Figure 11-13. Exposure has many aspects, but one of the most pervasive is simply the angle at which sunlight strikes the slope. If the Sun's rays arrive at

a high angle, they are much more effective in heating the ground and thus in evaporating available moisture. Such a Sun slope, called an **adret slope**, is hot and dry, and its vegetation is not only sparser and smaller than that on adjacent slopes having a different exposure to sunlight but is also likely to have a different species composition.

The opposite condition is a **ubac slope**, which is oriented so that sunlight strikes it at a low angle and is thus much less effective in heating and evaporating. This cooler condition produces more luxuriant vegetation of a richer diversity.

The difference between adret and ubac slopes decreases with increasing latitude, presumably because the ubac flora becomes impoverished under the cooler conditions that prevail as latitude increases, and now the relative warmth of the adret surface encourages plant diversity.

2. **Valley-bottom location.** In mountainous areas where a river runs through a valley, the vegetation associations growing on either side of the river have a composition that is significantly different from that found higher up on the slopes forming the valley. This floral gradient is sometimes restricted to immediate streamside locations and sometimes extends more broadly over the valley floor.

The difference is primarily a reflection of the perennial availability of subsurface moisture near the stream and is manifested in a more diversified and more luxuriant flora. This vegetative contrast is particularly prominent in dry regions, where streams may be lined with trees even though no other trees are to be found in the landscape. Such streamside growth is called **riparian vegetation** (Figure 11-14).

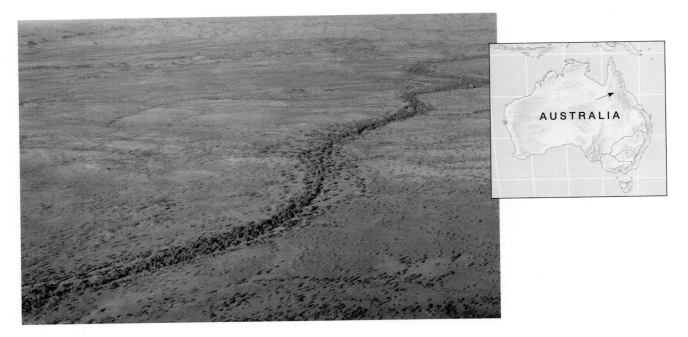

▲ **Figure 11-14**   Riparian vegetation is particularly prominent in dry lands. This stream in northern Queensland (Australia) would be inconspicuous in this photograph if it were not for the trees growing along it. *(Tom L. McKnight photo.)*

Terrestrial Fauna

Animals occur in much greater variety than plants over Earth. As objects of geographical study, however, they have been relegated to a place of lesser prominence for at least two reasons:

1. Animals are much less prominent than plants in the landscape. Apart from extremely localized situations—such as waterfowl flocking on a lake or an insect plague attacking a crop—animals tend to be secretive and inconspicuous.
2. Environmental interrelationships are much less clearly evidenced by animals than by plants. This is due in part to the inconspicuousness of animals, which renders them more difficult to study, and in part to the fact that animals are mobile and therefore more able to adjust to environmental variability.

This is not to say that fauna is inconsequential for students of geography. Under certain circumstances, wildlife is a prominent element of physical geography; and in some regions of the world, it is an important resource for human use and/or a significant hindrance to human activity. Moreover, it is increasingly clear that animals are sometimes more sensitive indicators than plants of the health of a particular ecosystem.

Characteristics of Animals

The diversity of animal life forms is not realized by most people. We commonly think of animals as being relatively large and conspicuous creatures that run across the land or scurry through the trees, seeking to avoid contact with humankind. In actuality, the term animal encompasses not only the larger, more complex forms, but also hundreds of thousands of species of smaller and simpler organisms that may be inconspicuous or even invisible. The variety of animal life is so great that it is difficult to find many unifying characteristics. The contrast, for example, between an enormous elephant and a microscopic protozoan is so extreme as to make their kinship appear ludicrous. Animals really have only two universal characteristics, and even these are so highly modified in some cases as to be almost unrecognizable:

1. Animals are motile, which means that they are capable of self-generated movement.
2. Animals must eat plants and/or other animals for sustenance. They are incapable of manufacturing their food from air, water, and sunlight, which plants can do.

Kinds of Animals

The vast majority of animals are so tiny and/or secretive as to be either invisible or extremely inconspicuous. Their size and habits, however, are not valid indicators of their significance for geographic study. Very minute and seemingly inconsequential organisms sometimes play exaggerated roles in the biosphere—as carriers of disease or as hosts of parasites, sources of infection, or providers of scarce nutrients. For example, no geographic assessment of Africa, however cursory, can afford to ignore the presence and distribution of the small

▲ **Figure 11-15** Insects, such as this moth, are arthropods, the largest group of invertebrate animals. *(Darrel Hess photo.)*

tsetse fly and the tiny protozoan called *Trypanosoma*, which together are responsible for the transmission of trypanosomiasis (sleeping sickness), a widespread and deadly disease for humans and livestock over much of the continent.

Zoological classification is much too detailed to be useful in most geographical studies. Therefore, presented in the paragraphs that follow is a brief summation of the principal kinds of animals that might be recognized in a general study of physical geography.

Invertebrates   Animals without backbones are called **invertebrates**. More than 90 percent of all animal species are encompassed within this broad grouping. Invertebrates include worms, sponges, mollusks, various marine animals, and a vast host of creatures of microscopic or near-microscopic size. Very prominent among invertebrates are the *arthropods*, a group that includes insects (Figure 11-15), spiders, centipedes, millipedes, and crustaceans (shellfish). With some 300,000 recognized species, beetles are the most numerous of animals, comprising about 40 percent of all insect species and more than one-fourth of all known animals.

Vertebrates   **Vertebrates** are animals that have a backbone that protects the main nerve (or spinal cord). Geographers generally follow biologists in recognizing five principal groups of vertebrates:

1. *Fishes* are the only vertebrates that can breathe under water (a few species are also capable of breathing in air). Most fishes inhabit either fresh water or salt water only, but some species are capable of living in both environments (such as the bull shark, *Carcharhinus leucas*), and several species, most notably salmon, spawn in freshwater streams but live most of their lives in the ocean.

2. *Amphibians* are semiaquatic animals. When first born, they are fully aquatic and breathe through gills; as adults, they are air-breathers by means of lungs and through their glandular skin. Most amphibians are either frogs or salamanders.

3. Most *reptiles* are totally land based. Ninety-five percent of all reptile species are either snakes or lizards. The remainder are mostly turtles and crocodilians.

4. *Birds* are believed to have evolved from reptiles; indeed, they have so many reptilian characteristics that they have been called "feathered reptiles." There are more than 9000 species of birds, all of which reproduce by means of eggs. Birds are so adaptable that some species can live almost anywhere on Earth's surface. They are **endothermic**, which means that, regardless of the temperature of the air or water in which they live, they maintain a constant body temperature.

5. *Mammals* are distinguished from all other animals by several internal characteristics as well as by two prominent external features. The external features are that only mammals produce milk with which they feed their young, and only mammals possess true hair. (Some mammals have very little hair, but no creatures other than mammals have any hair.) Mammals are also notable for being endothermic. Thus, the body temperature of mammals and birds stays about the same under any climatic conditions, which enables them to live in almost all parts of the world.

The great majority of all mammals are *placentals*, which means that their young grow and develop in the mother's body, nourished by an organ known as the *placenta*, which forms a vital connecting link with the mother's bloodstream (Figure 11-16). A small group of mammals (about 135 species) are *marsupials*, whose females have pouches in which the young, which are born in a very undeveloped condition, live for several

▲ **Figure 11-16** Most large land animals are placental mammals, as exemplified by this bull moose in Yellowstone Park. *(Tom L. McKnight photo).*

▲ **Figure 11-17** A red kangaroo joey (baby) peers out from its mother's pouch. *(Tom McHugh/Photo Researchers, Inc.)*

(a)

(b)

▲ **Figure 11-18** There are only two kinds of monotremes, or egg-laying mammals, in existence—the echidna and the duckbill platypus. **(a)** The echidna is found only in Australia and New Guinea. *(Tom L. McKnight photo.)* **(b)** The platypus is totally aquatic in its lifestyle. *(Tom McHugh, Taronga Park Zoo, Sydney, Australia/Photo Researchers, Inc.)*

weeks or months after birth (Figure 11-17). The most primitive of all mammals are the *monotremes,* of which only two types exist (Figure 11-18); they are egg-laying mammals.

Environmental Adaptations

As with plants, animals have evolved slowly and diversely through eons of time. Evolution has made it possible for animals to diverge remarkably in adjusting to different environments. Just about every existing environmental extreme has been met by some (or many) evolutionary adaptations that make it feasible for some (or many) animal species to survive and even flourish.

Physiological Adaptations The majority of animal adaptations to environmental diversity have been physiological, which is to say that they are anatomical and/or metabolic changes. A classic example is the size of fox ears. Ears are prime conduits for body heat in furred animals as they provide a relatively bare surface

for its loss. Arctic foxes (Figure 11-19a) have unusually small ears, which minimizes heat loss; desert foxes (Figure 11-19b) possess remarkably large ears, which are a great advantage during the blistering heat of desert summers.

There are several hundred species of mammals whose skin is covered with a fine, soft, thick, hairy coat referred to as *fur.* These mammals range in size from tiny mice and moles to the largest bears. An examination of their ranges reveals several generalized habitat preferences. Many fur-bearing species live in high-latitude and/or high-elevation locations, where winters are long and cold; a number of fur-bearing species live in aquatic environments; the remainder are widely scattered over the continents, occupying a considerable diversity of habitats. We can conclude tentatively that many fur-bearing species, including all those with the heaviest, thickest fur, live in regions where cold temperatures are common, but the climatic correlation in this case is partial and indistinct.

(a)

(b)

▲ **Figure 11-19** (a) An Arctic fox near Cape Churchill in the Canadian province of Manitoba. Its tiny ears are an adaptation to conserve body heat in a cold environment. *(Dan Guravich/Photo Researchers, Inc.)* (b) Desert foxes have large ears, the better to radiate away body heat. This is a bat-eared fox in northern Kenya. *(Tom L. McKnight photo.)*

The catalog of similar adaptations is almost endless: webbing between toes to make swimming easier; broad feet that won't sink in soft snow; increase in size and number of sweat glands to aid in evaporative cooling; and a host of others.

Behavioral Adaptations An important advantage that animals have over plants, in terms of adjustment to environmental stress, is that the former can move about and therefore modify their behavior in order to minimize the stress. Animals can seek shelter from heat, cold, flood, or fire; they can travel far in search of relief from drought or famine; and they can shift from daytime (diurnal) to nighttime (nocturnal) activities to minimize water loss during hot seasons. Such techniques as migration (periodic movement from one region to another), *hibernation* (spending winter in a dormant condition), and *estivation* (spending a dry–hot period in a torpid state) are behavioral adaptations employed regularly by many species of animals.

Reproductive Adaptations Harsh environmental conditions are particularly destructive to the newly born. As partial compensation for this factor, many species have evolved specialized reproductive cycles or have developed modified techniques of baby care. During lengthy periods of bad weather, for example, some species delay mating or postpone nest building. If fertilization has already taken place, some animal reproductive cycles are capable of almost indefinite delay, resulting in a protracted egg or larval stage or even total suspension of embryo development until the weather improves.

If the young have already been born, they sometimes remain longer than usual in nest, den, or pouch, and the adults may feed them for a longer time. When good weather finally returns, some species are capable of hastened *estrus* (the period of heightened sexual receptivity by the female), nest building, den preparation, and so on, and the progeny produced may be in greater than normal numbers.

Example of Animal Adaptations to Desert Life The desert is a classic illustration of a stressful environment for biotic life, as well as the many adaptations on the part of animals.

The simplest and most obvious adaptation to life in an arid land is for the animals to remain near a perpetual source of water. Thus, the permanent streams and enduring springs of the desert attract a resident faunal population that is often rich and diverse. Birds are more dependent on an open source of water than any other nonaquatic animal, so they often remain near such features throughout the day, or at least visit the water with some frequency. Many other kinds of animals also congregate near open water, although usually not as overtly as birds. Even in areas where open water is not available, it is rare for the desert to be uniformly inhospitable. There are usually some small pockets of localized favorable habitat that permit remnant populations of animals to survive until more propitious conditions allow them to recolonize large areas or to move on.

Often animals cannot remain near permanent water in a vast arid region, so the next best thing is to follow the rains in nomadic fashion. Many species demonstrate remarkable instincts for knowing where precipitation has occurred and will travel tens or

FOCUS Desert Adaptations of the Amazing Camel

Of all animals, perhaps the *dromedary* or one-humped camel (*Camelus dromedarius*) has developed the most remarkable series of adjustments to the desert environment, allowing it to survive and prosper under conditions of aridity that would be fatal to almost all other large animals (Figure 11-A).

Camels have a number of anatomical adaptations to desert life. The summer coat of the dromedary is relatively light-colored and shiny, reflecting solar radiation. Although the hair is short, it lies flat and serves as an effective barrier against heat gain from the environment. The upper lip of the dromedary is deeply cleft, with a groove that extends to this cleft from each nostril, presumably so that any moisture expelled from the nostrils can be caught in the mouth rather than being wasted. The nostrils consist of horizontal slits that can be closed tightly to keep out blowing dust and sand. The eyes are

set beneath shaggy, beetling brows, which help to shield them from the Sun's glare; the eyes are further protected from blowing sand by a complex double set of eyelids. The feet are broad and distended into pads that provide insulation from hot ground, and their firm but elastic tissue gives excellent traction on either sand or stony pebbles.

Physiological adaptations also are important for the dromedary. The heat balance of dromedaries is distinguished by a remarkable daily fluctuation of body temperature during hot weather. Humans and most other large animals have body temperatures that fluctuate by only 1° to 2°C (2° to 4°F) on hot days, whereas the range for dromedaries is 7°C (12°F). This means that the dromedary sweats little except during the very hottest hours, while a human in the same environment perspires almost from sunrise to sunset, the resultant

evaporative cooling irretrievably using up body water.

Dromedaries are also extremely economical in water use through producing only a small volume of urine and voiding very little water in their feces. Moreover, they are able to maintain bloodstream moisture during extreme heat stress (by a mechanism not clearly understood) nearly three times more efficiently than any other large mammal, which means that they can tolerate extreme dehydration without their body temperature rising to a fatal level. The remarkable efficiency of their heat and water budgets allows them to go without drinking for long periods (although they cannot "store" water in their hump, as was once believed), and when they do begin to drink, they are capable of rapid and complete rehydration in only a short time.

◀ **Figure 11-A** Camels are ideal pack animals in arid environments. This scene is from the Sudan. (*John Serafin.*)

even hundreds of kilometers to take advantage of locally improved conditions. This trait is again most prominently displayed by birds, which have greater powers of mobility than other animals. A high proportion of desert bird species can be classed as nomads, in contrast to the large proportion of sedentary migratory species in other parts of the world. Some of the larger mammals also have rain-following habits. Some African antelopes and Australian kangaroos have been observed to double in numbers almost overnight after a good rain, a feat impossible except by rapid, large-scale movement from one area to another.

Apart from mobility, a number of other behavioral techniques have been adopted by various kinds of animals to ensure survival in the desert. A significant method used by smaller creatures is to spend a great deal of time underground beneath the level of desiccating heat. Most desert rodents and reptiles live in underground burrows, and many lesser creatures do the same. Desert frogs, while not numerous, are noted burrowers; some have been found as deep as 2 meters (6 feet) underground. Freshwater crayfish and crabs often survive long dry spells by burying themselves. Most desert ants and termites live in underground nests. Most desert animals except birds, ungulates, and

▲ **Figure 11-20**   Ord kangaroo rat, Arizona. The kangaroo rat can live its entire life without taking a drink. *(John Cancalosi.)*

many flying insects are almost completely *nocturnal.* There is clearly much more wildlife activity at night than in the daytime.

A few species of rodents, most notably kangaroo rats (Figure 11-20), can exist from birth to death without ever taking a drink, surviving exclusively on moisture ingested with their food.

Perhaps the most astounding of all faunal adaptations to arid conditions is one that is overtly very similar to a vegetational adaptation—the ability to delay reproductive processes over long dry periods until more favorable conditions occur, at which time rapid breeding or birth can allow remarkable population regeneration. Australian desert kangaroos, for example, are capable of "delayed implantation," in which a fertilized *blastocyst* can remain in an inactive state of development in the uterus during a period of difficult living and then spontaneously resume normal development after conditions have improved. Desert birds may experience enormous die-offs when waters dry up during a prolonged drought, but when rains finally come, the survivors may begin nest construction within a week and ovulation within a fortnight. Moreover, clutch size (the number of eggs laid) may increase, as may the number of clutches produced.

Invertebrates, too, can take advantage of a favorable weather change to proliferate their numbers extraordinarily. Many of them survive the dry period in an egg or larval stage that is extremely resistant to desiccation; when the drought breaks, the egg hatches or the larva develops into an active stage that may not be at all drought resistant. Development continues with great rapidity until the adult form can breed and more drought resistant eggs can be laid. This is a commonplace circumstance for brine shrimp, crayfish, grasshoppers, locusts, flies, mosquitoes, and various other desert arthropods; cases have been known in which more than a quarter of a century passed between successive generations of these tiny creatures in which the adult life cycle lasts for only a few weeks!

Competition among Animals

Competition among animals is even more intense than that among plants because the former involves not only indirect competition in the form of rivalry for space and resources but also the direct antagonism of predation. Animals with similar dietary habits compete for food and occasionally for territory. Animals in the same area also sometimes compete for water. And animals of the same species often compete for territory and for mates. Across this matrix of ecological rivalry is spread a prominent veneer of predator–prey relationships.

Many animals live together in social groups of varying sizes, generally referred to as *herds, flocks,* or *colonies.* This is a common, but by no means universal, behavioral characteristic among animals of the same species (Figure 11-21), and sometimes a social group encompasses several species in a communal relationship, such as zebras, wildebeest, and impalas living together on an East African savanna. Within such groupings, there may be a certain amount of cooperation among unrelated animals, but competition for both space and resources is likely to be prominent as well.

Competition among animals is a major part of the general struggle for existence that characterizes natural relationships in the biosphere. Individual animals are concerned either largely or entirely with their own survival (and sometimes with that of their mates) in response to normal primeval instincts. In some species, this concern is broadened to include their own young, although such maternal (and, much more rarely, paternal) instinct is by no means universal among animals. Still fewer species show individual concern for the group, as represented in colonies of ants or prides of lions. For the most part, however, animal survival is a matter of every creature for itself, with no individual helping another and no individual deliberately destroying another apart from normal predatory activities.

Cooperation among Animals

Symbiosis is the arrangement in which two dissimilar organisms live together. There are three principal forms:

1. *Mutualism* involves a mutually beneficial relationship between the two organisms, as exemplified by the tickbirds that are constant companions of many African *ungulates* (hoofed animals). The birds aid the mammals by removing ticks and other insects that infest the latter's skin, and the birds benefit by having a readily available supply of food (Figure 11-22).
2. *Commensalism* involves two dissimilar organisms living together with no injury to either, as represented by burrowing owls sharing the underground home of prairie dogs.

▲ **Figure 11-21** Seals and sea lions are among the most gregarious of mammals. This "hauling-out" beach near Point Año Nuevo on the central coast of California is crowded with elephant seals. *(Tom L. McKnight photo.)*

3. *Parasitism* involves one organism living on or in another, obtaining nourishment from the host, which is usually weakened and sometimes killed by the actions of the parasite. Mistletoe, for example, is a parasite of forest trees that is widespread in North America and Europe.

▲ **Figure 11-22** There is often a symbiotic relationship between hoofed animals and insectivorous birds. In this scene from South Africa's Kruger National Park two red-billed oxpeckers are riding on a zebra as they look for tasty morsels. *(Tom L. McKnight photo.)*

Zoogeographic Regions

The distribution of animals over the world is much more complex and irregular than that of plants, primarily because animals are mobile and therefore capable of more rapid dispersal. As with plants, however, the broad distributions of animals are reflective of the general distribution of energy and of food diversity. Thus, the richest faunal assemblages are found in the permissive environment of the humid tropics, and the dry lands and cold lands have the sparsest representations of both species and individuals.

When considering the global patterns of animal geography, most attention is usually paid to the distribution of terrestrial vertebrates, with other animals being given only casual notice. The classical definition of world zoogeographic regions is credited to the nineteenth-century British naturalist A. R. Wallace, whose scheme is based on the work of P. L. Sclater. As shown in Figure 11-23, nine **zoogeographic regions** are generally recognized, but you should understand that this or any other system of faunal regions represents average conditions and cannot portray some common pattern in which different groups of animals fit precisely. It is simply a composite of many diverse distributions of contemporary fauna.

The *Ethiopian Region* is primarily tropical or subtropical and has a rich and diverse fauna. It is separated from other regions by an oceanic barrier on three sides and a broad desert on the fourth. Despite its isolation, however, the Ethiopian Region has many faunal affinities with the Oriental and Palearctic regions. Its vertebrate fauna is the most diverse of all the zoogeographic regions and includes the greatest number of mammalian

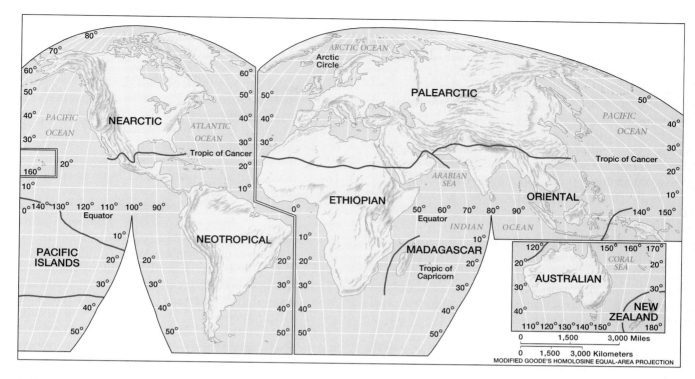

▲ **Figure 11-23** Zoogeographic regions of the world.

families, many of which have no living relatives outside Africa.

The *Oriental Region* is separated from the rest of Eurasia by mountains. Its faunal assemblage is generally similar to that of the Ethiopian Region, with somewhat less diversity. The Oriental Region has some *endemic* groups (endemic means these groups are found nowhere else) and a few species that are found only in the Oriental, Palearctic, and Australian regions. Many brilliantly colored birds live in the Oriental Region, and reptiles are numerous, with a particularly large number of venomous snakes.

The *Palearctic Region* includes the rest of Asia, all of Europe, and most of North Africa. Its fauna as a whole is much poorer than that of the two regions previously discussed, which is presumably a function of its location in higher latitudes with a more rigorous climate. This region has many affinities with all three bordering regions, particularly the Nearctic. Indeed, the Palearctic has only two minor mammal families (both rodents) that are endemic, and almost all its birds belong to families that have a very wide distribution.

The *Nearctic Region* consists of the nontropical portions of North America. Its faunal assemblage (apart from reptiles, which are well represented) is relatively poor and is largely a transitional mixture of Palearctic and Neotropical groups. It has few important groups of its own except for freshwater fishes. The considerable similarities between Palearctic and Nearctic fauna have persuaded some zoologists to group them into a single superregion, the *Holarctic*, which had a land connection in the recent geologic past when glaciation lowered

global sea level—the Bering land bridge across which considerable faunal dispersal took place (Figure 11-24).

The *Neotropical Region* encompasses all of South America and the tropical portion of North America. Its fauna is rich and distinctive, which reflects both a variety of habitats and a considerable degree of isolation from other regions. Neotropic faunal evolution often followed a path different from that in other regions. It contains a larger number of endemic mammal families

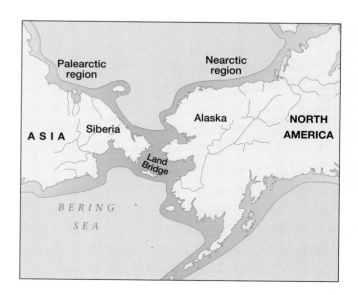

▲ **Figure 11-24** The Bering Land Bridge facilitated the interchange of animals between the Palearctic and Nearctic regions when sea level was lower during recent glaciations. Most of the dispersal was from the former to the latter.

than any other region. Moreover, its bird fauna is exceedingly diverse and conspicuous.

The *Madagascar Region,* restricted to the island of that name, has a fauna very different from that of nearby Africa. The Madagascan fauna is dominated by a relic assemblage of unusual forms in which primitive primates (lemurs) are notable.

The *New Zealand Region* has a unique fauna dominated by birds, with a remarkable proportion of flightless types. It has almost no terrestrial vertebrates (no mammals; only a few reptiles and amphibians).

The *Pacific Islands Region* includes a great many far-flung islands, mostly quite small. Its faunal assemblage is very limited.

The *Australian Region* is restricted to the continent of Australia and some adjacent islands, particularly New Guinea. Its fauna is by far the most distinctive of any major region, due primarily to its lengthy isolation from other principal landmasses. Its vertebrate fauna is noted for its paucity, but the lack of variety is made up for by uniqueness. There are only nine families of terrestrial mammals, but eight of them are unique to the region. The bird fauna is varied, and both pigeons and parrots reach their greatest diversity here. There is a notable scarcity of freshwater fishes and amphibians.

The Australian Region has a moderate amount of reptiles, mostly snakes and lizards, including the largest lizard of all: the Komodo dragon. Within the region, there are many significant differences between the fauna of Australia and that of New Guinea.

So why is the Australian Region so different from the other zoogeographic regions? The answer will become clearer when we discuss plate tectonics in Chapter 14, but for now, a quick explanation.

The Unique Biota of Australia The unusual faunal and floristic developments of Australia are largely the result of isolation. During long periods of time in the geologic past, while most of the continents were connected, the climate was more equitable, allowing for a vast evolution of plant species. As the continents began to separate about two hundred million years ago, climatic changes occurred requiring new adaptation and continued evolution. Australia became isolated from the rest of the continents, and so evolution continued with little genetic influence from the outside. This has engendered specialized evolutionary development among the isolated flora and fauna of Australia.

The most notable vegetation distinction is that nearly all the native trees in Australia—more than 90 percent of

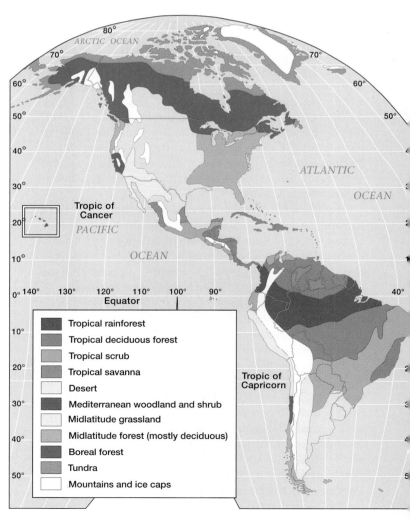

▶ **Figure 11-25** Major biomes of the world.

the total—are members of a single genus, *Eucalyptus.* Moreover, the eucalypts, of which there are more than 400 species, are native to no other continent but Australia. The shrubs and bushes of Australia are also dominated by a single genus, *Acacia,* which encompasses about half of the intermediate level (between grasses and trees) flora of the continent. Australia has several unusual grasses as well, but their distinctiveness is less pronounced.

If the flora of Australia is unusual, the fauna is absolutely unique; its assemblage of terrestrial animal life is completely without parallel in other parts of the world. This, too, is primarily the result of isolation. Through a chain of varied geological events and biological repercussions, the Australian continent functioned for millions of years as a faunal asylum, where rare and vulnerable species were able to flourish in relative isolation from the competitive and predatory pressures that influenced animal evolution in other parts of the world. The results of this isolation are bizarre, especially with regard to the highest forms of animal life—the mammals.

Unlike all other continents, the Australian fauna is dominated by a single primitive mammalian order, the marsupials (see Figure 11-17), an order that has long disappeared from most other parts of the world. Australia also provides the only continental home for an even more primitive group, the monotremes (see Figure 11-18). More remarkable, perhaps, is what is lacking in Australia—placental mammals, so notable elsewhere, are limited and inconspicuous. Australia is completely without representatives from such common groups as cats, dogs, bears, monkeys, hoofed animals, and many others. Partially because of the specialized character of the native mammals, feral livestock have become established in the wild in much greater profusion in Australia than elsewhere on Earth. Nine feral species exist in numbers that aggregate to several millions. In addition to the remarkable nature of the mammalian fauna, there are also unusual aspects to the bird, reptile, and invertebrate populations of Australia.

The biota of Australia, then, has many singular aspects, due primarily to the circumstances of isolated evolution, with significant recent human-induced modifications.

The Major Biomes

The major biomes of the world (Figure 11-25) are described below. As we learned earlier, most biomes are named for their dominant vegetation association, but

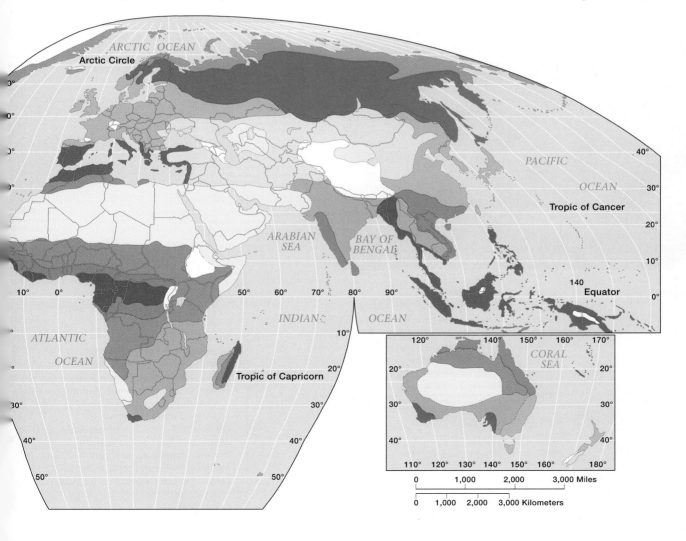

the biome concept also encompasses fauna as well as interrelationships with soil, climate, and topography.

Tropical Rainforest

You are probably familiar with the term *tropical rainforest* because it is used so often these days in the media. As we've seen, another name for this biome is *selva* (the Portuguese–Spanish word for "forest"), and the two terms are used interchangeably in this discussion. The distribution of this biome is closely related to climate—consistent rainfall and relatively high temperatures. Thus, there is an obvious correlation with the location of tropical wet (Af) and some tropical monsoon (Am) climatic regions (Figure 11-26).

The rainforest is probably the most complex of all terrestrial ecosystems, and the one with the greatest *species diversity* (many different species are found in an area, but often relatively few individuals of each species are present). It contains a bewildering variety of trees growing in close conjunction. Mostly they are tall, high-crowned, broadleaf evergreen species that never experience a seasonal leaf fall because seasons are unknown in this environment of continuous warmth and moistness (Figure 11-26a). The selva has a layered structure; the second layer down from the top usually forms a complete canopy of interlaced branches that provides continuous shade to the forest floor. Bursting through the canopy to form the top layer are the forest giants—tall trees that often grow to great heights above the general level. Beneath the canopy is an erratic third layer of lower trees, palms and tree ferns, able to survive in the shade. Sometimes still more layers of increasingly shade-tolerant trees grow at lower levels.

Undergrowth is relatively sparse in the tropical rainforest because the lack of light precludes the survival of most green plants. Only where there are gaps in the canopy, as alongside a river, does light reach the ground, resulting in the dense undergrowth associated with a jungle. *Epiphytes* like orchids and bromeliads hang from or perch on tree trunks and branches. Vines and lianas often dangle from the arching limbs.

(a)

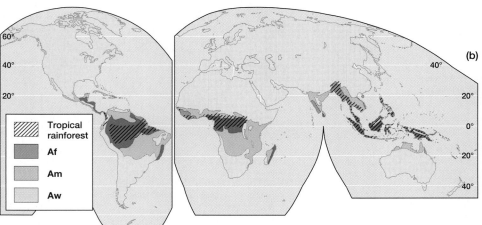

(b)

◀ **Figure 11-26** Tropical rainforest biome. **(a)** Mist rises from the forest canopy after heavy rains in the upper reaches of the Amazon basin in Ecuador. *(Dr. Morley Read/Science Photo Library/Photo Researchers, Inc.)* **(b)** World distribution of tropical rainforest. The colors show the three A climates from Figure 8-4; the diagonal lines indicate the rainforest, which occurs in tropical wet (Af) and tropical monsoonal (Am) climates.

The interior of the rainforest, then, is a region of heavy shade, high humidity, windless air, continuous warmth, and an aroma of mold and decomposition. As plant litter accumulates on the forest floor, it is acted on very rapidly by plant and animal decomposers. The upper layers of the forest are areas of high productivity, and there is a much greater concentration of nutrients in the vegetation than in the soil. Indeed, most selva soil is surprisingly infertile.

Rainforest fauna is largely arboreal (tree dwelling) because the principal food sources are in the canopy rather than on the ground. Large animals are generally scarce on the forest floor, although there are vast numbers of invertebrates. The animal life of this biome is characterized by creepers, crawlers, climbers, and flyers—monkeys, arboreal rodents, birds, tree snakes and lizards, and multitudes of invertebrates (Figure 11-27).

Tropical Deciduous Forest

The distribution of the *tropical deciduous forest* biome is shown in Figure 11-28. The locational correlation of this

▲ **Figure 11-27** Scarlet macaw in tropical rainstorm. *(Gregory G. Dimijian/Photo Researchers, Inc.)*

biome with specific climatic types is irregular and fragmented, indicating complex environmental relationships, although many tropical deciduous forests are found in the transition zone between tropical wet (Af) and tropical savanna (Aw) climates; such regions have high temperatures all year, but generally less—or more seasonal rainfall patterns—than in the tropical rainforest biome.

There is structural similarity between the selva and the tropical deciduous forest, but several important differences are usually obvious (Figure 11-28a). In the tropical deciduous forest, the canopy is less dense, the trees are somewhat shorter, and there are fewer layers, all these details being a response to either less total precipitation or less periodic precipitation. As a result of a pronounced dry period that lasts for several weeks or months, many of the trees shed their leaves at the same time, allowing light to penetrate to the forest floor. This light produces an understory of lesser plants that often grows in such density as to produce classic jungle conditions. The diversity of tree species is not as great in this biome as in the selva, but there is a greater variety of shrubs and other lesser plants.

The faunal assemblage of the tropical deciduous forest is generally similar to that of the rainforest. Although there are more ground-level vertebrates than in the selva, arboreal species such as monkeys, birds, bats, and lizards are particularly conspicuous in both biomes.

Tropical Scrub

The *tropical scrub* biome is widespread in drier portions of tropical savanna (Aw) climate and in some areas of subtropical steppe (BSh) climate (Figure 11-29). It is dominated by low-growing, scraggly trees and tall bushes, usually with an extensive understory of grasses (Figure 11-29a). The trees range from 3 to 9 meters (10 to 30 feet) in height. Their density is quite variable, with the trees sometimes growing in close proximity to one another but often spaced much more openly. Species diversity is much less than in the selva and tropical deciduous forest biomes; frequently just a few species comprise the bulk of the taller growth over vast areas. In the more tropical and wetter portions of the tropical scrub biome, most of the trees and shrubs are evergreen; elsewhere most species are deciduous. In some areas, a high proportion of the shrubs are thorny.

The fauna of tropical scrub regions is notably different from that of the two biomes previously discussed. There is a moderately rich assemblage of ground-dwelling mammals and reptiles, and of birds and insects.

Tropical Savanna

As Figure 11-30 shows, there is an incomplete correlation between the distribution of the *tropical savanna*

(a)

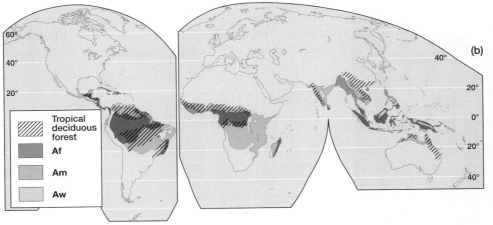

(b)

◀ **Figure 11-28** Tropical deciduous forest biome. **(a)** A tropical deciduous forest scene at about 2100 meters (7000 feet) elevation in central Mexico. *(Tom McHugh/Photo Researchers, Inc.)* **(b)** World distribution of tropical deciduous forest (diagonal lines) compared with distribution of A climates.

biome (also called the *tropical grassland* biome) and that of the tropical savanna (Aw) climate. The correlation tends to be most noticeable where seasonal rainfall contrasts are greatest, a condition particularly associated with the broad-scale annual shifting of the intertropical convergence zone (ITCZ).

Savanna lands are dominated by tall grasses (Figure 11-30a). Sometimes the grasses form a complete ground cover, but sometimes there is bare ground among dispersed tufts of grass in what is called a bunchgrass pattern. The name "savanna" without any modifier usually refers to areas that are virtually without shrubs or trees, but this type of savanna is not the most common. In most cases, a wide scattering of both types dots the grass-covered terrain,

and this mixture of plant forms is often referred to as *parkland* or *park savanna.*

In much of the savanna, the vegetation is degenerate because it has been created by human interference with natural processes. A considerable area of tropical deciduous forest and tropical scrub, and perhaps some tropical rainforest, has been converted to savanna over thousands of years through fires set by humans and through the grazing and browsing of domestic animals.

The savanna biome has a very pronounced seasonal rhythm. During the wet season, the grass grows tall, green, and luxuriant. At the onset of the dry season, the grass begins to wither, and before long the above-ground portion is dead and brown. At this time, too,

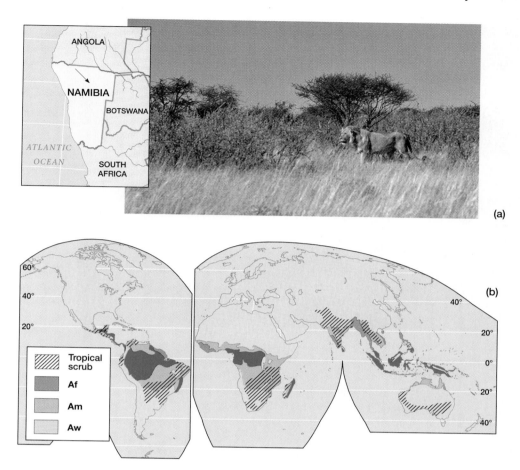

▲ **Figure 11-29**   Tropical scrub biome. **(a)** A tropical scrub scene in northern Namibia. *(Tom L. McKnight photo.)* **(b)** World distribution of tropical scrub (diagonal lines) compared with distribution of A climates. Much tropical scrub is found in Aw climates.

many of the trees and shrubs shed their leaves. The third "season" is the time of wildfires. The accumulation of dry grass provides abundant fuel, and most parts of the savannas experience natural burning every year or so. The recurrent grass fires are stimulating for the ecosystem, as they burn away the unpalatable portion of the grass without causing significant damage to shrubs and trees. When the rains of the next wet season arrive, the grasses spring into growth with renewed vigor.

Savanna fauna varies from continent to continent. The African savannas are the premier "big game" lands of the world, with an unmatched richness of large animals, particularly *ungulates* (hoofed animals) and carnivores (meat-eaters), but also including a remarkable diversity of other fauna. The Latin American savannas, on the other hand, have only a sparse population of large wildlife, with Asian and Australian areas intermediate between these two extremes.

FG9

Desert

In previous chapters, we noted a general decrease in precipitation as one moves away from the equator in

the low latitudes. This progression is matched by a gradation from the selva biome of the equator to the *desert* biome of the subtropics. The desert biome also occurs extensively in midlatitude locations in Asia, North America, and South America with a fairly close correlation to subtropical desert (BWh) and midlatitude desert (BWk) climates (Figure 11-31).

Desert vegetation is surprisingly variable (Figure 11-31a). It consists largely of xerophytic plants such as succulents and other drought-resisting plants with structural modifications that allow them to conserve moisture and drought-evading plants capable of hasty reproduction during brief rainy times. The plant cover is usually sparse, with considerable bare ground dotted by a scattering of individual plants. Typically the plants are shrubs, which occur in considerable variety, each with its own mechanisms to combat the stress of limited moisture. Succulents are common in the drier parts of most desert areas, and many desert plants have either tiny leaves or no leaves at all as a moisture-conserving strategy. Grasses and other herbaceous plants are widespread but sparse in desert areas. Despite the dryness, trees can be found sporadically in the desert, especially in Australia.

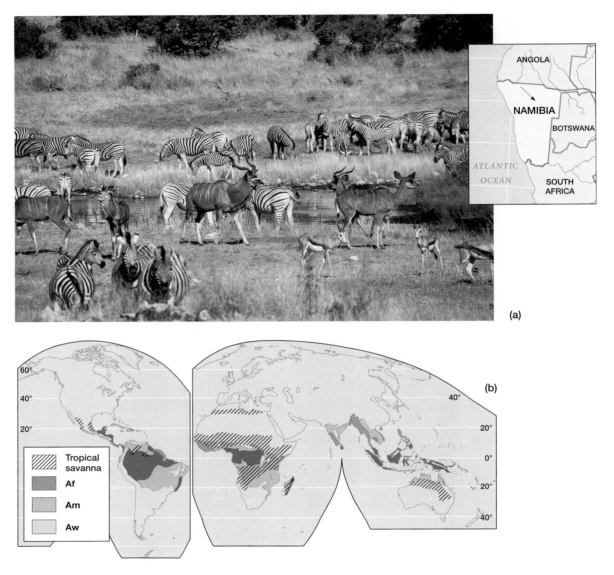

▲ **Figure 11-30** Tropical savanna biome. **(a)** A mixed array—zebra, kudu, and springbok—of ungulates surround a waterhole in a typical savanna landscape in Namibia's Etosha National Park. *(Tom L. McKnight photo.)* **(b)** World distribution of tropical savanna (diagonal lines) compared with distribution of A climates.

Animal life is exceedingly inconspicuous in most desert areas, leading to the erroneous idea that animals are nonexistent. In actuality, most deserts have a moderately diverse faunal assemblage, although the variety of large mammals is limited. A large proportion of desert animals avoid the principal periods of desiccating heat (daylight in general and the hot season in particular) by resting in burrows or crevices during the day and prowling at night (Figure 11-32).

Generally speaking, life in the desert biome is characterized by an appearance of stillness. In favorable times and in favored places (around water holes and oases), however, there is a great increase in biotic activities, and sometimes the total biomass is of remarkable proportions. Favorable times are at night, and particularly after rains. For example, a heavy rain might trigger the germination of wildflower seeds that had remained dormant for decades.

Mediterranean Woodland and Shrub

As Figure 11-33 shows, the *mediterranean woodland and shrub* biome is found in six widely scattered and relatively small areas of the midlatitudes, all of which experience the pronounced dry summer–wet winter precipitation typical of mediterranean (Cs) climates. In this biome, the dominant vegetation associations are physically very similar to each other but taxonomically quite varied. The biome is dominated mostly by a dense growth of woody shrubs known as a *chaparral* in North America, but having

(a)

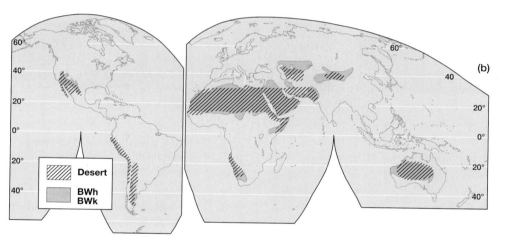

(b)

▲ **Figure 11-31** Desert biome.
(a) Natural vegetation typically
is spindly and thorny in deserts,
as in this scene from Red Rock
Canyon in California's Mojave
Desert. *(Darrel Hess photo.)*
(b) World distribution of desert
(diagonal lines) compared with
distribution of B climates.

▲ **Figure 11-32** This fierce-looking thorny devil lizard in
Western Australia is just 10 centimeters (4 inches) long. *(Tom L.
McKnight photo.)*

other names in other areas; chaparral includes
many species of *sclerophyllous* plants, adapted to the
prominent summer dry season by the presence of
small, hard leaves that inhibit moisture loss. A second significant plant association of mediterranean
regions is an open grassy woodland, in which the
ground is almost completely grass covered but has
a considerable scattering of trees as well.

The plant species vary from region to region. Oaks
of various kinds are by far the most significant genus in
the Northern Hemisphere mediterranean lands, sometimes occurring as prominent medium-sized trees but
also appearing as a more stunted, shrubby growth. In
all areas, the trees and shrubs are primarily broadleaf
evergreens. Their leaves are mostly small and have a
leathery texture or waxy coating, which inhibits water
loss during the long dry season. Moreover, most plants
have deep roots.

(a)

(b)

(c)

(d)

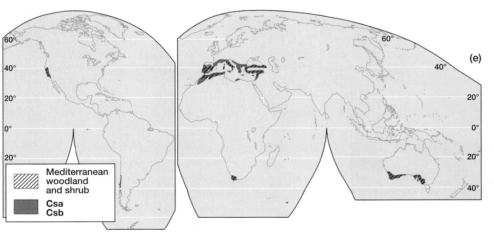

(e)

▲ **Figure 11-33** Mediterranean woodland and shrub biome. Wildfires are a natural and recurrent event in many biomes, but the seasonal rhythm in mediterranean lands is particularly notable. These four photographs record the annual pattern in the Mount Lofty Ranges of South Australia. **(a)** Winter is moist, mild, and green. **(b)** Early summer is hot, dry, and brown. **(c)** Then comes the fire season. **(d)** Late summer is the black time. *(Tom L. McKnight photos.)* **(e)** World distribution of mediterranean woodland and shrub (diagonal lines) compared with distribution of Cs climates.

Summer is a virtually rainless season in mediterranean climates, and so summer fires are relatively common. Many of the plants are adapted to rapid recovery after a wildfire has swept over the area (Figure 11-33d). Indeed, as noted in Chapter 10, some species have seeds that are released for germination only after the heat of a fire has caused their seedpods to open. Part of the seasonal rhythm of this biome is that winter floods sometimes follow summer fires, as slopes left unprotected by the burning away of grass and lower shrubs are susceptible to abrupt erosive runoff if the winter rains arrive before the vegetation has a chance to resprout.

The fauna of this biome is not particularly distinctive. Seed-eating, burrowing rodents are common, as are some bird and reptile groups. There is a general overlap of animals between this biome and adjacent ones.

Midlatitude Grassland

Vast *midlatitude grasslands* occur widely in North America and Eurasia (Figure 11-34). In the Northern Hemisphere, the locational coincidence between this biome and the steppe (BSh and BSk) climatic type is very pronounced. The smaller Southern Hemisphere areas (mostly the *pampa* of Argentina and the *veldt* of South Africa) have less distinct climatic correlations.

The vegetation typical of a grassland biome is a general response either to a lack of precipitation sufficient to support larger plant forms or to the frequency of fires (both natural and human induced) that prevent the growth of tree or shrub seedlings. In the wetter areas of a grassland biome, the grasses grow tall and the term *prairie* is often applied in North America. In drier regions, the grasses are shorter; such growth is often referred to as *steppe* (Figure 11-34a). Sometimes a continuous ground cover is missing, and the grasses grow in discrete tufts as bunchgrass or tussock grass.

Most of the grass species are perennials, lying dormant during the winter and sprouting anew the following summer. Trees are mostly restricted to riparian locations, whereas shrubs and bushes occur sporadically on rocky sites. Grass fires are fairly common in summer, which helps to explain the relative scarcity of shrubs. The woody plants cannot tolerate fires and can generally survive only on dry slopes where there is little grass cover to fuel a fire.

Grasslands provide extensive pastures for grazing animals, and before encroachment by humans drastically changed population sizes, the grassland fauna comprised large numbers of relatively few species. The larger herbivores were often migratory prior to human

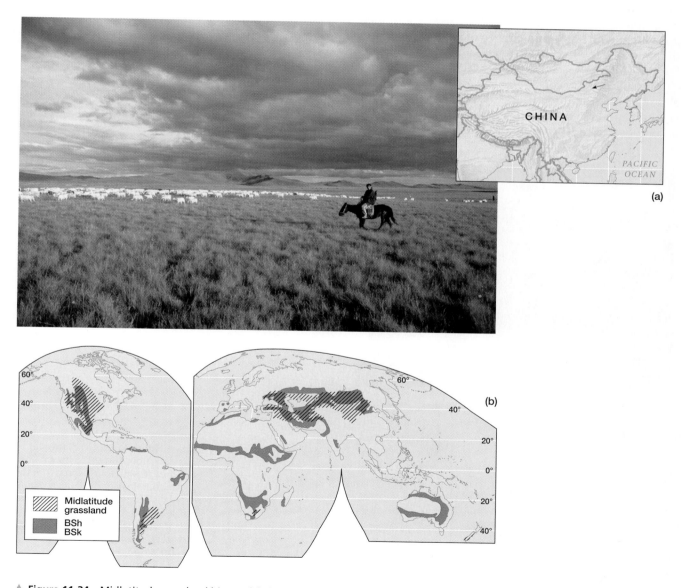

▲ **Figure 11-34** Midlatitude grassland biome. **(a)** Shepherd and flock of sheep on the steppe of China. *(© Tiziana and Gianni Baldizzone/CORBIS.)* **(b)** World distribution of midlatitude grassland (diagonal lines) compared with distribution of BS climates.

settlement. Many of the smaller animals spend all or part of their lives underground, where they find some protection from heat, cold, and fire.

Midlatitude Deciduous Forest

Extensive areas on all Northern Hemisphere continents, as well as more limited tracts in the Southern Hemisphere, were originally covered with a forest of largely broadleaf deciduous trees (Figure 11-35). Except in hilly country, a large proportion of this *midlatitude deciduous forest* has been cleared for agriculture and other types of human use, so that very little of the original natural vegetation remains.

The forest is characterized by a fairly dense growth of tall broadleaf trees with interwoven branches that provide a complete canopy in summer. Some smaller trees and shrubs exist at lower levels, but for the most part, the forest floor is relatively barren of undergrowth. In winter, the appearance of the forest changes dramatically, owing to the seasonal fall of leaves (Figure 11-35a).

Tree species vary considerably from region to region, although most are broadleaf and deciduous. The principal exception is in eastern Australia, where the forest is composed almost entirely of varieties of eucalyptus,

which are broadleaf evergreens. Northern Hemisphere regions have a northward gradational mixture with needleleaf evergreen species. An unusual situation in the southeastern United States finds extensive stands of pines (needleleaf evergreens) rather than deciduous species occupying most of the well-drained sites above the valley bottoms. In the Pacific Northwest of the United States, the forest association is primarily evergreen coniferous rather than broadleaf deciduous.

This biome generally has the richest assemblage of fauna to be found in the midlatitudes, although it does not have the diversity to match that of most tropical biomes. It has (or had) a considerable variety of birds and mammals, and in some areas reptiles and amphibians are well represented. Summer brings a diverse and active population of insects and other arthropods. All animal life is less numerous (partly due to migrations and hibernation) and less conspicuous in winter.

Boreal Forest

One of the most extensive biomes is the *boreal forest*, sometimes called *taiga* after the Russian word for the northern fringe of the boreal forest in that country (paralleling the way these synonyms are used to describe

(a)

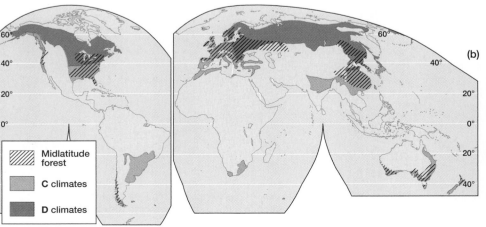

(b)

◀ **Figure 11-35** Midlatitude deciduous forest biome. **(a)** This midlatitude forest scene is in the mountains near Shizuoka, Japan. As is common in some midlatitude locations, the forest here consists of both deciduous and evergreen trees. *(Darrel Hess photo.)* **(b)** World distribution of midlatitude forest (diagonal lines) before human activities made significant changes in this biome. The colors indicate distribution of C and D climates.

climates, as mentioned in Chapter 8). The boreal forest occupies a vast expanse of northern North America and Eurasia (Figure 11-36). There is very close correlation between the location of the boreal forest biome and the subarctic (Dfc) climatic type, with a similar correlation between the locations of the tundra climate and the tundra biome.

This great northern forest contains perhaps the simplest assemblage of plants of any biome (Figure 11-36a). Most of the trees are conifers, nearly all needleleaf evergreens, with the important exception of the tamarack or larch which drops its needles in winter. The variety of species is limited to mostly pines, firs, and spruces extending broadly in homogeneous stands. In some places, the coniferous cover is interrupted by areas of deciduous trees. These deciduous stands are also of limited variety (mostly birch, poplar, and aspen) and often represent a seral situation following a forest fire.

The trees grow taller and more densely near the southern margins of this biome, where the summer growing season is longer and warmer. Near the northern margins, the trees are spindly, short, and more openly spaced. Undergrowth is normally not dense beneath the forest canopy, but a layer of deciduous shrubs sometimes grows in profusion. The ground is usually covered with a complete growth of mosses and lichens, with some grasses in the south and a considerable accumulation of decaying needles overall.

Poor drainage is typical in summer, due partially to permanently frozen subsoil, which prevents downward percolation of water, and partially to the derangement of normal surface drainage by the action of glaciers during the recent Pleistocene ice age. Thus, bogs and swamps are numerous, and the ground is generally spongy in summer. During the long winters, of course, all is frozen.

The immensity of the boreal forest gives an impression of biotic productivity, but such is not the case. Harsh climate, floristic homogeneity, and slow plant growth produce only a limited food supply for animals. Faunal species diversity is limited, although the

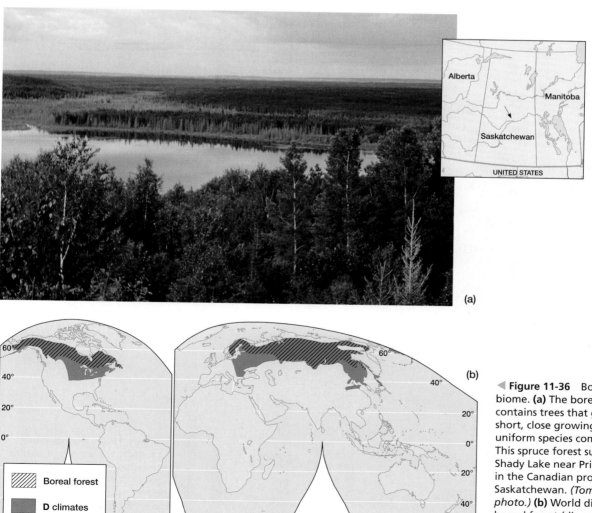

(a)

(b)

◀ **Figure 11-36** Boreal forest biome. **(a)** The boreal forest contains trees that generally are short, close growing, and of uniform species composition. This spruce forest surrounds Shady Lake near Prince Albert in the Canadian province of Saskatchewan. *(Tom L. McKnight photo.)* **(b)** World distribution of boreal forest (diagonal lines) compared with distribution of D climates.

number of individuals of some species is astounding. With relatively few animal species in such a vast biome, populations sometimes fluctuate enormously within the space of only a year or so. Mammals are represented prominently by fur-bearers (Figure 11-37) and by a few species of ungulates. Birds are numerous and fairly diverse in summer, but nearly all migrate to milder latitudes in winter. Insects are totally absent in winter but superabundant during the brief summer.

Tundra

The *tundra* is essentially a cold desert or grassland in which moisture is scarce and summers so short and cool that trees are unable to survive. This biome is distributed along the northern edge of the Northern Hemisphere continents, correlating closely to the distribution of tundra (ET) climate (Figure 11-38). The plant cover consists of a considerable mixture of species, many of them in dwarf forms (Figure 11-38a). Included are grasses, mosses, lichens, flowering herbs, and a scattering of low shrubs. These plants often occur in a dense, ground-hugging arrangement, although some

▲ **Figure 11-37** Bears live in diverse habitats, but mostly in cold climates. This grizzly bear inhabits Katmai National Park in Alaska. *(Tom L. McKnight photo.)*

(a)

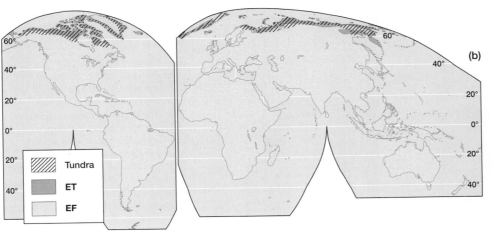

(b)

◄ **Figure 11-38** Tundra biome.
(a) A luxuriant growth of tundra vegetation in the short Arctic summer. The Alaska Range is in the background. *(Charlie Ott/ Photo Researchers, Inc.)*
(b) World distribution of tundra (diagonal lines) compared with distribution of E climates.

▲ **Figure 11-39**   Alpine tundra vegetation high in the Rocky Mountains. *(Darrel Hess photo.)*

places have a more sporadic cover with considerable bare ground interspersed. The plants complete their annual cycles hastily during the brief summer, when the ground is often moist and waterlogged because of inadequate surface drainage and particularly inadequate subsurface drainage.

Animal life is dominated by birds and insects during the summer. Extraordinary numbers of birds flock to the tundra for summer nesting, migrating southward as winter approaches. Mosquitoes, flies, and other insects proliferate astoundingly during the short warm season, laying eggs that can survive the bitter winter. Other forms of animal life are scarcer—a few species of mammals and freshwater fishes but almost no reptiles or amphibians.

Alpine Tundra   An alpine version of tundra is found in many high-elevation areas. Many mountain areas above the timberline exhibit areas with a sparse cover of vegetation consisting of herbaceous plants, grasses, and low shrubs (Figure 11-39).

Human Modification of Natural Distribution Patterns

Thus far in our discussion of the biosphere, most of our attention has been focused on "natural" conditions, that is, events and processes that take place in nature without the aid or interference of human activities. Such natural processes have been going on for millennia, and their effects on floral and faunal distribution patterns have normally been very slow and gradual. The pristine environment, uninfluenced by humankind, experiences its share of abrupt and dramatic events, to be sure, but environmental changes generally proceed at a gradual pace. When *Homo sapiens* appear, however, the tempo changes dramatically.

People are capable of exerting extraordinary influences on the distribution of plants and animals. Not only is the magnitude of the changes likely to be great, but also the speed with which they are affected is sometimes exceedingly rapid. In broadest perspective, humankind exerts three types of direct influences on biotic distributions: physical removal of organisms, habitat modification, and artificial translocation of organisms.

Physical Removal of Organisms

One of humankind's most successful skills is in the elimination of other living things. As human population increases and spreads over the globe, there is often a wholesale removal of native plants and animals to make way for the severely modified landscape that is thought necessary for civilization. The natural plant and animal inhabitants are cut down, plowed up, paved over, burned, poisoned, shot, trapped, and otherwise eradicated in actions that have far-reaching effects on overall distribution patterns.

Habitat Modification

Habitat modification is another activity in which humankind excels. The soil environment is changed by farming, grazing, engineering, and construction practices (Figure 11-40); the atmospheric environment is degraded by the introduction of impurities of various kinds; the waters of the planet are impounded, diverted, and polluted. All these deeds influence the native plants and animals in the affected areas.

Among the most dramatic recent human-initiated changes to global habitat have involved the removal of vast areas of tropical rainforest.

Tropical Rainforest Removal   Throughout most of history, rainforests were relatively inaccessible and as a consequence they were little affected by human activities. Since the twentieth century, however, rainforests have been exploited and devastated at an accelerating pace, and over the past 25 years or so, tropical deforestation has become one of Earth's most serious environmental problems. The exact rate of deforestation around the world is not precisely known, but conservative estimates suggest that tropical rainforest is currently being lost at a rate of about 11 million hectares (27 million acres) per year; this amounts to a loss of 30,000 hectares (74,000 acres) per day or 21 hectares (51 acres) each minute. More than half of the original African rainforest is now gone, about 45 percent of Asia's rainforest no longer exists, and the proportion in Latin America is approaching 40 percent.

▲ **Figure 11-40** An overgrazed range in the Colorado high country illustrates human-induced habitat modification caused by overstocking of livestock in the area to the right of the fence. The locale is near Central City. *(Tom L. McKnight photo.)*

The current situation varies in the five major rainforest regions:

1. The rate of deforestation is highest in southern and southeastern Asia, primarily associated with commercial timber exploitation, especially for teak and mahogany.
2. The current rate of deforestation is relatively low in central Africa.
3. Timber harvesting and agricultural expansion are responsible for a continuing high rate of forest clearing in West Africa. Nigeria has lost about 90 percent of its forests, Ghana, 80 percent.
4. Deforestation of the Amazon region as a percentage of the total area of rainforest has been moderate (perhaps 15 percent of the total has been cleared), but it continues at a rapid pace.
5. Much of the very rapid deforestation in Central America has been due to expanded cattle ranching (Figure 11-41).

As the forest goes, so goes its habitability for both indigenous peoples and native animal life. In the mid-1980s it was calculated that tropical deforestation was responsible for the extermination of one species per day; by the mid-1990s it was estimated that the rate was two species per hour. Moreover, loss of the forests contributes to accelerated soil erosion, drought, flooding, water quality degradation, declining agricultural productivity, and greater poverty for rural inhabitants. In addition, atmospheric carbon dioxide continues to be increased because burning trees as a way of clearing forest releases carbon to the air.

The irony of tropical deforestation is that the anticipated economic benefits are usually illusory. Much of the forest clearing is in response to the social pressure of overcrowding and poverty in societies where many people are landless. The governments open "new lands" for settlement in the rainforest. The settlers clear the land for crop or livestock. The result is almost always an initial nutrient pulse of high soil productivity, followed in only two or three years by a pronounced fertility decline as the nutrients are quickly leached and cropped out of the soil, weed species rapidly invade, and erosion becomes rampant (Figure 11-42). Sustainable agriculture can generally be expected only with continuous heavy fertilization, a costly procedure.

The forests, of course, are renewable. If left alone, they can regenerate, providing there are seed trees in the vicinity and the soil has not been stripped of all its nutrients. The loss of *biodiversity*, however, is a much more serious problem because extinction is irreversible. Valuable potential resources—pharmaceutical products, new food crops, natural insecticides, industrial materials—may disappear before they are even discovered. Wild plants and animals that could be combined with domesticated cousins to impart resistance to disease, insects, parasites, and other environmental stresses may also be lost.

Much concern has been expressed about tropical deforestation, and some concrete steps have been taken. The development of *agroforestry* (planting crops with trees, rather than cutting down the trees and replacing them with crops) is being fostered in many areas. The United Nations Educational, Scientific, and Cultural

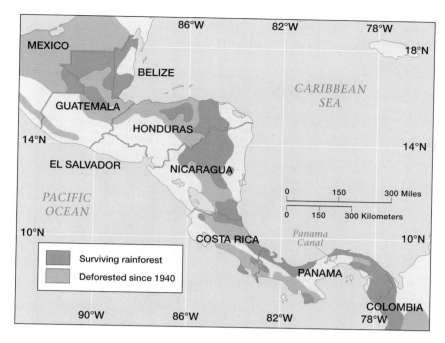

◀ **Figure 11-41** Shrinkage in the Central American rainforest since 1940. This region has one of the fastest rates of deforestation in the world.

Organization (UNESCO) administers the *Man and the Biosphere Programme* that coordinates an international effort to establish and protect biosphere reserves. The goal of this project is to set aside tracts of largely pristine land—including regions of tropical rainforest—to preserve biodiversity before it is lost to development.

▲ **Figure 11-42** When rainforests are cleared for agriculture, the results are often small yields and accelerated soil erosion. This scene is from central Thailand. *(Holt Studios International [Nigel Cattlin]/Photo Researchers, Inc.)*

PEOPLE AND THE ENVIRONMENT Rainforest Loss in Brazil

The country of Brazil contains about one-third of the world's tropical forest, most of it part of the vast rainforest spreading across the Amazon River basin. Although the rainforest has supported a sparse human population for thousands of years, over the last half century large tracts of the forest have been opened up for settlers. As a consequence, the pristine forest is being cleared for settlements, agriculture, ranching, and logging.

The Brazilian government completed construction of the Cuiabá-Port Velho highway across the province of Rondônia in 1960. Although the road opened up the region to immigrants and development, the forest was still relatively unchanged 15 years later (Figure 11-B). But by the late 1980s, the rate of deforestation had increased substantially and the region had taken on a "fishbone" pattern as forest was cleared along an expanding network of roads. By 2001 the extent of deforestation was extraordinary (Figure 11-C). Deforestation of this scale is taking place in a number of areas in the Amazon basin. In the year 2004, in Brazil alone more than 26,000 square kilometers (10,000 square miles) of rainforest were lost.

Such widespread deforestation is leading to a loss of both habitat and species, and in the end, many of the uses of the cleared land are simply not sustainable. In Rondônia, less than 10 percent of agricultural land use has gone toward potentially sustainable perennial crops such as cacao and coffee; much of the rest is either used for cattle grazing or annual crops—and this land must usually be abandoned in a few years after the generally poor tropical soils are depleted of nutrients. Once abandoned for agriculture, it may be decades before the forest can grow back to near its original density and composition.

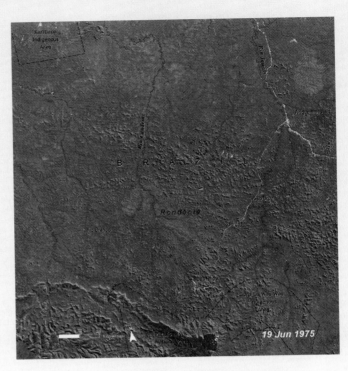

▲ **Figure 11-B** The Brazilian state of Rondônia in 1975. *(Landsat image courtesy of the United Nations Environmental Programme.)*

▲ **Figure 11-C** The same region of Rondônia in 2001. *(Landsat image courtesy of the United Nations Environmental Programme.)*

At present, about 300 reserves have been established in more than 75 countries, encompassing about 12 million hectares (30 million acres) of land.

Meanwhile, the sounds of ax, chain saw, and bull-dozer continue to be heard throughout the tropical forest lands.

Artificial Translocation of Organisms

People are capable of elaborate rearrangement of the natural complement of plants and animals in almost every part of the world. This is shown most clearly with domesticated species—crops, livestock, pets. There is now, for example, more corn than native grass-es in Iowa, more cattle than native gazelles in the Sudan, more canaries than native thrushes in Detroit. More importantly for our discussion here, humans have also accounted for many introductions of wild plants and animals into "new" habitats; such organisms are called **exotic species** in their new homelands.

In some cases, the introduction of exotic species was deliberate. A few examples among a great many in-clude the taking of prickly-pear cactus from Arizona to Australia; crested wheat grass from Russia to Kansas; European boar from Germany to Tennessee; prong-horn antelope from Oregon to Hawaii; and red fox from England to New Zealand. Frequently, however, the introduction of an exotic species was an accidental result of human carelessness. The European flea, for example, has become one of the most widespread crea-tures on Earth because it has been an unseen accompa-niment to human migrations all over the world. Similarly, the English sparrow and European brown rat have inadvertently been introduced to all inhabited continents by traveling as stowaways on ships.

One other type of human-induced translocation of animals involves the deliberate release or accidental escape of livestock to become established as a "wild" (properly termed *feral*) population. This has happened in many parts of the world, most notably in North America and Australia (Figure 11-43).

In many parts of the world, natural biotic distribu-tion patterns have been rearranged through deliberate and accidental human efforts to translocate plants and animals. When an exotic (nonnative) species is released in a new area, the results are usually one of two ex-tremes. Either it dies out in a short time because of en-vironmental hazards and/or competitive–predatory pressures, or the introduced species finds both a benign climate and an unfilled ecologic niche and is able to flourish extraordinarily. When the latter situation oc-curs, the results are occasionally salutary, but in many cases they are unsatisfactory and sometimes absolutely disastrous.

The world abounds with examples that could be cited—sparrows and starlings, rabbits and pigs, mon-gooses and mynas, lantana and prickly pear, mesquite and broomweed, Australia and New Zealand, Hawaii and Mauritius; the list of things and places is virtually endless. An argument could be made, however, that the recent and contemporary biotic history of Florida rep-resents one of the worst examples of all, made all the more frightening because the cumulative impact will almost surely be much worse in the near future than it is already.

Biotic Rearrangement: The Sad Case of Florida

Florida is a very attractive place for human settlement. Particularly in the last three decades, it has experienced one of the highest rates of in-migration of people ever known anywhere in the world. The major inducement is climate. A mild winter more than compensates for a hot summer, particularly when the latter can be ameliorated by artificial air-conditioning. Florida's

▲ **Figure 11-43** Burros are prominent feral animals in much of the southwestern desert area of the United States. This group is in the Panamint Mountains of California. *(Tom L. McKnight photo.)*

▲ **Figure 11-44**   Hydrilla-choked canal near Everglades National Park, Florida. *(William F. Campbell/Time Life Pictures/Getty Images.)*

subtropical climate is also very suitable for many plants and animals. The tropical regions of the world contain an incredible variety of biota. Only a small fraction of this total is native to Florida, but a great many alien tropical species are capable of survival and proliferation in the Sunshine State if they can but gain a foothold.

Humankind has been energetically and capriciously willing to help in providing that foothold. In the last few years, Florida has become the major world center for the animal-import industry, and it is almost as important as a focus for plant imports as well. It is inevitable that many of these organisms escape from confinement and try their luck at survival in the wild. Others are deliberately turned loose—by fishers who want new quarry, pet owners who are tired of their pets, gardeners who would like a new shrub in the backyard. Still others are brought in inadvertently, in the holds of freighters or the baggage of travelers. Through these and similar events, which have been accelerating year by year, Florida has become what has been termed a "biological cesspool" of introduced life forms. More than 50 species of exotic animals, not counting invertebrates, have now taken up residence in Florida, and exotic plants are almost too numerous to count.

Not all the introduced species have established viable, breeding populations in the wild, but many of them have, and some occur in plague proportions. Exotics are most likely to prosper in a new environment when the natural ecosystems of the host region are unstable. Florida has experienced massive disruption of its ecosystems in recent years due to the explosive human population increment and the associated accelerated changes in land use. Particularly contributory has been the modification of drainage systems in this flattish state of normally expansive water surfaces (lakes, swamps, marshes, everglades). In contemporary Florida, human interference has destabilized the

natural ecosystems, and human-induced introductions provide a large and steady source of exotic plants and animals on a year-round basis.

Dozens of species of exotic plants have become widespread, and almost all of them are continually expanding their ranges. Prominent among them is the melaleuca tree from Australia. Seeds from these "paperbark" trees were deliberately sown by airplane in the 1930s in the hope of developing a timber industry in the swamplands of southwestern Florida. Only recently have they begun to spread extensively, in response to increased artificial drainage and to wildfires. They prosper and flourish in disturbed land much better than the native species do. The spread of melaleuca has changed swamp to forest, radically altering the entire regional ecosystem, but the lumber potential has turned out to be negligible.

Much more extensive and deleterious in impact has been the spread of exotic aquatic weeds, which now infest more than 200,000 hectares (a half million acres) of Florida's waters. The two most significant are the water hyacinth and the hydrilla.

1. The Amazon water hyacinth grows incredibly fast. A single plant can double its mass in two weeks under ideal conditions. These plants grow so thickly as to impede boat traffic and shade out other flora, sometimes to the extent that the water receives virtually no oxygen, and biological deserts are created. They are very difficult to cut out, and even when this is done, the decay of displaced portions puts more nutrients into the water, which promotes even lusher growth.

2. The hydrilla is a native of tropical Africa and Southeast Asia that was brought to Florida as an aquarium plant but has now spread vastly in the wild (Figure 11-44). It has the form of long green tentacles, growing 2.5 centimeters (an inch) a day, which can become intertwined and form dense mats that will stop an outboard motor propeller dead. It overwhelms native plants and can even thrive in deep water where there is almost total darkness. Tiny pieces, when broken off, can regenerate into a new plant, so it is easily spread by birds, boat propellers, and other things that move from lake to lake. It has already clogged more than 60,000 hectares (150,000 acres) of waterways in Florida and has become established in almost all other southeastern states.

Exotic animals are less overwhelming in their occurrence, but many species are already well established and some are spreading rapidly. A sampling of nonaquatic species includes Mexican armadillos, Indian rhesus monkeys, Australian parakeets, Cuban lizards, Central American jaguarundi cats, South American giant toads, Great Plains jack rabbits, Amazonian parrots, and many others.

▲ **Figure 11-45** A walking catfish in Florida. *(Bruce Coleman, Inc.)*

canals; thus any introduced freshwater species now has access to most of the stream systems of the state. Moreover, Florida has a great abundance of springs that have stable water temperatures throughout the year, providing havens for many tropical fish that would otherwise find winter water temperatures below their tolerance limits.

South American acaras are already the dominant canal fish throughout southern Florida, and African tilapias are the most numerous fish in many lakes in the central part of the state. The greatest present and potential threat, however, is the so-called walking catfish from Southeast Asia, which numbers in the millions throughout the state and is considered to be "out of control," with "no practical method of eradication" (Figure 11-45). These catfish eat insect larvae until the insects are gone; then they eat other fish. They are overwhelming rivals of almost all the native fish, eventually reducing the entire freshwater community to a single species—the walking catfish. They are significantly hardier than other fish because if they don't like the local waters, or if the waters dry up, they can simply hike across land, breathing directly from the air, until they find a new lake or stream.

Exotic fish are much more numerous than their terrestrial counterparts and pose even more serious problems, primarily through fierce competition with native species. Most of the drainage systems of Florida are interconnected by numerous irrigation and drainage

Chapter 11 Learning Review

Key Terms

Before answering the study questions below, review the definitions of the following key terms (page references are provided for you):

adret slope *(p. 321)*
angiosperm *(p. 315)*
annual (plant). *(p. 314)*
biome *(p. 313)*
broadleaf tree *(p. 315)*
climax vegetation *(p. 317)*
conifer *(p. 315)*
deciduous tree *(p. 315)*
desert *(p. 319)*
ecosystem *(p. 313)*
ecotone *(p. 314)*
endothermic *(p. 323)*

evergreen tree *(p. 315)*
exotic species *(p. 347)*
forest *(p. 318)*
grassland *(p. 319)*
gymnosperm *(p. 315)*
herbaceous plant *(p. 315)*
hydrophyte *(p. 316)*
hygrophyte *(p. 316)*
invertebrate *(p. 323)*
needleleaf tree *(p. 315)*
perennial (plant) *(p. 314)*
riparian vegetation *(p. 321)*

shrubland *(p. 318)*
symbiosis *(p. 327)*
treeline *(p. 321)*
tundra *(p. 319)*
ubac slope *(p. 321)*
vertebrate *(p. 323)*
vertical zonation *(p. 320)*
wetland *(p. 320)*
woodland *(p. 318)*
woody plant *(p. 315)*
xerophytic adaptation *(p. 316)*
zoogeographic regions *(p. 328)*

Study Questions for Key Concepts

After studying this chapter, you should be able to answer the following questions:

Ecosystems and Biomes (p. 313)
1. Contrast and explain the concepts of *ecosystem* and *biome.*
2. What is an *ecotone*?

Terrestrial Flora (p. 314)
3. What is the difference between a *perennial* and an *annual*?

4. Explain the difference between a *gymnosperm* and an *angiosperm*. Name trees that are examples of each.
5. Explain the difference between a *deciduous* tree and an *evergreen* tree. Name trees that are examples of each.
6. Explain the difference between a *broadleaf* tree and a *needleleaf* tree. Name trees that are examples of each.

7. Describe some typical *xerophytic* adaptations of plants.
8. Describe some typical *hygrophytic* adaptations of plants.
9. Explain the concept of *climax vegetation.*
10. Why do trees require so much more moisture to survive than grass?
11. What is the difference between *forest* and *woodland*?
12. What are the similarities and differences among *savanna, prairie,* and *steppe*?
13. In what ways is an increase in altitude similar to an increase in latitude?
14. What is the *treeline*?
15. What generally happens to the elevation of the treeline going from the equator toward the poles? Why?
16. What is the difference between an *adret slope* and a *ubac slope*? How and why is vegetation likely to be different on an adret slope and a ubac slope?
17. What is *riparian* vegetation?

Terrestrial Fauna (p. 322)

18. What are some basic characteristics that distinguish plants from animals?
19. Contrast *invertebrates* with *vertebrates*. Provide one example of each.
20. Describe the distinguishing characteristics of *mammals.*
21. What are the advantages for an animal to be *endothermic*?
22. Distinguish among the three ways (physiological, behavioral, reproductive) animals adapt to the environment.
23. Describe and explain at least one animal adaptation to desert life.

24. What is meant by *symbiosis*?
25. Distinguish between *mutualism* and *parasitism.*

Zoogeographic Regions (p. 328)

26. Explain the concept of *zoogeographic regions.*
27. Why are the flora and fauna of the Australian Region so distinctive?

The Major Biomes (p. 331)

28. What climate characteristics are most closely associated with the *tropical rainforest* biome?
29. Contrast the general characteristics of the *tropical rainforest, tropical deciduous forest,* and *tropical scrub* biomes.
30. Describe the seasonal patterns of the *tropical savanna* biome.
31. Discuss the general climate characteristics and types of vegetation associated with the *mediterranean woodland and shrub* biome.
32. What are the general differences in climate associated with the tropical savanna and *midlatitude grassland* biomes?
33. Describe and explain the global distribution of the *desert* biome.
34. What are the general differences in climate associated with the *midlatitude deciduous forest* and *boreal forest* biomes?
35. Refer to the climate map (Figure 8-4) and biomes map in the textbook (Figure 11-25). The *boreal forest* biome generally corresponds to the distribution of which climate type?
36. Contrast the general *species diversity* in the tropical rainforest and boreal forest biomes.
37. Describe the general vegetation cover found in the *tundra* biome.

Human Modification of Natural Distribution Patterns (p. 343)

38. Why is it usually difficult to maintain productive agriculture year after year in a cleared area of tropical rainforest?

39. What is an *exotic species*?

40. Describe and explain one example of an exotic species that has disrupted a region's natural ecosystem.

Additional Resources

Books:

Park, Chris C. *Tropical Rainforests.* New York: Routledge, 1992.

Terborgh, John. *Diversity and the Tropical Rain Forest.* New York: Scientific American Library, 1992.

Tivy, Joy. *Biogeography: A Study of Plants in the Ecosphere,* 3rd ed. London: Longman Group, 1993.

Internet Sites:

The Earth Observatory

http://earthobservatory.nasa.gov/

The Earth Observatory is National Aeronautics and Space Administration's (NASA's) Internet site that provides information and images of Earth.

The National Map

http://www.nationalmap.usgs.gov/

The National Map is an interactive map service that provides access to a wide range of geospatial data.

U.S. Fish and Wildlife Service

http://www.fws.gov/

This site provides information about environmental quality, endangered species, and habitat conservation in the United States.

12
Soils

The final major component in our study of Earth's environment is the lithosphere. This fourth sphere is just as complex as the atmosphere, biosphere, or hydrosphere but contrasts with these other realms in its enormity and particularly in its seeming stability.

It is easy to observe change in the three other spheres—clouds forming, flowers blooming, rivers flowing—but the dynamics of the lithosphere, with a few spectacular exceptions, operate with such incredible slowness that Earth's crust often appears changeless. Most laypersons consider the phrase "the everlasting hills" a literal expression aptly describing the permanence of Earth's topography, whereas in reality the phrase is merely hyperbole that fails to recognize the remarkable alterations that take place over time.

A few lithospheric processes, such as earthquakes and volcanic eruptions, occur abruptly, but the vast majority operate so slowly as to be unrecognizable by the casual observer. Thus, the student of topographic change must search for clues about the ponderous processes that shape the land, clues from the past that help us interpret the landscape of the present and predict that of the future. Our goal in the remaining chapters of this book is to understand the contemporary character of Earth's surface and to explain the processes that have caused it to be as it is.

Soil and Regolith

Although the lithosphere encompasses the entire planet, from surface to core,[1] the part that holds our attention here is soil, the topmost layer. Soil is the essential medium in which most terrestrial life is nurtured. Almost all land plants sprout from this precious medium that is spread so thinly across the continental surfaces, with an average worldwide depth of only about 15 centimeters (6 inches).

Despite the implication of the well-known simile "as common as dirt," soil is extremely complex. It is an infinitely varying mixture of weathered mineral particles, decaying organic matter, living organisms, gases, and liquid solutions.

Preeminently, however, soil is a zone of plant growth. Although the concept almost defies definition, **soil** can be conceptualized as a relatively thin surface

◀ Wheat fields at Steptoe Butte, eastern Washington. *(Photo Researchers, Inc.)*

---

[1]In this chapter we use the word *lithosphere* as a general term for the solid part of Earth. In Chapter 13 we will see that the term lithosphere has a more limited definition when discussing plate tectonics.

layer of mineral matter that normally contains a considerable amount of organic material and is capable of supporting living plants. It occupies that part of the outer skin of Earth that extends from the surface down to the maximum depth to which living organisms penetrate, which means basically the area occupied by plant roots. Soil is characterized by its ability to produce and store plant nutrients, an ability made possible by the interactions of such diverse factors as water, air, sunlight, rocks, plants, and animals.

Although thinly distributed over the land surface, soil functions as a fundamental interface where atmosphere, lithosphere, hydrosphere, and biosphere meet. The bulk of most soil is inorganic material, so soil is usually classified as part of the lithosphere, but its relationship to the other three spheres is both intimate and complex (Figure 12-1).

Soil development begins with the physical and chemical disintegration of rock exposed to the atmosphere and to the action of water percolating down from the surface. This disintegration is called *weathering*. As we shall learn in Chapter 15, the basic result of weathering is the weakening and breakdown of solid rock, the fragmentation of coherent rock

▲ **Figure 12-1** Fields in Lancaster County, Pennsylvania. *(© Larry Lefevere/Grant Heilman Photography.)*

masses, the making of little rocks from big ones. The principal product is a layer of loose inorganic material called **regolith** ("blanket rock") because it lies like a blanket over the unfragmented rock below (Figure 12-2). Typically then, the regolith consists of material that has weathered from the underlying rock and that has a crude gradation of particle sizes, with the largest and least fragmented pieces at the bottom, immediately adjacent to the bedrock. Sometimes, however, the regolith consists of material that was transported from elsewhere by the action of wind, water, or ice. Thus, the regolith may vary significantly in composition from place to place.

The upper half meter or so of the regolith normally differs from the material below in several ways, most notably in the intensity of biochemical weathering. This upper portion is soil, which is composed largely of finely fragmented mineral particles, the ultimate product of weathering. It normally also contains an abundance of living plant roots, dead and rotting plant parts, microscopic plants and animals both living and dead, and a variable amount of air and water. Soil is not the end product of a process, but rather a stage in a never-ending continuum of physical–chemical–biotic activities (Figure 12-3).

Soil as a Component of the Landscape

The surface of the lithosphere is usually, but not always, represented by soil. Although extremely pervasive, soil is an inconspicuous component of the landscape because it is beneath our feet, and its presence is normally masked by either vegetation or human constructed features.

We recognize soil in the landscape mostly by its color, which can often be seen through the filigree of plant life that covers it. A second main aspect of soil—its depth—becomes obvious only where some of its vertical

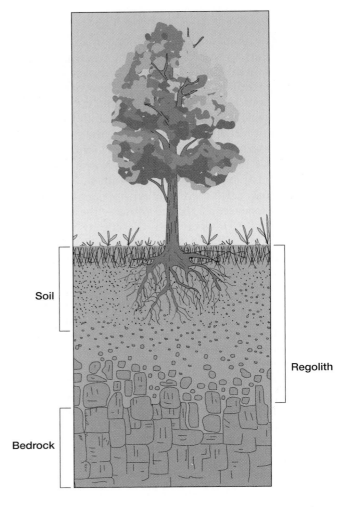

▲ **Figure 12-2** Vertical cross section from surface to bedrock, showing the relationship between soil and regolith.

dimension is exposed by gully erosion, road cuts, or some other type of excavation.

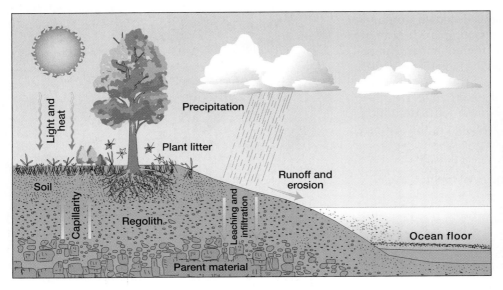

◄ **Figure 12-3** Soil develops through a complex interaction of physical, chemical, and biological processes. Parent-material bedrock weathers to regolith, and then plant litter combines with the regolith to form soil. Some of that soil washes to the ocean floor, where, over the eons of geologic time, it is transformed to sedimentary rock. Some day that ocean floor will be uplifted above sea level and the exposed sedimentary rock will again be weathered into soil.

Soil-Forming Factors

Five variables are the principal soil-forming factors: geology, climate, topography, biology, and time. Geology, topography, and time are passive factors, and climate and biology are active factors.

The Geologic Factor

The source of the rock fragments that make up soil is **parent material**, which may be either bedrock or loose sediments transported from elsewhere by water, wind, or ice. Whatever the parent material, it is sooner or later disintegrated and decomposed at and near Earth's surface, providing the raw material for soil formation.

The nature of the parent material often influences the characteristics of the soil that develops from it, and, particularly in the early stages of soil formation, this factor sometimes dominates all others. The chemical composition of parent material is obviously reflected in the resulting soil, and parent-material physical characteristics may also be influential in soil development, particularly in terms of texture and structure. Bedrock that weathers into large particles (as does sandstone, for example) normally produces a coarse-textured soil, one easily penetrated by air and water to some depth. Bedrock that weathers into minute particles (shale, for example) yields fine-textured soils with a great number of pores but of very small size, which inhibits air and water from easily penetrating the surface.

Young soils are likely to be very reflective of the rocks or sediments from which they were derived. With the passage of time, however, other soil-forming factors become increasingly important, and the significance of the parent material diminishes. Eventually the influence of the parent material may be completely obliterated, so that it is sometimes impossible to ascertain the nature of the rock from which the soil evolved.

The Climatic Factor

Temperature and moisture are the climatic variables of greatest significance to soil formation. As a basic generalization, both the chemical and biological processes in soil are usually accelerated by high temperatures and abundant moisture and are slowed by low temperatures and lack of moisture. One predictable result is that soils tend to be deepest in warm, humid regions and shallowest in cold, dry regions.

It is difficult to overemphasize the role of moisture moving through the soil. The flow is mostly downward because of the pull of gravity, but it is sometimes lateral in response to drainage opportunities and sometimes, in special circumstances, even upward. Wherever and however water moves, it always carries dissolved chemicals in solution and usually also carries tiny particles of matter in suspension. Thus, moving water is ever engaged in rearranging the chemical and physical components of the soil, as well as contributing to the variety and availability of plant nutrients.

In terms of general soil characteristics, climate is likely to be the most influential factor in the long run. This generalization has many exceptions, however, and when soils are considered on a local scale, climate is likely to be less prominent as a determinant.

The Topographic Factor

Slope and drainage are the two main features of topography that influence soil characteristics. Wherever soil develops, its vertical extent undergoes continuous, if usually very slow, change. This change comes about through a lowering of both the bottom and top of the soil layer (Figure 12-4). The bottom slowly gets deeper as weathering penetrates into the regolith and parent material and as plant roots extend to greater depths. At the same time, the soil surface is being lowered by sporadic removal of its uppermost layer through normal erosion, which is the removal of individual soil particles by running water, wind, and gravity.

Where the land is flat, soil tends to develop at the bottom more rapidly than it is eroded away at the top. This does not mean that the downward development is speedy; rather it means that surface erosion is extraordinarily slow. Thus, the deepest soils are usually on flat land. Where slopes are relatively steep, surface erosion is more rapid than soil deepening, with the result that such soils are nearly always thin and immaturely developed (Figure 12-5).

Because most soils are well drained, moisture relationships are relatively unremarkable factors in soil development. Some soils have inefficient natural drainage, however, a condition that imparts significantly different characteristics. For example, a waterlogged

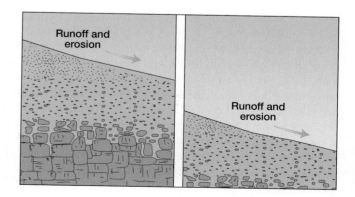

▲ **Figure 12-4**   Over time, the extent of soil undergoes slow, continuous change. The bottom of the soil layer is lowered by the break-up of parent material as weathering processes extend deeper into the regolith and bedrock. At the same time, the top of the soil layer can be lowered through erosional processes.

▲ **Figure 12-5** Slope is a critical determinant of soil depth. On flat land, soil normally develops more deeply with the passage of time because there is very little erosion washing away the topmost soil. On a slope, the rate of erosion is equal to or greater than the rate at which soil is formed at the bottom of the soil layer, with the result that the soil remains shallow.

soil tends to contain a high proportion of organic matter, and the biological and chemical processes that require free oxygen are impeded (because air is the source of the needed oxygen and a waterlogged soil contains essentially no air). Most illdrained soils are in valley bottoms or in some other flat locale because soil drainage is usually related to slope.

In some cases, such subsurface factors as permeability and the presence or absence of impermeable layers are more influential than slope.

The Biological Factor

From a volume standpoint, soil is about half mineral matter and about half air and water, with only a small fraction of organic matter. However, the organic fraction, consisting of both living and dead plants and animals, is of utmost importance. The biological factor in particular gives life to the soil and makes it more than just dirt. Every soil contains a quantity (sometimes an enormous quantity) of living organisms, and every soil incorporates some (sometimes a vast amount of) dead and decaying organic matter.

Vegetation of various kinds growing in soil performs certain vital functions. Plant roots, for instance, work their way down and around, providing passageways for drainage and aeration, as well as being the vital link between soil nutrients and the growing plants.

Many kinds of animals contribute to soil development as well. Even such large surface-dwelling creatures as

elephants and bison affect soil formation by compaction with their hooves, rolling in the dirt, grazing the vegetation, and dropping excreta. Ants, worms, and all other land animals fertilize the soil with their waste products and contribute their carcasses for eventual decomposition and incorporation into the soil.

Many smaller animals spend most or all of their lives in the soil layer, tunneling here and there, moving soil particles upward and downward, and providing passageways for water and air (Figure 12-6). Mixing and plowing by soil fauna is sometimes remarkably extensive. Ants and termites, as they build mounds, also transport soil materials from one layer to another. The mixing activities of animals in the soil, generalized under the term *pedoturbation,* tend to counteract the tendency of other soil-forming processes to accentuate the vertical differences among soil layers.

The abundance and variety of animal life connected with the soil are quite surprising. Such organisms vary in size from the gigantic to the microscopic, and in numbers from a few per hectare to billions per gram. The organic life of the soil ranges from almost impalpable protozoans existing in colloidal slime to larger animals that may accidentally alter certain soil characteristics. Of all creatures, however, it is probable that the earthworm is the most important to soil formation and development.

Earthworms The cultivating and mixing activities of earthworms are of great value in improving the structure, increasing the fertility, lessening the danger of accelerated erosion, and deepening the profile of

▲ **Figure 12-6** Like other burrowing animals, prairie dogs contribute to soil development by bringing subsoil to the surface and providing passageways for air and moisture to get underground. *(Tom McHugh/Photo Researchers, Inc.)*

the soil. The distinctive evidence of this value is that the presence of many well-nourished earthworms is almost always a sign of productive, or potentially productive, soil.

The mere presence of earthworms does not guarantee that a soil will be highly productive, as there may be other kinds of inhibiting factors such as a high water table. Nevertheless, an earthworm-infested soil has a higher potential productivity than similar soils lacking earthworms. In various controlled experiments, the addition of earthworms to wormless soil has enhanced plant productivity by several hundred percent.

At least seven beneficial functions have been attributed to earthworms:

1. Their innumerable tunnels facilitate drainage and aeration and the deepening of the soil profile.

2. The continual movement of the creatures beneath the surface tends to bring about the formation of a crumby structure, which is generally favorable for plant growth.

3. The soil is further mixed by material being carried and washed downward into their holes from the surface. This is notably in the form of leaf litter dragged downward by the worms, which fertilizes the subsoil.

4. The digestive actions and tunneling of earthworms form aggregate soil particles that increase porosity and resist the impact of raindrops, helping to deter erosion.

5. Nutrients in the soil are increased by the addition of *casts* excreted by earthworms, which have been shown to be 5 times richer in available nitrogen, 7 times richer in available phosphates, and 11 times richer in available potash than the surrounding soil.

6. They rearrange material in the soil, especially by bringing deeper matter to the surface, where it can be weathered more rapidly. Where earthworms are numerous, they may deposit as much as 9000 kg/hectare (25 tons/acre) of casts on the surface in a year.

7. Nitrification is also promoted by the presence of earthworms, due to increased aeration, alkaline fluids in their digestive tracts, and the decomposition of earthworm carcasses.

In many parts of the world, of course, earthworms are lacking. They are, for example almost totally absent from arid and semiarid regions. In these dry lands, some of the earthworm's soil-enhancing functions are carried out by ants and earth-dwelling termites, but much less effectively.

Microorganisms in the Soil Another important component of the biological factor are microorganisms, both plant and animal, that occur in uncountable billions. An estimated three quarters of a soil's metabolic activity is generated by microorganisms. These microbes help release nutrients from dead organisms for use by live ones by decomposing organic matter into **humus**, a dark adhesive of minute particles, and by converting nutrients to forms usable by plants. Algae, fungi, protozoans, actinomycetes, and other minuscule organisms all play a role in soil development, but bacteria probably make the greatest contribution overall. This is because certain types of bacteria are responsible for the decomposition and decay of dead plant and animal material and the consequent release of nutrients into the soil.

The Chronological Factor

For soil to develop on a newly exposed land surface requires time, with the length of time needed varying according to the nature of the exposed parent material and the characteristics of the environment. Soil-forming processes are generally very slow, and many centuries may be required for a thin layer of soil to form on a newly exposed surface. A warm, moist environment is conducive to soil development. Normally of much greater importance, however, are the attributes of the parent material. For example, soil develops from sediments relatively quickly and from bedrock relatively slowly.

Most soil develops with geologic slowness—so slowly that changes are almost imperceptible within a human life span. It is possible, however, for a soil to be degraded, either through the physical removal associated with accelerated erosion or through depletion of nutrients, in only a few years (Figure 12-7). In the grand

▲ **Figure 12-7** Accelerated erosion cutting a deep gully in the Coast Ranges of central California. (*Richard R. Hansen/Photo Researchers, Inc.*)

FOCUS Earthworms in the Soil

Several dozen varieties of segmented worms—ranging in size from those that are only 1 mm (1/25 inch) long to those that are up to 3 meters (10 feet) in length—are often referred to as earthworms (sometimes called *night crawlers*), but by far the most widespread and important is the "common earthworm," *Lumbricus terrestris* (Figure 12-A). These organisms are not widely distributed over the world; they are generally restricted to humid regions that have temperate or cool temperature regimes. Although they are common in eastern North America and most of Europe, in other parts of the world their occurrence is sometimes patchy and localized.

Their preferred habitat is a heavy, compact soil with moderate acidity. They are unable to live in soils with a high alkaline content; and if the soil has a pH value of less than 6, earthworms are almost certain to be absent. Where conditions are favorable, they may number in the hundreds of thousands per hectare; in such areas they may comprise as much as 80 percent by weight of the total soil fauna. Indeed, in some prime New Zealand pasture land, the weight of earthworms beneath the surface has been found to amount to as much as the total weight of sheep on the surface!

Almost every activity undertaken by earthworms has some sort of direct effect on the soil. They move about beneath the surface by means of tiny tunnels that they construct as they progress. The tunnels, however, are not "dug" in the ordinary sense of the word. Rather, the earthworm pushes its way through soft earth and literally eats its way through firmer soil. It obtains nourishment from the organic matter that is ingested, but it also takes into its alimentary canal large amounts of inorganic material, which is subsequently excreted in the form of *casts*. These casts consist of earthy matter bound together with decomposed organic residues, and they contribute considerable fertility to the soil and furnish a suitable environment for many microorganisms. Both the chemical and physical nature of the casts are important to the soil, whether on the surface or beneath it. The deposition of casts on the surface, which is particularly noticeable after a rain or heavy dew, involves the transportation of great quantities of subsurface material upward. Earthworms also drag leaves and other organic matter down into their tunnels.

The precise importance of earthworms to soil development is difficult to assess, but there can be no question that soil productivity is significantly increased by their activities. Thus, the impact of the earthworm on agricultural output is beyond measure. Charles Darwin conducted a classic study of earthworm activity more than a century ago and reached the conclusion that they may have played a more important role in the history of the world than any other type of animal. This is perhaps too sweeping an assertion, although many people are probably willing at least to modify the old aphorism concerning dogs to state, "A farmer's best friend is the earthworm."

▲ **Figure 12-A** Common earthworm in underground burrow. (© *David M. Dennis/Animals Animals/Earth Scenes.*)

scale of geologic time, then, soil can be formed and reformed, but in the dimension of human time, it is a nonrenewable resource.

Soil Components

Soil is made up of a variety of natural components existing together in myriad combinations. All these components can be classified, however, into just a few main groups: inorganics, organics, air, and water.

Inorganic Materials

As mentioned earlier, the bulk of most soils is mineral matter, mostly in the form of small but macroscopic particles. Inorganic material also occurs as microscopic clay particles and as dissolved minerals in solution.

About half the volume of an average soil is small, granular mineral matter called *sand* and *silt*. These particles may consist of a great variety of minerals, depending on the nature of the parent material from which they were derived, and are simply fragments of the wasting rock. Most common are bits of quartz, which are composed of silica (SiO_2) and appear in the soil as very resistant grains of sand. Other prominent minerals making up sand and silt are some of the feldspars and micas.

The smallest particles in the soil are *clay,* which is usually a combination of silica and of oxides of aluminum and iron found only in the soil and not in the parent material. Clay has properties significantly different from those of larger (sand and silt) fragments. Most clay particles are *colloidal* in size, which means they are larger than molecules but too small to be seen with the naked eye. They are usually flat platelets, as Figure 12-8 illustrates, and therefore have a relatively large surface area. For this reason, clay has an important influence on chemical activity in the soil because many chemical reactions occur at the surfaces of soil particles. The platelets group together in loose, sheetlike assemblages, and water moves easily between these sheets. Substances dissolved in the water are attracted to and held by the sheets. Since the sheets are negatively charged, they attract positively charged ions called **cations**. Many essential plant nutrients occur in soil solutions as cations, with the result that clay is an important reservoir for plant nutrients, just as it is for soil water.

Organic Matter

Although organic matter generally constitutes less than 5 percent of total soil volume, it has an enormous influence on soil characteristics and plays a fundamental role in the biochemical processes that make soil an effective medium of plant growth. Some of the organic

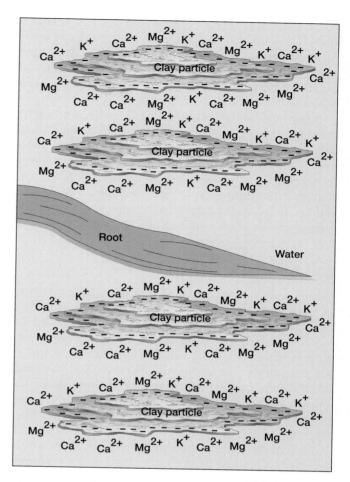

▲ **Figure 12-8** Clay particles offer a large surface area on which substances dissolved in soil water can cling. The particles are negatively charged and therefore attract cations (positively charged ions) from the water. These cations held by the clay are then absorbed by plant roots and become nutrients for the plant.

matter is living organisms, some is dead but undecomposed plant parts and animal carcasses, some is totally decomposed and so has become humus, and some is in an intermediate stage of decomposition.

Apart from plant roots, evidence of the variety and bounty of organisms living in the soil may be inconspicuous or invisible, but most soils are seething with life. A half hectare (about one acre) may contain a million earthworms, and the total number of organisms in 28 grams (an ounce) of soil is likely to exceed 100 trillion. Microorganisms far exceed more complex life forms, both in total numbers and in cumulative mass. They are active in rearranging and aerating the soil and in yielding waste products that are links in the chain of nutrient cycling. Some make major contributions to the decay and decomposition of dead organic matter, and others make nitrogen available for plant use.

Leaves, twigs, stalks, and other dead plant parts accumulate at the soil surface, where they are referred to collectively as **litter**. The eventual fate of most litter is decomposition, in which the solid parts are broken down into chemical elements, which are then either absorbed into the soil or washed away. In cold, dry areas, litter may remain undecomposed for a very long time; where the climate is warm and moist, however, decomposition may take place almost as rapidly as litter accumulates.

After most of the residues have been decomposed, a brown or black, gelatinous, chemically stable organic matter remains; this is referred to as *humus*. This "black gold" is of utmost importance to agriculture because it loosens the structure and lessens the density of the soil, thereby facilitating root development. Moreover, humus, like clay, is a catalyst for chemical reactions and a reservoir for plant nutrients and soil water.

Soil Air

Nearly half the volume of an average soil is made up of pore spaces (Figure 12-9). These spaces provide a labyrinth of interconnecting passageways, called *interstices*, among the soil particles. This labyrinth lets air and water penetrate into the soil. On the average, the pore spaces are about half filled with air and half with water, but at any given time and place, the amounts of air and water are quite variable, the quantity of one varying inversely with that of the other (Figure 12-10).

The characteristics of air in the soil are significantly different from those of atmospheric air. Soil air is found in openings generally lined with a film of water, and since this air exists in such close contact with water and is not exposed to moving air currents, it is saturated with moisture. Soil air is also very rich in carbon dioxide and poor in oxygen because plant roots and soil organisms remove oxygen from, and respire carbon dioxide into, the pore spaces. The carbon dioxide then slowly escapes into the atmosphere.

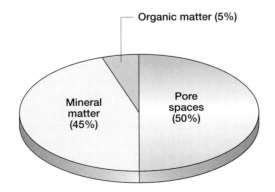

▲ **Figure 12-9** The best soil for plant growth is about half solid material (by volume) and about half pore spaces. Most of the solids are mineral matter, with only a small amount being organic. On average, about half of the pore spaces in an ideal soil are filled with air and the other half are filled with water.

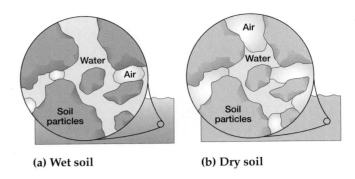

(a) Wet soil	(b) Dry soil

▲ **Figure 12-10** The relative amounts of water and air in soil pores vary from place to place and from time to time. **(a)** The interstices of wet soil contain much water and little air. **(b)** In dry soil there is much air and little water.

Soil Water

Water comes into the soil largely by percolation of rainfall and snowmelt, but some is also added from below when groundwater is pulled up above the water table by capillary action (Figure 12-11). Once water has penetrated the soil, it envelops in a film of water each solid particle that it contacts, and it either wholly or partially fills the pore spaces. Water can be lost from the soil by percolation down into the groundwater, by upward capillary movement to the surface followed by evaporation, or by plant use (transpiration).

Four forms of soil moisture are generally recognized (Figure 12-12).

Gravitational Water (Free Water) Gravitational water is temporary in that it results from prolonged infiltration from above (usually due to prolonged precipitation) and is pulled downward by gravity, through the interstices toward the groundwater zone. Thus, this water stays in the soil only for a short time and is not very effective in supplying plants because it drains away rapidly once the external supply ceases.

Gravitational water accomplishes significant functions during its passage through the soil, however. It is the principal agent of *eluviation* and *illuviation* (discussed below) and is therefore a translocation agent that makes the top soil coarser and more open-textured and the subsoil denser and more compact.

Capillary Water (Water of Cohesion) Capillary water, which remains after gravitational water has drained away, consists of moisture held at the surface of soil particles by surface tension, which is the attraction of water molecules for each other (discussed in Chapter 6, this is the same property that causes water to form rounded droplets rather than dispersing in a thin film). Capillary water is by far the principal source of moisture for plants. In this form of soil

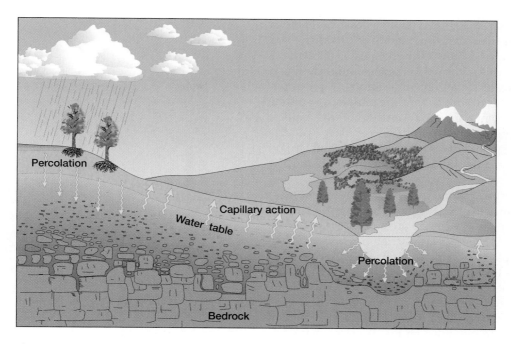

▲ **Figure 12-11**   Water is added to the soil layer by the percolation of rainwater and snowmelt from above. Additional moisture enters the soil from below as groundwater is pulled up above the water table by capillary action.

moisture, the surface-tension forces are stronger than the downward pull of gravity, so this water is free to move about equally well in all directions in response to capillary tension. It tends to move from wetter areas toward drier ones, which accounts for the upward movement of capillary water when no gravitational water is percolating downward.

Hygroscopic Water (Water of Adhesion)   Hygroscopic water consists of a microscopically thin film of moisture bound rigidly to all soil particles by adhesion, which is the attraction of water molecules to solid surfaces. Hygroscopic water adheres so tightly to the particles that it is normally unavailable to plants.

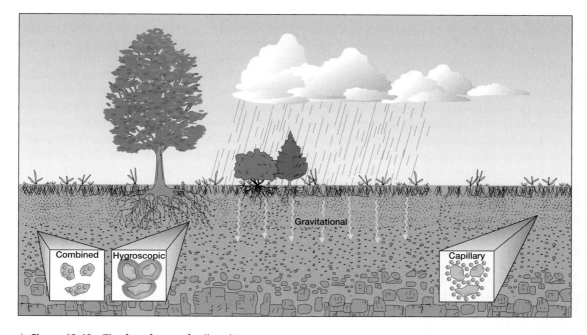

▲ **Figure 12-12**   The four forms of soil moisture.

Combined Water Combined water is least available of all. It is held in chemical combination with various soil minerals and is freed only if the chemical is altered.

For plants, capillary water is the most important and gravitational water is largely superfluous. After gravitational water has drained away, the remaining volume of water represents the *field capacity* of the soil. If drought conditions prevail and the capillary water is all used up by plants or evaporated, the plants are no longer able to extract moisture from the soil, and the *wilting point* is reached.

Water performs a number of important functions in the soil. It is an effective solvent, dissolving essential soil nutrients and making them available to plant roots. These dissolved nutrients are carried downward in solution, to be partly redeposited at lower levels. This process, called **leaching**, tends to deplete the topsoil of soluble nutrients. Water is also required for many of the chemical reactions of clay and for the actions of the microorganisms that produce humus. In addition, it can have considerable influence on the physical characteristics of soil by moving particles around.

As water percolates into the soil, it picks up fine particles of mineral matter from the upper layers and carries them downward in a process called **eluviation** (Figure 12-13). These particles are eventually deposited at a lower level, and this deposition process is known as **illuviation**.

Soil-Water Budget The moisture added to the soil by percolation of rainfall or snowmelt is diminished largely through evapotranspiration. The dynamic relationship between these two processes is referred to as the **soil–water balance**. It is influenced by a variety of factors, including soil and vegetation characteristics, but is primarily determined by temperature and humidity.

How much water is available to plants is much more important to an ecosystem than is the amount of precipitation. Much water derived from rainfall or snowmelt becomes unavailable to plants because of evaporation, runoff, deep infiltration, or other processes. At any given time and place, there is likely to be either a surplus or a deficit of water in the soil. Such a condition is only temporary, and it varies in response to changing weather conditions, particularly those related to seasonal changes. Generally speaking, warm weather causes increased evapotranspiration, which diminishes the soil–water supply, and cool weather slows evapotranspiration, allowing more moisture to be retained in the soil.

In a hypothetical Northern Hemisphere midlatitude location, January is a time of surplus water in the soil because low temperatures inhibit evaporation and there is little or no transpiration from plants. The soil is likely to be at or near **field capacity** at this time, which means that most of the pore spaces are filled with water. With the arrival of spring, temperatures rise and

Eluviation (fine particles carried by percolating water to deeper soil)

Illuviation (deposition of the particles eluviated from above)

Bedrock

▲ **Figure 12-13** In the process of eluviation, fine particles in upper soil layers are picked up by percolating water and carried deeper into the soil. In the process of illuviation, these particles are deposited in a lower soil layer.

plant growth accelerates, so that both evaporation and transpiration increase. The soil–water balance tips from a water surplus to a water deficit. This deficit builds to a peak in middle or late summer, as temperatures reach their greatest heights and plants need maximum water. Heavy use and diminished precipitation may combine to deplete all the moisture available to plants, and the **wilting point** is reached. Thus, the amount of soil moisture available for plant use is essentially the difference between field capacity and wilting point.

In late summer and fall, as air temperature decreases and plant growth slackens, evapotranspiration diminishes rapidly. At this time, the soil–water balance shifts once again to a water surplus, which continues through the winter. Then the cycle begins again.

Figure 12-14 illustrates the annual sequence just described. Such variation in the soil–water balance through time is called a **soil–water budget**.

Soil Properties

As one looks at, feels, smells, tastes, and otherwise examines soils, various physical and chemical characteristics appear useful in describing, differentiating, and

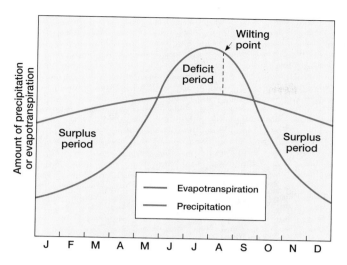

▲ **Figure 12-14** Hypothetical soil–water budget for a Northern Hemisphere midlatitude location. From January through May, there is more precipitation than evapotranspiration, and consequently the soil contains a surplus of water, more than sufficient for any plant needs. From mid-May to mid-September, the evapotranspiration curve rises above the precipitation curve, indicating that more water leaves the soil than enters it. About the first of August, so much water has been removed from the soil that plants begin to wilt. After mid-September, the evapotranspiration curve again dips below the precipitation curve and there is again a surplus of water in the soil.

classifying them. Some soil properties are easily recognized, but most can be ascertained only by precise measurement.

Color

The most conspicuous property of a soil is usually its color, but color is by no means the most definitive property. Soil color can provide clues about the nature and capabilities of the soil, but the clues are sometimes misleading. Soil scientists recognize 175 gradations of color. The standard colors are generally shades of black, brown, red, yellow, gray, and white. Soil color occasionally reflects the color of the unstained mineral grains, but in most cases, color is imparted by stains on the surface of the particles; stains caused by either metallic oxides or organic matter.

Black or dark brown usually indicates a considerable humus content; the blacker the soil, the more humus it contains. Color gives a strong hint about fertility, therefore, because humus is an important catalyst in releasing nutrients to plants. Dark color is not invariably a sign of fertility, however, because it may be due to other factors, such as poor drainage or high carbonate content.

Reddish and yellowish colors generally indicate iron oxide stains on the outside of soil particles. These colors are most common in tropical and subtropical regions, where many minerals are leached away by water moving under the pull of gravity, leaving insoluble iron compounds behind. In such situations, a red color bespeaks good drainage, and a yellowish hue suggests imperfect drainage. Red soils are also common in desert and semidesert environments, where the color is carried over intact from reddish parent materials rather than representing a surface stain (Figure 12-15).

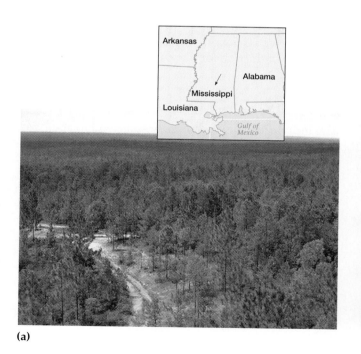

(a)

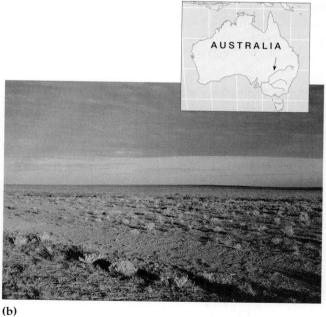

(b)

▲ **Figure 12-15** A red soil means different things in different places. **(a)** In this Mississippi forest, the soluble minerals have been leached away, leaving the insoluble iron to impart its reddish color to the soil. **(b)** In this Australian desert, the reddish color reflects the iron content of the underlying bedrock. *(Tom L. McKnight photos.)*

▲ **Figure 12-16**   The relative sizes of sand, silt, and clay particles.

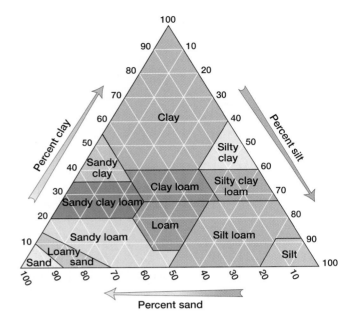

▲ **Figure 12-17**   The standard soil-texture triangle.

Gray and bluish colors typically indicate poor drainage, whereas mottling indicates saturated conditions for part of the year. In humid areas, a light color implies so much leaching that even the iron has been removed, but in dry climates, it indicates an accumulation of salts. It may also indicate simply a lack of organic matter.

Texture

All soils are composed of myriad particles of various sizes, as Figure 12-16 shows, although smaller particles usually predominate. Rolling a sample of soil about between the fingers can provide a feel for the principal particle sizes. Table 12-1 shows the standard classification scheme for particle sizes; in this scheme, the size groups are called **separates**. The gravel, sand, and silt separates are fragments of the weathered parent material and are mostly the grains of minerals found commonly in rocks, especially quartz, feldspars,

and micas. These coarser particles are the inert materials of the soil mass, its skeletal framework. As noted above, only the clay particles take part in the intricate chemical activities that occur in the soil.

Because no soil is made up of particles of uniform size, the texture of any soil is determined by the relative amounts of the various separates present. The *texture triangle* (Figure 12-17) shows the standard classification scheme for soil texture; this scheme is based on the percentage of each separate by weight. Near the center of the triangle is **loam**, the name given to a texture in which none of the three principal separates dominates the other two. This fairly even-textured mix is generally the most productive for plants.

Structure

The individual particles of most soils tend to aggregate into clumps called **peds**, and it is these clumps that determine soil structure. The size, shape, and stability of peds have a marked influence on how easily water, air, and organisms (including plant roots) move through the soil, and consequently on soil fertility. Peds are classified on the basis of shape as spheroidal, platy, blocky, or prismatic, with these four shapes giving rise to seven generally recognized soil structure types (Figure 12-18). Aeration and drainage are usually facilitated by peds of intermediate size; both massive and fine structures tend to inhibit these processes.

Some soils, particularly those composed largely of sand, do not develop a true structure, which is to say that the individual grains do not aggregate into peds. Silt and clay particles readily aggregate in most instances. Other things being equal, aggregation is usually greatest in moist soils and least in dry ones.

TABLE 12-1 Standard U.S. Classification of Soil Particle Size	
Separate	Diameter
Gravel	Greater than 2 mm (0.08 in.)
Very coarse sand	1–2 mm (0.04–0.08 in.)
Coarse sand	0.5–1 mm (0.02–0.04 in.)
Medium sand	0.25–0.5 mm (0.01–0.02 in.)
Fine sand	0.1–0.25 mm (0.004–0.01 in.)
Very fine sand	0.05–0.1 mm (0.002–0.004 in.)
Coarse silt	0.02–0.05 mm (0.0008–0.002 in.)
Medium silt	0.006–0.02 mm (0.00024–0.0008 in.)
Fine silt	0.002–0.006 mm (0.00008–0.00024 in.)
Clay	0.002 mm (less than 0.00008 in.)

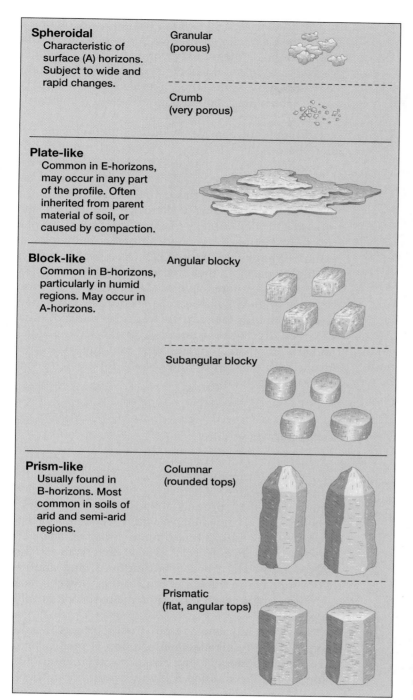

Structure is an important determinant of a soil's *porosity* and *permeability*. As we learned in Chapter 9, porosity refers to the amount of pore space between soil particles or between peds (Figure 12-19). We can define it as

$$porosity = \frac{volume\ of\ voids}{total\ volume}$$

Porosity is usually expressed as a percentage or a decimal fraction. It is a measure of a soil's capacity to hold water and air.

The relationship between porosity and permeability is not simple; that is, the most porous materials are not necessarily the most permeable. Clay, for example, is the most porous separate, but it is the least permeable because it soaks up water rather than allowing it to pass through.

Soil Chemistry

The effectiveness of soil as a growth medium for plants is based largely on the presence and availability of nutrients, which are determined by an intricate series of

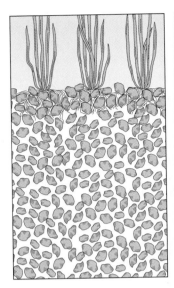
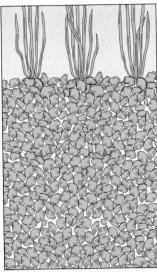

▲ **Figure 12-19** The contrast between a porous soil and a nonporous one.

chemical reactions. Soil chemistry is an extraordinarily complex subject that revolves primarily around microscopic particles and electrically charged atoms or groups of atoms called *ions*.

Colloids

Particles smaller than about 0.1 micrometer in diameter are called **colloids**. Inorganic colloids consist of clay in thin, crystalline, platelike forms created by the chemical alteration of larger particles; organic colloids represent decomposed organic matter in the form of humus; and both types are the chemically active soil particles. When mixed with water, colloids remain suspended indefinitely as a homogeneous, murky solution. Some have remarkable storage capacities, and consequently colloids are major determinants of the water-holding capacity of a soil. They function as a virtual sponge, soaking up water, whereas the soil particles that are too large to be classified as colloids can maintain only a surface film of water.

Both inorganic and organic colloids attract and hold great quantities of ions.

Cation Exchange

As was just noted, cations are positively charged ions. Elements that form them include calcium, potassium, and magnesium, which are all essential for soil fertility and plant growth.

Colloids carry mostly negative electrical charges on their surfaces, and these charges attract swarms of nutrient cations that would be leached from the soil if their ions were not retained by the colloids (see Figure 12-8).

The combination of colloid and attached cations is called the *colloidal complex,* and it is a delicate mechanism. If it holds the nutrients strongly, they will not be leached away, yet if the bond is too strong, they cannot be absorbed by plants. Thus, a fertile soil is likely to be one in which the cation–colloid attraction is intricately balanced.

Adding to the complexity of the situation is the fact that some types of cations are bound more tightly than others. Cations that tend to bond strongly in the colloid complex may replace those that bond less strongly. For example, basic ions are fairly easily replaced by metal ions or hydrogen ions, and this process is called *cation exchange.* The capability of a soil to attract and exchange cations is known as its **cation exchange capacity (CEC)**. As a generalization, the higher the CEC, the more fertile the soil. Soils with a high clay content have a higher CEC than more coarsely grained soils because the former have more colloids. Humus is a particularly rich source of high-CEC activity because humus colloids have a much higher CEC than inorganic clay minerals. The most fertile soils, then, tend to be those with a notable clay and humus content.

Acidity/Alkalinity

An *acid* is a chemical compound that produces hydrogen ions (H^+) or hydronium ions (H_3O^+) when dissolved in water, whereas a *base* is a chemical compound that produces hydroxide ions (OH^-) when dissolved in water. An acid reacts with a base to form a salt. Solutions that contain dissolved acids are described as being *acidic.* Those that contain dissolved bases are called *basic* solutions, and another word for basic in this context is *alkaline.* Any chemical solution can be characterized on the basis of its *acidity* or *alkalinity.*

Nearly all nutrients are provided to plants in solution. An overly alkaline soil solution is inefficient in dissolving minerals and releasing their nutrients. However, if the solution is highly acidic, the nutrients are likely to be dissolved and leached away too rapidly for plant roots to absorb them. The optimum situation, then, is for the soil solution to be neutral, neither too alkaline nor too acidic. The acidity/alkalinity of a soil is determined to a large extent by its CEC.

The chemist's symbol for the measure of the acidity/alkalinity of a solution is pH, which is based on the relative concentration of hydrogen ions (H^+) in the solution. The scale ranges from 0 to 14. The lower end represents acidic conditions; higher numbers indicate alkaline conditions (Figure 12-20). Neutral conditions are represented by a value of 7, and it is soil having a pH of about 7 that is most suitable for the great majority of plants and microorganisms.

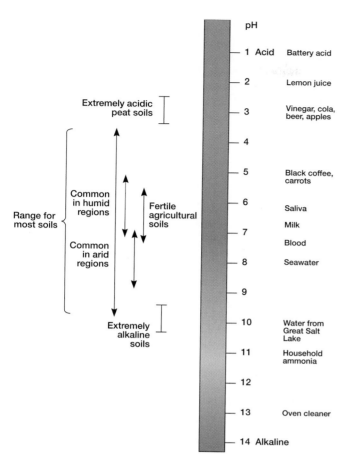

▲ Figure 12-20 The standard pH scale.

almost infinite variety of soils in the world are usually grouped and classified on the basis of differences exhibited in their profiles.

Figure 12-22 presents an idealized sketch of a well-developed soil profile, in which six horizons are differentiated:

- The **O horizon** is sometimes the surface layer, and in it organic matter, both fresh and decaying, makes up most of the volume. This horizon results essentially from litter derived from dead plants and animals. It is common in forests and generally absent in grasslands. It is actually more typical for soils not to possess an O horizon; the surface horizon of most soils is the A horizon.

- The **A horizon**, colloquially referred to as *topsoil,* is a mineral horizon that also contains considerable organic matter. It is formed either at the surface or immediately below an O horizon. A horizons generally contain enough partially decomposed organic matter to give the soil a darker color than underlying horizons. They are also normally coarser in texture, having lost some of the finer materials by erosion and eluviation. Seeds germinate mostly in the A horizon.

- The **E horizon** is normally lighter in color than either the overlying A or the underlying B horizon. It is essentially an eluvial layer from which clay, iron, and aluminum have been removed, leaving a concentration of abrasion-resistant sand or silt particles.

- The **B horizon**, usually called *subsoil,* is a mineral horizon of illuviation where most of the materials removed from above have been deposited. A collecting zone for clay, iron, and aluminum, this horizon is usually of heavier texture, greater density, and relatively greater clay content than the A horizon.

- The **C horizon** is unconsolidated parent material (regolith) beyond the reach of plant roots and most soil-forming processes except weathering. It is lacking in organic matter.

- The **R horizon** is bedrock, with little evidence of weathering.

True soil, which is called **solum,** only extends down through the B horizon.

As we learned earlier in the chapter, time is a critical passive factor in profile development, but the vital active factor is surface water. If there is no surface water, from rainfall or snowmelt or some other source, to infiltrate the soil, there can be no profile development. Descending water carries material from the surface downward, from topsoil into subsoil, by eluviation and leaching. This transported material is mostly deposited a few tens of centimeters (a few feet) below the surface. In the usual pattern, topsoil (A) becomes a somewhat depleted

Soil Profiles

The development of any soil is expressed in two dimensions: depth and time. There is no straight-line relationship between depth and age, however; some soils deepen and develop much more rapidly than others.

There are four processes that deepen and age soils: *addition, loss, translocation,* and *transformation* (Figure 12-21). The five soil-forming factors discussed earlier—geologic, climatic, topographic, biological, chronological—influence the rate of these four processes, the result being the development of various soil horizons and the soil profile.

The vertical variation of soil properties is not random but rather an ordered layering with depth. Soil tends to have more or less distinctly recognizable layers, called **horizons,** each with different characteristics. The horizons are positioned approximately parallel with the land surface, one above the other, normally, but not always, separated by a transition zone rather than a sharp line. A vertical cross section (as might be seen in a road cut or the side of a trench dug in a field) from the Earth's surface down through the soil layers and into the parent material is referred to as a **soil profile.** The

ADDITION
- Water as precipitation, condensation, and runoff
- Oxygen and carbon dioxide from atmosphere
- Nitrogen, chlorine, and sulfur from atmosphere and precipitation
- Organic matter
- Sediments
- Energy from sun

LOSS
- Water by evapotranspiration
- Nitrogen by denitrification
- Carbon as carbon dioxide from oxidation of organic matter
- Soil by erosion
- Energy by radiation

TRANSLOCATION
- Clay and organic matter carried by water
- Nutrients circulated by plants
- Soluble salts carried in water
- Soil carried by animals

TRANSFORMATION
- Organic matter converted to humus
- Particles made smaller by weathering
- Structure and concretion formation
- Minerals transformed by weathering
- Clay and organic matter reactions

LOSS
- Water and materials in solution or suspension

◀ **Figure 12-21** The four soil-forming processes: addition, loss, translocation, transformation. Geologic, climatic, topographic, biological, and chronological soil-forming factors influence the rate at which these four processes occur and therefore the rate at which soil is formed.

horizon through eluviation and leaching, and subsoil (B) develops as a layer of accumulation due to illuviation.

A profile that contains all horizons is typical of a humid area on well-drained but gentle slopes in an environment that has been undisturbed for a long time. In many parts of the world, however, such idealized conditions do not pertain, and the soil profile may have one horizon particularly well developed, one missing altogether, a *fossil horizon* formed under a different past climate, an accumulation of a hardpan (a very dense and impermeable layer), surface layers removed through accelerated erosion, or some other variation. Moreover, many soils are too young to have evolved a normal profile. A soil containing only an A horizon atop partially altered parent material (C horizon) is said to be *immature.* The formation of an illuvial B horizon is normally an indication of a *mature* soil.

Pedogenic Regimes

Soil-forming factors and processes interact in almost limitless variations to produce soils of all descriptions. Fundamental to an understanding of soil classification

and distribution is the realization that only five major **pedogenic regimes** ("soil-forming" regimes) exist: *laterization, podzolization, gleization, calcification,* and *salinization.* These regimes can be thought of as environmental settings in which certain physical–chemical–biological processes prevail.

Laterization

Laterization is named for the brick-red color of the soil it produces (*Later:* Latin, "brick"). The processes associated with this regime are typical of the warm, moist regions of the world, and a significant annual moisture surplus is a requisite condition. The soil formed by laterization is most prominent, then, in the tropics and subtropics, in regions dominated by forest, shrub, and savanna vegetation.

A laterization regime is characterized by rapid weathering of parent material, dissolution of nearly all minerals, and speedy decomposition of organic matter. Probably the most distinctive feature of laterization is the leaching away of silica, the most common constituent of most rock and soil and a constituent that is usually highly resistant to being dissolved. That

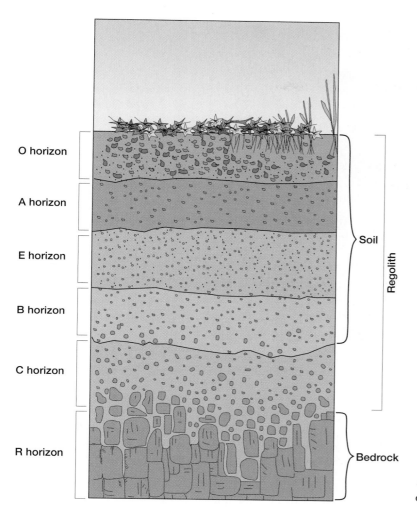

O horizon

A horizon

E horizon

B horizon

C horizon

R horizon

Soil

Regolith

Bedrock

◀ **Figure 12-22** Idealized soil profile. The true soil, or solum, consists of the O, A, E, and B horizons.

silica is indeed removed during laterization indicates the extreme effectiveness of chemical weathering and leaching under this regime. Most other minerals are also leached out rapidly, leaving behind primarily iron and aluminum oxides and barren grains of quartz sand. This residue normally imparts to the resulting soil the reddish color that gives this regime its name (Figure 12-23). The A horizon is highly eluviated and leached, whereas the B horizon has a considerable concentration of illuviated materials.

Because plant litter is rapidly decomposed in places where laterization is the predominant regime, little humus is incorporated into the soil. Even so, plant nutrients are not totally removed by leaching because the natural vegetation, particularly in a forest, quickly absorbs many of the nutrients in solution. If the vegetation is relatively undisturbed by human activities, this regime has the most rapid of nutrient cycles, and the soil is not totally impoverished by the speed of mineral decomposition and leaching. Where the forest is cleared for agriculture or some other human purpose, however, most base nutrients are likely to be lost from the cycle because the tree roots that would bring them up are gone. The soil then rapidly becomes impoverished, and hard crusts of iron and aluminum compounds are likely to form.

The general term applied to soils produced by laterization is **latosols**. These soils sometimes develop to depths of several meters because of the strong weathering activities and the fact that laterization continues year-round in these benign climates. Most latosols have little to offer as agricultural soils, for the reasons noted above, but laterization often produces such concentrations of iron and aluminum oxides that mining them can be profitable.

Podzolization

Podzolization is another regime named after the color of the soil it produces; in this case, gray (*podzol:* Russian for "like ashes"). It also occurs in regions having a positive moisture balance and involves considerable leaching, but beyond those two characteristics, it bears little similarity to laterization. Podzolization occurs primarily in areas where the vegetation has limited nutrient requirements and where the plant litter is acidic. These conditions are most prominent in mid- and high-latitude locales having a coniferous forest cover. Thus, podzolization is largely a Northern Hemisphere phenomenon because there is not much

▲ **Figure 12-23** In the wet tropics, laterization is the dominant soil-forming regime, and most soils are reddish as a result of the prominence of iron and aluminum compounds. Lateritic soils are exposed in this road cut near Savusavu on the Fijian island of Vanua Levu. *(Tom L. McKnight photo.)*

land in the higher midlatitudes south of the equator. The typical location for podzolization is under a boreal forest in subarctic climates, which is found only in the Northern Hemisphere.

In these cool regions, chemical weathering is slow, but the abundance of acids, plus adequate precipitation, makes leaching very effective. Mechanical weathering from frost action is relatively rapid during the unfrozen part of the year. Moreover, much of the land was bulldozed by Pleistocene glaciers, leaving an abundance of broken rock debris at the surface. Bedrock here consists mostly of ancient crystalline rocks rich in quartz and aluminum silicates and poor in the alkaline mineral cations important in plant nutrition. The boreal forests, dominated by conifers, require little in the way of soil nutrients, and their litter returns few nutrient minerals when it decays. The litter is largely needles and twigs, which accumulate on the surface of the soil and decompose slowly. Microorganisms do not thrive in this environment, and so humus production is retarded. Moisture is relatively abundant in summer, so that leaching of whatever nutrient cations are present in the topsoil, along with iron oxides, aluminum oxides, and colloidal clays, is relatively complete.

Podzolization, then, produces soils that are shallow and acidic and have a fairly distinctive profile. There is usually an O horizon. The upper part of the A horizon is eluviated to a silty or sandy texture and is so leached as to appear bleached. It is usually the ashy, light gray color that gives this regime its name, a color imparted by its high silica content. The illuviated B horizon is a receptacle for the iron–aluminum oxides and clay

minerals leached from above and has a sharply contrasting darker color (sometimes with an orange or yellow tinge). Soil fertility is generally low, and a crumbly structure makes the soil very susceptible to accelerated erosion if the vegetation cover is disturbed, whether by human activities or by such natural agencies as wildfire. Soils produced by podzolization often are referred to collectively as **podzols**.

Gleization

Gleization is a regime restricted to waterlogged areas, normally in a cool climate. (The name comes from *glej*, Polish for "muddy ground.") Although occasionally widespread, it is generally much more limited in occurrence than laterization and podzolization. The poor drainage that produces a waterlogged environment can be associated with flat land, but it can also result from a topographic depression, a high water table, or various other conditions. In North America, gleization is particularly prominent in areas around the Great Lakes, where recent glacial deposition has interrupted preglacial drainage patterns.

The general term for soils produced by gleization is **gley soils**. They characteristically have a dark, highly organic A horizon, where decomposition proceeds slowly because bacteria are inhibited by the lack of oxygen in a waterlogged situation. This slow decay yields organic acids that cannot oxidize iron to produce reddish colors, and the pH is invariably low. The B horizon in a true gley soil is poorly developed, but where waterlogging is more limited, a distinctive B horizon may show various colors.

Gley soils are usually too acidic and oxygen poor to be productive for anything but water-tolerant vegetation. If drained artificially, however, and fertilized with lime to counteract the acid, their fertility can be greatly enhanced.

Calcification

In semiarid and arid climates, where precipitation is less than potential evapotranspiration, leaching is either absent or transitory. Natural vegetation in such areas consists of grasses or shrubs. **Calcification** (so called because many calcium salts are produced in this regime) is the dominant pedogenic process in these regions, as typified by the drier prairies of North America, the steppes of Eurasia, and the savannas and steppes of the subtropics.

Both eluviation and leaching are restricted by the absence of percolating water, and so materials that would be carried downward in other regimes become concentrated in the soil where calcification is at work. Moreover, there is considerable upward movement of water by capillary action in dry periods. Calcium carbonate ($CaCO_3$) is the most important chemical compound active in a calcification regime. It is carried downward by limited leaching after a rain and is often concentrated in the B horizon to form a dense layer of *hardpan*, then brought upward by capillary water and by grass roots, and finally returned to the soil when the grass dies. Little clay is formed because of the limited amount of chemical weathering. Organic colloidal material, however, is often present in considerable quantity.

Where calcification takes place under undisturbed grassland, the resulting soils are likely to have remarkable agricultural productivity. Humus from decaying grass yields abundant organic colloidal material, imparting a dark color to the soil and contributing to a structure that can retain both nutrients and soil moisture. Grass roots tend to bring calcium up from the B horizon sufficiently to inhibit or delay the formation of calcic hardpans. Where shrubs are the dominant vegetation, roots are fewer but deeper, so that nutrients are brought up from deeper layers, and little accumulates at the surface with less humus being incorporated into the soil.

Where a calcification regime is operative in true deserts, the soils tend to be shallower and sandier, calcic hardpans may form near the surface, little organic matter accumulates either on or in the soil, and the soils are not very different from the parent material.

Salinization

In arid and semiarid regions, it is fairly common to find areas with inadequate drainage, particularly in enclosed valleys and basins. Moisture is drawn up-

ward and into the atmosphere by intense evaporation. The evaporating water leaves behind various salts in or on the surface of the soil, sometimes in such quantity as to impart a brilliant white surface color to the land, and the pedogenic regime is called **salinization**. These salts, which are mostly chlorides and sulfates of calcium and sodium, are toxic to most plants and soil organisms, and the resulting soil is able to support very little life apart from a few salt-tolerant grasses and shrubs.

Soils developed in a salinization (*salin:* Latin for "salt") regime can be sometimes made productive through careful water management, but artificial drainage is equally necessary or else salt accumulation will be intensified. Indeed, human-induced salinization has ruined good agricultural land in various parts of the world many times in the past.

Climate and Pedogenic Regimes

The regimes are distinguished primarily on the basis of climate as reflected in temperature and moisture availability (Figure 12-24) and secondarily on the basis of vegetation cover. In regions where there is normally a surplus of moisture—which is to say annual precipitation exceeds annual evapotranspiration—water movement in the soil is predominantly downward and leaching is a prominent process. In such areas where temperatures are relatively high throughout the year, laterization is the dominant regime; where winters are long and cold, podzolization predominates; and where the soil is saturated most of the time due to poor drainage,

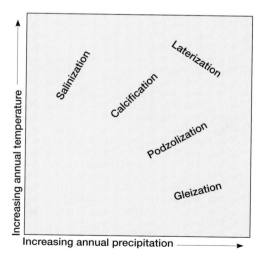

▲ **Figure 12-24** Temperature–moisture relationships for the five principal pedogenic regimes. Where temperature is high but precipitation low, salinization is the main method of soil formation. Where temperature is low but precipitation high, gleization predominates. Laterization occurs where both temperature and precipitation are high. Calcification and podzolization take place in less extreme environments.

gleization is notable. A broadly valid generalization is that gleization can occur in any of the pedogenic regimes, as it is more dependent on local topography than on macroclimate. In regions having a moisture deficit, the principal soil moisture movement is upward (through capillarity) and leaching is limited. Calcification and salinization are the principal pedogenic regimes under these conditions.

Soil Classification

Some of the most significant products of scholarly studies are classification systems. If phenomena can be classified meaningfully, it becomes easier to remember them and to understand the relationships among them. Our consideration thus far has included various classifications (for example, climate and biomes). In no other subdiscipline of physical geography, however, is the matter of classification more complicated than with soil.

The Soil Taxonomy

Over the past century, various soil classifications have been devised in the United States and other countries. As the knowledge of soil characteristics and processes has become greater, so have the efforts at soil classification become more sophisticated. Several different systems have been developed in other countries, particularly in Canada, the United Kingdom, Russia, France, and Australia. Moreover, United Nations agencies have their own classification schemes. The system that is presently in use in the United States is called simply **Soil Taxonomy**.

The basic characteristic that sets Soil Taxonomy apart from previous systems is that it is *generic*, which means it is organized on the basis of observable soil characteristics. The focus is on the existing properties of a soil rather than on the environment, genesis, or properties it would possess under virgin conditions. The logic of such a generic system is theoretically impeccable: soil has certain properties that can be observed, measured, and at least partly quantified.

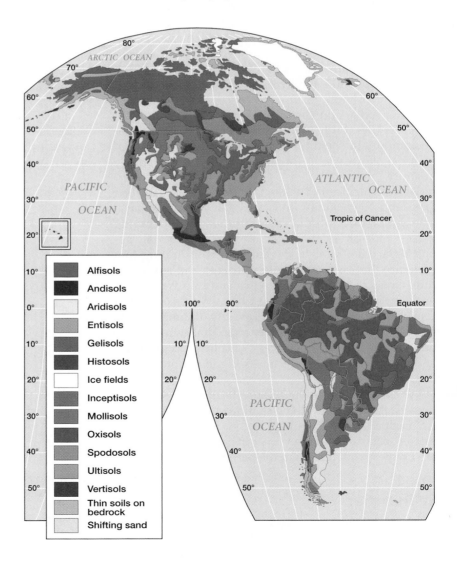

▶ **Figure 12-25** Soils of the world.

Like other logical generic systems, the Soil Taxonomy is a hierarchical system, which means that it has several levels of generalization, with each higher level encompassing several members of the level immediately below it. There are only a few similarities among all the members of the highest level category, but the number of similarities increases with each step downward in the hierarchy, so that in the lowest-level category, all members have mostly the same properties. (See Appendix VII for details.)

At the highest level (the smallest scale of generalization) of the Soil Taxonomy is **soil order**, of which only 12 are recognized worldwide (Table 12-2). The soil orders, and many of the lower-level categories as well, are distinguished from one another largely on the basis of certain diagnostic properties, which are often expressed in combination to form *diagnostic horizons*. The two basic types of diagnostic horizon are the *epipedon* (based on the Greek word *epi*, meaning "over" or "upon"), which is essentially the A horizon or the combined O/A horizon, and the *subsurface horizon*, which is roughly equivalent to the B horizon. (Note

that all A and B horizons are not necessarily diagnostic, and so the terms and concepts are not synonymous.)

Soil orders are subdivided into *suborders*, of which about 50 are recognized in the United States. The third level consists of *great groups*, which number about 250 in the United States. Successively lower levels in the classification are subgroups, families, and series. About 19,000 soil series have been identified in the United States to date, and the list will undoubtedly be expanded in the future. For the purpose of comprehending general world distribution patterns, however, we need to concern ourselves only with orders and suborders (Figure 12-25).

The Mapping Question

Maps are a basic tool of geographic study, and one of the fundamental problems that confronts any geographic inquiry is how the phenomena under study should be mapped. There are precise techniques for mapping features that are located at specific points or for mapping phenomena that are spread uniformly

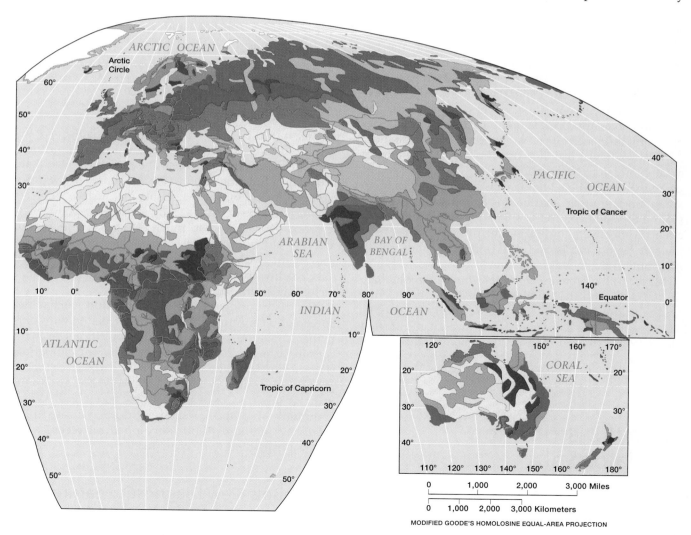

MODIFIED GOODE'S HOMOLOSINE EQUAL-AREA PROJECTION

TABLE 12-2 Name Derivations of Soil Orders	
Order	Derivation
Alfisols	"al" for aluminum, "f" for iron (chemical symbol Fe), two prominent elements in these soils
Andisols	andesite, rock formed from type of magma in Andes Mountains volcanoes; soils high in volcanic ash
Aridisols	Latin *aridus*, "dry"; dry soils
Entisols	last three letters in "recent"; these are recently formed soils
Gelisols	Latin *gelatio*, "freezing"; soils in areas of permafrost
Histosols	Greek *histos*, "living tissue"; these soils contain only organic matter
Inceptisols	Latin *inceptum*, "beginning"; young soils at the beginning of their "life"
Mollisols	Latin *mollis*, "soft"; soft soils
Oxisols	soils with large amounts of oxygen containing compounds
Spodosols	Greek *spodos*, "wood ash"; ashy soils
Ultisols	Latin *ultimus*, "last"; soils that have had the last of their nutrient bases leached out
Vertisols	Latin *verto*, "turn"; soils in which material from O and A horizons falls through surface cracks and ends up below deeper horizons; the usual horizon order is inverted

over an area. However, if the object of study is a generalized abstraction, its depiction on a map is necessarily imprecise, and choice of the mapping technique becomes more subjective. Because the higher levels of the Soil Taxonomy do not represent phenomena that actually exist but rather are generalized abstractions of average or typical conditions over broad areas, the selection of an appropriate mapping technique can significantly influence our understanding of the situation.

Most soil maps use the same timeworn technique of areal expression. If one soil type (at whatever level of generalization is being studied) is more common in an area than any other, that area is classified by the prevailing type and colored or shaded appropriately. Such a map is effective in indicating the principal type of soil in each region and is useful in portraying the general distribution of the major soil types.

Maps of this type are compiled through generalization of data, and the smaller the scale, the greater the generalization needed. Thus, more intricate patterns can be shown on the larger scale map of the United States (Figure 12-39) than on the smaller scale world map (Figure 12-25). In either case, the map is only as good as its generalizations are meticulous.

Global Distribution of Major Soils

There are 12 orders of soils, which are distinguished largely on the basis of properties that reflect a major course of development, with considerable emphasis on the presence or absence of notable diagnostic horizons. We consider each of the 12 orders in sequence, beginning with those characterized by little profile development and progressing to those with the most highly weathered profiles, as represented left to right in Figure 12-26.

Entisols (Very Little Profile Development)

The least well developed of all soils, **Entisols** have experienced little mineral alteration and are virtually without pedogenic horizons. Their undeveloped state is usually a function of time (the very name of the order connotes recency); most Entisols are surface deposits that have not been in place long enough for pedogenetic processes to have had much effect. Some, however, are very old, and in these soils the lack of horizon development is due to a mineral content that does not alter readily, to a very cold climate, or to some other factor totally unrelated to time.

The distribution of Entisols is therefore very widespread and cannot be specifically correlated with particular moisture or temperature conditions or with certain types of vegetation or parent materials (Figure 12-27). In the United States, Entisols are most prominent in the dry lands of the West but are found in most other parts of the country as well. They are commonly thin and/or sandy and have limited productivity, although those developed on recent alluvial deposits tend to be quite fertile.

Inceptisols (Few Diagnostic Features)

Another immature order of soils is the **Inceptisols**. Their distinctive characteristics are relatively faint, not yet prominent enough to produce diagnostic horizons

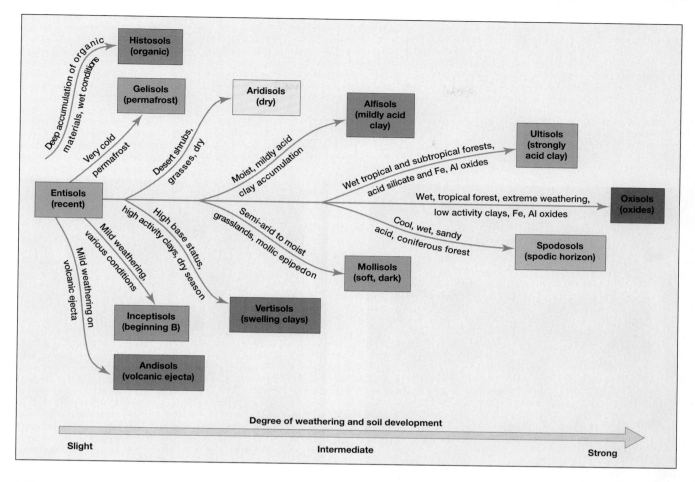

▲ **Figure 12-26**   The general relationship among the soil orders, in terms of degree of weathering, soil development, and broad environmental conditions. *(After Nyle C. Brady and Ray R. Weil,* The Nature and Properties of Soils, *© 1999. Reprinted by permission of Prentice-Hall, Inc., Upper Saddle River, NJ.)*

(Figure 12-28). If the Entisols can be called youthful, the Inceptisols might be classified adolescent. They are primarily eluvial soils and lack illuvial layers.

Like Entisols, Inceptisols are widespread over the world in various environments. Also like Entisols, they include a variety of fairly dissimilar soils whose common characteristic is lack of maturity. They are most common in tundra and mountain areas but are also notable in older valley floodplains. Their world distribution pattern is very irregular. This is also true in the United States, where they are most typical of the Appalachian Mountains, the Pacific Northwest, and the lower Mississippi Valley.

Andisols (Volcanic Ash Soils)

Having developed from volcanic ash, **Andisols** have been deposited in relatively recent geological time. They are not highly weathered, therefore, and there has been little downward translocation of their colloids. There is minimum profile development, and the upper layers are dark (Figure 12-29). Their inherent fertility is relatively high.

Andisols are found primarily in volcanic regions of Japan, Indonesia, and South America, as well as in the very productive wheat lands of Washington, Oregon, and Idaho.

Gelisols (Permafrost Layer)

Gelisols are young soils with minimal profile development (Figure 12-30). They develop only slowly because of cold temperatures and frozen conditions. These soils typically have a permafrost layer that is a defining characteristic. Also commonly found in Gelisols is *cryoturbation* or frost churning, which is the physical disruption and displacement of soil material by freeze–thaw action in the soil. Most of the soil-forming processes in Gelisols take place above the permafrost in the active layer that thaws every year or so.

Gelisols are the dominant soils of arctic and subarctic regions. They occur in association with boreal forest and tundra vegetation; thus, they are primarily found in Russia, Canada, and Alaska and are prominent in the Himalaya Mountain country of central

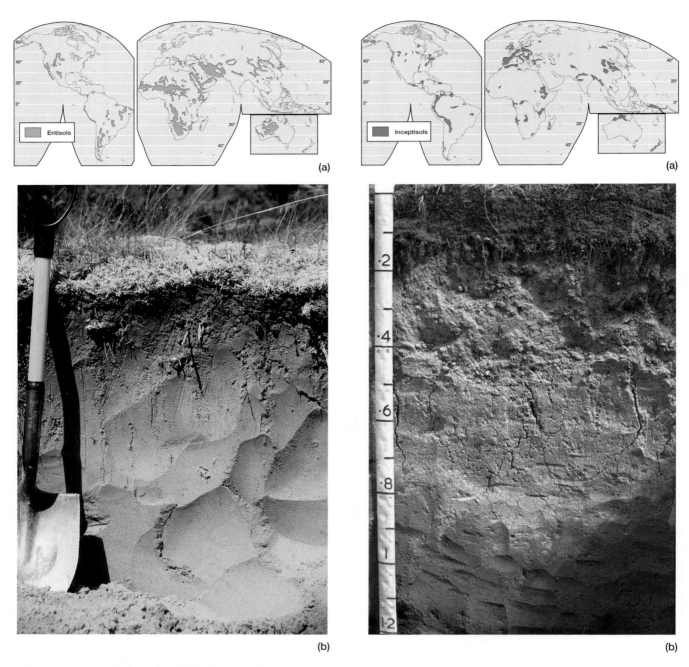

▲ **Figure 12-27** Entisols. **(a)** World distribution of Entisols. **(b)** Profile of an Entisol in northern Michigan. This weakly developed soil evolved from sandy parent material and is very droughty. *(Randy Schaetzl photo.)*

▲ **Figure 12-28** Inceptisols. **(a)** World distribution of Inceptisols. **(b)** Profile of a New Zealand Inceptisol with a distinctive B horizon of white pebbly material. The scale is in meters. *(U.S. Department of Agriculture.)*

Asia. Altogether nearly 9 percent of Earth's land area has a Gelisol soil cover.

Histosols (Organic Soils)

Least important among the soil orders are the **Histosols**, which occupy only a small fraction of Earth's land surface, a much smaller area than any other order. These are organic rather than mineral soils,

and they are invariably saturated with water all or most of the time. They may occur in any waterlogged environment but are most characteristic in mid- and high-latitude regions that experienced Pleistocene glaciation. In the United States, they are most common around the Great Lakes, but they also occur in southern Florida and Louisiana. Nowhere, however, is their occurrence extensive (Figure 12-31).

Some Histosols are composed largely of undecayed or only partly decayed plant material, whereas others

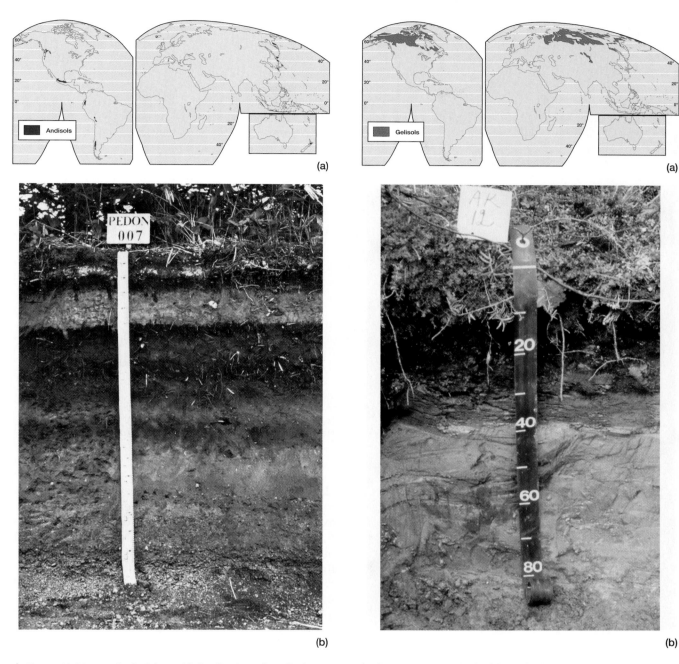

▲ **Figure 12-29**   Andisols. **(a)** World distribution of Andisols. **(b)** Profile of an Andisol in Washington state. The various horizons are very clearly delineated. *(Loyal A. Quandt, National Soil Survey Center.)*

▲ **Figure 12-30**   Gelisols. **(a)** World distribution of Gelisols. **(b)** Profile of a Gelisol. *(Courtesy of USDA Natural Resources Conservation Service, National Soil Survey Center.)*

consist of a thoroughly decomposed mass of muck. The lack of oxygen in the waterlogged soil slows down the rate of bacterial action, and the soil becomes deeper mostly by growing upward, that is, by more organic material being added from above.

Histosols are usually black, acidic, and fertile only for water-tolerant plants. If drained, they can be very productive agriculturally for a short while. Before long, however, they are likely to dry out, shrink, and oxidize, a series of steps that leads to compaction, susceptibility to wind erosion, and danger of fire.

Aridisols (Dry Soils)

Nearly one-eighth of Earth's land surface is covered with **Aridisols**, one of the most extensive spreads of any soil order (Figure 12-32). They are preeminently soils of the dry lands, occupying environments that do not have enough water to remove soluble minerals from the soil. Thus, their distribution pattern is largely correlated with that of desert and semidesert climate.

Aridisols are typified by a thin profile that is sandy and lacking in organic matter, characteristics clearly

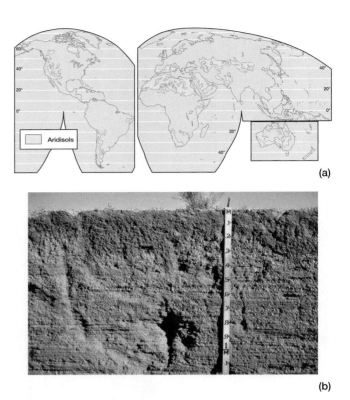

▲ **Figure 12-32** Aridisols. **(a)** World distribution of Aridisols. **(b)** The typical sandy profile of an Aridisol, in this case from New Mexico. *(U.S. Department of Agriculture.)*

▲ **Figure 12-31** Histosols. **(a)** World distribution of Histosols. **(b)** Histosols are characteristically dark in color and composed principally of organic matter. *(Randy Schaetzl photo.)*

associated with a dry climate and a scarcity of penetrating moisture. The epipedon is almost invariably light in color. There are various kinds of diagnostic subsurface horizons, nearly all distinctly alkaline. Most Aridisols are unproductive, particularly because of lack of moisture; if irrigated, however, some display remarkable fertility. The threat of salt accumulation is ever present, however.

Vertisols (Swelling and Cracking Clays)

Vertisols contain a large quantity of clay that becomes a dominant factor in the soil's development. The clay of Vertisols is described as "swelling" or "cracking"

clay. This clay-type soil has an exceptional capacity for absorbing water: when moistened, it swells and expands; as it dries, deep, wide cracks form, sometimes 2.5 centimeters (an inch) wide and as much as 1 meter (a yard) deep. Some surface material falls into the cracks, and more is washed in when it rains. When the soil is wetted again, more swelling takes place and the cracks close. This alternation of wetting and drying and expansion and contraction produces a churning effect that mixes the soil constituents (the name Vertisol connotes an inverted condition), inhibits the development of horizons, and may even cause minor irregularities in the land surface (Figure 12-33).

An alternating wet and dry climate is needed for Vertisol formation because the sequence of swelling and contraction is necessary. Thus, the wet–dry climate of tropical and subtropical savannas is ideal, but there must also be the proper parent material to yield the clay minerals. Consequently, Vertisols are widespread in distribution but are very limited in extent. The principal occurrences are in eastern Australia, India, and a small part of East Africa. They are uncommon in the United States, although prominent in some parts of Texas and California.

The fertility of Vertisols is relatively high, as they tend to be rich in nutrient bases. They are difficult to till, however, because of their sticky plasticity, and so they are often left uncultivated.

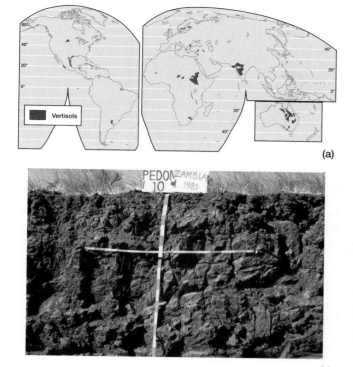

▲ **Figure 12-33** Vertisols. **(a)** World distribution of Vertisols. **(b)** A dark Vertisol profile from Zambia. Many cracks are typically found in Vertisols. *(U.S. Department of Agriculture.)*

Mollisols (Dark, Soft Soils of Grasslands)

The distinctive characteristic of **Mollisols** is the presence of a mollic epipedon, which is a mineral surface horizon that is dark and thick, contains abundant humus and basic cations, and retains a soft character (rather than becoming hard and crusty) when it dries out (Figure 12-34). Mollisols can be thought of as transition soils that evolve in regions not dominated by either humid or arid conditions. They are typical of the midlatitude grasslands and are thus most common in central Eurasia, the North American Great Plains, and the pampas of Argentina.

The grassland environment generally maintains a rich clay–humus content in a Mollisol soil. The dense, fibrous mass of grass roots permeates uniformly through the epipedon and to a lesser extent into the subsurface layers. There is almost continuous decay of plant parts to produce a nutrient-rich humus for the living grass.

Mollisols on the whole are probably the most productive soil order. They are generally derived from loose parent material rather than from bedrock and tend to have favorable structure and texture for cultivation. Because they are not overly leached, nutrients are generally retained within reach of plant roots. Moreover, Mollisols provide a favored habitat for earthworms, which contribute to softening and mixing the soil.

▲ **Figure 12-34** Mollisols. **(a)** World distribution of Mollisols. **(b)** A Mollisol profile from Nebraska. It has a typical mollic epipedon, a surface horizon that is dark and replete with humus. *(Loyal A. Quandt, National Soil Survey Center.)*

Alfisols (Clay Accumulation with High Bases)

The most wide ranging of the mature soils, **Alfisols** occur extensively in low and middle latitudes, as Figure 12-35 shows. They are found in a variety of temperature and moisture conditions and under diverse vegetation associations. By and large, they tend to be associated with transitional environments and are less characteristic of regions that are particularly hot or cold or wet or dry. Their global distribution is extremely varied. They are also widespread in the United States, with particular concentrations in the Midwest.

Alfisols are distinguished by a subsurface clay horizon and a medium to generous supply of plant nutrients and water. The epipedon is ochric (light-colored), as Figure 12-35b shows, but beyond that, it has no characteristics that are particularly diagnostic and can be considered an ordinary eluviated horizon. The relatively moderate conditions under which Alfisols develop tend to produce balanced soils that are reasonably fertile. Alfisols rank second only to Mollisols in agricultural productivity.

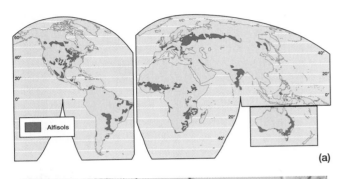

(a)

(b)

▲ **Figure 12-35** Alfisols. **(a)** World distribution of Alfisols. **(b)** Profile of an Alfisol in east-central Illinois. The soil has reddened, clay-rich B horizon. It formed under forest vegetation and is heavily cropped with corn and soybeans. *(Randy Schaetzl photo.)*

Ultisols (Clay Accumulation with Low Bases)

Ultisols are roughly similar to Alfisols except that the former are more thoroughly weathered and more completely leached of nutrient bases. They have experienced greater mineral alteration than any other soil in the midlatitudes, although they also occur in the low latitudes. Many pedologists believe that the ultimate fate of Alfisols is to degenerate into Ultisols.

Typically, Ultisols are reddish as a result of the significant proportion of iron and aluminum in the A horizon. They usually have a fairly distinct layer of subsurface clay accumulation. The principal properties of Ultisols have been imparted by a great deal of weathering and leaching (Figure 12-36). Indeed, the

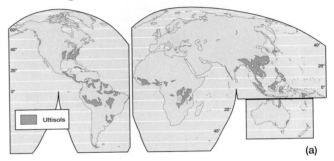

(a)

(b)

▲ **Figure 12-36** Ultisols. **(a)** World distribution of Ultisols. **(b)** A tropical Ultisol from Thailand. It is reddish throughout its profile, indicative of much leaching and weathering. *(U.S. Department of Agriculture.)*

▲ **Figure 12-37**   Spodosols. **(a)** World distribution of Spodosols. **(b)** Profile of a Spodosol in northern Michigan. This weakly developed soil was formed in sandy material under coniferous forest vegetation and contains few nutrients. *(Randy Schaetzl photo.)*

▲ **Figure 12-38**   Oxisols. **(a)** World distribution of Oxisols. **(b)** Oxisols are impoverished tropical soils that usually are heavily leached. The horizons typically are indistinct. This sample is from Hawaii. *(Randy Schaetzl photo.)*

connotation of the name (derived from the Latin ultimos) is that these soils represent the ultimate stage of weathering in the conterminous United States. The result is a fairly deep soil that is acidic, lacks humus, and has a relatively low fertility due to the lack of bases.

Ultisols have a fairly simple world distribution pattern. They are mostly confined to humid subtropical climates and to some relatively youthful tropical land surfaces. In the United States, they are restricted largely to the southeastern quarter of the country and to a narrow strip along the northern Pacific Coast.

Spodosols (Acid, Sandy Forest Soils)

The key diagnostic feature of a **Spodosol** is a spodic subsurface horizon, an illuvial dark or reddish layer where organic matter, iron, and aluminum accumulate. The upper layers are light-colored and heavily leached (Figure 12-37). At the top of the profile is usually an O horizon of organic litter. Such a soil is a typical result of podzolization.

Spodosols are notoriously infertile. They have been leached of useful nutrients and are acidic throughout. They do not retain moisture well and are lacking in humus and often in clay.

Spodosols are most widespread in areas of coniferous forest where there is a subarctic climate. Alfisols, Histosols, and Inceptisols also occupy these regions, however, and Spodosols are sometimes found in other environments, such as poorly drained portions of Florida.

Oxisols (Highly Weathered and Leached)

The most thoroughly weathered and leached of all soils are the **Oxisols**, which invariably display a high degree of mineral alteration and profile development. They occur mostly on ancient landscapes in the humid tropics, particularly in Brazil and equatorial Africa, and to a lesser extent in Southeast Asia (Figure 12-38, p. 381). The distribution pattern is often spotty, with Oxisols mixed with less-developed Entisols, Vertisols, and Ultisols. Oxisols are totally absent from the United States, except for Hawaii, where they are common.

Oxisols are essentially the products of laterization (and in fact were called Latosols in the older classification systems). They have evolved in warm, moist

TABLE 12-3 Approximate Proportional Extent of Soil Orders

Order	Percentage of Land Area Occupied	
	United States	World
Alfisols	14.5	9.7
Andisols	1.7	0.7
Aridisols	8.8	12.1
Entisols	12.2	16.3
Gelisols	7.5	8.6
Histosols	1.3	1.2
Inceptisols	9.1	9.9
Mollisols	22.4	6.9
Oxisols	—	7.6
Spodosols	3.3	2.6
Ultisols	9.6	8.5
Vertisols	1.7	2.4

Source: Nyle C. Brady and Ray R. Weil, *The Nature and Properties of Soils*, Upper Saddle River, NJ: Prentice Hall, 1999, p. 86.

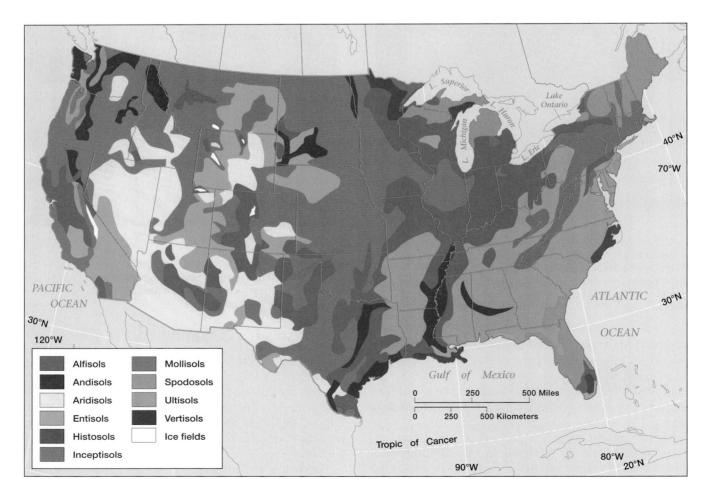

▲ **Figure 12-39** Distribution of predominant soil orders in the conterminous United States.

climates, although some are now found in drier regions, an indication of climatic change since the soils developed. The diagnostic horizon for Oxisols is a subsurface dominated by oxides of iron and aluminum and with a minimal supply of nutrient bases (this is called an *oxic* horizon). These are deep soils but not inherently fertile. The natural vegetation is efficient in cycling the limited nutrient supply, but if the flora is cleared (to attempt agriculture, for example), the nutrients are rapidly leached out, and the soil becomes impoverished.

Distribution of Soils in the United States

The distribution of the various soils in the United States is quite different from that of the world as a whole. This difference is due to many factors, the most important

being that the United States is essentially a midlatitude country, and it lacks significant expanses of area in the low and high latitudes (Figure 12-39). Table 12-3 compares the relative areas occupied by the 12 soil orders, nationally and globally. The statistics are generalized estimates prepared by the Soil Conservation Service of the U.S. Department of Agriculture and should not be considered definitive.

Mollisols are much more common in the United States than in the world as a whole; they are the most prevalent soil order throughout the Great Plains and in much of the West. Also significantly more abundant in the United States than in other parts of the world are Inceptisols and Ultisols. Almost totally lacking from this country are Oxisols, and Aridisols and Entisols are proportionally less extensive.

Chapter 12 Learning Review

Key Terms

Before answering the study questions below, review the definitions of the following key terms (page references are provided for you):

A horizon (*p. 367*)
Alfisol (*p. 379*)
Andisol (*p. 375*)
Aridisol (*p. 377*)
B horizon (*p. 367*)
calcification (*p. 371*)
cations (*p. 359*)
cation exchange capacity (CEC) (*p. 366*)
C horizon (*p. 367*)
colloid (*p. 366*)
E horizon (*p. 367*)
eluviation (*p. 362*)
Entisol (*p. 374*)
field capacity (*p. 362*)
Gelisol (*p. 375*)
gleization (*p. 370*)

gley soil (*p. 370*)
Histosol (*p. 376*)
horizon (soil horizon) (*p. 367*)
humus (*p. 357*)
illuviation (*p. 362*)
Inceptisol (*p. 374*)
laterization (*p. 368*)
latosol (*p. 369*)
leaching (*p. 362*)
litter (*p. 359*)
loam (*p. 364*)
Mollisol (*p. 379*)
O horizon (*p. 367*)
Oxisol (*p. 382*)
parent material (*p. 355*)
pedogenic regime (*p. 368*)
peds (*p. 364*)

podzol (*p. 370*)
podzolization (*p. 369*)
regolith (*p. 354*)
R horizon (*p. 367*)
salinization (*p. 371*)
separates (*p. 364*)
soil (*p. 353*)
soil order (*p. 373*)
soil profile (*p. 367*)
Soil Taxonomy (*p. 372*)
soil–water balance (*p. 362*)
soil–water budget (*p. 362*)
solum (*p. 367*)
Spodosol (*p. 381*)
Ultisol (*p. 380*)
Vertisol (*p. 378*)
wilting point (*p. 362*)

Study Questions for Key Concepts

After studying this chapter, you should be able to answer the following questions:

Soil and Regolith (p. 353)
1. What is the relationship between weathering and regolith?
2. What is the difference between *soil* and *regolith*?

Soil-Forming Factors (p. 355)
3. Briefly describe the five principal soil-forming factors.

4. Explain the importance of parent material to the nature of the overlying soil.
5. Why does soil tend to be deepest on flat land?
6. What are some of the roles of animals in soil formation?
7. Why are earthworms generally considered beneficial to humans?

8. What roles do microorganisms play in the soil?

Soil Components (p. 359)

9. Explain the importance of clay as a constituent of soil.
10. What is the difference between *litter* and *humus*?
11. Describe and explain the four forms of soil moisture.
12. Explain the processes of *eluviation* and *illuviation*.
13. What is the *soil-water balance*?
14. Distinguish between *field capacity* and *wilting point*.
15. What is the role of temperature in the soil-water budget?

Soil Properties (p. 362)

16. What can you learn about a soil from its color?
17. Distinguish between soil *texture* and soil *structure*.
18. What is meant by *loam*?
19. Explain the difference between *porosity* and *permeability*.

Soil Chemistry (p. 365)

20. Explain what is meant by the *cation exchange capacity* (CEC) of a soil?

Soil Profiles (p. 367)

21. What is a *soil profile*?
22. Briefly describe the six possible soil *horizons*.

Pedogenic Regimes (p. 368)

23. Briefly describe and explain the five major pedogenic regimes:
    * Laterization
    * Podzolization
    * Gleization
    * Calcification
    * Salinization
24. Why do tropical rainforests usually have poor soils?

Soil Classification (p. 372)

25. How does the Soil Taxonomy differ from previous soil classification schemes?
26. Why is it so difficult to portray soil distribution with reasonable accuracy on a small-scale map?

Global Distribution of Major Soils (p. 374)

27. Using the map of soil distribution in the United States (Figure 12-39) or the map showing the world distribution of soils (Figure 12-25), choose one of the soil orders that is found nearby your home and describe that order's general distribution and characteristics.

28. For each of the following circumstances, indicate which soil order is mostly likely to be found and the reasons for this:
   - Regions of permafrost
   - Areas with coniferous forest
   - Deserts

Additional Resources

Books:

Brady, Nyle C. and Ray R. Weil. *Elements of the Nature and Properties of Soils,* 2nd ed. Upper Saddle River, NJ: Pearson-Prentice Hall, 2004.

Soil Survey Staff. *Soil Taxonomy: A Basic System of Soil Classification for Making and Interpreting Soil Surveys,* 2nd ed. Washington, D.C.: USDA Natural Resources Conservation Service, 1999.

————. *Keys to Soil Taxonomy.* Washington, D.C.: USDA Natural Resources Conservation Service, 1998.

Internet Site:
National Cooperative Soil Survey
http://soils.usda.gov/

The National Cooperative Soil Survey is a good starting point for finding information about soils.

13
Introduction to Landform Study

In this chapter, we turn our attention more directly to the study of the solid portion of Earth. Thoughtful beginning students of physical geography may be daunted by the magnitude of their object of study because Earth is enormous from the human viewpoint. Its diameter of about 12,800 kilometers (about 8000 miles) and circumference of 40,000 kilometers (about 25,000 miles) are distances well beyond our normal scale of living and thinking. To comprehend the nature of such a massive body is a colossal task. Our endeavor is greatly simplified, however, because we can largely concentrate our attention on the surface—as geographers, we want to know about Earth's interior because it helps us to comprehend the nature and characteristics of the processes shaping Earth's surface features.

We begin our task with a description of the structure of Earth as a whole. We then turn to a discussion of rocks—the solid material from which the planet is made. We conclude the chapter by introducing some fundamental concepts that we will use in our study of Earth's surface features.

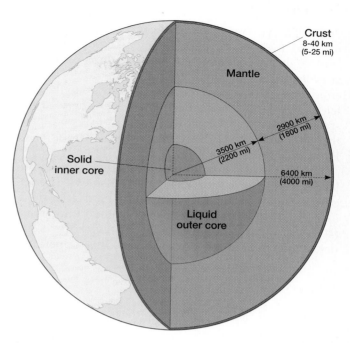

▲ **Figure 13-1** The presumed vertical structure of Earth's interior.

The Structure of Earth

Our knowledge of the interior of Earth is based largely on indirect evidence. No human activity has explored more than a minute fraction of the vastness beneath the surface. No person has penetrated as much as one-thousandth of the radial distance from the surface to the center of Earth; the deepest existing mine shaft extends a mere 3.8 kilometers (2.4 miles). Nor have probes extended much deeper; the deepest drill holes from which sample cores have been brought up have penetrated only a modest 12 kilometers (8 miles) into Earth. Earth scientists, in the colorful imagery of John McPhee, "are like dermatologists: they study, for the most part, the outermost two per cent of the earth. They crawl around like fleas on the world's tough hide, exploring every wrinkle and crease, and try to figure out what makes the animal move."[1]

Even so, a considerable body of inferential knowledge concerning Earth's interior has been amassed by geophysical means, primarily by monitoring patterns of the shock waves transmitted through Earth from

◀ Navajo Sandstone in the Paria Canyon Wilderness, Arizona. *(Kump-Kasting-Crane.)*

[1]McPhee, John, *Assembling California,* p. 36, New York: Farrar, Straus and Giroux, 1993.

earthquakes or from human-made explosions. Such seismic waves change their speed and direction whenever they cross a boundary from one type of material to another. Analysis of these changes, augmented by related data on Earth's magnetism and gravitational attraction, has enabled Earth scientists to develop a model of Earth's internal structure.

Figure 13-1 is one rendition of this inferred structure. It has been deduced that Earth has a heavy inner core surrounded by three concentric layers of various compositions and density. Starting at the surface and moving inward, these four regions are called the *crust,* the *mantle,* the *outer core,* and the *inner core.*

The Crust

The **crust**, the outermost shell, consists of a broad mixture of rock types. Beneath the oceans the crust has an average thickness of only 5 kilometers (3 miles), whereas beneath the continents the thickness averages more than five times as much. There is a gradual increase in density with depth in this rigid outer shell. Altogether, the crust makes up less than 1 percent of Earth's volume and about 0.4 percent of Earth's mass.

At the base of the crust there is a significant change in mineral composition. This relatively narrow zone of change is called the **Mohorovičić discontinuity**, or simply the **Moho** for short, named for the Croatian seismologist Andrija Mohorovičić (1857–1936) who discovered it.

The Mantle

Beneath the Moho is the **mantle**, which extends downward to a depth of approximately 2900 kilometers (1800 miles). Volumetrically, the mantle is by far the largest of the four shells. Although its depth is only about one-half the distance from the surface to the center of the Earth, its location on the periphery of the sphere gives it a vast breadth. It makes up 84 percent of the total volume of Earth and about two-thirds of Earth's total mass.

Earth scientists now think that there are three sublayers within the mantle, as Figure 13-2 shows. The uppermost zone is relatively thin but hard and rigid, extending down to a depth of 65 to 100 kilometers (40 to 60 miles)—somewhat deeper under the continents than under the ocean floors. This uppermost mantle zone together with the overlying crust is called the **lithosphere**.[2]

Beneath this rigid zone, and extending downward to a depth of possibly 350 kilometers (200 miles), is a zone in which the rocks are so hot that they lose much of their strength and are easily deformed, somewhat like tar. This is called the **asthenosphere** ("weak sphere"). Below the asthenosphere is the *lower mantle*, where the rocks are believed to be largely rigid again.

The Inner and Outer Cores

Beneath the mantle is the **outer core**, thought to be molten (liquid) and extending to a depth of about 5000 kilometers (3100 miles).

The innermost portion of Earth is the **inner core**, an evidently solid and very dense mass having a radius of about 1450 kilometers (900 miles). Both the inner and outer cores are thought to be made of iron/nickel or iron/silicate. These two zones together make up about 15 percent of Earth's volume and 32 percent of its mass.

Earth's *magnetic field* is generated primarily in the outer core—circulation within the liquid outer core induces the magnetic field of our planet. Interestingly, the magnetic field of Earth changes over time. The location of the north magnetic pole doesn't exactly match the true geographic North Pole, changing slowly year by year (the north magnetic pole is currently located at about 83° N, 114° W). In addition, for reasons that are not completely understood, at irregular intervals of thousands of years, the polarity of Earth's magnetic field reverses, with the north magnetic pole becoming the south. As we will see in Chapter 14, a record of these magnetic polarity reversals has been recorded in the iron-rich rocks of the ocean floor.

Plate Tectonics and the Structure of Earth

The generalized model of Earth's interior shown in Figures 13-1 and 13-2 is a useful starting point for understanding physical geography. However, many details of the processes taking place within the interior of Earth are still being worked out by scientists. The fragility of our understanding of the interior of Earth was dramatically revealed in the 1960s when the notion of "continental drift," first propounded in the early 1900s but held in disdain by most scientists for the next half-century, was revived and expanded into the present-day theory of *plate tectonics*—a theory that is now accepted by virtually all Earth scientists. Geological,

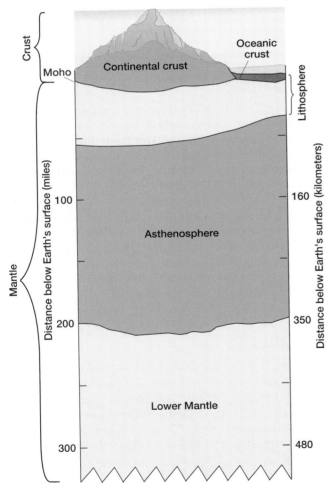

▲ **Figure 13-2** Idealized cross section through Earth's crust and part of the mantle. The crust and uppermost mantle, both rigid zones, are together called the *lithosphere*. In the asthenosphere, the mantle is hot and therefore weak and easily deformed. In the lower mantle, the rock is generally rigid again. The lower mantle is much deeper than shown here, extending to about 2900 kilometers (1800 miles) below Earth's surface.

---

[2] For the remainder of our study of landforms, the term *lithosphere* will have a more restricted meaning than earlier in the book when we introduced the four "spheres." For our purposes now, lithosphere refers specifically to the crust and upper rigid mantle, or simply the "plates" of plate tectonics.

paleontological, seismic, and magnetic evidence makes it clear that the lithosphere of Earth is broken into large, sometimes continent-sized slabs, commonly called "plates," that are slowly moving over the warm, soft asthenosphere below. These enormous plates are quite literally pulling apart, colliding or sliding past each other. Many internal processes such as faulting, folding, and volcanic activity are directly linked to the action taking place along the boundaries of these plates.

We will explore the dynamics of plate tectonics in much greater detail in Chapter 14. For the remainder of this chapter, however, we set the stage for that discussion by introducing some key concepts in the study of the surface features of Earth, such as rocks, geologic time, and the doctrine of uniformitarianism.

The Composition of Earth

About 100 natural chemical elements are found in Earth's crust, mantle, and core, occasionally as discrete elements but usually bonded with one or more other elements to form compounds. These naturally formed compounds and elements of Earth are called *minerals*— the building blocks of *rocks*, which are in turn the building blocks of the landscape itself.

Minerals

In order for a substance to be considered a **mineral**, it must:

- Be solid
- Be naturally found in nature
- Be inorganic
- Have a specific chemical composition wherever found that varies only within certain limits
- Contain atoms arranged in a regular pattern to form solid crystals

Although about 100 elements have been defined in nature, only about one-fourth of them are involved in the formation of minerals to any significant magnitude. Approximately 4400 minerals have been identified, with new types identified almost every year. The majority of known minerals are found only in the crust; a more limited number of minerals are found within the mantle or have been identified in extraterrestrial rocks such as meteorites or those brought back from the Moon.

Of the more than 4000 recognized minerals, only a few dozen are of much importance as constituents of the rocks of Earth's crust. Some of the most common rock-forming minerals are listed in Table 13-1. Mineral nomenclature is very unsystematic. Some names reflect the mineral's chemical composition or a physical property, some names are based on a person or a place, and some appear to have been chosen at random.

The rock-forming minerals can be grouped into seven principal categories or families based on their chemical properties and internal structure.

Silicates The largest and most important mineral family consists of the **silicates**. The bulk of the rocks of the crust are composed of silicate minerals, which combine the two most abundant chemical elements in the lithosphere, oxygen (O) and silicon (Si). Most silicates are hard and durable. The major subcategories of this group are *ferromagnesian silicates* and *nonferromagnesian silicates*, which are distinguished from one another by the presence or absence of iron and magnesium in their composition. Feldspars and quartz (Figure 13-3) are the most abundant of the silicate minerals. Quartz itself is composed of pure *silica* (SiO_2).

Oxides An *oxide* is an element combined with oxygen. Only a relatively few elements are able to do so. The most widespread of the oxides are those that combine with iron, particularly hematite, magnetite, and limonite, all three of which are major sources of iron ore as well as being common rock-forming minerals. (Although quartz has the chemical composition of an oxide, it is classified as a silicate because of its internal structure.)

Sulfides *Sulfides* are composed of sulfur in some combination with one or more other elements. Pyrite (Figure 13-4), for example, is a combination of iron and sulfur (FeS_2). Many of the most important ore minerals—such as galena (lead), sphalerite (zinc), and chalcopyrite (copper)—are sulfides. This group is common in many types of rock and may be abundant in veins.

▲ **Figure 13-3** Quartz crystal. *(G. Tompkinson/Photo Researchers, Inc.)*

TABLE 13-1 Some Common Rock Forming Minerals

Group	Mineral	Chemical Composition	Common Characteristics
Silicate (Ferromagnesian)	Olivine	$(Mg, Fe)_2SiO_4$	Green to brown color; glassy luster; gem peridot
	Pyroxene group (Augite)	$(Mg, Fe)SiO_3$	Green to black color; commonly has two cleavage planes at 90°
	Amphibole group (Hornblende)	$Ca_2(Fe, Mg)_5Si_8O_{22}(OH)_2$	Black or dark green color; often appear as elongated rod-shaped crystals
	Biotite mica	$K(Mg, Fe)_3AlSi_3O_{10}(OH)_2$	Black or brown; often appear as hexagonal crystals in thin sheets
Silicate (Nonferromagnesian)	Muscovite mica	$KAl_2(AlSi_3O_{10})(OH)_2$	Colorless or brown; splits into thin, translucent sheets
	Potassium feldspar (Orthoclase)	$KAlSi_3O_8$	White to gray or pink color; good cleavage in two planes at 90°
	Plagioclase feldspar	$(Ca, Na)AlSi_3O_8$	White to gray color; striations often appear along cleavage planes
	Quartz	SiO_2	Commonly colorless; forms six-sided elongated crystals
Oxide	Hematite	Fe_2O_3	Red to silver-gray color; type of iron ore
	Magnetite	Fe_3O_4	Black with metallic luster; magnetic
	Corundum	Al_2O_3	Brown or blue color; gems sapphires and rubies
Sulfide	Galena	PbS	Black to silver metallic luster; lead ore
	Pyrite	FeS_2	Brassy or golden yellow color; often seen in well formed cubes
	Chalcopyrite	$CuFeS_2$	Brassy or yellow metallic luster; copper ore
Sulfate	Gypsum	$CaSO_4 \cdot 2H_2O$	White or transparent; used in plaster and wallboard
Carbonate	Calcite	$CaCO_3$	White or colorless; cleavage in 3 planes forms rhombohedra; fizzes in dilute acid
	Dolomite	$CaMg(CO_3)_2$	White or transparent; cleaves into rhombohedra; powdered form fizzes in dilute acid
Halide	Halite	$NaCl$	Transparent or white; table salt
	Fluorite	CaF_2	Transparent purple, green, or yellow color; fluorine ore

Sulfates   The *sulfate* group includes minerals such as gypsum that contain sulfur and oxygen in combination with some other element. Calcium is the principal combining element. The sulfate minerals are usually light-colored and are mostly found in sedimentary rocks.

Carbonates   *Carbonates* are also light-colored (or colorless) minerals that are common constituents of sedimentary rocks such as limestone (largely made from calcium carbonate [$CaCO_3$] in its mineral form of *calcite*). Carbonates in general are composed of one or more elements in combination with carbon and oxygen.

▲ **Figure 13-4** Iron pyrite crystals. (*Breck P. Kent.*)

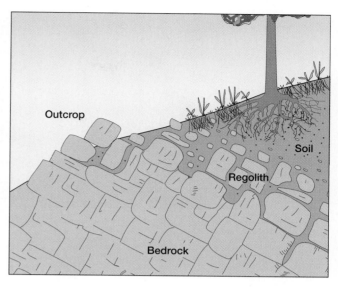

▲ **Figure 13-5** Bedrock is usually buried under a layer of soil and regolith but occasionally appears as an outcrop.

Halides The *halide* group is the least widespread of any. The name is derived from a word meaning "salt." Halide minerals are notably salty—such as halite, or common table salt (NaCl).

Native Elements A few minerals may occur as discrete elements (not combined chemically with another element) in nature. These are referred to as native elements. Included are such precious metals as gold and silver.

Rocks

Rocks are composed of mineral material—sometimes just one kind of mineral, but usually several different minerals. Rocks occur in bewildering variety and complexity in the lithosphere, although fewer than 20 minerals account for more than 95 percent of the composition of all continental and oceanic crustal rocks.

Solid rock is sometimes found right at the surface, in which case it is called an **outcrop** (Figure 13-5). Over most of Earth's land area, though, solid rock exists as a buried layer called *bedrock* and covered by a layer of broken rock called *regolith*. Soil, when present, comprises the upper portion of the regolith (see Chapter 12).

The enormous variety of rocks can be classified systematically. A detailed knowledge of *petrology* (the characteristics of different kinds of rocks) is unnecessary for our purposes here, however, so we restrict coverage to a survey of the three major rock classes—*igneous, sedimentary,* and *metamorphic*—and their basic attributes (Figure 13-6 and Table 13-2).

Igneous Rocks

The word *igneous* signifies a "fiery inception." **Igneous rocks** are formed by the cooling and solidification of molten rock (Figure 13-6a). **Magma** is a general term for molten rock beneath the surface of Earth, while the term **lava** refers to molten rock when it flows out on, or is squeezed up onto, the surface. Most igneous rocks form directly from the cooling of magma or lava; however, some igneous rocks develop from the "welding" of tiny pieces of solid volcanic rock, called **pyroclastics**, that have been explosively ejected out onto the surface by a volcanic eruption.

The classification of igneous rocks is based largely on *mineral composition* and *texture*. The composition of an igneous rock is determined by the "chemistry" of the magma—in other words, by the particular combination of molten mineral material in the magma. As we will see, one of the most important variables of magma composition is the relative amount of *silica* (SiO_2) present. Magmas with relatively large amounts of silica generally cool to form *felsic* igneous rocks that contain large portions of light-colored silicate minerals such as quartz and feldspar (the word felsic comes from *fel*dspar and *si*lica [quartz]). Magmas with relatively low amounts of silica generally cool to form *mafic* igneous rocks that contain large portions of dark-colored silicate minerals such as olivine and pyroxene (mafic comes from *ma*gnesium and *f*errum [Latin for iron]). The texture of an igneous rock is determined primarily by where and how the molten material cools; for example, the slow cooling of magma beneath the surface leads to a coarse-grained texture, while the rapid cooling of lava on the surface leads to a fine-grained texture. Thus, one particular kind of magma can produce a number of quite different igneous rocks depending on whether the material cools below the surface, on the surface as a lava flow, or on the surface as an accumulation of pyroclastics.

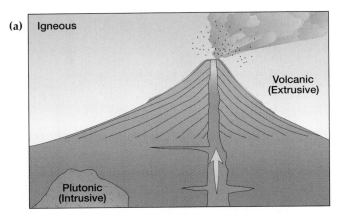

(a) Igneous

Volcanic (Extrusive)

Plutonic (Intrusive)

(b) Sedimentary

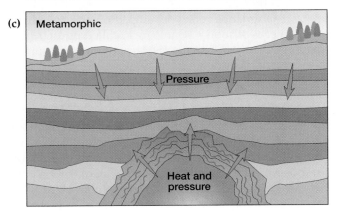

(c) Metamorphic

Pressure

Heat and pressure

▲ **Figure 13-6** The three rock classes. **(a)** Igneous rocks are formed when magma cools. **(b)** Sedimentary rocks result from consolidation of deposited particles. **(c)** Metamorphic rocks are produced when heat and/or pressure act on existing igneous and sedimentary rocks.

Igneous rocks are generally subdivided into two main categories based on where the rocks form: **volcanic**, or **extrusive igneous rocks,** form from the cooling of lava or the bonding of pyroclastic materials on the surface, whereas **plutonic**, or **intrusive igneous rocks**, form from the cooling of magma below the surface. Some common plutonic and volcanic rocks are shown in Figure 13-7.

Plutonic (Intrusive) Rocks Plutonic rocks cool and solidify beneath Earth's surface, where surrounding rocks serve as insulation around the intrusion of magma that greatly retards the rate of cooling. Because the magma may require many thousands of years for complete cooling, the individual mineral crystals in a plutonic rock can grow to a relatively large size—large enough to see with the naked eye—giving the rock a very coarse-grained texture. Although originally buried, plutonic rocks may subsequently become important to topographic development by being pushed upward to the surface or by being exposed by erosion.

The most common and well-known plutonic rock is **granite**, a generally light-colored, coarse-grained igneous rock (Figure 13-8). Granite is made of a combination of light- and dark-colored minerals such as quartz, plagioclase feldspar, potassium feldspar, hornblende, and biotite (granite is a felsic igneous rock; see Figure 13-7). Granite makes up the core of many mountain ranges, such as the Sierra Nevada in California, as well as the deep interior "shield" of many continents.

Volcanic (Extrusive) Rocks Volcanic rocks form on the surface of Earth, either from the cooling of lava or from the accumulation of pyroclastic material such as volcanic ash and cinders. When lava cools rapidly on Earth's surface, the solidification may be complete within hours, and so the mineral crystals in many volcanic rocks are so small as to be invisible without microscopic inspection. On the other hand, volcanic rocks that form from the accumulation of pyroclastics may clearly show tiny fragments of shattered rock that was explosively ejected from a volcano.

Of the many kinds of volcanic rocks, by far the most common is the black or dark gray, fine-grained rock called **basalt** (Figure 13-9). Basalt forms from the cooling of lava and is comprised only of dark-colored minerals such as plagioclase feldspar, pyroxene, and olivine (basalt is a mafic igneous rock; see Figure 13-7). Basalt is the most common volcanic rock in Hawaii and is widespread in parts of some continents—such as in the Columbia Plateau of the northwestern United States. Basalt also makes up the bulk of the ocean floor crust.

There are many other well-known volcanic rocks. *Obsidian* is a type of volcanic glass (meaning that there is no organized mineral crystal structure)—typically black in color—that forms from extremely rapid cooling of lava; *pumice* forms from the rapid cooling of frothy, gas-rich molten material (a piece of pumice is sometimes light enough to float on water!); *Tuff* is a volcanic rock consisting of welded pyroclastic fragments (see Figure 13-15b).

TABLE 13-2 Rock Classification

Class	Subclass	Rock	General Characteristics
Igneous	Plutonic (Intrusive)	Granite	Coarse-grained; "salt & pepper" appearance; high silica content; plutonic equivalent of rhyolite
		Diorite	Coarse-grained; intermediate silica content; plutonic equivalent of andesite
		Gabbro	Coarse-grained; black or dark gray color, low silica content; plutonic equivalent of basalt
		Peridotite	Common mantle rock consisting primarily of olivine and/or pyroxene
	Volcanic (Extrusive)	Rhyolite	Light color; high silica content; volcanic equivalent of granite
		Andesite	Typically gray in color; intermediate silica content; volcanic equivalent of diorite
		Basalt	Usually black in color; low silica content; volcanic equivalent of gabbro
		Obsidian	Volcanic glass; typically black in color and rhyolitic in composition
		Pumice	Volcanic glass with frothy texture; often rhyolitic in composition
		Tuff	Rock made from volcanic ash or pyroclastic flow deposits
Sedimentary	Clastic (Detrital)	Shale	Composed of very fine-grained sediments; typically thin bedded
		Sandstone	Composed of sand-sized sediments
		Conglomerate	Composed of rounded, pebble-sized sediments in a fine-textured matrix
		Breccia	Composed of coarse-grained, angular, sediments; typically thin bedded poorly-sorted fragments
	Chemical and Organic	Limestone	Composed of calcite; may contain shells or shell fragments
		Travertine	Limestone deposited in caves or around hot springs; often deposited in banded layers
		Chert	Common chemical sedimentary rock composed of microcrystalline quartz
Metamorphic	Foliated	Slate	Fine-grained; typically forms from the low-grade metamorphism of shale
		Schist	Thin, flaky layers of platy minerals
		Gneiss	Coarse-grained; granular texture; distinct mineral layers; high-grade metamorphism
	Nonfoliated	Quartzite	Composed primarily of quartz; often derived from sandstone
		Marble	Composed principally of calcite; typically derived from limestone
		Serpentinite	Greenish-black color; slippery feel; from hydrothermal alteration of peridotite

▲ **Figure 13-7** Common igneous rocks. Granite and rhyolite are sometimes called *felsic* igneous rocks—they consist largely of light-colored silicate minerals such as quartz and feldspar ("felsic" comes from combination of *f*eldspar & *si*lica [quartz]); these minerals tend to have relatively lower densities and lower melting temperatures than mafic minerals. Basalt and gabbro are sometimes called *mafic* igneous rocks—they consist largely of dark-colored, magnesium- and iron-rich silicate minerals such as olivine and pyroxene, along with plagioclase feldspar ("mafic" comes from *ma*gnesium and *f*errum, Latin for iron). Andesite and diorite are sometimes called *intermediate* igneous rocks, forming from magma that is intermediate in silica content between high-silica granitic magma and relatively low silica basaltic magma. Notice that felsic rocks form from magma with relatively high amounts of silica, while mafic rocks form from magma with relatively low amounts of silica. *(Photos of granite, diorite, gabbro, rhyolite, and andesite by Breck P. Kent/Earth Sciences; basalt by Animals Animals/Earth Sciences.)*

Sedimentary Rocks

External processes, mechanical and chemical, operating on rocks cause them to disintegrate. This disintegration produces fragmented mineral material, some of which is removed by water, wind, ice, gravity, or a combination of these agents. Much of this material is transported by water moving in rivers or streams as sediment. Eventually the sediment is deposited somewhere in a quiet body of water, particularly on the floor of an ocean (Figure 13-6b). Over a long period of time, sedimentary deposits can build to a remarkable thickness—many thousands of meters. The sheer weight of this massive overburden exerts an enormous pressure, which causes individual particles in the sediment to adhere to each other and to interlock. In addition, chemical cementation normally takes place. Various cementing agents—especially silica, calcium carbonate, and iron oxide—precipitate from the water into the pore spaces in the sediment (Figure 13-10). This combination of pressure and cementation consolidates and transforms the sediments to **sedimentary rock**.

During sedimentation, materials are often sorted roughly by size; the finer particles are carried farther than the heavier particles. Other variations in the composition of the sediments may be due to factors such as different rates of deposition, changes in climatic conditions, or patterns of sediment movement in the oceans. Most sedimentary deposits are built up

▲ **Figure 13-8** **(a)** Massive outcrops of granite at Sylvan Lake in the Black Hills of South Dakota. Granite is an intrusive igneous rock that solidified beneath Earth's surface and was subsequently exposed by erosion. *(Tom L. McKnight photo.)* **(b)** A sample of Vermont granite, showing glassy quartz grains and black biotite mica. *(Breck P. Kent.)*

▲ **Figure 13-9** **(a)** Several horizontal layers of flood basalt are exposed on the wall of the Snake River Canyon near Twin Falls, Idaho. *(Tom L. McKnight photo.)* **(b)** A porous chunk of gray basalt. *(Donna Tucker.)*

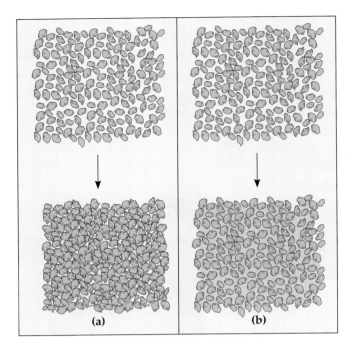

▲ **Figure 13-10** Sedimentary rocks are composed of small particles of matter deposited by water or wind in layers and then consolidated by compaction and/or cementation. **(a)** Compaction consists of the packing of the particles as a result of the weight of overlying material. **(b)** Cementation involves the infilling of pore spaces among the particles by a cementing agent, such as silica, calcium carbonate, or iron oxide.

in more or less distinct horizontal layers called **strata** (Figure 13-11), which vary in thickness and composition (wind-deposited sediments are a notable exception to the horizontal layers of most sediments). The resulting parallel structure, or stratification, is a characteristic feature of most sedimentary rocks. Although originally deposited and formed in horizontal orientation, the strata may later be uplifted, tilted, and deformed by pressures from within Earth (Figure 13-12).

Sedimentary rocks are generally classified into two subcategories based on how they were formed.

Clastic Sedimentary Rocks Sedimentary rocks composed of fragments of preexisting rocks in the form of boulders, gravel, sand, silt, or clay are known as *clastic* or *detrital* sedimentary rocks. By far the most common of these rocks are *shale* (or *mudstone*) that is composed of very fine silt and clay particles, and *sandstone* that is made up of compacted, sand-size grains (Figure 13-13). When the rock is composed of rounded, pebble-size fragments it is called *conglomerate.*

Chemical and Organic Sedimentary Rocks Chemically accumulated sedimentary rocks are usually formed by the precipitation of soluble materials or sometimes by more complicated chemical reactions. Calcium carbonate ($CaCO_3$) is a common component of such rocks, and *limestone* is the most widespread result (see Figure 13-11). *Chert* forms in a similar way to limestone but is composed of silica (SiO_2) instead of calcium carbonate.

Organically accumulated sedimentary rocks, including *coal*, are formed from the accumulated remains of dead plants or animals. Limestone can also be formed in this fashion from skeletal remains of coral and other lime-secreting sea animals.

▲ **Figure 13-11** **(a)** Nearly horizontal strata of limestone and shale in a road cut near Lyons, Colorado. *(Tom L. McKnight photo.)*
(b) A sample of limestone containing an abundance of small fossil mollusks. *(Joyce Photographics/Photo Researchers, Inc.)*

▲ **Figure 13-12** Sedimentary strata (mostly limestone and shale) that have been folded and tilted into an almost vertical orientation on Mount Angeles in the Olympic Mountains of Washington. *(Tom L. McKnight photo.)*

▲ **Figure 13-13** **(a)** The structure of these abrupt sandstone cliffs in southeastern Utah is easy to see. *(Tom L. McKnight photo.)* **(b)** A typical light-colored piece of sandstone. *(Richard M. Busch.)*

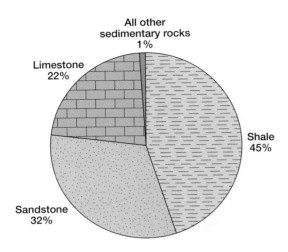

All other
sedimentary rocks
1%

Limestone
22%

Shale
45%

Sandstone
32%

▲ **Figure 13-14** The estimated relative abundance of various types of sedimentary rocks.

There is considerable overlap among these formation methods, with the result that, in addition to there being many different kinds of sedimentary rocks, there also are many gradations among them. Taken together, however, the vast majority of all sedimentary rocks are shale, sandstone, or limestone (Figure 13-14).

Metamorphic Rocks

Metamorphic Rock Foliation

Originally either igneous or sedimentary, **metamorphic rocks** are those that have been drastically changed by heat and/or pressure. The effects of heat and pressure on rocks are complex, being strongly influenced by such things as the presence or absence of fluids in the rocks and the length of time the rocks are heated and/or subjected to high pressure. Metamorphism can be a virtual "cooking" process that heats the rock, causing its mineral components to be recrystallized and rearranged (Figure 13-15). The metamorphic result is often quite different from the original rock; the rocks are changed in structure, texture, composition, and appearance.

Metamorphism can take place in a number of different circumstances. For example, metamorphism can occur beneath the surface of Earth where magma comes in contact with surrounding rocks, altering the surrounding rocks through heat and pressure. Because of such **contact metamorphism** (see Figure 13-6c), it is common to find exposed metamorphic rocks adjacent to plutonic rocks, such as granite. **Regional metamorphism** takes place where large volumes of rock deep within the crust are subjected to heat

▲ **Figure 13-15** **(a)** This bedrock exposure in northeastern California, near Alturas, shows a light brown basalt (a common extrusive igneous rock) overlying a colorful layer of tuff (an extrusive igneous rock formed by consolidation of volcanic ash). The basalt was extruded onto the tuff in molten form, and its great heat "cooked," or metamorphosed, the upper portion of the tuff. Visual evidence of the metamorphosis is seen in the difference in color between the metamorphosed and unmetamorphosed part of the tuff stratum. *(Tom L. McKnight photo.)* **(b)** A representative sample of tuff, which is formed by the consolidation of volcanic ash. *(Richard M. Busch.)*

(a)

(b)

▲ **Figure 13-16** **(a)** A large outcropping of schist in California's Merced River Valley. Parallel layers of micaceous minerals are characteristic. *(© Kennan Ward/Corbis.)* **(b)** A close-up of a chunk of schist showing mica and garnet. *(© Breck P. Kent.)*

and/or pressure over long periods of time. As we will see in Chapter 14, metamorphism is also common along many of the boundaries between lithospheric plates.

If the minerals in a metamorphic rock show a prominent alignment or orientation, we say that the rock is *foliated.* Such rocks may have a platy, wavy, or banded texture. If the original rock was dominated by a single mineral (as in some sandstones or limestones), such foliation is less common.

Some rocks, when metamorphosed, change in predictable fashion. Thus, limestone usually becomes *marble,* sandstone normally is changed to *quartzite,* and shale to *slate.* In many cases, however, the metamorphosis is so great that it is difficult to ascertain the nature of the original rock; in this case, metamorphic rocks are identified according to their physical characteristics and appearance. Among the most common metamorphic rocks are *schist,* in which the foliations are very narrow (Figure 13-16), and *gneiss,* which has broad, banded foliations (Figure 13-17), both of which represent a high degree of metamorphism.

The Rock Cycle

As the preceding description suggests, over long periods of time, the minerals in one rock might well end up in a different rock: igneous rocks can be broken down into sediments that might then form a sedimentary

(a)

(b)

▲ **Figure 13-17** **(a)** An outcrop of banded gneiss in Greenland. This particular formation is one of the oldest on Earth; its age is 3.8 billion years. *(Kevin Schafer/Peter Arnold, Inc.)* **(b)** A typical piece of gneiss, showing contorted foliation. *(Richard M. Busch.)*

rock, which in turn might undergo metamorphism, only to be worn back again into sediments. This ongoing "recycling" of lithospheric material is sometimes referred to as the **rock cycle** (Figure 13-18).

Continental and Ocean Floor Rocks

The lithosphere has a very uneven distribution of the three principal rock classes. Sedimentary rocks compose the most commonly exposed bedrock (perhaps as much as 75 percent) of the continents (Figure 13-19). The sedimentary cover is not thick, however, averaging less than 2.5 kilometers (1.5 miles), and sedimentary rocks accordingly constitute only a very small proportion (perhaps 5 percent) of the total volume of the crust (Figure 13-20). The bulk of the continents consist of granite (along with an unknown proportion of metamorphic rocks such as gneiss and schist). Continental crust is often referred to as *sial* after its common constituents, *si*lia and *al*uminum. On the other hand, the ocean floor crust is composed almost entirely of basalt (covered by a relatively thin veneer of oceanic sediments). Oceanic crust is sometimes called *sima* because of its two most prominent components *si*lica and *ma*gnesium.

The distinction between the dominant rocks of the ocean floors and continents is important. Basalt is a denser rock than granite (the density of basalt is about 3.0 g/cm^3 while that of granite is about 2.7 g/cm^3), and for this reason, continental lithosphere is less dense than oceanic lithosphere. Continental lithosphere "floats" quite easily on the denser asthenosphere below, while oceanic lithosphere is dense enough that it can actually be pushed down, or *subducted*, into the asthenosphere—the consequences of this are discussed at length in the following chapter.

Isostasy

Isostasy

Related to the recognition of differences between oceanic crust, continental crust, and the mantle, is the principle of **isostasy**. In simplest terms, the crust is floating on the denser, deformable, mantle below. Isostasy means that the addition of a significant amount of mass onto a portion of the crust causes the crust to sink, whereas the removal of a large mass allows the crust to rise.

All of the details of isostasy are not clear. For example, the depth of the sinking is not always known; it

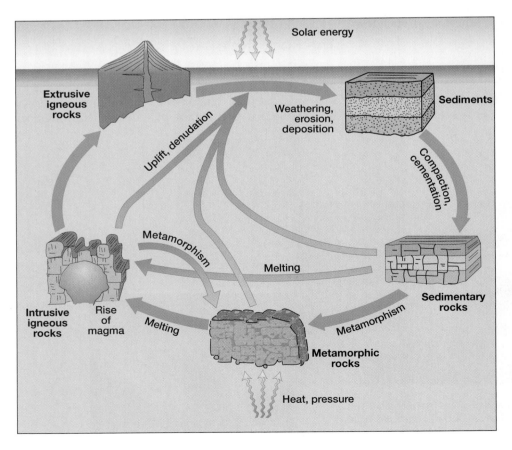

◀ **Figure 13-18** The rock cycle, showing the relationships among the three classes of rocks.

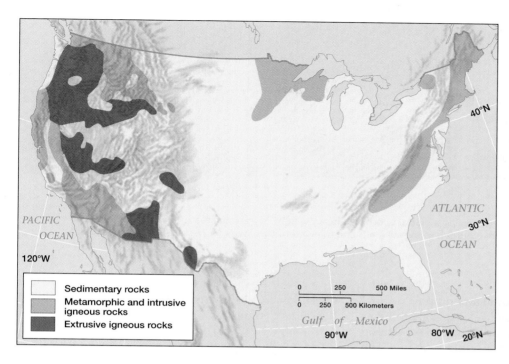

Sedimentary rocks
Metamorphic and intrusive igneous rocks
Extrusive igneous rocks

◀ **Figure 13-19** Surface distribution of rock classes in the conterminous United States. Sedimentary rocks clearly dominate, and this trend also holds true for the rest of the world.

may involve only the surface section in contact with the added mass, or it may extend through to the base of the lithosphere. Another puzzle is what determines the areal extent of an isostatic adjustment: some adjustments cover only a few hundred square kilometers, whereas others extend over half a continent. Also unclear is the immediacy of the isostatic response. In some cases, the raising or lowering seems to take place just as soon as a mass is added or removed; in others, there is a lengthy lag before the adjustment begins. In any case, the eventual topographic results are obvious—the raising or lowering of some portion of the surface.

Isostatic reactions have a variety of causes. The crust may be depressed, for example, by deposition of a large amount of sediment on a continental shelf, or by the accumulation of a great mass of glacial ice on a landmass, as illustrated in Figure 13-21, or even by the weight of water trapped behind a large dam. Depressed crust may rebound to a higher elevation as material is eroded away, as an ice sheet melts, or as a large body of water drains. Florida, for example, has experienced recent isostatic uplift because of the mass removed as groundwater dissolved the extensive limestone bedrock underlying the state.

The Study of Landforms

Our attention for the remainder of this book is directed primarily to **topography**—the surface configuration of

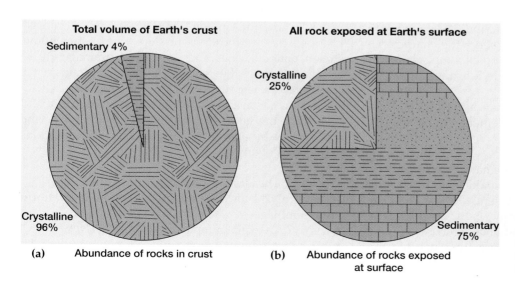

Total volume of Earth's crust
Sedimentary 4%

Crystalline 96%

(a)   Abundance of rocks in crust

All rock exposed at Earth's surface
Crystalline 25%

Sedimentary 75%

(b)   Abundance of rocks exposed at surface

◀ **Figure 13-20** Relative abundances of sedimentary and crystalline (igneous and metamorphic) rocks **(a)** in Earth's crust and **(b)** exposed at Earth's surface.

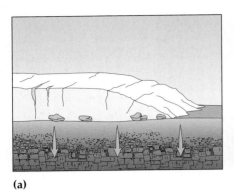

(a)

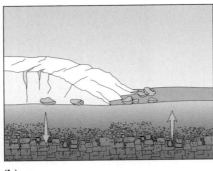

(b)

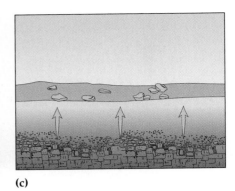

(c)

▲ **Figure 13-21** Isostatic adjustment. **(a)** During a glacial epoch, the heavy weight of accumulated ice depresses the crust. **(b)** Deglaciation removes the weighty overburden as the ice melts and the water flows away. **(c)** The crust rises, or "rebounds," after the weight is removed.

Earth. A **landform** is an individual topographic feature, of any size. Thus, the term could refer to something as minor as a cliff or a sand dune, as well as to something as major as a peninsula or a mountain range. The plural—landforms—is less restrictive and is generally considered synonymous with topography. Our focus, then, is a field of study known as **geomorphology**, the study of the characteristics, origin, and development of landforms.

To assert that the geographer's task in studying landforms is simplified by being only marginally concerned with Earth's interior does not, by any stretch of the imagination, mean that the task is simple. Although our focus is on Earth's surface, that surface is vast, complex, and often obscured. Even without considering the 70 percent of our planet covered with oceanic waters, we must realize that more than 150 million square kilometers (58 million square miles) of land are scattered over seven continents and innumerable islands. This area encompasses the widest possible latitudinal range and the full diversity of environmental conditions. Moreover, much of the surface is obscured from view by the presence of vegetation, soil, or the works of humankind. We must try to penetrate those obstructions, observe the characteristics of the lithospheric surface, and encompass the immensity and diversity of a worldwide landscape. This is far from a simple task.

To organize our thinking for such a complex endeavor, we can isolate certain basic elements for an analytic approach:

Structure *Structure* refers to the nature, arrangement, and orientation of the materials making up the feature being studied. Structure is essentially the geologic underpinning of the landform. Is it composed of bedrock or not? If so, what kind of bedrock and in what configuration? If not, what are the nature and orientation of the material? With a structure as clearly visible as that shown in Figures 13-12 and 13-13, these questions are easily answered, but such is not always the case, of course.

Process *Process* considers the actions that have combined to produce the landform. A variety of forces—usually geologic, hydrologic, atmospheric, and biotic—are always at work shaping the features of the lithospheric surface, and their interaction is critical to the formation of the feature(s). For example, a landscape resulting from the processes of *glaciation* is shown in Figure 13-22.

Slope *Slope* is the fundamental aspect of shape for any landform. The angular relationship of the surface is essentially a reflection of the contemporary balance among the various components of structure and process (Figure 13-23). The inclinations and lengths of the slopes provide details that are important both in describing and analyzing the feature.

Drainage *Drainage* refers to the movement of water (from rainfall and snowmelt), either over Earth's surface or down into the soil and bedrock. Although moving water is an outstanding force under the "process" heading, the ramifications of slope wash, streamflow, stream patterns, and other aspects of drainage are so significant that the general topic of drainage is considered a basic element in landform analysis.

Once these basic elements have been recognized and identified, the geographer is prepared to analyze the topography by answering the fundamental questions at the heart of any geographic inquiry:

- What? The *form* of the feature or features
- Where? The *distribution* and *pattern* of the landform assemblage
- Why? An explanation of *origin* and *development*
- So what? The *significance* of the topography in relationship to other elements of the environment and to human life and activities.

▲ **Figure 13-22**   The spectacular terrain of Montana's Glacier National Park was produced by a variety of interacting processes, but the contemporary topography is particularly due to glaciation. This view is across St. Mary Lake toward Mount Jackson. *(Tom L. McKnight photo.)*

Some Critical Concepts

One term used frequently in the following pages is **relief**, which refers to the difference in elevation between the highest and lowest points in an area. The term can be used at any scale. Thus, as we saw in Figure 1-7,

the maximum world relief is approximately 20 kilometers (12 miles), which is the difference in elevation between the top of Mount Everest and the bottom of the Mariana Trench. At the other extreme, the *local relief* in some places like Florida can be a matter of merely a few meters.

▲ **Figure 13-23**   Slope is a conspicuous visual element of some landscapes. The abrupt cliffs of the volcanic backbone of the island of Bora-Bora (in French Polynesia) dominate this scene. *(Tom L. McKnight photo.)*

Internal and External Geomorphic Processes

The relief we see in a landscape is temporary. It represents the momentary balance of two largely opposing sets of processes that are operating to shape and re-shape the surface of Earth: *internal processes* and *external processes* (Figure 13-24). These processes are relatively few in number but extremely varied in nature and operation. The great variety of Earth's topography reflects the complexity of interactions between these processes and the underlying structure of the surface.

Internal Processes   The **internal processes** originate from within Earth, energized by internal heat that generates forces that apparently operate outside of any surface or atmospheric influences. These processes result in crustal movements through folding, faulting, and volcanic activity of various kinds. In general, they are constructive, uplifting, building processes that tend to increase the relief of the land surface.

External Processes   In contrast, the **external processes** are largely subaerial (meaning that they operate at the base of the atmosphere) and draw their energy mostly from sources above the lithosphere, either in the atmosphere or in the oceans. Unlike some of the internal processes, external processes are generally well understood and their behavior is often predictable. Moreover, their behavior may be significantly influenced by the existing topography, particularly its shape and the nature of the surface materials. The external processes may be thought of generally as wearing-down or destructive processes that eventually tend to diminish topographic irregularities and decrease the relief of Earth's surface.

In succeeding chapters, we consider these various processes—their nature, dynamics, and effects—in detail, but it is useful here to summarize them so that they can be glimpsed in totality before we treat them one at a time. Table 13-3 presents such an overview. Note, however, that our classification scheme is imperfect; some items are clearly separate and discrete, whereas others overlap with each other. The table, then, represents a simple, logical way to begin a study of the processes, but is not necessarily the only or ultimate framework.

Thus, internal and external processes work in more or less direct opposition to one another—in some landscapes, both operating at the same time. Their battle-ground is Earth's surface, the interface between lithosphere and atmosphere, where this remarkable struggle has persisted for billions of years and may continue endlessly into the future.

Uniformitarianism

Fundamental to an understanding of internal and external processes and topographic development is familiarity with the doctrine of **uniformitarianism**, which holds that "the present is the key to the past." This means that the processes that are shaping the contemporary landscape are the same processes that formed the topography of the past—and are the same processes that will shape the topography of the future. Therefore, by understanding the geomorphic processes we see working today, we can study a landscape and begin to comprehend the history of its development. The development of landforms is a virtually endless event, with the topography at any given time simply representing one moment in a continuum of change. The processes involved are mostly ongoing and slow acting, although some of these processes reveal change rather episodically—an earthquake, a volcanic eruption, a flood.

Because many of the internal and external processes operate very slowly by human standards, they may be difficult to grasp. For example, the enormous lithospheric plates that we will discuss in Chapter 14 are moving, on average, about as fast as your fingernails

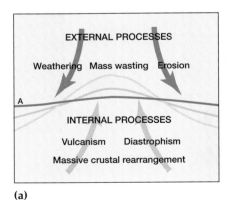
(a)

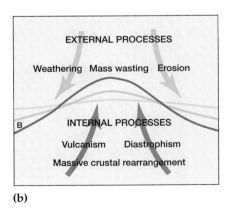
(b)

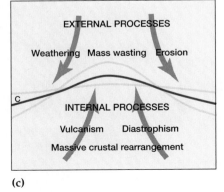
(c)

▲ **Figure 13-24** Schematic relationship between external and internal geomorphic processes. **(a)** A surface that has been worn down by external forces but not uplifted by internal forces. **(b)** A surface that has been uplifted by internal forces but not worn away by external forces. **(c)** A "normal" surface that has been both uplifted by internal forces and worn away by external forces.

TABLE 13-3 A Summary of Geomorphic Processes

Internal

    Crustal rearrangement (plate tectonics)

    Vulcanism

        Extrusive

        Intrusive

    Diastrophism

        Folding

        Faulting

External

    Weathering

    Mass Wasting

    Erosion/deposition

        Fluvial (running water)

        Aeolian (wind)

        Glacial (moving ice)

        Solution (ground water)

        Waves and currents (oceans/lakes)

grow. In order to understand how sometimes imperceptibly slow processes work to alter the landscape, we must stretch our concept of time.

Geologic Time

Probably the most mind-boggling concept in all physical geography is the vastness of geologic time (Figure 13-25). In our daily lives, we deal with such brief intervals of time as hours, months, years, and sometimes centuries, which does nothing to prepare us for the scale of Earth's history. The colossal sweep of geologic time encompasses epochs of millions and hundreds of millions of years.

The concept of *geologic time* refers to the vast periods of time over which geologic processes operate. For uniformitarianism to work as a basic premise for interpreting Earth history, that history must have occurred over a span of time vast enough to allow feats of considerable magnitude to be accomplished by means of processes infinitesimally slow when measured on a human time scale.

How can we grasp the grandiose sweep of geologic time? To state that Earth has existed for about 4.6 billion years, or that the Age of Dinosaurs persisted for some 160 million years, or that the Rocky Mountains were initially uplifted approximately 65 million years

ago is to enumerate temporal expanses of almost unfathomable scope.

Analogy offers at least the momentary illusion of comprehension: If we could envision the entire 4.6-billion-year history of Earth compressed into a single calendar year, each day would be equivalent to 12.6 million years, each hour to 525,000 years, each minute to 8,750 years, and each second to 146 years. On such a scale, the planet was lifeless for the first four months, with primal forms of one-celled life not appearing until early May. These primitive algae and bacteria had the world to themselves until early November, when the first multicelled organisms began to evolve. The first vertebrate animals, antediluvian fishes, appeared about November 21; and before the end of the month, amphibians began establishing themselves as the first terrestrial vertebrates. Vascular plants, mostly tree ferns, club mosses, and horsetails, appeared about November 27, and reptiles began their era of dominance about December 7. Mammals arrived about December 14, with birds on the following day. Flowering plants would first bloom about December 21, and on Christmas Eve would appear both the first grasses and the first primates. The first hominids walked upright in midafternoon on New Year's Eve, and *Homo sapiens* appeared on the scene about an hour before midnight. The age of written history encompassed the last minute of the year—just the last 60 ticks of the clock!!

Only with such an extraordinary time scale as this can one give credence to the doctrine of uniformitarianism or accept that the Grand Canyon is a youthful feature carved by that relatively small river seen deep in its inner gorge or accept that Africa and South America were once joined together and have drifted 3200 kilometers (2000 miles) apart. Indeed, the remainder of this book can be considered only as fanciful fiction unless one can rely on the concept of geologic time. The geomorphic processes generally operate with excruciating slowness, but the vastness of geologic history provides a suitable time frame for their accomplishments.

> If daunted by the noxious stench
> Exhaled from Time's abyss,
> Retreat into some lesser trench
> Where ignorance is bliss.
>
> Claude C. Albritton, Jr.,
> *The Abyss of Time*

Scale and Pattern

Before we proceed with our systematic study of geomorphic processes, two final concepts should be kept in mind—scale and pattern.

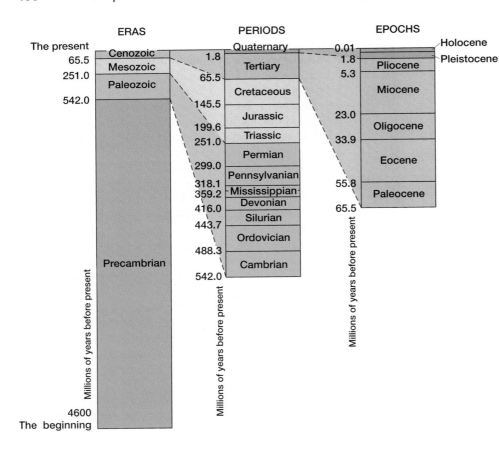

Figure 13-25 The relative length of geologic time intervals. Geologic history is divided into four major units, called *eras*. The eras are subdivided into *periods*, and the more recent periods are further subdivided into *epochs*. Notice that the Precambrian era was seven or eight times longer than the other three eras combined. The dates given are from the revision of the geologic time scale approved by the *International Commission on Stratigraphy* in 2005 (at the time of this revision, a proposal was made to eliminate the term *Quaternary* in reference to the Holocene and Pleistocene, although "Quaternary" still remains in widespread use).

An Example of Scale

The question of scale is fundamental in geography. Regardless of the subject of geographic inquiry, recognizable features and associations are likely to vary considerably depending on the scale of observation. This simply means that the aspects of the landscape one observes in a close-up view are different from those observed from a more distant view.

As an example of the complexity and significance of scale, let us focus our attention on a particular place on Earth's surface and view it from different perspectives. The location is north-central Colorado within the boundaries of Rocky Mountain National Park, some 13 kilometers (8 miles) due west of the town of Estes Park. It encompasses a small valley called Horseshoe Park, through which flows a clear mountain stream named Fall River and adjacent to which is the steep slope of Bighorn Mountain (Figure 13-26).

1. To illustrate the largest scale of ordinary human experience, we will hike northward from the center of Horseshoe Park up the side of Bighorn Mountain. At this level of observation, the first topographic feature of note is a smooth stretch of Fall River we must cross. We walk over a small sandbar at the south edge of the river, wade for a few steps in the river, and step up a half-meter (20-inch) bank onto the mountainside, noting the dry bed of a small intermittent pond on our

left. After 20 minutes or so of steep uphill scrambling, we reach a rugged granite outcrop (locally called Hazel Cone or Poop Point), which presents us with an almost vertical cliff face to climb.

2. At a significantly different scale of observation, we might travel for 20 minutes by car in this same area. The road through Horseshoe Park is part of U.S. Highway 34, which here is called the Trail Ridge Road. After 20 minutes, we reach a magnificent viewpoint high on the mountain to the southwest of Horseshoe Park. From this vantage point, our view of the country through which we have hiked is significantly enlarged. We can no longer recognize the sandbar, the bank, or the dry pond, and even the rugged cliff of Hazel Cone appears as little more than a pimple on the vast slope of Bighorn Mountain. Instead, we see that Fall River is a broadly meandering stream in a flat valley and that Bighorn Mountain is an impressive peak rising high above.

3. Our third observation of this area might take place from a plane flying at 12 kilometers (39,000 feet) on a run between Omaha and Salt Lake City. From this elevation, Fall River is nearly invisible, and only careful observation reveals Horseshoe Park. Bighorn Mountain is now merged indistinguishably as part of the Mummy Range, which is seen to be a minor offshoot of a much larger and more impressive mountain system called the Front Range.

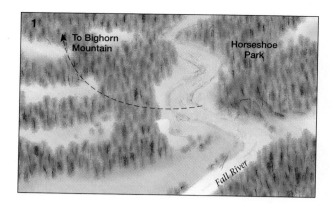

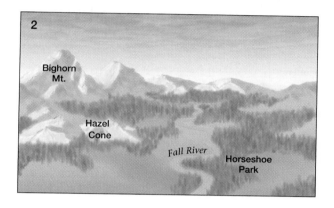

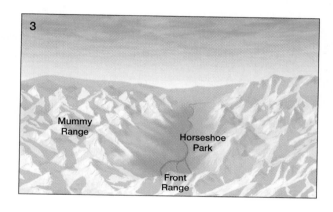

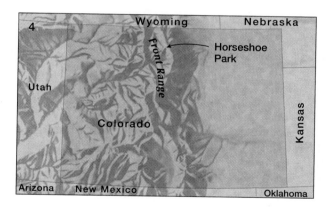

▲ **Figure 13-26** An experience with change of scale: (1) A close view of Horseshoe Park, Colorado, from the west. The dashed line shows our hiking route. (2) Looking down on Horseshoe Park from Trail Ridge Road. (3) An aerial view of the Mummy Range and part of the Front Range. (4) A high-altitude look at Colorado. (5) North America as it might be seen from a distant spacecraft.

4. A fourth level of observation would be available to us if we could hitch a ride on a satellite orbiting 160 kilometers (100 miles) above Earth. Our brief glimpse of northern Colorado would probably be inadequate to distinguish the Mummy Range, and even the 400-kilometer (250-mile) long Front Range would appear only as a component of the mighty Rocky Mountain cordillera, which extends from New Mexico to northern Canada.

5. At the smallest scale, the final viewpoint possible to humans could come from a spacecraft rocketing toward some distant heavenly body. Looking back in the direction of Horseshoe Park from a near-space position, one might possibly recognize the Rocky Mountains, but the only conspicuous feature in this small-scale view would be the North American continent.

The Pursuit of Pattern

A prime goal of any geographic study is to detect patterns in the areal distribution of phenomena. If

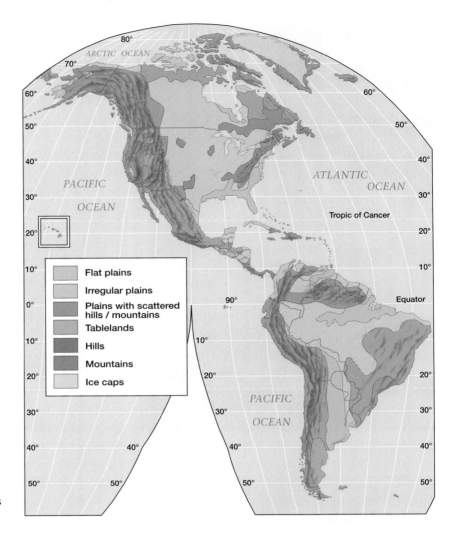

▶ **Figure 13-27**   Major landform assemblages of the world.

features have a disordered and apparently haphazard distribution, it is more difficult to comprehend the processes that formed them and the relationships that exist among them. If there is some perceptible pattern to their distribution, however—some more or less predictable spatial arrangement—it becomes simpler for us to understand both the reasons for the distribution pattern and the interrelationships that pertain.

In previous portions of this book, we were concerned with geographic elements and complexes having some predictability to their distribution patterns. For example, one can say with some assurance that, at about latitude 45° on the western coasts of continents, there can be found a certain type of climate (*marine west coast*, you may recall), a particular association of natural vegetation and native animal life (the *midlatitude forest* biome), and a set of roughly predictable soil-forming processes. These relatively orderly arrangements have been helpful, and perhaps even comforting, in our studies thus far.

Now, alas, we enter into a part of physical geography in which orderly patterns of distribution are much more difficult to discern, as the landform distribution pattern in Figure 13-27 so readily shows. There are a few aspects of predictability; for example, one can anticipate that in desert areas, certain geomorphic processes are more conspicuous than others and certain landform features are likely to be found. Overall, however, the global distribution of topography is very disordered and irregular. The pursuit of a predictable pattern is, for the most part, a thankless endeavor, and to comprehend the world distribution of landforms requires an unfortunate degree of sheer memorization.

Largely for this reason, the geomorphology portion of this book concentrates less on distribution and more on process. Comprehending the dynamics of topographic development is more important to an understanding of systematic physical geography than any amount of detailed study of landform distribution.

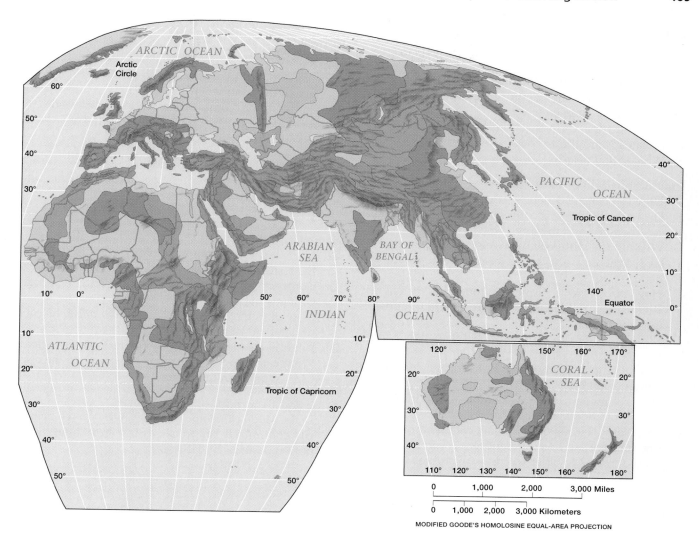

Chapter 13 Learning Review

Key Terms

Before answering the study questions, review the definitions of the following key terms (page references are provided for you):

asthenosphere *(p. 388)*
basalt *(p. 392)*
contact metamorphism *(p. 398)*
crust *(p. 387)*
external (geomorphic) processes *(p. 404)*
geomorphology *(p. 402)*
granite *(p. 392)*
igneous rock *(p. 391)*
inner core *(p. 388)*
internal (geomorphic) processes *(p. 404)*
isostasy *(p. 400)*

landform *(p. 402)*
lava *(p. 391)*
lithosphere *(p. 388)*
magma *(p. 391)*
mantle *(p. 388)*
metamorphic rock *(p. 398)*
mineral *(p. 389)*
Mohorovičić discontinuity (Moho) *(p. 387)*
outcrop *(p. 391)*
outer core *(p. 388)*
plutonic (intrusive) igneous rock *(p. 392)*

pyroclastics *(p. 391)*
regional metamorphism *(p. 398)*
relief *(p. 403)*
rock *(p. 391)*
rock cycle *(p. 400)*
sedimentary rock *(p. 394)*
silicate (silicate minerals) *(p. 389)*
strata *(p. 396)*
topography *(p. 401)*
uniformitarianism *(p. 404)*
volcanic (extrusive) igneous rock *(p. 392)*

Study Questions for Key Concepts

After studying this chapter, you should be able to answer the following questions:

The Structure of Earth (p. 387)

1. Briefly describe the overall structure of Earth, noting the four main layers.
2. What are the differences between the *lithosphere* ("plates") and the *asthenosphere*?
3. What is the *Moho*?

The Composition of Earth (p. 389)

4. How is a *mineral* different from a *rock*?
5. Describe the general differences among igneous, sedimentary, and metamorphic rocks.
6. What is the difference between a *plutonic* (intrusive) igneous rock and a *volcanic* (extrusive) igneous rock?
7. How can one kind of magma (one kind of magma chemistry) produce two or more different kinds of igneous rocks?
8. What are the main differences between *granite* and *basalt*?
9. Why do most sedimentary rocks form in flat, horizontal layers?
10. Why are metamorphic rocks often found in contact with plutonic rocks such as granite?
11. Over long periods of time, how can the minerals in one rock end up in a different rock (or in a different kind of rock)? In other words, explain the *rock cycle*.

12. Why are sedimentary rocks so common on the surface of the continents?
13. Contrast the composition and characteristics of *oceanic lithosphere* with that of *continental lithosphere*.
14. Explain the concept of *isostasy*.

The Study of Landforms (p. 401)

15. Briefly define the terms *topography, landform,* and *geomorphology*.
16. What is meant by the *structure* of a landform?

Some Critical Concepts (p. 403)

17. In the context of geomorphology, what is meant by the term *relief*?
18. Contrast the concepts of "internal" and "external" geomorphic processes.
19. How does the doctrine of *uniformitarianism* help us understand the history of Earth?
20. What is generally meant by the term *geologic time*?
21. What is the importance of geologic time to the doctrine of uniformitarianism?

Scale and Pattern (p. 405)

22. In the study of geomorphology, why do we primarily concentrate on processes rather than on distribution patterns by latitude?

Additional Resources

Books:

Albritton, Claude C., Jr. *The Abyss of Time.* San Francisco: Freeman, Cooper, 1980.

McPhee, John. *Annals of the Former World.* New York: Farrar, Strauss and Giroux, 1998.

Powell, James Lawrence. *Mysteries of Terra Firma: The Age and Evolution of the Earth.* New York: Free Press, 2001.

Internet Sites:

The Earth Observatory

http://earthobservatory.nasa.gov/

The Earth Observatory is National Aeronautics and Space Administration's (NASA's) Internet site that provides information and images of Earth.

National Geophysical Data Center

http://www.ngdc.noaa.gov/

The National Geophysical Data Center is a great starting point for finding information about glaciology, marine geology, paleoclimatology, solar–terrestrial physics, and geophysics.

U.S. Geological Survey

http://www.usgs.gov/

The U.S. Geological Survey home page provides links to information on a wide range of Earth science topics, including earthquakes, volcanoes, landslides, floods, and other natural hazards. The page also has links to sites where topographic maps, geological maps, research papers, and publications of general interest may be viewed or purchased.

14
The Internal Processes

The forces operating within Earth are complex and of unimaginable strength. As a result of geophysical and geologic research, each year we come to understand more and more of the energetics and dynamics of Earth's internal processes.

The Impact of Internal Processes on the Landscape

In our endeavor to understand the development of the earthly landscape, no pursuit is more rewarding than a consideration of the internal processes, for they are the supreme builders of terrain. Energized by awesome forces within Earth, the internal processes actively reshape the crustal surface. The crust is buckled and bent, land is raised and lowered, rocks are fractured and folded, solid material is melted, and molten material is solidified. These actions have been going on for billions of years and are fundamentally responsible for the gross shape of the lithospheric landscape at any given time. They do not always act independently and separately, but in this chapter we isolate them in order to simplify our analysis.

From Rigid Earth to Plate Tectonics

The shapes and positions of the continents may seem fixed at the time scale of human experience, but at the geologic time scale, measured in millions or tens of millions of years, continents are quite mobile. Continents have moved, collided and merged, and then been torn apart again; ocean basins have formed, widened, only to be eventually closed off. These changes on the surface of Earth continue today, so that the contemporary configuration of the ocean basins and continents is by no means the ultimate one. It is only in the last half century, however, that Earth scientists have come to understand how all of this could actually happen.

Until the mid-twentieth century, most Earth scientists assumed that the planet's crust was rigid, with continents and ocean basins fixed in position and significantly modified only by changes in sea level and periods of mountain building. The uneven shapes and irregular distribution of the continents were a puzzlement, but it

◀ Kilauea Volcano, Hawaii. *(Jim Sugar/Science Faction/Getty Images, Inc.)*

was generally accepted that the present arrangement was emplaced in some ancient age when Earth's crust cooled from its original molten state.

The idea that the continents had changed position over time, or that a single "supercontinent" once existed before separating into large fragments, has been around for a long time. Various naturalists, physicists, astronomers, geologists, botanists, and geographers from a number of countries have been putting forth this idea since the days of geographer Abraham Ortelius in the 1590s and philosopher Francis Bacon in 1620. Until fairly recently, however, the idea was generally unacceptable to the scientific community at large.

Wegener's Continental Drift

During the second and third decades of the twentieth century, the notion of **continental drift** was revived, most notably by the German meteorologist and geophysicist Alfred Wegener. Wegener put together the first comprehensive theory to describe and partially explain the phenomenon, publishing his landmark book, *Die Entstehung der Kontinente and Ozeane* (*The Origin of Continents and Oceans*), in 1915. Wegener postulated a massive supercontinent, which he called **Pangaea** (Greek for "whole land"), as having existed about 250 million years ago and then breaking apart into several large sections—the present-day continents—that have continued to move away from one another to this day (Figure 14-1).

Wegener accumulated a great deal of evidence to support his hypothesis, most notably the remarkable number of close affinities of geologic features on both sides of the Atlantic Ocean. He found the continental margins of the subequatorial portions of Africa and South America fit together with jigsaw-puzzle-like precision (Figure 14-2a). He also determined that the petrologic records on both sides of the Atlantic show many distributions—such as ancient coal deposits—that would be continuous if the ocean did not intervene. Moreover, when the continents are placed back in their Pangaean configuration, mountain belts in Greenland, Scandinavia, and the British Isles match up with the Appalachian Mountains in eastern North America (Figure 14-2b).

Supporting evidence came from paleontology: the fossils of some dinosaur species, such as the *Mesosaurus*, are found on both sides of the southern Atlantic Ocean, but nowhere else in the world (Figure 14-3). Fossilized plants, such as the fernlike *Glossopteris*, are found in similar-aged rocks in South America, South Africa, Australia, India, and Antarctica—its seeds too large and heavy to have been carried across the expanse of the present-day oceans by wind.

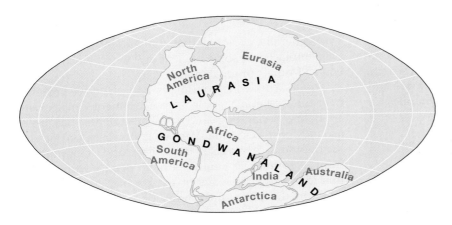

◀ **Figure 14-1** The presumed arrangement of the supercontinent Pangaea about 250 million years ago. The initial separation produced Laurasia, containing what is now North America and Eurasia (excluding India), and Gondwanaland, composed of all the present-day Southern Hemisphere continents plus India.

Wegener worked with climatologist Vladimir Köppen to study the past climate patterns of Earth. For example, they studied glacial deposits that indicated that large portions of the southern continents and India were extensively glaciated about 280 million years ago. The pattern of deposits made sense if the continents had been together in Pangaea when this glaciation took place (Figure 14-4).

Wegener's accumulated evidence could be most logically explained by continental drift. His ideas attracted much attention in the 1920s—and generated much controversy. Some Southern Hemisphere geologists, particularly in South Africa, responded with enthusiasm. The general response to Wegener's hypothesis, however, was disbelief. Despite the vast number of distributional

coincidences, most scientists felt that two difficulties made the theory improbable if not impossible: (1) Earth's crust was believed to be too rigid to permit such large-scale motions—after all, how could solid rock plow through solid rock? (2) Further, no suitable mechanism could be conceived of that would provide enough energy to displace such large masses for a long journey. For these reasons, most Earth scientists ignored or even debunked the idea of continental drift for the better part of half a century after Wegener's theory was presented.

Although certainly discouraged that his ideas on continental drift were rejected by most scientists, Wegener continued his other scientific work—most notably in meteorology and polar research, where his contributions

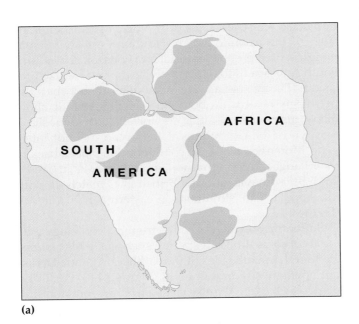

(a)

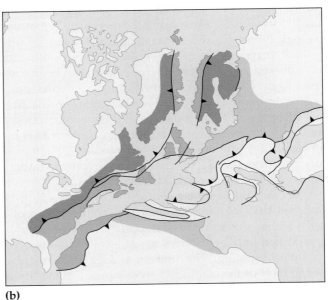

(b)

▲ **Figure 14-2** Some of the most decisive evidence for continental drift comes from the transatlantic connection. **(a)** The matching of the coasts of Africa and South America is persuasive. The ancient continental blocks of the two continents are shown in darker tone, with the younger areas (mostly regions of sedimentary deposition and volcanic activity) shown in lighter tone. **(b)** Across the North Atlantic are zones of similar geological activity, including mountain belts that are very difficult to correlate unless Europe, North America, and North Africa were once together.

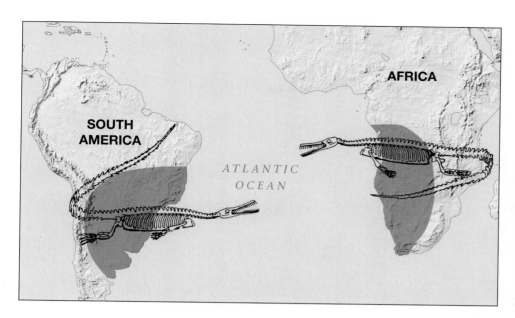

◀ **Figure 14-3** *Mesosaurus* fossils have been found in southeastern South America and southwestern Africa. These animals were alive at the time that present-day South America and Africa were together as part of a larger landmass in the geologic past. *(After Tarbuck and Lutgens,* Earth Sciences, *11th ed., Upper Saddle River, NJ: Prentice Hall, 2006.)*

are widely acknowledged.[1] In 1930, Wegener was leading a meteorological expedition to the ice cap of Greenland. After delivering supplies to scientists stationed in the remote research outpost of Eismitte in the middle of the ice cap (see Figure 8-38b for a climograph of this station), Wegener and a fellow expedition member set out by skis and dogsled to return to their base camp near the coast, but neither arrived. Wegener's body was found six months later buried in the snow—he died decades before his ideas on continental drift would receive serious attention by the majority of Earth scientists.

Plate Tectonics

The questionable validity of continental drift notwithstanding, throughout the middle of the twentieth century, continuing research revealed more and more about crustal mechanics.

The Evidence

1. Plate Boundaries
2. Seafloor Spreading
3. Paleomagnetism
4. Convection and Plate Tectonics

Among the many gaps in scientific knowledge at the time of Alfred Wegener was an understanding of the dynamics of the ocean floors. By the 1950s, geologists, geophysicists, seismologists, oceanographers, and physicists had accumulated a large body of data about the ocean floor and the underlying crust.

One of the most intriguing early findings came when thousands of depth soundings from the oceans of the world were used to construct a detailed map of ocean floor topography (Figure 14-5). The result was remarkable: vast abyssal plains were seen dotted with chains of

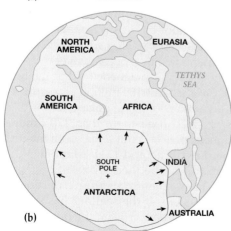

▲ **Figure 14-4** About 280 million years ago extensive areas of Pangaea were glaciated. When the continents are placed back in their former positions, the patterns of ice movement and glacial deposition make sense. *(After Tarbuck and Lutgens,* Earth Sciences, *11th ed., Upper Saddle River, NJ: Prentice Hall, 2006.)*

[1]Before Wegener developed his ideas on continental drift, his 1911 textbook, *The Thermodynamics of the Atmosphere,* had become a standard in German universities. The Swedish meteorologist Tor Bergeron openly acknowledged Wegener's contribution to our understanding of the raindrop formation process known today as the *Bergeron process* (see Chapter 6).

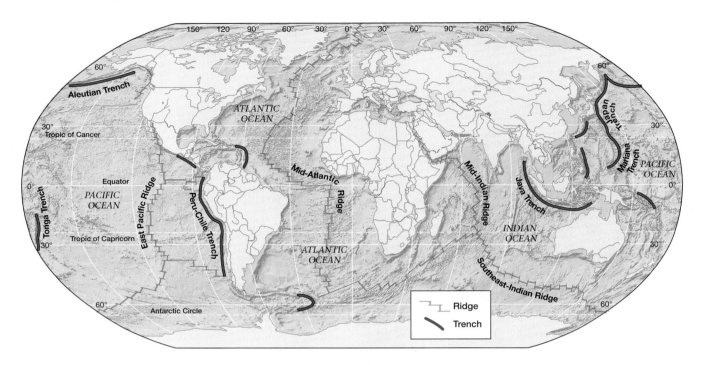

▲ **Figure 14-5**   A continuous system of ridges runs across the floor of the world ocean. In addition to the ridges, this schematic map also shows the major deep oceanic trenches, which lie along many of the world's coasts.

undersea volcanoes known as *seamounts*. Narrow, deep oceanic trenches occurred in many places, often around the margins of the ocean basins. Perhaps most stunning of all was a continuous ridge system running across the floors of all the oceans for 64,000 kilometers (40,000 miles)—wrapping around the globe like the stitching on a baseball. The mid-Atlantic segment of this midocean ridge system is especially striking, running exactly halfway between—and matching the shape of—the coastlines on both sides, almost as if a giant seam had opened up in the ocean floor between the continents.

By the 1960s a world network of seismographs was able to pinpoint the location of every significant earthquake in the world. When earthquake locations were mapped, it was clear that earthquakes don't occur randomly around the world; instead, most earthquakes occur in bands, often coinciding with the pattern of the midocean ridge system and deep oceanic trenches (Figure 14-6).

Seafloor Spreading   In the early 1960s, a new theory was propounded, most notably by the American oceanographer Harry Hess and geologist Robert S. Dietz, that could explain the significance of the midocean ridges, the deep oceanic trenches, the pattern of earthquakes—and could provide a possible mechanism for Wegener's continental drift. Known as **seafloor spreading**, this theory said that midocean ridges are formed by currents of magma rising up from the mantle; volcanic eruptions create new basaltic ocean

floor, that then spreads away laterally from the ridge (Figure 14-7). Thus, the midocean ridges contain the newest crust formed on the planet. At other places in the ocean basin—at the deep oceanic trenches—older lithosphere descends into the asthenosphere in a process called **subduction**, where it is ultimately "recycled." The amount of new seafloor created is compensated for by the amount lost at subduction zones.

Verification of Seafloor Spreading   The validity of seafloor spreading was confirmed by two lines of evidence: *paleomagnetism* and *ocean floor core sampling*.

When any rock containing iron is formed—such as iron-rich ocean floor basalt—it is magnetized so that the iron-rich grains become aligned with Earth's magnetic field. This orientation then becomes a permanent record of the polarity of Earth's magnetic field at the time the rock solidified. Over the last 100 million years, for reasons that are not fully understood, the polarity of Earth's magnetic field has reversed itself more than 170 times—with the north magnetic pole becoming the south magnetic pole.

In 1963, Fred Vine and D.H. Matthews used **paleomagnetism** to test the theory of seafloor spreading by studying paleomagnetic data from a portion of the midocean ridge system. If the seafloor has spread laterally by the addition of new crust at the oceanic ridges, there should be a relatively symmetrical pattern of magnetic orientation—normal polarity, reverse polarity, normal polarity, and so on—on both sides of the ridges (Figure 14-8). Such was the case, as Figure 14-9 clearly shows.

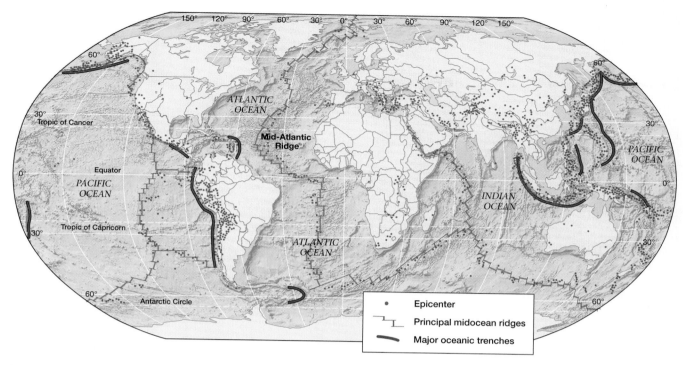

▲ **Figure 14-6**   The distributions of epicenters for all earthquakes of at least 5.5 magnitude over a 15-year period. Their relationship to midocean ridges and deep oceanic trenches is striking.

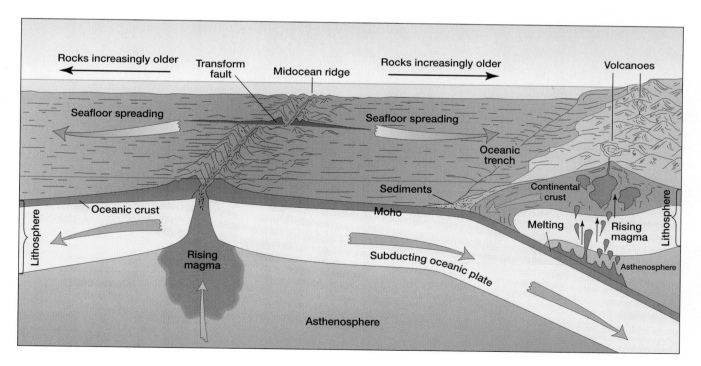

▲ **Figure 14-7**   Seafloor spreading. Convection currents bring magma from the asthenosphere up through fissures in the oceanic crust. The cooled and therefore solidified magma becomes a new portion of ridge along the ocean floor, and the two sides of the ridge spread away from each other, as indicated by the arrows. Where denser ocean lithosphere converges with lighter continental lithosphere, the oceanic plate slides under the continental plate in a process called subduction. Magma produced by this subduction rises to form volcanoes and igneous intrusions.

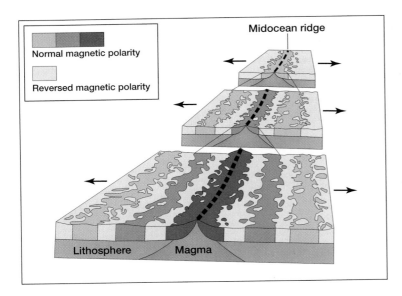

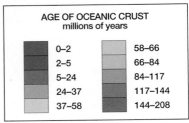

◄ **Figure 14-8**   New basaltic ocean floor is magnetized according to the existing magnetic field of the Earth. As ocean floor spreads away from a ridge, a symmetrical pattern of normal and reverse magnetic polarity develops on both sides of the spreading center. *(Adapted with the permission of W. H. Freeman and Company from R. L. Larson and others,* The Bedrock Geology of the World, *© 1985.)*

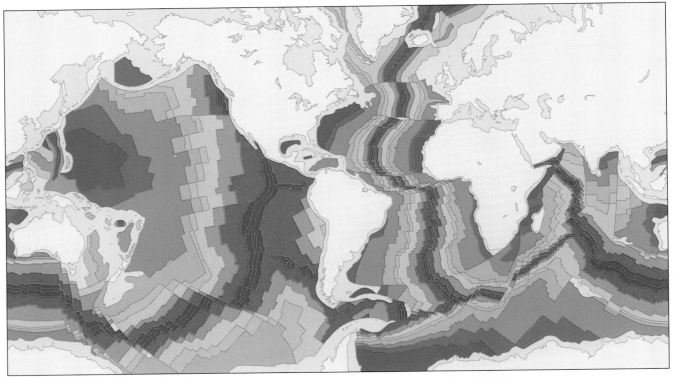

AGE OF OCEANIC CRUST
millions of years

0–2	58–66
2–5	66–84
5–24	84–117
24–37	117–144
37–58	144–208

▲ **Figure 14-9**   The age of the ocean floors. The patterns of magnetic reversals recorded in the ocean floor as it spreads away from midocean ridges have helped establish the age of oceanic crust. The youngest ocean floor is found at midocean ridges, while ocean floor farther from the ridges is the oldest. *(Adapted with the permission of W. H. Freeman and Company from R. L. Larson and others,* The Bedrock Geology of the World, *© 1985.)*

Final confirmation of seafloor spreading was obtained from core holes drilled into the ocean floor by the research ship, the *Glomar Challenger* in the late 1960s. Several thousand **ocean floor core samples** of sea-bottom sediments were analyzed, and it was evident from this work that, almost invariably, sediment thickness and age increase with increasing distance from the midocean ridges, indicating that sediments farthest from the ridges are oldest. At the ridges, ocean floor material is almost all igneous, with little accumulation of sediment—any sediment near the ridges is thin and young.

Thus, the seafloors can be likened to gigantic conveyor belts, moving ever outward from the midocean ridges toward the trenches. Oceanic crust has a relatively short life at Earth's surface. New crust is formed at the oceanic ridges, and within 200 million years is returned to the mantle by subduction. Because lower density continental crust cannot be subducted, once it forms it is virtually permanent. The continual recycling of oceanic crust means that its average age is only about

100 million years, whereas the average age of continental crust is 20 times that. Indeed, some fragments of continental crust have been discovered that are 4 billion years old—about four-fifths of the age of Earth!

So, as it turns out, Alfred Wegener was wrong about one detail in his theory of continental drift: it isn't just the continents that are drifting. The continents are embedded in the thicker lithospheric plates, carried along by the action of seafloor spreading.

Plate Tectonics By 1968, on the basis of these details and a variety of other evidence, the theory of **plate tectonics**, as it had become known, was being accepted by the scientific community. Plate tectonics provides a framework with which we can understand and relate a wide range of internal processes and topographic patterns around the world.

The lithosphere is a mosaic of rigid lithospheric plates floating over the underlying plastic asthenosphere (Figure 14-10). The plates vary considerably in

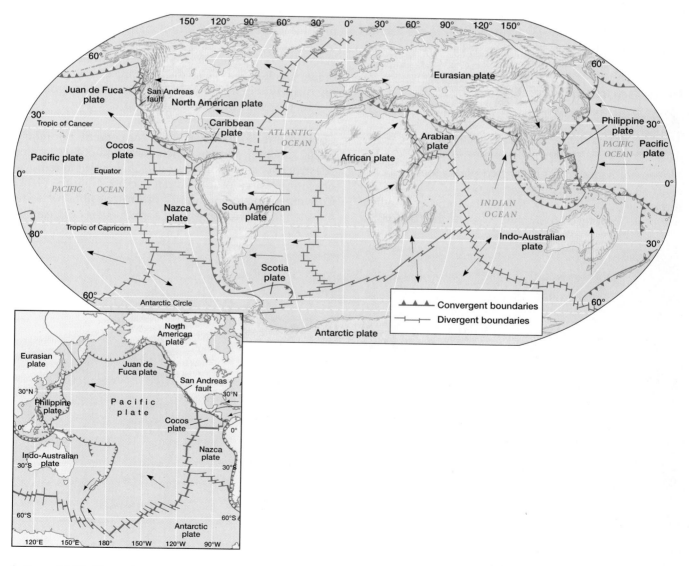

▲ **Figure 14-10** The major contemporary tectonic plates and their generalized direction of movement.

areal extent: some are almost hemispheric in size, whereas others are much smaller. The number of plates and some of their boundaries are not completely clear. About a dozen major plates, and perhaps an equal number of smaller ones, are postulated. Many of the smaller plates are remnants of once larger plates that are now being subducted. These plates are about 65 to 100 kilometers (40 to 60 miles) thick, and most consist of both oceanic and continental crust.

The driving mechanism for plate tectonics is convection within Earth's mantle (the process of convection was discussed in Chapter 4 in the context of atmospheric processes). A very sluggish thermal convection system appears to be operating within the planet, bringing deep-seated heated rock slowly to the surface. Plates may be "pushed" away from midocean ridges to a certain extent, but it appears that much of the motion is a result of the plates being "pulled" along by the subduction of dense oceanic lithosphere down into the asthenosphere.

These plates move slowly over the asthenosphere. The rates of seafloor spreading vary from less than 1 cm (0.4 in.) per year in parts of the Mid-Atlantic Ridge to as much as 10 cm (4 in.) per year in the Pacific-Antarctic Ridge.

Plate Boundaries

1. Divergent Boundaries
2. Subduction Zones
3. Collision of India with Eurasia
4. Transform Faults and Boundaries

Movement sometimes brings two plates together on a collision course. The plates are rigid and therefore deformed significantly only at the edges and only where one plate impinges on another. Most of the "action" in

plate tectonics takes place along such plate boundaries. Only three types of contact between plates are possible: two plates may diverge from one another, converge toward one another, or slide laterally past one another (Figure 14-11).

Divergent Boundaries At a **divergent boundary**, magma from the asthenosphere wells up in the opening between plates. This upward flow of molten material produces a continuous line of active volcanoes that spill out basalt onto the ocean floor. A divergent boundary is usually represented by a **midocean ridge** (Figure 14-12). Most of the midocean ridges of the world are either active or extinct spreading ridges. Such *spreading center* locations are associated with *shallow-focus earthquakes* (meaning that the ruptures that generate the earthquakes are within about 70 kilometers [45 miles] of the surface), volcanic activity, and hydrothermal metamorphism. Divergent boundaries are said to be "constructive" because material is being added to the crustal surface at such locations.

Divergent boundaries can also develop within a continent (Figure 14-13), resulting in a **continental rift valley** such as the great East African Rift Valley that extends from Ethiopia southward through Mozambique. The Red Sea is also the outcome of spreading taking place within a continent—in this case the spreading has been great enough to form a "proto-ocean."

Convergent Boundaries At a **convergent boundary**, plates collide and as such are sometimes called "destructive" boundaries because they result in removal or compression of the surface crust (Figure 14-14). Convergent plate boundaries are responsible for some of the most massive and spectacular of earthly

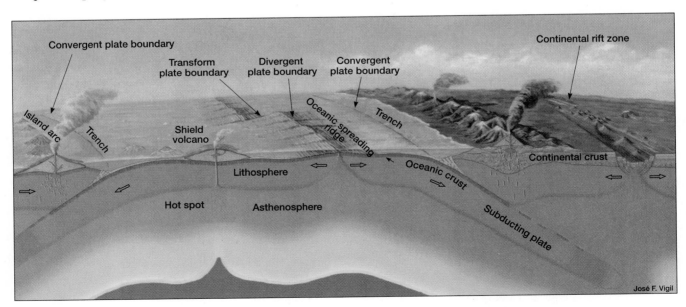

▲ **Figure 14-11** Three kinds of plate boundaries. The edges of lithospheric plates move apart at divergent boundaries, come together at convergent boundaries, and slide past each other along transform boundaries. *(After "This Dynamic Planet,"* U.S. Geological Survey, 1994.)

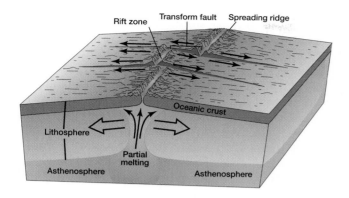

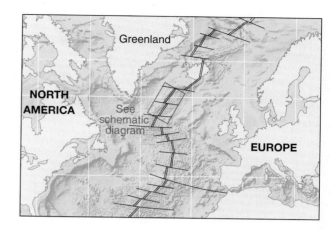

▲ **Figure 14-12** Midocean ridge spreading center. Seafloor spreading involves the rise of magma from within Earth and the lateral movement of new ocean floor away from the zone of upwelling. This gradual process moves the older material farther away from the spreading center as it is replaced by newer material from below.

landforms: major mountain ranges, volcanoes, and deep oceanic trenches. There are three types of convergent boundary: *oceanic–continental convergence, oceanic–oceanic convergence,* and *continental–continental convergence.*

1. **Oceanic–continental convergence:** Because oceanic lithosphere includes dense basaltic crust, it is denser than continental lithosphere, and so oceanic lithosphere always underrides continental lithosphere when the two collide (Figure 14-14a). The dense oceanic plate slowly and inexorably sinks into the asthenosphere in the process of subduction. The subducting slab pulls on the rest of the plate—such "slab pull" is probably the main cause of most plate movement, pulling the rest of the plate in after itself, as it were. Wherever such an oceanic–continental convergent boundary exists, a mountain range is formed on land (the Andes range of South America is one notable example; the Cascades in northwestern North America is another) and a parallel deep **oceanic trench** develops as the seafloor is pulled down by the subducting plate.

Earthquakes take place along the margin of a subducting plate. Shallow-focus earthquakes are common at the trench, but as the subducting plate descends into the mantle, the earthquakes become progressively deeper (Figure 14-15), with some subduction zones generating earthquakes as deep as 600 kilometers (375 miles) below the surface.

Volcanoes develop from magma generated in the subduction zone. Early researchers thought that a subducted plate would melt when pushed down into the hot asthenosphere. However, more recent calculations indicate that such a result is unlikely. Oceanic crust is relatively cold when it approaches a subduction zone and would take a long time to become hot enough to melt. A more likely explanation is that beginning at a depth of about 100 kilometers (about 60 miles) water is driven off from the oceanic crust as it is subducted, and this water lowers the melting point of the mantle rock above, causing it to melt. This magma rises through the overriding plate, producing both extrusive and intrusive igneous rocks. The chain of volcanoes that develops in association with an

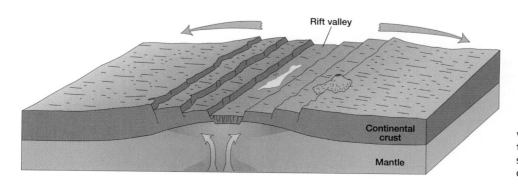

◀ **Figure 14-13** A continental rift valley develops where divergence takes place within a continent. As spreading proceeds, blocks of crust drop down to form a rift valley.

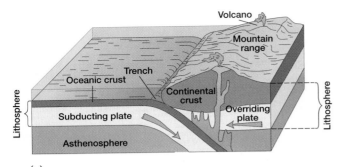

(a)

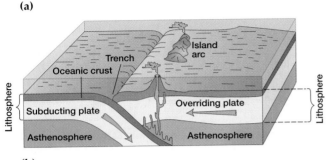

(b)

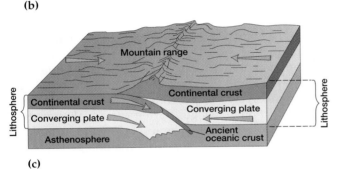

(c)

▲ **Figure 14-14** Idealized portrayals of convergent plate boundaries: **(a)** Where an oceanic plate converges with a continental plate, the oceanic plate is subducted and a deep oceanic trench and coastal mountains with volcanoes are usually created. **(b)** Where oceanic plate meets oceanic plate, a deep oceanic trench and volcanic island arc result. **(c)** Where continental plate meets continental plate, no subduction takes place, but mountains are generally thrust upward.

oceanic–continental plate subduction zone is sometimes referred to as a *continental volcanic arc*. As we will see later in this chapter, such subduction zone volcanoes frequently erupt explosively.

Metamorphic rocks often develop in association with subduction zones. The margin of a subducting oceanic plate is subjected to increasing pressure, although relatively modest heating, as it begins to descend—this can lead to the formation of high–pressure, low–temperature metamorphic rocks, such as *blueschist*. In addition, the magma generated in the subduction zone may cause contact metamorphism as it rises through the overlying continental rocks.

2. **Oceanic–oceanic convergence:** If the convergent boundary is between two oceanic plates, subduction also takes place, as in Figure 14-14b. As one of the oceanic plates subducts beneath the other an oceanic trench is formed, shallow- and deep-focus earthquakes occur, and volcanic activity is initiated with volcanoes forming on the ocean floor. With time, a **volcanic island arc** (such as the Aleutian Islands and Mariana Islands) develops; such an arc may eventually become a more mature island arc system (such as Japan and islands of Sumatra and Java in Indonesia are today).

3. **Continental–continental convergence:** Where there is a convergent boundary between two continental plates, no subduction takes place because continental crust is too buoyant to subduct. Instead, huge mountain ranges, such as the Alps, are built up (Figure 14-14c). The most dramatic present-day example of continental collision has resulted in the formation of the Himalayas. The Himalayas began to form about 35 million years ago, when the subcontinent of India started its collision with the rest of Eurasia. Under the conditions of continental collision, volcanoes are rare, but shallow-focus earthquakes and regional metamorphism are common.

Transform Boundaries At a **transform boundary**, two plates slip past one another laterally. This slippage occurs along great vertical fractures called *transform faults* (a type of *strike-slip fault* to be discussed in more detail later in this chapter). A transform boundary is classified as "conservative" because the plate movements are basically parallel to the boundary, a situation that neither creates new crust nor destroys old. Transform faults are associated with a great deal of seismic activity, commonly producing shallow-focus earthquakes.

Most transform faults are found along the mid-ocean ridge system where they form short offsets in the ridge perpendicular to the spreading axis (see Figure 14-12). However, in some places, transform faults extend for great distances, occasionally through continental lithosphere. For example, the most famous fault system in the United States, the San Andreas Fault in California, is on a transform boundary between the Pacific and North American plates (Figure 14-16).

The Rearrangement

 Assembly and Breakup of Pangaea

Plate tectonics provides us with a grand framework for understanding the extensive crustal rearrangement that has apparently taken place during the relatively recent history of Earth. Wegener's Pangaea is now accepted as having existed. There is substantial evidence

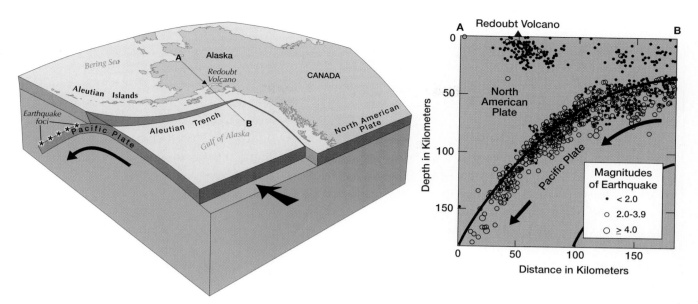

▲ **Figure 14-15** Earthquake patterns in a subduction zone. **(a)** Here the Pacific plate is being thrust below the North American plate along the Aleutian trench. **(b)** Earthquake activity associated with the Aleutian subduction zone during the decade of the 1980s. Earthquake foci become progressively deeper as the Pacific plate subducts below the North American plate. *(After U.S. Geological Survey.)*

to indicate that 450 million years ago—before Pangaea was assembled—five continents existed; these continents "sutured" together to form Pangaea. For the next 200 million years or so, Earth had but a single major continent and a single world ocean. About 200 million years ago, Pangaea began to break up, first into two massive pieces—*Laurasia* in the Northern Hemisphere and *Gondwanaland* in the Southern Hemisphere (see Figure 14-1)—and then into a number of smaller pieces (Figure 14-17). The absolute original locations of the plates are not precisely known, but their relative positions in the past can be determined by matching such features as rocks, fossils, and paleomagnetic patterns. The various plates, along with their attached continents and parts of continents, became separated and drifted in various directions, their divergence often associated with seafloor spreading and their convergence frequently involving collision, subduction, and mountain building.

A brief summary of continental rearrangement might highlight the following:

- Two hundred twenty-five million years ago, all the continents were assembled together into one supercontinent called Pangaea. At the same time, there was only one ocean. Pangaea began to fragment in a continuing process. Antarctica is the only continent that has remained near its original position.

- One hundred thirty-five million years ago, continental fragmentation was well under way. The North Atlantic Ocean was beginning to open, and the South Atlantic began to separate South America from Africa. The expansive Mediterranean Sea

began to close as Africa rotated northward toward Asia.

- Sixty-five million years ago, the North and South Atlantic Oceans joined, and South America was a new and isolated continent that was rapidly moving westward. The Andes were growing as South America overrode the Pacific Ocean Basin, the Rockies were starting to rise, but the Sierra Nevada was still far in the future.

- Today, South America has connected with North America. North America has separated from Europe, Australia has split from Antarctica, and India has collided with Eurasia to thrust up the Himalayas. All continents except for Antarctica are still in motion. Africa is splitting along the Great Rift Valley and slowly rotating counterclockwise.

- If current plate movement continues, 50 million years into the future Australia will straddle the equator as a huge tropical island. Africa may pinch the Mediterranean shut while East Africa becomes a new large island like Madagascar. The Atlantic will widen while the Pacific will shrink. Southern California, now a chilly island, will pass San Francisco en route to its ultimate destiny in the Aleutian Trench in the Gulf of Alaska.

One of the great triumphs of the theory of plate tectonics is that it explains topographic patterns. It can account for the formation of many mountains, midocean ridges, oceanic trenches, island arcs, and the associated earthquake and volcanic zones. Where these features appear, there are usually plates either colliding or separating. Perhaps nowhere in the

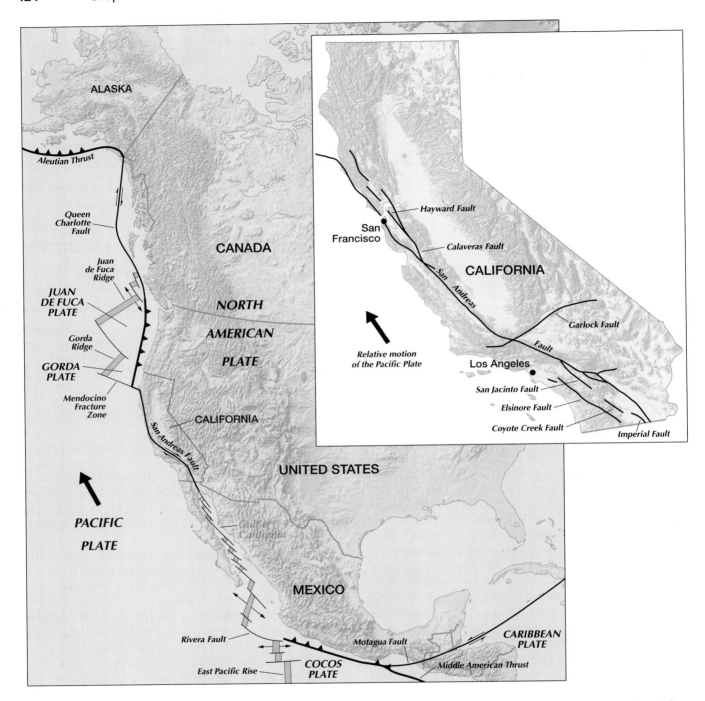

▲ **Figure 14-16** The San Andreas fault system of California is the major component of the transform boundary between the Pacific plate and North American plate. Notice that north of the San Andreas Fault system, subduction of several small oceanic plates is taking place; this subduction is associated with the Cascade volcanoes. *(After Tarbuck and Lutgens,* Earth Sciences, *11th ed., Upper Saddle River, NJ: Prentice Hall, 2006.)*

world are the consequences of tectonic and volcanic activity associated with plate boundaries more vividly displayed than around the rim of the Pacific Ocean.

The Pacific Ring of Fire

For many decades, geologists noted the high number of earthquakes and active volcanoes occurring around the rim of the Pacific Ocean basin. About three-quarters of

all active volcanoes in the world lie within the Pacific Rim, but it was only in the late 1960s that the model of plate tectonics provided an explanation for this pattern. Plate boundaries are found all of the way around the Pacific basin—primarily subduction zones, along with segments of transform and divergent boundaries. It is along these plate boundaries that the many volcanoes and earthquakes take place in what is now called the **Pacific Ring of Fire** (Figure 14-18).

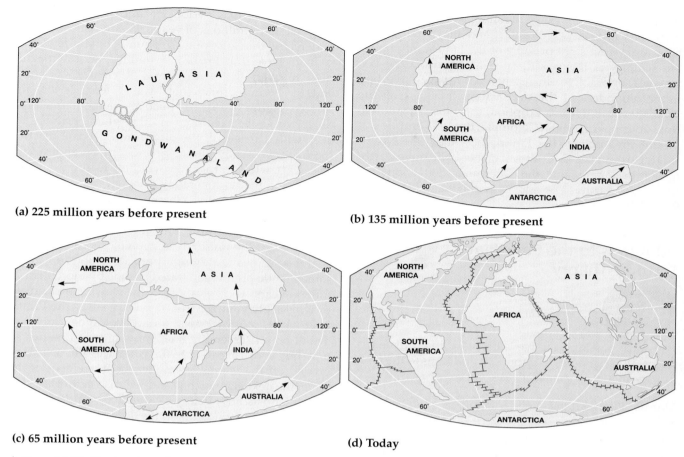

(a) 225 million years before present

(b) 135 million years before present

(c) 65 million years before present

(d) Today

▲ **Figure 14-17**   The breakup of Pangaea beginning about 225 million years ago. Part (d) is essentially the contemporary arrangement.

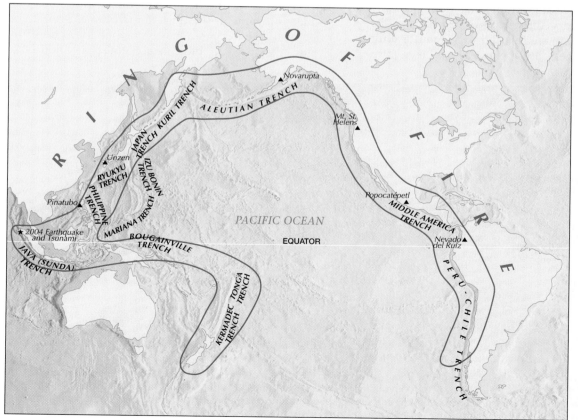

◄ **Figure 14-18**
The Pacific Ring
of Fire.

The Pacific Rim is home to millions of people. Active or potentially active volcanoes and major faults systems are within sight of some of the largest metropolitan regions in the world, such as Mexico City, Los Angeles, and Tokyo. In recent decades we have had many reminders of the ever-active Ring of Fire: the 1980 Mount St. Helens eruption; the 1985 Nevado del Ruiz volcano tragedy in Colombia; the 1991 eruption of Mount Pinatubo in the Philippines; the 1994 Northridge earthquake in California; the 1995 Kobe earthquake in Japan; and the December 2004 Sumatra, Indonesia, earthquake and tsunami that killed more than 270,000 people.

Additions to the Basic Plate Tectonic Theory

FG2
FG4

1. Mantle Plumes
2. Terrane Formation

With each passing year, we learn more about plate tectonics. Two examples of important additions to the plate tectonic model are *mantle plumes* and *accreted terranes*.

Mantle Plumes One augmentation to plate tectonic theory was introduced at the same time as the original model. The basic model of plate tectonics can explain tectonic and volcanic activity along the margins of plates, however, there are many places on Earth where magma from deep in the mantle comes either to or almost to the surface at locations that are not anywhere near a plate boundary; these spots of volcanic activity in the interior of a plate are referred to as **mantle plumes** or **hot spots**. They are believed to be relatively

stationary over long periods of time (in some cases, as long as tens of millions of years). We do not completely understand the cause of these plumes, but more than 50 of them have thus far been identified. As the magma rises through the plate above, it creates volcanoes and/or hydrothermal (hot water) features on the surface (Figure 14-19). The plate above the plume is on the move, so the volcanoes or other plume features are eventually carried off the plume and become inactive (perhaps eventually submerging to form an underwater *seamount*), while in turn new volcanic features develop over the plume, so generating a *hot spot trail*.

One striking result of a mantle plume are the Hawaiian Islands, where the ancient volcanic remnants of Midway Island are now 2500 kilometers (1600 miles) northwest of the presently active volcanoes on the Big Island of Hawaii, although both developed over the same mantle plume, separated in time by more than 27 million years. The volcanoes of the Hawaiian chain are progressively younger from west to east; as the Pacific plate drifts northwestward new volcanoes are produced on an "assembly line" moving over one persistent hot spot (Figure 14-20). After the Big Island is carried off the mantle plume by the movement of the plate, the next Hawaiian island will rise in its place—in fact, scientists are already studying the undersea volcano Loihi as it builds up on the ocean floor just southeast of the Big Island. Other well-known hot spot locations are Yellowstone National Park, Iceland, and the Galapagos Islands.

Mantle plumes help explain volcanic activity in the middle of plates, and help reveal the rate and direction of plate movement—because many plumes seem to be effectively fixed in position for long periods of time, the "trails" they produce indicate absolute plate motion.

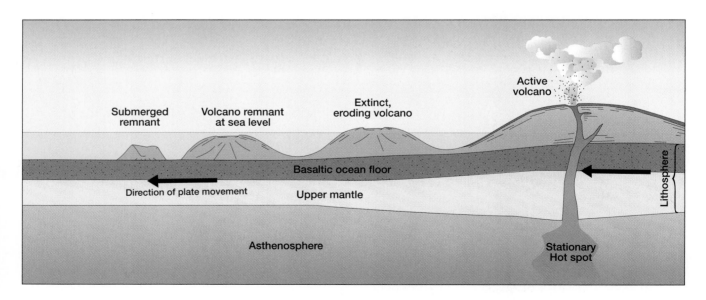

▲ **Figure 14-19**   Magma rises from a mantle plume and a volcano is formed. The plate on which the volcano is being formed is moving leftward in this drawing, while the "hot spot" in the mantle remains stationary. As the plate carries a volcano off the hot spot, it becomes extinct; as the plate cools, it becomes denser and subsides. So what is now a submerged volcano remnant (a *seamount*) at the extreme left was once a newly formed, active volcano at the extreme right.

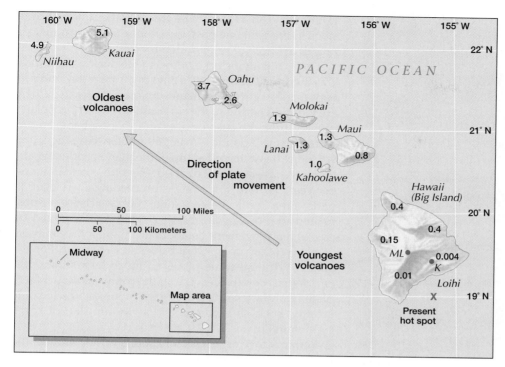

▶ **Figure 14-20** The Hawaiian hot spot. A mantle plume has persisted here for many millions of years. As the Pacific plate moved northwest, a progression of volcanoes was created and then died as their source of magma was shut off. Among the earliest known was at Midway. Later volcanoes developed down the chain. The numbers on the eight main islands indicate dates of the basalt that formed the volcanic cones, in millions of years before the present. The only recently active volcanoes are on the Big Island of Hawaii; Mauna Loa (ML on the map) and Kilauea (K) have been repeatedly active during historic times. Loihi, an underwater volcano in the southeastern corner, is the next volcanic island being built.

Recent research indicates that the complete explanation of hot spots may turn out to be more complex than once thought. *Seismic tomography*—a technique that uses earthquake waves to produce a kind of "ultrasound" of the Earth—suggests that the magma source of at least some mantle plumes is quite shallow, while the source for others is quite deep. Further, some researchers cite evidence suggesting that several mantle plumes may have changed location in the geologic past. For example, the Emperor Seamounts—a chain of seamounts to the northwest of Midway Island—are part of the Hawaiian hot spot trail, but they appear to divert quite significantly in direction from the straight line of the rest of the Hawaiian chain. This "bend" in the hot spot trail is due either to a significant change in direction of the Pacific Plate about 43 million years ago or to the migration of the hot spot itself—perhaps both. As additional information is gathered, a more complete understanding of mantle plumes and midplate volcanic activity will likely emerge.

Accreted Terranes A more recent discovery has helped explain the often perplexing amalgam of lithology seen along the margins of some continents. A **terrane** is a small-to-medium mass of lithosphere that may have been carried a long distance by a drifting plate that eventually converges with another plate. The terrane is too buoyant to be subducted in the collision and instead is fused ("accreted") to the other plate, often being fragmented in the process. In some cases, slices of oceanic lithosphere have accreted in terranes (including the accumulated sediment in what is called the *accretionary wedge* of a subduction zone); in other cases, it appears that entire old island arcs have fused with the margin of a continent (Figure 14-21).

Terranes are distinctive geologically because their lithologic complement (types of rock) is generally quite different from that of the plate to which they are accreted. It is generally believed that every continent has grown outward by the accumulation of accreted terranes on one or more of its margins. North America is a prominent example, as Figure 14-22 shows: Most of Alaska and much of western Canada and the western United States consist of a mosaic of several dozen accreted terranes, some of which have been traced to origins south of the equator.

(a)

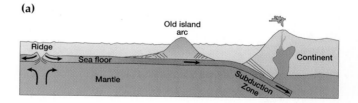

(b)

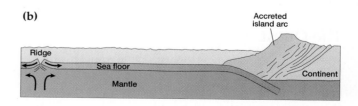

▲ **Figure 14-21** One way an accreted terrane can form. **(a)** A moving oceanic plate carries along an old island arc. The oceanic plate converges with a continental plate. **(b)** The oceanic plate begins to be subducted under the continental plate, but the island arc is too buoyant for subduction. The oceanic plate is completely subducted, and the island arc is now accreted to the continental plate.

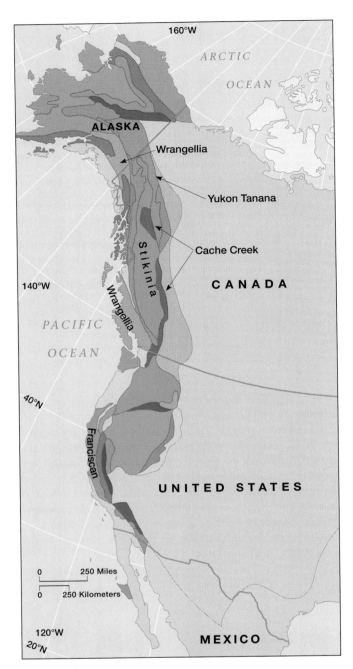

▲ **Figure 14-22** The western part of North America consists of a complicated mixture of terranes that have been accreted to the North American plate.

The Questions

Although plate tectonic theory has advanced our understanding of the internal processes of Earth dramatically, a number of questions remain. For example, despite the correlation of mountain building with plate convergence, the contemporary pattern of plates does not explain all mountain belts. Many of the major mountain ranges of North America and Europe are in the middle of plates rather than in boundary zones. The genesis of some midplate ranges, such as the Appalachians in North America and the Ural mountains in Eurasia, can evidently be traced to continental collisions in the geologic past, but other midplate mountain ranges are not yet fully understood.

There is convincing evidence that during some past eras there were fewer plates than there are today and perhaps during other eras there were more plates than there are today. In addition, the sizes and shapes of past plates differed from the current sizes and shapes. For example, there was no Atlantic Ocean 250 million years ago, and yet today it is a major feature of the planet, widening at a long-term average rate of about 5 centimeters (2 inches) per year. Seafloor spreading is proceeding even faster in parts of the Pacific. Indeed, some geophysicists have postulated that oceans are being created and removed by crustal rearrangement on about a 100-million-year cycle.

Many other unanswered questions remain. For example: Why are some plates so much larger than others? What determines the zones of weakness where plate boundaries first develop? What explains tectonic activity, such as earthquakes, in the middle of some continental plates?

Perhaps the most basic questions center around the mechanism of plate tectonics. While convection of heated material within the mantle provides the general mechanism for plate movement, the details of heat flow within Earth and the relationship of mantle plumes to these overall patterns are still being worked out.

The present state of our knowledge about plate tectonics, however, is ample to provide a firm basis for understanding the gross patterns of most of the world's major relief features—the size, shape, and distribution of the continents and ocean basins and many of the *cordilleras* (chains of mountains, often encompassing many ranges). To understand more detailed topographic features, we must now turn to less spectacular, but no less fundamental, internal processes that are often directly associated with tectonic movement.

Vulcanism

Vulcanism is a general term that refers to all the phenomena connected with the origin and movement of molten rock. These phenomena include the well-known explosive volcanic eruptions that are among the most spectacular and terrifying events in all nature, along with much more quiescent events, such as the slow solidification of molten material below the surface.

We noted in Chapter 13 the distinction between volcanic (extrusive) and plutonic (intrusive) igneous rocks; a similar differentiation is made between extrusive and intrusive vulcanism. When magma is expelled onto Earth's surface while still molten, the activity is extrusive and is called *volcanism*; when magma solidifies in the shallow crust near the surface, it is an intrusive process; when magma solidifies deep inside Earth far below the surface, the process is called *plutonic activity*. Thus, vulcanism is the general category, and *volcanism* (extrusive), *intrusive vulcanism* (shallow), and *plutonic activity* (intrusive, very deep) are three types of vulcanism.

Volcanism

Magma (molten mineral material below the surface) extruded onto Earth's surface is called **lava** (Figure 14-23). The ejection of lava into the open air is sometimes volatile and explosive, devastating the area for many kilometers around; in other cases, it is gentle and quiet, affecting the landscape more gradually. All eruptions, however, alter the landscape because the fiery lava is an inexorable force until it cools, even if it is expelled only slowly and in small quantities.

The explosive eruption of a volcano is an awesome spectacle. In addition to an outward flow of lava, such solid matter as rock fragments, solidified lava blobs, ashes, and dust—collectively called **pyroclastic** material—as well as gas and steam, may be hurled upward in prodigious quantities. In some cases, the volcano literally explodes, disintegrating in an enormous self-destructive blast. The supreme example of such self-destruction within historic times was the final eruption of Krakatau, a volcano that occupied a small island in Indonesia between Sumatra and Java. When it exploded in 1883, the noise was heard 2,400 kilometers (1500 miles) away in Australia, and 20 cubic kilometers (6 cubic miles) of material was blasted into the air. The island disappeared, leaving only open sea where it had been. The *tsunamis* (great seismic sea waves) it generated drowned more than 30,000 people, and sunsets in various parts of the world were colored by fine volcanic dust for many months afterward.

Volcano Distribution A volcano is considered active if it has erupted at least once within historical times and is considered likely to do so again. There are about 550 active volcanoes in the world. On average, about 15 of them will erupt this week, 55 this year, and perhaps 160 this decade. Moreover, there will be one or two eruptions per year from volcanoes with no historic activity. In addition to surface eruptions on continents and islands, there is a great deal of underwater volcanic

▲ **Figure 14-23** Eruption of Kilauea volcano, Hawaii. Note the stream of very fluid basaltic lava flowing away from the vent toward the right. *(© E. R. Degginer/Photo.)*

activity; indeed, it is estimated that more than three-fourths of all volcanic activity is undersea activity such as at midocean ridge spreading centers.

Within the conterminous 48 United States prior to the 1980 eruption of Mount St. Helens, there was only one volcano classified as active—Lassen Peak in California, which last erupted in 1917 but still occasionally produces gas and steam. A number of other volcanoes, notably California's Mount Shasta and Washington's Mount Baker and Mount Rainier, show signs of potential activity but have not erupted in recorded time, and there are hundreds of extinct volcanoes, primarily in the West Coast states. Both Alaska and Hawaii have many volcanoes, both active and inactive.

Areas of volcanism are widespread over the world, but as Figure 14-24 shows, their distribution is highly irregular, with many volcanoes in some regions and none in others. Volcanic activity is primarily associated with plate boundaries. At a divergent boundary, magma wells up from the interior both by eruption from active volcanoes and by flooding out of fissures. At convergent boundaries where subduction is taking place, volcanoes are formed in association with the generation of magma and the crustal crumpling that result from the subduction of oceanic lithosphere. Mantle plumes are responsible for volcanic and hydrothermal activity in many places such as Yellowstone, Hawaii, and the Galapagos Islands.

It is apparent from Figure 14-24 that the most notable area of volcanism in the world is around the margin of the Pacific Ocean in the *Pacific Ring of Fire*—also called the *Andesite Line* because the volcanoes consist primarily of the volcanic rock andesite. About 75 percent of the world's volcanoes, both active and inactive, are associated with the Pacific Rim.

Magma Chemistry and Styles of Eruption The nature of a volcanic eruption apparently is determined largely by the chemistry of the magma that feeds it, although the relative strength of the surface crust and the degree of confining pressure to which the magma is subjected may also be important. The chemical relationships are complex, but the critical component seems to be the relative amount of silica (SiO_2) in the magma. Recall that common magmas include relatively high-silica *felsic* magma (such as produces the volcanic rock rhyolite and the plutonic rock granite), intermediate-silica andesitic magma (such as produces the volcanic rock andesite and the plutonic rock diorite), and relatively low-silica *mafic* magma (such as produces the volcanic rock basalt and the plutonic rock gabbro). See Figure 13-7 in Chapter 13 for a review of igneous rocks resulting from different magma chemistries.

In high-silica felsic magmas, long chains consisting of silicate structures can develop even before crystallization of minerals begins, greatly increasing the *viscosity* (thickness or "stickiness") of the magma. A high silica content also usually indicates cooler magma in which some of the heavier minerals have already crystallized and a considerable amount of gas has already separated. Some of this gas is trapped in pockets in the magma under great pressure. Unlike the more fluid lavas, gas bubbles can rise only slowly through viscous felsic magma. As the magma approaches the surface, the confining pressure is diminished and the pent-up gases are released explosively, generating an

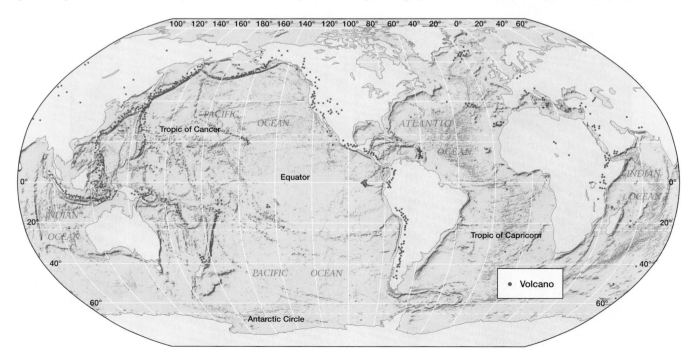

▲ **Figure 14-24**   Distribution of volcanoes known to have erupted at some time in the recent geological past. The Pacific Ring of Fire is quite conspicuous.

FOCUS Mount St. Helens

Eruption of Mount St. Helens

In the spring of 1980, Mount St. Helens in Washington, one of the most beautiful volcanic peaks of the Cascades, suddenly came back to life after lying dormant for 123 years. On the morning of May 18, after several months of seismic activity, swelling, and sporadic eruptions of steam and ash, the volcano unleashed a devastating eruption (Figure 14-A).

With little warning, an earthquake unhinged the entire north slope of the mountain in an enormous landslide. The landslide depressurized the magma within the volcano, triggering a powerful lateral blast that leveled trees more than 24 kilometers (15 miles) north of the volcano, completely devastating an area of more than 500 square kilometers (200 square miles). At the foot of the volcano, Spirit Lake, once one of the most scenic bodies of water in North America, was instantly laden with debris and dead trees. Immediately following the lateral blast, a strong vertical explosion of ash and steam began, forming an eruption column that rose to an altitude of 19 kilometers (12 miles) in less

than 10 minutes. Over the course of the day, more than 470 billion kilograms (520 million tons) of ash were carried to the east by the prevailing winds. Spokane, Washington, 400 kilometers (250 miles) from the volcano, was in darkness at midday. During the course of the eruption, a series of *pyroclastic flows* rolled down the mountain, reaching as far as 8 kilometers (5 miles) north of the volcano. Volcanic mudflows, or *lahars,* some created when the eruption melted snow and ice that capped the volcano, poured down nearby river valleys. The largest of these lahars carried tons of mud and debris into the Toutle River, where the raging mudflow knocked out every bridge for 48 kilometers (30 miles), overwhelmed the Cowlitz River valley, and clogged the Columbia River shipping channel to less than half of its normal depth of 12 meters (40 feet).

The cataclysmic eruption of May 18, 1980, reduced the elevation of Mount St. Helens by more than 390 meters (1300 feet), removed about 2.8 cubic kilometers (0.67 cubic miles) of rock from the volcano, spread volcanic ash over an area of 56,000 square kilometers (22,000 square miles), caused more than $1 billion in property and economic losses, and killed 57 people.

It is sobering to realize that the 1980 eruption of Mount St. Helens was not an extraordinarily large volcanic eruption. The 1991 eruption of Mount Pinatubo in the Philippines was more than 10 times larger, and the 1912 eruption of Novarupta in Alaska 30 times larger. The geologic record shows that Mount St. Helens has had much larger eruptions in the past, as have many other volcanoes in the Cascades—the catastrophic eruption of 7700 years ago that formed present-day Crater Lake in Oregon was 20 times larger than the 1980 eruption of Mount St. Helens.

Now more than 25 years after its last major eruption, Mount St. Helens continues to show activity. By late 2004, the volcano was having small eruptions. A new lava dome was building up inside the old crater, indicating that a plug of near-solid rock was being pushed up from the magma chamber below. Glaciers inside the crater that had grown back since the 1980 eruption were being pushed aside by the bulging new dome. Whether another major eruption comparable to the one in 1980 will occur anytime soon is unclear, although in the long run, Mount St. Helens is quite likely to vigorously erupt again.

(a)

(b)

▲ **Figure 14-A** (a) Mount St. Helens prior to the 1980 eruption. The peak in the background is Mt. Adams. (b) Mount St. Helens after the 1980 eruption. Its posteruption elevation is 400 meters (1300 feet) less than the pre-eruption elevation. *(Tom L. McKnight photos.)*

eruption in which large quantities of pyroclastic material are ejected from the volcano. Any lava flows are likely to be very thick and slow moving.

On the other hand, mafic magma is likely to be hotter and considerably more fluid because of its lower silica content. Dissolved gases can bubble out of very fluid mafic magma much more easily than from viscous felsic magma. The resulting eruptions usually yield a great outpouring of lava, quietly and without explosions or large quantities of pyroclastic material. ("Quietly" is a descriptive term that is relative and refers to the nonexplosive flow of fluid lava.) The highly active volcanoes of Hawaii erupt in this fashion.

Volcanoes with intermediate-silica content andesitic magmas erupt in a style somewhat between that of felsic and mafic magmas: periodically venting fairly fluid andesitic lava flows and periodically having explosive eruptions of pyroclastic material. Many of the major volcanoes associated with subduction zones are of this type.

Volcanic Activity All volcanoes are temporary features of the landscape. Some may have an active life of only a few years, whereas others are sporadically active for thousands of centuries. At the other end of the scale, new volcanoes are spawned from time to time. One of the more spectacular recent developments was the birth of Surtsey, which rose out of the sea as a new island above a mantle plume off the coast of Iceland in 1964.

Despite the destruction they cause, volcanoes do provide vital services to the planet. Just as our blood carries nutrients that nourish our bodies, so volcanoes do the same for the "skin" of Earth. Magma contains the major elements—phosphorus, potassium, calcium, magnesium, sulfur—required for plant growth. When this magma is extruded as lava that hardens into rock, the weathering that releases the nutrients into soil may require decades or centuries (Figure 14-25). When the magma is blasted out as ash, however, nutrients can be leached into the soil within months. It is no coincidence that Java, one of the most volcanically active parts of the planet, is also one of the world's most fertile areas.

As is the case with all other internal processes, volcanism can produce an almost infinite variety of terrain features. Four particular landforms are distinctively associated with volcanic activity, however: lava flows, volcanic peaks, calderas, and volcanic necks.

Lava Flows Whether originating from a volcanic crater or a crustal *fissure,* a lava flow spreads outward at an attitude approximately parallel with the surface over which it is flowing, and this parallelism is maintained as the lava cools and solidifies. Although some viscous flows cling to relatively steep slopes, the vast majority eventually solidify in a horizontal orientation that grossly resembles the stratification of sedimentary rock, particularly if several flows have accumulated on top of one another.

The topographic expression of a lava flow, then, is often a flattish plain or plateau. The strata of sequential flows may be exposed by erosion as streams usually incise very steep-sided gullies into lava flows (Figure 14-26). The character of the flow surface varies with the nature of the lava and with the extent

▲ **Figure 14-26** Lava flows displayed on the walls of the narrow gorge of the Rio Grande, near Taos, New Mexico. *(C.W. Bledel, M.D./Photri.)*

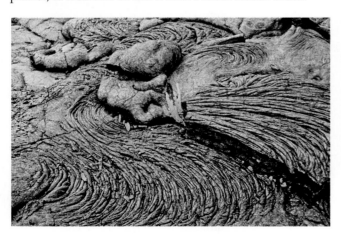

▲ **Figure 14-25** Young basalt of the Big Island of Hawaii. *(Darrel Hess photo.)*

▲ **Figure 14-28** Two extensive outpourings of flood basalt: **(a)** the Deccan Plateau in India and **(b)** the Columbia Plateau in the northwestern United States.

Idaho (Figure 14-28). Larger outpourings are evidenced on other continents, most notably the Deccan Plateau of India (520,000 square kilometers [200,000 square miles]; Figure 14-28a), and even more extensive flood basalts probably occupy much of the ocean floors. Over the world as a whole, more lava has issued quietly from fissures than from the combined outpourings of all volcanoes.

Volcanic Peaks

 1. Volcanoes
2. Formation of Crater Lake

Volcanoes are surface expressions of subsurface igneous activity. Often starting small, a volcano may grow into a conspicuous hill or a massive mountain. Most volcanic peaks take the form of a cone that has a symmetrical profile. A common denominator of nearly all volcanic peaks is a crater normally set conspicuously at the apex of the cone. Frequently, smaller subsidiary cones develop around the base or on the side of a principal peak, or even in the crater. Generally, differences in magma, and therefore eruption style, result in different types of volcanic peaks (Table 14-1 and Figure 14-29).

Shield Volcanoes Basaltic lava tends to flow quite easily over the surrounding surface, forming broad, low-lying **shield volcanoes**, built up of layer upon layer of solidified lava flows with relatively little pyroclastic material. Some shield volcanoes are very high, but they are never steep-sided (Figure 14-29b).

The Hawaiian Islands are composed of numerous shield volcanoes. Produced by the Hawaiian "hot spot," Mauna Loa on the Big Island of Hawaii is the world's largest volcano—it is more than 9 kilometers (6 miles) high from its base on the floor of the ocean to the top of its summit (Figure 14-30). Kilauea, currently the most active of the Hawaiian shield volcanoes, is on the southeast flank of Mauna Loa (Figure 14-31, p. 436).

▲ **Figure 14-27** Basalt cliffs in Devils Postpile National Monument, California. Note the hexagonal columns—a common result when a fluid lava flow cools uniformly. *(John Gerlach/Earth Scenes.)*

of erosion, but as a general rule the surface of relatively recent lava flows tends to be extremely irregular and fragmented. When flows of fluid lava such as basalt cool uniformly, a distinctive pattern of joints frequently develops resulting in hexagonal columns (Figure 14-27).

Many of the world's most extensive lava flows were not extruded from volcanoes but rather issued quietly from midocean ridges and mantle plumes. The lava that flows out of these fissures is nearly always basaltic and frequently comes forth in great volume. The term **flood basalt** is applied to the vast accumulations of lava that build up, layer upon layer, sometimes covering tens of thousands of square kilometers to depths of many hundreds of meters. A prominent example of flood basalt in the United States is the Columbia Plateau, which covers 130,000 square kilometers (50,000 square miles) in Washington, Oregon, and

TABLE 14-1 Principal Types of Volcanoes

Volcano Type	Shape and Size	Structure	Magma and Eruption Style	Examples
Shield	Broad, gently sloping mountain; much broader than high; size varies greatly.	Layers of lava flows.	Magma usually basaltic; characterized by quiet eruptions of fluid lava.	Hawaiian Islands; Tahiti
Composite (Stratovolcano)	Large, steep-sided symmetrical cone; heights to over 3700 m (12,000 ft).	Layers of lava flows, pyroclastics, and hardened mudflow deposits.	Magma usually intermediate in chemistry, often andesitic; long life span; characterized by both explosive eruptions of pyroclastics and quiet eruptions of lava.	Mt. Fuji, Japan; Mt. Rainier, Washington; Mt. Shasta, California; Mt. Vesuvius, Italy; Mt. St. Helens, Washington
Lava Dome (Plug Dome)	Usually small, typically less than 600 m (2000 ft) high; sometimes irregular shape.	Solidified lava that was thick and viscous when molten; plug of lava often covered by pyroclastics; frequently occur within the crater of composite volcano.	Magma usually high in silica, often rhyolitic; dome grows by expansion of viscous lava from within; explosive eruptions common.	Lassen Peak, California; Mono Craters, California
Cinder Cone	Small, steep-sided cone; maximum height 500 m (1500 ft).	Loose pyroclastic material; may be composed of ash or cinder-size pieces.	Chemistry of magma varies, often basaltic; short life span; pyroclastics ejected from central vent; occasionally produce lava flows.	Paricutin, Mexico; Sunset Crater, Arizona

Composite Volcanoes Volcanoes that emit higher silica "intermediate" lavas such as andesite often erupt explosively and tend to develop into symmetrical, steep-sided volcanoes known as **composite volcanoes** or *stratovolcanoes* (Figure 14-29d). These mountains build up steep sides by having layers of ejected pyroclastics (ash and cinders) from explosive eruptions alternate with lava flows from nonexplosive eruptions. The pyroclastic material tends to produce the steep slopes, while the lava flows hold this loose material together. Famous examples of composite volcanoes include Mt. Fuji in Japan, Mt. Rainier in Washington, and Volcán Popocatépetl near Mexico City (Figure 14-32, p. 436)

Lava Domes Lava domes—also called **plug domes**—have masses of very viscous lava such as high-silica rhyolite that are too thick and pasty to flow very far. Instead, lava bulges up from the vent, and the dome grows largely by expansion from below and within (Figure 14-29c). The Mono Craters are a chain of young rhyolitic plug domes just to the east of the Sierra Nevada and Yosemite National Park in California—the most recent activity taking place just a few hundred years ago (Figure 14-33, p. 437).

Lava domes may also develop within the craters of composite volcanoes when viscous lava moves up into the vent. Shortly after the large eruption of Mount St. Helens in 1980, such a lava dome began to develop.

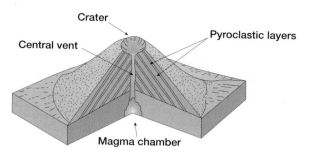

(a) Cinder cone

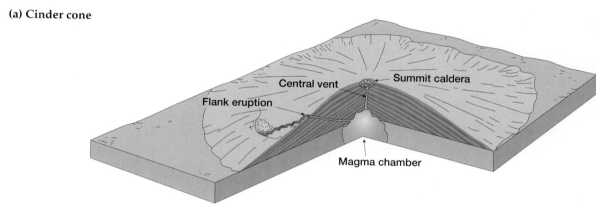

(b) Shield volcano

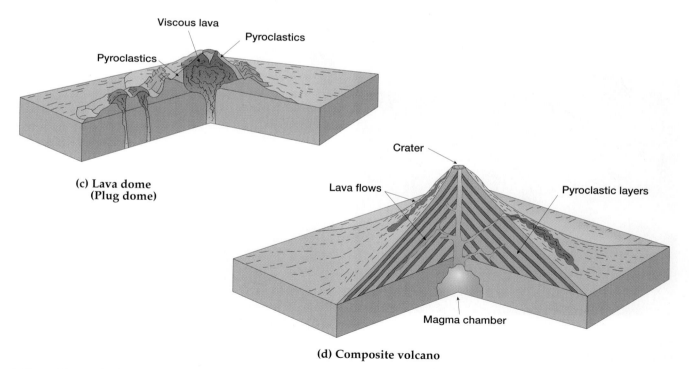

(c) Lava dome (Plug dome)

(d) Composite volcano

▲ **Figure 14-29** The four principal types of volcanic cones.

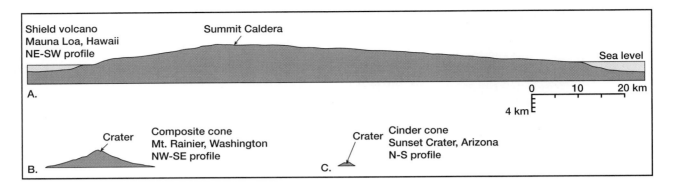

Shield volcano
Mauna Loa, Hawaii
NE-SW profile

Summit Caldera

Sea level

A.

0   10   20 km

4 km

Crater   Composite cone
Mt. Rainier, Washington
NW-SE profile

B.

Crater   Cinder cone
Sunset Crater, Arizona
N-S profile

C.

▲ **Figure 14-30**   Profiles of volcanoes drawn at identical scales. **(a)** Mauna Loa, Hawaii—a shield volcano. **(b)** Mt. Rainier, Washington—a composite volcano. **(c)** Sunset Crater, Arizona—a cinder cone. *(After Tarbuck and Lutgens,* Earth Sciences, *11th ed., Upper Saddle River, NJ: Prentice Hall, 2006.)*

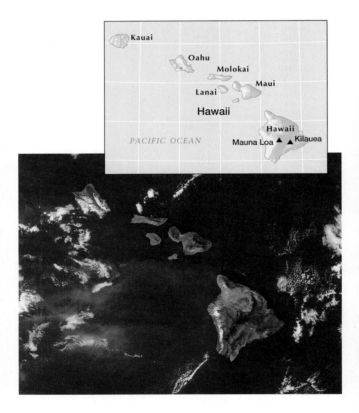

▲ **Figure 14-31**   The Hawaiian Islands consist of a series of large shield volcanoes. Kilauea and Mauna Loa, currently the most active Hawaiian volcanoes, are on the southeast side of the Big Island. *(Jacques Descloitres, MODIS Rapid Response Team, NASA/GSFC/Visible Earth.)*

▶ **Figure 14-32**   Volcán Popocatépetl near Mexico City erupting in November 1998. The Church of Our Lady of Remedies is in the foreground. *(AP Photo/Ulises Ruiz.)*

▲ **Figure 14-33**   Crater Mountain is the highest peak in the Mono Craters chain of rhyolitic plug domes in California. *(Darrel Hess photo.)*

Cinder Cones Cinder cones are the smallest of the volcanic mountains. Their magma chemistry varies, but basaltic magma is most common. They are cone-shaped peaks built by the pyroclastic materials that are ejected from the volcanic vent (Figure 14-29a). The size of the particles being ejected determines the steepness of the slopes. Tiny particles ("ash") can support slopes as steep as 35 degrees, whereas the larger ejecta ("cinders") will produce slopes up to about 25 degrees. Cinder cones are generally less than 450 meters (1500 feet)

high and are often found in association with other volcanoes (Figure 14-34).

Calderas Uncommon in occurrence but spectacular in result is the formation of a **caldera**, which is produced when a volcano explodes, collapses, or does both. The result is an immense basin-shaped depression, generally circular, that has a diameter many times larger than that of the original volcanic vent or vents. Some calderas are tens of kilometers in diameter.

▲ **Figure 14-34**   Sunset Crater, in northern Arizona near Flagstaff, is a classic example of a cinder cone volcano. *(Tom L. McKnight photo.)*

(a)

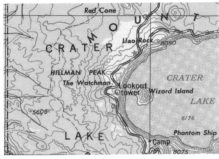

(b)

 Figure 14-35 Oregon's Crater Lake occupies an immense caldera. Wizard Island represents a more recent subsidiary volcanic cone. *(Tom L. McKnight photo.)*

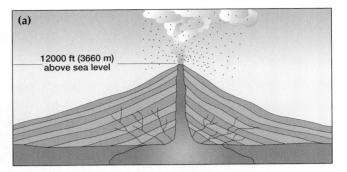

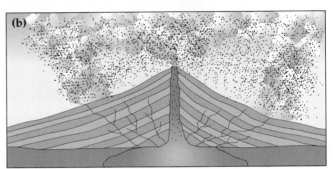

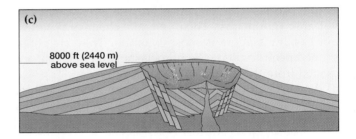

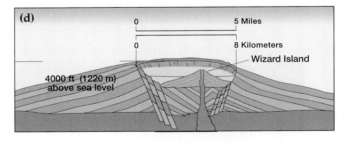

▲ **Figure 14-36** Formation of Crater Lake. **(a)** Mount Mazama about 7700 years ago. **(b)** Enormous eruptions of ash flows emptied the magma chamber. **(c)** The top of the volcano collapsed, forming a caldera 1220 meters (4000 feet) deep. **(d)** A new fissure allows magma to flow again, and the volcano known as Wizard Island is created.

North America's most famous caldera is Oregon's misnamed Crater Lake (Figure 14-35). About 7700 years ago, a mountain on this site, Mount Mazama, was a volcanic cone that reached an estimated elevation of 3660 meters (12,000 feet) above sea level. During a major eruption, the magma chamber was emptied (Figure 14-36). Once magma ceased to flow out from the top of this volcano, pressure built up and the walls weakened because they were no longer supported by the upflowing magma. The final, cataclysmic eruption removed—by explosion and collapse—the upper 1220 meters (4000 feet) of the peak and produced a caldera whose bottom is 1220 meters (4000 feet) below the crest of the remaining rim. Later, half this depth filled with water, creating one of the deepest lakes in North America. A subsidiary volcanic cone has subsequently built up from the bottom of the caldera and now breaks the surface of the lake as Wizard Island (Figure 14-37).

Shield volcanoes may develop summit calderas in a different way. When large quantities of fluid lava are vented from rift zones along the sides of a volcano, the magma chamber below the summit can empty and collapse, forming a relatively shallow caldera. Both

Mauna Loa and Kilauea on the Big Island of Hawaii have calderas that formed in this way.

Volcanic Necks More limited still but very prominent where it does occur is a volcanic neck, a small, sharp spire that rises abruptly above the surrounding land. It represents the pipe, or throat, of an old volcano that

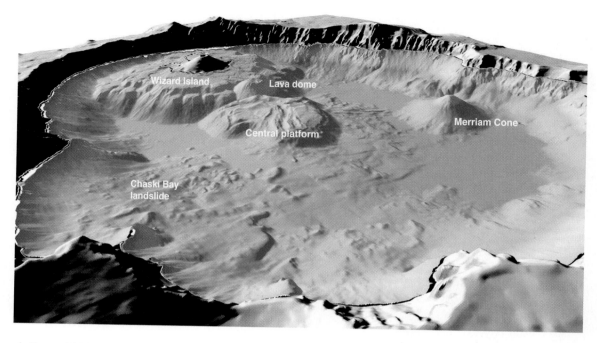

▲ **Figure 14-37** Bathymetry of Crater Lake. This detailed map of the floor of Crater Lake in Oregon shows evidence of postcollapse volcanic activity and massive landslides. *(From U.S. Geological Survey Fact Sheet 092–02, "Mount Mazama and Crater Lake: Growth and Destruction of a Cascade Volcano," 2002.)*

filled with solidified lava after its final eruption. Millennia of erosion have removed the less resistant material that made up the cone, leaving the harder, lava-choked neck as a conspicuous remnant (Figure 14-38).

Volcanic Hazards

Millions of people around the world live in close proximity to active or potentially active volcanoes. In the United States alone, there are more than 50 volcanoes that have erupted within the last 200 years, and some of these volcanoes are located near population centers in Washington, Oregon, California, Alaska, and Hawaii. Future eruptions could expose large numbers of people to a wide range of volcanic hazards (Figure 14-39).

Volcanic Gases A volcano emits large quantities of gas during an eruption. Water vapor makes up the bulk of the gas emitted, but other volcanic gases include carbon dioxide, sulfur dioxide, hydrogen sulfide, and fluorine. The hazards resulting from these gases vary. For example, sulfur dioxide may combine with water in the atmosphere to form a mist of sulfuric acid that falls to the surface as acid rain, harming vegetation and causing corrosion. High in the atmosphere, these same droplets may reflect incoming solar radiation, altering global weather. As we described in Chapter 8, the large quantities of sulfur dioxide emitted by Mount Pinatubo in the Philippines

in 1991 reduced insolation enough to lower global temperatures slightly for more than a year.

Lava Flows Perhaps surprisingly, lava flows rarely cause loss of life, although they can produce significant property damage. The speed and distance covered by a lava flow depends mostly on its viscosity, which in turn depends on its silica content. Low-silica basaltic lava

▲ **Figure 14-38** Shiprock in northwestern New Mexico is a prime example of a volcanic neck. *(Darrel Hess photo.)*

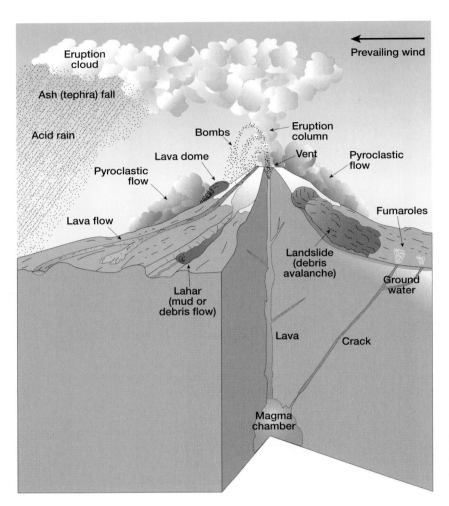

Eruption cloud

Ash (tephra) fall

Prevailing wind

Acid rain

Bombs

Eruption column

Lava dome

Vent

Pyroclastic flow

Pyroclastic flow

Lava flow

Fumaroles

Landslide (debris avalanche)

Ground water

Lahar (mud or debris flow)

Lava

Crack

Magma chamber

◄ Figure 14-39 The hazards associated with a typical composite volcano. Some of these hazards may also occur with other kinds of volcanoes. *(After U.S. Geological Survey Fact Sheet 002–97, "What are Volcano Hazards?" 1997.)*

associated with shield volcanoes, such as those on Hawaii, tends to be quite fluid and fast moving. Although most basaltic lava flows move more slowly than a person can walk, some flows travel at speeds of over 25 kilometers (15 miles) per hour and cover distances of more than 120 kilometers (75 miles) before congealing. Since the paths taken by lava flows tend to be predictable they cause few injuries, although many dozens of homes have been destroyed by lava flows from Kilauea Volcano in Hawaii over the last few decades.

Higher-silica lava, such as the andesitic lava associated with the many composite volcanoes around the rim of the Pacific, tends to be thicker and more sluggish than basaltic lava, usually moving only short distances down the slopes of the volcano. Very viscous rhyolitic lava often does little more than squeeze out of a vent, bulging up to form a lava dome. While lava flows from intermediate- and high-silica magmas rarely represent a direct danger to people, the explosive nature of these volcanoes does often produce a number of significant hazards.

Eruption Column and Clouds It is common for composite volcanoes and lava domes to erupt explosively. The violent ejection of pyroclastic material and gases from a volcano can form an *eruption column* reaching altitudes of 16 kilometers (10 miles) or more.

Large fragments of solid rock, called volcanic "bombs," drop to the ground immediately around the volcano, while smaller fragments of volcanic ash and dust form an enormous eruption cloud from which great quantities of ash may fall. A heavy covering of ash can damage crops and even cause the collapse of buildings.

Pyroclastic Flows The collapse of a lava dome or the explosive eruption of a composite volcano can lead to a terrifying high-speed avalanche of searing hot gases, ash, and rock fragments known as a **pyroclastic flow**. A pyroclastic flow (sometimes called a *nuée ardente*) can travel down a volcano at speeds of more than 160 kilometers (100 miles) per hour, burning and burying everything in its path (Figure 14-40). Probably the most famous example of a pyroclastic flow took place in 1902 on the Caribbean island of Martinique. An explosive eruption of Mont Pelée sent a massive pyroclastic flow down onto the port city of St. Pierre, destroying the town and killing nearly all of its 28,000 inhabitants in a matter of moments.

More recently, the Unzen volcano complex on the Japanese island of Kyushu began a series of eruptions in 1990. After a period of escalating seismic activity, a lava dome formed in Fugen–dake, a peak adjacent to the large Mayu–yama dome. By the spring of 1991, lava

◀ **Figure 14-40**   Eruption of Mount St. Augustine, Alaska. A pyroclastic flow is moving down the slopes of the volcano to the left of the summit. *(Steve Kaufman/DRK.)*

blocks were collapsing off the dome, generating hundreds of pyroclastic flows, some of which traveled more than 5 kilometers (3 miles) off the flanks of the volcano (Figure 14-41). By 1993, pyroclastic flows and volcanic mudflows had destroyed 2000 structures, forced the evacuation of as many as 12,000 local

◀ **Figure 14-41**   Aerial view of Unzen volcano in Japan showing the path of pyroclastic flows that moved down toward the town of Shimabara in 1993. *(© Michael S. Yamashita/CORBIS.)*

PEOPLE AND THE ENVIRONMENT Monitoring Volcanic Hazards

The recent eruptions of Mount St. Helens, Mount Pinatubo, Nevado del Ruiz, Unzen, and Volcán Popocatépetl may appear to be unusual, brief, and isolated sequences of events; but such is not the case. Formed by ongoing plate convergence around the rim of the Pacific basin, these are just a few of the many active volcanoes associated with the subduction zones of the Andes, Central America, the Cascades, Alaska, Japan, and the islands of the western Pacific. Individual volcanoes may lie dormant for hundreds of years between major eruptions, and so the volcanic hazards in the surrounding regions are not always evident. In North America, the Cascade range alone contains more than a dozen potentially active volcanoes, including seven that have exhibited activity since the late 1700s (Figure 14-B). Because of rapidly expanding populations here and elsewhere around the Pacific Rim, increasing numbers of people are now exposed to the same volcanic hazards that have killed thousands in the past.

By the 1970s, a concerted international effort was underway to both assess volcanic hazards and to gain enough knowledge to anticipate the onset of major volcanic eruptions. In the United States, the U.S. Geological Survey and research universities are looking at past historical eruptions as well as evidence from the geological record to map out the most likely paths of pyroclastic flows and lahars from volcanoes such as Mt. Shasta in California, Mt. Hood in Oregon, and Mt. Rainier in Washington.

The monitoring of active volcanoes includes measuring slight changes in the slope of a mountain using sensitive "tiltmeters" that can detect swelling of a volcano with magma, measuring variations in gas composition and quantity vented from a volcano that may indicate changes in magma, and monitoring earthquake activity below a volcano—swarms of small earthquakes may indicate the filling of the magma chamber below a volcanic peak. Remote cameras can produce time-lapse movie sequences that document changes to lava domes and other crater features. Especially promising research is pointing toward distinctive seismic patterns that often accompany the onset of major eruptions. It is hoped that this growing knowledge will enable authorities to make more informed choices about when and where to evacuate local populations when the next volcano erupts.

▲ Figure 14-B Prominent volcanoes (active, dormant, and extinct) of the Cascade Range.

---

residents, and taken the lives of 43 people, including the well-known French filmmakers and volcanologists Maurice and Katia Krafft.

Volcanic Mudflows (Lahars) One of the most common hazards associated with composite volcanoes are **volcanic mudflows**—also known by their Indonesian name, **lahar**. A loose mantle of ash and pyroclastic flow deposits on the slopes of a volcano can be mobilized easily by heavy rain or by the melting of snow and glaciers during an eruption. The water mixes with unconsolidated pyroclastic material to produce a fast-moving—and sometimes hot—slurry of mud and boulders, flowing with the consistency of wet concrete. Lahars typically flow down stream valleys off the slopes of a volcano, leaving the valley floor buried in thick mud and debris. They can reach speeds of over 50 kilometers (30 miles) per hour and travel distances of over 80 kilometers (50 miles). One of the most tragic examples of a lahar took place in 1985 when the Nevado del Ruiz volcano in Colombia produced a mudflow that inundated the town of Armero nearly 50 kilometers (30 miles) away, killing more than 20,000 people.

Igneous Features

Igneous Features

When magma solidifies below Earth's surface, it produces igneous rock. If this rock is pushed upward into the crust either before or after solidification, it is called an **igneous intrusion.** Most such intrusions have no effect on the surface landscape, but sometimes the igneous mass is raised high enough to deform the overlying material and change the shape of the surface. In many cases, the intrusion is exposed at the surface. When intrusions are thus exposed to the external processes, they often become conspicuous because they are usually resistant to erosion and with the passage of time stand up relatively higher than the surrounding land.

Intrusions come in all shapes, sizes, and compositions. Moreover, their relationship to overlying or surrounding rock is also quite variable. The intrusive process is usually a disturbing one for preexisting rock. Rising magma makes room for itself by a process called *stoping* (a mining term for ore removal by working

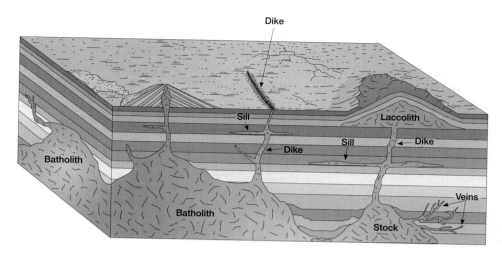

◀ **Figure 14-42** The six typical forms of igneous intrusions.

upward). The molten, invading magma can assimilate the rock being invaded or heat it enough to make it flow out of the way or either split or bow it upward. Adjacent to the area the magma has invaded, the invaded rock usually experiences contact metamorphism from being exposed to the heat and pressure of the rising intrusion.

In rare cases, there may be little or no disturbance, as with a small intrusion that inserts itself between preexisting sedimentary beds with little deformation or metamorphism. Although there is almost infinite variety in the forms assumed by igneous intrusions, most can be broadly classified according to a scheme that contains only a half-dozen types (Figure 14-42).

Batholiths By far the largest and most amorphous intrusion is the **batholith**, which is a subterranean igneous body of indefinite depth and enormous size (it must have a surface area of at least 100 square kilometers [40 square miles] to be a batholith). Batholiths often form the core of major mountain ranges, their intrusive uplift being a fundamental part of the mountain-building process. Such notable ranges as the Sierra Nevada in California, Idaho's Sawtooth Mountains, and Colorado's Front Range were created at least partially by the uplift of massive batholiths. Almost all the bedrock exposed in the high country of these ranges consists of batholithic granite, which was originally covered by an extensive overburden of other rocks that has since been eroded away (Figure 14-43).

Stocks Similar to a batholith but much smaller is a *stock*. It is also amorphous and of indefinite depth, but it has a surface area of only a few square kilometers at most. Many stocks apparently are offshoots of batholiths.

Laccoliths A specialized form of intrusion is the *laccolith*, which is produced when slow-flowing, viscous magma is forced between horizontal layers of preexisting rock. Although continuing to be fed from some subterranean source, the magma resists flowing and instead builds up into a mushroom-shaped mass

that domes the overlying strata. If this dome is near enough to Earth's surface, a rounded hill will rise, like a blister, above the surrounding area. Many laccoliths are small, but some are so large as to form the cores of hills or mountains in much the same fashion as batholiths. The Black Hills of South Dakota, for

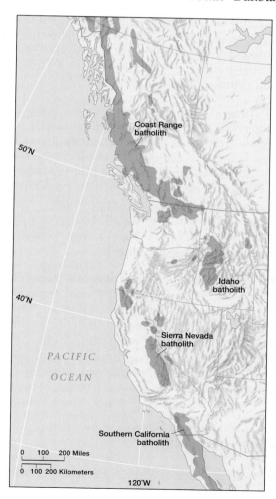

▲ **Figure 14-43** The major batholiths of western North America. These extensive intrusions are mostly associated with the former subduction boundary along the western edge of the North American plate.

example, have a laccolithic core, as do several of the geologically famous mountain groups (Henry, Abajo, LaSal) in southern Utah.

Batholiths, stocks, and laccoliths are sometimes grouped under the general heading **plutons**, which simply means any large, intrusive igneous body.

Dikes Probably the most widespread of all intrusive forms is the **dike**, a vertical or nearly vertical sheet of magma thrust upward into preexisting rock, sometimes forcing its way into vertical fractures and sometimes melting its way upward. Dikes are notable because they are vertical, narrow (a few centimeters to a few meters wide), and usually quite resistant to erosion. As with most other igneous intrusions, their depth is indeterminate; they often serve as conduits through which deep-seated magma can reach the surface. In some cases, dikes are quite long, extending for kilometers or even tens of kilometers in one direction. When exposed at the surface by erosion, they commonly form sheer-sided walls that rise above the surrounding terrain, as Figure 14-44 shows. Dikes are often found in association with volcanoes, occurring as radial walls extending outward from the volcano like spokes of a wheel. Notable examples of radial dike development can be seen around Shiprock in northwestern New Mexico and around the Spanish Peaks in south-central Colorado.

Sills A *sill* is also a long, thin intrusive body, but its orientation is determined by the structure of the preexisting rocks. It is formed when magma is forced between strata that are already in place; the result is often a horizontal igneous sheet between horizontal sedimentary layers. Sills are much less common than dikes, and their landscape expression is usually inconspicuous except where a sill serves as a caprock protecting softer rocks underneath, which can produce a steep-walled mesa, butte, or cliff.

Veins Least prominent among igneous intrusions but widespread in occurrence are thin *veins* of magma that may occur individually or in profusion. They are commonly formed when molten material forces itself into small fractures in the preexisting rocks, but they can also result from melting by an upward surge of magma. Intrusive veins may take very irregular shapes, but they normally have a generally vertical orientation.

Diastrophism

Diastrophism is a general term that refers to the deformation of Earth's crust. The term covers various kinds of crust movement and implies that the material is solid and not molten. The rocks may be bent or broken in a variety of ways in response to great pressures exerted either in the mantle or crust. Some of these vast

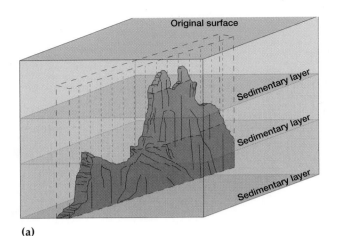

(a)

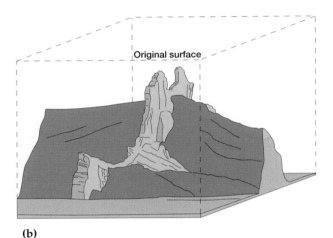

(b)

(c)

▲ **Figure 14-44** **(a)** An igneous dike was intruded into softer bedrock. **(b and c)** Subsequent erosion has left the resistant dike standing as an abrupt natural wall. This scene is in southern Colorado near LaVeta. *(Tom L. McKnight photo.)*

pressures clearly result from plate movement, but others appear to be unrelated directly to plate boundary activity. Some are caused by the rise of molten material from below, either intrusively or extrusively, but most seem to have no causal relationship with magma.

Whatever the causes of diastrophic pressures, the results are often conspicuous in the landscape. Diastrophic movements are particularly obvious in sedimentary rocks because nearly all sedimentary strata are initially deposited in a horizontal or near-horizontal attitude—so if they now are bent, broken, or nonhorizontal, they have clearly experienced some sort of diastrophic deformation.

For purposes of description and analysis, diastrophic movements can be separated into two types—*folding* and *faulting*—although the separation in nature is not always so discrete and clear-cut.

Folding

Folding

When crustal rocks are subjected to certain forces, particularly lateral compression, they are often deformed by being bent in a process called **folding** (Figure 14-45). The notion of folding is sometimes difficult to conceptualize. Our common experience is that rocks are hard and

brittle. If subjected to stresses, they might be expected to break—bending is harder to visualize. In nature, however, when great pressure is applied for long periods, particularly in an enclosed, buried, subterranean environment, the result is often a slow plastic deformation that can produce folded structures of incredible complexity. Folding can occur in any kind of rock, but it is obviously most recognizable in sedimentary strata.

Folding can take place at almost any scale. Some folds can be measured in no more than centimeters, whereas others can develop over such broad areas that crest and trough are tens of kilometers apart.

The configuration of the folds can be equally variable. In some cases, the folding is simple and symmetrical; elsewhere it may be of extraordinary complexity and totally without symmetry. Moreover, the structure may become even more complex by breakage of the rock (faulting), which the stresses may engender in addition to the complicated folding.

Structural geologists recognize many kinds of folds, with a lengthy nomenclature to classify them. For

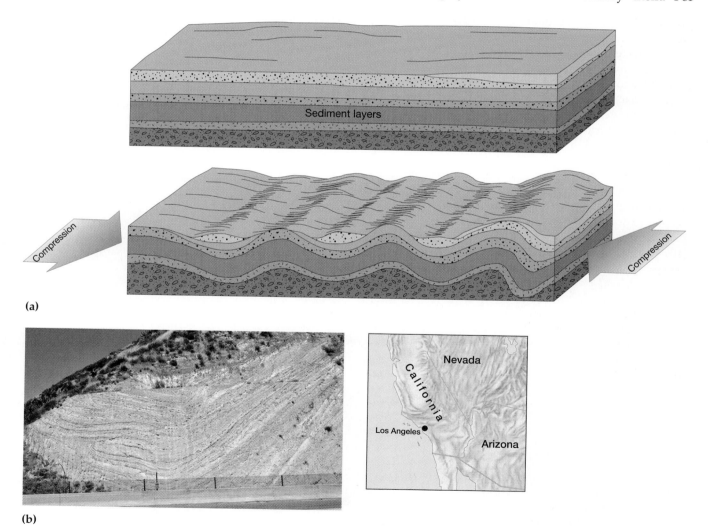

(a)

(b)

▲ **Figure 14-45** (a) Compressive lateral pressures cause sedimentary strata that are initially horizontal to fold, much as pushing on a tablecloth causes it to bunch up into folds. (b) Tightly folded sedimentary strata in a road cut near Los Angeles. *(Tom L. McKnight photo.)*

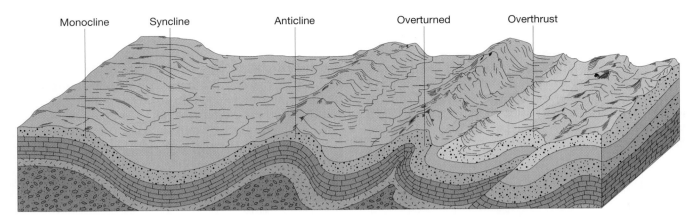

Monocline Syncline Anticline Overturned Overthrust

▲ **Figure 14-46** The basic types of folds.

introductory physical geography, however, only a few terms are necessary (Figure 14-46). A *monocline* is a one-sided slope connecting two horizontal or gently inclined strata. A simple symmetrical upfold is an **anticline**, and a simple downfold is a **syncline**. Also relatively common is an upfold that has been pushed so vigorously from one side that it becomes oversteepened enough to have a reverse orientation on the other side; such a structure is referred to as an **overturned fold**. If the pressure is enough to break the oversteepened limb and cause a shearing movement, the result is an *overthrust fold,* which causes older rock to ride above younger rock.

Folds frequently occur in multiples rather than individually, as enormous forces crumple the land surface.

When sedimentary strata are subjected to lateral compression, a series of simple parallel folds is often formed, with an alternating sequence of anticlines and synclines. If the folding takes place near enough to the surface, or if it is subsequently exposed by uplift and/or erosion, the topographic result is likely to be a series of long, narrow, parallel ridges and valleys.

The simplest relationship between structure and topography, and one that often occurs in nature, finds the upfolded anticlines producing ridges and the downfolded synclines forming valleys. The converse relationship is also possible, however, with valleys developing on the anticlines and ridges on the synclines (Figure 14-47). This inverted topography is most easily

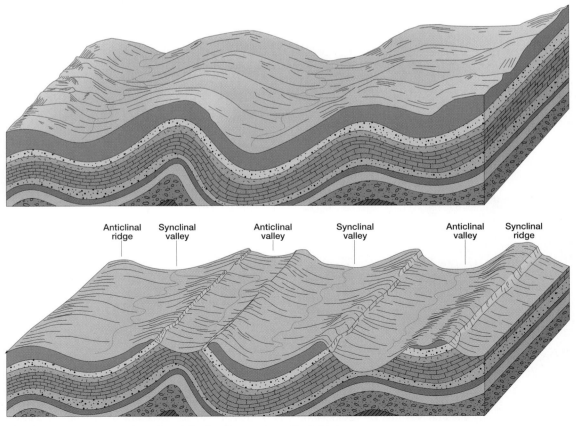

Anticlinal ridge Synclinal valley Anticlinal valley Synclinal valley Anticlinal valley Synclinal ridge

▲ **Figure 14-47** Formation of anticlinal valleys and synclinal ridges.

noted for its remarkably parallel sequence of mountains and valleys developed on folds (Figure 14-48). The section extends for about 1600 kilometers (1000 miles) in a northeast–southwest direction across parts of nine states, with a width that varies from 40 to 120 kilometers (25 to 75 miles).

The geometry of complex folding is of infinite variability, with extremes of crumpling and overturning. The resultant topographic features can be equally variable depending, as always, on the actions of the external processes. One example of this complexity is portrayed in Figure 14-49, which displays some of the remarkable compressional folding that has taken place in the Swiss Alps and the generalized topographic profile that has resulted.

The landforms that result from folding are even more varied than the folds themselves because other processes are involved in the final shaping of the surface. Most folding takes place in a constricted subterranean environment; when the structures are exposed at the surface, erosion modifies them in a variety of ways.

▲ **Figure 14-48** Satellite image of the intensely folded Appalachian topography of the eastern United States. *(Worldsat International Inc./Science Photo Library/Photo Researchers, Inc.)*

Faulting

Another prominent result of crustal stresses is the breaking apart of rock material. When rock is broken with accompanying displacement (i.e., actual movement of the crust on one or both sides of the break), the action is called **faulting** (Figure 14-50). The movement can be vertical or horizontal or a combination of both. Faulting usually takes place along zones of weakness in the crust; such an area is referred to as a *fault zone*, and the intersection of that zone with Earth's surface is called a *fault line*.

Movement of crust along a fault zone is sometimes very slow, but it may also occur as a sudden slippage. A single slippage may result in a displacement of only a few centimeters or so, but in some cases the movement may

explained by the effects of tension (pulling apart) and compression (pushing together) on the folded strata. Where a layer is arched over an upfold, tension cracks can form and provide easy footholds for erosional forces to remove materials and incise downward into the underlying strata. Conversely, the compression that acts on the downfolded beds increases their density and therefore their resistance to erosion. Thus, over a long period of time, the upfolds may be eroded away faster than the downfolds, producing anticlinal valleys and synclinal ridges.

All these types of folding, as well as many variations, are found in what is called the ridge-and-valley section of the Appalachian Mountains, a world-famous area

◀ **Figure 14-49** Cross section through the Swiss Alps, showing the enormous complexity of fold structures.

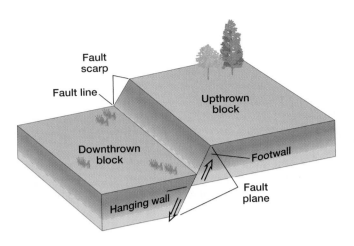

▲ **Figure 14-50** A simple fault structure.

▲ **Figure 14-51** The steep east side of the Sierra Nevada mountains in California is a prominent fault scarp. *(Darrel Hess photo.)*

be as much as 5 or 10 meters (15 or 30 feet). Successive slippages may be years or even centuries apart, but the cumulative displacement over millions of years could conceivably amount to hundreds of kilometers horizontally and tens of kilometers vertically.

Major faults penetrate many kilometers into Earth's crust. Indeed, the deeper fault zones apparently serve as conduits to allow both water and heat from inside Earth to approach the surface. Frequently springs are found along fault lines, sometimes with hot water gushing forth. Volcanic activity is also associated with some fault zones as magma forces its way upward in the zone of weakness.

Fault lines are often marked by other prominent topographic features. Most notable are **fault scarps** (see Figure 14-50), which are steep cliffs that represent the edge of a vertically displaced block. Some fault scarps are as much as 3 kilometers (2 miles) high and extend for more than 150 kilometers (100 miles) in virtually a straight line. The abruptness of their rise, the steepness of their slope, and the linearity of their orientation combine to make some fault scarps extremely spectacular features in the landscape, as exemplified by the eastern face of California's Sierra Nevada (Figure 14-51) and the western face of Utah's Wasatch Range.

Types of Faults

Faulting

Although structural geologists recognize more than two dozen kinds of faults, they can be generalized into four principal types on the basis of direction and angle of movement (Figure 14-52). Two types involve

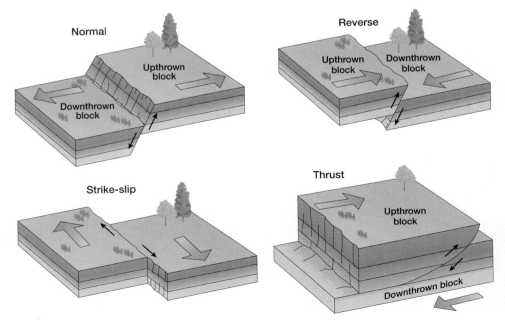

◀ **Figure 14-52** The principal types of faults. The large arrows show the direction of stress.

displacement that is mostly vertical, a third encompasses only horizontal movement, and the fourth includes both horizontal and vertical offsets:

1. **Normal faults:** A **normal fault** results from *tension stresses* (pulling apart) in the crust. It produces a very steeply inclined fault, with the block of land on one side being faulted up, or upthrown, relative to the down block on the other side. A prominent cliff or scarp is usually formed. A prominent fault scarp is produced from the upthrown block rising relative to the downthrown block, so that the fault scarp may be severely oversteepened if erosion ... smooth the slope somewhat. ... company reverse faulting.

2. **Reverse faults** ... complicated in structure and ... in their dynamics are **thrust faults** ... ults), in which compression forces the ... k to override the downthrown block

3. ... low angle, sometimes for many kilo-... thrusting occurs frequently in mountain ... sulting in unusual geologic relationships ... der strata being piled on top of younger ... th thrust faults and reverse faults are com-... associated with subduction zones.

...ike-slip faults: In a **strike-slip fault** the movement is horizontal, with the adjacent blocks being displaced laterally relative to each other (Figure 14-53). Strike-slip faults are a consequence of *shear stresses*. Transform faults described earlier in this chapter are one variety of strike-slip fault.

Landforms Associated with Normal Faulting

Certain conspicuous fault associations recur frequently in various parts of the world, causing a very notable gross configuration of the terrain. The following examples describe some of the landforms that commonly develop from normal faulting.

Tilted Fault-Block Mountains Under certain stresses, a surface block may be severely faulted and upthrown on one side without any faulting or uplift on the other. When this happens, the block is tilted asymmetrically, producing a steep slope along the fault scarp and a relatively gentle slope on the other side of the block. The classic example of such a **tilted fault-block mountain** range (also simply called a *fault-block mountain*) is California's Sierra Nevada (Figure 14-54), an immense block nearly 640 kilometers (400 miles) north–south and about 96 kilometers (60 miles) east–west. The spectacular eastern face is a fault scarp that has a vertical relief of about 3 kilometers (about 2 miles) in a horizontal distance of only about 20 kilometers (12 miles) (also see Figure 14-51). In contrast, the general slope of the western flank of the range, from crest to hinge line (the line along which the gentle side begins to rise), has a vertical dimension of about 3 kilometers (about 2 miles) spread over a horizontal distance of nearly 80 kilometers (50 miles). The shape of the range has of course been modified by other processes, but its general configuration was determined by block faulting.

Horst and Graben Another frequent occurrence ... nature is the uplift of a block of land between ... parallel faults, an action that produces a structure ca... a **horst** (Figure 14-55). The same result can be achi... if the land on both sides has been downthrow... either case, the horst is a block elevated ab... surrounding land. It may take the form of a plat... mountain mass with two steep, straight sides.

At the other extreme is a **graben**—a bloc... bounded by parallel faults in which the bloc... downthrown, producing a distinctive struc... with a straight, steep-sided fault scarp on e... world-famous graben is Death Valley in C...

▲ **Figure 14-53** The Calaveras Fault, one of the strike-slip faults in the San Andreas Fault system, runs through the town of Hollister, California. Dramatic evidence of its activity is shown by this offset wall and sidewalk. *(Tom L. McKnight photo.)*

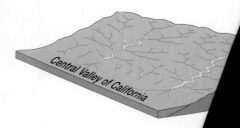

▲ **Figure 14-54** The western slope o... and gentle, whereas the eastern slop... gentle-steep combination is the resu... faulting on the eastern side.

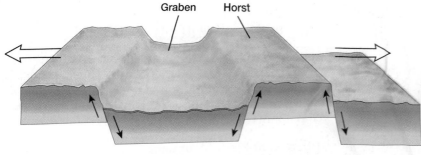

Graben   Horst

Grabens and horsts and/or tilted fault-block mountains often occur side by side. The *basin-and-range* country of the western interior of the United States is a vast sequence of horsts and grabens, mixed with fault-block ranges and some more complex structures, encompassing most of Nevada and portions of surrounding states.

Rift Valleys Downfaulted grabens occasionally extend for extraordinary distances as linear valleys enclosed between steep fault scarps. Such lengthy trenches are called rift valleys (see Figure 14-13), and they comprise some of Earth's most notable structural lineaments, particularly the Great Rift Valley in East Africa.

...ndforms Associated with Strike-Slip
...ting

...riety of landforms can result from strike-slip ...gure 14-56). The surface trace of a large ...It may be marked by a **linear fault trough** ...d by repeated movement and fracturing ... fault zone. Small depressions known ...ugh the settling of rock within the ...ecome filled with water to form ...s and scarps trending parallel to

◀ Figure ...
as a result ...
The large a... Horst and graben can form
stress. ...l (extensional) faulting.
...the direction of

the trace of the fault may deve...
displacement that may occur alo...
Perhaps the most conspicuous lan...
strike-slip faulting is an **offset** ...t vertical
drainage channel). Streams flowing ac... fault.
displaced by periodic fault movement or... ...by
a *shutter ridge* is faulted in front of a drai...

FG2
FG3

Earthquakes

1. Earthquake Waves
2. Seismographs

Usually, but not exclusively, associated with faulting is the abrupt shaking of the crust known as an earthquake. The movement varies from mild, imperceptible tremors to wild shaking that persists for many seconds.

An **earthquake** is essentially a vibration in the Earth produced by shock waves resulting from a sudden displacement along a fault (earthquakes may also develop from the movement of magma or sudden ground subsidence). The fault movement allows an abrupt release of energy, usually after a long, slow accumulation of strain. While a fault rupture can take place at the surface, displacement can also take place at considerable

Sag
Pond   Linear
          ridge   Offset drainage
                     channel   Linear valley
                                  or trough

                                              Shutter
                                              ridge

Mono
basin

...k of land
...k has been
...tural valley
...ither side. A
...alifornia.

...e the Sierra Neva...
...e is short and st...
...t of enormous

◀ **Figure 14-56**   Common landforms produced by strike-slip faults. *(After U.S. Geological Survey.)*

depth—as deep as 600 kilometers (375 miles) beneath the surface in the case of subduction zones.

Earthquake Waves The energy released in an earthquake moves through Earth in several different kinds of seismic waves that originate at the center of fault motion, called the *focus* of the earthquake (Figure 14-57). These waves travel outward in widening circles, like the ripples produced when a rock is thrown into a pond, gradually losing momentum with increasing distance from the focus. The strongest shocks, and greatest crustal vibration, are often felt on the ground directly above the focus, at the location known as the **epicenter** of the earthquake.

The fastest moving earthquake waves, and the first to be felt during an earthquake, are known as *P* or *primary waves*. P waves move through the Earth in the same fashion as sound waves, by alternately compressing and relaxing the medium through which they are traveling. The initial jolt of the P waves is followed by the strong side-to-side and up-and-down shearing motion of the slower-moving *S* or *secondary waves*. Both P waves and S waves travel through the body of the Earth (so they are also known as *body waves*), while the motion of a third type of earthquake wave is limited to the surface. These *surface waves* typically arrive immediately after the S waves and produce strong side-to-side movement as well as the up-and-down "rolling" motion often experienced during a large earthquake.

Because P waves and S waves travel at different speeds—at the surface P waves travel through bedrock at about 6 kilometers (3.7 miles) per second, while S waves travel at about 3.5 kilometers (2.2 miles) per second—it is possible to determine the distance to an earthquake's focus. The farther away an earthquake, the greater the time lag between the arrival of the P waves and the S waves. By using a network of *seismographs* (instruments used to record earthquakes) and comparing arrival times

of the seismic waves, seismologists can pinpoint the focus of an earthquake with great precision.

Earthquake Magnitude Perhaps the most widely mentioned—and most widely misunderstood—aspect of an earthquake is its **magnitude**. Magnitude describes the relative amount of energy released during an earthquake. Magnitudes are calculated on a logarithmic scale, with an energy increase from one magnitude to the next of about 32 times. The difference in size between small earthquakes (magnitudes less than 3) and large earthquakes (magnitude 7 and higher) is enormous. A magnitude 4 earthquake releases about 32 times more energy than a magnitude 3; a magnitude 5 releases 1,000 times more energy than a magnitude 3; and a magnitude 7 releases 1,000,000 times more energy than a magnitude 3.

The most commonly quoted magnitude is the *Richter scale*, devised in 1935 by Charles Richter at the California Institute of Technology in Pasadena. While the Richter scale magnitude is relatively easy for seismologists to calculate, it is not ideal for comparing the sizes of very large earthquakes (magnitude 7 and higher). The more recently devised *moment magnitude* is now the most commonly used scale to describe the size of large quakes, although the Richter scale (also known as the *local magnitude scale*) and other scales are still in use. Because the method of calculation varies among the magnitude scales, slightly different magnitude numbers are often reported for the same earthquake.

In any given year, tens of thousands of earthquakes occur around the world (Table 14-2). The vast majority of these are too small to be felt by people, but perhaps 60 or 70 are large enough to cause damage or loss of life (commonly magnitude 6 or higher). Great earthquakes—those with magnitude 8 or higher—might occur only once every few years. The two largest earthquakes yet recorded were the 1960 Chile earthquake with a moment magnitude of 9.5, and the 1964 Alaska earthquake with a moment magnitude of 9.2. The great Sumatra earthquake of December 2004 had a moment magnitude of 9.0. For comparison, the famous 1906 San Francisco earthquake had a moment magnitude of 7.7, the 1989 Loma Prieta earthquake a moment magnitude of 7.0, and the 1994 Northridge earthquake a moment magnitude of 6.8.

Shaking Intensity While each earthquake can be assigned a single magnitude number to describe its relative size, every earthquake generates a wide range of local ground shaking intensities—and it is the strength of local ground shaking that directly influences the amount of damage that results from an earthquake. Local variations in the shaking intensity of an earthquake can be quantitatively measured—usually as the peak horizontal ground acceleration expressed as a percentage of gravity—but the most widely used intensity scale was originally devised in 1902 by the Italian geologist Giuseppe Mercalli. Updated by the

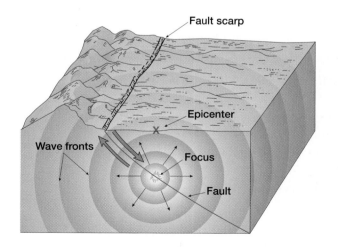

▲ **Figure 14-57** Relationship among focus, epicenter, and seismic waves of an earthquake. The waves are indicated by the concentric circles.

TABLE 14-2 Worldwide Earthquake Frequency	
Magnitude	Number per Year
<3.4	800,000
3.5–4.2	30,000
4.3–4.8	4800
4.9–5.4	1400
5.5–6.1	500
6.2–6.9	100
7.0–7.3	15
7.4–7.9	4
>8.0	1 every 5–10 years

U.S. Coast and Geodetic Survey, the **modified Mercalli intensity scale** assigns the strength of local shaking to one of 12 categories, based on the observed effects and damage (Table 14-3). The modified Mercalli scale is also used by seismologists to describe the anticipated intensity of ground shaking that may occur during future earthquakes in a region.

Earthquake Hazards Most of the damage from an earthquake is due to ground shaking. Generally, the strength of ground shaking decreases with increasing distance from the epicenter of the earthquake, but this pattern can be significantly modified by the local geology. Loose, unstable soils and sediments tend to amplify ground shaking—buildings on such "soft" ground will shake much more strongly than those located on bedrock the same distance from the epicenter. In addition, loose, water-saturated sediments, such as coastal landfill, may undergo **liquefaction**—during the shaking of an earthquake, the water-saturated material turns fluid, resulting in subsidence, fracturing, and horizontal sliding of the ground surface. A great deal of the damage in the 1989 Loma Prieta earthquake and in the 1995 Kobe earthquake was due to amplified ground shaking and liquefaction in artificial fill (Figure 14-58).

Landslides are often triggered by earthquakes. During the 1964 Alaska earthquake, for example, dozens of homes in the Turnagain Heights residential area outside of Anchorage were destroyed when a 2.6-kilometer (1.6-mile) wide section of the development moved toward the sea in a series of massive landslides.

Another kind of hazard associated with earthquakes involves water movements in lakes and oceans. Abrupt crustal movement can set great waves (known as *seiches*) in motion in lakes and reservoirs, causing them to overflow shorelines or dams in the same fashion that water can be sloshed out of a dishpan. Much more significant, however, are great seismic sea waves called *tsunami* (the Japanese term for these large waves), which are sometimes generated by undersea earthquakes or landslides. These waves, often occurring in a sequential train, move quickly across the ocean. They are barely perceptible in deep water, but when they reach shallow coastal waters, they sometimes build up

TABLE 14-3 Modified Mercalli Intensity Scale

I. Not felt except by very few people under especially favorable circumstances

II. Felt only by a few persons at rest, especially on upper floors of buildings

III. Felt quite noticeably indoors, especially on upper floors of buildings, but many people do not recognize it as an earthquake

IV. During the day felt indoors by many, outdoors by few; sensation like heavy truck striking building

V. Felt by nearly everyone, many awakened; disturbances of trees, poles, and other tall objects sometimes noticed

VI. Felt by all; many frightened and run outdoors; some heavy furniture moved; few instances of fallen plaster or damaged chimneys; damage slight

VII. Everybody runs outdoors; damage negligible in buildings of good design and construction; slight to moderate in well-built ordinary structures; considerable damage in poorly built or badly designed structures

VIII. Damage slight in specially designed structures; considerable in ordinary substantial buildings, with partial collapse; great in poorly built structures; fall of chimneys, factory stacks, columns, monuments, and other vertical features

IX. Damage considerable in specially designed structures; buildings shifted off foundations; ground cracked conspicuously

X. Some well-built wooden structures destroyed; most masonry and frame structures destroyed with foundations; ground badly cracked

XI. Few, if any, masonry structures remain standing; bridges destroyed; broad fissures in ground

XII. Damage total; waves seen on ground surfaces; objects thrown upward into the air

PEOPLE AND THE ENVIRONMENT Earthquake Forecasting

Earthquakes may occur anywhere, even in the middle of apparently stable continental areas. Most, however, take place in the boundary zones of the great lithospheric plates, particularly along the midocean ridges, in the subduction zones associated with the deep oceanic trenches and along transform boundaries such as the San Andreas Fault system. The greatest concentrations of earthquakes are found around the rim of the Pacific Ocean (see Figure 14-18). Because large populations in these areas are at risk from future earthquakes, considerable attention has been focused in recent years on the topics of earthquake prediction and forecasting.

The goal of earthquake prediction is to provide warnings far enough in advance to enable people to minimize loss of life and property. Such short-term predictions hinge on the existence of "precursors" or warning signs of an impending earthquake. Many such possible warning signs are being studied, including patterns of small earthquakes that sometimes occur before major quakes ("foreshocks"), changes in water-well levels, changes in the amount of dissolved radon gas in groundwater, variations in electrical conductivity of rocks, the bulging of the ground surface, and changes in the behavior of animals.

One of the world's most elaborate earthquake research projects has been underway since 1985 in the tiny California town of Parkfield, which sits atop the San Andreas Fault in the central part of the state. Since the mid-1800s this segment of the fault has ruptured at fairly regular intervals—1857, 1881, 1901, 1922, 1934, and 1966—each time producing an earthquake of about magnitude 6. The U.S. Geological Survey (USGS) and dozens of university and industry researchers began intensive monitoring of the fault here in hopes of "capturing" the next earthquake as it happens. They especially wanted to have enough monitoring equipment in place to detect any precursors before the quake; such precursors might lead seismologists closer to short-term predictions of earthquakes. The Parkfield earthquake came on September 28, 2004—a number of years later than expected, but it yielded a great deal of data for the scientists to analyze.

Just a few months before the quake, drilling was started on the *San Andreas Fault Observatory at Depth* (SAFOD), a project that is installing instruments 2 to 3 kilometers (1.2–1.9 miles) deep in the active fault zone of the San Andreas (Figure 14-C). The project was not complete at the time of the September 2004 Parkfield earthquake, but once fully operational SAFOD should provide seismol-ogists with valuable data on fault-zone rocks and fluids.

Currently, there is no reliable method of predicting earthquakes, and some seismologists think it unlikely that the short-term prediction of earthquakes will ever exist. However, seismologists have made great strides toward long-term *forecasts* of earthquakes: the probability of an earthquake occurring along a given segment of a fault within a period of several decades.

Long-term probabilities are based on the balance of two processes: the loading of strain onto faults, and the slip along the faults (which should, over time, release the strain). By recognizing seismic "gaps" where little strain has been released in recent decades, seismologists can identify which fault segments are most likely to rupture in the future. For example, the USGS recently concluded that in the San Francisco Bay region, there is a 62 percent probability of at least one magnitude 6.7 or greater earthquake occurring before the year 2033. Although such forecasts do not state the likelihood of a quake coming in any particular month or year, long-term forecasts can help local governments, businesses, and the general public to establish priorities for retrofitting structures and for disaster preparation.

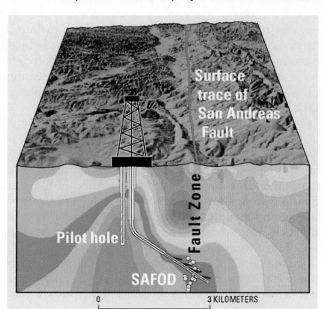

◀ **Figure 14-C** A schematic cross section of the San Andreas Fault zone at Parkfield, California. The San Andreas Fault Observatory at Depth instrument bore extends diagonally into the active fault zone. The colors below the surface represent differences in electrical resistivity in the rocks. The lowest resistivity is shown with red—the zone above the SAFOD instruments may represent a fluid-rich zone in the fault. *(From USGS Fact Sheet 049-02, "The Parkfield Experiment—Capturing What Happens in an Earthquake," 2004.)*

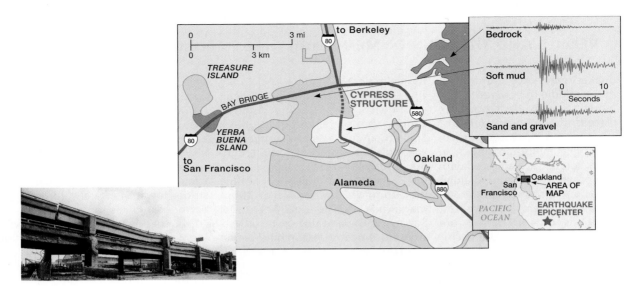

▲ **Figure 14-58** The portion of the Cypress freeway structure in Oakland, California that collapsed during the 1989 magnitude 7.0 Loma Prieta earthquake stood on soft mud (dashed red line). Adjacent parts of the structure built on firmer ground (solid red line) remained standing. Seismograms in the upper right show that ground shaking was more severe on the soft mud than on the nearby bedrock. *(After U.S. Geological Survey Fact Sheet 176–95, "Saving Lives Through Better Design Standards," 1995; Roger Hess photo.)*

to heights of more than 15 meters (50 feet) and crash onto the shoreline with devastating effect (where they are often incorrectly called tidal waves). Most of the deaths from the 1964 Alaska earthquake were the result of tsunami—even as far away as Crescent City, California, 12 people were killed when a 6-meter (19-foot) high tsunami came on shore. In December 2004, more than 270,000 people were killed when a tsunami generated by a subduction zone earthquake off the Indonesian island of Sumatra spread through the Indian Ocean. A detailed description of tsunami formation and the 2004 Indian Ocean tsunami disaster is found in Chapter 20, where we discuss the dynamics of ocean waves.

The Complexities of Crustal Configuration

Considering each internal process in turn as we have just done is a helpful way to systematize knowledge. Doing so presents an artificial and misleading picture, however, because in nature these processes are inter-related. To attempt a more balanced assessment, let us consider a highly simplified statement of the origin of the gross contemporary topographic features of a small part of Earth's surface—a mountainous section of northwestern Montana that encompasses the spectacular scenery of Glacier National Park.

This area, now part of the northern Rocky Mountains, was below sea level for many millions of years. Most of the rocks in the region were formed in the Precambrian era, when much of the area now occupied

by the Rocky Mountain cordillera consisted of a large, shallow, seawater-filled trough. Muds and sands were washed into this Precambrian sea for millennia, and a vast thickness of sedimentary strata built up. These limestones, shales, and sandstones accumulated as six distinct formations, each with a conspicuous color variation known collectively as the Belt Series.

Occasionally during this lengthy epoch of sedimentary accumulation, igneous activity added variety. Most notable was a vast outpouring of flood basalt that issued from fissures in the ocean floor and was extruded in the form of a submarine lava flow. Further sediments were then deposited on top of the lava flow.

Igneous intrusions were also injected from time to time, including one large sill and a number of dikes. The igneous rocks, both the flood basalt and the various intrusions, initiated contact metamorphism, whereby the tremendous heat of the igneous material converted some of the adjacent sedimentary rocks into metamorphic rocks (mostly changing limestone to marble and sandstone to quartzite).

After a long gap in the geologic record, during which the Rocky Mountain region was mostly above sea level, the land once again sank below the ocean during the Cretaceous period and another thick series of sediments was deposited. This was followed by a period of mountain building so significant that it has been named the Rocky Mountain Revolution. In the Glacier National Park area, the rocks were compressed and uplifted, converting the site of the former sea into a mountainous region.

Along with uplift came extreme lateral pressure from the west, convoluting the gently downfolded strata into a prominent anticline. Continuing pressure then

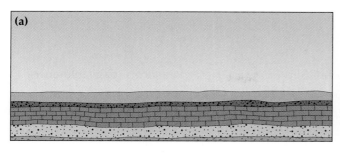

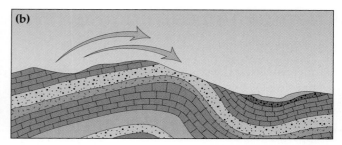

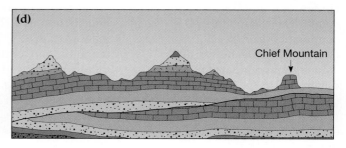

▲ **Figure 14-59** Sequential development of the Lewis Overthrust. **(a)** Initial sea-bottom deposition of sediments. **(b)** Uplift and folding. **(c)** Continued pressure from the west causes overturning of the fold and faulting along the eastern limb of the anticline. **(d)** Subsequent erosion produces the present topography, with Chief Mountain as a residual outlier to the east of the range.

overturned the anticline toward the east, with a lengthening western limb and a truncating eastern limb. This additional strain on the rock and the persistent crustal pressure eventually caused a vast rupture and faulting. The entire block was then pushed eastward by one of the greatest thrust faults known, the Lewis Overthrust (Figure 14-59). This remarkable fault forced the Precambrian sedimentaries out over the Cretaceous strata that underlie the plains to the east by as much as 30 kilometers (about 20 miles). The plane of the thrust fault was only slightly above the horizontal, nowhere exceeding a dip of 10°. This had the peculiar effect of placing older rock layers on top of much younger strata. The terrain thus produced is referred to as mountains without roots. Chief Mountain is world famous as a rootless mountain because of its conspicuous location as an erosional outlier east of the main range (Figure 14-60).

▲ **Figure 14-60** Chief Mountain sits in splendid isolation because of the massive movement associated with the Lewis Overthrust and subsequent erosion. *(Tom L. McKnight photo.)*

Chapter 14 Learning Review

Key Terms

Before answering the study questions below, review the definitions of the following key terms (page references are provided for you):

anticline *(p. 446)*
batholith *(p. 443)*
caldera *(p. 437)*
cinder cone *(p. 437)*
composite volcano *(p. 434)*
continental drift *(p. 413)*
continental rift valley *(p. 420)*
convergent boundary *(p. 420)*
diastrophism *(p. 444)*
dike *(p. 444)*
divergent boundary *(p. 420)*
earthquake *(p. 450)*
epicenter (of earthquake) *(p. 451)*
faulting *(p. 447)*
fault scarp *(p. 448)*
flood basalt *(p. 433)*
folding *(p. 445)*
graben *(p. 449)*
horst *(p. 449)*

igneous intrusion *(p. 442)*
lava *(p. 429)*
lava dome (plug dome) *(p. 434)*
linear fault trough *(p. 450)*
liquefaction *(p. 452)*
magma *(p. 429)*
magnitude (of earthquake) *(p. 451)*
mantle plume (hot spot) *(p. 426)*
midocean ridge *(p. 420)*
modified Mercalli intensity scale
  (p. 452)
normal fault *(p. 449)*
ocean floor core samples *(p. 419)*
oceanic trench *(p. 421)*
offset stream *(p. 450)*
overturned fold *(p. 446)*
Pacific Ring of Fire *(p. 424)*
paleomagnetism *(p. 416)*
Pangaea *(p. 413)*

plate tectonics *(p. 419)*
plutons *(p. 444)*
pyroclastic flow *(p. 440)*
pyroclastics *(p. 429)*
reverse fault *(p. 449)*
sag pond *(p. 450)*
seafloor spreading *(p. 416)*
shield volcano *(p. 433)*
strike-slip fault *(p. 449)*
subduction *(p. 416)*
syncline *(p. 446)*
terrane *(p. 427)*
thrust fault *(p. 449)*
tilted fault block mountain *(p. 449)*
transform boundary *(p. 422)*
volcanic island arc *(p. 422)*
volcanic mudflow (lahar) *(p. 442)*
vulcanism *(p. 428)*

Study Questions for Key Concepts

After studying this chapter, you should be able to answer the following questions:

From Rigid Earth to Plate Tectonics (p. 413)

1. Describe and explain at least two lines of evidence that Alfred Wegener used to support his theory of "continental drift."
2. Why was Wegener's theory of continental drift rejected for so long?

Plate Tectonics (p. 415)

3. What lines of evidence confirm that *seafloor spreading* has been taking place? You should be able to explain both *paleomagnetic* evidence and that of *ocean floor core samples.*
4. What is the general relationship between global earthquake activity and plate boundaries?
5. Describe and explain the general process within Earth that is responsible for lithospheric plate movement.
6. Describe the fundamental differences among *divergent, convergent,* and *transform* plate boundaries.
7. Describe and explain the tectonic activity, volcanic activity, and general topographic features associated with the two kinds of divergent plate boundary: *midocean ridges* and *continental rift valleys.* Mention at least one present-day example of each of these kinds of divergent boundary.

8. Describe and explain the tectonic activity, volcanic activity, and general topographic features associated with the three kinds of convergent plate boundary: *oceanic–continental plate subduction, oceanic–oceanic plate subduction,* and *continental plate collision.* Mention at least one present-day example of each of these kinds of convergent boundary.
9. Why doesn't subduction take place in a continental plate collision zone?
10. How does the San Andreas Fault system fit in with the model of plate tectonics?
11. Why are *deep-focus earthquakes* (those originating many hundreds of kilometers below the surface) associated with subduction zones, but not with divergent boundaries and transform boundaries?
12. Why is there such a concentration of volcanoes and earthquakes around the margin of the Pacific Ocean (the region referred to as the *Pacific Ring of Fire*)?
13. What is a *mantle plume* ("hot spot")? Name at least one present-day example of a mantle plume.
14. In what ways don't mantle plumes fit in with the basic model of plate tectonics and plate boundaries?
15. In what ways have mantle plumes been used to verify that plate motion is taking place?
16. What is a *terrane* and how does one form?

Vulcanism (p. 428)

17. Define and contrast the following: *magma, lava,* and *pyroclastics.*
18. Explain the general differences in silica content and style of volcanic eruption (i.e., quiet lava flows versus explosive eruptions of pyroclastics) associated with basaltic magma, andesitic magma, and rhyolitic magma.
19. Describe and explain the general formation, shape, and structure of the following kinds of volcanic peaks: *shield volcanoes, composite volcanoes,* and *lava domes* (*plug domes*).
20. Explain the formation of a *caldera* such as Crater Lake in Oregon.
21. Describe and explain the origin and characteristics of *volcanic mudflows* ("lahars") and *pyroclastic flows.*
22. What are the differences between a *batholith* and a *dike*?

Folding (p. 445)

23. What is a *syncline*? What is an *anticline*?
24. How is it possible for a syncline to be associated with a topographic ridge and for an anticline to be associated with a topographic valley?

Faulting (p. 447)

25. Explain the differences in stress direction and displacement among the four basic kinds of faults: *normal faults, reverse faults, thrust faults,* and *strike-slip faults.*
26. Describe and explain the formation of landforms that result from normal faulting (such as *grabens, horsts,* and *tilted fault-block mountains*).
27. Describe and explain the formation of landforms that result from strike-slip faulting (such as *linear fault troughs, sag ponds,* and *offset streams*).
28. What is the difference between the *focus* of an earthquake and the *epicenter* of an earthquake?
29. About how much more energy is released during a magnitude 6 earthquake than during a magnitude 5 earthquake?
30. Briefly describe the differences among the *P waves, S waves,* and *surface waves* of an earthquake.
31. Why do areas far away from the epicenter sometimes experience greater damage during an earthquake than areas closer to the epicenter? (Consider factors other than differences in building construction.)

Additional Resources

Books:

Bruce, Victoria. *No Apparent Danger: The True Story of the Volcanic Disaster at Galeras and Nevado del Ruiz.* New York: Harper Collins, 2001.

Hough, Susan Elizabeth. *Earthshaking Science: What We Know (and Don't Know) about Earthquakes.* Princeton, New Jersey: Princeton University Press, 2002.

Sieh, K., and S. LeVay. *The Earth in Turmoil: Earthquakes, Volcanoes, and Their Impact on Humankind.* New York: W. H. Freeman and Company, 1998.

Wallace, Robert E., ed. *The San Andreas Fault System, California.* U.S. Geological Survey Professional Paper 1515. Washington, D.C.: U.S. Government Printing Office, 1990.

Winchester, Simon. *A Crack in the Edge of the World: America and the Great California Earthquake of 1906.* New York: Harper Collins, 2005.

Internet Sites:

U.S. Geological Survey

http://www.usgs.gov/

> The U.S. Geological Survey home page provides links to information on a wide range of Earth science topics, including earthquakes, volcanoes, landslides, floods, and other natural hazards. The page also has links to sites where topographic maps, geological maps, research papers, and publications of general interest may be viewed or purchased.

Earthquake Hazards Program

http://earthquake.usgs.gov/

> This site offers near-real-time maps and information about the locations and magnitudes of earthquakes around the world, as well as information about seismic hazards and current earthquake research.

The IRIS Consortium

http://www.iris.edu

> The Incorporated Research Institutions for Seismology (IRIS) is a university research consortium that collects and distributes seismographic data.

National Geophysical Data Center

http://www.ngdc.noaa.gov/

> The National Geophysical Data Center is a great starting point for finding information about glaciology, marine geology, paleoclimatology, solar–terrestrial physics, and geophysics.

Smithsonian Global Volcanism Program

http://www.volcano.si.edu/gvp/

> This site provides information about volcanoes and current volcanic activity around the world.

Volcano Hazards Program

http://volcanoes.usgs.gov/

> This site furnishes links to volcano observatories around the world.

15
Preliminaries to Erosion: Weathering and Mass Wasting

If the internal processes of landscape formation are overwhelming, the external processes are inexorable. During all the time that lithospheric plates are moving, the crust is bending and breaking, and volcanoes are erupting and intrusions forming, another suite of natural forces is simultaneously at work. These are the external forces, often mundane and even minuscule in contrast to those described in the preceding chapter. Yet the cumulative effect of the external processes is awesome; they are capable of wearing down anything the internal forces can erect. No rock is too resistant and no mountain too massive to withstand their unrelenting power. Ultimately, the detailed configuration of peaks, slopes, valleys, and plains is molded by the work of gravity, water, wind, and ice.

Denudation

The overall effect of the disintegration, wearing away, and removal of rock material is generally referred to as **denudation**, a term that implies a lowering of continental surfaces. Denudation is accomplished by the interaction of three types of activities:

- **Weathering** is the breaking down of rock into smaller components by atmospheric and biotic agencies.
- **Mass wasting** involves the relatively short-distance downslope movement of broken rock material due to gravity.
- **Erosion** consists of more extensive and generally more distant removal, transportation, and eventual deposition of fragmented rock material.

All three processes are illustrated in Figure 15-1.

The Impact of Weathering and Mass Wasting on the Landscape

The most readily observable landscape effect of weathering is the fragmentation of bedrock—the reduction of large rock units into more numerous and less cohesive smaller units. This activity occurs in place, without conspicuous displacement of the rocks.

Mass wasting always involves the downslope movement of rock material. Its impact on the landscape is normally twofold: an open scar may be left on the surface that was vacated, and an accumulation of debris is deposited somewhere downslope from the scar.

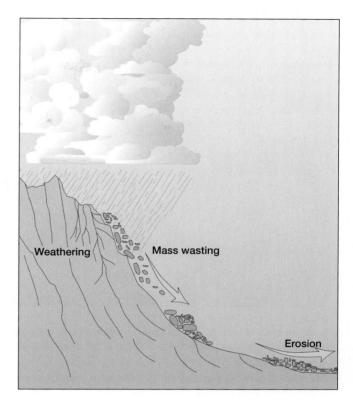

▲ **Figure 15-1** Denudation, the lowering of continental surfaces, is accomplished by a combination of weathering, mass wasting, and erosion.

Although weathering and mass wasting are often deemphasized as processes of landform modification and shaping, the role they play is critical. Take the Grand Canyon of the Colorado River, for example. One of the most impressive landscape features of the world, the canyon is usually attributed only to the erosive powers of the river. However, most of what we see in the Grand Canyon are forms produced by weathering and mass wasting (Figure 15-2). Besides deepening its channel, the river's main role is to transport the sediment loosened by weathering and pulled into the stream by gravity and mass wasting.

Weathering and Rock Openings

The first step in the shaping of Earth's surface by external processes is *weathering*, the mechanical disintegration and/or chemical decomposition that destroys the coherence of bedrock and begins to fragment rock masses into progressively smaller components. Fast or slow, mechanical and chemical weathering occurs wherever the lithosphere and atmosphere meet. It occurs with

▲ **Figure 15-2** The Colorado River, shown here in Arizona's Grand Canyon, is the principal erosive force, but weathering and mass wasting have also contributed significantly to the carving of the massive canyon. *(Tom L. McKnight photo.)*

great subtlety, however, breaking chemical bonds, separating grain from grain, pitting the smooth, and fracturing the solid. It is the aging process of rock surfaces, the process that must precede the other, more active, forms of denudation.

Whenever bedrock is exposed, it weathers. It often has a different color or texture than neighboring unexposed bedrock. Most significant from a topographic standpoint, exposed bedrock is likely to be looser and less coherent than the underlying rock. Blocks or chips may be so loose that they can be detached with little effort. Sometimes pieces are so "rotten" that they can be crumbled by finger pressure. Slightly deeper in the bedrock, there is firmer, more solid rock, although along cracks or crevices weathering may extend to considerable depths. In some cases, the weathering may reach as much as several hundred meters beneath the surface. This penetration is made possible by open spaces in the rock bodies and even in the mineral grains. Subsurface weathering is initiated along these openings, which can be penetrated by such weathering agents as water, air, and plant roots. As time passes, the weathering effects spread from the immediate vicinity of the openings into the denser rock beyond (Figure 15-3).

Openings in the surface and near-surface bedrock are frequently microscopic, but they may also be large enough to be conspicuous and are sometimes huge. In any case, they occur in vast numbers and provide avenues along which weathering agents can attack the bedrock and break it apart. Broadly speaking, five types of openings are common:

1. **Microscopic openings:** Microscopic openings in the rock surface occur in profusion. Although tiny,

they are so numerous that they can be responsible for extensive weathering. They may consist of spaces between crystals of igneous or metamorphic rocks, pores between grains of sedimentary rocks, or minute fractures within or alongside mineral grains in any kind of rock.

2. **Joints:** The most common structural features of the rocks of the lithosphere are **joints**—cracks that develop as a result of stress—but the rocks show no appreciable displacement parallel to the joint walls. Joints are innumerable in most rock masses, dividing them into blocks of various sizes. Because of their ubiquity, joints are the most important of all rock openings in facilitating weathering.

3. **Faults:** Faults are breaks in bedrock along which there is relative displacement of the walls making up the crack (Figure 15-4). Faults are generally individual or occur only in small numbers, whereas joints normally are multitudinous. A further difference between faults and joints is that faults sometimes appear as major landscape features, extending for tens or even hundreds of kilometers, whereas joints are normally minor structures extending only a few meters. Faults allow easy penetration of weathering agents into subsurface areas because not only fracturing but also displacement is involved.

4. **Lava vesicles:** Lava *vesicles* are holes of various sizes, usually small, that develop in cooling lava when gas is unable to escape as the lava solidifies.

5. **Solution cavities:** *Solution cavities* are holes formed in calcareous rocks (particularly limestone) as the soluble minerals are dissolved and carried away by percolating water. Most solution cavities are small,

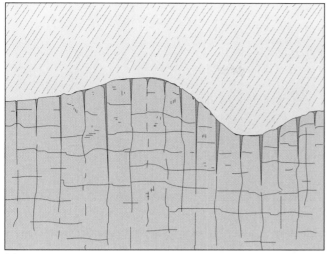

(a)

(b)

⬛ **Figure 15-3** How deep weathering develops in bedrock containing many cracks **(a)** before weathering; **(b)** after weathering.

but sometimes huge holes and even massive caverns are created when large amounts of solubles are removed. (A more lengthy description of solution processes and topography appears in Chapter 17.)

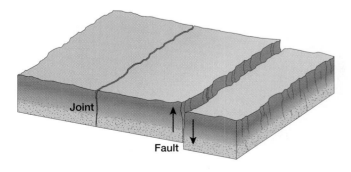

⬛ **Figure 15-4** The essential difference between joints and faults is that joints exhibit no displacement along either side of the crack.

The Importance of Jointing

Almost all lithospheric bedrock is jointed, resulting sometimes from contractive cooling of molten material, sometimes from contraction of sedimentary strata as they dry, and sometimes from diastrophic tension. At Earth's surface, the separation between blocks on either side of a joint may be conspicuous because weathering emphasizes the fracture. Below the surface, however, the visible separation is minimal.

Joints are relatively common in most rock, but they are clearly more abundant in some places than in others. Where numerous, they are usually arranged in sets, each set comprising a series of approximately parallel fractures. Frequently, two prominent sets intersect almost at right angles; such a combination constitutes a *joint system* (Figure 15-5). A well-developed joint system, particularly in sedimentary rock having prominent natural bedding planes, can divide stratified rock into a remarkably regular series of close-fitting blocks. Generally speaking, jointing is more regularly patterned, and the resulting blocks are more sharply defined in fine-grained rocks than in coarse-grained ones.

In some places, large joints or joint sets extend for long distances and through a considerable thickness of rocks; these are termed **master joints** (Figure 15-6). Master joints play a role in topographic development by functioning as a plane of weakness, a plane more susceptible to weathering and erosion than the rock around it. Thus, the location of large features of the landscape, such as valleys and cliffs, may be influenced by the position of master joints.

Weathering Agents

Most weathering agents are atmospheric. Because it is gaseous, the atmosphere is able to penetrate readily into all cracks and crevices in bedrock. From a chemical standpoint, oxygen, carbon dioxide, and water vapor are the three atmospheric components of greatest importance in rock weathering.

Temperature changes are a second important weathering agent. Most notable, however, is water, which can penetrate downward effectively into openings in the bedrock. Biotic agents also contribute to weathering, in part through the burrowing activities of animals and the rooting effects of plants, but especially through the production of chemical substances that attack the rock.

The total effect of these agents is complicated and is influenced by a variety of factors: the nature and structure of the bedrock, the abundance and size of openings in it, the surface configuration, prevailing climatic conditions, the vegetative cover, and the variety and abundance of digging animals. For analytical purposes, however, it is convenient to recognize three principal categories of weathering—mechanical, chemical, and

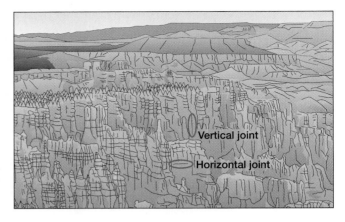

▲ **Figure 15-5** Photograph and matching drawing of the badlands topography of Bryce Canyon in southern Utah from Inspiration Point. The closely spaced joint systems contribute to intricate sculpturing by weathering and erosion. *(Tom L. McKnight photo.)*

biotic. Although we now consider each of them in turn, we should bear in mind that they usually act in concert.

Mechanical Weathering

 Mechanical Weathering

Mechanical weathering is the physical disintegration of rock material without any change in its chemical composition. In essence, big rocks are mechanically weathered into little ones by various stresses that cause the rock to fracture into smaller fragments. Most mechanical weathering occurs at or very near the surface, but under certain conditions it may occur at considerable depth.

Frost Wedging Probably the most important single agent of mechanical weathering is the freeze–thaw action of water. When water freezes, it expands by almost 10 percent. Moreover, the upper surface of the water freezes first, which means that the principal force of expansion is exerted against the wall of the confining rock rather than upward. This expanding wedge of ice splits the rock, as shown in Figure 15-7.

Even the strongest rocks cannot withstand frequent alternation of freezing and thawing. Repetition is the key to understanding the inexorable force of **frost wedging** or *frost shattering* (Figure 15-8). Regardless of its size, if an opening in rock contains water, when the temperature falls below 0°C (32°F) ice forms, wedging its way downward. When the temperature rises above freezing, the ice melts and the water sinks farther into the slightly enlarged cavity. With renewed freezing, the

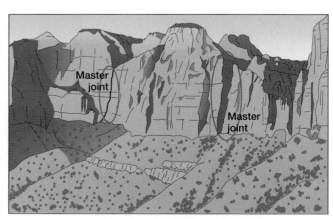

▲ **Figure 15-6** Photograph and matching drawing of mighty monoliths in Utah's Zion National Park. Master joints are widely spaced in this area, allowing for the development of massive blocks and precipitous cliffs. *(Tom L. McKnight photo.)*

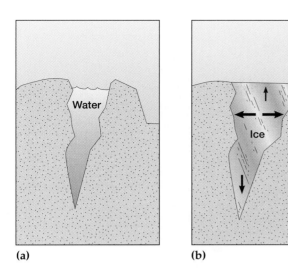

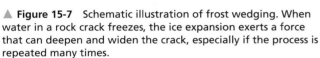

▲ **Figure 15-7** Schematic illustration of frost wedging. When water in a rock crack freezes, the ice expansion exerts a force that can deepen and widen the crack, especially if the process is repeated many times.

(a)   (b)

wedging is repeated. Such a freeze–thaw pattern may be repeated millions of times through the eons of Earth history, providing what is literally an irresistible force.

Frost wedging in large openings may produce large boulders, whereas that occurring in small openings may granulate the rock into sand and dust particles, with every size gradation in between. A common form of breakup in coarse-grained crystalline rocks is a shattering caused by frost wedging between grains. This type of shattering produces gravel or coarse sand in a process termed *granular disintegration.*

The physical characteristics of the rock are important determinants of the rate and magnitude of mechanical weathering, as are temperature and moisture variations. The process is most effective where freezing is prolonged and intense—in high latitudes, in midlatitudes during winters, and at high elevations. It is most conspicuous above the treeline of mountainous areas (Figure 15-9), where broken blocks of rock are likely to be found in profusion everywhere except on slopes that are too steep to allow them to lie without sliding downhill.

Salt Wedging   Related to frost wedging but much less significant is **salt wedging**, which happens when salts crystallize out of solution as water evaporates. In areas of dry climate, water is often drawn upward in rock openings by capillary action (*capillarity* was discussed in Chapter 6). This water nearly always carries dissolved salts. When the water evaporates, as it commonly does, the salts are left behind as tiny crystals. With time, the crystals grow, prying apart the rock and weakening its internal structure, much in the fashion previously described for freezing water, although less intensely (Figure 15-10). In humid areas, salt wedging is inconsequential because the soluble salts are flushed away by percolating groundwater.

Temperature Changes   Temperature changes not accompanied by freeze–thaw cycles also weather rock mechanically, but they do so much more gradually than the processes just described. The fluctuation of temperature from day to night and from summer to winter can cause minute changes in the volume of most

▲ **Figure 15-8** An example of the powerful force of freeze–thaw action on a granite boulder in Colorado's Forest Canyon. *(Tom L. McKnight photo.)*

▲ **Figure 15-9** Frost wedging is an especially pervasive force on mountaintops above the treeline, as with these granite boulders on Australia's highest peak, Mount Kosciusko, in New South Wales. *(Tom L. McKnight photo.)*

mineral particles, forcing expansion when heated and contraction when cooled. This volumetric variation weakens the coherence of the mineral grains and tends to break them apart. Millions of repetitions are normally required for much weakening or fracturing to occur, although the intense heat of forest fires or brushfires can speed up the process. This factor is most significant in arid areas and near mountain summits, where direct solar radiation is intense during the day and radiational cooling is prominent at night.

Exfoliation One of the most striking of all weathering processes is **exfoliation**, in which curved layers peel off bedrock. (We saw in Chapter 13 that the term *foliation* refers to the parallel alignment of textural and structural

▲ **Figure 15-10** Salt wedging. This crystalline rock is being shattered by salt wedging near the floor of Death Valley in California. *(Darrel Hess photo.)*

features of a rock; exfoliation involves the stripping away of roughly parallel, concentric rock slabs.) Curved and concentric sets of joints, usually minor and inconspicuous, develop in the bedrock, and parallel shells of rock break away in succession, somewhat analogous to the way layers of an onion separate. The sheets that split off are sometimes only a millimeter or so thick; in other cases, however, they may be several meters thick (Figure 15-11).

Exfoliation occurs mainly in granite and related intrusive rocks, but under certain circumstances it is also common in sandstone and other sedimentary strata.

The results of exfoliation are conspicuous. If the rock mass is a large one, such as Half Dome or one of the other granite monoliths overlooking Yosemite Valley, California, its surface consists of imperfect curves punctuated by several partially fractured shells of the surface layers, and the mass is referred to as an **exfoliation dome** (Figure 15-12). Exfoliation may also occur on detached boulders in which case the result is usually a rounder shape, with each layer of shelling revealing a smaller spherical mass (Figure 15-13, p. 466).

The dynamics of exfoliation are not fully understood. The most widely accepted explanation of massive exfoliation is that the rock cracks after an overlying weight has been removed, a process called *unloading* or pressure release. The intrusive bedrock may originally have been deeply buried beneath a heavy overburden. When the overlying material is stripped away by erosion, the release of pressure allows expansion in the rock. The outer layers are unable to contain the expanding mass, and the expansion can be absorbed only by cracking along the sets of joints.

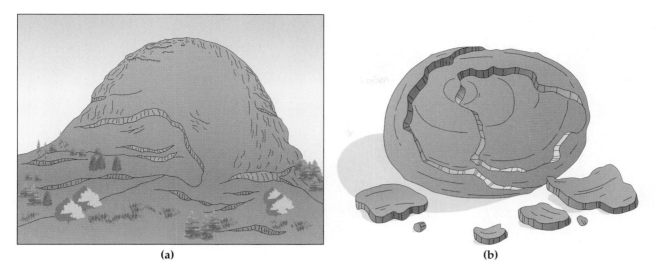

(a)   (b)

▲ **Figure 15-11**   Example of exfoliation at different scales. **(a)** A massive exfoliation dome. **(b)** An individual boulder.

Other processes, however, are likely at work to produce the very thin exfoliation layers seen on boulders. Fracturing resulting from temperature variations may be an important component of the mechanism, although exfoliation is also found in areas where temperature fluctuations are not marked. Volumetric changes in minerals, which set up strains in the rock, may also be involved. Such changes are most notably produced by *hydration*, in which water molecules become attached to other substances and then the added water causes the

▲ **Figure 15-12**   Two large exfoliation domes in Yosemite National Park, California. *(© Bob Newman/Visuals Unlimited, Inc.)*

▲ **Figure 15-13** An exfoliated boulder in California's Joshua Tree National Park. *(Tom L. McKnight photo.)*

original substance to swell without any change in its chemical composition. This swelling weakens the rock mass and is usually sufficient to produce some fracturing.

Other Mechanical Weathering Processes Chemical changes (discussed in more detail in the next subsection) also contribute to mechanical weathering. Various chemical actions can cause an increase in volume of the affected mineral grains. This swelling sets up strains that weaken the coherence of the rock and cause fractures.

Some biotic activities also contribute to mechanical weathering. Most notable is the penetration of growing plant roots into cracks and crevices, which exerts an expansive force that widens the openings. This factor is especially conspicuous where trees grow out of joint or fault planes, with their large roots showing amazing

tenacity and persistence as wedging devices. Additionally, burrowing animals sometimes are factors in rock disintegration. The total effect of these biotic actions is probably significant, but it is difficult to assess because it is obscured by subsequent chemical weathering.

When acting alone, mechanical weathering breaks up rock masses into ever smaller pieces, producing boulders, cobbles, pebbles, sand, silt, and dust (Figure 15-14).

Chemical Weathering

Mechanical weathering is usually, but not always, accompanied by **chemical weathering**, which is the decomposition of rock by the chemical alteration of its minerals. Almost all minerals are subject to chemical alteration when exposed to atmospheric and biotic

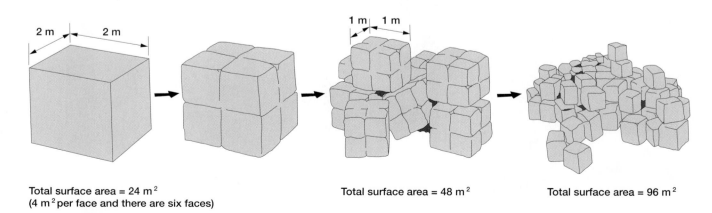

2 m   2 m

1 m   1 m

Total surface area = 24 m²
(4 m² per face and there are six faces)

Total surface area = 48 m²

Total surface area = 96 m²

▲ **Figure 15-14** As mechanical weathering fragments rock, the amount of surface area exposed to further weathering is increased. Each successive step shown here doubles the surface area of the preceding step. *(After William M. Marsh and Jeff Dozier,* Landscape: An Introduction to Physical Geography, *Reading, MA: Addison-Wesley, 1981. By permission of John Wiley & Sons.)*

agents. Some minerals, such as quartz, are extremely resistant to chemical change, but many others are very susceptible. There are very few rocks that cannot be significantly affected by chemical weathering because the alteration of even a single significant mineral constituent can lead to the eventual disintegration of an entire rock mass.

One important effect of mechanical weathering is to expose bedrock to the forces of chemical weathering. The greater the surface area exposed, the more effective the chemical weathering. Thus, finer-grained materials decompose more rapidly than coarser-grained materials of identical composition because in the former there is more exposed surface area.

Virtually all chemical weathering requires moisture. Thus, an abundance of water enhances the effectiveness of chemical weathering, and chemical processes operate more rapidly in humid climates than in arid areas. Moreover, chemical reactions are more rapid under high-temperature conditions than in cooler regions. Consequently, chemical weathering is most efficient and conspicuous in warm climates. In cold lands, there is less chemical weathering (although the removal of dissolved salts is sometimes notable), and the influence of mechanical weathering is dominant.

Some of the chemical reactions that affect rocks are very complex, but others are simple and predictable. The principal reacting agents are oxygen, water, and carbon dioxide, and the most significant processes are oxidation, hydrolysis, and carbonation. These processes often take place more or less simultaneously, largely because they all involve water that contains dissolved atmospheric gases. Water percolating into the ground acts as a weak acid because of the presence of these gases and of decay products from the local vegetation;

the presence of these impurities increases the water's capacity to drive chemical reactions.

Oxidation   When the oxygen dissolved in water comes into contact with certain rock minerals, the minerals undergo **oxidation**, in which the oxygen atoms combine with atoms of various metallic elements making up the minerals in the rock and form new products. The new substances are usually more voluminous, softer, and more easily eroded than the original compounds.

When iron-bearing minerals react with oxygen (i.e., become oxidized), *iron oxide* is produced:

$$4Fe + 3O_2 \rightarrow 2Fe_2O_3$$

Iron   Oxygen   Iron Oxide (Hematite)

This reaction, probably the most common oxidation in the lithosphere, is called *rusting,* and the prevalence of rusty red stains on the surface of many rocks attests to its widespread occurrence (Figure 15-15). Similar effects are produced by the oxidation of aluminum. Since iron and aluminum are very common in Earth's crust, a reddish brown color is seen in many rocks and soils, particularly in tropical areas because there oxidation is the most notable chemical weathering process. Rusting contributes significantly to weathering because oxides are usually softer and more easily removed than the original iron and aluminum compounds from which the oxides were formed.

Hydrolysis   **Hydrolysis** is the chemical union of water with another substance to produce a new compound that is nearly always softer and weaker than the original. Igneous rocks are particularly susceptible to hydrolysis because their silicate minerals combine readily with water. Hydrolysis invariably increases the volume of the

▲ **Figure 15-15**   Iron oxide (rust) stains on a cliff in Capitol Reef National Park in Utah. *(Charlie Ott/Photo Researchers, Inc.)*

mineral, and this expansion can contribute to mechanical disintegration. In tropical areas, where water frequently percolates to considerable depth, hydrolysis often occurs far below the surface.

Carbonation Carbonation is the reaction between the carbon dioxide in water (which forms *carbonic acid* [H_2CO_3], a mild acid) and carbonate rocks such as limestone to produce a very soluble product (calcium bicarbonate) that can readily be removed by runoff or percolation and can also be deposited in crystalline form if the water is evaporated. We will discuss this process in greater detail in Chapter 17.

These and other less common chemical weathering processes are continuously at work at and beneath Earth's surface. Most chemically weathered rocks are changed physically, too. Their coherence is weakened, and the loose particles produced at Earth's surface are quite unlike the parent material. Beneath the surface, the rock holds together—but in a chemically altered condition. The major eventual products of chemical weathering are clays.

Biological Weathering

As already mentioned, plants frequently and animals occasionally contribute to weathering, and such processes involving living organisms are called **biological weathering**. Most notable is the penetration of growing plant roots into cracks and crevices, as in Figure 15-16, with the result that the opening is expanded. Roots are especially effective as weathering agents where trees grow out of joint or fault planes, with their large roots showing amazing tenacity and persistence as wedging devices.

Lichens are primitive organisms that consist of algae and fungi living as a single unit. Typically they live on bare rock, bare soil, or tree bark (Figure 15-17). They draw minerals from the rock by ion exchange, and this leaching can weaken the rock. Moreover, expansion and contraction of lichens as they get alternately wet and dry flake off tiny particles of rock.

Burrowing by animals mixes soil effectively and is sometimes a factor in rock disintegration (for example, see Figure 12-6 in Chapter 12).

The total effect of all these biotic actions is probably significant but difficult to evaluate because it is obscured by subsequent chemical weathering.

Climate and Weathering

Geomorphic research tells us more and more every year about how climate influences weathering. The basic generalization is that weathering, particularly chemical weathering, is enhanced by a combination of high temperatures and abundant precipitation. Of these two factors, the moisture is usually more important than temperature. For example, we'll see in Chapter 18

▲ **Figure 15-16**   Roots can serve as formidable natural tools to enlarge cracks and crevices in bedrock. **(a)** Grass growing out of a vertical cliff of basalt near Cairns, Queensland, Australia. **(b)** Juniper trees that have managed to find footholds in bare sandstone surfaces near Tuba City in northern Arizona. *(Tom L. McKnight photos.)*

(The Topography of Arid Lands) that in most desert regions, because of a general lack of precipitation, mechanical weathering tends to be more conspicuous than chemical weathering. As we saw in Chapter 12 (Soils), the climatic regime significantly influences patterns of soil development.

There are many variations in the connection between weathering and climate; Figure 15-18 represents a generalized model of relevant relationships.

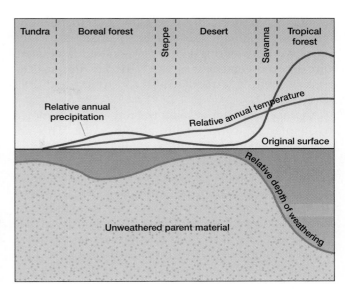

▲ **Figure 15-18**   Relationship between important climatic elements and depth of weathering. The extreme effectiveness of weathering in the humid tropics is clearly shown. Humid midlatitude regions are omitted from this diagram because the relationships are more complex there.

▲ **Figure 15-17**   Rocks covered with multicolored lichens in the Lake District of England. *(Martin Bond/Science Photo Library/Photo Researchers, Inc.)*

Mass Wasting

Mass Wasting

As we learned above, the denudation of Earth's surface is accomplished by weathering followed by mass wasting followed by erosion. The ultimate destiny of all weathered material is to be carried away by erosion, a topic we cover in the remaining chapters of this book. The remainder of this chapter is concerned with *mass wasting*, the process whereby weathered material is moved a relatively short distance downslope under the direct influence of gravity. Although it is sometimes circumvented when erosive agents act on weathered material directly, mass wasting is normally the second step in a three-step denudation process.

Throughout our planet, gravity is inescapable; everywhere, it pulls objects toward the center of Earth. Where the land is flat, the influence of gravity on topographic development is minimal. Even on gentle slopes, however, minute effects are likely to be significant in the long run, and on steep slopes the results are often immediate and conspicuous. Any loosened material is impelled downslope by gravity—in some cases falling abruptly or rolling rapidly, in others flowing or creeping with imperceptible gradualness.

The materials involved in these movements are all the varied products of weathering. Gigantic boulders respond to the pull of gravity in much the same fashion as do particles of dust, although the larger the object, the more immediate and pronounced the effect. Of particular importance, however, is the implication of "mass" in mass wasting; the accumulations of material moved—fragmented rock, regolith, soil—are often extremely large and contain enormous amounts of mass.

All rock materials, from individual fragments to cohesive layers of soil, lie at rest on a slope if undisturbed unless the slope has a certain steepness. The steepest angle that can be assumed by loose fragments on a slope without downslope movement is called the **angle of repose**. This angle, which varies with the nature and internal cohesion of the material, represents a fine balance between the pull of gravity and the cohesion and friction of the rock material. If additional material accumulates on a debris pile lying on a slope that is near the angle of repose, the newly added material may upset the balance (because the added weight overcomes the friction force that is keeping the pile from sliding) and may cause all or part of the material to slide downward.

If water is added to the rock material through rainfall, snowmelt, or subsurface flow, the mobility is usually increased, particularly if the rock fragments are small. Water is a lubricating medium, and it diminishes friction between particles so that they can slide past one another more readily. Water also adds to the buoyancy and weight of the weathered material, which makes for a lower angle of repose and adds momentum once movement is under way. For this reason, mass wasting is particularly likely during and after heavy rains.

Another facilitator of mass wasting is *clay.* As noted in Chapter 12, clays readily absorb water. This absorbed water combined with the fine-grained texture of the material makes clay a very slippery and mobile substance. Any material resting on clay can often be set in motion by rainfall or an earthquake shock, even on very gentle slopes. Indeed, some clay formations are called *quick clays* because they spontaneously change from a relatively solid mass to a near-liquid condition as the result of a sudden disturbance or shock.

In subarctic regions and at high latitudes, mass wasting is often initiated by the heaving action of frozen groundwater. The presence of thawed, water-saturated ground in summer overlying permanently frozen subsoil (*permafrost*) also contributes to mass wasting in such regions. Some geomorphologists assert that, in the subarctic, mass wasting is the single most important means of transport of weathered material.

Although some types of mass wasting are rapid and conspicuous, others are slow and gradual. The principles involved are generally similar, but the extent of the activity and particularly the rate of movement are quite variable. In our consideration here, we proceed from the most rapid to the slowest, discussing the characteristics of each as if they were discrete movements, although in nature the various types often overlap (Figure 15-19).

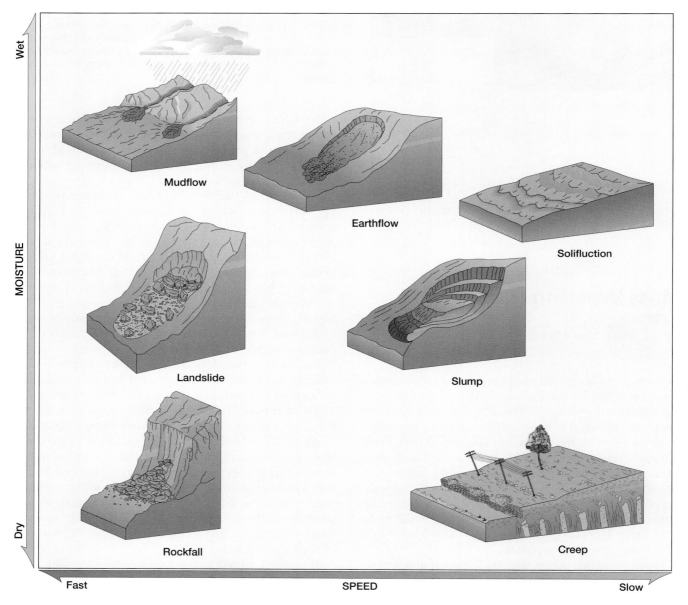

▲ **Figure 15-19**   Speed and moisture relationships for the various types of mass wasting.

▲ **Figure 15-20** An accumulation of talus at the base of a steep slope near Tioga Pass in the Sierra Nevada of California. *(Tom L. McKnight photo.)*

Fall

The simplest and most obvious form of mass wasting is **rockfall**, or simply **fall**, the falling of pieces of rock downslope. When loosened by weathering on a very steep slope, a rock fragment may simply be dislodged and fall, roll, or bounce down to the bottom of that segment of slope. This is a very characteristic event in mountainous areas, particularly as a result of frost wedging (Figure 15-20). Normally the fragments do not

travel far before they become lodged, although the lodging may be unstable and temporary.

Pieces of unsorted, angular rock that fall in this fashion are referred to collectively as **talus** or **scree**. Sometimes the fragments accumulate relatively uniformly along the base of the slope, in which case the resultant landform is called a *talus slope* or *talus apron*. More characteristically, however, the dislodged rocks collect in sloping, cone-shaped heaps called **talus cones** (Figure 15-21). This cone pattern is commonplace because most

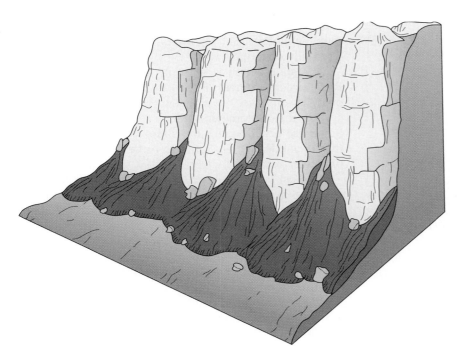

◄ **Figure 15-21** Talus cones at the foot of a steep slope.

steep bedrock slopes and cliffs are seamed by vertical ravines and gullies that funnel the falling rock fragments into piles directly beneath the ravines, usually producing a series of talus cones side by side along the base of the slope or cliff. Some falling fragments, especially larger ones with their greater momentum, tumble and roll to the base of the cone. Most of the new talus, however, comes to rest at the upper end of the cone. The cone thereby grows up the mountainside.

The angle of repose for talus is very high, generally about 35° and sometimes as great as 40°. The slope of a talus accumulation is gently concave upward, with the steepest angle near the apex of the cone. New material is frequently added to the top of the cone, where the fragments are invariably in delicate equilibrium, and each new piece that bombards down from above may cause a readjustment, with considerable downhill sliding. The freshest blocks, then, tend to be at the upper end of the cone. There is sometimes a rough sorting of fragments according to size, however, with the larger pieces rolling farther downslope and the smaller bits lodging higher up. With the passage of time, all talus slowly migrates downslope, encouraged by the freeze–thaw action of water in the many open spaces of the cones and aprons. All may be further reduced in size by more weathering.

In some rugged mountain areas, talus accumulates in great masses, and these masses may move slowly downslope under their own weight. As we shall see in Chapter 19, glaciers move in this same way, and for this reason these extremely slow flows of talus are called **rock glaciers**. The flow in rock glaciers is caused primarily by the pull of gravity, aided by freeze–thaw temperature changes and may largely be independent of any lubricating effect of water. Rock glaciers occur primarily in glacial environments; many are found in midlatitude mountains that are relics of periods of glaciation. They are normally found on relatively steep slopes but sometimes extend far down-valley and even out onto an adjacent plain.

Slide

Eruption of Mount St. Helens

In mountainous terrain, landslides carry large masses of rock and soil downslope abruptly and often catastrophically. A **landslide** is essentially an instantaneous collapse of a slope (a type of *slope failure*) and does not necessarily involve the lubricating effects of water or clay (Figure 15-22). In other words, the sliding material represents a rigid mass that is suddenly displaced without any fluid flow. The presence of water may contribute to the action, however; many slides are triggered by rains that add weight to already overloaded

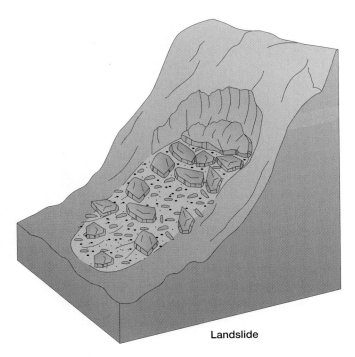

Landslide

▲ **Figure 15-22** Landslide is a type of slope failure that entails the rapid downslope movement of masses of weathered rock.

slopes. Landslides may be activated by other stimuli as well, most notably by earthquakes. Slides are also sometimes initiated simply by lateral erosion of a stream that undercuts its bank and thus oversteepens the slope above.

Some slides move only regolith, but many large slides also involve masses of bedrock detached along joint planes and fracture zones. The rapid downslope surge invariably involves the violent disintegration of much of the material, regardless of the size of the blocks originally dislodged.

Landslide action is not only abrupt but also rapid. Precise measurement of the rate of movement is obviously impossible, but eyewitness accounts affirm speeds of 160 kilometers (100 miles) per hour. Thunderous noise accompanies the slide, and the blasts of air that the slide creates can strip leaves, twigs, and even branches from nearby trees.

As most landslides occur in steep, mountainous terrain, the great mass of material (displaced volume is sometimes measured in cubic kilometers) that roars downslope may choke the valley at the bottom. Moreover, the momentum of the slide may push material several hundred meters up the slope on the other side of the valley. One characteristic result is the creation of a natural dam across the width of the valley, blocking the valley-bottom stream and producing a new lake, which becomes larger and larger until it either overtops the dam or cuts a path through it.

People and the Environment The Madison Valley Landslide

Just before midnight in the late summer of 1959, the geologically unstable area of Yellowstone National Park was rocked by a major earthquake (magnitude 7.8). Of the many striking geomorphic results of the shock, by far the most conspicuous and tragic took place in the narrow valley of the Madison River a few kilometers west of the park in Montana. Hebgen Lake, a reservoir in the valley 11 kilometers (7 miles) long, experienced a series of *seiches*—abrupt wave actions in which sudden oscillations of the surface caused a surge of water to flow across the lake. An enormous quantity of water was hurled over the dam as if sloshed out of a dishpan, and it swept down the valley as a flash flood.

The wall of water sped 11 kilometers (7 miles) downstream, almost to the point where the constricted canyon opened out into rolling wheat and grazing land. Just as the surge approached the canyon mouth, a resistant buttress of sedimentary rock on the steep south slope gave way, releasing an enormous mass of unstable rock that had been retained above and behind it. Some 33 million cubic meters (43 million cubic yards) of debris cascaded down the slope, filled the valley bottom (Figure 15-A),

▲ **Figure 15-A** The scar from the Madison Valley landslide of 1959 is seen in the distance beyond Quake Lake. *(Darrel Hess photo.)*

spurted up the opposite hillside, and sprawled up and down the canyon for about 2.5 kilometers (1.5 miles). A U.S. Forest Service campground, crowded with sleeping vacationers, was partly buried by the landslide.

The slide dammed the river and forced the surging water back into the unburied portion of the campground. Thus the campers who had escaped being crushed were further endangered by the force of the ricocheting water and then the inexorable flooding as a new lake formed behind the natural dam. The final death toll from this tragic episode may never be known. Nine bodies were found, and indirect evidence (mostly reports from families and friends of people thought

to be in the area at the time) indicated that at least 19 other people were buried in the slide.

An immediate result of the cataclysm was the creation of a continuously enlarging lake, called Quake Lake, upstream from the blocking debris (Figure 15-B). Not only did this impoundment produce pressures that might rupture the natural dam, but its upstream end would eventually lap against the foundations of Hebgen Dam, quite possibly undermining it. The down-valley area, which includes three towns, thus faced the threat of abrupt flooding from two broken dams. The memories of a post-landslide tragedy that took place a quarter century earlier in the Gros Ventre River valley nearby in Wyoming to the southeast of Yellowstone were much in the minds of officials. (In 1925 a huge landslide blocked the Gros Ventre River, forming a lake 8 kilometers [5 miles] long; two years later the landslide dam was breached and a wall of water rushed downstream, killing 9 people as the flood washed away the town of Kelly.) Consequently, nearly $2 million was spent in the next 10 weeks to construct a deep channel across the top of the slide, allowing the Madison River to resume its normal flow regime.

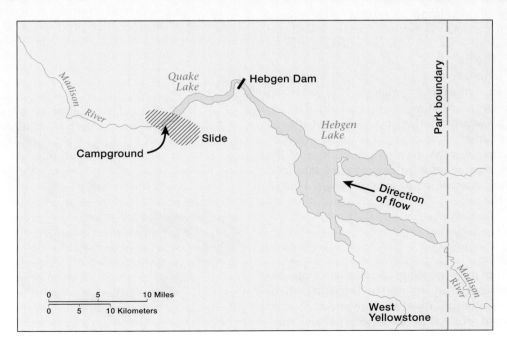

▲ **Figure 15-B** The temporary formation of Quake Lake behind the landslide dam.

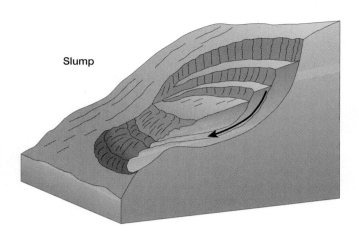

Slump

▲ **Figure 15-23**   Slump involves movement along a curved sliding plane.

The immediate topographic result of a landslide is threefold:

1. On the hill where the slide originated, there is a deep and extensive *scar*, usually exposing a mixture of bedrock and scattered debris.
2. In the valley bottom where the slide material comes to rest, there is a massive pile of highly irregular debris, usually in the form of either a broad ridge or low-lying cone. Its surface consists of a jumble of unsorted material, ranging from immense boulders to fine dust.
3. On the up-valley side of the debris, a lake may form.

Slump   An extremely common form of mass wasting is the type of slide called a **slump**. Slumping involves slope failure in which the rock or regolith moves downward and at the same time rotates outward along a curved slide plane that has its concave side facing upward (for this reason, a slump is sometimes called a *rotational slide*). The upper portion of the moving material tilts down and back, and the lower portion moves up and out. The top of the slump is usually marked by a crescent-shaped scarp face, sometimes with a steplike arrangement of smaller scarps and terraces below. The bottom of the slumping block consists of a bulging lobe of saturated debris protruding downslope or into the valley bottom (Figure 15-23).

Flow

FG9

In another form of mass wasting, a sector of a slope becomes unstable, normally owing to the addition of water, and flows gently downhill. In some cases, the flow is fairly rapid, but it is in others gradual and sluggish. Usually the center of the mass moves more rapidly than the base and sides, which are retarded by friction.

Many flows are relatively small, often encompassing an area of only a few square meters. More characteristically, however, they cover several tens or hundreds of hectares. Normally, they are relatively shallow phenomena, including only soil and regolith, but under certain conditions a considerable amount of bedrock may be involved.

As with other forms of mass movement, gravity is the impelling force. Water is an important catalyst to the movement; the surface materials become unstable with the added weight of water, and their cohesion is diminished by waterlogging, so that they are more responsive to the pull of gravity. The presence of clay also promotes flow, as clay minerals become very slippery when lubricated with any sort of moisture.

Earthflow   The most common flow movement is **earthflow**, in which a portion of a water-saturated slope moves a limited distance downhill, normally during or immediately after a heavy rain. At the place where the flow originates, there is usually a distinct interruption in the surface of the preflow slope, either cracks or a prominent oversteepened scarp face. An earthflow is most conspicuous in its lower portion, where a bulging lobe of material pushes out onto the valley floor (Figure 15-24).

This type of slope failure is relatively common on hillsides that are not densely vegetated and often results in blocked transportation lines (roads, railways) in valley bottoms. Property damage is occasionally extensive, but the rate of movement is usually so sluggish that there is no threat to life.

Mudflow   A **mudflow** originates in drainage basins in arid and semiarid country when a heavy rain following a long dry spell produces a cascading runoff too voluminous to be absorbed into the soil. Fine

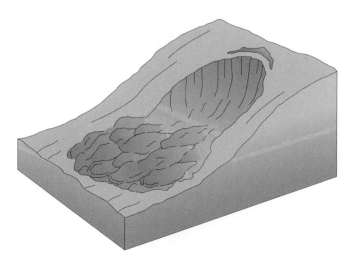

▲ **Figure 15-24**   Earthflow takes place on hillsides when very wet surface material begins to flow downslope.

debris is picked up from the hillsides by the runoff and concentrated in the valley bottoms, where it flows down-valley with the consistency of wet concrete. The leading edge of the mudflow continues to accumulate load, becoming increasingly stiff and retarding the flow of the more liquid upstream portions, so that the entire mudflow moves haltingly down the valley. When a mudflow reaches the mouth of the valley and abruptly leaves its confining walls for the more open slopes of the piedmont zone, the pent-up liquid behind the glutinous leading edge breaks through with a rush, spreading muddy debris into a wide sheet. Mudflows often pick up large rocks, including huge boulders, and carry them along as part of their load. In some cases, the large pieces are so numerous that the term **debris flow** is used in preference to mudflow (Figure 15-25).

An important distinction between earthflow and mudflow is that mudflows move along the surface of a slope and down established drainage channels, whereas earthflow involves a slope collapse and has no relationship to the drainage network. Moreover, mudflows are normally much more rapid, with a rate of movement intermediate between the sluggish surge of an earthflow and the rapid flow of a stream of water. Mudflows are potentially (and actually) more dangerous to humans than earthflows because of the more rapid movement, the larger quantity of debris involved, and the fact that the mudflow often discharges abruptly across a piedmont zone, which is likely to be a favored area for human settlement and intensive agriculture.

As we will see in Chapter 18, mudflow and debris flow are especially important mass wasting processes in arid regions. In the mountain areas of deserts, an intense, local thunderstorm can quickly mobilize loose, weathered material; the flow will move rapidly down a desert canyon, depositing the mud and debris at the foot of the mountains.

Creep

The slowest and least perceptible form of mass wasting, **creep**—or **soil creep**—consists of a very gradual downhill movement of soil and regolith so unobtrusive that it can normally be recognized only by indirect evidence. Generally the entire slope is involved. Creep is such a pervasive phenomenon that it occurs all over the world on sloping land. Although most notable on steep, lightly vegetated slopes, it also occurs on gentle slopes that have a dense plant cover. Wherever weathered materials are available for movement on land that is not flat, creep is a persistent form of mass wasting.

Creep is universal. Infinite numbers of tiny bits of lithospheric material, as well as many larger pieces, march slowly and sporadically downslope from the places where they were produced by weathering or deposited after erosion. When free water is present in the

▲ **Figure 15-25** The city of Caraballeda in Venezuela after a series of debris flows in 1999. *(Photo by L.M. Smith, Waterways Experiment Station, U.S. Army Corps of Engineers.)*

surface material, creep is usually accelerated because the lubricating effect allows individual particles to move more easily and because water adds to the weight of the mass.

Creep is caused by the interaction of various factors, the most significant being alternation of freeze–thaw and wet–dry conditions. When water in the soil freezes, soil particles tend to be displaced upward and in the direction perpendicular to the ground surface, as Figure 15-26 shows. After thawing, however, the particles settle downward, not directly into their original position but rather pulled slightly downslope by gravity. With countless repetitions, this process can result in downhill movement of the entire slope.

Many other agents also contribute to creep. Indeed, any activity that disturbs soil and regolith on a sloping surface is a contributor because gravity affects every rearrangement of particles, attracting them downslope. For example, burrowing animals pile most of their excavated material downslope, and subsequent infilling of burrows is mostly by material from the upslope side. As plant roots grow, they also tend to displace particles downslope. Animals that walk on the surface exert a downslope movement as well. Even the shaking of earthquakes or thunder produces disturbances that stimulate creep.

Whenever it occurs, creep is a very slow process, but its rate of movement is faster under some circumstances than others. The principal variables are slope angle, vegetative cover, and moisture supply. Creep operates faster on steep slopes than on gentle ones, for obvious reasons. Deep-rooted and dense-growing vegetation inhibits creep because the roots bind the soil. Also, as mentioned previously, creep is generally faster on water-saturated slopes than on dry ones. Although extreme creep rates of up to 5 centimeters (2 inches) per year have been reported, much more common are rates of just a fraction of a centimeter per year.

Whatever the creep rate, it is much too slow for the eye to perceive and the results are all but invisible. Creep is usually recognized only through the displacement of human-built structures—most commonly when fence posts and utility poles are tilted downhill. Retaining walls may be broken or displaced, and even roadbeds may be disturbed (Figure 15-27).

Unlike the other forms of mass wasting, creep produces few distinctive landforms. Rather it induces an imperceptible diminishing of slope angles and gradual lowering of hilltops—in other words, a widespread but minute smoothing of the land surface.

Under certain conditions, and usually on steep grassy slopes, grazing animals accentuate soil creep through the formation of a network of hillside ridges known as *terracettes*. Over time, the entire hillside

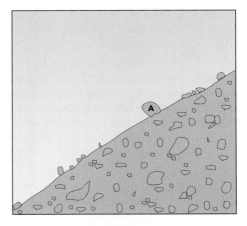

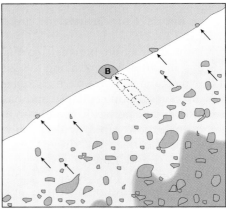

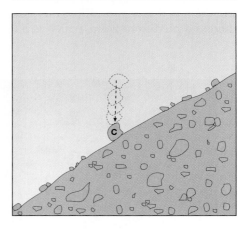

▲ **Figure 15-26**   The movement of a typical rock particle in a freeze–thaw situation. Freezing lifts the particle perpendicular to the slope (from A to B); upon thawing, the particle settles slightly downslope (from B to C).

may be covered with a maze of these terracettes (Figure 15-28).

Solifluction   A special form of creep that produces a distinctive surface appearance is **solifluction** (meaning "soil flowage"), a process largely restricted to tundra

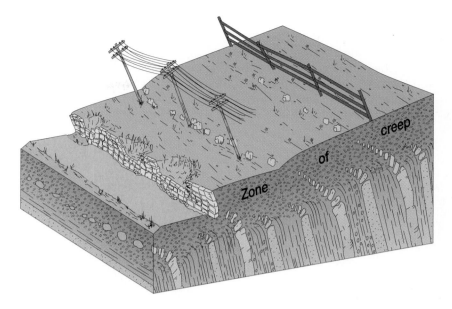

▲ **Figure 15-27** Visual evidence of soil creep: displacement and/or bending of fences, utility poles, and retaining walls.

▲ **Figure 15-28** A hillside laced with terracettes near Palmerston North, on the North Island of New Zealand. Heavy use of the slope by sheep accentuates the ridges. *(Tom L. McKnight photo.)*

landscape beyond the tree line (Figure 15-29). During the summer, the near-surface portion of the ground (called the *active layer*) thaws, but the meltwater cannot percolate deeper because of the permafrost below. The spaces between the soil particles become saturated, and the heavy surface material sags slowly downslope. Movement is erratic and irregular, with lobes overlapping one another in a haphazard, fish-scale pattern. The lobes move only a few centimeters per year, but they remain very obvious in the landscape, in part because of the scarcity of vegetation. Where solifluction occurs, drainage channels are usually scarce because water flow during the short summer is mostly lateral through the soil rather than across the surface.

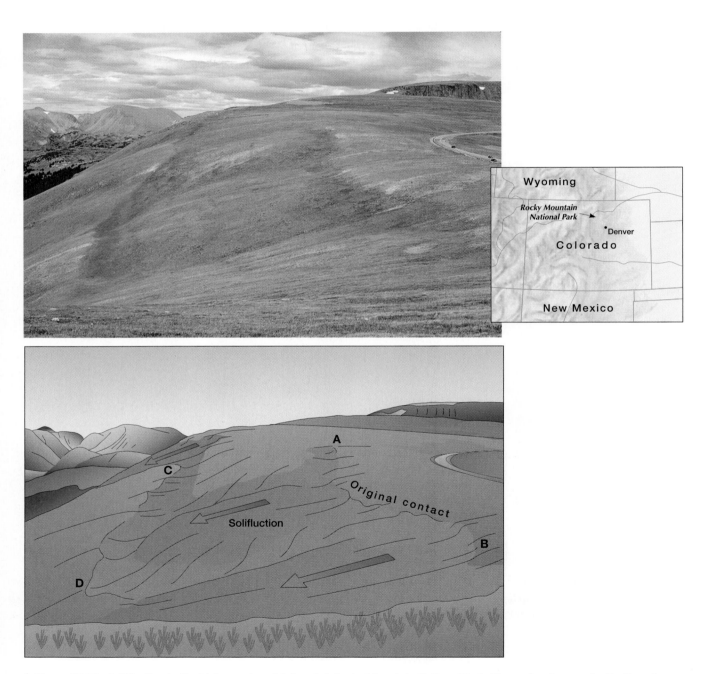

▲ **Figure 15-29** Solifluction in the high country of Colorado's Rocky Mountain National Park. The surface has gradually slipped downslope about 60 meters (200 feet). A–B and C–D were originally in contact with each other. *(Tom L. McKnight photo.)*

Chapter 15 Learning Review

Key Terms

Before answering the study questions below, review the definitions of the following key terms (page references are provided for you):

angle of repose *(p. 469)*
biological weathering *(p. 468)*
carbonation *(p. 468)*
chemical weathering *(p. 466)*
creep (soil creep) *(p. 475)*
debris flow *(p. 475)*
denudation *(p. 459)*
earthflow *(p. 474)*
erosion *(p. 459)*
exfoliation *(p. 464)*

exfoliation dome *(p. 464)*
frost wedging *(p. 462)*
hydrolysis *(p. 467)*
joints *(p. 460)*
landslide *(p. 472)*
mass wasting *(p. 459)*
master joints *(p. 461)*
mechanical weathering *(p. 462)*
mudflow *(p. 474)*
oxidation *(p. 467)*

rockfall (fall) *(p. 471)*
rock glaciers *(p. 472)*
salt wedging *(p. 463)*
scree *(p. 471)*
slump *(p. 474)*
solifluction *(p. 476)*
talus *(p. 471)*
talus cones *(p. 471)*
weathering *(p. 459)*

Study Questions for Key Concepts

After studying this chapter, you should be able to answer the following questions:

Denudation (p. 459)
1. Distinguish among *weathering, mass wasting,* and *erosion.*

Weathering and Rock Openings (p. 459)
2. What is the difference between a *joint* and a *fault*?
3. What roles can joints play in the weathering of rock?
4. Explain how it is possible for weathering to take place beneath the surface of bedrock.

Weathering Agents (p. 461)
5. What are the general differences between *mechanical weathering* and *chemical weathering*?
6. Explain the mechanics of *frost wedging.*
7. Explain the weathering process of *exfoliation* ("unloading") that is responsible for features such as *exfoliation domes.*
8. What is the relationship between *oxidation* and *rust*?
9. Describe and explain one example of *biological weathering.*

10. Why is chemical weathering more effective in humid climates than in arid climates?

Mass Wasting (p. 469)
11. What is the relationship between gravity and mass wasting?
12. How does the *angle of repose* affect mass wasting?
13. What is the role of *clay* in mass wasting?
14. In what ways can moisture expedite mass wasting?
15. Describe the process of *rockfall.*
16. What is a *talus cone*?
17. What roles may heavy rain play in triggering a *landslide*?
18. How is a *slump* different from other kinds of landslide?
19. What are the differences between a landslide and a *mudflow*?
20. How is *earthflow* different from mudflow?
21. Explain the process of *soil creep.*
22. In what kinds of environments is *solifluction* common?

Additional Resources

Books:
Bland, Will, and David Rolls. *Weathering: An Introduction to the Scientific Principles.* New York: Oxford University Press, 1998.
McPhee, John. "Los Angeles Against the Mountains," in *The Control of Nature.* New York: Farrar, Straus and Giroux, 1989.

Internet Sites:
U.S. Geological Survey
http://www.usgs.gov/
    The U.S. Geological Survey home page provides links to information on a wide range of Earth science

topics, including earthquakes, volcanoes, landslides, floods, and other natural hazards. The page also has links to sites where topographic maps, geological maps, research papers, and publications of general interest may be viewed or purchased.

16
The Fluvial Processes

Land is shaped by a variety of agents functioning in concert. In Chapter 14, we considered internal landshaping agents, and in Chapter 15, we studied the external processes called weathering and mass wasting. In Chapters 16 through 20, we concentrate on the external land-shaping agents that work by erosion and deposition: running water, subsurface waters, wind, moving ice, and coastal waters. By far the most important of these external agents is running water moving over the land—**fluvial processes**—the topic of this chapter.

Running water probably contributes more to shaping landforms than all other external agents combined. This is true not because running water is more forceful than other agents (moving ice and pounding waves often apply much greater amounts of energy per unit area), but rather because running water is ubiquitous: it exists everywhere except in Antarctica. (Wind is ubiquitous, too, but trivial in its power as a terrain sculptor.)

The Impact of Fluvial Processes on the Landscape

Moving water is so widespread and so effective as an agent of erosion and deposition that its impact on the landscape is usually prominent, if not dominant. With few exceptions, the shapes of valleys are either determined or significantly modified by the water that runs over them (Figure 16-1). Areas above the valleys are less affected by running water, but even there flowing water may significantly influence the shape of the land.

The basic landscape-sculpturing effect of running water is to smooth irregularities—in simplest terms, to wear down the hills by erosion and fill up the valleys by deposition. Before achieving these results, however, fluvial action often creates deep canyons and steep slopes that persist for very long periods of time.

Streams and Stream Systems

Streams and their valleys dissect the land in myriad patterns. However, there are some important threads of similarity, and the study of individual streams can produce additional generalities to aid in our understanding of topographic development. Before we get into the specifics of fluvial processes and their topographic results, we need to introduce a few basic concepts.

◀ Lower Sylvian Falls in the Blue Mountains, New South Wales, Australia. *(Photolibrary.Com.)*

▲ **Figure 16-1** The erosive work of some rivers is very conspicuous. This gorge carved out by the Green River in northeastern Utah is called Whirlpool Canyon. *(Tom L. McKnight photo.)*

Streamflow and Overland Flow

Fluvial processes, defined as those that involve running water, encompass both the unchanneled downslope movement of surface water, called **overland flow**, and the channeled movement of water along a valley bottom, or **streamflow**.

Valleys and Interfluves

All the surfaces of the continents can be considered to consist of two topographic elements—*valleys* and *interfluves*. The distinction between the two is not always obvious in nature, but the conceptual demarcation is clear. A **valley** is that portion of the terrain in which a drainage system is clearly established (Figure 16-2). It

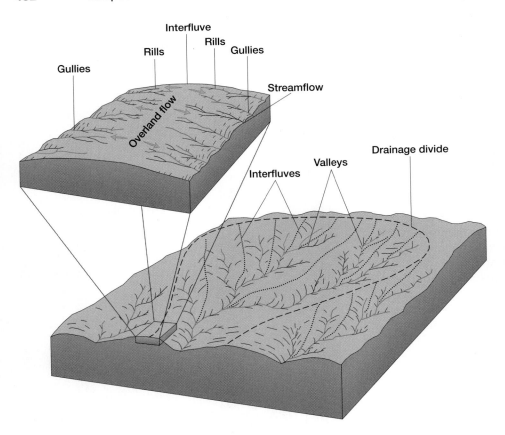

◀ **Figure 16-2** Valleys and interfluves. Valleys normally have clear-cut drainage systems; interfluves do not.

includes the valley bottom, which is the lower, flatter area that is partially or totally occupied by the channel of a stream, as well as the valley sides, the steeper slopes that rise above the valley bottom on either side. Some valley bottoms are narrow, elongated, and limited in area, while others are broad and extensive. Valley sides are also variable, with slopes that are steep or gentle and an extent that is limited or expansive. The upper limit of a valley is not always readily apparent, but it can be clearly conceptualized as a lip or rim at the top of the valley sides above which drainage channels are either absent or indistinct.

An **interfluve** (from Latin, *inter*, "between," and *fluvia*, "rivers") is the higher land above the valley sides that separates adjacent valleys. Some interfluves consist of ridgetops or mountain crests with precipitous slopes, but others are simply broad and flattish divides between drainage systems. Conceptually, all parts of the terrain not in a valley are part of an interfluve. We can envision that on an interfluve water will move downslope through unchanneled overland flow until it reaches the lip of the interfluve; there, as the water drops off the lip of the interfluve into the first small gullies of the valley system, streamflow begins.

These simplistic definitions are not always applicable in nature, as some terrain elements defy classification. Swamps and marshes, for example, may be on interfluves but are usually in valleys, although with no clearly established drainage system. Such exceptional cases, however, should not inhibit our acceptance of the valley–interfluve concept.

Drainage Basins

The **drainage basin** or **watershed** of a particular stream is all the area that contributes overland flow and groundwater to that stream. In other words, the drainage basin consists of a stream's valley bottom, valley sides, and those portions of the surrounding interfluves that drain toward the valley. Conceptually, the drainage basin terminates at a **drainage divide**, which is the line of separation between runoff that descends in the direction of the drainage basin in question and runoff that goes toward an adjacent basin.

Every stream of any size has its own drainage basin, but for practical purposes the term is often reserved for major streams. The drainage basin of a principal river encompasses the smaller drainage basins of all its tributaries; consequently, larger basins include a hierarchy of smaller tributary basins (Figure 16-3).

Stream Orders

In every drainage basin, small streams come together to form successively larger ones, and small valleys join more extensive ones. This relationship, although variable in detail, holds true for drainage basins of any size. This systematic characteristic makes it possible to recognize a natural organization within a watershed, and the concept of **stream order** has been devised to describe the arrangement (Figure 16-4).

A *first-order stream*, the smallest unit in the system, is one without tributaries. Where two first-order streams

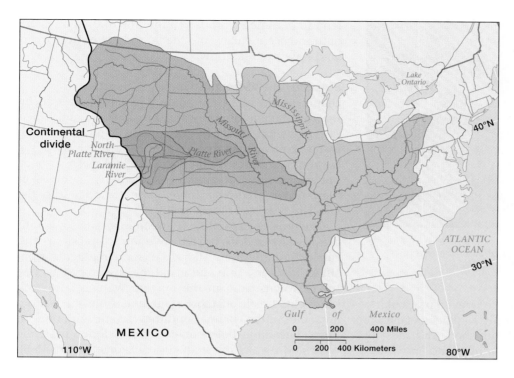

◀ **Figure 16-3** A nested hierarchy of drainage basins: the Laramie River flows into the North Platte; the North Platte drains into the Platte; the Platte is a tributary of the Missouri; the Missouri flows into the Mississippi; finally, the Mississippi empties into the Gulf of Mexico.

unite, a *second-order stream* is formed. At the confluence of two second-order streams, a *third-order stream* begins, and this uniting principle applies through successively higher orders.

Note from Figure 16-4 that the joining of a lower-order stream with a higher-order stream does not increase the order below that junction. For example, the confluence of a first-order stream and a second-order one does not produce a third-order stream. A third-order stream is formed only by the joining of two second-order streams.

The concept of stream order is more than simply a numbers game, as several significant relationships are involved. In a well-developed drainage system, for example, one can predict with some certainty that first-order streams and valleys are more numerous than all others combined and that each succeeding higher order is represented by fewer and fewer streams. Some other predictable relationships are that average stream length increases regularly with increasing order, that average watershed area increases regularly with increasing order, and that average stream gradient decreases with increasing order.

Fluvial Erosion and Deposition

Stream Sediment Movement

All external forces remove fragments of bedrock, regolith, and soil from their original positions (erosion), transport them to another location, and set them down (deposition). The fluvial processes, our concern in this chapter, produce one set of landforms by erosion and another quite different set by deposition.

Erosion by Overland Flow   On the interfluve, fluvial erosion begins when rain starts to fall. Unless the impact of rain is absorbed by vegetation or some other protective covering, the collision of raindrops with the ground is strong enough to blast fine soil particles upward and outward, shifting them a few millimeters laterally. On sloping ground, most particles move downhill by this *splash erosion* (Figure 16-5).

In the first few minutes of a rain, much of the water infiltrates the soil, and consequently there is little *runoff.*

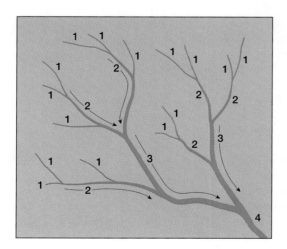

▲ **Figure 16-4** Stream orders. The branching component of a stream and its tributaries can be classified into a hierarchy of segments, ranging from smallest to largest (in this case, from 1 to 4).

▲ **Figure 16-5** The awesome impact of a raindrop produces splash erosion. *(U.S. Department of Agriculture.)*

During heavy or continued rain, however, particularly if the land is sloping and has only a sparse vegetative cover, infiltration is greatly diminished, and most of the water moves downslope as overland flow. The water flows across the surface as a thin sheet, transporting material already loosened by splash erosion, in a process termed *sheet erosion.* As overland flow moves downslope and its volume increases, the resulting turbulence tends to break up the sheet flow into multitudinous tiny channels called *rills.* This more concentrated flow loosens additional material and scores the slope with numerous parallel seams; this sequence of events is termed *rill erosion.* If the process continues, the rills begin to coalesce into fewer and larger channels called *gullies,* and *gully erosion* becomes recognizable. As the gullies get larger and larger, they

tend to become incorporated into the drainage system of the adjacent valley, and the flow changes from overland flow to streamflow.

Erosion by Streamflow Once surface flow is channeled, its ability to erode is greatly increased by the increased volume of water. Erosion is accomplished in part by the direct hydraulic power of the moving water, which can excavate and transport material at the bottom and sides of the stream. Banks can also be undermined by streamflow, particularly at times of high water, dumping more loose material into the water to be swept downstream.

The erosive capability of streamflow is also significantly enhanced by the abrasive tools it picks up and carries along with it. All sizes of rock fragments, from silt to boulders, chip and grind the stream bed as they travel downstream in the moving water. These rock fragments break off more fragments from the bottom and sides of the channel, and they collide with one another, becoming both smaller and rounder from the wear and tear of the frequent collisions (Figure 16-6). The eventual result of this abrasion is to reduce almost all stream-carried debris to very small silt particles.

A certain amount of chemical action also accompanies streamflow, and some chemical weathering processes—particularly solution action and hydrolysis—also help erode the stream channel by *corrosion.*

The erosive effectiveness of streamflow varies enormously from one situation to another, determined primarily by the speed and turbulence of the flow on the one hand, and by the resistance of the bedrock on the other. Flow speed is governed by the gradient (slope angle) of the streambed (the steeper the gradient, the

▲ **Figure 16-6** Rock particles transported by streams are inevitably rounded by frequent collisions. These streamworn rocks are in the bed of the Aluna River in the Southern Highlands of Papua New Guinea. *(Tom L. McKnight photo.)*

faster the flow) and by the volume of flow (more water normally means higher speed). The degree of turbulence is determined in part by the flow speed (faster flows are more turbulent) and in part by the roughness of the stream channel (an irregular channel surface increases turbulence).

Transportation Any water moving downslope, whether moving as overland flow or as streamflow, can transport rock material. At any given time and place, the load carried by overland flow is likely to be small in comparison with what a stream can transport. In total, however, the amount of material transported by overland flow is incredibly large. Eventually, most of this great mass of material reaches the streams in the valley bottoms, where it is added to the stream-eroded debris to constitute the **stream load**.

Essentially, the stream load contains three fractions (Figure 16-7):

1. Some minerals, mostly salts, are dissolved in the water and carried in solution as the **dissolved load**.
2. Very fine particles of clay and silt are carried in suspension, moving along with the water without ever touching the streambed. These tiny particles, called the **suspended load**, have a very slow settling speed, even in still water. (Fine clay may require as much as a year to sink 30 meters [100 feet] in perfectly quiet water.)
3. Sand, gravel, and larger rock fragments constitute the **bedload**. The smaller particles are moved along with the general streamflow in a series of jumps or bounces collectively referred to as *saltation*. Coarser pieces are moved by *traction*, which is defined as rolling or sliding along the streambed.

As a general rule, most of the material transported by a stream is in the suspended load and the least amount is in the bedload. The load is normally moved

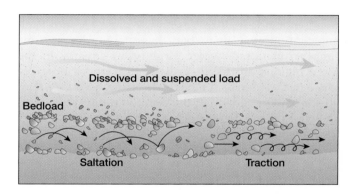

▲ **Figure 16-7** A stream moves its load in three ways. The dissolved and suspended loads are carried in the general water flow. The bedload is moved by traction (dragging) and saltation (bouncing).

spasmodically: debris is transported some distance, dropped, then picked up later and carried farther.

Geomorphologists employ two concepts—*competence* and *capacity*—in describing the load a stream can transport. **Competence** is a measure of the particle size a stream can transport, expressed by the diameter of the largest particles that can be moved. Competence depends mainly on flow speed, with the power of the water generally increasing by the square of its speed. In other words, if the flow speed is doubled, the size of the largest movable particle is increased fourfold (2^2); if the flow speed triples, the force increases ninefold (3^2)—as stream speed increases even moderately, the largest moveable particle increases significantly. Thus, a stream that normally can transport only sand grains, might easily be able to move large boulders during a flood.

Capacity is a measure of the amount of solid material a stream has the potential to transport, normally expressed as the volume of material passing a given point in the stream channel during a given time interval. Capacity may vary tremendously over time, depending mostly on fluctuations in volume and flow speed but also on the characteristics of the load (particularly the mix of coarse and fine sediments). It is difficult to overemphasize the significance of the greatly expanded capacity of a stream to transport material at flood time.

Deposition Whatever is picked up must eventually be set down, which means that erosion is inevitably followed by deposition. Moving water, whether moving as overland flow or as streamflow, carries its load downslope or down-valley toward an ultimate destination—either ocean, lake, or interior drainage basin. A large volume of fast-moving water can carry its debris a great distance, but sooner or later deposition will take place as either flow speed or water volume decreases. Diminished flow is often the result of a change in gradient, but it may also occur when a channel either widens or changes direction. Therefore, stream deposits are found at the mouths of canyons, on floodplains, and along the inside bank of river bends. Eventually, however, most waterborne debris is dumped by moving water (stream or river) into quiet water (ocean or lake).

The general term for stream-deposited debris is **alluvium**; it is characterized by a sorting of particles on the basis of size—that is, an alluvial deposit is often comprised of rocks of just about the same size. Sorting can occur when the speed of water flow diminishes—as stream competence drops, the heaviest (and therefore largest) rocks are deposited first, while smaller rocks are carried away to be deposited elsewhere.

Alluvial material is typically smooth and round due to the battering the particles receive from each other as they flow downstream. Further, alluvial deposits often display distinct strata or layers, due to episodes of deposition following periodic floods.

▲ **Figure 16-8** Most desert streams are either intermittent or ephemeral, carrying water only rarely. This dry bed is near Wiluna in Western Australia. *(Tom L. McKnight photo.)*

The Role of Floods

Our discussion of factors associated with effective stream erosion and deposition leads us to an important concept in fluvial geomorphology—the role of floods. Most of us have stood on a bridge or on the brink of a canyon looking at a small stream far below and wondered how that meager flow could have carved the enormous gorge we see spread beneath us. On such occasions, we might be tempted to discount uniformitarianism and consider some brief, catastrophic origin as a more logical linking of what we can see with what we can imagine. Such reasoning, however, is erroneous, for uniformitarianism easily accounts for the existence of tiny streams in extensive valleys by invoking two geomorphic principles: (1) the extraordinary length of geologic time and (2) the remarkable effectiveness of floods.

We have already discussed the incredible expanse of time involved in the evolution of topography (Chapter 13). This vast temporal sweep provides the opportunity for countless repetitions of an action, and the repetitive movement of even a tiny flow of water can wear away the strongest rock.

Of perhaps equal importance is that the amount of water flowing is not always tiny. Most streams have very erratic regimes, with great fluctuation in **discharge**, or volume of flow. Most of the world's streams carry a relatively small amount of water during most of the year and a relatively large volume during flood time. In some streams, flood flow occurs for several weeks or even months each year; but in the vast majority, the duration of high-water flow is much more restricted. In many cases, the "wet season" may be only one or two days a year. Yet the amount of denudation that can be accomplished during high-water flow is supremely greater than that done during periods of normal discharge. The epic work of streams—the carving of great valleys, the forming of vast floodplains—is primarily accomplished by flood flows.

We tend to think of rivers as permanent, but in fact many of the world's streams do not flow year-round. In humid regions, the large rivers and most tributaries are **perennial streams**—that is, permanent—but in less well-watered parts of the world, many of the major streams and most tributaries carry water only part of the time, either during the wet season or during and immediately after rains. These impermanent flows are called **ephemeral streams** if they carry water only during and immediately after a rain and **intermittent streams** if they flow for only part of the year, although the term intermittent is sometimes applied to both cases (Figure 16-8).

Even in humid regions, many first-order and second-order streams are only intermittent. These are generally short streams with relatively steep gradients and small watersheds. If rain is not frequent, or snowmelt not continuously available, these low-order streams simply run out of water. High-order streams in the same regions are likely to have permanent flow because of their larger drainage areas and because previous rainfall or snowmelt that sank into the ground can emerge in the valleys as groundwater runoff long after the rains have ceased.

Stream Channels

Overland flow is a relatively simple process. It is affected by such factors as rainfall intensity and duration, vegetative cover, surface characteristics, and slope shape, but its general characteristics are straightforward and easily understood. Streamflow is much more complicated, in part because streams represent not only a process of denudation but also an element of the landscape—an active force as well as an object of study.

Channel Flow

A basic characteristic of streamflow, and one that distinguishes it from the randomness of overland flow, is that it is normally confined to channels, which gives it a three-dimensional nature with scope for considerable complexity. In any channel having even a slight gradient, gravitational pull overcomes friction forces to move the water down-channel. Except under unusual circumstances, however, this movement is not straight, smooth, and regular. Rather it tends to be unsystematic and irregular, with many directional components and with different speeds in different parts of the channel.

A principal cause of flow irregularity is the retarding effect of friction along the bottom and sides of the channel, which causes the water to move most slowly there and fastest in the center of the stream (Figure 16-9). The amount of friction is determined by the width and depth of the channel and the roughness of its surface. A narrow, shallow channel with a rough bottom has a much greater retarding effect on streamflow than a wide, deep, smooth-bottomed one. One effect of friction is that it uses up much of the stream's energy, decreasing the amount available for erosion and transportation.

Turbulence   In turbulent flow, the general downstream movement is interrupted by irregularities in the direction and speed of the water. Such irregularities produce momentary currents that can move in any direction, including upward. Turbulence in streamflow is caused partly by friction, partly by internal shearing stresses between currents within the flow, and partly by surface irregularities in the channel. Stream speed also contributes to the development of turbulence, with faster streams more turbulent than slow-moving ones.

Eddies and whirlpools are conspicuous results of turbulence, as is the roiling whitewater of rapids. Even streams that appear very placid and smooth on the surface, however, are often turbulent at lower levels.

The effect of turbulence is varied because it is a selective process. In some places, it slows the stream's velocity, thus reducing erosion. In other locations, it may increase erosion due to the complexity of water currents and the churning of water at that spot.

Turbulent flow creates a great deal of frictional stress as the numerous internal currents interfere with one another. This stress dissipates much of the stream's

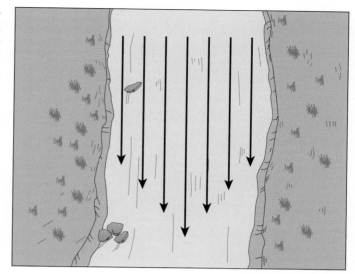

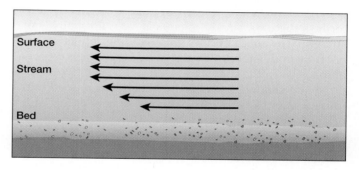

▲ **Figure 16-9**   Friction between the solid and liquid surfaces cause a stream to flow fastest in the middle and at the surface. **(a)** Overhead view. The water speed is proportional to arrow length, fastest in the center of the stream and slowest near the two banks. **(b)** Cross section through center of stream. The arrow lengths indicate that water speed is greatest at the surface, where the water is farthest from any solid surfaces, and least at the bottom, where the water drags along the streambed.

energy, decreasing the amount available to erode the channel and transport sediment. On the other hand, turbulence contributes to erosion by creating flow patterns that pry and lift rock materials from the streambed.

Stream Channel Patterns

Irregularities in streamflow are manifested in various ways, but perhaps most conspicuously by variations in channel patterns. If streamflow were smooth and regular, one might expect stream channels to be straight and direct. Few natural stream channels are straight and uniform for any appreciable distance, however. Instead, they wind about to a greater or lesser extent, sometimes developing remarkable sinuosity. In some

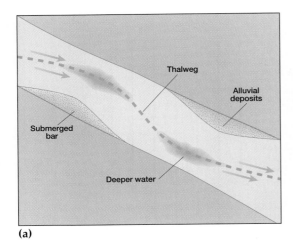

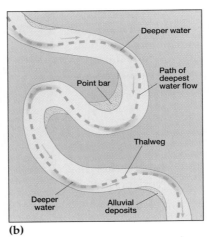

◀ **Figure 16-10** **(a)** Straight and **(b)** meandering channels. Pools of deeper water and alluvial deposits often occur on opposite sides of the channel from one another. Where the channel curves in part **(b)**, there is usually a deeper water pool on the outside of the curve and an alluvial deposit on the inside.

instances, this winding is a response to the underlying geologic structure, but even in areas of perfectly uniform structure, stream channels are normally not straight. The mechanics of this winding tendency are not fully understood, although we discuss some aspects of this later in the chapter.

Stream channel patterns are generally grouped into four categories—straight, sinuous, meandering, and braided—each with variations:

1. **Straight channels** are short and uncommon and usually indicative of strong control by the underlying geologic structure. A straight channel does not necessarily mean straight flow, however. A line running in the direction of the water and indicating the deepest parts of the channel, called the *thalweg* (German: *Thal,* "valley," and *Weg,* "way"), rarely follows a straight path midway between the stream banks; rather it wanders back and forth across the channel, as Figure 16-10 shows. Opposite the place where the thalweg approaches one bank, a deposit of alluvium is likely to be found. Thus, straight channels are likely to have many of the characteristics of sinuous channels.

2. **Sinuous channels** are much more common than straight ones. They are winding channels and are found in almost every type of topographic setting (Figure 16-11). Their curvature is usually gentle and irregular. Stream channels are likely to be sinuous even when the gradient of the stream is high (in other words, when flowing down a steep slope); where gradients are low (over flatter land), stream channels will tend to develop greater sinuosity and begin to *meander.*

3. **Meandering channels** exhibit an extraordinarily intricate pattern of smooth curves in which the stream follows a serpentine course, twisting and contorting and turning back on itself, forming tightly curved loops and then abandoning them, cutting a new, different, and equally tortuous course. Meandering generally occurs when the land is flat and the

gradient is low, and in a stream that has an unhurried flow but is moving with enough force to erode its banks and carry sediment (Figure 16-12). A meander shifts its location almost continuously. This is accomplished by erosion on the outside of curves and deposition on the inside. In this fashion, meanders

▲ **Figure 16-11** The sinuous channel of the Merced River flowing out of Yosemite Valley in California. *(Darrel Hess photo.)*

▲ **Figure 16-12** Floodplain of the Trinity River in Big Thicket National Preserve, Texas. *(Photo © Michael Collier.)*

migrate across the floodplain and also tend to shift down-valley, producing rapid and sometimes abrupt changes in the channel. (Landforms that develop along a meandering river channel will be discussed later in this chapter.)

4. **Braided streams** consist of a multiplicity of interwoven and interconnected channels separated by low bars or islands of sand, gravel, and other loose debris (Figure 16-13). Braiding takes place when a very flat stream channel has a heavy load of alluvium and a period of low discharge. At any given time, the active channels of a braided stream may cover less than one-tenth of the width of the entire channel system, but in a single year most or all of the surface sediments may be reworked by the flow of the laterally shifting channels.

Structural Relationships

Many factors affect stream development, and perhaps the most important is the geologic–topographic structure over or through which the stream must make its way

▲ **Figure 16-13** A typical braided stream on the South Island of New Zealand. This is the valley of the Lower Matukituki River. *(© Bill Bachman; Photo Researchers, Inc.)*

and carve its valley. Each stream faces particular structural obstacles as it seeks the path of least resistance in its descending course to the sea. Most streams respond directly and conspicuously to structural controls, which is to say that their courses are guided and shaped by the nature and arrangement of the underlying bedrock.

Although streams change in pattern and flow characteristics, they may persist through eons of time, outlasting mountain ranges and other topographic assemblages that are more temporary occupants of continental surfaces. Thus, sometimes a relationship can be seen between the location of a stream and the contemporary structure of the land over which it flows, although sometimes it is necessary to delve into the geomorphic history of a region before the location of a drainage channel can be comprehended.

There are hundreds of millions of streams in the world, and each channel (and valley) has its own particular characteristics. Nevertheless, the extensive replication of situations enables us to use brief terms to describe important development relationships. Chief among these categories are the following.

Consequent Streams The simplest and most common relationship between underlying structure and channel development is one in which the stream follows the initial slope of the land. Such a **consequent stream** is normally the first to develop on newly uplifted land, and many streams remain consequent throughout their evolutionary development.

Subsequent Streams Streams that develop along zones of structural weakness are termed **subsequent streams**. They may excavate their channels along an outcrop of weak bedrock, or perhaps follow a fault zone or a master joint. Subsequent streams often trend at right angles to other drainage channels.

Antecedent Streams Sometimes an established drainage system will be interrupted by an uplift of land that is so slow that the stream is able to maintain its previously established course by downward erosion. In many cases, this results in a deep gorge carved through hills or mountains. As the stream antedates (predates) the existence of the uplift, it is called an **antecedent stream** (Figure 16-14).

Superimposed Streams A **superimposed drainage system** is one originally established on a higher sequence of land that has been entirely or largely eroded away, so that the original drainage pattern becomes incised into an underlying sequence of rocks of quite different structure. The result may be a drainage system that bears no relation at all to the present surface structure.

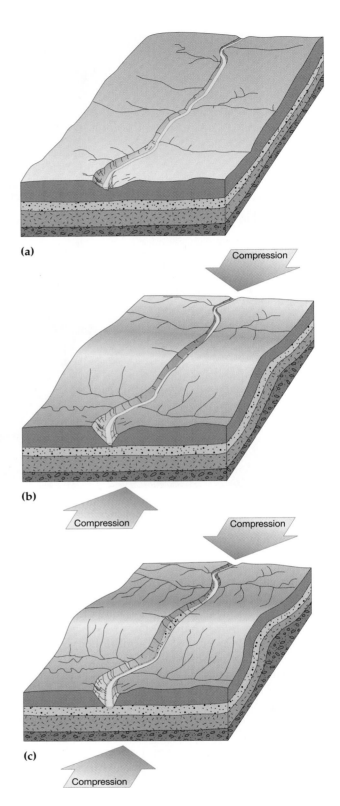

▲ **Figure 16-14** The development of an antecedent stream. **(a)** Stream course established before uplift begins. **(b and c)** Stream maintains its course and erodes through slowly rising ridge.

Many other categories of stream types are based on structural relationships, but those which are identified above are the most widely recognized. In addition, many streams fit into no clearly defined structural category.

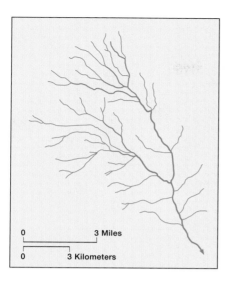

▲ **Figure 16-15** A dendritic drainage pattern in the Pat O'Hara Mountain (Wyoming) topographic quadrangle.

Stream Drainage Patterns

Stream systems are frequently orderly, forming conspicuous drainage patterns in the landscape. These patterns develop largely in response to the underlying structure and slope of the land surface. Geologic–topographic structure can often be deduced from a drainage pattern, and, conversely, drainage pattern often can be predicted from structure.

Dendritic Pattern   The most common drainage pattern over the world is a treelike, branching one called a **dendritic drainage pattern** (Figure 16-15). It consists of a random merging of streams, with tributaries joining larger streams irregularly but always at an angle smaller than 90°. The pattern resembles branches on a tree or veins on a leaf. The relationship between drainage pattern and land structure is negative, which is to say that the underlying structure does not control the evolution of the drainage pattern. Dendritic patterns are more numerous than all others combined and can be found almost anywhere.

Trellis Pattern   A **trellis drainage pattern** usually develops as a response to an underlying structure consisting of alternating bands of tilted hard and soft strata, with long, parallel streams linked by short, right-angled segments. Two regions of the United States are particularly noted for their trellis drainage patterns: the ridge-and-valley section of the Appalachian Mountains and the Ouachita Mountains of western Arkansas and southeastern Oklahoma.

In the ridge-and-valley section, which extends northeast–southwest for more than 1280 kilometers (800 miles) from New York to Alabama, the drainage pattern developed in response to tightly folded Paleozoic sedimentary strata forming a world-famous series of parallel

▲ **Figure 16-16** A trellis drainage pattern in the Norris (Tennessee) topographic quadrangle.

ridges and valleys. Parallel streams flow in the valleys between the ridges, with short, right-angled connections here and there cutting through the ridges (Figure 16-16).

The marked contrast between trellis and dendritic patterns is shown dramatically by the principal streams of West Virginia (Figure 16-17). The folded structures of the eastern part of the state produce trellising, whereas the nearly horizontal strata of the rest of the state are characterized by dendritic patterns.

Radial Pattern   A **radial drainage pattern** is usually found when streams descend from some sort of concentric uplift, such as an isolated volcano. Figure 16-18 shows one example: Mount Egmont on the North Island of New Zealand.

Centripetal Pattern   A **centripetal drainage pattern**, essentially the opposite of a radial one, is usually associated with streams converging in a basin. Occasionally, however, centripetal drainage develops on a much grander scale. Shown in Figure 16-19 is the northeastern part of Australia, where rivers from hundreds of kilometers away converge toward the Gulf of Carpentaria, a basin partially inundated by the sea.

Annular Pattern   More complex is an **annular drainage pattern**, which can develop either on a dome or in a basin where dissection has exposed alternating concentric bands of tilted hard and soft rock. The principal streams follow curving courses on the softer

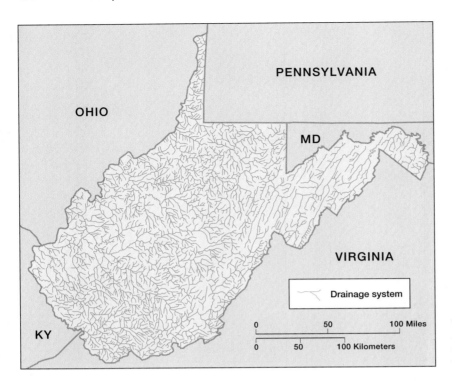

◀ **Figure 16-17** Drainage pattern contrasts in West Virginia. The trellis systems in the east are a response to parallel folding; the dendritic drainages in the west have developed because there are no prominent structural controls.

material, occasionally breaking through the harder layers in short, right-angled segments. The Maverick Spring Dome of Wyoming portrays a prominent example of annular drainage (Figure 16-20). This dome of ancient crystalline rocks was pushed up through a sedimentary overlay and has been deeply eroded, thus exposing crystallines in the higher part of the hills, with upturned concentric sedimentary ridges (called *hogbacks*) around the margin. The streams are mostly incised into the softer layers.

The Shaping and Reshaping of Valleys

Running water shapes terrain partly by overland flow on interfluves but mostly by streamflow in the valleys. Thus, by focusing our attention on the processes through which streams shape and reshape their valleys, we can understand the development of fluvial landforms in general. The shaping of valleys and their

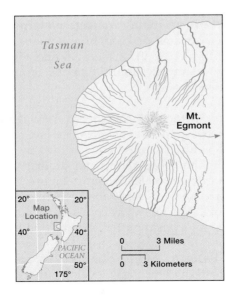

▲ **Figure 16-18** The extraordinary radial drainage pattern of Mount Egmont in New Zealand.

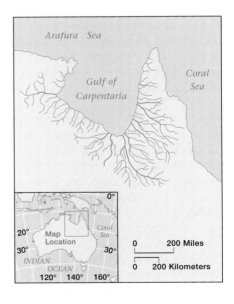

▲ **Figure 16-19** The centripetal drainage pattern of the region around the Gulf of Carpentaria in northeastern Australia.

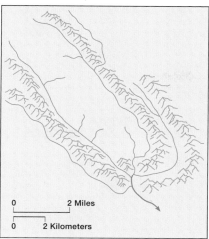

▲ **Figure 16-20**   An annular drainage pattern in the Maverick Spring Dome (Wyoming) topographic quadrangle.

almost continuous modification through time produce a changing balance between valleys and interfluves and consequently an ongoing dynamism in the configuration of most parts of the continental surfaces.

Valley Deepening

Wherever it has either a relatively rapid speed or a relatively large volume, a stream expends most of its energy in **downcutting**. This lowering of the streambed involves the hydraulic power of the moving water, the prying and lifting capabilities of turbulent flow, and the abrasive effect of the stream's bedload as it rolls, slides, and bounces along the channel. Downcutting is most frequent in the upper reaches of a stream, where the gradient is usually steep and the valley narrow. The general effect of downcutting is to produce a deep valley with steep sides and a V-shaped cross section (Figure 16-21).

Base Level   A stream excavates its valley by eroding the channel bed. If only downcutting were involved, the resulting valley would be a narrow, steep-sided gorge. Such gorges sometimes occur, but usually other factors are at work also and the result is a wider valley. In either case, there is a lower limit to how much downcutting a stream can do, and this limit is called the **base level** of the stream. Base level is an imaginary surface extending underneath the continents from sea level at the coasts (Figure 16-22). This imaginary surface is not simply a horizontal extension of sea level, however; inland it is gently inclined at a gradient that

◀ **Figure 16-21**   The Yellowstone River has carved a conspicuous V-shaped valley through downcutting. *(Darrel Hess photo.)*

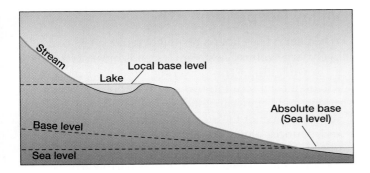

▲ **Figure 16-22** Comparison of sea level, base level, and local base level.

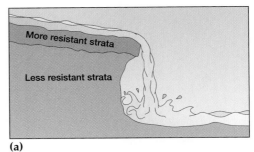

(a)

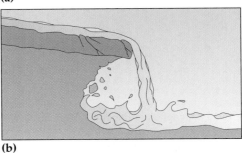

(b)

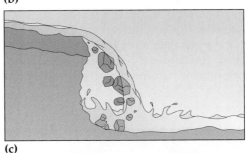

(c)

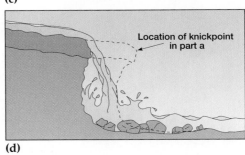

(d)

▲ **Figure 16-23** **(a)** Knickpoint formed where a stream flows over a resistant layer of rock. **(b)** The water flow undercuts the lip and **(c)** causes it to collapse. **(d)** Position of knickpoint has migrated upstream.

allows streams to maintain some flow. Sea level, then, is the absolute, or ultimate base level, or lower limit of downcutting.

As Figure 16-22 shows, there are also local, or temporary, base levels, which are limits to downcutting imposed on particular streams or sections of streams by structural or drainage conditions. For example, no tributary can cut deeper than its level of confluence with the higher-order stream it joins, and so the level of their point of junction is a local base level for the tributary. Similarly, a lake normally serves as the temporary base level for all streams that flow into it.

Some valleys have been downfaulted to elevations below sea level (Death Valley in California is one example), a situation producing a temporary base level lower than the ultimate base level. This can occur because the stream does not reach the ocean but terminates in an inland basin or body of water that is itself below sea level.

The longitudinal profile of a stream (the downvalley change in elevation from source to mouth) is ultimately restricted by base level, but the profile at any given time depends on a variety of factors. The long-term tendency is toward a smooth profile in which all factors are balanced. This hypothetical condition is called a *graded stream,* defined as one in which the gradient just allows the stream to transport its load. A graded stream is more theoretical than actual because equilibrium is so difficult to achieve and so easy to upset.

Knickpoint Migration Waterfalls and rapids are often found in valleys where downcutting is prominent. They occur in steeper sections of the channel, and their faster, more turbulent flow intensifies erosion. These irregularities in the channel are collectively termed **knickpoints**. They may originate in various ways but are commonly the result of abrupt changes in bedrock resistance. The more resistant material inhibits downcutting, and as the water plunges over the waterfall or rapids with accelerated vigor, it tends to scour the channel above and along the knickpoint and fill the channel immediately downstream. This intensified action eventually wears away the harder material, so that the knickpoint migrates upstream with a successively lower profile until it finally disappears and the channel gradient is smoothed (Figure 16-23).

This principle of **knickpoint migration** is important in understanding fluvial erosion because it illustrates dramatically the manner in which valley shape often develops first in the lower reaches and then proceeds progressively upstream, even though the water obviously flows downstream.

FOCUS Niagara Falls

Niagara Falls is a particularly good example of knickpoint migration on a massive scale and in a spectacular setting that is so easily available and so readily interpreted to the visiting public (Figure 16-A).

The entire natural drainage of the Great Lakes works its way toward the Atlantic Ocean through short, connecting rivers from lake to lake. The Niagara River forms the connecting link between Lake Erie and Lake Ontario. As the contemporary drainage system became established in this area, following the last retreat of Pleistocene ice sheets about 12,000 years ago, Lake Ontario was about 50 meters (about 150 feet) higher than its present level, and the Niagara River had no falls. However, an easterly outlet, the Mohawk Valley, developed for Lake Ontario, and the lake drained down to approximately its present level, exposing a prominent escarpment directly across the course of the river. The Niagara Escarpment is formed by a

▲ **Figure 16-A** Niagara Falls from the American side. *(AP Worldwide.)*

massive bed of resistant limestone that dips gently toward Lake Erie and is underlain by similarly dipping but softer strata of shale, sandstone, and limestone (Figure 16-B).

As the river pours over the escarpment, the swirling water undermines the hard limestone by erosion of the weaker beds beneath, leaving a lip of resistant rock projecting without support. Through the years, the lip has collapsed, with block after block of limestone tumbling into the gorge below. After each collapse, rapid undermining takes place again, leading to further collapse. In this fashion the falls has gradually retreated upstream, moving southward a distance of about 11 kilometers (7 miles) from its original position along the trend of the escarpment, the retreat being marked by a deep gorge.

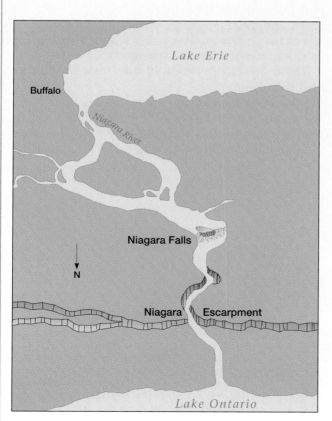

◄ **Figure 16-B** The situation of Niagara Falls. The falls was originally located where the Niagara River crosses the Niagara Escarpment, but it has retreated upstream to its present location.

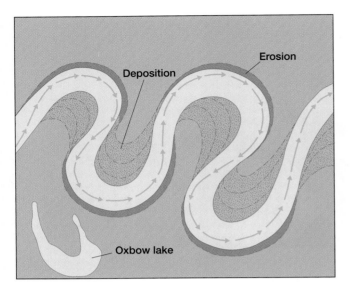

▲ **Figure 16-24** Lateral erosion in a meandering stream. Erosion occurs on the outside of bends, whereas deposition is common on the inside. If the neck of a meander is cut through by the stream, an oxbow lake is formed. *(After Sheldon Judson, Marvin E. Kauffman, and L. Don Leet, Physical Geology, 7th ed., Englewood Cliffs, NJ: Prentice Hall, 1987, p. 264.)*

Valley Widening

Where a stream gradient is steep and the channel well above the local base level, downcutting is the dominant activity; as a result, valley widening is likely to be slow. Even at this stage, however, some widening takes place as the combined action of weathering, mass wasting, and overland flow removes material from the valley sides. In the valley bottom, downcutting diminishes with time and eventually ceases as the stream develops a gentle profile. The stream's energy is then increasingly diverted into a meandering flow pattern. As the stream sways from side to side, **lateral erosion** begins: the main flow of the current swings from one bank to the other, eroding where the water speed is greatest

and depositing where it is least. The water moves fastest on the outside of curves, and there it undercuts the bank; on the inside of a curve where water is moving most slowly, alluvium is likely to accumulate (Figure 16-24), forming a *point bar* along the inside bank of the stream.

The channel often shifts position, so that undercutting is not concentrated in just a few locations. Rather, over a long period of time, most or all parts of the valley sides are undercut (Figure 16-25). The undercutting allows material to slump into the stream. All this time the valley floor is being widened, mass wasting and overland flow also help wear down the valley sides. In addition, similar processes along tributary streams also contribute to the general widening of the main valley.

Valley Lengthening

A stream may lengthen its valley in two quite different ways: (1) by *headward erosion* at the upper end or (2) by *delta formation* at the lower end.

Headward Erosion   No concept is more fundamental to an understanding of fluvial processes than **headward erosion** because it is the basis of rill, gully, and valley formation and extension. The upper perimeter of a valley is the line where the gentle slope of an interfluve changes to the steeper slope of a valley side. Overland flow from the interfluve drops abruptly over this slope break, and the fast-moving water tends to undercut the rim of the perimeter, weakening it and often causing a small amount of material to collapse (Figure 16-26).

The result of this action is a decrease in interfluve area and a commensurate increase in valley area. As the overland flow of the interfluve becomes part of the streamflow of the valley, there is a minute but distinct extension of rills and gullies into the drainage divide of the interfluve—in other words, a headward

(a)   (b)   (c)

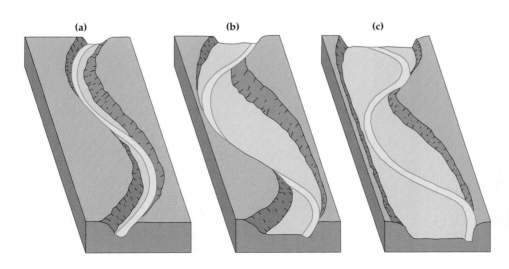

◀ **Figure 16-25** A meandering stream widens its valley by lateral erosion, producing an increasingly broader valley floor by undercutting the bluffs on the sides of the valley. The flattish valley floor develops into a floodplain.

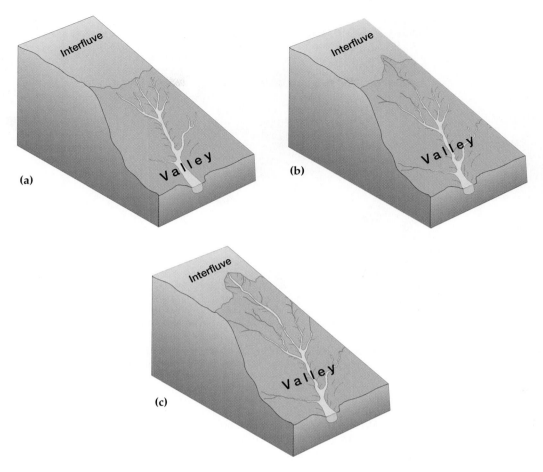

▲ **Figure 16-26** **(a)** Headward erosion occurs at the upper end of a stream where overland flow pours off the lip of the interfluve into the valley. **(b)** The channeled streamflow wears back the lip of the interfluve. **(c)** Over time, this erosion extends the valley headward at the expense of the interfluve.

extension of the valley. Although minuscule as an individual event, when multiplied by a thousand gullies and a million years, this action can lengthen a valley by tens of kilometers and the expansion of a drainage basin by hundreds of square kilometers. Thus, the valley lengthens at the expense of the interfluve (Figure 16-27).

Stream Capture Headward erosion is illustrated dramatically when a portion of the drainage basin of one stream is diverted into the basin of another stream by natural processes. This event, called **stream capture** or **stream piracy,** is relatively uncommon in nature, but evidence that it does sometimes occur is found in many places.

As a hypothetical example, let us consider two streams flowing across a coastal plain, as shown in Figure 16-28. Their valleys are separated by an interfluve, which for this example can be thought of as an undulating area of low relief. Stream A is shorter than stream B but is also more powerful, and A's valley is aligned so that headward extension will project it in the direction of B's valley.

Owing to its orientation, stream A lengthens its valley headward at the expense of the interfluve. As the valley becomes larger and the interfluve smaller, the drainage divide between the two valleys is shifted toward stream B. As the process continues, the headwaters of stream A eventually extend completely into the valley bottom of stream B and the flow from the upper reaches of B is diverted into A. In the parlance of the geographer, A has "captured" part of stream B. Stream A is called the *captor stream,* the lower part of B is the *beheaded stream,* the upper part of B is the *captured stream,* and the abrupt bend in the stream channel where the capture took place is called an **elbow of capture**.

Stream capture on a grand scale can be detected on a map of West Africa. The mighty Niger River has its headwaters relatively near the Atlantic Ocean, but it flows inward rather than seaward. After flowing northeast for nearly 1600 kilometers (1000 miles), it makes an abrupt turn to the southeast and then continues in that direction for another 1600 kilometers before finally emptying into the Atlantic. At some time in the past, the upper reaches of what is now the Niger was a separate river, one that did not change course but rather

▲ **Figure 16-27** This Wisconsin scene illustrates headward erosion. The grassy area being enjoyed by the horses is an interfluve that is being cut into by headward erosion of the irregular gorgelike valley in the foreground. *(Tom L. McKnight photo.)*

flowed northeast until it reached a great inland lake in what is now the central Sahara (Figure 16-29). This river was beheaded by the ancestral Niger, producing a great elbow of capture and leaving the beheaded stream to wither and dry up as the climate became more arid.

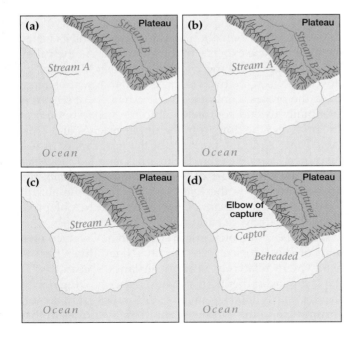

▲ **Figure 16-28** A hypothetical stream-capture sequence. The valley of stream A is extended by headward erosion until stream A captures and beheads stream B.

The map of Africa provides us with still another major point of interest concerning stream capture, but in this case the capture has not yet taken place. The Chari River of central Africa flows northwesterly into Lake Chad. Because its lower course has a very flat gradient, the stream flows sluggishly there without any power for downcutting. West of the Chari is an active and powerfully downcutting river in Nigeria, the Benue, a major tributary of the Niger. Some of the tributary headwaters of the Benue originate in a flat, swampy interfluve only a short distance from the floodplain of the Chari. Since the Benue is more active than the Chari and its alignment is such that headward erosion cuts directly into the Chari drainage, the Benue is likely to behead the Chari before our very eyes, so to speak, provided we can wait a few thousand years.

Delta Formation A valley can also be lengthened at its seaward end—in this case, by deposition. Flowing water slows down whenever it enters the quiet water of a lake or ocean and deposits its load. Most of this debris is dropped right at the mouth of the river in a landform called a **delta**, after a fancied resemblance to the Greek capital letter delta, Δ (Figure 16-30). The classic triangular shape is maintained in some deltas, but it is severely modified in others because of imbalances between the amount of sediment deposited by rivers and the removal of those sediments by ocean waves and currents. At some river mouths, the local coastal currents are so vigorous that no delta is formed, the stream sediment is simply swept away to be deposited elsewhere along the coast or offshore (Table 16-1).

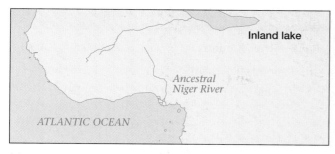

(a)

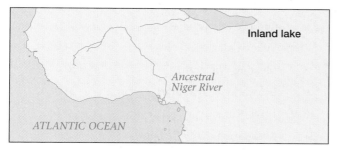

(b)

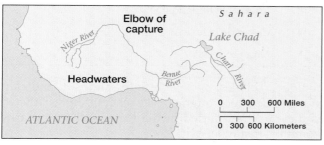

(c)

▲ **Figure 16-29** Stream capture, actual and anticipated in West Africa. **(a)** The upper course of the Niger River was once part of an unnamed stream that flowed into a large lake in what is now the Sahara. **(b)** This ancient stream was captured by headward erosion of the ancestral Niger. **(c)** At present, headward erosion on the Benue River gives promise of capturing the Chari River just a few tens or hundreds of centuries from now.

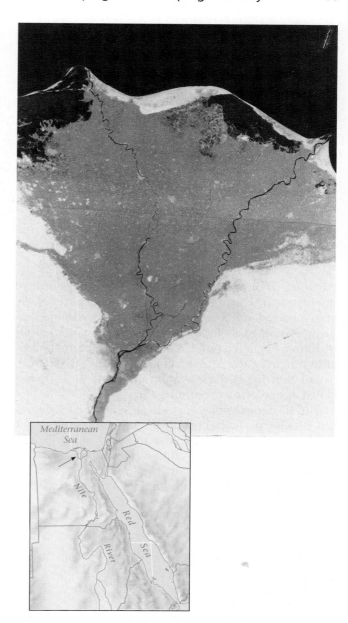

▲ **Figure 16-30** The full extent of the Nile River delta is shown clearly in this high-altitude false-color infrared image because almost the entire area of the delta is devoted to irrigated farming. The view is northward, with the Nile entering from the bottom and the Mediterranean Sea at the top. *(Photri.)*

Often, however, a prominent and clear-cut delta does form (Table 16-2 and Figure 16-31). The stream slows down, losing both competence and capacity, and drops much of its load, which partially blocks the channel and forces the stream to seek another path (Figure 16-32, p. 501). Later this new path is likely to become clogged, and the pattern is repeated. As a result, deltas usually consist of a maze of roughly parallel channels called *distributaries* through which the water flows slowly toward the sea. Continued deposition builds up the surface of the delta so that it is at least partially exposed above sea level. Rich alluvial sediments and an abundance of water favor the establishment of vegetation, which provides a base for further expansion of the delta. In this fashion, the stream valley is extended downstream.

Deposition in Valleys

Thus far, we have emphasized the prominence of erosion in the formation and shaping of valleys, but deposition, too, has a role in these processes.

Nearly every stream continuously rearranges its sediment in response to variations in flow speed and volume. Alluvium can be deposited almost anywhere in a valley bottom: on the stream bottom, on the sides, in the center, at the base of knickpoints, in overflow areas, and in a variety of other locations.

During high-water periods, when flow is fast and voluminous, the stream scours its bed by detaching

Rank*	River (Country)
1	Amazon (Brazil)
2	Congo (Democratic Republic of Congo)
6	Yenisey (Russia)
10	Paraná (Argentina)
11	St. Lawrence (Canada)
15	Tocantins (Brazil)
20	Columbia (United States)
21	Zambezi (Mozambique)

TABLE 16-1 The World's Largest Deltaless Rivers

*In terms of average discharge.

TABLE 16-2 The World's Largest Deltas

Rank	River (Country)	Area (km² × 1000)
1	Indus (Pakistan)	163.0
2	Nile (Egypt)	160.0
3	Hwang Ho (China)	127.0
4	Yangtze (China)	124.0
5	Ganges/Brahmaputra (Bangladesh)	91.0
6	Orinoco (Venezuela)	57.0
7	Yukon (Alaska)	54.0
8	Mekong (Vietnam)	52.0
9	Irrawaddy (Myanmar)	31.0
10	Lena (Russia)	28.5
11	Mississippi (United States)	28.0
12	Chao Phraya (Thailand)	24.6
13	Rhine (Netherlands)	22.0
14	Colorado (Mexico)	19.8
15	Niger (Nigeria)	19.4

particles from it and shifting most or all sediment downstream. During low-water periods, particularly after a period of flood flow, the flow is slowed and sediment is more likely to settle to the bottom, which results in filling of the channel. Under some circumstances, alluvium may accumulate on the streambed to such an extent that the bed's elevation is raised in a process called **aggradation** (Figure 16-33).

Fluvial deposits may include all sizes of rock debris, but smaller particles constitute by far the bulk of the total primarily because most soil and surface sediment are either silt or clay. In addition, all particles get smaller as they are transported downstream because the constant battering and buffeting eventually reduces

boulders, cobbles, and pebbles to sand, silt, and clay. Moreover, all rock fragments are chemically weathered as they are transported in the water and temporarily stored in stream deposits.

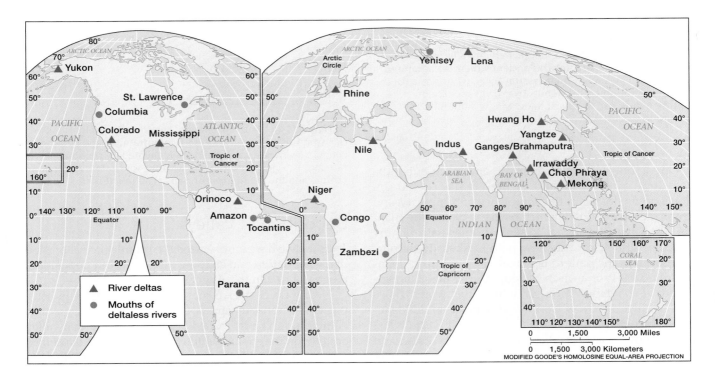

▲ **Figure 16-31**   Locations of the world's largest deltas and of the mouths of the largest deltaless rivers.

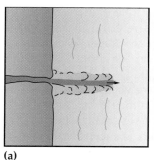
(a)

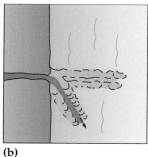
(b)

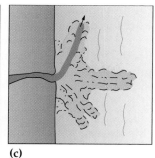
(c)

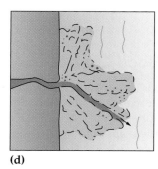
(d)

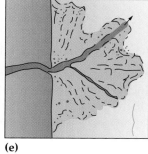
(e)

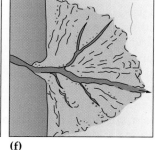
(f)

◀ **Figure 16-32** Hypothetical sequence showing the formation of a simple delta.

Floodplains

1. Meandering Streams
2. Floods and Natural Levee Formation

Special attention needs to be given to an important assemblage of fluvial landforms. The most prominent depositional landscape is the **floodplain**—a low-lying, nearly flat alluvial valley floor that is periodically inundated with flood waters. Floodplains are frequently formed where a meandering stream flows across a wide, nearly level valley floor.

Floodplain Landforms

The frequent shifting of stream meanders produces an increasingly broader, flattish valley floor largely or completely covered with deposits of alluvium. At any given time, a stream is likely to occupy only a small portion of the flatland, although during periods of flood flow, the entire floor may be flooded. For this reason, the valley bottom is properly termed a floodplain. The outer edges of the floodplain are usually bounded by a slope, marking the outer limit of lateral erosion and undercutting where the flat terrain abruptly changes to a line of **bluffs**. Valley widening and floodplain development can extend for great distances; the

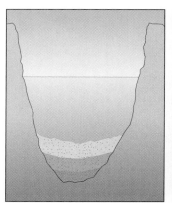
(a) Normal flow-slight filling

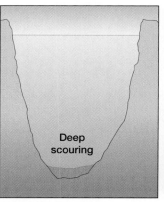
Deep scouring

(b) Flood flow-deep scouring

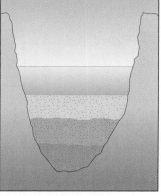
(c) Receding water after flood-filling

◀ **Figure 16-33** Changing channel depth and shape during a flood: **(a)** Normal flow with slight filling. **(b)** Flood flow significantly deepens the channel by scouring. **(c)** As the flood recedes, considerable filling raises the channel bed again.

floodplains of many of the world's largest rivers are so broad that a person standing on the bluffs at one side cannot see the bluffs on the other.

The most conspicuous feature of a floodplain is often the meandering channel of its river (Figure 16-34). A meandering river swings back and forth in ever expanding loops. Eventually, when the radius of a loop reaches about 2.5 times the stream's width, the loop stops growing. Often a loop is short-circuited as the stream cuts a new channel across its neck and starts meandering again, leaving the old meander loop as a **cutoff meander**. The cutoff portion of the channel may remain for a period of time as an **oxbow lake**, so named because its rounded shape resembles the bow part of yokes used on teams of oxen. Oxbow lakes gradually fill with sediment and vegetation to become oxbow swamps and eventually retain their identity only as **meander scars** (Figure 16-35).

A floodplain is slightly higher along the banks of the stream channel. As the stream overflows at floodtime, the current, as it leaves the normal channel, is abruptly slowed by friction with the floodplain surface. This slowdown causes the principal deposition to take place along the margins of the main channel, producing **natural levees** (from the Old French word *levée*, "act of raising," derived from the Latin *levare*, "to raise") on each side of the stream (Figure 16-36). The natural levees merge outwardly and almost imperceptibly with the less well-drained and lower portions of the floodplain, generally referred to as *backswamps* (Figure 16-37).

Sometimes a tributary stream entering a floodplain that has prominent natural levees cannot flow directly into the main channel and so flows down-valley in the backswamp zone, running parallel to the main stream for some distance before finding an entrance. A tributary stream with such a pattern is referred to as a **yazoo stream**, after Mississippi's Yazoo River, which flows parallel to the Mississippi River for about 280 kilometers (175 miles) before joining it.

Although the landforms we've just described are most prominently displayed on the floodplains of large streams, nearly identical processes and landforms may also be found where a stream is meandering over a nearly flat surface and down a gentle slope. Thus, examples of cutoff meanders and oxbow lakes might well be seen on the valley floor of a small creek meandering across a flat alpine meadow.

Modifying Rivers for Flood Control

There are obvious attributes—flat land, abundant water, productive soils—that attract humans to valley bottoms, and therefore such areas are often places of intensive agriculture, transportation routes, and urban development. However, fluvial processes are always ongoing in valley bottoms, with the result that nature and humans coexist in an uneasy juxtaposition shrouded by the specter of flood. We have seen that every river is subject to at least occasional flooding, and thus the existence of a floodplain, so very attractive for human settlement, is incontrovertible evidence that floods do occur from time to time.

Accordingly, wherever humans have settled in considerable concentrations in river valleys, they have gone to extraordinary lengths to mitigate potential flood damage. The principal means for averting disaster are

▲ **Figure 16-34** The floodplain of the Bear River near Brigham City, Utah. As with all other floodplains, the meandering river channel is the most conspicuous feature. In this case, snow cover highlights the pattern. *(Tom L. McKnight photo.)*

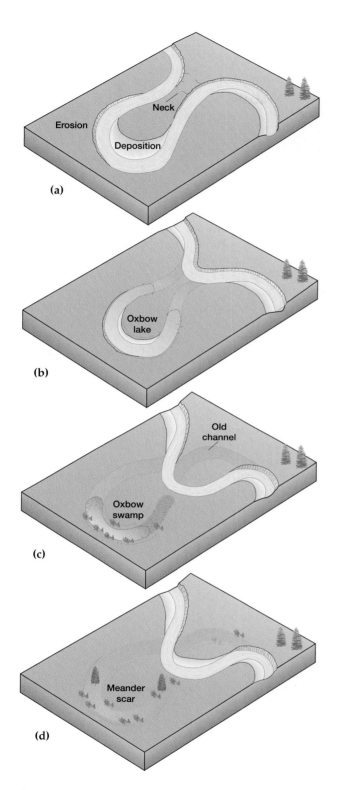

(a)

Erosion   Neck

Deposition

(b)

Oxbow
lake

(c)

Old
channel

Oxbow
swamp

(d)

Meander
scar

▲ **Figure 16-35** The formation of a cutoff meander on a floodplain. As the river cuts across the narrow neck of a meander, the river bend becomes an oxbow lake, which becomes an oxbow swamp, which becomes a meander scar.

sizable earthwork or concrete water-containment and diversion structures in the form of *dams, artificial levees,* and *overflow floodways.* As an example of the remarkable

efforts that go into such endeavors, we might consider the major river system of North America: the Mississippi.

Flood Control on the Mississippi River The Mississippi originates in Minnesota and flows more or less directly southward to the Gulf of Mexico below New Orleans (Figure 16-38, p.506). It is joined by a number of right-bank tributaries along the way, of which the Missouri is by far the most important. There are also many left-bank tributaries, of which the Ohio, with its tributary the Tennessee, is the most notable. (Tributary streams are designated as "right bank" or "left bank" from the perspective of an observer looking downstream.)

All four of these rivers have been thoroughly dammed, largely for flood control but also for such other benefits as hydroelectricity production, navigation stabilization, and recreation. On the Mississippi, there are 27 low dams between St. Louis and the head of navigation at Minneapolis, most equipped with hydroelectricity facilities and each with locks to allow barges and other shallow-draft boats to pass. The Missouri has fewer but larger dams, six in all, widely scattered from Montana to Nebraska. They are primarily flood-control dams. The Ohio is punctuated by more than three dozen low dams, whose primary purpose is maintenance of pools deep enough for barge navigation, with flood control as a secondary consideration. Most thoroughly dammed is the Tennessee, whose nine mainstream dams have reduced it to a series of quiet reservoirs for its entire length, apart from the upper headwaters. These are Tennessee Valley Authority (TVA) dams built during the 1930s particularly for flood control but with various subsidiary benefits.

These four river valleys contain an extensive series of artificial levees designed to protect the local floodplain and move floodwaters downstream. There is a vicious-circle aspect to levee building: anytime a levee is raised in an upstream area most downstream locales require higher levees to pass the floodwaters on without overflow. These levees are usually the highest parts of the landscape, particularly in the ever-flatter and more extensive floodplains downstream. In addition, while the system of artificial levees may work to contain flooding in most years, if the levees should fail, the results can be catastrophic for the population living on the adjacent floodplain. (Many experienced hydrologists and geologists say, somewhat cynically, that there are only two kinds of flood control levees: "those that have failed, and those that will fail.")

At the lower end of the Mississippi system, in southern Louisiana, river control is extremely complicated and the results of human efforts are ambiguous. This region, which receives the full flow of the continent's mightiest river system, is exceedingly flat and thus has poor natural drainage. During the past 2000 years, the lower course of the river has shifted several times, producing at least seven subdeltas that are the principal

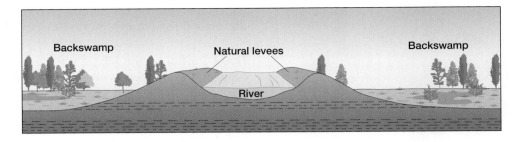

▲ **Figure 16-36** Cross section of a stream channel bordered by natural levees.

elements of the present complicated **bird's-foot delta** of the Mississippi—a series of narrow, sediment-lined distributary channels. The main flow of the river during the past 600 years or so has been along its present course, southeast from New Orleans. This portion of the delta was built out into the Gulf of Mexico at a rate of more than 10 kilometers (6 miles) per century in that period.

Under the normal pattern of deltaic fluctuations, the main flow of the river would now be shifting to the shorter and slightly steeper channel of the Atchafalaya River, a prominent distributary of the ancestral delta a few kilometers west of the present main channel of the Mississippi. However, an enormous flood-control structure was erected above Baton Rouge in an effort (thus far successful) to prevent the river from abandoning its present channel and delta.

Another major disruption of the natural fluvial pattern has produced particularly serious effects on the lower delta. The Herculean artificial-drainage and river-channeling efforts to provide a dry surface for human settlement in southeastern Louisiana have restricted the Mississippi and its distributaries to relatively narrow channels, thus keeping both silt and fresh water from getting to the extensive surrounding marshlands. In addition, a maze of canals dredged to drain potential farmland and provide for increased boat traffic accelerates erosion and allows salt water to encroach. The result is a continuing diminution of land at a rate that is unprecedented on the North American coastline. The delta is both washing away and sinking. The amount of marsh continues to decrease, as Figure 16-39 shows, and the amount of open water in the delta continues to expand. Over the last four decades, the land loss has averaged about 100 square kilometers (40 square miles) annually. The freshwater and brackish ecosystems suffer, and some of the higher land containing human settlements is sinking.

The eternal battle between humans and rivers continues. Can people live on a floodplain without being flooded? Immense efforts are necessary to "control" rivers and mitigate flood damage. In every case the economic costs are exorbitant, and the ecological costs are sometimes equally high.

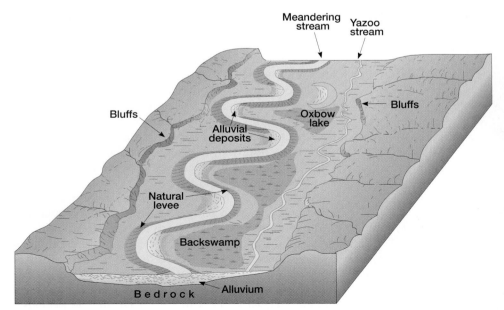

◀ **Figure 16-37** Typical landforms in a floodplain.

PEOPLE AND THE ENVIRONMENT The Bird's-foot of the Mississippi

Since the end of the last ice age, the "bird's-foot" delta of the Mississippi River has changed its form many times and occupied different locations along a 320 kilometer (200 mile) stretch of the gulf coastline. It has been in its current position for about the last 600 years.

The size, shape, and configuration of the delta are the outcome of a number of different processes. The Mississippi River supplies sediment to the delta, deposited when the velocity of the river decreases as it flows into the Gulf of Mexico (Figure 16-C). At the same time, however, the delta slowly subsides into the gulf. Before dams and other kinds of human manipulation of the Mississippi-Missouri River system began decreasing the sediment load of the river, the delta was growing faster than it was sinking. Today the delta is sinking faster than sediments can replenish it (see Figure 16-39).

The slight increase in sea level that has occurred over the last century has also led to increased erosion of the delta. As saltwater moves farther into the formerly freshwater marshes of the delta, the marsh vegetation dies, leaving the delta more susceptible to erosion. Over the last few decades, lengthening of the navigation channels has also changed the pattern of the "toes" of the delta somewhat.

Before the shipping channels were as extensively lined with artificial levees as they are today, floodwaters would regularly deposit sediment into the marshes of the delta. With time, the sediment compacted around the roots of the marsh plants—the delta would subside, but a continuing supply of sediment would replenish the marshes (Figure 16-D). Once the artificial levees cut off much of the sediment supply to the marshes just outside

▲ **Figure 16-C** Landsat image of the Mississippi River Delta in 2003. *(USGS.)*

the shipping channels, the marsh vegetation became discontinuous and much more susceptible to damage from storms. Once damaged from storms—as happened in many areas of the delta as a result of Hurricane Katrina in 2005—the marshlands degrade even more.

Scientists and policy makers have been struggling for years to come up with a practical way to restore the wetlands of the delta, but no approach can be agreed upon by all. One promising strategy involves controlled diversions of water into the marshes, but it's too early to tell if that will be enough

to restore some of the marshlands—or even stop the ongoing decline.

▲ **Figure 16-D** Freshwater marsh near Mississippi River delta, Louisiana. *(D. Donne Bryant.)*

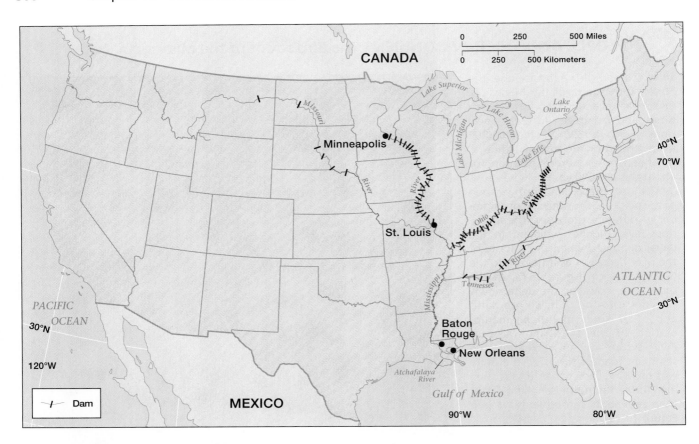

▲ **Figure 16-38** Dams on the Mississippi, Missouri, Ohio, and Tennessee rivers.

Stream Rejuvenation

Stream Rejuvenation

All parts of the continental surfaces experience episodes, sometimes frequent and sometimes rare, when their elevation relative to sea-level changes. This change is occasionally caused by a drop in sea level (as occurred throughout the world during the various ice ages when frozen water accumulated on the land, diminishing the amount of water in the oceans), but it is much more commonly the result of tectonic uplift of the land surface. When such uplift occurs, it "rejuvenates" the streams in the area. The increased gradient causes the streams to flow faster, which provides renewed energy for downcutting (a dramatic, sustained increase in discharge may also rejuvenate a stream). Vertical

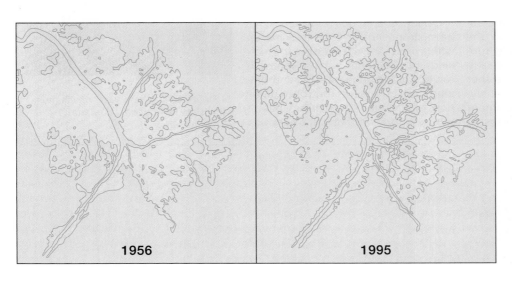

◄ **Figure 16-39** Land loss in the lower Mississippi delta. Much of the marshland shown in the left map (1956) had sunk or been washed away by the intruding ocean by 1995.

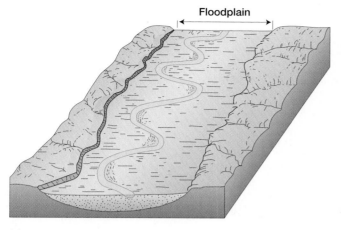

(a) Before uplift

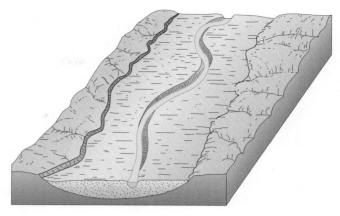

(b) Uplift

Floodplain

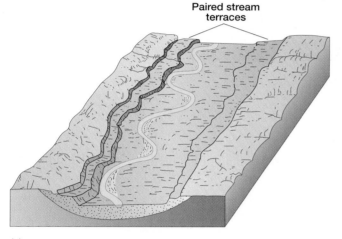

Paired stream
terraces

(c) After uplift

▲ **Figure 16-40** Stream terraces normally represent sequences of uplift and rejuvenation. **(a)** Before uplift a river meanders across an alluvial floodplain. **(b)** During period of uplift, the stream begins to downcut into its original floodplain. **(c)** After uplift the river again widens out a floodplain, leaving remnants of the original valley floor as a pair of stream terraces.

incision, which may have long been dormant, is initiated or intensified by **stream rejuvenation**.

Stream Terraces If a stream occupied a broad floodplain prior to rejuvenation, rejuvenation cuts a steep-walled gorge (Figure 16-40). This means that the floodplain can no longer function as an overflow area and instead becomes an abandoned stretch of flat land overlooking the new gorge. This remnant of the previous valley floor is called a **stream terrace**. Terraces often, but not always, occur in pairs, one on either side of the newly incised stream channel.

Entrenched Meanders Under certain circumstances, rejuvenative uplift has a different and even more conspicuous topographic effect: **entrenched meanders** (Figure 16-41). These topographic features are formed when an area containing a meandering stream is uplifted slowly and the stream incises downward while still retaining the meandering course. In some cases, such meanders may become entrenched in narrow gorges hundreds of meters deep.

Theories of Landform Development

Slope is the basic element of landforms. In the final analysis, all topographic study is the study of how slopes change through time. In the long run, slopes are ever changing, and our understanding of topography is predicated largely on how well we can comprehend the nature, extent, and causes of these changes.

The various internal and external processes operating on Earth's surface produce an infinite variety of landscapes. Systematizing this vast array of facts and relationships into a coherent body of knowledge has been the goal of many students of geomorphology. If principles can be recognized, theories and models can be formulated. The theories and models can then be tested, and out of this procedure we can hope to gain a broader understanding of the features of the terrain and of the processes that produced them. Many scholars have contributed to this organizational task, and several comprehensive theories of terrain evolution have been devised, three of which we discuss here.

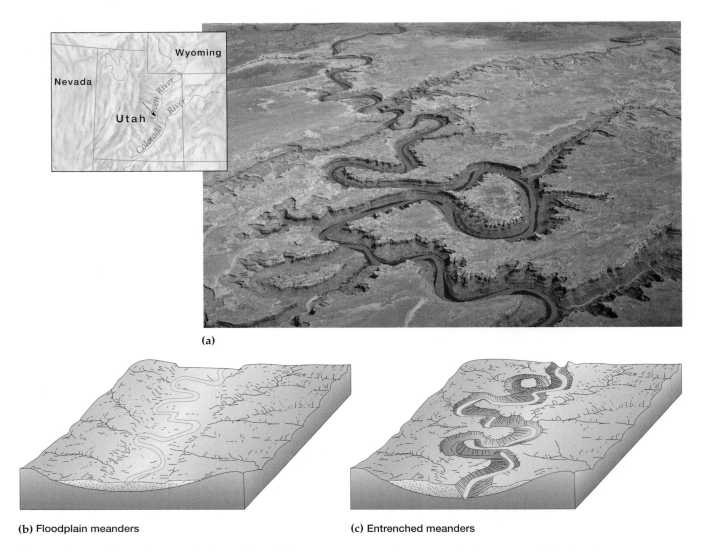

(a)

(b) Floodplain meanders

(c) Entrenched meanders

▲ **Figure 16-41** **(a)** Deeply entrenched meanders of the Green River in southeastern Utah. *(Tom L. McKnight photo)* **(b)** Floodplain meanders sometimes become rejuvenated by uplift. **(c)** If the stream maintains its meandering pattern during uplift, renewed downcutting can produce entrenched meanders.

Davis' Geomorphic Cycle

The first, and in many ways most influential, model of landscape development was propounded by William Morris Davis, an American geographer/geomorphologist active in the 1890s and early 1900s. He called it the *geographical cycle*, but many of his students considered the adjective too generalized, and so the theory came to be known as the *cycle of erosion*. This term in turn was considered too restrictive because weathering and deposition are also involved, and so the Davisian theory is now usually referred to as the *geomorphic cycle.*

Davis envisioned a continuous sequence of terrain evolution in which a relatively flat surface is uplifted, then incised by fluvial erosion into a landscape of slopes and valleys, and finally denuded until it is once again a flat surface at low elevation (Figure 16-42). He metaphorically likened this sequence to the life cycle of

an organism, recognizing stages of development he called youth, maturity, and old age.

Davis stressed that any landscape can be comprehended by analyzing structure, process, and stage. Structure refers to the type and arrangement of the underlying rocks and surface materials, process is concerned with the internal and external forces that shape the landforms, and stage is the length of time during which the processes have been at work.

Davis postulated that the initial surface is uplifted relatively rapidly, so that erosion has little time to act until the uplift is complete. Thus, the initial surface consists of relatively flat land far above sea level. He further assumed no significant subsequent crustal movement or deformation for the duration of the cycle as well as a stable base level during all stages.

Youth During the youthful stage of development, streams become established and a drainage pattern

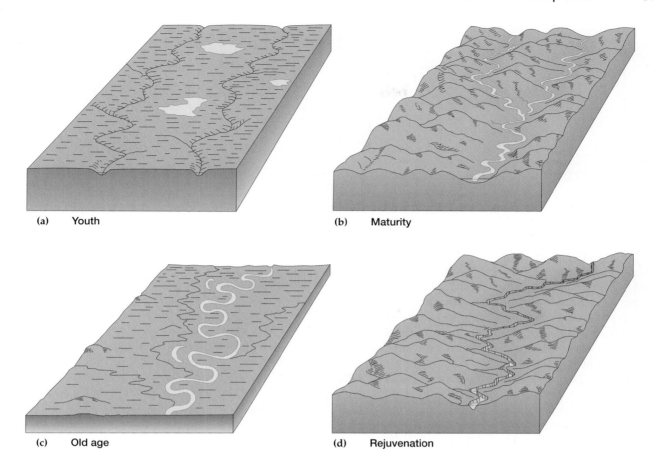

(a)   Youth

(b)   Maturity

(c)   Old age

(d)   Rejuvenation

▲ **Figure 16-42**   The Davisian geomorphic cycle.

begins to take shape. These streams, which incise deep, narrow, steep-sided, V-shaped valleys, flow rapidly and have irregular gradients marked by waterfalls and rapids. During this stage, most of the initial surface is broad, flattish interfluves, largely unaffected by stream erosion and encompassing shallow lakes and swamps because of the incomplete drainage system.

Maturity   In the mature stage, the main streams approach an equilibrium condition, having worn away the falls and rapids and developed smooth profiles. Vertical erosion ceases in the main valleys, the streams begin to meander, floodplains are formed, and the drainage system is more extensive than in the youth stage. The interfluves are thoroughly dissected during this stage, their lakes and swamps drained by headward erosion, and their remnants existing only as narrow drainage divides between valleys. Whereas youth is characterized by the presence of a vast area of initial surface, maturity is marked by the absence of initial surface.

Old Age   With the passage of a vast amount of time, erosion reduces the entire landscape to near base level. Sloping land is virtually absent, and the entire region is dominated by extensive floodplains over which a

few major streams meander broadly and slowly. The end product of the geomorphic cycle is a flat, featureless landscape with minimal relief. Davis called this a *peneplain* (*paene* is Latin for "almost"; hence, "almost a plain"). He envisioned occasional remnants of exceptionally resistant rock rising slightly above the peneplain surface; such erosional remnants are dubbed *monadnocks* after a mountain of this name in New Hampshire.

Rejuvenation   Because Davis recognized that the extraordinarily long time without crustal deformation required by his model is unlikely, his theory also covered rejuvenation, whereby regional uplift could raise the land and interrupt the cycle at any stage. This tectonic activity would reenergize the system, initiate a new period of downcutting, and restart the cycle.

Penck's Theory of Crustal Change and Slope Development

The second theory of terrain evolution we consider grew out of critical analysis of Davis' geomorphic cycle. Davis was both a prolific writer and a persuasive teacher, and his theory had a profound influence for many decades, especially in the United States.

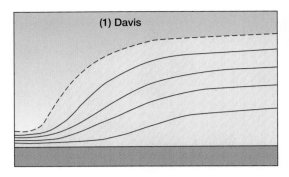
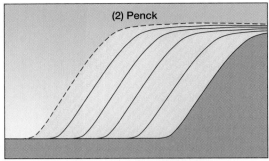

▲ **Figure 16-43**   Slope retreat in **(a)** the Davis model and **(b)** the Penck model. The Davis concept proposes a continually diminishing angle of slope, whereas Penck theorized parallel retreat in which the slope angle remains approximately the same over time.

Even in the early days, however, there were strong dissenters. Other geomorphologists recognized imperfections in some of his assumptions and questioned some of his conclusions. For example, apparently no intact peneplains exist; remnants of peneplain surfaces are recognized in some areas, but nowhere does an actual peneplain occur. A more important difficulty with Davis's model concerns his idea that little erosion takes place while the initial surface is being uplifted, a notion unacceptable to most geomorphologists. Moreover, the causal interplay between uplift and erosion is open to varying interpretations. Finally, there are serious doubts about sequential development, and some people feel that the biological analogy may be more misleading than helpful.

The sequential aspect of the geomorphic cycle is very appealing because it provides an orderly, evolutionary, and predictable train of development. Moreover, many areas in nature have the appearance of youthful, mature, or old-age topography. However, no proof has ever been found that one stage commonly precedes another in regular fashion, and even in a single valley the terrain characteristic of the various stages is often jumbled. For landform analysis, therefore, it is probably better to use the terms youth, maturity, and old age as descriptive summaries of regional topography rather than as distinct implications of sequential development.

In the Davisian cycle, drainage divides waste away in a steady and predictable pattern. As a slope retreats, it becomes less steep and more rounded, always maintaining a convex form. In nature, however, not all slopes are convex; some are straight and others are concave. Walther Penck, a young German geomorphologist and a prominent early critic of Davis, pointed out in the 1920s that slopes assume various shapes as they erode. Penck stressed that uplift stimulates erosion immediately and that slope form is significantly influenced by the rate of uplift or other crustal deformation. He argued

that steep slopes, particularly, maintain a constant angle as they erode, retaining their steepness as they diminish in a sort of "parallel retreat" rather than being worn down at a continually lower slope angle. He viewed eroding slopes as retreating rather than being reduced overall, which means that some initial surface is retained long after it would have been worn away in the Davisian concept (Figure 16-43). Many, but not all, of Penck's ideas have been substantiated by subsequent workers, and his ideas have come to be called the *theory of crustal change and slope development*.

Equilibrium Theory

The third model of landform development is called *equilibrium theory*. In the last four decades or so, many geomorphologists have been studying the mechanics of landform development. This approach emphasizes the delicate balance between form and process in the landscape. It is believed that the influence of crustal movement and the resistance of the underlying rock vary significantly from place to place and that these variations are as significant as differences in process in determining terrain. Thus, equilibrium theory suggests that slope forms are adjusted to geomorphic processes so that there is a balance of energy—the energy provided is just adequate for the work to be done. For example, harder rock develops steeper slopes and higher relief, and softer rock has gentler slopes and lower relief. The uniformity inherent in both the Davis and Penck theories is thus called into question.

A prime example of the application of equilibrium theory can be seen in any hilly area where the land is being simultaneously uplifted tectonically and eroded fluvially, as is happening in the Alps and the Himalayas today (Figure 16-44). If the slopes are in equilibrium, they are being wasted away at the same rate as they are being regenerated by uplift. Thus, the rocks are

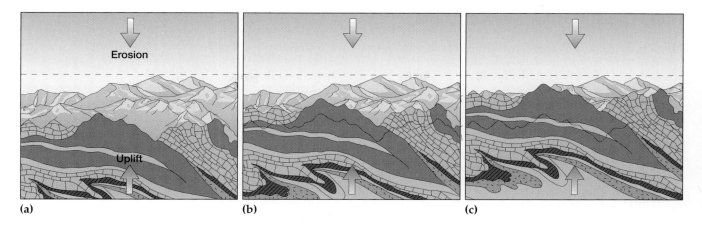

(a)   (b)   (c)

▲ **Figure 16-44** The dynamic equilibrium concept. This vertical cross section through an area of the Swiss Alps shows that erosion reduces relief just about as rapidly as uplift raises the land, with the result that the elevation of the mountains remains essentially constant over time. The surface rocks are continually changing through uplift and erosion, but the shape of the surface remains approximately the same because removal and replacement are in balance.

being changed through erosion from above and uplift from below, but the form of the surface remains the same; the landscape is in dynamic equilibrium. A change in either the rate of erosion or the rate of uplift forces the landscape through a period of adjustment until the slopes again reach a gradient at which the rate of erosion equals the rate of uplift.

Equilibrium theory has serious shortcomings in areas that are tectonically stable or have limited streamflow (deserts, for example). It does, however, focus more precisely than our other two models on the relationship between geomorphic processes and surface forms and for this reason has dominated fluvial geomorphology since the 1960s.

Chapter 16 Learning Review

Key Terms

Before answering the study questions, review the definitions of the following key terms (page references are provided for you):

aggradation *(p. 500)*
alluvium *(p. 485)*
annular drainage pattern *(p. 491)*
antecedent stream *(p. 490)*
base level *(p. 493)*
bedload *(p. 485)*
bird's-foot delta *(p. 504)*
bluffs *(p. 501)*
braided stream (braided channel pattern) *(p. 489)*
capacity (of a stream) *(p. 485)*
centripetal drainage pattern *(p. 491)*
competence *(p. 485)*
consequent stream *(p. 490)*
cutoff meander *(p. 502)*
delta *(p. 498)*
dendritic drainage pattern *(p. 491)*
discharge *(p. 486)*
dissolved load *(p. 485)*

downcutting *(p. 493)*
drainage basin *(p. 482)*
drainage divide *(p. 482)*
elbow of capture *(p. 497)*
entrenched meanders *(p. 507)*
ephemeral stream *(p. 486)*
floodplain *(p. 501)*
fluvial processes *(p. 481)*
headward erosion *(p. 496)*
interfluve *(p. 482)*
intermittent stream *(p. 486)*
knickpoint *(p. 494)*
knickpoint migration *(p. 494)*
lateral erosion *(p. 496)*
meandering channel pattern *(p. 488)*
meander scar *(p. 502)*
natural levee *(p. 502)*
overland flow *(p. 481)*
oxbow lake *(p. 502)*

perennial stream *(p. 486)*
radial drainage pattern *(p. 491)*
sinuous channel pattern *(p. 488)*
straight channel pattern *(p. 488)*
stream capture (stream piracy) *(p. 497)*
streamflow *(p. 481)*
stream load *(p. 485)*
stream order *(p. 482)*
stream rejuvenation *(p. 507)*
stream terraces *(p. 507)*
subsequent stream *(p. 490)*
superimposed drainage system *(p. 490)*
suspended load *(p. 485)*
trellis drainage pattern *(p. 491)*
valley *(p. 481)*
watershed *(p. 482)*
yazoo stream *(p. 502)*

Study Questions for Key Concepts

After studying this chapter, you should be able to answer the following questions:

Streams and Stream Systems (p. 481)
1. What is the difference between *streamflow* and *overland flow*?
2. What are the differences between an *interfluve* and a *valley*?
3. What is a *drainage basin*? A *drainage divide*?
4. What factors influence the erosional effectiveness of a stream?
5. What are the abrasive tools used by a stream in its erosive activities?
6. What are the components of a stream's *load*?
7. What is the difference between stream *capacity* and *competence*?
8. What factor determines the competence of a stream?
9. How does a stream sort alluvial material by size?
10. Why are deposits of alluvium often rounded and stratified?
11. Explain how *talus* (from rockfall; Chapter 15) is likely to look different from a deposit of *alluvium*.
12. Why are floods so important in the development of fluvial landforms?

Stream Channels (p. 486)
13. Under what circumstances is a stream likely to have a *meandering channel pattern*?
14. Under what circumstances is a stream likely to have a *braided channel pattern*?

Structural Relationships (p. 489)
15. What is an *antecedent stream* and how might one form?
16. Describe and explain the circumstances under which *dendritic stream drainage* patterns develop, and the conditions under which *trellis stream drainage* patterns develop.
17. Describe *radial stream drainage* patterns and one kind of location where such a drainage pattern might be found.

The Shaping and Reshaping of Valleys (p. 492)
18. Explain the process of valley deepening through *downcutting*.
19. What is meant by *base level*?
20. What prevents a stream from downcutting to sea level throughout its entire course?
21. Why would few depositional features be found in most V-shaped stream valleys?
22. Describe and explain the process of *knickpoint migration*.
23. Explain how a meandering stream widens its valley through the process of *lateral erosion*.
24. Describe and explain the process of *headward erosion*.
25. Explain the process of *stream capture* (stream piracy).
26. Describe the formation of a *delta*.
27. Why don't all large rivers form deltas where they enter the ocean?

Floodplains (p. 501)

28. What are *natural levees* and how do they form?
29. Why might meandering rivers make poor political boundaries?
30. Describe and explain the formation process and consequences of a *cutoff meander*.
31. What explains the presence of a *yazoo stream* on a floodplain?

Stream Rejuvenation (p. 506)

32. Describe and explain the formation of *stream terraces*.

33. How is it possible for stream meanders to become deeply entrenched?

Theories of Landform Development (p. 507)

34. Describe and explain at least one problem with Davis' *geomorphic cycle* model of fluvial landform development.
35. How does *equilibrium theory* differ from earlier theories of topographic development?

Additional Resources

Books:

Barry, John M. *Rising Tide: The Great Mississippi Flood of 1927 and How It Changed America.* New York: Simon & Schuster, 1997.

McPhee, John, "Atchafalaya." *The Control of Nature.* New York: Farrar, Straus and Giroux, 1989.

Smith, Gary A., and Aurora Pun. *How Does Earth Work?: Physical Geology and the Process of Science.* Upper Saddle River, NJ: Pearson Prentice Hall, 2006.

Internet Sites:

The National Map

http://www.nationalmap.usgs.gov/

The National Map is an interactive map service that provides access to a wide range of geospatial data.

Water Resources of the United States

http://water.usgs.gov/

This site has links to data and information about water quality, acid rain, and stream flow.

U.S. Geological Survey

http://www.usgs.gov/

The U.S. Geological Survey home page provides links to information on a wide range of Earth science topics, including earthquakes, volcanoes, landslides, floods, and other natural hazards. The page also has links to sites where topographic maps, geological maps, research papers, and publications of general interest may be viewed or purchased.

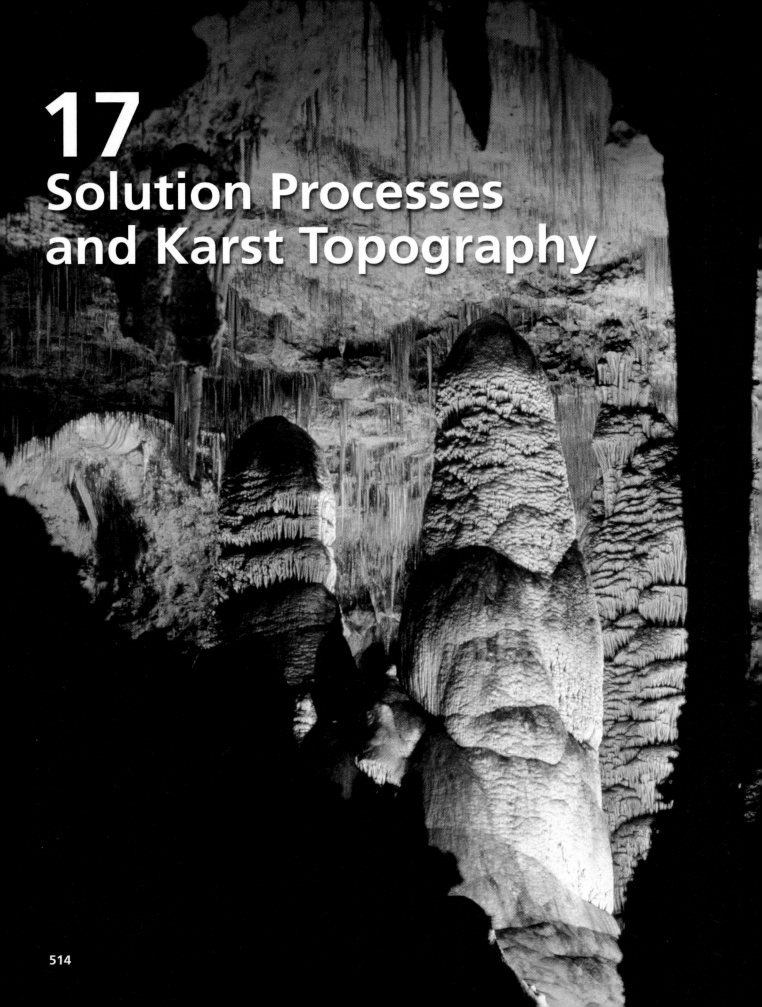

17
Solution Processes and Karst Topography

In studying topographic development, we pay a great deal of attention to the role of water. We noted that water running across the ground is the most significant external shaper of terrain, and we will see that coastal waters produce distinctive landforms around the margins of oceans and lakes. In both cases, the water moves rapidly, and much energy is expended in erosion, transportation, and deposition.

In this brief chapter, we focus on underground water, which, because it is confined, functions in a much more restricted fashion than surface water. Underground water is largely unchanneled and therefore generally diffused, and it moves very slowly for the most part. Consequently, it is almost totally ineffective in terms of hydraulic power and other kinds of mechanical erosion.

The Impact of Solution Processes on the Landscape

The mechanical effects of underground water have only a limited influence on topographic development. Some subsurface mechanical weathering does take place, but the surface landscape is rarely directly affected by it, although certain forms of mass wasting (such as earthflows and slumps) are facilitated when loose materials are lubricated by underground water.

Through its chemical action, however, underground water is an effective shaper of the topographic landscape. Water is a solvent for certain rock-forming chemicals, dissolving them from rock and then carrying them away in solution and depositing them elsewhere. Under particular circumstances, the aboveground results of this dissolution are widespread and distinctive.

Underground water also affects surface topography via the creation of such hydrothermal features as hot springs and geysers, formed when hot water from underground is discharged at the ground surface.

Solution and Precipitation

The chemical reactions involving underground water are relatively simple. Although pure water is a poor solvent, almost all underground water is laced with enough chemical impurities to make it a good solvent for the compounds that make up a few common minerals (Figure 17-1). Basically, underground water is a

◀ Carlsbad Caverns, New Mexico. *(Getty Images, Inc.—Stone Allstock.)*

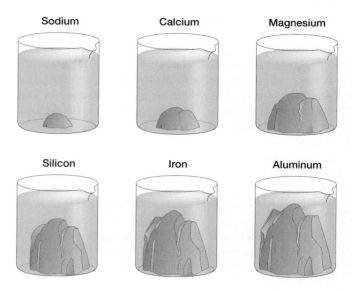

▲ **Figure 17-1** Relative solubility in water of some common rock-forming elements. The darker portion of each diagram indicates the proportion of the element that is insoluble in water. Sodium and calcium can be almost completely dissolved, for instance, whereas iron and aluminum are essentially insoluble.

weak solution of **carbonic acid** (H_2CO_3) because it contains dissolved carbon dioxide gas.

Dissolution Processes **Dissolution** is an important weathering–erosion process for all rocks, but it is particularly effective on carbonate sedimentary rocks, especially limestone. A common sedimentary rock, limestone is composed largely of calcium carbonate, which reacts strongly with carbonic acid solution to yield calcium bicarbonate, a compound that is very soluble in (and thus easily removed by) water. Other limy rocks, such as gypsum and chalk, undergo similar reactions. Dolomite is a calcium magnesium carbonate rock that dissolves almost as quickly as limestone. The pertinent chemical equations (in simplified form) for the dissolving of limestone and dolomite are as follows:

$$CaCO_3 + H_2O + CO_2 \rightarrow Ca(HCO_3)_2$$
calcium carbonate · · · water · · · carbon dioxide · · · calcium bicarbonate

$$CaMg(CO_3)_2 + 2H_2O + 2CO_2 \rightarrow Ca(HCO_3)_2 + Mg(HCO_3)_2$$
dolomite · · · water · · · carbon dioxide · · · calcium bicarbonate · · · magnesium bicarbonate

These reactions are the most notable dissolution processes. Water percolating down into a limy bedrock dissolves and carries away a part of the rock mass. Since limestone and related rocks are largely composed of soluble minerals, great volumes of rock are sometimes dissolved and removed, leaving conspicuous voids in the bedrock. This action occurs more rapidly and on a vaster scale in a humid climate, where abundant precipitation provides plenty of the aqueous medium necessary for dissolution. In arid regions, dissolution action is unusual except for relict features dating from a more humid past.

Although reactions with carbonic acid are the most common processes involved in the dissolution of carbonate rocks, recent studies suggest that in some locations sulfuric acid (H_2SO_4) may also be important. For example, it appears that Lechuguilla Cave in New Mexico was at least in part enlarged through dissolution of limestone by sulfuric acid, formed when hydrogen sulfide (H_2S) from deeper petroleum deposits combined with oxygen in the groundwater.

Role of the Bedrock Structure Bedrock structure is also a factor in dissolution. A profusion of joints and bedding planes permits groundwater to penetrate the rock readily. That the water is moving also helps because, as a given volume of water becomes saturated with dissolved calcium bicarbonate, it can drain away and be replaced by fresh unsaturated water that can dissolve more rock. Such drainage is enhanced by some outlet at a lower level, such as a deep subsurface stream.

Most limestone is resistant to mechanical erosion and often produces rugged topography. Thus, its ready solubility contrasts notably with its mechanical durability—a vulnerable interior beneath a durable surface.

Precipitation Processes Complementing the removal of lime is its precipitation from solution. Mineralized water may trickle in along a cavern roof or wall. The reduced air pressure in the open cavern induces precipitation of whatever minerals the water is carrying.

One other type of precipitation is worth mentioning despite its scarcity, because of its dramatic distinctiveness. Hot springs and geysers nearly always provide an accumulation of precipitated minerals, frequently brilliant white but sometimes orange, green, or some other color due to associated algae. Wherever it comes in contact with magma, underground water becomes heated, and this water sometimes finds its way back to the surface through a natural opening so rapidly that it is still hot when it reaches the open air. Hot water is generally a much better solvent than cold, and so a hot spring or geyser usually contains a significant quantity of dissolved minerals. When exposed to the open air, the hot water precipitates much of its mineral content as its temperature and the pressure on it decrease, as the dissolved gases that helped keep the minerals in solution dissipate, and as algae and other organisms living in it secrete mineral matter. These deposits (such as *travertine*, *tufa*, and *sinter*) contain a variety of calcareous minerals and take the form of mounds, terraces, walls, and peripheral rims.

It should be noted, however, that the solubility of carbon dioxide increases as water temperature declines. Thus, cool water often is more potent than hot water as a solvent for calcium carbonate.

Caverns and Related Features

Some of the most spectacular landforms produced by dissolution are not visible at Earth's surface. Solution along joints and bedding planes in limestone beneath the surface often creates large open areas called **caverns**. The largest of these openings are usually more expansive horizontally than vertically, indicating a development along bedding planes. In many cases, however, the cavern pattern has a rectangularity that demonstrates a relationship to the joint system (Figure 17-2).

Caverns are found anywhere there is a massive limestone deposit at or near the surface. The state of Missouri, for example, has more than 6000. Caverns often are difficult to find because their connection to the surface may be extremely small and obscure. Beneath the surface, however, some caverns are very extensive, with an elaborate system of galleries and passageways, usually very irregular in shape and sometimes including massive openings ("rooms") scattered here and there along the galleries. A stream may flow along the

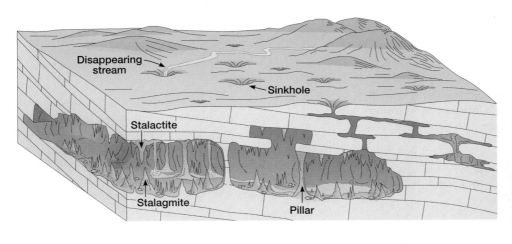

◄ **Figure 17-2** Caverns are formed by solution action of underground water as it trickles along bedding planes and joint systems.

▲ **Figure 17-3**   A multitude of stalactites hang from the ceiling of this room in New Mexico's Carlsbad Caverns. Some of them have joined with stalagmites to form pillars. *(David Muench Photography, Inc.)*

floor of a large cavern, adding another dimension to erosion/deposition.

There are two principal stages in cavern formation. First there is the initial excavation, wherein percolating water dissolves the limy bedrock and leaves voids. This dissolution is followed by a "decoration stage" in which ceilings, walls, and floors are decorated with a wondrous variety of **speleothems** (Figure 17-3). These forms are deposited when water leaves behind the compounds (principally carbon dioxide and calcite) it was carrying in solution. Once out of solution, the carbon dioxide gas diffuses into the cave atmosphere, and calcite is deposited. Much of the deposition occurs on the sides of the cavern, but the most striking features are formed on the roof and floor. Where water drips

from the roof, a pendant structure grows slowly downward like an icicle—a **stalactite**. Where the drip hits the floor, a companion feature, a **stalagmite**, grows upward. Stalactites and stalagmites may extend until they meet to form a *pillar* (Figure 17-4).

Karst Topography

In many areas where the bedrock is limestone or similarly soluble rock, dissolution has been so widespread and effective that a distinctive landform assemblage has developed at the surface, in addition to whatever caves may exist underground. The term **karst** (a Germanized form of an ancient Slavic word) is applied to this topography. The name derives from the Karst (meaning "barren land") region of the former Yugoslavia, a rugged hilly area that has been shaped almost entirely by solution action in limestone formations (Figure 17-5).

The term karst connotes both a set of processes and an assemblage of landforms. The word is used as the catchall name of a cornerstone concept that describes the special landforms that develop on exceptionally soluble rocks, although there is a broad international vocabulary to refer to specific features in specific regions.

Typical landforms in karst regions include sinkholes, disrupted surface drainage, and underground drainage networks that have openings formed from solution action. The openings range in size from enlarged cracks to huge caverns.

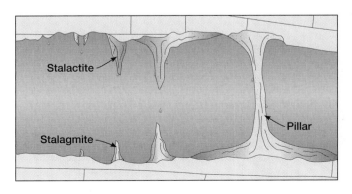

▲ **Figure 17-4**   The development of stalagmites, stalactites, and pillars.

▲ **Figure 17-5**   Irregular topography is prominent in the namesake karst region of the former Yugoslavia. *(Alex S. MacLean/Peter Arnold, Inc.)*

Karst landscapes usually evolve where there is massive limestone bedrock. However, karstic features may also occur where other highly soluble rocks—dolomite, gypsum, or halite—predominate. Karst landforms are worthy of study not only because of their dramatic appearance but also because of their abundance. It is estimated that about 10 percent of Earth's land area has soluble carbonate rocks at or near the surface; in the conterminous United States, this total rises to 15 percent (Figure 17–6).

The most common surface features of karst landscapes are **sinkholes** (also called *dolines*), which occur by the hundreds and sometimes by the thousands. Sinkholes are rounded depressions formed by the dissolution of surface carbonate rocks, typically (but by no means always) at joint intersections. The sinkholes

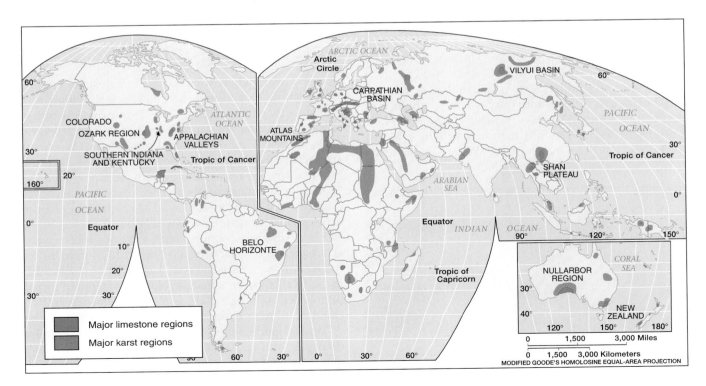

▲ **Figure 17-6**   Major limestone and karst regions of the world.

erode more rapidly than the surrounding area, forming closed depressions. Their sides generally slope inward at the angle of repose (usually 20° to 30°) of the adjacent material, although some have more gentle side slopes. A sinkhole that results from the collapse of the roof of a subsurface cavern is called a **collapse doline**; these may have vertical walls or even overhanging cliffs (Figure 17–7).

Sinkholes range in size from shallow depressions a few meters in diameter and a few centimeters deep to major features kilometers in diameter and hundreds of meters deep. The largest are associated with tropical regions, where they develop rapidly and where adjacent holes often intersect.

The bottom of a sinkhole may lead into a subterranean passage, down which water pours during a rainstorm. More commonly, however, the subsurface entrance is blocked by rock rubble, soil, or vegetation, and rains form temporary lakes until the water percolates away. Indeed, sinkholes are the karst analog of

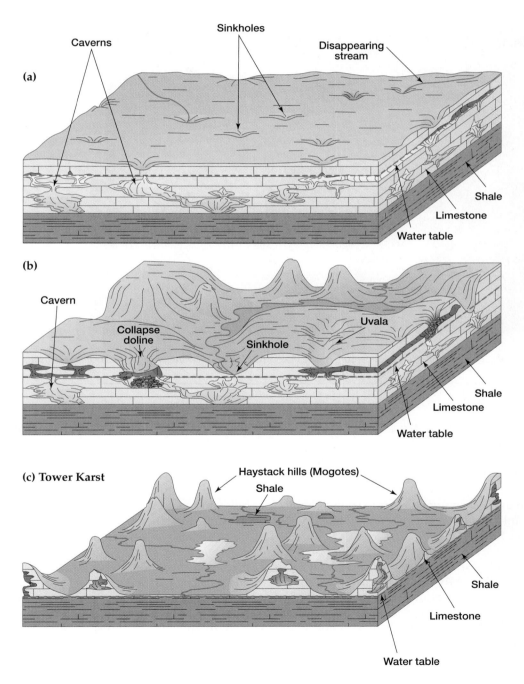

▲ **Figure 17-7** Sequential development of karst topography, from early sinkholes to eventual mogotes.

People and the Environment Sinkholes in Florida

Most of central Florida is underlain by massive limestone bedrock, which is particularly susceptible to the formation of *sinkholes* and *collapse dolines*, and the process is accelerated when the water table drops. Sinkholes have been forming in Florida for a long time, with several thousand of them having appeared in the twentieth century. Indeed, most of central Florida's scenic lakes began as sinkholes.

The frantic population growth that Florida has experienced in recent decades has put a heavy drain on its underground water supply. This depletion was exacerbated by several years of below-normal rainfall in the 1970s, which caused accelerated drawdown of the water table. As a result, the number and size of Florida sinkholes increased at a disturbing pace (Figure 17-A). New sinkholes materialized somewhere in the state at a rate of about one per day during the early 1980s, although the tempo has slowed since then.

▲ **Figure 17-A** The sinkhole that swallowed a house in central Florida. *(St. Petersburg Times/Gamma-Liaison, Inc.)*

river valleys, in that they are the fundamental unit of both erosion and weathering.

Where sinkholes occur in profusion, they often channel surface runoff into the groundwater circulation, leaving networks of dry valleys as relict surface forms. The Serbo-Croatian term **uvala** refers to such a chain of intersecting sinkholes. In many cases, sinkholes evolve into uvala over time.

In many karst locations, depressions dominate the landscape. Sinkholes are commonplace in central Florida and parts of the Midwest, particularly Kentucky, Illinois, and Missouri. For example, at the University of Missouri in Columbia, both the football stadium and the basketball fieldhouse are built in sinkholes, and parking lots around them occasionally sink.

Apart from the ubiquity of sinkholes, karst areas show considerable topographic diversity. Where the relief is slight, as in central Florida, sinkholes are the dominant features. Where the relief is greater, however,

cliffs and steep slopes alternate with flat-floored, streamless valleys. Limestone bedrock exposed at the surface tends to be pitted, grooved, etched, and fluted with a great intricacy of erosive detail.

Residual karst features, in the form of very steep-sided hills, dominate some parts of the world (Figure 17-8). These formations are sometimes referred to as **tower karst** because of their almost vertical sides and conical or hemispheric shapes. Such towers are sometimes riddled with caves. The tower karst of southeastern China and adjacent parts of northern Vietnam is world famous for its spectacular scenery, as are the *mogotes* (haystack hills) of western Cuba.

In many ways, the most notable feature of karst regions is what is missing—surface drainage. Most rainfall and snowmelt seep downward along joints and bedding planes, enlarging them by dissolution. Surface runoff that does become channeled does not usually go far before it disappears into a sinkhole or joint

▲ **Figure 17-8**   Spectacular tower karst hills in Guilin, China. *(© Wolfgang Kaehler.)*

crack—such streams are often termed **disappearing streams**. The water that collects in sinkholes generally percolates downward, but some sinkholes have distinct openings at their bottom, called **swallow holes**, through which surface drainage can pour directly into an underground channel, often to reappear at the surface through another hole some distance away. Where dissolution has been effective for a long time, there may be a complex underground drainage system that has superseded any sort of surface drainage net. An appropriate generalization concerning surface drainage in karst regions is that valleys are relatively scarce and mostly dry.

Hydrothermal Features

In many parts of the world, there are small areas where hot water comes to the surface through natural openings. Such outpouring of hot water, often accompanied by steam, is known as **hydrothermal activity** and usually takes the form of either a hot spring or a geyser.

Hot Springs

The appearance of hot water at Earth's surface usually indicates that the underground water has come in contact with heated rocks or magma and has been forced upward through a fissure by the pressures that develop when water is heated anywhere (Figure 17-9). The usual result at the surface is a **hot spring**, with water bubbling out either continuously or intermittently. The

hot water invariably contains a large amount of dissolved mineral matter, and a considerable proportion of this load is precipitated out as soon as the water reaches

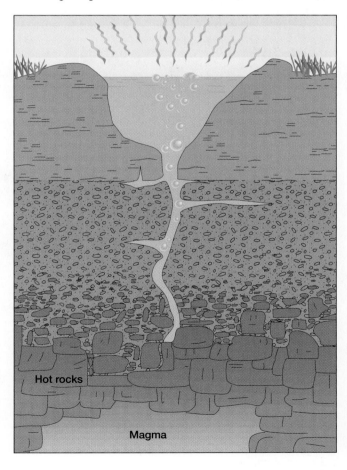

▲ **Figure 17-9**   Cross section through a hot spring.

the surface and its temperature and the pressure on it both decrease.

The deposits around and downslope from hot springs can take many forms. If the opening is on sloping land, terraces are usually formed. Where the springs emerge onto flat land, there may be cones, domes, or irregular concentric deposits. Since lime is so readily soluble in water containing carbonic acid, the deposits of most springs are composed largely of massive (*travertine*) or porous (*tufa* or *sinter*) accumulations of calcium carbonate. Various other minerals are also contained in the deposits on occasion, especially silica, but are much less common than calcium compounds.

Sometimes the water bubbling out of a hot spring builds a continually enlarging mound or terrace. As the structure is built higher, the opening through which the hot water comes to the surface also rises, so that the water is always emerging above the highest point. As the water flows down the sides of the structure, more deposition takes place there, thus broadening the structure as well, often with brilliantly colored algae, which add to the striking appearance as well as contribute mineral secretions to the deposit (Figure 17-10).

Geysers

A special form of intermittent hot spring is the **geyser**. Hot water usually issues from a geyser only sporadically, and most or all of the flow is a temporary ejection (called an *eruption*) in which hot water and steam spout upward. Then the geyser subsides into apparent inactivity until the next eruption.

The basic principle of geyser activity involves the building up of pressure within a restricted subterranean tube until that pressure is relieved by an eruption. The process begins when underground water seeps into subterranean openings that are connected in a series of narrow caverns and shafts. Heated rocks and/or magma are close enough to these storage reservoirs to provide a constant source of heat. As the water accumulates in the reservoirs, it is heated to 200°C (400°F) or higher, which is much above the boiling point at sea level and normal pressure. (Such superheating is possible because of the high underground water pressure.) At these high temperatures, much of the water becomes steam. The accumulation of steam deep in the tube and of boiling water higher in the

▲ **Figure 17-10** The sides and bottoms of hot springs are often brilliantly colored by algal growth. This is Beauty Pool in Yellowstone National Park. The black area at the bottom of the pool is the opening to the fissure that brings hot water to the surface. *(Darrel Hess photo.)*

tube eventually causes a great upward surge that sends water and steam showering out of the geyser vent. This eruption releases the pressure, and when the eruption subsides, underground water again begins to collect in the reservoirs in preparation for a repetition of the process.

A tremendous supply of heat is essential for geyser activity. Recent studies in Yellowstone Park's Upper Geyser Basin indicate that the heat emanating from that basin is at least 800 times greater than the heat flowing from a nongeyser area of the same size. This extraordinary flow of extra heat has been going on for at least 40,000 years.

Some geysers erupt continuously, indicating that they are really hot springs that have a constant supply of water through which steam is escaping. Most geysers are only sporadically active, however, apparently depending on the accumulation of sufficient water to force an eruption. Some eruptions are very brief, whereas others continue for many minutes. The interval between eruptions for most geysers is variable. Most erupt at intervals of a few hours or a few days, but some wait years or even decades between eruptions. The temperature of the erupting water generally is near the boiling point for pure water (100°C or 212°F at sea level). In some geysers, the erupting water column goes up only a few centimeters in the air, whereas in others the column rises to more than 45 meters (150 feet).

Geyser comes from the Icelandic word *geysir* ("to gush" or "to rage"), the Great Geysir in southern Iceland being the namesake origin for this term. The most famous of all geysers is Old Faithful in Yellowstone Park (Figure 17-11). Its reputation is based partly on the force of its eruptions (the column goes more than 30 meters or 100 feet high) but primarily on its regularity. Since first timed by scientists more than a century ago, Old Faithful had maintained an average interval of 65 minutes between eruptions, day and night, winter and summer, year after year. In the early 1980s, however, several consecutive earthquakes on the Yellowstone plateau apparently upset the geyser's internal plumbing. During the 1990s, Old Faithful's average interval between eruptions expanded to 77 minutes, with variations as great as 30 to 120 minutes. Thus, Old Faithful is becoming more erratic, which is to say, more like other geysers.

The deposits resulting from geyser activity are usually much less notable than those associated with hot springs. Some geysers erupt from open pools of hot water, throwing tremendous sheets of water and steam into the air but usually producing relatively minor depositional features. Other geysers are of the "nozzle" type and consequently build up a depositional cone and erupt through a small opening in it (Figure 17-12). Most deposits resulting from geyser activity are simply sheets of precipitated mineral matter spread irregularly over the ground.

▲ **Figure 17-11** Old Faithful geyser in all its eruptive grandeur. *(Tom L. McKnight photo.)*

Fumaroles

A third hydrothermal feature is the **fumarole**, a surface crack directly connected to a deep-seated heat source (Figure 17-13). For some reason, very little water drains into the tube of a fumarole. The water that does drain in is instantly converted to steam by the heat, and a cloud of steam is then expelled from the opening. Thus, a fumarole is marked by steam issuing either continuously or sporadically from a surface vent; in essence, a fumarole is simply a hot spring that lacks water.

Hydrothermal Features in Yellowstone

Hydrothermal features are found in many volcanic areas, being particularly notable in Iceland, New Zealand, Chile, and Siberia's Kamchatka Peninsula. By far the largest concentration, however, occurs in Yellowstone

▲ **Figure 17-12**   Most geysers erupt from vents or hot pools, but some build up prominent depositional "nozzles" through which water is expelled. This is Lone Star Geyser in Yellowstone Park. *(Tom L. McKnight photo.)*

is almost entirely volcanic materials, and although no volcanic cones are in evidence, we know that this is clearly a region of extensive recent volcanism.

The uniqueness of Yellowstone's geologic setting stems from the presence of a large, shallow magma chamber beneath the plateau—believed by most geologists to be a result of a *mantle plume*, or hot spot, rising from the mantle below. Test boreholes reveal an abnormally high thermal gradient, in which the temperature increases with depth at a rate of about 67°C per 100 meters (36°F per 100 feet), indicating molten material less than 1.6 kilometers (1 mile) below the surface. This shallow magma pool provides a remarkable heat source—the most important of the three conditions necessary for the development of hydrothermal features.

The second requisite is an abundance of water that can seep downward and become heated. Yellowstone receives copious summer rain and a deep winter snowpack (averaging more than 250 centimeters or 100 inches).

The third necessity for hydrothermal development is a weak or broken ground surface that allows water to move up and down easily. Here, too, Yellowstone fits the bill, for the ground surface there is very unstable and subject to frequent earthquakes, faulting, and volcanic activity. Consequently, many fractures and weak zones provide easy avenues for vertical water movement.

The park contains about 225 geysers, more than 3000 hot springs, and 7000 other thermal features (fumaroles, steam vents, hot-water terraces, hot-mud cauldrons, and so forth). There are five major geyser basins, a half dozen minor ones, and an extensive scattering of individual or small groups of thermal features.

The principal geyser basins are all in the same watershed on the western side of the park (Figure 17-15). The

National Park, located mostly in northwestern Wyoming, which contains about 225 of the world's 425 geysers as well as more than half of the world's other hydrothermal phenomena. The area consists of a broad, flattish plateau bordered by extensive mountains (the Absaroka Range) on the east and by more limited highlands (particularly the Gallatin Mountains) on the west (Figure 17-14). The bedrock surface of the plateau

▲ **Figure 17-13**   A fumarole is like a geyser except that it erupts no water; it sends out only steam. This scene is from Iceland. *(Torleif Svensson/The Stock Market.)*

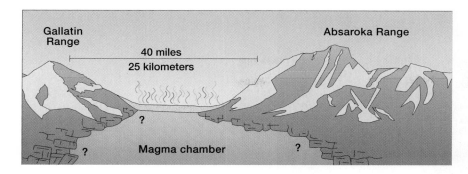

◀ **Figure 17-14** Schematic west–east cross section through the Yellowstone Plateau.

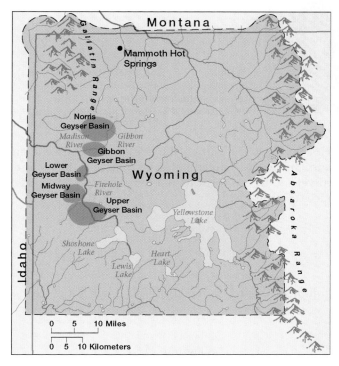

▲ **Figure 17-15** Yellowstone National Park and its major geyser basins.

Gibbon River from the north and the Firehole River from the south unite to form the Madison River, which flows westerly into Montana, eventually to join two other rivers in forming the Missouri (a 1959 earthquake in the Yellowstone area triggered a major landslide in the Madison River valley just to the west of Yellowstone; see Chapter 15). The Gibbon River drains the Norris and Gibbon geyser basins, whereas the Firehole drains the Upper, Midway, and Lower basins. The Firehole River derives its name from the great quantity of hot water fed into it from the hot springs and geysers along its way. Approximately two-thirds of the hydrothermal features of Yellowstone are in the drainage area of the Firehole River.

All the major geyser basins consist of gently undulating plains or valleys covered mostly with glacial sediments and large expanses of whitish siliceous material called *geyserite*. Each basin contains from a few to several dozen geysers, some of which are inconspicuous holes in the geyserite, but others of which are built-up cones that rise a few meters above the basin. In addition, each basin contains a number of hot springs and fumaroles.

Yellowstone's geysers exhibit an extraordinary range of behavior. Some erupt continually; others have experienced only a single eruption in all history. Most, however, erupt irregularly several times a day or week. Some shoot their hot water only a few centimeters into the air, but the largest (Steamboat, Excelsior) erupt to heights of 100 meters (300 feet), with clouds of steam rising much higher.

In the northwestern portion of the park is the most remarkable aggregation of hot-water terraces in the world—the Mammoth Hot Springs Terraces (Figure 17-16). There, groundwater percolates down from surrounding hills into thick layers of limestone. Hot water, carbon dioxide, and other gases rise from the heated magma to mingle with the groundwater and produce a

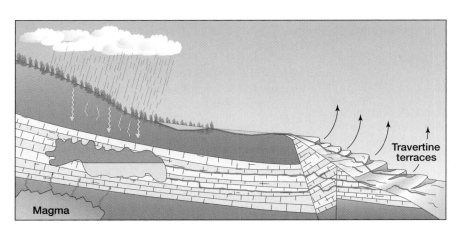

◀ **Figure 17-16** Jupiter Terrace at Mammoth Hot Springs, Yellowstone Park. Water from rainfall and snowmelt percolates down into the underlying limestone, where it is heated from below and seeps downslope. Some of the hot water issues onto the surface and precipitates travertine deposits when exposed to the air.

◀ **Figure 17-17** This is neither snow nor ice, but rather a small portion of the travertine terraces at Mammoth Hot Springs in Yellowstone Park. *(Tom L. McKnight photo.)*

mild carbonic acid solution that rapidly dissolves great quantities of the limestone. Saturated with lime, the temporarily carbonated water seeps downslope until it gushes forth near the base of the hills as the Mammoth Hot Springs. The carbon dioxide escapes into the air, and the lime is precipitated as massive deposits of travertine in the form of flat-topped, steep-sided terraces (Figure 17-17).

Chapter 17 Learning Review

Key Terms

Before answering the study questions below, review the definitions of the following key terms (page references are provided for you):

carbonic acid *(p. 515)*
cavern *(p. 516)*
collapse doline *(p. 519)*
disappearing stream *(p. 521)*
dissolution *(p. 515)*
fumarole *(p. 523)*

geyser *(p. 522)*
hot spring *(p. 521)*
hydrothermal activity *(p. 521)*
karst *(p. 517)*
sinkhole *(p. 518)*
speleothems *(p. 517)*

stalactite *(p. 517)*
stalagmite *(p. 517)*
swallow hole *(p. 521)*
tower karst *(p. 520)*
uvala *(p. 520)*

Study Questions for Key Concepts

After studying this chapter, you should be able to answer the following questions:

Solution and Precipitation (p. 515)
1. What kinds of rock are most susceptible to solution processes? Why?
2. How is it possible for percolating groundwater to both erode and deposit?

Caverns and Related Features (p. 516)
3. What is the importance of jointing and bedding planes to the underground structure of caverns?
4. Describe and explain the formation of *speleothems* such as *stalactites, stalagmites,* and *pillars.*

Karst Topography (p. 517)
5. Explain how a *sinkhole* is formed.

6. Why is there a scarcity of surface drainage in karst areas?
7. What is a *swallow hole*? A *disappearing stream*?

Hydrothermal Features (p. 521)
8. What are the differences among a *hot spring*, a *geyser*, and a *fumarole*? What causes these differences?
9. Briefly explain the eruption sequence of a typical geyser.
10. What three conditions are necessary in order for hydrothermal features to develop?
11. What is the importance of jointing and bedding planes to the development of hot springs and geysers?

Additional Resources

Books:

Fournier, R. O., R. L. Christiansen, R. A. Hutchinson, and K. L. Pierce. *A Field-Trip Guide to Yellowstone National Park, Wyoming, Montana, and Idaho: Volcanic, Hydrothermal, and Glacial Activity in the Region.* U.S. Geological Survey Bulletin 2099. Washington, D.C.: U.S. Government Printing Office, 1994.

Lineback, Neal G. "That Sinking Feeling." *Focus.* Vol. 45. Summer/Fall 1998, p. 14.

Internet Sites:

The Earth Observatory

http://earthobservatory.nasa.gov/

The Earth Observatory is National Aeronautics and Space Administration's (NASA's) Internet site that provides information and images of Earth.

Water Resources of the United States

http://water.usgs.gov/

This site has links to data and information about water quality, acid rain, and stream flow.

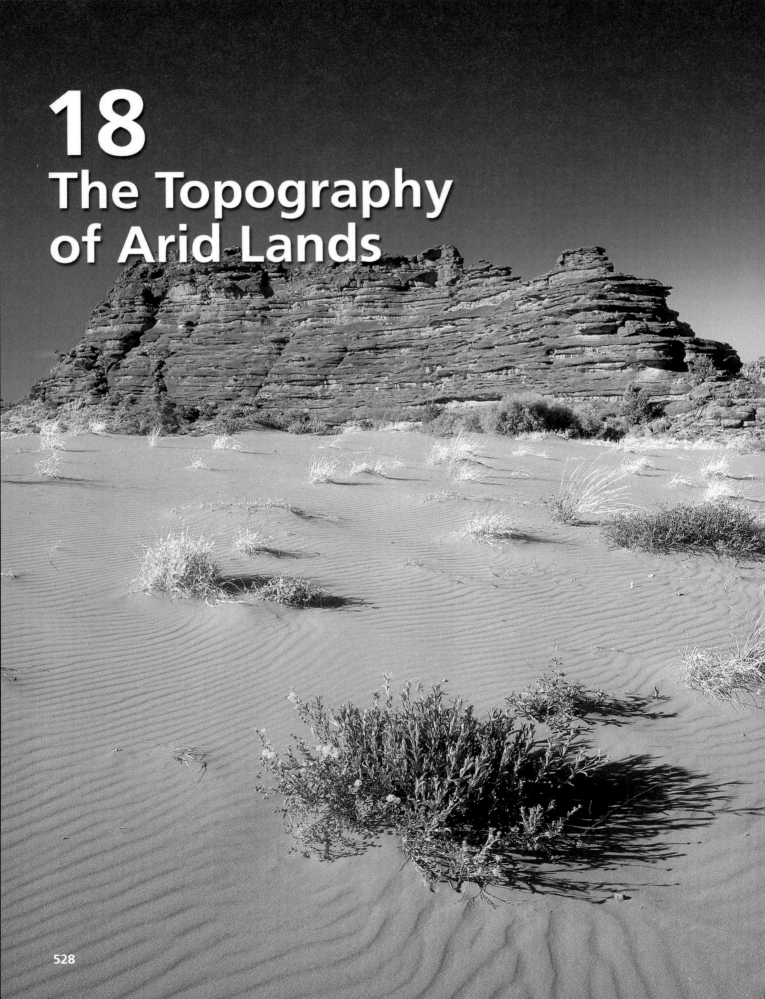

18
The Topography of Arid Lands

A rid lands are in many ways distinctive from humid ones, but there are no obvious boundaries to separate the two. In this chapter, we focus on the dry lands of the world without attempting to establish precise definitions or borders. We are concerned not with where such borders lie, but rather with the processes that shape desert landscapes. It should be understood, however, that both the processes and the landforms of desert landscapes occur more widely than the term *desert* might imply. Thus, although this chapter is about deserts, much of what is discussed is also applicable to semiarid, subhumid, and even some humid regions.

A Specialized Environment

As we learned in Chapter 11, desert terrain is usually stark and abrupt, unsoftened by regolith, soil, or vegetation. Despite the great difference in appearance between arid lands and humid, however, most of the terrain-forming processes active in humid areas are also at work in desert areas. There are, however, special conditions found in deserts that do significantly influence landform development.

Special Conditions in Deserts

The desert landforms are often conspicuously different from those found in wetter locations. These differences are largely the result of a variety of factors and special conditions found in arid regions. The most important of these special conditions include:

1. **Weathering:** In dry lands, mechanical weathering is dominant (whereas chemical weathering often dominates in humid regions). This predominance of mechanical weathering results not only in a generally slower rate of total weathering in deserts, but also in the production of more angular particles of weathered rock. For example, weathering processes such as *salt wedging* are more common in arid regions than in humid ones (see Figure 15-10).
2. **Soil and regolith:** In deserts, the covering of soil and regolith is either thin or absent in most places, a condition that exposes the bedrock to erosion and contributes to the stark, rugged, rocky terrain (Figure 18-1).
3. **Soil Creep:** Soil creep is a relatively minor phenomenon on most desert slopes. This is due partly

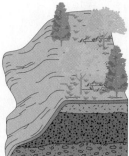

Dry climate

Moist climate

▲ **Figure 18-1** Slope comparisons in dry and moist climates. The steep relief is more easily seen in a dry climate because there is very little obscuring vegetation cover. In a humid climate, the steep faces are to some degree obscured by vegetation.

to the lack of soil but primarily to the lack of the lubricating effects of water. Creep is a smoothing phenomenon in more humid climates, and its lack in deserts accounts in part for the angularity of desert slopes.

4. **Impermeable surfaces:** A relatively large proportion of the desert surface is impermeable to percolating water, permitting little moisture to seep into the ground. *Caprocks* (resistant bedrock surfaces) and *hardpans* (hardened and generally water-impermeable subsurface soil layers) of various types are widespread, and what soil has formed is usually thoroughly compacted. Such impermeable surfaces lead to high runoff when it rains. Other kinds of impermeable surfaces, such as *desert pavement*, are discussed later in this chapter.
5. **Sand:** Some deserts have an abundance of sand in comparison with other parts of the world (Figure 18-2). This is not to say that deserts are mostly sand covered; indeed, the notion that deserts consist of great seas of sand is quite erroneous. Nevertheless, the relatively high proportion of sand in deserts has three important influences on topographic development: (1) A sandy cover allows water to infiltrate the ground and inhibits drainage via streams and overland flow, (2) sand is readily moved by heavy rains, and (3) it can be shifted and shaped by the wind.
6. **Rainfall:** Much of the rainfall in desert areas is intense, often coming from convective thunderstorms, which means that runoff is usually rapid. Floods, although often brief and covering only a limited area, are the rule rather than the exception. Thus, fluvial erosion and deposition, however sporadic and rare, are remarkably effective and conspicuous.
7. **Fluvial deposition:** Almost all streams in desert areas are *ephemeral*, flowing only during and immediately after a rain. Such streams are effective

▲ **Figure 18-2** Many deserts contain considerable accumulations of sand, which sometimes builds up to form conspicuous dunes. Here, tourists explore dunes in the extreme southeastern corner of California. *(Tom L. McKnight photo.)*

agents of erosion, shifting enormous amounts of material in a short time. This is mostly short-distance transportation, however. A large volume of unconsolidated debris is moved to a nearby location, and as the stream dries up, the debris is dumped on slopes or in valleys, where it is readily available for the next rain. As a consequence, depositional features of alluvium are unusually common in desert areas.

8. **Wind:** Another fallacy associated with deserts is that their landforms are produced largely by wind action. This is not true, even though high winds are characteristic of most deserts and even though sand and dust particles are easily shifted.

9. **Basins of interior drainage:** Desert areas contain many watersheds that do not drain ultimately into any ocean. For most continental surfaces, rainfall has the potential of flowing all the way to the sea. In dry lands, however, drainage networks are frequently underdeveloped, and the terminus of a drainage system is often a basin or valley with no external outlet, as Figure 18-3 shows for the United States. Any rain that falls in Nevada, for example, except in the extreme southeastern and northeastern corners of the state, has no hope of reaching the sea.

10. **Vegetation:** All the previous environmental factors have important effects on topographic development, but perhaps the single most obvious feature of dry lands is the lack of a continuous vegetative cover. The plant cover consists mostly of widely spaced shrubs or sparse grass, which provide little protection from the force of raindrops and function inadequately to bind the surface material with roots (Figure 18-4).

Running Water in Waterless Regions

Probably the most fundamental fact of desert geomorphology is that running water is by far the most important external agent of landform development. The erosional and depositional work of running water accounts for the shape of the terrain surface almost everywhere outside areas of extensive sand accumulation. The lightly vegetated ground is defenseless to whatever rainfall may occur, and erosion by rain splash, sheetwash, rilling, and streamflow is enormously effective. Despite the rarity of precipitation, its intensity and the presence of impermeable surfaces produce abrupt runoff, and great volumes of sediment can be moved in a very short time.

The steeper gradients of mountain streams increase the capacity of these streams for carrying large loads, of course, but the sporadic flow of mountain streams in arid lands results in an unpredictable imbalance between erosion and deposition. At any given time, therefore, much transportable rock debris and alluvium sit at rest in the dry stream bed of a desert mountain, awaiting the next flow. Loose surface material is either thin or absent on the slopes, and bedrock is often clearly

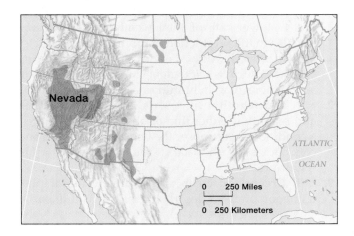

▲ **Figure 18-3** The basins of interior drainage in the United States are all in the western part of the nation. By far the largest area of interior drainage is in Nevada and the adjoining states.

▲ **Figure 18-4**   In most arid regions, the vegetation is sparse and spindly. This is a Death Valley, California, scene. *(Tom L. McKnight photo.)*

exposed, with the more resistant strata standing out as caprocks and cliff faces.

Where slopes are gentle in an arid land, the streams rapidly become choked with sediment as the brief flood time subsides. Here stream channels are readily subdivided by braiding, and main channels often break up into distributaries in the basins. Much silt and sand are thus left on the surface for the next flood to move, unless wind moves them first.

Surface Water in the Desert

Surface water in deserts is conspicuous by its absence. These are lands of sandy streams and dusty lakes, in which the presence of surface water is usually episodic and brief.

Exotic Streams Permanent streams in dry lands are few, far between, and, with scarce exceptions, *exotic*, meaning they are sustained by water that originates outside the desert. This water that feeds **exotic streams** comes from an adjacent wetter area or a higher mountain area in the desert and has sufficient volume to survive passage across the dry lands. The Nile River of North Africa is the classic example of an exotic stream (Figure 18-5). Its water comes from the mountains and lakes of central Africa and Ethiopia in sufficient quantity to survive a 3200-kilometer (2000-mile) journey across

▶ **Figure 18-5**   The world's preeminent example of an exotic stream, the Nile River, flows for many hundreds of kilometers without being joined by a tributary.

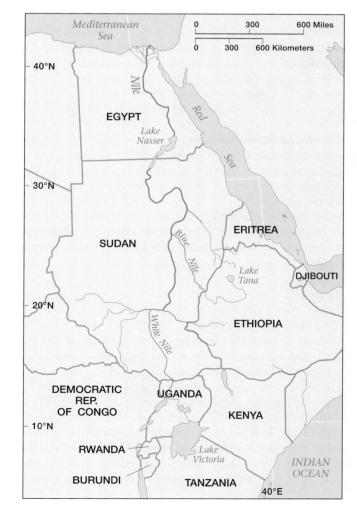

▲ **Figure 18-6** An ephemeral streambed in central New Mexico. It carries water only a few days each year. *(Dr. E. R. Degginger photo.)*

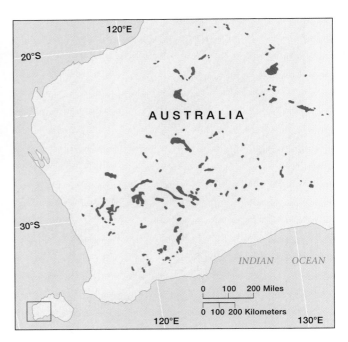

▲ **Figure 18-7** Dry lake beds are often numerous in desert areas. This map shows the principal playas and salinas in Western Australia.

the desert without benefit of tributaries. In North America, the Colorado River is a prominent example of an exotic stream.

In humid regions, a river becomes larger as it flows downstream, nourished by tributaries and groundwater inflow. In dry lands, however, the flow of exotic rivers diminishes downstream because the water seeps into the riverbed, evaporates, and is diverted for irrigation.

Ephemeral Streams Although almost every desert has a few prominent exotic rivers, more than 99 percent of all desert streams are **ephemeral** (Figure 18-6). The brief periods during which these streams flow are times of intense erosion, transportation, and deposition, however. Most ephemeral desert streamflow eventually dissipates through seepage and evaporation, although sometimes such a stream is able to reach the sea, a lake, or an exotic river.

Desert Lakes Although lakes are uncommon in desert areas, dry lake beds are not (Figure 18-7). We have already noted the prevalence of basins of interior drainage in dry lands; most of them have a lake bed occupying their area of lowest elevation, which functions as the local base level for that basin. These dry lake beds are called **playas** (Figure 18-8), although the term **salina** may be used if there is an unusually heavy concentration of salt in the lake-bed sediments. If a playa surface is heavily impregnated with clay, the formation is called a *claypan*. On rare occasions, the intermittent streams may have sufficient flow to bring water to the playa, forming a temporary *playa lake*.

Playas are among the flattest and most level of all landforms—in some cases they are several kilometers across, but with a local relief of only a few centimeters. A playa develops such a flat surface when it is periodically covered with water as a playa lake. The suspended silt in the shallow lake eventually settles out and the water evaporates, leaving a flat layer of dried mud. Through repeated episodes such as this, over the centuries a playa attains its flat surface.

A few desert lakes are permanent. The smaller ones are nearly always the product of either subsurface structural conditions that provide water from a permanent spring or exotic streams or from streams flowing down from nearby mountains. Many permanent lakes in desert areas are **saline lakes**—high rates of evaporation relative to the inflow and/or basins of interior drainage lead to the accumulation of dissolved salts in such lake waters.

Many of the largest natural desert lakes are remnants of still larger bodies of water that formed in a previously wetter climate. Utah's Great Salt Lake is the outstanding example in this country. Although it is the second largest lake wholly in the United States (after Lake Michigan), it is a mere shadow of the former Lake Bonneville, which was formed during the wetter conditions of Pleistocene times (see Figure 19-2).

Fluvial Erosion in Arid Lands

Although fluvial erosion takes place in desert areas only during a small portion of each year, it does its work rapidly and effectively, and the results are conspicuous. In

◁ **Figure 18-8**   Desert playa in central Nevada. Playas are among the flattest of all landforms. *(Dennis Flaherty, Getty Images, Inc./Image Bank.)*

desert areas of any significant relief, large expanses of exposed bedrock are common because of the lack of soil and vegetation. During the rare rains, this bedrock is both mechanically weathered and eroded by running water, and the result of the latter process is steep, rugged, rocky surfaces.

A typical circumstance leading to fluvial erosion in a desert might first entail a brief but intense thunderstorm, perhaps over a mountain drainage basin. The localized thunderstorm puts lots of water on the ground, but because the desert surface is either exposed bedrock or some other kind of relatively impermeable surface, most of the water quickly runs off into a nearby dry ephemeral stream channel. This stream channel quickly fills up with water, perhaps developing into a *flash flood* or a debris flow that travels for many kilometers down out of the desert mountains onto a basin floor. Such flash floods and debris flows can move a remarkable amount of material in just a few minutes. It is through such localized but infrequent events that most change takes place in the desert.

Flash floods and debris flows also pose a significant hazard to humans in arid lands—travelers are cautioned against camping or parking in dry stream washes, since such floods can arrive with little local warning.

Differential Erosion   Whenever a land surface erodes, variations in rock type and structure produce differences in the slope and shape of the resulting landform, a process called **differential erosion** (Figure 18-9). In many cases, rocks resistant to erosion form the cliffs, pinnacles, spires, and other sharp crests, while softer rocks wear away more rapidly to produce gentler slopes. Differential erosion is very common in sedimentary landscapes because there are significant differences in resistance from one stratum to the next; such areas often have vertical escarpments (precipitous clifflike slopes) and abrupt changes in slope angle. In areas dominated by igneous or metamorphic bedrock, however, there is not much differential erosion because there is not much difference in resistance from one part of the bedrock to another.

The steep rock faces that are evidence of differential erosion are more noticeable in dry lands than in humid lands. The reason for this difference is that in humid areas the lush vegetation overgrows the faces and obscures their steepness (see Figure 18-1).

Residual Erosional Surfaces   Scattered throughout the arid and semiarid lands of the world are isolated landforms that rise abruptly from the surrounding plains. Such steep-sided mountains, hills, or ridges are referred to as **inselbergs** ("island mountains") because they resemble rocky islands standing above the surface of a broad sea. A notable type of inselberg is the **bornhardt**, which is composed of highly resistant rock and has a rounded form (Figure 18-10). Differential weathering and erosion lower the surrounding terrain, leaving the resistant bornhardt standing high (Figure 18-11). Bornhardts are very stable and may persist for tens of millions of years.

Along the lower slopes of desert mountains and hills, a distinctive kind of surface often develops. This gently inclined bedrock platform, called a **pediment**, is a "residual" surface (i.e., a surface created by erosion rather than deposition) extending outward from the mountain front (Figure 18-12). Pediments have a complicated origin that is still incompletely understood. They develop as desert mountains are worn down and

▲ **Figure 18-9**   The effects of differential erosion are conspicuous on the Red Cliffs near Gateway in western Colorado. The more resistant layers near the top form an abrupt escarpment, whereas the softer layers below are weathered and eroded into gentler slopes. *(Tom L. McKnight photo.)*

back by weathering and erosion. Many geomorphologists believe that pediments were formed in previous periods of wetter climate and are only marginally related to present-day erosion. In any case, they seem to have been produced by a complex of fluvial processes that wear away the lower slopes, although we do know that stream dissection is not a critical agent in pediment formation because the pediment surface is relatively smooth and has few lines of concentrated drainage. As the slopes of the upland erode, the pediment becomes more extensive.

Pediments are found in almost all deserts and are sometimes the dominant terrain feature. They are not easily recognizable, however, because almost invariably they are covered with a veneer of debris deposited by water and wind.

▲ **Figure 18-10**   Kata Tjuta (the Olgas) is a massive bornhardt in the desert of central Australia. *(Tom L. McKnight photo.)*

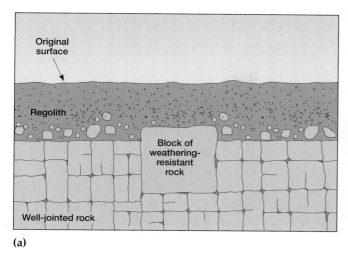

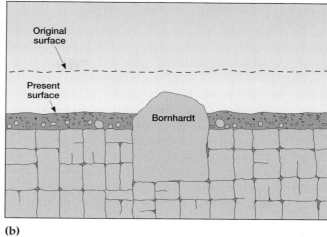

(a)   (b)

▲ **Figure 18-11**   The development of a bornhardt. **(a)** The well-jointed rock is more susceptible to weathering and erosion than the resistant block in the center. **(b)** As a result, the bornhardt emerges as a conspicuous result of erosion.

Desert Stream Channels   The normally dry beds of ephemeral streams typically have flat floors, sandy bottoms, and steep sides (Figure 18-13). In the United States, they are variously referred to as *arroyos, gullies, washes,* or *coulees.* In North Africa and Arabia, the name *wadi* is common; in South Africa, *donga;* in India, *nullah.*

Stream channels in desert areas tend to be deep. Both mountain canyons and flatland arroyos typically have flat, narrow bottoms and steep, often near-vertical sides. Deep accumulations of sand and other loose debris usually cover the channel bed, although flash floods sometimes scour away all alluvial fill right down to the bedrock.

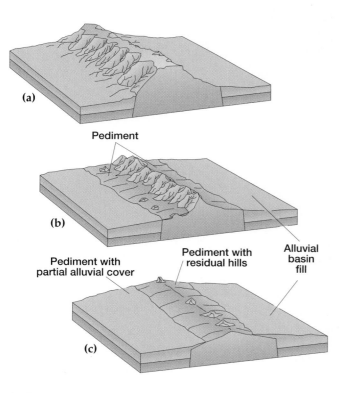

▲ **Figure 18-12**   The development of a pediment as a desert mountain range is worn down by erosion. The residual hills are sometimes called inselbergs.

▲ **Figure 18-13**   Ephemeral stream channel in the Mojave Desert near Baker, California. *(Darrel Hess photo.)*

Fluvial Deposition in Arid Lands

Except in hills and mountains, depositional features are more notable than erosional ones in a desert landscape. Depositional features consist mostly of talus accumulations at the foot of steep slopes and deposits of alluvium and other fragmented debris in ephemeral stream channels, the latter representing bedload left behind with the subsidence of the last flood.

Piedmont is a generic term meaning any zone at the foot of a mountain range. (Do not confuse it with *pediment*, which comes from the same Latin root but refers to a specific landform.) The piedmont zone of a desert mountain range is one of the most prominent areas of fluvial deposition. There is normally a pronounced change in the angle of slope at the mountain base (the *piedmont angle*), with a steep slope giving way abruptly to a gentle one (Figure 18-14). This is a logical area for significant accumulation of rock debris because the break in slope greatly reduces the speed of any sheetwash or streamflow that crosses the piedmont angle. Moreover, the streams issue more or less abruptly from canyons onto the more open piedmont and so are freed from lateral constraint. The resulting fluvial deposition in the piedmont often reaches depths of hundreds of meters.

The flatter portions of desert areas, particularly in basins of interior drainage, also hold a prominent accumulation of water-deposited material. Any sheetwash or streamflow that reaches into such low-lying flatlands usually had to travel a considerable distance over low-angle slopes, which means that both flow volume and flow speed are likely to be limited. Consequently, larger rock fragments are rarely transported into the basins; instead, they are covered with fine particles of sand, silt, and clay, sometimes to a considerable depth.

Characteristic Desert Surfaces—Ergs, Regs, and Hamadas

There are three types of landscape surfaces found only in desert areas: the *erg*, the *reg*, and the *hamada*.

Erg—A Sea of Sand

The most notable desert surface is the **erg**, the classic "sea of sand" often associated in the public mind with the term desert (Figure 18-15). An erg (Arabic for "sand") is a large area covered with loose sand generally arranged in some sort of dune formation by the wind. The accumulation of the vast amount of sand necessary to produce an erg is not easily explained. Since desert weathering processes are very slow, it is probable that ergs have developed only where a more

▲ **Figure 18-15** Sand dunes in an erg area of the Namib Desert, Sossusvlei National Park, Namibia. *(Walter Bibikow/Getty Images.)*

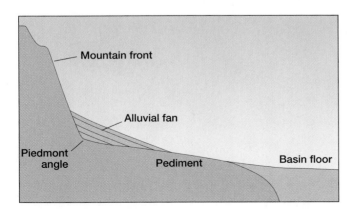

▲ **Figure 18-14** An idealized cross section of a desert piedmont zone.

PEOPLE AND THE ENVIRONMENT Desertification

Desertification is sure to appear on almost any shortlist of major world environmental problems. Although coined much earlier, the term *desertification* has come into prominent use in the last four decades to refer to the expanding of desert conditions into areas previously not desert. Desertification is occurring today all over the world: southern Africa, the Middle East, India, western China, southern Australia, Chile and Peru, northeastern Brazil, the southwestern United States, Mexico, and other places. The United Nations Environment Program (UNEP) estimates that perhaps 21 million hectares (8100 square miles) of land is desertified each year.

The concept of deserts progressively and clearly moving over productive land, usually in the form of a readily recognizable front of mobile sand dunes, may be appealing in its simplicity and its potential for raising political and public awareness, but it is not the form that desertification commonly takes. The United Nations describes desertification as a type of land degradation: "the loss of the land's biological productivity, caused by human-induced factors and climate change."

Deserts can enlarge through entirely natural causes, primarily through climate change that leads to recurrent drought. However, deserts can also expand as a result of human activity: overgrazing of livestock, imprudent agricultural practices, deforestation, and improvident use of water resources.

Desertification is normally associated with the margins of existing deserts and implies an expansion of an already-existing desert, but this is not always the case. For example, "dust bowl" conditions in the North American Great Plains in the 1930s were not peripheral to any existing desert, yet they represented a clear and spectacular case of desertification long before the term was in common use.

The specter of desertification was brought to worldwide attention in the late 1960s by the onset of a cruel six-year drought in the African Sahel. This subhumid to semiarid region on the southern margin of the Sahara

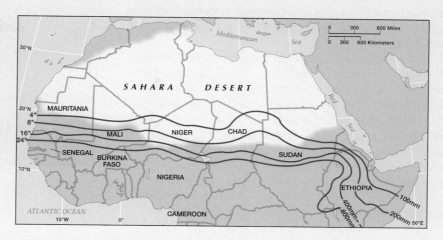

▲ **Figure 18-A** The Sahel Region of Africa. The isolines are isohyets of average annual rainfall. Only the Sahelian countries are named.

occupies parts of 10 countries, from the Atlantic Ocean on the west to the Ethiopian highlands on the east (Figure 18-A). It has an east–west expanse of more than 4800 kilometers (3000 miles), and a north–south extent that varies from 480 to 800 kilometers (300 to 500 miles).

As the Sahelian drought intensified from 1968 to 1974, vegetation disappeared, millions of livestock perished, tens of thousands of people died, and there was a prominent outflow of surviving humans to an uncertain future in already overcrowded lands, particularly cities to the south of the drought-stricken region. Since the 1970s the grip of the drought has been less intense, but almost every year the Sahel has had below-average rainfall, and the cumulative effect has been awesome

(Figure 18-B). Although more than $10 billion in aid has come into the region to ease famine, there are no major success stories in the continuing, exhausting, complex problem of combating Sahelian desertification.

In an effort to gain international recognition for the problem of desertification, as well as to seek cooperative long-term solutions to help the millions of mostly impoverished people displaced by it, in 1994 the United Nations (UN) adopted the *United Nations Convention to Combat Desertification*. More recently, the General Assembly of the UN designated 2006 as the International Year of Deserts and Desertification (IYDD). The goals of the IYDD include raising awareness of desertification so that the urgency of the problem is more generally recognized around the world.

▲ **Figure 18-B** Cattle raising clouds of dust on desertified land in Sudan. *(Y. Artus/Peter Arnold, Inc.)*

humid climate originally formed the weathering products. After being formed, these products were carried by streams into an area of accumulation. Then the climate became drier and consequently wind, rather than water, became the principal agent of transportation and deposition.

Several large ergs occur in the Sahara and Arabian deserts, and smaller ergs are found in most other deserts. The Australian deserts are dominated by large accumulations of sand, including extensive dunefields, but these are not true ergs because most of the sand is anchored by vegetation and therefore not free to move with the wind. Relict ergs (usually in the form of sand dunes covered with vegetation) are sometimes found in nonarid areas, indicative of a drier climate in the past. Much of western Nebraska has such relicts.

Reg—Stony Deserts

A second type of desert landscape surface is the **reg**, a tight covering of coarse gravel, pebbles, and/or boulders from which all sand and dust have been removed by wind and water. A reg (Arabic for "stone"), then, is a stony desert, although the surface covering of stones may be very thin (in some cases, it is literally one pebble deep). The finer material having been removed, the surface pebbles often fit closely together, sealing whatever material is below from further erosion. For this reason, a reg is often referred to as **desert pavement** or *desert armor* (Figure 18-16). In Australia, where regs are widespread, they are called *gibber plains*.

A striking feature of some deserts, one particularly but not exclusively associated with regs, is **desert varnish**. This is a dark, shiny coating, consisting mostly of iron and manganese oxides, that forms on the surface of pebbles, stones, and larger outcrops after long exposure to the desert air (see Figure 18-16). Desert varnish is characterized by a high content of iron and manganese oxides along with wind-delivered clay. The relatively high concentrations of manganese in desert varnish seem to be a consequence of a biochemical process involving bacteria. Desert varnish is an important dating tool for geomorphologists because the longer a rock surface has been exposed to weathering, the greater is the concentration of the oxide coating and thus the darker the color.

Hamada—Barren Bedrock

A third desert landscape surface is the **hamada** (Arabic for "rock"), a barren surface of consolidated material. A hamada surface usually consists of exposed bedrock, but it is sometimes composed of sedimentary material that has been cemented together by salts evaporated from groundwater. In either case, fragments formed by weathering are quickly swept away by the wind, so that little loose material remains.

▲ **Figure 18-16** Desert pavement in California's Panamint Valley. Note the dark brown coating of desert varnish on the larger rocks. *(Darrel Hess photo.)*

Ergs, regs, and hamadas are all limited to plains areas. Regs and hamadas are exceedingly flat, whereas ergs are as high as the sand dunes built by the wind. The boundaries of these landscapes are often sharp because of the abrupt change in friction-layer speed as the wind moves from a sandy surface to a nonsandy surface. For example, wind passing from an erg to a reg or hamada is no longer slowed by the drag of loose sand and so can speed up and sweep the hard surface clean. On the other hand, wind moving from a barren reg or hamada to a sandy erg is slowed down perceptibly, and deposition results.

Although the extent of ergs, regs, and hamadas is significant in some desert areas, the majority of the arid land in the world contains only a limited number of these surfaces. For example, only one-third of the Arabian Desert, the sandiest desert of all, is covered with sand, and much of that is not in the form of an erg.

The Work of the Wind

The irrepressible winds of the desert create spectacular sand and dust storms and continuously reshape minor details of the landscape (Figure 18-17). However, the effect of wind as a sculptor of terrain is very limited, with the important exception of such relatively impermanent features as sand dunes.

The term wind is theoretically restricted to horizontal air movement. Some turbulence is nearly always

▲ **Figure 18-17** The wind is sometimes a prominent force in rearranging loose particles. This scene is near Barrow Creek in the Northern Territory of Australia. *(Tom L. McKnight photo.)*

involved, however, so there is usually a vertical component of flow as well. In general, the motion of air passing over the ground is similar to that of water flowing over a streambed, and that similarity is the cause of the turbulence. In a thin layer right at the ground surface, wind speed is zero, just as the speed of the water layer touching the banks and bed of a stream is zero, but wind speed increases with distance above the ground. The shear developed between different layers of air moving at different speeds causes turbulence similar to that in a stream of water. Wind turbulence can also be caused by heating from below, which causes the air to expand and move upward.

Aeolian processes are those related to wind action (Aeolus was the Greek god of the winds). They are most pronounced, widespread, and effective wherever fine-grained unconsolidated sedimentary material is exposed to the atmosphere, without benefit of vegetation, moisture, or some other form of protection—in other words, in deserts and along sandy beaches. Our focus here is wind action in desert regions.

Aeolian Erosion

The erosive effect of wind can be divided into two categories: deflation and abrasion.

Deflation **Deflation** is the shifting of loose particles as a result of their being blown either through the air or along the ground. Except under extraordinary circumstances, the wind is not strong or buoyant enough to move anything more than dust and small sand grains, and therefore no significant landforms are created by deflation. Sometimes a **blowout**, or *deflation hollow*, may be formed; this is a shallow depression from which an abundance of fine material has been deflated. Most blowouts are small, but some exceed 1.5 kilometers (1 mile) in diameter. Along with fluvial erosion, deflation is also a factor in the formation of a reg surface.

Abrasion *Aeolian abrasion* is analogous to fluvial abrasion, except that the aeolian variety is much less effective. Whereas deflation is accomplished entirely by air currents, abrasion requires "tools" in the form of airborne sand and dust particles. The wind drives these particles against rock and soil surfaces in a form of natural sandblasting. Wind abrasion does not construct or even significantly shape a landform; it merely sculptures those already in existence. The principal results of aeolian abrasion are the pitting, etching, faceting, and polishing of exposed rock surfaces and the further fragmenting of rock fragments. Rocks so faceted by wind sandblasting are called *ventifacts* (Figure 18-18).

▲ **Figure 18-18** A sand-blasted rock, or ventifact. This piece of basalt is in Death Valley, near Badwater. *(Darrel Hess photo.)*

Aeolian Transportation

Wind Transportation of Sediment

Rock materials are transported by wind in much the same fashion as they are moved by water, but less effectively. The finest particles are carried in suspension as dust. Strong, turbulent winds can lift and carry thousands of tons of suspended dust. Some dust storms extend for hundreds of meters above Earth's surface and may move material through more than 1600 kilometers (1000 miles) of horizontal distance.

Particles larger than dust are moved by wind through *saltation* and *traction*, just as in streamflow (Figure 18-19). Wind is unable to lift particles larger than the size of sand grains, and even these are likely to be carried less than one meter above the surface. Indeed, most sand, even when propelled by a strong wind, leaps along in the low, curved trajectory typical of saltation, striking the ground at a low angle and bouncing onward. Larger particles move by *traction*, being rolled or pushed along the ground by the wind. It is estimated that three-fourths of the total volume of all wind-moved material in dry lands is shifted by saltation and traction, particularly the former. At the same time, the entire surface layer of sand moves slowly downwind as a result of the frequent impact of the saltating grains; this process is called *creep*, but it should not be confused with soil creep.

Because the wind can lift particles only so high, a true sandstorm is a cloud of horizontally moving sand that extends for only a few centimeters or feet above the ground surface. Persons standing in its path have their legs peppered by sand grains, but their heads are most likely above the sand cloud. The abrasive impact of a sandstorm, while having little erosive effect on the terrain, may be quite significant for the works of humans near ground level; unprotected wooden poles and posts can be rapidly cut down by the sandblasting, and cars traveling through a sandstorm are likely to suffer etched windshields and chipped paint.

Aeolian Deposition

Desert Sand Dunes

Sand and dust moved by the wind are eventually deposited when the wind dies down. The finer material, which may be carried long distances, is usually laid down as a thin coating of silt and has little or no landform significance. The coarser sand, however, is normally deposited locally. Sometimes it is spread across the landscape as an amorphous sheet called a *sandplain*. The most notable of all aeolian deposits, however, is the **sand dune**, in which loose, windblown sand is heaped into a mound or low hill.

Desert Sand Dunes In some instances, dunefields are composed entirely of unanchored sand that is mostly uniform grains of quartz (occasionally gypsum, rarely some other minerals) and usually brownish-gray colored, although sometimes a brilliant white. Unanchored dunes are deformable obstructions to airflow. Because they are unanchored, they can move, divide, grow, or shrink. They develop sheltered air pockets on their leeward sides that slow down and baffle the wind, so that deposition is promoted there.

Unanchored dunes are normally moved by local winds. The wind erodes the windward slope of the dune, forcing the sand grains up and over the crest to be deposited on the steeper leeward side, or **slip face** (Figure 18-20). The slip face of a dune typically maintains an angle of 32° to 34°—the angle of repose of dry sand. If the wind prevails from one direction for many days, the dune may migrate downwind without changing shape. Such migration is usually slow, but in some cases dunes can move tens of meters in a year.

Not all dunes are unanchored, however, and another characteristic dunefield arrangement is one in which the dunes are mostly or entirely anchored and therefore no longer shifting with the wind. Various agents can anchor dunes, the primary one being vegetation. Dunes provide little nourishment or moisture for plant

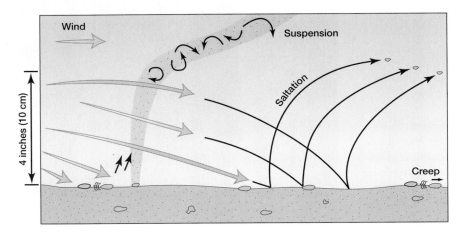

◀ **Figure 18-19** Wind carries tiny dust particles in suspension; larger particles are moved by saltation and traction.

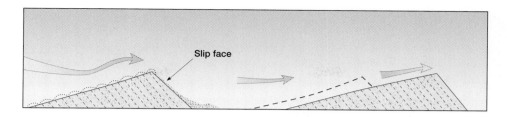

▲ **Figure 18-20**   Sand dunes migrate downwind as sand grains move up the gentle windward slope and are deposited on the steep slip face.

growth, but desert vegetation is remarkably hardy and persistent and often able to survive in a dune environment. Where vegetation manages to gain a foothold, it may proliferate and anchor the dunes.

Dune patterns are almost infinite in their variety. Several characteristic dune forms are widespread in the world's deserts, their configuration largely a consequence of the relative amount of sand present and the persistence of the wind direction. Here we consider three of the most common:

1. Best known of all dune forms is the **barchan**, which usually occurs as an individual dune migrating across a nonsandy surface, although barchans may also be found in groups. A barchan is crescent-shaped, with the horns of the crescent pointing downwind (Figures 18-21a and 18-22). Sand movement in a barchan is not only over the crest, from windward side to slip face, but also around the edges of the crescent to extend the horns. Barchans form where strong winds blow consistently from one direction. They tend to be the fastest moving of all dunes and are found in all deserts except those of Australia. They are most widespread in the deserts of central Asia (Thar and Takla Makan) and in parts of the Sahara.

2. **Transverse dunes**, which are also crescent-shaped but less uniformly so than barchans (Figure 18-21b), occur where the supply of sand is much greater than that found in locations that have barchans; normally the entire landscape leading to transverse-dune formation is sand covered. As with a barchan, the convex side of a transverse dune faces the prevailing wind direction. In a formation of transverse dunes, all the crests are perpendicular to the wind direction, and the dunes are aligned in parallel waves across the land. They migrate downwind just as barchans do, and if the sand supply decreases, they are likely to break up into barchans.

3. **Seifs** are long, narrow dunes that usually occur in multiplicity and in a generally parallel arrangement (Figures 18-21c and 18-23). They are typically a few dozen to a few hundred meters high, a few tens of meters wide, and kilometers or even tens of kilometers long. Their origin is still not well understood, although their lengthy, parallel orientation

apparently represents an intermediate direction between two dominant wind directions. Seifs are rare in American deserts but may be the most common dune forms in other parts of the world.

In some locations what are sometimes called "fossil" sand dunes are found. For example, in some regions of the southwestern United States vast deposits of sandstone exhibit the characteristic "cross-bedding" of wind-deposited sand, rather than the more typical horizontal strata (Figure 18-24).

Coastal Dunes   Winds are also active in dune formation along many stretches of ocean and lake coasts, whether the climate is dry or otherwise. On

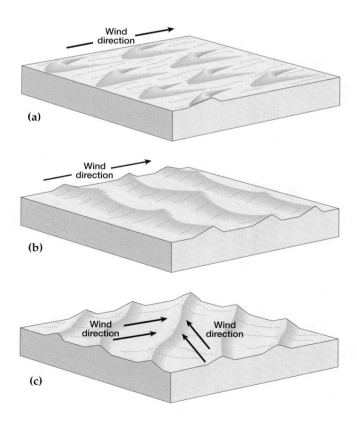

▲ **Figure 18-21**   Common desert sand dune types: **(a)** barchans; **(b)** transverse dunes; **(c)** seifs.

▲ **Figure 18-22**   The characteristic crescent shape of a big barchan dune in Namibia's Namib-Naukluft National Park. *(Tom L. McKnight photo.)*

almost all flattish coastlines, ocean waves deposit sand along the beach. A prominent onshore wind can blow some of the sand inland, often forming dunes. In some areas, particularly if vegetative growth is inhibited, the dunes slowly migrate inland, occasionally inundating forests, fields, roads, and buildings. Most coastal dune aggregations are small, but they sometimes cover extensive areas. The largest area is probably along the Atlantic coastline of southern France, where dunes extend for 240 kilometers (150 miles) along the shore and reach inland for 3 to 10 kilometers (2 to 6 miles).

Loess   A form of aeolian deposit not associated with dry lands is **loess**, a wind-deposited silt that is fine grained, calcareous, and usually buff colored. (Pronounced *luhss* to rhyme with "hearse" if one left out the "r," this is a German word derived from the name of a village in Alsace.) Despite its depositional

▲ **Figure 18-23**   The parallel linearity of seifs is characteristic of many desert areas. This scene is from the Simpson Desert of central Australia. *(Tom L. McKnight photo.)*

▲ **Figure 18-24** Cross-bedded sandstone in "fossil" sand dunes near Zion National Park in Utah. *(Darrel Hess photo.)*

Prominent bluffs are often produced as erosional surfaces in loess deposits.

The formational history of loess is varying, complicated, and not completely understood. Its immediate origin is clearly aeolian deposition, but the materials can apparently be derived from a variety of sources. Much of the silt was produced in association with Pleistocene glaciation. During both glacial and interglacial periods, rivers carried large amounts of debris-laden meltwater from the glaciers, producing many broad floodplains. During periods of low water, winds whipped the smaller, dust-sized particles from the floodplains and dropped them in some places in very thick deposits. Much loess also seems to have been generated by deflation of dust from desert areas, especially in central Asia.

Most deposits of loess are in the midlatitudes, where some are very extensive, particularly in the United States, Russia, China, and Argentina (Figure 18-26). Indeed, some 10 percent of Earth's land surface is covered with loess, and in the conterminous United States the total approaches 30 percent. Loess deposits provide fertile possibilities for agriculture, for they serve as the parent material for some of the world's most productive soils, especially for growing grain.

The loess areas have been particularly significant in China because of their agricultural productivity. The Yellow River (Hwang Ho) received its name from the vast amount of buff-colored sediment it carries, as did its destination, the Yellow Sea. Also, numerous cave dwellings have been excavated in the Chinese loess because of its remarkable capability for standing in

origin, loess lacks horizontal stratification. Perhaps its most distinctive characteristic is its great vertical durability, which results from its fine grain size, high porosity, and vertical jointlike cleavage planes. The tiny grains have great molecular attraction for one another, making the particles very cohesive. Moreover, the particles are angular, which increases porosity. Thus, loess accepts and holds large amounts of water. Although relatively soft and unconsolidated, when exposed to erosion loess maintains almost vertical slopes because of its structural characteristics, as though it were firmly cemented rock (Figure 18-25).

▲ **Figure 18-25** Loess has a remarkable capability for standing in vertical cliffs, as seen in this road cut near Maryville, Missouri. *(Tom L. McKnight photo.)*

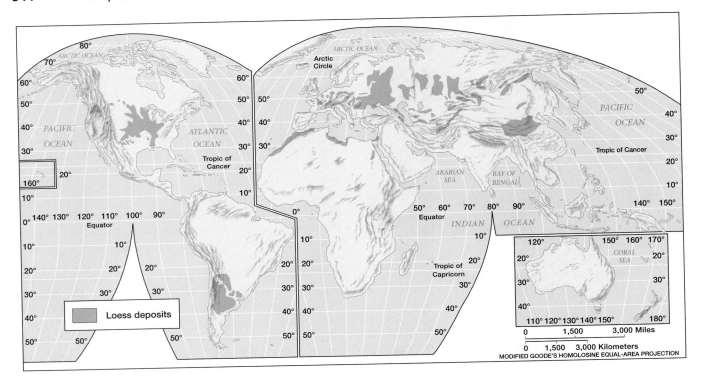

▲ **Figure 18-26** Major loess deposits of the world.

vertical walls. Unfortunately, however, this region is also prone to earthquakes, and the cave homes collapse readily when tremors occur; thus, some of the world's greatest earthquake disasters in terms of loss of life have taken place there.

Two Characteristic Desert Landform Assemblages

Surface features vary considerably from one desert to the next. Overall, however, the most common desert landform is a mountain or mountain range, and the most frequently recurring desert profile is a mountain flanked by plains.

Two particular assemblages of landforms are the most common in the deserts of the United States: basin-and-range terrain and mesa-and-scarp terrain. Their pattern of development is repeated time and again over thousands of square kilometers of the American Southwest (Figure 18-27). Both of these landform assemblages are good representative examples of the outcome of the special conditions and desert landform-shaping processes we have just described.

Basin-and-Range Terrain FG9

As Figure 18-27 shows, most of the southwestern interior of the United States is characterized by basin-and-range topography. This is a land largely without external drainage, with only a few exotic rivers (notably the

Colorado and Rio Grande) flowing through or out of the region. This region of North America has undergone extensive normal faulting, leaving a landscape consisting of numerous fault-block mountain ranges surrounding a series of interior drainage basins, including many down-dropped grabens.

Basin-and-range terrain has three principal features: ranges, piedmont zones, and basins (Figure 18-28).

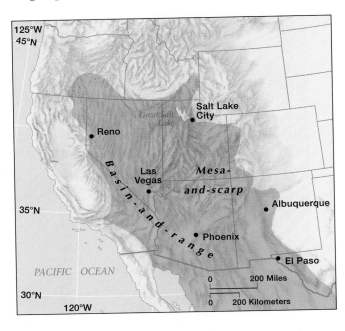

▲ **Figure 18-27** The southwestern interior of the United States contains two principal assemblages of landforms: basin-and-range and mesa-and-scarp.

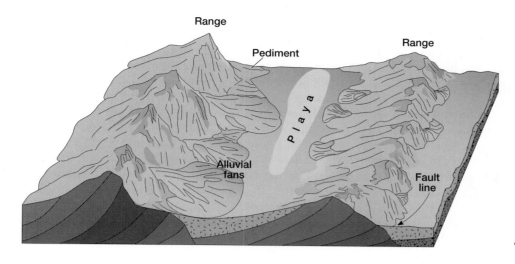

◀ **Figure 18-28** A typical basin-and-range landscape.

The Ranges If we stand in the basin of any basin-and-range landscape, the mountain ranges dominate the horizon in all directions. Some of the ranges are high and some quite low, but the prevalence of steep and rocky slopes presents an aura of ruggedness. Although the diastrophic origins of these mountains vary (most have been uplifted by faulting, but others were formed by folding, by vulcanism, or in a more complex fashion), their surface features have been shaped almost entirely by weathering, mass wasting, and fluvial processes.

Ridge crests and peaks are usually sharp, steep cliffs are common, and rocky outcrops protrude at all elevations. The mountain ranges of a basin-and-range formation are usually long, narrow, and parallel to one another. Most of them are seamed by numerous gullies, gorges, and canyons that rarely house flowing streams. These dry drainage channels are usually narrow and steep sided and have a V-shaped cross section. Typically the channel bottoms are well supplied with sand and other loose debris.

In some areas, the ranges have been eroding for a long time and have consequently been worn down to a very low relief. Where this has happened, slopes are gentler, summits more rounded, and gorges less incised. Bare rock outcrops are still prominent, however. If the range stands in isolation and the alluvial plains and basins roundabout are extensive, the term inselberg is applied to the mountain remnant (see Figure 18-12).

The Piedmont Zone At the base of the ranges, there is usually a sharp break in slope (the *piedmont angle*) that marks the change from range to piedmont (see Figure 18-14). The piedmont is a transition area from the steep slopes of the ranges to the near-flatness of the basins. Slope angles vary in any given piedmont but are generally gentle, with a somewhat steeper upper margin.

Much of the piedmont is underlain by an erosional pediment, although the pediment is rarely visible. It is normally covered with several meters of unconsolidated

debris because the piedmont is particularly well suited for deposition. During the occasional rainfall, flash floods and debris flows come roaring out of the gullies and gorges of the surrounding ranges, heavily laden with sedimentary material. As they burst out of the mouths of the confining canyons onto the piedmont, their speed and load capacity drop abruptly. Significant deposition is the inevitable result.

One of the most prominent and widespread topographic features to be found in any desert area is the **alluvial fan**, particularly characteristic of a basin-and-range piedmont. As a stream leaves the narrow confines of a mountain gorge and debouches into the open piedmont, it abruptly loses both capacity and competence and breaks into distributaries that wend their way down the piedmont slope, sometimes cutting shallow new channels in the loose alluvium but frequently depositing more debris atop the old (Figure 18-29). Channels become choked and overflow, developing new ones. In this fashion, a moderately sloping, fan-shaped deposit is constructed at the mouth of the canyon.

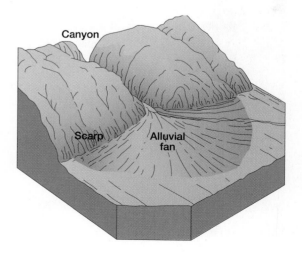

▲ **Figure 18-29** An alluvial fan develops at the mouth of a canyon.

When one part of the fan is built up, the channeled flow shifts to another section and builds that up. This means that the entire fan is eventually covered more or less symmetrically with sediment. As deposition continues, the fan is extended outward across the piedmont and onto the basin floor.

The material in an alluvial fan is not well sorted. Instead, the fan may have a heterogeneous mixture of particle sizes because volumes of water flow vary, often considerably, from year to year. Thus, there is not the neat sorting that occurs in a delta. In general, however, large boulders are dropped near the apex of the fan and finer material around the margins, with a considerable mixture of particle sizes throughout. The dry drainage channels across the fan surface frequently shift their positions as well as their balance between erosion and deposition.

As alluvial fans become larger, neighboring ones often overlap and are called *coalescing alluvial fans*. Continued growth and more complete overlap may eventually result in a continuous alluvial surface all across the piedmont, in which case it is difficult to distinguish between individual fans. This feature is known as either a *piedmont alluvial plain* or a **bajada**. Near the mountain front, a bajada surface is undulating, with convex sections near the canyon mouths and concave sections in the overlap areas between the canyons. In the portion of the bajada away from the range and out on the basin floor, however, no undulations occur because the component fans have coalesced so thoroughly.

The Basin Beyond the piedmont is the flattish floor of the basin, which has a very gentle slope from all sides toward some low point (Figure 18-30). This low point is usually in a playa (or claypan or salina, depending on the nature of the surface). Drainage channels across the basin floor are sometimes clear cut, but more often shallow and ill defined, frequently disappearing before reaching the low point. This low point thus functions as the theoretical drainage terminal for all overland and streamflow from the near sides of the surrounding ranges, but only sometimes does much water reach it. Most is lost by evaporation and seepage long before.

Salt accumulations are commonplace on the playa surrounding the low point of a desert basin because of all the water-soluble minerals washed out of the surrounding watershed. Once out of the mountains and in the basin, the water evaporates or seeps away, but the salts cannot evaporate and are only marginally involved in seepage. There is usually sufficient water to allow flow across the outer rim of the basin floor and into the playa area, however, and so salts become increasingly concentrated in the playa, which is then more properly called a salina. The presence of the salt usually gives a brilliant whitish color to the playa–salina surface. Many different salts can be involved, and their accumulations are sometimes large enough to support a prosperous mining enterprise.

In the rare occasions when water does flow into a playa, the formation becomes a *playa lake*. Such lakes may be extensive, but they are usually very shallow and normally persist for only a few days or weeks. Saline lakes are marked by clear water and a salty froth around the edges, whereas shallow freshwater lakes have muddy water because they lack salt to make the silt settle.

▲ **Figure 18-30** Looking across the playa of Owens Lake toward California's Sierra Nevada range. Note the alluvial fan at the base of the canyon in the center of the photo. *(Tom L. McKnight photo.)*

The basin floor is covered with very fine-grained material because the contributory streams are too weak to transport large particles. Silt and sand predominate and sometimes accumulate to remarkable depths. Indeed, the normal denudation processes in basin-and-range country tend to raise the floor of the basins. Debris from the surrounding ranges has nowhere to go but the basin of interior drainage. Thus, as the mountains are being worn down, the basin floor is gradually rising.

The fine material of basin floors is very susceptible to the wind, with the result that small concentrations of sand dunes are often found in some corner of the basin. Free-moving sand is rarely found in the center of the basin because winds push it to one side or another.

Death Valley: A Primer of Basin-and-Range Terrain

California's Death Valley is a vast topographic museum, a veritable primer of basin-and-range terrain. Located in east-central California, close to the Nevada border, the valley is a classic graben, with extensive and complex fault zones both east and west of the valley floor (Figure 18-31). The trough is about 225 kilometers (140 miles) long, in a general northwest–southeast orientation; its width ranges from 6 to 26 kilometers (4 to 16 miles). The downfaulting has been so pronounced that nearly 1425 square kilometers (550 square miles) of the valley floor is below sea level, reaching a depth of -86 meters (-282 feet) Lengthy, upfaulted mountain

ranges border the valley on either side. The Panamint Mountains on the west are the most prominent; their high point at Telescope Peak 3368 meters or 11,049 feet above sea level is only 29 kilometers (18 miles) due west from the low point of the valley. The Amargosa Range on the east is equally steep and rugged, but a bit lower overall.

The most conspicuous topography associated with Death Valley is the surrounding mountains. The ranges have all the characteristic features of desert mountains, being rugged, rocky, and generally barren. Their erosional slopes are steep and their escarpments steeper. The canyons that seam the ranges are invariably deep, narrow, V-shaped gorges. Many of those in the Amargosa Range and some in the Panamints are *wineglass canyons*. The cup of the glass is the open area of dispersed headwater tributaries high in the range, the stem is the narrow gorge cut through the mountain front, and the base is the fan that opens out onto the piedmont.

The piedmont at the foot of the Panamints and the Amargosas is almost completely alluviated in one of the most extensive fan complexes imaginable (Figure 18-32). Every canyon mouth is the apex either of a fan or a fan-shaped debris flow deposit, and most of the fans overlap with neighbors to the north and south. The fans on the western side of the valley (those formed by debris from the Panamints) are much more extensive than those on the eastern side. For the most part, the Panamint fans are

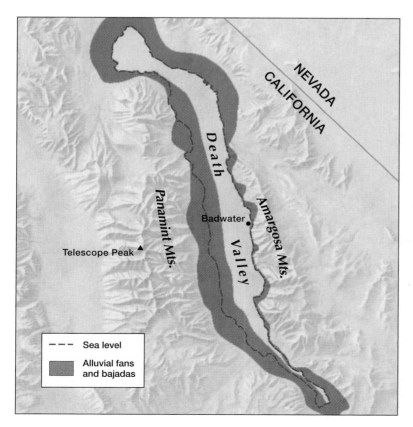

▲ **Figure 18-31** The setting of Death Valley.

◀ **Figure 18-32**   Alluvial fans at Tucki Wash, Death Valley, California. *(Photo © Michael Collier.)*

thoroughly coalesced into a conspicuous bajada that averages about 8 kilometers (5 miles) wide, with the outer margin of the bajada as much as 610 meters (2000 feet) lower than the canyon mouths.

The Amargosa fans are much smaller, primarily because the fault pattern of the graben has tilted the valley eastward so that its lowest portions are nestled close to the base of the Amargosa Range. Thus, the west-side fans have been able to extend outward onto the valley floor, whereas tilting has reduced the size of the east-side fans by creating shorter slopes (and therefore, smaller drainage basins to supply sediment), and by facilitating their partial burial by valley-floor deposits. The Amargosa fans, then, are mostly short, steep, and discrete so there is no bajada on the eastern side of Death Valley, although some of the fans do overlap with one another.

The floor of Death Valley is also of great topographic interest, although its flatness makes the features less easy to see and understand. The valley is filled with an incredible depth of alluvium, most of which has been washed down from the surrounding mountains; in places the fill is estimated to consist of 900 meters (3000 feet) of young alluvium resting atop another 1800 meters (6000 feet) of tertiary sediment. The surface of the valley floor has little relief and slopes gently toward the low point near Badwater, a permanent salt pond. Drainage channels appear irregularly on the valley floor, trending toward Badwater. In some places, distinct braided channels appear; in other locations, the channels disappear in sand or playa.

There are several extensive crusty-white *salt pans*, particularly in the middle of the valley (Figure 18-33), along with several sand accumulations, with one area of mobile dunes covering 36 square kilometers (14 square miles).

During the most recent ice age, Death Valley was occupied by an immense lake. Lake Manly was more than 160 kilometers (100 miles) long and 180 meters (600 feet) deep. It was fed by three rivers that flowed into the valley from the west, carrying meltwater from Sierra Nevada glaciers. As the climate became drier and warmer, the lake eventually disappeared through evaporation and seepage, but traces of its various shoreline levels can still be seen at several places on the lower slopes. Much of the salt accumulated in the valley is due to the evaporating waters of Lake Manly as well as lakes that existed more recently.

Mesa-and-Scarp Terrain

The other major landform assemblage of the American Southwest is mesa-and-scarp terrain. It is most prominent

▲ **Figure 18-33**   The Death Valley "salt pan" here consists mostly of ordinary table salt (NaCl). The polygonal ridges form as salt crystals grow through the evaporation of water from a salty "slush" just below the surface. *(Darrel Hess photo.)*

▲ **Figure 18-34** The stair-step pattern of mesa-and-scarp terrain is shown on an imposing scale in Arizona's Grand Canyon. *(Tom L. McKnight photo.)*

in Four Corners country, the place where Colorado, Utah, Arizona, and New Mexico come together (Figure 18-34). **Mesa** is Spanish for "table" and implies a flat-topped surface. **Scarp** is short for "escarpment" and pertains to steep, more or less vertical cliffs.

Mesa-and-scarp terrain is normally associated with horizontal sedimentary strata. Such strata invariably offer different degrees of resistance to erosion, and so abrupt changes in slope angle are characteristic of this terrain. The most resistant layers, typically limestone or sandstone, often play a dual role in the development of a mesa-and-scarp terrain. They form an extensive *caprock*, which becomes the mesa; and at the eroded edge of the caprock, the hard layer protects underlying strata and produces an escarpment. Thus, it is the resistant layers that are responsible for both elements of slope (mesa and scarp) that describe this terrain type.

Often mesa-and-scarp topography has a broad and irregular stair-step pattern. Figure 18-35 shows a cross section through a typical formation. An extensive, flat erosional platform (the mesa) in the topmost resistant layer of a sedimentary accumulation terminates in an escarpment (the scarp) that extends downward to the bottom of the resistant layer(s). From here, another slope, steep but not as steep as the escarpment, continues down through softer strata. This inclined slope extends downward as far as the next resistant layer, which forms either another escarpment or another mesa ending in an escarpment.

The erosional platforms are properly referred to as **plateaus** if they are bounded on one or more sides by a prominent escarpment. If a scarp edge is absent or relatively inconspicuous, the platform is called a *stripped plain*.

The escarpment edge is worn back by fluvial erosion. The cliffs retreat, maintaining their perpendicular faces, as they are undermined by the more rapid erosion of the less resistant strata (often shale) beneath the caprock. Much of the undermining is accomplished by a process called **sapping**, in which groundwater seeps and trickles out of the scarp face, eroding fine particles and weakening the cohesion of the face. When thus undermined, blocks of the caprock break off, usually along vertical joint lines. Throughout this process, the harder rocks are the cliff-formers, and the less resistant beds develop more gently inclined slopes. Talus often accumulates at the base of the slope.

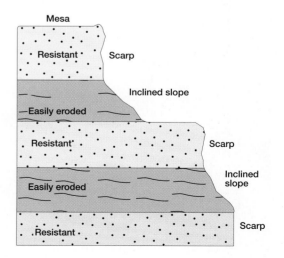

▲ **Figure 18-35** Cross section of a mesa-and-scarp formation. Differential erosion shows up prominently: The resistant strata weather and erode into mesas or scarps, whereas the more easily eroded strata yield gentler inclined slopes.

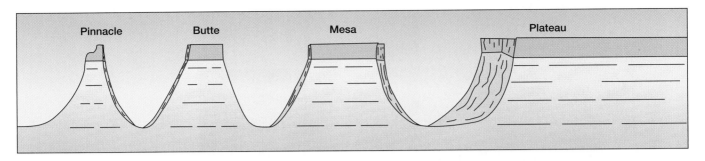

▲ **Figure 18-36** Typical development of residual landforms in horizontal sedimentary strata with a hard caprock. With the passage of time, larger features are eroded into smaller features.

Although the term mesa is applied generally to many flat surfaces in dry environments, it properly refers to a particular landform: a flat-topped, steep-sided hill with a limited summit area. It is a remnant of a formerly more extensive surface, most of which has been worn away by erosion (Figure 18-36). Sometimes it stands in splendid isolation as a final remnant in an area where most of the previous surface has been removed, but more commonly it occurs as an outlying mass not very distant from the retreating escarpment face to which it was once connected. A mesa is invariably capped by some sort of resistant material that helps keep the summit flat even as the bulk of the rock mass is reduced by continuing erosion of its rimming cliffs.

A related but smaller topographic feature is the **butte**, an erosional remnant having a very small surface area and cliffs that rise conspicuously above their surroundings. Some buttes have other origins, but most are formed by the mass wasting of mesas (Figure 18-37). With further erosion, a still smaller

residual feature, usually referred to as a **pinnacle** or *pillar*, may be all that is left—a final spire of resistant caprock protecting weaker underlying beds. Buttes, mesas, and pinnacles are typically found not far from some retreating escarpment face (see Figure 18-36).

Badlands One of the most striking topographic features of arid and semiarid regions is the intricately rilled and barren terrain known as **badlands** (Figure 18-38). In areas underlain by horizontal strata of shale and other clay formations that are poorly consolidated, overland flow after the occasional rains is an extremely effective erosive agent. Innumerable tiny rills that develop over the surface rapidly evolve into ravines and gullies that dissect the land in an extraordinarily detailed manner. A maze of short but very steep slopes is etched in a filigree of rills, gullies, and gorges, with a great many ridges, ledges, and other erosional remnants scattered throughout. Erosion is too rapid to permit soil to form or plants to grow, and so badlands are barren, lifeless wastelands of almost

▲ **Figure 18-37** The spectacular starkness of arid-land topography is demonstrated dramatically in the view of the Mitten Buttes in Arizona's Monument Valley. *(Tom L. McKnight photo.)*

▲ **Figure 18-38** Badlands are characterized by innumerable ravines and gullies dissecting the land and forming a maze of low but very steep slopes. This scene is in western Wyoming, near Dubois. *(Tom L. McKnight photo.)*

impassable terrain. They are found in scattered locations (most of them mercifully small) in every western state, the most famous areas being in Bryce Canyon National Park in southern Utah and in Badlands National Park in western South Dakota.

Arches and Natural Bridges Mesa-and-scarp terrain is also famous for numerous minor erosional features, most produced by a combination of weathering and fluvial erosion. An *arch* (Figure 18-39) can form when the lower portions of a narrow "fin" of sedimentary rock weaken and collapse, leaving an arch of more resistant rock above. A *natural bridge* can form anytime the rock over which water flows changes from an erosion-resistant type to a less resistant type. One place a natural bridge frequently forms is where an entrenched meander wears away the rock in a narrow neck between meander loops (see Figure 16-41 in Chapter 16).

Pedestals and pillars, sometimes larger at the top than at the bottom, rise abruptly above their surroundings, their caps resistant material but their narrow bases continuously weathered by rainwater trickling

▲ **Figure 18-39** Delicate Arch in Utah's Arches National Park. *(Darrel Hess photo.)*

TABLE 18-1 Basic Characteristics of Arid Region Landforms		
Landform	Process	Composition
Alluvial fan	Fluvial deposition	Alluvial debris
Badlands	Fluvial erosion	Soft bedrock
Bajada	Fluvial deposition	Alluvial debris
Barchan dune	Aeolian deposition	Sand
Bornhardt	Fluvial erosion	Bedrock
Butte	Fluvial erosion	Bedrock
Claypan	Fluvial deposition	Fine alluvium
Erg	Aeolian deposition	Sand
Hamada	Erosion	Bedrock
Inselberg	Fluvial erosion	Bedrock
Mesa	Fluvial erosion	Bedrock
Pediment	Fluvial erosion	Bedrock
Playa	Fluvial deposition	Fine alluvium
Reg	Erosion	Pebbles, etc.
Salina	Fluvial deposition	Fine alluvium
Sand dune	Aeolian deposition	Sand
Scarp	Fluvial erosion	Bedrock
Seif dune	Aeolian deposition	Sand
Transverse dune	Aeolian deposition	Sand

down the surface. This water dissolves the cementing material that holds the sand grains together, and the loosened grains are easily blown or washed away.

One other notable characteristic of mesa-and-scarp terrain is vivid colors. The sedimentary outcrops and sandy debris of these regions are often resplendent in various shades of red, brown, yellow, and gray, due mostly to iron compounds.

Table 18-1 summarizes basic characteristics of arid region landforms.

Chapter 18 Learning Review

Key Terms

Before answering the study questions, review the definitions of the following key terms (page references are provided for you):

aeolian processes (p. 539)
alluvial fan (p. 545)
badlands (p. 550)
bajada (p. 546)
barchan dune (p. 541)
blowout (p. 539)
bornhardt (p. 533)
butte (p. 550)
deflation (p. 539)
desert pavement (p. 538)
desert varnish (p. 538)

differential erosion (p. 533)
ephemeral stream (p. 532)
erg (p. 536)
exotic stream (p. 531)
hamada (p. 538)
inselberg (p. 533)
loess (p. 542)
mesa (p. 549)
pediment (p. 533)
piedmont (p. 536)
pinnacle (p. 550)

plateau (p. 549)
playa (p. 532)
reg (p. 538)
salina (p. 532)
saline lake (p. 532)
sand dune (p. 540)
sapping (p. 549)
scarp (p. 549)
seif dune (p. 541)
slip face (p. 540)
transverse dune (p. 541)

Study Questions for Key Concepts

After studying this chapter, you should be able to answer the following questions:

A Specialized Environment (p. 529)

1. List several ways in which topographic development in arid lands is different from that in humid regions.
2. What is meant by an *impermeable surface* and how does such a surface influence the results of rainfall in a desert?
3. What is a *basin of interior drainage*?
4. Why are basins of interior drainage particularly prevalent in desert areas?

Running Water in Waterless Regions (p. 530)

5. What is the difference between an *ephemeral stream* and an *exotic stream* in a desert?
6. Although there is very little rainfall in deserts, running water is still the most important process of erosion and deposition in arid environments. Describe and explain at least two special conditions in deserts that tend to increase the likelihood of fluvial erosion whenever it does rain.
7. What is a *playa* and why does one form?
8. What is the difference between a playa and a *salina*?
9. Why are playas so flat and level?
10. Explain the concept of *differential erosion*.
11. Describe the formation of an *inselberg*.
12. What is the difference between *pediment* and *piedmont*?
13. Why are depositional features of alluvium so prominent in many desert regions?

Characteristic Desert Surfaces—Ergs, Regs, and Hamadas (p. 536)

14. Distinguish between *erg* and *reg*.

15. Describe and explain the formation of *desert pavement* and *desert varnish*.

The Work of the Wind (p. 538)

16. Contrast aeolian *deflation* and aeolian *abrasion*.
17. How important is wind in the sculpturing of desert landforms?
18. Describe and explain the general cross section of an unanchored desert sand dune. Be sure to contrast the windward side with the *slip face* of the dune.
19. Explain the general shape and movement of *barchan sand dunes*.
20. How are *transverse dunes* different from *seif dunes*?
21. Most *loess* is not found in arid regions; why is it discussed in this chapter?

Two Characteristic Desert Landform Assemblages (p. 544)

22. What is an *alluvial fan* and why are they so prevalent in the basin-and-range desert area of North America?
23. How does an alluvial fan differ from a delta?
24. How is a *bajada* different from an alluvial fan?
25. Why are some playas in the basin-and-range desert so salty?
26. Why are there few deep stream channels cutting across basin floors in the basin-and-range desert?
27. How does a *plateau* differ from a *mesa*?
28. Describe and explain the processes involved that can change a mesa into a *butte* or *pinnacle*.
29. What is distinctive about *badlands* terrain? How did it come to be that way?

Additional Resources

Books:

Cooke, Ron, Andrew Warren, and Andrew Goudie. *Desert Geomorphology*. London: University College London Press, 1993.

Livingstone, Ian, and Andrew Warren. *Aeolian Geomorphology: An Introduction*. Essex, UK: Longman, 1996.

Walker, A. S. *Deserts: Geology and Resources*. U.S. Geological Survey publication 1992 0–305–515. Washington, D.C.: U.S. Government Printing Office, 1992.

Internet Sites:

The National Map

http://www.nationalmap.usgs.gov/

    The National Map is an interactive map service that provides access to a wide range of geospatial data.

U.S. Geological Survey

http://www.usgs.gov/

    The U.S. Geological Survey home page provides links to information on a wide range of Earth science topics, including earthquakes, volcanoes, landslides, floods, and other natural hazards. The page also has links to sites where topographic maps, geological maps, research papers, and publications of general interest may be viewed or purchased.

19
Glacial Modification of Terrain

In the long history of our planet, ice ages have occurred an unknown number of times. The cause or causes of the climate changes that led to these ice ages are still incompletely understood, a topic we discuss further at the end of the chapter. With one outstanding exception, however, nearly all evidence of past glacial periods has been eradicated by subsequent geomorphic events, with the result that only the most recent ice age has influenced contemporary topography. Consequently, when referring to the Ice Age, capitalized, we usually mean this most recent ice age, which is the main feature of the geologic epoch known as *the Pleistocene*, a period that began about 2 million years ago and ended less than 10,000 years ago.

In this chapter, we are concerned with Pleistocene events both because they significantly modified pre-Pleistocene topography and because their results are so thoroughly imprinted on many parts of the continental terrain today. Glacial processes are still at work, to be sure, but their importance is much less now than it was just a few thousand years ago simply because so much less glacial ice is present today.

The Impact of Glaciers on the Landscape

A glacier begins to develop when there is a net year-to-year accumulation of snow—that is, when the amount of snow that falls in a winter is greater than the amount that melts the following summer over a period of years. The snow that falls the next winter weighs down on the old snow and turns it to ice. After many years of such accumulation, the ice mass begins to move under the pull of gravity. Wherever glaciers have developed, they have had an overwhelming impact on the landscape simply because moving ice grinds away almost anything in its path. Human-built structures and preexisting vegetation are destroyed, most soil is bulldozed away, and bedrock is polished, scraped, gouged, plucked, and abraded. In short, preglacial topography is significantly reshaped. Moreover, when the glacier ceases its advance, and even before, under certain circumstances, the debris that it picked up is deposited in a new location, further changing the shape of the terrain.

About 7 percent of all contemporary erosion is accomplished by glaciers. This is a paltry total in comparison with fluvial erosion, to be sure, but considering how small a land area is covered by glacial ice today, it

◀ Mendenhall Glacier, Alaska. *(Getty Images, Inc.—Taxi.)*

is clear that glaciers make a respectable contribution to continental denudation. It has been calculated that glaciation increases the erosion rate on a mountain by at least 10 times over the rate on a comparable unglaciated mountain.

Glaciation modifies flat landscapes greatly, with the result that postglacial slope, drainage, and surficial material are likely to be totally different from what they were before the glacier passed by. In mountainous areas, the metamorphosis of the landscape may be less complete, but the topography is deepened, steepened, and sharpened throughout.

Glaciations Past and Present

The amount of glacial ice on Earth's surface has varied remarkably over the last few million years, with periods of accumulation interspersed with periods of melting and times of ice advance alternating with times of ice retreat. A great deal of secondary evidence was left behind by the moving and melting ice, and scientists have been remarkably perspicacious in piecing together the chronology of past glaciations. Nevertheless, the record is incomplete and often approximate. As is to be expected, the more recent events are best documented; the farther one delves into the past, the murkier the evidence becomes.

Pleistocene Glaciation

1. End of the Last Ice Age
2. Isostasy

The precise boundaries of the **Pleistocene epoch** (see Figure 13-25) are unknown. It began at least 1.8 million years ago, but geochronologists have pushed the starting date of the glaciations further and further back (evidence suggests, for example, that Antarctica was covered by an ice cap similar in size to today's as long ago as perhaps 10 million years). The most recent findings tell us that by about 2.5 million years ago the "amplitude" of climate fluctuations—from glacial period to interglacial period—had increased and some parts of the Northern Hemisphere were covered by glaciers.

New evidence has also changed the date of the close of the Pleistocene, with glaciologists now believing that the last major ice retreat took place more recently than 9000 years ago. Even this most recent estimate for the close date cannot be cast in stone, however, because the Ice Age may not yet have ended at all, a possibility we consider later in the chapter. For now, let us just say that, to the best of present knowledge, the Pleistocene epoch occupied almost all of the most recent two million years of Earth's history.

The dominant environmental characteristic of the Pleistocene was the refrigeration of high-latitude and high-elevation areas, so that a vast amount of ice accumulated in many places. However, the epoch was by no means universally icy. During several lengthy periods, most or all of the ice melted, only to be followed by intervals of ice accumulation. In broad terms, the Pleistocene consisted of an alternation of *glacial* (times of ice accumulation) and *interglacial* (times of ice retreat) periods. Current evidence suggests as many as 18 or 19 glacial episodes took place during the Pleistocene.

The end of the Pleistocene epoch coincided with the conclusion of what is known in North America as the "Wisconsin" glacial stage (known as the "Würm" in the Alps), approximately 10,000 years ago. The period since then is identified as the *Holocene epoch.* Conceptually, then, the Holocene is either a postglacial epoch or the latest in a series of interglacial interludes.

At its maximum Pleistocene extent, ice covered one-third of the total land area of Earth—nearly 47,000,000 square kilometers (19 million square miles), as Figure 19-1 shows. Table 19-1 shows the maximum extent of the Wisconsin–Würm glaciation. Ice thickness varied and can be estimated only roughly,

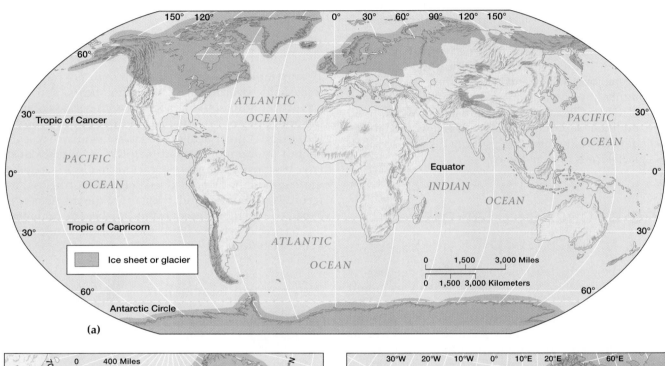

(a)

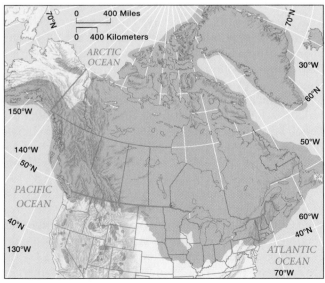

(b)

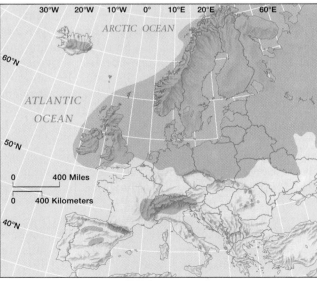

(c)

▲ **Figure 19-1** The maximum extent of Pleistocene glaciation: **(a)** worldwide; **(b)** in North America; **(c)** in Western Eurasia.

TABLE 19-1 Maximum Extent of Wisconsin–Würm Ice		
	Area Covered	
Region	Square Kilometers	Square Miles
North America	16,964,000	6,550,000
Eurasia: Europe	4,926,000	1,902,000
Asia	4,740,000	1,830,000

but we do know that in some areas it reached a depth of several thousands of meters.

The greatest total area of ice-covered land was in North America. The *Laurentide* ice, which covered most of Canada and a considerable portion of the northeastern United States, was the most extensive Pleistocene ice mass; its area was slightly larger than that of the present glacier covering Antarctica. It extended southward into the United States to approximately the present location of Long Island, the Ohio River, and the Missouri River. Most of western Canada and much of Alaska were covered by an interconnecting network of smaller glaciers. For reasons we do not fully understand, however, a small area in northwestern Canada as well as extensive portions of northern and western Alaska were never glaciated during the Pleistocene. Moreover, a small area (29,000 square kilometers, 11,200 square miles) in southwestern Wisconsin and parts of three adjoining states was also left uncovered, as Figure 19-1b shows. This area, referred to as the *Driftless Area,* apparently never existed as an island completely surrounded by ice; rather, ice encroached first on one side and then on another side during different glacial advances.

More than half of Europe was overlain by ice during the Pleistocene (Figure 19-1c). Asia was less extensively covered, presumably because in much of its subarctic portion there was not enough precipitation for the ice to last. Nevertheless, ice covered much of Siberia, and extensive glaciation occurred in most Asian mountain ranges.

In the Southern Hemisphere, Antarctic ice was only slightly more extensive than it is today, a large ice complex covered southernmost South America, and the South Island of New Zealand was largely covered with ice. Other high mountain areas all over the world—in central Africa, New Guinea, Hawaii—experienced more limited glaciation.

The accumulation of ice and the movement and melting of the resulting glaciers had an enormous effect on topography and drainage, a topic we discuss later in the chapter. In addition, however, there were several indirect effects of Pleistocene glaciation:

1. **Periglacial processes:** Beyond the outermost extent of ice advance is an area of indefinite size called the **periglacial zone**, which was never touched by glacial ice but where indirect influence of the ice was felt. The most important periglacial process was the erosion and deposition done by the prodigious amounts of meltwater released as the glaciers melted. Also important were frost weathering caused by the low temperatures in the periglacial zone and the associated *solifluction* of frozen subsoil (see Chapter 15 for a review of solifluction). It is estimated that periglacial conditions extended over more than 20 percent of the Earth's land area. (Periglacial landforms are discussed later in this chapter.)

2. **Sea-level changes:** The buildup of ice on the continents meant that less water was available to drain from the continents into the oceans, a condition that resulted in a worldwide lowering of sea level during every episode of glacial advance; when the glaciers retreated, sea level would again rise as meltwater returned to the oceans. At the peak of the Pleistocene glaciations, global sea level was about 130 meters (430 feet) lower than it is today. These fluctuations in the amount of drainage water caused a significant difference in drainage patterns and topographic development on seashores and coastal plains (the influence of Pleistocene sea level changes on coastal topography will be discussed in Chapter 20).

3. **Crustal depression:** The enormous weight of accumulated ice on the continents caused portions of Earth's crust to sink, in some cases by as much as 1200 meters (4000 feet). After the ice melted, the crust slowly began to rebound. This *isostatic adjustment* has not yet been completed, and some portions of Canada and northern Europe are still rising as much as 20 centimeters (8 inches) per decade. Isostasy is discussed in detail in Chapter 13 (for example, see Figure 13-21).

4. **Pluvial (increased rain) developments:** During the Pleistocene glaciations, there was, on almost all areas of the continents, a considerable increase in the amount of moisture available. This increase was caused by a combination of meltwater runoff, increased precipitation, and decreased evaporation. A prominent result of these **pluvial effects** was the creation of many lakes in areas where none had previously existed. Most of these lakes have subsequently been drained or significantly reduced in size, but they have left lasting imprints on the landscape. Pleistocene lakes in the western part of the United States are shown in Figure 19-2. The present-day Great Salt Lake in Utah is a tiny remnant of a much larger Pleistocene lake known as Lake Bonneville, and today's Bonneville Salt Flats were once the floor of this enormous lake.

Contemporary Glaciation

In marked contrast to Pleistocene glaciation, the extent of ice covering the continental surfaces today is very

▲ **Figure 19-2** Pleistocene lakes of the intermontane region of the United States. Today's Great Salt Lake (Utah) is shown outlined in blue inside the boundaries of the ancestral Lake Bonneville.

limited (Figure 19-3). About 10 percent of Earth's land surface—some 15 million square kilometers (6 million square miles)—is covered with ice today, but more than 96 percent of that total is in Antarctica and Greenland.

Something more than two-thirds of all the world's fresh water is at this moment frozen into glacial ice.

Antarctic Ice Cap Antarctic ice is by far the most extensive ice cap on Earth. At present, about 98 percent of its surface is covered with glacial ice, representing about 85 percent of the world's land–ice total. This ice is more than 4000 meters (13,000 feet) thick in some places and more than 1500 meters (5000 feet) thick over most of the continent.

Physically the continent and its ice sheets can be thought of as consisting of two unequal sections separated by the wide upland belt of the Transantarctic Mountains, which extend for some 4000 kilometers (2500 miles) (Figure 19-4, p. 560). West Antarctica, the smaller of the two sections, is generally mountainous (Figure 19-5, p. 560). It contains, however, a few interior valleys that are curiously ice free. The "Dry Valleys" area consists of about 3900 square kilometers (1500 square miles) which, because winds blast away snow and keep precipitation out, does not build ice. The three major parallel valleys contain several large lakes, a number of ponds, and a river that flows for one or two months each year.

If West Antarctica were to lose its ice, it would appear as a considerable number of scattered islands. East Antarctica is more extensive, and its subglacial relief is less varied, appearing to be largely a broad plateau with scattered mountains. The ice is considerably deeper in West Antarctica, and the surface of the ice is generally at a greater elevation than in the eastern section. Most of the surface of West Antarctica exceeds 2.4 kilometers (8000 feet) above sea level, and a

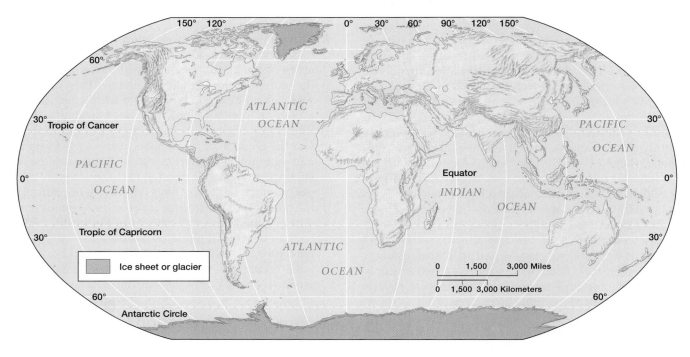

▲ **Figure 19-3** World distribution of glacial ice today.

PEOPLE AND THE ENVIRONMENT Disintegration of Antarctic Ice Shelves

Despite its remoteness, Antarctica exerts a prominent influence on the world's environment—global sea level, oceanic temperature, ocean nutrient content, and patterns of atmospheric circulation all are affected by conditions in Antarctica. At the same time, the global environment exerts its own influence on the conditions in Antarctica. As is true in the Arctic, the ice sheets of Antarctica appear to be sensitive indicators of changes in global climate. Over the last half century, average temperatures in the Antarctic have increased by about 2.5°C (4.5°F)—much more than the average increase in temperature worldwide. As a consequence, Antarctic ice has been undergoing changes.

If all 30,000,000 cubic kilometers (7,200,000 cubic miles) of Antarctic ice were to melt, the sea level around the world would rise by about 73 meters (240 feet)—up to the nose of the Statue of Liberty. While the complete melting of the Antarctic icecap is unlikely, the long-term equilibrium

between accumulation and wastage of the ice does appear to be changing significantly as a response to higher global temperatures. Some of the most dramatic changes are occurring in Antarctica's ice shelves.

The Antarctic ice sheets flow outward from the interior of the continent in nearly all directions toward the sea, which means that icebergs are being calved (broken off) into the sea more or less continuously around the perimeter of the continent. Some of these icebergs originate through outlet glaciers, but many are broken off from *ice shelves.* There are several of these great plates of floating ice, particularly in West Antarctica, with the Ross Ice Shelf being the largest (520,000 square kilometers or 200,000 square miles) (see Figure 19-4). On the Antarctic Peninsula, a number of smaller ice shelves are found, such as the Larsen Ice Shelves on the eastern side of the peninsula.

Over the last few years, large sections of the ice shelves along the

Antarctic Peninsula have disintegrated—about 8000 square kilometers (3100 square miles) of ice shelf have disappeared since 1993. After slowly retreating for many years, in 1995 the Larsen-A ice shelf simply collapsed and disappeared. In 2002, the Larsen-B ice shelf collapsed in little more than a month (Figure 19-A). The larger Larsen-C ice shelf is currently losing mass as a result of both higher air temperatures above and higher water temperatures below.

Although the loss of ice shelves does not raise global sea level (for the same reason that a floating ice cube doesn't raise the level of the water in a glass as it melts), changing ice shelves can trigger a change in the flow of land-based ice off the continent. To a certain extent, an intact ice shelf holds back the flow of continental ice into the ocean. Once an ice shelf is gone, the continental ice may flow faster into the ocean, and with land-based ice entering the ocean at a greater rate than before, sea level will rise.

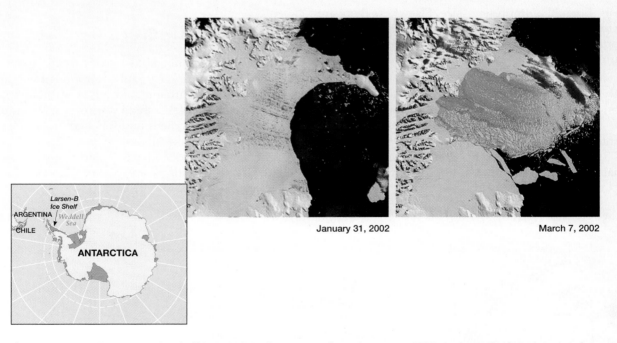

▲ **Figure 19-A** The Larsen-B ice shelf in Antarctica began to collapse in January 2002, as shown in these images taken by NASA's Terra satellite. On January 31, 2002, blue "melt ponds" are seen on top of the ice shelf. By March 7, 2002, the ice shelf had disintegrated. The blue area shows the shattered ice from the shelf. *(AP Photo/NASA, National Snow and Ice Data Center, University of Colorado, Ted Scambos.)*

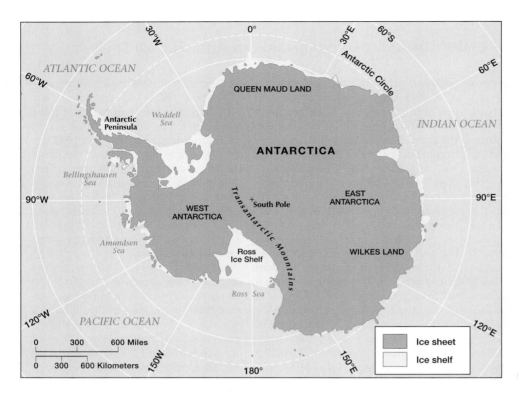

◀ **Figure 19-4** The Antarctic ice sheet and ice shelves.

considerable portion is more than 3 kilometers (10,000 feet) in altitude.

Greenland Ice Cap Greenland ice is much less extensive—1,740,000 square kilometers (670,000 square miles)—but still of impressive size. Elsewhere there are only relatively small ice masses on certain islands in the Canadian Arctic, Iceland, and some of the islands north of Europe.

North American Glaciers In the conterminous United States, most glaciers are in the Pacific Northwest, and more than half of these are in the North Cascade Mountains of Washington (Figure 19-6). In Alaska, there are 75,000 square kilometers (29,000 square miles) of glacial ice, amounting to about 4 percent of the total area of the state. The largest Alaskan glacier is the Bering Glacier, near Cordova, which covers 5830 square kilometers (2250 square miles) and is more than twice the size of Rhode Island.

Types of Glaciers

A glacier is more than a block of ice filling up a mountain valley; it is a finely tuned environment with a delicately balanced nourishment budget. Although glacial ice behaves in similar fashion wherever it accumulates, its pattern of movement and its effect on topographic shaping can vary considerably depending on the quantity of ice involved and particularly on the environment. These variations are best understood by first

◀ **Figure 19-5** The Transantarctic Mountains. *(Howard Platt photo.)*

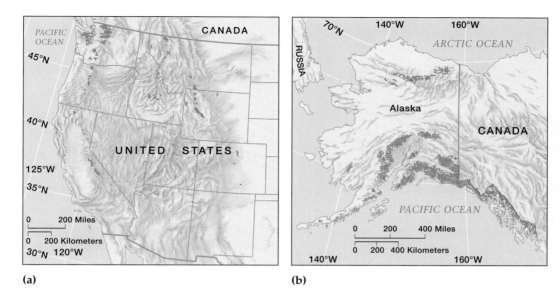

(a)   (b)

▲ **Figure 19-6** The location of contemporary glaciers in **(a)** the conterminous western United States and **(b)** Alaska.

considering the different types of glaciers: ice sheets and mountain glaciers.

Continental Ice Sheets

Glaciers that formed in nonmountainous areas of the continents are called **continental ice sheets**. During the Pleistocene these were vast blankets of ice that completely inundated the underlying terrain to depths of hundreds or thousands of meters. Because of their immense size, ice sheets have been the most significant agents of glaciation across the land surface. Only two true ones exist today, in Antarctica and Greenland. The ice in an ice sheet accumulates to great depths in the interior of the sheet but is much thinner at the outer edges. Around the margin of the sheet, some long tongues of ice, called *outlet glaciers*, extend between rimming hills to the sea (Figure 19-7). In other places, the ice reaches the ocean along a massive front, where it sometimes projects out over the sea as an ice shelf. Great chunks of ice frequently

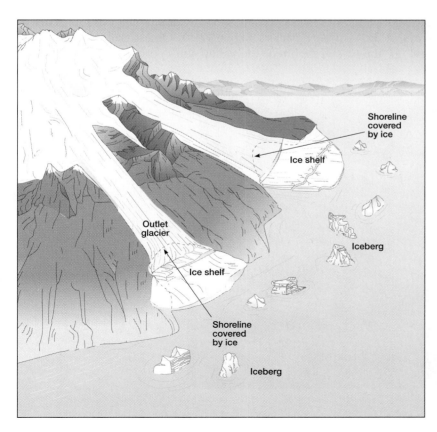

◀ **Figure 19-7** When either an ice sheet or an outlet glacier reaches the ocean, some of the ice may extend out over the water as an ice shelf. Icebergs form when the hanging ice of the shelf breaks off and floats away, a process called calving.

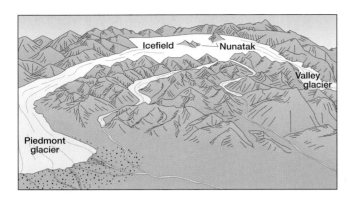

▲ **Figure 19-8** Icefield, nunataks, valley glaciers, and a piedmont glacier in a mountainous region.

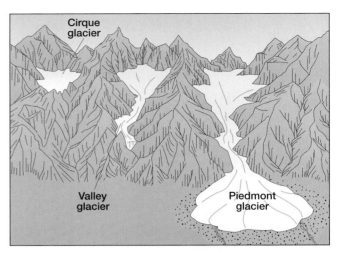

▲ **Figure 19-9** The three basic types of alpine glaciers. In addition to forming this way when an alpine glacier overflows its cirque, valley and piedmont glaciers can also originate from an icefield, as we saw in Figure 19-8.

break off, both from the ice shelves and from the ends of outlet glaciers, fall into the sea, and float away. These huge floating ice masses are *icebergs.*

Mountain Glaciers

Two types of glaciers form in the high country: *icefields* and *alpine glaciers.*

Highland Icefields   In a few high-mountain areas, ice accumulates in an unconfined sheet that may cover a few hundred or few thousand square kilometers, submerging all the underlying topography except perhaps for some protruding pinnacles (called *nunataks*) (Figure 19-8). Such **highland icefields** are notable in parts of the high country of western Canada and southern Alaska and on various Arctic islands (particularly Iceland). Their outlets are often tongues of ice that travel down valleys in the mountains and so are called **valley glaciers.** If the

leading edge of a valley glacier reaches a flat area and so escapes from the confines of its valley walls, it is called a **piedmont glacier**.

Alpine Glaciers   Alpine glaciers are those that develop individually high in the mountains rather than as part of a broad icefield, usually at the heads of valleys (Figure 19-9). Very small alpine glaciers confined to the basins where they originate are called **cirque glaciers** (because the basin is called a *cirque,* as we shall see later in the chapter). Normally, however, alpine glaciers spill out of their originating basins and flow down-valley as long, narrow valley glaciers (Figure 19-10). Occasionally they extend to the mouth of the valley and become piedmont glaciers.

▲ **Figure 19-10**   Alpine glaciers in southeastern Alaska near Skagway. A half-dozen small valley glaciers in the high country have united to form the very large Davidson Glacier, which extends off the bottom of the photo. *(Tom L. McKnight photo.)*

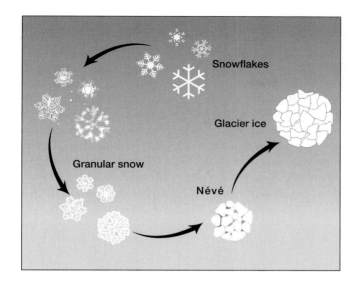

▲ **Figure 19-11** Snow is changed to ice by compression and coalescence, following a sequence from snowflake to granular snow to névé to glacier ice.

Glacier Formation and Movement

Snow falls and ice accumulates in many parts of the world, but glaciers do not always develop from these events. Glaciers require certain circumstances to form and then depend on just the right combination of temperature and moisture to survive. A slight warming or drying trend for a few decades can cause even the most extensive ice sheet to disappear. The persistence of any glacier depends on the balance between **accumulation** (addition of ice by incorporation of snow) and **ablation** (wastage of ice through melting and sublimation).

Changing Snow to Ice

Snow is not merely frozen water; rather, it is a substance that has crystallized directly from water vapor in the atmosphere and floats to Earth as lacy, hexagonal crystals that are only about one-tenth as dense as liquid water. Sooner or later (within a few hours if the temperature is near freezing, but only over a period of years in very cold situations), crystalline snow is compressed by overlying snow into granular form, and in the process its density is approximately doubled. With more time and further compression, the granules are packed more closely and begin to coalesce, the density increasing steadily until it is about half the density of water (Figure 19-11). This material is called **névé** or **firn**. As time passes, the pore spaces with their trapped air among the whitish névé crystals gradually diminish as the air is squeezed out by the weight of the overlying snow; the density approaches 90 percent of that of liquid water, and the material takes on the bluish tinge of glacial ice. This ice continues to change, although very slowly, with more air being forced out, the density increasing slightly, and the crystals increasing in size.

Every glacier can be divided into two portions on the basis of the balance between accumulation and ablation, as shown in Figure 19-12. The upper portion is called the **accumulation zone** because here the amount

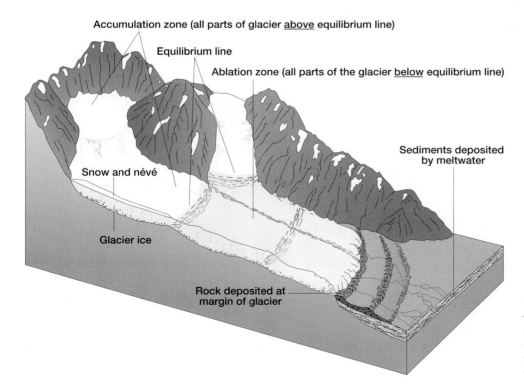

Accumulation zone (all parts of glacier <u>above</u> equilibrium line)

Equilibrium line

Ablation zone (all parts of the glacier <u>below</u> equilibrium line)

Sediments deposited by meltwater

Snow and névé

Glacier ice

Rock deposited at margin of glacier

◀ **Figure 19-12** Cross section through an alpine glacier. The upper portion is an area of net ice accumulation. Below the equilibrium line there is more ablation than accumulation.

of new ice from snowfall added each year exceeds the amount lost by melting and sublimation. The lower portion is called the **ablation zone** because here the amount of new ice added each year is less than the amount lost. Separating the two zones is a theoretical **equilibrium line**, along which accumulation exactly balances ablation.

Glacial Movement

Flow of Ice Within a Glacier

Despite the fact that glaciers are often likened to rivers of ice, there is very little similarity between liquid flow and glacial movement. The "flow" of a glacier involves an orderly sliding of ice molecules one over the other, quite unlike the disordered, pell-mell movement of molecules in flowing water.

We usually think of ice as being a brittle substance that breaks rather than bends and resists any sort of deformation. This is generally true for surface ice, as evidenced by the cracks and *crevasses* that often appear at the surface of a glacier. However, ice under considerable confining pressure, as below the surface of a glacier, behaves quite differently: it deforms rather than breaks. Moreover, partial melting, due to the stresses within and the pressure at the bottom of the glacier, aids movement because the meltwater sinks to the bottom of the glacier and becomes a slippery layer on which the glacier can slide.

When a mass of ice attains a thickness of about 50 meters (165 feet)—less on steep slopes—it begins to flow in response to the overlying weight. The entire mass does not move; rather, there is an oozing outward from around the edge of an ice sheet or down-valley from the toe of an alpine glacier. There is also *laminar flow* along internal planes which causes different portions of the glacier to move with different speeds. A third type of movement is **basal slip** at the bottom of the glacier, in which the entire mass slides over its bed on a lubricating film of water. The glacier more or less molds itself to the shape of the terrain over which it is riding, although it simultaneously reshapes the terrain significantly by erosion.

Glaciers usually move very slowly; indeed, the adjective "glacial" is synonymous with "exceedingly slow." The movement of most glaciers can be measured in a few centimeters per day, although an advance of several meters per day would not be unusual, and extreme examples of nearly 30 meters (100 feet) in a 24-hour period have been recorded. Also, the flow is often erratic, with irregular pulsations and surges over a short span of time. As might be expected, all parts of a glacier do not move at the same rate. The fastest-moving ice is that at and near the surface, and if the glacier is confined, the way a valley glacier is, for instance, the center of the surface ice moves faster than the sides, which is similar to streamflow patterns.

Glacier Flow versus Glacier Advance In discussing glacier movement, it is important to distinguish between glacier *flow* and glacier *advance*. As long as a glacier exists, the ice in it is flowing, either laterally outward or downhill. This does not necessarily mean that the outer edge of the ice is advancing, however. The ice in a glacier always moves forward, but the outer margin of the glacier may or may not be advancing, depending on the balance between accumulation and ablation (Figure 19-13). Even in a retreating glacier (which is one whose outer margin is retracting toward its point of origin due to heavy ablation), the ice is flowing forward.

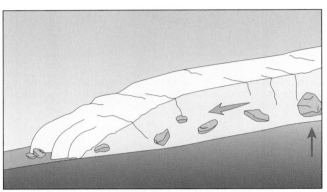

(a)

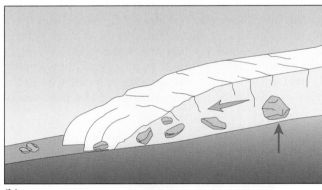

(b)

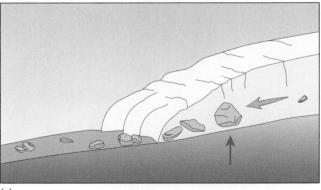

(c)

▲ **Figure 19-13** A flowing glacier is not necessarily an advancing glacier. In this sequential illustration, the front of the glacier is clearly retreating, but the ice continues to flow forward. The boulder marked by the red arrow illustrates the principle.

During wetter or cooler periods when there is a great accumulation of ice, a glacier can flow farther before it finally wastes away, and so the outer margin of the glacier advances. During warmer or drier periods when the rate of ablation is increased, the glacier continues to flow, but it wastes away sooner, and so the end or *terminus* of the glacier retreats.

The Effects of Glaciers

Glacial Processes

As glaciers move across a landscape, they can reshape the topography through the erosion, transportation, and deposition of rock.

Erosion by Glaciers

As with streams, volume and speed determine the effectiveness of glacial erosion. The amount of erosion caused by a glacier is roughly proportional to the thickness of the ice and its rate of flow. The depth of the erosion is limited in part by the structure and texture of the bedrock and in part by the relief of the terrain. Erosion by glaciers is inhibited by low relief and enhanced by high relief. On flat land the changes are minor, but in mountainous areas they may be striking.

Glacial Plucking   The direct erosive power of moving ice is greater than that of flowing water but not remarkably so. As the slowly moving ice scrapes against bedrock, friction between rock and ice causes the lowermost ice to melt, and the layer of water created reduces the pressure on the rock. This water can refreeze around rocky protrusions, however, and the refrozen ice can exert a significant force as it is pushed by the ice behind it. Probably the most significant erosive work of glacial ice is accomplished by this **glacial plucking**. Rock particles beneath the ice are grasped as meltwater refreezes in bedrock joints and fractures where frost wedging further loosens the rock. As the ice moves along, these particles are plucked out and dragged along. This action is particularly effective on leeward slopes (slopes facing away from the direction of ice movement).

Glacial Abrasion   Glaciers also erode by abrasion, in which the bedrock is worn down by the rock debris being dragged along in the moving ice (Figure 19-14). Abrasion mostly produces minor features, such as

(a)

(b)

◀ **Figure 19-14   (a)** Grooves and striae caused by glacial abrasion near Cuzco, Peru. *(Walter H. Hodge/Peter Arnold, Inc.)* **(b)** Striations on limestone bedrock caused by glacial abrasion in Canada's Jasper National Park. *(Tom L. McKnight photo.)*

polished surfaces when the bedrock is of highly resistant material and striations (fine parallel indentations) and grooves (indentations deeper and larger than striations) in less resistant bedrock. Whereas plucking tends to roughen the underlying surface, abrasion tends to polish it and dig striations and grooves.

In plains areas, the topography produced by glacial erosion is inconspicuous. Prominences are smoothed and small hollows may be excavated, but the general appearance of the terrain changes little. In hilly areas, however, the effects of glacial erosion are much more notable. Mountains and ridges are sharpened, valleys are deepened and steepened and made more linear, and the entire landscape becomes more angular and rugged.

Transportation by Glaciers

Glaciers are extremely competent, as well as indiscriminate, in their ability to transport rock debris. Being solid bodies, they can move immense blocks of rock, literally the size of houses. Moreover, they may transport these gigantic pieces for dozens or even hundreds of kilometers. Most of a glacier's load, however, is not such huge blocks but rather a heterogeneous collection of particles of all sizes. Perhaps the most typical component of the load is **glacial flour**, which is rock material that has been ground very fine.

Most of the material transported by a glacier is plucked or abraded from the underlying surface and so is carried along at the base of the ice. Thus, there is a narrow zone at the bottom of the glacier that is likely to be well armored by miscellaneous rock debris frozen into it, with most of the rest of the glacial ice relatively free of rock fragments. In alpine glaciers, some material is also transported on top of the ice, as mass wasting or surface erosion causes debris to fall down from the surrounding slopes. Also, a certain amount of debris is pushed along in front of an advancing glacier, in a sort of bulldozer effect.

A glacier transports its load outward or down-valley at a variable speed. The rate of flow usually increases in summer and slows in winter but also depends on variations in ice accumulation and in the gradient of the underlying slopes.

One other important aspect of transportation by glaciers is the role of flowing water on, in, and under the ice. During the warmer months, streams of meltwater normally flow along with the moving ice (Figure 19-15). Such streams may run along the surface of the glacier until they find cracks or crevasses into which to plunge, continuing their flow as subglacial streams either within the ice or along the interface between glacier and bedrock. Wherever such streams flow, they transport rock debris, particularly smaller particles and glacial flour, providing an effective mechanism for shifting debris from the ice surface to a position within or at the bottom of the glacier.

Even if a glacier is retreating, the debris inside it is still carried forward because of the ice flow taking place all through the glacier. The transport function of a glacier persists indefinitely unless and until the ice becomes so thin that subglacial obstacles, such as a hill, prevent further flow.

▲ **Figure 19-15**   A meltwater stream flowing over the surface of Athabaska Glacier in the Canadian Rockies. *(Tom L. McKnight photo.)*

Deposition by Glaciers

Probably the major role of glaciers in landscape modification is to remove lithospheric material from one area and take it to some distant region, where it is left in a fragmented and vastly changed form. This is clearly displayed in North America, where an extensive portion of central Canada has been glacially scoured of its soil, regolith, and much of its surface bedrock, leaving a relatively barren, rocky, gently undulating surface dotted with bodies of water. Much of the removed material was taken southward and deposited in the midwestern part of the United States, producing an extensive plains area of remarkably fertile soil. Thus, the legacy of Pleistocene ice sheets for the Midwest was the evolution of one of the largest areas of productive soils ever known, at the expense of central Canada, which was left impoverished of soil by those same glaciers. (On the other hand, many valuable Canadian mineral deposits were exposed when the glaciers removed soil and regolith.)

The general term for all material moved by glaciers is **drift**, a misnomer coined in the eighteenth century when it was believed that the vast debris deposits of the Northern Hemisphere were leftovers from biblical floods. Despite the erroneous thinking that led to the name, the term is fully accepted today as applicable to all materials carried by glaciers and/or their meltwater.

Rock debris deposited directly by moving or melting ice, with no meltwater flow or redeposition involved, is given the more distinctive name **till** (Figure 19-16). Direct deposition by ice is usually the result of melting around the margin of an ice sheet or near the lower end of an alpine glacier, but it is also accomplished whenever debris is dropped on the ground beneath the ice, especially in the ablation area. In either case, the result is an unsorted and unstratified agglomeration of fragmented rock material. Most of the fragments are angular because they have been held in position while carried in the ice and consequently have had little opportunity to become rounded by frequent impact the way pebbles in a stream would. Sometimes outsized boulders are included in the glacial till; such enormous fragments, which may be very different from the local bedrock, are called **glacial erratics** (Figure 19-17).

Deposition by Meltwater

Glacial runoff has several peculiarities—peak flows in midsummer, distinct day-and-night differences in volume, large silt content, and occasional floods—that set meltwater streams apart from other kinds of natural waterways. Much of the debris carried by glaciers is eventually deposited or redeposited by meltwater. In some cases, this is accomplished by subglacial streams issuing directly from the ice and carrying sedimentary material washed from positions in, on, or beneath the glacier. Much meltwater deposition, however, involves debris that was originally deposited by ice and subsequently picked up and redeposited by the meltwater well beyond the outer margin of the ice. Such **glaciofluvial deposition** occurs around the margins of all glaciers, as well as far out in some periglacial zones.

▲ **Figure 19-16**   Unsorted glacial till in a roadcut near Bridgeport, California. *(Tom L. McKnight photo.)*

▲ **Figure 19-17**   A glacial erratic carried many kilometers before being deposited by a Pleistocene glacier in what is now Yellowstone National Park. The ice has long since melted, and a forest has grown up around the erratic. *(Tom L. McKnight photo.)*

Continental Ice Sheets

Apart from the oceans and continents, continental ice sheets are the most extensive features ever to appear on the face of the planet. Their actions during Pleistocene time significantly reshaped both the terrain and the drainage of nearly one-fifth of the total surface area of the continents.

Development and Flow

Pleistocene ice sheets, with the exception of the one covering Antarctica, did not originate in the polar regions. Rather, they developed in subpolar and midlatitude locations and then spread outward in all directions, including poleward. Several (perhaps several dozen) centers of original ice accumulation have been identified. The accumulated snow/névé/ice eventually produced such a heavy weight that the ice began to flow outward from each center of accumulation.

The initial flow was channeled by the preexisting terrain along valleys and other low-lying areas, but in time the ice developed to such depths that it overrode almost all preglacial topography. In many places, it submerged even the highest points under thousands of meters of ice. Eventually the various ice sheets coalesced into only one, two, or three massive sheets on each continent. These vast ice sheets flowed and ebbed as the climate changed, always modifying the landscape with their enormous erosive power and the great masses of debris they deposited. The elaborate result was nothing less than a total reshaping of the land surface and a total rearrangement of the drainage pattern.

Erosion by Ice Sheets

Except in mountainous areas of great initial relief, the principal topography resulting from the erosion caused by an ice sheet is a gently undulating surface. The most conspicuous features are valley bottoms gouged and deepened by the moving ice. Such U-shaped troughs are deepest where the preglacial valleys were oriented parallel to the direction of ice movement, particularly in areas of softer bedrock. A prime example of such development is the Finger Lakes District of central New York, where a set of parallel stream valleys was reshaped by glaciation into a group of long, narrow, deep lakes (Figure 19-18). Even where the preglacial valley was not oriented parallel to the direction of ice flow, however, glacial gouging and scooping normally produced a large number of shallow excavations that became lakes after the ice disappeared. Indeed, the postglacial landscape in areas of ice-sheet erosion is notable for its profusion of lakes.

Hills are generally sheared off and rounded by the moving ice. A characteristic shape produced by both continental ice sheets and mountain glaciers is the **roche moutonnée**, which is often produced when a bedrock hill is overridden by moving ice (Figure 19-19). (The origin of this French term is unclear. It is often translated as "sheep's back," but some authorities believe it is based on a fancied resemblance to wavy wigs that were fashionable in France in the late 1700s and were known as *moutonnées* because they were pomaded with mutton tallow.) The *stoss side* (facing in the direction from which the ice came) of a roche moutonnée is smoothly rounded and streamlined by grinding

▲ **Figure 19-18**   The Finger Lakes of upstate New York occupy glacial valleys that were gouged out by ice sheets moving from north–northwest to south–southeast. The large body of water at upper left is Lake Ontario. This false-color composite image was taken from an altitude of about 920 kilometers (570 miles) by the ERTS-1 satellite. *(NASA/Photri.)*

abrasion as the ice rides up the slope, but the lee side (facing away from the direction from which the ice came) is shaped largely by plucking, which produces a steeper and more irregular slope (Figure 19-20).

The postglacial landscape produced by ice sheets is one of relatively low relief but not absolute flatness. The principal terrain elements are ice-scoured rocky knobs and scooped-out depressions. Soil and weathered materials are largely absent, with bare rock and lakes dominating the surface. Stream patterns are erratic and inadequately developed because the preglacial drainage net was deranged by ice erosion. Once eroded by the passing ice sheet, however, most of this landscape was subjected to further modification by glacial deposition. Thus, the starkness of

the erosional landscape is modified by depositional debris.

Deposition by Ice Sheets

In some cases, the till transported by ice sheets is deposited heterogeneously and extensively, without forming any identifiable topographic features; a veneer of unsorted debris is simply laid down over the preexisting terrain. This veneer is sometimes quite shallow and does not mask the original topography. In other cases, till is deposited to a depth of several hundred meters, completely obliterating the shape of the preglacial landscape. In either case, deposition tends to be uneven, producing an irregularly undulating surface of broad,

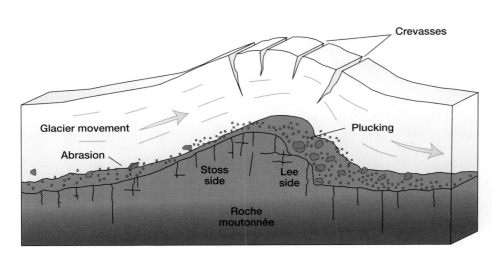

◀ **Figure 19-19**   The formation of a roche moutonnée. The glacier rides over a resistant bedrock surface, smoothing the stoss side by abrasion and steepening the lee side by plucking. When the ice has melted, an asymmetrical hill is the result.

◀ **Figure 19-20** Lembert Dome in Yosemite National Park is an example of a roche moutonnée. The glaciers moved from right to left (from east to west) across this granite dome. *(Darrel Hess photo.)*

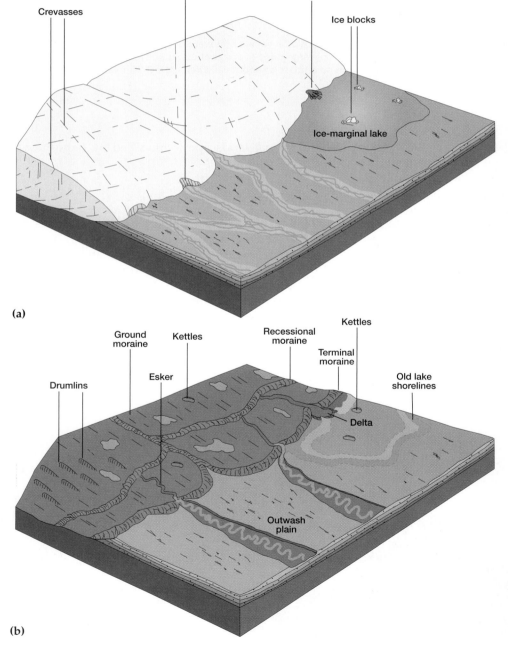

◀ **Figure 19-21** Glacier-deposited and glaciofluvially deposited features of a landscape **(a)** covered by a continental ice sheet and **(b)** after the ice sheet has retreated.

low rises and shallow depressions. Such a surface is referred to as a **till plain**.

In many instances, glacial sediments are laid down in more precise patterns, creating characteristic and identifiable landforms (Figure 19-21). **Moraine** is a general term for glacier-deposited landforms composed entirely or largely of till. They typically consist of irregular rolling topography rising some small height above the surrounding terrain. Moraines are usually much longer than they are wide, although the width can vary from a few tens of meters to as much as several kilometers. Some moraines are distinct ridges, whereas others are much more irregular in shape. Their relief is not great, varying from a few meters to a few hundred meters. When originally formed, moraines tend to have relatively smooth and gentle slopes, which become more uneven with the passage of time, as the blocks of stagnant ice, both large and small, included within the till eventually melt, leading to the collapse of the surface of the moraine.

Three types of moraines are particularly associated with deposition from continental ice sheets, although all three may be produced by alpine glaciers as well. A **terminal moraine** is a ridge of till that marks the outermost limit of glacial advance. It can vary in size from a conspicuous rampart tens of meters high to a low, discontinuous wall of debris. A terminal moraine is formed when a glacier reaches its equilibrium point and so is wasting at the same rate that it is being nourished. Although the toe of the glacier is not advancing, the interior continues to flow forward, delivering a supply of till. As the ice melts around the margin, the till is deposited, and the moraine grows (Figure 19-22).

Behind the terminal moraine (in other words, facing the direction from which the ice advanced), **recessional moraines** may develop. These are ridges that mark positions where the ice front was temporarily stabilized during the final retreat of the glacier. Both terminal and recessional moraines normally occur in the form of concave arcs that bulge outward in the direction of ice movement, indicating that the ice sheets advanced not along an even line but rather as a connecting series of great tongues of ice, each with a curved front (Figure 19-23).

The third type of moraine is the **ground moraine**, formed when large quantities of till are laid down from underneath the glacier rather than from its edge. A ground moraine usually means gently rolling plains across the landscape. It may be shallow or deep and often consists of low knolls and shallow *kettles*. **Kettles** form when large blocks of ice left by a retreating glacier become surrounded or even covered by glacial drift; after the ice block melts, the morainal surface collapses, leaving an irregular depression (Figure 19-24).

Another prominent feature deposited by ice sheets is a low, elongated hill called a **drumlin**, a term that comes from *druim*, an old Irish word for "ridge." Drumlins are much smaller than moraines but composed of

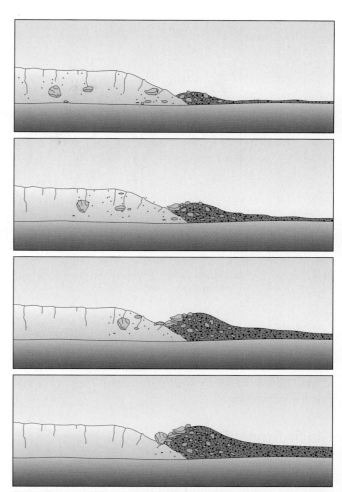

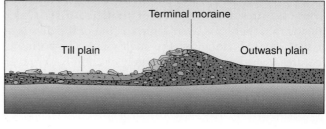

▲ **Figure 19-22** Terminal moraine growth at the toe of a stable glacier. The movement of a large boulder is shown from the time it is plucked from the bedrock until it is deposited as part of the moraine. The final diagram represents the situation after the ice has melted. (*After Sheldon Judson, Marvin E. Kauffman, and L. Don Leet,* Physical Geology, *Englewood Cliffs, NJ: Prentice Hall, 1987.*)

similarly unsorted till. The long axis of the drumlin is aligned parallel with the direction of ice movement. The end of the drumlin facing the direction from which the ice came is blunt and slightly steeper than the opposite end. Thus, the configuration is the reverse of that of a roche moutonnée. The origin of drumlins is complex, but most of them are apparently the result of ice readvance into an area of previous glacial deposition. In other words, they are depositional features subsequently shaped by erosion. Drumlins usually occur in groups, sometimes numbering in the hundreds, with all

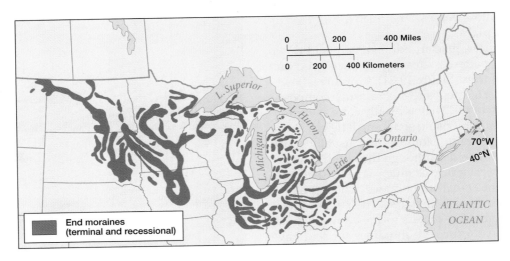

▲ **Figure 19-23** Terminal and recessional moraines in the United States resulting from the Wisconsin glaciation.

drumlins in a group oriented parallel to each other (Figure 19-25). The greatest concentrations of drumlins in the United States are found in central New York and eastern Wisconsin.

Glaciofluvial Features

The deposition or redeposition of debris by ice-sheet meltwater produces certain features both where the sheet covered the ground and in the periglacial region. These features are composed of **stratified drift**, which means that there has been some sorting of the debris as it was carried along by the meltwater. Glaciofluvial features, then, are composed largely or entirely of gravel, sand, and silt because meltwater is incapable of moving larger material.

The most extensive glaciofluvial features are **outwash plains**, which are smooth, flat alluvial aprons deposited beyond recessional or terminal moraines by streams issuing from the ice (see Figure 19-21). Streams of water, heavily loaded with reworked till or with debris washed directly from the ice, issue from the melting glacier to form a braided pattern of channels across the area beyond the glacial front. As they flow away from the ice, these braided streams, choked with debris, rapidly lose their speed and deposit their load. Such outwash deposits sometimes cover many hundreds of square kilometers.

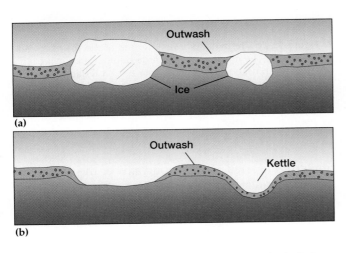

▲ **Figure 19-24** The formation of kettles. During deglaciation isolated masses of ice are often mixed in with the glacial debris and outwash and only melt slowly because of the insulation provided by the surrounding debris. When the ice does eventually melt, sizable depressions known as kettles may pit the surface of the outwash.

▲ **Figure 19-25** Drumlin west of Rochester, New York. The glacier flowed from right to left. (*Ward's Natural Science Establishment.*)

Focus Shrinking Alaskan Glaciers

Glaciers are sensitive indicators of environmental change. As we have seen, the size of a glacier is a delicate balance between the accumulation of ice and the ablation of ice. A relatively small increase in summer temperature or decrease in winter precipitation for a number of years may lead to the retreat of a glacier. But the relationships are sometimes counterintuitive: a glacier might also advance if slightly higher temperatures lead to an increase in winter precipitation.

Throughout most of Alaska and the rest of the world glaciers are retreating, and some of the most striking evidence for this comes not from specialized instruments or satellite measurements, but from old-fashioned photographs. Bruce Molina of the U.S. Geological Survey (USGS) has compared photographs of Alaskan glaciers taken from the 1890s to the 1970s with new photographs he's taken from the exact same locations. The contrast between pairs of images taken just decades apart in some cases is remarkable (Figure 19-B). Not only have glaciers been shrinking, but the photographs also reveal that vegetation patterns have been changing. In some areas where little vegetation was visible in the past, an extensive plant cover is now obvious.

The causes of the observed changes in glaciers and vegetation are certainly linked to global climate change. Although a few scientists are reluctant to conclude that the changes in Alaska's glaciers are a result of human-induced global warming alone, many researchers see the findings as some of the most convincing evidence yet of the human impact on global climate.

▲ **Figure 19-B** Change in the Muir Glacier and Riggs Glacier in Alaska's Glacier Bay National Park and Preserve. In 1941 the Muir and Riggs Glaciers filled Muir Inlet. By 2004, the Muir Glacier had retreated out of view and lush vegetation is now growing on the hillsides in the foreground. The "trimline" along the mountain front of the left side of the photograph indicates that the Muir Glacier was at least 600 meters (2000 feet) thick in 1941. (*USGS/Bruce Molina.*)

They are occasionally pitted by kettles that often become ponds or small lakes. Beyond the outwash plain, there is sometimes a lengthy deposit of glaciofluvial alluvium confined to a valley bottom; such a deposit is termed a **valley train**.

Less common than outwash plains, but more conspicuous, are long sinuous ridges of stratified drift called **eskers**, named from *eiscir,* another Irish word for "ridge." These landforms are composed largely of glaciofluvial gravel and are thought to have originated when streams flowing through tunnels in the interior of the ice sheet became choked off during a time in which the ice was neither flowing nor advancing. These streams beneath the stagnating sheet often carry a great deal of debris, and as the ice melts, the streams deposit much of their load in the tunnel. Eskers are this debris exposed once the ice melts away. They are usually a few dozen meters high, a few dozen meters wide, and may be a few dozen kilometers (or up to 160 kilometers [a hundred miles]) long (Figure 19-26).

Small, steep mounds or conical hills of stratified drift are found sporadically in areas of ice-sheet deposition. These **kames** (the word derives from *comb,* an old Scottish word referring to an elongated steep ridge) appear to be of diverse origin, but they are clearly associated with meltwater deposition in stagnant ice. They are mounds of poorly sorted sand and gravel that probably formed within glacial fissures or between the glacier and the land surface (Figure 19-27). Many seem to have been built as steep fans or deltas against the edge of the ice that later collapsed partially when the ice melted. Morainal surfaces containing a number of mounds and depressions are called *kame-and-kettle topography.*

Lakes are very common in areas that were glaciated during the Pleistocene. The old stream systems were obliterated by the ice sheets, and water remains ponded in the many erosional basins and kettles, and behind morainal dams. One has only to compare the northern and southern parts of the United States to recognize this fact (Figure 19-28). Most of Europe

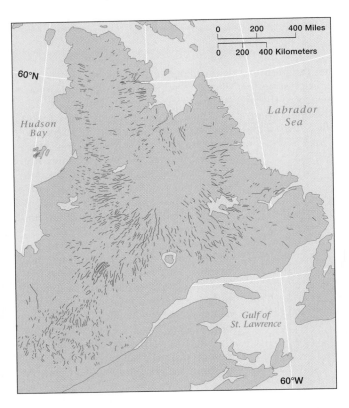

▲ **Figure 19-26** The distribution of eskers in eastern Canada.

▲ **Figure 19-27** A kame in southeastern Wisconsin, near Dundee. *(Tom L. McKnight photo.)*

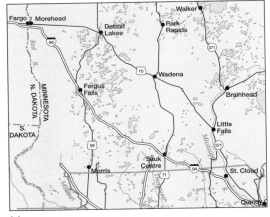

(a)

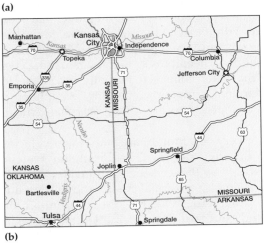

(b)

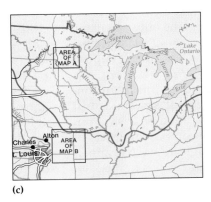

(c)

◀ **Figure 19-28** There is an abundance of natural lakes in the region north of the Ohio and Missouri rivers, a result of glacial action. South of these rivers, however, there was no glaciation and consequently natural lakes are almost unknown.

and the northern part of Asia demonstrate a similar correlation between past glaciation and present-day lakes.

Mountain Glaciers

Most of the world's high-mountain regions experienced extensive Pleistocene glaciation, and many mountain glaciers exist today. Mountain glaciers do not usually reshape the terrain as completely as the ice sheets did, partly because some portions of the mountains protrude above the ice and partly because the movement of mountain glaciers is channeled by the mountains. However, the effect of glacial action, particularly erosion, on mountainous topography is to create slopes that are steeper and relief that is greater than the preglacial slope and relief. This action, of course, is in contrast to ice-sheet action, which smoothes and rounds the terrain.

Development and Flow

A highland icefield can extend broadly across the high country, submerging all but the uppermost peaks and finding its outlet in a series of lobes that issue from the icefield and move down adjacent drainage channels (Figure 19-29). Individual alpine glaciers usually form in sheltered depressions near the heads of stream valleys (often far below the level of the peaks). Glaciers from either source advance downslope, pulled by gravity and normally finding the path of least resistance along a preexisting stream valley. A system of merging glaciers usually develops, with a trunk glacier in the

main valley joined by tributary glaciers from smaller valleys.

Erosion by Mountain Glaciers

Erosion by highland icefields and alpine glaciers reshapes the topography in dramatic fashion, as Figure 19-30 shows. It remodels the peaks and ridges and thoroughly transforms the valleys leading down from the high country.

In the High Country   The basic landform feature in glaciated mountains is the **cirque**, a broad amphitheater hollowed out at the head of a glacial valley (Figure 19-31). It has very steep, often perpendicular, head and side walls and a floor that is either flat or gently sloping or else gouged enough to form a basin. A cirque marks the place where an alpine glacier originated. It is the first landform feature produced by alpine glaciation, essentially being quarried out of the mountainside. The shifting of the equilibrium line back and forth as a result of minor climatic changes may generate much of this quarrying action, abetted by plucking, mass wasting, and frost wedging. By the middle of summer, a large crevice known as the *bergschrund* opens at the top of the glacier, exposing part of the headwall to frost wedging. The shattered rock from the headwall is eventually incorporated into the glacial ice. As the glacier grows, its erosive effectiveness within the cirque increases, and when the glacier begins to extend itself down-valley out of the cirque, quarried fragments from the cirque are carried away with the flowing ice (Figure 19-32). Cirques vary considerably in size, ranging from a few hectares to a

(a)

(b)

▲ **Figure 19-29**   (a) Topographic map of the icefield at the top of Mt. Rainier in the Cascade Range in Washington. Note the tongues of valley glaciers radiating from the central field. (b) The ice-covered peak of Mt. Rainier, the highest volcano in the Cascade Range. (*Tom L. McKnight photo.*)

▲ **Figure 19-30** The Grand Teton Mountains of Wyoming have been spectacularly modified by the action of mountain glaciers. *(Darrel Hess photo.)*

few square kilometers in extent. Many large cirques apparently owe their development to repeated episodes of glaciation.

A cirque grows steeper as its glacier plucks rock from the head and side walls. Where cirques are close together, the upland interfluve between neighboring

▲ **Figure 19-31** Only a small remnant glacier remains in this cirque on the north side of Wheeler Peak in Nevada's Great Basin National Park. *(Tom L. McKnight photo.)*

cirques is reduced to little more than a steep rock wall. Where several cirques have been cut back into an interfluve from opposite sides of a divide, a narrow, jagged, serrated spine of rock may be all that is left of the ridge crest; this is called an **arête** (French for "fishbone"; derived from the Latin *arista,* "spine") (Figure 19-33). If two adjacent cirques on opposite sides of a divide are being cut back enough to remove part of the arête between them, the sharp-edged pass or saddle through the ridge is referred to as a **col** (*collum* is Latin for "neck") (Figure 19-34). An even more prominent feature of glaciated highland summits is a **horn**, a steep-sided, pyramidal rock pinnacle formed by expansive quarrying of the headwalls where three or more cirques intersect (Figure, 19-35, p. 578). The name is derived

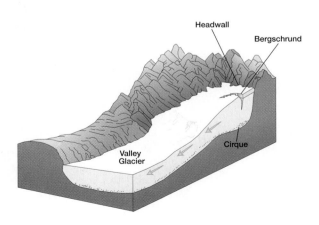

▲ **Figure 19-32** The development of a cirque at the head of a valley glacier.

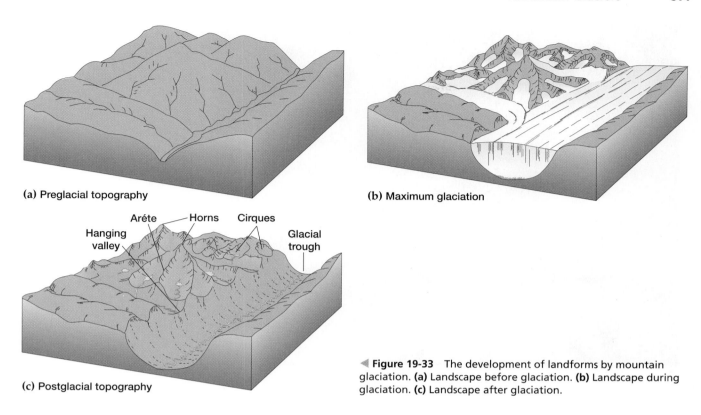

(a) Preglacial topography

(b) Maximum glaciation

Aréte   Horns   Cirques

Hanging
valley

Glacial
trough

(c) Postglacial topography

◀ **Figure 19-33**   The development of landforms by mountain glaciation. **(a)** Landscape before glaciation. **(b)** Landscape during glaciation. **(c)** Landscape after glaciation.

from Switzerland's Matterhorn, the most famous example of such a glaciated spire.

When the glacial ice in a cirque has melted away, there is often enough of a depression formed to hold water. Such a cirque lake is called a **tarn**.

In the Valleys   Some alpine glaciers, such as those shown in Figure 19-36, never leave their cirques, presumably because of insufficient accumulation of ice to force a down-valley movement, and as a result the valleys below are unmodified by glacial erosion. Most

Wyoming

Rocky Mountain
National Park →   •Denver

C o l o r a d o

New Mexico

Col

▲ **Figure 19-34**   A heavily glaciated section of the Front Range in north-central Colorado. A *col* is seen in the center of the photograph between the sharp peaks on either side in this scene from Rocky Mountain National Park. *(Tom L. McKnight photo.)*

▲ **Figure 19-35** Mount Aspiring is a prominent horn in the Southern Alps of New Zealand. *(Tom L. McKnight photo.)*

alpine glaciers, however, as well as those issuing from highland icefields, flow down preexisting valleys and reshape them (Figure 19-37).

A glacier moves down a mountain valley with much greater erosive effectiveness than a stream. The glacier is denser, carries more abrasive tools, and has an enormously greater volume. It erodes by both abrasion and plucking. The lower layers of the ice can even flow uphill for some distance if blocked by resistant rock on the valley floor, permitting rock fragments to be dragged out of depressions in the valley floor.

The principal erosive work of a valley glacier is to deepen, steepen, and widen its valley. Abrasion and plucking take place not only on the valley floor but along the sides as well. The cross-sectional profile is changed from its stream-cut "V" shape to an ice-eroded "U" shape flared at the top (Figure 19-38). Moreover, the general course of the valley is straightened

▲ **Figure 19-36** Three little cirques lined up in a row at about the 3300-meter (11,000-foot) level on Mount Nebo in central Utah. From the shape of the valleys below the cirques, it appears that the original cirque glaciers never moved out to become valley glaciers. *(Tom L. McKnight photo.)*

▲ **Figure 19-37** The magnificent glacial landscape of Yosemite, looking past Half Dome up the U-shaped Tenaya Valley. *(Tom L. McKnight photo.)*

because the ice does not meander like a stream; rather it tends to grind away the protruding spurs that separate side canyons, creating what are called *truncated spurs,* and thereby replacing the sinuous course of the stream with a straight, U-shaped **glacial trough** (see Figure 19-33).

As might be expected, a glacier grinding along the floor of a glacial trough does not produce a very smooth surface. Valley glaciers do not erode a continuously sloping channel because differential erosion works with ice as well as with water. Therefore, resistant rock on the valley floor is gouged less deeply than weaker or more fractured rock. As a result, the long profile of the glaciated valley floor is irregular, with parts that are gently sloping, flat, or steep, and with some excavated depressions alternating in erratic sequence—landforms known as **glacial steps** (Figure 19-39).

The resulting landscape of the glacial trough, after the ice has melted away, usually shows an irregular series of rock steps or benches, with steep (although usually short) cliffs on the down-valley side and small lakes in the shallow excavated depressions of the benches. The postglacial stream that flows down-valley out of the cirque has a relatively straight course but a fluctuating gradient. Rapids and waterfalls are common, particularly on the cliffs below the benches. The various shallow lakes occur in a sequence called **paternoster lakes**, after a fancied resemblance to beads on a rosary.

▲ **Figure 19-38** The Hollyford Valley in New Zealand's South Island has been carved by glacial erosion. The U-shaped cross section is conspicuous. *(Tom L. McKnight photo.)*

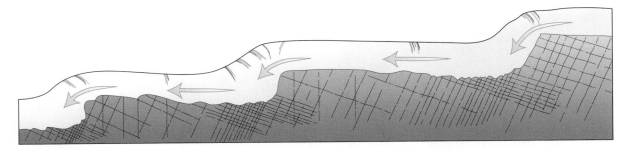

▲ **Figure 19-39** A longitudinal cross section of a glaciated valley in hilly or mountainous terrain showing a sequence of glacial steps. *(After François Matthes, U.S. Geological Survey, Professional Paper 160.)*

As we will discuss in Chapter 20, some of the most spectacular glacial troughs occur along coastlines where valleys have been partly drowned by the sea to create *fjords*.

Our focus in the last few paragraphs has been on major valleys occupied by trunk glaciers. The same processes are at work and the same features produced in tributary valleys, although usually on a lesser scale. However, one important distinction between main valleys and tributary valleys is the amount of glacial erosion. Erosive effectiveness is determined largely by the amount of ice that passes through the valley; thus, the smaller ice streams of tributary valleys cannot widen and deepen as much as the main valley glaciers.

When occupied by glaciers and thus covered by a relatively level field of ice, main and tributary valleys may appear equally deep. When the ice melts, however, that valleys are of different depths becomes obvious; the mouths of the tributary valleys are characteristically perched high along the sides of the major troughs, forming **hanging valleys** (see Figure 19-33). Typically, streams that drain the tributary valleys must plunge

over waterfalls to reach the floor of the main trough. Several of the world-famous falls of Yosemite National Park are of this type (Figure 19-40).

Deposition by Mountain Glaciers

Depositional features are less significant in areas of mountain glaciation than in areas where continental ice sheets have been at work. The high country is almost totally devoid of drift; only in the middle and lower courses of glacial valleys can much deposition be found.

The principal depositional landforms associated with mountain glaciation are moraines. Terminal and recessional moraines form just as they do with ice sheets. Moraines resulting from mountain glaciation are much smaller and less conspicuous, however, because they are restricted to glacial troughs (Figure 19-41).

The largest depositional features produced by mountain glaciation are **lateral moraines**; these are well-defined ridges of unsorted debris built up along the sides of valley glaciers (Figure 19-42). The debris is

▲ **Figure 19-40** Bridalveil Creek plunges out of a hanging valley in California's Yosemite National Park. *(Darrel Hess photo.)*

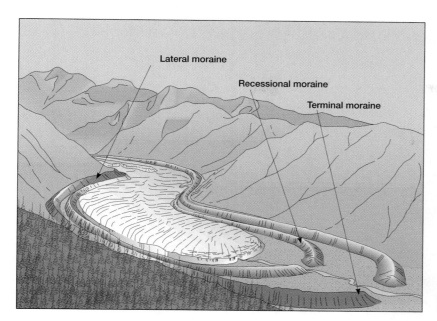

◀ **Figure 19-41** Common types of moraines in mountainous areas. *(After François Matthes, U.S. Geological Survey, Professional Paper 160.)*

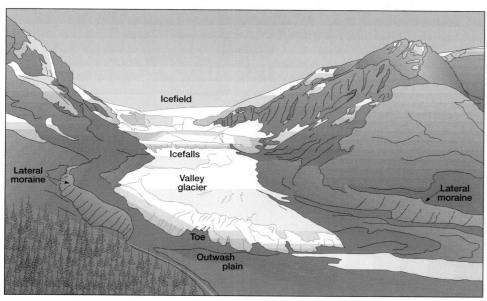

◀ **Figure 19-42** The Athabaska valley glacier issuing from a highland icefield in the Canadian Rockies. The distance from the highest icefall to the toe is about 11 kilometers (7 miles). The glacier has heaped up conspicuous lateral moraines along both sides. *(Tom L. McKnight photo.)*

▲ **Figure 19-43**   Emerald Bay on the California side of Lake Tahoe is nearly closed off from the rest of the lake by the arms of two lateral moraines left by Pleistocene glaciers. *(Darrel Hess photo.)*

partly material deposited by the glacier and partly rock that falls or is washed down the valley walls (Figure 19-43).

Where a tributary glacier joins a trunk glacier, their lateral moraines become united at the intersection and often continue together down the middle of the combined glacier as a dark band of rocky debris known as a **medial moraine** (Figure 19-44). Medial moraines are sometimes found in groups of three or four running together, indicating that several glaciers have joined to produce a candy-cane effect of black (moraine) and white (ice) bands extending down the valley. The debris left by meltwater below mountain glaciers is similar to that bordering ice sheets because similar outwash is produced.

Table 19-2 summarizes the landforms associated with glaciation.

▲ **Figure 19-44**   Prominent medial moraines on McBride Glacier, near Glacier Bay in southeastern Alaska. *(Tom L. McKnight photo.)*

TABLE 19-2 Landforms Produced by Glacial and Glaciofluvial Processes

Landform	Process	Agent*	Composition
Arête	Glacial erosion	MG	Bedrock
Cirque	Glacial erosion	MG	Bedrock
Col	Glacial erosion	MG	Bedrock
Drumlin	Glacial deposition & erosion	CIS	Till
Esker	Glaciofluvial deposition	CIS	Stratified drift
Fjord	Glacial erosion	MG	Bedrock
Glacial steps	Glacial erosion	MG	Bedrock
Glacial trough	Glacial erosion	MG	Bedrock
Ground moraine	Glacial deposition	MG, CIS	Till
Hanging valley	Glacial erosion	MG	Bedrock
Horn	Glacial erosion	MG	Bedrock
Kame	Glaciofluvial deposition	MG, CIS	Stratified drift
Kettle	Glaciofluvial deposition	MG, CIS	Stratified drift
Lateral moraine	Glacial deposition	MG	Till
Medial moraine	Glacial deposition	MG	Till
Nunatak	Glacial erosion	MG	Bedrock
Outwash plain	Glaciofluvial deposition	MG, CIS	Stratified drift
Recessional moraine	Glacial deposition	MG, CIS	Till
Roche moutonnée	Glacial erosion	MG, CIS	Bedrock
Terminal moraine	Glacial deposition	MG, CIS	Till
Till plain	Glacial deposition	MG, CIS	Till
Valley train	Glaciofluvial deposition	MG, CIS	Stratified drift

*MG = mountain glacier; CIS = continental ice sheet

The Periglacial Environment

The term *periglacial* means "on the perimeter of glaciation." More than 20 percent of the world's land area is presently periglacial, but most of this was covered by ice on one or more occasions during the Pleistocene epoch.

Periglacial lands are found either in high latitudes or in high elevations. Almost all are in the Northern Hemisphere because the Southern Hemisphere continents either do not extend far enough into the high latitudes to be significantly affected by contemporary glaciation (Africa, South America, Australia) or are mostly ice covered (Antarctica).

Nonglacial land-shaping processes function in periglacial areas, but in addition the pervasive cold imparts some distinctive characteristics, the most notable of which is *permafrost* (discussed in Chapter 9).

Either continuous or discontinuous permafrost occurs over most of Alaska and more than half of Canada and Russia. There are also extensive high-altitude areas of permafrost in Asia, Scandinavia, and the western United States. In some cases, the frozen ground extends to extraordinary depths; a thickness of 1000 meters (3000 feet) has been found in Canada's Northwest Territories and 1500 meters (4500 feet) in north-central Siberia.

The most unique and eye-catching periglacial terrain is **patterned ground**, the generic name applied to various geometric patterns that repeatedly appear over large areas in the Arctic (Figure 19-45). The patterns are varied, with their formation related to frost action. The principal significance of patterned ground is that it demonstrates the mobility of periglacial surfaces, emphasizing the role of soil ice in producing geomorphic activities largely unknown in warmer regions.

▲ **Figure 19-45** Polygonal ground patterns near Prudhoe Bay, Alaska. *(© Peter Dunwiddle/Visuals Unlimited.)*

Another sometimes conspicuous development in periglacial regions is **proglacial lakes** (*pro* here means "marginal to" or "in advance of"). Where ice flows across a land surface, the natural drainage is either impeded or blocked, and meltwater from the ice can become impounded against the ice front, forming a proglacial lake. Such an event sometimes occurs in alpine glaciation but is much more common along the margin of continental ice sheets, particularly when the ice stagnates.

Most proglacial lakes are small and quite temporary because subsequent ice movements cause drainage changes and because normal fluvial processes, accelerated by the growing accumulation of meltwater in the lake, cut spillways or channels to drain the impounded waters. Sometimes, however, proglacial lakes are large and relatively long lived. Such major lakes are characterized by considerable fluctuations in size due to the changing location of the receding or advancing ice front. Several huge proglacial lakes were impounded along the margins of the ice sheets as they advanced and retreated during the Pleistocene epoch in North America, Europe, and Siberia.

Among the most dramatic consequences of a lake once impounded by continental glaciers is found in eastern Washington near Spokane. A series of great floods during the Pleistocene scoured eastern Washington's "channeled scablands" when enormous volumes of water were periodically let loose from an ice sheet-dammed lake near present-day Missoula, Montana. Several times during the Pleistocene, a lobe of the continental ice sheets blocked the Clark Fork River, forming Pleistocene Lake Missoula, which at times was more than 300 meters (1000 feet) deep. When the ice dam failed, a wall of water surged across the landscape, scouring deep channels and leaving enormous ripple marks before the water eventually drained into the Columbia River (Figure 19-46).

Causes of the Pleistocene

Ice ages are fascinating not only because of the landscape changes they bring about but also because of their mystery. What initiates massive accumulations of ice on the continental surfaces, stimulates their advances and retreats, and finally causes them to disappear? Scientists and other scholars have pondered these questions for decades. They have developed many scenarios, postulated many theories, and constructed many models in attempts to explain the sporadic glaciation and deglaciation of our planet.

Any satisfactory theory of the causes of the Pleistocene must be able to account for four main glacial characteristics:

1. The accumulation of ice masses more or less simultaneously at various latitudes in both hemispheres but without uniformity (e.g., much less in Siberia and Alaska than in similar latitudes in Canada and Scandinavia)

▲ **Figure 19-46** The channeled scablands of Washington, shown here where the Lower Palouse River Canyon enters the Snake River. *(John Marshall.)*

2. The apparently concurrent development of pluvial conditions in dryland areas
3. Multiple cycles of ice advance and retreat, including both minor fluctuations over decades and centuries and major glaciations and deglaciations over tens of thousands of years (Figure 19-47)
4. Eventual total deglaciation, either actual (in past geologic eras) or potential (for the Pleistocene epoch)

It is easy enough to state that glaciers develop when there is a net accumulation of snow over a period of time and that glaciers waste away when summer melting exceeds winter snowfall. Beyond that simplistic statement, however, in some cases it isn't always clear whether a colder climate would be more conducive to glaciation than a warmer but wetter one! Although colder conditions would inhibit summer wastage and thus enhance the longevity of the winter accumulation, cold air cannot hold much water vapor. Hence, warmer winters would favor increased snowfall, whereas cooler summers are needed for decreased melting. Even a theory that accommodated either significantly increased snowfall or significantly decreased melting, or a combination of both, would still have to take into account the advance and retreat of the ice.

A lot is known about many of the factors associated with the Pleistocene, but certainly not all of the factors. As we discussed in Chapter 8, cyclical variations in Earth–Sun relations, often referred to as *Milankovitch cycles*, played a part. The combination of slight variations in the inclination of Earth's axis and the eccentricity of Earth's orbit, as well as the changing orientation of Earth's axis relative to the stars (known as the "precession of the equinoxes"), seem to correlate fairly well with some—but certainly not all—of the major glacial advances and retreats during the Pleistocene.

Other factors that have been postulated as triggers or components of glacial episodes include variations in the energy output of the Sun; variations in the level of carbon dioxide in the atmosphere; the changing positions of continents and the configuration of ocean basins and ocean circulation patterns; atmospheric circulation changes due to increased elevation of continental masses after a period of tectonic upheaval; and reductions in insolation reaching the surface due to particulates released during massive volcanic eruptions.

We make no attempt here to offer details of these many theories, primarily because none of them alone or in combination provides a complete explanation of

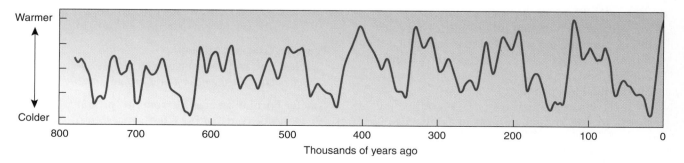

▲ **Figure 19-47** Global temperature fluctuations from 800,000 years ago to the present. Many glacial and interglacial periods are easily recognizable. *(After Aguado and Burt,* Understanding Weather and Climate, *4th ed. Upper Saddle River, NJ: Prentice Hall, 2005.)*

the climate changes during the Pleistocene. The search for a complete explanation continues.

Are We Still in an Ice Age?

One significant outgrowth of our study of what causes a glacial age is the further puzzle of whether or not Earth's most recent ice age has actually ended. Are we now living in a postglacial period or in an interglacial period? Has the Pleistocene epoch closed? Are we now in the early centuries of a new geologic era or have the glaciers merely "gone back to get some more rocks"? Can the Ice Age be over when nearly 7 percent of the ocean surface is sheathed by ice in winter, 10 percent of the land surface remains covered by glaciers, an additional 20 percent is underlain by permafrost, seasonal snow covers the continents throughout the midlatitudes, and higher mountain summits are snow capped even at the equator? Based on the climate patterns of the last two million years, it is quite possible that Earth will enter another period of glaciation within a few tens of thousands of years; however, might human-enhanced greenhouse effect and global warming "postpone" the onset of this glacial period?

We are, of course, much too close to the event in a temporal sense to obtain a definitive answer.

Chapter 19 Learning Review

Key Terms

Before answering the study questions below, review the definitions of the following key terms (page references are provided for you):

ablation (of glacial ice) *(p. 563)*
ablation zone *(p. 564)*
accumulation (of glacial ice) *(p. 563)*
accumulation zone *(p. 563)*
arête *(p. 576)*
basal slip *(p. 564)*
cirque *(p. 575)*
cirque glacier *(p. 562)*
col *(p. 576)*
continental ice sheet *(p. 561)*
drift (glacial drift) *(p. 567)*
drumlin *(p. 571)*
equilibrium line *(p. 564)*
erratic (glacial erratic) *(p. 567)*
esker *(p. 573)*
glacial flour *(p. 566)*

glacial plucking *(p. 565)*
glacial steps *(p. 579)*
glacial trough *(p. 579)*
glaciofluvial deposition *(p. 567)*
ground moraine *(p. 571)*
hanging valley *(p. 580)*
highland ice field *(p. 562)*
horn *(p. 576)*
kame *(p. 573)*
kettle *(p. 571)*
lateral moraine *(p. 580)*
medial moraine *(p. 582)*
moraine *(p. 571)*
névé (firn) *(p. 563)*
outwash plain *(p. 572)*
paternoster lakes *(p. 579)*

patterned ground *(p. 583)*
periglacial zone *(p. 557)*
piedmont glacier *(p. 562)*
Pleistocene epoch *(p. 555)*
pluvial effects *(p. 557)*
proglacial lake *(p. 584)*
recessional moraine *(p. 571)*
roche moutonnée *(p. 568)*
stratified drift *(p. 572)*
tarn *(p. 577)*
terminal moraine *(p. 571)*
till *(p. 567)*
till plain *(p. 571)*
valley glacier *(p. 562)*
valley train *(p. 573)*

Study Questions for Key Concepts

After studying this chapter, you should be able to answer the following questions:

Glaciations Past and Present (p. 555)

1. Why is the Pleistocene epoch so important to physical geography, whereas other ice ages are not?
2. Briefly describe the world-wide extent of ice cover during the peak of the Pleistocene glaciations.
3. Explain how and why global sea level fluctuated during the Pleistocene.
4. What is the relationship of large continental ice sheets to the crustal depression associated with *isostatic adjustment* (isostasy)?
5. What is meant by the *pluvial effects* of the Pleistocene?

6. Describe and explain the formation of large *Pleistocene lakes* in western North America.
7. Describe the global extent of glaciers today.

Types of Glaciers (p. 560)

8. Describe and contrast *continental ice sheets, highland ice fields, valley glaciers,* and *cirque glaciers.*

Glacier Formation and Movement (p. 563)

9. Describe and contrast the processes of glacial ice *accumulation* and *ablation.*
10. Describe the metamorphosis from snow to glacial ice.

11. Explain how the balance between ice accumulation and ablation influences the "advance" or "retreat" of a glacier. (In other words, explain what causes glaciers to grow larger or to become smaller.)
12. Discuss the different components of glacial movement.
13. Why can a glacier continue to erode and transport rock even while it is retreating?

The Effects of Glaciers (p. 565)
14. Contrast the erosional processes of *glacial plucking* and *glacial abrasion*.
15. Describe the characteristics of glacial *till*.
16. How is a deposit of till likely to look different from a deposit of alluvium?
17. What is a *glacial erratic*?
18. How does *glaciofluvial deposition* differ from deposition directly by glacial ice?

Continental Ice Sheets (p. 568)
19. Describe and explain the formation of a *roche moutonnée*.
20. Explain the formation of *terminal moraines* and *recessional moraines*.

21. Describe and explain the formation of a *kettle*.
22. What is meant by *stratified drift*?
23. Describe the formation of a *glacial outwash plain*.
24. Why are there so many lakes in areas that were glaciated by continental ice sheets during the Pleistocene?

Mountain Glaciers (p. 575)
25. Why are mountainous areas that have experienced glaciation usually quite rugged?
26. Contrast the general cross-sectional shape of a stream valley with that of a *glacial trough* (glacial valley).
27. Describe the general downvalley profile of a glacial trough.
28. Describe and explain the formation of *cirques*, *horns*, and *hanging valleys*.
29. What are *paternoster lakes* and why do they form?
30. What is a *lateral moraine*?
31. How does a *medial moraine* form?

The Periglacial Environment (p. 583)
32. Briefly describe *patterned ground* in periglacial areas.
33. What is a *proglacial lake*?

Additional Resources

Books:
French, H. M. *The Periglacial Environment*, 2nd ed. London: Longman, 1995.
Huber, N. King. *The Geologic Story of Yosemite National Park*. U.S. Geological Survey Bulletin 1595. Washington, D.C.: U.S. Government Printing Office, 1987.
Sharp, Robert P. *Living Ice: Understanding Glaciers and Glaciation*. New York: Cambridge University Press, 1991.
Williams, Richard S. *Glaciers: Clues to Future Climate?* U.S. Geological Survey publication 1990 0–273–468 QL 2. Washington, D.C.: U.S. Government Printing Office, 1990.

Internet Sites:
National Geophysical Data Center
http://www.ngdc.noaa.gov/
   The National Geophysical Data Center is a great starting point for finding information about glaciology, marine geology, paleoclimatology, solar–terrestrial physics, and geophysics.

National Oceanic and Atmospheric Administration (NOAA)
http://www.noaa.gov/
   The National Oceanic and Atmospheric Administration (NOAA) oversees a number of government agencies, including the National Weather Service. NOAA's home page provides links to sites about weather, climate, weather satellites, the oceans, and coastlines.

NOAA Arctic Theme Page
http://www.arctic.noaa.gov/
   NOAA provides current information and data about the Arctic region of Earth.

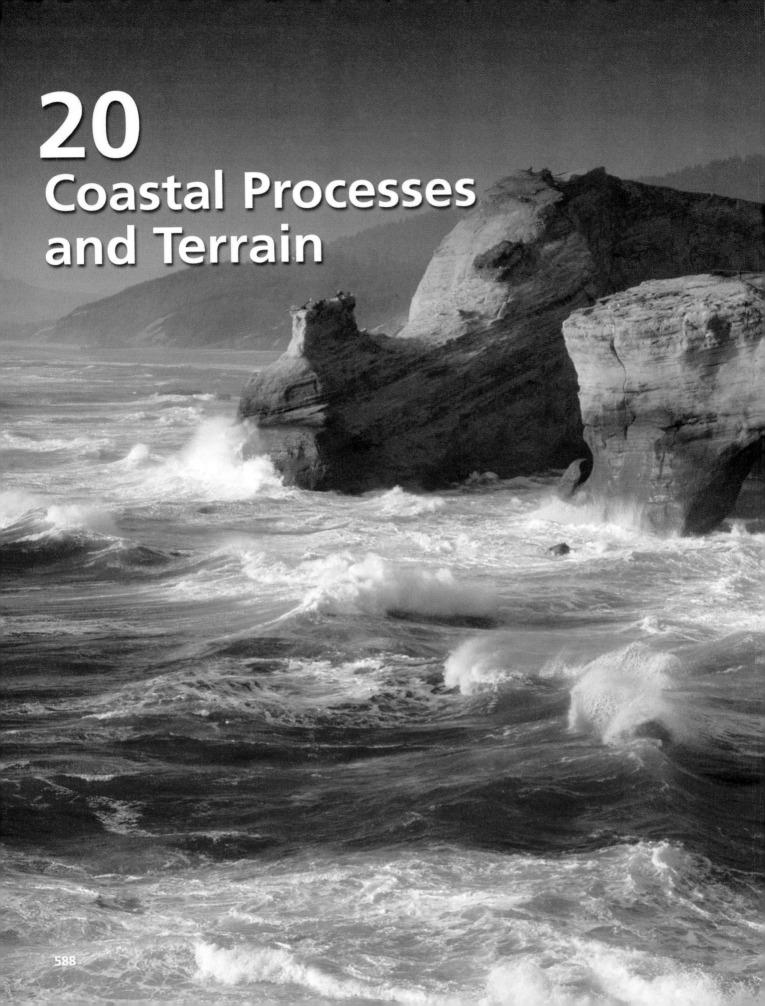

20
Coastal Processes and Terrain

In addition to running water, two other forms of moving water—waves and ocean currents—shape the land. Coastlines are shaped by the agitated waters crashing or lapping against them, with the result that coastal terrain is often quite different from the landscape just a short distance from shore.

The Impact of Waves and Currents on the Landscape

Coastal processes affect only a tiny fraction of the total area of Earth's surface, but they create a landscape that is almost totally different from any other on the planet. Although there is some overlap, in essence waves are agents of erosion, and currents are agents of transportation and deposition. The most notable land features created by waves are rocky cliffs and headlands (promontories of sloping land projecting into the sea). Depositional features are diverse in form, but by far the most common are beaches and sandbars.

Beaches along the shorelines of both oceans and lakes are the most distinctive aspect of coastal landscapes. They provide a transition from land to water and are usually impermanent features of the landscape, built up during times of "normal" weather and eroded during storms.

Coastal Processes

The coastlines of the world's oceans and lakes extend for hundreds of thousands of kilometers. Every conceivable variety of structure, relief, and topography can be found somewhere along these coasts. The distinctiveness of the coastal milieu, however, is that it is at the interface of three major components of Earth's environment: hydrosphere, lithosphere, and atmosphere. This interface is dynamic and highly energetic, primarily because of the restless motions of the waters (Figure 20-1).

We saw in Chapter 18 that wind is sometimes an important shaper of landforms on the continents. Along coastlines, the wind has an even greater influence on topography because the surface of a large body of water can be deformed abruptly and rapidly by wind action. This deformation of the water surface is what creates waves and ocean currents, both of which shape coastlines, producing topographic features found throughout the world in all latitudes and in a variety of climates.

The wind is not the only force causing water to move, of course, but from the standpoint of geomorphic effects it

▲ **Figure 20-1** A coastline is the place where hydrosphere, lithosphere, and atmosphere meet. It is often an interface of ceaseless movement and energy transfer. Pounding waves do not always erode evenly and smoothly. Stacks and cliffs testify to the principle of differential erosion in this scene from Port Campbell National Park, Victoria, Australia. *(Tom L. McKnight photo.)*

◀ Cape Kiwanda State Park, Oregon. *(© Ric Ergenbright/CORBIS.)*

is the most important. Oceanic coastlines also experience daily tidal fluctuations which often move enormous quantities of water. Diastrophic events, particularly earthquakes, contribute to water motion, as does volcanic activity upon occasion. Even more fundamental are long-term variations in sea or lake level caused by tectonic forces and *eustatic sea-level change* (sea-level change entirely due to an increase or decrease in the amount of water in the world ocean) and to a lesser extent by the actions of continental ice sheets.

The forces that shape the topography of oceanic coastlines are similar to the forces acting on lakeshores, with three important exceptions:

1. Along lakeshores, the range of tides is so small that they are insignificant to landform development.
2. The causes of sea-level fluctuations are quite different from the causes of lake-level fluctuations.
3. Coral reefs are built only in tropical and subtropical oceans, not in lakes.

With these exceptions, the topographic forms produced on seacoasts and lakeshores are generally similar. Even so, the larger the body of water, the greater the effects of the coastal processes. Thus, topographic features developed along seacoasts are normally larger, more conspicuous, and more distinctive than those found along lakeshores.

There are a number of processes that contribute to the shaping of coastal features. These are discussed in the following subsections.

Waves

1. Wave Motion and Wave Refraction
2. Tsunami

Waves entail the transfer of energy through a cyclical rising and falling motion in a substance. Our interest here is in water waves, which are simply undulations in the surface layers of a water body. Although water waves appear to move water horizontally, this appearance is misleading: in open water, the form of the wave (and therefore its energy) moves along through the water, although the water itself is shifted only very slightly; as we will see, this motion changes in shallow water, where waves crest and break.

Most water waves are wind generated, set in motion largely by the friction of air blowing across the water. This transfer of energy from wind to water initiates wave motion. Some water waves (called *forced waves*) are generated directly by wind stress on the water surface; they can develop to considerable size if the wind is strong and turbulent but usually last for only a limited time and do not travel far. Water waves become **swells** when they escape the influence of the generating wind, and swells can travel enormous distances. A small number of all water waves are generated by something other than the wind, such as a tidal surge, volcanic activity, or undersea diastrophic movement (discussed later in this chapter).

Waves of Oscillation and Translation As a wave passes a given point on the water surface, the water at that point makes a small circular or oscillatory movement, with very little forward motion (to oscillate means to move back and forth over the same space time and again). Waves that cause water to move this way are called **waves of oscillation**. As the wave passes, the water moves upward, producing a *wave crest*, as shown in Figure 20-2. Then crest formation is followed by a sinking of the surface that creates a *wave trough*. The horizontal distance from crest to crest or from trough to trough is called the *wavelength*. The vertical dimension of wave development is determined by the circular orbit of the surface water particles as the wave form passes; the vertical distance from crest to trough is equivalent to the diameter of this orbit and is called the **wave height**. The height of any wave depends on wind speed, wind duration, water depth, and *fetch* (the area of open water). *Wave amplitude* is one-half the height, in other words, the vertical distance from the still-water level either upward to the crest or downward to the trough.

The passage of a wave of oscillation normally moves water only very slightly in the direction of flow. Thus an object floating on the surface simply bobs up and

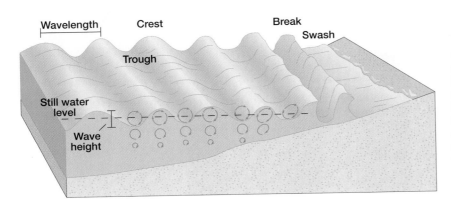

◀ **Figure 20-2** In deep water, the passage of a wave involves almost circular movements of individual water particles. Agitation diminishes rapidly with increasing depth, as shown here by decreasing orbital diameter downward. As the wave moves into shallow water, the orbits of the revolving particles become more elliptical, the wavelength becomes shorter, and the wave becomes steeper. Eventually the wave "breaks" and dissipates its remaining energy as it washes up onto the beach.

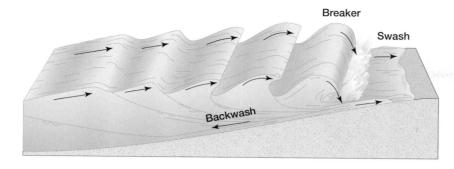

Figure 20-3 A breaking wave. In shallow water the ocean bottom impedes oscillation, causing the wave to become increasingly steeper until it is so oversteepened that it collapses and tumbles forward as a breaker. The surging water then rushes up the beach as swash, and then drains off the beach below the waves as backwash.

down without advancing, except as it may be pushed by the wind. The influence of wave movement diminishes rapidly with depth; even very high waves stir the subsurface water to a depth of only a few tens of meters.

Waves often travel great distances across deep water with relatively little change in speed or shape. As they roll into shallow water, however, a significant metamorphosis occurs. When the water depth becomes equal to about half the wavelength, the wave motion begins to be affected by frictional drag on the sea bottom. The waves of oscillation then rapidly become changed into **waves of translation**, and the result is significant horizontal movement of the surface water. Friction retards the progress of the waves so that they are slowed and bunch together, marking a decrease in wavelength, while at the same time their height is increased. As the wave becomes higher and steeper, frictional drag becomes even greater, which causes the wave to tilt forward and become more and more unstable. Soon and abruptly the wave *breaks* (Figure 20-3), collapsing into whitewater surf or plunging forward as a breaker or, if the height is small, perhaps simply surging up the beach without cresting.

When a wave breaks, the motion of the water instantly becomes turbulent, like that of a swift river. The breaking wave rushes toward shore or up the beach as **swash**. This surge can carry sand and rock particles onto the beach, and it can pound onto rocky headlands and sea cliffs with considerable force (Figure 20-4). When the wave is spent, the return flow sweeps seaward, carrying loose material with it. The momentum of the surging swash is soon overcome by friction, and a reverse flow, called **backwash**, drains much of the water seaward again, usually to meet the oncoming swash of the next wave.

Wave Refraction Waves often change direction as they approach the shore, a phenomenon known as **wave refraction**. It occurs because a line of waves does not approach exactly parallel to the shore, either because the coastline is uneven or because of irregularities in water depth in the near-shore zone. For one or more of these reasons, one portion of a wave reaches shallow water sooner than other portions and is thus slowed down. This slowing down causes the wave line to bend (*refract*) as it pivots toward the obstructing area. The wave energy then becomes concentrated in

Figure 20-4 The continuous pounding of waves can erode even the most resistant coastal rocks. This scene is near Port Edward on the Natal coast of South Africa. *(Tom L. McKnight photo.)*

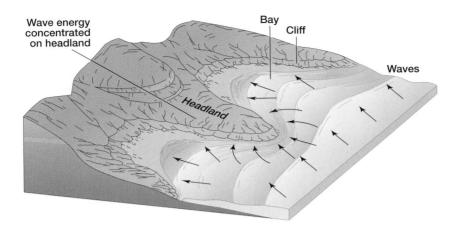

Wave energy concentrated on headland

Bay

Cliff

Waves

Headland

◀ **Figure 20-5** Refraction of waves on an irregular coastline. The waves approach the headland first and then pivot toward it. Thus wave energy is concentrated on the headlands and is diminished in the bays.

the vicinity of the obstruction and is diminished in other areas (Figure 20-5).

The most conspicuous geomorphic result of wave refraction is the focusing of wave action on headlands (Figure 20-6), subjecting them to the direct onslaught of pounding waves, whereas an adjacent bay experiences much gentler, low-energy wave action. Other things being equal, the differential effect of wave refraction tends to smooth the coastal outline by wearing back the headlands and increasing sediment accumulation in the bays.

Wave Erosion The most notable erosion along coastlines is accomplished by wave action. The incessant pounding of even small waves is a potent force in wearing away the shore, and the enormous power of storm waves almost defies comprehension—it is often large storm waves that accomplish most of the erosion along a shoreline. Waves break with abrupt and dramatic impact, hurling water, debris, and air in a thunderous crash onto the shore. Spray from breaking waves

commonly moves as fast as 115 kilometers (70 miles) per hour, and small jets have been measured at more than twice that speed. This speed, coupled with the sheer mass of the water involved in such hydraulic pounding, is responsible for much coastal erosion, which is made much more effective by the abrasive rock particles carried by the waves.

Wherever the land along a shore is rocks or cliffs rather than sand, there is another dimension to wave erosion: the air forced into cracks in the rock as the wave hits the shore. The resulting compression is abruptly released as the water recedes, allowing instant expansion of the air. This pneumatic action is often very effective in loosening rock particles of various sizes.

Chemical action also plays a part in the erosion of rocks and cliffs because most rocks are to some extent soluble in seawater. In another form of chemical action, salts from seawater crystallize in the crevices and pores of onshore rocks and cliffs, and this deposition is a further mechanism for weakening and breaking up the rock.

AUSTRALIA

Victoria

▲ **Figure 20-6** The incessant pounding of waves on this soft-rock headland on the southern coast of the state of Victoria, Australia, produced a double arch that eventually eroded into a single arch. The double-arch photograph was taken in 1985 and the single-arch one in 1992. The view is in Port Campbell National Park. *(Tom L. McKnight photos.)*

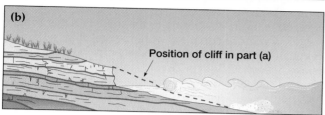

▲ **Figure 20-7**   **(a)** Waves pounding an exposed rocky shoreline erode the rock most effectively at water level, with the result that a notch may be cut in the face of the headland. **(b)** The presence of this notch undermines the higher portion of the headland, which may subsequently collapse **(c)**, producing a steep cliff. **(d)** The notching/undercutting/collapse sequence may be repeated many times, causing the cliff face to retreat.

On shores made up of cliffs, the most effective erosion takes place just at or slightly above sea level, so that a notch is cut in the base of the cliff. The cliff face then retreats as the slope above the undercutting collapses (Figure 20-7). The resulting debris is broken, smoothed, and made smaller by further wave action, and eventually most of it is carried seaward.

Where a shoreline is composed of sand or other unconsolidated material, currents and tides may also cause rapid erosion. Storms greatly accelerate the erosion of sandy shores; a violent storm can remove an entire beach in just a few hours, cutting it right down to bedrock.

Tsunami   Occasionally, major oceanic wave systems are triggered by a sudden disruption of the ocean floor. These waves are called **tsunami** (from the Japanese *tsu* for harbor and *nami* for wave) or *seismic sea waves* (improperly called "tidal waves"). Most tsunami are a consequence of abrupt movement along an ocean floor fault—especially from the vertical displacement caused by reverse or thrust faulting along a subduction zone. Tsunami may also result from underwater volcanic eruptions and major underwater landslides.

The great destructive power unleashed by some tsunami comes from the way in which the ocean is disrupted to form such a wave. Recall that with wind-generated waves, only the surface of the ocean exhibits significant movement—the orbital movement of the water only extends down to a depth of about one-half the wavelength of the wave (rarely more than a few tens of meters). On the other hand, when fault rupture on the ocean floor generates a tsunami, the entire water column—from the floor of the ocean to the surface—is disrupted, displacing an enormous volume of water (Figure 20-8, p.595).

Out in the open ocean, tsunami are usually quite inconspicuous because they are low and have very long wavelengths (in the open sea a tsunami might have a wave height of only 0.5 meter [1.5 feet] with a wavelength of perhaps 200 kilometers [125 miles]), although they can travel at speeds exceeding 700 kilometers an hour (435 miles per hour). When tsunami reach shallow water, however, they change considerably. As a tsunami approaches a coast, it slows—as do all waves—causing the wavelength to decrease and the wave height to increase.

When they strike a shoreline, tsunami rarely form towering breaking waves; instead, most tsunami arrive as a very rapidly advancing surge of water, sometimes up to 40 meters (130 feet) high. In many cases, before a tsunami arrives, the water withdraws from the coast, appearing like a very sudden, very low tide—this happens when the trough of the tsunami arrives. Unfortunately, people sometimes venture out on the freshly exposed subtidal areas to collect shellfish or stranded fish, only to be caught a few minutes later by the rapid surge of water when the crest of the tsunami comes onshore. Frequently, there will be a series of surges and withdrawals, with the largest surge not necessarily the first to arrive.

Tsunami can usually be anticipated long enough in advance to allow time for evacuation of the impact area. Since they often originate from sudden fault displacement in a subduction zone, the resulting earthquakes are readily detectable by seismographs. However, as the great northern Sumatra earthquake and tsunami disaster of December 2004 revealed, if local warning systems are not in place, there may be no way to get evacuation orders to coastal populations in time.

Whether they are awesome tsunami or mild swells, the peculiar contradiction of water waves is that they normally pass harmlessly under such fragile things as boats or swimmers in open water but can wreak devastation on even the hardest rocks of a shoreline. In other words, a wave of oscillation is a relatively gentle phenomenon, but a wave of translation can be a powerful force of destruction.

PEOPLE AND THE ENVIRONMENT The Sumatra Earthquake and Tsunami of 2004

On December 26, 2004, one of the greatest natural disasters in recent history was triggered after a magnitude 9.0 earthquake—the largest in 40 years—shook the northern coast of Sumatra in Indonesia. A 1200 kilometer- (750 mile-) long section of the *interplate thrust fault* (or "megathrust"), formed where the Indo-Australian Plate is subducting beneath the Burma Plate, ruptured, uplifting the ocean floor by as much as 4.9 meters (16 feet). The sharp movement of the ocean floor displaced a massive column of ocean water all of the way up to the surface, generating a tsunami that spread away in all directions.

About 28 minutes after the earthquake struck, a 24 meter- (80 foot-) high wave rushed onshore at the city of Banda Aceh on the northern tip Sumatra, just 100 kilometers (60 miles) from the epicenter of the earthquake. Along a 100 kilometer (60 mile) stretch of coastline in northwestern Sumatra, wave heights of 20 to 30 meters (65 to 100 feet) were documented.

The tsunami also raced away from Sumatra to the west across the Indian Ocean at about 800 kilometers an hour (500 mph). Although almost unnoticeable in the open water because of its great wavelength, whenever the tsunami reached shallow water wave height grew (Figure 20-A). Two hours after the earthquake, waves as high as 14 meters (45 feet) struck Sri Lanka. Three and a half hours after the earthquake, waves as high as 4 meters (13 feet) reached the Maldives Islands southwest of India. Seven hours after the earthquake, 1.2 meter (4 foot) waves reached the coast of Somalia in northeast Africa. In most places, at least three waves came on shore; in some locations, there were more than three.

The results were astonishing. The exact death toll will likely never be known, but estimates now suggest that 270,000 to 300,000 people died and many tens of thousands more were seriously injured. In a few locations, entire villages were quite

literally washed away. Devastation in some cities extended inland from the coast for more than a kilometer (Figure 20-B). The recovery will take years.

Adding to the tragedy is that some scientists were aware that a large tsunami was likely moving across the Indian Ocean shortly after the earthquake occurred—but there was no way to issue a tsunami warning in the region. In the Pacific basin, where about 85 percent of the world's tsunami occur, a well-organized tsunami warning system is in place: earthquakes are carefully monitored; data buoys are in place to detect changes in the ocean movement; warnings can be relayed to government officials around the Pacific Rim. After the 2004 tsunami in the Indian Ocean, an international effort was started to establish a tsunami warning system for the region had such a system been in place in December of 2004, thousands of lives would likely have been saved.

▲ **Figure 20-A** Tsunami coming onshore at Hat Rai Lay Beach, near Krabi, Thailand, on December 26, 2004. (*Getty Images, Inc.—Agence France Presse.*)

▲ **Figure 20-B** Damage from the December 26, 2004 tsunami in Banda Aceh, Indonesia. (*Getty Images, Inc.—Agence France Presse.*)

Tides

Tides

As we learned in Chapter 9, the waters of the world ocean oscillate in a regular and predictable pattern called *tides,* resulting from the gravitational influence of the Sun and Moon. The tides rise and fall in a cycle

that takes about 12 hours, producing two high tides and two low tides a day on most (but not all) seacoasts.

Despite the enormous amount of water moved by tides and despite the frequency of this movement, the topographic effects are surprisingly small. Tides are significant agents of erosion only in narrow bays, around the margin of shallow seas, and in passages between islands, where they produce currents strong enough to scour the bottom and erode cliffs and shorelines (Figure 20-9).

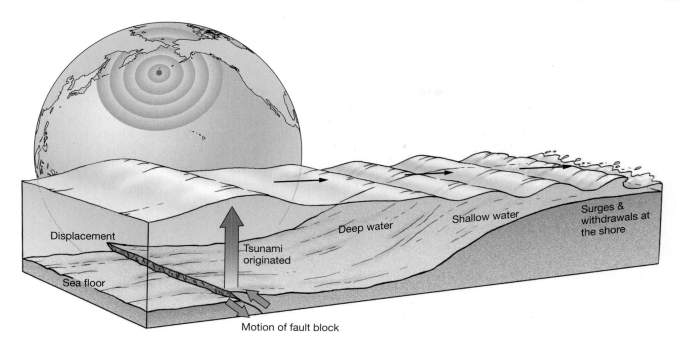

▲ **Figure 20-8**   The formation of a tsunami. A vertical disruption of the ocean floor, such as from faulting, displaces the entire water column from the ocean floor to the surface. In the open ocean, the tsunami may be almost indistinguishable because of its great wavelength. Once it reaches shallow water, however, wave height increases and the tsunami comes onshore as a series of surges and withdrawals. *(After Trujillo and Thurman,* Essentials of Oceanography, *8th ed., Upper Saddle River, NJ: Prentice Hall, 2005.)*

Changes in Sea Level and Lake Level

Sea-level changes can result either from the uplift/sinking of a landmass (tectonic cause) or from an increase/decrease in the amount of water in the oceans—**eustatic sea-level change**. During Earth's recent history, there have been many changes in sea level, sometimes worldwide and sometimes only around one or a few continents or islands. The eustatic changes of greatest magnitude and most extensive effect are those associated with seawater volume before, during, and after the Pleistocene glaciations. As we saw in Chapter 19, at the peak of the Pleistocene glaciations, sea level

▲ **Figure 20-9**   Under certain circumstances, tidal flow can be strong enough to shape landforms. These gigantic pedestal rocks on the edge of the Bay of Fundy in New Brunswick, Canada, were carved by the highest tides in the world. For scale, the spruce trees on top of the rocks are about 9 meters (30 feet) tall. *(Tom L. McKnight photo.)*

around the world was as much as 130 meters (430 feet) lower than today.

As a result of both tectonic and eustatic sea level changes, many present-day ocean coastlines show emergent characteristics, in which shoreline topography of the past is now situated well above the contemporary sea level (Figure 20-10), while others show submergence characteristics, with a portion of a previous landscape now underwater.

Most water-level changes in lakes are less extensive and less notable than those along ocean shorelines. These changes are usually the result of the total or partial drainage of a lake, and their principal topographic expression is exposed ancestral beach lines and wave-cut cliffs above present lake levels.

Global Warming and Sea-Level Change   In Chapters 4 and 8, we discussed the consequences of global warming, including the rise in sea level associated with the thermal expansion of ocean water and the increase in volume from the melting of continental glaciers and ice caps. If worldwide temperature trends continue to warm, we can anticipate an ongoing period of deglaciation, with the ice sheets of Antarctica and Greenland slowly melting. Such a situation would cause a global eustatic rise in sea level that would inundate many islands and coastal plains of the world, and would expose coastal populations to greater risks from storm waves such as those generated by hurricanes.

Should the ice caps of Antarctic and Greenland melt completely, global sea level would rise by about 80 meters (260 feet). However, even a modest increase in global sea level will be potentially devastating to populations now living in low-lying coastal areas. Given the anticipated levels of greenhouse gases and the associated temperature rise due to global warming, in 2001 the Intergovernmental Panel on Climate Change forecast perhaps a 0.5 meter (20 inch) rise in global sea level by the end of this century. Such an increase in sea level would cause shorelines around the world to retreat on average more than 30 meters (about 100 feet)—eliminating thousands of square kilometers of coastal land in North America alone. With such an increase in global sea level, some island countries would literally disappear.

Ice Push

The shores of bodies of water that freeze over in winter are sometimes significantly affected by ice push, which is usually the result of the contraction and expansion that occurs when the water freezes and thaws as the weather changes. As more and more water turns to ice—and therefore expands in volume (recall the discussion of *frost wedging* in Chapter 15)—near-shore ice is shoved onto the land, where it can deform the shoreline by pushing against it, more or less in the fashion of a small glacial advance.

Ice push is usually unimportant on seashores outside the Arctic and Antarctic, but it can be responsible for numerous minor alterations of the shorelines of high-latitude or high-elevation lakes.

Organic Secretions

Several aquatic animals and plants produce solid masses of rocklike material by secreting calcium carbonate.

▲ **Figure 20-10**   A tectonically active coastline has helped produce the sharp cliffs in this scene along the north coast of California. *(Darrel Hess photo.)*

By far the most significant of these organisms is the *coral polyp,* a tiny animal that builds a hard external skeleton of calcium carbonate and then lives inside it. Coral polyps are of many species, and they cluster together in social colonies of uncounted billions of individuals. Under favorable conditions (clear, shallow, salty warm water), the coral can accumulate into enormous masses, forming reefs, platforms, and atolls, all commonplace features in tropical and subtropical oceans. (Coral reef structures will be discussed later in this chapter.)

Stream Outflow

The outflow of streams and rivers into oceans and lakes is included here in our discussion of shore-shaping forces because these outflows are important feeders of sediments to oceans and lakes. They provide much of the sand and other sedimentary material that is moved around and deposited by coastal waters (Figure 20-11). As we will discuss later in this chapter, should the source of sediment from stream outflow be disrupted, beaches along a coastline may begin to shrink.

Currents and Coastal Sediment Transport

 Coastal Sediment Transport

Currents consist of large volumes of water moving horizontally. Many kinds of currents flow in the oceans and lakes of the world, usually confined to surface areas but sometimes deeper. Nearly all movement of sediment along coastlines is accomplished by wave action and local currents.

Longshore Currents   Coastal topography is affected most by **longshore currents**, in which the water moves roughly parallel to the shoreline. (Think of longshore as a contraction for "along the shore.") Longshore currents develop just offshore and are set up by the action of the waves striking the coast at a slight angle (Figure 20-12). Since most waves are generated by wind, the direction of longshore current typically reflects the local wind direction. Longshore currents are prominent transporters of sand and other sediment along many shorelines.

▲ **Figure 20-11**   The sediment plume of the Betsiboka River of Madagascar spreads broadly into the blue waters of the Mozambique Channel, which separates the island of Madagascar from the African coast. *(NASA Headquarters.)*

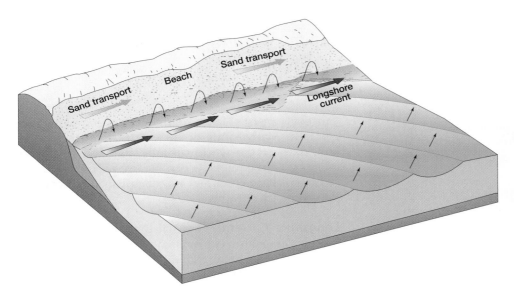

Figure 20-12 ... (continued below)

Figure 20-12 Beach drifting involves a zigzag movement of sand along the coast. Sand is brought obliquely onto the beach by the wave and is then returned seaward by the backwash. Longshore currents develop just offshore and move sediment parallel to the coastline. Since most waves develop in response to the wind, longshore currents and beach drifting typically move sediment in a general downwind direction along a shore.

Beach Drifting Another significant mechanism of coastal sediment transport involves the short-distance shifting of sand directly onshore by breaking waves and directly offshore by the retreating water. The debris (mostly sand) that advances and retreats with the repeated surging and ebbing of the waves abrades and smoothes the beach, while the continuous abrasion reduces the size of the particles.

This movement may take the form of **beach drifting** along a coastline, a zigzag movement of particles that results in downwind displacement parallel to the coast (see Figure 20-12). Nearly all waves approach the coast obliquely rather than at a right angle (Figure 20-13), and therefore the sand and other debris carried onshore by the breaking wave move up the beach at an oblique angle. Some of the water soaks into the beach, but much of it returns seaward directly downslope, which is normally at a right angle to the shoreline. This return flow takes some of the debris with it, much of which is picked up by the next surging wave and carried shoreward again along an oblique path. This infinitely repetitious pattern of movement shifts the debris farther and farther along the coastline longitudinally. Because wind is the driving force for wave motion, the strength, direction, and duration of the wind are the principal determinants of beach drifting.

▲ **Figure 20-13** Here a series of waves rolls in obliquely to the beach at Cape Byron, on the eastern coast of Australia. *(Tom L. McKnight photo.)*

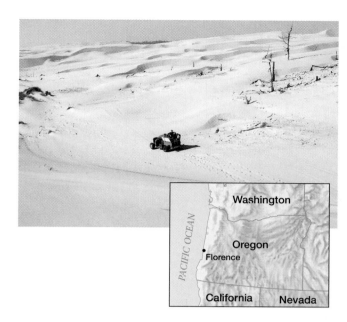

▲ **Figure 20-14** Sand is sometimes heaped into dunes that cover extensive areas. One of the largest sand accumulations in North America is along the central coast of Oregon, near Florence. *(Tom L. McKnight photo.)*

Tides are not very effective in moving coarser debris, but where channels are narrow and relatively shallow, tides can move fine material.

Some debris transport along shorelines is accomplished directly by the wind. Wherever waves have carried or hurled sand and finer-grained particles to positions above the water level, these particles can be picked up by a breeze and moved overland. This type of movement frequently results in dune formation and sometimes moves sand a considerable distance inland (Figure 20-14).

Coastal Deposition

Although the restless waters of coastal areas accomplish notable erosion and transportation, in many cases the most conspicuous topographic features of a shoreline are formed by deposition. Just as in streamflow over the surface of a continent, marine deposition occurs wherever the energy of moving water is diminished.

Maritime deposits along coastlines tend to be more ephemeral than noncoastal deposits. This is due primarily to the composition of marine deposits, which typically consist of relatively small particles (sand and gravel), and to the fact that the sand is not stabilized by a vegetation cover. Most coastal deposits are under constant onslaught by agitated waters which can rapidly wash away portions of the sediment. Consequently, the **sediment budget** must be in balance if the deposit is to persist; for the budget to be in balance, removal of sand must be offset by addition of sand. Most marine deposits have a continuing sediment flux, with debris arriving in some places and departing in others. During storms, the balance is often upset, with the result that the deposit is either significantly reshaped or totally removed.

Coastal Landforms FG2 FG8

Certain coastal landforms are widespread on Earth. How they develop illustrates many of the processes we have just discussed.

Depositional Landforms

Coastal Stabilization Structures

Beaches   The most widespread marine depositional feature is the **beach**, which is an exposed deposit of loose sediment adjacent to a body of water. Although the sediment can range in size from fine sand to large cobbles, it is usually relatively homogeneous in size on a given section of beach. Beaches composed of smaller particles (which is to say sand, because silt and clay get carried away in suspension and do not form beaches) are normally broad and slope gently seaward, whereas those formed of larger particles (gravel, cobbles) generally slope more steeply.

Beaches occupy the transition zone between land and water, sometimes extending well above the normal sea level into elevations reached only by the highest storm waves. On the seaward side, they generally extend down to the level of the lowest tides and can often be found at still lower levels, where they merge with muddy bottom deposits. Figure 20-15 portrays an idealized beach profile. The *backshore* is the upper part of the beach, landward of the high-water line. It is usually dry, being covered by waves only during severe storms. It contains one or more *berms*, which are flattish wave-deposited sediment platforms. The *foreshore* is the zone that is regularly covered and uncovered by the rise and fall of tides. The *offshore* is the zone that is permanently underwater; it is the place where waves break and where surf action is greatest.

Beaches sometimes extend for dozens of kilometers along straight coastlines, particularly if the relief of the land is slight and the bedrock unresistant. Along irregular shorelines, beach development may be restricted largely or entirely to bays, with the bays frequently alternating with rocky headlands.

Beach shape may change greatly from day to day and even from hour to hour. Normally beaches are built up during quiet weather and removed rapidly during storms. Most beaches are longer and wider in summer and greatly worn away by the storminess of winter.

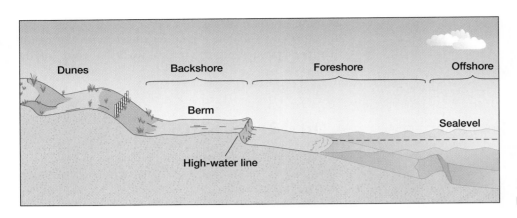

◀ **Figure 20-15** An idealized beach profile.

Spits Near-shore ocean waters normally contain a considerable amount of fine-grained sediment that is shifted about by waves, currents, and tides. At the mouth of a bay, sediment may be moved by longshore currents into deeper water. There the flow speed is slowed and the sediment is deposited. The growing bank of land guides the current farther into the deep water, where still more material is dropped. Any such linear deposit attached to the land at one end and extending into open water in a down-current direction is called a **spit** (Figure 20-16).

Although most spits are straight, sandy peninsulas projecting out into a bay or other coastal indentation, the vicissitudes of currents, winds, and waves often give them other configurations. In some cases, the spit becomes extended clear across the mouth of a bay to connect with land on the other side, producing what is called either a *bay barrier* or a **baymouth bar** and transforming the bay to a lagoon. Another common modification of spit shape is caused by conflicting water movements in the bay which can cause the deposits to curve toward the mainland, forming a *hook* at the outer end of the spit (Figure 20-17). A less common but even more distinctive development is a **tombolo**. This is a spit formed when waves converging in two directions on the landward side of a near-shore island deposit their sand, so that the bar connects the island to the land (Figure 20-18).

Barrier Islands Another prominent coastal deposition is the **barrier island** (Figure 20-19), a long, narrow sandbar built up in shallow offshore waters, sometimes only a few hundred meters from the coast but often several kilometers at sea. Barrier islands are always oriented approximately parallel to the shore. They are believed to result from the heaping up of debris where large waves (particularly storm waves) begin to break in the shallow waters of continental shelves. However, many larger barrier islands may have more complicated histories linked to the lowered sea level that resulted when a large amount of seawater was locked up in glaciers during the Pleistocene.

Barrier islands often become the dominant element of a coastal terrain. Although they usually rise at most

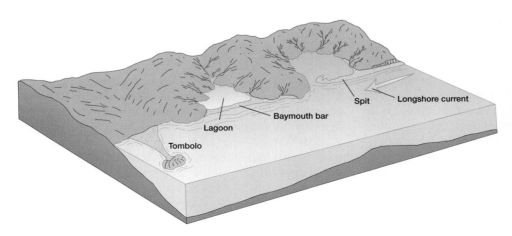

◀ **Figure 20-16** Common depositional landforms along a coastline include spits, baymouth bars, and tombolos. Note the orientation of the spit to the direction of the longshore current.

▲ **Figure 20-17** Spit at Cape Henlopen, Delaware. *(Prof. Stewart Farrell.)*

only a few meters above sea level and are typically only a few hundred meters wide, they may extend many kilometers in length. Most of the Atlantic and Gulf of Mexico coastline of the United States, for instance, is paralleled by lengthy barrier islands, several more than 50 kilometers (30 miles) long (Figure 20-20).

▲ **Figure 20-18** A famous tombolo is found on the northwestern coast of France. A large rock, called Mont Saint Michel, is tied to the mainland by a narrow sandbar. The village of Mont Saint Michel has been built on the rock. *(Cotton Coulson/National Geographic Society.)*

An extensive barrier island isolates the water between itself and the mainland, forming a body of quiet salt or brackish water called a **lagoon**. Over time, a lagoon becomes increasingly filled with water-deposited sediment from coastal streams, wind-deposited sand from the barrier island, and tidal deposits if the lagoon has an opening to the sea. All three of these sources contribute to the buildup of *mudflats* on the edges of the lagoon. Unless tidal inlets across the barrier island permit vigorous tides or currents to carry lagoon debris seaward, therefore, the ultimate destiny of most lagoons is to slowly be transformed, first to marshes and then to meadows (Figure 20-21).

In addition to infilling by sediment, another factor contributes to a lagoon's disappearance. After a barrier island becomes a certain size, it often begins to migrate slowly shoreward as waves wear away its seaward shore and sediments accumulate to build up its landward shore. Eventually, if the pattern is not interrupted

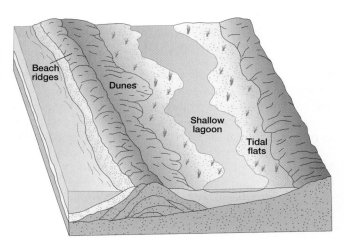

▲ **Figure 20-19** A typical relationship between ocean, barrier island, and lagoon.

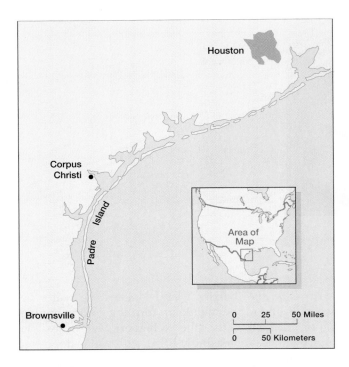

▲ **Figure 20-20**   The longest of the barrier islands off the Gulf Coast of the United States is Texas's Padre Island. *(National Park Service.)*

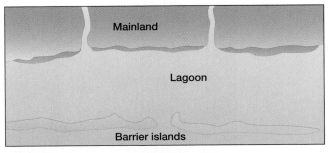

(a)

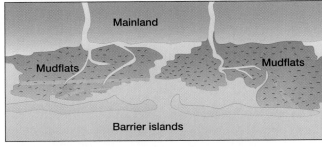

(b)

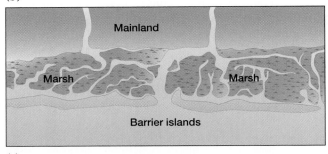

(c)

▲ **Figure 20-21**   Barrier islands are separated from the mainland by lagoons. With the passage of time, the lagoons often become choked with sediment and become converted to marsh, mudflat, or meadow.

by such things as changing sea level, the island and the mainland shore will merge.

Human Alteration of Coastal Sediment Budgets

Over the last half-century, human activity has disrupted the sediment budgets of beaches along many shorelines of the world—this has been especially true in many coastal areas of North America. For example, dams built along rivers for flood control or hydroelectric power generation effectively act as sediment traps. With less sediment reaching the mouths of rivers, there is less sediment to be transported along the shoreline by longshore currents and beach drifting, and so the downcurrent beaches begin to shrink. In addition, artificial structures built by one community to increase or stabilize their beaches, may reduce the amount of sediment transported

farther down a shoreline, thus causing downcurrent beaches to be reduced in size.

Local communities have taken a number of different approaches to solving the problem of shrinking beaches. One direct, but relatively expensive, approach is to "nourish" a beach by dumping tons of sand just slightly upcurrent of the beach. Unfortunately, since longshore currents and beach drifting will eventually transport the sand away, such nourishment must be undertaken repeatedly in order to maintain the beach at a desired size.

Another approach to maintaining beaches is the use of "hard" stabilization structures. For example, a **groin** is a short wall or dam built out from a beach to impede the longshore current and force sand deposition on the upcurrent side of the structure (Figure 20-22). While groins do trap sediment on their upcurrent side, erosion tends to take place on their downcurrent side; to reduce this erosion, another groin can be built just downcurrent. In some locations, a series of groins, known as a *groin field,* has been built.

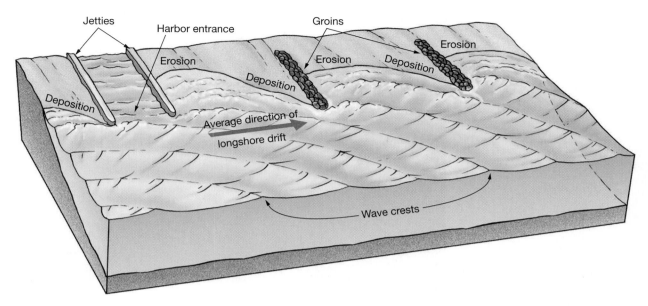

▲ **Figure 20-22**   Jetties and groins along a shoreline trap sediment on their upcurrent side, while erosion tends to remove sediment on their downcurrent side. *(After Trujillo and Thurman,* Essentials of Oceanography, *8th ed., Upper Saddle River, NJ: Prentice Hall, 2005.)*

Jetties are usually built in pairs on either side of a river or harbor entrance. The idea is to confine the flow of water to a narrow zone, thereby keeping the sand in motion and inhibiting its deposition in the navigation channel. Jetties tend to interfere with longshore currents in the same way as groins, trapping sand on the upcurrent side while causing erosion on the downcurrent side.

Even after undertaking such expensive projects as building groin fields and carrying out regular beach nourishment, some communities are finding that it's a losing proposition—the beaches continue to shrink and there seems to be no clear solution available to them.

Shorelines of Submergence

In the recent geological past, sea level has fluctuated sharply. For example, during a warmer climatic interval in an interglacial period, 125,000 years ago, sea level was about 6 meters (20 feet) higher than it is today. During the last glacial peak (about 20,000 years ago), sea level is estimated to have been about 120 meters (400 feet) lower than it is at present.

Almost all the world's oceanic coastlines show evidence of submergence during the last 15,000 years or so, a result of the melting of the Pleistocene ice sheets. As water from melting glaciers returned to the oceans, rising sea level caused widespread submergence of coastal zones.

Ria Shorelines   The most prominent result of submergence is the drowning of previous river valleys, which produces estuaries, or long fingers of seawater projecting inland. A coast along which there are numerous estuaries is called a **ria shoreline**. A ria (from

the Spanish *ría,* "river") is a long, narrow inlet of a river that gradually decreases in depth from mouth to head (Figure 20-23). If a hilly or mountainous coastal area is submerged, numerous offshore islands may indicate the previous location of hilltops and ridge crests.

Fjorded Coasts   The most spectacular coastlines occur where high-relief coastal terrain has undergone extensive glaciation. Troughs once gouged out either by glaciers or by ice sheets have been cut so deep that their bottoms are presently far below sea level. Gradually, therefore, as the ice has melted, the troughs have filled up with seawater. In some localities these deep, sheer-walled coastal indentations—called **fjords**—are so

▲ **Figure 20-23**   Landsat image of Chesapeake Bay. On the left, the flooded mouth of the Patuxent River can be seen running parallel to the Bay; on the right the flooded mouth of the Choptank River connects with the Bay. *(NASA/Goddard Space Flight Center Scientific Visualization Studio.)*

▲ **Figure 20-24**   Entrance to fjords at Milford Sound, New Zealand. *(Getty Images, Inc.–Peter Hendrie.)*

numerous that they create an extraordinarily irregular coastline, often with long, narrow fingers of saltwater reaching more than 160 kilometers (100 miles) inland.

The most extensive and spectacular fjorded coasts are in Norway, western Canada, Alaska, southern Chile, the South Island of New Zealand, Greenland, and Antarctica (Figure 20-24).

Shorelines of Emergence and Erosion

Evidence of previously higher sea levels is sometimes related to ice melting during past interglacial ages but is more often associated with tectonic uplift. The clearest topographic result of coastal emergence is shoreline features raised well above the present water level. Often the emerged portion of a continental shelf appears as a broad, flat coastal plain.

Wave-Cut Cliffs and Platforms   One of the most common coastal landform complexes comprises wave-cut cliffs, wave-cut benches, and wave-built terraces. As discussed earlier, as waves eat away at a rocky headland, steep wave-cut cliffs are formed, and these cliffs receive the greatest pounding at their base, where the power of the waves is concentrated. A combination of hydraulic pounding, abrasion, pneumatic push, and chemical solution at the cliff base frequently cuts a notch at the high-water level. As the notch is enlarged,

▲ **Figure 20-25**   A conspicuous wave-cut notch in resistant coralline rock on the Fiji island of Vanua Levu. *(Tom L. McKnight photo.)*

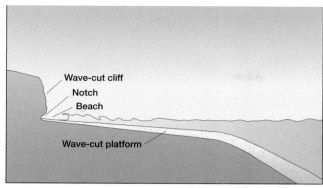

(a)

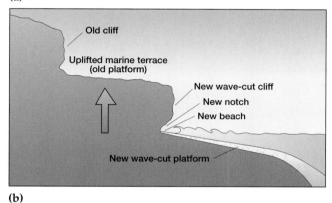

(b)

▲ **Figure 20-26** A marine terrace develops when a wave-cut platform is tectonically uplifted above sea level.

▲ **Figure 20-27** Uplifted marine terraces, well above the present shoreline. This scene is on the north coast of California near Fort Ross. *(Darrel Hess photo.)*

the overhang sporadically collapses, and the cliff recedes as the ocean advances (Figure 20-25).

Seaward of the cliff face, the pounding and abrasion of the waves create a broad erosional platform called a *wave-cut bench* or **wave-cut platform**, usually slightly below water level. The combination of wave-cut cliff and wave-cut bench produces a profile that resembles a letter "L," with the steep vertical cliff descending to a notched base and the flat horizontal bench extending seaward (Figure 20-26a).

The debris eroded from cliff and bench is mostly removed by the swirling waters. The larger fragments are battered into smaller and smaller pieces until they are small enough to be transportable. Some of the sand and gravel produced in this fashion may be washed into an adjacent bay to become, at least temporarily, a part of the beach. Much of the debris, however, is shifted directly seaward, where a great deal of it is deposited just beyond the wave-cut bench as a *wave-built terrace.* With the passage of time and the wearing away of the cliff by weathering and erosion, the terrace may become so large that it buries the bench entirely. Here the result is formation of a beach that extends to the base of the cliff.

Marine Terraces When a wave-cut platform is uplifted along tectonically rising coast, a **marine terrace** is

formed (Figure 20-26b). Along some shorelines of the world, a series of marine terraces is present, reflecting several episodes of terrace formation (Figure 20-27).

Coral Coasts

In tropical oceans, nearly all continents and islands are fringed with either *coral reefs* or some other type of coralline formation (Figure 20-28). Coralline structures are built by a complicated series of events that involve animals, algae, and various physical and chemical processes.

The critical element in the development of coral reefs is a group of anthozoan animals (members of the class *Anthozoa* that are closely related to jellyfish and sea anemones) called *stony corals.* These tiny creatures (most are only a few millimeters long) live in colonies of countless individuals, attaching themselves to one another both with living tissue and with their external skeletons (Figure 20-29). Each individual *coral polyp* extracts calcium carbonate from the seawater and secretes a limy skeleton around the lower half of its body. Most polyps withdraw into their skeletal cups during the day and extend their armlike feeding structures at night. At the top of the body is a mouth surrounded by rings of tentacles, which gives them a blossomlike appearance that for centuries caused biologists to believe that they were plants rather than animals. They feed on minute animal and plant plankton. Although the coral polyp is an animal, most varieties of hard coral are hosts to symbiotic algae that provide additional food for the coral polyp through photosynthesis.

The ubiquity of coral reefs in shallow tropical waters is a tribute to the remarkable fecundity of the polyps

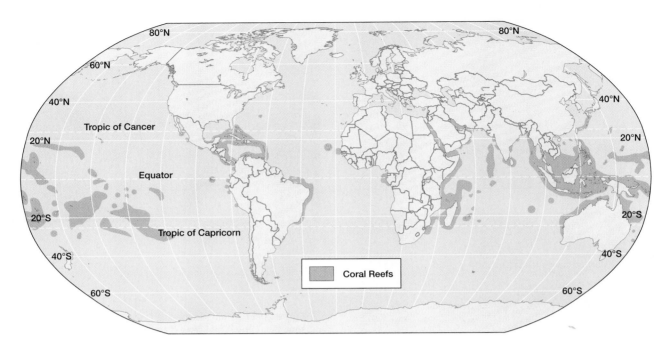

▲ **Figure 20-28**   Distribution of coral reefs and other coralline structures in the oceans of the world.

because they are not actually very hardy creatures. They cannot survive in water that is very cool or very fresh or very dirty. Moreover, they require considerable light, so they cannot live more than a few tens of meters below the surface of the ocean.

Coral polyps can build coralline formations almost anywhere in shallow tropical waters where a coastline provides a stable foundation. Coral reefs in the shallows off the coasts of Florida, for instance,

are built on such stable bases. The famous Great Barrier Reef off the northeastern coast of Australia is an immense shallow-water platform of bedrock largely, but not entirely, covered with coral. Its enormously complex structure includes many individual reefs, irregular coral masses, and a number of islands (Figure 20-30).

One favored location for coral reefs is around a volcanic island in tropical waters; as the volcano forms

▲ **Figure 20-29**   Coral comes in an extraordinary variety of sizes, shapes, forms, and species. This closeup reef scene in the Bahamas shows a "Christmas tree" worm in a colony of coral. *(Roger Hess photo.)*

FOCUS Bleaching of Coral Reefs

All species of coral contain *zooxanthellae*, a type of algae that lives in a symbiotic relationship with the coral polyp. Through photosynthesis, the algae provides nutrients to the coral—it is also the algae that gives coral its beautiful color.

For reasons that are not completely understood, when coral is stressed it expels the algae, leaving its exoskeleton of calcium carbonate a translucent white color. This phenomenon is known as *coral bleaching* (Figure 20-C). In some cases, bleached corals die within just a few weeks if the zooxanthellae are not replaced.

Bleaching events have been observed for decades, caused by such factors as a sharp decrease in water salinity, sedimentation, pollution, and abrupt changes in temperature; but it became clear to researchers in

the 1980s that stress from high water temperature was the most common cause. The warming of coastal waters during the 1982–83 El Niño was observed to cause bleaching of coral in Panama; the 1997–98 El Niño was even stronger and caused bleaching in reefs around the world. In recent years, some researchers have started pointing to higher sea surface temperatures (SST) associated with global warming as at least one of the causes of the rising number of coral bleaching incidents.

In 2005 a major bleaching event occurred in the Caribbean. At one monitoring station south of St. John in the U.S. Virgin Islands, 30 percent of the coral died within a six-month period. The National Oceanic and Atmospheric Administration (NOAA) monitors stress on coral reefs through

a program known as the *Coral Reef Early Warning System* (CREWS). CREWS evaluates the SST, the intensity of solar radiation, and the wind speed, and issues a Coral Bleaching Alert when stress levels are high. The 2005 heat stress levels were the highest observed since satellite monitoring of reefs began 20 years ago.

The loss of coral reefs through bleaching and other natural and human-produced causes is alarming many researchers. When coral dies, an entire ecosystem is at risk: the fish and other creatures that depend on coral for survival are stressed, local fisheries can decline, the protection from storm waves offered to low-lying islands fringed with reefs is diminished, and, of course, the loss of species and biodiversity may be irreparable.

▲ **Figure 20-C**   Bleached coral in the Great Barrier Reef, Australia. *(SeaPics.)*

and then subsides, the following different types of reefs grow upward. When the volcano first forms, as, for example, over the Hawaiian hot spot described in Chapter 14, coral accumulates on the part of the mountain flank just below sea level because it is in these shallow waters that polyps live. The result is a reef built right onto the volcano, as shown in Figure 20-31a; such an attached reef is called a **fringing reef** (Figure 20-32).

As new layers are laid down over old, the coral builds upward around the volcano as a cylinder of irregular

height. At the same time, the volcano is sinking and pulling the original reef base downward. When the coral has been built up enough and the volcano has sunk enough, the result at the water surface is a coral ring separated by a lagoon from the part of the volcano still above water, as in Figure 20-31b. This ring of coral, which may be a broken circle because of the varying thickness of the coral, appearing to float around a central volcanic peak (but is actually attached to the flanks of the sinking mountain far below

◀ **Figure 20-30** A view of Australia's Great Barrier Reef. *(Tony Roberts/Sportshot/Photo Researchers, Inc.)*

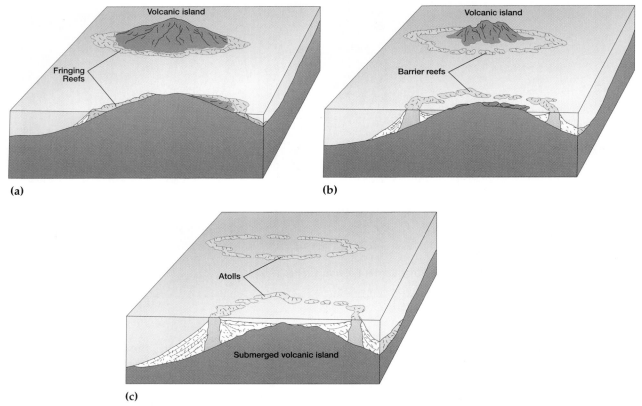

▲ **Figure 20-31** Coral reef formation around a sinking volcano. **(a)** Around a newly formed volcano rising above the water of a tropical ocean, secretions from coral polyps living along the shallow-water flanks of the volcano accumulate into a fringing reef attached to the mountain. **(b)** As the volcano becomes dormant and begins to sink, the coral continues to grow upward over the original base, essentially a cylinder surrounding the mountain. Breaks in the coral ring allow water in, and a lagoon forms between coral and mountain. Such a reef separated from its mainland by a lagoon is a barrier reef. **(c)** Once the volcano is completely submerged, the coral surrounding a landless lagoon is called an atoll reef.

▲ **Figure 20-32** A part of the fringing reef on the island of Moorea in French Polynesia. *(Jack Fields/Photo Researchers, Inc.)*

the water surface), is called a **barrier reef**. The surface of a barrier reef is usually right at sea level, with some portions projecting upward into the air.

Coral polyps continue to live in the upper, shallow-water portions of a barrier reef, and so the reef continues to grow upward. Once the top of the volcano sinks below the water surface, the reef surrounding a now

landless lagoon is called an **atoll** (Figure 20-31c). The term atoll implies a ring-shaped structure. In actuality, however, the ring is rarely unbroken; rather it consists of a string of closely spaced coral islets separated by narrow channels of water. Each individual islet is called a *motu*.

Chapter 20 Learning Review

Key Terms

Before answering the study questions below, review the definitions of the following key terms (page references are provided for you):

atoll *(p. 609)*	fringing reef *(p. 607)*	swash *(p. 591)*
backwash *(p. 591)*	groin *(p. 602)*	swell *(p. 590)*
barrier island *(p. 600)*	jetty *(p. 603)*	tombolo *(p. 600)*
barrier reef *(p. 609)*	lagoon *(p. 601)*	tsunami *(p. 593)*
baymouth bar *(p. 600)*	longshore current *(p. 597)*	wave-cut platform *(p. 605)*
beach *(p. 599)*	marine terrace *(p. 605)*	wave height *(p. 590)*
beach drifting *(p. 598)*	ria shoreline *(p. 603)*	wave of oscillation *(p. 590)*
eustatic sea-level change *(p. 595)*	sediment budget *(p. 599)*	wave of translation *(p. 591)*
fjord *(p. 603)*	spit *(p. 600)*	wave refraction *(p. 591)*

Study Questions for Key Concepts

After studying this chapter, you should be able to answer the following questions:

Coastal Processes (p. 589)
1. Contrast the characteristics of ocean waves in deep water with waves in shallow water.
2. Describe and explain the process of *wave refraction*.

3. What factors influence the erosional power of waves striking a coastline?
4. How does air serve as a tool of erosion in wave action?

5. Explain the formation and characteristics of a *tsunami*.
6. What effect did Pleistocene glaciation have on sea level?
7. Describe the formation and characteristics of *longshore currents*.
8. Describe the process of *beach drifting*.
9. Explain the concept of the *sediment budget* of a coastal depositional landform such as a beach.

Coastal Landforms (p. 599)

10. What causes beaches to change shape and size?
11. Describe and contrast a coastal *spit* and a *baymouth bar*.
12. What happens to most *coastal lagoons* with the passage of time?

13. What will likely happen to a downcurrent beach when a major river flowing into the ocean is dammed? Why?
14. Why are *shorelines of submergence* so common today?
15. Explain the formation of a *ria coast* and a *fjorded coast*.
16. Explain how a *wave-cut cliff* forms.
17. Describe the formation of a *marine terrace* along a *shoreline of emergence*.
18. Explain how a *fringing coral reef* forms and how it can subsequently become transformed first to a *barrier reef* and then to an *atoll*.

Additional Resources

Books:

Dean, Cornelia. *Against the Tide: The Battle for America's Beaches.* New York: Columbia University Press, 1999.

Oldale, Robert N. *Geologic History of Cape Cod, Massachusetts.* U.S. Geological Survey publication 1992–332–682. Washington, D.C.: U.S. Government Printing Office, 1992.

Sunamura, Tsuguo. *Geomorphology of Rocky Coasts.* New York: John Wiley & Sons, 1992.

Trujillo, Alan P., and Harold V. Thurman. *Essentials of Oceanography*, 8th ed. Upper Saddle River, NJ: Prentice Hall, 2005.

Internet Sites:

International Tsunami Information Center

http://www.prh.noaa.gov/itic/

The International Tsunami Information Center in Hawaii provides information about tsunami and current tsunami warnings.

National Oceanic and Atmospheric Administration (NOAA)

http://www.noaa.gov/

The National Oceanic and Atmospheric Administration (NOAA) oversees a number of government agencies, including the National Weather Service.

NOAA's home page provides links to sites about weather, climate, weather satellites, the oceans, and coastlines.

National Undersea Research Program

http://www.noaa.gov/ocean.html

This site has information about current ocean conditions and current marine research.

Appendix I
The International System of Units (SI)

With the major exception of the United States, the system of weights and measures used worldwide both in scientific work and in everyday life is the International System, usually abbreviated SI from its French name, *Système Internationale.* The system has seven base units and supplementary units for angles (Table I-1). The beauty of the system lies in its reliance on multiples of the number 10, with the prefixes shown in Table I-2 being used to cover a magnitude range from the astronomically large to the infinitesimally small. Table I-3 lists the most frequently used conversion factors.

TABLE I-1 SI Units

Quantity	Unit	Symbol
Base Units		
Length	Meter	m
Mass	Kilogram	kg
Time	Second	s
Electric current	Ampere	A
Temperature	Kelvin	K
Amount of substance	Mole	mol
Luminous intensity	Candela	Cd
Supplementary Units		
Plane angle	Radian	rad
Solid angle	Steradian	Sr

TABLE I-2 Common Multiples and SI Prefixes

Multiple	Value	Prefix	Symbol
1 000 000 000 000	10^{12}	tera	T
1 000 000 000	10^{9}	giga	G
1 000 000	10^{6}	mega	M
1000	10^{3}	kilo	K
100	10^{2}	hecto	H
10	10^{1}	deka	Da
0.1	10^{-1}	Deci	D
0.01	10^{-2}	centi	C
0.001	10^{-3}	Milli	M
0.000001	10^{-6}	micro	μ
0.000000001	10^{-9}	nano	n
0.000000000001	10^{-12}	Pico	P

TABLE I-3 SI—English Conversion Units

Multiply	By	To Get
Length		
Inches	2.540	Centimeters
Foot	0.3048	Meters
Yards	0.9144	Meters
Miles	1.6093	Kilometers
Millimeters	0.039	Inches
Centimeters	0.3937	Inches
Meters	3.281	Foot
Kilometers	0.6214	Miles

(continued)

TABLE I-3 (continued)

Area

Square inches	6.452	Square centimeters
Square feet	0.0929	Square meters
Square yards	0.836	Square meters
Square miles	2.590	Square kilometers
Acres	0.4047	Hectares
Square centimeters	0.155	Square inches
Square meters	10.764	Square feet
Square meters	1.196	Square yards
Square kilometers	0.386	Square miles
Hectares	2.471	Acres

Volume

Cubic inches	16.387	Cubic centimeters
Cubic feet	0.028	Cubic meters
Cubic yards	0.7646	Cubic meters
Fluid ounces	29.57	Milliliters
Pints	0.47	Liters
Quarts	0.946	Liters
Gallons	3.785	Liters
Cubic centimeters	0.061	Cubic inches
Cubic meters	35.3	Cubic feet
Cubic meters	1.3	Cubic yards
Milliliters	0.034	Fluid ounces
Liters	1.0567	Quarts
Liters	0.264	Gallons

Mass (Weight)

Ounces	28.35	Grams
Pounds	0.4536	Kilograms
Tons (2000 lb)	907.18	Kilograms
Tons (2000 lb)	0.90718	Tonnes
Grams	0.035	Ounces
Kilograms	2.2046	Pounds
Kilograms	0.0011	Tons (2000 lb)
Tonnes	1.1023	Tons (2000 lb)

Appendix II
U.S. Geological Survey Topographic Maps

The U.S. Geological Survey (USGS) is one of the world's largest mapping agencies and is primarily responsible for the country's National Mapping Program. The USGS produces a broad assortment of maps, but its topographic "quadrangles" are by far the ones most widely used by geographers. The quadrangles come in various sizes and scales (from 1:24,000 to 1:1,000,000), but all are rectangles bordered by parallels and meridians rather than by political boundaries. For many years the quadrangles were produced by surveys on the ground. Today, however, they are created from aerial photographs, satellite imagery, and computer rectification.

The USGS has produced more than 55,000 topographic quadrangles as well as about 220,000 digital orthorectified aerial images. These are valuable resources, but many are outdated. The average topographic map sheet is about 23 years old. In 2001, the USGS outlined an ambitious 10-year plan that is the agency's largest mapping endeavor to date—to develop a seamless, continuously maintained, nationally consistent set of online, public-domain, geographic based information for the United States. Both the program and the resulting publications are known as The National Map. Relevant documents are now available via the USGS World Wide Web site at http://www.nationalmap.usgs.gov.

Elevation Contour Lines

USGS topographic map quadrangles use elevation contour lines to portray the relief of the land—its shape, slope, and elevation (Figure II-1). The following guidelines are followed when interpreting contour lines:

1. A contour line connects points of equal elevation.
2. The difference in elevation between two contour lines is called the *contour interval*.
3. Usually every fourth or fifth contour line is a darker *index contour*.
4. Elevations on one side of a contour line are higher than on the other side.
5. Contour lines never touch or cross one another (except at some cliffs).

6. Contour lines have no beginning or end—every line closes on itself, either on or off the map.
7. Uniformly spaced contours indicate a uniform slope.
8. If spaced far apart, contour lines indicate a gentle slope; if spaced close together, they represent a steep slope.
9. Contour lines bend upstream in a "V" shape when crossing a stream valley, gully, or "draw" (the "V" points uphill).
10. Along a spur or ridge running down a hillside, a contour line forms a "V" pointing downhill.
11. A contour line that closes within the limits of the map represents a hill or rise. The land inside that contour is higher than the elevation of the closed contour itself.
12. A depression may be represented by a closed contour that is hachured on the side leading into the depression—the elevation of such a *depression contour* is the same as that of the adjacent lower regular contour (unless otherwise marked).

Topographic Map Symbols

Topographic quadrangles also portray a variety of other features using symbols and colors. Standard colors are used to distinguish various kinds of map features:

- **Brown:** contour lines and other topographic features
- **Blue:** hydrographic (water) features
- **Black:** features constructed or designated by humans, such as buildings, roads, boundary lines, and names
- **Green:** areas of vegetation, such as woodlands, forests, orchards, and vineyards
- **Red:** important roads and lines of the public land survey system
- **Gray or red tint:** urban areas
- **Purple:** features added from aerial photos during map revision

The principal standard symbols used on USGS topographic maps are shown in Figure II-2. Note that in a few cases more than one kind of symbol is used to show the same kind of feature.

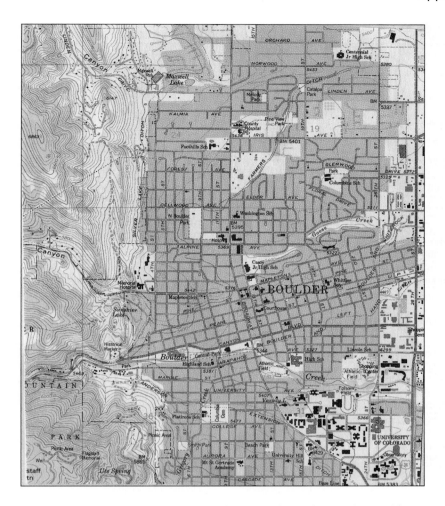

▲ **Figure II-1**   A typical USGS topographic map. Shown here is the Boulder, Colorado, quadrangle; scale 1:62,500; contour interval 40 feet (13 meters). *(Source: U.S. Geological Survey, U.S. Department of the Interior.)*

BATHMETRIC FEATURES

Area exposed at mean low tide; sounding datum line***	
Channel***	
Sunken rock***	

BOUNDARIES

National	
State or territorial	
County or equivalent	
Civil township or equivalent	
Incorporated city or equivalent	
Federally administered park, reservation, or monument (external)	
Federally administered park, reservation, or monument (internal)	
State forest, park, reservation, or monument and large county park	
Forest Service administrative area*	
Forest Service ranger district*	
National Forest System land status, Forest Service lands*	
National Forest System land status, non-Forest Service lands*	
Small park (county or city)	

BUILDINGS AND RELATED FEATURES

Building	
School; house of worship	
Athletic field	
Built-up area	
Forest headquarters*	
Ranger district office*	
Guard station or work center*	
Racetrack or raceway	
Airport, paved landing strip, runway, taxiway, or apron	
Unpaved landing strip	
Well (other than water), windmill or wind generator	
Tanks	
Covered reservoir	
Gaging station	
Located or landmark object (feature as labeled)	
Boat ramp or boat access*	
Roadside park or rest area	
Picnic area	
Campground	
Winter recreation area*	
Cemetery	

COASTAL FEATURES

Foreshore flat	
Coral or rock reef	
Rock, bare or awash; dangerous to navigation	
Group of rocks, bare or awash	
Exposed wreck	
Depth curve; sounding	
Breakwater, pier, jetty, or wharf	
Seawall	
Oil or gas well; platform	

CONTOURS

Topographic

Index	
Approximate or indefinite	
Intermediate	
Approximate or indefinite	
Supplementary	
Depression	
Cut	
Fill	
Continental divide	

Bathymetric

Index***	
Intermediate***	
Index primary***	
Primary***	
Supplementary***	

CONTROL DATA AND MONUMENTS

Principal point**	
U.S. mineral or location monument	
River mileage marker	

Boundary monument

Third-order or better elevation, with tablet	
Third-order or better elevation, recoverable mark, no tablet	
With number and elevation	

Horizontal control

Third-order or better, permanent mark	
With third-order or better elevation	
With checked spot elevation	
Coincident with found section corner	
Unmonumented**	

▲ **Figure II-2** Topographic map symbols used on USGS quadrangles. *(Source: U.S. Geological Survey, U.S. Department of the Interior.)*

CONTROL DATE AND MONUMENTS — *continued*

Vertical control

Third-order or better elevation, with tablet	BM $\times$ 5280
Third-order or better elevation, recoverable mark, no tablet	$\times$ 528
Bench mark coincident with found section corner	BM + 5280
Spot elevation	$\times$ 7523

GLACIERS AND PERMANENT SNOWFIELDS

Contours and limits	
Formlines	
Glacial advance	
Glacial retreat	

LAND SURVEYS

Public land survey system

Range or Township line	
Location approximate	
Location doubtful	
Protracted	
Protracted (AK 1:63,360-scale)	
Range or Township labels	R1E T2N R3W T4S
Section line	
Location approximate	
Location doubtful	
Protracted	
Protracted (AK 1:63,360-scale)	
Section numbers	1 - 36 1 - 36
Found section corner	
Found closing corner	
Witness corner	WC
Meander corner	MC
Weak corner*	

Other land surveys

Range or Township line	
Section line	
Land grant, mining claim, donation land claim, or tract	
Land grant, homestead, mineral, or other special survey monument	
Fence or field lines	

MARINE SHORELINES

Shoreline	
Apparent (edge of vegetation)***	
Indefinite or unsurveyed	

MINES AND CAVES

Quarry or open pit mine	
Gravel, sand, clay, or borrow pit	$\times$
Mine tunnel or cave entrance	
Mine shaft	
Prospect	X
Tailings	Tailings
Mine dump	
Former disposal site or mine	

PROJECTION AND GRIDS

Neatline	3915 ´ 9037 30 ˝
Graticule tick	55´
Graticule intersection	
Datum shift tick	

State plane coordinate systems

Primary zone tick	640 000 FEET
Secondary zone tick	247 500 METERS
Tertiary zone tick	260 000 FEET
Quaternary zone tick	98 500 METERS
Quintary zone tick	320 000 FEET

Universal transverse metcator grid

UTM grid (full grid)	273
UTM grid ticks*	269

RAILROADS AND RELATED FEATURES

Standard guage railroad, single track	
Standard guage railroad, multiple track	
Narrow guage railroad, single track	
Narrow guage railroad, multiple track	
Railroad siding	
Railroad in highway	
Railroad in road	
Railroad in light duty road*	
Railroad underpass; overpass	
Railroad bridge; drawbridge	
Railroad tunnel	
Railroad yard	
Railroad turntable; roundhouse	

RIVERS, LAKES, AND CANALS

Perennial stream	
Perennial river	
Intermittent stream	
Intermittent river	
Disappearing stream	
Falls, small	
Falls, large	
Rapids, small	
Rapids, large	
Masonry dam	
Dam with lock	
Dam carrying load	

▲ **Figure II-2**   *(continued)*

RIVERS, LAKES, AND CANALS — *continued*

Perennial lake/pond	
Intermittent lake/pond	
Dry lake/pond	
Narrow wash	
Wide wash	
Canal, flume, or aqueduct with lock	
Elevated aqueduct, flume, or mud pot	
Aqueduct tunnel	
Water well, geyser, fumarole, or mud pot	
Spring or creep	

ROADS AND RELATED FEATURES

Please note: Roads on Provisional-edition maps are not classified as primary, secondary, or light duty. These roads are all classified as improved roads and are symbolized the same as light duty roads.

Primary highway	
Secondary highway	
Light duty road	
Light duty road, paved*	
Light duty road, gravel*	
Light duty road, dirt*	
Light duty road, unspecified*	
Unimproved road	
Unimproved road*	
4WD road	
4WD road*	
Trail	
Highway or road with median strip	
Highway or road under construction	
Highway or road underpass; overpass	
Highway or road bridge; drawbridge	
Highway or road tunnel	
Road block, berm, or barrier*	
Gate on road*	
Trailhead*	

  * USGS-USDA Forest Service Single-Edition
 ** Provisional-Edition maps only.
*** Topographic Bathymetric maps only.

▲ **Figure II-2** *(continued)*

SUBMERGED AREAS AND BOGS

Marsh or swamp	
Submerged marsh or swamp	
Wooded marsh or swamp	
Submerged wooded marsh or swamp	
Land subject to inundation	

SURFACE FEATURES

Levee	
Sand or mud	
Disturbed surface	
Gravel beach or glacial moraine	
Tailings pond	

TRANSMISSION LINES AND PIPELINES

Power transmission line; pole, tower	
Telephone line	
Aboveground pipeline	
Underground pipeline	

VEGETATION

Woodland	
Shrubland	
Orchard	
Vineyard	
Mangrove	

Appendix III
Meteorological Tables

Determining Relative Humidity

A *psychrometer* is an instrument used for measuring relative humidity. It consists of two thermometers mounted side by side. One of these is an ordinary thermometer (called a *dry bulb*), which simply measures air temperature. The other thermometer (called a *wet bulb*) has its bulb encased in a covering of muslin or gauze which is saturated with distilled water prior to use. The two thermometers are then thoroughly ventilated either by being whirled around (this instrument has a handle around which the thermometers can be whirled and is referred to as a *sling psychrometer*) or by fanning a current of air past them. This ventilation encourages evaporation of water from the covering of the wet bulb at a rate

that is directly related to the humidity of the surrounding air. Evaporation is a cooling process, and the temperature of the wet bulb drops. In dry air there is more evaporation, and therefore more cooling, than in moist air. The difference between the resulting wet-bulb and dry-bulb temperatures (called the *depression of the wet bulb*) is an expression of the relative saturation of the surrounding air. A large difference indicates low relative humidity; a small difference means that the air is near saturation. If the air is completely saturated, no net evaporation will take place; thus the two thermometers would have identical readings.

To determine relative humidity, measure the wet-bulb and dry-bulb temperatures using a sling psychrometer. Then use these two values to read the relative humidity from Table III-1 (for degrees Celsius) or Table III-2 (for degrees Fahrenheit).

TABLE III-1 Relative Humidity Psychrometer Tables (°C)

Air Temp. °C	Depression of Wet-Bulb Thermometer (°C)																					
	1	2	3	4	5	6	7	8	9	10	11	12	13	14	15	16	17	18	19	20	21	22
−4	77	54	32	11																		
−2	79	58	37	20	1																	
0	81	63	45	28	11																	
2	83	67	51	36	20	6																
4	85	70	56	42	27	14																
6	86	72	59	46	35	22	10	0														
8	87	74	62	51	39	28	17	6														
10	88	76	65	54	43	33	24	13	4													
12	88	78	67	57	48	38	28	19	10	2												
14	89	79	69	60	50	41	33	25	16	8	1											
16	90	80	71	62	54	45	37	29	21	14	7	1										
18	91	81	72	64	56	48	40	33	26	19	12	6	0									
20	91	82	74	66	58	51	44	36	30	23	17	11	5									
22	92	83	75	68	60	53	46	40	33	27	21	15	10	4	0							
24	92	84	76	69	62	55	49	42	36	30	25	20	14	9	4	0						
26	92	85	77	70	64	57	51	45	39	34	28	23	18	13	9	5						
28	93	86	78	71	65	59	53	45	42	36	31	26	21	17	12	8	4					
30	93	86	79	72	66	61	55	49	44	39	34	29	25	20	16	12	8	4				
32	93	86	80	73	68	62	56	51	46	41	36	32	27	22	19	14	11	8	4			
34	93	86	81	74	69	63	58	52	48	43	38	34	30	26	22	18	14	11	8	5		
36	94	87	81	75	69	64	59	54	50	44	40	36	32	28	24	21	17	13	10	7	4	
38	94	87	82	76	70	66	60	55	51	46	42	38	34	30	26	23	20	16	13	10	7	5

Relative Humidity (%)

TABLE III-2 Relative Humidity Psychrometer Tables (°F)

Air Temp. °F	Depression of Wet-Bulb Thermometer (°F)																													
	1	2	3	4	5	6	7	8	9	10	11	12	13	14	15	16	17	18	19	20	21	22	23	24	25	26	27	28	29	30
0	67	33	1																											
5	73	46	20																											
10	78	56	34	13	15																									
15	82	64	46	29	11																									
20	85	70	55	40	26	12																								
25	87	74	62	49	37	25	13	1																						
30	89	78	67	56	46	36	26	16	6																					
35	91	81	72	63	54	45	36	27	19	10	2																			
40	92	83	75	68	60	52	45	37	29	22	15	7																		
45	93	86	78	71	64	57	51	44	38	31	25	18	12	6																
50	93	87	74	67	61	55	49	43	38	32	27	21	16	10	5															
55	94	88	82	76	70	65	59	54	49	43	38	33	28	23	19	11	9	5												
60	94	89	83	78	73	68	63	58	53	48	43	39	34	30	26	21	17	13	9	5	1									
65	95	90	85	80	75	70	66	61	56	52	48	44	39	35	31	27	24	20	16	12	9	5	2							
70	95	90	86	81	77	72	68	64	59	55	51	48	44	40	36	33	29	25	22	19	15	12	9	6	3					
75	96	91	86	82	78	74	70	66	62	58	54	51	47	44	40	37	34	30	27	24	21	18	15	12	9	7	4	1		
80	96	91	87	83	79	75	72	68	64	61	57	54	50	47	44	41	38	35	32	29	26	23	20	18	15	12	10	7	5	3
85	96	92	88	84	81	77	73	70	66	63	59	57	53	50	47	44	41	38	36	33	30	27	25	22	20	17	15	13	10	8
90	96	92	89	85	81	78	74	71	68	65	61	58	55	52	49	47	44	41	39	36	34	31	29	26	24	22	19	17	15	13
95	96	93	89	86	82	79	76	73	69	66	63	61	58	55	52	50	47	44	42	39	37	34	32	30	28	25	23	21	19	17
100	96	93	89	86	83	80	77	73	70	68	65	62	59	56	54	51	49	46	44	41	39	37	35	33	30	28	26	24	22	21
105	97	93	90	87	84	81	78	75	72	69	66	64	61	58	56	53	51	49	46	44	42	40	38	36	34	32	30	28	26	24

Relative Humidity (%)

For example, if the dry-bulb temperature is 20°C and the wet-bulb temperature is 14°C, the depression of the wet bulb is 6°C. In Table III-1, find 20°C in the *Air Temperature* column; move across to the 6° column under *Depression of the Wet-Bulb Thermometer*, at the point of intersection, read the relative humidity, 51 percent.

The Beaufort Scale of Wind Speed

Admiral Beaufort of the British Navy developed, early in the nineteenth century, a scale of wind speed widely used in the English-speaking world. It has been modified through the years, but the essentials have not changed. The scale is shown in Table III-3.

Wind Chill

Wind chill is the popular name used to describe what cold weather feels like at various combinations of low temperature and high wind. On a cold, windless day, one's body heat is conducted sluggishly to a thin layer of atmospheric molecules near the skin. These heated molecules diffuse away slowly, to be replaced by other, cooler molecules. One's body thus comes into contact with a relatively small number of cool molecules, and one's body heat dissipates slowly.

TABLE III-3 Beaufort Scale

| Beaufort Force | Speed | | | Description |
	Kilometers per Hour	Miles per Hour	Knots	
0	<1	<1	<1	Calm
1	1–5	1–3	1–3	Light air
2	6–11	4–7	4–6	Light breeze
3	12–19	8–12	7–10	Gentle breeze
4	20–29	13–18	11–16	Moderate breeze
5	30–38	19–24	17–21	Fresh breeze
6	39–49	25–31	22–27	Strong breeze
7	50–61	32–38	28–33	Near gale
8	62–74	39–46	34–40	Gale
9	75–87	47–54	41–47	Strong gale
10	88–101	55–63	48–55	Storm
11	102–116	64–72	56–63	Violent storm
12	117–132	73–82	64–71	Hurricane
13	133–148	83–92	72–80	Hurricane
14	149–166	93–103	81–89	Hurricane
15	167–183	104–114	90–99	Hurricane
16	184–201	115–125	100–108	Hurricane
17	202–219	126–136	109–118	Hurricane

With a rise in wind speed, however, body heat dissipates much more rapidly, as the protective layer of warmer molecules is speedily removed and supplanted by a continually renewing supply of cold air molecules against the skin. Up to a certain speed, the greater the wind velocity, the greater the cooling effect on one's body. Wind chill affects only organisms that contain heat; inanimate objects have no heat to lose, so their temperatures are not affected at all by wind movement.

The term wind chill was apparently first used in 1939 by Paul Siple, a geographer and polar explorer. Meteorologists from the National Weather Service of the United States and from the Meteorological Services of Canada have refined the calculations several times, most recently in 2002. The revised wind-chill index currently in use accounts for the wind effects at face level (the "old" system relied on observed winds 10 meters [33 feet] above the ground) and a better calculation for body heat loss.

The updated index also includes a new frostbite chart, which shows how long skin can safely be exposed to the air given varying temperatures and wind (Tables III-4 and III-5).

The Heat Index

Sensible temperatures may be significantly influenced by humidity, which can make the weather seem either colder or warmer than it actually is—although humidity is more likely to impinge on our lives in hot weather. Quite simply, high humidity makes hot weather seem hotter.

The National Weather Service has developed a *heat index* that combines temperature and relative humidity to produce an "apparent temperature" that quantifies how hot the air feels to one's skin. A sample heat index chart is given in Table III-6.

To this index has been added a general *heat stress index* to indicate heat-related dangers at various apparent temperatures, as shown in Table III-7.

TABLE III-4 Wind Chill (°C)

Actual Air Temperature °C

Wind Speed (km/h) / Calm	5	0	−5	−10	−15	−20	−25	−30	−35	−40
5	4	−2	−7	−13	−19	−24	−30	−36	−41	−47
10	3	−3	−9	−15	−21	−27	−33	−39	−45	−51
15	2	−4	−11	−17	−23	−29	−35	−41	−48	−54
20	1	−5	−12	−18	−24	−31	−37	−43	−49	−56
25	1	−6	−12	−19	−25	−32	−38	−45	−51	−57
30	0	−7	−13	−20	−26	−33	−39	−46	−52	−59
35	0	−7	−14	−20	−27	−33	−40	−47	−53	−60
40	−1	−7	−14	−21	−27	−34	−41	−48	−54	−61
45	−1	−8	−15	−21	−28	−35	−42	−48	−55	−62
50	−1	−8	−15	−22	−29	−35	−42	−49	−56	−63
55	−2	−9	−15	−22	−29	−36	−43	−50	−57	−63
60	−2	−9	−16	−23	−30	−37	−43	−50	−57	−64
65	−2	−9	−16	−23	−30	−37	−44	−51	−58	−65
70	−2	−9	−16	−23	−30	−37	−44	−51	−59	−66
75	−3	−10	−17	−24	−31	−38	−45	−52	−59	−66
80	−3	−10	−17	−24	−31	−38	−45	−52	−60	−67

Wind Speed (kilometers per hour)

Frostbite within 30 minutes

Frostbite within 10 minutes

Frostbite within 5 minutes

TABLE III-5 Wind Chill (°F)

Actual Air Temperature °F

Wind Speed (mph) / Calm	40	35	30	25	20	15	10	5	0	−5	−10	−15	−20	−25	−30	−35	−40
5	36	31	25	19	13	7	1	−5	−11	−16	−22	−28	−34	−40	−46	−52	−57
10	34	27	21	15	9	3	−4	−10	−16	−22	−28	−35	−41	−47	−53	−59	−66
15	32	25	19	13	6	0	−7	−13	−19	−26	−32	−39	−45	−51	−58	−64	−71
20	30	24	17	11	4	−2	−9	−15	−22	−29	−35	−42	−48	−55	−61	−68	−74
25	29	23	16	9	3	−4	−11	−17	−24	−31	−37	−44	−51	−58	−64	−71	−78
30	28	22	15	8	1	−5	−12	−19	−26	−33	−39	−46	−53	−60	−67	−73	−80
35	28	21	14	7	0	−7	−14	−21	−27	−34	−41	−48	−55	−62	−69	−76	−82
40	27	20	13	6	−1	−8	−15	−22	−29	−36	−43	−50	−57	−64	−71	−78	−84
45	26	19	12	5	−2	−9	−16	−23	−30	−37	−44	−51	−58	−65	−72	−79	−86
50	26	19	12	4	−3	−10	−17	−24	−31	−38	−45	−52	−60	−67	−74	−81	−88
55	25	18	11	4	−3	−11	−18	−25	−32	−39	−45	−54	−61	−68	−75	−82	−89
60	25	17	10	3	−4	−11	−19	−26	−33	−40	−48	−55	−62	−69	−76	−84	−91

Wind Speed (miles per hour)

Frostbite within 30 minutes

Frostbite within 10 minutes

Frostbite within 5 minutes

TABLE III-6 Heat Index (Apparent Temperature)

					Relative Humidity				
Temperature	10%	20%	30%	40%	50%	60%	70%	80%	90%
46°C	44°C	49°C	57°C	66°C					
115°F	111°F	120°F	135°F	151°F	*	*	*	*	*
43°C	41°C	44°C	51°C	58°C	66°C				
110°F	105°F	112°F	123°F	137°F	150°F	*	*	*	*
41°C	38°C	41°C	45°C	51°C	57°C	65°C			
105°F	100°F	105°F	113°F	123°F	135°F	149°F	*	*	*
38°C	35°C	37°C	40°C	43°C	49°C	56°C	62°C		
100°F	95°F	99°F	104°F	110°F	120°F	132°F	144°F	*	*
35°C	32°C	34°C	36°C	38°C	42°C	46°C	51°C	58°C	
95°F	90°F	93°F	96°F	101°F	107°F	114°F	124°F	136°F	*
32°C	29°C	31°C	32°C	34°C	36°C	38°C	41°C	45°C	50°C
90°F	85°F	87°F	90°F	93°F	96°F	100°F	106°F	113°F	122°F
29°C	27°C	28°C	29°C	30°C	31°C	32°C	34°C	36°C	39°C
85°F	80°F	82°F	84°F	86°F	88°F	90°F	93°F	97°F	102°F
27°C	24°C	25°C	26°C	26°C	27°C	28°C	29°C	30°C	31°C
80°F	75°F	77°F	78°F	79°F	81°F	82°F	85°F	86°F	88°F

*Temperature–relative humidity conditions rarely observed in the atmosphere.

TABLE III-7 General Heat Stress Index

Danger Category	Heat Index	Heat Syndrome
IV. Extreme Danger	Above 54°C (130°F)	Heat/sunstroke highly likely with continued exposure.
III. Danger	40–54°C (105–130°F)	Sunstroke, heat cramps, or heat exhaustion likely; heatstroke possible with prolonged exposure and/or physical activity.
II. Extreme Caution	32–40°C (90–105°F)	Sunstroke, heat cramps, or heat exhaustion possible with prolonged exposure and/or physical activity.
I. Caution	27–32°C (80–90°F)	Fatigue possible with prolonged exposure and/or physical activity.

Appendix IV
The Weather Station Model

Weather data are recorded at regular intervals for a great many locations on Earth, each location being called a *weather station*. These data are then plotted on weather maps according to a standard format and code. The format for a standard station model is shown in Figure IV-1, along with an explanation of the code. Figure IV-2 shows the same model but with the codes replaced by sample data, and Figures IV-3 and IV-4 list some of the codes and symbols used by meteorologists. Tables IV-1 through IV-3 give additional codes and symbols, and Figure IV-5 is a sample weather map.

The wind symbol (Table IV-3) gives two pieces of information. Wind direction is indicated by an arrow shaft entering the station circle from the direction in which the wind is blowing, as at the one-o'clock position in Figure IV-2, and wind speed is indicated by the number of "feathers" and half-feathers protruding from the shaft; each half-feather represents a 5-knot increase in speed (a knot is one nautical mile per hour, which is the same as 1.15 statute miles per hour or 1.85 kilometers per hour).

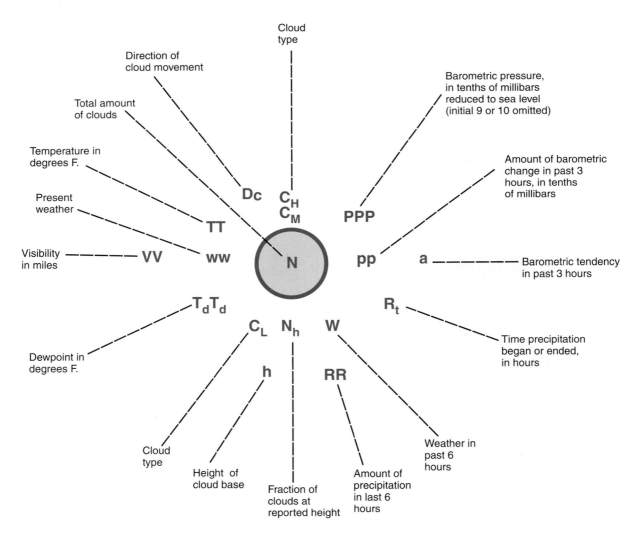

▲ **Figure IV-1** A standard weather station model. (No symbol for wind speed and direction is shown here because there is no one assigned place for this symbol; instead, its position on the model depends on wind direction.)

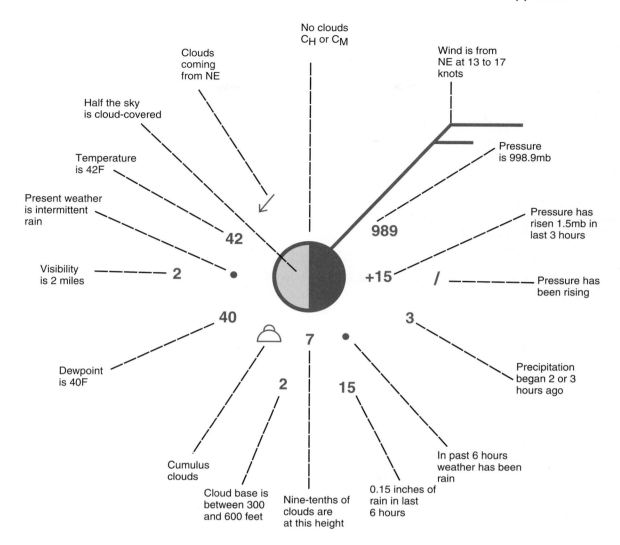

▲ **Figure IV-2**   A standard weather station model with the codes replaced by sample data.

TABLE IV-1 Standard Cloud Height Codes		
	Approximate Cloud Height	
h (height of cloud base)	*Meters*	*Feet*
0	0–49	0–149
1	50–99	150–299
2	100–199	300–599
3	200–299	600–999
4	300–599	1000–1999
5	600–999	2000–3499
6	1000–1499	3500–4999
7	1500–1999	5000–4699
8	2000–2499	6500–7999
9	>2500 or no clouds	>8000 or no clouds

TABLE IV-2 Standard Precipitation Codes	
R_t *Code*	*Time of Precipitation*
0	No precipitation
1	Less than 1 hour ago
2	1 to 2 hours ago
3	2 to 3 hours ago
4	3 to 4 hours ago
5	4 to 5 hours ago
6	5 to 6 hours ago
7	6 to 12 hours ago
8	More than 12 hours ago
9	Unknown

C_L Clouds of type C_L	C_M Clouds of type C_M	C_H Clouds of type C_H	W Past Weather	N_h* No clouds.	a Barometer characteristics
0 No Sc, St, Cu, or Cb clouds.	**0** No Ac, As or Ns clouds.	**0** No Ci, Cc, or $\overline{C}s$ clouds.	**0** Clear or few clouds.	**0** No clouds.	**0** Rising then falling. Now higher than 3 hours ago.
1 Cu with little vertical development and seemingly flattened.	**1** Thin As (entire cloud layer semitransparent).	**1** Filaments of Ci, scattered and not increasing.	**1** Partly cloudy (scattered) or variable sky.	**1** Less than one-tenth or one-tenth.	**1** Rising, then steady; or rising, then rising more slowly. Now higher than, as, 3 hours ago.
2 Cu of considerable development, generally towering, with or without other Cu or Sc; bases all at same level.	**2** Thick As, or Ns.	**2** Dense Ci in patches or twisted sheaves, usually not increasing.	**2** Cloudy (broken or overcast).	**2** Two- or three-tenths.	**2** Rising steadily, or unsteady. Now higher than, 3 hours ago.
3 Cb with tops lacking clear-cut outlines, but distinctly not cirriform or anvil-shaped; with or without Cu, Sc or St.	**3** Thin Ac; cloud elements not changing much and at a single level.	**3** Ci, often anvil-shaped, derived from or associated with Cb.	**3** Sandstorm, or dust-storm, or drifting or blowing snow.	**3** Four-tenths.	**3** Falling or steady, then rising; or rising, then rising more quickly. Now higher than, 3 hours ago.
4 So formed by spreading out of Cu; Cu often present also.	**4** Thin Ac in patches; cloud elements and/or occurring at more than one level.	**4** Ci, often hook-shaped, gradually spreading over the sky and usually thickening as a whole.	**4** Fog, or smoke, or thick dust haze.	**4** Five-tenths.	**4** Steady. Same as 3 hours ago.§
5 Sc not formed by spreading out of Cu.	**5** Thin Ac in bands or in a layer gradually spreading over sky and usually thickening as a whole.	**5** Ci and Cs, often in converging bands, or Cs alone; the continuous layer not reaching 45° altitude.	**5** Drizzle.	**5** Six-tenths.	**5** Falling, then rising. Same or lower than 3 hours ago.
6 St or Fs or both, but not Fs of bad weather.	**6** Ac formed by the spreading out of Cu.	**6** Ci and Cs, often in converging bands, or Cs alone; the continuous layer exceeding 45° altitude.	**6** Rain.	**6** Seven- or eight-tenths.	**6** Falling, then steady; or falling, then falling more slowly. Now lower than 3 hours ago.
7 Fs and/or Fc of bad weather (scud) usually under As and Ns.	**7** Double-layered Ac or a thick layer of Ac, not increasing; or As and Ac both present at same or different levels.	**7** Cs covering the entire sky.	**7** Snow, or rain and snow mixed, or ice pellets (sleet).	**7** Nine-tenths or overcast with openings.	**7** Falling steadily, or unsteady. Now lower than 3 hours ago.
8 Cu and Sc (not formed by spreading out of Cu) with bases at different levels.	**8** Ac in the form of Cu-shaped tufts or Ac with turrets.	**8** Cs not increasing and not covering entire sky; Ci and Cc may be present.	**8** Shower(s).	**8** Completely overcast.	**8** Steady or rising, then falling; or falling, then falling more quickly. Now lower than 3 hours ago.
9 Cb having a clearly fibrous (cirriform) top, often anvil-shaped, with or without Cu, Sc, St, or scud.	**9** Ac of a chaotic sky, usually at different levels; patches of dense Ci are usually present also.	**9** Cc alone or Cc with some Ci or Cs, but the Cc being the main cirriform cloud present.	**9** Thunderstorm, with or without precipitation.	**9** Sky obscured.	**9**

*Fraction representing how much of the total cloud cover is at the reported base height.

▲ **Figure IV-3**   Standard symbols used to indicate cloud conditions, past weather, and barometer characteristics. The numbers in the upper-left-hand corner of the cells are used in a standard model and the icons are used on weather maps.

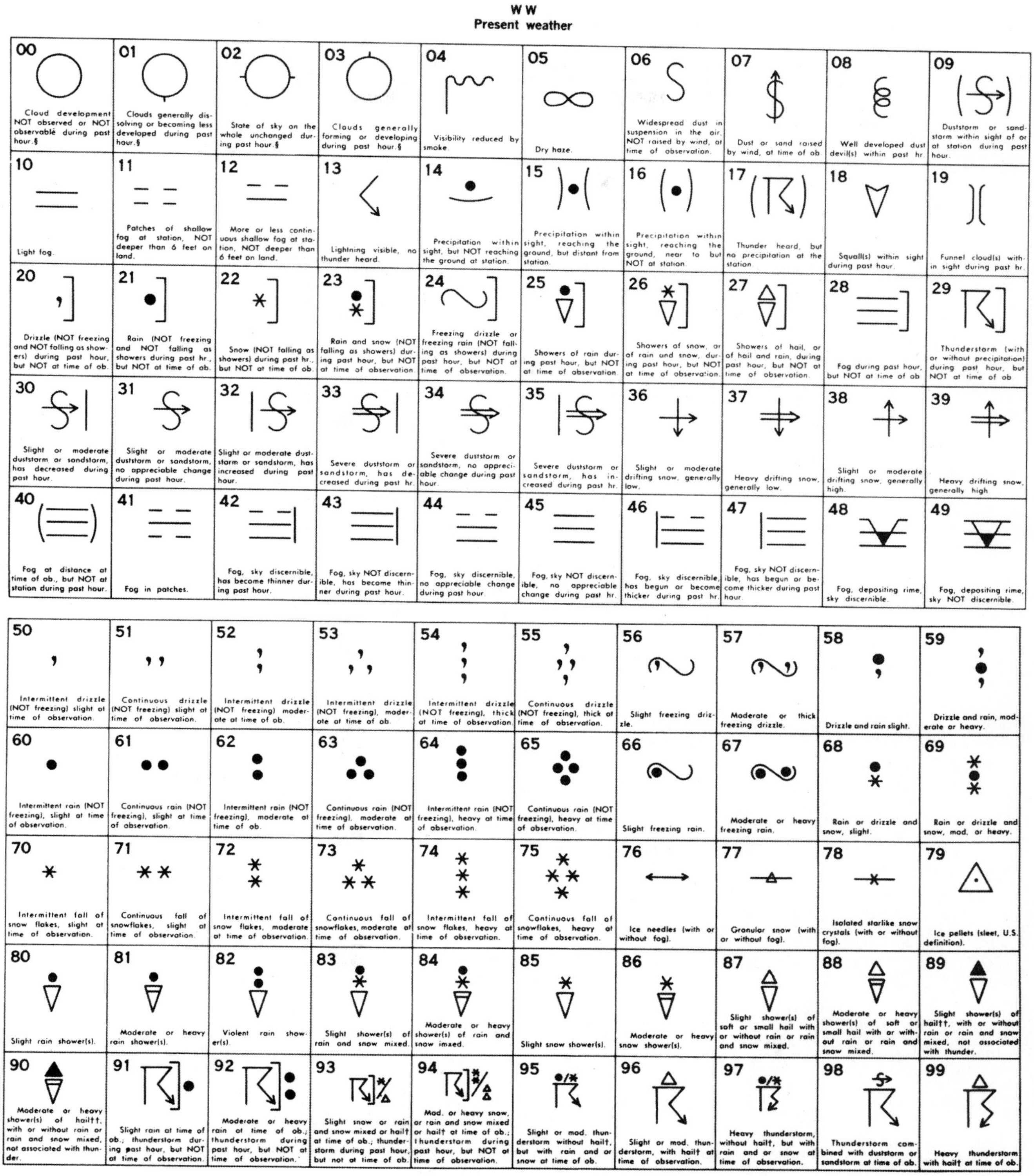

WW
Present weather

00 Cloud development NOT observed or NOT observable during past hour.§	**01** Clouds generally dissolving or becoming less developed during past hour.§	**02** State of sky on the whole unchanged during past hour.§
03 Clouds generally forming or developing during past hour.§	**04** Visibility reduced by smoke.	**05** Dry haze.
06 Widespread dust in suspension in the air, NOT raised by wind, at time of observation.	**07** Dust or sand raised by wind, at time of ob.	**08** Well developed dust devil(s) within past hr.
09 Duststorm or sandstorm within sight of or at station during past hour.	**10** Light fog.	**11** Patches of shallow fog at station, NOT deeper than 6 feet on land.
12 More or less continuous shallow fog at station, NOT deeper than 6 feet on land.	**13** Lightning visible, no thunder heard.	**14** Precipitation within sight, but NOT reaching the ground at station.
15 Precipitation within sight, reaching the ground, but distant from station.	**16** Precipitation within sight, reaching the ground, near to but NOT at station.	**17** Thunder heard, but no precipitation at the station.
18 Squall(s) within sight during past hour.	**19** Funnel cloud(s) within sight during past hr.	**20** Drizzle (NOT freezing and NOT falling as showers) during past hour, but NOT at time of ob.
21 Rain (NOT freezing and NOT falling as showers during past hr., but NOT at time of ob.	**22** Snow (NOT falling as showers) during past hr., but NOT at time of ob.	**23** Rain and snow (NOT falling as showers) during past hour, but NOT at time of observation.
24 Freezing drizzle or freezing rain (NOT falling as showers) during past hour, but NOT at time of observation.	**25** Showers of rain during past hour, but NOT at time of observation.	**26** Showers of snow, or of rain and snow, during past hour, but NOT at time of observation.
27 Showers of hail, or of hail and rain, during past hour, but NOT at time of observation.	**28** Fog during past hour, but NOT at time of ob	**29** Thunderstorm (with or without precipitation) during past hour, but NOT at time of ob
30 Slight or moderate duststorm or sandstorm, has decreased during past hour.	**31** Slight or moderate duststorm or sandstorm, no appreciable change during past hour.	**32** Slight or moderate duststorm or sandstorm, has increased during past hour.
33 Severe duststorm or sandstorm, has decreased during past hr.	**34** Severe duststorm or sandstorm, no appreciable change during past hour.	**35** Severe duststorm or sandstorm, has increased during past hr.
36 Slight or moderate drifting snow, generally low.	**37** Heavy drifting snow, generally low.	**38** Slight or moderate drifting snow, generally high.
39 Heavy drifting snow, generally high.	**40** Fog at distance at time of ob., but NOT at station during past hour.	**41** Fog in patches.
42 Fog, sky discernible, has become thinner during past hour.	**43** Fog, sky NOT discernible, has become thinner during past hour.	**44** Fog, sky discernible, no appreciable change during past hour.
45 Fog, sky NOT discernible, no appreciable change during past hr.	**46** Fog, sky discernible, has begun or become thicker during past hr.	**47** Fog, sky NOT discernible, has begun or become thicker during past hour.
48 Fog, depositing rime, sky discernible.	**49** Fog, depositing rime, sky NOT discernible.	
50 Intermittent drizzle (NOT freezing) slight at time of observation.	**51** Continuous drizzle (NOT freezing) slight at time of observation.	**52** Intermittent drizzle (NOT freezing) moderate at time of ob.
53 Continuous drizzle (NOT freezing), moderate at time of ob.	**54** Intermittent drizzle (NOT freezing), thick at time of observation.	**55** Continuous drizzle (NOT freezing), thick at time of observation.
56 Slight freezing drizzle.	**57** Moderate or thick freezing drizzle.	**58** Drizzle and rain slight.
59 Drizzle and rain, moderate or heavy.	**60** Intermittent rain (NOT freezing), slight at time of observation.	**61** Continuous rain (NOT freezing), slight at time of observation.
62 Intermittent rain (NOT freezing), moderate at time of ob.	**63** Continuous rain (NOT freezing), moderate at time of observation.	**64** Intermittent rain (NOT freezing), heavy at time of observation.
65 Continuous rain (NOT freezing), heavy at time of observation.	**66** Slight freezing rain.	**67** Moderate or heavy freezing rain.
68 Rain or drizzle and snow, slight.	**69** Rain or drizzle and snow, mod. or heavy.	**70** Intermittent fall of snow flakes, slight at time of observation.
71 Continuous fall of snowflakes, slight at time of observation.	**72** Intermittent fall of snow flakes, moderate at time of observation.	**73** Continuous fall of snowflakes, moderate at time of observation.
74 Intermittent fall of snow flakes, heavy at time of observation.	**75** Continuous fall of snowflakes, heavy at time of observation.	**76** Ice needles (with or without fog).
77 Granular snow (with or without fog).	**78** Isolated starlike snow crystals (with or without fog).	**79** Ice pellets (sleet, U.S. definition).
80 Slight rain shower(s).	**81** Moderate or heavy rain shower(s).	**82** Violent rain shower(s).
83 Slight shower(s) of rain and snow mixed.	**84** Moderate or heavy shower(s) of rain and snow mixed.	**85** Slight snow shower(s).
86 Moderate or heavy snow shower(s).	**87** Slight shower(s) of soft or small hail with or without rain or rain and snow mixed.	**88** Moderate or heavy shower(s) of soft or small hail with or without rain or rain and snow mixed.
89 Slight shower(s) of hail††, with or without rain or snow mixed, not associated with thunder.	**90** Moderate or heavy shower(s) of hail††, with or without rain or rain and snow mixed, not associated with thunder.	**91** Slight rain at time of ob.; thunderstorm during past hour, but NOT at time of observation.
92 Moderate or heavy rain at time of ob.; thunderstorm during past hour, but NOT at time of observation.	**93** Slight snow or rain and snow mixed or hail at time of ob.; thunderstorm during past hour, but not at time of ob.	**94** Mod. or heavy snow, or rain and snow mixed or hail at time of ob.; thunderstorm during past hour, but not at time of ob.
95 Slight or mod. thunderstorm without hail, but with rain and or snow at time of observation.	**96** Slight or mod. thunderstorm, with hail at time of observation.	**97** Heavy thunderstorm, without hail, but with rain and or snow at time of observation.
98 Thunderstorm combined with duststorm or sandstorm at time of ob.	**99** Heavy thunderstorm with hail at time of ob.	

§ The symbol is not plotted for "ww" when "00" is reported. When "01, 02, or 03" is reported for "ww," the symbol is plotted on the station circle. Symbols are not plotted for "a" when "3 or 8" is reported.

† Refers to "hail" only.

††Refers to "soft hail," "small hail," and "hail."

▲ **Figure IV-4** Standard weather map symbols used to indicate present weather.

TABLE IV-3 Wind Speed/Direction Symbols	
Symbol	Wind Speed(knots)
◎	Calm
(barb symbol)	1–2
(barb symbol)	3–7
(barb symbol)	8–12
(barb symbol)	13–17
(barb symbol)	18–22
(barb symbol)	23–27
(barb symbol)	28–32
(barb symbol)	33–37
(barb symbol)	38–42
(barb symbol)	43–47
(barb symbol)	48–52
(barb symbol)	53–57
(barb symbol)	58–62
(barb symbol)	63–67
(barb symbol)	68–72
(barb symbol)	73–77

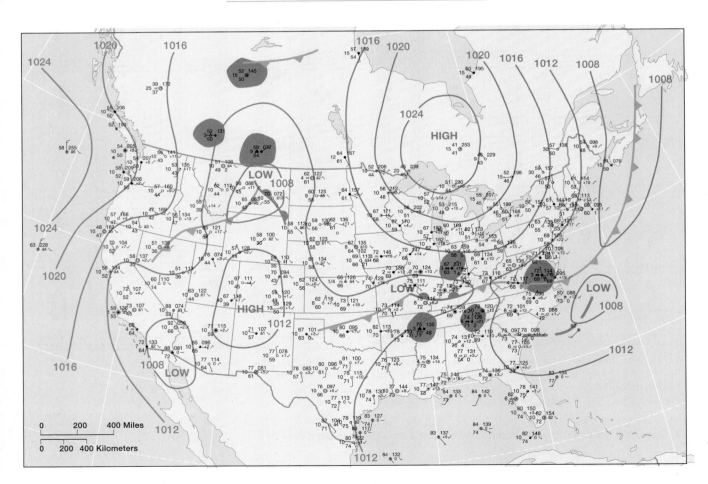

▲ Figure IV-5   A sample weather map. (From Daily Weather Maps, National Weather Service/NOAA.)

Appendix V
Köppen Climate Classification

Table V-1 provides the definitions of the code letters used in the modified Köppen climate classification system. The exact classification of a climate using the Köppen system may require additional calculations, and so the definitions of each letter given here may be approximate. For more detailed directions for classifying climates with the Köppen system, see the *Laboratory Manual* for *Physical Geography: A Landscape Appreciation*, 9th edition, by Darrel Hess.

TABLE V-1 Code Letters of the Modified Köppen Classification System

Letters				
1st	2nd	3rd	*Description*	*Definitions*
A			Low-latitude humid climates	Average temperature of each month above 18°C (64°F)
	f		No dry season [German: *feucht* ("moist")]	Average rainfall of each month at least 6 cm (2.4 in.)
	m		Monsoon; short dry season compensated by heavy rains in other months	1 to 3 months with average rainfall less than 6 cm (2.4 in.)
	w		Winter dry season (low-Sun season)	3 to 6 months with average rainfall less than 6 cm (2.4 in.)
B			Dry climates	Evaporation exceeds precipitation
	W		Desert (German: *wüste* ["desert"])	Average annual precipitation generally less than 38 cm (15 in.) in low latitudes; 25 cm (10 in.) in midlatitudes
	S		Steppe (semiarid)	Average annual precipitation generally between 38 cm (15 in.) and 76 cm (30 in.) in low latitudes; between about 25 cm (10 in.) and 64 cm (25 in.) in midlatitudes; without pronounced seasonal concentration
		h	Low-latitude (subtropical) dry climate (German: *heiss* ["hot"])	Average annual temperature more than 18°C (64°F)
		k	Midlatitude dry climate (German: *kalt* ["cold"])	Average annual temperature less than 18°C (64°F)
C			Mild midlatitude climates	Average temperature of coldest month between 18°C (64°F) and −3°C (27°F); average temperature of warmest month above 10°C (50°F)
	s		Summer dry season	Wettest winter month has at least 3× precipitation of driest summer month

(continued)

TABLE V-1 (continued)

1st	2nd	3rd	Description	Definitions
	w		Winter dry season	Wettest summer month has at least 10× precipitation of driest winter month
	f		No dry season (German: *feucht* ["moist"])	Does not fit either s or w above
		a	Hot summers	Average temperature of warmest month more than 22°C (72°F)
		b	Warm summers	Average temperature of warmest month below 22°C (72°F); at least 4 months with average temperature above 10°C (50°F)
		c	Cool summers	Average temperature of warmest month below 22°C (72°F); less than 4 months with average temperature above 10°C (50°F); coldest month above −38°C (−36°F)
D			Humid midlatitude climates with severe winters	Warmest month above 10°C (50°F); coldest month below −3°C (27°F)
			(2nd and 3rd letters same as in C climates)	
		d	Very cold winters	Average temperature of coldest month less than −38°C (−36°F)
E			Polar climates; no true summer	No month with average temperature more than 10°C (50°F)
	T		Tundra climates	At least one month with average temperature more than 0°C (32°F) but less than 10°C (50°F)
	F		Ice cap climates ("frost")	No month with average temperature more than 0°C (32°F)
H			Highland Climates	Significant climatic changes within short horizontal distances due to altitudinal variations

Appendix VI
Biological Taxonomy

Taxonomy is the science of classification. As a term it was originally applied to the classification of plants and animals, although its meaning has been broadened to encompass any sort of systematic classification. Our concern here is only with biological taxonomy. People have attempted to devise meaningful classifications of plants and animals for thousands of years. One of the most useful of the early classifications was designed by Aristotle 2300 years ago, and this system was in general use for nearly 20 centuries. In the late 1700s, the Aristotelian classification was finally replaced by a much more comprehensive and systematic one developed by the Swedish naturalist Carolus Linnaeus. Linnaeus made use of ideas from other biologists, but the system is largely his own work.

The *Linnaean system of classification* is generic, hierarchical, comprehensive, and binomial. *Generic* means that it is based on observable characteristics of the organisms it classifies, primarily their anatomy, structures, and details of reproduction. *Hierarchical* means that the organisms are grouped on the basis of similar characteristics, with each lower level of grouping having a larger number of similar characteristics and therefore containing fewer individuals in the group. *Comprehensive* means that all plants and animals, existing and extinct, can be encompassed within the system. *Binomial* means that every kind of plant and animal is identified by two names.

The binomial naming of organisms is highly systematized. Each type of living thing has a name with two parts. The first part, in which the first letter is capitalized, designates the *genus*, or group; the second part, which is not capitalized, indicates the *species*, or specific kind of organism. The combination of genus and species is referred to as the scientific name; it is always in Latin, although many of the words have Greek derivations.

Each type of organism, then, has a scientific name that distinguishes it from all other organisms. Although the popular name may be variable, or even indefinite, the scientific name is unvarying. Thus, in different parts of the Western Hemisphere, the large native cat may be called a mountain lion, cougar, puma, panther, painter, or leon, but its scientific name is always *Felis concolor*.

The intellectual beauty of the Linnaean system is twofold: (1) every organism that has ever existed can be fitted into the scheme in a logical and orderly manner for the system is capable of indefinite expansion, and (2) the various hierarchical levels in the system provide a conceptual framework for understanding the relationships among different organisms or groups of organisms. This is not to say the system is perfect. Linnaeus believed that species were unchanging entities, and his original system had no provision for variations. The concept of subspecies was a major modification of the system that was introduced subsequently to accommodate observed conditions of evolution.

Nor is the system even completely objective. Whereas its concept and general organization are accepted by scientists throughout the world, details of the classification depend on judgments and opinions made by biologists. These judgments and opinions are based on careful measurements and observations of plant and animal specimens, but there is often room for differing interpretations of the relevant data. Consequently, some details of biological taxonomy are disputed and even controversial.

Despite confusion about some of the details, the generally accepted Linnaean system provides a magnificent framework for biological classification. The seven main levels of the system, in order from largest to smallest, are (1) kingdom, (2) phylum, (3) class, (4) order, (5) family, (6) genus, and (7) species.

Kingdom is the broadest category and contains the largest number of organisms. Until recently, the system recognized only two kingdoms: one encompassing all plants and the other including all animals. Increasingly, however, taxonomists encountered difficulty in accommodating the many varieties of one-celled and other simple microscopic organisms into such a two-kingdom system. It is now widely, but by no means universally, accepted that six kingdoms exist at the highest level of taxonomic distinction.[1]

1. *Archaea* are simple organisms that live in harsh environments such as underwater hydrothermal vents, hot sulfur springs, and hypersaline water. Some may also live in the open ocean and can be either autotrophs or heterotrophs.
2. *Eubacteria* are true, one-celled bacteria.
3. *Protista* consist of other one-celled organisms and some simple multicelled algae, most of which were formerly classed as plants.

---

[1]Until a few years ago only five kingdoms were recognized: *Monera, Protista, Fungi, Plantae,* and *Animalia.* The new six-kingdom classification is not recognized by all biologists.

4. *Fungi* were also previously classified as plants, but it is now recognized that they differ in origin, direction of evolution, and primary nutrition from plants and therefore deserve separation.

5. *Plantae* include the multicelled green plants and higher algae.

6. *Animalia* consist of the multicelled animals.

Phylum is the second major level of the system. Of the two or three dozen phyla within the animal kingdom, one, *Chordata*, includes all animals with backbones, which means almost every animal more than a few centimeters in length (Figure VI-1). In the plant kingdom, the term *division* is often used in place of phylum. Most large plants belong to the division *Tracheophyta*, or vascular plants, which have efficient internal systems for transporting water and sugars and a complex differentiation of organs into leaves, stem, and roots.

The third principal level is *class*. Among the several dozen animal classes, the most important are *Mammalia* (mammals), *Aves* (birds), *Reptilia* (reptiles), *Amphibia* (amphibians), and two classes that encompass fishes.

There are somewhat fewer classes of plants, of which the most notable is *Angiospermae*, the flowering plants.

The fourth level of the classification is called *order*, and the three lower levels are *family, genus,* and *species*. As in all levels of the hierarchy, each succeeding lower level contains organisms that are increasingly alike. Species is the basic unit of the classification. In theory, only members of the same species are capable of breeding with one another. In practice, however, interbreeding is possible among just a few species (always within the same genus), although the offspring of such interspecific breeding are nearly always infertile (i.e., totally incapable of reproducing). In some cases, species are further subdivided into subspecies, also called varieties or races (Figure VI-2).

The relative diversity of living and extinct species is worthy of note. About 1,500,000 species of living organisms have been identified and described. From 3 to 10 million additional species, mostly microscopic in size, may not yet be identified. An estimated 500 million species have become extinct in Earth's history. Thus, more than 95 percent of all evolutionary lines have already completely disappeared.

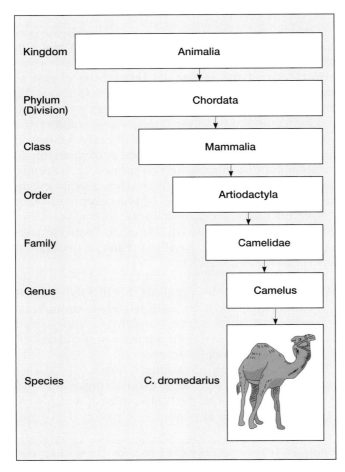

Kingdom	Animalia
Phylum (Division)	Chordata
Class	Mammalia
Order	Artiodactyla
Family	Camelidae
Genus	Camelus
Species	C. dromedarius

▲ **Figure VI-1**   The taxonomic classification of an animal, as illustrated by the Arabian camel, or dromedary.

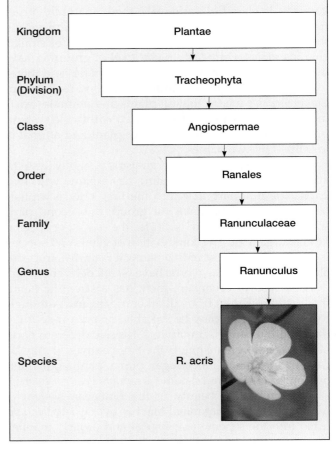

Kingdom	Plantae
Phylum (Division)	Tracheophyta
Class	Angiospermae
Order	Ranales
Family	Ranunculaceae
Genus	Ranunculus
Species	R. acris

▲ **Figure VI-2**   The taxonomic classification of a plant, as illustrated by the buttercup.

Appendix VII
The Soil Taxonomy

The Soil Taxonomy, described in Chapter 12, utilizes a nomenclature "invented" for the purpose. This nomenclature consists of "synthetic" names, which means that syllables from existing words are rearranged and combined to produce new words for the names of the various soil types. The beauty of the system is that each newly coined name is highly descriptive of the soil it represents.

The awkwardness of the nomenclature is threefold:

1. Most of the terms are new and have never before appeared in print or in conversation. Thus they look strange, and the words do not easily roll off the tongue. It is almost a new language.
2. Many of the words are difficult to write, and great care must be taken in the spelling of seemingly bizarre combinations of letters.
3. Many of the syllables sound so much alike that differences in pronunciation are often slight, although enunciating these slight differences is essential if the new nomenclature is to serve its purpose.

Nevertheless, the Soil Taxonomy has a sound theoretical base, and once the user is familiar with the vocabulary, every syllable of every word gives important information about a soil. Almost all the syllables are derived from Greek or Latin roots, in contrast to the English and Russian terms used in previous systems. In some cases, the appropriateness of the classical derivatives may be open to question, but the uniformity and logic of the terminology extend throughout the system.

The Hierarchy

The top level in the Soil Taxonomy hierarchy is *soil order*. The names of orders are made up of three or four syllables, the last of which is always *sol* (from the Latin word *solum*, "soil"). The next-to-last syllable consists of a single linking vowel, either *i* or *o*. The syllable (or two) that begins the word contains the formative element of the name and gives information regarding some distinctive characteristic of the order. Thus the names of the 12 soil orders contain 12 syllables that (1) serve as formative elements for the order names and (2) appear in all names in the next three levels of the hierarchy.

Suborder is the second level in the hierarchy. All suborder names contain two syllables: The first indicates some distinctive characteristic of the suborder; the second identifies the order to which the suborder belongs. For example, *aqu* is derived from the Latin word for "water," and so *Aquent* is the suborder of wet soils of the order Entisols. The names of the four dozen suborders are constructed from the two dozen root elements shown in Table VII-1.

The third level of the hierarchy contains *great groups*, the names of which are constructed by grafting one or more syllables to the beginning of a suborder name. Hence, a *Cryaquent* is a cold soil that is a member of the Aquent suborder of the Entisol order (*cry* comes from the Greek word for "coldness"). The formative prefixes for the great group names are derived from about 50 root words, samples of which are presented in Table VII-2.

The next level is called *subgroup*, and there are more than 1000 subgroups recognized in the United States. Each subgroup name consists of two words: the first derived from a formative element higher up in the hierarchy (with a few exceptions), the second the same as that of the relevant great group. Thus, a *Sphagnic Cryaquent* is of the order Entisol, the suborder Aquent, the great group *Cryaquent*, and it contains sphagnum moss (derived from the Greek word *sphagnos*, "bog").

The *family* is the penultimate level in the hierarchy. It is not given a proper name but is simply described by one or more lowercase adjectives, as "a skeletal, mixed, acidic family."

Finally, the lowest level of the hierarchy is the *series*, named for geographic location. Table VII-3 gives a typical naming sequence.

Summary of Soil Suborders
Alfisols

Alfisols have five suborders. *Aqualfs* have characteristics associated with wetness. *Boralfs* are associated with cold boreal forests. *Udalfs* are brownish or reddish soils of moist midlatitude regions. *Ustalfs* are similar to Udalfs in color but subtropical in location and usually have a hard surface layer in the dry season. *Xeralfs* are found in mediterranean climates and are characterized by a thick, hard surface horizon in the dry season.

TABLE VII-1 Name Derivations of Soil Suborders

Root	Derivation	Connotation	Example of Suborder Name
alb	Latin *albus*, "white"	Presence of bleached eluvial horizon	Alboll
and	Japanese *ando*, a volcanic soil	Derived from pyroclastic material	Andept
aqu	Latin *aqua*, "water"	Associated with wetness	Aquent
ar	Latin *arare*, "to plow"	Horizons are mixed	Arent
arg	Latin *argilla*, "white clay"	Presence of a horizon containing illuvial clay	Argid
bor	Greek *boreas*, "northern"	Associated with cool conditions	Boroll
ferr	Latin *ferrum*, "iron"	Presence of iron	Ferrod
fibr	Latin *fibra*, "fiber"	Presence of undecomposed organic matter	Fibrist
fluv	Latin *fluvius*, "river"	Associated with floodplains	Fluvent
fol	Latin *folia*, "leaf"	Mass of leaves	Folist
hem	Greek *hemi*, "half"	Intermediate stage of decomposition	Hemist
hum	Latin *humus*, "earth"	Presence of organic matter	Humult
ochr	Greek *ochros*, "pale"	Presence of a light-colored surface horizon	Ochrept
orth	Greek *orthos*, "true"	Most common or typical group	Orthent
plag	German *plaggen*, "sod"	Presence of a human-induced surface horizon	Plaggept
psamm	Greek *psammos*, "sand"	Sandy texture	Psamment
rend	Polish *rendzino*, a type of soil	Significant calcareous content	Rendoll
sapr	Greek *sapros*, "rotten"	Most decomposed stage	Saprist
torr	Latin *torridus*, "hot and dry"	Usually dry	Torrox
trop	Greek *tropikos*, "of the solstice"	Continuously warm	Tropert
ud	Latin *udud*, "humid"	Of humid climates	Udoll
umbr	Latin *umbro*, "shade"	Presence of a dark surface horizon	Umbrept
ust	Latin *ustus*, "burnt"	Of dry climates	Ustert
xer	Greek *xeros*, "dry"	Annual dry season	Xeralf

TABLE VII-2 Name Derivations for Great Groups

Root	Derivation	Connotation	Example of Great Group Name
calc	Latin *calcis*, "lime"	Presence of calcic horizon	Calciorthid
ferr	Latin *ferrum*, "iron"	Presence of iron	Ferrudalf
natr	Latin *natrium*, "sodium"	Presence of a natric horizon	Natraboll
pale	Greek *paleos*, "old"	An old development	Paleargid
plinth	Greek *plinthos*, "brick"	Presence of plinthite	Plenthoxeralf
quartz	The German name	High quartz content	Quartzipsamment
verm	Latin *vermes*, "worm"	Notable presence of worms	Vermudoll

TABLE VII-3	A Typical Soil Taxonomy Naming Sequence
Order	Entisol
Suborder	Aquent
Great group	Cryaquent
Subgroup	Sphagnic Cryaquent
Family	Skeletal, mixed, acidic, Sphagnic Cryaquent
Series	Aberdeen

Andisols

Seven suborders are recognized in the Andisols, five of which are distinguished by moisture content. *Aquands* have abundant moisture, often with poor drainage. *Torrands* are associated with a hot, dry regime. *Udands* are found in humid climates, *Ustands* in dry climates with hot summers. *Xerands* have a pronounced annual dry season. In addition, *Cryands* are found in cold climates, and *Vitrands* are distinguished by the presence of glass.

Aridisols

Two suborders are generally recognized on the basis of degree of weathering. *Argids* have a distinctive subsurface horizon with clay accumulation, whereas *Orthids* do not.

Entisols

There are five suborders of Entisols. *Aquents* occupy wet environments where the soil is more or less continuously saturated with water; they may be found in any temperature regime. *Arents* lack horizons because of human interference, particularly that involving large agricultural or engineering machinery. *Fluvents* form on recent water-deposited sediments that have satisfactory drainage. *Orthents* develop on recent erosional surfaces. *Psamments* occur in sandy situations, where the sand is either shifting or stabilized by vegetation.

Gelisols

The three suborders of Gelisols—*Histels*, *Orthels*, and *Turbels*—are distinguished largely on the basis of quantity and distribution of organic material.

Histosols

The four suborders of Histosols—*Fibrists*, *Folists*, *Hemists*, and *Saprists*—are differentiated on the basis of degree of plant-material decomposition.

Inceptisols

The six suborders of Inceptisols—*Andepts*, *Aquepts*, *Ochrepts*, *Plaggepts*, *Tropepts*, and *Umbrepts*—have relatively complicated distinguishing characteristics.

Mollisols

The seven suborders of Mollisols—*Albolls*, *Aquolls*, *Borolls*, *Rendolls*, *Udolls*, *Ustolls*, and *Xerolls*—are distinguished largely, but not entirely, on the basis of relative wetness/dryness.

Oxisols

The five suborders of Oxisols—*Aquox*, *Humox*, *Orthox*, *Torrox*, and *Ustox*—are distinguished from one another primarily by what effect varying amounts and seasonality of rainfall have on the profile.

Spodosols

Of the four suborders of Spodosols, most widespread are the *Orthods*, which represent the typical Spodosols. *Aquods*, *Ferrods*, and *Humods* are differentiated on the basis of the amount of iron in the spodic horizon.

Ultisols

Five suborders of Ultisols—*Aquults*, *Humults*, *Udults*, *Ustults*, and *Xerults*—are recognized. The distinction among them is largely on the basis of temperature and moisture conditions and on how these parameters influence the epipedon.

Vertisols

The four principal suborders of Vertisols are distinguished largely on the frequency of "cracking," which is a function of climate. *Torrerts* are found in arid regions, and the cracks in these soils remain open most of the time. *Uderts* are found in humid areas, and in these soils cracking is irregular. *Usterts* are associated with monsoon climates and have a relatively complicated cracking pattern. *Xererts* occur in mediterranean climates and have cracks that open and close regularly once each year.

Glossary

ablation Wastage of glacial ice through melting and sublimation.

ablation zone The lower portion of a glacier where there is a net annual loss of ice due to melting and sublimation.

abrasion (fluvial abrasion) The chipping and grinding effect of rock fragments as they are swirled or bounced or rolled downstream by moving water.

absolute humidity A direct measure of the water vapor content of air, expressed as the mass of water vapor in a given volume of air, usually as grams of water per cubic meter of air.

absorption The ability of an object to assimilate energy from electromagnetic waves that strike it.

accumulation (glacial ice accumulation) Addition of ice into a glacier by incorporation of snow.

accumulation zone The upper portion of a glacier where there is a greater annual accumulation of ice than there is wastage.

acid rain Precipitation with a pH less than 5.6. It may involve dry deposition without moisture.

adiabatic cooling Cooling by expansion, such as in rising air.

adiabatic warming Warming by compression, such as in descending air.

adret slope A slope oriented so that the Sun's rays arrive at a relatively direct angle. Such a slope is relatively hot and dry, and its vegetation will not only be sparser and smaller but is also likely to have a different species composition from adjacent slopes with different exposures.

advection Horizontal movement of air across the Earth's surface.

advectional inversion An inverted temperature gradient caused by a horizontal inflow of colder air into an area; usually colder air "draining" downslope into a valley or by cool maritime air blowing into a coastal locale.

advection fog The condensation that results when warm, moist air moves horizontally over a cold surface.

aeolian processes Processes related to wind action that are most pronounced, widespread, and effective in dry lands.

aerial photograph A photograph taken from an elevated "platform," such as a balloon, airplane, rocket, or satellite.

aggradation The process in which a stream bed is raised as a result of the deposition of sediment.

A horizon Upper soil layer in which humus and other organic materials are mixed with mineral particles.

air The colloquial term for the mixture of gases and impurities that make up the atmosphere.

air drainage The sliding of cold air downslope to collect in the lowest spots, usually at night.

air mass An extensive body of air that has relatively uniform properties in the horizontal dimension and moves as an entity.

albedo The reflectivity of a surface. The fraction of total solar radiation that is reflected back, unchanged, into space.

Alfisol A widely distributed soil order distinguished by a subsurface clay horizon and a medium-to-generous supply of plant nutrients and water.

alluvial fan A fan-shaped deposition feature laid down by a stream issuing from a mountain canyon.

alluvium Any stream-deposited sedimentary material.

alpine glacier Individual glacier that develops near a mountain crest line and normally moves down-valley for some distance.

altocumulus Middle-level clouds, between about 2 and 6 kilometers (6500 and 20,000 feet), which are puffy in form and are composed of liquid water.

altostratus Middle-level clouds, between 2 and 6 kilometers (6500 and 20,000 feet), which are layered and are composed of liquid water.

amphibians Semiaquatic vertebrate animals. In the larval stage they are fully aquatic and breathe through gills; as adults they are air-breathers by means of lungs and through glandular skin.

andesite A volcanic rock intermediate in silica content between basalt and rhyolite; composed largely of a distinctive mineral association of plagioclase feldspar.

Andisol Soil order derived from volcanic ash.

anemometer An instrument that measures wind speed.

angiosperms Plants that have seeds encased in some sort of protective body, such as a fruit, a nut, or a seedpod.

angle of incidence The angle at which the Sun's rays strike Earth's surface.

angle of repose Steepest angle that can be assumed by loose fragments on a slope without downslope movement.

animalia The kingdom of organisms that consists of all multicellular animals.

annuals (annual plant) Plants that perish during times of climatic stress but leave behind a reservoir of seeds to germinate during the next favorable period.

annular drainage pattern A network in which the major streams are arranged in a ringlike, concentric pattern in response to a structural dome or basin.

Antarctic Circle The parallel of 66.5° south latitude.

antecedent stream Stream that predates the existence of the hill or mountain through which it flows.

anthropogenic Human-induced.

anticline A simple symmetrical upfold in the rock structure.

anticyclone A high-pressure center.

antitrade winds Tropical upper-air westerly winds that blow toward the northeast in the Northern Hemisphere and toward the southeast in the Southern Hemisphere.

aphelion The point in Earth's elliptical orbit at which the Earth is farthest from the Sun (about 152,171,500 kilometers or 94,555,000 miles).

apogee The point at which the Moon is farthest from Earth in its elliptical orbit.

aquiclude An impermeable rock layer that is so dense as to exclude water.

aquifer A permeable subsurface rock layer that can store, transmit, and supply water.

arboreal Tree-dwelling.

Arctic Circle The parallel of 66.5° north latitude.

arête A narrow, jagged, serrated spine of rock; remainder of a ridge crest after several glacial cirques have been cut back into an interfluve from opposite sides of a divide.

arid Dry; receiving limited precipitation (generally less than 25 centimeters [10 inches] annually).

Aridisol A soil order occupying dry environments that do not have enough water to remove soluble minerals from the soil; typified by a thin profile that is sandy and lacking in organic matter.

arroyo The term used in the United States for the normally dry bed of an intermittent stream.

artesian well The free flow that results when a well is drilled from the surface down into the aquifer and the confining pressure is sufficient to force the water to the surface without artificial pumping.

ascent Large-scale upward movement of air.

association (plant) An assemblage of plants living in close inter-dependence, with similar habitat requirements, and with one or more dominant species that may be used to denote it.

asthenosphere Plastic layer of the upper mantle that underlies the lithosphere. Its rock is very hot and therefore weak and easily deformed.

atmosphere The gaseous envelope surrounding Earth.

atmospheric pressure The force exerted by the atmosphere on a surface.

atoll Coral reef in the general shape of a ring or partial ring that encloses a lagoon.

autumnal equinox Equinox that occurs about September 23 in the Northern Hemisphere and March 21 in the Southern Hemisphere.

average annual temperature range Difference in temperature be-tween the average temperature of the hottest and coldest months for a location.

average lapse rate The average rate of temperature decrease with height in the troposphere—about 6.5°C per 1000 meters (3.6°F per 1000 feet).

axis (Earth's axis) The diameter line around which Earth rotates; con-nects the points of maximum flattening on Earth's surface.

azimuthal projection A family of maps derived by the perspective extension of the geographic grid from a globe to a plane that is tan-gent to the globe at some point. Also called plane projections.

backshore The upper part of the shore, beyond the reach of ordinary waves.

backswamp Area of low, swampy ground on a floodplain between the natural levee and the bluffs.

backwash Water moving seaward after the momentum of the wave swash is overcome by gravity and friction.

badlands Intricately rilled and barren terrain of arid and semiarid regions, characterized by a multiplicity of short, steep slopes.

baguio The term used for a tropical cyclone affecting the Philippines.

bajada (piedmont alluvial plain) A continual alluvial surface that ex-tends across the piedmont zone, slanting from the range toward the basin, in which it is difficult to distinguish between individual fans.

bar Ridge of sand or gravel deposited offshore or in a river.

barchan dune A crescent-shaped sand dune with cusps of the cres-cent pointing downwind.

barometer Instrument used to measure atmospheric pressure.

barrier island Narrow offshore island composed of sediment; gener-ally oriented parallel to shore.

barrier reef A prominent ridge of coral that roughly parallels the coastline but lies offshore, with a shallow lagoon between the reefs and the coast.

basal slip The term used to describe the sliding of the entire mass at the bottom of a glacier over its bed on a lubricating film of water.

basalt Fine-grained, dark volcanic rock; low silica content.

base element A chemical element that is an important plant nutrient, such as calcium and potassium.

base level An imaginary surface extending underneath the conti-nents from sea level at the coasts and indicating the lowest level to which land can be eroded.

batholith The largest and most amorphous of igneous intrusions.

baymouth bar A spit that has become extended across the mouth of a bay to connect with a headland on the other side, transforming the bay into a lagoon.

beach An exposed deposit of loose sediment, normally composed of sand and/or gravel, and occupying the coastal transition zone between land and water.

beach drifting See **longshore drift**.

bedload Sand, gravel, and larger rock fragments moving in a stream by saltation and traction.

bedrock Residual rock that has not experienced erosion.

benthos Animals and plants that live at the ocean bottom.

berm The relatively flat part of a backshore beach, composed of wave-deposited material.

B horizon Mineral soil horizon located beneath the A horizon.

binomial classification scheme A taxonomic classification scheme that consists of a generic and a specific name.

Biogeography The study of the distribution patterns of plants and animals, and how these patterns change over time.

biological weathering Rock weathering processes involving the action of plants or animals.

biomass The total mass (or weight) of all living organisms in an ecosystem or per unit area.

biome A large, recognizable assemblage of plants and animals in functional interaction with its environment.

biosphere The living organisms of Earth.

biota The total complex of plant and animal life.

bird's-foot delta A delta that has long, projecting distributary chan-nels branching outward like the toes or claws of a bird.

blackbody A body that emits the maximum amount of radiation possible, at every wavelength, for its temperature.

blowout (deflation hollow) A shallow depression from which an abundance of fine material has been deflated.

bluff A relatively steep slope at the outer edge of a floodplain.

boreal Northern, especially referring to the expanses of northern coniferous forest.

boreal forest (taiga) An extensive needleleaf forest in the subarctic regions of North America and Eurasia.

bornhardt A rounded or domal inselberg composed of very resistant rock that stands above the surrounding terrain because of differen-tial erosion and weathering.

brackish Slightly saline, with a salt content less than that of sea water.

braided channel pattern (braided stream) A stream that consists of a multiplicity of interwoven and interconnected shallow channels separated by low islands of sand, gravel, and other loose debris.

breakwater A structure protecting a nearshore area from breaking waves.

broadleaf trees Trees that have flat and expansive leaves.

bryophytes Mosses and liverworts.

butte An erosional remnant of very small surface area and clifflike sides that rises conspicuously above the surroundings.

Buys-Ballot's law A physical principle stating that if one stands with one's back to the wind in the Northern Hemisphere, low pressure is on the left and high pressure is on the right. Directions are re-versed in the Southern Hemisphere.

calcification One of the dominant pedogenic regimes in areas where the principal soil moisture movement is upward because of a mois-ture deficit. This regime is characterized by a concentration of cal-cium carbonate ($CaCO_3$) in the B horizon forming a hardpan, an upward movement of $CaCO_3$ by capillary water by grass roots, and a return of $CaCO_3$ when grass dies.

caldera Large, steep-sided, roughly circular depression resulting from the explosion and collapse of a large volcano.

capacity (stream capacity) The maximum load that a stream can transport under given conditions.

capacity (water vapor capacity) Maximum amount of water vapor that can be present in the air at a given temperature.

capillarity The action by which water can climb upward in restricted confinement as a result of its high surface tension, and thus the ability of its molecules to stick closely together.

capillary water Moisture held at the surface of soil particles by sur-face tension.

caprock A flattish erosional surface formed of the most resistant layers of horizontal sedimentary or volcanic strata.

carbonate A category of minerals composed of carbon and oxygen combined with another element or elements.

carbonates Minerals that are carbonate compounds of calcium or magnesium.

carbonation A process in which carbon dioxide in water reacts with carbonate rocks to produce a very soluble product (calcium bicarbonate), which can readily be removed by runoff or percolation, and which can also be deposited in crystalline form if the water is evaporated.

carbon cycle The change from carbon dioxide to living matter and back to carbon dioxide.

carbon dioxide CO_2; Minor gas in the atmosphere; one of the greenhouse gases; by-product of combustion and respiration.

carbonic acid Mild acid formed when carbon dioxide dissolves in water; H_2CO_3.

carnivore A flesh-eating animal.

cartographer A mapmaker.

cartography The construction and production of maps.

cation An atom or group of atoms with a positive electrical charge.

cation exchange capacity (CEC) Capability of soil to attract and exchange cations.

cavern Large opening or cave, especially in limestone; often decorated with speleothems.

centripetal drainage pattern A basin structure in which the streams converge toward the center.

chaparral Shrubby vegetation of the mediterranean climatic region of North America.

chemical weathering The chemical decomposition of rock by the alteration of rock-forming minerals.

chinook A localized downslope wind of relatively dry and warm air, which is further warmed adiabatically as it moves down the leeward slope of the Rocky Mountains.

chlorofluorocarbons (CFCs) Synthetic chemicals commonly used as refrigerants and in aerosol spray cans; destroy ozone in the upper atmosphere.

chordata The phylum within the animal kingdom that includes all animals with backbones.

C horizon Lower soil layer composed of weathered parent material that has not been significantly affected by translocation or leaching.

cinder cone Small, common volcano that is composed primarily of pyroclastic material blasted out from a vent in small but intense explosions. The structure of the volcano is usually a conical hill of loose material.

circle of illumination The edge of the sunlit hemisphere that is a great circle separating Earth into a light half and a dark half.

cirque A broad amphitheater hollowed out at the head of a glacial valley by ice erosion.

cirque glacier A small glacier confined to its cirque and not moving down-valley.

cirriform cloud A cloud that is thin and wispy, composed of ice crystals rather than water particles, and found at high elevations.

cirrocumulus High cirriform clouds arranged in a patchy pattern.

cirrostratus High cirriform clouds that appear as whitish, translucent veils.

cirrus cloud High cirriform clouds of feathery appearance.

clay Very small inorganic particles produced by chemical alteration of silicate minerals.

claypan A playa surface that is heavily impregnated with clay.

cliff Sheer residual rock face.

climate An aggregate of day-to-day weather conditions over a long period of time.

climax vegetation A stable plant association of relatively constant composition that develops at the end of a long succession of changes.

climograph (climatic diagram) Chart showing the average monthly temperature and precipitation for a weather station.

cloud seeding The introduction of particles (usually dry ice or silver iodide) into clouds for the purpose of altering the cloud's normal development, usually in an effort to enhance precipitation.

col A pass or saddle through a ridge produced when two adjacent glacial cirques on opposite sides of a divide are cut back enough to remove part of the arête between them.

cold-air-drainage inversion Temperature inversion developing when cooler air slides down a slope into valley displacing slightly warmer air.

cold front The leading edge of a cool air mass actively displacing warm air.

collapse doline A sinkhole produced by the collapse of the roof of a subsurface cavern.

colloids Organic and inorganic microscopic particles of soil that represent the chemically active portion of particles in the soil.

color infrared (color IR) film Photographic film sensitive to radiation in the infrared region of the spectrum.

combined water Water held in chemical combination with various soil minerals.

competence The size of the largest particle that can be transported by a stream.

composite volcano Volcanoes with the classic symmetrical, cone-shaped peak, produced by a mixture of lava outpouring and pyroclastic explosion.

condensation Process by which water vapor is converted to liquid water; a warming process because latent heat is released.

condensation nuclei Tiny atmospheric particles of dust, bacteria, smoke, and salt that serve as collection centers for water molecules.

conditional instability A lapse rate somewhere between the dry and saturated adiabatic rates; rising air becomes unstable after condensation releases latent heat.

conduction The movement of energy from one molecule to another without changing the relative positions of the molecules. It enables the transfer of heat between different parts of a stationary body.

cone of depression The phenomenon whereby the water table has sunk into the approximate shape of an inverted cone in the immediate vicinity of a well as the result of the removal of a considerable amount of the water.

conformality The property of a map projection that maintains proper shapes of surface features.

conformal map projection A projection that maintains proper angular relationships over the entire map; over limited areas shows the correct shapes of features shown on a map.

conglomerate Sedimentary rock composed of pebbles or larger particles in a matrix of finer material.

conic projection A family of maps in which one or more cones is set tangent to, or intersecting, a portion of the globe and the geographic grid is projected onto the cone(s).

conifer See gymnosperm.

consequent stream Stream following the initial slope of the land.

contact metamorphism Metamorphism of surrounding rocks by contact with magma.

continental drift Theory that proposed that the present continents were originally connected as one or two large landmasses that have broken up and literally drifted apart over the last several hundred million years.

continental ice sheet Large ice sheet covering a portion of a continental area.

continentality Tendency of areas remote from the ocean, especially in high and midlatitudes, to have large annual and daily temperature ranges.

continental rift valley Fault-produced valley resulting from spreading or rifting of continent.

continental shelf Submerged margin of continents.

contour line (elevation contour line) A line joining points of equal elevation.

controls of weather and climate The most important influences acting upon the elements of weather and climate.

convection Vertical movements of parcels of air due to density differences.

convection cell Closed pattern of convective circulation.

convective lifting Air lifting as a result of convection.

convective precipitation Showery precipitation resulting from the convective lifting of air.

convergent [plate] boundary Location where two lithospheric plates collide.

convergent lifting Air lifting as a result of air convergence.

convergent precipitation Showery precipitation that occurs as a result of the forced uplift of air due to crowding in areas of air convergence.

coral reef A coralline formation that fringes continents and islands in warm-water tropical oceans.

cordillera A chain of mountains, often encompassing many ranges.

core Spherical central portion of Earth, divided into a molten outer layer and a solid inner layer.

Coriolis effect (Coriolis force) The apparent deflection of free-moving objects to the right in the Northern Hemisphere and to the left in the Southern Hemisphere, in response to the rotation of Earth.

corrosion Chemical reactions (especially hydrolysis and solution action) associated with streamflow that assist in erosion.

crater The depression at the summit of a volcano, or a depression caused by the impact of a meteorite.

creep (soil creep) The slowest and least perceptible form of mass wasting, which consists of a very gradual downhill movement of soil and regolith.

crust The outermost solid layer of Earth.

cryosphere Subsphere of the hydrosphere that encompasses water frozen as snow or ice.

cryoturbation (frost churning) The physical disruption and displacement of soil material by freeze–thaw action in the soil.

cultural geography The study of the human and/or cultural elements of geography.

cumuliform cloud A cloud that is massive and rounded, usually with a flat base and limited horizontal extent, but often billowing upward to great heights.

cumulonimbus Cumuliform cloud of great vertical development, often associated with a thunderstorm.

cumulus cloud Puffy white cloud that forms from rising columns of air.

cumulus stage The early stage of thunderstorm formation in which updrafts prevail and the cloud continues to grow.

cutoff meander A sweeping stream channel curve that is isolated from streamflow because the narrow meander neck has been cut through by stream erosion.

cycle of erosion See **geomorphic cycle**.

cyclone Low-pressure center.

cylindrical projection A family of maps derived from the concept of projection onto a paper cylinder that is tangential to, or intersecting with, a globe.

debris flow Streamlike flow of muddy water heavily laden with sediments of various sizes; a mudflow containing large boulders.

December solstice Day of the year when the vertical rays of the Sun strike the Tropic of Capricorn; on or about December 21.

deciduous tree A tree that experiences an annual period in which all leaves die and usually fall from the tree, due either to a cold season or a dry season.

decomposers Mainly microscopic organisms such as bacteria that decompose dead plant and animal matter.

deflation The shifting of loose particles by wind blowing them into the air or rolling them along the ground.

delta A landform at the mouth of a river produced by the sudden dissipation of a stream's velocity and the resulting deposition of the stream's load.

dendritic drainage pattern A treelike, branching pattern that consists of a random merging of streams, with tributaries joining larger streams irregularly, but always at acute angles.

dendrochronology Study of past events and past climate through the analysis of tree rings.

denitrification The conversion of nitrates into free nitrogen in the air.

density Mass of a substance per unit volume.

denudation The total effect of all actions that lower the surface of the continents.

desert Climate, landscape, or biome associated with extremely arid conditions.

desertification Degradation of the soil and biota due to a combination of drought and improper land use.

desert pavement Hard and relatively impermeable desert surface of tightly packed small rocks.

desert varnish A dark shiny coating of iron and manganese oxides that forms on rock surfaces exposed to desert air for a long time.

dew The condensation of beads of water on relatively cold surfaces.

dew point temperature (dew point) The critical air temperature at which water vapor saturation is reached.

diastrophism A general term that refers to the deformation of Earth's crust.

differential erosion The process whereby different rocks or parts of the same rock erode at different rates.

dike A vertical or nearly vertical sheet of magma that is thrust upward into preexisting rock.

disappearing stream Stream that abruptly disappears from the surface where it flows into an underground cavity; common in karst regions.

discharge Volume of flow of a stream.

dissolution Removal of bedrock through chemical action of water; includes removal of subsurface rock through action of groundwater.

dissolved load The minerals, largely salts, that are dissolved in water and carried invisibly in solution.

distributaries Branching stream channels that cross a delta.

diurnal Daily.

divergent [plate] boundary Location where two lithospheric plates spread apart.

doldrums Belt of calm air associated with the region between the trade winds of the Northern and Southern hemispheres, generally in the vicinity of the equator. The region of the intertropical convergence zone (ITCZ).

Doppler effect Shift in the frequency of a sound wave or an electromagnetic wave due to either the movement of the observer or the source of the waves.

downcutting Action of stream to erode a deeper channel; occurs when stream is flowing swiftly and/or flowing down a steep slope.

downdraft Small-scale downward movement of air.

drainage basin An area that contributes overland flow and groundwater to a specific stream (also called a watershed or catchment).

drainage density The ratio of the total length of all stream segments in a drainage basin to the area of the basin.

drainage divide The line of separation between runoff that descends into two different drainage basins.

drainage net The complex of streams within a drainage basin.

drift (glacial drift) All material carried and deposited by glaciers.

dripstone Features formed by precipitated deposits of minerals that decorate the walls, floor, and roof of a cavern.

drumlin A low, elongated hill formed by ice-sheet deposition. The long axis is aligned parallel with the direction of ice movements, and the end of the drumlin that faces the direction from which the ice came is somewhat blunt and slightly steeper than the narrower and more gently sloping end that faces in the opposite direction.

dry adiabatic rate (dry adiabatic lapse rate) The rate at which a parcel of unsaturated air cools as it rises (10°C per 1000 meters [5.5°F per 1000 feet]).

dynamic high High pressure cell associated with prominently descending air.

dynamic low Low pressure cell associated with prominently rising air.

dyne The force needed to accelerate 1 gram of mass 1 centimeter per second per second.

earthflow Mass wasting process in which a portion of a water-saturated slope moves a short distance downhill.

earthquake Vibrations generated by abrupt movement of Earth's crust.

easterly wave A long but weak migratory low-pressure trough in the tropics.

ebb tide A periodic falling of sea level during a tidal cycle.

ecosystem The totality of interactions among organisms and the environment in the area of consideration.

ecotone The transition zone between biotic communities in which the typical species of one community intermingle or interdigitate with those of another.

edaphic factors Having to do with soil.

E horizon A light-colored, eluvial layer that usually occurs between the A and B horizons.

elbow of capture Sharp bend in river course that develops where one stream captures another stream.

electromagnetic radiation Flow of energy in the form of electromagnetic waves; radiant energy.

electromagnetic spectrum Electromagnetic radiation, arranged according to wavelength.

elements of weather and climate The basic ingredients of weather and climate—temperature, pressure, wind, and moisture.

elevation contour line See **contour line**.

elliptical projection A family of map projections in which the entire world is displayed in an oval shape. Also called pseudocylindrical projection.

El Niño Periodic atmospheric and oceanic phenomenon of the tropical Pacific that typically involves the weakening or reversal of the trade winds and the warming of surface water off the west coast of South America.

eluviation The process by which gravitational water picks up fine particles of soil from the upper layers and carries them downward.

endemic Organism found only in a particular area.

endothermic [animal] Warm-blooded animal.

energy The capacity to do work.

ENSO (El Niño/Southern Oscillation) Linked atmospheric and oceanic phenomenon of pressure and water temperature. Commonly called simply El Niño. See **El Niño** and **Southern Oscillation**.

Entisol The least developed of all soil orders, with little mineral alteration and no pedogenic horizons. These soils are commonly thin and/or sandy and have limited productivity, although those developed on recent alluvial deposits tend to be quite fertile.

entrenched meanders A winding, sinuous stream valley with abrupt sides; possible outcome of the rejuvenation of a meandering stream.

environmental lapse rate The observed vertical temperature gradient of the troposphere.

ephemeral stream A stream that carries water only during the "wet season" or during and immediately after rains.

epicenter Location on the surface directly above the center of fault rupture during an earthquake.

epiphytes Plants that live above ground level out of contact with the soil, usually growing on trees or shrubs.

equal area projection See **equivalence**.

equator The parallel of 0 latitude.

Equatorial Countercurrent An east-moving ocean current, between the two equatorial currents.

equilibrium line A theoretical line separating the ablation zone and accumulation zone of a glacier along which accumulation exactly balances ablation.

equilibrium theory Idea that slope forms are adjusted to geomorphic processes so that there is a balance of energy; the energy provided is just adequate for the work to be done.

equinox The time of the year when the perpendicular rays of the Sun strike the equator, the circle of illumination just touches both poles, and the periods of daylight and darkness are each 12 hours long all over Earth.

equivalence The property of a map projection that maintains equal areal relationships in all parts of the map. Such maps are also called equal area maps.

equivalent map projection A projection that maintains constant area (size) relationships over the entire map; also called an "equal area projection."

erg "Sea of sand." A large area covered with loose sand, generally arranged in some sort of dune formation by the wind.

erosion Detachment and removal of fragmented rock material.

erratic See **glacial erratic**.

escarpment An abrupt slope that breaks up the general continuity of the terrain.

esker Long, sinuous ridge of stratified glacial drift composed largely of glaciofluvial gravel and formed by the choking of subglacial streams during a time of glacial stagnation.

estivation The act of spending a dry/hot period in a torpid state.

estuary A finger of the sea projecting inland along drowned river valleys.

eustatic sea-level change Change in sea level due to an increase or decrease in the amount of water in the world ocean, also known as eustasy.

evaporation Process by which liquid water is converted to gaseous water vapor; a cooling process because latent heat is stored.

evaporation fog The condensation that results from the addition of water vapor to cold air that is already near saturation.

evapotranspiration The transfer of moisture to the atmosphere by transpiration from plants and evaporation from soil and plants.

evergreen A tree or shrub that sheds its leaves on a sporadic or successive basis but at any given time appears to be fully leaved.

exfoliation Weathering process in which curved layers peel off bedrock in sheets. This process commonly occurs in granite and related intrusive rocks. Also referred to as "unloading."

exfoliation dome A large rock mass with a surface configuration that consists of imperfect curves punctuated by several partially fractured shells of the surface layers; result of exfoliation.

exosphere The highest zone of Earth's atmosphere.

exotic species (exotics) Organisms that are introduced into "new" habitats in which they did not naturally occur.

exotic stream A stream that flows into a dry region, bringing its water from somewhere else.

extinction The dying out of the entire population of a taxa.

external geomorphic processes Destructive processes that serve to denude or wear down the landscape. Includes weathering, mass wasting, and erosion.

extrusive rock Molten rock ejected onto Earth's surface, solidifying quickly in the open air; also called volcanic rock.

eye (eye of tropical cyclone) The nonstormy center of a tropical cyclone, which has a diameter of 16 to 40 kilometers (10 to 25 miles) and is a singular area of calmness in the maelstrom that whirls around it.

eye wall Peripheral zone at the edge of a tropical cyclone eye where winds reach their highest speed.

fall Mass wasting process in which pieces of weathered rock fragments fall to the bottom of a cliff or steep slope; also called rockfall.

fault A fracture or zone of fracture where the rock is forcefully broken with an accompanying displacement, that is, an actual movement of the crust on one or both sides of the break. The movement can be horizontal or vertical, or a combination of both.

fault-block mountain (tilted-fault-block mountain) A mountain formed under certain conditions of crustal stress, whereby a surface block may be severely faulted and upthrown on one side without any faulting or uplift on the other side. The block is tilted asymmetrically, producing a steep slope along the fault scarp and a relatively gentle slope on the other side of the block.

faulting See **fault**.

fault line The intersection of a fault zone with Earth's surface.

fault plane Interface along which movement occurs in faulting.

fault scarp Cliff formed by faulting.

fault zone Zone of weakness in the crust where faulting may take place.

fauna Animals.

feral A domesticated creature that has reverted to a wild existence, or the progeny thereof.

ferromagnesian Containing iron and/or magnesium as a major constituent.

field capacity The maximum amount of water that can be retained in the soil after the gravitational water has drained away.

firn (névé) Snow granules that have become packed and begin to coalesce due to compression, achieving a density about half as great as that of water.

first-order relief The largest scale of relief features, consisting of continental platforms and ocean basins.

fix (the verb) To make firm or stable; example: to fix nitrogen.

fjord A glacial trough that has been partly drowned by the sea.

flood basalt A large-scale outpouring of basaltic lava that may cover an extensive area of Earth's surface.

floodplain A flattish valley floor covered with stream-deposited sediments (alluvium) and subject to periodic or episodic inundation by overflow from the stream.

flood tide The movement of ocean water toward the coast in a tidal cycle—from the ocean's lowest surface level the water rises gradually for about 6 hours and 13 minutes.

flora Plants.

flow A category of mass wasting processes. A gentle, smooth motion as when a sector of a slope becomes unstable, normally due to an addition of water, and slips gently downhill.

fluvial Running water including both overland flow and streamflow.

fluvial processes Processes involving the work of running water on the surface of Earth.

foehn See **chinook**. The word foehn is used particularly in Europe.

fog A cloud whose base is at or very near ground level.

folding The bending of crustal rocks by compression and/or uplift.

foliation Bending that gives a wavy layered appearance to metamorphic rock.

food chain Sequential predation in which organisms feed upon one another, with organisms at one level providing food for organisms at the next level, and so on. Energy is thus transferred through the ecosystem.

food pyramid See also **food chain**. Another conceptualization of energy transfer through the ecosystem from large numbers of "lower" forms of life through succeedingly smaller numbers of "higher" forms, as the organisms at one level are eaten by the organisms at the next higher level.

forbs Broadleaf herbaceous plants.

foreshore The lower shore zone of a beach, generally between the levels of high and low tide.

forest An assemblage of trees growing closely together so that their individual leaf canopies generally overlap.

fractional scale (fractional map scale) Ratio of distance between points on a map and the same points on Earth's surface, expressed as a ratio or fraction.

freezing Change from liquid to solid state.

friction layer Zone of the atmosphere, between Earth's surface and about 1000 meters (3300 feet), where most frictional resistance is found.

fringing reef A coral reef built out laterally from the shore, forming a broad bench that is only slightly below sea level, often with the tops of individual coral "heads" exposed to the open air at low tide.

front A zone of discontinuity between unlike air masses.

frontal lifting Forced lifting of air along a front.

frontal precipitation Precipitation associated with the lifting of air along a front.

frost churning See **cryoturbation**.

frost wedging Fragmentation of rock due to expansion of water that freezes in rock openings.

Fujita tornado intensity scale Classification scale of tornado strength, with F0 being the weakest tornadoes and F5 being the most powerful.

fumarole A hydrothermal feature consisting of a surface crack that is directly connected with a deep-seated source of heat. The little water that drains into this tube is instantly converted to steam by heat and gases, and a cloud of steam is then expelled from the opening.

fungi Kingdom of organisms that lack vascular tissue and chlorophyll, such as mushrooms.

funnel cloud Funnel-shaped cloud extending down from a cumulonimbus cloud; a tornado is formed when the funnel cloud touches the surface.

Gelisol Soil order that develops in areas of permafrost.

general circulation model (GCM) Computer simulation of the atmosphere; models based on physical processes operating in the atmosphere.

genus The usual major subdivision of a family in the taxonomy of plants and animals, normally consisting of more than one species.

geographic information systems (GIS) Computerized systems for the capture, storage, retrieval, analysis, and display of spatial data.

geomorphic cycle (cycle of erosion) A conceptual model of landscape development that was propounded by William Morris Davis. Davis envisioned a circular sequence of terrain evolution in which a relatively flat surface was uplifted from a lower to a higher elevation, where it was incised by fluvial erosion into a landscape of slopes and valleys and then thoroughly denuded until it became a flat surface at low elevation. He recognized three stages: "youth," "maturity," and "old age."

geomorphology The study of the characteristics, origin, and development of landforms.

geostrophic wind A wind that moves parallel to the isobars as a result of the balance between the pressure gradient force and the Coriolis effect.

geyser A specialized form of intermittent hot spring with water issuing only sporadically as a temporary ejection, in which hot water and steam are spouted upward for some distance.

geyserite Whitish-colored siliceous sinter that often covers a geyser basin.

gibber plain A gravel-covered desert in Australia.

glacial erratic Outsize boulder included in the glacial till, which may be very different from the local bedrock.

glacial flour Rock material that has been ground to the texture of very fine talcum powder by glacial action.

glacial plucking Action in which rock particles beneath the ice are grasped by the freezing of meltwater in joints and fractures and pried out and dragged along in the general flow of a glacier. Also called glacial quarrying.

glacial steps Series of level or gently sloping bedrock benches alternating with steep drops in the down-valley profile of a glacial trough.

glacial trough A valley reshaped by an alpine glacier, usually U-shaped.

glacier A large natural accumulation of land ice that flows either downslope or outward from its center of accumulation.

glaciofluvial deposition The action whereby much of the debris that is carried along by glaciers is eventually deposited or redeposited by glacial meltwater.

glaze Rain that turns to ice the instant it collides with a solid object.

gleization The dominant pedogenic regime in areas where the soil is saturated most of the time due to poor drainage.

gley soils The general term for soils produced by gleization.

global conveyer-belt circulation Slowly moving circulation of deep ocean water that forms a continuous loop from the North Atlantic to the Antarctic, into the Indian and Pacific Oceans, and back into the North Atlantic.

Global Positioning System (GPS) A satellite-based system for determining accurate positions on or near Earth's surface.

global warming Popular name given to the recent warming of Earth's climate due to human-released greenhouse gases.

gneiss One of the most common metamorphic rocks; it is characterized by broad foliations and a banded appearance.

Gondwanaland Presumed Southern Hemisphere supercontinent resulting from the initial breakup of Pangaea.

graben A block of land bounded by parallel faults in which the block has been downthrown, producing a distinctive structural valley with a straight, steep-sided fault scarp on either side.

graded stream A stream that is at equilibrium with its load; the stream is just able to transport the load.

gradient Horizontal rate of variation of some quantity, such as atmospheric pressure or elevation of stream bed.

granite The most common and well-known plutonic (intrusive) rock; coarse-grained rock consisting of both dark- and light-colored minerals.

graphic scale (graphic map scale) The use of a line marked off in graduated distances as a map scale.

grassland Plant association dominated by grasses and forbs.

graticule The network of parallels and meridians on a map.

gravitational water Soil water that is temporary in occurrence, in that it results from prolonged infiltration from above (usually due to prolonged precipitation) and is pulled downward through the interstices toward the groundwater zone below by gravitational attraction.

great circle Circle on a globe formed by the intersection of Earth's surface with any plane that passes through Earth's center.

greenhouse effect The warming in the lower troposphere because of differential transmissivity for shortwave and longwave radiation through the gases in the atmosphere; the atmosphere easily transmits shortwave radiation from the Sun but inhibits the transmission of longwave radiation from the surface.

greenhouse gases Gases with the ability to transmit incoming shortwave radiation from the Sun but absorb outgoing terrestrial radiation. The most important greenhouse gases are water vapor and carbon dioxide.

Greenwich Mean Time (GMT) Time in the Greenwich time zone. Today more commonly called UTC or Universal Time Coordinated.

groin A short wall built perpendicularly from the beach into the shore zone to interrupt the longshore current and trap sand.

ground fog See **radiation fog**.

ground moraine A moraine consisting of glacial till deposited widely over a land surface beneath an ice sheet.

groundwater Water found underground in the zone of saturation.

groundwater flow Water that moves through the groundwater system below the water table.

gully erosion Overland flow that erodes conspicuous channels in the soil.

gymnosperms (naked seeds) Seed-reproducing plants that carry their seeds in cones.

Hadley cells Two complete vertical convective circulation cells between the equator, where warm air rises in the ITCZ, and 25° to 30° of latitude, where much of the air subsides into the subtropical highs.

hail Rounded or irregular pellets or lumps of ice produced in cumulonimbus clouds as a result of active turbulence and vertical air currents. Small ice particles grow by collecting moisture from supercooled cloud droplets.

halide A category of minerals that is notably salty.

Halley, Edmund An English astronomer and cartographer who, in his published map of 1700, was the first person to use isolines that appeared in print. His map showed isogonic lines in the Atlantic Ocean.

hamada A barren desert surface of consolidated material that usually consists of exposed bedrock but is sometimes composed of sedimentary material that has been cemented together by salts evaporated from groundwater.

hanging valley A tributary glacial trough, the bottom of which is considerably higher than the bottom of the principal trough that it joins.

hardpan A thin hard stratum within or beneath the soil surface.

hardwoods Angiosperm trees that are usually broad-leaved and deciduous. Their wood has a relatively complicated structure, but it is not always hard.

headland A promontory with a steep cliff face projecting into the sea.

headward erosion Erosion that cuts into the interfluve at the upper end of a gully or valley.

heat Energy that transfers from one object or substance to another because of a difference in temperature. Sometimes the term thermal energy is used interchangeably with the term heat. A form of energy associated with the random motion of molecules. Things can be made hotter by the collision of the moving molecules.

heat index A calculation of apparent temperature (how hot the air feels to one's skin) from temperature and relative humidity data.

herbaceous plants Plants that have soft stems, mostly grasses, forbs, and lichens.

herbivore An animal that feeds on vegetation.

heterosphere That portion of the atmosphere above the homosphere where there is an irregular layering of gases in accordance with their molecular weights.

hibernation The act of spending winter in a dormant state.

high [pressure cell] Area of relatively high atmospheric pressure.

highland climate High mountain climate where altitude is dominant control. Designated H in Köppen system.

highland ice field Largely unconfined ice sheet in high mountain area.

Histosol A soil order characterized by organic, rather than mineral, soils, which is invariably saturated with water all or most of the time.

homosphere A zone of homogenous composition comprising the lowest 80 kilometers (50 miles) of the atmosphere, where the principal gases have a uniform pattern of vertical distribution.

hook A curving sandbar at the outer end of a spit, produced by conflicting water movements in a bay that guide deposition in a curved fashion toward the coast.

horizon (soil horizon) The more or less distinctly recognizable layer of soil, distinguished from one another by differing characteristics and forming a vertical zonation of the soil.

horn A steep-sided, pyramidal rock pinnacle formed by expansive glacial quarrying of the headwalls where three or more cirques intersect.

horse latitudes Areas in the subtropical highs characterized by warm, tropical sunshine and an absence of wind.

horst An uplifted block of land between two parallel faults.

hot spot See **mantle plume**.

hot spring Hot water at Earth's surface that has been forced upward through fissures or cracks by the pressures that develop when underground water has come in contact with heated rocks or magma beneath the surface.

humid continental climate Severe midlatitude climate characterized by hot summers, cold winters, and precipitation throughout the year.

humid subtropical climate Mild midlatitude climate characterized by hot summers and precipitation throughout the year.

humidity Water vapor in the air.

humus A dark-colored, gelatinous, chemically stable fraction of organic matter on or in the soil.

hurricane A tropical cyclone with wind speeds of 64 knots or greater affecting North or Central America.

hurricane warning Notification issued by the Weather Service when hurricane conditions are expected in a specified area within 24 hours or less.

hurricane watch Notification issued by the Weather Service when hurricane conditions are expected in a specified area within 24 to 36 hours.

hydration The process whereby water molecules become attached to other substances and cause a wetting and swelling of the original substance without any change in its chemical composition.

hydrogen bond Attraction between water molecules in which the negatively charged oxygen side of one water molecule is attracted to the positively charged hydrogen side of another water molecule.

hydrography The study of the waters of Earth.

hydrologic cycle A series of storage areas interconnected by various transfer processes, in which there is a ceaseless interchange of moisture in terms of its geographical location and its physical state.

hydrology Study of water on or below the surface of Earth.

hydrolysis A chemical union of water with another substance to produce a new compound that is nearly always softer and weaker than the original.

hydrophyte A "water-loving" plant that is adapted to living more or less permanently immersed in water.

hydrosphere Total water realm of Earth, including the oceans, surface waters of the lands, groundwater, and water held in the atmosphere.

hydrothermal activity The outpouring or ejection of hot water, often accompanied by steam, which usually takes the form of either a hot spring or a geyser.

hygrometer Any instrument for measuring humidity.

hygrophyte A water-tolerant plant that requires a saturated or semisaturated environment.

hygroscopic particles Tiny particles suspended in the atmosphere that act as nuclei for water vapor condensation.

hygroscopic water A microscopically thin film of moisture that is bound rigidly to soil particles by adhesion.

iceberg A great chunk of floating ice that breaks off an ice shelf or the end of an outlet glacier.

icecap A small ice sheet, normally found in the summit area of high mountains.

ice cap climate Polar climate characterized by temperatures below freezing throughout the year.

ice floe A mass of ice that breaks off from larger ice bodies (ice sheets, glaciers, ice packs, and ice shelves) and floats independently in the sea. This term is generally used with large, flattish, tabular masses.

ice pack The extensive and cohesive mass of floating ice that is found in the Arctic and Antarctic oceans.

ice sheet A vast blanket of ice that completely inundates the underlying terrain to depths of hundreds or thousands of meters.

ice shelf A massive portion of an ice sheet that projects out over the sea.

igneous intrusion Features formed by the emplacement and cooling of magma below the surface.

igneous rock Rock formed by solidification of molten magma.

illuviation The process by which fine particles of soil from the upper layers are deposited at a lower level.

Inceptisol An immature order of soils that has relatively faint characteristics; not yet prominent enough to produce diagnostic horizons.

inclination [of Earth's axis] The tilt of Earth's rotational axis relative to its orbital plane (the plane of the ecliptic).

infiltration Downward movement of water into the soil and regolith.

infrared radiation Electromagnetic radiation in the wavelength range of about 0.7 to 1000 micrometers; wavelengths just longer than visible light.

inertia Resistance to change of motion; remaining at rest.

inner core The solid, dense, innermost portion of Earth, believed to consist largely of iron and nickel.

inselberg ("island mountain") Isolated summit rising abruptly from a low-relief surface.

insolation Incoming solar radiation.

interflow Water that infiltrates from the land surface above and then moves laterally in the soil or rock below.

interfluve The higher land or ridge above the valley sides that separates adjacent valleys.

intermittent stream A stream that carries water only part of the time, during the "wet season" or during and immediately after rains.

internal geomorphic processes Geomorphic processes originating below the surface; include vulcanism, folding, and faulting.

International Date Line The line marking a time difference of an entire day from one side of the line to the other. Generally, this line falls on the 180th meridian except where it deviates to avoid separating an island group.

international system of measurement (SI) Popularly known as the "metric system" of measurement.

interpolate To insert something additional between other things, particularly by estimation.

interstices The pore spaces; a labyrinth of interconnecting passageways among the soil particles that makes up nearly half the volume of an average soil.

intertropical convergence zone (ITCZ) The region near or on the equator where the northeast trades and the southeast trades converge.

interval (isoline interval) The numerical difference between one isoline and the next.

intrusive rock Rocks that cool and solidify beneath Earth's surface; also called plutonic rock.

invertebrates Animals without backbones.

ionosphere A deep atmospheric layer containing electrically charged molecules and atoms in the upper mesosphere and lower thermosphere.

island arc (volcanic island arc) Chain of volcanic islands associated with an oceanic plate–oceanic plate subduction zone.

isobar A line joining points of equal atmospheric pressure.

isogonic line A line joining points of equal magnetic declination.

isohyet A line joining points of equal numerical value of precipitation.

isoline A line on a map connecting points that have the same quality or intensity of a given phenomenon.

isostasy Maintenance of the hydrostatic equilibrium of Earth's crust.

isotherm A line joining points of equal temperature.

isotopes Atoms of the same element but with different numbers of neutrons.

ITCZ See **intertropical convergence zone**.

jet stream A rapidly moving current of air concentrated along a quasi-horizontal axis in the upper troposphere or in the stratosphere, characterized by strong vertical and lateral wind shears and featuring one or more velocity maxima.

jetty A wall built into the ocean at the entrance of a river or harbor to protect against sediment deposition, storm waves, and currents.

joints Cracks that develop in bedrock due to stress, but in which there is no appreciable movement parallel to the walls of the joint.

jungle A type of forest that is overgrown with dense vegetation, usually found in tropical or subtropical regions.

June solstice Day of the year when the vertical rays of the Sun strike the Tropic of Cancer; on or about June 21.

kame A relatively steep-sided mound or conical hill composed of stratified drift found in areas of ice-sheet deposition and associated with meltwater deposition in close association with stagnant ice.

karst Topography developed as a consequence of subsurface solution.

katabatic wind A wind that originates in cold upland areas and cascades toward lower elevations under the influence of gravity.

kettle An irregular depression in a morainal surface created when blocks of stagnant ice eventually melt.

kilopascal Equivalent to 10 millibars.

kinetic energy The energy of movement.

knickpoint A sharp irregularity (such as a waterfall, rapid, or cascade) in a stream-channel profile.

knickpoint migration Upstream shift in location of a knickpoint due to erosion.

knot A unit of speed equal to 1 nautical mile, or 1.15 statute miles, per hour; 1.85 kilometers per hour.

Köppen climate classification system A climatic classification of the world devised by Wladimir Köppen.

laccolith An igneous intrusion produced when slow-moving, viscous magma is forced between horizontal layers of preexisting rock. The magma resists flowing and builds up into a mushroom-shaped mass that domes the overlying strata. If near enough to Earth's surface, a rounded hill will rise above the surrounding area.

lagoon A body of quiet salt or brackish water in an area between a barrier island or a barrier reef and the mainland.

lahar Volcanic mudflow; a fast-moving muddy flow of volcanic ash and rock fragments.

lake A body of water surrounded by land.

land breeze Local wind blowing from land to water, usually at night.

landform An individual topographic feature, of any size.

landforms Topography.

Landsat A series of unmanned satellites that orbit Earth at an altitude of 915 kilometers (570 miles) and are capable of imaging all parts of Earth, except the polar regions, every nine days.

landslide An abrupt and often catastrophic event in which a large mass of rock and earth slides bodily downslope in only a few seconds or minutes. An instantaneous collapse of a slope.

langley (ly) The unit of measure of radiation intensity that is 1 calorie per square centimeter.

La Niña Atmospheric and oceanic phenomenon associated with cooler than usual water off the west coast of South America. Sometimes described as the opposite of El Niño.

lapse rate The rate of temperature decrease with height in the troposphere. The average lapse rate has been calculated to be about 6.5°C per 1000 meters (3.6°F per 1000 feet).

large-scale map A map with a scale that is a relatively large representative fraction and therefore portrays only a small portion of Earth's surface, but in considerable detail.

latent heat Energy stored or released when a substance changes state. For example, evaporation is a cooling process because latent heat is stored and condensation is a warming process because latent heat is released.

latent heat of condensation Heat released when water vapor condenses back to liquid form.

latent heat of evaporation Energy stored when liquid water evaporates to form water vapor.

latent heat of vaporization Stored energy absorbed by escaping molecules during evaporation or boiling.

lateral erosion Erosion that occurs when the principal current of a stream swings laterally from one bank to the other, eroding where the velocity is greatest and depositing where it is least.

lateral moraine Well-defined ridge of unsorted debris built up along the sides of valley glaciers, parallel to the valley walls.

laterization The dominant pedogenic regime in areas where temperatures are relatively high throughout the year and which is characterized by rapid weathering of parent material, dissolution of nearly all minerals, and the speedy decomposition of organic matter.

latitude Location described as an angle measured north and south of the equator.

latosol The general term applied to soils produced by laterization.

Laurasia Presumed Northern Hemisphere supercontinent resulting from the initial breakup of Pangaea.

lava Molten magma that is extruded onto the surface of Earth, where it cools and solidifies.

lava dome (plug dome) Dome or bulge formed by the pushing up of viscous magma in a volcanic vent.

lava vesicles Holes of various sizes, usually small, that develop in cooling lava when gas is unable to escape during solidification.

leaching The process in which gravitational water dissolves soluble materials and carries them downward in solution to be redeposited at lower levels.

lifting condensation level (LCL) The altitude at which rising air cools sufficiently to reach 100 percent relative humidity at the dew point temperature, and condensation begins.

lightning A luminous electric discharge in the atmosphere caused by the separation of positive and negative charges associated with cumulonimbus clouds.

limestone A common, chemically accumulated sedimentary rock composed largely of calcium carbonate.

limiting factor Variable that is important or most important in determining the survival of an organism.

linear fault trough Straight-line valley that marks the surface position of a fault, especially a strike-slip fault; formed by the erosion or settling of crushed rock along the trace of a fault.

Linnaean system A biological classification that focuses on the morphology of the organisms and groups them on the basis of structural similarity.

liquefaction Phenomenon observed during an earthquake when water-saturated soil or sediments become soft or even fluid during the time of strong ground shaking.

lithosphere Tectonic plates consisting of the crust and upper rigid mantle. Also used as a general term for the entire solid Earth.

litter The collection of dead plant parts that accumulate at the surface of the soil.

loam A soil texture in which none of the three principal soil separates—sand, silt, and clay—dominates the other two.

loess A fine-grained, wind-deposited silt. Loess lacks horizontal stratification, and its most distinctive characteristic is its ability to stand in vertical cliffs.

longitude Location described as an angle measured (in degrees, minutes, and seconds) east and west from the prime meridian on Earth's surface.

longshore current (littoral current) A current in which water moves roughly parallel to the shoreline in a generally downwind direction.

longshore drift (beach drifting) The zigzag movement of beach particles in which the net result is a displacement parallel to the coast in a general downwind direction.

longwave radiation Wavelengths of thermal infrared radiation emitted by Earth and the atmosphere; also referred to as terrestrial radiation.

low [pressure cell] Area of relatively low atmospheric pressure.

loxodrome (rhumb line) A true compass heading; a line of constant compass direction.

magma Molten material below Earth's surface.

magnetic declination The angular difference between a magnetic north line and a true north line, expressed as degrees east or west of the meridian in question.

magnetic north The direction in which a magnetic compass needle points.

magnitude [of an earthquake] Scale used to describe the relative amount of energy released during an earthquake. Several different magnitude scales are in current use. Also see **Richter scale** and **moment magnitude.**

mammals The highest form of animal life, distinguished from all other animals by several internal characteristics and two prominent external features: the production of milk to feed their young and the possession of true hair.

mantle The portion of Earth beneath the crust and surrounding the core.

mantle plume (hot spot) A location where molten mantle magma rises to, or almost to, Earth's surface.

map A flat representation of Earth at a reduced scale, showing only selected detail.

map projection A systematic representation of all or part of the three-dimensional Earth surface on a two-dimensional flat surface.

map scale Relationship between distance measured on a map and the actual distance on Earth's surface.

marble Metamorphosed limestone.

March equinox One of two days of the year when the vertical rays of the Sun strike the equator; every location on Earth has equal day and night; occurs on or about March 20th each year.

marine west coast climate Mild midlatitude climate characterized by mild temperatures and precipitation throughout the year.

marine terrace A platform of marine erosion that has been uplifted above sea level.

maritime Of or pertaining to the sea.

marsh Flattish surface area that is submerged in water at least part of the time but is shallow enough to permit the growth of water-tolerant plants, primarily grasses and sedges.

marsupials A small group of mammals whose females have pouches in which the young, born in a very undeveloped condition, live for several weeks or months after birth.

mass wasting The downslope movement of broken rock material by gravity, sometimes lubricated by the presence of water.

master joints Major joints that run for great distances through a bedrock structure.

meandering channel pattern (meandering stream channel) Highly twisting or looped stream channel pattern.

meander scar A former stream meander through which the stream no longer flows.

mechanical weathering The physical disintegration of rock material without any change in its chemical composition.

medial moraine A dark band of rocky debris down the middle of a glacier created by the union of the lateral moraines of two adjacent glaciers.

mediterranean climate Mild midlatitude climate characterized by dry summers and wet winters.

Mercalli intensity scale Scale to evaluate the intensity of earthquake shaking on the basis of damage caused. Also see **modified Mercalli intensity scale.**

Mercator projection A cylindrical projection mathematically adjusted to attain complete conformality which has a rapidly increasing scale with increasing latitude; straight lines on a Mercator projection are lines of constant compass heading.

meridian An imaginary line of longitude extending from pole to pole, crossing all parallels at right angles, and being aligned in true north–south directions.

mesa A flat-topped, steep-sided hill with a limited summit area.

mesocyclone Cyclonic circulation of air within a severe thunderstorm; diameter of about 10 kilometers (6 miles).

mesopause Transition zone at the top of the mesosphere.

mesosphere Atmospheric layer above the stratopause, where temperature decreases with height; also refers to the rigid part of the deep mantle, below the asthenosphere.

metamorphic rock Rock that was originally something else but has been drastically changed by massive forces of heat and/or pressure working on it from within Earth.

midlatitude anticyclone An extensive migratory high-pressure cell of the midlatitudes that moves generally with the westerlies.

midlatitude cyclone Large migratory low-pressure system that occurs within the middle latitudes and moves generally with the westerlies. Also known as extratropical cyclones and wave cyclones.

midlatitude desert climate Desert climate characterized by warm summers but cold winters.

midlatitude steppe climate Semiarid climate characterized by warm summers but cold winters.

midocean ridge A lengthy system of deep-sea mountain ranges, generally located at some distance from any continent; formed by divergent plate boundaries on the ocean floor.

Milankovitch cycles Combination of long-term astronomical cycles involving Earth's inclination, precession, and eccentricity of orbit; believed at least partially responsible for major periods of glaciation and deglaciation. Named for Milutin Milankovitch, an early twentieth century Yugoslavian astronomer, who studied these cycles.

millibar An "absolute" measure of pressure, consisting of one-thousandth part of a bar, or 1000 dynes per square centimeter.

mineral A naturally formed solid inorganic substance that has a specified chemical composition.

mistral A cold, high-velocity wind that sometimes surges down France's Rhone Valley, from the Alps to the Mediterranean Sea.

modified Mercalli intensity scale Qualitative scale from I to XII used to describe the relative strength of ground shaking during an earthquake.

mogote A steep-sided hill of residual limestone bedrock formed largely by solution action.

Mohorovičić discontinuity The boundary between Earth's crust and mantle. Also known simply as the Moho.

Mollisol A soil order characterized by the presence of a mollic epipedon, which is a mineral surface horizon that is dark, thick, contains abundant humus and base nutrients, and retains a soft character when it dries out.

moment magnitude Scale used to describe the relative amount of energy released during an earthquake; most useful magnitude scale for describing moderate to large earthquakes.

monera The kingdom of organisms that comprises the simplest known organisms: one-celled bacteria and blue-green algae.

monocline A one-limbed fold connecting horizontal or gently inclined strata.

monotremes Egg-laying mammals.

monsoon A seasonal reversal of winds; a general onshore movement in summer and a general offshore flow in winter, with a very distinctive seasonal precipitation regime.

moraine The largest and generally most conspicuous landform feature produced by glacial deposition, which consists of irregular rolling topography that rises somewhat above the level of the surrounding terrain.

morphology Form or shape or structure.

motus Coral islets that are closely spaced and separated by narrow channels of water and that together form a ring-shaped atoll.

mountain breeze Downslope breeze from a mountain due to chilling of air on its slopes at night.

mudflow Downslope movement of a thick mixture of soil and water.

multispectral scanning system (MSS) A remote sensing instrument that collects multiple digital images simultaneously in different bands.

natural levee An embankment of slightly higher ground fringing a stream channel in a floodplain; formed by deposition during floodtime.

natural selection The Darwinian theory of "the survival of the fittest," which explains the origin of any species as a normal process of descent, with variation, from parent forms.

nautical mile A unit of distance in sea and air navigation equal to 1852 meters or 6076 feet; 1.15 statute miles.

neap tides The lower-than-normal tidal variations that occur twice a month as the result of the alignment of the Sun and Moon at a right angle to one another.

nebula A cloud of interstellar gas and dust, perhaps one light-year in diameter.

needleleaf trees Trees adorned with thin slivers of tough, leathery, waxy needles rather than typical leaves.

nekton The term applied to animals that swim freely in the oceans.

net primary productivity The net photosynthesis of a plant community over a period of one year, usually measured in the amount of fixed carbon per unit area (kilograms of carbon per square meter per year).

névé See firn.

nimbostratus A low, dark cloud, often occurring as widespread overcast and normally producing precipitation.

nitrogen cycle An endless series of processes in which nitrogen moves through the environment.

nitrogen fixation Conversion of gaseous nitrogen into forms that can be used by plant life.

nocturnal Active at night.

nonferromagnesian Lacking iron and magnesium in its chemical composition.

normal fault The result of tension (extension) producing a steeply inclined fault plane, with the block of land on one side being pushed up, or upthrown, in relation to the block on the other side, which is downthrown.

North Pole Latitude of 90° north.

nunatak A rocky pinnacle protruding above an ice field.

occluded front A complex front formed when a cold front overtakes a warm front.

occlusion Process of cold front overtaking a warm front to form an occluded front.

ocean current Surface movement of ocean water along generally well-defined path.

ocean floor core samples Rock and sediment samples removed from ocean floor.

oceanic trench (deep oceanic trench) Deep linear depression in the ocean floor where subduction is taking place.

offset stream A stream course displaced by lateral movement along a fault.

offshore That portion of the shore zone seaward from the low-tide line and extending to the area where wave erosion and deposition do not occur.

offshore bar (barrier bar) Long, narrow sandbar built up in shallow offshore waters.

offshore flow Wind movement from land to water.

O horizon The immediate surface layer of a soil profile, consisting mostly of organic material.

onshore flow Wind movement from water to land.

orographic fog See upslope fog.

orographic lifting Uplift of air over a topographic barrier.

orographic precipitation Precipitation that occurs when air, forced to ascend over topographic barriers, cools to the dew point.

orthophoto map A map produced through computerized rectification of aerial imagery.

oscillation A swinging movement to and fro.

outcrop Surface exposure of bedrock.

outer core The liquid shell beneath the mantle that encloses Earth's inner core.

outlet glacier A tongue of ice around the margin of an ice sheet that extends between rimming hills to the sea.

outwash plain Extensive glaciofluvial feature that is a relatively smooth, flattish alluvial apron deposited beyond recessional or terminal moraines by streams issuing from ice.

overland flow The general movement of unchanneled surface water down the slope of the land surface.

overthrust fault (thrust fault) A fault created by compression forcing the upthrown block to override the downthrown block at a relatively low angle.

overthrust fold A fold in which the pressure was great enough to break the oversteepened limb and cause a shearing movement.

overturned fold An upfold that has been pushed so vigorously from one side that it becomes oversteepened enough to have a reverse orientation on the other side.

oxbow lake A cutoff meander that initially holds water.

oxbow swamp An oxbow lake that has been at least partly filled with sediment and vegetation.

oxidation The chemical union of oxygen atoms with atoms from various metallic elements to form new products, which are usually more voluminous, softer, and more easily eroded than the original compounds.

oxide A category of minerals composed of oxygen combined with another element.

Oxisol The most thoroughly weathered and leached of all soils. This soil order invariably displays a high degree of mineral alteration and profile development.

oxygen cycle The movement of oxygen by various processes through the environment.

ozone A gas composed of molecules consisting of three atoms of oxygen, O_3.

ozone layer A layer of ozone between 16 and 40 kilometers (10 and 25 miles) high, which absorbs ultraviolet solar radiation.

ozonosphere Zone of relatively rich concentration of ozone in the atmosphere.

Pacific ring of fire Name given to the rim of the Pacific Ocean basin due to widespread volcanic and seismic activity; associated with lithospheric plate boundaries.

paleoclimatology The study of past climates.

paleomagnetism Past magnetic orientation.

Pangaea The massive supercontinent that Alfred Wegener postulated to have existed about 200 million years ago. He visualized Pangaea as breaking up into several large sections that have continually moved away from one another and that now comprise the present continents.

parallel A circle resulting from an isoline connecting all points of equal latitude.

parallel drainage pattern A drainage pattern that can emerge in areas of pronounced regional slope, particularly if the gradient is gentle, with long consequent streams flowing parallel to one another.

parasites Organisms of one species that infest the body of a creature of another species, obtaining their nutriment from the host, which is almost invariably weakened and sometimes killed by the actions of the parasite.

parent material The source of the weathered fragments of rock from which soil is made; solid bedrock or loose sediments that have been transported from elsewhere by the action of water, wind, or ice.

particulate Composed of distinct tiny particles or droplets suspended in the atmosphere; also known as aerosols.

pascal (Pa) A pressure of 1 newton per square meter (1 newton is the force that must be exerted on a mass of 1 kilogram in order to accelerate it at a rate of 1 meter per second per second).

paternoster lakes A sequence of small lakes found in the shallow excavated depressions of a glacial trough.

patterned ground Polygonal patterns in the ground that develop in areas of seasonally frozen soil and permafrost.

pediment A gently inclined bedrock platform that extends outward from a mountain front, usually in an arid region.

pedogenic regimes Soil-forming regimes that can be thought of as environmental settings in which certain physical/chemical/biological processes prevail.

ped A larger mass or clump that individual soil particles tend to aggregate into and that determines the structure of the soil.

peneplain A flat and relatively featureless landscape with minimal relief; considered to be the end product of the geomorphic cycle. Peneplain means "almost a plain."

percolate To filter through a porous substance.

perennial plants (perennials) Plants that can live more than a single year despite seasonal climatic variations.

perennial stream A permanent stream that contains water the year-round.

perigee The point at which the Moon is closest to Earth in its elliptical orbit—370,000 kilometers (231,200 miles).

periglacial zone An area of indefinite size beyond the outermost extent of ice advance that was indirectly influenced by glaciation.

perihelion The point in its orbit at which a planet is nearest the Sun.

permafrost Permanent ground ice or permanently frozen subsoil.

permeability A soil or rock characteristic in which there are interconnected pore spaces through which water can move.

phases of the Moon The recurring appearances of the Moon or a planet with regard to the form of its illuminated disk.

photochemical smog Form of secondary air pollution caused by the reaction of nitrogen compounds and hydrocarbons to ultraviolet radiation in strong sunlight.

photogrammetry The science of obtaining reliable measurements from photographs and, by extension, mapping from aerial photos.

photoperiodism The response of an organism to the length of exposure to light in a 24-hour period.

photosynthesis The basic process whereby plants produce stored chemical energy from water and carbon dioxide and which is activated by sunlight.

phreatic zone (zone of saturation) The second hydrologic zone below the surface of the ground, whose uppermost boundary is the water table. The pore spaces and cracks in the bedrock and regolith of this zone are fully saturated.

physical geography Study of the physical elements of geography.

piedmont Zone at the "foot of the mountains."

piedmont angle The pronounced change in the angle of slope at a mountain base, with a steep slope giving way abruptly to a gentle one.

piedmont glacier A valley glacier that extends to the mouth of the valley and spreads out broadly over the flat land beyond.

piezometric surface The elevation to which water will rise under natural confining pressure in a well.

pillar An erosional remnant in the form of a steep-sided spire that has a resistant caprock; normally found in an arid or semiarid environment; also speleothem column.

pinnacle See **pillar**.

pixel An individual picture element of a remote sensing image.

placental mammals Mammals whose young grow and develop in the mother's body, nourished by an organ known as the placenta, which forms a vital connecting link with the mother's bloodstream.

plane of the ecliptic The imaginary plane that passes through the Sun and through Earth at every position in its orbit around the Sun; the orbital plane of Earth.

plane of the equator The imaginary plane that passes through Earth perpendicular to its rotation axis; the equator is the surface location of the plane of the equator.

plane projection A family of maps derived by the perspective extension of the geographic grid from a globe to a plane that is tangent to the globe at some point.

plankton Plants and animals that float about, drifting with the currents and tides; mostly microscopic in size.

plantae The kingdom of organisms that includes the green plants and higher algae.

plant respiration Stored energy in carbohydrates consumed directly by the plant itself; carbohydrates are oxidized, releasing water, carbon dioxide, and heat energy.

plant succession The process whereby one type of vegetation is replaced naturally by another.

plateau Flattish erosional platform bounded on at least one side by a prominent escarpment.

plate suturing The crushing together and joining of two continental plates when they collide.

plate tectonics A coherent theory of massive crustal rearrangement based on the movement of continent-sized lithospheric plates.

playa Dry lake bed in a basin of interior drainage.

playa lake Shallow and short-lived lake formed when water flows into a playa.

Pleistocene epoch An epoch of the Cenozoic era between the Pliocene and the Holocene; from 1.8 million to 10,000 years ago.

plucking (glacial plucking) Action in which rock particles beneath the ice are grasped by the freezing of meltwater in joints and fractures and pried out and dragged along in the general flow of a glacier. Also called glacial quarrying.

pluton A large, intrusive igneous body.

plutonic activity Processes involving the intrusion of magma deep below the surface of Earth.

plutonic rock Igneous rock formed below ground from the cooling and solidification of magma.

pluvial (pluvial effects) Pertaining to rain; often used in connection with a past rainy period.

podzol General term for a soil formed by podzolization.

podzolization The dominant pedogenic regime in areas where winters are long and cold, and which is characterized by slow chemical weathering of soils and rapid mechanical weathering from frost action, resulting in soils that are shallow, acidic, and with a fairly distinctive profile.

polar easterlies A global wind system that occupies most of the area between the Polar Highs and about 60° of latitude. The winds move generally from east to west and are typically cold and dry.

polar front The contact between unlike air masses in the subpolar low-pressure zone.

polar front jet stream Upper troposphere jet stream typically found at a latitude of about 55° N and S at an elevation of 9 to 12 kilometers (30,000 to 40,000 feet).

polar high A high-pressure cell situated over either polar region.

polarity [of rotation axis] A characteristic of Earth's axis wherein it always points toward Polaris (the North Star) at every position in Earth's orbit around the Sun. Also called parallelism.

pond A lake of very small size.

porosity The amount of pore space between the soil particles and between the peds, which is a measure of the capacity of the soil to hold water and air.

potential evapotranspiration The maximum amount of moisture that could be lost from soil and vegetation if the water were available.

prairie A tall grassland in the midlatitudes.

precipitation Drops of liquid or solid water falling from clouds.

precipitation variability Expected departure from average annual precipitation in any given year.

pressure [of a gas] The force exerted by a gas on a surface or walls of a container.

pressure gradient Change in atmospheric pressure over some horizontal distance.

primary consumer Animals that eat plants as the first stage in a food pyramid or chain.

primates Humans and such humanlike mammals as apes and monkeys.

prime meridian The meridian passing through the Royal Observatory at Greenwich (England), just east of London, and from which longitude is measured.

producers Organisms that produce their own food through photosynthesis; plants.

proglacial lake A lake formed when ice flows across or against the general slope of the land and the natural drainage is impeded or completely blocked so that meltwater from the ice becomes impounded against the ice front.

protista The kingdom of organisms that consists of one-celled organisms outside the Monera Kingdom, and some simple multicelled algae.

pseudocylindrical projection (elliptical projection) A family of map projections in which the entire world is displayed in an oval shape.

pteridophytes Spore-bearing plants such as ferns, horsetails, and clubmosses.

pyroclastic flow High-speed avalanche of hot gases, ash, and rock fragments emitted from a volcano during an explosive eruption; also known as a nuée ardente.

pyroclastics (pyroclastic material) Solid rock fragments thrown into the air by volcanic explosions.

quartz A mineral composed of silicon dioxide.

quartzite A metamorphosed rock derived from sandstone or another rock composed largely of quartz.

quick clays Clay formations that spontaneously change from a relatively solid mass into a near-liquid condition as the result of a sudden disturbance or shock.

radar Radio detection and ranging.

radial drainage pattern Drainage pattern in which consequent streams flow outward in all directions from a central dome or peak.

radiant energy Electromagnetic radiation.

radiation The process by which energy is emitted from a body, the flow of energy in the form of electromagnetic waves.

radiation inversion Surface inversion that results from rapid radiational cooling of lower air, typically on cold winter nights.

radiation fog A fog produced by condensation near the ground, where air is cooled to the dew point by contact with the colder ground.

rain The most common and widespread form of precipitation, consisting of drops of liquid water.

rain gauge An instrument used to measure the amount of rain that has fallen.

rain shadow Area of low rainfall on the leeward side of a topographic barrier.

recessional moraine A glacial deposit formed during a pause in the retreat of the ice margin.

rectangular drainage pattern Pattern where streams are essentially all subsequents that follow sets of faults and/or joints, with prominent right-angled relationships.

reef A mass of rock with its surface at or just below the low-tide line.

reflection The ability of an object to repel waves without altering either the object or the waves.

refraction Change of direction, for example, the bending of ocean waves or light waves.

reg A desert surface of coarse material from which all sand and dust have been removed by wind and water erosion. Often referred to as desert pavement or desert armor.

regime Seasonal pattern or sequential process.

regional metamorphism Widespread subsurface metamorphism of rock as a result of prolonged exposure to heat and high pressure.

regolith A layer of broken and partly decomposed rock particles that covers bedrock.

rejuvenation Concept that regional uplift could raise the land and interrupt the geomorphic cycle at any stage by reenergizing the degradational processes.

relative humidity An expression of the amount of water vapor in the air in comparison with the total amount that could be there if the air were saturated. This is a ratio that is expressed as a percentage.

relief The difference in elevation between the highest and lowest points in an area; the vertical variation from mountaintop to valley bottom.

remote sensing Study of an object or surface from a distance by using various instruments.

representative fraction (r.f.) The ratio that is an expression of a fractional map scale that compares map distance with ground distance.

reptiles Cold-blooded vertebrates, of which most are land-based.

residual landform A topographic feature caused by the erosion of bedrock.

reverse fault A fault produced from compression, with the upthrown block rising steeply above the downthrown block, so that the fault scarp would be severely oversteepened if erosion did not act to smooth the slope.

R horizon The consolidated bedrock at the base of a soil profile.

rhumb line See **loxodrome**.

ria shoreline An embayed coast with numerous estuaries; formed by the flooding of stream valleys by the sea.

Richter scale A scale of earthquake magnitudes, devised by California seismologist Charles F. Richter, in 1935, to describe the amount of energy released in a single earthquake.

ridge Linear or elongated area of relatively high atmospheric pressure.

rift valley A downfaulted graben structure extended for extraordinary distances as linear structural valleys enclosed between typically steep fault scarps.

rill erosion A more concentrated flow than that of sheet erosion, which loosens additional material and scores the slope with numerous parallel seams.

rills Tiny drainage channels.

riparian vegetation Anomalous streamside growth, particularly prominent in relatively dry regions, where stream courses may be lined with trees, although no other trees are to be found in the landscape.

roche moutonnée A characteristic glacial landform produced when a bedrock hill or knob is overridden by moving ice. The stoss side is smoothly rounded and streamlined by grinding abrasion as the ice rides up the slope, but the lee side is shaped largely by plucking, which produces a steeper and more irregular slope.

rock Solid material composed of aggregated mineral particles.

rock cycle Term given to the long-term "recycling" of mineral material from one kind of rock to another.

rockfall (fall) Mass wasting process in which weathered rock drops to the foot of a cliff or steep slope.

rock glacier An accumulated talus mass that moves slowly but distinctly downslope under its own weight.

Rossby wave A very large north–south undulation of the upper-air westerlies and jet stream.

runoff Flow of water from land to oceans by overland flow, streamflow, and groundwater flow.

rusting Production of reddish/yellowish/brownish iron oxide minerals by oxidation.

Saffir-Simpson Hurricane Scale Classification system of hurricane strength with category 1 the weakest and category 5 the strongest.

sag pond A pond caused by the collection of water from springs and/or runoff into sunken ground, resulting from the crushing of rock in an area of fault movement.

salina Dry lake bed that contains an unusually heavy concentration of salt in the lake-bed sediment.

saline lake Salt lake; commonly caused by interior stream drainage in an arid environment.

salinity A measure of the concentration of dissolved salts.

salinization One of the dominant pedogenic regimes in areas where principal soil moisture movement is upward because of a moisture deficit.

saltation Process in which small particles are moved along by streamflow or wind in a series of jumps or bounces.

salt wedging Rock disintegration caused by the crystallization of salts from evaporating water.

sand dune A mound, ridge, or low hill of loose, windblown sand.

sandplain An amorphous sheet of coarse sand spread across the landscape with no particular surface shape or significant relief.

sandstone A common mechanically accumulated sedimentary rock composed largely of sand grains.

sandstorm A cloud of generally horizontally moving sand that extends for only a few centimeters or meters above the surface.

Santa Ana winds Name given to dry, usually warm, and often very powerful winds blowing offshore in southern California region.

sapping An erosional process in which soil particles are removed from a slope by the seepage or trickling out of underground water.

saturated adiabatic rate (saturated adiabatic lapse rate) The diminished rate of cooling, averaging about 6°C per 1000 meters (3.3°F per 1000 feet) of rising air above the lifting condensation level.

saturation [with water vapor] Circumstance in which the air contains the maximum amount of water vapor for a given tempera-

ture; condensation typically will begin when the air is saturated with water vapor.

saturation vapor pressure The maximum pressure that can be exerted by water vapor at a given temperature; the pressure exerted by water vapor when the air is saturated.

savanna A low-latitude grassland characterized by tall forms.

scale [of a map] The relationship between length measured on a map and the actual distance represented on Earth.

scarp A steep escarpment; nearly vertical cliff.

scattering A change in direction, but not in wavelength, of light waves.

schist One of the most common metamorphic rocks in which the foliations are very narrow.

scree See **talus**.

sea breeze A wind that blows from the sea toward the land, usually during the day.

seafloor spreading The pulling apart of lithospheric plates to permit the rise of deep-seated magma to Earth's surface in midocean ridges.

seawall A strong wall or embankment built along the shore to act as a breakwater.

secondary consumer Animals that eat other animals, as the second and further stages in a food pyramid or chain.

second-order relief Major mountain systems and other extensive surface formations of subcontinental extent.

sediment Small particles of rock debris or organic material deposited by water, wind, or ice.

sediment budget [of a beach] The balance between the sediment being deposited on a beach and the sediment that is being transported away from a beach.

sedimentary rock Rock formed of sediment that is consolidated by the combination of pressure and cementation.

seep (the noun) A small spring or pool where liquid from the ground has oozed to the surface.

seep (the verb) To ooze gradually.

seif (longitudinal dune) Long, narrow desert dunes that usually occur in multiplicity and in parallel arrangement.

seismic sea wave See **tsunami**.

seismograph Instrument used to measure and record earthquakes.

selva (tropical rainforest) A distinctive assemblage of tropical vegetation that is dominated by a great variety of tall, high-crowned trees.

semiarid Characterized by a small amount of annual precipitation (generally between 25 and 50 centimeters [10 and 20 inches]).

sensible temperature A concept of the relative temperature that is sensed by a person's body.

separates The size groups within the standard classification of soil particle sizes.

September equinox One of two days of the year when the vertical rays of the Sun strike the equator; every location on Earth has equal day and night; occurs on or about September 22nd each year.

seral A stage that is not the final stage in an ecological succession.

shale A common mechanically accumulated sedimentary rock composed of silt and clay.

sheet erosion The transportation by water flowing across the surface as a thin sheet of material already loosened by splash erosion.

shield volcanoes Volcanoes built up in a lengthy outpouring of very fluid basaltic lava. Shield volcanoes are broad mountains with gentle slopes.

shortwave radiation Wavelengths of radiation emitted by the Sun, especially ultraviolet, visible, and short infrared radiation.

shrub Woody, low-growing perennial plant.

shrubland Plant association dominated by relatively short woody plants.

sial A discontinuous igneous rock layer apparently underlying only the continental masses, where it sits as immense bodies of rock embedded in the sima beneath. "Sial" is named for its common constituents of silica and aluminum.

sidereal day A complete rotation of Earth with respect to the stars (23 hours, 56 minutes, and 4.099 seconds).

silica Silicon dioxide (SiO_2) in any of several mineral forms.

silicate mineral (silicates) A category of minerals composed of silicon and oxygen combined with another element or elements.

sill A long, thin intrusive body that is formed when magma is forced between parallel layers of preexisting rock to solidify eventually in a sheet.

sima An igneous rock layer that underlies the ocean basins and portions of some continents. "Sima" is named for its two most prominent mineral compounds, silica and magnesium.

sinkhole (doline) A small, rounded depression that is formed by the dissolution of surface limestone, typically at joint intersections.

sinuous channel pattern (sinuous stream channel) Gently curving or winding stream channel pattern.

slate Metamorphosed shale.

sleet Small raindrops that freeze during descent.

slip face Steeper leeward side of a sand dune.

slump A slope collapse with a backward rotation.

small circle Circle on a globe formed by the intersection of Earth's surface with any plane that does not pass through Earth's center.

small-scale map A map whose scale is a relatively small representative fraction and therefore shows a large portion of Earth's surface in limited detail.

snow Solid precipitation in the form of ice crystals, small pellets, or flakes, which is formed by the direct conversion of water vapor into ice.

snowline The elevation above which some winter snow is able to persist throughout the year.

softwoods Gymnosperm trees; nearly all are needleleaved evergreens with wood of simple cellular structure but not always soft.

soil An infinitely varying mixture of weathered mineral particles, decaying organic matter, living organisms, gases, and liquid solutions. Soil is that part of the outer "skin" of Earth occupied by plant roots.

soil order The highest (most general) level of soil classification in the Soil Taxonomy.

soil profile A vertical cross section from Earth's surface down through the soil layers into the parent material beneath.

Soil Taxonomy The system of soil classification currently in use in the United States. It is genetic in nature and focuses on the existing properties of the soil rather than on environment, genesis, or the properties it would possess under virgin conditions.

soil water Water found in the phreatic zone.

soil–water balance The relationship between gain, loss, and storage of soil water.

soil–water budget An accounting that demonstrates the variation of the soil–water balance over a period of time.

solar altitude Angle of the Sun above the horizon.

solar constant The fairly constant amount of solar insolation received at the top of the atmosphere, about 1372 watts per square meter (W/m^2) or slightly less than 2 calories per square centimeter per minute, or 2 langleys per minute.

solar day A complete rotation of Earth with respect to the Sun (24 hours).

solifluction A special form of soil creep in tundra areas that produces a distinctive surface appearance. During the summer the near-surface portion of the ground thaws, but the meltwater cannot percolate deeper because of the permafrost below. The spaces between the soil particles become saturated, and the heavy surface material sags slowly downslope.

solstice One of those two times of the year in which the Sun's perpendicular rays hit the northernmost or southernmost latitudes (23.5°) reached during Earth's cycle of revolution.

solum The true soil that includes only the top four horizons: O, the organic surface layer; A, the topsoil; E, the eluvial layer; and B, the subsoil.

sonar Sound navigation and ranging.

source region (air mass source region) A part of Earth's surface that is particularly suited to generate air masses.

South Pole Latitude of 90° south.

Southern Oscillation Periodic seesaw of atmospheric pressure in the tropical southern Pacific Ocean basin; associated with El Niño. Also see **El Niño/Southern Oscillation**.

species The major subdivision of a genus, regarded as the basic category of biological taxonomic classification.

specific heat The amount of energy required to raise the temperature of 1 gram of a substance by 1°C.

specific humidity A direct measure of water-vapor content expressed as the mass of water vapor in a given mass of air (grams of vapor/kilograms of air).

speleothem A feature formed by precipitated deposits of minerals on the wall, floor, or roof of a cave.

spit A linear deposit of marine sediment that is attached to the land at one or both ends.

splash erosion The direct collision of a raindrop with the ground, which blasts fine particles upward and outward, shifting them a few millimeters laterally.

Spodosol A soil order characterized by the occurrence of a spodic subsurface horizon, which is an illuvial layer where organic matter and aluminum accumulate, and which has a dark, sometimes reddish, color.

spring A stream of surface water that emerges from the ground.

spring tide A time of maximum tide that occurs as a result of the alignment of Sun, Moon, and Earth.

squall line A line of intense thunderstorms.

stable [air] Air that rises only if forced.

stalactite A pendant structure hanging downward from a cavern's roof.

stalagmite A projecting structure growing upward from a cavern's floor.

stationary front The common boundary between two air masses in a situation in which neither air mass displaces the other.

statute mile A unit of distance on land equal to 5280 feet or 1760 yards (1693 meters).

steppe A plant association dominated by short grasses and bunchgrasses of the midlatitudes.

stock A small body of igneous rock intruded into older rock, amorphous in shape and indefinite in depth.

storm surge A surge of wind-driven water as much as 8 meters (25 feet) above normal tide level, which occurs when a hurricane pounds into a shoreline.

straight channel pattern A straight or nearly straight stream channel; unusual except over relatively short distances.

strata Distinct layers of sediment.

stratified drift Drift that was sorted as it was carried along by the flowing glacial meltwater.

stratiform cloud A cloud form characterized by clouds that appear as grayish sheets or layers that cover most or all of the sky, rarely being broken into individual cloud units.

stratocumulus Low clouds, usually below 2 kilometers (6500 feet), which sometimes occur as individual clouds but more often appear as a general overcast.

stratopause The top of the stratosphere elevation, about 48 kilometers (30 miles), where maximum temperature is reached.

stratosphere Atmospheric layer directly above the troposphere.

stratus clouds Low clouds, usually below 2 kilometers (6500 feet), which sometimes occur as individual clouds but more often appear as a general overcast.

stream capture (stream piracy) An event where a portion of the flow of one stream is diverted into that of another by natural processes.

streamflow Channeled movement of water along a valley bottom.

stream load Solid matter carried by a stream.

stream order Concept that describes the hierarchy of a drainage network.

stream rejuvenation When a stream gains downcutting ability, usually through regional tectonic uplift.

stream terrace Remnant of a previous valley floodplain of a rejuvenated stream.

striations Marks in a bedrock surface produced by the direct impact of glacial ice and its load of abrasive debris, which parallel the direction of ice movement.

strike-slip fault A fault produced by shearing, with adjacent blocks being displaced laterally with respect to one another. The movement is entirely horizontal.

stripped plain A flattish erosional platform where the scarp edge is absent or relatively inconspicuous.

structure Nature, arrangement, and orientation of the materials.

subaerial Occurring or forming on Earth's surface.

subarctic climate Severe midlatitude climate found in high latitude continental interiors, characterized by very cold winters and an extreme annual temperature range.

subartesian well The free flow that results when a well is drilled from the surface down into a confined aquifer and which requires artificial pumping to raise the water to the surface because the confining pressure forces the water only partway up the well shaft.

subduction Descent of the edge of an oceanic lithospheric plate under the edge of an adjoining plate.

sublimation The process by which water vapor is converted directly to ice, or vice versa.

subpolar low A zone of low pressure that is situated at about 50° to 60° of latitude in both Northern and Southern hemispheres (also referred to as the polar front).

subsequent stream Stream that develops along zones of structural weakness.

subsidence Large-scale downward movement of air.

subsidence inversion A temperature inversion that occurs well above Earth's surface as a result of air sinking from above.

subtropical Bordering on the tropics; between tropical and temperate regions.

subtropical gyres The closed-loop pattern of surface ocean currents around the margins of the major ocean basins; the flow is clockwise in the Northern Hemisphere and counterclockwise in the Southern Hemisphere.

subtropical desert climate A hot desert climate; generally found in subtropical latitudes, especially on the western sides of continents.

subtropical high (STH) Large, semipermanent, high-pressure cells centered at about 30° latitude over the oceans, which have average diameters of 3200 kilometers (2000 miles) and are usually elongated east–west.

subtropical jet stream Upper troposphere jet stream typically found at a latitude of about 30° N & S at an elevation of 15 kilometers (50,000 feet).

subtropical steppe climate A hot semiarid climate found in the subtropics.

succulents Plants that have fleshy stems that store water.

sulfate A category of minerals composed of sulfur and oxygen, combined with another element or elements.

sulfide A category of minerals composed of sulfur, combined with another element or elements.

summer solstice The dates that represent the most poleward extent of the perpendicular rays of the Sun. (Northern Hemisphere—23.5° N on about June 21; Southern Hemisphere—23.5° S on about December 21).

supercooled water Water that persists in liquid form at temperatures below freezing.

superimposed drainage system Stream system that has incised into an underlying structure.

supersaturated [air] Air in which the relative humidity is greater than 100 percent but condensation is not taking place.

surf The swell of the sea that breaks upon a reef or a shore.

surface tension Because of electrical polarity, liquid water molecules tend to stick together—a thin "skin" of molecules forms on the surface of liquid water causing it to "bead."

suspended load The very fine particles of clay and silt that are in suspension and move along with the flow of water without ever touching the streambed.

swallow hole The distinct opening at the bottom of some sinks through which surface drainage can pour directly into an underground channel.

swamp A flattish surface area that is submerged in water at least part of the time but is shallow enough to permit the growth of water-tolerant plants—predominantly trees.

swash The cascading forward motion of a breaking wave that rushes up the beach.

swell A water wave, usually produced by stormy conditions, that can travel enormous distances away from the source of the disturbance.

symbiosis A mutually beneficial relationship between two organisms.

syncline A simple downfold in the rock structure.

taiga (boreal forest) The great northern coniferous forest.

talus (scree) Pieces of weathered rock, of various sizes, that fall directly downslope.

talus cone Sloping, cone-shaped heaps of dislodged talus.

talus slope (talus apron) The fragments of rocks (talus) that accumulate relatively uniformly along the base of the slope.

tarn Small lake in the shallow excavated depression of rock benches of a glacial trough or cirque.

taxonomy The science of classification.

tectonic activity Crustal movements of various kinds.

teleconnection The coupling or relationship of weather and/or oceanic events in one part of the world with those in another.

temperature Description of the average kinetic energy of the molecules in a substance; the more vigorous the jiggling of the molecules (and therefore the greater the internal kinetic energy), the higher the temperature of a substance; in popular terms, a measure of the degree of hotness or coldness of a substance.

temperature inversion A situation in which temperature increases upward and the normal condition is inverted.

terminal moraine A glacial deposit that builds up at the outermost extent of ice advance.

terracettes A complicated terracing effect, resembling a network of faint trails, which is produced by grazing animals on hillside where soil creep is at work; usually seen on steep grassy slopes.

terrane A mass of lithosphere that has become accreted to a lithospheric plate margin with different lithologic characteristics from those of the terrane; often comprised of lithosphere that is too buoyant to subduct.

terrestrial Growing or living on the ground.

terrestrial radiation Longwave radiation emitted by Earth's surface or atmosphere.

thalweg A line connecting the deepest points of a stream channel.

thermal energy See **heat.**

thermal high High pressure cell associated with cold surface conditions.

thermal infrared radiation (thermal IR) The middle and far infrared part of the electromagnetic spectrum.

thermal layers [of atmosphere] Layers of the atmosphere largely defined by differences in thermal characteristics.

thermal low Low pressure cell associated with warm surface conditions.

thermocline The boundary between near-surface and cold deep ocean waters.

thermohaline circulation Slow circulation of deep ocean water because of differences in water density that arise from differences in salinity and temperature.

thermometer An instrument designed for the measurement of temperature.

thermosphere The highest recognized thermal layer in the atmosphere, above the mesopause, where temperature remains relatively uniform for several kilometers and then increases continually with height.

third-order relief Specific landform complexes of lesser extent and generally of smaller size than those of the second order.

thrust fault See **overthrust fault.**

thunder The sound that results from the shock wave produced by the instantaneous expansion of air that is abruptly heated by a lightning bolt.

thunderstorm A relatively violent convective storm accompanied by thunder and lightning.

tidal bore A wall of seawater several centimeters to several meters in height that rushes up a river as the result of enormous tidal inflow.

tidal range The vertical difference in elevation between high and low tide.

tides The rise and fall of the coastal water levels caused by the alternate increasing and decreasing gravitational pull of the Moon and the Sun on varying parts of Earth's surface.

till Rock debris that is deposited directly by moving or melting ice, with no meltwater flow or redeposition involved.

till plain An irregularly undulating surface of broad, low rises and shallow depressions produced by the uneven deposition of glacial till.

tilted fault block mountain See **fault-block mountain**.

tombolo A spit formed by sand deposition of waves converging in two directions on the landward side of a nearshore island, so that a spit connects the island to the land.

topography Surface configuration of Earth.

tornado A localized cyclonic low-pressure cell surrounded by a whirling cylinder of violent wind; characterized by a funnel cloud extending below a cumulonimbus cloud.

tower karst Tall, steep-sided hills in an area of karst topography.

traction Process in which coarse particles are rolled or slid along the streambed.

trade winds The major easterly wind system of the tropics, issuing from the equatorward sides of the subtropical highs and diverging toward the west and toward the equator.

transform [plate] boundary Two plates slipping past one another laterally.

transmission The ability of a medium to allow electromagnetic waves to pass through it.

transpiration The transfer of moisture from plant leaves to the atmosphere.

transverse dune A crescent-shaped dune that has convex sides facing the prevailing direction of wind and which occurs where the supply of sand is great. The crest is perpendicular to the wind vector and aligned in parallel waves across the land.

travertine Massive accumulation of calcium carbonate.

treeline The elevation above (or below) sea level, in which trees do not grow.

trellis drainage pattern A drainage pattern that is usually developed on alternating bands of hard and soft strata, with long parallel subsequent streams linked by short, right-angled segments and joined by short tributaries.

tropical cyclone A storm most significantly affecting the tropics and subtropics, which is intense, revolving, rain-drenched, migratory, destructive, and erratic. Such a storm system consists of a prominent low-pressure center that is essentially circular in shape and has a steep pressure gradient outward from the center. When wind speed reaches 64 knots, they are called hurricanes in North America and the Caribbean.

tropical depression By international agreement, an incipient tropical cyclone with winds not exceeding 33 knots.

tropical disturbance A term used by the National Weather Service for a cyclonic wind system in the tropics that is in its formative stage.

tropical monsoon climate Tropical humid climate with a pronounced winter dry season and a very wet summer rainy season; associated with monsoon wind pattern.

tropical rainforest See **selva**.

tropical savanna climate Tropical humid climate with a dry winter season and a moderately wet summer season; associated with the seasonal migration of the ITCZ.

tropical storm By international agreement, an incipient tropical cyclone with winds between 34 and 63 knots.

tropical wet climate Tropical humid climate that is wet all year; usually under the influence of the ITCZ all year.

tropical year The amount of time it takes for Earth to revolve completely around the Sun (365.25 days).

Tropic of Cancer The parallel of 23.5° north latitude, which marks the northernmost location reached by the vertical rays of the Sun in the annual cycle of Earth's revolution.

Tropic of Capricorn The parallel of 23.5° south latitude, which marks the southernmost location reached by the vertical rays of the Sun in the annual cycle of Earth's revolution.

tropopause A transition zone at the top of the troposphere, where temperature ceases to decrease with height.

troposphere The lowest thermal layer of the atmosphere, in which temperature decreases with height.

trough Linear or elongated band of relatively low atmospheric pressure.

true (geographic) north The actual direction toward the North Pole from any point, measured along the meridian that passes through that point.

tsunami Very long wavelength oceanic wave generated by submarine earthquake, landslide, or volcanic eruption; also called seismic sea wave.

tufa (sinter) Porous accumulations of calcium carbonate.

tundra A complex mix of very low-growing plants, including grasses, forbs, dwarf shrubs, mosses, and lichens, but no trees. Tundra occurs only in the perennially cold climates of high latitudes or high altitudes.

tundra climate Polar climate in which no month of the year has an average temperature above 10°C (50°F).

turbulent flow The general downstream movement that is interrupted by continuous irregularities in direction and speed, producing momentary currents that can move in any direction, including upward.

typhoon The term used for tropical cyclones affecting the western North Pacific region.

ubac slope A slope oriented so that sunlight strikes it at a low angle and hence is much less effective in heating and evaporating than on the adret slope, thus producing more luxuriant vegetation of a richer diversity.

Ultisol A soil order similar to Alfisols, but more thoroughly weathered and more completely leached of bases.

ultraviolet (UV) radiation Electromagnetic radiation in the wavelength range of 0.1 to 0.4 micrometers.

ungulates Hoofed mammals.

uniformitarianism The concept that the present is the key to the past in geomorphic processes. The processes now operating have also operated in the same way in the past.

Universal Time Coordinated (UTC) or Coordinated Universal Time The world time standard reference; previously known as Greenwich mean time (GMT).

unstable [air] Air that rises without being forced.

updraft Small-scale upward movement of air.

upslope fog Condensation that occurs when humid air is caused to ascend a topographic slope and consequently cools adiabatically.

upwelling Cold, deep ocean water that rises to the surface where wind patterns deflect surface water away from the coast; especially common along the west coasts of continents in the subtropics and midlatitudes.

urban heat island Higher temperatures in the air over a city than over adjacent rural areas.

uvala A compound doline or chain of intersecting dolines.

vadose zone (zone of aeration) The topmost hydrologic zone within the ground, which contains a fluctuating amount of moisture (soil water) in the pore spaces of the soil (or soil and rock).

valley That portion of the total terrain in which a drainage system is clearly established.

valley breeze Upslope breeze up a mountain due to heating of air on its slopes during the day.

valley glacier A long, narrow feature resembling a river of ice, which spills out of its originating basins and flows down-valley.

valley train A lengthy deposit of glaciofluvial alluvium confined to a valley bottom beyond the outwash plain.

vapor pressure The pressure exerted by water vapor in the atmosphere.

vein Small igneous intrusions, usually with vertical orientation.

verbal scale [of a map] Scale of a map stated in words; also called a word scale.

vernal equinox The spring equinox that occurs about March 20 in the Northern Hemisphere and September 22 in the Southern Hemisphere.

vertebrates Animals that have a backbone that protects their spinal cord—fishes, amphibians, reptiles, birds, and mammals.

vertical zonation The horizontal layering of different plant associations on a mountainside or hillside.

Vertisol A soil order comprising a specialized type of soil that contains a large quantity of clay and has an exceptional capacity for absorbing water. An alternation of wetting and drying, expansion and contraction, produces a churning effect that mixes the soil constituents, inhibits the development of horizons, and may even cause minor irregularities in the surface of the land.

visible light Waves in the electromagnetic spectrum in the narrow band between about 0.4 and 0.7 micrometers in length; wavelengths of electromagnetic radiation to which the human eye is sensitive.

volcanic ash Fine particles of pyroclastic material blown out of a volcanic vent.

volcanic island arc Chain of volcanic islands associated with an oceanic plate–oceanic plate subduction zone.

volcanic mudflow A fast-moving, muddy flow of volcanic ash and rock fragments; also called a lahar.

volcanic neck Small, sharp spire that rises abruptly above the surrounding land. It represents the pipe or throat of an old volcano, filled with solidified lava after its final eruption. The less resistant material that makes up the cone is eroded, leaving the harder, lava-choked neck as a remnant.

volcanic rock Igneous rock formed on the surface of Earth; also called extrusive rock.

volcano A conical mountain or hill from which extrusive material is ejected.

vulcanism General term that refers to movement of magma from the interior of Earth to or near the surface.

wadi The normally dry beds of an intermittent stream. This term is used in the Sahara Desert region.

Walker Circulation General circuit of air flow in the southern tropical Pacific Ocean; warm air rises in the western side of the basin (in the updrafts of the ITCZ), flows aloft to the east where it descends into the subtropical high off the west coast of South America; the air then flows back to the west in the surface trade winds. Named for the British meteorologist Gilbert Walker (1868–1958) who first described this circumstance.

warm front The leading edge of an advancing warm air mass.

waterfall Abrupt descent of a stream over a prominent knickpoint.

waterless zone The fifth and lowermost hydrologic zone that generally begins several kilometers or miles beneath the land surface and is characterized by the lack of water in pore spaces due to the great pressure and density of the rock.

waterspout A funnel cloud in contact with the ocean or a large lake; similar to a weak tornado over water.

watershed See **drainage basin**.

water table The top of the saturated zone within the ground.

water vapor The gaseous state of moisture.

wave amplitude One-half the wave height; that is, the vertical distance from still-water level, either upward to the crest or downward to the trough.

wave-built terrace Submarine deposit of sand at the outer margin of an erosional platform or bench.

wave crest Highest point of a wave.

wave-cut notch An indentation in a sea cliff cut at water level by the combined effects of hydraulic pounding, abrasion, pneumatic push, and solution action.

wave-cut platform Gently sloping, wave-eroded bedrock platform that develops just below sea level; common where coastal cliff is being worn back by wave action; also called wave-cut bench.

wave height The vertical distance from wave crest to trough.

wavelength The horizontal distance from wave crest to crest or from trough to trough.

wave of oscillation Motion of wave in which the individual particles of the medium (such as water) make a circular orbit as the wave form passes through.

wave of translation The horizontal motion produced when a wave reaches shallow water and finally "breaks" on the shore.

wave refraction Phenomenon whereby waves change their directional trend as they approach a shoreline.

wave trough Lowest part of a wave.

weather The short-term atmospheric conditions for a given time and a specific area.

weathering The physical and chemical disintegration of rock that is exposed to the weather.

westerlies The great wind system of the midlatitudes that flows basically from west to east around the world in the latitudinal zone between about 30° and 60° both north and south of the equator.

wetland Landscape characterized by shallow, standing water all or most of the year, with vegetation rising above the water level.

wilting point The point at which plants are no longer able to extract moisture from the soil because the capillary water is all used up or evaporated.

wind Horizontal air movement.

wind chill Description of what cold weather feels like at various combinations of low temperature and high wind.

wind shear (vertical wind shear) Significant change in wind direction or speed in the vertical dimension.

winter solstice The dates at which the most poleward extent of the perpendicular rays of the Sun occur in the opposite hemisphere.

woodland Tree-dominated plant association in which the trees are spaced more widely apart than those of forests and do not have interlacing canopies.

woody plants Plants that have stems composed of hard fibrous material—mostly trees and shrubs.

word scale [of a map] Scale of a map stated in words.

xerophytic adaptations Plants that are structurally adapted to withstand protracted dry conditions.

yazoo stream A tributary unable to enter the main stream because of natural levees along the main stream.

zone of aeration (vadose zone) The topmost hydrologic zone within the ground, which contains a fluctuating amount of moisture (soil water) in the pore spaces of the soil (or soil and rock).

zone of confined water The third hydrologic zone below the surface of the ground, which contains one or more permeable rock layers (aquifers) into which water can infiltrate and is separated from the zone of saturation by impermeable layers.

zone of saturation (phreatic zone) The second hydrologic zone below the surface of the ground, whose uppermost boundary is the water table. The pore spaces and cracks in the bedrock and the regolith of this zone are fully saturated.

zoogeographic regions Division of land areas of the world into major realms with characteristic fauna.

Index

Note: Pages in *italic* locate figures and tables. Page numbers followed by an *n* are for footnotes.

California Field Guides

Edited By

Darrel Hess
City College of San Francisco

To Accompany the California Edition of *Physical Geography,*
***A Landscape Appreciation*, Ninth Edition**

The California Cascades: Lassen Volcanic National Park and Mount Shasta

Les Rowntree, University of California, Berkeley

Introduction

The Cascade Range is composed of volcanic landforms stretching from southern British Columbia to northern California and is part of the **Pacific Ring of Fire** circumscribing the Pacific Basin. At least six North American Cascade Range volcanoes are considered active because of eruptions during historical time and only a few are characterized as geologically extinct. While the 1980 Mount St. Helens eruption in southern Washington State is the most recent, major Cascade volcanoes such as Mount Baker, Mount Rainier and Mount Shasta are active enough to be considered hazardous, and therefore are monitored constantly for a possible eruption.

Tectonically, the Cascade Range is linked to the **convergent boundary** between the North American, Gorda, and Juan de Fuca Plates just offshore from northern California, Oregon, Washington, and British Columbia (see textbook Figure 14-10).

In northern California the Cascade geologic province is expressed in a wide variety of volcanic landforms, ranging from undulating lava flows and small cinder cones to the major composite volcano of Mount Shasta and the lava dome of Lassen Peak. California's Cascade Range can be experienced readily in a two- or, better, three-day field trip to the area.

Location

Both Lassen Volcanic National Park and Mount Shasta are accessed from Interstate 5 (I-5) in northern California. The Shasta area, for example, is 220 miles north of Sacramento, or a bit over three hours driving time. Count on just over four hours of driving time from the San Francisco Bay Area.

Campgrounds abound in Lassen Park itself, along California Highway 89 to the north, and even in the Shasta area. Beds and other creature comforts are available in the numerous motels and cafes of Mt. Shasta City, a picturesque small town nestled at the western flanks of the mountain with its own unique social geography.

Visiting this area is best done in late spring, summer, or early autumn since Highway 89 through Lassen Park closes with the first significant snowfall, which can come in late October, and remains closed until snowplows clear the road in May or early June.

Background

Formation of Lassen Peak: The foundation for Lassen Peak was laid down half a million years ago with the formation of Mount Tehama, an 11,000-foot (3,350 m) high **composite volcano** (or *stratovolcano*; see textbook Figure 14-29d). Later, around 350,000 years ago, following a series of violent eruptions, Mount Tehama collapsed into itself, forming a large **caldera** (see textbook Figure 14-36). Brokeoff Mountain, the second highest peak in the area at 9,235 feet (2,815 m), is one of the best preserved remnants of ancient Mount Tehama.

Then, roughly 27,000 years ago, a **lava dome** (or **plug dome;** see textbook Figure 14-29c) with an active vent pushed its way through the northeastern portion of the caldera to become the current

Figure FG1-1   Lassen Peak from Lake Helen near field guide Site 1, Stop 2. Eagle Peak is the low peak on the left. *(Darrel Hess photo.)*

10,457-foot (3,187 m) high Lassen Peak (Figure FG1-1). This new mountain was subsequently modified by late **Pleistocene** glaciation. Today, though, unlike on Mount Shasta, there are no living glaciers on the mountain.

Volcanic activity has continued into the present with smaller lava domes (such as Chaos Crags) appearing in the last eleven hundred years. Cinder Cone in the northeast corner of the Park reportedly appeared only in the mid-eighteenth century. More recently, Lassen Peak itself erupted in 1914 and remained active for several years. This activity was punctuated by violent eruptions on May 19 and 22, 1915, which created a new crater on the peak and also sent a superheated **volcanic mudflow (lahar)** and **pyroclastic flow** down the northern flank of the mountain to create the Devastated Area.

Formation of Mount Shasta: Mount Shasta, a composite volcano, like Lassen Peak was built upon the remnants of a collapsed (yet unnamed) predecessor dating back 600,000 years. The modern mountain has been formed within the past 200,000 years from four separate volcanic vents. Lava and **pyroclastic** material from numerous eruptions have coalesced to form the present day 14,160-foot (4,316 m) high Mount Shasta.

Remnants of these four vents can be seen near the mountain's summit. The Sargents Ridge cone, southeast of the summit, and dated to 200,000 years ago, is the oldest. Part of its crater forms Thumb Rock, a prominent feature at the top of Avalanche Gulch (see Bunny Flat, Site 2, Stop 3). The Misery Hill cone is next oldest, dating back to 30,000 to 50,000 years ago, and makes up a large part of the upper mountain. The Shastina cone actually forms a separate peak of 12,330 feet (3,758 m) attached to the western flank of Mount Shasta, and volcanologists date its origin back 9,000 years. The fourth and most recent vent is Hotlum on the northeastern side of the mountain, and the dome that fills its crater forms the current summit of Mount Shasta. Although the Hotlum vent originated at the same time as Shastina, most of the cone has grown within the last 6,000 years. Even more recently, the Hotlum cone was responsible for an explosion about 200 years ago when it exhaled an ash cloud that covered the northern flanks of the mountain.

Mount Shasta's Growing Glaciers: There are at least seven living glaciers on Mount Shasta's flanks, with three more small ice fields whose status is debated. For our purposes we'll stick with those glaciers recognized by the U.S. Geological Survey in their 1986 mapping of the mountain. Most of the glaciers are on the colder, more shadowed north side of the mountain, and on a topographic map are, from west to east: Whitney—the longest glacier; Bolam; Hotlum—the largest in terms of area and volume; Wintun; Watkins; Konwakiton; and Mud Creek.

Scientists believe the larger Pleistocene glaciers that shaped so much of Mount Shasta's landscape melted away completely during the early Holocene (10,000 years ago to present) warming, and that the current glaciers formed during the *Little Ice Age* (~1550-1850 AD), when global climates cooled for several centuries.

Interestingly enough, Mount Shasta's five main glaciers have grown during the last several decades, unlike most of the world's glaciers, which have retreated as the global climate has warmed. Several explanations are offered to account for the growth of Mount Shasta's glaciers, including the fact that the mountain makes is own weather because of its isolation from other mountain ranges; a northward shift of Pacific storm tracks, bringing more snow to Mount Shasta; the warming of the Pacific Ocean, which adds more moisture to the storms visiting northern California—or a combination of all or some of those various factors.

Site Descriptions

Approaching the area from the south on Interstate 5, a loop trip to see Lassen Peak and Mount Shasta can be made by taking California Highway 36 east from Red Bluff to California Highway 89, which then enters Lassen Volcanic National Park at the southwest entrance, traverses the park close to Lassen Peak, then exits at the northern Park boundary near Manzanita Lake. Continuing northwest on Highway 89 for 106 miles (170 km) brings one to Mt. Shasta City at the foot of this spectacular volcano.

Site 1—Lassen Volcanic National Park

Driving California Highway 89 through Lassen Volcanic National Park is an extraordinary introduction to an array of volcanic processes and landforms and will occupy at least one full day (Figure FG1-2). As at all National Parks, there is an entrance fee, so be prepared. A number of the trails, exhibits and campgrounds in the Park are wheelchair accessible—check the Park Web site on page F-8 for details.

When entering the Park at the southwestern entrance, your first stop should be at the new Kohm Yah-mah-nee Visitor Center that opened in October 2008; the Center's name comes from the local Native American tribe's name for "snow mountain." There, visitors can see displays about the physical and cultural geography of the region, watch films and videos, and buy books and maps that will guide one through the Park.

Here are just a few highlights of the Highway 89 drive across the Park:

Stop 1—Sulphur Works (40°26'55"N, 121°32'08"W): The Sulfur Works are 1.1 miles from the southwest entrance to the Park. A one-quarter-mile self-guided nature trail leads through this active hydrothermal area. Because it's one of the most visited areas in the Park, try for an early morning or early evening visit. Boardwalks provide safe passage around hydrothermal features thought to be remains of the central vent of ancient Mount Tehama. **Fumaroles,** boiling **hot springs** (see textbook Figure 17-9), and mudpots abound.

Stop 2—Bumpass Hell Trailhead (40°28'27"N, 121°30'21"W): About 5.7 miles from the southwest Park entrance is the parking area for Bumpass Hell. This is the largest of the Park's hydrothermal areas and in sixteen acres one will find an array of steaming fumaroles, gurgling mud pots, and boiling hot springs. Again, the crowds can be thick and the parking lot packed, so try for an early or late visit. The main hydrothermal area is 1.4 miles from the trailhead. Bumpass Hell is the result of fissures that connect to volcanic heat three miles (4.8 km) deep.

Stop 3—Lassen Peak Trailhead (40°25'27"N, 121°30'20"W): The trailhead for Lassen Peak is 6.9 miles from the southwest entrance to the Park. The 2.5-mile trail begins at 8,500 feet (2,590 m), and zigzags to the 10,457-foot summit of Lassen Peak. This is another popular trail, so don't expect to be alone, although because of altitude and steepness many hikers drop by the wayside before the halfway point. At about 9,200 feet (2,800 m), you pass the last of the dwarf Mountain Hemlocks *(Tsuga mertensiana)* and enter into the alpine zone.

From the summit one can better visualize ancient Mount Tehama, whose summit once stood about two miles south-southwest. Only parts of Tehama's flanks can be seen, primarily Brokeoff Mountain about four miles southwest and Mount Diller, the long sloping ridge just north of Brokeoff.

Stop 4—Devastated Area Interpretive Trail (40°30'56"N, 121°27'55"W): This 0.4-mile wheelchair-accessible trail loop begins 18.7 miles from the Park's southwest entrance.

On May 19, 1915, hot lava spilled over the crater rim of Lassen Peak onto a thick snowfield layered with volcanic ash from previous minor eruptions, creating a slow-moving mudflow or lahar down the northeast slope of the mountain. Three days later, a massive eruption sent a blast of superheated air and ash (pyroclastic flow) down the same path, leveling a swath of forest one mile wide and three miles long. Thousands of downed evergreen trees were blown over like matchsticks, all pointing away from the source of the blast. Although the Devastated Area has been healing for almost a century, this is still a vivid portrait of nature's power of destruction (Figure FG1-3).

▲ **Figure FG1-2** Regional map of Lassen Volcanic National Park showing Site 1 field guide stops.

▲ **Figure FG1-3** The northeastern side of Lassen Peak showing the mature forest in the foreground before the eruptions of 1915 (left). The Devastated Area after the eruptions of May 1915 (right). The large boulder in the foreground can still be seen on the Devastated Area Interpretive Trail at Site 1, Stop 4. *(Photographs courtesy of the National Park Service.)*

Site 2—Mount Shasta

To reach the Mount Shasta area, take the Mt. Shasta City central exit off I-5 and head east on West Lake Street into Mt. Shasta City (Figure FG1-4). Continue east toward Mount Shasta itself, passing through several stoplights; after crossing North Mt. Shasta Boulevard—the town's main street—West Lake Street changes to East Lake Street. Continue several blocks until East Lake Street dead-ends into North Washington Drive; turn left and head north, passing Mt. Shasta High School on your right. At this point North Washington Drive turns into the Everitt Memorial Highway, also signed Siskiyou County Route A-10.

This 15.2-mile highway goes up the southern flank of Mount Shasta, taking you from 3,500 feet (1,065 m) to almost 8,000 feet (2,440 m). Not only does it provide a spectacular close-up of Mount Shasta itself, but it also provides a fascinating look at the biogeography of the mountain as one travels from dry chaparral scrub lands at the lower elevations, into coniferous forests between 4,000 and 7,000 feet (1,220–2,130 m), then terminating at the treeline with alpine meadows at 8,000 feet above sea level.

Stop 1 (rolling stop)—The Everitt Memorial Highway from Mt. Shasta City (41°19′33″N, 122°18′23″W): Going up the mountain, look for small U.S. Forest Service signs on the right-hand side that provide elevation and mileage information.

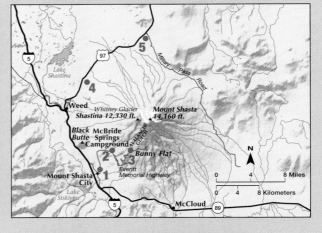

▲ **Figure FG1-4** Regional map of Mount Shasta area showing Site 2 field guide stops.

Before going too far up the road, pull over to the right shoulder and stop to ponder the landscape (Figure FG1-5). Most impressive, of course, is snow-covered Mount Shasta itself, rising before you to 14,162 feet, with Shastina, the more recent volcanic cone, to the left. On the north flank of Mount Shasta, in the gap between it and Shastina, you can see the head of Whitney Glacier. Note also, on the summit of Mount Shasta, the several promontories that compose the four different volcanic vents from past eruptions. These will become even more prominent as you travel up the highway and get different views of the summit area.

Figure FG1-5   View of Mount Shasta from Mt. Shasta City at Site 2, Stop 1. *(Les Rowntree photo.)*

Figure FG1-6   Avalanche Gulch on Mount Shasta from Bunny Flat at Site 2, Stop 3. *(Les Rowntree photo.)*

Stop 2—McBride Springs Campground

(41°20′56″N, 122°16′45″W): McBride Springs Campground is about four miles up the highway, on your left, at an elevation of 4,880 feet (1,487 m). This is a good place to get acquainted with the different **coniferous trees** found on Mount Shasta. Between the town of Mt. Shasta and the campground you've passed through an extensive second-growth Ponderosa Pine forest (*Pinus ponderosa; see Field Guide #4—Sierra Nevada via Tioga Pass*, Figure FG4-3). The original old growth was cut for timber in the early part of the twentieth century. Once the forest was gone, different chaparral species expanded into the area. But in 1957, the U.S. Forest Service began planting rows and rows of Ponderosa Pine—note that the trees are in fairly straight lines, giving clue to their heritage as planted seedlings.

But at McBride Springs Campground you'll be leaving the Ponderosa Pine belt and entering into the zone of fir trees, which will continue unbroken to near the treeline when the Whitebark Pine (*Pinus albicaulis*) appears around 7,500 feet (2,300 m). If you have the time and inclination, and are equipped with a good tree identification book, you'll be able to identify the different kinds of firs—Red Fir (*Abies magnifica*), White Fir (*Abies concolor*), and the endemic Shasta Fir (*Abies magnifica var. shastensis*)— as well as the Whitebark Pine.

As you proceed up the mountain, pull over frequently to admire the view beyond Mount Shasta. To the southwest, the jagged rocks of the Castle Crags State Park remind you that you're on the border between the volcanic Cascade Range and the metamorphic rock of the Klamath Massive to the west. Looking to the south you'll see snow-capped Lassen Peak and Mount Brokeoff. Additionally, as you drive higher on Mount Shasta, notice the volcanic ash and pyroclastic material in the roadcuts.

Stop 3—Bunny Flat (41°21′14″N, 122° 14′00″W):

Twelve miles up Everitt Memorial Highway at an elevation of 6,900 feet (2,100 m) is Bunny Flat, the trailhead for hikers and climbers going up the mountain. Even if you're not interested in hiking, the view up Avalanche Gulch to the summit is definitely worth the stop. The Bunny Flat parking area is hard to miss, so find an empty space and park.

From Bunny Flat you look across a small alpine meadow and then up Avalanche Gulch to a glacial **cirque.** Running laterally across the upper cirque are the Red Banks, an outcrop of reddish tephra that separates the cirque from the summit plateau at 12,000 feet (3,660 m). To the right of Red Banks is Thumb Rock, a remnant of the Sargents Ridge cone. The summit itself is barely visible above the left side of Red Banks (Figure FG1-6).

Avalanche Gulch itself was originally carved into the soft volcanic material by a Pleistocene glacier that has long since melted. As noted earlier, today Mount Shasta's largest glaciers are all on the colder north side of the mountain, protected somewhat from the Sun's direct rays.

A short 1.7-mile hike from Bunny Flat will take you up a thousand feet to Horse Camp, the Sierra Club stone shelter, a spring, and solar-composting toilets; this area serves as base camp for climbers and hikers. This hike shouldn't take more than an hour and offers a closer look at the treeline environment of forest and meadows.

From Bunny Flat the road continues for another two miles past Panther Meadows to an old ski area that was wiped out by a huge avalanche in 1978. Although the U.S. Forest Service removed the debris in the 1980s, traces of the avalanche pathway can still be seen in the hundreds of downed and uprooted mature trees; young seedlings that have grown up since 1978 fill the pathway, with older forests on either side.

Stop 4—North Side of Mount Shasta

(41°19'14"N, 122°20'17"W): Mount Shasta's glaciers are best seen by driving around to the north side of the mountain where one can ponder the mountain from a distance on a paved state highway. Get even closer by driving on an unimproved dirt road, or, for the truly adventurous, hike to the foot of several glaciers from remote trailheads.

To get to the north side of the mountain, return to Interstate 5 and drive north (passing close to Black Butte on the route) eight miles to the Central Weed exit. Take this exit through town to U.S. Highway 97, noting your mileage, then drive northeast a couple of miles until you find a safe place to pull off, park, and view Mount Shasta (Figure FG1-7).

From any vantage point along Highway 97 at least three of Shasta's seven glaciers can be seen. From Shastina going east, one sees first, Whitney glacier (the mountain's longest glacier); Bolum glacier; and then Hotlum glacier.

Stop 5 (rolling stop)—An Off-road Adventure: Military Pass Road

(41° 33'32"N, 122°12'33"W): For those driving a high-clearance vehicle (preferably 4WD) and carrying a good supply of food and drink, as well as a good map of the area (namely the *Shasta-Trinity National Forest* map), a closer view of Mount Shasta and its glaciers can be had by turning off Highway 97 onto an unimproved Forest Service dirt road, the Military Pass Road, signed U.S. Forest Service road 43N19. Driving east on Highway 97, this road is about thirteen miles from Weed, and is marked by a small sign on the right.

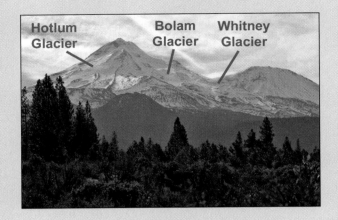

▲ **Figure FG1-7**   North side of Mount Shasta at Site 2, Stop 4, showing glaciers. *(Les Rowntree photo.)*

Since there are dozens of small dirt roads intersecting 43N19, pay close attention to all signs so that you don't end up on a dead-end logging road. And even though the first several miles of Military Pass Road are relatively smooth, later on there are many areas where deep ruts and protruding boulders will require you to creep along at a snail's pace.

But by the time you're four miles in from Highway 97, the views of Shasta and its glaciers will be absolutely spectacular as you get closer and closer to the mountain. Hotlum glacier dominates the view early on, with Wintum glacier becoming visible after eight miles from the paved highway.

For the truly adventurous (and well prepared), turn off Military Pass Road to either the North Gate or Brewer Creek trailheads, then hike to the foot of either glacier. A trail guide is strongly recommended in both cases.

Additional Resources

Textbook:

McKnight, Tom L., and Darrel Hess. *Physical Geography: A Landscape Appreciation*, 9th ed. Upper Saddle River, NJ: Pearson/Prentice Hall, 2008. Chapters 6, 11, 14, 17 and 20.

Further Reading:

Alt, David, and Donald W. Hyndman. *Roadside Geology of Northern and Central California*. Missoula, MT: Mountain Press, 2000.

Selters, Andy, and Michael Zanger. *The Mt. Shasta Book*, 3rd ed. Berkeley, CA: Wilderness Press, 2006.

White, Mike. *Lassen Volcanic National Park: A Complete Hiker's Guide*, 4th ed. Berkeley, CA: Wilderness Press, 2008.

Web Sites:

Lassen Volcanic National Park
http://www.nps.gov/lavo/

Mount Shasta Companion, College of the Siskiyous
http://www.siskiyous.edu/shasta/index.htm

Textbook Page References for Key Terms

caldera *(p. 437)*
cirque *(p. 575)*
composite volcano
  (stratovolcano) *(p. 434)*
coniferous trees *(p. 315)*
convergent boundary *(p. 420)*

fumaroles *(p. 523)*
hot spring *(p. 521)*
lava *(p. 391)*
Pacific Ring of Fire *(p. 424)*
Pleistocene epoch *(p. 555)*
pyroclastic flow *(p. 440)*

pyroclastic material *(p. 391)*
treeline *(p. 321)*
vertical zonation *(p. 320)*
volcanic mudflow (lahar)
  (p. 442)

Field Guide #2

Point Reyes National Seashore

Barbara A. Holzman, San Francisco State University

Introduction

The Point Reyes National Seashore (PRNS) reaches out into the Pacific Ocean, greeting the Gray Whales that pass by on their annual migration between December and April. The geography of the Peninsula's mysterious fog-drenched landscape is characterized by the critical role of geologic time, moving tectonic plates, mild mediterranean climate, and human impact on the land. The Peninsula is defined by its distinct geographic boundaries, most notably the San Andreas Fault and Inverness Ridge that run along its eastern flank. Situated approximately at latitude 38° N, it comprises over 100 square miles of biologically rich diversity not found in the rest of Marin County.

Location

Point Reyes National Seashore is located 35 miles north of San Francisco in Marin County, along the west coast of California. PRNS is located just west of the Coast Highway (California Highway 1). The easiest way to get there from San Francisco is to take U.S. Highway 101 north across the Golden Gate Bridge to the Sir Frances Drake Boulevard exit and head west through several Marin County towns until you reach Highway 1 at Olema (Figure FG2-1). Turn right on Highway 1 and then left onto Bear Valley Road to the Bear Valley Visitor Center. A more winding approach is to drive across the Golden Gate Bridge and take the

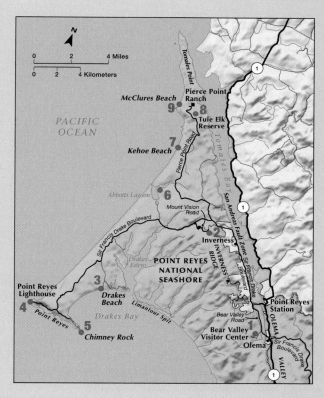

▲ **Figure FG2-1** Regional map of Point Reyes National Seashore showing field guide stops.

exit to Highway 1 and Stinson Beach. From there travel along Highway 1 until you reach Olema and PRNS. The views from this road are fantastic on a clear day, but the road is only two lanes and very winding.

Parts of the PRNS may also be reached by public transportation with Golden Gate Transit and West Marin Stagecoach—see *Additional Resources* on F-17.

Park hours are sunrise to sunset. The Bear Valley Visitor Center is open 9 AM to 5 PM on weekdays and 8 AM to 5 PM on weekends and holidays. The lighthouse and its Visitor Center are open 10 AM to 4:30 PM, Thursday through Monday, but closed during high winds. There is no car camping inside the park, and only a few walk-in camps. If you want to camp at PRNS you must go to the Visitor Center to check in and get your camping permit. Reservations are advised, as camping is very limited and fills quickly. Many exhibits and trails in Point Reyes National Seashore are wheelchair accessible—check the PRNS Web site on F-17 for details.

Background

Point Reyes National Seashore is well known in the San Francisco Bay Area as a place to view coastal forests, a great diversity of spring wildflowers and native plants, and Gray Whales on their migration north and south. What underlies these wonders is as interesting as what lies above them.

Geologic History: The exact origin of the Point Reyes Peninsula is still unclear. It is a geologic anomaly compared to its neighboring inland landscape. Beneath the spiny, tree-covered Inverness Ridge and gradually sloping rangelands lies a very distinct geology that separates the Peninsula from the rest of the nearby California coastline. Like coastal Santa Barbara County to the south and Bodega Head to the north, the Point Reyes Peninsula is a geologic "island." It is part of the northwesterly moving Pacific Plate and separated from the rest of California by the San Andreas Fault system. The fault cuts through Tomales Bay, Olema Valley, and Bolinas Lagoon, passes into the Pacific Ocean, and then returns east and inland just south of San Francisco.

The rest of California and the United States are part of the slower, westerly-moving North American Plate (see textbook Figure 14-16). These plate movements result in periodic seismic activity along the San Andreas Fault. On average, the Pacific Plate moves in a northwesterly direction about 2 inches (5 cm) per year. The San Andreas Fault, running alongside the east border of Point Reyes (along Highway 1) is an example of a **strike-slip fault,** and is the main component of the **transform boundary** between the Pacific and North American Plates. The Pacific Plate and North American Plate glide past each other in fits and starts, causing earthquakes.

The epicenter of the famous 1906 San Francisco earthquake was located along this fault, and Olema Valley, just outside the park boundary, was the site of maximum observed displacement.

The most notable geologic difference between the Point Reyes Peninsula and the remainder of the California coast is the presence of *Salinian* **granite** basement rock and the absence of the *Franciscan Complex* (greywacke [sandstone], shale, greenstone [metamorphosed basalt], and chert) commonly found east of the San Andreas Fault. The Peninsula's granite is overlain with marine deposits thought to be from the late Jurassic and Cretaceous Periods (about 65 to 150 million years ago). However, the granite probably originated from much deeper in Earth and several hundred miles south of its current location. Some other widespread geologic formations found on top of the granitic basement rock include Laird Sandstone, Monterey Shale, and the Purisima Formation (Figure FG2-2). With the exception of the granite, most of the Peninsula's geologic formations are from the Tertiary Period (1.8 to 65.5 million years ago)—younger than many other formations found along the California coast.

Weather and Climate: The Point Reyes Peninsula, similar to the rest of California, is characterized by winter rains and summer drought. The temperature varies little between seasons (average ranges from 50°–55°F [10–13°C]). Rainfall varies dramatically on the Peninsula. The interior Olema Valley receives approximately 40 inches (102 cm) of rain per year, while during the same period, the Point Reyes Headlands may receive only 20 inches (51 cm). The weather at Point Reyes can get very windy and cold along the coast. Often fog will envelop the whole coast. It is best to check weather forecasts before traveling here.

▲ **Figure FG2-2** The cliffs along Drakes Beach near Stop 3 consist of sedimentary rocks of the Purisima Formation. *(Darrel Hess photo.)*

Site Descriptions

Most of these sites can be reached by automobile. Several sites require a short hike, and they will be noted below. Many of these sites can be reached in one day, but it is more advisable to take only one of the options and spend the entire day in that area, returning to PRNS on another day to visit the other sites. There are two general routes described below. Both start at the Bear Valley Visitor Center. *Option 1* heads to the most western point, the headlands and the Point Reyes Lighthouse, and *Option 2* to the farthest northern point, Pierce Point Ranch.

Stop 1—Bear Valley Visitor Center and Earthquake Trail

(38°02'29"N, 122°48'01"W): The Bear Valley Visitor Center and Park Headquarters are located near the town of Olema. It is the best place to start your Point Reyes adventure. The center provides brochures, maps, and books for sale, as well as an exhibit about the area's ecosystems, wildlife, and cultural history.

The Visitor Center is located near the aboveground rupture of the San Andreas Fault caused by the famous 1906 earthquake. The National Seashore maintains a short Earthquake Loop Trail to the 1906 fault rupture zone. The wheelchair-accessible Earthquake Trail starts at the Visitor Center parking lot. There are signs and displays along the trail that provide information on plate tectonics, earthquakes, and the San Andreas Fault. As you walk along the half-mile loop trail, the **fault scarp** is clearly visible. Along the trail, a historic fence offset caused by the 1906 earthquake was reconstructed. The original offset was about 18 feet (5.5 m). Along with the fence, blue posts trace the surface rupture of the 1906 earthquake. There is a longer, four-mile Rift Zone Trail from the Visitor Center south to the trailhead at Five Brooks in Olema, which follows the trace of the 1906 rupture. (For additional information see *Field Guide #3—The San Andreas Fault.*)

Option 1—Western Point Reyes: From the Visitor Center, continue along Bear Valley Road until it intersects Sir Francis Drake Boulevard; continue north along Sir Francis Drake, turning left before you reach the bridge that leads to Point Reyes Station. Continue north on Sir Francis Drake Boulevard into the park and stay to your left following signs to the lighthouse. It is about 20 miles to the lighthouse.

Stop 2—Mount Vision, Inverness Ridge, and the 1995 Mount Vision Fire

(38°06'03"N, 122°53'08"W): Your first stop is the Bishop Pine forest and Inverness Ridge. Turn left off the main road onto Mount Vision Road. Mount Vision Road winds uphill for four miles along the crest of Inverness Ridge. This narrow, winding road leads through mature Bishop Pine forests and into the fire area. Bishop Pine (*Pinus muricata*) is a closed-cone pine that needs fire or heat to release seeds from its resinous cones.

On October 3, 1995, the Mount Vision fire was started by an improperly extinguished illegal campfire on State Park lands adjacent to the National Seashore. The fire swept through the area, at a rate of up to 3,100 acres per hour. It burned over 12,000 acres, mostly inside the PRNS boundary. It took two weeks to bring the fire under control, and 45 homes along Inverness Ridge were destroyed. The fire consumed a majority of the Bishop Pine forest, along with Douglas Fir forests and coastal strand communities. It traveled from the top of the ridge to the Pacific Ocean. On a clear day, Mount Vision Road provides spectacular views of Point Reyes and the extent of the fire. The road ends in a parking lot, next to a fire road that is closed to vehicles. Walk along the fire road to see a new Bishop Pine forest developing. The stand of new trees is dense and difficult to walk through. Additional trees that either stump-sprouted or germinated after the fire include Madrone, California Bay, and Coast Live Oak, and these, as well as many native shrubs like *Ceanothus* ("California Lilac"), California Coffeeberry, Huckleberry, and Sticky Monkey Flower, have returned. Unlike the mature forest you passed on the way up, the new forest has little understory vegetation due to the dense cover of young Bishop Pine trees. As the forest naturally thins out, more light will become available for understory species.

From the fire site, take Mount Vision Road back to Sir Francis Drake Boulevard and continue toward the lighthouse. As you can see, the area you are passing through is largely used for cattle grazing. These ranches were here prior to PRNS and have been allowed to continue ranching. Grass covers about 50 percent of Point Reyes, and, like much of California's grasslands, many native perennial grasses have been replaced with non-native annuals. The gullying and erosion you see on the rolling hills are examples of some of the effects of heavy grazing in these grasslands.

Stop 3—Drakes Bay and Beach

(38°01'40"N, 122°57'45"W): Drakes Bay is accessed along a road left off Sir Francis Drake Boulevard,

Figure FG2-3 Walking along Drakes Beach at Stop 3. The cliffs are exposed porcellanite, mudstones, sandstones, and siltstones of the Purisima Formation. *(Barbara Holzman photo.)*

Figure FG2-4 Point Reyes Conglomerate from Stop 4 at the lighthouse. *(Barbara Holzman photo.)*

5.8 miles north of the lighthouse. From the beach, you can see exposed white cliffs of *porcellanite* (an impure chert with an appearance similar to unglazed porcelain) and *glauconitic* mudstones, siltstones, and sandstones, which include fossils of Miocene age (5.3 to 23.0 million years ago; Figure FG2-3). These sedimentary rocks formed from material deposited under the sea while the landmass was submerged offshore as the Pacific Plate moved northward. These cliffs are part of the Santa Margarita Sandstone and Purisima Formation that can also be seen along the Santa Cruz coast and the San Francisco peninsula. The exposed cliffs near the east end of Drakes Bay unveil a **syncline** and adjacent **anticline** (see textbook Figure 14-46). As you walk along the beach, you can examine marine beds, sea cliffs, and a **wave-cut platform** (*wave-cut bench*; see textbook Figure 20-26) near the Visitor Center.

After visiting this area, return to Sir Francis Drake Boulevard and follow signs to the lighthouse.

Stop 4—The Point Reyes Lighthouse

(37°59′44″N, 123°01′23″W): From the lighthouse parking lot, a stairway of 300 steps takes you to the lighthouse, Visitor Center, and museum. Along the stairway and above the Visitor Center are examples of Point Reyes Conglomerate (Figure FG2-4). These outcrops have been dated from the Paleocene and Eocene (33.9 to 65.5 million years ago). The conglomerates are colorful, and consist of white and black granodiorite clasts, purple and black porphyritic volcanic clasts, light-colored quartzite pebbles, red chert, and green pebbles, most of volcanic origin. This area consists of both conglomerates and sandstones deposited as *turbidites* (deposits from

underwater sand flows) and debris flows in deep water. These beds were deposited in a submarine channel that was cut into the underlying granodiorite. It is the oldest marine sediment found atop the granitic bedrock.

The lighthouse projects about ten miles into the Pacific Ocean, providing great views of the entire peninsula, and making the headlands of the Point Reyes Peninsula a great spot to view Gray Whales (*Eschrictius robustus*). The Gray Whales pass Point Reyes during their winter migration (November and December) to the southern waters of Baja California, and return along the same route in March and April on their journey back to Alaska. It is possible to see mothers and calves close to shore during the spring migration. While there are many potential locations for whale watching in the Point Reyes area, the lighthouse is considered one of the best.

Stop 5—Chimney Rock (37°59′42″N, 122°58′47″W): The Chimney Rock and Sea Lion Overlook trails start at the Chimney Rock parking lot east of the lighthouse. The trail to the Chimney Rock overlook is about one mile. From the overlook, you can see several sea *stacks*; the one that looks like a chimney is the namesake of the area (Figure FG2-5). There is also a sea arch in view from the overlook. These are made from Salinian granite. A short loop trail leads over the bluffs and provides great views of the ocean as well as the beaches below, where Elephant Seals and Harbor Seals often haul out.

▲ **Figure FG2-5** Chimney Rock from Stop 5. The cliffs and sea stacks are granite. *(Barbara Holzman photo.)*

Continuing on the trail, you will see more sea stacks and a sea arch on the eastern side. Be very careful near the cliffs as they are in a constant state of erosion. The Chimney Rock area resembles a mesa. It is capped by a gravel-covered **marine terrace** (see textbook Figures 20-26 and 20-27). The gravel is overlain by sand and a thin layer of rich organic soil, which provides the perfect habitat for a coastal prairie type ecosystem with a grand showing of native wildflowers in the spring.

Another trail, heading north from the parking lot, leads you to the Sea Lion Overlook where you can see the white cliffs that surround Drakes Bay mentioned at the last stop. From the overlook you can also see a cobble-strewn beach where Northern Elephant Seals *(Mirounga angustirostris)* and Harbor Seals *(Phoca vitulina)* frequently haul out and give birth in the protected bay. The beach has no public access.

Returning along Sir Francis Drake Boulevard, visit North or South Beach and watch the wave action of the Pacific. These areas have several types of sand dunes; some are dominated by non-native species introduced to stabilize dunes, such as European Beachgrass *(Ammophila arenaria)* and Ice Plant *(Caprobrotus species)*. Prior to these introductions, this dune community was dominated by American Dune Grass *(Leymus mollis)* and coastal plants like Dune Lupine *(Lupinus chamissonis)*, and Sand Verbena *(Abronia umbellata)*. This coastal beach and dune area is characterized by stretches of loose, windswept, sandy dunes that vary in width from a few to several hundred feet. If you hike on the dunes, you will find examples of continually shifting foredunes (nearest the shore), sparsely vegetated central dunes, and stable and densely vegetated hind dunes.

Option 2—Northern Point Reyes: Another way to explore Point Reyes National Seashore geography is to take a more northern route, along Pierce Point Road to Abbotts Lagoon, Kehoe Beach, and the Tule Elk Reserve ending at Pierce Point Ranch and McClure Beach. After starting at the Bear Valley Visitor Center, continue north along Bear Valley Road until it intersects Sir Francis Drake Boulevard, continue north along Sir Francis Drake, then turn left before you reach the bridge that leads to Point Reyes Station. Continue to follow Sir Francis Drake Boulevard into the Park and stay to your right, turning onto Pierce Point Road.

At the intersection of Sir Francis Drake and Pierce Point Road, Bishop Pine and Douglas Fir forests dominate the landscape on the more exposed granitic basement rock. Farther north, there are several cattle and dairy farms along the road, taking advantage of the hilly grasslands. These areas represent a change in geology to Laird Sandstone, a medium- to coarse-grained rock of Middle Miocene origin (about 12 million years ago), deposited by the sea. Also visible is the Monterey Formation capped by Santa Margarita Sandstone. The Monterey Formation is made up of sandstone, chert, and organic shales, and the outcrops turn white when bleached by the Sun. These changes in lithology are represented by changes in vegetation.

Stop 6—Abbotts Lagoon (38°09'05"N, 122°56'21"W): Three and one-half miles from the Pierce Point Road intersection lies Abbotts Lagoon. From the dirt parking lot, a two-mile trail winds around a 200-acre brackish lagoon that is connected by a spillway to two freshwater ponds. Alternatively, a short, wheelchair-accessible trail leads to an overlook of the lagoon.

This is a submerged valley blocked by coastal dunes and beaches. A hilly escarpment of Monterey Formation capped by Santa Margarita Sandstone can be seen along the south side of lagoon (Figure FG2-6).

▲ **Figure FG2-6** Abbotts Lagoon at Stop 6. The cliff consists of Monterey Shale capped with Santa Margarita Sandstone. *(Barbara Holzman photo.)*

Beyond the ponds are green cattle pastures, endless huge drifting sand dunes, and the ocean. Keep a lookout for the abundant wildlife that inhabits the area, such as Grey Fox, Striped Skunk, Badger, Mule Deer, and a wide variety of bird species including California Quail and Northern Harrier. Herons and grebes can be seen in the ponds and lagoon, and Brown and White Pelicans are common closer to the ocean. It is rare to find both pelican species together, but Abbotts Lagoon and the ponds attract them.

Stop 7—Kehoe Beach (38°09'10"N, 122° 56'21"W):
About two miles north of Abbotts Lagoon is Kehoe Beach. Kehoe Beach provides an opportunity to see several geomorphic features. From the parking lot, a 1.5-mile trail along a freshwater marsh leads to the beach. Monterey Formation underlies the pasture lands of the area, and the formation is exposed in the cliffs on the beach. Further north, cliffs of Laird Sandstone meet Salinian granitic rocks. The sandstone formation and the granitic lower layer are visible from the beach. Sea stacks can be seen from the beach. The exposed rock is a mix of several types, including quartz diorite, schist, and gneiss among others. The cliffs are heavily fractured, displaying incidents of ancient and historic faulting. These rocks are highly erodible due to wave action and should not be climbed upon.

Stop 8 (rolling stop)—Tule Elk Reserve:
As you continue north along Pierce Point Road, about two miles from Kehoe Beach you will cross several cattle guards and enter the Tule Elk Reserve. Tule Elk (*Cervus elaphus nannodes*) were reintroduced to Point Reyes National Seashore in 1978. They have grown from ten animals to over 550, making it one of the largest populations in California. There are two separate herds of Tule Elk at Point Reyes: A small group recently transferred to the southern grasslands, and this larger herd at Tomales Point, a 2,600-acre fenced reserve at the north end of the PRNS. The elk are easy to see from the road as they graze freely on the grassy hills of the reserve.

Stop 9—McClures Beach and Tomales Point (38°11'19"N, 122°57'28"W):
Continue through the Elk Reserve to the end of the road and Upper Pierce Point Ranch. McClures Beach is reached by a 0.5-mile trail to the west. The Salinian basement rock discussed previously is well exposed at the beach. Towards the end of the trail, there is a clear demarcation between that ancient granite and the overlying dune deposits from the Quaternary Period (less than 1.8 million years ago) that accumulated in what appears to have been a valley. These dunes are heavily eroded due to wave action from rising sea level that followed the last glaciation.

From upper Pierce Point Ranch, a four-mile trail (one way) leads to Tomales Point with great views of the granitic headlands on the Pacific side. The trail is very cold and windy in the winter, but the spring brings views of wildflowers as well as whales offshore.

There are other routes and many other geographic features to explore throughout Point Reyes. You are encouraged to come back to PRNS many times, in different seasons. Each time you are sure to discover something new and fascinating.

Additional Resources

Textbook:
McKnight, Tom L., and Darrel Hess. *Physical Geography: A Landscape Appreciation*, 9th ed. Upper Saddle River, NJ: Pearson/Prentice Hall, 2008. Chapters 11, 14 and 20.

Further Reading:
Brown, M., and Barbara Holzman. *Point Reyes Peninsula and Vicinity Ecosystem Field Trip.* Online, 1997. http://www.sfsu.edu/~geog/bholzman/ptreyes/welcome.htm

Evens, Jules, G. *Natural History of the Point Reyes Peninsula.* Berkeley, CA: University of California Press, 2008.

McConnaughey, Bayard H., and Evelyn McConnaughey. *The Audubon Society Nature Guides: Pacific Coast.* New York, New York: Alfred A. Knopf, Inc., 1985.

Stoffer, Phillip. "Geology at Point Reyes National Seashore and Vicinity, California: A Guide to San Andreas Fault Zone and the Point Reyes Peninsula," in *The San Andreas Fault in the San Francisco Bay Area, California: A Geology Fieldtrip Guidebook to Selected Stops on Public Lands.* U.S. Geological Survey: Open-File Report 2005-1127, 2005. Online. http://pubs.usgs.gov/of/2005/1127/chapter9.pdf

Whitnah, Dorothy L. *Point Reyes: A Guide to the Trails, Roads, Beaches, Campgrounds, Lakes Trees, Flowers, and Rocks of Point Reyes National Seashore.* Berkeley, CA: Wilderness Press, 1985.

Web Sites:

Golden Gate Transit Bus & Ferry Service
http://goldengatetransit.org/

West Marin Stagecoach
http://www.marintransit.org/stage.html

Point Reyes National Seashore
http://www.nps.gov/pore/

Textbook Page References for Key Terms

anticline *(p. 446)*
fault scarp *(p. 448)*
granite *(p. 392)*

marine terrace *(p. 605)*
syncline *(p. 446)*
strike-slip fault *(p. 449)*

transform boundary *(p. 422)*
wave-cut platform *(p. 605)*

The San Andreas Fault

Darrel Hess, City College of San Francisco

Introduction

The San Andreas Fault is probably the world's most famous fault. It cuts through California for a distance of 800 miles (1,300 km), from the Gulf of California in the south to Cape Mendocino in the north. It has generated many large earthquakes, including the 1906 San Francisco and 1989 Loma Prieta Earthquakes. Movement along the San Andreas and related faults continues to shape the topography of coastal California—and rattle the nerves of Californians. This field guide describes five locations along the San Andreas Fault where its features may easily be seen.

Location

The five sites in this field guide will likely be visited at different times, although Sites 1 and 2—the Point Reyes Peninsula and the San Francisco Peninsula—in the northern part of the state may be visited in one day. Sites 4 and 5—Tejon Pass and Palmdale—in the southern part of the state, although separated by a distance of about 60 miles (100 km), could also be visited within a day. Site 3 in the southern Coast Range's Carrizo Plain National Monument deserves special mention. It is the most remote—although perhaps most interesting—location described in this field guide. There are few services in the vicinity, so be sure top off your gas tank and fill up your water bottles before leaving the major freeways for the Carrizo Plain.

Background

Plate Tectonics and the San Andreas Fault: Although the San Andreas Fault is sometimes called the "plate boundary" between the North American Plate and the Pacific Plate (see textbook Figure 14-16), this is somewhat simplistic. The San Andreas Fault itself is the most important component of this **transform plate boundary** that includes many other faults in the San Andreas system such as the Hayward and Calaveras Faults in northern California, and the San Jacinto and Elsinore Faults in southern California. Overall, about 60% of the 2.2 inches (5.6 cm) per year of relative motion between the North American and Pacific Plates is released along the San Andreas Fault. Most of this plate motion is released during fault rupture events that unload many decades of accumulated strain in a matter of seconds—and generate large earthquakes as a result.

The San Andreas Fault is a **strike-slip fault** (see textbook Figure 14-52), so the predominant displacement is lateral (although a slight amount of "dip-slip" or vertical displacement is not uncommon as well). The San Andreas, and nearly all of the other mostly parallel faults in the system, are *right-lateral strike-slip faults*—this means that looking across the fault, the displacement of features on the other side is to the right. (The Garlock Fault, which splinters off of the San Andreas near Site 4 at Tejon Pass, is an example of a left-lateral strike-slip fault.)

Origin: The origin of the San Andreas Fault is associated with a significant change in the plate boundary along the west coast of North America beginning about 30 million years ago. For many tens of millions of years before that time, a **mid-ocean ridge** was present to the west of what is today California. Out of this spreading center, the ancestral Pacific Plate moved to the northwest (as it continues to do today) while a southeast-moving oceanic plate, called the Farallon Plate, subducted beneath the west-moving North American Plate. Much of the magma generated in this **subduction zone** cooled below the surface to form the granites of the Sierra Nevada batholith (see *Field Guide #4—Sierra Nevada via Tioga Pass*).

By about 30 million years ago, the Farallon Plate was almost entirely "consumed" by subduction, and the North American Plate began to override the midocean ridge to the west. At that point, a transform boundary developed between the North American Plate and the Pacific Plate, forming the ancestral San Andreas Fault (Figure FG3-1). By 20 million years ago, the San Andreas Fault was growing in length as the two "triple junctions" between the North American Plate, Pacific Plate, and the old Farallon Plate migrated north and south.

Today, remnants of the Farallon Plate are still subducting beneath the North American Plate: North of the Mendocino Triple Junction, subduction of the Juan de Fuca and Gorda Plates is associated with the Cascade volcanoes; south of the Rivera Triple Junction near Baja, subduction of the Cocos Plate is associated with the volcanoes of central Mexico.

Earthquakes: Most of the relative motion between the Pacific Plate and the North American Plate is released episodically through abrupt fault ruptures along the San Andreas Fault system—each time, the Pacific Plate side of the fault system (which includes Los Angeles, Monterey Bay and Point Reyes) jumps a little closer to the subduction zone of the Aleutian Islands. In a very simplistic sense, the size of an earthquake is determined by the length of fault rupture and amount of offset, which in turn are generally related to how many years that fault segment remained "locked" and strain accumulated before the rupture.

In the last 150 years or so, there have been two "great" earthquakes along the San Andreas Fault. The January 9, 1857, Great Fort Tejon Earthquake was a rupture of the southern section of the San Andreas Fault—from roughly Parkfield in the north to Cajon Pass in the south—a distance of more than 200 miles (320 km), with a maximum offset of about 30 feet (9.5 m) in the area of the Carrizo Plain. The April 18, 1906, San Francisco Earthquake was a rup-

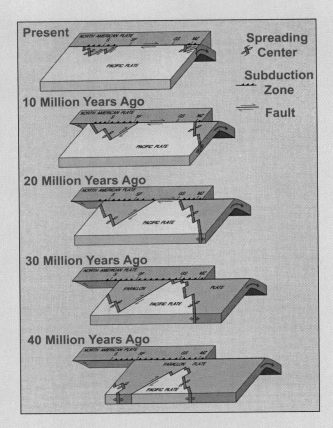

▲ **Figure FG3-1** Development of the San Andreas Fault system as the North American Plate overrode the spreading center of the Pacific and Farallon Plates. *(Adapted from U.S. Geological Survey Professional Paper 1515.)*

ture of the northern segment of the fault—from Cape Mendocino in the north to San Juan Bautista in the south—a distance of about 270 miles (430 km), with a maximum observed offset of about 20 feet (6 m) in the area of Point Reyes. Both earthquakes had **magnitudes** of about 8 (roughly one magnitude, or 32 times larger, than the 1989 Loma Prieta and 1994 Northridge earthquakes). Contemporary estimates put the *moment magnitude* of the 1857 earthquake at 7.8 and the 1906 earthquake at 7.7.

Topographic Features: The location of a strike-slip fault such as the San Andreas Fault is often revealed by linear features in the landscape (see textbook Figure 14-56). For example, the surface location of a strike-slip fault is often marked by a narrow *linear fault trough* or valley that forms in the zone of crushed rock along the fault plane. In some places—such as along the San Francisco Peninsula and the Point Reyes Peninsula (Sites 1 and 2 described below)—a wide fault zone is present. In such places multiple breaks of the fault are found, and a wide valley—in some cases more than a half-mile across—has developed.

Where small depressions form in the fault zone, sags or **sag ponds** may be formed. Linear ridges and *fault scarps* may develop parallel to the fault from either compression or slight vertical displacement. A hill may be displaced by fault movement to close off a valley with a *shutter ridge.* Perhaps the most conspicuous feature formed by a strike-slip fault is an **offset stream,** formed when repeated movement along the fault displaces the course of a stream flowing across it.

Site Descriptions

Unlike the site descriptions found in most of the other field guides in this collection, the five sites for the San Andreas Fault are separated by great distances. The following sites are described from north to south in the state, and they may be visited in any order. Each site includes two or more local stops (or "rolling stops" where features may be observed from the road).

Site 1—Point Reyes Peninsula

It was in the vicinity of the Point Reyes Peninsula—especially within the Olema Valley—that the significance of the San Andreas Fault to the 1906 San Francisco earthquake was realized and studied extensively. Because much of the region is part of the Point Reyes National Seashore, large areas within the fault zone remain undeveloped, and so many fault features can be easily observed here.

There are a number of ways to reach the Point Reyes National Seashore (Figure FG3-2). If traveling north from San Francisco on U.S. 101, after crossing the Golden Gate Bridge take the Stinson Beach exit just past Sausalito and follow California Highway 1 for sixteen winding, but very scenic, miles to Stinson Beach. Alternatively, you can take Sir Francis Drake Boulevard the 21 miles from U.S. 101 at San Rafael to the town of Olema. Parts of the Point Reyes National Seashore may also be reached by public transportation with Golden Gate Transit and West Marin Stagecoach—see *Additional Resources* on F-27.

The stops described below take you from Stinson Beach in the south, to Tomales Bay in the north.

Stop 1—Stinson Beach (37°53′48″N, 122°38′26″W): From one of the roadside turnouts on Highway 1 just above the town of Stinson Beach, or from the beach parking area (where there are public restrooms), you can observe the San Andreas Fault zone where it comes onshore after leaving land at Mussel Rock south of San Francisco. Bolinas Lagoon itself formed in the zone of crushed rock along the fault.

Stinson Beach is a **spit** (see textbook Figure 20-16) that nearly closes off the lagoon from Bolinas Bay. The 1906 trace of the San Andreas Fault cut through the spit near its western end (Figure FG3-3), although all evidence of the rupture quickly disappeared.

Traveling north from Stinson Beach on Highway 1, for the next 4.5 miles you drive along Bolinas Lagoon. The main trace of the San Andreas Fault runs along, or just offshore of, the western side of the lagoon. North of Bolinas Lagoon you enter the Olema Valley—a linear trough produced by repeated displacement along the San Andreas Fault.

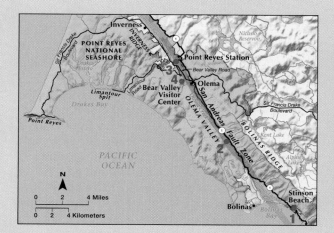

▲ **Figure FG3-2** Regional map of the Point Reyes Peninsula, showing Site 1 field guide stops.

▲ **Figure FG3-3** View northwest across Bolinas Bay showing Stinson Beach and the location of the San Andreas Fault (SAF) at Site 1, Stop 1. *(Darrel Hess photo.)*

Although little direct evidence of the 1906 rupture remains, traveling through Olema Valley toward Point Reyes Station you can see many examples of shutter ridges, fault scarps and seasonal sag ponds. Use caution when driving or cycling along the highway here—the road is narrow and twisting.

Stop 2 (rolling stop)—Olema Valley
(37°58'37"N, 122°44'01"W): About 7.5 miles north of Stinson Beach, you pass a prominent linear ridge running down the middle of the valley. Drainage patterns in the fault zone have been so disrupted that Olema Creek, which runs next to the highway, flows to the north, while Pine Gulch Creek only 1,200 feet (165 m) away on the other side of the ridge flows to the south.

Stop 3 (rolling stop)—1906 Road Offset Location (38°03'47"N, 122°48'45"W):
About fifteen miles north of Stinson Beach, you pass through the town of Olema. Two miles beyond Olema at Point Reyes Station, turn left (west) onto Sir Francis Drake Boulevard. About 0.3 miles down this stretch of road you'll pass over the fault where the maximum offset of 20 feet (6 m) from the 1906 earthquake was observed (the road has since been repaired). To your right (north) is Tomales Bay—a flooded portion of the San Andreas Fault zone.

Continue a short distance to Bear Valley Road and turn left (south).

Stop 4—Bear Valley Visitor Center and Earthquake Trail (38°02'29"N, 122° 48'01"W):
About two miles south of Sir Francis Drake Boulevard, turn right onto the road leading to the Bear Valley Visitor Center of the Point Reyes National Seashore. At the Visitor Center you can see natural history displays and purchase maps and other publications.

A short distance south of the Visitor Center is a sign directing you to the Earthquake Trail. This short, wheelchair-accessible, self-guided interpretive trail takes you past the location where a fence was offset by 18 feet (5.5 m) during the 1906 earthquake (38°02'28"N, 122°47'46"W). The fence has since been reconstructed, but a series of blue posts clearly marks the location of the 1906 surface rupture along the fault scarp here.

From the Bear Valley Visitor Center, you can expand your exploration of the Point Reyes area with *Field Guide #2—Point Reyes National Seashore*.

▲ **Figure FG3-4**   Regional map of the San Francisco Peninsula, showing Site 2 field guide stops.

Site 2—San Francisco Peninsula

Along the peninsula south of San Francisco the San Andreas Fault has produced one of its largest and most prominent features anywhere in the state: a wide, linear fault trough, made all the more obvious by the presence of two long reservoirs that flood portions of this valley (Figure FG3-4). The fault valley of the San Andreas is so large here that it may be difficult to recognize from ground level—but it is often easily seen from the air by passengers flying in or out of San Francisco International Airport.

It is along the San Francisco Peninsula, too, that the San Andreas Fault passes closest to a major metropolitan area. Over the last century, housing development, transportation networks and urban water delivery projects have all expanded within, or adjacent to, the fault zone.

Stop 1—Crystal Springs Reservoir Vista Point (37°28'42"N, 122°17'50"W):
Interstate 280 runs along or within the fault zone of the San Andreas from roughly Woodside in the south, to South San Francisco in the north. A convenient vantage point to observe the fault zone is the Vista Point off northbound Interstate 280 about three miles south of the Interstate 280/California 92 junction (if you're traveling southbound on I-280, to reach this Vista Point you'll need to drive a few miles south to the Edgewood Road exit and return northbound on I-280).

The broad fault zone of the San Andreas is clearly seen here. Sawyer Ridge (on the far side of the reservoir) runs parallel to both the San Andreas Fault and the Pilarcitos Fault (on the western side of Sawyer Ridge). Looking across the fault zone at Sawyer Ridge, notice that many of the stream valleys have had their courses deflected slightly to the south by periodic fault movement.

The earliest development of Crystal Springs Reservoir area dates back to the 1860s when the Spring Valley Water Company began delivering water from the watersheds here to San Francisco. The dam at the south end of the reservoir was first constructed in 1888, but was enlarged in 1890 and 1911 to its present height of 149 feet. By 1934 both Crystal Springs Reservoir and San Andreas Lake farther north, had been incorporated into San Francisco's Hetch Hetchy Aqueduct water delivery system (see *Field Guide #4—Sierra Nevada via Tioga Pass* for additional information). The 1906 rupture of the San Andreas Fault ran though the reservoir close to the far (western) shore, but didn't damage the dam itself.

A causeway for California Highway 92 separates Crystal Springs into Lower and Upper reservoirs. The 1906 earthquake offset the original road embankment there by 8 feet (2.4 m), but the dam at Lower Crystal Springs was undamaged.

Stop 2—San Andreas Lake (37°34'49"N, 122°24'39"W):

Traveling north on Interstate 280, drive about 6.8 miles north of the I-280/CA-92 junction, then take the Millbrae Avenue/Hillcrest Boulevard exit. Continue straight for 0.3 miles, and then turn left on Hillcrest Boulevard. (If you're traveling southbound on I-280, take the Hillcrest Boulevard exit and turn left at the bottom of the offramp.) You may park below the freeway. Just to the west is the trailhead for the Sawyer Camp Trail along San Andreas Lake, and if you have time to visit only one place along the San Francisco Peninsula, this is a good choice.

From the fenced area at the trailhead (37°35'19"N, 122°24'47"W), walk south along the paved but moderately steep and twisting Sawyer Camp Trail for about one mile until you reach the dam at the southeast end of San Andreas Lake.

The San Andreas Fault was named after this lake in 1895 by geologist Andrew C. Lawson, who recognized the fault in the San Francisco Peninsula—although the full extent of the fault was not realized until after the 1906 earthquake. Originally a large sag pond in the fault zone, San Andreas Lake was enlarged in 1868 with a dam. During the 1906 earthquake, the dam was damaged but did not fail. The trace of the 1906 rupture was through the eastern

▲ **Figure FG3-5**   View northwest across San Andreas Lake showing the location of the San Andreas Fault (SAF) at Site 2, Stop 2. *(Darrel Hess photo.)*

side of the dam (where it is marked with a stone monument) and along the eastern shore of the lake (Figure FG3-5). From near the center of the dam, you can look south and see Upper Crystal Springs Reservoir. The wooded valley below the dam is typical of the wide and remarkably straight fault zone in this area.

After leaving San Andreas Lake, if you continue north on Interstate 280 and then on Skyline Boulevard toward Pacifica, for the next few miles you're traveling in or next to the San Andreas Fault zone. The **epicenter** of the 1906 earthquake was offshore of San Francisco, a few miles northeast of Mussel Rock—the San Andreas Fault actually never crosses San Francisco itself.

Site 3—Carrizo Plain

The Carrizo Plain is the most dramatic place in California to see features of the San Andreas Fault. Here the fault has a fairly simple configuration: Rather than a wide fault zone, in many places the fault here has a single active trace with a clear topographic expression that is easily recognized from ground level. Although it isn't possible to straddle the San Andreas Fault and really have one foot on the North American Plate and one foot on the Pacific Plate, the Carrizo Plain comes closest to letting you do that. Since the Carrizo Plain is undeveloped and fairly dry, many subtle strike-slip fault features are visible here that are obscured in urbanized regions or in areas with denser vegetation.

Figure FG3-6   Regional map of the Carrizo Plain, showing Site 3 field guide stops.

Figure FG3-7   View southeast across Wallace Creek, showing the location of the San Andreas Fault (SAF) at Site 3, Stop 1. *(Darrel Hess photo.)*

To reach Carrizo Plain National Monument, travel west on California Highway 58 from Interstate 5 at Buttonwillow, through the town of McKittrick and its surrounding oil fields, and over the Temblor Range on a steep and windy road to the Carrizo Plain (Figure FG3-6). About 35 miles west of Interstate 5 (about 55 miles east of Santa Margarita if you're coming from U.S. 101) you'll come to the foot of the Temblor Range where Highway 58 turns sharply to the west (to the right, if you're coming from I-5). At the bend in the highway continue straight, leaving Highway 58 and going on to Seven Mile Road. After 0.3 miles turn left (southwest) onto Elkhorn Road.

Elkhorn Road is a graded dirt road that is easily driven with ordinary passenger vehicles in dry weather but becomes impassible during rainy weather (in some cases even to four-wheel drive vehicles). The road follows the foot of the Temblor Range, and in places runs exactly along the trace of the fault. From Seven Mile Road, proceed for 4.2 miles along Elkhorn Road until you see a sign and small parking area for Wallace Creek. The "walking" stops at Wallace Creek are visited on a round-trip hike of about three miles. Wear sturdy shoes and be alert to the possibility that you might surprise a rattlesnake.

Stop 1—Wallace Creek (35°16′16″N, 119°49′38″W): A hike of about one-quarter mile along a well-worn dirt trail takes you up the hillside to an overlook of Wallace Creek—probably the most famous (and most studied) offset stream in the world (Figure FG3-7).

Named for the U.S. Geological Survey geologist Robert E. Wallace, who spent decades studying the San Andreas Fault in this area, Wallace Creek is an **ephemeral stream** that has been offset 430 feet (130 m) by movement along the San Andreas Fault. Wallace and others determined that this offset occurred over a period of approximately 3,700 years, meaning that the average long-term rate of displacement along the fault in this area is about 1.4 inches (34 mm) per year. However, movement along this part of the San Andreas Fault occurs only intermittently: When the fault ruptures, it produces many feet of offset as decades of accumulated energy is suddenly released during an earthquake.

The last major earthquake along this segment of the San Andreas Fault was the 1857 Great Fort Tejon Earthquake. Lateral offset of about 31 feet (9.5 m) from this earthquake was measured here on the Carrizo Plain.

There is a short self-guiding nature trail at Wallace Creek with several signs pointing out features of the fault. Visit the five "Posts" along the trail in the area of Wallace Creek. As you walk along the trail south of Wallace Creek, notice the steep scarp produced by vertical displacement along the fault. Notice also that there are many small gullies that run down this scarp that stop abruptly at the bottom. If you look carefully, you may be able to find the offset continuations of some of these gully channels below the fault (for example, at Post 4; 35°16′09″N, 119°49′30″W).

If you do match the gullies on the scarp with their offset continuations, you'll see that the smallest amount of displacement for any of these offset streams is about 30 feet. This suggests that there hasn't been any movement along this part of the

San Andreas since the 1857 earthquake. In fact, most channels you see here (and those farther south along the fault trace) have been offset for distances that are roughly multiples of 30 feet—suggesting that this part of the San Andreas tends to produce fault rupture displacements of about the same length each time.

Once you reach Post 5, if you're up for a longer walk, continue south along the fault for another mile or so. There is no trail, but it's easy to find the way. Do, however, watch your step on the uneven ground.

Stop 2 (walking stop)—Shutter Ridge

(35°15′45″N, 119°49′06″W): About 0.8 miles south of Wallace Creek, you come to a long, low shutter ridge, with deposits of alluvium dammed behind it. A short distance farther, you come to a prominent "beheaded" stream channel, cutoff by displacement along the fault (35°15′40″N, 119°48′59″W).

Stop 3 (walking stop)—Offset Streams

(35°15′33″N, 119°48′53″W): A short distance beyond the beheaded stream, you cross two prominent offset ephemeral stream channels. The second one (the larger of the two) is offset about 65 feet (20 m)—the total offset of this stream is a combination of displacement from the Great Fort Tejon Earthquake and the large earthquake that preceded it.

Stop 4 (walking stop)—Sag (35°15′25″N,

119°48′45″W): Finally, about 1.5 miles south of Wallace Creek, you come to a "sag" along the fault trace. Here the surface probably dropped down between to parallel segments of the fault, forming a miniature version of what is known as a *pull-apart basin* (see Figure FG9-2 in *Field Guide #9—Death Valley* for a diagram showing how pull-apart basins form). In wet years, a temporary sag pond forms in this depression.

Site 4—Tejon Pass

Tejon Pass is one of the few places in California where the San Andreas Fault is easily seen along a commonly-traveled major freeway (Figure FG3-8). At the southwestern end of the Tehachapi Mountains, Tejon Pass is located along what is called the "Big Bend" segment of the San Andreas Fault.

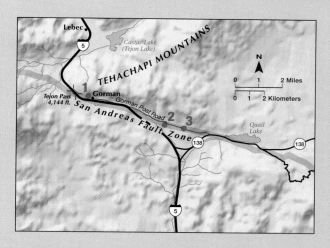

Figure FG3-8 Regional map of Tejon Pass, showing Site 4 field guide stops.

In this part of the state the fault takes a decidedly east-west turn, deviating from its generally northwest-southeasterly trend south and north of here. In the most basic sense, the uplift of the Transverse Ranges (such as the San Gabriel Mountains and San Bernardino Mountains) is a result of compression along this bend where southern California southwest of the fault converges into the land northeast of the fault. The last major fault rupture here occurred during the Great Fort Tejon Earthquake of 1857.

Tejon Pass is reached on Interstate 5, just south of the "Grapevine" section of the freeway where it climbs steeply out of the Central Valley into the mountains; snow occasionally closes the freeway in winter. The San Andreas Fault crosses Interstate 5 almost exactly at the small freeway sign marking Tejon Pass (4,144 feet; 1,263 m), but there is no safe place to pull off the freeway and little to see here. Whether you are traveling north or south on I-5, take the Gorman exit (about 1.5 miles south of Tejon Pass) and drive north one block to the cluster of gas stations and other buildings along the Gorman Post Road (if you've been traveling northbound on I-5, turn right after exiting the freeway; if you've been traveling southbound, turn left and drive under the freeway).

Stop 1—Gorman (34°47′49″N, 118°51′46″W):

Turn left on Gorman Post Road and drive northwest until it dead-ends in a turnaround about 0.6 miles from the freeway exit. Look back toward the tiny town of Gorman. The steep hillside here (with the water tank that says "Gorman") is a scarp produced by the San Andreas Fault (Figure FG3-9). In the distance, about four miles to the southeast,

Figure FG3-9 View southeast to Gorman and Interstate 5 near Tejon Pass, showing the location of the San Andreas Fault (SAF) at Site 4, Stop 1. *(Darrel Hess photo.)*

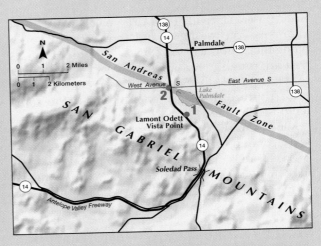

Figure FG3-10 Regional map of Palmdale, showing Site 5 field guide stops.

you see a notch in the mountains where Gorman Post Road and Interstate 5 begin to run parallel to each other toward you—both are following the trace of the San Andreas Fault.

Stop 2 (rolling stop)—Sag Ponds

(34°46'57"N, 118°48'24"W): Retrace your path to the southeast along Gorman Post Road, continuing past the Gorman freeway exit. For the next few miles, Gorman Post Road parallels the freeway, running along the path of the San Andreas Fault. About 2.6 miles from Gorman you pass a small sag pond, and 0.2 miles beyond this, you come to a much larger sag pond.

Stop 3—Fault Valley

(34°46'44"N, 118° 47'32"W): Continuing 0.9 miles from the large sag pond (3.7 miles from the Gorman freeway exit) is a turnout on the left (north) side of the road where you can park. From this parking area, walk a short distance north to the top of the small rise and look back in the direction of Gorman. The San Andreas Fault runs through the valley below toward you, marked roughly by the series of "notches" in the hills in the distance.

From here you can return to Gorman and Interstate 5. If you continue east, Gorman Post Road soon merges with California Highway 138 (one of the ways to reach *Site 5—Palmdale*), which in turn passes Quail Lake—one of the reservoirs in the California Water Project—impounded in the fault trough of the San Andreas and a likely location of an old natural sag pond.

Site 5—Palmdale

The city of Palmdale is located at the northern foot of the San Gabriel Mountains at the edge of the Mojave Desert, about 60 miles (95 km) north of downtown Los Angeles (Figure FG3-10). Palmdale is a great place to see major topographic features of the San Andreas Fault, and it has a spectacular road-cut exposing severely deformed rocks in the fault zone.

To reach Palmdale, travel north on California Highway 14 (the Antelope Valley Freeway) from San Fernando, or south from the nearby desert city of Lancaster. A good first stop is the Lamont Odett Vista Point, about one mile south of Palmdale (about two miles north of Soledad Pass) along Highway 14. The Vista Point can be reached only when traveling northbound on Highway 14; if traveling southbound from Lancaster you'll need to drive past the Vista Point on the other side of the freeway, then travel several miles to an exit where you can return on the freeway toward Palmdale.

Stop 1—Lamont Odett Vista Point

(34°32'27"N, 118°07'22"W): The Lamont Odett Vista Point offers a panoramic view of Palmdale, the California Aqueduct, and the fault zone below you. The lake you see is Lake Palmdale—an old sag pond that has been extensively modified for human use. The active trace of the San Andreas Fault runs just along the northern (far) shore of the lake. Extending both northwest and southeast (to the right and left) of Lake Palmdale—and generally aligned with the north shore of the lake—is a low, linear ridge. This ridge is the fault scarp of the San Andreas. Just west (left) of the lake, where the freeway cuts through this ridge, is your next stop.

Stop 2—Roadcut in California Highway 14 (34°33′29″N, 118°08′03″W):
Continue north from the Vista Point on Highway 14 for 1.2 miles to the Avenue S exit in Palmdale. Turn left (west) on Avenue S, driving under the freeway, and then park in a dirt pullout just west of the freeway. Walk up the hill west of the freeway about one-quarter mile, for a view of perhaps the most famous roadcut in California (Figure FG3-11).

The short, steep slope you first encounter when walking to the top of the roadcut is the fault scarp of the San Andreas. When you reach the middle of the roadcut (34°33′45″N, 118°08′00″W), you have a great view across Highway 14 to the east wall of the roadcut. Most of the exposure consists of interbedded layers of sandstone and shale, severely folded by compression in the San Andreas Fault zone. Although you can see a number of minor faults in the roadcut, the main trace of the San Andreas itself

▲ **Figure FG3-11** View southeast across California Highway 14 in Palmdale, showing the location of the San Andreas Fault (SAF) at Site 5, Stop 2. *(Darrel Hess photo.)*

is at the far southern end of the roadcut—at the steep scarp at the end of the roadcut.

Use caution when walking along the roadcut and don't stand too close to its edge. The slope of the roadcut is somewhat unstable, especially beyond the halfway point.

Additional Resources

Textbook:
McKnight, Tom L., and Darrel Hess. *Physical Geography: A Landscape Appreciation*, 9th ed. Upper Saddle River, NJ: Pearson/Prentice Hall, 2008. Chapter 14.

Further Reading:
Hough, Susan Elizabeth. *Finding Fault in California: An Earthquake Tourist's Guide.* Missoula: Mountain Press Publishing Company, 2004.

Wallace, Robert E., editor. *The San Andreas Fault System, California.* U.S. Geological Survey Professional Paper 1515. Washington, D.C.: U.S. Government Printing Office, 1990.

Web Sites:
Carrizo Plain National Monument
http://www.blm.gov/ca/st/en/fo/bakersfield/Programs/carrizo/html

Golden Gate Transit Bus & Ferry Service
http://goldengatetransit.org/

Point Reyes National Seashore
http://www.nps.gov/pore/

West Marin Stagecoach
http://www.marintransit.org/stage.html

U.S. Geological Survey, Recent California Earthquakes
http://quake.usgs.gov/recenteqs/

Textbook Page References for Key Terms

ephemeral stream *(p. 532)*
epicenter *(p. 451)*
magnitude (of an earthquake) *(p. 451)*

midocean ridge *(p. 420)*
offset stream *(p. 450)*
sag pond *(p. 450)*
spit *(p. 600)*

strike-slip fault *(p. 449)*
subduction zone *(p. 416)*
transform plate boundary *(p. 422)*

Field Guide #4

Sierra Nevada via Tioga Pass

Darrel Hess, City College of San Francisco

Introduction

The Sierra Nevada is one of the most stunning mountain ranges in North America. Four hundred miles (650 km) long from north to south, it rises from near sea level along its foothills at the Central Valley to an elevation of over 14,000 feet (4300 m) at its crest less than 70 miles (110 km) to the east. Travelers crossing the Sierra see dramatic examples of the work of faulting, volcanoes, streams, and glaciers, and pass through a wide range of habitats that include oak savanna, montane forest, subalpine forest, piñon-juniper woodland and sagebrush scrub.

This field guide highlights features you can see traveling across the Sierra along California Highway 120 from the foothills at the edge of the Central Valley, across the high country of Yosemite National Park to Tioga Pass, and down into the Mono Lake basin.

Location

If you're traveling out of the Central Valley, take California Highway 120 east from California Highway 99 near the town of Manteca. The highway winds through the communities of Escalon and Oakdale before climbing up into the foothills of the Sierra along the south bank of the Stanislaus River (Figure FG4-1). If you're traveling from Mono Lake, take California 120 west toward Tioga Pass from U.S. Highway 395 at the town of Lee Vining.

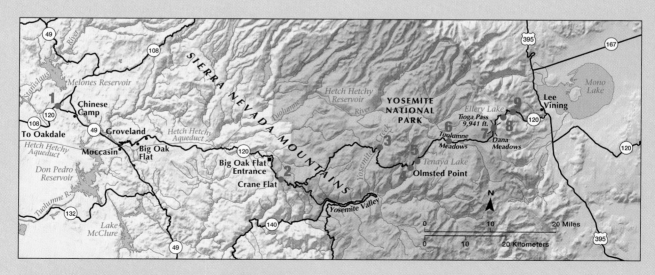

▲ **Figure FG4-1** Regional map of Sierra Nevada showing California Highway 120 and field guide stops.

Gasoline and supplies are available in most towns in the Central Valley's western foothills and in Lee Vining; however, facilities are limited once you enter Yosemite National Park and begin your drive along the 57-mile (92-km) "Tioga Pass Road" portion of the highway. At the western side of the Park, gasoline is available in Crane Flat (about eight miles east of the Big Oak Flat Entrance to Yosemite National Park), and at Tuolumne Meadows, but nowhere else along the Tioga Pass Road. The speed limit through much of the Park is 45 mph—but lower in areas with many pedestrians.

During the summer, bus service is available from Yosemite Valley to Tuolumne Meadows and Lee Vining via the Tioga Pass Road with the Yosemite Area Regional Transportation System—see *Additional Resources* on F-36.

Most of the Forest Service campgrounds outside the Park do not take reservations, but if you arrive early, especially in the middle of the week, you should be able to find a campsite. However, reservations are recommended if you want to stay in the Park at either the Crane Flat or Tuolumne Meadows campgrounds.

A number of exhibits, campgrounds and trails within Yosemite National Park are wheelchair accessible—see the Park Web site on F-36 for details.

Although Yosemite National Park remains open all year, the Tioga Pass Road usually closes with the first heavy snow of the season, and doesn't open again until summer (typically by early June, but in some heavy snow years the pass remains closed until late June).

Summer temperatures are likely to be hot in the Central Valley (often over 100°F [38°C]), but mild in the high country. However, because of the high elevations (Tioga Pass is at 9,941 feet [3,030 m]), nighttime temperatures can drop below freezing any time of year. In late summer, be aware of thunderstorms when hiking in exposed high country areas, especially above the timberline. Because of the thinner atmosphere, in higher elevations everyone should take precautions against sunburn by wearing a hat and applying sun cream.

Background

Geologic History: The geologic history of the Sierra Nevada is complex, but the basic outline of events is clear. About 200 million years ago—around the time that the supercontinent of *Pangaea* was beginning to break apart—the plate boundary of western North America was quite different from today. Rather than the **transform boundary** of the San Andreas Fault system, a **midocean ridge** was west

of the continent, and an oceanic plate (called the Farallon Plate) was subducting beneath the west coast of ancestral North America (see textbook Figure 14-7). The coastline, however, was much farther east than it is now, perhaps near the location of the present foothills of the Sierra. Magma generated in this subduction zone rose to form a series of volcanoes, much like the present-day Cascade Range north of the Sierra (see *Field Guide #1—The California Cascades*). Much of this magma, however, cooled deep below the surface, forming the plutonic rocks such as granite (see textbook Figure 13-8) that we see exposed in the Sierra today. By about 80 million years ago the intrusion of granitic plutons into the Sierra Nevada **batholith** stopped, leaving an ancestral Sierra Nevada mountain range that was perhaps a bit lower than the present range.

The subduction zone would occasionally "jam" as slices of unsubducted lithosphere were added to the margin of California. As ancestral California grew through the accretion of such **terranes** (see textbook Figure 14-21), the coastline increasingly shifted westward to its present location.

By about 65 million years ago, erosion had removed enough overlying rock to begin to expose the granites of the batholith and to reduce the ancestral Sierra to a gently rolling highland. Today, some of the rocks that existed before the Sierran granites formed remain as metamorphic rocks. The western metamorphic belt runs along the western foothills of the range, and includes the famous *Mother Lode* region; the eastern metamorphic belt is found near the crest of the Sierra.

By about 25 million years ago, the Farallon Plate was entirely "consumed" by subduction, and the North American Plate began to override the mid-ocean ridge to the west—this eventually resulted in the development of the present-day transform boundary of the San Andreas Fault system (see *Field Guide #3—The San Andreas Fault* for additional information). The change of plate boundary also changed the direction of stress; the western part of the continent began to stretch, and the resulting faulting (especially *normal faulting*) initiated the uplift of the modern Sierra as well as the faulting throughout the Basin-and-Range province to the east. The uplift of the Sierra along its eastern side continues today, at a long-term rate of about 1½ inches (3.8 cm) per 100 years. This faulting has left one of the world's best examples of a **tilted fault-block mountain** (see textbook Figure 14-54).

Between about 15 and 5 million years ago, extensive volcanic eruptions, especially in the northern Sierra, covered large areas with lava flows, *volcanic mudflows (lahars)* and pyroclastics such as volcanic ash.

Glaciation: With the onset of the **Pleistocene epoch** about 2 million years ago, the Sierra underwent a series of extensive glaciations, at their peak covering the Sierra with a highland icefield 100 miles (160 km) long. Today, the mark of glacial erosion and deposition is found throughout the Sierra (see *Field Guide #5—Yosemite Valley* for additional information about glaciation in the Sierra).

Weather and Climate: The great mountain barrier of the Sierra Nevada dramatically influences the climate, and so the entire biogeography, of the region. Westerly winds encounter the range and are forced to rise, yielding high rainfall and snowfall in winter. The slow melting of the winter snow pack provides much of California with its water supply. By removing much of the moisture of the westerlies on its west side, the Sierra creates a **rain shadow** east of the range, leaving the Mono Basin, Owens Valley and most of Nevada with a *desert* or *steppe* climate.

Plant Communities: Traveling from west to east over the range, you pass through a sequence of vegetation zones, beginning in the foothills with the valley grassland and oak savanna; with increasing elevation you move into the montane forests of Ponderosa Pine and Incense Cedar, and finally into the subalpine forests of Lodgepole Pine, Red Fir and Whitebark Pine as you approach Tioga Pass. Dropping down from the crest to the east side of the Sierra, you pass through the piñon-juniper woodland, and finally down into the arid zone of sagebrush scrub (see textbook Figure 11-10).

Site Descriptions

The following stops describe major features along California 120 traveling across the Sierra from west to east from Oakdale in the Central Valley to Lee Vining in the Mono Basin. (The approximate mileage between each stop is provided to make following the field guide easier if you're traveling from east to west.) The total distance is about 130 miles (210 km), so it is possible to visit all of these sites in one day, but more time is needed if you wish to explore some of the other locations you'll pass along the way.

About 22 miles east of Oakdale, notice the thin slabs of rock that are standing up on end in the grassy hills among the oak trees—these are known as the "tombstone" rocks. They are metamorphosed 140-million-year-old ocean floor volcanic rocks, and although they look like they're rising out of the ground, the opposite is actually true: the softer rock that once surrounded them has since eroded away—an example of *differential erosion.*

Stop 1—Table Mountain (37°53'27"N, 120°29'17"W): About 25 miles east of Oakdale pull off the road where California 120 splits to the right (southeast) from California 108 and temporarily joins California Highway 49.

About nine million years ago, a volcano near the crest of the ancestral Sierra in the area of Sonora Pass erupted, sending lava flowing for 60 miles (95 km) down a channel of the ancestral Stanislaus River. The lava cooled and solidified into the resistant rock *latite* (a volcanic rock very similar to basalt). Over time, the softer rock that once surrounded the river channel eroded away, leaving the dark-colored volcanic rock as a ridge. This is known as the Stanislaus Table Mountain (Figure FG4-2), and it is one of the world's best examples of "inverted topography" (what was once the lowest part of the landscape is now the highest part of the landscape). Table Mountain is best preserved here in the foothills, but remnants can be seen well up the western slope of the Sierra along California Highway 108.

Continue east on California 120/49 through Chinese Camp. At its peak in the early 1850s, about 5,000 Chinese mine workers—many of them indentured servants—lived in this community. Thirteen miles from Table Mountain you reach Moccasin, where water from the Tuolumne River drops in penstocks to a powerhouse before continuing along in the 167-mile-long Hetch Hetchy Aqueduct system to San Francisco. At this elevation, Gray Pines *(Pinus sabiniana),* recognized by their long, sparse needles and forked trunks, increasingly replace the oaks of the lower foothills.

At Moccasin, Highway 120 turns sharply uphill, climbing up the steep Priest Grade where you pass a sequence of road cuts exposing dark brown rocks of the western metamorphic belt. A short distance from here you pass through the southern section of

▲ **Figure FG4-2** Stanislaus Table Mountain near Stop 1. *(Darrel Hess photo.)*

| Douglas Fir | Ponderosa Pine | Incense Cedar | Black Oak | Jeffrey Pine | Lodgepole Pine | (young) (mature) White Fir | Red Fir |

Montane Forest

Upper Montane and Subalpine Forest

▲ **Figure FG4-3** Characteristic silhouettes of common Sierra Nevada montane forest trees and upper montane/subalpine forest trees. *(Adapted from P.V. Peterson and P.V. Peterson, Jr.,* Native Trees of the Sierra Nevada. California Natural History Guide #36. Berkeley: University of California Press, 1975.)

the Mother Lode—a 120-mile-long band of gold-bearing quartz that runs along the foothills of the Sierra (California Highway 49 roughly follows the Mother Lode north to south). More than 100 million years ago, hydrothermal fluids containing gold and other elements circulated into the cracks of the hard metamorphic rocks next to the cooling Sierra batholith, leaving veins of quartz with concentrations of gold.

Three miles beyond the top of Priest Grade, you pass through the old gold rush town of Groveland. As you continue east on Highway 120 toward Buck Meadows, you've gained enough elevation to begin to move into the montane forest zone of Douglas Fir (*Pseudotsuga menziesii*), Incense Cedar (*Calocedrus decurrens*), and Ponderosa Pine (*Pinus ponderosa*; Figure FG4-3).

About 35 miles east of Table Mountain you begin passing road cuts of granite. The granite here was not glaciated, and it is slowly weathering into coarse sand called *grus*. About 44 miles from Table Mountain (1.2 miles west of the entrance to Yosemite National Park), you pass the turnoff for the winding, seventeen-mile Evergreen Road through Mather to the Hetch Hetchy Reservoir—the source of much of San Francisco's drinking water.

Forty-five miles east of Table Mountain is the Big Oak Flat Entrance to Yosemite National Park (37°48′01″N, 119°52′32″W). In addition to the ranger station where you'll need to pay the Park entrance fee, there are restrooms and other visitor facilities here.

Stop 2—Crane Flat, Yosemite National Park (37°48′09″N, 119°47′51″W): About 53 miles east of Table Mountain on California 120 (7.7 miles from the Big Oak Flat Entrance to Yosemite National Park) you arrive at Crane Flat. There is a campground here (reservations are required), as well as gasoline and basic groceries.

At the intersection just beyond the campground entrance, turn left (north) onto the Tioga Pass Road segment of California 120. You may want to reset your trip odometer to zero in order to read the field guide mileage to stops along the Tioga Pass Road. (If you continue straight on the Big Oak Flat Road for another ten miles, you reach Yosemite Valley [*Field Guide #5—Yosemite Valley*].)

About 0.6 miles from Crane Flat along the Tioga Pass Road you pass the parking area for the Tuolumne Grove. A one-mile hike (with an elevation drop of about 500 feet), takes you to the Tuolumne Grove of Big Trees—the Giant Sequoia (*Sequoiadendron giganteum*)—where there is a short, self-guided nature trail.

Stop 3 (rolling stop)—Yosemite Creek

(37°51'06"N, 119°34'02"W): About nineteen miles from Crane Flat, you pass over Yosemite Creek. Seven miles south of here the creek drops 2,425 feet (739 m) out of a **hanging valley** to the floor of Yosemite Valley—the highest waterfall in the park (see Hike C in *Field Guide #5—Yosemite Valley*).

Stop 4—Olmsted Point (37°48'39"N, 119°29'06"W):

Twenty-nine miles from Crane Flat (ten miles from Yosemite Creek), take the right (south) pullout to the parking lot for Olmsted Point. This is one of the best stops anywhere along the Tioga Pass Road. There is a great view of Half Dome and other features from the wheelchair-accessible exhibits near the parking area, but it's worth the effort to hike the quarter-mile-long trail out to Olmsted Point itself—a gently sloping exposure of granite with a wonderful view of Tenaya Canyon (Figure FG4-4).

The granitic bedrock here is the Half Dome Granodiorite, one of the last plutons to be emplaced in the Yosemite area, about 87 million years ago. Notice that the granite here contains many small *inclusions* of darker rock. Some of this dark rock was derived from preexisting rock that dropped down in to the magma, while some probably was derived from globs of darker magma that chilled before the lighter rock around it solidified.

At the peak of the Pleistocene glaciations, this area was thoroughly scoured by ice. As you walk over the granite here, you see fine examples of glacial polish and striations. Glacial polish is sometimes incorrectly pointed out as a demonstration of the erosional power of glaciers, but the opposite is actually true—it indicates that the rock was quite resistant to erosion. Much of the rock removed by glaciers is from *plucking*. The amount of plucking is in part dependent upon *jointing* and other fractures in the rock within which *frost wedging* can loosen material (see textbook Figure 15-7). Notice that the granodiorite in this area is relatively free of joints, and so offered great resistance to the ice. Notice also that much of the glacial polish is now peeling off as *weathering* proceeds. In a short time geologically, this polish will disappear.

Glacial **erratics** are all around you at Olmsted Point. These large boulders were left behind as the Pleistocene glaciers retreated (Figure FG4-5). Erratics are sometimes different from the rock on which they rest, making it possible in some cases to trace their origin back up-valley to their source.

Olmsted Point is a great location to see examples of **exfoliation,** in which curved layers of rock are peeling off like the layers of an onion. Exfoliation is thought to be the consequence of the unloading of pressure from formerly buried rocks such as granite. As the overlying rock is removed, the release of pressure causes the rock to expand slightly, and so joints develop roughly parallel to the surface. Exposed knobs of granite tend to become rounded over time, forming *exfoliation domes* (see textbook Figure 15-12). In a similar way, valley walls also tend to be smoothed by exfoliation.

Down Tenaya Canyon toward Yosemite Valley is perhaps the most distinctive landmark in the Park, Half Dome—a granite monolith rising 4,748 feet (1,447 m) above the valley floor (the elevation of the

▲ **Figure FG4-4** Tenaya Canyon and Half Dome from Olmsted Point at Stop 4. *(Darrel Hess photo.)*

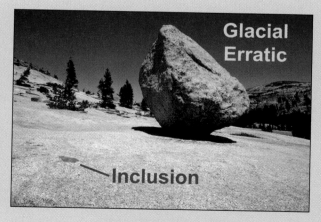

▲ **Figure FG4-5** Glacial erratic near Olmsted Point at Stop 4. Note the inclusion of darker plutonic rock in the granite. *(Darrel Hess photo.)*

summit is 8,842 feet [2,695 m]). The shape of Half Dome is due to jointing and exfoliation: The 2,000-foot (600 m) vertical cliff face is associated with a prominent set of vertical joints that cut through the batholith here, roughly aligned with Tenaya Canyon; the rounded back side of Half Dome is due to exfoliation. Glaciers did skirt Half Dome, carrying away the *talus* that would have accumulated below the vertical face, but the ice probably didn't get much higher than about 700 feet (210 m) below the top of the dome.

Clouds Rest is another example of exfoliation in granitic rock that is undergoing pressure release. The gently undulating surface illustrates the general tendency of the sheet joints of exfoliation to align parallel to the exposed surface of rock.

Return to the Olmsted Point parking lot and continue east on the Tioga Pass Road. As you gain elevation, you move through the mixed coniferous and upper montane forest of Jeffrey Pine *(Pinus jeffreyi)* and White Fir *(Abies concolor)*, and eventually into the subalpine forest of Red Fir *(Abies magnifica)*, and Lodgepole Pine *(Pinus contorta;* see Figure FG4-3).

Stop 5 (rolling stop)—Tenaya Lake

(37°56'01"N, 119°27'35"W): About 31 miles from Crane Flat (1.8 miles from Olmsted Point) is Tenaya Lake. The lake rests in a basin scoured by the series of Pleistocene glaciers that flowed from near Tioga Pass, past Half Dome, and into the Yosemite Valley. Notice that Tenaya Canyon here has the characteristic broad U-shape of a glacial trough (see textbook Figure 19-33). Tenaya Lake and Tenaya Canyon were named for Chief Tenaya of the Yosemite Indians. In June of 1851, Captain John Boling led a surprise attack here with the Mariposa Battalion of the U.S. Army, capturing the band of Indians led by Chief Tenaya. Chief Tenaya himself wasn't captured until a month later.

Stop 6—Tuolumne Meadows (37° 52'53"N, 119°23'59"W): Thirty-seven miles from Crane Flat (6.1 miles from Tenaya Lake) you arrive at the western end of Tuolumne Meadows. At an elevation of 8,600 feet (2,620 m) it is the largest meadow in the High Sierra. There are many places to stop and explore here. Gasoline and groceries are available in the summer months in the visitor area near the eastern end of the meadow.

During the Pleistocene, this entire area was buried beneath the enormous Tuolumne Icefield. A large glacier flowed out of this region to the northwest about fifteen miles to carve the "Grand Canyon of the Tuolumne" and the Hetch Hetchy Valley—the "sister"

valley to Yosemite. Hetch Hetchy Valley was blocked by O'Shaughnessy Dam in 1938 to form Hetch Hetchy Reservoir—the penstocks at Moccasin (between Stops 1 and 2) are part of the aqueduct system that transports this drinking water to San Francisco.

Other glaciers extended down from this area into Yosemite Valley—one glacier down Tenaya Canyon, and another down "Little Yosemite Valley"—the canyon of the upper Merced River; these two glaciers then joined to flow through Yosemite Valley. At the height of the Pleistocene glaciations only the highest peaks in the area stood above the ice. After the Pleistocene, a succession of shallow lakes remained in the area of present-day Tuolumne Meadows, slowly filling with sand and gravel transported by streams.

Two prominent granite domes are found at Tuolumne Meadows on the north side of the road—one on the western end, and the other on the eastern end. The western dome is Pothole Dome (37°52'53"N, 119°23'59"W). Pothole Dome is a **roche moutonnée,** formed when a glacier flows over a resistant hill of bedrock. Ice flows up the "stoss" side, smoothing and polishing the rock through glacial abrasion, leaving a gentle slope. As the glacier pulls away from the lee side of the hill, glacial plucking leaves a steeper, blocky slope (see textbook Figure 19-19). The orientation of Pothole Dome clearly shows that the ice flowed from east to west.

The larger, eastern dome at Tuolumne Meadows is Lembert Dome (37°52'39"N, 119°21'12"W)—it is also a roche moutonnée (Figure FG4-6).

Both domes make nice day hikes—Lembert Dome offers a wonderful view of Tuolumne Meadows and the surrounding area, while the western side of Pothole Dome has a series of "potholes" carved and polished by meltwater streams that flowed below the glacial ice.

▲ **Figure FG4-6** Lembert Dome is a roche moutonnée at the eastern end of Tuolumne Meadows at Stop 6. The glaciers moved from right to left (east to west) through this area. *(Darrel Hess photo.)*

Stop 7—Tioga Pass and Dana Meadows

(37°54'39"N, 119°15'29"W): Forty-four miles east of Crane Flat (6.9 miles from Lembert Dome at the eastern end of Tuolumne Meadows) you reach Tioga Pass. At 9,941 feet (3,030 m) this is the highest highway pass in the Sierra. There is a parking area just west of the Tioga Pass Entrance Station to Yosemite National Park (where you'll pay the Park entrance fee if you're arriving from the east). Many of the trees you see here are the five-needled Whitebark Pine (*Pinus albicaulis*).

Dana Meadows is the gently rolling grassy meadow south of the road. The little lakes and depressions you see on the meadow are **kettles**—depressions left by melting blocks of ice from the retreating glaciers (see textbook Figure 19-24).

Across Dana Meadows to the southeast is the northern shoulder of Mt. Dana (13,053 feet; 3,979 m). The western slope of Mt. Dana and the Dana Plateau to the east were not glaciated during the Pleistocene—these are thought to be "residual" surfaces, remnants of the original landscape surface before it was uplifted into the modern Sierra.

From Tioga Pass, the highway begins its drop of about 3,400 feet (1,000 m) down to the Mono Lake basin to the east. The original trail from Mono Lake to Tioga Pass was the Indian trail up through Bloody Canyon and Mono Pass, about five miles south of here. (On the east side of the Sierra you have a nice view of Bloody Canyon from Stop 2 in *Field Guide #6—Mono Lake*.) The first modern road up Lee Vining Canyon from Mono Lake was completed in 1911; the present highway was completed in 1963.

Stop 8—Ellery Lake

(37°56'11"N, 119°14'05"W): As you continue east from Tioga Pass, you first pass Tioga Lake, and then, about three miles east of Tioga Pass (47 miles east of Crane Flat), you come to Ellery Lake. There are several automobile pull-outs on the south side of the road along the lake. Ellery Lake sits in a basin carved by Pleistocene glaciers that flowed from the Conness Icefield that existed north of here, and then down Lee Vining Canyon to the east.

Look across the lake to the large slope of talus along the southern side of the lake (see textbook Figure 15-20). Notice that the color of the rocks to the left (east) is light gray—this is granite. The rocks to the right (west) are reddish brown. These reddish brown rocks are part of the eastern metamorphic belt, and are probably at least 250 million year old. This is one of the most distinctive contacts between the relatively younger plutonic rocks of the Sierra Nevada batholith, and the older metamorphic rocks into which the granitic magma intruded. Much of the metamorphic rock here is called *hornfels*—a catch-all term for fine-grained metamorphic rocks that formed from the recrystalization of sedimentary or volcanic rocks. The old geologic term *roof pendants* is still used to describe these metamorphic rocks that appear to "hang down" into the younger granite.

Continue down Tioga Pass toward the Mono Lake basin. Once past Ellery Lake, Lee Vining Canyon takes a steep drop down. This is an example of a **glacial step**—an abrupt drop in the floor of a glacial valley (see textbook Figure 19-39). Water from Ellery Lake falls 1,640 feet (500 m) through a penstock to power turbines in the powerhouse below.

Stop 9—Lee Vining Canyon

(37°57'01"N, 119°12'30"W): As you continue down the canyon, the road becomes steeper. This is typical of the east-side passes of the Sierra. The steep eastern face is the eroded *fault plane* along which the Sierra was uplifted. There are several turnouts on the way down where you can safely stop and look at the topography (for example, there is one about 1.3 miles from Ellery Lake; 48.2 miles from Crane Flat).

Looking toward the south wall of Lee Vining Canyon you see several short hanging valleys that originate in **cirques** eroded into the Dana Plateau (Figure FG4-7). During the Pleistocene, small tributary glaciers entered the main Lee Vining glacier from these valleys, but were unable to erode as deeply as the main glacier (see textbook Figure 19-33). Notice also the large **talus cones** along the south wall of the canyon. This debris has accumulated since the glaciations ended about 10,000 years ago.

▲ **Figure FG4-7** Seen from Stop 9, a hanging valley along the south side of Lee Vining Canyon originates in a cirque eroded into the Dana Plateau. A talus cone has developed below the hanging valley. *(Darrel Hess photo.)*

As you continue down Lee Vining Canyon, notice that some of the roadcuts expose glacial **till** deposited by Pleistocene glaciers. Near the bottom of the canyon, especially along the south wall, you see large **lateral moraines** left by the glaciers (see textbook Figure 19-41). The glaciers that flowed down this canyon were the largest in this part of the eastern Sierra, more than 700 feet (210 m) thick. The highest lateral moraine ridge was left by the "Tahoe" stage glaciation, about 70,000 years ago. Inside and below this rim is another smaller ridge of till from the "Tioga" stage glaciation, about 20,000 years ago (see *Field Guide #5—Yosemite Valley,* for more information about stages of glaciation during the Pleistocene). Near the bottom the canyon, the lateral moraines begin to converge together—these are the eroded remnants of *recessional moraines* left by the terminus of the glaciers as they receded at the end of a glacial advance.

By the time you've reached the lower parts of Lee Vining Canyon, notice that the vegetation has changed considerably from just a few miles higher—here the piñon-juniper woodland becomes visible, with the sagebrush scrub dominating the lower parts of the arid Mono Basin in the distance.

This field guide ends at the junction of the Tioga Pass Road (California 120) and U.S. Highway 395, near the town of Lee Vining. *Field Guide #6—Mono Lake* describes this region of California.

Additional Resources

Textbook:

McKnight, Tom L., and Darrel Hess. *Physical Geography: A Landscape Appreciation,* 9th ed. Upper Saddle River, NJ: Pearson/Prentice Hall, 2008. Chapters 14 and 19.

Further Reading:

Ditton, Richard P., and Donald E. McHenry. *Yosemite Road Guide.* Yosemite National Park, CA: Yosemite Association, 1989.

Hill, Mary. *Geology of the Sierra Nevada,* revised edition. California Natural History Guide, 80. Berkeley: University of California Press, 2006.

Huber, N. King. *The Geologic Story of Yosemite National Park.* U.S. Geological Survey Bulletin 1595, 1987.

Web Sites:

Yosemite Area Regional Transportation System
http://www.yarts.com

Yosemite National Park
http://www.nps.gov/yose

Textbook Page References for Key Terms

batholith *(p. 443)*
cirque *(p. 575)*
erratic (glacial erratic) *(p. 567)*
exfoliation *(p. 464)*
glacial steps *(p. 579)*
hanging valley *(p. 580)*

kettle *(p. 571)*
lateral moraine *(p. 580)*
midocean ridge *(p. 420)*
Pleistocene epoch *(p. 555)*
rain shadow *(p. 168)*
roche moutonnée *(p. 568)*

talus cone *(p. 471)*
terrane *(p. 427)*
till *(p. 567)*
tilted fault-block mountain *(p. 449)*
transform boundary *(p. 422)*

Field Guide #5

Yosemite Valley

Darrel Hess, City College of San Francisco

Introduction

In the words of naturalist John Muir, Yosemite is the "Incomparable Valley." It has sheer granite cliffs, towering waterfalls, cascading streams, quiet meadows and lush forest. Within the valley you can see evidence of the remarkable sequence of events and processes that shaped the region. This field guide describes many of the most popular sights within Yosemite Valley. All of these sites can be visited in one day; however, you'll be rewarded by taking the extra time to explore some of the less-crowded locations and trails within the valley as well.

▲ **Figure FG5-1** Regional map of Yosemite Valley, showing California Highway 140 and field guide stops. Letters indicate locations of "Hikes" within the valley.

Location

This field guide starts in Yosemite Valley about seven miles east of the Arch Rock entrance to Yosemite National Park. The valley is reached by following California Highway 140 east from the Central Valley town of Merced for 75 miles (120 km; Figure FG5-1). You may also reach Yosemite Valley from Crane Flat to the north via the New Big Oak Flat Road (see *Field Guide #4—Sierra Nevada via Tioga Pass*), or from the south via California Highway 41/ Wawona Road.

Yosemite Valley may also be reached with Amtrak train/motorcoach service, and locally with the Yosemite Area Regional Transportation System—see *Additional Resources* on F-43.

Yosemite Valley is one of the most popular tourist destinations in the country, and so expect large crowds during the peak summer tourist season. Reservations for lodging and campsites within the valley should be made well in advance. Yosemite Village is the service center for the valley—restaurants, groceries and other visitor services are found here.

Parking is limited or restricted in most parts of the valley—the Park Service encourages visitors to leave their vehicles in day-use parking lots, and then if possible walk, ride bicycles, or take the free Yosemite Valley Shuttle Bus—especially in the crowded east end of the valley. Many exhibits, campgrounds, and trails in Yosemite Valley are wheelchair accessible, as are the Yosemite Valley Shuttle Buses—check the Park Web site on F-43 for details.

Yosemite Valley is open throughout the year. Summer is the most popular season, although smaller crowds make visits during the other seasons of the year especially satisfying. Summers are usually warm during the day, but cool—or even cold—at night (the elevation of the valley floor is 4,000 feet [1,220 m]). Fall and spring are generally mild, but occasionally wet, while winter is cold with frequent heavy snow. Tire chains for snow may be required as early as October.

Observe all Park Service guidelines regarding bears. Bears are strong, fast and smart. They will exert remarkable effort to get inside your car, tent or backpack if they see or smell anything that even resembles food (including non-food items such as sun cream and insect repellant), as well ice chests and empty food containers or soft drink cans.

Background

Geologic History: Yosemite Valley is sometimes described as a "classic" glacial valley, but this really isn't the case. In some regards it is an "extreme" example of a glacial trough—the valley walls are steeper, the valley floor flatter, and the hanging valleys and waterfalls much higher than those of most glacial valleys. The reasons for these differences include the characteristics of the rocks and the geologic history of the valley.

Yosemite Valley is made of granite (see textbook Figure 13-8) and similar plutonic rocks such as granodiorite, ranging in age from about 80 million years to 140 million years. This granite was emplaced deep below the surface through series of "pulses" of magma that cooled into the collection of *plutons* that comprise the Sierra Nevada **batholith.**

By perhaps 25 million years ago, as the continental crust of North America east of here began to pull apart, the ancient Sierra was uplifting through faulting along its eastern side. As the mountain range rose, the overlying volcanic and metamorphic rock was increasingly removed by erosion. Over the last few million years, the rate of uplift along the eastern faults seems to have accelerated, leaving the modern Sierra as one of the world's best examples of a *tilted fault-block mountain range* (see textbook Figure 14-54). As the Sierra Nevada rose along its eastern edge, streams, such as the ancestral Merced River, downcut "V-shaped" valleys. (For a more detailed description of the early geologic history of the Sierra, see *Field Guide #4—Sierra Nevada via Tioga Pass*).

Glaciation: During the **Pleistocene epoch,** from roughly 2 million years ago to 10,000 years ago, glaciers formed in the higher parts of the Sierra. The glaciers flowed down the western and eastern sides of the range, largely following the paths of existing stream valleys. At the peak of the Pleistocene glaciations, however, a highland ice-field 100 miles (160 km) long covered the High Sierra, in some areas to depths of hundreds of feet, with ice more than 3,000 feet (900 m) deep in some valleys.

The Pleistocene glaciers reshaped the old stream valleys through which they flowed. Glaciers tend to deepen, steepen and widen an existing valley, usually transforming the V-shaped stream valley into a U-shaped glacial trough. Glaciers also often straighten sinuous stream valleys, but leave irregular *glacial steps* in the down-valley profile (see textbook Figure 19-39).

Yosemite Valley underwent multiple glaciations. The names and time periods for each of these glaciations have been subject to debate and revision by geologists over the last few decades—and may well be revised again as new evidence is deciphered. The most extensive of the Pleistocene glaciations in the Yosemite area took place about 1,000,000 years ago and is known as the Sherwin glaciation (the Sherwin and earlier glaciations are often collectively referred to as "pre-Tahoe" glaciations). During the Sherwin glaciation, glaciers completely filled Yosemite Valley to a depth of more than 2,000 feet (600 m) in places, flowing as far west as El Portal (Figure FG5-2). During the more recent Tahoe and Tioga glaciations (the Tahoe glaciation took place between about 70,000 and 150,000 years ago, and the Tioga glaciation between about 19,000 and 26,000 years ago), glaciers in the valley advanced only as far as El Capitan. Following the retreat of the Tioga glaciers, a lake (called Ancient Lake Yosemite by geologists) occupied the valley floor, before filling up with sediment and turning into a meadow.

Weather and Climate: The present-day climate of Yosemite Valley is largely the consequence of two important factors. (1) The influence of the seasonal migration of the *subtropical high:* As with the coastal **mediterranean climate** to the west, the summer influence of the subtropical high leads to stability and generally dry conditions in the Yosemite area. During the winter, the subtropical high migrates equatorward, allowing the *westerlies* to bring in *midlatitude cyclones.* In the Sierra as a whole, winter is the wet season, although summer thunderstorms also bring some rain. (2) The role of altitude: Because of the greater cooling of air that results when storms are given an *orographic* lift up the west slope of the Sierra, much of the precipitation during the winter falls as snow. The winter snow pack melts in the spring and summer, draining into reservoirs (such as into the Hetch Hetchy Valley to the north of

▲ **Figure FG5-2** Artist's depiction of glaciation in Yosemite Valley. **(A)** Pre-Tahoe glaciation about 1,000,000 years ago. **(B)** Tioga glaciation about 20,000 years ago. **(C)** Ancient Lake Yosemite after retreat of Tioga glaciers. *(From U.S. Geological Survey Bulletin 1595.)*

Yosemite) providing the water supply for much of California.

Plant Communities: The high elevation generally leads to cooler summers than in lower areas as well—which in turn influences the patterns of vegetation in the Sierra (see textbook Figure 11-10). Vegetation changes from the valley grassland and oak savanna in the western foothills into the montane forests of Ponderosa Pine (*Pinus ponderosa*) and Incense Cedar (*Calocedrus decurrens*) on the floor of Yosemite Valley. In the higher areas above the rim of the valley, the vegetation transitions into subalpine forests of Lodgepole Pine (*Pinus contorta*) and Red Fir (*Abies magnifica*).

Site Descriptions

If you're traveling east from Merced along Highway 140, notice that for much of the way, the Merced River Canyon is generally "V" shaped—this indicates that it was cut primarily through stream erosion, not glaciation. Once in Yosemite Valley, however, the walls become much steeper and the valley floor flatter and wider—indication that processes other than stream erosion have been at work. About 69 miles east of Merced you reach the Arch Rock Entrance Station to Yosemite National Park, where you'll need to pay the Park entrance fee. About five miles beyond the Park entrance, you enter Yosemite Valley itself.

Once in the valley, you'll generally loop around the valley floor in a counterclockwise direction (following the one-way-road loop). Because many of the sites in the valley are reached by short walks, once you've reached the Visitor Center (Stop 5), sites are described through a series of "Hikes." These hikes, of course, may be taken in any order.

Once you enter the far western end of Yosemite Valley, road signs direct you to turn right (southeast) onto a one-way road that curves east into the valley's Southside Drive. Less than a mile after the turnoff (about 6.7 miles east of the Arch Rock Entrance Station), follow the signs and make a sharp right turn (heading west) onto the Wawona Road that climbs out of the valley. In 1.6 miles pull off at the parking lot at the Yosemite Valley Overlook (often simply called the Wawona "Tunnel View").

Stop 1—Wawona Tunnel View (37° 42'23"N, 119°40'39"W): This is one of the best views of Yosemite Valley, and a great starting point to see many features of the valley you'll visit at other stops (Figure FG5-3).

The exposed rock of the valley walls consists of the plutonic rocks granite and granodiorite. The valley was originally deepened by the ancestral Merced River as the Sierra slowly uplifted along its eastern side. During the Pleistocene, glaciers reshaped the stream valley through a series of advances and retreats.

Most glacial valleys (or more correctly, glacial troughs) are generally U-shaped—having been widened, deepened and steepened by glacial abrasion and glacial *plucking* along the sides and bottom of the glacier. Notice that Yosemite Valley isn't really U-shaped—it has a flat floor and nearly vertical walls.

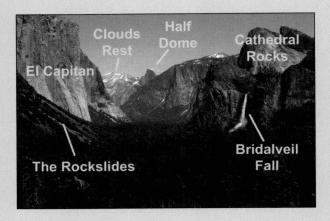

▲ **Figure FG5-3**   Yosemite Valley from Wawona Tunnel View at Stop 1. *(Darrel Hess photo.)*

The vertical walls are due primarily to **jointing** in the granite. Prominent, widely-spaced vertical *master joints* in otherwise unjointed, resistant rock influenced where weathering, mass wasting, and erosion could easily remove rock. Yosemite's enormous granite monoliths such as El Capitan and Half Dome remain as nearly vertical cliffs because they are largely unjointed, and so resist erosion. On the other hand, more closely-jointed rock, such as the source of **talus** that makes up the Rockslides just to the west of El Capitan, is much more susceptible to weathering and mass wasting. **Rockfall** is a continuing process within Yosemite Valley. In October of 2008, two rockfalls forced the permanent closure of about one-third of the guest accommodations at Curry Village at the far eastern end of the valley.

The floor of Yosemite Valley is unusually flat for a glacial valley. The bottom of the U-shaped trough left by glacial erosion has been filled with as much as 2,000 feet (600 m) of sediment. As ancient Lake Yosemite silted up with alluvium following the last glaciation, it leveled the valley floor, which was eventually covered with meadow and forest.

In the far distance, you see Half Dome. The flat face of Half Dome is due to a prominent vertical joint that runs through the pluton in this area (see textbook Figure 19-37). Contrary to popular misconception, Half Dome was not cut in half by glaciers. Glaciers flowed down Tenaya Canyon past Half Dome, removing rock that broke off its face along the vertical jointing plane. The rounded top and back side of Half Dome—as well and the gently undulating surface of Clouds Rest farther up canyon—is due to **exfoliation** (also see Figure FG4-4 in Field Guide #4). The unloading of pressure on these formerly buried rocks caused the rock to crack along curved joints parallel to the surface (see textbook Figures 15-11 and 15-12). Over time, layer after layer of rock peeled off, gently rounding and

smoothing exposed granite into domes and valley walls.

A short distance from Wawona Tunnel View along the south side of the valley is Bridalveil Fall, dropping from one of the world's most spectacular examples of a **hanging valley** (see textbook Figure 19-33). During the peak of the Pleistocene glaciations, tributary glaciers entered the main glacier flowing down Yosemite Valley. These smaller tributary glaciers couldn't deepen their valleys as much as the main glacier, so today these tributary valleys enter high up on the main valley walls. Because the walls of Yosemite Valley are nearly vertical, streams flowing out of these hanging valleys form many of the most beautiful waterfalls in the Park, such as Bridalveil Fall (Stop 2) and Yosemite Falls (Hike C).

Considering the great amount of glacial erosion that has taken place in Yosemite Valley, there are relatively few areas in the valley itself where glacial **till** remains. Unlike the eastern side of the Sierra Nevada, only poorly developed **moraines** are found in Yosemite Valley, probably because the amount of meltwater was so great that debris melted out of the glaciers was immediately transported by streams down into the Central Valley.

Stop 2—Bridalveil Fall (37°42'12"N, 119° 38'52"W):
Retrace your route back down the Wawona Road toward the valley floor. Near where the Wawona Road intersects Southside Drive is the parking lot and trailhead for Bridalveil Fall. A trail from the east end of the parking lot takes you 0.2 miles to an observation area near the bottom of the fall.

Bridalveil Fall forms where Bridalveil Creek drops 620 feet (189 m) out of a hanging valley (see textbook Figure 19-40). The fall has its peak flow during the late spring and early summer, but has water all year. The steep spire to the right (west) of Bridalveil Fall is the Leaning Tower, and the three peaks just to the left (east) are the Cathedral Rocks.

Stop 3—El Capitan View (37°43'15"N, 119°38'53"W):
From the Bridalveil Fall parking lot, continue east on Southside Drive for 0.5 miles where there are long pullouts on both sides of the road (with a wooden post labeled "V14"). From here, there are great views of Bridalveil Fall to the south and El Capitan across the valley to the north.

El Capitan, "The Chief," is a sheer granite wall rising 3,000 feet (910 m) above the valley floor—perhaps the highest uninterrupted cliff face in the world. It is made from nearly unjointed granite which resisted both stream and glacial erosion, and constricted the valley width here. The Cathedral Rocks on the opposite side of the valley are made of the same resistant granite, and similarly resisted erosion.

About halfway down the eastern side of El Capitan (and better seen from vantage points farther east of here) is a patch of the darker plutonic rock called diorite, which was intruded as a **dike** into the El Capitan granite. This dark patch reminds some people of a map of North America.

Toward the far western end of this parking area, you may recognize an exposure of glacial till. This till is part of a moraine that marks the terminus of the last glacier in Yosemite Valley. This moraine helped dam the valley floor, producing Lake Yosemite before it disappeared several thousand years ago.

Stop 4—Three Brothers View (37° 43'18"N, 119°37'28"W): About 1.3 miles farther east on the Southside Drive, you reach a small pullout (designated by a wooden post labeled "V16"). This spot provides a good view of the Three Brothers on the opposite side of the valley. The tallest, Eagle Peak, rises more than 3,800 feet (1,160 m) above the valley floor and is the highest peak along the north rim of Yosemite Valley. Notice that these three dramatic peaks share the same geometry: All three formed along a prominent set of parallel diagonal joints in the granite, and each ends with a parallel vertical cliff. On the south side of the valley, opposite the Three Brothers, you may be able to recognize rocks with similar jointing patterns.

Stop 5—Visitor Center at Yosemite Village (37°44'55"N, 119°35'17"W): Continue east on Southside Drive, past the Yosemite Chapel, until you come to the day-use parking area at Yosemite Village. To reach the Visitor Center or other sites in the often congested eastern part of the valley, you may walk, bicycle or take the free Yosemite Valley Shuttle Bus that loops around the valley floor from Yosemite Lodge in the west to Curry Village and Happy Isles in the east. Many day hikes are possible from this part of the valley, ranging from short and easy to long and strenuous. The following are among the most popular and interesting easy hikes:

Hike A—Vernal Fall Footbridge (37° 43'34"N, 119°33'06"W): From Shuttle Bus Stop #16 at Happy Isles, hike 0.8 miles along the cascading Merced River to the footbridge near the bottom of Vernal Fall. A short distance along the Merced River after leaving the Bus Stop, you pass the U.S. Geological Survey Happy Isles Bridge Stream Gage Station. Data on the flow of the Merced River—unaltered by human action upstream from here—has been gathered continuously since 1915 (view near-real time streamflow data from the Web site listed on F-43).

From the stream gage station, the paved but steep trail climbs along a talus slope at the foot of the north side of the Merced River Canyon. In most places trees are growing among the large moss-covered boulders. Many of the trees here are oaks, along with smaller willows—which thrive in wet areas such as this. Notice, however, that in a few places along the trail there are no trees among the rocks—these are areas of relatively recent rockfall and trees haven't had a chance to become established.

After an elevation gain of about 400 feet (120 m), you reach a footbridge crossing the Merced River. From this location, Vernal Fall can be seen upstream in the distance. Vernal Fall forms where the Merced River drops 317 feet (97 m) off one of the glacial steps in Merced Canyon. Glaciers deepen their valleys (primarily through glacial plucking) where the bedrock is weaker or more closely jointed, but leave flatter benches or "steps" in areas where the rock is stronger (see textbook Figure 19-39).

From the footbridge you may continue up the "Mist Trail" an additional 0.7 miles, climbing more than 600 steps along the south wall of the canyon to the top of Vernal Fall. About 1.3 miles beyond Vernal Fall, you reach Nevada Fall where it drops 594 feet (181 m) off the lip of another glacial step in Merced Canyon. Use great caution when hiking up the Mist Trail—in addition to getting hikers quite wet from the windblown spray, the trail can be extremely slippery. Also, be careful at the top of Vernal Fall where strong currents have swept hikers off the rocks.

If you walk or take the Shuttle Bus from the start of the Vernal Fall trail (Shuttle Bus Stop #16) to Shuttle Bus Stop #17 (Hike B to Mirror Lake) you'll pass over a gentle rise in the road—you can see in the small roadcut that this rise consists of till. Although sometimes called "Medial Moraine," it is more likely a **lateral moraine** left by the last glacier that flowed down Tenaya Canyon into Yosemite Valley.

Hike B—Mirror Lake (37°44'47"N, 119° 33'03"W): Take the Shuttle Bus to the trailhead for Mirror Lake at Shuttle Bus Stop #17. From there, it's a one-mile hike up a paved trail to Mirror Lake at the foot of Half Dome (Figure FG5-4). Visitors with Accessibility Placards may drive to Mirror Lake.

Figure FG5-4   Half Dome above Mirror Lake on Hike B. *(Darrel Hess photo.)*

Named for the beautiful reflections of the surrounding valley walls, Mirror Lake is slowly disappearing. The low rock dam built by visitors in the late 1800s to try to preserve the lake divides Mirror Lake into upper and lower pools. During the fall and winter, sand builds up in the lower pool, but this sand is scoured away by the spring floods. By early autumn, Mirror Lake is usually nearly dry. Although some hydrologists hypothesize that Mirror Lake will remain a seasonal pool in Tenaya Creek, others expect that silt deposited by Tenaya Creek will gradually fill the shallow lake, eventually turning it into a meadow.

Half Dome rises 4,748 feet (1,447 m) from the valley floor above you to the southeast. The 2,000 foot (600 m) vertical face of Half Dome was accentuated when Pleistocene glaciers carried away slabs of rock that broke off along the master joint in the granite here, while the rounded summit and back side is due to exfoliation. Glaciers themselves never went higher than about 700 feet (210 m) below its summit, and it's doubtful there ever was a "full dome" exposed.

If you want a slightly longer hike, instead of a round-trip to Shuttle Bus Stop #17, about halfway back you can follow the bike trail west to Yosemite Village. This will give you a closer view of the Royal Arches along the north wall of the Valley—these great arcs in the granite were formed by exfoliation.

Hike C—Lower Yosemite Falls (37° 45′00″N, 119°35′43″W): Just west of the Visitor Center, at Shuttle Bus Stop #6, is an easy half-mile hike along a well-maintained loop trail to a bridge near the foot of Yosemite Falls. The eastern part of the loop is wheelchair accessible. Yosemite Falls is one of the highest waterfalls in the world, dropping a total of 2,425 feet (739 m) from the hanging val-

Figure FG5-5   Yosemite Falls on Hike C. *(Darrel Hess photo.)*

ley of Yosemite Creek to the valley floor below (see *Field Guide #4—Sierra Nevada via Tioga Pass,* Stop 3, for a description of Yosemite Creek along the Tioga Pass Road). Yosemite Falls is at its most spectacular in the late spring and early summer, and will often go dry by early autumn.

The Upper Fall drops 1,430 feet (436 m) down a near-vertical wall of granite until it strikes a narrow rock ledge marked by a line of trees (Figure FG5-5). This ledge forms along a joint that runs through the pluton here. The Middle Cascade drops 675 feet (206 m) through a narrow gorge to another wooded ledge, again formed by a horizontal joint in the granite. After the final 320-foot (98 m) drop of the Lower Fall, Yosemite Creek empties into the Merced River.

Hike D—Cook's Meadow and Merced River (37°44′36″N, 119°35′36″W): From Shuttle Bus Stop #6 ("Yosemite Falls"), cross the road to the south along a trail and boardwalk that take you across Cook's Meadow to the Merced River. In the late 1800s, Cook's Hotel was established near here, and cattle grazed in this meadow until the 1920s.

First, follow the path across the meadow to the footbridge crossing the Merced River. The river is fed by the snow pack along the crest of the High Sierra, nearly 20 miles (30 km) to the east. Although it is tempting to swim in the Merced River during a hot summer day, use extreme caution: The water is very cold and the current is much stronger than it first appears.

From the footbridge, backtrack a short distance to where the boardwalk forks and you can turn east out into the open area of Cook's Meadow. In order to improve hunting and gathering conditions, the Miwok Indians used fire to keep the valley floor meadows open. Since that time, forest has increasingly encroached on the meadows, although the Park Service does undertake prescribed burns to keep the ecosystem healthy. Common trees on the valley floor include the deciduous California Black Oak (*Quercus kelloggii*), Ponderosa Pine, and Incense Cedar (see Figure FG4-3 in *Field Guide #4*). In late spring and early summer, you may see the blossoms of the Western Azalea (*Rhododendron occidentale*) in places along the banks of the Merced River.

About midway along the path across Cook's Meadow, notice the elongated, low grassy depression—this is an abandoned channel of the Merced River. During the spring floods, this channel has flowing water, but for most of the rest of the year, only a shallow pond contains water.

If you continue along the boardwalk to the eastern end of the meadow, you come to a parking area and Shuttle Bus Stop #11. From here it is a short walk to Sentinel Bridge—a stone bridge across the Merced River that offers a wonderful view of Half Dome in the distance.

Additional Resources

Textbook:
McKnight, Tom L., and Darrel Hess. *Physical Geography: A Landscape Appreciation*, 9th ed. Upper Saddle River, NJ: Pearson/Prentice Hall, 2008. Chapters 14 and 19.

Further Reading:
Ditton, Richard P., and Donald E. McHenry. *Yosemite Road Guide.* Yosemite National Park, CA: Yosemite Association, 1989.
Guyton, Bill. *Glaciers of California.* California Natural History Guide, 59. Berkeley: University of California Press, 1998.
Huber, N. King. *The Geologic Story of Yosemite National Park.* U.S. Geological Survey Bulletin 1595. Washington, D.C.: United States Government Printing Office, 1987.

Web Sites:
Amtrak Train and Motorcoach Service
http://www.amtrak.com

Merced River Stream Gage, Happy Isles
http://waterdata.usgs.gov/nwis/uv?11264500

Yosemite Area Regional Transportation System
http://www.yarts.com

Yosemite National Park
http://www.nps.gov/yose

Textbook Page References for Key Terms

batholith *(p. 443)*
dike *(p. 444)*
exfoliation *(p. 464)*
hanging valley *(p. 580)*
joint *(p. 460)*
lateral moraine *(p. 580)*
mediterranean climate *(p. 229)*
moraine *(p. 571)*
Pleistocene epoch *(p. 555)*
rockfall *(p. 471)*
talus *(p. 471)*
till *(p. 567)*

Field Guide #6

Mono Lake

Darrel Hess, City College of San Francisco

Introduction

The Mono Basin offers some of the most varied and fascinating natural history of any place in California. It includes Mono Lake itself—a salt lake with a specialized ecosystem and dramatic tufa towers—as well as a chain of young volcanoes and steep glacial canyons carved into the spectacular eastern face of the Sierra Nevada.

This field guide highlights features you can easily see in one day around Mono Lake.

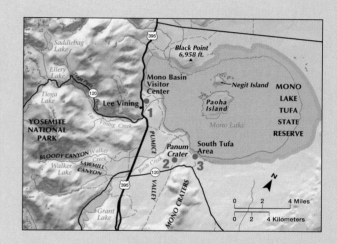

▲ **Figure FG6-1** Regional map of Mono Lake area showing field guide stops.

Location

Lee Vining, the largest town in the Mono Basin, is reached via U.S. Highway 395 or California Highway 120 (Figure FG6-1). (*Field Guide #4—Sierra Nevada via Tioga Pass* describes the trip across the Sierra to Lee Vining along California Highway 120.)

During the summer, bus service is available from Yosemite Valley to Tuolumne Meadows and Lee Vining via the Tioga Pass Road with the Yosemite Area Regional Transportation System—see *Additional Resources* on F-49.

Gasoline, groceries, restaurants and lodging are available in Lee Vining. Several small campgrounds are located a few miles away off California 120 in the lower portion of Lee Vining Canyon. The Mono Basin Scenic Area Visitor Center is about one mile north of Lee Vining off U.S. 395. The Visitor Center is wheelchair accessible and includes a natural history museum, a ranger information counter, and a museum store where you can purchase maps and additional guide books for the region. The Visitor Center is closed during winter months.

Winters here are cold and often snowy. Tioga Pass usually remains closed until June, but sections of U.S. 395 may also close during snowstorms, so check road conditions before traveling here in winter months. The summers are warm and pleasant, but often punctuated by thunderstorms. Because of the relatively high elevation of Mono Lake (6,382 feet; 1,945 m) take precautions against sunburn in summer by wearing a hat and sun cream, and be sure to drink plenty of water to avoid dehydration.

Background

Geologic History: Mono Lake is found at the western edge of the Basin-and-Range province of North America. The down-dropped Mono Basin was formed through the same processes of crustal extension and faulting that uplifted the Sierra Nevada (see *Field Guide #4—Sierra Nevada via Tioga Pass*) and down-dropped Death Valley (see *Field Guide #9—Death Valley*). The eastern face of the Sierra Nevada was uplifted and the Mono Basin down-dropped along a series of high-angle faults (see textbook Figure 14-54). The basin itself is structurally much deeper than it appears, having been filled in some places with more than 3,000 feet (900 m) of sediments deposited by glacial streams and ash ejected from nearby volcanoes.

This region has experienced geologically-recent volcanic activity, at least in part associated with the faulting and crustal extension in the Basin-and-Range region over the last few million years. The Mono Craters are a young chain of **plug dome** volcanoes (see textbook Figure 14-29c), some erupting less than 1,000 years ago. Just south of the Mono Basin, a catastrophic eruption 730,000 years ago blanketed much of western North America with volcanic ash and formed the Long Valley **caldera**. It is likely that **magma** remains just a few miles below the surface in the region, and future eruptions are expected by geologists.

Like most of the down-dropped basins in the Basin-and-Range, the Mono Basin is a *basin of interior drainage*—streams here have no natural outlet to the sea. Water enters Mono Lake from streams flowing from the east slope of the Sierra, but leaves only through evaporation. Because of this, over time the waters of Mono Lake became naturally salty.

Hydrology: Mono Lake is one of the oldest lakes in North America, formed at least 700,000 years ago. During the **Pleistocene epoch,** a wetter and cooler climate allowed the formation of large glaciers in the Sierra Nevada; it also allowed the formation of many large lakes in basins of interior drainage. At the peak of the Pleistocene glaciations, Mono Lake—known to geologists as Lake Russell—was at least 400 feet (120 m) deeper than today. Lake Russell filled the Mono Basin, then overflowed into the Owens Valley to the south, which also filled as a lake and overflowed into the Searles Basin and Panamint Valley farther south—which in turn overflowed into Death Valley to form Pleistocene Lake Manly (see *Field Guide #9—Death Valley*). When the Sun is right, you can still see the marks of the wave-cut shorelines of Pleistocene Lake Russell on the mountain face of the Sierra to the west.

Water Diversion: Mono Lake shrank naturally after the end of Pleistocene about 10,000 years ago, but the white alkali "bathtub ring" you see around the lake today was exposed more recently. In 1913, the Los Angeles Aqueduct began transporting water from Owens Valley south of here to Los Angeles, 233 miles (370 km) away. By the mid-1930s, Los Angeles was purchasing water rights in the Mono Basin as well, and by the early 1940s water was diverted from four streams entering Mono Lake.

As soon as the water diversion from the Mono Basin began, the level of Mono Lake began to drop, threatening the delicate ecosystem of the lake. In 1978 the Mono Lake Committee was formed to help protect Mono Lake. Through a legal ruling in 1994, the Los Angeles Department of Water and Power was mandated to reduce diversions and let the lake level rise and stabilize at an elevation of 6,392 feet (1,948 m)—about 20 feet (6 m) higher than its lowest diversion-era level of 6,372 feet (1,942 m), but lower than its original pre-diversion level that fluctuated between 6,400 and 6,425 feet (1,951 m and 1,958 m).

Weather and Climate: The arid climate of the Mono Basin is due to the Sierra Nevada to the west. The moist westerlies (often carrying midlatitude cyclones in winter) are lifted **orographically** along the windward west slope of the Sierra. The forced lifting results in high precipitation (especially winter snowfall) on the west slope of the Sierra, while a **rain shadow** develops on the leeward side (see textbook Figure 6-32b).

Plant Communities: The dominant types of vegetation in the Mono Basin reflect the generally arid conditions here, although vertical zonation patterns reveal surprising diversity. High on the eastern slope of the Sierra subalpine forest is found, while piñon-juniper woodland typically covers the lower elevations along the mountain front. In the lowest parts of the basin, sagebrush scrub dominates the landscape (see textbook Figure 11-10), with salt-tolerant alkali sink scrub vegetation found along the shore of Mono Lake itself.

Site Descriptions

These stops can be visited in any order, but the Mono Basin Visitor Center is a good starting point. In addition to its exhibits, it has an overlook of Mono Lake where you can view the entire basin before heading off to the other stops. Stops 2 and 3 are reached via graded dirt roads that are passable in dry weather with ordinary passenger automobiles.

Stop 1—Mono Basin Visitor Center

(37°58'01"N, 119°07'12"W): About one mile north of Lee Vining on U.S. 395, turn right (east) into the Mono Basin Scenic Area Visitor Center. From the outside overlook you can see many features around the lake.

On the hills above Lee Vining you see piñon-juniper woodland. This plant community is dominated by the Piñon Pine (*Pinus monophylla*) recognized by its single needles, along with the Utah Juniper (*Juniperus osteosperma*) with its scaly needles and small, blue cones.

The large island in the middle of Mono Lake is Paoha Island, and the smaller one in the north is Negit Island. Both of the islands are the result of volcanic eruptions—as is Black Point along the northern shore (which originally formed from an underwater volcanic eruption). Negit Island is an andesitic volcano that last erupted only 270 years ago. Although Paoha Island had volcanic eruptions along its north shore (and still has active steam vents), it largely originated from lake bed deposits that were uplifted along faults.

The islands were named by geologist Israel Russell in the 1870s (for whom Pleistocene Lake Russell is named). He used words from the language of the Paiute Indians for the islands. "Negit" is the Paiute word for gull—quite appropriate considering the large number of gulls often found nesting there. "Paoha" refers to spirits with wavy long hair thought to rise in the vapor from hot springs, such as those found on the island.

Because of water diversion to southern California, by 1979 the level of Mono Lake had dropped so much that a land bridge developed between the mainland and Negit Island. The California National Guard in cooperation with California Fish and Game used dynamite to blast a channel between island and the mainland, but eventually coyotes crossed over and killed thousands of nesting birds.

Directly south of the lake you see the northern end of the Mono Craters volcanoes (described at Stop 2). The highest peak in the chain is Crater Mountain (see textbook Figure 14-33), with an elevation of 9,172 feet (2,796 m). In several places along the shore of the lake, you can see the famous white towers of tufa (which you'll visit at Stop 3).

Return to U.S. 395, turn left (south), and drive back through Lee Vining.

Stop 2—Panum Crater

(37°55'32"N, 119°02'56"W): Drive south from Lee Vining on U.S. 395. About 4.7 miles south of the turnoff for Tioga Pass, turn left (east) onto California 120 East. After 3.1 miles, turn left (north) on to a graded gravel road, following the signs 0.9 miles to the parking area at Panum Crater.

The plant community around you here is sagebrush scrub. The most common plant you see is the fragrant Big Sagebrush (*Artemisia tridentata*), probably North America's most abundant shrub (although it smells similar, this sagebrush is not in the same genus as the sage used for cooking). The other very common shrub you see is the Bitterbrush (*Purshia tridentata*), recognized by its yellow flowers in early summer and the three little "teeth" on its leaves.

Panum is the youngest and the northern-most volcano of the Mono Craters chain (although the volcanic islands in Mono Lake also appear related). The term "craters" is a bit of a misnomer, since the chain is really a series of plug domes, lava flows and explosion pits that began forming perhaps only 35,000 years ago. Roughly twenty domes make up the Mono Craters-Inyo Craters volcanic chain that extends in a gentle arc south into the Mammoth Lake basin. These volcanoes are composed of solidified **lava** and explosively ejected **pyroclastics** such as pumice. The composition of the lava is mostly rhyolite and dacite—volcanic rocks that have the same mineral composition as the plutonic rocks granite and granodiorite respectively.

From the parking lot, hike the short distance up to the outer rim of the volcano. Panum erupted as recently as 640 years ago, and is quite typical of rhyolitic plug domes. You see that Panum consists of two parts: an outer ring of pumice that was exploded out of the volcano, and an inner plug of solidified lava (Figure FG6-2).

The first stage in the life of a volcano like Panum is a series of explosive events that produce the outer ring of light-colored pumice. Pumice is a type

▲ **Figure FG6-2** Panum Crater at Stop 2 showing inner plug of solidified rhyolitic lava and the outer ring of pyroclastics. *(Darrel Hess photo.)*

of volcanic glass that forms when molten material cools so quickly there is no crystalline mineral structure—the molecules simply "freeze" in place. Because this magma was thick and frothy with gases, pumice is full of tiny open spaces—often a piece of pumice is light enough to float on water. A layer of pumice several feet thick blankets the region around the Mono Craters (an area appropriately named Pumice Valley).

After its explosive phase, Panum went into another phase of formation. A plug of viscous, pasty rhyolitic lava—molten rock with the consistency of toothpaste—slowly pushed up into the throat of the volcano, where it cooled. The inner plug of Panum consists of the volcanic rock rhyolite as well as rhyolitic obsidian—another kind of volcanic glass that forms from the rapid solidification of lava that isn't frothy with gas.

If you hike a short distance around the rim of Panum toward the east, you can get a good view of the other Mono Craters volcanoes to the south. During the eruption of the plug dome just south of you, rhyolitic lava poured over the edge of the crater, leaving a thick flow of rhyolitic obsidian called a "coulee." Coulees are very rugged, steep and blocky since the surface hardens while the interior of the flow is still molten, pushing out at the edges of the flow.

Walk back along the rim of Panum a short distance to where you have a good view of the Sierra. Looking west you may be able to see the Farrington Siphon along the hills near Lee Vining. This pipe takes water from Lee Vining Creek, down to Grant Lake in the south; an aqueduct then takes the water in a tunnel beneath the Mono Craters into Long Valley to the south.

A short distance farther to the south along the crest of the Sierra, you see Mono Pass and Bloody Canyon—the location of the old Mono Trail up into the Sierra (described in *Field Guide #4—Sierra Nevada via Tioga Pass*, Stop 7). Two pairs of large **lateral moraines** are found at the bottom of Bloody Canyon (Figure FG6-3), each formed by a different glacial advance during the Pleistocene (see *Field Guide #5—Yosemite Valley* for additional information about glaciation in the Sierra).

The earliest advance about 130,000 to 140,000 years ago (probably during the beginning of the Tahoe-stage glaciations or what is sometimes called the "Mono Basin" glaciation) left the pair of moraines to the left (south), forming Sawmill Canyon. The second, larger advance came perhaps 70,000 years ago (probably toward the end of the Tahoe-stage glaciations, although some studies suggest these moraines are only slightly younger than the Sawmill moraines)—this time, the glacier turned

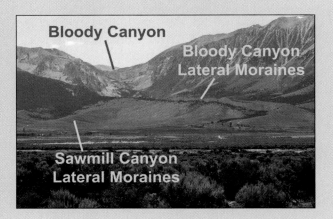

▲ **Figure FG6-3** Bloody Canyon and Sawmill Canyon lateral moraines seen from Stop 2. *(Darrel Hess photo.)*

north at the bottom of the canyon, cutting off the Sawmill Canyon moraines. Out of sight behind the lateral moraines of the larger advance, more recent glacial advances (Tioga-stage glaciations and a slightly older stage locally called the "Tenaya" glaciation) left smaller moraines that created the natural dam impounding Walker Lake.

From Panum Crater, return to California 120 and turn left (east).

Stop 3—South Tufa Area (37°56'20"N, 119°01'38"W):
About 1.6 miles east of the road to Panum Crater (4.7 miles east of U.S. 395), turn left onto a graded gravel road, following the signs about one mile to the South Tufa Area parking lot. Here you can pay a nominal entrance fee and take a short walk along a self-guided accessible boardwalk and nature trail that loops through tufa towers to the lake, and then back again to the parking lot. Please remember that tufa is quite fragile, so please do not climb on any of the towers—and no collecting of any kind is allowed.

Because Mono Lake has no natural outlet, its waters have become salty. All streams carry very small concentrations of dissolved salts and minerals. These substances are naturally concentrated in the lake as freshwater evaporates. If you were to taste the water of Mono Lake, you would find it both salty and bitter. The salty taste is mostly from sodium chloride ($NaCl$)—common table salt. The bitter taste is from carbonates—such as, sodium carbonate (Na_2CO_3), which is similar to baking soda—and other natural alkaline chemicals that give the water its "slippery" feel. The lake also contains relatively large amounts of sulfates such as sodium sulfate (Na_2SO_4). Mono Lake is about three times as salty as the ocean, and 80 times as alkaline.

If you look closely at the water, you may see some glistening or "oily" looking patches of water just off-shore. These are the upwellings from freshwater springs that come out of the lake bottom. The fresh-water doesn't mix immediately with the saltwater of the lake, producing the "shiny" looking water.

The most famous features of Mono Lake are the towers of tufa you see all around you at the lake shore (Figure FG6-4). The tufa towers are made of calcium carbonate ($CaCO_3$)—the chemical from which limestone is made. Tufa forms beneath the lake surface where freshwater springs enter the water. The freshwater contains dissolved calcium compounds, which combine with the carbonate-rich lake water to form calcium carbonate. It also appears that algae play at least a minor role in the form and texture of the tufa. These limestone towers build up as calcium carbonate precipitates out around the springs. In the quiet waters below the surface of the lake, the towers gradually extend themselves higher and higher.

Most of the tufa towers you see here at the South Tufa Area were not visible until the level of Mono Lake began dropping as a result of water diversions in the 1940s. Some of the tufa towers are 30 feet (9 m) high, visual evidence of the lake's former level. The towers exposed here are probably only 500 years old. Much older tufa formations are found along the ancient shorelines of the lake—especially along the north shore—some dating back as much as 13,000 years.

Although the waters of Mono Lake may at first seem rather lifeless, a fascinating ecosystem exists here. At the bottom of the food chain are micro-scopic, single-celled algae that live in the lake. The algae support two animal species: brine shrimp and brine flies. The shrimp and flies reproduce in

Figure FG6-4   Tufa towers in South Tufa Area at Stop 3. *(Darrel Hess photo.)*

extraordinary numbers, providing food for the many species of migratory water birds that visit the lake—some estimates suggest that as many as 900,000 birds stop or nest at Mono Lake each year.

The brine shrimp (*Artemia monica*) thrive during the summer months. After laying their eggs in September, the adults die. A new generation of brine shrimp hatches in the spring. During the winter, the lake water turns green because shrimp aren't pres-ent to eat the algae. In summer, when the numbers of brine shrimp are at their peak, the lake waters are usually quite clear.

The brine flies (*Ephydra hians*) around the lake shore are harmless. They were gathered for food by the Kuzedika Paiute people of the Mono Basin. You may also notice how birds catch large numbers of the flies: by running into a swarm along the shore with their mouths open.

Additional Resources

Textbook:
McKnight, Tom L., and Darrel Hess. *Physical Geography: A Landscape Appreciation*, 9th ed. Upper Saddle River, NJ: Pearson/Prentice Hall, 2008. Chapters 14, 18 & 19.

Further Reading:
Hill, Mary. *Geology of the Sierra Nevada*, revised edition. California Natural History Guide, 80. Berkeley: University of California Press, 2006.

Teirney, Timothy. *Geology of the Mono Basin*. Lee Vining, CA: Kutsavi Press, 1995.

Web Sites:
Inyo National Forest
http://www.fs.fed.us/r5/inyo

Mono Lake Committee
http://www.monolake.org

Yosemite Area Regional Transportation System
http://www.yarts.com

Textbook Page References for Key Terms

caldera *(p. 437)*
granite *(p. 392)*
lateral moraine *(p. 580)*
lava *(p. 429)*

magma *(p. 391)*
orographic lifting *(p. 168)*
Pleistocene epoch *(p. 555)*
plug dome *(p. 434)*

pyroclastic *(p. 429)*
rain shadow *(p. 168)*

Field Guide #7

Santa Ana Winds

Edward Aguado, San Diego State University

Introduction

The coastal areas of southern California generally avoid extreme temperatures; summers don't usually get extremely hot and subfreezing temperatures are rare at the lower elevations. But temperatures can become surprisingly high during the fall and winter months due to a phenomenon known as Santa Ana winds. People from other parts of the United States might envy reports of 85°F (29°C) temperatures in January, but the winds sometimes have catastrophic consequences in the way of massive wildfires. This field guide departs from the format of the others in this collection; rather than describing a particular region, it will explain how one of the most important weather conditions arises in southern California.

Location

While Santa Anas are associated with southern California, similar warm, dry winds can occur elsewhere. For example, **foehn winds** (locally called *Chinooks*) often bring hot and dry conditions in the plains east of the Rocky Mountains, causing rapid snowmelt and extremely rapid changes in temperature. And northern California can get descending, warm winds out of the east. But the term *Santa Ana* is primarily associated with southern California.

Site Description

Across the California coast there is a tendency for winds, especially in the afternoon, to blow from west to east. This is due to a combination of the state's position in the westerly wind belt and the classic **sea and land breeze** system. Santa Ana winds bring a major departure from this pattern, bringing winds out of the northeast rather than the west.

Santa Ana winds develop as part of a larger-scale pattern wherein a large **anticyclone** (high pressure cell) migrates from the Pacific into the Great Basin. Surface-level winds in the Northern Hemisphere rotate clockwise out of high pressure cells toward areas of low pressure. If low pressure occurs offshore near southern California, winds can move from the interior states, across southern California, and even into the eastern Pacific.

To understand the high temperatures associated with Santa Anas, we need to consider the topography of the western United States and the idea of **adiabatic warming.** Nevada, Utah, and western Colorado occupy a large part of the Great Basin, whose elevation is mostly above 4,000 feet (1,200 m). As air flows southwestward out of the region to the southern California coastal area, it descends as it moves across the lowering surface. This is extremely important because sinking air undergoes compression, and this compression in turn causes the air's temperature to increase. (If you find this hard to imagine, take a hand pump and hold the base of it while you inflate a ball or bicycle tire— the base of the pump will feel warm because of the air's compression.)

If unsaturated air sinks, it warms at the **dry adiabatic rate** of 5.5°F per thousand feet (10°C/ 1,000 m). So if air starts out at an elevation of 6,000 feet with a temperature of 40°F, its temperature will rise 33 degrees by the time it reaches the Los Angeles or San Diego coast. This air is not only cool before it leaves the Great Basin, it is also dry, and as its temperature increases its **relative humidity** automatically decreases. Thus the air approaches southern California both warm and dry.

The local topography of southern California also plays a major role in the behavior of the Santa Anas. The region is bounded by several high mountain chains that have numerous lower-elevation passes. The Santa Ana winds funnel into these passes, and in so doing undergo major increases in wind speed—often with greater than 50 miles per hour (80 kph) sustained winds and even faster gusts.

Coastal southern California has a climate typical of west-coast areas with latitudes of about 30 to 40 degrees north and south, known as a **mediterranean climate.** This climate, named for the Mediterranean region of southern Europe and north Africa, is marked by generally mild winter and summer temperatures, moderate levels of humidity, and dry summers that can give way to sometimes very rainy winters. Such a climate favors natural vegetation that can tolerate the annual summer drought by having dry, waxy leaves and short, scrubby stems and branches that retard water loss. This type of vegetation, known as **chaparral** (Figure FG7-1), not only tolerates the dry season but has also adapted to withstand the natural fires that can sweep through these regions. But while these fires may leave no permanent mark on the vegetation, they can be catastrophic to the people who live in these areas.

Typical Santa Ana Airflow Patterns: Figure FG7-2 shows the weather pattern over the western United States at the peak of a Santa Ana wind event on October 23, 2007. The high pressure over southern Idaho, Utah and Nevada is very well developed and lower pressure is found off the southern California coast. This event generated very strong winds over the entire southern California region.

Figure FG7-3 shows the local wind flow pattern brought on during a different Santa Ana event. Notice that air enters the Los Angeles basin from the north and northeast through several canyons and, most notably, through Cajon Pass, which separates the San Gabriel Mountains from the San Bernardino Mountains. The winds not only flow from the northeast over much of the Los Angeles basin but even extend some distance offshore.

Residents of southern California have no trouble discerning Santa Ana winds from the normal wind patterns that otherwise dominate the region. The usual wind pattern over the area is dominated by the classic sea breeze and land breeze complex (see textbook Figure 5-35). Sea breezes form during the late morning in response to the low pressure inland generated by solar heating. This surface warming causes air to rise and spread out at higher altitudes, reducing the amount of air over the local area and creating a low pressure system. The offshore waters do

▲ **Figure FG7-1** Chaparral vegetation in coastal southern California. *(Edward Aguado photo.)*

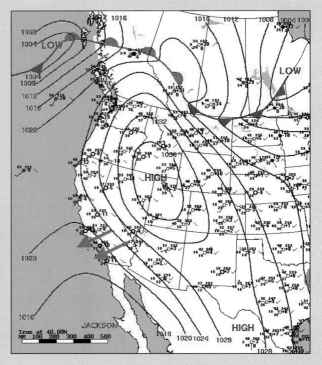

▲ **Figure FG7-2** Weather map during peak of the October 23, 2007 Santa Ana wind event. *(Adapted from National Weather Service.)*

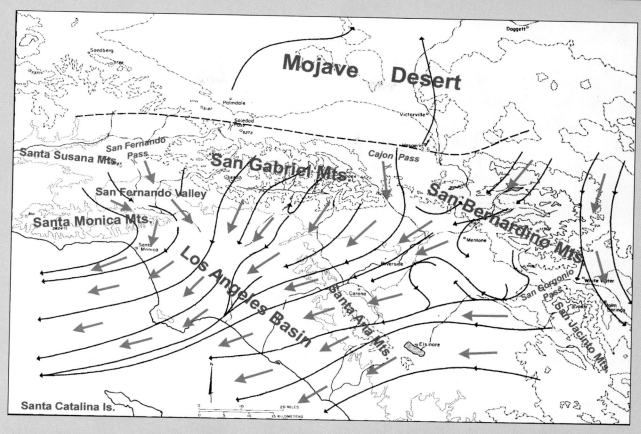

▲ **Figure FG7-3**   Typical wind flow pattern in southern California during a Santa Ana wind event. *(Adapted from M.A. Fosberg, C.A. O'Dell, and M.J. Schroeder, Some Characteristics of the Three-Dimensional Structure of Santa Ana Winds. U.S. Forest Service Research Paper PSW—30. Forest Service, U.S. Department of Agriculture, 1966.)*

not undergo such warming, so the air stays cooler and more dense. The result is a greater air pressure offshore and a west-to-east wind. Because the sea breeze originates over cool waters, it tends to bring moderate temperatures and humidities—a far cry from the dry northeasterly Santa Ana winds.

Frequency and Timing of Santa Ana Winds: Almost all Santa Ana winds occur between the months of September through April, and they are infrequent during the summer months. While Santa Ana wind conditions represent a departure from the normal wind conditions in southern California, they cannot be considered rarities. A recent study analyzing the weather over a 33-year period has found that an average of 20 Santa Ana events occur each year, each typically lasting several days.

December is the month having the greatest average number of Santa Anas, closely followed by November and January. But Santa Anas are almost as frequent in October and are often far more significant. This is partly because Santa Ana events in the late fall and winter normally don't bring the intensely hot conditions that their October counter-

parts do. But October Santa Anas also follow the normally dry summer months associated with mediterranean climates. Thus they can bring hot, dry conditions to an area dominated by dry vegetation. The combination of intense temperature and humidity conditions, dry vegetation, and strong winds provides the perfect situation for catastrophic wildfires. Such was the case in the Octobers of 2003 and 2007.

Impacts of Santa Ana Winds: The October 2007 weather map shown in Figure FG7-2 was selected because the Santa Ana event triggered an outbreak of major wildfires across San Diego County. The fires burned about 560 square miles of land (Figure FG7-4), taking with them some 1,600 homes and forcing the evacuation of a half million people. The conflagration had one other noteworthy aspect: It followed an even worse outbreak only four years earlier. In that event, several major fires burned large portions of southern California, especially in San Diego and San Bernardino counties. Those fires caused the destruction of over 3,500 homes and the loss of 40 lives.

Figure FG7-4 Satellite image showing southern California fires on October 23, 2007. *(Image courtesy of NASA/MODIS Rapid Response.)*

Fire ecology specialists have had a long debate about the role of fire suppression's impact on the spread of uncontrollable wildfires in chaparral regions. Some have argued that when humans extinguish relatively small wildfires, they allow the amount of chaparral to grow so much that it provides a greater amount of fuel for subsequent fires. The subsequent fires, they believe, can become unmanageable and destined to destroy huge areas. Other experts argue that chaparral fuel builds up to these levels very quickly and that fire suppression therefore has little effect on the development of huge burns such as those of 2003 and 2007.

It should be noted that much of the area burned in 2007 had already been burned in 2003. Thus the vegetation that had been part of the huge 2007 fires had regenerated in only four years. This lends support to the notion that fire suppression is not a major factor in the threat of major conflagrations.

Additional Resources

Textbook:
McKnight, Tom L., and Darrel Hess. *Physical Geography: A Landscape Appreciation*, 9th ed. Upper Saddle River, NJ: Pearson/Prentice Hall, 2008. Chapters 5 and 6.

Further Reading:
Aguado, Edward, and James E. Burt. *Understanding Weather & Climate*, 5th edition. Upper Saddle River, NJ: Pearson/Prentice Hall, 2010.
Raphael, M.N. "The Santa Ana Winds of California" in *Earth Interactions*, v. 7, issue 8, 2003, pp. 1–13 (Available online through the American Meteorological Society: *http://www.ametsoc.org/*).

Web Sites:
NASA Satellite Movies of 2007 Fires
http://www.nasa.gov/mov/194204main_goes-20071024-small.mov

San Diego State University 2007 Fires Web page
http://www.nasa.gov/vision/earth/lookingatearth/socal_wildfires_oct07.html

Textbook Page References for Key Terms

adiabatic warming *(p. 85)*
anticyclone *(p. 112)*
chaparral *(p. 336)*

dry adiabatic rate *(p. 153)*
Foehn/chinook winds *(p. 131)*
mediterranean climate *(p. 229)*

relative humidity *(p. 149)*
sea/land breeze *(p. 128)*

Southern Coast: Dana Point to La Jolla

Patricia Deen, Palomar College

Introduction

The coast of southern California from Dana Point to La Jolla provides an opportunity to explore a variety of coastal processes, landforms, and ecosystems. Changes in sea level from repeated ice ages and active uplift along faults have resulted in an extraordinary cliffed coastline with intervening stream valleys and coastal lagoons.

Urbanization has taken its toll on the coastal zone. Construction of dams and coastal structures such as seawalls and jetties has decreased sand supply and increased rates of bluff erosion. Construction of highways and railroads across lagoons has decreased tidal flow, degrading the health of wetland ecosystems. However, several recent projects have been initiated to minimize some of these human impacts. This field guide surveys natural processes that have shaped this coastline, the impacts of urbanization, and the ongoing battle to restore the quality of this coastal region.

Location

Dana Point is located in Orange County, California, about halfway between Los Angeles and San Diego. Figure FG8-1 shows the general location of field guide stops. Specific directions with mileages are provided; the total distance is about 65 miles (104 km). All seven stops can be visited in one day; however, you may find it more enjoyable to linger on the beach or at the tide pools, making a two-day trip optimal.

The mild climate makes this field trip possible at any time of the year; however, warm summer weather brings large crowds and parking problems to beach areas. Note that beach access and tide pools are best at low tide, so check a tide table before you go (see *Additional Resources* on F-60).

Background

Beach Compartments: Beaches are deposits of wave-worked sediment along the coast. In southern California, beaches are divided into *beach compartments*. The rocky headland at Dana Point is the beginning of the Oceanside Beach Compartment (see Figure FG8-1). Sand is delivered to the coast by streams and erosion of coastal bluffs. Wave energy generates **longshore currents** that transport sand southward along the coast (see textbook Figure 20-12). The Oceanside Beach Compartment ends 50 miles (80 km) down the coast where sand is drained off the beach through La Jolla Submarine Canyon, which extends to a depth of over 3,000 feet (1,000 meters).

Sandy beaches are valuable not only for their recreational use but also for the protection they provide to coastal bluffs. Construction of harbors and jetties diverts sand from the coastal **sediment budget,** leaving downstream beaches and coastal cliffs prone to erosion.

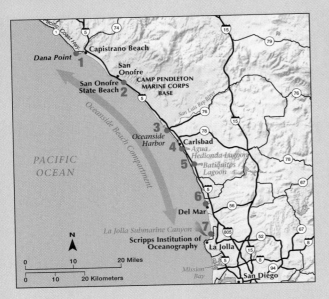

Figure FG8-1 Regional map of the southern California Coast from Dana Point to San Diego, showing field guide stops and the Oceanside Beach Compartment.

Site Descriptions

To reach Stop 1 from Interstate 5 (I-5) take Exit #79 (California Highway 1—the Pacific Coast Highway or PCH) near the town of Capistrano Beach. Turn left onto Dana Point Harbor Drive and continue 1.3 miles to where the road dead-ends into the parking lot of the Ocean Institute.

Stop 1—Ocean Institute at Dana Point (33°27′42″N, 117°42′23″W): In 1835, Richard Henry Dana, Jr. described the tall cliffs, rocky shore, and dangerous landing at Dana Point in his epic tale *Two Years Before the Mast*. In the 1960s, Dana Cove became legendary to surfers for **wave refraction** around the point (see textbook Figure 20-5), building into the surf break known as "Killer Dana." In 1968, a breakwater was built to provide safe harbor for recreational boats, spelling the end of the "Killer Dana" surf break. Today, Dana Point Harbor is the home of the Ocean Institute, a wheelchair-accessible facility which offers a variety of public programs including whale-watching trips aboard its research vessel R/V *Sea Explorer*. A reproduction of the brig *Pilgrim*, which carried Dana on his voyage, helps to transport visitors back in time to the days of early California. Check the Ocean Institute's Web site for a schedule of activities. If the tide is low, investigate the tide pools below the rocky point.

Tourist attractions aside, Dana Point marks a significant place along the southern California coastline; its rock promontory or *headland* marks the beginning of the Oceanside Beach Compartment. Just south of the harbor, San Juan Creek delivers sand to Doheny State Beach. Sand is carried by longshore currents down the coast where it will eventually drain out of the beach system through La Jolla Submarine Canyon.

Stop 2—San Onofre State Beach (33°21′43″N, 117°32′26″W): From the Ocean Institute, travel east on Dana Point Harbor Drive for 1.2 miles. Turn right onto PCH/Highway 1, and after one mile enter southbound Interstate 5. After 7.6 miles take Exit 71 (Basilone Road) and turn right at the end of the offramp. Continue for 3.2 miles to the San Onofre State Beach entrance station; stop and pay the entrance fee. Park in the lot for *Beach Trail #1*.

Beach Trail #1 leads to a spectacular overlook. (For a wheelchair-accessible path, instead of parking next to Beach Trail #1, continue 100 yards and park by the entrance to a gravel access road—from there it is about 50 yards to the overlook.). The flat surface along the top of the bluffs is a **marine terrace,** eroded by waves 125,000 years ago and then uplifted by faulting (see textbook Figure 20-26). Looking north, you can see the San Onofre Nuclear Generating Station (SONGS). Like other power plants along the coast, SONGS uses seawater as part of its cooling system. Seawater that is drawn into the power plant contains large numbers of small fish and microscopic plants and animals. The destruction of these organisms has been linked to the decline of fisheries along the coast. Legislation mandates that coastal users mitigate the negative effects of their activities. As a result, SONGS has helped to pay for many projects including lagoon restoration and fish stock enhancement. In order to combat the negative effects of its warm water outfall on kelp growth, an artificial kelp reef has recently been constructed to the north of the plant.

The amphitheater-shaped scarps in the bluff are from **landslide** activity. Nearly 80% of the bluffs between SONGS and Marine Corps Base Camp Pendleton to the south are fronted by landslides. To see the reason for this, follow the trail downhill and walk north along the beach about 0.25 miles. Note the change from contorted landslide deposits to a light-colored vertical sandstone cliff (Figure FG8-2). This marks the location of the Christianitos Fault. The Christianitos Fault is a normal fault (see textbook Figure 14-52) that brings erosion-resistant sandstone into contact with landslide-prone mudstones. Although there has been no recent movement on the fault, it is still considered active. As such, its proximity to SONGS has caused some concern.

▲ **Figure FG8-2** View looking north along San Onofre State Beach at Stop 2. *(Patricia Deen photo.)*

▲ **Figure FG8-3** Oceanside Harbor area at Stop 3. *(Image adapted from Google Earth.)*

The beach here can be difficult to walk along. Although sand dominates the beach in summer, winter waves uncover cobbles composed of an amazing assortment of igneous and metamorphic rocks. The variety of colors and crystals in these rocks will certainly catch your eye.

Stop 3—Oceanside Harbor (33°12′11″N, 117°23′31″″W):
From the San Onofre State Beach entrance, return to Interstate 5 and continue south. After 16.5 miles take Exit 54C (Harbor Drive) and turn right at the end of the offramp. Turn left onto Harbor Drive South (a "T" intersection) and left again at the "Y" to stay on Harbor Drive South. Continue for about 0.5 miles past restaurants and shops until you reach Parking Lot #10 where there is two-hour free parking

Oceanside Harbor is located between Marine Corps Base Camp Pendleton to the north and a chain of coastal cities to the south (Figure FG8- 3). The **jetty** was built in 1942 to protect Del Mar Boat Basin, which was used for amphibious training exercises during World War II. A civilian small-craft marina was added in 1958. The Santa Margarita River, located just north of the harbor, delivers huge volumes of sand to the coast. Longshore currents pile up sand against the north side of the jetty providing Camp Pendleton with one of the widest beaches in the region. Sand is transported around the jetty and deposited in the harbor entrance where it must be dredged regularly. Sand is pumped from the harbor entrance back into the longshore current system south of the harbor. In addition, the jetty deflects a large quantity of sand offshore. Ever since its construction, Oceanside Harbor has severely impeded coastal sand transport and has resulted in less sand on beaches down the coast.

The long rock wall structure along the south side of Parking Lot #10 marks the north bank of the San Luis Rey River. This river is a major source of sand for beaches south of Oceanside Harbor. However, due to the region's dry climate and upstream development, sand rarely reaches the coast from its large inland watershed. It is only during exceptionally wet years that floods deliver a significant volume of sand to the beaches. The newly constructed Pacific Street Bridge is a testament to flooding of the San Luis Rey River; the City of Oceanside will no longer have to periodically rebuild Pacific Street, which was once laid over the sand at the river's mouth.

Stop 4—Agua Hedionda Lagoon (33°08′30″N, 117°20′28″W):
Return to Interstate 5 via Harbor Drive South and continue south on I-5. After 5.0 miles, take Exit 49 (Tamarack Avenue) and turn right at the end of the offramp. Turn left onto Carlsbad Boulevard and go 0.5 miles. Park along the street near lifeguard tower #32.

Agua Hedionda Lagoon is one of several coastal **lagoons** in San Diego County; its development and successful multi-use history is unique to the region. This relatively deep-water lagoon stretches inland 1.5 miles (2.4 km); it is divided into three sections by Interstate 5 and the railroad. The eastern section contains a small boat launch and dock for recreational users. The central section is home to a YMCA youth aquatics camp.

From your position, you can see the activities in the western basin. The rows of barrel-shaped floats suspend mussels and oysters grown commercially by Carlsbad Aquafarms. Carlsbad Aquafarms has recently partnered with Scripps Institution of Oceanography scientists to culture abalone, a highly prized yet severely depleted resource along our coast. On the north shore of the lagoon is a low building with green circles; this is the Leon Raymond Hubbard Marine Fish Hatchery, which is operated by the Hubbs-SeaWorld Research Institute. Inside the building, wild adult White Seabass (*Astractoscion nobilis*) are spawned to produce eggs. Eggs are then raised into juvenile seabass, which are then released into the ocean. The goal of this program is to increase the population of White Seabass, whose numbers have decreased substantially due to overfishing. So far, the hatchery has released more than 1.3 million juvenile White Seabass along the southern California coast.

All of these activities are made possible by the Encina Power Plant. The deepened lagoon is the result of dredging to accommodate sufficient circulation of seawater for use in the plant's cooling system. Two pairs of jetties allow water to flow through the lagoon. Seawater flows into the lagoon through the north pair of jetties; the inflow captures sand, which must be dredged regularly and placed back on the beach. The south pair of jetties is locally known as "warm-water jetties" due to the outflow of warm seawater from the power plant.

The Encina Power Plant is also the future site of the Poseidon Resources Desalination Project. Upon completion in 2010, 50 million gallons of fresh drinking water will be produced daily, which constitutes 9% of San Diego's freshwater needs. Currently, over 95% of the county's freshwater is imported.

Stop 5—Batiquitos Lagoon and Nature Center (33°05'37"N, 117°18'05"W): From Agua Hedionda Lagoon continue south on Carlsbad Boulevard. After 0.6 miles turn south onto Cannon Road, and then after 0.4 miles turn right onto southbound Interstate 5. After 2.1 miles take Exit 45 (Poinsettia Lane) and turn left at the end of the offramp; after 0.6 miles turn right onto Batiquitos Drive, and after 0.5 miles turn right onto Gabbiano Lane. Drive about 0.3 miles and park at the end of Gabbiano Lane. This is a residential area.

Batiquitos Lagoon is the site of the first major lagoon restoration project on the West Coast. Tidal flow had been severely restricted by the construction of Pacific Coast Highway, the railroad, and Interstate 5. The lagoon had also been sectioned off for salt evaporation ponds, and, up until the 1970s, used for sewage discharge. By 1980, the lagoon was an odorous, mosquito-ridden mudflat that posed a health risk to humans. The City of Carlsbad, in cooperation with other government agencies, developed a plan to restore tidal flushing and enhance wildlife habitat. The Batiquitos Lagoon Enhancement Plan was put into action with mitigation funds largely from the Port of Los Angeles and was completed in 1996. Since then, biological monitoring has shown a marked increase in the number of marine fish and bird species. Nesting of endangered bird species, including the Least Tern (Sterna antillarum) and Snowy Plover (*Charadrius alexandrinus*), has also proven a success.

The Batiquitos Lagoon Foundation operates a wheelchair-accessible nature center where you can learn more about the restoration project, lagoon ecology, and the hundreds of species of birds that can be seen at Batiquitos Lagoon throughout the year. Pick up a lagoon trail guide and take a leisurely stroll to experience a healthy coastal lagoon environment.

Stop 6—Del Mar Shores (33°58'51"N, 117°16'22"W): Retrace your route back to I-5 via Gabbiano Lane, Batiquitos Drive, and Poinsettia Lane, then turn left onto southbound Interstate 5. After 9.0 miles take Exit 36 (Via de la Valle) and turn right at the end of the offramp. About 1.2 miles after exiting the freeway, continue straight across S-21/Old Highway 101 (the street name becomes Border Avenue). After 0.1 mile turn right onto Sierra Avenue, then immediately left onto Del Mar Shores Terrace. Park along the street.

From the "Coastal Access" sign next to the Del Mar Shores condominium complex, follow the alleyway to the stairs overlooking the beach. This section of coastal cliffs is composed of fractured sandstone overlain by poorly cemented sandy terrace deposits. The lack of beach sand makes access difficult except at low tide. At high tide, waves undermine the base of the cliffs, accelerating their retreat. Heed the warning signs to keep your distance from the base of the cliffs!

Walk along the beach to the north and south to observe erosional features such as sea caves, small landslides, and gullies from runoff erosion. Also note the remnants of staircases that have been destroyed by storms. A variety of methods have been used to protect the base of the cliffs from wave erosion (Figure FG8-4); these include seawalls, riprap, and concrete plugs that fill sea caves. Crib walls and plaster coatings, called *gunite*, have also been installed to hold the upper portion of the bluff in place. One homeowner has piled decades of yard waste in an attempt to protect the upper portion of the bluff!

Armoring coastal bluffs against wave attack is very controversial. Opponents note that structures take up large sections of public beach and are visu-

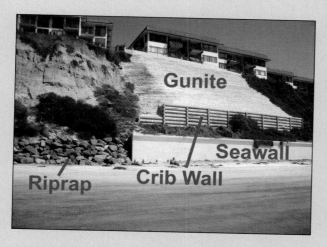

Figure FG8-4 Structures armoring bluffs in Solana Beach near Stop 6. *(Patricia Deen photo.)*

ally unappealing. In addition, scientists have recently determined that up to 50% of beach sand in the Oceanside Beach Compartment is derived from bluff erosion; armoring the cliffs therefore accelerates disappearing beaches. Current legislation mandates that new construction must be properly set back from the edge of a cliff. However, structures built in the coastal zone before passage of the California Coastal Act in 1976 can be granted a permit to build a seawall.

A new approach to prevent bluff erosion is the addition of sand to the beach in a process called "beach nourishment." In 2001, the San Diego Regional Beach Sand Project spent $17 million to add two million cubic yards of sand onto twelve sections of San Diego County beaches. The project utilized sand from former river channels and offshore beach deposits and transported the sand via barge to the beach. The newly widened beaches lasted about two years; the longshore current system has long since carried the sand down the coast. However, the value of sand to promote tourism and protect coastal bluffs has made beach nourishment a viable policy option. The next large-scale beach nourishment project is slated to begin in 2010.

Stop 7—Scripps Institution of Oceanography and the Birch Aquarium (33° 51'59"N, 117°14'5"W): From Del Mar Shores turn left onto Sierra Avenue and then left again onto Border Avenue. In 0.2 miles turn right onto Old Highway 101 and drive south through the city of

Del Mar (the street name becomes Camino del Mar). Continue past Torrey Pines State Reserve (the street name becomes North Torrey Pines Road). After about 6.5 miles turn right to continue on North Torrey Pines Road. In 1.4 miles turn right onto Expedition Way; note the sign for the Birch Aquarium. After 0.5 miles turn left into the Birch Aquarium parking lot. Parking is free for three hours.

The Birch Aquarium at Scripps provides an opportunity to explore marine ecosystems from the Pacific Northwest, southern California, Mexico, and the tropical Pacific. Displays also highlight oceanographic research at Scripps Institution of Oceanography (SIO). The aquarium is well worth a visit and is wheelchair accessible. However, begin by walking downhill along Downwind Way toward Scripps pier and the beach. Use the pedestrian bridge to cross La Jolla Shores Drive; you can then use a series of elevators or stairs to walk through the campus towards the pier.

The platform next to the pier provides a beautiful place from which to view La Jolla Cove and the surrounding area. To the south, Mount Soledad rises 822 feet (250 meters) along the Rose Canyon Fault, which is part of an active fault system that parallels the coast northward into Los Angeles. La Jolla Submarine Canyon follows the fault out into the bay and marks the end of the Oceanside Beach Compartment. Sand that enters the Oceanside Beach Compartment is drained off here through La Jolla Submarine Canyon.

As you look out on the bay, you will probably notice large areas of Giant Kelp (*Macrocystis pyrifera*) offshore. La Jolla Cove and the area around Point La Jolla have a robust forest of kelp due to cold, nutrient-rich water rises to the surface. Under ideal conditions, Giant Kelp can grow up to two feet (0.6 meters) per day! Giant Kelp is the foundation for a biologically rich ecosystem that stretches all along the California coast. In 2005, La Jolla Cove was designated the La Jolla State Marine Conservation Area, part of a state-wide network of reserves created to protect critical marine habitats.

If the tide is low, you can walk down to the beach and north of the pier for some good tide pooling. The 200-foot (60-meter) cliffs provide a look at channeled conglomerates and contorted mudstones that are similar to those being deposited beyond La Jolla Submarine Canyon today. Further north, you can see the tall cliffs of Torrey Pines, which are subject to massive landslides.

Additional Resources

Textbook:

McKnight, Tom L., and Darrel Hess. *Physical Geography: A Landscape Appreciation*, 9th ed. Upper Saddle River, NJ: Pearson/Prentice Hall, 2008. Chapter 20.

Further Reading:

Dana, Richard Henry Jr. *Two Years Before the Mast: A Personal Narrative of Life at Sea,* introduction by Gary Kinder. New York: Modern Library Paperback Edition, 2001.

Griggs, Gary, Kiki Patsch, and Lauret Savoy. *Living With the Changing California Coast*. Berkeley: University of California Press, 2005.

Sheldon, Ian. *Seashore of Southern California*. Auburn, WA: Lone Pine Publishing International Inc., 2007.

Web Sites:

Batiquitos Lagoon Foundation
http://www.batiquitosfoundation.org

Birch Aquarium
http://aquarium.ucsd.edu

Carlsbad Desalination Project
http://www.carlsbad-desal.com

Hubbs SeaWorld Research Institute
http://www.hswri.org/index.cfm

Ocean Institute
http://www.ocean-institute.org

Tidelines Online
http://www.tidelinesonline.com

Textbook Page References for Key Terms

beach *(p. 599)*
jetty *(p. 603)*
lagoon *(p. 601)*

landslide *(p. 472)*
longshore current *(p. 597)*
marine terrace *(p. 605)*

normal fault *(p. 449)*
sediment budget *(p. 599)*
wave refraction *(p. 591)*

Field Guide #9

Death Valley

Darrel Hess, City College of San Francisco

Introduction

Death Valley offers some of the most spectacular examples of desert processes and landforms in the world. It is the driest and hottest location in the United States, with an average annual rainfall of less than 2.0 inches (5.1 cm) and summertime high temperatures that regularly exceed 120°F (49°C). Death Valley's July 10, 1913 temperature of 134°F (56.7°C) is the second highest temperature ever recorded in the world.

Death Valley National Park encompasses not only Death Valley itself, but also portions of surrounding desert valleys, including Saline Valley, Eureka Valley, and northern Panamint Valley. This field guide describes a number of easily-reached sites within the Park that provide a wide sampling of Basin-and-Range desert features such as alluvial fans, sand dunes, a fascinating display of evaporative salt and mineral deposits, evidence of recent tectonic activity, and remarkable examples of plant and animal adaptations to the desert environment.

Figure FG9-1 Regional map of Death Valley showing field guide stops.

Location

The main Visitor Center for Death Valley National Park is at Furnace Creek (36°27′43″N, 116°51′59″W), reached by traveling east on California Highway 190 from U.S. 395 or traveling west on Highway 190 from California Highway 127 (Figure FG9-1). In addition to the Visitor Center where you can pay the Park entrance fee, the Furnace Creek area has several campgrounds (reserve your campsite ahead of time or you're likely to end up in the "overflow" Sunset campground that doesn't have picnic tables or fire rings). Gasoline, groceries, restaurants, and water are available near the campgrounds and Visitor Center. Lodging is available in the two private resorts in the area—Furnace Creek Ranch and Furnace Creek Inn—as well as in Stovepipe Wells to the north.

The Furnace Creek Visitor Center and many campgrounds in the Park are wheelchair accessible. However, a limited number of trails in Death Valley are fully accessible—check the Park Web site below for details.

Spring is the most popular time to visit Death Valley. The weather is warm, but not oppressively hot—and you may be lucky enough to see a wildflower bloom (see *Additional Resources* on F-66). Be prepared for cool nights (or even snow in the surrounding mountains), and expect that at least a few of the days will be very windy.

There are three important cautions for travelers in Death Valley: (1) Even if temperatures are not especially high, because of the extremely dry air you can quickly lose a great deal of fluid through perspiration without realizing it. To avoid dehydration be sure to drink lots of water. (2) Flash floods and debris flows can be hazards any time of year. Watch the sky for growing thunderstorms and avoid narrow canyons if you see storm clouds developing over the surrounding mountains—a flash flood or debris flow can fill up a dry canyon in a matter of seconds with almost no warning. (3) Nearly every year visitors are injured in single-vehicle accidents that occur when a quickly-moving vehicle's passenger-side tires veer off the pavement onto the lower "soft shoulder." If this happens to you, *do not* brake hard or turn sharply to get back up on the pavement—this may cause your car to overturn. Instead, gradually slow down before reentering the road.

Background

Geology and Landforms: Death Valley is part of the Basin-and-Range province of North America (see textbook Figure 18-27). Although called a "valley," Death Valley was not produced by stream erosion—this region of the continent has been undergoing tectonic extension for several million years, resulting in a series of down-dropped **grabens** and uplifted **tilted-fault block mountains** and **horsts** (see textbook Figures 14-54 and 14-55). Although much of the structure of Death Valley is due to such **normal faulting**, at least part of the valley is thought to be a *pull-apart basin*, formed where land drops between two parallel **strike-slip faults** (Figure FG9-2).

Death Valley itself is the deepest of the desert grabens in North America, with more than 500 square miles (1,300 square kilometers) of the basin floor below sea level. Like most basins in the region, Death Valley is a *basin of interior drainage*, with no stream outlet to the sea. Ongoing deposition from the surrounding mountains has filled the basin with great thickness of sediment, and active **alluvial fans**

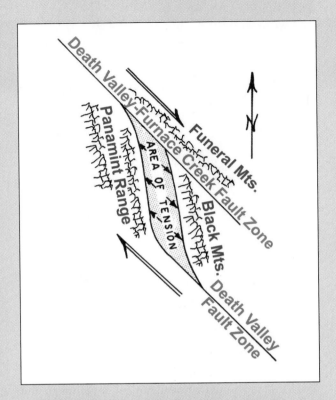

▲ **Figure FG9-2** Extension is taking place between two parallel strike-slip faults in Death Valley, forming a pull-apart basin. *(Adapted from California Division of Mines and Geology, Special Report 106.)*

are found at the mouths of nearly every canyon (see textbook Figure 18-28). Rather than the more typical desert **playa**, the lowest part of Death Valley has a *salt pan*—an expanse of dry salt deposits.

While the basin itself is relatively young geologically—and is still undergoing faulting—the rocks in Death Valley vary enormously in age. In the salt pan *evaporite* rocks are still forming, while in other parts of the Park rocks as old as 1.7 billion years are exposed.

Weather and Climate: The dryness of Death Valley is primarily a result of its position in a "quadruple" **rain shadow** formed by the mountain ranges to the west—especially the Sierra Nevada. By the time the moist air of the westerlies coming off Pacific Ocean reaches the valley, it's been forced to rise and cool several times by mountain ranges, condensing out almost all of the moisture. Over the last 95 years, Death Valley rainfall has averaged less than 2.0 inches (5.1 cm) per year, although over the last 30 years rainfall has increased to 2.5 inches (6.4 cm) per year.

When it does rain in Death Valley, it often comes in the form of a localized thunderstorm, which in turn may trigger a flash flood or **debris flow**. It is through such episodic events that most change takes place in desert areas such as this. It may seem paradoxical in such an arid location, but evidence of both fluvial erosion and fluvial deposition are common sights in Death Valley.

The high summer temperatures are due to the lack of moderating water bodies nearby, and to the great total *insolation* produced by the high Sun and clear skies. It also appears that convection within the deep valley circulates warm air back down to the basin floor, without much cooling.

Plant Communities: The common glossy green shrub you see growing on the slopes of the alluvial fans is the Creosote Bush (*Larrea tridentata*). Along the bottom edges of the alluvial fans, especially in the driest and saltiest areas, Desert Holly (*Atriplex hymenelytra*) grows. Stands of Honey Mesquite (*Prosopis juliflora*) are found around the lower parts of the fans where freshwater is close to the surface—such as in the area of Furnace Creek.

Site Descriptions

The following stops can be reached easily by ordinary automobiles. Although it is possible to visit all of these sites in one day, it's best to spend at least a couple of days in the Park, perhaps going to sites east and south of Furnace Creek on the first day (Stops 1 through 6), and sites north and west on the second day (Stops 7 through 9). Along the way, you'll find many other interesting spots to explore.

Stop 1—Dantes View (36°13′15″N, 116°43′35″W):
A good starting point for first-time visitors to the Park is the high mountain overlook of Dantes View. Drive southeast from Furnace Creek on California 190, climbing up off the valley floor along the dry Furnace Creek Wash. About eleven miles from Furnace Creek, a sign directs you to turn right (south) onto a road that will take you the final thirteen miles up to Dantes View (the last few miles of the road are very steep). This 5,475-foot (1,669 m) high vantage point in the Black Mountains offers spectacular views of the valley and surrounding mountains (Figure FG9-3). It is typically very windy at Dantes View, and usually more than 20°F (12°C) cooler than at Badwater 5,700 feet below you—recall that the **average lapse rate** is about 3.6°F/1000 feet (6.5°C/1000 m).

Directly below you at the foot of the Black Mountains are Badwater (Stop 5) and the Badwater alluvial fan (Stop 6). The Death Valley salt pan stretches across valley floor to the enormous **bajada**

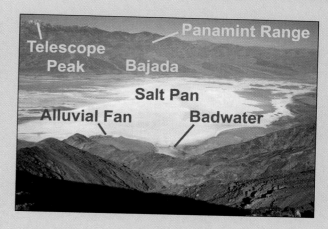

▲ **Figure FG9-3** View northwest across Death Valley from Dantes View at Stop 1. *(Darrel Hess photo.)*

running along the foot of the Panamint Range to the west. Telescope Peak (11,049 feet; 3,368 m) is the high point in the Panamints 21 miles across the valley.

Several times during the **Pleistocene epoch**, Death Valley was filled with water as a freshwater lake (called Lake Manly) as much as 600 feet (180 m) deep (see textbook Figure 19-2 and *Field Guide #6—Mono Lake* for more information about Pleistocene lakes). If the season has been especially wet, the salt pan may be temporarily covered with a shallow salty lake that can take weeks to completely evaporate.

Stop 2—Zabriskie Point (36°25′13″N, 116°48′40″W):
As you retrace your path back down to the valley floor, about four miles before Furnace Creek, you'll come to a turnout for Zabriskie Point. This is a great location to see **badlands** topography. Here, three- to nine-million-year-old lake bed deposits have been heavily dissected by ephemeral streams into this stark landscape. The dark-colored material was derived mostly from lava flows and volcanic ash, while the lighter tan and yellow material was derived mostly from weathered iron-rich deposits. Zabriskie Point is a popular spot to view the sunset.

Stop 3—Fault Scarp (36°26′15″N, 116°51′05″W):
Continue west on Highway 190. Just past the Furnace Creek Inn turn left (south) onto the Badwater Road—the main road along the east side of the valley. After traveling south about 0.7 miles, pull off the road and look to the left (east). Notice the six-foot (two m) high fault scarp running parallel to the road along the front of the Black Mountains (Figure FG9-4).

This fault scarp was produced by a prehistoric fault rupture along the east side of the valley (perhaps 2,000 years ago). During the large earthquake

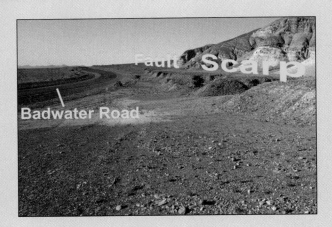

▲ **Figure FG9-4** Fault scarp along Badwater Road at Stop 3. *(Darrel Hess photo.)*

produced by this fault rupture, the basin floor dropped down more than six feet relative to the Black Mountains—indication of geologically-recent tectonic activity in Death Valley. As you continue south on the Badwater Road, you'll see evidence of this and similar fault scarps cutting through the tops of some of the alluvial fans.

Stop 4—Ventifacts (36°19'48"N, 116°49'48"W): Continue south on the Badwater Road for about 7.8 miles until you see the turn-off for Artists Drive (Artists Drive and Golden Canyon, which you passed north of here, are very popular destinations in the Park). However, instead of turning left (east) onto Artists Drive, pull off the road and walk right (to the west) up along a low ridge that extends toward the valley floor. The large rocks you see are mostly **basalt**. As you approach the crest of the ridge, notice that most of the rocks have been fluted through sand-blasting by the wind (see textbook Figure 18-18). Although wind is not generally a very powerful process of erosion, these rocks, known as "ventifacts," are the most conspicuous evidence of the wind erosion of rock in the valley. (Recall that sand dunes, which you'll visit at Stop 8, are primarily the consequence of wind deposition, not wind erosion.)

Stop 5—Badwater and the Death Valley Salt Pan (36°13'49"N, 116°46'01"W): Continue south on the Badwater Road another eight miles until you reach the parking lot at Badwater. The elevation here is about 280 feet (85 m) below sea level. The official weather station for Death Valley is at Furnace Creek, but summer temperatures here at Badwater typically run one or two degrees hotter. In fact, some researchers suggest that during the summer Badwater may be the hottest place on Earth.

If you look back to the Black Mountains just north of Badwater, you will see the gently rounded, convex surface of the Badwater *turtleback* extending slightly away from the generally straight mountain front. This turtleback (and two others just south of here) have been studied and debated for decades by geologists (they're called turtlebacks because they resemble the shape of a turtle shell). Turtlebacks along the Black Mountains consist of very old rock (probably more than one billion years old), exposed relatively recently by faulting along curved fault planes.

The salty pond that gives Badwater its name originates from freshwater issuing out of the Black Mountains into the salty valley floor. The water isn't poisonous—just salty.

Walk along the path out onto the salt pan. Out in the middle of the valley floor, a few miles to the northwest of you, is the lowest spot in North America: 282 feet (86 m) below sea level. However, the structural floor of the valley is as much as 8,000 feet (2,500 m) below the present elevation of the salt pan, having been filled with sediments washed down from the surrounding mountains.

Although the lowest part of most desert basins contains a playa consisting of dried mud, because of great volumes of water that have occupied the floor of Death Valley from time to time, a "salt pan" is found here—a layer of salt averaging two to three feet (60 to 90 cm) thick. Some of the salt in the salt pan accumulated from the evaporation of Pleistocene Lake Manly; however, most of the salt here was left by the evaporation of more recent lakes on the basin floor.

The streams that flow into Death Valley contain a variety of dissolved salts. As this water evaporates, the salts crystallize out in a sequence that reflects their solubility. From the center to near its edges (including where you're standing now) the salt pan consists of nearly pure table salt (NaCl). However, around the outer edge of the salt pan a discontinuous ring of deposits of less soluble sulfates are found. In some places, deposits of even less soluble carbonates are seen. Near Furnace Creek to the north, in the Cottonball Basin, deposits of borate minerals derived from volcanic sediments are found—these borate deposits were mined beginning in the 1880s and transported out of the valley by the famous twenty-mule teams.

The polygonal ridges you see on the salt pan form as salt crystals grow through the evaporation of water from a salty slush just below the surface (textbook Figure 18-33). If you visit the Devils Golf Course on the way back to Furnace Creek, you can see other examples of the formation and expansion of salt crystals on the basin floor. On a hot day, you may be able to hear the hard salt crust crack as it expands.

Stop 6—Alluvial Fan (36°13'30"N, 116° 46'17"W):

While parked at Badwater, you may want to walk south across the road onto the alluvial fan at the foot of the Black Mountains. This is a typical isolated alluvial fan, built up from deposits left by periodic debris flows and flash floods (see textbook Figure 18-32). As you hike up the fan toward its mouth at the mountain front, notice the gravels and cobbles that make up the fan. There is almost no **desert varnish** or **desert pavement** on this fan, indicating that this fan is quite active—recall that it takes hundreds, if not thousands, of years for desert varnish and desert pavement to develop. If you travel across the valley to the large fans and bajada at the foot of the Panamint Range, you'll find much more varnish and desert pavement. The gravel and cobbles on the Badwater alluvial fan are somewhat angular—this alluvium simply hasn't traveled far enough to become smooth and rounded. Also notice the abrupt low fault scarp along the top of the fan—this scarp is associated with the same faulting that you saw at Stop 3.

If you continue to hike up to the top the fan, you come to the mouth of a narrow canyon at the foot of the Black Mountains. You can hike into in the steep-walled canyon for a short distance until it dead-ends at a dry waterfall (remember to watch the sky above for potential thunderstorms). In the springtime, be sure to look for tiny "belly" flowers as you walk up the fan and into the canyon—often the only wildflowers you'll find in Death Valley are those you need to get down on your belly to see.

Return to Furnace Creek.

On the second day, travel north from Furnace Creek on Highway 190 toward the settlement of Stovepipe Wells, about 28 miles from Furnace Creek. There are guest facilities there, a Park ranger station, and a campground.

Stop 7—Salt Creek (36°35'31"N, 116° 59'17"W):

About fifteen miles north of Furnace Creek, take the turnoff to the left (west) for Salt Creek. From the parking area, follow the wheelchair-accessible boardwalk with its self-guided nature trail. Salt Creek is one of several streams originating at the foot of the Panamint Mountains to the west. Along the edges of the creek and in the surrounding flat valley bottom you see a crust of salts built up through the ongoing evaporation of creek water. The water in Salt Creek is about as salty as in the ocean, and a creature that lives here is one of the most intriguing in Death Valley. At the end of the Pleistocene, as freshwater Lake Manly dried up and became saltier, only a few organisms were able to adapt to the changing environment. The Salt Creek

▲ **Figure FG9-5**   Large dunes in the Mesquite Flat sand dune field near Stovepipe Wells at Stop 8. *(Darrel Hess photo.)*

Pupfish (*Cyprinodon salinus*) is a tiny fish found nowhere else in the world (several different species of pupfish are found in other parts of the desert Southwest). In spring and early summer, you'll see the tiny bright blue male pupfish defending their territories in the shallow water, trying to attract spawning females.

Stop 8—Sand Dunes (36°36'20"N, 117° 06'45"W):

About 26 miles from Furnace Creek (about 1.2 miles before Stovepipe Wells) you come to the pull-out parking area for the Mesquite Flat sand dunes. This extensive field of sand dunes is the most accessible and popular in the Park (Figure FG9-5). Morning is a nice time to visit the dunes—you can make the first footprints on the dunes, wiped smooth by the wind the night before. Distances are deceiving here—the tallest dunes in the distance are about a mile from the road, so be sure to take plenty of water.

Most of the lower dunes are configured in short, irregular transverse ridges. Between many dunes you'll see dried fine-grain mud, probably deposited by periodic mudflows coming out of the nearby mountains and now partially covered by the shifting sand. You'll also see mesquite and creosote bushes among the dunes.

You can usually tell the most recent persistent wind direction by comparing the steepness of the dune slopes—the gentler slope tends to develop on the windward side, where sand bounces up until it reaches the crest of the dune. On the leeward or *slip face* of the dune, the sand falls down, leaving a slope that is at the *angle of repose* for dry sand (about 32-34°; see textbook Figure 18-20). As you hike up and over the dunes, you'll find that the slip face is much harder to climb than the windward side, since the slip face is steeper and consists of less compacted sand.

The largest sand dunes here are a type of dune known as a "star dune." Star dunes develop in areas where the wind comes from several directions during the year. The configuration of the smaller **transverse dune** ridges (as well as isolated *barchan* dunes such as are found in other desert areas) generally reflects the most recent dominant wind direction (see textbook Figure 18-21).

Stop 9—Mosaic Canyon (36°34'19"N, 117°08'39"W): Return to Highway 190 and continue west to Stovepipe Wells. About 0.2 miles beyond Stovepipe Wells, turn left (south) following the sign to the Mosaic Canyon parking area, 2.4 miles up an alluvial fan on a well-graded gravel road. Mosaic Canyon is one of the most scenic and interesting short day hikes in Death Valley.

From the parking area, walk up the flat floor of the canyon's wash toward the mouth of Mosaic Canyon. Notice the cliffs cut from alluvium brought down by flash floods and debris flows. The gravel layers in which most of the stones are well sorted by size—or in which the small platy stones are mostly lined up parallel with each other—were left by running water such as a flash flood. However, the gravel layers in which the larger stones came to rest at all angles, especially deposits in which the large rocks came to rest without touching each other, were left by debris flows—water with a large amount of sand-size material and large rocks flowing with the consistency of wet concrete. You can find evidence of deposits left by both running water and debris flows in Mosaic Canyon itself.

As you walk up the narrow canyon, you'll begin to see the nearly vertical walls of the Noonday Dolomite and the Noonday Dolomite *breccia*—a sedimentary rock formed from the cemented angular fragments of 700-million-year-old marine carbonate deposits—scoured and polished by periodic floods

▲ **Figure FG9-6**   The narrow polished walls of lower Mosaic Canyon at Stop 9. *(Darrel Hess photo.)*

and debris flows (Figure FG9-6). As you walk up the canyon, you'll see patches of this breccia, plastered and cemented onto the canyon walls, indicating that Mosaic Canyon has undergone repeated episodes of both cutting and filling.

The lowest half-mile of Mosaic Canyon is the most spectacular, but you may want to continue your hike farther up where the walls begin to open into a wider valley floor. Even in the driest years, you're likely to see spring wildflowers blooming in some of the small side canyons.

Additional Resources

Textbook:
McKnight, Tom L., and Darrel Hess. *Physical Geography: A Landscape Appreciation*, 9th ed. Upper Saddle River, NJ: Pearson/Prentice Hall, 2008. Chapters 14 and 18.

Further Reading:
Decker, Robert, and Barbara Decker. *Road Guide to Death Valley National Park*, 4th ed. Mariposa, CA: Double Decker Press, 2004.

Hunt, Charles B. *Death Valley: Ecology, Archaeology*. Berkeley: University of California Press, 1975.

Sharp, Robert P., and Allen F. Glazner. *Geology Underfoot in Death Valley and Owens Valley*. Missoula, MT: Mountain Press Publishing Company, 1997.

Web Sites:
Death Valley National Park
http://www.nps.gov/deva

DesertUSA Wildflower Report
http://www.desertusa.com/wildflo/ca_dv.html

Textbook Page References for Key Terms

alluvial fan *(p. 545)*
average lapse rate *(p. 98)*
badlands *(p. 550)*
bajada *(p. 546)*
basalt *(p. 392)*
debris flow *(p. 475)*

desert pavement *(p. 538)*
desert varnish *(p. 538)*
graben *(p. 449)*
horst *(p. 449)*
normal fault *(p. 449)*
Pleistocene epoch *(p. 555)*

playa *(p. 532)*
rain shadow *(p. 168)*
tilted-fault block mountain
   (p. 449)
transverse dune *(p. 541)*
strike-slip fault *(p. 449)*